SPECIAL POPULATIONS
IN
CAREER AND TECHNICAL
EDUCATION

AMERICAN TECHNICAL PUBLISHERS, INC.
HOMEWOOD, ILLINOIS 60430-4600

Michelle Sarkees-Wircenski
John L. Scott

American Technical Publishers, Inc. Editorial Staff

Copy Editors:
    Aimée M. Brucks
    Catherine A. Mini

Layout:
    Tina T. Biegel
    Aimée M. Brucks
    Robert J. Deisinger
    Catherine A. Mini

Illustrators:
    Carl R. Hansen
    Ellen E. Pinneo

CD-ROM Development:
    Robert J. Deisinger
    Valerie A. Deisinger
    Carl R. Hansen

1 2 3 4 5 6 7 8 9 – 03 – 9 8 7 6 5 4 3 2 1

Printed in the United States of America

ISBN 0-8269-4007-2

Acknowledgments

The author and publisher would like to acknowledge the assistance provided by the following individuals in the development of *Special Populations in Career and Technical Education.*

For content development and review:

Ellie Bicanich
Director
Special Vocational Services in Pennsylvania
Penn State McKeesport Campus
101 Ostermayer
McKeesport, PA 15132

Dr. Jim Brown
Professor and Director
Minnesota Research and Development Center
  for Vocational Education
Department of Work, Community, and Family Education
College of Education and Human Development
The University of Minnesota
1954 Buford Avenue
St. Paul, MN 55108

Dr. Nick Elksnin
Consultant
233 Coinbow Circle
Mt. Pleasant, SC 29464

Dr. Donnella Hess-Grabill
Director
Illinois Center for Specialized Professional Support
Illinois State University
Corporate Center East
2203 East Empire, St. B
Bloomington, IL 61704

Dr. Jim Greenan
Professor and Chair
Division of Vocational Education
Purdue University
1442 Liberal Arts and Education Bldg.
West Lafayette, IN 49707

Dr. John Gugerty
Senior Outreach Specialist
Center on Education and Work
University of Wisconsin
1025 West Johnson Street, #964
Madison, WI 53706

Dr. Lynda West
Professor
Department of Teacher Preparation and Special Education
Graduate School of Education and Human Development
The George Washington University
2134 G Street, NW #306
Washington, DC 20052

Dr. Jerry Wircenski
Professor
Department of Technology and Cognition
College of Education
The University of North Texas
P.O. Box 311337
Denton, TX 76203

For assistance in manuscript development:

Mrs. Mary Chandler
University of North Texas

Mrs. Pam Gentry
University of North Texas

Table of Contents

CD-ROM Contents

- Using the CD-ROM
- Quick Quizzes
- Interactive Glossary
- Forms
- Reference Material

Introduction

Many learners leaving high school today are unable to compete for jobs or enter postsecondary institutions. A significant number of these learners are from special populations. Career and technical education programs can provide learners from special populations with avenues for achievement as well as the skills needed for future education and employment. *Special Populations in Career and Technical Education* was written to help special population teachers, special population teacher educators, counselors, career and technical education instructors, school administrators, and human resource development specialists meet the needs of these learners.

The book contains 12 chapters covering all aspects of integrating learners from special populations into career and technical education programs. Extensive text and graphics cover such topics as identification of learners from special populations, recent legislation, assessment practices, instructional delivery strategies, individualized education programs (IEPs), curriculum modification, and the transition process. Each chapter begins with objectives and key terms and ends with self-assessment questions and activities.

The CD-ROM in the back of the book is designed as a self-study aid to enhance book content. It includes Quick Quizzes, an Interactive Glossary, Forms, and Reference Material. The Quick Quizzes provide an interactive review of topics covered in the chapters. The Interactive Glossary provides a helpful reference to key terms included in the text. The Reference Material button accesses links to web sites and other useful related material. The Forms included on the CD-ROM can be individually customized for use by educators and institutions for documentation efficiency. Instructions for using the CD-ROM can be found on the last page of the book.

The Publisher

About the Authors

Michelle Sarkees-Wircenski

Michelle Sarkees-Wircenski is a professor in Applied Technology, Training and Development in the College of Education at the University of North Texas. A past president of the National Association of Vocational Education Special Needs Personnel, Dr. Sarkees-Wircenski has authored and coauthored books related to career and technical education and training. She has also authored numerous articles covering such topics as special populations, learning styles, vocational assessment, student organizations, curriculum modification, authentic assessment, and ageism in the workforce. Dr. Sarkees-Wircenski serves on the editorial board of several professional journals and has delivered in-service and professional development sessions in forty-five states.

John L. Scott

John L. Scott is an associate professor in the Technological Studies Program, Department of Occupational Studies in the College of Education at the University of Georgia. With an extensive background in career and technical education, Dr. Scott has taught at the middle school, high school, and university levels. He has authored and coauthored numerous publications in the field. He has also consulted with state departments of education and local school districts on preparing teachers to work with learners from special populations. Dr. Scott is active with SkillsUSA-VICA and has served as president of both the National Association of Industrial and Technical Teacher Educators and the National Association of Trade and Industrial Education.

Special Populations in the Workforce

INTRODUCTION

We have a national dilemma. Dropouts from secondary school programs are unable to compete for jobs or enter postsecondary institutions for further education and training. Adults who need to be trained and retrained cannot remain in or reenter the workforce. Individuals who lack basic academic skills and employability skills have fallen through the cracks of our nation's educational system and have nowhere to go.

Important economic and educational reasons exist for providing career and technical education for learners with special needs, as evidenced by recent statistical reports citing its benefits. It is more cost effective to educate these individuals than to provide high cost public assistance for the rest of their lives. Individuals from special populations have a legal right to participate in career and technical education programs in order to develop marketable skills. These learners have the same needs and desires as anyone else to develop workplace skills, enter the labor force, and become contributing members of society.

During the past few decades, considerable progress has been made in allowing learners with special needs to access career and technical education programs. Educators must work collaboratively with other school-based personnel and with outside agencies to help learners from special populations succeed. This chapter presents a rationale for integrating learners from special populations into career and technical education programs and provides a glimpse into the methods of assuring their success in these programs.

OUTLINE

INDIVIDUALS FROM SPECIAL POPULATIONS
FACTORS AFFECTING INDIVIDUALS FROM SPECIAL POPULATIONS
EDUCATIONAL REFORM—CHALLENGES
CONSTRUCTING EFFECTIVE EDUCATIONAL ENVIRONMENTS FOR ALL LEARNERS
PATTERNS AND ISSUES IN EDUCATIONAL REFORM
STANDARDS—AN ESSENTIAL ELEMENT IN EDUCATIONAL REFORM
EDUCATIONAL REFORM AND LEARNERS FROM SPECIAL POPULATIONS
INDIVIDUALS FROM SPECIAL POPULATIONS IN CAREER AND TECHNICAL PROGRAMS
COMPETENCIES NEEDED BY CAREER AND TECHNICAL INSTRUCTORS
THE ROLE OF CAREER AND TECHNICAL EDUCATION IN DROPOUT PREVENTION
CAREER AND TECHNICAL PROGRAMS AND SPECIAL POPULATIONS
CAREER AND TECHNICAL SPECIAL NEEDS PROGRAMS—EXEMPLARY COMPONENTS
LEGISLATIVE FOUNDATION
MAKING FEDERAL LEGISLATION RELEVANT AT LOCAL LEVELS
SUMMARY
SELF-ASSESSMENT
ASSOCIATED ACTIVITIES
REFERENCES

OBJECTIVES

Afer completing this chapter, the reader should be able to accomplish the following:

1. Describe the characteristics of individuals from special populations.
2. Identify the economic factors affecting individuals from special populations.
3. Identify the educational factors affecting individuals from special populations.

4. Identify the key legislative mandates that provide individuals from special populations the right to develop their career potential.
5. List various ways to make federal legislation relevant at the local level.
6. Describe educational reform and its impact on those working with individuals from special populations in career and technical programs.
7. Identify the characteristics of effective schools that provide successful learning environments for learners with special needs.
8. Supply a rationale for providing individuals from special populations with opportunities to enroll and succeed in career and technical programs.
9. Identify the components of exemplary career and technical special needs programs.
10. State the basic rationale for including or integrating learners from special populations in existing career and technical programs.
11. List several successful methods for including or integrating learners from special populations in career and technical programs.
12. Identify the competencies needed by career and technical instructors who work with learners with special needs.

TERMS

criminal offender
economically disadvantaged
educationally disadvantaged
educational reform
equal access

essential functions
foster children
full participation
limited English-proficient learner
migrant

qualified individual with a disability
reasonable accommodation
related services
transition services
undue hardship

INDIVIDUALS FROM SPECIAL POPULATIONS

Over the past years, there has been much debate about the definition, nature, and needs of individuals from special populations, about those who are most at risk in our educational institutions and in our society. There is no easy way to describe or characterize individuals who are at risk. A review of the literature cited by Lehr and Harris (1988) revealed labels that have been used to characterize learners who have special needs:

- disadvantaged
- culturally deprived
- underachiever
- nonachiever
- low ability
- slow learner
- low socioeconomic status
- alienated
- dropout prone
- disenfranchised
- underprivileged
- low-performing
- language impaired
- impoverished
- remedial education

Frymier and Gansneder (1989) described being at risk as:

A function of when bad things happen to a child, how severe they are, how often it happens, and what else happens in the child's immediate environment. Moreover, being at risk is not solely a phenomenon of adolescence. Children of all ages are at risk. If we think of human existence as a continuum that ranges from healthy (or good) to unhealthy (or bad), then being at risk shows up on half of the continuum. The good end of the continuum tends in the general direction of health, adjustment, adequacy, happiness, high self-esteem, achievement, and pro-social or life-oriented behavior. The bad end of the continuum points in the direction of illness, maladjustment, low self-esteem, and antisocial or death-oriented behavior. (p. 142)

Hixson and Tinzmann (1990) discussed the various definitions and characteristics of at-risk learners:

- Historically, "at-risk" learners were primarily those whose appearance, language, culture, values, communities, and family structures did not match those of the dominant white culture that schools were designed to serve and support. These learners—primarily minorities, the poor, and immigrants—were considered culturally or educationally disadvantaged or deprived.
- Learners who have certain kinds of conditions, such as living with one parent, being a member of a minority group, or having limited English proficiency, are de-

fined as at risk because, statistically, learners in these categories are more likely to be in the lowest achievement groups or drop out of school altogether.

- Learners who are already performing poorly or failing in school are at risk because they have not been able to successfully take advantage of the "regular" school program and will likely fall further behind or drop out. This method of identification reflects a monitoring/intervention strategy. In attempting to get away from the use of predisposing indicators, this approach waits until school-related problems occur and then identifies the learner as at risk. A major difficulty with this approach, however, is that identification of a learner's problems often occurs after a pattern of poor performance, and the expectations of both teachers and learners that it will continue have become severe enough to make successful intervention/remediation less likely. In addition, even if problems are identified early, the typical intervention involves ancillary programs that do not promote changes in the regular program, intensify the impact of negative labeling and isolation of less successful learners from important peer role models and support systems, and tend to slow down learner progress and thereby exacerbate the degree to which learners fall behind and further diminish their belief that they will ever "catch up."

There is an emerging body of research that looks at school factors as potential causes of "at-riskness." School characteristics that have been identified as hindering the academic achievement of many learners include inflexible schedules; narrow curricula; a priority focus on basic/lower-order skills; inappropriate, limited, and rigid instructional strategies; inappropriate texts and other instructional materials; over-reliance on standardized tests to make instructional and curricular decisions; tracking; isolated pull-out programs; and the beliefs and attitudes of teachers and administrators toward both learners and their parents.

Among all races and income groups and in communities nationwide, many children are in jeopardy. They grow up in families in turmoil. Their parents are too stressed and too drained to provide the nurturing, structure, and security necessary to protect them and prepare them for adulthood. Some children are unloved and ill-tended, while others are unsafe at home and in their neighborhoods. Many are poor and some are homeless and hungry. The harshness of these children's lives and their tenuous hold on tomorrow cannot be countenanced by a wealthy nation, a caring people, or a prudent society. America's future depends on these children. (The National Commission on Children, 1991).

Davis and McCaul (1991) described the wide range of individuals from special populations as

- dropping out of school (1 million annually);
- living below the poverty line (about 20-25%);
- dependent upon alcohol or drugs or having immediate family members with substance abuse problems (approximately 3 million);
- homeless (about 100,000);

- having no access to regular and appropriate medical care (nearly 10 million);
- latchkey kids with no after-school support (estimated to be 7 million below age 10);
- abused and/or neglected by family members (more than 2,200,000 cases annually);
- living in single-parent families (15,300,000 or 90% live with their mothers);
- becoming pregnant during the teenage years (1,500,000 annually); and
- having different cultural backgrounds and, in many cases, having limited English-speaking abilities.

Many of these individuals are at risk of not succeeding in our educational institutions. Kershner and Connolly (1991) described an individual who is at risk as a person who comes from a low socioeconomic background that may include various forms of family stress or instability. If that person is consistently discouraged by the educational system because he or she receives signals about academic inadequacies and failures, perceives little interest or caring from instructors, and sees the institution's discipline system as both ineffective and unfair, then it is not unreasonable to expect that the learner will become alienated and uncommitted to completing an education.

Children brought up with one or more of these factors . . .
- poverty or economic disadvantage
- physical or learning disability
- limited language proficiency
- victim of crime
- victim of abuse or neglect
- alcoholic or substance abusing parent
- geographic disadvantage
- victim of racial or ethnic prejudice

…can be at greater risk for involvement in one or more of these…
- alcohol, tobacco, or other drug use
- drinking and driving
- low educational achievement
- antisocial, violence or gangs
- school truancy or dropping out
- running away
- teen pregnancy
- depression or suicide. See Figure 1-1.

A more recent term for individuals who are at risk is *individuals from special populations*. The term *special populations* means
- individuals with disabilities;
- individuals from economically disadvantaged families, including foster children;
- individuals preparing for nontraditional training and employment;
- single parents, including single pregnant women;
- displaced homemakers; and
- individuals with other barriers to educational achievement, including individuals with limited English proficiency (American Vocational Association, 1998).

INFLUENCES THAT AFFECT LEARNERS FROM SPECIAL POPULATIONS IN EDUCATIONAL SETTINGS

THE FOLLOWING LIST OF VARIABLES CAN NEGATIVELY AFFECT LEARNER PROGRESS:
- Substance abuse (self, friends, family members)
- Affiliations outside of school (gangs, school dropouts)
- Lack of worker role models
- History of sporadic employment
- No emphasis at home on success at school
- Low parent/family expectations
- Few opportunities to break social stigma
- Public assistance/public housing
- Lack of respect for authority
- Low self-esteem, lack of self-confidence
- Health problems
- Teen parent/single parent/pregnant
- Lack of peer group acceptance
- Low grade point average (GPA)
- Poor performance on standardized tests
- Low basic skills levels (reading, math, communication)
- Difficulty in mastering basic competencies
- Behavior disorders/problems
- Cultural diversity (different language, religion, etc.)
- Lack of financial resources
- Others dependent on them for support/assistance
- Sees only minimum wage opportunities
- Generally interested in short-term goals
- Desire for immediate gratification
- Loner
- Poor hygiene
- Antisocial behavior

Figure 1-1. A variety of school related and family/home related factors that can affect the educational performance of individuals from special populations.

The following predictions, made a decade ago, influence the societal and educational situation that we must deal with now:
- The wide cultural diversity reaching our shore will generate a distinct culture of its own that will be neither traditional American nor identical to the country of origin.
- Immigration will account for half of all U.S. population growth by 2015. Without volatile birth, death, and immigration rates, the U.S. population will peak at about 300 million about 2038 and begin to decline for the first time ever. However, unless increased immigration from Asia, Latin America, and Eastern Europe is checked, a decline is highly unlikely.

- U.S. immigration is approaching the record levels of the early 1900s. While Asian-Americans grow at a rate eight times that of whites, Hispanic immigration and birth will increase at a rate four times that of whites and will double that rate in the next decade. African-Americans, currently the largest minority group, are also growing at a rate faster than that of whites but not as fast as Asians and Hispanics.
- In 2040, whites will have a median age of 45, while Hispanics will have a median age of 28, reinforcing the tendency for diverse groups to stay apart from each other. The growth of separate ethnic groups and gangs will provide the social backdrop in our schools and universities. The loss of the traditional American way of life, coupled with political impotence to reverse the trend, will spawn a conservative backlash over the next decade.
- Hispanics will surpass African-Americans as the largest U.S. minority group by 2015. Though Hispanics will continue to have an ever-increasing share of poverty, they will also show strong increases in the number of upper- and middle-class families.
- Record numbers of Americans will stay single longer, lessening the family influence on society. The percentage of people who will never marry will triple in the next decade. By 2005, single people will account for more than half the U.S. population. Of those who are single today, 25% are separated or divorced and 56% have never married. We will see rapid growth in the number of roommates and singles as members of the baby boomer generation begin their adult lives. Getting voter support for education and family service initiatives will be more difficult as the number of single people increases.
- Important characteristics of single parents include a busy lifestyle, lower-than-average incomes, lower-than-average spending on most things and a greater likelihood of dwelling as renters. Households of related people not headed by married couples, referred to by the Census Bureau as "other families," are divided into two major groups. The households with children under 18 are known as single parents, and the remaining households are a conglomeration of siblings, grandparents and other relatives living together. The total number of households classified as other families could reach almost 19 million by 2010. Single parents represent 56% of other families, and single mothers comprise 85% of single parents. Single mothers are expected to grow 18% between 1990 and 2010 and will remain the majority of all single parents in 2010 at nearly 8 million households (Minkin, 1995).

Other factors have had a significant influence on the growth of special populations:
- There has been a marked reduction in the salience of the family. Since 1960, the proportion of women not marrying has doubled; the probability of divorce has risen to 50%. Rates of childbearing have declined steadily over the past two centuries, from a total fertility rate of 7 in 1800 to 1.8 today, with one interruption—the post–World War II baby boom (Eisenberg, 1991).
- In the model American family of the 1980s and 1990s, both parents are at work outside the home. This has major consequences for family life, consequences captured by the phrase "time poverty." Economist Victor Fuchs has calculated that between 1960 and 1986, the opportunity for children to spend time with parents declined by 10 hours per week for the average white child, and 12 hours for the black child. The principal reason is the increase in the proportion of mothers holding paid jobs; not far behind is the increase in one-parent households. Fathers in intact families can offset the loss in hours of mothering by doing more fathering; however, there is little evidence that they do (Eisenberg, 1991).
- The myth that family and work occupy separate spheres is fast fading in the face of tremendous demographic and economic changes. Smaller families, increasing numbers of working women, nontraditional family patterns, and changing values are spurring a growing awareness of the interdependence of work and family life. Although the composition of the labor force and family structures have both changed rapidly, attitudes and institutions have been slower to evolve. Many workplace rules and practices remain based on a male, single-earner workforce, and many families still act under role-sharing assumptions based on the presence of full-time homemakers, despite the fact that fewer than 7% of families fit that model (Kerka, 1991).
- Few issues concern Americans more than what has happened to the role of the family in caring for children. Almost one in four of the nation's youngsters under 18 lives with only one parent, almost always the mother. If the youngster is African-American, the ratio rises to one in two. The divorce ratio has tripled and the percentage of out-of-wedlock births among teenage women has doubled over the past 15 years (Eisenberg, 1991).
- Twenty percent of all children in the United States live in poverty. In any randomly assigned classroom in the country, one would find at least one third of the learners living at or below 20% of the poverty level. In some states it is more than half, and in some rural and urban school districts it could be virtually all. Though progress was made in lowering the poverty rate in the late 1900s, the decrease was measured only in tenths of a percent. And, although the poverty rate for African-Americans (26.5%) and Hispanics (27.1%) exceeds that of whites, the experience of all economically disadvantaged children is fairly the same regardless of race. They all enter elementary school at a disadvantage and face the same type of future. For example, both black and white learners who must repeat the first grade are equally likely to drop out of school (Gray & Herr, 2000).

- There is a great need for measures to protect young mothers and their children against poverty. It is not single parenthood alone, but the poverty associated with it that accounts for much of the pathology in the children in such families. In the U.S., the typical public assistance grant provides an income well below the poverty line. Intended as a spur to work, the payment locks mothers into a cycle of dependency due to the fact that the earnings from the part-time, low-paying work available to them are confiscated. The payments offer nothing to parents who keep just above the poverty line. Health care coverage is variable and uncertain, as though our nation believes that children of indigent parents do not deserve health care. Medicaid covers half of the cost of health care at best (Eisenberg, 1991).

- Today, 21% of U.S. children grow up in poverty. For children in young families—that is, with parents under 30—the figure is 35%. These data reflect the decline in real dollar incomes for young families and the growing percentage of single-parent families. From 1979 to 1987, the average family income of the poorest fifth of U.S. families declined by 10%, and that of the poorest fifth of African-American families by 20%. During the same period, family income for the top fifth grew by 16%. The news is even grimmer for young single-parent families; 75% of their children live in poverty (Eisenberg, 1991).

- Every day, approximately 5,600 people in this country celebrate their 65th birthday, and the fastest-growing segment of the U.S. population is the one over 85 years of age. Of the latter, only one in four can live alone without difficulty. Families are being forced to choose between paying for a nursing home for an aged parent or paying the college tuition for their son or daughter. It is the "sandwich" generation—squeezed between the demands of the young and the old—and when the baby boomers retire, the demands will only worsen. By 2030 the entire baby boomer generation, a full one-third of today's U.S. population, will be 65 or older. Four-generation families—great-grandparents, grandparents, parents, and children—will become the norm, and there will be great-great-grandparents in some families. The "sandwich" is destined to get more layers, and each layer will only add to the demands for care (Bureau of Labor Statistics, 1999).

- The 21st century may be known as the era of lifelong learning and lifelong working. Retirement, the end stage of a linear working life, may be replaced with a learning, working, leisure, working, learning life cycle. In a cyclical living and working model, participating in the workforce never ceases but is interspersed with periods of leisure and learning. Full-time work may be interspersed with periods of flexible working arrangements such as part-time, seasonal, occasional, and project work. The traditional notion of retirement may be replaced with lifelong working—in various positions and in varying amounts of time throughout adult life. In the future, a declining birthrate may result in a shortage of skilled and knowledgeable employees, making the notion of retirement for older workers a serious drain on organizational productivity. Increasing demands for work force productivity, a projected shortage of skilled and experienced workers, and older adults who are healthier and living longer than previous generations are powerful societal forces shaping future employment practices (Stein, 2000).

FACTORS AFFECTING INDIVIDUALS FROM SPECIAL POPULATIONS

There are important reasons for focusing on the problems affecting learners from special populations and providing necessary support services in our educational programs. Some of the concerns are economic. Others originate from educational factors that have implications for our country's future. Still other reasons have a legal base. Regardless of the motive behind changing attitudes and restructuring educational programs, accommodations for these learners must be made if they are to become contributing members of society.

Educational Considerations

The National Center for Education Statistics (2000) reported the following:

- Changes in the racial-ethnic composition of learner enrollments can alter the amount of diversity of language and culture in the nation's schools. Although variety in learner backgrounds can enhance the learning environment, it can also create new or increased challenges for schools, making it necessary for them to accommodate the needs of this wide variety of learners. Knowledge of these shifts in the racial-ethnic distribution of public school learners in grades 1-12 may help schools plan for this change.

- In 1998, 37% of public school learners enrolled in these grades were considered to be part of a minority group, an increase of 15 percentage points from 1972. This increase was largely due to the growth in the proportion of Hispanic learners. In 1998, black and Hispanic learners accounted for 17% and 15% of the public school enrollment respectively, up 2 and 9 percentage points from 1972. The percentage of learners from other racial-ethnic groups also increased, from 1% in 1972 to 5% in 1998.

- Parents' educational attainment is related to learner achievement and other dimensions of educational participation and outcomes. In 1999, a higher percentage of white children compared with African-American and Hispanic children ages 6-18 had parents who had attained at least a high school education. The same is true for the percentage who had attained at least a bachelor's degree.

- Between 1974 and 1999, the percentage of children ages 6-18 whose parents had at least a high school education increased among all racial-ethnic groups. However, the rates of increase differed by racial-ethnic groups. While fewer African-American children ages 6-18 had parents who completed at least a high school education compared with their white peers, the attainment gap between the percentage of white and black children whose parents attained this level of education narrowed considerably between 1974 and 1999.
- This large reduction in the gap was due to a large increase in the percentage of African-American children with parents who attained at least a high school education compared with their white peers. In contrast, the gap between the percentages of white and Hispanic children whose mothers attained at least a high school education did not change, while the gap between the percentages of white and Hispanic children whose fathers attained this level of education increased.

Our nation still faces the dilemma of the rising dropout rate. The following can be used by all schools to define a dropout: a pupil who leaves school, for any reason except death, before graduation or completion of a program of studies and without transferring to another school or institution. Within this definition are categories of learners including those

- in grades 9 or 10-12 (or in a special ungraded program equivalent to these grades) who leave during the school year and do not return within a specified length of time;
- who do not return to school after a break, summer vacation, or suspension;
- who are runaways or whose whereabouts are unknown;
- those who enter the military, a trade or business school, prison, or any other program not qualifying as an elementary or secondary school; and
- who are expelled.

Potential dropouts tend to be retained in the same grade, have poor academic grades, and feel disengaged from school. They are more likely to come from low socioeconomic status families where parents did not get very far in their schooling. They tend to be part of a large peer group, to be involved in passive activities, to adhere frequently to deviant norms, to manifest behavior problems, to be arrested frequently by the police, and to exhibit psychological vulnerability (Duttweiler, 1997).

There are several ways to measure dropout rates. One, called the event dropout rate, is the proportion of learners who were enrolled in one year who were not enrolled in the following year and did not earn a high school credential in the intervening year. According to this measure, 5% of all young people 15–24 years old who were enrolled in school dropped out of grades 10–12 in 1998. However, in urban areas, the dropout rate was about 6%, compared with about 4% in suburban areas. Learners in urban areas also appeared to drop out at a higher rate than rural learners (National Center for Education Statistics, 2000). See Figure 1-2.

While any one or even several factors do not necessarily place learners at risk, combinations of the following circumstances identify the potential to drop out:

School Related
- conflict between home/school culture
- ineffective discipline system
- lack of adequate counseling
- negative school climate
- lack of relevant curriculum
- passive instructional strategies
- inappropriate use of technology
- disregard of learner learning styles
- retentions/suspensions
- low expectations
- lack of language instruction

DROPOUT AND COMPLETION RATES

Dropout and completion measures	Total	White, non-Hispanic	Black, non-Hispanic	Hispanic	Asian/Pacific Islander
Percentage of youth ages 15 – 24 who dropped out of grades 10 – 12, October 1998 to October 1999 (event dropout rate)	5.0	4.0	6.5	7.8	5.0
Percentage of youth ages 16 – 24 who were dropouts in 1999 (status dropout rate)	11.2	7.3	12.6	28.6	4.3
Percentage of youth ages 18 – 24 who were high school completers in 1999 (completion rate)	85.9	91.2	83.5	63.4	94.0

Source: National Center for Educations Statistics, 2000.

Figure 1-2. Percentage of 15- through 24-year-olds who dropped out of grades 10–12, percentage of 16- through 24-year-olds who dropped out, and percentage of 18- through 24-year-olds who completed high school, by race/ethnicity, in the 1998–1999 school year.

Community Related
• lack of community support services or response
• lack of community support for schools
• high incidences of criminal activities
• lack of school/community linkages

Learner Related
• poor school attitude
• low ability level
• attendance/truancy
• behavior/discipline problems
• pregnancy
• drug abuse
• poor peer relationships
• nonparticipation
• friends have dropped out
• illness/disability
• low self-esteem/low self-efficacy

Family Related
• low socioeconomic status
• dysfunctional home life
• lack of parental involvement
• low parental expectations
• non-English-speaking home
• ineffective parenting/abuse
• high mobility

The National Center for Education Statistics (1996) revealed the following facts about the dropout situation in this country:

• Five out of every 100 young adults enrolled in high school in 1995 left school before October of 1996 without successfully completing a program. This estimate of 5% is on a par with those reported over the last 10 years.
• Although dropout rates were highest among learners age 19 or older, about three-fourths of the current year dropouts were ages 15 through 18; moreover, 43% of the 1996 dropouts were 15 through 17 years of age.
• A larger percentage of Hispanic learners, compared with white learners, leave school short of completing a high school program. Although the 6.7% rate for African-American learners falls between the rate of 9% for Hispanics and 4.1% for whites, the differences are not significant.
• In 1996, young adults living in families with incomes in the lowest 20% of all family incomes were five times as likely as their peers from families in the top 20% of the income distribution to drop out of high school. Two-thirds of this gap was due to differences between learners in the lowest and middle income groups.
• Learners who remain in school after the majority of their age cohort has left drop out at higher rates than their younger peers.
• Over the past 50 years, the value of a high school education has changed dramatically. During the 1950s, a high school degree was considered a valued asset in the labor market, and through the 1970s, a high school diploma continued to open doors to many promising career opportunities. In recent years, however, advances in technology have fueled the demand for a highly skilled labor force, transforming a high school education into a minimum requirement for entry into the labor market.
• Because high school completion has become a requirement for accessing additional education, training, or the labor force, the economic consequences of leaving high school without a diploma are severe. On average, dropouts are more likely to be unemployed than high school graduates and to earn less money when they eventually secure work. High school dropouts are also more likely to receive public assistance than high school graduates who do not go on to college. This increased reliance on public assistance is likely due, at least in part, to the fact that young women who drop out of school are more likely to have children at younger ages and more likely to be single parents than high school graduates. The individual stresses and frustrations associated with dropping out have social implications as well: Dropouts make up a disproportionate percentage of the nation's prison and death row inmates.
• Secondary schools in today's society are faced with the challenge of increasing curricular rigor to strengthen the knowledge base of high school graduates, while at the same time increasing the proportion of all learners who successfully complete a high school program. Monitoring high school dropout and completion rates provides one measure of progress toward meeting these goals.

The twelfth annual dropout report from the National Center for Education Statistics (NCES) spans the 28-year time period from 1972 through 1999. Data from the October 1999 Current Population Survey (CPS) of the U.S. Census Bureau are used to compute national high school dropout and completion rates and rates by background characteristics such as sex, race/ethnicity, family income, and region of the country. The report revealed the following about the dropout situation in this country:

• Over the last decade, between 347,000 and 544,000 10th through 12th grade learners left school each year without successfully completing a high school program. Status dropout rates represent the proportion of young adults ages 16 through 24 who are out of school and who have not earned a high school credential. Status rates are higher than event rates because they include all dropouts in this age range, regardless of when they last attended school.
• Five out of every 100 young adults enrolled in high school in October 1998 left school before October 1999 without successfully completing a high school program. This estimate was similar to the estimates reported over the last 10 years, but lower than those reported in the early 1970s.
• Hispanic learners were more likely than white learners to leave school before completing a high school program; in 1999, 7.8% of Hispanic learners were event dropouts, compared with 4% of white learners. However,

the event dropout rate of white learners was not significantly different from those of African-American learners (6.5%) or Asian learners (5%).

- In 1999, young adults living in families with incomes in the lowest 20% of all family incomes were five times as likely as their peers from families in the top 20% of the income distribution to drop out of high school.

- Although dropout rates were highest among learners age 19 or older, about two-thirds (67.3%) of the current-year dropouts were ages 15 through 18; moreover, about two-fifths (43.2%) of the 1999 dropouts were ages 15 through 17.

- In October 1999, some 3.8 million young adults were not enrolled in a high school program and had not completed high school. These youths accounted for 11.2% of the 34.1 million 16 through 24-year-olds in the United States in 1999. This estimate is consistent with the estimates reported over the last 10 years but lower than those reported in the early 1970s.

- The status dropout rate of whites remains lower than that of African-Americans, but over the past quarter of a century, the difference between the rates of whites and African-Americans has narrowed. In addition, Hispanic young adults in the United States continue to have a higher status dropout rate than whites or African-Americans.

- In 1999, the status dropout rate for Asian/Pacific Islander young adults was 4.3% compared with 28.6% for Hispanics, 12.6% for African-Americans, and 7.3% for whites.

- In 1999, 44.2% of Hispanic young adults born outside the United States were high school dropouts. Hispanic young adults born in the United States were much less likely to drop out. However, when looking at just those young adults born in the United States, Hispanic youths were still more likely to drop out than other young adults.

- High school graduates, on the average, earn $6,415 more per year than high school dropouts.

- Each year's class of dropouts will cost the country over $200 billion during their lifetime in lost earnings and unrealized tax revenue.

- Eighty-two percent of America's prisoners are high school dropouts.

- In October of 1989, 35% of those who had dropped out of school were not employed—only about one-half of those who had dropped out in the previous 12 months were employed.

- Learners from low-income families are 2.4 times more likely to drop out of school than are children from middle-income families and 10.5 times more likely than learners from high-income families. See Figure 1-3.

Monitoring the various aspects of learner performance is the crucial element in identifying at-risk learners and helping them progress through school. These aspects include the following:

- Attendance–Since poor attendance often foreshadows dropping out, personal attention from the school is needed at the first sign of excessive absenteeism.

- Testing–New sensitive testing devices can be used to identify learners' learning strengths and weaknesses so that compensatory measures can be taken early.

- Educational history–By maintaining comprehensive academic profiles of learners, educators can facilitate their placement in proper compensatory programs based on their past experience and can facilitate appropriate placement in new schools of transferees.

During the past three decades, more national and state attention has been directed toward dropout prevention than at any point in our history. The problem has intensified with major shifts in the workplace, a new social order, the advent of technology, and globalization of the economy.

Changes in the educational system will have to take place in order to adequately address the dropout problem and identified issues related to it:

- The central lesson we have had reinforced is that young people are the sum total of the experiences they bring to the school. Teachers can change, reinforce, and get maximum potential from young people. Of all the professional service providers, teachers are the most effective change agents. The challenge is to provide competent and caring teachers. In this millennium, all young people should have access to quality instructional programs and qualified teachers at every level.

- We have learned that programs do not make a difference; people make a difference. Any success we have had with eradicating the dropout problem has been because of a caring significant adult, usually a teacher. Young people who were at risk of dropping out of school often refer to a teacher or an administrator who helped to make the difference in their lives. In far too many places we have experimented with young people who are at risk by purchasing and installing new programs often without any input from the teachers or staff who will implement the programs. A major investment in the professional development of personnel who work with young people is the highest priority. We should not overlook the fact that many young people who do not complete high school are capable of doing excellent school work. The missing ingredient for them is a teaching force that is able to recognize their potential and get maximum results from their efforts regardless of poverty or other limiting factors.

- In this millennium, there should be an expectation that every learner will succeed, and there should be resources to make this a reality. All learners should be taught by teachers who are competent in the subject area being taught. The traditional model of grades 1–12 should gradually diminish for some learners, and there should emerge new models that should be based on learner strengths and interest such as theme schools (magnet or charter) with a particular curricular focus (i.e. vocational/technical, art, music, etc.). The typical school schedule should change, and there should be places in the community for young people of school age to be involved in service learning endeavors.

• We should recognize and celebrate individual differences and honor diversity, ceasing in our quest to "normalize" everybody. There is documented evidence that learners respond to projected expectations. There should be a full recognition and utilization of those institutions and places beyond the walls of the school that "teach" and effectively reach young people. The present alternative school that is used primarily as a means of removing disruptive learners from regular schools should cease to exist. When learners' academic and social needs and interests are met, there will be no need for this expensive alternative model that has proven to be ineffective.

• This millennium should usher in a major shift in education that will incorporate valuing and celebrating diversity and ensuring that learners are able to experience a smooth transition through each level of the educational system. In this millennium, there should be a renewed commitment to providing a quality education, void of labels and failures and reflective of relevance and excellence.

DROPOUT RATE CHARACTERISTICS

Characteristic	Status dropout rate (percent)	Number of status dropouts (thousands)	Population (thousands)	Percent of all dropouts	Percent of population
Total	11.2	3,829	34,173	100.0	100.0
Sex					
Male	11.9	2,032	17,106	53.1	50.1
Female	10.5	1,797	17,066	46.9	49.9
Race/ethnicity					
White, non-Hispanic	7.3	1,636	22,408	42.7	65.6
Black, non-Hispanic	12.6	621	4,942	16.2	14.5
Hispanic	28.6	1,445	5,060	37.7	14.8
Asian/Pacific Islander	4.3	65	1,515	1.7	4.4
Age					
16	3.5	139	3,995	3.6	11.7
17	6.7	278	4,137	7.3	12.1
18	12.6	489	3,870	12.8	11.3
19	13.6	559	4,121	14.6	12.1
20 through 24	13.1	2,366	18,050	61.8	52.8
Recency of immigration					
Born outside the 50 states and the District of Columbia					
Hispanic	.44.2	994	2,250	26.0	6.6
Non-Hispanic	7.0	133	1,909	3.5	5.6
First generation					
Hispanic	16.1	240	1,494	6.3	4.4
Non-Hispanic	5.0	94	1,893	2.5	5.5
Second generation or more					
Hispanic	16.0	211	1,316	5.5	3.9
Non-Hispanic	8.5	2,156	25,130	56.3	74.1

Source: National Center for Education Statistics, 2000.

Figure 1-3. Status dropout rates and number and distribution of 16- through 24-year-olds who dropped out, by background characteristics, in the 1998–1999 school year.

Workforce Considerations

The U.S. Department of Labor (1999) reported the following on the American workforce:

- In an economy where what we earn very much reflects what we learn, there is important new evidence on the kinds of skills that matter in the labor market. A wide range of skills is important in the new economy: Formal education and workforce experience, on-the-job training, and a variety of competencies needed to perform different occupations all are rewarded. Workers must enter the workforce with strong basic and job-related skills, and they must be prepared to learn new skills continuously in their places of employment, over the course of their lives.

- Despite the progress of the last several years, certain groups continue to experience weak attachment to the labor market or high unemployment. For instance, African-American teens still suffer unemployment rates of nearly 30%, just as they did 20 years ago during an earlier boom. And while welfare recipients have entered the labor market in record numbers, many experience frequent job turnover and low earnings, while those on the rolls increasingly reflect a hard-to-employ population. Programs that raise the skills of these groups and enable them to enter and prosper in the mainstream economy should be among our highest priorities. And those workers who have been displaced by new technology, international trade, and other sources of workplace restructuring must be ensured access to the kinds of reemployment services that will enable them to regain the earnings and employment that they have lost through no fault of their own.

The attitudes of young people leaving the education system reflect in part their experiences at home and in school. One life goal consistently rated 'very important' by young men and women was 'being successful in work.' A survey of 1992 high school seniors found that 89% of the men and 90% of the women rated 'being successful in work' as a 'very important goal.' Two of the other most highly rated goals in the 1992 survey were 'finding steady work' ('very important' for 87% of men and 89% of women) and 'having strong friendships' ('very important' for 80% of both men and women). Two years later in 1994, these values continued to be highly rated by the former high school seniors. Another value that was highly rated two years after high school was 'providing better opportunities for my children' which was cited by 91% of the young adults as 'very important' (Bureau of Labor Statistics, 1999).

The difficulties in entering the job market for dropouts, and youth in general, are highlighted by examining their labor force and unemployment status. About 57% of 1998-99 dropouts were in the labor force (employed or looking for work), and 26% of those were unemployed. Of the 1998 high school graduates who were not in college, 84% were in the labor force, and 18% of those in the labor force were unemployed (Bureau of Labor Statistics, 1999).

By the year 2005, we're going to see quite a different workforce than we see today, a much more diverse workforce in the United States. Many more women and many more so-called minorities will be a part of the workforce. By 2010, the average person getting a technology degree will be a female or a minority male or female. Companies are going to have to learn how to thrive with a much more diverse workforce than we have today.

As more women and two-parent working families enter into the workforce, we will have to come up with more flexibility to accommodate both the work and personal demands of these people so that they can raise families as well as hold down careers. Today, we still think about a normal workday and a five-day workweek. Flexible work hours and job-sharing to accommodate and benefit people with significant demands outside the workplace exist only in a small fraction of the jobs (Minkin, 1995).

By 2005, we're going to have to have a different view of how people accomplish work. The communications revolution and new technologies will make it easier to accomplish work off-site and on a schedule that is more accommodating to the rest of the worker's life responsibilities. It will be easier to do productive work and stay connected to colleagues when away from the office or working outside a normal eight to five time frame (Minkin, 1995).

The level of education required in this new workforce will also change. The fastest-growing occupations are those that employ knowledgeable workers, where a college education is a minimum requirement. A picture of an older, more educated, and higher-paid workforce emerges, one that will have different attitudes and expectations about the relationship of people to their jobs (Grantham, 2000).

Though the United States keeps spending more on learners, performance keeps declining. An identifiable rise in illiteracy among the youth is also producing a growing segment of the population with limited skills in mathematics, English, history, geography, and general culture. A recent study of mathematics proficiency of the country's 12th graders showed that only a very small percent are operating at the highest level and less than half are able to handle the math traditionally taught in the first few years of high school. Yet many occupations projected to grow most rapidly by 2005 will require at least this level of proficiency in mathematics. These include not only science and engineering, but also many of the occupations in health care and the highly skilled blue-collar trades such as tool-and-die making (Minkin, 1995).

In 1995, Boyett provided this challenging look at the American labor force:

- There is no doubt that the American workforce has changed in dramatic ways. Not so very long ago the American workforce was predominantly white male. Non-Hispanic white males once represented nearly two-thirds of the U.S. workforce. As America approaches the end of the twentieth century, that is no longer the case. Since the 1960s, the proportion of the workforce that is non-Hispanic white male has been declining steadily. If current trends continue, white males will represent less than 40% of the workforce by the year 2005, down from 60% in 1960.

- One of the reasons white males no longer dominate the workforce is that women have entered the workforce in record numbers. In 1950, only a little more than one-third of all U.S. adult women over the age of 16 held jobs or were actively looking for work. By 1980, half of them were. The Bureau of Labor Statistics estimated that by the year 2000 over 60% of U.S. adult women will be in the workforce. The higher participation rates of women means that by the year 2000, nearly half of the American workforce will be female.

- As more women and mothers entered the workforce, the structure of the American family changed. Since 1960, the proportion of two-income families has almost doubled, and the proportion of what were considered traditional families—those in which the husband was in the labor force and the wife wasn't—has dropped from 61% to just 26%. Perhaps more importantly, the proportion of children in two-parent families with both parents in the labor force has grown from 36% to 61%.

- If it is no longer possible for employees to neatly separate work and family, career and the rest of life, then it is equally unrealistic for employers to expect their employees to do so. The family baggage, like it or not, sits right there on the factory floor or in the middle of the office. And there is a lot of baggage.

- Today, over one-half of all first marriages in the United States end in divorce and nearly 60% of all of the people getting divorced have children under the age of 18. One million children a year experience the trauma of seeing their parents' marriage dissolve, often in an ugly and protracted dispute in which the children themselves become barter in the struggle. If current trends continue, fully one-third of all children who were born in the 1980s will see their parents divorce.

- The high divorce rate and the explosion of out-of-wedlock birth means that many American children live in single-parent households. The percentage of white children living with one parent has almost tripled over the last three decades, and the number of African-American children living in one-parent households has doubled. Now, nearly 20% of all white children and over half of all black children live in one-parent families.

- Over one-fourth of all children born in the United States today are born to unmarried mothers. Two out of every three black children are born out of wedlock, and one out of every five white children are born out of wedlock. Fourteen hundred teenage girls per day become mothers. Two-thirds of these girls are unmarried and only 60% will ever receive a high school diploma. Given current trends, by age 20, 44% of all girls in the United States and 63% of all black girls will become pregnant at least once. Twenty percent of these teen

pregnancies will even be planned. The United States has the dubious distinction of having one of the highest birthrates for 15-to 19-year-olds of all Western industrialized countries.

- Frequently, single-parent homes are also poor homes. Almost 45% of single-parent households that are headed by a woman—and most are headed by women—fall below the poverty line, compared to only 7.8% of two-parent households. Correspondingly, approximately one-half of all children in single-parent families live in poverty, and three-fourths can expect to live in poverty for some period of time, possibly an extended period of time, before they reach 18 years of age.

- If children in single-parent homes have difficulties, children in two-parent households don't find their lives to be too much better. There may be two parents in the family, but they aren't around during most of the day, since both are usually working. Consequently, many children end up caring for themselves. By some estimates, nearly 1.4 million children ages 5 to 14 are latchkey kids, left to fend for themselves during much of the day, and as many as 3.4 million kids in roughly the same age group take care of themselves either before or after school for several hours each day.

- Then, of course, there is the problem of youth violence. American kids are killing, dying, and bleeding. Homicide by firearms is the third leading cause of death for 15- to 19-year-old white youths and *the* leading cause of death for 15- to 19-year-old black youths. The number of children dying from homicide has increased 48% since 1984. The number of children arrested for murder each year has jumped 55% in the last 10 years. More adolescents now die from violence, especially violence involving firearms, than from any other cause, and guns are a factor in 75% of all adolescent homicides and over half of all adolescent suicides.

Lerman and Schmidt (1999) offered an assessment of broad social, economic, and demographic trends and the effects of these trends on the present and future labor force. They focus on demographic trends, work and family issues, health and pension patterns, technical change, adjustment to low unemployment, globalization, and the plight of low-skilled workers:

- Important demographic trends will take place in the workforce over the next 10–15 years. The emerging patterns are the result of ups and downs in birthrates (low in the late 1920s and early 1930s, high in the late 1940s through the early 1960s, and modest in the late 1970s through the early 1990s). The population and labor force will continue to diversify, as immigration continues to account for a sizable part of population growth. Projections suggest that the Hispanic and Asian shares of the population will rise from 14% in 1995 to 19% in 2020.

- Bureau of Labor Statistics projections imply that over the next decade, 40 million people will enter the workforce, about 25 million will leave the workforce, and 109 million will remain. Although only a modest reduction will take place in the overall growth in the workforce (from 1.3% per year to 1.1% per year), the composition of growth will generate rising shares of young (under 25) and older (45 and over) workers and a decline in the share of middle-age workers.

- The specific trends in the age composition of the workforce vary with future time periods and are subject to uncertainty related to labor force participation rates. The aging of the population is largely the result of a boom in births during the 1946–64 period. Over the coming decade (through 2005), substantial growth will occur among 45 to 64-year-olds, but the number over age 65 will increase only modestly (by 5%). However, between 2005 and 2010, the population of 65 to 69-year-olds will rise by 17% and then explode by another 37% in the 2010–2020 period.

- After declining by 9% from 1986 to 1996 and not growing between 1976 and 1986, the youth labor force will keep pace with the overall labor force with an expected 15% increase over the next decade. More dramatic are the changing patterns of growth among prime-age workers and older workers. The prime-age group of 25 to 54-year-olds accounted for virtually all the workers added to the labor force over the last two decades.

- Between 1976 and 1996, 38 million prime-age workers and 1.7 million workers 55 and over joined the labor force, while reductions in the youth labor force amounted to about 2.1 million. Over the next decade, instead of having nearly all increases in employment coming from the 25 to 54-year-old age group, fewer then one in three (31%) of the added workers will be in this category. Nearly half of the additional workers will come from the 55-and-older category, while about one in five will come from the youth labor force.

- Shifts in the ethnic composition of the workforce will continue the patterns of recent decades. Immigrants will account for as much as half of net population growth over the next decades. Between 1996 and 2006, white non-Hispanic entrants will make up 49% of new labor force entrants, up from 43% during the previous U.S. decade, but well below the 1995 level of 76%. As a result, the share of non-Hispanic whites will fall to 73% in 2005. Of the nearly 15 million worker increase in the 1996–2006 period, about 7 million will be Hispanic or Asians. Hispanic-Americans will raise their share of new workers slightly from 29% to 31%, as will Asian-Americans, whose share will grow from 14.5% to 15.7%. By 2020, white non-Hispanic workers will make up only 68% of the workforce.

- One concern about the changing ethnicity is the potential impact on the educational structure of the workforce. Hispanic workers have the lowest educational attainment of any major ethnic group: Only 55% of the Hispanic population over age 25 had completed high school as of 1997, well below the 85% completion levels among non-Hispanics. Thus, unless Hispanic youth and immigrants raise their educational attainment, their growing presence in the job market will lower the educational base of the labor force at the very time when the demand for skills is continuing to increase.

- The expanding share of Asians in the labor force will moderate this trend, since their educational attainment is higher than the rest of the workforce. As of 1997, 42% of Asians over 25 had at least a bachelor's degree, well above the 23% rate for the overall population. As a whole, immigrants have an education profile that embodies higher proportions lacking a high school diploma but the same share of college graduates as non-immigrants.

- While the last two decades witnessed significant increases in the share of women in the workforce (rising from 40.5% in 1976 to 46.2% in 1996), the female share will barely increase over the next decade. Still, by 2006 women will account for nearly half (47%) of the workforce. However, given the age composition shift away from the 25 to 44-year-olds, a declining share of women workers will be mothers with young children.

- Working parents, especially working mothers, report a great deal more stress in their lives than other workers. Journalists and academics argue that the very structure of the workplace contributes to that stress; few jobs allow workers the flexibility of dealing with family responsibilities during normal business hours. Some employers have adopted policies to make the workplace more "family-friendly," including flex-time, job sharing, generous parental leave following the birth of a child, and on-site child care. Evidence on the success of these programs in reducing stress is mixed. A rising share of workers are choosing self-employment, consulting, temporary work, or other forms of contingent work, which gives them more flexibility in balancing work and family responsibilities. Moreover, an increasing share of men and women are providing assistance to elderly relatives. Women provide the majority of eldercare, and many providing eldercare are part of the so-called "sandwich generation," caring for children and elderly relatives at the same time.

- Unmarried mothers living in poverty often face particular difficulties managing their work and family responsibilities. Because of the lack of affordable child care, these women often must place their children in poor-quality care. States do provide some subsidized child care, but the programs in several large states have long waiting lists and cannot provide subsidies to all who apply. In addition, women who rely on public transportation often face long and logistically difficult trips getting from home to child care and work.

- Recent research has shown that poor-quality child care could ultimately take a toll on children. Research on the brain development shows that the first three years of life are key in developing a child's full intellectual and emotional potential. Poor-quality care reduces a child's future cognitive abilities and emotional health.

- With the economy apparently running out of skilled workers, since nearly all were already employed earlier in the business cycle, employers must turn to less-qualified workers to fill the new jobs. These pressures are good for the disadvantaged: Firms are more willing to take inexperienced, less educated workers, to expand training, and to lower hiring standards. But shortages of high-skilled workers could lead to inflationary wage increases, while adding low-skilled workers could lower productivity and raise costs.

- The growth in information technology and changes in work organization have likely contributed to the rising demand for and return to higher-order cognitive skills. Anecdotal evidence shows that new technologies and workplace practices often require workers to have good writing and verbal skills, good math skills, and good problem-solving skills. In addition, given the increased autonomy and responsibilities in many environments, there is evidence that so-called soft skills—motivation, work habits, and so on—have become more important.

EDUCATIONAL REFORM—CHALLENGES

The restructured school is based in part on a recognition that the United States and other nations are entering into a new economic and information era and that industrial analogies for schooling are not working and will not be useful for our children in the 21st century. The model for the restructured school is based upon the assumption that the world we are entering will be governed by information, not manufacturing technologies. The model presupposes that meaningful learning is a personal experience involving self, readiness, understanding, and inquiry. The graduate of the restructured new American school is a continuous learner, a flexible, caring person who is competent, can solve problems, take responsibility, process information, and make decisions. The development of such capacities is a necessary condition for forming successful persons who can function in an effective and just society (Hill, 1992).

The futures of our free and democratic society and our free-market economy depend on public education. So do the individual futures of millions of children, who will need to live fulfilling lives, serve as good citizens, and contribute to our economy. Public education faces a great many challenges for the following reasons:

- Technology has influenced school, work, and home life.
- Children are threatened by crime, violence, ignorance, and poverty.
- Communities are changing and becoming more diverse.
- Mass media grips our children, giving them more knowledge at an earlier age.
- Children shun authority, traditional values, and responsibilities.
- A "hurry-up" society often lacks a sense of community.

- Changing workplace demands create a need for higher levels of literacy.
- Knowledge about learning styles demands new kinds of education.
- Peers exert a powerful influence on values.

Against this backdrop of social disarray, conditions affecting the nation's children have steadily gotten worse, making education in the classroom even more difficult. In the early 1990s, 25% of American children under six lived in poverty, compared to 14.5% of Americans of all ages. That fact alone is an indication that we desperately need to care even more for and about our children.

While these growing challenges may seem overwhelming, the nation's schools are committed to taking learners as they are and to making sure they are well-prepared for life in the 21st century (Uchida, 1996).

The characteristics of schools that have been successful in promoting achievement have become the focus of a body of research that characterizes effective schools. These characteristics are the foundation of campus improvement efforts across the country. Effective schools are those in which all learners master priority learning objectives. See Figure 1-4.

CHARACTERISTICS OF EFFECTIVE SCHOOLS

- A postitive atmosphere and supportive peer culture
- High but effective expectations for students
- Diverse opportunities for achieving success
- Basic skills development integrating the use of basic and vocational skills
- Minimal structure and high flexibility
- Opportunities to orient students to the broader world outside school (i.e., showing the correlation between education and work)
- Opportunities for students to become aware of their potential as workers and define clear, realistic goals
- Extensive guidance and counseling services
- Specific individualized educational plan for each student
- A high degree of student participation in extracurricular activities
- Intimate and caring work environment for staff and students alike
- Parents and community volunteers as mentors
- Individualized and small-group instructional materials and practices (e.g., cooperative learning, peer coaching)

Source: Bhaerman, R., & Kopp, K. (1998). *The School's Choice: Guidelines for Dropout Prevention at the Middle and Junior High School.* Columbus, OH: The Ohio State University, National Center for Research in Vocational Education.

Figure 1-4 An overview of characteristics of schools that succeed in meeting the needs of learners who are at risk of dropping out.

The Committee for Economic Development (1987) stated that no two good schools are exactly alike. However, in a statement developed by their Research and Policy Committee, the following key characteristics for providing a successful learning environment for at-risk learners were provided:

- School must be a place where learners want to learn.
- Character building should be emphasized through a positive, invisible curriculum.
- Administrators need to develop better leadership and management skills.
- Schools should encourage greater parental involvement.
- English language proficiency should be a primary objective of the school-wide program.
- Instructors should be given a more important role while being held far more accountable for learner progress and achievement.
- Extracurricular activities should become a more integral part of the school-wide program.
- Comprehensive social services and health care are needed to address problems that interfere with learning.

There is a broad-based agreement that the education we provide for our children will determine America's future role in the community of nations, the character of our society, and the quality of our individual lives. Thus, education has become the most important responsibility of our nation and our state, with an imperative for bold new directions and renewed commitments.

To meet the global challenges this responsibility presents, schools will need to provide the leadership necessary to guarantee access to a system of high-quality public education. This system will develop in all learners the knowledge, understanding, skills and attitudes that will enable all residents to lead productive and fulfilling lives in a complex and changing society. All learners should be provided appropriate and adequate opportunities to learn to

- communicate with words, numbers, visual images, symbols, and sounds;
- think analytically and creatively, and be able to solve problems to meet personal; social, and academic needs;
- develop physical and emotional well-being;
- contribute as citizens in local, state, national, and global communities;
- work independently and cooperatively in groups;
- understand and appreciate the diversity of our world and the interdependence of its peoples;
- contribute to the economic well-being of society; and
- continue to learn throughout their lives (Uchida, 1996).

The most prevalent elements of an effective school were identified by Wilson (1989) as follows:

- Instructional leadership–The school leadership defines the school's mission, frames the school's goals, and communicates these goals to staff, parents, students, and the community. Effective school leaders make it their business to ensure that all effective school correlates are present, promoted, and improved upon as necessary.

- Safe, orderly school climate–There is an orderly, purposeful school atmosphere free from threat of physical harm. The school climate is not oppressive. It is conducive to teaching and learning. Physical facilities are clean and attractive. Building repairs are made promptly.
- High expectations for student achievement–Teachers believe all students can learn, enthusiastically accepting the challenge to teach them. These high expectations are conveyed to both students and parents. Grading scales and student mastery standards are developed in order to promote academic excellence.
- Focus on instruction–The school's purpose is clearly focused on instruction which is understood by teachers, students, and parents. The curriculum serves as a blueprint for teaching and learning. It includes goals and objectives that present a clear picture of what students are expected to learn and how teachers can help them learn. Instruction is the basis for all major decisions made by the school administration and staff. Curriculum and instructional programs are interrelated so that school goals, grade-level and classroom objectives, instructional content and activities, and measures of academic performance are all carefully coordinated.
- Monitoring and measuring progress–Regular assessment and evaluation of students, programs, and staff provide information about whether the school is meeting its goals and whether these goals need revision. Evaluation of the school's effectiveness is based on student learning outcomes. A wealth of information about the student population is produced by multiple assessment methods such as tests, student work samples, and mastery skills checklists. These instruments are obtained and utilized according to a well-planned schedule. Testing results are used for decision-making in order to improve both individual student performance and the instructional program.
- Parent and community support–Parents and other members of the larger community understand, support, and are involved in the basic mission of the school. They are provided with avenues or significant roles for achieving this mission. (pp. 1-2)

CONSTRUCTING EFFECTIVE EDUCATIONAL ENVIRONMENTS FOR ALL LEARNERS

The development of school environments that meet the needs of all learners is based first on acceptance of the fact that, for the most part, traditional approaches have failed to change substantively overall patterns of learner achievement. In most schools, those categories of learners who have performed least well as a whole generally continue to do so. School-based educators and district or state level policymakers should understand, however, that such an admission is not an indictment, but rather simply a recognition that current organizational structures and patterns of practice are not matched to the needs of the school's current learners. Therefore, a change is in order—no more, no less. Open acceptance of this reality is an essential prerequisite for initiating the other changes that will be necessary to establish a more broadly successful educational environment. (Hixson & Tinzmann, 1990)

This process of change involves four strategic initiatives:
- redefining the cultural norms of the school
- refocusing the content, methods, and priorities of the instructional program
- attending to the personal/affective needs of learners and staff
- establishing new relationships between the school and learner's homes and the broader school community

PATTERNS AND ISSUES IN EDUCATIONAL REFORM

Much of the push for systemic educational reform stems from a recognition that the nation's social and economic structure has changed. The changes in traditional family structure, an increase in child poverty, the inadequacy of social-welfare and social-service programs, and a decreased sense of civic responsibility are among the factors that are directly or indirectly placing new expectations on educators (Conley, 1993). Economic forces and educational equity issues have combined to heighten calls for improved education for all learners. Although society's needs have changed radically since public schools were first instituted in America, many outdated and ineffectual purposes and methods have been retained by schools.

As workers are increasingly expected to weather multiple career changes, it is imperative for schools to emphasize the importance of lifelong learning, strengthen learners' thinking and problem-solving skills, and increase their adaptability. Reformers hope that by totally rethinking the very structure of the education system, schools will be better prepared to meet the needs of all children and the communities in which they live.

Conley's conceptualization of educational restructuring (1993) dovetails with the goals of systemic reform. He sets forth a framework of 12 dimensions of educational restructuring that are grouped into three subsets: central, enabling, and supporting variables. Leaner outcomes, curriculum, instruction, and assessment make up the central variables, labeled as such because they have a powerful direct effect on learning. Enabling variables— also closely related to instruction—consist of learning environment, technology, school-community relations, and time. Supporting variables, those further removed from the classroom, consist of governance, teacher leadership, personnel structures, and working relationships.

The Cross City Campaign for Urban School Reform (2001) provided the following snapshot of public high schools in the U.S.:
- Current enrollment: 12.8 million (net increase of 9 percent from 1985-1999)

- Drop-out rates: White, non-Hispanic, 8 percent; African-American, 14 percent; Hispanic, 30 percent (1998)
- Number of teachers: 1.5 million
- Average class size: 24 (teachers from public schools with a high minority enrollment had a slightly larger average class size than public teachers from schools with a low minority enrollment)
- Teacher qualifications: Students attending high schools in which African-Americans and Latinos comprise 90 percent or more of the student population are more than twice as likely to be taught by teachers without certification than their counterparts in schools where Whites comprise 90 percent or more of the student population. (High Schools in Focus)

The Cross City Campaign for Urban School Reform (2001) explains why smaller "schools" meet the special needs of students at risk. Indeed it is in small schools across the nation's major urban areas that the largest number of poor and working class youth are getting a challenging and rigorous education in an environment where they are well known and supported. A small school is characterized by the following:
- intent
- small size: preferably no more than 350 students in elementary schools, 500 in high schools
- cohesive, consistent, self-selected faculty
- substantial autonomy
- coherent curricular focus that provides continuous educational experience
- inclusive admissions
- consistent student body
- contiguous space, and
- vision....
- Students attending smaller high schools are more likely to pass their courses, accumulate credits, and attain a higher level of education than students who attend larger schools.
- Dropout rates are consistently, and often strikingly, lower in small schools. In New York City, for example, the dropout rate of schools with 2,000 students is twice as high as schools with 600 or fewer students.
- The average achievement of students as measured by standardized tests tends to be higher in small schools than in large schools....
- There is a consistent and often strong relationship between small school size and more equitable academic achievement across ethnicity and socioeconomic background—9 of the 11 reviewed studies found this relationship. Smaller school size predicts higher academic achievement among minority students and students from low-income families.
- Smaller high school size reduces the gaps between the average achievement levels of white students and students of color; and, between students from high and low socioeconomic backgrounds who attend the same school....

- Students in small schools are suspended less often, feel safer at school, use drugs less often, and are truant from school less often than students in larger schools.
- Smaller schools have fewer discipline problems in the classroom and principals report fewer problems such as assault and vandalism.
- Nine out [of] 11 studies found a positive relationship between smaller school size and lower levels of drug abuse, truancy, vandalism, and student victimization. *No studies* found a positive relationship between larger school size and lower levels of school violence and disorder....
- Small schools are more cost effective. When dividing educational costs by the number of graduates rather than the number of total students, small schools are found to be fiscally efficient. (Small Schools)

Conley (1992) described trends in school restructuring:

- The learner is being moved to the center of the instructional process by playing the roles of worker/client/customer/partner/participant. Learners must be actively involved in constructing meaning. They simply do not retain information for which there is no structure or reason. Learning must have utility. Often this is accomplished by linking learning to the world outside of the school or by having learning occur outside the school.
- The emphasis is on success, and instruction is being adapted to be congruent with the needs, capabilities, and motivations of the learner. Interestingly enough, this leads to a substantial increase, rather than a decrease, in the amount of content that can be taught.
- There is a resurgence in attempts to individualize instruction, although it might be more accurate to say "personalize" instruction. The emphasis is on the learner developing meaningful learning experiences in partnership with others. Teams are one means by which this is accomplished. Learners set individual and group learning goals and are held accountable for them. Learning can be achieved by helping others, tutoring, providing advice, and by studying new material independently. Team learning is personal and interactive, is developed in relation to goals, has utility, and leads to demonstrable outcomes.
- Assessment is becoming an integral part of the teaching/learning process as opposed to evaluation, which stands apart from it. Assessment provides a larger amount of feedback to learners, allowing them to continually improve their performance, rather than simply to judge performance at some arbitrary ending point. Learning is being analyzed in a more integrated fashion through an increasingly larger constellation of skills and abilities. This parallels changes in curriculum and instructional techniques. The emphasis is on the performance of the learner as an individual (or team member) in relation to predetermined standards and not necessarily in relation to the performance of national norming groups. If learners can master and apply certain identified skills, it is not necessary for some to fail in order to create a "normal distribution."
- Distinctions between subject areas in the curriculum are being reexamined. There are numerous attempts to redesign curriculum so that learners can be actively involved in constructing meaning, rather than having the structure determined solely by the teacher (or the textbook publishing company). The content, too, is under scrutiny. Is it relevant, accurate, meaningful? Is there a compelling reason for children to know the material? Can it be structured to allow all learners to achieve higher levels of mastery?
- The world around the school is becoming a source for curriculum. Local issues, problems, and resources are being integrated. Information from around the world, available to teachers and learners via technology, serves as the framework within which local issues can be understood and examined, creating curriculum that allows learners to understand global events in relation to the world in which they live.
- Learning environments are being redefined. All the structural boundaries of the current model are being challenged. Learners are staying with the same teacher or group of teachers for extended periods of time within the day, the school year, and from year to year, in both elementary and secondary schools. Multiage groupings of varying combinations, in which learners can proceed at developmentally appropriate paces and can serve as tutors for one another, are proliferating. The idea that learning can occur only within four walls when 25 young people interact with one certified teacher is rapidly being replaced with models in which varying combinations of adults and children interact both inside and outside of school.
- The community at large also plays a new role. Businesses and civic groups, local government, and social service agencies all have vital roles to play by offering services; coordinating their programs with those in the public schools; serving as volunteers and tutors; offering educational opportunities at work sites; helping teachers develop new skills and knowledge; and, most importantly, perceiving themselves as centrally involved in the education of the community's youth.

STANDARDS—AN ESSENTIAL ELEMENT IN EDUCATIONAL REFORM

Fletcher (2001) made the following observations about the national dropout dilemma in relationship to increasing graduation requirements and state standards:

- After decades of improvement, the nation's school completion rate has stagnated over the past 15 years despite the large amount of money and attention focused on education. Nearly one-quarter of the nation's students fail to graduate, though some go on to earn GEDs and other alternative credentials.

- Dropouts are 50 percent more likely to be unemployed than high school graduates, according to the National Center for Education Statistics. When they are employed, high school dropouts earn about 25 percent less than high school graduates.
- In 1940, only 38 percent of the nation's 25 to 29-year-olds had completed high school, partly because a diploma was not crucial for the agricultural and factory jobs that dominated the economy. By the mid-1980s, that number—which includes recipients of conventional high school diplomas and those who receive alternative credentials such as GEDs—had increased to 86 percent, where it has remained since.
- That figure masks a recent drop in the percentage of students who earn conventional high school diplomas, a credential researchers call essential in today's job market. That number has gone from roughly 80 percent to about 75 percent in the past 15 years.
- Now, as the national debate focuses on raising standards and tightening accountability, some experts say too little attention is being paid to students who will leave school before they can even begin to reap the benefits of the education reform movement.
- As states impose new standards and high-stakes tests for graduation and promotion, some predict that our dropout problem will only get more dire.
- Our challenge is to raise academic standards for all student, while simultaneously ensuring that at-risk students receive the supports they need to meet the standards and stay in school.
- The dropout problem is most severe in big cities. Crushing social problems and poor academic preparation often eliminate huge percentages of students from the rolls before they make it to graduation.
- Programs that divide huge high schools into smaller units, create more familiarity with staff and offer intensive remedial instruction to ninth-graders show promise. But they have not been widely implemented, even as more educators grow concerned about implications of the dropout problem. (Fletcher, 2001, p.4A)

Characteristics of schools in the education reform movement include the following:

- They are comprehensive in their approach; address all core academic subject areas, address all types of school organization and all grade levels; and align all resources (human, financial, and technological).
- They incorporate best-practices research and are the subjects of ongoing evaluation aimed at continued improvement.
- They provide faculty and community with a shared vision, focus, and organizing framework to shape and direct reform efforts.
- They provide high-quality professional development.
- They offer innovative and effective ways to involve parents and community in schooling.
- They aim to help all learners reach high standards.

The overwhelming challenge facing the American high school is to do a first-class job of the new basics—to make sure that all learners really master the academic subjects in the core curriculum and are able to apply what they know to the kind of real-world, complex problems they will routinely encounter as adults. If this is to happen, the standards that learners must meet will have to be defined, the learners will have to be motivated to take the necessary courses and to work hard enough to meet the standards, and the schools will have to have the resources needed to get these motivated learners to the standards (Marsh & Codding, 1999).

There is ample evidence to suggest that when learners are encouraged to work with challenging content under optimum teaching and learning conditions, they will make far greater progress than those learners who receive basic skills instruction. Standards that assume all learners can learn more and can learn at high levels help guard against the self-fulfilling prophecy of low achievement that low standards produce. Further, standards are an effective defense against parental complacency that undermines learner achievement. By adopting high standards and weaving them into the whole fabric of the education system, a basis is provided for implementing reforms and schools are able to reclaim their unique role of educating learners (Markham, 1993).

When implementing school reform, issues of financing, class size, and the condition of educational facilities must also be taken into consideration. Further, educators may require additional training as traditional teaching methods give way to new modes of learning. Learners should not be held to higher standards until the resources are in place to facilitate such achievement. It is also important to remember that developing standards is not a one-time undertaking but is a dynamic, self-renewing process. The change in American schools to reflect higher standards will not take place overnight. It will be the result of persistent effort over time.

Bottge and Yehle (1999) described the process which all educators should use in order to align curriculum with current standards:

- To ensure that teachers and administrators make the necessary adjustments in their curriculum, some states have test-based requirements for high school graduation. In addition to traditional testing, some states require learners to show what they have learned in demonstrations.
- In the wake of these pressures, all 50 states, the District of Columbia, and Puerto Rico have established standards to which local school districts must align their curriculum and instruction.
- Despite frustration over the time and effort needed to develop instruction matched to the assessments, the standards movement can help educators and community members articulate the skills that learners should acquire in order to lead productive lives at home and at work.

- Once there is agreement on these skills, teachers can plan lessons that have value both in and beyond school by linking pedagogy that promotes learner understanding to the standards described in Goals 2000, the SCANS report, state standards, and workforce competencies.
- Teachers should examine each level of standards (national, state, and local) in relation to workforce competencies and learn how they can map their standards using the "standards funnel." See Figure 1-5.

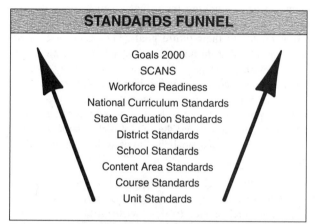

STANDARDS FUNNEL

Goals 2000
SCANS
Workforce Readiness
National Curriculum Standards
State Graduation Standards
District Standards
School Standards
Content Area Standards
Course Standards
Unit Standards

Source: Bottge, B., & Yehle, A. (1999, Fall). Making Standards-Based Instruction Meaningful for All. *The Journal for Vocational Special Needs Education, 22*(1), 23–32.

Figure 1-5. "Standards funnel" of national, state, school, and classroom standards.

EDUCATIONAL REFORM AND LEARNERS FROM SPECIAL POPULATIONS

To present a picture of the dropout situation, researchers at the Policy Information Center of the Educational Testing Service (ETS) analyzed national information, data from states, cities, other sources, and results of surveys of high school learners. Based on this research, Schwartz (1995) characterized the dropout population as follows:

1. Overall–Calculating the accurate dropout rate is nearly impossible, since some learners return to school, and schools differ in their definitions and counting methods. Nearly two-thirds of the dropouts leave before the tenth grade, 20% drop out by the eighth grade, and 3% do not even complete the fourth grade.
2. Ethnic differences–Hispanic learners are slightly more likely to drop out than African-Americans; Asian-American and white learners are less likely to drop out than both those groups. Nearly 40% of Hispanic learners who drop out do so before the eighth grade.
3. The urban rate–The dropout rate in large urban districts remains high, although it has decreased slightly in the last few years. In some districts it is double the national average. Also, as opposed to the national trend, the rate for African-American and Hispanic learners is increasing in some urban areas.

4. High school equivalency candidates–Each year, nearly half a million people get a high school equivalency General Educational Development (GED) certificate. The average age of GED candidates is 26, and more than 60% of them plan to continue their schooling after receiving a certificate.
5. Income and earnings potential–With respect to lifetime wages, the gap between dropouts and more educated adults is widening steadily as opportunities expand for higher skilled workers and disappear for the lesser skilled. For example, it is estimated that, overall, the 1993 dropout pool will earn $212,000 less than high school graduates, and $812,000 less than college graduates. Further, in the last 20 years, the earnings level for dropouts doubled while it nearly tripled for college graduates, a trend that is likely to intensify in the future.
6. Marital status and parenthood–About one-fifth of the dropouts in the study (approximate age 18) were married, living as married, or divorced, with females more likely than males to be married. Nearly 40% had a child or were expecting one. Nearly one-third of the females who dropped out cited pregnancy as the reason. Interestingly, some youth said they dropped out because they wanted to have a family (12% of the females and 6% of the males).
7. School and home stability–More than half the dropouts moved during the four-year study period, compared with 15% of the graduates. Nearly a quarter of the dropouts changed schools two or more times. Twice as many dropouts as graduates ran away from home: 12% and 6%.
8. School experiences–A large majority of dropouts were enrolled in a general high school program, with very few in a college preparatory program. Almost one-fifth were held back a grade, and almost half failed a course. They were also more likely than the persisters to have been enrolled in special education or alternative programs. Dropouts reported the following information about personal behavior during their last two years in school:
- Almost one-half missed at least 10 days of school.
- One-third cut class at least 10 times.
- One-quarter were late at least 10 times.
- One-third were put on in-school suspension, suspended or put on probation.
- Six percent were transferred to another school for disciplinary reasons.
- Eleven percent were arrested.
- Eight percent spent time in a juvenile home or shelter.
9. Attitudes and expectations–Dropouts tended to believe that they don't have control over their lives, that chance and luck are important, and that something always seemed to stop them from getting ahead. Conversely, graduates felt that they had a great deal of control over their lives, a belief known to promote educational achievement.

Dropouts did not differ significantly from graduates in their sense of self-concept, with both expressing some negative personal feelings. Nearly one-half felt "useless at times," one-third thought they were "no good at all," and nearly one-quarter "didn't have much to be proud of."

Despite leaving school, 85% of the dropouts planned to attain at least a high school education. About one-fifth expected to attend a career education school; a third expected to attend college, with 11% looking forward to getting a degree; and 5% expected to get a master's degree.

10. Reasons for dropping out–As reported, usually a variety of school problems and personal factors combined to cause a learner to drop out. Dropouts cited the following reasons most frequently:

- didn't like school in general or a particular transfer school
- was failing, getting poor grades, or couldn't keep up with school work
- didn't get along with teachers and/or learners
- had disciplinary problems, was suspended or expelled
- didn't fit in
- didn't feel safe
- got a job, had a family to support, or had trouble managing both school and work
- got married, got pregnant (one-third were pregnant when they left), became a parent, wanted to have a family, or had a family to take care of
- had friends who dropped out.
- wanted to travel
- had a drug or alcohol problem

Among the principal barriers to full participation by all learners in everything that the school has to offer are

- inflexible school structures and schedules based more on history and inertia than learner or family needs;
- abuses of tracking and ability grouping that often serve simply to separate learners on the basis of perceived differences in ability, interest, or potential rather than to promote improved educational attainment;
- misuses of testing where tests become used more as vehicles for sorting learners or allocating rewards and benefits than as a database for program planning;
- narrowness of curriculum and teaching practices, allowing many learners to become frustrated and disconnected from the basic instructional activities of the school;
- lack of support services for youth, reflecting a lack of understanding on the part of many educators of (1) the clear and direct connection between learners' life circumstances and their interest or ability to participate in any meaningful way in the school's instructional or other programs and (2) the vested interests of the school in seeing that learners' personal, emotional, and social needs are addressed;
- lack of early childhood programs similarly reflecting the unwillingness of many educators and policymakers to invest in prevention initiatives rather than remediation programs that could be made unnecessary; and finally
- lack of democratic governance, coupled with cumbersome and generally inefficient bureaucracies in most schools and districts, serving to further isolate and alienate those parents and community residents who need most to be involved in intimate partnerships with their children's schools—both for their children's benefit and their own (Hixson and Tinzmann, 1990).

For at-risk learners, the key to success in high school seems to be convincing them that a satisfying future is within their grasp and then showing them how their education relates to their future goals. People do not invest effort in tasks that do not lead to valued outcomes even if they know they can perform the task successfully. Learners who don't see a connection between high school and future success are doomed to spend their school years in a 'neutral' position. The way to turn on turned-off learners is to help them understand the role of high school achievement in reaching their goals in life as well as in education and employment.

> 'If you can give young people a reason to believe that they can change their future, then it is much easier to deal with violence and substance abuse and teenage pregnancy,' Dr. David Satcher, director of the Centers for Disease Control and Prevention, told the *New York Times* recently. 'We've found that those were not the problems; they were the symptoms. When young people don't have any hope for the future, they'll do anything.' (Academic Innovations, 2000)

There are seven basic reasons why special attention to the problem of at-risk children and youth is not only important, but essential, to the long-term success of the broader and more general drive to restructure schools.

1. Quality and equality–Research findings underscore the need for a new priority in the school reform agenda that recognizes that true educational quality and equality are inseparable. In his book, *A Place Called School*, Goodlad noted the continuing denial of equal access to knowledge for all learners in nominally desegregated schools. There is a similar danger if restructuring efforts are driven only by the normative needs of learners as a whole without specific and overt attention to the particular needs of those learners who have historically been least well-served by most public schools.

2. Escalation of the problem–Each year, increasing numbers of learners are entering schools from circumstances and with needs that schools are not prepared (or in some cases are unwilling) to accommodate. This requires that increased understanding and sensitivity to these new contexts for schooling become a more integral part of the national dialogue about educational reform than is currently the case.

3. Demands of the work force–The combined trends of a decreasing proportion of youth and increasing educational requirements for jobs at all levels require us to ensure that a significantly larger percentage of learners attain higher levels of intellectual skills and knowledge if we are to continue to be a first-level participant in the world economy.

4. Social development–A significant number of social problems are, at least in part, the result of inadequate education. The failure to educate millions of children is turning the potential for social profit into grave deficit, the cost of which American taxpayers will bear both financially and socially in terms of increased dependency and the loss of a common sense of purpose. Society, therefore, can avoid more costly problems in the future by investing more heavily in the development of all of its youth today.

5. New role of the school–Changing societal realities and expectations now require that schools attend to issues that were traditionally addressed by families and other community institutions. This is particularly evident in the increasing number of young parents who were themselves unsuccessful in school and, therefore, need additional support and assistance to support their own children's educational efforts.

6. Restrictive attitudes toward learner capabilities–Though attitudes are changing, there still remain a large number of educators as well as policymakers and members of the general public who believe that school failure can be primarily attributed to characteristics of learners and their families. While most teachers attributed the much reported success of Asian learners to hard work, they attributed the failure of American minorities (primarily African-Americans and Hispanics) to lack of capability.

7. Legal responsibilities–Lastly, it is important that, in designing strategies for school restructuring, educators and others are mindful that providing equitable education for all learners is also a legal requirement. Titles VI, IX, and Section 504 of the Civil Rights Act all provide broad-reaching standards for complying with equity and non-discrimination aspects of the law as it applies to education (Hixson & Tinzmann, 1990).

Baas (1991) identified positive elements for schools to implement in order to decrease the dropout numbers:

- Prevention must begin early—in kindergarten or first grade. Dollars spent on early intervention can yield up to a six-fold savings in potential future costs of dealing with children who drop out.
- Aggressive leadership "by school boards, superintendents, principals, and teachers" is needed to make things happen.
- Parents are crucial. Incorporate them any way you can.
- Specific solutions must be school-based, rather than delivered from above and should be woven into a comprehensive K-12 program.

- Remedial programs are out. Teachers should stress high ethical and intellectual standards matched to realistic, attainable goals.
- Teachers and principals need the training, encouragement, and "empowerment" to become active decision-makers. All participants should understand precisely how they fit within a clear, predictable structure in which strategies can be adapted to meet each learner's specific needs.
- Teaching should focus on continuous progress in language skills and emphasize problem-solving and teamwork. Teachers need to be tough, compassionate, and professional. They also need to possess a strong sense of how to relate to the particular cultures represented in their learners.
- Classes (and, when possible, schools) need to be smaller to facilitate interaction and one-on-one contact with learners.
- Districts and state departments of education should serve as resources and encourage decision-making to be made where it counts—at the local level. Principals should be freed from bureaucratic tasks to work more closely with teachers and learners.
- Learners should never be allowed to disappear into anonymity. The school environment should be a place in which learners are esteemed for their unique abilities and strengths.
- Educators should integrate their services and goals with those of the basic social and health services in the community.
- School leaders need to mobilize the entire community. Businesses, senior citizens, clubs, and service groups can all provide extra funding, resources, and volunteers to work with learners.

INDIVIDUALS FROM SPECIAL POPULATIONS IN CAREER AND TECHNICAL PROGRAMS

General goals for all career and technical programs were outlined by Boyett (1995):

- Career and technical learning must emphasize intellectual skills as well as teach learners skills they will need on the job. Learners must know how to perform tasks that use thinking, estimation, reasoning, and judgment.
- Career and technical education must stress a number of skills within an area rather than teach a learner to do one job. They must "learn how to learn."
- Developing good career and technical education skills requires two years of training beyond high school. Community colleges play an important part in this reform.
- Learners should go to job sites to understand how the technologies they are learning are applied to the real world. By linking study and work through partnerships and apprenticeship programs, the theoretical aspects of education quickly become real.
- Business leaders and workers must help teachers and administrators plan career and technical education programs. These groups must be in constant communication.

Rather than learn only specific skills, learners must be versed in all aspects of a particular area. To be capable of adapting to a changing workplace, learners must know the full history and practice of a trade or industry.

It may be more comfortable to look the other way, but as educators and responsible citizens, it is imperative that American educators address the major learning problems of learners from special populations. Such a task will not be resolved overnight, but the immediate needs seem self-evident. Although schools are the target of discontent, due to their inability to meet the needs of these learners, it is clear that these individuals are the products of conditions that go far beyond the educational system. It will take the collaboration of many agencies, including health, social services, and education, to even begin to understand the extent of the problems, let alone find the solutions.

Kochhar and Deschamps (1992) stated that the educational community needs to unite to ensure that public policies preserve access for special populations to the full range of educational options. They proposed a "Bill of Rights 2000 for Youth With Special Needs" to include the following:

1. The right to accommodation of special learners in the full range of mainstream and special educational programs and services, including regular education, vocational education, transition services, job training, placement opportunities, and articulated postsecondary placement assistance.
2. The right to receive a comprehensive vocational assessment as part of transition services.
3. The right to be protected from economic arguments that current funding is inadequate to provide support services and access to mainstream programs and services for special needs students.
4. The right to be protected from program funding reductions that disproportionately impact special needs learners.
5. The right to have the needs of learners from special populations addressed in relation to national standards for education and job training.
6. The right to expect employers to support parent involvement in their children's education and preparation for work and independence, and to eliminate work-place barriers and disincentives to such involvement. (p. 19)

COMPETENCIES NEEDED BY CAREER AND TECHNICAL INSTRUCTORS

Career and technical instructors are faced with a great challenge as a result of the equal rights legislation for members of special populations. Learners with special needs enrolled in career and technical education programs will require assistance through appropriate resources and support services. The laws and guarantees are here to stay. Educators must begin to provide these learners with opportunities to develop their vocational potential. With staff development training and cooperative planning among professional personnel and agencies, preparing these individuals for competitive employment or postsecondary education can be a shared task.

Case Study . . . José

José is a learner with emotional problems. He is integrated into regular educational programs and works with a special education teacher periodically. He is very hyperactive and finds it difficult to concentrate on tasks or to remain in his seat for long periods of time. He often wanders around the room during class and laboratory activities. His actions are often haphazard and his behavior is frequently random, both in school and at home. There are times when he knows what he is doing. At other times he appears to be totally unaware of his behavior and its impact on others. José has average intelligence, but his grades in school have always been significantly below average. Because of this, his self-concept is poor. He has been having problems with his peers in the class. His mother has contacted Miss Gabriel, the guidance counselor at the school, because she is afraid that José is becoming involved with the neighborhood gang. Miss Gabriel has worked with Ms. Ramierez, the career and technical education instructor, to identify a volunteer peer in the classroom who can spend time with José working on laboratory team assignments. José has also been encouraged by Ms. Ramierez to become involved in the career and technical student organization. There are also plans for an industry mentor to meet with Jose once a month to provide encouragement and support.

In the beginning, Ms Ramierez was not very optimistic about José's chances of success in the program. A conference was recently held between José, Ms. Ramierez, Miss Gabriel, and Mr. Valencia (the special education teacher). The class rules and regulations were firmly emphasized and the consequences were discussed. Later, Mr. Valencia worked cooperatively with Ms. Ramierez to establish a system of behavior management techniques that would include José and could be reinforced by both the career and technical and special education instructors. As José's behavior becomes more appropriate, there are plans for him to become involved in some shadowing experiences in the community at several job sites that reflect the skills he is learning in the career and technical education program.

A student-teacher contract system was developed for José's participation in the career and technical education program. The contracts were set up so that the work would be self-paced. Since José contributed to the development of the contract, he feels more confident about his ability to complete the contract assignments. The contract system has proven to be effective in motivating him. His behavior has been steadily improving. His test grades have all been good since the collaborative planning began.

There have been many reasons for the reluctance of career and technical education teachers to work with learners with special needs in the past. Reasons commonly cited for this reluctance include negative attitudes, stereotypical thinking, and misconceptions.

Another contributing factor for the reluctance in working with these learners has been the practice of placing learners into career and technical education programs without adequately preparing either the learner or the instructor. In some cases, information about the learner has been withheld from these teachers. Often appropriate support services have been lacking.

Today, the level of commitment of career and technical education teachers toward serving learners from these special populations is rapidly increasing. These teachers, along with special needs personnel, counselors, school administrators, and interested members of the community at the local level are learning how to work together effectively to meet the challenge of educating these individuals. Within the past decade, the preparation of school personnel, including career and technical teachers, has emerged as a top priority. Many state and local school systems have recognized the need for professional development for those who work with or will be working with learners with special needs. Numerous in-service and staff development programs have been conducted to assist educators in understanding the need for their participation in this endeavor. Teacher preparation programs have focused on the development of the competencies necessary for working with learners from special populations. Effective curriculum materials have also been developed.

Providing learners with special needs with career and technical education opportunities is often accomplished through inclusion or integration of these learners into existing programs. Not every learner with special needs can or will be integrated into regular program activities. However, each learner, as an individual, must be given the chance to develop his or her vocational potential to the maximum degree.

As local schools respond to the mandates of equal access and equal rights legislation, efforts to include learners in regular programs are increasing. The philosophy of "inclusion" or "integration" recognizes that all learners are different from each other. Some learners have special learning problems, but this does not justify their exclusion from being educated with their peers in regular program activities. Bradley (1993) stated that inclusive schools provide services for learners within a unified educational system. This includes all learners in the school community—those with disabilities, those at risk of failing or dropping out, and those considered average.

Inclusion is a method of assuring equal access to career and technical programs for individuals from special populations. It is not, however, a practice of "dumping" learners with special needs into regular class settings without providing accommodations for their success.

Inclusion of learners from special populations means that proper support services and resources must be provided. This will make the task of providing appropriate educational experiences for these learners much easier for career and technical education instructors. The total responsibility for preparing learners should be shared. The technical knowledge and skills represented in career and technical education programs must be combined with the expertise of special needs coordinators, special education personnel, counselors, basic skills teachers, and agency representatives.

An effective process for including learners with special needs in career and technical programs should incorporate the following elements:

- development of a positive attitude on the part of teachers, administrators, and educational personnel
- assessment of the abilities and limitations of each learner (e.g., learner interest inventories, behavioral information, academic performance, work experiences, prevocational background, career development experiences)
- development of a work ethic concept by learners (i.e., work as a positive reinforcer and contribution to society)
- development of realistic career goals developed by teachers, support personnel, parents, and the learner
- removal of overgeneralized labels and substitution of a solid profile of individual abilities and limitations
- sharing of appropriate information among professionals working with learners with special needs and use of these data to develop effective instructional programs
- development and implementation of instructional arrangements through individualized learning plans
- availability of flexible scheduling and extended time in a program to develop required competencies
- utilization of instructional techniques that match the learning styles of learners with the instructional strategies used by instructors
- frequent assessment of learner progress through competency-based measures

Career and technical instructors should demonstrate certain professional competencies that are beneficial in working with learners with special needs. Generally, they have developed a high level of knowledge and skills in their particular area of expertise. Therefore, they should be able to identify the component parts that make up each work task. Learners with special needs often need to receive instruction in smaller, more basic steps. Because of their concrete, cumulative nature, many vocational tasks readily lend themselves to task analysis. Instructors should also provide ongoing reinforcement of learner performance. The tangible nature of vocational tasks allows teachers to design appropriate learning experiences for learners with special needs and to continuously observe learner performance. This provides an excellent opportunity to provide immediate and continuous reinforcement to them.

The education of learners with special needs requires the cooperative efforts of teachers, system-wide support personnel, parents, and the community. Career and technical education teachers, being committed to the goal of providing the best possible education for their learners, welcome the opportunity to work with other educators, community volunteers, and parents in helping these learners develop knowledge and skills required to become independent workers and contributing members of society.

Some specific competencies that are helpful for career and technical education personnel who work with learners with special needs include the ability to

- prepare members of the class for the inclusion of learners with special needs so that a positive learning environment is established;
- gather information to determine the educational and social needs of each learner;
- evaluate each learner's present level of functioning;
- determine individual goals for each learner that are appropriate, realistic, and measurable;
- work with parents to help reinforce career goals at home;
- determine group goals for the class as a whole as well as for small working groups within the class;
- assist learners in defining goals and objectives that are realistic in terms of their abilities and limitations;
- provide career counseling;
- develop a system for reinforcing learners that is both positive and effective;
- develop the ability to build the self-confidence in learners with special needs by identifying their hidden strengths and channeling them in positive directions;
- design a system of teaching procedures that provides for individual differences in learners;
- acquire, adapt, and develop materials necessary to achieve learning goals;
- determine successful methods to evaluate learners by individual achievements and abilities without lowering standards for the entire class (e.g., competency-based instruction);
- organize a system to collect and record data by which to evaluate learner progress toward established goals;
- develop a feedback system that will furnish continuous data to the learner, other teachers, and parents relative to learner progress;
- utilize the evaluation data to measure outcomes and set new goals;
- provide placement and follow-up services; and
- provide transition services with the assistance of other professionals and agencies. See Figure 1-6.

THE ROLE OF CAREER AND TECHNICAL EDUCATION IN DROPOUT PREVENTION

The education reform movement has placed career and technical education in a precarious position. For some time many within and outside the field have argued that career and technical education must play an increasingly important role in the enhancement and reinforcement of learners' basic skills and in the practical application and use of higher-order skills. To do this, however, career and technical education must develop an organized, comprehensive approach to addressing the challenges of changes in the world of work, in the workforce, and in national priorities and policies.

FACILITATORS FOR INTEGRATING LEARNERS FROM SPECIAL POPULATIONS IN CAREER AND TECHNICAL EDUCATION PROGRAMS

- Positive administrative policy with provision of support services, funding for materials and equipment, flexible scheduling policy, and professional development of staff
- Student assessment including profile of academic, social, psychomotor, career development, and career and technical education background information
- Career and technical assessment information such as interest inventories, aptitude tests, work samples, situational assessments, learning style inventories, behavioral checklists, and basic skills
- Cooperative development of career and technical component of the individualized learning plan
- Examination of course content including units to be covered, time limitations, licensure requirements, and open entry/open exit
- Realistic career goal assessment with examination of career and technical program, program exit points, entry-level competencies, physical demands of jobs, and opportunities for advancement on career ladder
- Positive learning environment with positive attitude of teacher, opportunities for interaction with peers, and positive reinforcement
- Instructional techniques and material matching academic levels of students, with appropriate comprehension levels, consideration of learning styles of students, and use of a variety of teaching and evaluation techniques
- Sequencing of skills to be taught including amount to be presented at one time and rate of presentation
- Support services such as cooperative planning with in-school resources, industry-sponsored resources, parents, volunteers, community-based organizations, and advisory committees and agencies
- Competency-based evaluation of learner progress using such items as the student's portfolio or competency profile
- Job development, placement, and follow-up assistance in conjunction with necessary transition services

Figure 1-6. An overview of practices that facilitate the successful integration of learners from special populations in career and technical education programs.

In 1992, the Office of Vocational and Adult Education, U.S. Department of Education, funded 10 demonstration sites around the country for a three-year study of the role of career and technical education in preventing at-risk youth from dropping out.

Although no two of the demonstration sites were alike, they shared a number of successful strategies and practices that could be identified across projects and fit into a common framework. This framework, which includes the best elements of all projects and yet is flexible enough to meet the needs of a variety of learners, consists of both a curriculum component and an educational support system. This enhanced program is based on the experiences the sites had in integrating the best of vocational education with a variety of successful policies, practices, and strategies to reach learners who have not graduated from school, who might not graduate, and who might graduate with too few effective skills to sustain them in a competitive and changing job market.

Curriculum Component

Imel (1993) reported the enhanced program as follows:
1. Academics–Regardless of their goals following graduation, all learners need to be competent in such academic areas as communicating, computing, problem solving, group living, and economic self-sufficiency.
2. Vocational-technical education–A core set of occupational training activities and experiences is an integral part of an enhanced career and technical education program. Although offerings varied across sites, each included several choices from the eight main areas of career and technical education: trade and industrial education, business education, agriculture, home economics, marketing education, technical education, technology education, and health occupations. Also important are courses that count in the diploma track or lead to certification, on-the-job training, and career and technical education and career exploration for middle school or early high school learners as well as for at-risk high school learners who are not ready to enter an occupational training program.
3. Employability skills training–In addition to academic and occupational education, demonstration sites found that learners also needed employability skills training to help them develop appropriate work-related characteristics and habits. Specific skills covered by this training include searching for a job (e.g., completing applications, preparing for interviews), adhering to employers' schedules, exhibiting initiative and motivation, participating as a team member, exercising leadership, and working with people from diverse backgrounds.
4. Life-coping skills training–This unique feature of enhanced vocational education curricula offers learners training designed to deal with the personal and social issues of daily living, both in and out of school, in the present and the future. Although this particular component of the comprehensive curriculum has not received as much attention as the others, project findings indicated that it was a critical element for success in school and on the job. Specific life-coping skills include developing a well-defined personal identity, identifying and dealing with personal fears, coping with different feelings and emotions, making wise choices, dealing positively with values conflicts, and choosing ethical courses of action.

Educational Support System

The comprehensive curriculum described here must be supported by an equally comprehensive educational support system to ensure that the curriculum is available to learners over an extended period. Results of the project indicated that an enhanced vocational education support system should address the following: program location and organization; learner recruitment, selection, and orientation; instructional strategies; counseling and guidance; learner management and discipline; community collaboration; parental and family involvement; staff selection and development; flexible scheduling; summer school; small class size; transportation; and district commitment and support.

CAREER AND TECHNICAL PROGRAMS AND SPECIAL POPULATIONS

Brown (1998) synthesized research on the role that career and technical programs make in working with individuals from special populations:
- Any number of career and technical education programs have been targeted to solve the education and employment problems of the nations high-risk populations (the dropout prone, persons with disabilities, educationally and economically disadvantaged persons, and so forth). Some have realized successful outcomes; others have not.
- Although in-school retention is a goal of career and technical education programs targeted to at-risk youth, it is not the most significant outcome. Data from the evaluation of a three-year demonstration program funded by the Carl D. Perkins Vocational Education Act reflect a broader perspective on program success. In summarizing the outcomes of the 12 evaluated projects, Hayward and Tallmadge (1995) reported that only 4 of the 12 showed a significant reduction in numbers of dropouts. The most successful outcome was the improved school performance of program participants. Ten of the 12 projects showed an increase in learners grade point averages; 7 of the 12 showed a reduction in number of courses failed.
- In a review of the literature regarding the impact of career and technical education on student retention, Hill and Bishop (1993) acknowledge that, although

there is some evidence that career and technical education programs and approaches have succeeded in keeping students in school, other research showed that career and technical education enhanced student retention only when it included other components such as work experience.

- Coordinating career and technical education programs with programs addressing the special conditions that place individuals at risk may provide better outcomes than programs solely devoted to vocational education.
- Not all programs achieve the goal of enhancing the employability of at-risk persons. Successful outcomes depend on the extent to which the programs meet the needs of those at risk.
- Many at-risk persons lack even the most basic academic skills, not to mention the higher order thinking, reasoning, and problem-solving skills required in today's workplace. They require programs that can help them develop good communication and social skills, think creatively, work well in teams, and take responsibility for their own learning and advancement. Career and technical education programs that contain formal ongoing coordination of academic and vocational content are more likely to prepare students with these skills, which is why the integration of academic and vocational education is increasingly recognized as a critical component of model programs for at-risk populations.
- Skill development (academic and vocational) is only one factor impeding the continued education and employment of at-risk populations. Teenage pregnancy and early parenting responsibilities; alcohol and drug dependency; emotional/psychological disorders; poverty; crime, violence and physical abuse; and dysfunctional family situations are just some of the other conditions that place persons at risk. Persons with these disadvantages need career and technical education programs to connect them to the support services that will help them improve their status in life.
- Woloszyk (1996) warned that limiting program focus to dropout prevention, for example, is a barrier to career and technical programs serving at-risk and out-of-school youth. Because learners leave school for many reasons, they need academic, occupational, and social supports that complement career and technical education as a remedy to the dropout problem. These supports could include attention to personal development and social skills, work experience, mentoring, and other efforts targeted to the problems that place individuals in the high-risk category.
- A general consensus of the role of career and technical education in serving at-risk populations as reported in the literature is one of facilitating learner skill development, retention in school, and employment. By itself, career and technical education cannot solve all the education and employment problems of the wide array of high-risk persons. However, its integration with other programs and connection with the community affords a greater potential for program success.
- Mentors are another way to extend learners' connections to the community. Mentoring at-risk learners has become one of the fastest growing and frequently used strategies in programs for at-risk youth.
- Career and technical education has long been acclaimed for its "hands-on" approach to education, for its ability to demonstrate a connection between what is learned in school and what is required for employment. Employers, mentors, and other community members, including parents, can augment career and technical education programs by helping at-risk persons bridge the gap between their current status and the realization of their life and work potential.

CAREER AND TECHNICAL SPECIAL NEEDS PROGRAMS—EXEMPLARY COMPONENTS

The Technical Assistance for Special Populations Program (TASSP)/Office of Special Populations of the National Center for Research in Vocational Education at the University of California-Berkeley conducted research to identify the components of an exemplary vocational special needs program. Burac and Bullock (1993) reported the results of this research, which were collected from professionals working in the area of career and technical programs serving learners with special needs; research studies of effective career and technical programs serving learners with special needs; studies by state boards of education on best practices; and literature on effective instruction, legislation, and textbooks.

The research team stressed that educators should search for strategies that produce positive outcomes for individuals from special populations. Examples provided include a decreased drop-out rate, increased number of drop-outs returning to school, increased employment percentage, increased percentage of learners continuing in postsecondary programs, and improved learner achievement. The exemplary framework resulting from this research consists of the following 20 components, grouped into five clusters:

Program Administration
- Strong administrative leadership and support–Strong hands-on leadership with such tools as an organizational chart or table identifying its operational elements and administrative personnel and a clear decision-making structure which is communicated to everyone;
- Sufficient financial support–Use of diverse funding sources or long-term stability if reliance on a single funding source is necessary and accurate records of personnel salaries, staff training costs, equipment, and material costs sufficient for successful program operation;
- Staff development–High quality preservice, inservice,

and/or continuing education programs (e.g., faculty retreats, conferences and workshops, summer internships in industry, and graduate studies) and incentives to encourage participation in these staff development activities;

- Formative program evaluation–Ongoing formative evaluation activities conducted by program staff and/or outside consultants (e.g., monthly/quarterly reports submitted by personnel, advisory committee feedback, input from agency collaboration, and use of feedback from students); and
- Summative program evaluation–Biannual or annual summative evaluations conducted internally or by an outside evaluator.

Formalized Articulations and Communications
- Family/parental involvement–Secondary programs have strong family support with proactive personnel who encourage parents and family members to become actively involved in the educational process;
- Notification of both students and parents regarding vocational [career and technical] education opportunities–Addressing the federal mandate (Carl Perkins Vocational and Applied Technology Act) to provide information about vocational program opportunities to all members of special populations and their parents (e.g., mailouts in the language spoken in their home, posting daily job listings, in-class announcements, school newsletter, and in-school meetings for students and family members);
- Career and technical educators involvement in individualized education planning–Involvement in the development and implementation of the Individualized Education Program/Individualized Transition Program (IEP/ITP) process required for students with disabilities in special education programs, attendance at IEP meetings, participation in curricular and placement decisions, and involvement in follow-up support when students leave school;
- Formalized transition planning–Formalized and individualized transition planning team involving parents, students, educators, and other appropriate representatives, identification of specific transition goals and objectives for each student from a special population, and periodic reviews to review and discuss progress toward the goals and objectives; and
- Intra- and inter-agency collaboration–Agencies and individuals involved in the educational planning for the special needs learner collaborate to avoid unnecessary duplication or gaps in services.

Curriculum and Instruction
- Individualized curriculum modifications–Modification of the curricula to meet the specific needs of individual learners (e.g., use of computers, adapting lesson plans, use of media, and use of teacher aides/tutors);
- Integration of academic and vocational curricula–Use of applied academic materials, collaborative working

relationships between vocational [career and technical] education and academic instructors, development of interrelated instructional materials, and use of new evaluation strategies;
- Appropriate instructional settings–Use of least restrictive environment/inclusion in career and technical programs to the fullest extent possible for members of special populations; and
- Cooperative learning experiences–Provision of opportunities for students to learn teaming skills through cooperative learning activities including group projects both in and out of the classroom, peer tutoring, and participation in vocational student organizations.

Comprehensive Support Services
- Assessment of individual's vocational interests and abilities–An appropriate vocational assessment process to provide information regarding the student's vocational abilities and interests so that an appropriate placement can be made, realistic goals can be developed and necessary support services can be provided;
- Instructional support services–The diversity of the student population should be matched with the diversity of available support services (e.g., tutors, mentors, psychologists, job coaches, adaptive devices, financial support, child care, career counseling, and note-takers); and
- Ongoing career guidance and counseling–Well-defined, structured guidance and counseling services are provided by credentialed individuals who understand the needs of individuals from special populations (e.g., assisting students to match their abilities and interests to an appropriate career goal, preparation of resumes, identification of job opportunities in the geographic area, preparation for job interviews, and identification of postsecondary opportunities in the community).

Occupational Experience
- Work experience opportunities–Students are provided with work experiences as soon as possible after entering a career and technical program, work experience opportunities are consistent with the interests and abilities of the student, and whenever possible, work experience opportunities are comprehensive rather than limited to a single skill;
- Job placement services–Strive to place students from special populations in jobs where they can succeed and advance, programs are proactive in contacting business and industry in the local area on the student's behalf, and appropriate job seeking skills are taught (e.g., resume instruction, interviewing techniques, and developing a networking system); and
- Follow-up of graduates and non-graduates–Data are collected for documentation and evaluation purposes (e.g., job retention rate, student promotion rate, salaries, and additional training/education received) (pp. 37-39). See Figure 1-7.

EXEMPLARY SPECIAL NEEDS PROGRAM COMPONENTS

PROGRAM ADMINISTRATION
- Strong administrative leadership and support
- Financial support
- Staff development
- Formative program evaluation
- Summative program evaluation

FORMAL ARTICULATION AND COMMUNICATION
- Family/parental involvement and support
- Notification of both students and parents regarding opportunities
- Career and technical educator's involvement in individualized educational planning
- Formalized transition planning
- Intra- and interagency collaboration

CURRICULUM AND INSTRUCTION
- Individualized curriculum modifications
- Integration of academic and technical curricula
- Appropriate instructional settings
- Cooperative learning experiences

COMPREHENSIVE SUPPORT SERVICES
- Assessment of individual's interests
- Instructional support services
- Ongoing career guidance and counseling

OCCUPATIONAL EXPERIENCE
- Work experience opportunities
- Job placement services
- Follow-up of graduates and nongraduates

Source: Burac, L., & Bullock, C. (1993). The Making of an Exemplary Program: Practices That Work. *The Journal for Vocational Special Needs Education 15*(2), 37.

Figure 1-7. The components of exemplary vocational programs that meet the needs of individuals from special populations.

LEGISLATIVE FOUNDATION

Since the Civil Rights Act of 1964, legislation has been passed to ensure the educational rights of individuals from special populations. Before these laws existed, many individuals with special needs were often ignored by society and were not considered to have the same rights as others. Pressure from advocate, consumer, and parent groups began to mount. These groups asserted that all human beings, as individuals, deserve to share the same rights. A great number of lawsuits were filed demanding equal educational opportunities. As a result, laws were passed to guarantee the rights of individuals from special populations.

Career and technical education is recognized as an important option for assisting individuals from special populations to bridge the gap between education and employment. Aaccess to these programs should be available to all learners in secondary and postsecondary programs.

During the past four decades, a number of pieces of legislation have been enacted to guarantee individuals from special populations the right to develop their vocational potentials. Although the definition of "individuals from special populations," "individuals with special needs," and "at-risk individuals" changes from one act to another, the fact remains that these individuals must be provided with equal access to career and technical education programs and the support services that will enable them to succeed in these programs.

Meers and Towne (1997) provide a perfect backdrop for the legislative foundation in workforce preparation that has been constructed over the past several decades.

> The work place is very different in the 1990s than it was in the 1970s. Change is constant. Preparation for a job has become preparation for a career. Employer/employee loyalty has fallen by the wayside. Global competition affects every nation's economy. Technological advances change the way and speed with which we work. Downsizing, rightsizing, outplacement, mergers, independent contractors, home-based employment, and a host of other variables impact jobs and careers. Accordingly, people with special needs– like the general population–must have educational experiences that enable them to be flexible in their career pursuits. Lifespan development must become a part of career planning. People moving into the work force in the next 20 years must know how to identify their options for career preparation and change. Special needs populations must have the support services and career planning opportunities necessary to facilitate lifespan development. Educators must continue the search for better educational strategies and meaningful interventions to insure that success will be a part of the life of each learner with special needs. Our do-more-with-less-faster-better global work place of the future promises more pressure, more change, more technology, more competition, more communication, etc. Through it all, there must be a consistent pattern of education and training that reflects the needs of *all* workers—including those with special needs. (p. 98)

Career and Technical Education Legislation

Since 1917 Congress has focused on the ability of our country to educate people for productive work and meaningful lives. Federal support for career and technical education has been expressed over the years through a series of enactments. The acts that specifically address the needs of individuals from special populations are reviewed below. See Figure 1-8.

CAREER AND TECHNICAL EDUCATION LEGISLATION		
Title	Public Law	Date Enacted
The Vocational Education Act of 1963	PL 88-210	1963
The Vocational Education Act Amendments of 1968	PL 90-576	1968
The Vocational Education Act Amendments of 1976	PL 94-482	1976
The Carl D. Perkins Vocational Education Act of 1984	PL 98-524	1984
The Carl D. Perkins Vocational and Applied Technology Act of 1990	PL 101-392	1990
The Carl D. Perkins Vocational and Technical Education Act of 1998	PL 105-332	1998

Figure 1-8. Career and technical education legislation affecting individuals from special populations.

The Vocational Education Act of 1963 (PL 88-210). This law recognized that individuals with special needs require assistance in order to achieve success in regular vocational programs. This was the beginning of a movement to provide opportunities for these learners to develop vocational potential in the form of salable skills for the competitive labor market. See Figure 1-9.

This act stated that vocational education should be available to "persons who have academic, socioeconomic, or other handicaps that prevent them from succeeding in the regular vocational education program." However, few vocational education resources were made available to learners with special needs as a result of this law. A national survey, conducted three years after the law went into effect, identified only 79 programs in 12 states that were preparing these learners with vocational skills. In reality, the law served primarily to focus attention on the need to provide vocational education opportunities for all people.

THE VOCATIONAL EDUCATION ACT OF 1963 (PL 88-210)

HIGHLIGHTS

- Authorized federal grants to states to assist them in maintaining, extending, and improving existing programs of vocational education so that persons of all ages . . . and those with special education handicaps . . . will have ready access to vocational training or retraining which is of high quality, which is realistic in the light of actual or anticipated opportunities for gainful employment, and which is suited to their needs, interest, and ability to benefit from such programs
- Recognized that individuals with special needs require assistance in regular vocational education programs

Figure 1-9. An overview of the highlights of the Vocational Education Act of 1963.

The Vocational Education Amendments of 1968 (PL 90-576). This legislation further emphasized the need to provide vocational education opportunities for learners with special needs. It identified two distinct categories of special populations—disadvantaged individuals and handicapped individuals. Separate vocational education programs were discouraged except when they were in the best interest of the learner. Otherwise, learners were expected to be integrated into regular programs and provided with appropriate support services and resources. See Figure 1-10.

In order to aid states in providing these services, the law allocated federal funds such that, for any fiscal year, a state had to use at least 10% of its basic vocational funds to provide programs for handicapped individuals and 15% of the basic vocational funds to provide programs for disadvantaged individuals. Funds were to be used to provide services over and above those available to all learners in vocational programs. Some resources provided included staff development, flexible scheduling, recruitment activities to reach potential employers, curriculum modifications, development of appropriate instructional materials, and additional staff to coordinate and supervise work-study programs.

The Vocational Education Amendments of 1976 (PL 94-482). This law emphasized the need to prepare all learners for employment or continuing vocational-technical education. It attempted to assure that handicapped and disadvantaged individuals were granted equal access to programs and services. States wishing to receive federal vocational education dollars were required by law to meet certain requirements.

States had to expend 10% of the funds from their basic state grants to provide vocational education opportunities for learners with disabilities and 20% for disadvantaged learners. These federal set-aside funds had to be matched on a 50-50 basis with state and local funds. All money was to be used to assist learners with special needs in regular vocational education programs.

THE VOCATIONAL EDUCATION AMENDMENTS OF 1968 (PL 90-576)

HIGHLIGHTS

- Further emphasized the need to provide vocational education skills for students with special needs
- Separated special needs populations into two distinct categories: disadvantaged students and handicapped students
- Earmarked federal funds to provide vocational education for students with special needs
- Promoted regular program placement (mainstreaming)
- Discouraged separate vocational programs for students with special needs except when the programs were in the best interest of the student
- Required states to expend 10% of their basic vocational funds to provide programs for handicapped students
- Required states to expend 15% of their basic vocational funds to provide programs for disadvantaged students

Figure 1-10. An overview of the highlights of the Vocational Education Act of 1968.

Set-aside funds allotted for vocational education for disadvantaged persons were to be used primarily in areas of high youth unemployment or school dropouts. Federal set-aside funds for vocational education for handicapped individuals were used for purposes that matched the goals stated in the Education of All Handicapped Children Act of 1975 (PL 94-142). As a result, learners with handicapping conditions were to be educated and enrolled in regular vocational education programs to the greatest extent possible in order to satisfy the requirement for educating them in the least restrictive environment. The specific nature of the vocational education program goals and objectives for each learner had to be planned and implemented according to the content of an individualized education program (IEP).

Specific provisions for providing programs and services for learners with disabilities and disadvantaged learners were included in annual and five-year state plans. National and state advisory councils for vocational education included one or more persons who had special knowledge about the needs of poor and disadvantaged individuals. The input from these advisory councils was essential because it affected decisions made about vocational education opportunities for individuals with special needs. See Figure 1-11.

The Carl D. Perkins Vocational Education Act of 1984 (PL 98-524). This act encompassed two broad themes:
- making vocational education programs accessible to all persons, including handicapped and disadvantaged persons, single parents and homemakers, adults in need

of retraining and training, persons participating in programs designed to eliminate gender bias and stereotyping, and incarcerated persons; and
- improving the quality of vocational education programs in order to give the nation's workforce the marketable skills needed to improve productivity and promote economic growth.

Under Title II, Part A, identified as the Vocational Education Opportunities Program, a state had to use 57% of the funds available for programs under the basic state grant for vocational education projects for special needs individuals. The specific breakdown of the mandated set-aside funds for individuals from special populations was as follows:
- handicapped individuals–10%
- disadvantaged individuals–22%
- adults in need of training or retraining–12%
- single parents and homemakers–8.5%
- individuals participating in programs to eliminate sex bias and stereotyping–3.5%
- criminal offenders–1%

THE VOCATIONAL EDUCATION AMENDMENTS OF 1976 (PL 94-482)

HIGHLIGHTS

- Increased funding formula for special needs programs and services
- Established cooperative working relationships between U.S. Department of Labor programs and vocational education
- Assured equal access to vocational programs for special needs individuals
- Emphasized educating special needs learners in existing vocational programs whenever possible
- Required states to expend 10% of their federal grant for vocational education to provide services to handicapped students
- Required states to expend 20% of their federal grant for vocational education to provide services for disadvantaged students
- Required that set-aside funds allocated for vocational education for disadvantaged individuals be used primarily in areas of high youth unemployment or dropout rates
- Required federal set-aside dollars to be matched on a 50-50 basis with state and local funds
- Required that national and state advisory councils for vocational education include one or more persons who had special knowledge about the needs of poor and disadvantaged individuals
- Required that all special needs students enrolled in vocational programs be prepared for employment or continuing vocational-technical education

Figure 1-11. An overview of the highlights of the Vocational Education Amendments.

Funds set aside for the handicapped and disadvantaged (the 10% and 22% set-aside funds, respectively) could only be used for supplemental or additional staff, equipment, materials, and services not provided to other individuals in vocational education programs.

This law required that handicapped and disadvantaged individuals participating in vocational education programs be provided with

1. equal access in recruitment, enrollment, and placement activities;
2. equal access to the full range of vocational education programs available to individuals without handicapping conditions or disadvantages;
3. assessment of individual interests, abilities, and special needs with respect to successful completion of the vocational education program;
4. special services, including adaptation of curriculum, instruction, equipment, and facilities designed to meet the special needs of these individuals;
5. guidance, counseling, and career development activities conducted by professionally trained counselors; and
6. counseling services designed to facilitate transition from school to employment or career opportunities. (Section 204)

In addition, the local educational agency had a responsibility to provide information to handicapped and disadvantaged learners and their parents about the available opportunities in vocational education at least one year before these learners were eligible to enter these programs.

Although the Vocational Education Amendments of 1976 (PL 94-482) allowed for the full costs of separate vocational education programs, this law provided for only 50% of the costs of services and activities for separate programs that exceeded the average per pupil expenditures of regular programs. Separate programs for handicapped and disadvantaged learners were discouraged. Mainstreaming learners with special needs in regular vocational education programs and providing them with support services was encouraged. See Figure 1-12.

Each state was allowed to use a portion of the 22% set-aside funds for disadvantaged individuals to design activities that would increase equal access to vocational education programs. This portion could also be used to pay the costs of services and activities applying the latest technological advances to instructional programs or to purchase state-of-the-art tools and equipment if the enrollment of the school was at least 75% economically disadvantaged.

A local district could contract with a community-based organization (CBO) if the vocational education programs in that district could not meet the needs of special needs learners or if the district decided that the CBO could better meet the needs of these learners. A CBO was defined as "a private nonprofit organization which is representative of the community or significant segments of communities and which provides job training services" (e.g., National Urban League, United Way, and Vocational Rehabilitation).

THE CARL D. PERKINS VOCATIONAL EDUCATION ACT OF 1984 (PL 98-524)

HIGHLIGHTS

- Assisted the states in raising the quality of vocational education programs
- Assured that persons who previously were inadequately served invocational education had access to quality programs
- Promoted greater cooperation between public agencies and the private sector
- Improved academic foundations of vocational students
- Required that the following be made available to all handicapped and disadvantaged students:
  - ~ vocational education services to train unemployed workers
  - ~ equal access to recruitment, enrollment, and placement
  - ~ vocational assessment to help assure success in vocational education programs
  - ~ any necessary special services
  - ~ professionally trained counselors for guidance, counseling, and career development activities
  - ~ counseling services to facilitate the transition from school to postschool employment

Figure 1-12. An overview of the highlights of the Carl D. Perkins Vocational Education Act.

The Carl D. Perkins Vocational and Applied Technology Act of 1990 (PL 101-392). Enacted in 1990 to amend the Carl D. Perkins Vocational Education Act, one of the primary purposes of this law was to enable our country to be more competitive in the world economy by more fully developing the academic and occupational skills of the population. Resources were to be concentrated on improving educational programs leading to academic and occupational skills development in order to train people who were capable of working in a technologically advanced society.

This act had several new directions, reflected in the mandated criteria used to assess quality career and technical programs. The criteria addressed the degree to which these programs

- integrate academic and vocational education;
- teach basic and higher order thinking skills;
- raise the quality of learning in schools having high percentages of poor and low-achieving learners;
- increase learner competency for workplace attainment and job placement;
- sequence courses of study that lead to both vocational and academic competence;
- increase linkages between secondary and postsecondary programs;
- provide learners with experiences in all aspects of an industry;

- reflect current and future labor market needs, including new and emerging technologies;
- meet the demands of the labor force through curriculum, equipment, and materials; and
- meet the needs of learners from special populations.

This legislation placed a strong emphasis on improving career and technical programs and services for individuals from special populations. States were required to ensure equal access and provide supplementary services for these learners. Special populations groups were identified to include

- individuals with disabilities;
- educationally and economically disadvantaged individuals (including foster children);
- individuals of limited English proficiency;
- individuals who participate in programs designed to eliminate sex bias;
- individuals in correctional institutions; and
- migrants.

With this act, individuals from special populations were guaranteed

1. equal access to recruitment, enrollment, and placement activities;
2. equal access to the full range of vocational education programs available to individuals who are not members of special populations, including occupationally specific courses of study, cooperative education, apprenticeship programs, and to the extent practicable, comprehensive career guidance and counseling services;
3. vocational education programs and activities for learners with disabilities provided in the least restrictive environment in accordance with the Education of the Handicapped Amendments (replaced by the Individuals with Disabilities Education Act, PL 101-476) and, whenever appropriate, included as a component of the individualized education program (IEP) with respect to vocational education programs; and
4. monitoring of vocational education to ensure that disadvantaged learners and individuals with limited English proficiency have access to programs in the most integrated setting possible.

Specifically, the act provides the following assurances for individuals from special populations:

- Each local educational agency shall provide information about vocational education opportunities at least one year before the students enter ninth grade or are of an appropriate age for the grade level in which vocational education programs are first generally available in the state, but in no event later than the beginning of the ninth grade. This information shall include opportunities available in vocational education, requirements for eligibility for enrollment in these programs, specific courses that are available, specific support services that are available, employment opportunities, and placement.
- Each eligible institution will provide information to individuals who request it concerning or seeking ad-

mission to vocational education programs offered by institutions, and when appropriate, assist in the preparation of applications relating to such admission.
- Information must be, to the extent practicable, in a language and form that parents and students understand. (The Carl Perkins Vocational and Applied Technology Act, Section 118 [b]).

This law provides critical guidelines for local education agencies in meeting the needs of individuals from special populations. Vocational assessment activities must be provided for all individuals from these populations in order to determine their abilities, interests, and special needs with respect to their successful participation in a vocational program in the most integrated setting possible. This information should be used to provide appropriate curriculum modifications, equipment modifications, classroom modifications, support personnel, and instructional aids and devices to assist the learner in succeeding.

Finally, guidance, counseling, and career development should be provided to facilitate a smooth transition from school to continuing education opportunities, postschool employment, and career opportunities. See Figure 1-13.

Carl D. Perkins Vocational and Technical Education Act of 1998 (PL 105-332). Some of the most important quality and equity principles of federal policy in vocational education and high school reform were preserved and extended through the Carl D. Perkins Vocational and Technical Education Act of 1998, signed into law on October 31, 1998.

The purpose of this act was to more fully develop the academic, vocational, and technical skills of learners enrolled in career and technical education programs by

1. building on the efforts of states and localities to develop challenging academic standards;
2. promoting the development of services and activities that integrate academic, vocational and technical instruction and that link secondary and postsecondary education for participating vocational and technical education learners;
3. increasing state and local flexibility in providing services and activities designed to develop, implement, and improve vocational and technical education, including tech-prep education; and
4. disseminating national research and providing professional development and technical assistance that will improve vocational and technical education programs, services and activities.

Known as Perkins III, PL 105-332 establishes some significant changes:

- Previous set-asides for the categories of Single Parent/Displaced Homemaker and Elimination of Sex Bias/Sex Equity have been eliminated. These categories have now been added to the definition of "special populations." (Special populations means individuals with disabilities; individuals from economically disadvantaged families, including foster children; individuals preparing for nontraditional training and employment; single parents, including single pregnant women; displaced homemakers; and individuals with other barriers to educational achievement, including individuals with limited English proficiency.)

- Secondary (section 131) and postsecondary (section 132) allocations have increased from 75% of the total state grant to 85%.
- There is no longer a targeting requirement to a limited number of sites or to a limited number of program areas. Increased local flexibility will determine the program(s) to be assisted with Perkins funds.
- The act requires the establishment of a state performance accountability system to assess the effectiveness of the state in achieving statewide progress in vocational and technical education.
- One of the required uses of funds at the local level is to develop and implement evaluations of the vocational and technical education programs, including an assessment of how the needs of special populations are being met.

Perkins III promotes reform, innovation, and continuous improvement in vocational and technical education to ensure that students acquire the skills and knowledge they need to meet challenging state academic standards and industry-recognized skill standards, and to prepare for postsecondary education, further learning, and a wide range of opportunities in high-skill, high-wage careers. Following are the focal areas of the act:

- Education reform–Perkins III supports the alignment of vocational and technical education with state and local efforts to reform secondary schools and improve postsecondary education. The implementation of the new law promises to make vocational and technical education programs an integral part of these efforts.
- Seamless education and workforce development systems–Together with the Workforce Investment Act of 1998, which restructures employment training, adult education, and vocational rehabilitation programs, Perkins III promotes the development of integrated, "one-stop" education and workforce development systems at the state and local level.

THE CARL D. PERKINS VOCATIONAL AND APPLIED TECHNOLOGY ACT OF 1990 (PL 101-392)

HIGHLIGHTS
- Defined three main themes as
  - ~ the integration of vocational and academic education
  - ~ equal access for special populations
  - ~ technical preparation
- Defined special populations as individuals with handicaps, educationally and economically disadvantaged individuals (including foster children), individuals of limited English proficiency, individuals who participate in programs designed to eliminate sex bias, individuals in correctional institutions, and migrants
- Provided members of special populations equal access to recruitment, enrollment, and placement activities and to the full range of vocational education programs
- Provided handicapped individuals with services in the least restrictive environment and afforded them certain rights and protections
- Coordinated vocational education planning for individuals with handicaps with special education and rehabilitation agencies
- Required that the provisions of vocational education be monitored to determine that the education provided was consistent with the IEP for each student and to ensure that disadvantaged students and students with limited English proficiency had access to education in the most integrated setting possible
- Required each local agency receiving funds to
  - ~ assist special populations students to enter vocational education programs, and with respect to students with handicaps, assist in providing certain transitional services
  - ~ assess the special needs of students participating in programs using Perkins funds, with respect to their successful completion of vocational education programs in the most integrated setting possible
  - ~ provide certain supplementary services to special populations students, including individuals with handicaps
  - ~ provide certain guidance, counseling, and career development activities
  - ~ provide counseling and instructional services designed to facilitate the transition from school to postschool employment and career opportunities

Figure 1-13. An overview of the highlights for individuals from special populations in the Carl D. Perkins Vocational and Applied Technology Education Act.

- Focus on quality–Perkins III focuses the Federal investment in vocational and technical education on high-quality programs that integrate academic and vocational education; promote student attainment of challenging academic and vocational and technical standards; provide students with strong experience in and understanding of all aspects of an industry; address the needs of individuals who are members of special populations; involve parents and employers; provide strong linkages between secondary and postsecondary education; develop, improve and expand the use of technology; and provide professional development for teachers, counselors, and administrators.

- Flexibility–A number of prescriptive administrative requirements and restrictions have been eliminated to give states, school districts, and postsecondary institutions greater flexibility to design services and activities that meet the needs of their learners and communities.

- Accountability–To promote continuous program improvement, Perkins III creates a state performance accountability system. The secretary and states reach agreement on annual levels of performance for a number of "core indicators" specified in the law. The indicators are learner attainment of challenging state established academic and vocational and technical skill proficiencies; learner attainment of a secondary school diploma or its recognized equivalent, a proficiency credential in conjunction with a secondary school diploma, or a postsecondary degree or credential; placement in, retention, and completion of postsecondary education or advanced training, placement in military service, or placement or retention in employment; and learner participation in and completion of vocational and technical education programs that lead to nontraditional training and employment.

Incentive grants will be awarded to states that exceed agreed-upon performance levels for Perkins III, the Adult Education and Family Literacy Act, and employment training services authorized under Title I of the Workforce Investment Act. Grants may be reduced to States that do not meet agreed-upon performance levels.

- Tech-prep–Perkins III reauthorizes tech-prep, an important catalyst for secondary school reform and postsecondary education improvement efforts. Perkins III promotes the use of work-based learning and new technologies in tech-prep programs and encourages partnerships with business, labor organizations, and institutions of higher education.

The Office of Vocational and Adult Education (OVAE) will give state and local recipients of funds the flexibility, guidance, and technical assistance needed to take advantage of the opportunities created by Perkins III. OVAE will collaborate with other offices of the Departments of Education and Labor and other federal agencies to promote the quality education and workforce systems. See Figure 1-14.

THE CARL D. PERKINS VOCATIONAL AND TECHNICAL EDUCATION ACT OF 1998 (PL 105-332)

HIGHLIGHTS
- De-emphasized targeting of programs
- Increased accountability
- Eliminated the 10.5% set-aside of the basic state grant that provided programs for single parents, displaced homemakers, single pregnant women, and sex equity.
- Changed the definintion for special populations; the new definintion added single parents, including single pregnant women and displaced homemakers, and replaced "individuals participating in programs designed to eliminate sex bias" with "individuals preparing for nontraditional training and employment." It dropped the reference to individuals in correctional facilities, dropped the terminology "academically disadvantaged individuals," and added "individuals with other barriers to educational achievement."
- Required that no less than $60,000 but no more than $150,000 of state leadership funds be used for services that prepared individuals for nontraditional training and employment
- Provided set-asides for individuals in state institutions, such as state correctional institutions and institutions that served individuals with disabilities (of an amount equal to not more than 1% of the amount alloted to the state)
- Required greater focus on professional development (including in-service and preservice training)
  Specified the participation of nonprofit private school career and technical educators in professional development
- Prohibited using Perkins funds for programs below the seventh grade
- Required that students must voluntarily choose career and technical education
- Prohibited using Perkins funds to carry out School-to-Work Opportunities Act provisions
- Allowed private or homeschool students to participate in public career and technical education programs and services

Figure 1-14. An overview of the highlights of the Carl D. Perkins Vocational and Technical Education Act.

Perkins III took effect in program year 2000, beginning July 1, 1999. OVAE gave states a variety of options for implementing the new law in the first year. States could submit a new five-year plan; a one-year transitional plan; an amendment to a Perkins II state plan; a consolidated plan that incorporates other federal elementary and secondary education programs; or a unified plan that incorporates other federal workforce development programs. Whichever option they chose, states had to submit a new plan by April 2, 1999.

Perkins III defines special populations as the following:

- individuals with disabilities
- individuals from economically disadvantaged families, including foster children
- individuals preparing for nontraditional training and employment
- single parents, including single pregnant women
- individuals with other barriers to educational achievement, including those individuals with limited English proficiency

Local districts, as a result of this act, must address its provisions to individuals from special populations. They must

1. describe efforts to review career and technical education programs and subsequent strategies adopted to overcome barriers that contributed to lowered rates of access or success in programs for each of the special populations listed above;
2. identify local programs or special activities that are designed to enable the special populations to meet the core indicators of performance;
3. describe how individuals who are members of the special populations will not be discriminated against on the basis of their status as members of special populations;
4. describe how opportunities for nontraditional training and employment will be provided; and
5. describe the activities conducted that eliminate gender bias and enhance gender equity in career and technical education programs.

Hess-Grabill and Bueno (2000) identified specific methods for serving special populations as follows:

- ensuring equal access for special populations
- encouraging work-based or work-site learning in conjunction with business and all aspects of industry
- providing support services for learner retention and completion
- providing career guidance and academic counseling

- supporting nontraditional training and employment activities
- requiring local and state agencies to develop and implement evaluations, including an assessment of how the needs of special populations are met
- providing programs for adults and school dropouts to complete secondary education
- involving parents, businesses, and labor organizations in planning, implementing, and evaluating career and technical education programs
- providing dependent-care and transportation costs
- offering mentoring, tutoring, and note-taking services
- providing special instructional materials/supplies or adaptive devices and equipment
- providing special populations personnel
- assisting with the cost of laboratory fees and supplies
- providing other activities required by this act

Workforce Preparation Legislation

Workforce legislation was passed in this country in response to education reforms that advocated an expanded curriculum to prepare youth and adults for careers, social mobility, and economic security. Specific acts that reinforce workforce preparation are reviewed below. See Figure 1-15.

The Comprehensive Employment and Training Act of 1973 (PL 93-203). The Comprehensive Employment and Training Act (CETA) was created to provide job training opportunities and employment for individuals who were identified as economically disadvantaged, underemployed, and/or unemployed. Administered by the United States Department of Labor, this legislation combined the resources and services of the Economic Opportunity Act and the Manpower Development and Training Act. It also required collaboration among providers of employment and training-related programs.

WORKFORCE PREPARATION LEGISLATION		
Title	**Public Law**	**Date Enacted**
The Comprehensive Employment and Training Act of 1973	PL 93-202	1973
The Job Training Partnership Act of 1982	PL 97-300	1982
The National Skill Standards Act of 1994: Title V of Goals 2000	PL 103-227	1994
The Personal Responsibility and Work Opportunity Act of 1996	PL 104-193	1996
The Workforce Investment Act of 1998	PL 105-220	1998

Figure 1-15. Workforce preparation legislation affecting individuals from special populations.

The CETA was amended in 1978 through PL 95-524. These amendments mandated that prime sponsors assist handicapped individuals by including descriptions of employment and training services for them in their master and annual plans. An affirmative action program for outreach, training, placement, and advancement had to be included in each annual plan. The act prohibited discrimination on the basis of handicap. Participation on planning, state employment, and training councils by handicapped individuals was also required (Berkell and Brown, 1989). The Comprehensive Employment and Training Act was replaced by the Job Training Partnership Act (PL 97-300) in 1982. See Figure 1-16.

THE COMPREHENSIVE EMPLOYMENT AND TRAINING ACT OF 1973 (PL 93-203)

HIGHLIGHTS
- Provided job training and employment for individuals identified as economically disadvantaged, unemployed, and/or underemployed
- Required collaboration among service providers of employment and training-related programs
- Prohibited discrimination on the basis of handicap
- Required prime sponsors to assist handicapped individuals by including descriptions of employment and training services in their master and annual plans
- Required that an affirmative action program for outreach, training, placement, and advancement be included in each annual plan
- Required participation of handicapped individuals on planning, state employment, and training councils

---

Figure 1-16. An overview of the highlights of the Comprehensive Employment and Training Act.

The Job Training Partnership Act (PL 97-300). The Job Training Partnership Act (JTPA) was passed by Congress in 1982. It was intended to replace and improve upon the Comprehensive Employment and Training Act (PL 93-203) and to increase the role of private business and industry in the training and employment of disadvantaged youth and adults.

The purpose of the JTPA was to establish programs to prepare youth and unskilled adults for entry into the labor force and to afford job training to economically disadvantaged individuals and others facing serious barriers to employment. This act represented a partnership between the public and private sectors. Federal funds are directed by states to local or regional service delivery areas (SDAs), each of which must have a private industry council (PIC). The PIC is responsible for deciding the type of training to be provided within the SDA and is composed of local business leaders and officials as well as representatives from organized labor, rehabilitation, employment, economic development, and education.

Funds available to states under this act can be used to provide eligible dislocated workers with needs-related payments so that they can participate in training or education programs. These payments can be offered to individuals who do not qualify or have ceased to qualify for unemployment compensation. To be eligible for such payments, a worker must be enrolled in training by the end of the 13th week of the initial unemployment compensation benefit period, or, if later, the end of the eighth week after the employee is informed that a short-term layoff will exceed six months.

Funds may be used to deliver, coordinate, and integrate basic readjustment and support services to eligible dislocated workers. These services may include the following:
- development of individual readjustment plans for participants in programs under JTPA
- outreach and intake
- early readjustment assistance
- job or career counseling
- testing
- orientation
- assessment, including evaluation of educational attainment, interests, and aptitudes
- determination of occupational skills
- provision of future world-of-work and occupational information
- job placement assistance
- labor market information
- job clubs
- job development
- supportive services, including child care, commuting assistance, and financial and personal counseling, which terminates no later than the 90th day after the participant has completed other services
- pre-layoff assistance
- relocation assistance
- programs conducted in cooperation with employers or labor organizations to provide early intervention in the event of closures of plants or facilities

Funds from the JTPA may also be used to provide training services to eligible dislocated workers. These services may include but are not limited to the following:
- classroom training
- occupational skill training
- on-the-job training
- out-of-area job search
- relocation
- basic and remedial education
- literacy and English for non-English speakers
- entrepreneurial training
- other appropriate training activities directly related to specific employment opportunities in the service delivery area

There are many opportunities for employment training available through the JTPA for individuals from special populations. Coordination will be necessary between educators and JTPA program personnel to make certain that there is no duplication of services or a lack in services between the school-based program and the individual's participation in JTPA activities (e.g., summer employment training). Educators should be aware of the services and opportunities available through the JTPA and should communicate these to individuals from special populations and their families. Information about the application process should also be shared. See Figure 1-17

On September 7, 1992, the Job Training Reform Amendments of 1992 (PL 102-367) were signed into law. These amendments modified the existing JTPA legislation. As a result, the direction and focus of the JTPA training and employment programs are on improving services to those facing serious barriers to employment; enhancing the quality of services provided; strengthening fiscal and program accountability; linking services provided and local labor market needs; and fostering a comprehensive and coherent system of human resource services.

THE JOB TRAINING PARTNERSHIP ACT OF 1982 (PL 97-300)

HIGHLIGHTS

- Replaced the Comprehensive Employment and Training Act (CETA) and provided funding and programs to assist economically disadvantaged individuals
- Promoted involvement of local business and industry in the training and employment of disadvantaged and unemployed individuals
- Provided funding and programs to assist in the employment of economically disadvantaged youth and adults
- Promoted involvement of local business and industry through the Private Industry Council (PIC)
- Provided job search assistance, including orientation, counseling, and referral; on-the-job training, remedial education, upgrading and retraining; supportive services such as health care, child care, residential support, and transportation; and payment of needs-based allowances to persons to cover expenses incurred in training or employment
- Provided that 10% of the persons served by adult programs did not have to be economically disadvantaged if they had other barriers to employment (e.g., handicapped, older workers, persons with limited English proficiency)

Figure 1-17. An overview of the highlights of the Job Training Partnership Act.

There are two key parts that relate to JTPA eligibility for persons with disabilities. The first is that for purposes of determining program eligibility, persons receiving supplemental security income under Title XVI of the Social Security Act will not have their SSI counted as income when determining eligibility. The second key part is that an individual with a disability may, for purpose of income eligibility determination, be considered to be an unrelated individual who is a family unit of one.

The U.S. Department of Labor published the Title II eligibility guidelines, which clarify how disability status will be determined by JTPA intake workers:
- letter from drug or alcohol rehabilitation agency
- letter from child study team stating specific disability
- medical records
- observable condition
- physician's statement
- psychiatrist's diagnosis
- psychologist's diagnosis
- rehabilitation evaluation
- school records
- sheltered workshop certification
- social service records
- Social Security Administration disability records
- Veterans Administration letter/records
- vocational rehabilitation letter
- workers' compensation record

Each state must submit the goals to be achieved and the services to be provided by school-to-work transition programs for inclusion in the governor's coordination and special services plan. This description should be developed jointly by the state's educational agency and the governor's office and should contain, at a minimum, information regarding the linkages that will be established between programs such as the Carl D. Perkins Act and the Individuals with Disabilities Education Act. This mandate should provide greater support for transition programs for individuals from special populations.

National Skill Standards Act of 1994: Title V of Goals 2000 (PL 103-227). The National Skill Standards Act of 1994 is incorporated as Title V of Goals 2000. This act establishes the National Skill Standards Board (NSSB) to oversee (a) the development of voluntary national skills standards, and (b) a system for certification of attainment of skill standards.

The National Skill Standards Act established the NSSB to serve as a catalyst to stimulate the development and adoption of a national system of voluntary skill standards and certification. The NSSB is composed of 27 members representing business, labor, education, government, and civil rights organizations. Its mission is to promote the creation of voluntary standards by industry in partnership with education, labor, and community stakeholders. Key tasks of the board in carrying out this mission are to identify broad clusters of major occupations that share characteristics appropriate for the development of skill standards; to promote the establishment of voluntary partnerships that will develop the standards; and to endorse the standards developed by these partnerships.

Skills standards identify what people need to know and what they must be able to do to successfully perform work-related functions within an industry sector. Specifically, standards define the work to be performed, how well the work must be done, and the level of knowledge and skill required.

The NSSB is building a voluntary national system of skill standards, assessment, and certification that will enhance the ability of the United States to compete effectively in a global economy. These skills are being identified by industry in full partnership with education, labor, civil rights, and community-based organizations. The standards will be based on high-performance work and will be portable across industry sectors. In a time of rapidly changing markets, a high-tech revolution, and increasing global competition, employers will need workers with specialized skills. The following are some industry-based projections:

- The information technology industry will need more than 1 million technicians by 2005.
- The health services industry will need 796,000 new workers by 2006.
- The retail industry will need 408,000 more skilled salespeople by 2006.

Because NSSB-endorsed skill standards must meet the highest professional criteria for development and use, the evolving certification system will help provide a clear road map to future security and success for employers and employees alike. In order that the industry-defined skill standard certifications meet or exceed the highest standards, the NSSB has developed the following quality controls for endorsement and benchmarking:

- Common language/format–The standards must be based on a common language and format so that they will be understood clearly across all industry sectors.
- Continuous improvement–The standards must be continually updated and improved so that the standards system keeps pace with the ever-changing American workplace and remains focused on the future.
- Portability–Centralized endorsement of skill standards by the NSSB will ensure that skills are recognized throughout the country and across all industries.
- Accessibility–The standards must remain consistent with civil rights laws and take into account the relevant regulations pertaining to health, safety, and the environment, and they must be accessible to all.

Following are benefits of national skills standards:

- Employers–A national system of skill standards increases competitiveness by boosting workforce quality; streamlines and reduces costs for employee recruitment, hiring, retention, and promotion; and encourages a high-performance workplace, improving the way work is organized and human resources are used.

- Current and future employees–The clear requirements set out by skill standards help raise wages by raising competencies and productivity; create long-term security by providing a personal, portable portfolio of skills and certifications; and improve opportunities by offering more complete learning options tied to real-world career information.
- The community–Everyone benefits from improved employment opportunities, a higher standard of living, and economic security. Labor unions, educators, job training programs, and other community organizations are all vital partners in skill standards development.

The Personal Responsibility and Work Opportunity Reconciliation Act of 1996 (PL 104-193). On August 22, President Clinton signed into law the Personal Responsibility and Work Opportunity Reconciliation Act of 1996 (PRWORA), a comprehensive bipartisan welfare reform plan that will dramatically change the nation's welfare system into one that requires work in exchange for time-limited assistance. The law contains strong work requirements, a performance bonus to reward states for moving welfare recipients into jobs, state maintenance of effort requirements, comprehensive child support enforcement, and supports for families moving from welfare to work—including increased funding for child care and guaranteed medical coverage.

This act ushered in a new era of welfare reform that emphasized economic self-sufficiency through a "work-first" approach designed to move welfare recipients into the workforce as quickly as possible. Known as a rapid-employment strategy, the work-first approach assumes that "the best preparation for work is work itself and that welfare recipients will gain experience in entry-level jobs and move on to better work." Education and training for welfare recipients and limited training sessions are provided after work for those who have found jobs. The work-first philosophy has created challenges for adult and vocational educators who provide education and training for welfare recipients.

Highlights of the Personal Responsibility and Work Opportunity Reconciliation Act of 1996 that relate to individuals from special populations follow:

- Support for families transitioning into jobs–This law provides funding to help more mothers move into jobs. It also guarantees that women on welfare continue to receive health coverage for their families, including at least one year of transitional Medicaid when they leave welfare for work.
- Work activities–To count toward state work requirements, recipients will be required to participate in unsubsidized or subsidized employment, on-the-job training, work experience, community service, or 12 months of vocational training or to provide child care services to individuals who are participating in community service. Up to six weeks of job search (no more than four consecutive weeks) would count toward the

work requirement. However, no more than 20% of each state's caseload may count toward the work requirement solely by participating in vocational training or by being a teen parent in secondary school. Single parents with a child under six who cannot find child care cannot by penalized for failure to meet the work requirements. States can exempt from the work requirement single parents with children under age one and disregard these individuals in the calculation of participation rates for up to 12 months.

- Job subsidies–The law allows states to create jobs by taking money now used for welfare checks and using it to create community service jobs or to provide income subsidies or hiring incentives for potential employers.
- Live at home and stay in school requirements–Unmarried minor parents will be required to live with a responsible adult or in an adult-supervised setting and participate in educational and training activities in order to receive assistance. States will be responsible for locating or assisting in locating adult-supervised settings for teens.
- Personal employability plans–Under the new plan, states are required to make an initial assessment of recipients' skills. States can also develop personal responsibility plans for recipients identifying the education, training, and job placement services they need to move into the workforce.

The current work-first environment does present challenges for adult and vocational educators wishing to serve welfare recipients. Educators should employ the following guidelines in developing welfare-to-work programs:

- Collaborate with local agencies–Interagency collaboration is a necessary ingredient of successful programs. It can provide a forum for interpreting and implementing state and local policies in ways that are favorable to education and can serve as the medium for providing essential support services such as transportation and child care. Interagency collaboration promotes service integration that in turn enhances the retention of participants.
- Focus on training for jobs that have potential in the local labor market–Program developers must understand the local labor market so that they can target training for jobs that have relatively high earnings, opportunities for advancement, and potential for growth in the local market. Unfortunately, the availability of low-skill, entry-level jobs in the current job market and the narrow scope of funding for education and training in most states' welfare reform policies have resulted in the placement of many welfare-to-work participants in occupations with limited opportunities. Educators should strive to overcome these limitations by working with local employers and the officials responsible for economic development.
- Include a combination of academic and occupational learning experiences designed to lead to further education and training–Evaluations of welfare-to-work pro-

grams conducted during the past two decades clearly show that the most effective programs are those that mix job search, basic skills education, job training through the development of occupational skills, and paid and unpaid work experience. These elements should be integrated, with the intensity of academic and occupational training tailored to the jobs targeted. Furthermore, these programs should be structured so that they lead to opportunities for further education and training when participants are ready.

- Attend to instruction–Instruction should be linked to the workplace and to further education and training. Unfortunately, instruction in many programs is delivered by inexperienced instructors or instructors who have no training in linking instruction to work. Therefore, professional development of instructors must be a priority.
- Work to change current policies–Finally, adult and career and technical educators should work to change policies that focus on ending welfare into policies that are oriented to ending poverty. Although a work-first approach might be a short-term solution to reducing the current welfare rolls, it does not represent the needs of learners and of educators, nor does it address the underlying structural problems that lead to poverty and joblessness (Imel, 2000).

The Workforce Investment Act of 1998 (PL 105-220). The Workforce Investment Act (WIA) was based on the premise that "all youth, particularly those out-of-school, acquire the necessary skills and work experience to successfully transition into adulthood, careers, and further education and training." This statement, together with the tenets of the act, frame the Department of Labor's vision for preparing youth for active participation in this nation's workforce and for real change in the ways in which such preparation occurs. The WIA is based on the premise that the right interventions at the right time in a young person's life will have a major impact in his or her future success. It reflects a core value that all youth can learn and acquire skills and that it is indeed possible to achieve parity among the employability prospects for youth of all backgrounds.

The purpose of the WIA is to consolidate, coordinate, and improve employment, training, literacy, and vocational rehabilitation programs in the United States. This act will consolidate and coordinate many of the employment and training programs (such as the Job Training Partnership Act) through a one-stop delivery system. The intent of this consolidation is to improve employment and training programs for all individuals, including those with disabilities, and to assist the consumer in identifying a range of workforce options through the one-stop delivery system.

The Workforce Investment Act (WIA) provides increased flexibility for state and local officials to establish broad-based labor market systems using federal job training funds for adults, dislocated workers, and youth. With this increased flexibility comes challenges and opportunities for organized labor. While the act does not "block grant" all training programs, the law mandates coordination among a range of federal job training programs, including the Employment Service, adult education and literacy programs, welfare-to-work, vocational education, and vocational rehabilitation. WIA's goal is to provide workforce development services to employers and workers through a universally accessible, information-driven, one-stop career center (OSCC) system.

One-stop career centers are the foundation for the delivery of services in a local workforce system. The state board sets the criteria for the one-stop system while local boards select one-stop operators. In selecting a one-stop operator, local boards may choose a collaborative model, a competitive model, or grandfather existing one-stops. Eligible one-stop operators can include the following:
- postsecondary institution
- nonprofit entity
- employment service
- government agency
- private-for-profit entity
- business organization (e.g. chamber of commerce)

One-stop centers are to provide access to core, intensive, and training services to adults and dislocated workers. Any worker (employed or unemployed) can receive core services, which include assessment, counseling, job search and placement, as well as information on the labor market and training providers. Workers who do not find jobs or who are in need of further assistance to maintain self-sufficiency, can receive intensive services and then training services.

Serving all youth within a one-stop system is neither a new nor revolutionary concept. After all, a full 60% of youth aged 16 to 18 are already in the labor market. Many such youth are already accessing job information through the local one-stop or through its partner agency, the employment service. Local entities across the country have already gone well beyond basic job finding services to promote access to the one-stop system by
- establishing linkages with schools, community-based youth service organizations, and school-to-work systems;
- conducting outreach efforts targeting out-of-school youth;
- conducting youth tours of one-stop centers; and
- creating separate youth resource areas and designating specific staff to work with youth.

It is important for youth who have begun to think about their careers, youth who are still in school but need additional support to remain there, and youth who have dropped out of school to see the value of one-stop services and be able to access them. Eligible youth may access various one-stop offerings and, after they reach age 18, participate in either youth or adult program offerings or both, depending upon individual assessments. Youth may then begin to tap into the services of a one-stop that will be available throughout their working lives. While the act does underscore focusing WIA youth funds on serving

eligible youth, particularly those most in need, it does not prohibit local program operators from encouraging any area youth to access the one-stop's self-service tools and to receive such assistance as basic labor market information.

Local areas are called upon to create opportunities for youth that move beyond traditional employment and training services and that infuse such principles as preparation for postsecondary opportunities, linkages between academic and occupational learning, connections to the local job market, and appropriate follow-up services into their youth systems.

The WIA brings new emphasis and substantive reform to how youth are served within the workforce investment system. It presents an opportunity to better prepare our young people and offer them a comprehensive array of services so that they are able to successfully transition to the workforce and to continued education and training.

A number of programmatic elements included in the act will foster inclusionary strategies for integrating workforce training, education, and other community offerings to local youth. Several of the program elements identified in the act focus on providing young people assistance in achieving a secondary school diploma or its equivalent. These elements include tutoring, study skills training, dropout prevention strategies, and alternative secondary school services. Other program elements outlined in the act—summer employment opportunities, paid and unpaid work experiences, and occupational skill training—seek to encourage exposing youth to the work world and to allow youth to apply what they learn in school or other training settings to various workplace experiences. Still other program elements serve to ensure that participating youth have adequate support in completing the learning and employment goals they have helped to set. These elements include the provision of supportive services, such as assistive technology for youth with disabilities; adult mentoring; appropriate follow-up services; and comprehensive guidance and counseling.

Legislation for Individuals With Disabilities-Special Education

Since 1975 there has been federal legislation to provide assurances and protective measures for individuals with disabilities in educational programs. As a result of these acts, services and programs are provided to meet the specific needs of each individual. A review of this legislation is presented below. See Figure 1-18.

The Education for All Handicapped Children Act (PL 94-142). This law, passed in 1975, expressed a national commitment to provide a free and appropriate public education for every handicapped person between the ages of 3 and 21. It assured more than 8 million learners in this country the right to develop their potential to the maximum extent possible. States and local school systems were required to provide all identified handicapped learners with an education designed to meet their needs and abilities as well as related services necessary to assist them in succeeding in their educational programs.

This far-reaching act contained six general themes:

1. A free, appropriate public education assured that a special education program with appropriate related services would be developed for each identified handicapped learner. These learners were to be provided with the same educational opportunities that all other learners enjoyed, including access to vocational education programs that were realistic in light of their abilities and interests.

2. The Individualized Education Program (IEP) was mandated for every handicapped learner each year. This plan specified long-range planning and short-term goals developed especially for the learner as well as identifying the support services required to meet these goals. Evaluation criteria were to be included in the IEP so that progress could be determined.

3. The provision of access to records gave parents of handicapped learners the right to view all records on file pertaining to their child. The parents also could ask to have changes made in the records if they believed the information was incorrect or misleading. Individuals 18 years or older had the right of access to their own records.

4. The right of due process guaranteed that a specific procedure had to be followed in thoroughly evaluating a learner thought to have a disability so that the decision regarding the proper educational placement would be in the learner's best interest. Parents were to be involved in all steps of this evaluation and decision-making process. This guarantee prevented schools from placing learners in special education programs who did not belong there.

5. Placement in the "least restrictive environment" gave handicapped learners the right to be placed in regular education programs whenever possible or programs that did not restrict their abilities.

6. The guarantee of nondiscriminatory testing meant that the tests used to evaluate learners could not be racially or culturally biased and had to be administered in the language spoken in the learner's home. This provision also stated that the results of more than one test had to be used to make a decision about placing a learner. A variety of test results had to be considered before an appropriate decision could be made. See Figure 1-19.

The Education of the Handicapped Act Amendments of 1983 (PL 98-199). PL 94-142 was amended by the Education Handicapped Act Amendments of 1983. This law addressed services in the following areas: development of transition strategies leading to independent living; establishment of demonstration models emphasizing vocational, transition, and job placement services; provision of demographic studies on numbers and types of disabling conditions and the related services that they require; provision for collaborative models between adult community service providers and educational agencies; and development of procedures for evaluating transition programs. Finally, these amendments mandated that data be collected and follow-up studies be performed regarding learners with disabilities who leave the educational system (Berkell and Brown, 1989).

The Education of the Handicapped Act Amendments of 1986 (PL 99-457). The Education Handicapped Act Amendments of 1986 reauthorized transition programs and allowed funded activities to serve learners who left school as well as those still enrolled. Focal points of these amendments included vocational and life skills development, demonstration projects, technical assistance in transition efforts, and follow-up studies.

INDIVIDUALS WITH DISABILITIES/SPECIAL EDUCATION LEGISLATION		
Title	**Public Law**	**Date Enacted**
The Education of All Handicapped Children Act of 1975	PL 94-142	1975
The Education of the Handicapped Act Amendments of 1983	PL 98-199	1983
The Education of the Handicapped Act Amendments of 1986	PL 99-457	1986
The Individuals with Disabilities Education Act of 1990	PL 101-476	1990
The Individuals with Disabilities Education Act Amendments of 1997	PL 105-17	1997

Figure 1-18. Special education legislation affecting individuals from special populations.

THE EDUCATION FOR ALL HANDICAPPED CHILDREN ACT OF 1975 (PL 94-142)

HIGHLIGHTS

- Provided necessary funding for public schools to ensure a free and appropriate education for all handicapped youth from ages 3 to 21
- Guaranteed to the student a free and appropriate education (including vocational education) occurring in the least restrictive environment
- Required that a comprehensive assessment be made of the student's functional abilities in all areas of development and achievement using nondiscriminatory testing and evaluation
- Guaranteed due process procedures to ensure that specific procedures were followed in evaluation of the student
- Required that every student with a handicap have an individualized education program (IEP) on record
- Guaranteed parents access to all records

Figure 1-19. An overview of the highlights of the Education of All Handicapped Children Act of 1975.

The Individuals with Disabilities Education Act of 1990 (PL 101-476). In 1990 Congress amended the Education of All Handicapped Act (PL 94-142). The new law was renamed the Individuals with Disabilities Education Act (IDEA). This law expanded the definition of special education to include instruction in all settings, including workplace and training sites. The IDEA put a new emphasis on meeting the needs of traditionally neglected populations (defined as "underrepresented") to include minority, poor, and limited-English proficient individuals with disabilities. Eligible learners were identified in the IDEA by disability condition and include those with mental retardation, specific learning disabilities, serious emotional disturbances (behavior disorders), speech or language impairments, visual impairments (including blindness), hearing impairments, orthopedic impairments, other health impairments, autism, and traumatic brain injury.

This act stipulated that learners with disabilities must receive any related services necessary to ensure that they benefit from their educational experience. Related services refer to special transportation and other support services, including speech pathology, psychological services, physical and occupational therapy, recreation, rehabilitation counseling, social work, and medical services. See Figure 1-20.

The IDEA provided the following assurances to individuals with disabilities through the age of 21:

- nondiscriminatory and multidisciplinary assessment of educational needs
- parental involvement in developing each individual's educational program

- the right to learn in the least restrictive environment consistent with academic, social, and physical needs through a continuum of placements, ranging from regular classrooms with support services to homebound and hospital programs

---

THE INDIVIDUALS WITH DISABILITIES EDUCATION ACT OF 1990 (PL 101-476)

HIGHLIGHTS

- Added autism and traumatic brain injury as new categories of disabilities
- Solicited public comments on providing special education services to students with attention deficit disorder (ADD)
- Expanded the definition of special education to encompass instruction in all settings, including the workplace and training centers
- Added rehabilitation counseling and social work services
- Placed a new emphasis on meeting the needs of traditionally neglected or underrepresented populations (minority, poor, and limited English proficiency)
- Included transition services in the definition of Special Education (Basic State Grants)
- Required that the IEP include a statement of needed transition services (beginning at age 14 or earlier, but no later than age 16) and, before the student leaves the school setting, a statement of interagency responsibilities or linkages
- Required that the IEP team reconvene if participating agencies failed to provide agreed upon transitional services

Figure 1-20. An overview of the highlights of the Individuals with Disabilities Education Act.

This law also provided a vehicle for developing an individualized education program (IEP) based on multidisciplinary assessment and designed to meet the individual needs of the learner. The IEP provides an opportunity for professional educators and parents to provide for continuity in the delivery of educational services. Each IEP contains information about the learner's present level of performance; annual goals; short-term instructional objectives; related services; percentage of time spent in regular education; beginning and ending dates for special education services; and an annual evaluation.

The IDEA added the following new requirements to the IEP assurance for each learner with a disability:

- Beginning at age 16, and at a younger age if determined appropriate, the IEP must include a statement of the needed transition services for the learner.

- The IEP should also include, if appropriate, a statement of each public agency's and each participating agency's responsibilities or linkages, or both, before the learner leaves the school setting.
- If the IEP team determines that services are not needed in one or more of the areas specified (i.e., instruction, community experiences, the development of employment, and other postschool adult living objectives), the IEP must include a statement to that effect and the basis upon which the determination was made.
- If a purpose of the IEP meeting is the consideration of transition services for a learner, the education agency should include the learner and a representative of any other agency that is likely to be responsible for providing or paying for transition services.
- If the learner does not attend the IEP meeting, the educational agency shall take other steps to ensure that the learner's preferences and interests are considered.
- If an agency invited to send a representative to an IEP meeting does not do so, the educational agency shall take other steps to obtain the participation of this agency in planning any transition services.
- If a participating agency fails to provide agreed-upon transition services contained in the IEP of a learner, the educational agency responsible for the learner's education shall, as soon as possible, initiate a meeting for the purpose of identifying alternative strategies to meet the transition objectives and, if necessary, for revising the learner's IEP. This does not relieve any participating agency, including a state vocational rehabilitation agency, of the responsibility to provide or pay for any transition service that the agency would otherwise provide to learners with disabilities who meet the eligibility criteria of that agency.

The act also addressed the issue of transition services. The IDEA defined transition as a "coordinated set of activities for a learner, designed within an outcome-oriented process, that promotes movement from school to postschool activities, including post-secondary education, vocational training, integrated employment (including supported employment), continuing and adult education, adult services, independent living, or community participation." The coordinated set of activities must be based on the individual learner's needs, taking into account his or her preferences and interests.

The definition for transition in the IDEA also contained a listing of in-school activities that must be provided and others that might be appropriate. Those that must be provided are

1. instruction;
2. community experience;
3. development of employment; and
4. other postschool adult living objectives.

Activities mentioned as possibly being appropriate are

1. acquisition of daily living skills; and
2. functional vocational evaluation.

The Individuals with Disabilities Education Act Amendments of 1997 (PL 105-17). On June 4, 1997, President Clinton signed the bill reauthorizing and amending the IDEA. The bill became Public Law 105-17, the Individuals with Disabilities Education Act Amendments of 1997. The law is frequently referred to as IDEA '97.

PL 105-17 retains the major provisions of earlier federal laws in this area, including the assurance of a free appropriate public education (FAPE) available to all children with disabilities, in the least restrictive environment (LRE) and the guarantee of all due-process procedures and procedural safeguards. It also includes modifications to the law. Some of the changes that affect special education practices nationwide include

- participation of learners with disabilities in state and district-wide assessment programs, with appropriate accommodations where necessary (the law also includes the development of guidelines for participation of children with disabilities in alternate assessments when those children cannot participate in regular assessments with accommodations and modifications);
- development and review of the individualized education program (IEP), including increased emphasis on participation of children and youth with disabilities in the general curriculum and the involvement of regular education teachers in developing, reviewing, and revising the IEP;
- enhanced parent participation in placement decisions;
- streamlined evaluation and re-evaluation requirements;
- a statement, beginning at age 14 and updated annually, of the transition service needs of the learner that focuses on the learner's courses of study;
- the availability of mediation as a means of more easily resolving parent-school differences (at a minimum, mediation must be available whenever a due-process hearing is requested);
- disciplinary procedures for learners with disabilities, including placement of certain learners with disabilities in appropriate interim alternative educational settings for up to 45 days; and
- allowance of children ages 3–9 (previously 3–5) to be identified as developmentally delayed, with the upper age limit at the discretion of the state and the local educational agency.

Following are some of the highlights of the new law:

Outcomes and Standards
- includes learners with disabilities in state and district-wide testing programs, with appropriate accommodations when necessary
- establishes performance goals and indicators for learners with disabilities

Evaluations and Curriculum
- requires a statement of any type of individual accommodation or modification that is needed for the learner to be able to participate in state- or district-wide assessments of learner achievement

- requires states to ensure that learners with disabilities have access to the general curriculum. If a learner will not be participating with nondisabled children in the regular classroom and extracurricular and other non-academic activities, an explanation in the learner's IEP is required
- requires at least one regular education teacher of the child to be a member of the IEP team if the learner is participating or might be participating in the regular education environment
- expressly requires that the IEP address positive behavioral intervention strategies, if appropriate, in the case of a learner whose behavior impedes his or her progress
- requires that parents be informed about the educational progress of their child, by means such as periodic report cards, at least as often as parents of nondisabled children
- specifies that a statement of transition services needs relating to the learner's course of study be included in the learner's IEP beginning at age 14 and updated annually
- adds "orientation and mobility services" to the definition of related services

Procedural Safeguards
- requires that the language used in delivering information to parents about their child's rights be as easily understood as possible
- requires that parents be given access to all records relating to their child, not just those "relevant" records on the identification, evaluation, and educational placement of their child

Discipline
- ensures that no learner with a disability is denied continuing educational services due to behavior (Schools must continue to provide educational services for learners with disabilities whose suspension or expulsion constitutes a change in placement.)
- gives schools the authority to remove learners with disabilities to the appropriate interim alternative educational setting (IAES) for behavior related to drugs, guns, and other dangerous weapons for up to 45 days
- allows schools to suspend learners with disabilities for up to 10 school days to the extent that such alternatives are used for children without disabilities
- requires the IEP team to conduct a "manifestation determination" once a disciplinary action for a learner with a disability is contemplated (The IEP team must determine—within 10 calendar days after the school decides to discipline a learner—whether the learner's behavior is related to the disability. If the behavior is not related to the disability, the learner may be disciplined in the same way as a learner without a disability, but the appropriate educational services must continue.)
- permits school personnel to report crimes allegedly committed by learners with disabilities to law enforcement authorities (Knoblauch & McLane, 1999).

Neubert (2000) identified specific transition related elements of the IDEA as follows:
- The IDEA Amendments of 1997 have far-reaching implications for including learners with disabilities in regular education settings for earlier transition planning, and for including learners with disabilities in education reform efforts that emphasize accountability and outcomes for all learners. In addition, interagency planning is required during the IEP process. Vocational rehabilitation personnel are often involved in interagency planning as learners make the transition from high school to work or adult service programs.
- The law mandate requires special educators, learners, and families to be aware of curricula and diploma options, prerequisites for vocational-technical programs, and college entrance requirements as early as the middle school years. For example, if a learner is college bound, the IEP team should determine what courses are needed throughout middle school and high school that will enable the learner to enter a postsecondary institution. The IDEA Amendments of 1997 also continued to mandate that a statement of needed transition services for the child, including, when appropriate, a statement of the interagency responsibilities or any needed linkages, be included in the IEP by age 16.
- The definition of transition services remained the same as in the IDEA of 1990, with the exception that the coordinated set of activities could include related services such as transportation and support services such as speech and language pathology and audiology services, psychological services, physical and occupational therapy, recreation, social work services, counseling services (including rehabilitation counseling), orientation and mobility services, and medical services (for diagnostic and evaluation purposes). Providing related services may be especially significant to learners with more significant disabilities who participate in community-based transition programs until the age of 21 (or 22). (p. 44)

Civil Rights Legislation

Civil rights legislation has been passed in this country since 1964. The intent of this legislation was to deal with basic human rights and responsibilities in our society. These acts focused on the assurances that all individuals, regardless of race, gender, national origin, or disability, would receive equal treatment in employment opportunities, voting rights, education, housing, and public accommodations. A review of civil rights legislation is presented below. See Figure 1-21.

The Rehabilitation Act of 1973 (PL 93-112). Sometimes referred to as "The Bill of Rights for the Handicapped," this legislation prohibited discrimination in programs receiving federal funds. Section 503 of this act represents a historic step to provide employment opportunities for handicapped individuals. Any employer receiving federal assistance in the form of contracts for $2,500 or more is required to develop an affirmative action plan to recruit, hire, train, and advance in employment qualified handicapped individuals. Employers receiving federal contracts for $50,000 or more and having 50 or more employees must develop and implement an affirmative action program within 120 days that outlines specific policies and procedures regarding handicapped individuals. This program must be reviewed and updated once a year.

Section 503 also required that employers make "reasonable accommodations" for handicapped individuals in the workforce. This means that specific changes must be made to the work environment to meet the specific need of each worker. These changes may require, for instance, that a worktable be raised or lowered to accommodate an individual who uses a wheelchair or that a visually impaired employee be provided with a tape recorder for assistance with job duties.

Section 504 of this act, passed in 1977, prohibited discrimination in educating handicapped individuals, admitting them to career and technical education programs, or providing them with equal employment opportunities. Specific requirements were set forth for secondary and adult education programs, postsecondary education programs, and employers.

The five basic requirements in Section 504 mandated that

1. handicapped persons, regardless of the nature or severity of their handicap, be provided a free appropriate public education;
2. handicapped learners be educated with non-handicapped learners to the maximum extent, appropriate to their needs;
3. educational agencies undertake to identify and locate all unserved handicapped children;
4. evaluation procedures be improved in order to avoid the inappropriate education that results from the misclassification of learners; and

5. procedural safeguards be established to enable parents and guardians to influence decisions regarding the evaluation and placement of their children.

Public elementary and secondary programs must provide handicapped individuals with the opportunity to participate in existing services such as regular program options, nonacademic services, extracurricular activities, school-sponsored interest groups and clubs, and counseling services. Evaluation procedures used to assess the aptitude or achievement levels of each learner must be appropriate and should be administered periodically. An individualized education program (IEP) must be developed and implemented for each handicapped learner. In addition, reasonable accommodation must be made to assure that programs, services, and facilities are accessible to everyone.

These learners must be placed in regular programs to the maximum extent possible with necessary supplementary aids and services. Possible adaptations in regular education settings under Section 504 include

- providing a structured learning environment;
- repeating and simplifying instructions about in-class and homework assignments;
- using behavioral management techniques;
- supplementing instructions with visual presentation;
- adjusting class schedules;
- modifying test delivery;
- providing computer-aided instruction;
- selecting modified textbooks or workbooks;
- tailoring homework assignments; and
- using note-takers.

Postsecondary programs are prohibited from discriminating against handicapped individuals in recruitment or admissions procedures. Admission quotas cannot be used. Any admissions test, including standardized tests, must be selected and administered so that they record the aptitude or achievement level of the learner rather than the disability.

CIVIL RIGHTS LEGISLATION		
Title	**Public Law**	**Date Enacted**
The Rehabilitation Act of 1973	PL 93-112	1973
The Rehabilitation Act Amendments of 1986	PL 99-506	1986
The Americans with Disabilities Act of 1990	PL 101-336	1990
The Rehabilitation Act Amendments of 1992	PL 102-569	1992
The Rehabilitation Act Amendments of 1998	PL 105-220	1998

Figure 1-21. Civil rights and rehabilitation legislation affecting individuals from special populations.

Reasonable accommodations must be made to ensure accessibility to postsecondary programs, services, and facilities. Modifications, such as extended time for completing a course or degree requirements or adapting the manner in which the course is taught, must be made according to the specific needs of the individual. In addition, support aids must be provided as necessary. These aids might include special equipment, interpreters, library readers, cassette recorders, note-takers, and taped texts. Often these aids can be provided by outside agencies or organizations.

Section 504 prohibits employers from discriminating against otherwise qualified handicapped individuals in recruitment, hiring, or promotion. Pre-employment medical examinations or specific questions regarding a disability are not allowed under these regulations. Employers are required to make facilities accessible, modify work schedules, restructure jobs, and provide for the modification of necessary equipment or devices. See Figure 1-22.

The Rehabilitation Act Amendments of 1986 (PL 99-506). The Rehabilitation Act Amendments, passed in 1986, revised the requirements for individualized written rehabilitation plans (IWRPs) to include a permanent section for supported employment programs. Supported employment, in this act, was defined as "paid work experience in business, industry, and government, supported by those services necessary to maintain the involvement and productivity of the individual to function in a specific work environment." In addition, collaborative transition planning was mandated between state education agencies and vocational rehabilitation agencies.

The Americans with Disabilities Act (PL 101-336). An estimated 43 million Americans have disabilities. They represent the most welfare-dependent minority in our country and are underrepresented in the labor market. Only 8% of individuals with disabilities are employed full time and about 7% are employed part-time (Rothwell, 1991). Historically, society has tended to isolate and segregate these individuals. Despite some improvements, such forms of discrimination against this population continue to be a serious social problem. Discrimination against individuals with disabilities exists in such crucial areas as employment, housing, public accommodations, education, transportation, communication, and health services. See Figure 1-23.

A report to Congress in 1992 revealed that individuals with disabilities constantly encounter various forms of discrimination, including outright exclusion; the discriminatory effects of architectural, transportation, and communication barriers; overprotective rules and policies; failure to make modifications to existing facilities and practices; exclusionary qualification standards and criteria; segregation; and relegation to lesser services, programs, activities, benefits, job, or other opportunities.

The Americans with Disabilities Act (ADA) was signed into law in 1990 and went into effect on January 26, 1992. The purpose of the ADA was to extend to the private sector

---

THE REHABILITATION ACT OF 1973 (PL 93-112)

SECTION 503 HIGHLIGHTS

- Promoted and expanded employment opportunities in the public and private sectors for handicapped persons
- Required employers receiving federal contracts of $2500+ to develop affirmative action plans to recruit, hire, train, and advance in employment persons with handicaps
- Required employers receiving federal contracts of $50,000+ to develop and implement affirmative action programs within 120 days
- Required employers to make "reasonable accommodation" in the work environment to meet the needs of workers with handicaps

SECTION 504 HIGHLIGHTS

- Prohibited discrimination on the basis of handicaps in all federally funded programs and activities
- Identified annually eligible persons with handicaps not receiving a free appropriate public education
- Placed students in their "least restrictive environment"
- Ensured comparable facilities for students with handicaps
- Used appropriate evaluative techniques and qualified people when planning handicapped student's placement
- Used specified safeguards to ensure rights of students with handicaps
- Provided nondiscriminatory guidance, counseling, and placement
- Required employers to provide recruitment, job assignments, and fringe benefits
- Required all new public facilities to provide recruitment, job assignments, and fringe benefits

Figure 1-22. An overview of the highlights of the Rehabilitation Act.

---

civil rights protections for individuals with disabilities. The legislation provided civil rights similar to those based on race, religion, national origin, and sex in the Civil Rights Act of 1974.

According to the Rehabilitation Act of 1973, whose definition has been used in the ADA, a person with a disability is defined as "an individual having a physical or mental impairment that substantially limits him or her in some major life activity and having experienced discrimination resulting from this physical or mental impairment."

Examples of individuals with disabilities who are covered in the ADA are

- persons with mobility impairments;
- persons who have lost one or more limbs;
- persons who have vision impairments;

- persons who have hearing impairments;
- persons who have mental or psychological disorders, including mental retardation, emotional and mental illness, and learning disabilities;
- persons with a psychological disorder, including depression and post traumatic stress syndrome;
- persons with cosmetic disfigurements (e.g., burn victims); and
- persons with serious diseases including AIDS, epilepsy, cancer, and tuberculosis.

THE AMERICANS WITH DISABILITIES ACT OF 1990 (PL 101-336)

HIGHLIGHTS
- Extended to people with disabilities civil rights similar to those now available through the Civil Rights Act of 1964
- Guaranteed equal opportunity in employment, public accommodations, transportation, state and local government services, and telecommunications
- **Title I:** Employment Provisions – No covered entity shall discriminate against a qualified individual with a disability in regard to job application procedures, hiring, advancement, or discharge of employees, or other terms, conditions, and privileges of employment. An employer must make reasonable accommodations for employees with a disability so they will enjoy benefits and privileges equal to the benefits and privileges enjoyed by other employees.
- **Title II:** Public Services – All government facilities, services, and communications must be accessible to individuals with disabilities; buses, trains, subways, and other transportation are required to be accessible.
- **Title III:** Public Accommodations – Places of public accommodations may not discriminate and must be accessible to individuals with disabilities.
- **Title IV:** Telecommunications – Any common carrier that offers telephone services to the public must make accommodations for people with disabilities.

Figure 1-23: An overview of the highlights of the Americans with Disabilities Act.

Five specific areas affected by the ADA include
1. employment;
2. transportation;
3. public accommodations;
4. telecommunications; and
5. state and local government operations.

Pertinent to educators are the following employment assurances in the Americans with Disabilities Act:
- Employers may not discriminate against an individual with a disability in hiring or promotion if the person is otherwise qualified for the job.

- Employers can ask about a person's ability to perform a job, but cannot inquire if someone has a disability or subject a person to any test that tends to screen out people with disabilities.
- Employers must provide "reasonable accommodations" to individuals with disabilities.
- Employers do not need to provide accommodations that impose an undue hardship on business operations.

Kochhar and Deschamps (1992) described the areas in which the ADA assurances will impact on the vocational preparation of individuals with disabilities:
- Assurances of equal access–ADA states that public services, including public schools, cannot discriminate against individuals with disabilities. If a learner with a disability in a vocational program funded by the Carl D. Perkins Vocational and Applied Technology Act is not being given a service needed to enjoy equal participation, then that learner could file a complaint under ADA. In addition, that local plan would not be in compliance with the Perkins Act.
- Guidance and counseling–In order for ADA to fulfill its purpose to prepare learners with disabilities in career and technical programs, knowledge about job descriptions and reasonable accommodations must be provided before individuals interview for specific jobs.
- Reasonable accommodation–According to the regulations of ADA, "reasonable accommodations" include modifications or adjustments to a job application process that enable a qualified applicant with a disability to be considered for the position the applicant desires. These include modifications or adjustments to the work environment, or to circumstances under which the work is customarily performed, that enable a qualified individual with a disability to perform the essential functions of that position. Helping learners to determine their own reasonable accommodations for different jobs should be a critical part of their preparation for employment.
- Job descriptions–Career and technical programs funded by the Carl Perkins Act can now prepare their learners for specific jobs by using descriptions of the job's essential functions, defined in ADA as "fundamental job duties." Employers are now required to make job descriptions with fundamental job duties available to all potential applicants. This will help vocational educators and transition personnel prepare learners for specific jobs and anticipate the need for reasonable accommodations.
- Supplementary services–In order for individuals with disabilities to participate fully in a career and technical program, supplementary services must be provided. These services may include curriculum modification, equipment modification, supportive personnel, and instructional aids and devices. Examples of accommodations which can be provided for learners with disabilities include sign language

interpreters, mobility assistance, note-takers, oral exams, extra time on tests, textbooks on tape, in-class aid, enlargements, and voice-synthesized computers.
- Job interview issues–Career and technical programs can and should teach individual learners about their strengths and limitations in order to prepare them for potential job interviews. To be considered qualified, the individual must, according to ADA, "satisfy the requisite skills, experience, and education and other job-related requirements of the employment position."

One important aspect of preparation for employment is how to appropriately inform employers about a disability. Even though an employer is not permitted to ask if an applicant has a disability, it is important for individuals with disabilities to know how their disability will affect the job, if at all, so they can explain this and present an accurate picture of themselves to the employer. Educators can play a critical role in preparing students for this responsibility.
- Testing issues–ADA prohibits tests for employment positions that are designed to exclude individuals based on a disability. This provision further emphasizes that individuals with disabilities are not to be excluded from jobs they can actually perform merely because a disability prevents them from taking a test, or negatively influences a test result that is a prerequisite of the job.
- Transition–The definition of transition services in the ADA specifies the movement from school to post-school activities including postsecondary education, vocational training, integrated employment, continuing and adult education, adult services, independent living, or community participation. Under this act, transition activities can include preparation for interviews, knowledge about reasonable accommodations, and written job descriptions stating the essential functions of the job. These activities are consistent with the intent of ADA to improve access to employment (pp. 17-18).

The Rehabilitation Act Amendments Of 1992 (PL 102-569). This act was signed into law by President George Bush on October 29, 1992. This law was based on the following five simple but critical principles:
1. Individuals with disabilities make up one of the most disadvantaged groups in society and still encounter daily discrimination in every facet of life.
2. Disability is a natural part of life and in no way diminishes the right of individuals to live independently, make choices, contribute to society, and pursue meaningful careers.
3. Increased employment of individuals with disabilities begins with increased access to needed training, supports and reasonable accommodations.
4. Individuals with disabilities should be afforded the tools to make informed choices and decisions and to achieve equality of opportunity, full inclusion, and integration in society.

5. Individuals with even the most significant disabilities should be presumed capable of gainful employment and provided the needed supports to do so.

This fifth principle is meant to transform the way state vocational rehabilitation (VR) agencies operate in our country. Up to now, an individual with a significant disability could be and often was found or presumed to be unemployable and, thus, ineligible for VR services.

The law tells people with disabilities and rehabilitation professionals alike: Don't focus on the severity of the disability; don't focus on the problem. Focus instead on the solutions and on getting people the tools that they need. Assistive technology, personal assistance, literacy training, job supports, and other reasonable accommodations are needed, not just to become and stay employed but to pursue careers of their own choosing and design as well.

The amendments also adopted the IDEA definition of transition services and required state rehabilitation agencies to establish policies and procedures to facilitate the transition of youth with disabilities from school to the rehabilitation service system.

The Rehabilitation Act Amendments of 1998 (PL 105-220). The Rehabilitation Act Amendments of 1998 comprise the major portion of Title IV of the Workforce Investment Act of 1998, which consolidates several employment and training programs into statewide systems of workforce development partnerships.

The Rehabilitation Amendments extend the state/federal vocational rehabilitation (VR) program for five years. Following are the principal provisions:
- Federal agencies are required to procure, maintain, and use electronic and information technology that provides individuals with disabilities comparable access to what is available to individuals who do not have disabilities.
- The governor must ensure that the state's VR agency enters into agreements with appropriate public entities, including the state's workforce investment system, to provide VR services more efficiently and comprehensively.
- The amendments provide for cooperative agreements with other parts of a state's workforce investment system to allow for such activities as staff training and technical assistance regarding VR services and eligibility and common customer service procedures such as intake and telephone hot lines.
- Consumer choice is enhanced through new language on the consumer's role in rehabilitation planning. Consumers must be provided with information and support services to assist them in exercising informed choice throughout the VR process.
- State VR agencies are encouraged to assist schools in identifying transition services and to participate in the cost of transition services for any learner with a disability who is determined eligible to receive VR services.
- Persons receiving SSI or SSDI benefits are automatically eligible for VR services.

- Individuals with the most severe disabilities are now called individuals with a significant disability.
- The individualized written rehabilitation program (IWRP) is renamed the individual plan for employment (IPE).
- The State Rehabilitation Advisory Council is now called the State Rehabilitation Council. Membership is expanded, responsibilities are increased, and the council and state agency are required to jointly develop, agree to, and review state goals and priorities.

Educational Reform Legislation

The 1990s initiated a number of legislative efforts to reform education as it was being delivered at that time. Foundation elements of this legislation included educating *all* learners together through inclusion, developing education and occupation skill standards to parallel the demands of the workforce, and providing transition skills through existing curricula to enable individuals to successfully move from school to postschool options. See Figure 1-24.

Goals 2000: Educate America Act (PL 103-227). The Goals 2000: Educate America Act (PL 103-227) was signed into law on March 31, 1994. The act provided resources to states and communities to ensure that all learners reach their full potential. It is based on the premise that all learners will reach higher levels of achievement when more is expected of them. Goals 2000 established a framework in which to identify world-class academic standards, measure learner progress, and provide the support that learners may need to meet the standards.

The purpose of the act is, in part, "to provide a framework for meeting the National Education Goals by supporting new initiatives at the federal, state, local, and school levels to provide equal educational opportunity for all learners to achieve high educational and occupational skill standards and to succeed in the world of employment and civic participation." One of the key aspects of the law is the development and adoption of a voluntary national system of skill standards and certification to serve as the cornerstone of the national strategy to enhance workforce skills. The statute calls for creating a unified system of standards for all learners, rather than separate sets of standards for different groups of learners.

Section 3(a) of the act defines the terms all learners and all children to mean

> (1)...students or children from a broad range of backgrounds and circumstances, including disadvantaged students and children, students or children with diverse racial, ethnic, and cultural backgrounds, American Indians, Alaska Natives, Native Hawaiians, students or children with disabilities, students or children with limited English proficiency, school-aged students or children who have dropped out of school, migratory students or children, and academically talented students and children.

The act codified in law the six original education goals concerning school readiness, school completion, learner academic achievement, leadership in math and science, adult literacy, and safe and drug-free schools. It added two new goals encouraging teacher professional development and parental participation. The National Education Goals to have been enacted by the year 2000 were as follows:

1. All children in America will start school ready to learn.
2. The high school graduation rate will increase to at least 90 percent.
3. All students will leave grades 4, 8, and 12 having demonstrated competency over challenging subject matter including English, mathematics, science, foreign languages, civics and government, economics, the arts, history, and geography, and every school in America will ensure that all students learn to use their minds well, so they may be prepared for responsible citizenship, further learning, and productive employment in our nation's modern economy.
4. United States students will be first in the world in mathematics and science achievement.
5. Every adult American will be literate and will possess the knowledge and skills necessary to compete in a global economy and exercise the rights and responsibilities of citizenship.
6. Every school in the United States will be free of drugs, violence, and the unauthorized presence of firearms and alcohol and will offer a disciplined environment conducive to learning.

EDUCATIONAL REFORM LEGISLATION		
Title	**Public Law**	**Date Enacted**
Goals 2000: Educate America Act of 1994	PL 103-227	1994
The School-to-Work Opportunities Act of 1994	PL 103-239	1994
The Improving America's Schools Act of 1994	PL 103-382	1994

Figure 1-24. Educational reform legislation affecting individuals from special populations.

7. The nation's teaching force will have access to programs for the continued improvement of their professional skills and the opportunity to acquire the knowledge and skills needed to instruct and prepare all American students for the next century.

8. Every school will promote partnerships that will increase parental involvement and participation in promoting the social, emotional, and academic growth of children. (Section 102)

The Goals 2000 legislation accomplished the following:

- set in law the original six national education goals–school readiness, school completion, learner academic achievement, leadership in math and science, adult literacy, and safe and drug-free schools–and added two new goals related to professional development and parental participation
- developed and adopted for the first time challenging national performance standards that define what all learners should know and be able to do in core subject areas such as science, math, history, and the arts and supported local reform efforts to make those standards a reality in every classroom
- strengthened and improved teacher training, textbooks, instructional materials, technologies and overall school services so that learners would have the tools to achieve higher standards
- encouraged the development of innovative learner performance assessments to gauge progress
- established the National Skills Standard Board to promote the development of occupational skill standards to define what workers will need to know and ensure that American workers will be better trained and internationally competitive
- increased flexibility for states, school districts, and schools by waiving rules and regulations (other than the IDEA) that might impede local reform and improvement

Action steps for insuring the inclusion of youth with disabilities in Goals 2000 include the following:

- monitoring the development of educational and occupational skill standards to ensure that they adequately encompass and address the needs and interests of young people with disabilities
- communicating the importance of school completion (National Education Goal 2) for learners with disabilities
- sharing facts and findings on school dropout rates for learners with disabilities with federal and state officials
- familiarizing educators, employers, human service professionals, parents, and youth with disabilities with the transition service requirements of Part B of the IDEA
- promoting collaborative joint training initiatives between general and special education, vocational rehabilitation, vocational education, employers, and others in an effort to broadly address the specific secondary and transition needs of youth with disabilities for work, independent living, participation in postsecondary education, and other facets of community life

- informing federal and state officials that learners with disabilities are presently entering postsecondary training institutions at lower rates than any other learners
- encouraging parents of learners with disabilities to become familiar with the intent and purposes of National Education Goal 8–Parental Participation
- providing information to the National Education Goals Panel concerning the status and needs of youth with disabilities involved in secondary education and transition services

The School-to-Work Opportunities Act of 1994 (PL 103-239). The School-to-Work Opportunities Act of 1994 was designed to facilitate the creation of a universal, high quality school-to-work transition system. The act uses federal funds as venture capital to underwrite the initial costs of planning and establishing statewide systems that will be maintained with other resources. These systems are to provide all learners with opportunities to participate in programs that integrate school- and work-based learning, vocational and academic education, and secondary and postsecondary education.

This legislation is distinct from other education reform initiatives because it does not create another separate program with federal mandates. Rather, the law helps states and localities to build on and advance existing programs and reforms. In building on existing programs and reform efforts, school-to-work links existing program reform efforts with workforce development and economic development by engaging diverse stakeholders in designing and implementing an integrated system. School-to-work is also linked with the Goals 2000: Educate America Act, which provides a framework for state efforts to improve learner academic achievement. Goals 2000 also establishes the National Skill Standards Board, which is developing a system of voluntary occupational skill standards.

Under the act, school-to-work systems must be designed to provide all learners with the opportunity to participate in programs that do the following:

- integrate school-based learning and work-based learning
- integrate academic and occupational education
- include and effectively link secondary and postsecondary education
- meet the same academic standards set by the state for all learners, prepare learners for postsecondary education, and award skills certificates
- provide learners with strong experience in and understanding of all aspects of the industry learners are preparing to enter, including planning; management; finances; technical and production skills; underlying principles of technology; labor and community issues; health and safety issues; and environmental issues
- provide all learners with equal access to the full range of program components and related activities
- give learners flexibility to develop new career goals over time, to change career majors, and to transfer between education and training programs

"All learners" is defined as meaning

> both male and female students from a broad range of backgrounds and circumstances, including disadvantaged students, students with diverse racial, ethnic, or cultural backgrounds, American Indians, Alaska Natives, Native Hawaiians, students with disabilities, students with limited English proficiency, migrant children, school dropouts, and academically talented students. (School-to-Work Opportunities Act, 1994)

The school-to-work approach to learning is based on the fact that individuals learn best by doing and by relating what they learn in school to their experiences as workers. This approach has come to be accepted as a better way to educate all young people. Instead of traditional general track and vocational education programs that were based on the theory that learners who didn't go to college needed to be taught a skill they could use to make a living, the school-to-work approach is based on the concept that education for all should be made more relevant to multiple future careers and lifelong learning. Developed with the input of business, education, labor, and community-based organizations with a strong interest in how learners prepare for careers, the effort to create a national school-to-work system contains three fundamental elements: school-based learning, work-based learning, and activities connecting the two:

- School-based learning–School-to-work programs restructure the educational experience so that learners learn how academic subjects relate to the world of work. Teachers work together with employers to develop broad-based curricula that help learners understand the skills needed in the workplace. Learners actively develop projects and work in teams, much like the modern workplace. Teachers work in teams to integrate their usually separate disciplines and create projects that are relevant to work and life in the real world.
- Work-based learning–Employers provide learning experiences for learners that develop broad, transferable skills. Work-based learning provides learners with opportunities to study complex subject matter as well as vital workplace skills in a hands-on, "real-life" environment. Working in teams, solving problems, and meeting employers' expectations are workplace skills that learners learn best through doing and master under the tutelage of adult mentors.
- Connecting activities–Connecting schools and workplaces does not happen naturally. It requires a range of activities to integrate the worlds of school and work to ensure that the learner is not "the slender thread" that connects the two. Connecting activities provide program coordination and administration; integrate the worlds of school and work through, for example, school and business staff exchanges; and provide learner support, such as career counseling and college placements.

The Improving America's Schools Act of 1994 (PL 103-382). The final version of the Improving America's Schools Act of 1994 was signed into law on October 20, 1994. Selected key provisions that affect individuals from special populations include the following:

Title I–Helping Disadvantaged Children Meet High Standards

- Prevention and intervention programs for children and youth who are neglected, delinquent, or at risk of dropping out–State plans must describe how appropriate professional development will be provided to "other staff" and provide assurances that staff are trained to work with children with disabilities and learners with other special needs.
- Innovative elementary school transition projects–Projects are designed to assist children and their families in making a successful transition from preschool through early elementary grades. Project components include a support services team with family service coordinators to ensure delivery of comprehensive educational, health, nutritional, social and other services.
- School support teams–Teams will assist schools in the development of schoolwide plans, review learner progress toward meeting the state's content and learner performance standards, identify problems, and make recommendations for improvement.
- Parental involvement–Programs must include educational opportunities for working with parents as equal partners, implementing parental involvement programs, and building ties between home and school.

Title II–Dwight D. Eisenhower Professional Development Program

- Federal, state, and local levels–Where appropriate, school personnel are eligible to participate in a wide range of professional development programs and activities at the local, state, and federal levels. Examples include (1) professional development institutes that contain strong and integrated disciplinary pedagogical components; (2) preparation in collaborative skills needed to appropriately teach children with disabilities; (3) programs to ensure that girls and young women, minorities, limited English- proficient learners, individuals with disabilities, and economically disadvantaged learners have the full opportunity to meet challenging state content and learner performance standards; (4) professional development in the core academic subjects that are offered through professional associations, universities, community-based organizations, and other providers; and (5) preparation for working with parents and families.

Title IV–Safe and Drug-Free Schools and Communities

- Programs at the federal, state and local levels–Examples include (1) programs of drug prevention, comprehensive health education, pupil services, mentoring, and rehabilitation referral; (2) implementation of strategies such as conflict resolution and peer mediation; (3) family counseling and early intervention activities that prevent family dysfunction; (4) innovative education and training for school personnel; and (5) programs to prevent and reduce the incidence of hate crimes.

Title V – Promoting Equity

• School Dropout Assistance Act–Designed to decrease the number of school dropouts through early identification of and intervention for those at risk and to encourage the return of those who have already left school. Activities may include the development and implementation of efforts to identify and address factors in a learner's decision to drop out of school that are related to gender and family roles, including activities and services designed to meet the needs of pregnant and parenting teens.

Title XI – Coordinated Services

• Coordinated services–This program is designed to give learners and their families better access to the social, health, and educational services necessary for children to succeed in school. Projects, through community-wide partnerships, will link services provided by public and private agencies at a coordination site located in or near a school.

• 21st Century Community Learning Centers Act–Authorizes grants for rural and inner-city public schools to develop a comprehensive local plan that enables the school to serve as a center to address the educational, health, social services, cultural, and recreational needs of the community. Activities may include (1) integrated education, health, social service, recreational, and cultural programs; (2) parenting skills education programs; (3) services for individuals with disabilities; (4) day care services; and (5) support and training for day care providers.

• Urban and rural education assistance–Authorizes grants to urban and rural schools to assist in school improvement efforts and school reform. Activities may include (1) pupil services and other support services; (2) collaborative efforts with health and social service agencies to provide comprehensive services and facilitate the transition from home to school; and (3) services to decrease the use of drugs and alcohol among learners and enhance their physical and emotional health.

MAKING FEDERAL LEGISLATION RELEVANT AT LOCAL LEVELS

Weckstein (1993) stated that civil rights implications make it essential that learners, parents, advocates, and educators work collaboratively to monitor both the local responses to federal regulations for individuals from special populations and their impact on these learners. In essence, this means staying awake and alert to instances in which individuals are denied access to programs and services that are guaranteed through legislation. It also means observing and communicating with others about changes in availability of support personnel needed to assist learners in programs once they have been admitted. The following steps were suggested so that educators could determine the local response to federal assurances for special needs individuals:

• Meet with the school, district, and state level staff to clarify their interpretation of the legislation and the responsibilities of programs to provide needed services. Get program information and announcements that go to learners and parents and examine how local educational agencies and programs are interpreting the regulations.

• Become familiar with the requirements for learners with support services required to participate and succeed in the career and technical program. Provision of work-based programs, transition programs and support, and access to vocational education are now all addressed under the definition of special education.

• Rely on the Office of Civil Rights vocational education guidelines, which prohibit the denial of access to learners with disabilities based on the need for related aids or services, including modifications to equipment and courses.

• For limited-English proficient learners, rely on the Equal Education Opportunity Act of 1974 and Title VI of the Civil Rights Act of 1964, which require schools to take affirmative steps to assist learners in overcoming language barriers to their equal participation.

• Look at your state and local education agency applications for funds under the Carl Perkins Career and Technical Act as well as their evaluation and improvement process. The local application and any improvement application must be based upon an assessment of learner needs and must use the same equity and quality criteria in this act.

• Develop a team to discuss concerns about quality and access to vocational and tech-prep programs. Potential team members could include community development, corporation, labor unions, business, minority organizations, entrepreneurship training programs, employment and training programs, and university faculty (from education, planning, business management, or engineering schools).

• Communicate with others about your experiences and observations regarding local and state responses as programs respond to new regulations. Share information through newsletters, professional networks, and conferences. If necessary, use the available local and state due process, appeal, or mediation channels to obtain the needed services. (p. 3)

SUMMARY

There are many ways of describing an individual who is at risk. Regardless of the label used to categorize them, many of these individuals are at risk of not succeeding in our educational institutions. Kershner and Connolly (1991) described an individual who is at risk as a person who comes from a low socioeconomic background which may include various forms of family stress or instability. If that person is consistently discouraged by the educational system because he or she receives signals about academic inadequacies and failures, perceives little interest or caring from instructors, and sees the institution's discipline system as both ineffective and unfair, then it is not unreasonable to expect that the learner will become alienated and uncommitted to completing an education.

During the past few decades, the rights of individuals from special populations have been raised as a strong public issue. Since the Civil Rights Act of 1964, legislation has been passed to ensure the educational rights of individuals from special populations. Before these laws existed, many individuals with special needs were often ignored by society and were not considered to have the same rights as other citizens. Pressure from advocate, consumer, and parent groups began to mount. These groups asserted that all human beings, as individuals, deserved to share the same rights. Mandates have provided the incentive for public education institutions to provide access and equity to educational programs and services for all learners.

The characteristics of schools that have been successful in promoting learner achievement have become the focus of a body of research that characterizes effective schools. Effective schools are those in which all learners master priority learning objectives. The most prevalent elements of an effective school are (a) instructional leadership, (b) safe, orderly school climate, (c) high expectations for learner achievement, (d) focus on instruction, (e) monitoring and measuring progress, and (f) parent and community support.

Career and technical education is recognized as an important option for assisting individuals from special populations to bridge the gap between education and employment. During the past four decades, a number of pieces of legislation have been enacted to guarantee these learners the right to develop their vocational potential.

There are several major reasons why learners with special needs must be provided with opportunities to develop their vocational potential. Large numbers of these learners have left public schools without the competencies needed to secure a job. They often face unemployment and underemployment. Many remain dependent on society, which results in an economic drain as well as a great loss of undeveloped individual potential. It is imperative to prepare all learners, including those from special populations, with technical and other essential skills for success in the labor market.

Providing learners with special needs with a workforce preparation foundation is often accomplished through inclusion or integration into existing career and technical programs. Not every learner with special needs can or will be integrated into regular program activities. However, each learner must be given the chance to develop his or her vocational potential to the maximum degree.

Today, the level of commitment of career and technical instructors toward serving learners from special populations is rapidly increasing. Teachers, special needs personnel, counselors, school administrators, and interested members of the community at the local level are learning how to work together effectively to meet the challenge of educating these individuals.

SELF-ASSESSMENT

1. Identify some general characteristics of individuals from special populations and how these characteristics affect their ability to succeed in an educational setting.
2. Identify several educational factors that impact on the challenge to successfully serve individuals from special populations in our educational system.
3. Identify several economic factors that impact on the challenge to successfully serve individuals from special populations in our educational system.
4. List legislative mandates that have been passed regarding the vocational preparation of individuals from special populations. Include the key points from each law and discuss their implications for education and training programs.
5. Describe why individuals from special populations should be assured a full range of educational options.
6. Identify prevalent elements of an effective school.
7. Identify the primary characteristics of successful programs for learners who are at risk.
8. Describe why learners from special populations should be provided with equity and access to career and technical education programs.
9. Describe several demographic facts relating to individuals from special populations that will impact on the future workforce.
10. Identify several competencies that all workers will need in order to succeed in the labor force of the future.
11. Identify the components of exemplary career and technical special needs programs. Discuss the importance of each component and what would be needed in a school district to implement each.

12. Describe the effect that integrating individuals from special populations may have on career and technical education programs.
13. Describe the effect that integrating learners with special needs in career and technical education programs may have on our economy.
14. Identify several competencies that career and technical education instructors should have in order to successfully work with learners with special needs.

ASSOCIATED ACTIVITIES

1. Your administrator has asked you to talk to your colleagues at a staff development conference. You are to address the issue of integrating learners from special populations into existing career and technical education programs. Prepare an outline that includes the important points that you need to cover.
2. Meet with individuals in your school setting who work with learners from special populations. Discuss with them the problems that can arise in classroom settings and determine what support services are available within your institution, district, or campus. Develop an informal "guide" for your use so that you will know who to contact for what service(s). (A visit to the counselor's office is often a good place to start.)
3. List the barriers that learners with special needs might face when they attempt to enroll in career and technical education programs. Next, examine the career and technical programs in your school and identify the barriers that would make it difficult for these learners to enter and/or succeed in these programs. Prepare a plan to eliminate or modify these barriers.
4. You have been asked to submit a paper to a state or national journal. The title you are to address is "Strategies to Promote Success in Career and Technical Education Programs for Learners with Special Needs." Prepare a three-to-five page paper containing all important points for this potential publication.

REFERENCES

Academic Innovations. (2000). *At-risk students must believe*. [On-line]. Available: http://www.academicinnovations.com/believe.html

Americans with Disabilities Act of 1990, Pub. L. No. 101-336, United States Statutes at Large, (194), 327. Washington, DC: U.S. Government Printing Office.

American Vocational Association. (1998). *The official guide to the Perkins Acts of 1998*. Alexandria, VA: Author.

Baas (1991). *Promising strategies for at-risk youth*. Eugene, OR: ERIC Clearinghouse on Educational Management. ED 328958.

Berkell, D., & Brown, J. (1989). *Transition from school to work for persons with disabilities*. NY: Longman.

Bhaerman, R., & Kopp, K. (1998). *The school's choice: Guidelines for dropout prevention at the middle and junior high school*. Columbus, OH: The Ohio State University, National Center for Research in Vocational Education.

Bottge, B., & Yehle, A. (1999, Fall). Making standards-based instruction meaningful for all. *The Journal for Vocational Special Needs Education, 22*(1), 23-32.

Boyett, J. (1995). *Beyond workplace 2000*. New York: Penguin Books.

Bradley, L. (1993, March). Including students with disabilities in the mainstream. *Lincletter, 15* (3).

Brown, B. (1998). *Is vocational education working for high-risk populations*? ERIC Clearinghouse.

Burac, Z., & Bullock, C. (1993). The making of an exemplary program: Practices that work. *The Journal for Vocational Special Needs Education, 15*(2), 36-39.

Bureau of Labor Statistics. (1999). *Message from the Secretary of Labor: Report on the American workforce*. Washington, DC: U.S. Department of Labor.

Carl D. Perkins Vocational Education Act of 1984, Pub. L. No. 98-524, United States Statutes at Large, (98), 22435. Washington, DC: U.S. Government Printing Office.

Carl D. Perkins Vocational and Applied Technology Act of 1990, Pub. L. No. 101-392, United States Statutes at Large, (104), 753. Washington, DC: U.S. Government Printing Office.

Carl D. Perkins Vocational and Technical Education Act of 1998, Pub. L. No. 105-332, United States Statutes at Large, (12), 3077. Washington, DC: U.S. Government Printing Office.

Committee for Economic Development (1987). *Children in need: Investment strategies for the educationally disadvantaged*. Washington, DC: Research and Policy Committee.

Comprehensive Employment and Training Act of 1973, Pub. L. No. 93-203, United States Statutes at Large, (87), 839. Washington, DC: U.S. Government Printing Office.

Conley, D. (1992). *Some emerging trends in school restructuring*. ERIC Digest #67.

Conley, D. (1993). *Roadmap to restructuring: Policies, practices, and the emerging visions of schooling*. Eugene, OR: ERIC Clearinghouse on Educational Management, University of Oregon.

Cross City Campaign for Urban School Reform. (2001). *High schools in focus*. [On-line]. Available: http://www.crosscity.org/pubs/flashfacts2.htm

Cross City Campaign for Urban School Reform. (2001). *Small schools*. [On-line]. Available: http://www.crosscity.org/pubs/flashfacts1.htm

Davis, W. & McCaul, E. (1991). *The emerging crises: Current and projected status of children in the United States*. (Monograph). Orono, ME: Institute for the Study of At-Risk Students.

Duttweiler, P. (1997, Winter/Spring). Gay and lesbian youth at-risk. *The Journal of At-Risk Issues, 3*(2).

Education for All Handicapped Children Act of 1975, Pub. L. No. 94-142, United States Statutes at Large, (89), 773. Washington, DC: U.S. Government Printing Office.

Education of the Handicapped Amendments of 1983, Pub. L. No. 98-199, United States Statutes at Large, (97), 1357. Washington, DC: U.S. Government Printing Office.

Education of the Handicapped Act Amendments of 1986, Pub. L. No. 99-457, United States Statutes at Large, (100), 1145. Washington, DC: U.S. Government Printing Office.

Eisenberg, L. (1991). *What's happening to American families?* ED 330496.

Fletcher, M. (2001, March 5). Dropout rate puts educator to test. *Las Vegas Review–Journal*. Las Vegas, NV.

Frymier & Gansneder. (1989). *Phil Delta Kappan, 70*,142.

Goals 2000: Educate America Act of 1994, Pub. L. No. 103-227, United States Statutes at Large, (108), 125. Washington, DC: U.S. Government Printing Office.

Grantham, C. (2000). *The future of work.* New York: McGraw-Hill.

Gray, K., & Herr, E. (2000). *Other ways to win.* Thousand Oaks, CA: Corwin Press.

Hayward, B., & Tallmadge, G. (1995). *Strategies for keeping kids in school: Evaluation of dropout prevention and reentry projects in vocational education. Final report.* Washington, DC: U.S. Department of Education.

Hess-Grabill, D. & Bueno, S. (2000). *Roadmap to Perkins III: A guidebook for Illinois.* Bloomington, IL: Illinois Center for Specialized Professional Support.

Hill, S. & Bishop, H. (1993). *A review of the literature regarding the impact of vocational education student retention: A paper to support a research study regarding Georgia secondary school vocational instructors, vocational education supervisors, and principals.* ED 371219.

Hill, J. (1992). *The new American school.* Lancaster, PA: Technomic Publishing Company.

Hixon, J. & Tinzmann, M. (1990). *Who are the "at-risk" students of these 1990s?* Portland, OR: North Carolina Regional Educational Laboratory.

Imel, S. (1993). *Vocational education's role in dropout prevention.* Columbus, OH: ERIC Clearinghouse on Adult, Career, and Vocational Education. ED 355455.

Imel, S. (2000). *Welfare to work: Considerations for adult and vocational education programs.* Columbus, OH: ERIC Clearinghouse on Adult Career and Vocational Education. ED 440253.

Improving America's Schools Act of 1994, Pub. L. No. 103-382, United States Statutes at Large, (1108), 3518. Washington, DC: U.S. Government Printing Office.

Individuals with Disabilities Education Act of 1990, Pub. L. No. 101-476, United States Statutes at Large, (104), 1103. Washington, DC: U.S. Government Printing Office.

Individuals with Disabilities Education Act Amendments of 1997, Pub. L. No. 105-17, United States Statutes at Large, (111), 37. Washington, DC: U.S. Government Printing Office.

Job Training Partnership Act of 1982, Pub. L. No. 97-300, United States Statutes at Large, (96), 1322. Washington, DC: U.S. Government Printing Office.

Job Training Reform Amendments of 1992, Pub. L. No. 102-367 United States Statutes at Large, (106), 1021. Washington, DC: U.S. Government Printing Office.

Kerka, S. (1991). *Balancing work and family life.* ERIC Digest #110.

Kershner, K., & Connolly, J. (Eds.). (1991). *At-risk students and school restructuring.* Philadelphia: Research for Better Schools.

Knoblauch, B., & McLane, K. (June 1999). *An overview of the Individuals with Disabilities Education Act Amendments of 1997 (PL 105-17): Update 1999.* Arlington, VA: The ERIC Clearinghouse on Disabilities and Gifted Education.

Kochhar, C., & Deschamps, A. (1992). Public crossroads in preserving the right of passage to independence for learners with special needs. *The Journal for Vocational Special Needs Education, 14*(2 and 3), 9-19.

Lehr, J., & Harris, J. (1988). *At-risk, low-achieving students in the classroom.* Washington, DC: National Education Association.

Lerman, R. & Schmidt, S. (1999). *An overview of economic, social, and demographic trends affecting the U.S. labor market.* Washington, DC: The Urban Institute.

Markham, K. (1993). *Standards for student performance.* ERIC Digest, #81.

Marsh, D., & Codding, J. (Eds.). (1999). The new American high school. Thousand Oaks, CA: Corwin Press.

Meers, G., & Towne, V. (1997). Missions and milestones: Yesterday, today and tomorrow in vocational special needs education. *The Journal for Vocational Special Needs Education, 19*(3), 94-98.

Minkin, B. (1995). *Future in sight.* New York: Macmillan.

National Center for Education Statistics. (1996). *Dropout rates in the United States: 1996. Executive Summary.* Washington, DC: Author

National Center for Education Statistics. (1999). *Dropout rates in the United States: 1999. Executive Summary.* Washington, DC: Author.

National Center for Education Statistics. (2000). [On-line]. Available: http://nces.ed.gov/quicktables

National Commission on Children. (1991). *Beyond rhetoric: A new American agenda for children and family.* Washington, DC: U.S. Government Printing Office.

National Skill Standards Act of 1994 (Title V of Goals 2000: Educate America Act), Pub. L. No. 103-227. United States Statutes at Large, (108), 125. Washington, DC: U.S. Government Printing Office.

Neubert, D. (2000). Transition education and services guidelines. In P. Sitlington, G. Clark, & O. Kolstoe, *Transition education and services for adolescents with disabilities.* Boston, MA: Allyn and Bacon, 39-69.

Personal Responsibility and Work Opportunity Reconciliation Act of 1996, Pub. L. No. 104-193, United States Statutes at Large, (110), 2105. Washington, DC: U.S. Government Printing Office.

Rehabilitation Act of 1973, Pub. L. No. 93-112. United States Statutes at Large, (87), 355. Washington, DC: U.S. Government Printing Office.

Rehabilitation Act Amendments of 1986, Pub. L. No. 99-506, United States Statutes at Large, (100), 1807. Washington, DC: U.S. Government Printing Office.

Rehabilitation Act Amendments of 1992, Pub. L. No. 102-569, 42 USC 2000e-16; 29 USC 794a. Washington, DC: U.S. Government Printing Office.

Rehabilitation Act Amendments of 1998, Pub. L. No. 105-220, United States Statutes at Large, (112), 1581. Washington, DC: U.S. Government Printing Office.

Rothwell, W. (1991, August). HRD and the Americans with disabilities act. *Training and Development.*

Schwartz, W. (1995). *School dropouts: New information about an old problem.* ERIC/CUE Digest, #108.

School-to-Work Opportunities Act of 1994, Pub. L. No. 103-239, United States Statutes at Large, (108), 568. Washington, DC: U.S. Government Printing Office.

Stein, D. (2000). *The new meaning of retirement.* ERIC Digest #217.

Uchida, D. (1996). *Preparing students for the 21st century.* Arlington, VA: American Association of School Administrators.

Weckstein. (1993). What should education agencies and programs do now? *Capital Connection Policy Newsletter, 1* (1), p.3. Washington, DC: George Washington University, Division on Career Development and Transition.

Vocational Education Act of 1963, Pub. L. No. 88-210, United States Statutes at Large, (77), 403, 1-16. Washington, DC: U.S. Government Printing Office.

Vocational Education Amendments of 1968, Pub. L. No. 90-576, United States Statutes at Large, (82), 1064. Washington, DC: U.S. Government Printing Office.

Vocational Education Amendments of 1976, Pub. L. No. 94-482, United States Statutes at Large, (90), 2081. Washington, DC: U.S. Government Printing Office.

Wilson, D. (1989). *Effective schools research and dropout reduction.* Austin, TX: Texas Education Agency.

Woloszyk, C. (1996). *Models for at-risk youth. Final report.* Kalamazoo, MI: Upjohn Institute for Employment Research. ED 404-77.

Workforce Investment Act of 1998, Pub. L. No. 105-220, United States Statutes at Large, (112), 937. Washington, DC: U.S. Government Printing Office.

Overview of Career and Technical Education

INTRODUCTION

Career and technical education is the primary system through which youth and adults are prepared to enter competitive employment and continue lifelong learning. Career and technical education, an important component of the American education system, serves the purpose of providing learning experiences that help learners explore career areas and prepare for employment and independent living. Career and technical education curricula include materials that focus on the development of foundational skills, such as basic skills, thinking skills, and personal qualities, as well as a common core of workplace competencies and the specific skill competencies required for each occupational area. Career and technical education programs make use of real-life situations in classrooms and laboratories as well as supervised work experiences in internships, practicums, cooperative education, and apprenticeships. These programs are offered in many different forms at the secondary and postsecondary levels with some pre-career and technical programs provided in some school systems at the middle/junior high school level.

The vast majority of secondary learners and about half of the subbaccalaureate learners who are enrolled in postsecondary institutions take career and technical education courses. Career and technical education is delivered through a variety of general labor and specific labor market programs in both public and private secondary and postsecondary schools. Traditional program areas include agriculture, business, family and consumer sciences, health, marketing, trade and industry, and technical communications. These programs provide a variety of program areas and courses for those planning to take a concentration of courses required to enter a chosen labor market field. In addition to specific labor market preparation programs, career and technical education offers programs of general labor market preparation such as technology (formerly industrial arts), family and consumer sciences, general work experience, and computers. The U.S. Department of Education has established 16 career clusters as an organized framework for understanding and classifying workforce preparation programs such as those offered through career and technical education.

Career and technical education is being affected by the technological, social, and economic changes that are transforming our world, and educators at every level are responding by changing their curriculum and instructional practices to better prepare learners to compete in the job market and succeed in continuing education. Career and technical education teachers are professionals who are actively engaged in professional development activities like those offered by the Association for Career and Technical Education (ACTE), which has as its mission to provide educational leadership in developing a competitive American workforce. Career and technical education programs have changed a great deal in the last decade, and the separation between academic education and career and technical education is giving way to curriculum and instructional articulation that provides learners with both the academic and technical skills needed to function in the family, community, and workplace. Business and industry is becoming more actively involved in career and technical education programs through partnerships with educational institutions and through input into the standards, curriculum, and assessment practices used in career and technical education programs.

The current system of career and technical education in the United States is the product of an extended period of experimentation and development through an evolutionary process spanning thousands of years. Career and technical education as we know it today has been shaped by philosophical, educational, economic, societal, and political forces that continue to impact all education. For over 80 years, Congress has responded to these forces through federal legislation linked in a cooperative venture with state and local education agencies to provide funding and direction for career and technical education. The field has evolved from the three programs areas of agriculture, home economics (family and consumer sciences), and trade and industrial education to a broad area dedicated to preparing individuals at the secondary and postsecondary levels for an array of careers. The Carl D. Perkins Vocational and Technical Education Act of 1998 is the current legislation affecting career and technical education.

A review of the history of career and technical education will help those involved in it understand its inner workings. It is beyond the scope of this chapter to provide more than a summary of the history and development of career and technical education, but your authors have published a textbook entitled *Overview of Career and Technical Education* that provides readers with a detailed history of this important form of education.

OUTLINE

SUMMARY OF THE ROOTS OF CAREER AND TECHNICAL EDUCATION
FEDERAL WORKFORCE LEGISLATION
DEFINING CAREER AND TECHNICAL EDUCATION
CAREER AND TECHNICAL EDUCATION PROGRAM SETTINGS
SECONDARY CAREER AND TECHNICAL EDUCATION PROGRAMS AND CURRICULUM
POSTSECONDARY CAREER AND TECHNICAL EDUCATION PROGRAMS AND CURRICULUM
TRENDS FOR CAREER AND TECHNICAL EDUCATION
SNAPSHOT OF CAREER AND TECHNICAL EDUCATION PROGRAMS
CAREER AND TECHNICAL EDUCATION PROGRAMS
SUMMARY
SELF-ASSESSMENT
ASSOCIATED ACTIVITIES
REFERENCES

OBJECTIVES

After completing this chapter, the reader should be able to accomplish the following:

1. Describe the purposes of career and technical education programs at the middle/junior high school, high school, and postsecondary levels.
2. Describe the curriculum and instructional delivery system for a typical secondary and postsecondary career and technical education program.
3. Describe the special career and technical education programs of tech-prep, youth apprenticeship, cooperative education, internships and practicums as defined by the Carl D. Perkins Vocational and Technical Education Act of 1998 and how they operate.
4. Describe a typical job shadowing or school-based/enterprise that would complement a career and technical education program.
5. Describe some of the trends affecting career and technical education.
6. Describe the enrollment trends, popular programs, credits earned, and academic achievement of secondary career and technical concentrators, as well as the enrollment trends of subbaccalaureate learners in postsecondary institutions.
7. Identify the 16 career clusters established by the U.S. Department of Education and describe how they can be useful for program and curriculum development as well as for career guidance.
8. Describe some local programs that provide support services for career and technical education learners from special populations.
9. Describe the changes in career and technical education at the secondary level and the role of the federal government in improving education through partnerships with state and local educational agencies.
10. Describe the earliest forms of education for work, including apprenticeship, and how the work of European educational reformers impacted education in America.
11. Describe the development of universal education in America and the development of junior and comprehensive high schools.
12. Describe some of the early attempts to introduce practical subjects into the common and high school curricula.
13. Define the following terms: mechanics institute, American Lyceum, manual labor schools, trade schools, corporate schools, manual training, arts and crafts movement, practical arts, and career and technical education.
14. Describe the major elements of the Carl D. Perkins Vocational and Technical Education Act of 1998, the major provisions of the Individuals With Disabilities Education Act Amendments of 1998, and the Workforce Investment Act of 1998.

TERMS

American Lyceum	industrial arts	mechanics institute
apprenticeship	internship	practicum
arts and crafts movement	job shadowing	school-based enterprise
career academy	manual arts	technology education
career and technical education	manual labor	trade school
common school	manual training	universal education

SUMMARY OF THE ROOTS OF CAREER AND TECHNICAL EDUCATION

From the dawn of civilization to the present time, two kinds of education have emerged: education for work and education for culture. For many years education for work was carried on almost wholly through practical experiences with tools, materials, utensils, and machines in the home, field, shop, store, and factory and only recently through organized career and technical education programs offered in secondary and postsecondary institutions. In contrast, education for culture has always been delivered through the medium of books and through formalized instruction in the home by private tutors, in church-related schools, private schools, and later in history, through public schools.

For centuries these two types of education were widely separated and learners of each type of education differed widely in social and educational classes. In recent times, however, these types of education have been moving closer together and in many cases have combined to meet the modern view that what is needed in today's world is a fusion of the two. In fact, educational leaders of today are advocating a new pedagogy that combines academic and experiential education in a system of lifelong learning in school, community, and work. Although changes resulting in combining these two distinct types of education have been made only in recent times, they have not been the result of a sudden stroke of the pen but rather have been the subject of discussion, controversy, and experimentation for hundreds of years.

Much of what we know about ancient history is provided through artifacts of the tools and implements that early man used to survive. Very early, people learned that by using their intellect to develop tools, work could be performed more easily and the necessities of life (food, clothing, and shelter) could be provided with less effort. The constant search for a way to relieve the burden of work and improve living standards has led to the modern technological world. See Appendix.

Individuals have learned to work by various methods, perhaps first by accident, followed by imitation, trial and error, and eventually through planned learning experiences in an apprenticeship (a semi-formal method of education where a learner is instructed by a master craftsman), the earliest recorded form of planned learning. Proceeding apprenticeship was the practice of parents assuming the role of teaching their children how to use their heads and hands to provide the necessities of life. Although this parent-child form of education was an unconscious process of imitative learning, it was very effective, for it enabled primitive people to survive their unstable environment. The study of history is very much a study of how people learned to work, survive, advance, and the study of tools and implements that were developed along the way to make this work possible and more efficient. See Figure 2-1.

BRIEF HISTORY OF WORK EDUCATION THROUGH THE 1500s

Paleolithic period	Tools fashioned from stone
Neolithic period	Animals domesticated and crops cultivated
Agricultural civilization	Ox-drawn wooden plow utilized
Bronze Age	Tools and weapons fashioned from copper and bronze
Iron Age/Greek civilization	Tools, weapons, and utensils fashioned from iron; items for trade manufactured in Athens and Sparta
Roman civilization	Elementary, secondary, and higher education levels of schooling developed
Middle Ages	Merchants engaged in commerce; guilds governing apprenticeships and crafts created
Renaissance and Reformation	Culture engaged in learning and commerce

Figure 2-1. Examples of developments through different historical periods.

From the sixteenth to the nineteenth centuries, traditional ideas about educational theory and practice based on humanism (the teaching of classical literature from a purely grammatical and linguistic point of view) were supplemented by the views and experiments of educational reformers like Martin Luther, who advocated two hours of formal schooling each day with the remaining time allocated for ordinary economic duties and for learning a trade. Many other reformers were critical of the form of schooling provided in educational institutions of the time and recommended that school subjects could be learned more effectively through games, recreation, interaction with the natural environment, and manual labor.

Most reformers favored educational methods that promoted learning through experience and investigation. Many of the ideas and principles of these reformers have become basic principles of educational pedagogy today, such as the tenets of John Comenius that objects should be taught first and then the characteristics of the object and that words could be understood better when they were linked to objects familiar to the learner. Comenius was a leader of the sense-realism movement and developed nine tenets concerning education. He proposed levels of schooling beginning with an infant school, then a vernacular or elementary school, and finally a gymnasium or secondary school.

Francis Bacon was one of the first educational leaders to use the term *manual arts* in his discussion of how learning could be improved by studying nature and making observations and experiments of concrete, common objects and real-world experiences. He became one of the early leaders of the realism philosophy out of which developed the educational philosophy of pragmatism. Pragmatism has been the main philosophical thought guiding career and technical education in the United States since its inception. Many more principles and practices of education developed by European reformers were transported to America. See Figure 2-2.

Early Career and Technical Education in America

The foundations of the American educational system were built on the types of education that had evolved in Europe. In colonial America, the responsibility of providing education, both basic and vocational, fell on the extended family, with some instruction in reading and writing provided by the church. For over 150 years colonial America used an American version of apprenticeship as the chief source of education and training for the masses. As the factory system of production developed and millions of immigrants and rural Americans poured into the manufacturing cities to work at the same detailed tasks every day, the interest in apprenticeship, which featured comprehensive training, declined because these new tasks did not require much training. New systems of education and training were surfacing in a progressive America and apprenticeship was regulated to serving a small number of people in specific occupational areas. These new educational thrusts included the beginnings of universal education; the mechanics institute, American Lyceum, manual labor, and trade school movements; corporate schools; educational reforms in the common school; the manual training movement; the beginnings of the comprehensive high school; American sloyd; the arts and crafts movement; correspondence schools; and manual and industrial arts.

Education in the colonies fell chiefly to the church and family. These entities shouldered the responsibility of teaching children how to read and participate in church services. In addition, families served as the center for apprenticeship training, the only means of education available for most American families. Most families were engaged in agriculture or in trades such as blacksmithing, carpentry, leather tanning, spinning, etc., and imparted their skills through the father-son, mother-daughter informal apprenticeship system. Wealthy families established private schools for their children or hired tutors, and some even sent their children to Europe for formal schooling. Churches provided elementary education in reading, writing, and church doctrine so that children could read and understand the Bible and church theology, but the amount of elementary education many children received from their parents was limited because many parents were illiterate and therefore could only provide training in the things required to provide sustenance for the family. From the beginning, colonists sup-

EUROPEAN EDUCATIONAL REFORMERS WHO SHAPED AMERICAN PRACTICE	
Martin Luther	Advocated two hours of formal schooling each day with the remaining time allocated for ordinary economic duties and for learning a trade
John Comenius	Developed nine tenets concerning education and proposed levels for schooling; leader of the sense-realism movement
Francis Bacon	Used the term "manual arts" in his discussion of how learning could be improved by studying nature and making observations and experiments of concrete, common objects and real-world experiences
Richard Mulcaster	Introduced drawing as a subject
Samuel Hartlib	Proposed government agencies that became the predecessors of bureaus of education
Sir William Petty	Advocated publishing great encyclopedias for the arts and sciences
John Locke	Advocated a system of education that would fit youth for a practical life
August Franke	Advocated a seminary for training teachers
Johann Hecker	Developed the concept of a "realschule" that would change the curriculum and teaching methods to emphasize teaching realities and subjects believed to be useful for students later in life
Jean-Jacques Rousseau	Advocated an education system that emphasized nature study and the manual arts
Johann Pestalozzi	Developed educational principles grounded in psychology that became the basic principles of education today
Johann Herbart	Developed Herbartian psychology
Friedrich Froebel	Advocated Petalozzian principles of education; father of the kindergarten
Otto Salomon	Developed the sloyd system of hand tool work introduced in the elementary school
Gustaf Larson	Introduced sloyd into the manual training movement in America
Victor Della Vos	Developed a system of tool instruction in Russia that radically changed manual training in America

Figure 2-2. Accomplishments of several European educational reformers.

ported the idea of literacy for their children, first as a means of purifying the soul and later to promote social equality through the belief that literacy was the right of all people (Barlow, 1976).

American Apprenticeship

The early colonists imported the concept of apprenticeship to America and adjusted the concept to meet their needs. Two forms of apprenticeship emerged: voluntary and involuntary or compulsory. Voluntary apprenticeship involved an individual agreeing to be bound to a master to learn a trade or craft. Involuntary or compulsory apprenticeship involved a master becoming responsible for poor children and orphans, thus providing a means of meeting their personal and occupational needs.

In general, apprenticeship in colonial America followed the traditions of Europe, but town governments instead of guilds controlled apprenticeship through laws. These laws ensured that the children would receive an education and be prepared for productive work. It was only natural that town governments would regulate apprenticeship because all decisions regarding the town, e.g. political, educational, economic, and social, were made at the town meetings where people were invited and encouraged to attend and participate. Apprenticeship agreements provided for room and board; clothing; religious training; general education; knowledge, understanding, and experience in the trade skills; and finally, instruction in the "mysteries" of the trade or practices that had an elementary scientific basis. Both boys and girls were apprenticed beginning at age eight or nine for varying periods of time, with the norm being from 5 to 10 years. Girls usually served until the age of 18 or until they married.

Apprenticeship declined in importance in the colonial period and was dealt the heaviest blow by the factory system in the nineteenth century. There were a number of reasons for its decline: (1) the abundance of land, which encouraged young men and women to establish their own lives, (2) the long periods of apprenticeship (up to 10 years) in which marriage was forbidden, (3) the confusion of apprentices with indentured servants (individuals who were sold into binding work agreements to pay their way to America), (4) the mobility and freedom of the people, (5) the willingness of the frontier people to make do with handmade furniture and implements, (6) the immigration of mechanics and craftsworkers from Europe, and (7) the division of labor in household factories that no longer required workers to make complete products from scratch.

Apprenticeship served as the chief source of education and training for the masses for over 150 years. New systems of education and training were beginning to surface in a progressive America that would relegate apprenticeship to only a small number of people. While a small number of workers continued to be thoroughly trained through apprenticeship, most workers learned job skills from their parents or through on-the-job training (learning job skills through observation and imitation).

Beginnings of Universal Education

Apprenticeship in America was considered an educational institution and not solely a means to prepare skilled crafts workers. Very early on, however, colonial town leaders recognized that many masters could not read and write well enough to provide adequate instruction in these subjects, which lead to the development of schools to meet this educational need. In 1647, the general court of Massachusetts ordered towns of more than 50 households to employ a teacher to provide basic instruction in reading, writing, and arithmetic. Other colonies began to recognize the importance of elementary education to the survival and progress of a free society. In 1685, Thomas Budd developed an educational plan calling for seven years of compulsory education in Pennsylvania and New Jersey, which was to be funded by rent from 1,000 acres of land donated to the community to support a school. The proposed curriculum was a common core of reading, writing, arithmetic, and specialty areas for girls (spinning, weaving, sewing) and boys (joinery, turning, shoemaking). His proposal for education was not well accepted, but in 1747 the Moravian Brethren established a public school based on Budd's plan in Bethlehem, Pennsylvania (Walter, 1993).

Ben Franklin was concerned with broadening educational opportunities for common people and expanding the curriculum beyond the classics and religion to include in the same school instruction in the common trades. The Franklin Academy of Philadelphia opened its doors in 1751 but this new educational experiment was short lived, and in 1775 the school changed direction toward serving the elite. This academy later became the University of Pennsylvania (Barlow, 1976).

Franklin's experiment in combining academic subjects and those of a practical nature in the academy spread to other parts of the country and has continued into today. A takeoff on the concept of an academy is the career academies that are currently operating in some states. Career academies are programs designed to integrate academic and career and technical education curricula organized around a theme (occupation areas such as health, aerospace, etc.), which are taught as a "school-within-a-school" where learners take a sequence of courses together. Career academy programs encompass a set of jobs ranging from those that require no postsecondary education to those requiring an advanced degree.

Following the Revolutionary War, the need for a common system of education emerged as an essential element of a democratic society. Leaders of the new independent nation of America viewed education as important in promoting nationalism and balancing freedom and order. They saw the need for the development of moral character in its citizens in order to promote a society that would have social and political order.

According to Spring (1990), a new belief grew out of the Lancasterian system of instruction, which contended that moral character was shaped by the way learners interacted in schools as well as through the learning of didactic materials. This belief of the importance of institutional arrangements in the development of moral character led to the conclusion that all children should be educated in a common school system. The notion of developing moral character as well as intelligence through common schooling was supported by proponents of faculty psychology. Faculty psychology maintained that the human mind was divided into different parts, such as intelligence and morality, and that these different parts (faculties) were natural components of the individual and could be influenced by environment (schooling).

Powerful leaders like Benjamin Rush, the leading physician of the late 1700s and the father of American psychiatry, and Horace Mann, the father of the common school, were strong supporters of faculty psychology and the belief that virtuous functioning of the moral faculty is dependent upon how it is cultivated. Both of these leaders argued that discipline and exercise of the various faculties of the mind where necessary for proper development toward the goal of the perfectibility of the human being and that controlling the institutional environment was critical to this process (Spring, 1990).

Post–Revolutionary War formal education was chiefly supported and conducted by the church or through special schools (charity schools) established for poor and orphaned children by wealthy individuals or societies. At the same time, a process of change resulting from a variety of forces (philanthropic, political, economic, social) and moving control of education from churches and private ownership to the state was underway. According to Spring (1990) a number of charity schools and juvenile reformatories developed in the United States in the early 1800s to help reduce the crime and poverty that resulted from large concentrations of people in urban areas working long hours at industrial jobs and thus failing to provide a nurturing family environment. This charity school movement was important for it provided the framework for the later development of public schools and was the first attempt to use schools as a means of socializing children and preparing them for an industrious way of life.

Charity schools were established as a way of providing learners with instruction to create good moral character and to replace a weak family structure as well as a way of keeping children off the streets and away from criminal associations. Many charity schools adopted the Lancasterian system of instruction, which featured learners seated in rows receiving instruction from monitors. These monitors had previously received instruction from the master teacher who was seated at the front of the room. Monitors were selected from among the better learners in a class and wore badges indicating their achievement rank. The Lancasterian system of instruction for learners was similar to the factory system of production for adults and was called a "manufactory of knowledge" (Spring, 1990).

A learner's submission to this factory system of education was supposed to result in a sense of orderliness and obedience. Learners were constantly moving through materials with monitors that required discipline and order. Learners who did not comply or were idle suffered some unique punishment. Business and industry leaders advocated this system of instruction, for the virtues of submission, order, and industriousness were considered essential for functioning in the workplace. In addition, this system was appreciated because it was efficient, was inexpensive to operate, and could serve a large number of learners with one teacher. However, charity schools presented a problem in the socialization process; they created a division between the social classes, with the poor attending charity schools and the economically fortunate attending other private schools and public institutions.

According to Spring (1990), the belief in the ameliorating power of schooling became an essential part of the common school movement in the 1830s and 1840s. Charity schools provided a working model for the establishment of common school systems. It was hoped that the negative aspect of charity schools, which reinforced social class differences, would be overcome in the common school, where learners from different social classes would be mixed together in the same school facility. The emphasis on moral development that was the chief outcome of charity schools could be offered to all social classes in common schools. The Lancasterian system of factory-type education also carried over to the common school movement, resulting in the seating arrangement of learners and strict disciplinary control of instruction. Charity schools also paved the way for the belief that schools could be one of the best institutions to solve the problems of society and that belief continues to receive strong support from the general public today. Charity schools embodied the belief that education could end poverty and crime in society and this belief also carried over to the common school system that followed.

The American constitution had not addressed education directly, since education was considered a state responsibility. In time, education in America came to be viewed as a "concern of the federal government, a function of the state, and a responsibility of the local government" (Barlow, 1976). In the late 1700s and early 1800s church schools and private schools, including schools for the well-to-do as well as the charity and reform schools mentioned earlier, served those whose parents desired an education for them and those who needed a moral education to escape poverty and crime. There were no compulsory school laws, so the vast majority of children did not attend school and were taught the basics of living by their parents or through apprenticeship. Vast numbers of immigrants were coming from Germany, France, and other European countries and their children needed instruction in the American way of life.

There was considerable debate as to the type of education that was to be provided to learners of the new republic, but everyone agreed that democracy required an educated citizenry. The private schools simply could not handle all of these learners and leaders like Benjamin Franklin, Thomas Jefferson, Benjamin Rush, Samuel Harrison Smith, Samuel Knox, and later Horace Mann began to propose the formation of a common school system for all children.

Thomas Jefferson furthered the ideas and concepts proposed earlier by Benjamin Franklin that education should prepare a person for life in the business and social world. His plan for a universal, secular, public education system was proposed in 1779 in a bill to the Virginia Legislature entitled "A Bill for the More General Infusion of Knowledge." He believed in educational equality, secularization of school curriculum, separation of church and state, state systems of education, local educational initiative, and academic freedom. Jefferson's bill passed in the Virginia legislature in 1796 but was never implemented by the state. Jefferson's terms *public school* and *universal education* had different meanings to the 13 early states, and these two educational concepts received much discussion among educational philosophers and statesmen. While the idea of universal education and public expense continued to be debated, the movement to meet the basic educational needs of poor children through private or philanthropic efforts and apprenticeship continued (Martin, 1981).

Three important occurrences that were landmarks in the movement to establish universal public education at public expense were (1) the development of a system of public primary schools in Boston in 1818, (2) the establishment of a public high school in Boston in 1821, and (3) the passage in 1827 of a law in Massachusetts requiring the establishment of high schools in cities, towns, and districts of 500 families or more (Edwards and Richey, 1963). These three events, coupled with the semiprivate academies initiated by Benjamin Franklin that featured diversified and flexible curricula including English, classical studies, and practical studies, paved the way for a universal, public-supported educational system at the elementary and high school levels. Academies attracted all types of learners, but they charged tuition. This made it impossible for many working-class families to afford the kind of education they wanted for their children. What was needed for most American youth was a system of free public elementary and secondary education (Martin, 1981).

According to Spring (1990), the 1830s and 1840s are known as the decades of the common school movement in the United States. Before the common school period, a variety of public and private school organizations existed. For example, Boston had established the first system of urban education in the 1790s. States like New York and Pennsylvania supported a system of charity schools since a majority of learners in those states attended private schools. In 1821, Ohio law permitted the taxation of all

property in a district for the support of schools and the state created a permanent school fund in 1827. While these states and others had taken action to provide support for public education, they did not approximate the distinct features of the common school—a school under state control teaching a common body of knowledge to learners from diverse social and economic backgrounds.

Spring (1990) points out the three distinct aspects of the common school movement that made it different from other educational ventures. The first was an emphasis on educating all children in a common schoolhouse. It was argued that if learners attended a common school in which a common political and social ideology was taught, they would be prepared to deal with political and social problems and meet the expectation of national unity among diverse populations. A second aspect of the common school movement was the idea of using schools as a means of conveying government policies. Earlier schools were created to provide leaders and responsible citizens for the new republic, but the common school movement took this idea a step further by implementing government policy to solve and control social, economic, and political problems. This idea led to the concept of the common school as a panacea for society's problems. The third distinctive feature of the common school movement was the creation of state agencies to control local schools. This feature was necessary to carry out government social, political, and economic policies and to maintain some sense of uniformity in the ways schools were formed and operated.

While New York was the first state to create a position of state school superintendent in 1812 and while other states followed that lead, it was not until the 1830s that state supervision and control of schools was widely implemented (due in part to the tireless work of Horace Mann, the first secretary of the Massachusetts Board of Education in 1837). These three aspects of the common school originated with the idea that human nature could be formed, shaped, and given direction if learners were educated in a formally organized institution. The concept of a common school had popular support from most segments of society. The African-American community saw schooling as a means for economic and social improvement. Leaders of educational reform saw the government-operated common school as a place where children could be educated for a more perfect society. Political factions like liberals and conservatives battled over the creation of a school system that would be beneficial to all members of society (Spring, 1990).

From the early 1800s until the passage of the famous Kalamazoo Case in 1872, which paved the way for the right of states to collect taxes to support education, the movement to establish universal elementary and secondary education at public expense gained momentum under the untiring efforts of educational leaders like Horace Mann from Massachusetts. Mann was a firm believer in public support and control of education and felt that only through free, public, popular education could the excesses of a capitalistic democracy be eliminated. He believed strongly that education should be equally available to all classes and delivered through non-authoritarian and non-sectarian means. He further believed that the emphasis of school studies should be on the practical needs of the individual and that the individual should be actively involved in the learning process. Beginning in 1851 with Massachusetts, state after state began to pass legislation requiring the attendance of youth in state-supported schools until the eighth grade. By 1875, the nation's educational system became firmly established and attention began to focus on the high school curriculum, which was viewed by many to be too narrow and traditional. The high school was viewed as the people's school and the belief was that courses should be offered that met the needs of all learners. Some educational reformers were advocating expanding the curriculum to include the introduction of many new practical subjects like those offered in the early academies. It was through this reform movement, many years later, that vocational education (now career and technical education) had its beginning in the public schools of our nation (Martin, 1981).

Early Educational Efforts for Adults

While many children were receiving elementary education through church schools, secular Sunday schools serving all classes of learners, private academies, philanthropic institutions, apprenticeships, and eventually state-supported schools, older youth and adults also needed access to education to learn the basics and to improve their knowledge of democracy, citizenship, and work. The American labor force strongly supported the concept of free, public-supported schools for their children and the development of schools that could provide the educational advantages offered through apprenticeship but they also recognized the need to develop educational opportunities for employed workers. The mechanics institute movement, the American Lyceum movement, the manual labor movement, the early technical school movement and the trade school movement developed to provide education and training for adults.

Mechanics Institute. The mechanics institute movement in Europe and America arose as part of an effort to improve the economic and social conditions of industrial and agricultural workers and to provide a pool of educated and efficient workers for the merchant and manufacturing ruling class. These institutes were designed to provide adult workers with an education that encompassed technical and industrial instruction. The mechanics institutes were short-lived, with a few of them developing into technical or trade schools and the vast majority of them dying as a result of ineffective teaching and the formation of the land-grant colleges, American high schools, and private trade schools. These institutes conducted classes in the evenings for workers and played a significant role in the establishment of evening programs for adults in community colleges and the technical schools of today (Martin, 1981).

American Lyceum. The American Lyceum, created to serve towns in the country, was the counterpart of the mechanics institutes, which served cities and large towns. It was based on the concept that "men may improve themselves through sharing their knowledge and expertise." The lyceum was an organization in the towns of America where speeches were given to increase the knowledge of the common person. The lyceum movement, like the mechanics institute movement, was short-lived, but it served to popularize education for all and placed an emphasis on acquiring useful information. It perpetuated the idea that education was a community affair and responsibility, an idea that was critical to establishing publicly supported elementary and secondary schools (Martin, 1981).

Manual Labor Schools. In America, the manual labor movement was first introduced in order to integrate regular school subjects with agriculture training. Later, manual labor was used as a means of providing physical activity, reducing the cost of education by selling learner labor or the products of that labor, promoting a respect for all kinds of honest work, building individual character, promoting originality, stimulating intellectual development, and increasing the wealth of the country. Manual labor gained acceptance in a number of literary (higher education) institutions, such as the Oneida Institute in Whitesboro, New York, and in manual labor schools like those established in New Harmony, Indiana. Many private schools established for African-Americans, like the Hampton Institute in Virginia, established in 1868, and the Tuskegee Institute in Alabama, established in 1881, were manual labor schools that later incorporated manual training into their instructional programs. While manual labor schools were short-lived in the North, manual labor schools for African-Americans in the South continued to operate into the 1920s and beyond. The manual labor movement lasted for 15 years and then began to decline rapidly for a variety of reasons, including insufficient financial support from the institution or philanthropic society, manual work that was not educative, and manual work consisting of odd jobs not related to the learner's interest or later calling in life (Martin, 1981; Walter, 1993).

Early Technical Schools. The most popular subject for courses and lectures in the evening school programs of mechanics institutes and American Lyceums were those dealing with science and mathematics and their applications to agriculture and mechanical and manufacturing processes. As the teaching of science became more popular, a new type of full-time institution emerged. These institutions provided a curriculum to prepare individuals with advanced scientific knowledge in agriculture, the mechanic arts, and engineering. These schools were the early technical schools of our country and many of them later became engineering schools. One of the first of these was the Gardiner Lyceum in Maine, which opened in 1823, and was a full-time scientific and technical school at the college level.

After the Civil War, the idea of educated labor as opposed to just skilled labor gained wider acceptance. The public schools of that day resisted the inclusion of practical subjects, especially those that would prepare people for work. But the necessity of providing an education for the vast number of workers could not be overlooked. For over 50 years, private academies had included some practical subjects in the areas of business, domestic science (home economics), agriculture, and mechanical arts. Evening schools were established as a result of the mechanics institute and lyceum movements to provide related academic instruction to interested adult workers. Agriculture was promoted through a number of societies and departments of agriculture were established in academies, colleges, and universities The land-grant colleges and universities were established by the provisions of the Morrill Act of 1862 to provide instruction in agriculture, mechanical arts, and domestic science for higher education learners. The manual labor movement resulted in a number of institutions that attempted to meet the needs of the farmer and mechanic.

Early Trade Schools. The reconstruction period following the Civil War demanded a new type of school that could prepare people for employment in the rapidly expanding industrial economy. The trade school movement emerged to provide a workable system of industrial education for all Americans, regardless of the color of their skin. One of the first trade schools was Hampton Institute in Virginia, established in 1868 to provide both liberal education and trade training to African-Americans to improve character and social status. Learners devoted eight hours each day to the study of a trade through organized courses lasting for a three-year period, along with academic courses that required four years. If learners completed the entire four-year educational experience, they could earn a diploma. Booker T. Washington was one of the Hampton Institute's most famous graduates. He later became principal at the Tuskegee Institute in Alabama and had a distinguished educational career until his death in 1915 (Barlow, 1976).

The trade school was designed to provide specific trade training supplemented with directly related academic subjects. While the evening schools had attempted such training, they emphasized book learning and did not solve the need for an understanding of basic trade skills. Some trade schools were private tuition schools, some were free, and others were operated by manufacturing companies to train their employees.

Corporate Schools for Adults. Another type of trade school, the corporate school, was established by large manufacturing companies in an attempt to revise the old apprenticeship method of training high quality employees. It was believed that an apprenticeship program alone could not solve social and trade problems as well as a good trade school that incorporated academic instruction. One of the first corporate trade schools was established in 1872 by R. Hoe and Company—manufacturers of printing presses. The company needed an educated class of workers to produce improved machinery and responded to this need by establishing a school that met two evenings each week. The school was free to employees and although it was not compulsory, advancement opportunities were tied to participation. Modern companies are still using corporation schools to train workers.

Educational Reform in the Common School and Roots of the Comprehensive High School

Three major reform movements sought to introduce manual activity into the common schools (elementary schools) of America: the Oswego movement, the Quincy Plan, and the development of the American kindergarten. The Oswego movement was introduced in Oswego, New York, and adopted some of the teaching methods of Pestalozzi to train teachers to change their teaching methods from (1) memorization to reasoning and individual judgment, (2) book-centered to object-centered, (3) over-dependence on words in text to oral instruction using objects, (4) teachers "keeping school" to teachers teaching with skill, (5) textbook lessons to oral language lessons, (6) text-dictated lessons to teacher-planned lessons, and (7) reciting what was read to expressing ideas. (Wright, 1981).

The Quincy Plan was developed by Francis Parker in 1875 in Quincy, Massachusetts. The plan focused on an activity-oriented curriculum based on the needs and interests of children. Parker was able to Americanize Pestalozzi's ideas and develop a model of a child-centered curriculum that changed the teaching methods and curriculum of elementary education in this country. The American kindergarten was and remains the best example of a truly child-centered school. The kindergartens of America were based on the work of Friedrich Froebel and emphasized natural but directed self-activity and a focus upon educational, social, and moral ends. The kindergarten was intended to be a miniature ideal society—a place where people were courteous, helpful, and involved in cooperative activity. It emphasized doing, self-activity, individual expression, directed play, song, color, the story, nature study, gardening, and motor activity. Passive lessons were replaced with object lessons, stressing the use of concrete objects. The kindergarten had individual development as its primary aim, motor expression as its teaching method, and social cooperation as its means (Wright, 1981).

These three educational movements reshaped the elementary schools of America, but little progress was being made in including practical subjects in the high school curriculum. The academies modeled after Franklin's academy that once included practical subjects at the upper common school and high schools levels had all but eliminated these subjects (with the exception of some business subjects) and had become primarily academic. In 1890, high schools were highly selective and had programs mostly for young people preparing to become professionals, ministers, lawyers, doctors, teachers, and engineers. With the passage of compulsory school laws, the high schools of America had a much larger and diverse learner population to serve. Learners came to the high school with different social and cultural backgrounds, with low to high abilities, and with a wide variety of future job interests. The high school was no longer a transition school for those planning to enter college, it became a terminal school for the masses. Many high schools began to offer a two-tract curriculum, a practical one for terminal learners and a classical one for college-bound youth. The comprehensive high school that offered two parallel curriculums became the common high school model. There were, however, some special purpose high schools, such as the manual training high schools, and later, special high schools for commercial and agricultural pursuits (Smith, 1981).

The industrial revolution created a large working class that demanded new educational opportunities for their children. Industrialization was more than the growth of factories and urban areas: Industrialization was the foundation of the change in the whole structure of society. It created two classes of people: a working class and a non-working class. As time passed, the gap between these two classes continued to widen. Many of the children of the working class worked beside their parents in dangerous factories instead of attending school. The illiteracy rate of the working class soon became a problem. Parents who were illiterate and had limited practical skills could not pass on much of an education to their children. Crime was the second major problem plaguing society in the 1800s. It was out of these undesirable conditions of ignorance, delinquency, and human suffering that the drive to create a system of universal, free public schools was initiated. The working class wanted schools that would provide the basic academic skills for their children and would also include instruction in practical subjects that would prepare their children for better jobs than the ones they presently endured.

Drawing, initiated by Richard Mulcaster in England a hundred years earlier, had already been included in a number of high schools (it was a required subject in Boston high schools in 1836), but there was growing public sentiment in favor of including other types of practical subjects. Elementary schools had included more activity into their curriculum and some high schools had established programs in agriculture, general business, and domestic science (home economics) and more were being added as a result of land-grant universities. Technical schools at the college level had already experimented with combining shopwork with academic subjects in science and mathematics and found this curriculum vastly improved the

preparation of their engineering graduates. America was moving from an agricultural to an industrial society, and business and industry advocated the inclusion of subjects that would give learners, as part of their general education, the underlying principles and practices of industrial occupations so they would be better prepared to live in the new industrial society.

A great debate arose among educational leaders of the late 1800s over the inclusion of more practical subjects into the curriculum of the public high schools of America. Proponents argued that the lack of practical education in the public schools represented a deficiency in the school system and a lack of commitment to serving the majority of the learners. Opponents claimed that the introduction of practical subjects would interfere with the intellectual culture and that schools were not the place to prepare people for business and industry. From 1875 to 1900, the pages of educational literature covered the debate over what should be taught in the public schools—subjects preparing people for only culture or a mix of courses preparing people for both work and life. At the center of the debate was the new manual training movement championed by two engineering professors, Calvin Woodward, and John D. Runkle (Barlow, 1976).

Manual Training Movement. The manual training movement in America began at Washington University in St. Louis, Missouri and at the Massachusetts Institute of Technology (MIT). In 1878, Professor Calvin Woodward, dean of the Washington University Polytechnic faculty, implemented a program of shopwork for engineering learners so they could become more versed in the application of engineering principles through the use of tools and machines. He became convinced that secondary learners should have access to shop courses and that a combination of academics and shopwork would increase learner interest in school and provide a means of supplementing the mostly liberal education of the day. In 1880, with the philanthropic support of several prominent business leaders, the first manual training high school in America was established in St. Louis. It was a four-year institution that provided instruction in mathematics, science, drawing, language, and literature, as well as practice in the use of tools. Learners attended class six periods each day, one period for academic subjects and a double period for shopwork. The desired end of manual instruction was acquisition of skills in the use of tools and materials, not production of specific articles or direct preparation for the trades. The laboratory method of instruction was used. This consisted of graded lessons in the use (demonstrated by the instructor) of ordinary tools, with opportunities for learners to ask question and take notes, followed by the learners proceeding with their own work (Roberts, 1971).

In 1876, John Runkle, president of MIT, took a large party of learners and faculty to the Centennial Exposition in Philadelphia where he saw the solution to one of his most pressing problems: the methodology of providing practical training to his engineering learners. He and his learners were fascinated with the Russian exhibit of the Imperial Technical School of Moscow under the direction of Victor Della Vos. The four instructional directives of the Russian system that impressed them the most were: (1) separate instruction shops from construction shops, (2) provide only one kind of work in each shop, (3) provide as many workstations and tools for each station as a teacher can reasonably handle in one instructional period, and (4) graduate the instruction in each shop according to the difficulty and complexity of the operation. Upon Runkle's return from the exposition, he formulated and received approval from MIT to establish an American version of the Russian manual training system for his engineering learners at MIT. In addition, he established the School of Mechanic Arts, which was open to qualified grammar school learners (Barlow, 1976).

Woodward and Runkle soon became advocates for introducing manual training into the public schools of America. They proposed its inclusion because training in the manual arts was desirable and advantageous for all learners, regardless of their educational goals. They felt strongly that the education in the schools had been dealing too exclusively with the abstract and the remote and not enough with the concrete and the near at hand. They saw manual training as a way to improve the basic education of all youth. Woodward listed the following outcomes of manual training when combined with academic and moral training:

- longer attendance at school
- better intellectual development
- more wholesome moral education
- sound judgment of men and things
- better choice of occupation
- material success for the individual and the community
- elevation of the perception of manual occupations from brute, unintelligent labor to work requiring and rewarding both knowledge and skill
- basis for an individual career in the mechanical arts
- first step in the solution to labor problems
- basis for higher education

Woodward truly believed in manual activity as a way to enhance general education. He recognized that the overwhelming sentiment of educators was that vocational education had no place in the schools but should be the province of business and industry. He also recognized that business and industry wanted manual training to serve more of a vocational education purpose, but organized labor opposed manual training for fear it would flood the market with poorly trained workers who would be inferior to those produced through apprentice programs. He was keenly aware of the many critics that believed that anything manual could never be elevated to the same plane as the classics and made a part of the public school curriculum. Some educators supported the concept of manual training as long as it was conducted in a separate school

(Wright, 1981). The concept of manual training was first applied to industrial subjects to enhance general education. It was adopted by agriculture and home economic programs and later by business education programs and was commonly known as *practical arts*.

The success of the manual training school in St. Louis led to the establishment of manual training high schools in other cities and towns. Like the pioneer manual training school, most were established as separate and apart from academic high schools and supported as part of a higher education institution or through donations and tuition.

Arts and Crafts Movement. The arts and crafts movement, which began in England as a backlash against the poor quality of manufactured products, came to America after 1880 when Charles Leland introduced the plan into the schools of Philadelphia. The arts and crafts movement emphasized artistic design, practical skill development for vocational as well as for future work applications, the revival of artistic pursuits all but eliminated by industrial machinery, and the teaching of decorative arts to the abilities and interest of youngsters. Subjects in the arts and crafts included drawing, wood carving, clay modeling, mosaic work, leather carving, metal embossing, embroidery, carpentry, wood turning, wood inlaying, and ornamental wood sawing. Learners were given considerable freedom in the selection and designing of projects. The arts and crafts movement had little effect on manual training in America; however, it did broaden the materials and tasks used to train learner in tool usage, and it emphasized the importance of artistic design in the construction of useful projects. While the arts and crafts movement lasted into the early twentieth century, primarily through the efforts of various arts and craft societies, its application in schools declined as the public became more concerned with industrial skill development training (Smith, 1981). One result of the arts and crafts movement was that it eventually led to a change of name for manual training to *manual arts*, and manual arts programs were later called *industrial arts*.

Special Manual Training Schools Become Technical Schools. As manual training high schools grew in popularity, their curriculum included a broader range of courses and elective opportunities. This expansion of programs and curriculum in manual training high schools later led to the formation of the combined cosmopolitan high school (comprehensive high school) and the technical school. Some manual training schools in larger cities placed more emphasis on shopwork, drawing, and science and changed their names to technical schools. Among the first of these schools was the Technical School of Springfield, Massachusetts, established in 1898. This school provided instruction in the usual high school subjects together with the fundamentals of drawing, design, and hand and machine tools. Soon other technical schools were established in New York City, Detroit, and Chicago (Barlow, 1976).

Beginnings of Junior High and Comprehensive High Schools. In the early 1900s a complex set of social, economic, and educational conditions led to changes in the traditional high school, which was portrayed as an elite institution serving only a small minority of learners. At first, a small number of learners chose to attend high schools. They were typically learners preparing for higher education and entrance into the professions. As more and more learners entered high school, the one-track academic curriculum began to be challenged by learners, parents, and business and industry leaders. Early high schools were dedicated to providing learners with an academic and civic education along with a few opportunities to develop practical skills. Social conditions, however, forced learners and parents to exert pressure on schools to provide training for success in the job market as well. It was this emphasis on education to serve economic and social needs that shaped the development of the comprehensive high schools, which featured a differentiated curriculum to serve the vocational aspirations of learners. The result was establishment of a three-track curriculum: a college preparatory curriculum for those intending to enter higher education institutions, a more general curriculum for learners who planned to enter employment in the community immediately following high school, and in some schools, a vocational curriculum that would prepare learners for semi-skilled and skilled jobs in business and industry. The comprehensive high school was also challenged to take on more of the social development of youth through the addition of schools activities such as clubs, learner government, assemblies, organized athletics, and other social events (Spring, 1990).

In the early 1900s a great debate arose between those who advocated the older academic concepts of the high school and those who embraced the concept of social efficiency. Most business and industry leaders supported the doctrine of social efficiency and wanted education to produce individuals who were trained for a specific role in society and who were willing to work cooperatively in that role. First, advocates for social efficiency argued that school curricula should be organized to meet the future social needs of individual learners. Second, they argued that school activities should be designed to teach cooperation as preparation for future social activities. Third, social efficiency advocates proposed a differentiated curriculum based on the future social destination of the learner. In other words, social efficiency proponents wanted the high school curriculum to be based on the key concepts of cooperation, specialization, and equality of opportunity. They wanted high schools to increase their emphasis on cooperation and reduce competition. They felt that in the modern corporate society workers needed to learn to work together and not engage in battles with management in a competitive environment. They wanted learners trained in special areas for specialization. It was reasoned that efficiency would increase by allowing in-dividuals to concentrate fully on a single individual task. Finally, they wanted schools to ensure equality of opportunity in the labor market by objectively selecting learners for different educational programs. These doctrines of social efficiency ran counter to the traditional academic thrust of the high school embraced by many educators (Spring, 1990).

The National Education Association (NEA), founded in 1857 in Philadelphia, took up the challenge of advancing the cause of public education. Several important NEA committee reports paved the way for the modern comprehensive high school. In 1892, at the beginning of the rapid expansion of high schools, the NEA formed the Committee of Ten, which took up the debate over an educational system designed to provide everyone with a common education versus an educational system organized to provide everyone with a specific education based on a future social destination. This committee ruled against creating different curricula for the college-bound and non-college-bound high school learners and endorsed four different courses of study, all of which would meet college admission requirements. They were afraid that a two-track system of education would perpetuate a class system of education. With increasing numbers of youth attending high schools and the recognition that the preparation of American youth was critical to the future of the nation, pressure mounted for changes in the American high school. Social-efficiency educators who wanted to shape the high school to meet the needs of the corporate state stepped up their attack on academics in the high school (Spring, 1990).

Recognizing the need to address concerns about the American high school, the NEA organized the Commission on the Reorganization of Secondary Education in 1913. The report of this commission, *Cardinal Principles of Secondary Education*, established the framework for the organization of the comprehensive high school. It called for the creation of a high school that would include a variety of curricula designed to meet the needs of different types of learners. The commission ruled against the establishment of separate schools for special curricula and argued for the establishment of a comprehensive high school where all learners could come together and experience a variety of contacts to help them make intelligent choices as to the type of education and careers they wanted. The commission used the arguments of social efficiency to justify the comprehensive high school, namely the two important aspects of democracy—specialization and unification. The comprehensive high school became a mixture of planned social activities and a variety of curricula and was designed to prepare a new generation for a society based on large organizations and occupational specialization (Spring, 1990).

According to Spring (1990), vocational education, vocational guidance, and the establishment of the junior high school were key elements in the development of the comprehensive high school and its goal of developing human capital. Prior to 1900, little support existed for public education that would train learners for specific occupations. However, it was becoming increasingly clear that youth would have to receive training for jobs if the United States was going to enjoy favor in world markets relative to that enjoyed by other industrialized countries. Vocational education, with its promise of providing specialized training, was viewed as an important part of the comprehensive high school that would help promote industrial efficiency through proper selection and training of manpower. Early claims as to why vocational education needed to be included in the high school curriculum were articulated by the 1914 Commission on National Aid to Vocational Education. Vocational education (1) met the individual needs of learners for a meaningful curriculum, (2) provided opportunity for all learners to prepare for life and work, (3) helped foster a better teaching-learning process—learning by doing, and (4) introduced the idea of utility into education. The Commission argued that vocational education needed to be delivered by a competent, trained teacher.

Proponents of American sloyd proclaimed that the instructional system developed the learner physically, mentally, and morally; its manual regimentation employed the central nervous system, thereby enhancing learners' kinesthetic coordination, nurturing their neurological complexity, and developing their talents and habits. These advocates also proclaimed that participation in sloyd instruction would make school more interesting and encourage learners to stay in school longer (Kincheloe, 1999). The sloyd movement lasted only a few years, but it did change the way practical art subjects were taught. It also encouraged the use of trained teachers (Smith, 1981).

Status of Practical Arts Programs in 1900. In the early years of the twentieth century, the programs of agriculture education, business education, home economics education, industrial education, and industrial arts had been established in manual training schools, public elementary and secondary schools, and public and private colleges and universities. For the most part, these programs were viewed as having a cultural, social, and general education purpose, with vocational usage being an unplanned natural outcome. Special schools were created to offer instruction in these occupational areas for vocational purposes, including public and private trade schools, technical schools, evening schools, colleges of engineering and technology, and corporation schools.

Practical subjects were added to school curricula to supplement the purely academic content of most schools with the hope that these subjects would hold the interests of learners and help them better understand academic content through practical application. It was also hoped that this would reduce the dropout rate, which was estimated to be about 50% by the eighth grade. In addition, these subjects were believed to be important for preparation for life in an industrial economy (Barella, 1981).

The impact of industrialism was being felt in every phase of human life. Technological innovations created new industries and expanded existing ones, causing a tremendous need for semiskilled and skilled workers. The prevailing view of the day regarding business was that individuals had the right to regulate their economic affairs without government interference. This philosophy caused government to side with big business and adopt a hands-off policy concerning the regulation of business and industry. This in turn allowed big business to exploit its workers. For most people at this time in American history, the process of creating wealth seemed to be more important than religion, education, or politics. John Dewey understood the reality of corporate power and its abuses and spoke out about it. He also voiced his disdain of the inequitable distribution of wealth and the irrational system of production that placed major emphasis on making a profit and little emphasis on the human needs of workers. Most Americans accepted the belief that the individual was responsible for personal success, and this belief was reinforced in the schools of the day. Slogans like "America is the land of opportunity" revealed the belief that success was personal and not social. It was believed that economic inequality resulted from differences in an individual's ability and motivation and not his or her social circumstances. Hard work allegedly paid off and when it did not, individuals were assumed responsible for personal failures. Increasing production, employment, and income became the measures of community success and personal riches the result of hard work. Labor formed unions to protect themselves against the exploitation of workers and bitter battles occurred between management and labor over the employment of poorly trained workers, working conditions, and pay (Barella, 1981).

Kincheloe (1999) describes the plight of the worker in the early 1900s as very dismal. In the name of efficiency, scientific managers de-skilled most jobs by taking a particular activity and analyzing it to determine minute steps, then dividing the tasks into subtasks and assigning workers to do the subtask with little or no idea of the shape or form of the product being produced. Rarely were workers able to see how their everyday labor contributed to the larger goals of the business or to a better way of life. Workers were reduced to machine caretakers with little hope for advancement in jobs or society. Workers daily experienced the removal of thought and creativity from their work. What managers wanted included the following: (1) increased output without wage increases, (2) reduced labor turnover, (3) reduced conflict between labor and management, (4) more loyalty among workers, (5) workers who respected authority, and (6) workers who valued the work ethic. If workers did not fit this mold, they were fired, and few workers could afford to lose their jobs as they lacked the education and skills to obtain other jobs. Workers were forced to work in mindless jobs for long hours and low pay and often in dangerous and unhealthy conditions.

Workers were not compensated for injury or death. That idea was unheard-of in the late 1880s. While employers wanted skilled workers, they were often more interested in the attitudes of individuals. They wanted to employ dependable, passive, cheerful workers who would endure simplistic work that demanded little analysis or creativity. They began to see the public high schools as a place where learners could be prepared for these adult roles. They looked to the public schools and to practical arts programs in particular to provide learners with good work attitudes and a strong work ethic since these programs were generally not designed to produce skilled workers.

Business and industry leaders were not particular advocates of public education as the vehicle to produce an educated citizenry; they supported education primarily to protect their economic self-interests and need for workers with attitudes conducive to the industrial organization of labor. They were not necessarily strong supporters of manual training and later vocational education in public schools as a source of skilled workers but were motivated to gain some control over these types of educational programs in the hope that they could undermine union-controlled apprenticeship programs.

The United States had become the industrial giant of the world, and the demand for goods internally and across the seas spurred increased production and industrial activity. Even though many skilled workers were coming to this country from Europe as a result of relaxed immigration laws, American industry needed additional skilled workers and became very vocal about the need to better prepare workers in the public schools of this country. Pressured by business and industry, a growing number of educators were ready for a new type of education that included specific skills training. They began to endorse the idea, strongly supported by industry, of vocational education programs that would produce individuals with specific skill training and good attitudes toward work. It was hoped that vocational programs would impart to learners industrial values like respect for hard work, submission to authority, willingness to follow directions, and loyalty to the company and that by employing workers with these values political labor problems would be eliminated. No longer could educators ignore the issue of preparing learners for industrial occupations. Some form of vocational education was inevitable. What was needed was a thorough study of the interest in and need for more specific vocational training than was being offered through existing practical arts programs. This study came in the form of the Douglas Commission Report of Massachusetts in 1906, and the research of the National Association for the Promotion of Industrial Education and the Commission of National Aid to Vocational Education (Barella, 1981).

Douglas Commission of Massachusetts. Massachusetts had led the way for universal public education thanks to the leadership of educators like Horace Mann. According to Kincheloe (1999), Mann endorsed the concerns of business and industry leaders when he advanced his arguments for a common school that would teach a common core of values and support and promote industrial development. Mann promised that the common school would reduce the poor's hostility toward the wealthy and that it would prepare factory workers who were productive, respectful, easily supervised, and who would avoid participation in strikes or worker violence.

Massachusetts had been one of the first states to introduce practical subjects into the public school. It was among the leaders in the manual training movement and it had passed legislation opening the way for the establishment of industrial schools in 1872. Industrial progress and education were important to the leaders of Massachusetts, as evidenced by the re-evaluation of their education system in 1905 to see what needed to be done to better meet the needs of expanding industry. Governor Douglas, responding to a legislative mandate, appointed the Commission on Industrial and Technical Education, which consisted of nine representatives from manufacturing, agriculture, education, and labor, to investigate the need for industrial education (the term then used for vocational education), to determine the extent to which existing programs were meeting this need, and to make recommendations regarding how to modify existing programs to serve a vocational purpose (Barlow, 1976).

The commission released its report in 1906, which contained the following findings:

1. There was widespread interest in the general subject of industrial education or special training for vocations.
2. There was a practical and specific interest among manufacturers and wage earners because of personal need. Industry wanted workers with more than skill in manual operations; they wanted workers with "industrial intelligence."
3. There was a growing feeling of the inadequacy of the existing public school system to fully meet the needs of modern industrial and social conditions. Schools were found to be too exclusively literary in their spirit, scope, and methods.
4. There was no evidence that the people interested in industrial education had any concrete ideas as to its scope and method.
5. Their investigation had aroused the suspicion and hostility of many of the labor unions of the state.
6. There was little opposition to technical schools but significant opposition to trade schools.
7. There was general agreement that the financial support for technical education should be born wholly or in part by the state (Barlow, 1976).

The Douglas Commission Report concluded that the lack of industrial training for workers increased the cost of production. The report stated that workers with general intelligence, technical knowledge, and skill would command the world market. It emphasized that the foundation for technical success required a wider diffusion of industrial intelligence and that this foundation could only be acquired in connection with a general system of education in which it was an integral part of the curriculum from the beginning (Barlow, 1976).

The Douglas Commission Report generated considerable interest. It brought to the nation's attention the urgent need to introduce programs of vocational education into the nation's secondary schools to prepare workers for America's growing industries. The report was instrumental in starting a definite movement for the inclusion of vocational education in secondary schools, which would come some 11 years later with the passage of the Smith-Hughes Act of 1917.

National Society for the Promotion of Industrial Education. The widespread interest in industrial education discovered by the Douglas Commission prompted a group of 13 influential men to gather at a meeting of the Engineer's Club in New York City in 1906 to discuss the formation of a society to further the promotion of industrial education. Two leaders of manual training, James P. Haney and Professor Charles R. Richards, were responsible for arranging the meeting. Prior to adjournment, these men agreed on the need to establish an organization and appointed an ad hoc committee to plan a fall meeting at which organizational details would be discussed and a large group of industrialists and educators would be invited to discuss their views on industrial education. At the fall meeting, the National Society for Promotion of Industrial Education (NSPIE) was formed. Its mission was to promote industrial education by focusing public attention on the value of an educational system that could prepare young men and women to enter industrial pursuits. More specifically, the society wanted to unite all the forces of industrial education by providing them with opportunities for the study and discussion of mutual problems and by making them aware of experiences in industrial education both in this country and abroad (Barlow, 1976).

One of the first accomplishments of the society was to define the term industrial education. It was determined that industrial education referred to "that area of education between manual training and college engineering." Industrial education was intended to apply to vocational training of direct value to the industrial worker. While the focus of the society was originally on the development of education for trade and industrial workers, it broadened its scope to include other areas of vocational training (Barlow, 1976, p.53).

In 1908, the NSPIE formed state societies. These state societies would carry on the work of informing the citizens of their states about industrial education. The NSPIE realized that each state had different educational, industrial, and social conditions that would alter its views toward industrial education. Prior to the Smith-Hughes Act, these societies were most influential in the passage of state legislation favoring industrial education (Barlow, 1976).

The National Society for the Promotion of Industrial Education included some of the most informed and dynamic leaders in manufacturing, labor, education, business, and government. Included were James P. Haney, Charles Richards, David Sneeden, and the foremost leader in the development and promotion of vocational education in America, Charles Prosser. Prosser served as executive secretary of the NSPIE and was the person most influential in securing passage of the Smith-Hughes Act of 1917, which established the principle of federal support for vocational education in America. With passage of the act, the NSPIE changed its name to the National Society for Vocational Education, and in 1925 it combined with the Vocational Association of the Middle West to form the American Vocational Association (AVA), which continues to this day to meet the needs of vocational educators (Barlow, 1976). The AVA is now the Association of Career and Technical Education.

Commission on National Aid to Vocational Education. In 1914, President Woodrow Wilson responded to a joint resolution of Congress and appointed a special nine-member commission to study the issue of federal aid to vocational education. Senator Hoke Smith of Georgia was named as chairman, and Charles Prosser, executive director of the NSPIE was one of the members. Hearings, conferences, and reports were used to gather information to determine (1) the need for vocational education, (2) the need for federal grants, (3) the kinds of vocational education for which grants should be made, (4) the extent and conditions under which aid should be granted, and (5) the proposed legislation. Six months after its creation, the commission issued its report recommending grants for vocational education in agriculture and the trades. The report included the following important recommendations, which were included in the Smith-Hughes Act:

• Grants should be used for training vocational teachers, paying part of teachers' salaries, and making studies and investigations helpful to vocational education.

• Federal aid should be given to publicly supervised and controlled schools of less than college grade.

• Instruction should be limited to youths over age 14 and designed for profitable employment in agriculture and the trades.

• Three types of classes should be developed to provide vocational education: day school, part-time, and evening classes.

• A federal board should be established to oversee federal grants.

• State boards should be created to administer the grants and states should develop a state plans for administering vocational education programs.

The commission included a draft bill, which was brought before Congress in 1914 but was not acted upon until President Wilson urged its passage in 1916. Representative Dudley Hughes of Georgia introduced an important revision to the original bill that included home economics as a vocational program eligible for federal grants. With the help of the NSPIE, the American Federation of Labor (AFL), The National Association of Manufacturers (NAM), the National Education Association (NEA), the Chamber of Commerce of the United States, the Commission on Aid to Vocational Education, the Vocational Education Association of the Middle West, and the general will of the people, federal aid to vocational education became law in the form of the Smith-Hughes Act (Barlow, 1976).

FEDERAL WORKFORCE LEGISLATION

Federal legislation has always been enacted in order to help solve the major problems facing the nation as a whole or to address a cultural need, such as ensuring the constitutional rights of all Americans. The Smith-Hughes Act of 1917 demonstrated the concern in Congress that the security and the welfare of a nation are dependent not only upon the nation's ability to govern itself, but also upon its ability to educate its people for productive work and meaningful lives. As skills needed for work and living became more complex (a trend that continues today), the training of skilled workers became a continuous identified need. Congress responded to the need by providing support for vocational (career and technical) education. This began with the passage of the Morrill Act of 1862, which supported college and university programs of vocational education. With current career and technical legislation, Congress continues that support today. It continues to affirm its belief that federal support for career and technical education is an investment in the future of the nation's workforce. A highly skilled workforce is viewed as essential to maintaining the nation's standard of living, defense preparedness, economic strength, and leadership position in the free world.

As the nation progressed from a predominantly agrarian society in its early years to a highly industrialized, technological society, vast social, religious, philosophical, psychological, educational, and cultural changes took place requiring congressional action that could address the nation's needs. These needs were addressed over the years by educational legislation. The development of career and technical education has been influenced greatly by many federal enactments since the Smith-Hughes Act of 1917.

The state of the nation in the early 1900s raised concerns among leaders, for it was faced with a shortage of skilled workers in agriculture and industry. A continuous flow of people came from rural America to the cities to fill vacant positions in manufacturing jobs. A growing number of European immigrants also flowed into the cities in search of employment. Urban areas grew so rapidly that they could not provide adequate housing or services. Poor men and women entered agricultural and industrial jobs. Workers were forced to work long hours for low pay at repetitive jobs that afforded little opportunity for them to use their talents and creativity. Public high schools established in the late 1800s to provide classical education to only a small number of learners were being forced to serve an increasing number of learners from rural America and from foreign countries.

The narrow curriculum offered in high schools to prepare learners for the professions was deemed unsuitable for preparing the masses needed for the industrial age. Critics of public secondary schools were unhappy that only about 8% of learners graduated from high school, leaving many without an adequate general education and few skills that prepared them for work. Educational reformers began to advocate an expanded curriculum to include practical education, one designed to prepare workers for the type of jobs in which the masses of people could find employment. Business and industry leaders wanted a supply of young people to fill agricultural and industrial jobs so that they could compete in the market. They wanted individuals who respected authority, followed directions, and could fit into the organization of the workplace. Educational reformers, business and industry leaders, and government leaders began to form coalitions to press for federal legislation that would stimulate the development of federal-state partnerships and lead to the inclusion of practical subjects in the curricula to prepare young people for employment in the trade and industries, in agriculture, in commerce and commercial pursuits, and in occupations and roles related to home economics. A little over ten years later, the goal of this coalition of leaders was met with the passage of the Smith-Hughes Act.

Most career and technical educators associate the beginning of federal support for career and technical education with direct federal funding to programs as first provided by the Smith-Hughes Act, but federal support for career and technical education actually began with the passage of the Morrill Act of 1862, which authorized land grants for the establishment of educational institutions that included programs for agriculture and the mechanic arts. The Morrill Act initiated the Land Grant Universities of our country that have been a major source for career and technical education teachers.

Ever since the passage of the Smith-Hughes Act of 1917, which established the federal-state-local cooperative effort of providing career and technical education, the federal government has maintained an active interest in career and technical education. Federal policy from 1917 to the passage of the Vocational Act of 1963 focused on expanding and improving career and technical education programs and building career and technical education capacity to serve the corporate needs of business and industry. Accountability was the hallmark of the new legislation. Congress listened to a field that was demanding greater flexibility in administering programs and allocating federal funds and honored its request. In return for granting this flexibility, however, Congress established procedures that required the field to demonstrate results in terms of learner achievement, program completion, placement in postsecondary education and the workforce, and improved gender equity in program offerings. Educators will have to devise new state plans for administering vocational-technical education and develop systems to track learners more extensively than in the past. The new law is expected to strengthen academic and vocational-technical instruction, place more emphasis on professional development, and support career guidance activities along with other desirable outcomes (Hoachlander & Klein, 1999).

The 1998 Perkins Act is a direct response by Congress to the national concern that high school graduates lack the basic skills necessary to succeed in the global market place. Congress identified these skills for the new century as (1) strong basic and advanced academic skills, (2) computer and other technical skills, (3) theoretical knowledge and communication, (4) problem-solving, teamwork, and employability skills, and (5) the ability to acquire additional knowledge and skill throughout a lifetime. Congress wanted the Perkins funds to serve all learners at the public secondary and postsecondary levels who are interested in vocational and technical education programs. Section 2 of the act reveals the purpose or Congressional intent of the legislation. The purposes of the legislation are "to further develop the academic, vocational, and technical skills of vocational and technical education learners through high standards; link secondary and postsecondary programs; increase flexibility in the administration and use of funds provided under the act; disseminate national research about vocational and technical education; and provide professional development and technical assistance to vocational and technical educators." The new Perkins Act continues federal support for vocational and technical education that assists youth and adults to prepare for and make successful transitions to postsecondary education, employment and independent, satisfying adult life (American Vocational Association [AVA], 1998, p. 63).

There are similarities between the 1990 Perkins Act and the 1998 Perkins Act, such as the continuing focus on integrating academic and vocational education and expanding tech-prep. There are also a number of striking differences in the two pieces of legislation, especially with regard to increased state and local education agency flexibility in designing, delivering and funding career and technical education programs and the requirement of increased accountability for providing results in terms of improved learner learning and increased numbers of learners who continue their education beyond high school. The following are distinguishing features of the 1998 Perkins Act sometimes called Perkins III, which were identified by Hettinger (1999).

- Accountability–States will have to develop new data collection and reporting systems that differ significantly from those used in the past. States must report data on learner achievement using a common language that allows for nationwide comparisons. States will have to shoulder the burden of greater follow-up career and technical education programs and be able to document the impact of their programs. In particular states will have to work with the U. S Department of Education in setting expected performance levels for four categories: (1) learner attainment of vocational, technical, and academic skill proficiencies; (2) acquisition of secondary or postsecondary degrees or credentials; (3) placement and retention in postsecondary education or employment; and (4) completion of vocational and technical programs that lead to nontraditional training and employment. The performance indicators must include percentages or numbers that can be used to make data objective, quantifiable, and measurable. States will have to show progress toward improving the performance of career and technical education learners, and they will have to publicize their progress in a manner that allows state-by state comparisons.

- Funding formulas–Perkins III established the formula of 85% of state grants being allocated to local school districts, with states able to keep 10% for leadership activities and 5% or $250,000 (whichever is greater). States can reserve up to 10% of funds sent to local districts for rural areas, regions that have high numbers or percentages of career and technical education learners, and areas that receive less money because of changes made to the within-state secondary funding formula. The first year funding remained the same as the 1990 Perkins Act, but the second year funding formula switches to one based 70% on poverty and 30% on population.

- Tech-prep–Tech-prep programs are strengthened in Perkins III by requesting the use of consortia to develop longer-range plans, to use technology more in instruction, to improve communication among tech-prep partners, and to extend their plans outlining the development and implementation of their programs from three to five years. The expectation of the new legislation regarding tech-prep is that consortia will develop more thorough and complete plans that will serve learners from high school through an associate's degree, and on to work or even a four-year college. Specific instructional activities that can be offered through the new tech-prep regulations include preparing learners for the information technology field and using technology for the professional development and distance learning of career and technical educators involved in tech-prep activities.

- School-to-work–Congress sought to prevent Perkins Act funds from being used for school-to-work programs unless those funds were used for activities serving only learners eligible for career and technical education. Since there is considerable overlap between activities that are funded through the School-to-Work Act of 1994 and Perkins III, it will be somewhat difficult for states and local school districts to determine what is legal in the use of funds for activities such as curriculum integration, professional development, and career guidance. Most state and local school career and technical administrators interpret this portion of the law as continuing to allow Perkins III funds to enable learners to continue with work-site learning, career guidance, and other activities.

- Gender equity–Perkins III reduces required gender equity activities, eliminating the requirement for states to have a full-time equity coordinator, the requirement that states spend $60,000 on related activities, and the 10.5% set-aside for sex equity and programs serving single parents, single pregnant women and displaced homemakers. The act does give states the flexibility to continue equity programs if they choose and mandates that states spend between $60,000 and $150,000 of their leadership money on programs that prepare people for nontraditional training and employment.

- Learners with disabilities–Perkins III contains several important changes from earlier Perkins Acts, which are intended to better serve learners with disabilities by ensuring that they are not placed in career and technical education programs only so that school districts receive federal funding. Perkins II had established a funding formula that unintentionally became a quota system and led to the placement of learners with disabilities in vocational programs whether or not this was the best decision for the learners, so school districts could receive federal funding. Perkins III eliminates the quota for learners with disabilities in area vocational schools. Gone also is a loophole that allowed cities to strike deals with area vocational schools to distribute funding, which resulted in some area vocational schools being underfunded.

Perkins III intends for school systems to better serve learners with disabilities who choose career and technical education programs by eliminating specific requirements, which the school systems believed did not work well, and replacing them with greater flexibility for states to determine what are the best strategies for serving learner with disabilities. While some special education teachers may believe that the Perkins III Act reduces the emphasis on serving learners from special populations, the intent of the act is to force state and local school district educators to rethink how to best serve these learners in a more flexible manner while preserving accountability. Accountability provisions in the Perkins Act require states to report in quantifiable terms the progress that career and technical education learners with disabilities are making toward the new, state-established, academic and career and technical skill proficiencies. States will also have to track how many learners with disabilities obtain diplomas and advance to postsecondary education. In addition, state plans must describe how special populations are being provided equal access to vocational education programs and how they are being prepared for high-skill, high-wage careers.

The Perkins Act of 1998 ushered in a new area for federal funding of career and technical education, relaxing some of the specific requirements while giving states and local school districts considerable flexibility in determining how best to serve all learners who choose to enroll in the programs. In exchange for greater flexibility, however, states and local school districts are being held accountable for favorable results for all learners including contribution to learner achievement, program completion, placement in postsecondary education and the workforce, and improved gender equity in program offerings.

The Individuals with Disabilities Education Act Amendments of 1997 (PL 105-17)

Federal legislation for individuals from special populations began as early as 1935 with the passage of the Social Security Act, which provided for vocational training of the handicapped. Over the years, Congress has continued to provide funding to help individuals with disabilities prepare for work and productive citizenship.

The original act on which the Individuals with Disabilities Education Act Amendments of 1997 was based was The Education of All handicapped Children Act of 1975 (PL 94-142), which was amended in 1983 and 1986 and amended again in 1990 as PL 102-19 when its name was changed to the Individuals with Disabilities Education Act (IDEA). The IDEA, with its amendments signed into law on June 4, 1997, was the most important piece of federal legislation passed by Congress for educating children and youth with disabilities. This act strengthened academic expectations and accountability for the nation's 5.8 million children with disabilities and bridged the gap that had frequently existed between what children with disabilities learn and what is expected in a regular curriculum. Other legislative acts that had provisions for serving children with disabilities like the School-to-Work Act, Perkins III, and Americans with Disabilities (ADA) only provided limited guidance as to how to design the support services, modifications, and accommodations that individual learners in curricular experiences needed. The Individuals with Disabilities Act as amended, however, provided for individual planning and service design that helped accomplish the goals established by other supporting legislation.

The purposes of the IDEA as described in the act are: (1) to ensure that all children with disabilities have available to them a free appropriate public education that emphasizes special education and related services designed to meet their unique needs and prepare them for employment and independent living; (2) to assist states in the implementation of a statewide, comprehensive, coordinated, multidisciplinary, interagency system of early intervention services for infants and toddlers with disabilities and their families; (3) to ensure that educators and parents have the necessary tools to improve educational results for children with disabilities by supporting systemic-change activities, coordinated research and personnel preparation, coordinated technical assistance, dissemination, and support and technology development and media services; and (4) to assess, and ensure the effectiveness of, efforts to educate children with disabilities.

The IDEA is written to ensure that special education and related services are provided to eligible individuals under the age of 22 in addition to the general curriculum and not separate from it. The IDEA provides for individualized planning and service. It provides federal funds for children and youth with disabilities and delimits who is covered under the laws by identifying 13 types of disabilities persons must have that need special education. The IDEA reaffirms the right to a free appropriate education, including transition and planning services to eligible persons with disabilities. Special education is defined in the IDEA as "specially designed instruction...to meet the unique needs of a child with a disability," including instruction conducted in the classroom and other settings. The IDEA emphasizes that special education is a package of instructional techniques and services, not a place. Related services are to be provided that are defined as "any developmental, corrective, and other support services that a child may need to benefit from his or her education." Examples include transportation, rehabilitation counseling, physical and occupational therapy, etc. Transition services, which are a set of activities that promote movement from school to postschool activities, are to be provided and include such things as employment, postsecondary education and vocational training. The IDEA requires annual individualized education programs (IEPs) that contain detailed requirements for planning the education of individual learners. Learners must be provided with a comprehensive evaluation of their educational needs at least once every three years. Transition planning must begin by age 14, and the IEPs must include transition service needs. Schools are responsible for ensuring transition services, including those from outside agencies. The IDEA clarifies who participates in transition planning, including parents, learner, and agency participation. Finally, the IDEA provides detailed procedures to deal with any disputes that may occur between parents and schools regarding the planning and delivery of services to learners with disabilities (Ordover & Annexstein, 1999).

Knoblauch and McLane (1999) report the following changes that affect special education practice nationwide as a result of the new IDEA Amendments: (1) participation of learners with disabilities in state and district-wide assessment (testing) programs (including alternative assessment) with appropriate accommodations where necessary, (2) development and review of the IEP, including increased emphasis on participation of children and youth with disabilities in the general education curriculum and involvement of general education teachers in developing, reviewing, and revising the IEP, (3) enhanced parent par-

ticipation in eligibility and placement decisions, (4) streamlined learner evaluation/reevaluation requirements, (5) identification of transition service needed within a child's course of study beginning at age 14 and updated annually, (6) the availability of mediation services as a means of more easily resolving parent-school differences, (7) disciplinary procedures for learners with disabilities, including allowance for an appropriate interim alternative educational setting up to 45 days, and (8) allowing children ages 3-9 to be identified as developmentally delayed; previously, it was ages 3-5.

Career and technical educators should become familiar with the many details of services and accommodations of the IDEA so they can maximize their efforts in providing a free and appropriate education to learners with disabilities. There is a growing body of literature regarding the IDEA that is available in published form and on the Internet to assist career and technical teachers with providing services to learners with disabilities. One very good source of information for vocational education teachers is the textbook by Taymans, J.M., West, L.L. and Sullivan, M. (Eds.). (2000). *Unlocking Potential That Promotes the Concept of Self-Determination—An Individual's Ability to Define and Achieve Goals Based on Knowing and Valuing Him or Herself.*

The Workforce Investment Act (WIA) of 1998 (PL 105-220)

The federal government has a long history of providing programs to meet the needs of the unemployed. In the 1930s, the Civilian Conservation Corp (CCC) was established to provide work-study and vocational education to unemployed youth affected by the Great Depression. The 1960s was a period of high unemployment and social unrest, and Congress responded to economic and social problems by passing the first in a series of manpower legislation acts, beginning with the Area Redevelopment Act of 1961, which provided funds for retraining persons in defined redevelopment areas of the country that were severely depressed. A number of other enactments were passed in the 1960s, such as the Manpower Development and Training Act of 1962, which provided funds for training the underemployed and unemployed. Since the 1960s, Congress has continued to enact manpower legislation.

The Workforce Investment Act (WIA) was signed into law August 7, 1998 repealing the Job Training Partnership Act as of July 1, 2000. The WIA provides increased flexibility for state and local officials to establish broad-based labor market systems using job training funds for adults, dislocated workers, and youth. It is designed to establish a framework for a unique national workforce preparation and employment system that will better meet the needs of the nation's businesses, the needs of job seekers, and those who want to further their careers. The overall goal of WIA is to provide workforce development services to employers and workers through a highly accessible, information-driven, one-stop career center system. Specifically, the goals of WIA are (1) increase the employment, retention, and earnings of participants, (2) increase occupational skill attainment by participants, (3) improve the quality of the workforce, (4) reduce welfare dependency, and (5) enhance the productivity and competitiveness of our nation. Key principles of WIA include (1) streamlining services, (2) empowering individuals, (3) providing universal access, (4) increasing accountability, (5) creating new roles for local boards, (6) providing state and local flexibility, and (7) improving youth programs.

According to former Secretary of Labor Alexis M. Herman, the WIA brings a new emphasis and substantive reform to how youth are served within the workforce investment system. It provides the structure to prepare the nation's young people and offers an array of services so that they are able to successfully transition to the workforce and to continued education and training. The act challenges local communities to reach a higher level of collaboration among local workforce training providers, schools, community organizations, and others in an effort to align and leverage resources and to create community youth assistance strategies. The reforms of youth services are organized under four major themes: (1) the establishment of the local youth council, (2) comprehensive services based on individual assessment, (3) youth connections and access to the one-stop delivery system, and (4) performance accountability.

The road to the WIA is filled with a long history of legislation and movements to create jobs and provide income assistance for needy individuals. Kaufmann and Wills (1999) provide an historical account of the events and legislation that began with the Smith-Hughes Act of 1917 and the creation of the vocational rehabilitation system three years later to provide targeted services to individuals with disabilities, and ending with the Workforce Investment Act of 1998, which replaced the Job Partnership and Training Act passed in 1982. From the 1930s through the 1950s, the focus of federal support was on income support and job creation, such as with the Civilian Conservation Corps and the Work Progress Administration. Training was only incidental to these programs. Two pieces of legislation that did support training during this time were the National Apprenticeship Act of 1937 and the GI Bill. In the 1960s and 1970s, government workforce programs expanded to address the high level of unemployment that persisted after the Korean War.

Two of the major workforce preparation acts that refocused federal support for training were the Manpower Development and Training Act of 1962 and the Comprehensive Employment and Training Act of 1973. These acts attempted to consolidate several war-on-poverty programs and decentralize control of the programs to better serve the manpower needs of local governments. In the period between 1980 and 1984, President Ronald Reagan sought to eliminate costly and ineffective programs and reduce federal expenditure, which resulted in the passage of the Job Training and Partnership Act (JTPA) of 1982 that eliminated job creation efforts and emphasized support for training and related services. The JTPA gave state government and the business community stronger roles on how federal funds would be spent and established the Private Industry Councils (PICs) to coordinate all job preparation programs within a state's geographic areas.

The Workforce Investment Act of 1998 replaced the JTPA using some of the strong components of the JTPA such as PICs, which are now called Local Workforce Investment Boards, but placing overall responsibility of managing the workforce preparation component of the welfare system under the Department of Labor. The WIA makes some significant changes in the nation's employment and training programs and builds on themes that have emerged in past manpower legislation.

The WIA is a very comprehensive act with five main titles and many provisions in each. Kaufmann and Wills (1999) present nine key features of the act as follows:

- Designation of one-stop centers for delivery of services–The WIA makes the U.S. Department's one-stop career centers the central player of the workforce delivery system. These centers make it possible for job-seekers and employers to obtain information and services in one location instead of having to go from place to place to receive information and services as in the past. One-stop centers help individuals and employers determine who is eligible for various programs and provide services such as assessment, job search and placement, and all other needed services.
- Consolidation of workforce development activities–President Reagan began the movement to consolidate federal programs to assist the underemployed or unemployed with the creation of the JTPA Act of 1982, but despite this, the General Accounting Office reported 154 programs or funding streams designed to assist the unemployed, enhance worker skills, or create employment opportunities. The WIA still does not consolidate all the federal initiatives, but it does eliminate the JTPA, the Adult Education Act and the National Literacy Act of 1991 and consolidates their activities, along with activities of vocational rehabilitation.
- Realignment of existing programs–Legislation and programs not eliminated by the WIA are re-aligned in various ways through an optional state plan or through the designation of local areas by the governor of each state who determines the service areas within a state. For example, Job Corps, one of the successful programs of the JTPA, can be represented on youth councils and is a vital part of the state plan.
- Emphasis on youth programs–A separate title of the WIA is youth programs. In some cases under the JTPA, out-of-school youth did not receive enough attention from the local service delivery area that was responsible for both youth and adults. The WIA has a separate

section for youth activities and creates a youth council to coordinate activities and services. The summer youth employment and training programs that had to be offered under the JTPA are now allowable services that must be balanced with other youth services. Youth programs must have the following assessments: (1) individual assessment, (2) service strategies, (3) preparation for postsecondary educational opportunities, (4) linkages between academic and occupational learning, (5) preparation for jobs, and (6) connections to the job market for area employers.

There are a number of important provisions relating to youth: (1) eligible youth must be below income; (2) 5% of youth served may be other than low income if they face other barriers to school completion and employment; (3) categories under which the 5% with other barriers may be identified are school dropout, basic literacy skills deficient, homeless, runaway or foster child, pregnant or parenting, offender, or in need of help completing an educational program or securing and holding employment; (4) programs will link academic and occupational learning and skill development; (5) programs must include: tutoring, study skills and instruction leading to the completion of secondary school, mentoring, paid and unpaid work, leadership development, and other appropriate services; (6) participants must receive follow-up services for a minimum of one year; and (7) programs must provide summer employment opportunities linked to academic and occupational learning.

- Emphasis on customer information and choice–The WIA uses a new service delivery system that includes individual training accounts with vouchers that allow those seeking services to make informed choices among service providers regarding education and training. To ensure that those needing services are provided with them in an efficient manner, customer satisfaction surveys are part of the accountability measures in the law.
- New focus on program accountability–The demand for accountability of federal programs, which began in the Nixon administration and was emphasized even more in the Reagan administration, was a major consideration of the WIA. More responsibility for setting performance measures and providing accountability data is placed on state and local agencies. Providers of services are to be chosen based on their track record of performance.
- Difference in individual outcomes–The WIA has established different outcomes depending on who is being served. The appropriate outcome for youth is basic attainment or work readiness occupational skills and education. The outcomes for older youth and adults include both attainments of educational and occupational credentials as well as employment. The WIA provides different types and levels of services depending on the individual's skills and needs as they relate to workplace demands.

- Role of employers–The WIA, as with previous workforce preparation programs like the JTPA, recognizes the important role employers must play in a workforce development system. State employers associations like the Chamber of Commerce are recognized as important participants on the Workforce Investment Board (WIB) at the state level. Likewise, local workforce investment boards must involve private sector employers in providing connecting, brokering, and coaching activities along with other services.
- Longer periods of time for planning and service–The WIA recognizes that individuals with disabilities and other barriers to employment need assistance for longer periods of time than was provided by previous education/employment and training programs. Under the provisions of WIA, individuals are provided with extended mentorship services, longer follow-up on services, and longer planning periods. States must submit five-year plans for providing services in both the job training and adult education and literacy section of the WIA.

The WIA ushers in a new approach of a more complete workforce development system. The act builds on the most successful elements of previous federal legislation and adjusts or eliminates legislation that was not effective. It is based on extensive federal, state, and local research and evaluation studies of successful training and employment innovation over the last 10 years. The new law makes changes to the current funding streams, target populations, systems of delivery, long-term planning, labor market information system, and governance structure. Career and technical state and local educational leaders should become familiar with the many provision of the WIA and become actively involved in workforce investment board planning and activities.

Current Legislation Affecting Workforce Preparation Programs And Outlook

Only a few acts currently in force impact career and technical education. These include the original Smith-Hughes Act of 1917, which is a perpetual act that has been in force since its inception; the Education of All Handicapped Children Act of 1975 as amended in 1990 and 1997, which changed the name of the act to the Individuals with Disabilities Act (IDEA); the Developmental Disabilities Assistance and Bill of Rights Act of 1990; the Technology-Related Assistance Act for Individuals with Disabilities Act Amendments of 1994; the Goals 2000: Educate America Act of 1994; the School-to-Work Opportunities Act of 1994; the Personal Responsibility and Work Opportunities Act of 1996; the Balanced Budget Act of 1997; the Carl D. Perkins Act of 1998; the Workforce Investment Act of 1998; the Ticket to Work and Work Incentives Act of 1999; and the No Child Left Behind Act of 2001. See Appendix.

From the passage of the Smith-Hughes Act of 1917 to the Carl D. Perkins Act of 1998 and the Workforce Investment Act of 1998, Congress has attempted to solve some of the nation's most pressing social, political, and economic problems by enacting workforce legislation to assist states and local educational and training agencies as they design and implement programs that prepare individuals for meaningful, productive employment. The federal government has a long history of continuing support for career and technical education and understands the importance of investing in workforce education in order to ensure the career futures of American learners. At first, federal legislation was highly prescriptive; however, since the Vocational Education Act of 1963, most federal legislation has specified basic requirements but has given states and local agencies considerable flexibility on how to meet legislative mandates. Recent federal legislation has also sent more money to the local level, believing that local educational agencies are in the best position to identify problems and make adjustment to maximize learning for learners. In exchange for increased flexibility for states and local educational and training agencies, there is increased emphasis on accountability. Congress wants to see the results of career and technical education programs in terms of performance measures established by states for learners and clients. Congress has also attempted to consolidate many separate enactments affecting vocational education and workforce preparation programs into only a few that are active today. The Workforce Investment Act of 1998 consolidated a number of separate federal job training programs, but there are still others that will probably be targeted for consolidation in future congressional action.

Career and technical education programs are supported by a combination of federal, state, local and private funds, with most funding coming from state and local education budgets. The amount of federal financial support has remained fairly constant for many years at around 11%. While the federal share of financing for career and technical education is relatively small, federal support has driven much of the needed changes in programs to prepare people for work over the years. Federal legislation is not solely generated in Washington. Considerable input comes from individuals and groups that have a vested interest in workforce preparation at the state and local levels. Federal and state legislation can expand opportunities to improve career and technical education, or it can severely limit the ability of career and technical educators to prepare learners for the highly advanced workplace. It is important now more than ever for career and technical educators to become advocates for legislation and to provide input to the political leaders who will make the decisions that will affect career and technical education programs, opportunities for learners, and the careers of educators (Dykman, 1995).

It is difficult to predict what changes will be made in federal support for career and technical education, but many leaders believe that continuing federal support is dependent upon data provided to Congress that reports progress in terms of performance measures established by states. Congress wants to see data on learner achievement reported by states in a way that has never been done before. In other words, Congress has removed a number of reported barriers confronting career and technical education and has given states and local educational agencies considerable flexibility to improve services to learners, but it wants to see evidence of the effects that career and technical education programs have on preparing learners for productive employment or lifelong learning. It is important that career and technical educators understand the intent of federal legislation as well as the rules and regulations designed to implement Congressional intent. It is only through a full understanding of content and context of legislation that educators can ensure that expected outcomes of legislation are fully realized.

DEFINING CAREER AND TECHNICAL EDUCATION

The term *career and technical education* has evolved over the years from the generic *industrial education*, which at one time encompassed most forms of education for work, to *vocational education,* as defined in the Smith-Hughes Act of 1917. The Carl D. Perkins Act of 1990 identified vocational education as *vocational and applied technology education.* The Carl D. Perkins Vocational and Technical Education Act of 1998 used term *vocational-technical education.* Today the field is called career and technical education in the professional literature and as promoted by the Association for Career and Technical Education.

Career and technical education is a large and diverse educational enterprise spanning both secondary and postsecondary education. It encompasses a tremendous number of programs designed to prepare learners for employment and for living. Most people identify career and technical education at the secondary level with courses in one of the seven specific labor market program areas: agriculture, business, family and consumer sciences (formerly home economics), marketing (formerly distributive education), health, trade and industry (T&I), and technical/communications. Technology education (formerly industrial arts) is sometimes viewed to be a service area of career and technical education, but it is more appropriately viewed as a vital part of general and academic education. The most popular career and technical education courses are Business and T&I, with business enrolling over one-half of all learners and T&I enrolling one-third. Enrollment in the other service areas is roughly equal. Examples of courses in the service areas include agricultural science, carpentry, accounting, word processing, retailing, fashion, practical nursing, respiratory therapy, child care, electronics, computer programming, and food and nutrition (Boesel, Hudson, Deich, & Masten, 1994).

The career and technical education curriculum appeals to a diverse group of learners, with almost every high school learner earning at least some credits in career and technical education courses. These courses are also very popular at the postsecondary level, with nearly two-thirds of all learners enrolled in less than baccalaureate institutions enrolled in career and technical education programs. The majority of secondary learners preparing for college has taken at least one career and technical education course other than keyboarding. Almost 14,000,000 learners participate in career and technical education programs, which assist them in exploring career options and developing occupational skills for the workplace. These programs are offered by approximately 11,000 comprehensive high schools, several hundred vocational-technical high schools, and about 1,400 area vo-tech centers that serve learners from several "sending" high schools. About 9,400 postsecondary institutions offer technical programs, including community colleges, technical colleges, skills centers and other public and private two- and four-year colleges. Individuals from all racial-ethnic backgrounds and all levels of ability and socioeconomic status take career and technical education courses (Boesel, Hudson, Deich, & Masten, 1994). In addition, millions of adults enroll in these programs to acquire basic skills for employment or to retrain for new jobs in order to keep up with the changing technological requirements of the workplace (Association for Career and Technical Education, 2001).

Historically, the purpose of vocational (career and technical education) has been to prepare learners for entry-level jobs in occupations requiring less than a baccalaureate degree. Over the last decade, educational reform has reshaped the purpose of career and technical education into a broader preparation that develops the academic, vocational, and technical skills of learners. Among other reform efforts, this preparation now includes the integration of academic and career and technical education, an emphasis on all aspects of an industry, and the implementation of academic performance measures (Levesque, et al., 2000).

Career and technical education today is evolving into a multipurpose enterprise that seeks to impart not only occupational knowledge and skills for immediate employment bound learners, but also the academic skills required to function in both the world of work and postsecondary education. As previously mentioned, the vast majority of high school learners enroll in one or more courses (97% of high school learners in 1994). Most of these learners take more than 1.0 Carnegie unit of career and technical education and more than half take the equivalent of three or more yearlong courses. This dispels the belief that learners take only one course as an elective in their high school program. The flexibility provided by new course scheduling, as with the block schedule, has enabled more learners to enroll in the programs. In addition, the tech-prep and school-to-work programs have provided a way for traditional academic learners as well to enroll in career and technical education courses (Levesque et al., 2000).

The Carl D. Perkins Vocational and Technical Act of 1998 defined vocational and technical education as "organized educational activities that (1) offer a sequence of courses that provide individuals with the academic and technical knowledge and skills the individuals need to prepare for further education and for careers (other than careers requiring a baccalaureate, master's or doctoral degree) in current or emerging employment sectors and (2) include competency-based applied learning that contributes to the academic knowledge, higher-order reasoning and problem-solving skills, work attitudes, general employability skills, technical skills, and occupation-specific skills of an individual." This definition encompasses a wide variety of classes teaching academic skills, work habits and attitudes, general employability skills, and occupationally specific skills (American Vocational Association [AVA], 1998, p.92).

CAREER AND TECHNICAL EDUCATION PROGRAM SETTINGS

Most secondary career and technical education occurs in programs in comprehensive high schools that offer academic, personal use, and career and technical education classes. Programs of secondary career and technical education may be found in a variety of settings at the local school level in comprehensive high schools, vocational-technical high schools, and secondary area vocational-technical centers or area vocational-technical schools.

Area vocational-technical schools and centers provide career and technical education instruction for typically half a day to learners who are bussed in from comprehensive high schools. Area vocational-technical schools are more likely to be located in suburban rather than in urban or rural areas. A small number of learners are served in all-day vocational-technical schools, which are usually located in urban areas. These vocational-technical high schools deliver essential academic courses as well as career and technical education courses. Career and technical education for adults is also carried on during evening hours in some of these secondary vocational-technical schools (Adams, 1993).

Postsecondary career and technical education programs are conducted in community colleges, private proprietary schools, area vocational schools also serving secondary learners, technical colleges, specialized postsecondary schools, adult education centers, skill centers, correctional institutions, and four-year colleges and universities. Most postsecondary career and technical education is provided by community colleges, with the second largest provider being private proprietary schools, followed by technical colleges and area vocational-technical schools serving postsecondary learners. A number of four-year colleges continue to offer career and technical education programs, but the number is dwindling (Adams, 1993; Boesel & McFarland, 1994).

Career and technical education programs are also found in middle/junior high schools in the form of pre-career and technical education. These programs orient learners to the world of work, make them aware of career and occupational options, and give them opportunities to try out a variety of jobs in various fields at several levels. There are pre-career and technical programs in all seven of the career and technical education service areas, including technology education. These programs assist learners in selecting secondary and postsecondary career and technical education programs, provide opportunities for learners to apply academic skills to concrete occupational situations, and motivate learners not only to stay in school, but also to exert more effort.

From automotive technician to computer technician, career and technical education programs prepare both youth and adults for a broad range of careers that require varying levels of education, from high school to postsecondary certificates to two-year associate's degree programs and four-year college degrees. These programs are not just for the non-college bound learners but for all learners who need a foundation of skills that will enable them to be gainfully employed, either full-time following graduation or part-time as they continue their education. A blend of integrated academic and career and technical skills, which are made relevant through internships and cooperative work experiences, ensures that learners will be ready for entry-level employment as well as for entry into some form of postsecondary education. The Association of Career and Technical Education (2001) reports that nearly two-thirds of all high school graduates of career and technical education programs enter some form of postsecondary education program.

SEONDARY CAREER AND TECHNICAL EDUCATION PROGRAMS AND CURRICULUM

Career and technical education at the secondary level has traditionally consisted of courses that correspond to specific labor market preparation such as agriculture and renewable resources, business, marketing, health care, trade and industry, family and consumer sciences education, and general labor market preparation. This collection of courses typically included basic keyboarding, industrial arts (now reformed to as technology education), and career preparation and general work experience.

In its February 2000 report entitled *Vocational Education in the United States: Toward the Year 2000* by Levesque et al., the National Center for Educational Statistics (NCES) classifies high school courses into the categories of academic, vocational, enrichment/other, and special education. Under the category of vocational, the three units are family and consumer sciences education, general labor market preparation, and specific labor market preparation. Under the unit of specific labor market preparation, the career and technical education programs listed include agriculture and renewable resources, business, marketing and distribution, health care, public and protective services, trade and industry, technology and communications, personal and other services, food service and hospitality, and child care education.

Each of the specific labor market preparation programs consists of a number of occupational program areas and courses. For example, agriculture and renewable resources encompasses programs in agricultural technology and horticulture. The trade and industry classification consists of the construction trades, mechanics and repair, precision production, and transportation and material moving. The construction trades may be further divided into more specific programs such as carpentry, electricity, plumbing, and masonry (Levesque et al., 2000).

Some schools are beginning to change the course work in specific labor market programs by organizing courses around broad occupational clusters or specific industries. This allows learners to take a variety of courses as part of a blended preparation program. For example, blueprint reading is usually taught in a drafting program but learners enrolled in a building trades cluster program are required to take this course. Other schools are changing the name and scope of occupational programs by organizing courses under broad occupational or industry themes such as aviation, fashion, business and finance, health science, natural resources, communications, or technology. Still other configurations involve grouping occupational programs into clusters, majors, or pathways. School leaders may even organize their schools into magnet or theme schools or career academies (Levesque et al., 2000).

Regardless of the configuration of courses that make up a career and technical education program curriculum, learners enroll in regular academic classes and a sequence of introductory, advanced, and elective classes in occupational areas. With the expansion of work-based programs in most schools, learners now can enroll in job shadowing experiences, internships, practicums, cooperative education, and apprenticeships as part of their occupational program. Many schools also offer a tech-prep curriculum that consists of a sequence of courses that learners take during their junior and senior years and a sequence of courses they take at a postsecondary institution following graduation.

Secondary Career and Technical Education Instruction

A wide variety of instructional delivery systems are used in secondary career and technical education programs. In general, instruction consists of classroom teaching, laboratory applications, supervised work experience, and career and technical student organization activities. These classes are typically offered in one-, two-, and three-hour blocks of time. The basic component of instruction is the classroom, where learners learn concepts and theories dealing with a wide spectrum of topics, from basic career awareness to highly technical, job specific content. The lessons learned in the classroom form the basis for other types of instructional experiences. Classroom work is followed by supervised laboratory instruction where the concepts and theories are applied in typical job applications. Laboratory instruction is characterized by problem-solving and hands-on experiences that ensure that the skills learned are practical and usable in future work tasks. Learner progress is measured through a number of traditional and alternative assessment strategies with emphasis placed on performance assessments such as performance tests, performance projects, and portfolios. Learners are provided with the opportunity to further develop their computer skills as they use computers to obtain information, solve problems, and complete their assignments.

Career and technical education teachers use real-life situations to reinforce classroom and laboratory learning in order to develop realistic on-the-job skills. These real-life experiences may be live-work tasks that occur in the laboratory, or they may take the form of supervised work experience in internships, practicums, cooperative education, and apprenticeships at an actual worksite. Real-life experiences are not just work experience but are experiential, requiring learners to reflect on what happened during their experience by evaluating it. They write or orally present what they learned, what worked and what did not, what knowledge or skills they applied, what they need to do to become better future employees, and what they liked and did not like about the experience. Finally, career and technical education teachers use career and technical student organization activities as an integral, intracurricular component of their programs to teach leadership and occupational skills. The structured activities and incentives provided by the awards programs of career and technical student organizations lead to improved learner performance and to the development of future leaders.

As the United States enters the new century, the need to prepare the nation's future workforce is more challenging and important than ever before. The impact of technology, globalization, and cultural diversity is constant and permanent. Knowledge is growing exponentially and the changes that are occurring in every aspect of life will only accelerate. Lifelong learning is no longer a catchphrase but a fact of life. This exciting new time demands new skills and knowledge, but many Americans are not fully prepared to participate in the global economy. Employers continue to report difficulty in finding the skilled workers they need. America is not investing sufficiently in education and training for its people throughout a life span. Learners of today who graduate from high school and postsecondary schools or colleges must be prepared to adapt to change. They must learn how to learn so they can keep abreast of changes in every aspect of life, and they must possess the skills required to become productive workers. The U.S. system of career and technical education has served the nation well in

providing learners with the knowledge, skills, and attitudes required to successfully enter the workforce. However, beginning in the 1980s and continuing into the 1990s, report after report revealed the need for new skills or competencies for U.S. workers. The most often cited workplace competencies required for U.S. workers come from two reports, identified in the following section (U.S. Department of Labor, Employment and Training Administration, 1998).

Competencies Required for Work

Many career and technical education programs at the secondary and postsecondary levels have revised their curriculum and instructional programs to include the competencies identified in the American Society for Training and Development (ASTD) report *Workplace Basics: The Skills Employers Want* (1988) and the Secretary's Commission on Achieving Necessary Skills (SCANS) report *Learning a Living: A Blueprint for High Performance* (1992). Both of these reports identify the basic foundational skills that are needed in order to learn the specific skills required for the high-performance workplace. Technical changes on most jobs have drastically changed the basic skill requirements and are increasing the range of skills the worker needs to work in an increasingly technological environment. High-performance workers must have a solid foundation in basic literacy and computational skills and in the thinking skills required to apply knowledge at the work site. They must also possess the personal qualities that will enable them to function in an increasingly team-oriented environment and become dedicated and trustworthy workers. Following are the seven skill groups comprising the workplace basics identified in the ASTD report:

1. Foundation–Learning to Learn
2. Competence–Reading, Writing, and Computation
3. Communication–Listening and Oral Communication
4. Adaptability–Creative Thinking and Problem-solving
5. Personal Management–Self Esteem, Goal Setting/Motivation, and Personal/Career Development
6. Group Effectiveness–Interpersonal Skills, Negotiation, and Teamwork
7. Influence–Organizational Effectiveness and Leadership

The workplace know-how of the SCANS report is made up of a three-part list of foundational skills and personal qualities and a five-part list of competency areas that comprise the skills needed for effective job performance. These foundational skills and workplace competencies are as follows:

Foundation Skills

- Basic skills–writing, arithmetic, mathematics, speaking, and listening
- Thinking skills–ability to learn, reason, think creatively, make decisions, and solve problems
- Personal qualities–individual responsibility, self-esteem and self-management, sociability, and integrity.

Workplace Competencies

- Resources–know how to allocate time, money, materials, space, and staff
- Interpersonal skills–work on teams, teach others, serve customers, lead, negotiate, and work well with people from culturally diverse backgrounds
- Information–acquire and evaluate data, organize and maintain files, interpret and communicate, and use computers to process information
- Systems–understand social, organizational, and technological systems; monitor and correct performance; and design and improve systems
- Technology–elect equipment and tools, apply technology to specific tasks, and maintain and troubleshoot equipment

Tech-Prep Programs

According to the American Vocational Association (1998), tech-prep was a significant innovation in the educational reform of career and technical education programs in the 90s. It inspired a national program designed to offer strong comprehensive links between secondary and postsecondary institutions in order to prepare learners for high-skill technical jobs in business and industry. Tech-prep was an important part of the Carl D. Perkins Vocational and Applied Technology Education Act of 1990, was amended in the School-to-Work Opportunities Act of 1994, and was amended again in the Carl D. Perkins Vocational and Technical Education Act of 1998. Tech-prep is defined in the Carl D. Perkins Vocational and Technical Education Act of 1998 as

> a program that provides technical preparation in a career field such as engineering, applied science, a mechanical, industrial or practical art or trade, agriculture, health occupations, business, or applied economics, and must do the following: (1) combines at least two years of secondary and two years of postsecondary education in a sequential course of study without duplication of coursework, (2) integrates academic, vocational and technical education and, if appropriate and available, work-based learning, (3) provides technical preparation for careers, (4) builds student competence in core academic and technical areas, (5) leads to an associate's or baccalaureate degree or postsecondary certificate in a specific career field, and (6) leads to placement in appropriate employment or further education. (p. 79)

Tech-prep programs span the last two years in high school and the first two years of postsecondary education and lead to an associate's degree or certificate. The curriculum for tech-prep programs is jointly planned between secondary and postsecondary institutions. This planning results in an articulation agreement that spells out a sequence of academic and career and technical education courses to be taken while in high school and a sequence of courses to be taken at the postsecondary institution. These programs are intended to build learner competence in mathematics, communications, science, technology, and occupational skills through integration of academic and vocational education (The Office of Vocational & Adult Education [OVAE], 2000).

The Carl D. Perkins Vocational and Technical Education Act of 1998 requires that tech-prep programs have the following seven elements:

- an articulation agreement between secondary and postsecondary consortium participants
- a 2 + 2, 3 + 2, or a 4 + 2 design with a common core of proficiency in math, science, communication, and technology
- a specifically developed tech-prep curriculum
- joint in-service training of secondary and postsecondary teachers to implement the tech-prep curriculum effectively
- training of counselors to recruit learners and to ensure program completion and appropriate employment
- equal access of special populations to the full range of tech-prep programs
- preparatory services such as recruitment, career and personal counseling, and occupational assessment.

States receive federal funds to implement tech-prep programs and distribute these funds along with state funds to local tech-prep consortia that involve secondary and postsecondary institutions or an approved two-year apprenticeship program. According to the U. S. Office of Vocational and Adult Education, there were approximately 1,029 tech-prep consortia in 1995 and the number is increasing yearly. Tech-prep consortia are serving over 737,635 learners in the United States and the number continues to grow (OVAE, 2000).

Apprenticeship Programs

The apprenticeship method of instruction (structured learning on the job under the tutelage of a journeyperson) is the oldest method of formal instruction and is still used to prepare workers in the building trades, machine trades, and a variety of other trade areas. Only a small portion of American workers are prepared through formal apprenticeship programs and until recently, apprenticeship was not viewed as a viable training option for teenage youth since the average age of beginning apprentices is 25. Beginning in the late 1970s, the U.S. Department of Labor funded eight demonstration youth apprenticeship programs, which established apprenticeship as a workable training option for young people in certain occupational areas. According to the U.S. General Accounting Office (1991), there are approximately 400 school-to-apprenticeship programs serving over 3,500 learners with nearly half of these youth apprenticeship programs in machine trade occupations. Today, all states provide opportunities for local educational agencies to offer youth apprenticeship programs for junior and senior high school learners as part of their work-based education programs funded by the School-to-Work Opportunities Act of 1994.

Youth apprenticeship or school-to-apprenticeship programs are based on an employer-school partnership that integrates academic instruction, structured vocational training, and paid workplace experience. In the school-based component of apprenticeship, the classroom instruction the apprentice receives in academic and vocational subjects leads to a high school diploma and a certificate of competency. At the job-site, apprentices receive on-the-job training including technical knowledge and skills, employability skills, writing and speaking skills, and reasoning and problem-solving skills, as well as how to foster good work attitudes and habits. The expected program outcome is that youth apprentices will continue their vocational preparation in a postsecondary institution or that the apprenticeship will lead to journeyperson status and permanent employment.

Youth apprenticeship programs vary widely among states and local schools, but learners typically enter into a high school/youth apprenticeship in their junior or senior year. Each apprentice works on a part-time basis during the school year and usually full-time during the summer. The apprentice's work is monitored and evaluated by the employer, with occasional monitoring provided by the school work-based program coordinator. Related academic and career and technical instruction is coordinated to connect school and work-based instruction by a youth apprenticeship coordinator. After graduation, youth apprenticeship learners move into an adult apprenticeship program, which involves taking educational courses at a local technical/community college and continuing to work for an employer. When the apprentice successfully completes the required number of hours of work-based instruction and related classroom instruction, a certification of occupational and academic mastery is awarded that paves the way for the apprentice to enter the workforce or to continue his/her education.

Youth apprenticeship as a career and technical education program began slowly but is gaining momentum. Today, a growing number of educators and industry leaders are viewing it as an ideal vehicle for delivering the work-based learning necessary for school-to-work transition. In particular, youth apprenticeships provide a way to keep youth from floundering in the labor market, ensure that youth receive a meaningful educative work experience, increase earnings and educational attainment potential, and make the entire school experience more meaningful (Gregson, 1995). Evanciew and Rojewski (1999), indicate that apprenticeship has become an increasingly attractive option to prepare workers for today's high-tech, high-performance workplace with its demands

for a blend of technological, information, interpersonal, and lifelong learning skills.

Cooperative Education Programs

Cooperative education (co-op) is the oldest and most commonly available option for work-based learning in the United States. The cooperative education program was initiated in the 1930s by Herman Schneider, a University of Cincinnati professor of engineering, and it quickly found its way into secondary schools. There was a need then, as there is now, to provide programs to help learners earn money in jobs that enrich their educational experience, increase their work-related competence, and improve their general employability. This approach is more beneficial than having learners engaged in part-time jobs that do not relate to their school experience or prepare them to enter full-time employment in a meaningful way. Cooperative education received categorical federal support through the Vocational Education Amendments of 1968 (PL 90-576), which expanded the number of cooperative education programs nationwide.

According to the American Vocational Association (1998), cooperative education is defined in the Carl D. Perkins Vocational and Technical Education Act of 1998 as a

> method of instruction of education for individuals who, through written cooperative arrangements between a school and employers, receive instruction, including required academic courses and related vocational and technical instruction, by alteration of study in school with a job in any occupational field, which alteration shall be planned and supervised by the school and employer so that each contributes to the education and employability of the individual, and may include an arrangement in which work periods and school attendance may be on alternate half days, full days, weeks, or other periods of time in fulfilling the cooperative program. (p. 88)

While the definition included in the Perkins Act refers to cooperative education as a method of instruction, there are actually cooperative education programs in most major vocational and technical education fields, such as trade and industrial, family and consumer sciences, business, marketing, agriculture, and health occupations that operate at the local school level. These programs are a major component of the school-to-work initiatives being provided by secondary schools across the nation. Levesque et al. report that cooperative education is the most common work-based program, with 48% of secondary schools offering cooperative education programs. The percentage of high school graduates that have taken cooperative education courses has increased in the last 20 years to about

9.4% in 1994, with career and technical education concentrations exhibiting the highest rates of participation in cooperative education programs.

Co-op is a planned program that combines classroom study with arranged periods of paid, career-related work. Cooperative education is part of the school curriculum, and learners receive grades and earn credit toward graduation for their co-op work experience as well as their related classroom instruction. A cooperative education coordinator, usually with a career and technical education background, provides classroom instruction in generally related information about work and assists learners in obtaining specific information related to the jobs they are performing at the work site. A training plan is prepared cooperatively by the co-op coordinator and workstation supervisor (mentor) identifying the competencies needed on the job and the general and specific information that is to be provided for the co-op learner. Learners usually attend school in the morning and go to the training station (work site) in the afternoon. They are generally required to work a minimum of 15 hours per week and are periodically visited by the co-op coordinator to ensure that the training plan is being followed and that learners are receiving instruction in the many aspects of the occupation.

Interships, Practicums, School-Based Enterprises, and Job Shadowing

As part of their work-based program initiatives, a growing number of secondary schools are offering job shadowing, internships, practicums, and school-based enterprises in order to provide learners with opportunities to observe adults in work roles and to apply what they have learned in school-based instruction to real work settings.

Job shadowing is the term used for an activity that makes it possible for a learner to go to a work site and observe or shadow an employee for one or more days to learn about a job of interest to the learner. Job shadowing is a capstone type of experience that follows career awareness or career exploration instruction. Job shadowing is more widely used at the middle school level, but some high schools make it available primarily to ninth and tenth grade learners to help them explore careers and select a career focus area in which to take career and technical education courses later in their high school program. (Georgia Department of Education, 1999). NCES 2000 data reveal that 43% of public schools offer job shadowing experiences as part of their work-based programs.

Internships and practicums are similar in nature and involve arranging the placement of a learner for a specified period of time in a work setting where the learner can observe workers in various roles and actually participate in daily work routines. This allows them to interact with adult workers and to learn all aspects of an industry from them. Both internships and practicums continue career awareness and career exploration instruction, provided in schools, in the workplace. Learners can ask questions about a particular career and perform appropriate tasks under the watchful eye of a skilled worker, called a work site mentor, to see if they like a particular type of work and to further develop their employability skills. A school work site coordinator or a career and technical education teacher periodically visits and observes learners at work and discusses the internship or practicum experience with the mentor to ensure that a quality learning experience is being provided. The major expected outcome of internships and practicums is for learners to experience firsthand all aspects of a career/occupation/job, and not to develop technical job skills. In their *Standards and Guidelines for Work-Based Learning Programs in Georgia*, the Georgia Department of Education (1999) lists the following benefits of an internship or practicum:

* allows learners to observe a specific workplace and to develop initial workplace skills
* targets workplace experiences to a learner's program of study
* allows learners to learn work terminology, work environment, and business and industry protocol
* allows learners to apply school-based learning theories in an actual work setting
* allows learners to get firsthand professional experience.
* helps learners develop positive work habits and abilities
* offers opportunities to test for potential aptitudes for a specific career area prior to graduation

Internships and practicums are designed as a type of capstone experience. They usually occur near the end of an instructional program so that learners have an opportunity to practice what they have learned in school through direct application to actual work tasks and jobs. Learners participating in internships and practicums are generally not paid for their work productivity; the quality work-related experience is the expected outcome. NCES 2000 data reveal that about 25% of public schools offer internships or practicums.

School-based enterprises and school-sponsored enterprises provide learners with an opportunity to produce goods and services as part of their program of study and to develop knowledge and skills in all aspects of an industry. The primary purpose of school-based enterprises is to help learners learn all that is involved in establishing and operating a successful business in a career focus area. In school-based enterprises, school personnel assist learners in planning, implementing, conducting, and evaluating a business that is involved in producing goods and/or providing services. For example, a school-based enterprise may be setting up and operating a "sweets shop" as part of the commercial foods instructional program at a secondary school. Another example may include setting up a small manufacturing venture where learners design, produce, and market a product that is not readily available commercially. An example of an enterprise that provides a service might be the establishment of a seasonal enterprise to provide lost cost services for income tax preparation, or the establishment of a child-care center as part of a family and consumer sciences program (Georgia Department of Education, 1999).

Some school-based or school-sponsored enterprises involve public and private partnerships where private firms provide the equipment and materials necessary to operate the enterprise and the school system provides faculty and staff to instruct the learners and to supervise business operations. The primary goal of business and industry partners is not to produce goods and services in the competitive market but to provide learners with an authentic learning experience so they will be able to develop the knowledge, skills, and personal attributes required to function more effectively in an enterprise. Another goal is to give them initial knowledge and skills to start a company of their own at a later time in order to contribute to the local economy.

POSTSECONDARY CAREER AND TECHNICAL EDUCATION PROGRAMS AND CURRICULUM

Postsecondary career and technical education differs from secondary career and technical education in many respects, including the fact that instruction is provided in both public and private institutions. In the NCES 2000 report, Levesque et al. list six different types of institutions: (1) public four-year institutions, (2) public two-year institutions (sometimes called community colleges), (3) public less-than two-year institutions (sometimes referred to as vocational-technical institutes or technical colleges), (4) private, not-for-profit four-year institutions, (5) private, not-for-profit two-year institutions, and (6) private, for profit institutions.

Public postsecondary career and technical education institutions provide a broad range of career paths, such as educational programs leading to an associate's degree, a diploma, or an occupational certificate; continuing education programs; and economic development programs. For example, the Georgia Department of Technical and Adult Education manages a system of 33 technical colleges and institutes with 17 satellite campuses, as well as four university system institutions that offer postsecondary career and technical education programs. These institutions offer a variety of technical education programs as well as provide instruction and leadership for adult literacy and for a number of economic development programs (Georgia Department of Adult and Technical Education, 2001).

Postsecondary career and technical education institutions offer a wide variety of associate's degree, diploma, and certificate programs in a diverse range of occupational and career areas. The names of these programs vary among states but most of them are technology programs. For example, Georgia Postsecondary Technical Colleges

offer a number of instructional programs under the headings of agricultural/natural resource technologies, business technologies, engineering/science technologies, health technologies, industrial technologies, and personal/public service technologies. Example instructional programs under the business technologies area include accounting, computer programming, office technology management, legal assisting, Internet working, and others. One of the largest program areas in most postsecondary career and technical education institutions is industrial technologies with numerous instructional programs such as avionics, automotive repair, electronics, media production, welding, telecommunications, and many more (Georgia Department of Adult and Technical Education, 2001).

Postsecondary career and technical education differs from secondary in the schedule of classes as well as when classes are offered. Postsecondary classes are offered both in the day and evenings to accommodate learners who work different shifts or have family obligations, while secondary learners only attend classes during the regular school day. Postsecondary learners, like secondary learners, are required to take some academic courses, but generally only a small number and these courses are typically more occupationally related. The typical curriculum framework for postsecondary programs is made up of a sequence of courses beginning with general core courses, like general mathematics and English, and proceeding to fundamental occupational courses and then specific occupational courses. The number of hours postsecondary learners attend classes varies widely, with most day school learners attending about six hours and evening school learners varying from a few hours to as many as six hours an evening. Like secondary learners, some postsecondary learners can take advantage of work-based options like cooperative education, internship, practicums, and clinical experiences (an important component of many health technology programs).

Instructional programs consist of a blend of classroom and laboratory instruction and utilize a variety of educational technology including computerized, self-paced instruction and web-based courses. Postsecondary learners may have one or more teachers (instructors) to guide their learning in a program area. The focus of the instructional program is occupational preparation and occupational updating for those who are already employed in an area. Postsecondary learners are provided with a number of support services including career counseling, financial aid, and job placement.

According to the NCES 2000 report by Levesque et al., participation in postsecondary career and technical education increased slightly between 1992 and 1996. About one-half of all subbaccalaureate learners major in career and technical education programs. Business, health, and technical fields accounted for the majors of large numbers of learners. Postsecondary career and technical education learners tend to be older, have family responsibilities, receive financial aid, possess a previous postsecondary degree or certificate, and report higher grade-point averages than their academic counterparts. A majority of both academic and career and technical majors complete some type of degree, diploma, or certificate within a four-year period. One of the challenges facing postsecondary career and technical education is how to attract more career and technical concentrators following graduation, since this group is less likely to pursue postsecondary education than their academic counterparts. Postsecondary career and technical education institutions are responding to this challenge with intensive recruitment programs and increasing participation in tech-prep programs.

TRENDS FOR CAREER AND TECHNICAL EDUCATION

The field of career and technical education in the U.S. today is, as it has always been, in transition. Since its early development in the late 1880s, when battles were fought over the role of classical education and practical education in the public educational programs of the nation, career and technical education survived because it was recognized as essential for preparing people for the industrial age. In the early 1900s, proponents argued that a broader curriculum was needed in the public schools to encourage youth to complete high school and to give youth and adults a better chance at satisfying careers. The United States Congress became involved in 1914, authorizing the president to establish a commission to study national aid for vocational education. The commission found that there was an urgent social and educational need for vocational education in the public schools of the nation. President Woodrow Wilson signed the Smith-Hughes Vocational Act of 1917, which started federal funding for vocational education and the federal government continues to support career and technical education in the form of the Carl D. Perkins Vocational and Technical Education Act of 1998.

From the beginning, Congress has supported career and technical education as a vehicle to prepare youth and adults to develop the skills needed by business and industry. Congress is still concerned today with the lack of a technologically and technically skilled workforce. They have addressed their concerns in the new Perkins Act to ensure that career and technical education programs adjust to industry needs and that states enhance coordination between career and technical education programs and job training programs run by the federal government. Since the 1963 Vocational Education Act, federal legislation has focused on serving the needs of people, as well as business and industry needs.

Career and technical education today emphasizes a broader preparation for learners that includes developing academic, vocational, and technical skills. This preparation involves integrating academic and vocational education and emphasizing all aspects of an industry. Career and technical education policy now encourages high school learners to continue their schooling at the postsecondary level through tech-prep arrangements. The traditional focus of specific occupational preparation in a relatively small number of occupations is giving way to a broader purpose that includes emphasis on academic preparation and coverage of a wider range of career choices. Career and technical education programs are placing greater emphasis on critical thinking, personal responsibility, social skills, and leadership/follower skills to better prepare learners for modern workplace realities.

Changes in the economy and in education are altering the way business and industry works and have implications for the skills required of new employees. Increasing global competition has led to many mergers and the creation of high performance workplaces that rely on flexible and decentralized work practices and multiskilled workers. Career and technical education programs will need to continue preparing workers for more traditional workplaces, but even these work settings require a new set of skills. Career and technical education institutions will also have to expand their program offerings to prepare individuals for new and emerging occupations with a mindset of preparing learners with multiple skills. Career and technical education will have to implement more programs to prepare learners for jobs in the services and information industries, including health care and technology and communications among others (Levesque, et al., 2000).

SNAPSHOT OF CAREER AND TECHNICAL EDUCATION PROGRAMS

Career and technical education encompasses a large number of diverse programs that are designed to assist learners in developing the knowledge, attitudes, and skills required to enter and advance in occupational careers. Lynch (2000) reports that more than 35,000 public and private institutions offer career and technical education programs. He reports that one or more courses of career and technical education are offered in 93% of the nation's 15,200 comprehensive high schools and about 75% of all comprehensive high schools offer specialized labor market preparation programs for career and technical education concentrators (learners who take three or more sequenced career and technical education courses in one program area). Career and technical education programs are also offered in more than 250 career and technical high schools and in about 1,100 area career and technical centers where learners attend part of the school day in their home institution and part of the day at the center. Career and technical education is offered in a large number of postsecondary institutions, with over 720 degree-granting community colleges; 162 technical institutes or technical colleges that grant degrees in technical fields; 504 postsecondary area career and technical schools that do not grant degrees; 308 postsecondary schools serving only one industry; and 70 postsecondary skills centers for disadvantaged youth offering career and technical education programs and courses. In addition, approximately 2,400 private institutions offer career and technical education programs to prepare people for occupational careers.

Career and technical education programs fall under two major types: general labor market programs and specific labor market programs. In the National Center for Education Statistics (NCES) *Fast Facts* Report (2000), the number of Carnegie units earned by public school graduates is classified into general labor market preparation programs, consumer and homemaking education, and specific labor market preparation. Of all high school graduates, the average number of Carnegie units earned in all three categories was 3.99 with .61 earned in general labor market preparation programs, .51 earned in consumer and homemaking education, and 2.87 units earned in specific labor market preparation programs. The total number of Carnegie units earned by academic track learners was 2.22, as compared to the total number earned by vocational track learners of 9.12. Over two thirds of the Carnegie units earned by vocational track learners were in specific labor market preparation programs, or 6.97 out of 9.12 units.

Overall, research indicates that the number of credits earned by high school learners enrolled in career and technical education improves their chances of employment in their field of choice. However, occupation specific training is less beneficial to learners when they cannot find related employment. Therefore, Boesel and McFarland (1994), in the *National Assessment of Vocational Education: Final Report to Congress Volume I*, recommend an integration of academic education and career and technical education to provide learners with the opportunity to develop a range of skills in addition to their occupation specific training.

While most high school learners earn some Carnegie units of credit in career and technical education, the average number of career and technical education credits earned is declining, with the average number of courses in career and technical education areas completed by high school graduates dropping from 4.6 units in 1882 to 4.0 units in 1998. The decline described another way is that 34% of high school graduates concentrated in career and technical education programs in 1982, 28% in 1990, and 25% in 1994 (the latest year data available). There are a number of possible causes for the decline of enrollment of high school learners taking career and technical education courses, including reduced opportunity for high school learners to take elective career and technical education courses because of an increase in the number of required academic courses. Today, there is some evidence that this trend is leveling off as schools move toward new course schedules that allow learners more freedom to take elec-

tive courses as part of their high school program (National Center for Education Statistics [NCES], 2000).

According to *Career Tech 2000: Statistical Snapshot* (2000), which reports data on today's career and technical education learners, 97% of high school learners took at least one course in career and technical education in 1994, and 25% completed three or more courses. The United States Department of Education labels those learners who have completed three of more career and technical education courses as vocational concentrators.

The *Statistical Snapshot* includes findings that show enrollment in trade and industry and business programs dropped between the years 1982 and 1994, while enrollment in service programs such as health care, food services, and child care increased along with technology and communication programs, and marketing and agriculture programs. These findings correspond to shifts in the U.S. economy toward a service and information economy.

The *Statistical Snapshot* also shows that vocational concentrators are meeting new basic academic core requirements, with 33% meeting requirements in 1994 and an estimated 45% expected to meet core requirements in 1998. As more career and technical education learners complete basic academic core requirements, they are more likely to enroll in postsecondary education. This assumption has proven true, as there was an increase in the number of vocational concentrators enrolling in postsecondary education within two years of high school graduation, from 42% in 1982 to 55% in 1992. A picture of where they enrolled reveals that 50% enrolled in community colleges, 30% enrolled in four-year colleges and universities, and 20% enrolled in other postsecondary education.

The *Statistical Snapshot* reports that the vast majority of career and technical education concentrators graduating from high school are working one year after graduation. Four out of five high school career and technical concentrators who graduated in 1992 were working in 1993. In addition, among all high school graduates of the class of 1992 who enrolled in college, career and technical concentrators were more likely than their college-prep peers to work while enrolled—44% versus 17%.

About half of subbaccalaureate learners taking credit courses at postsecondary institutions declared a career and technical major. This statistic is a strong confirmation of interest in career and technical education at the postsecondary level, but it is actually a 5% decline since 1990. The most popular programs in which subbaccalaureate postsecondary learners enrolled were business and office, health, and engineering/science technologies. Between 1990 and 1996 the percentage of learners enrolling in health programs increased slightly while enrollments in business and office and engineering/science technologies declined slightly. Of the learners who declared a career and technical education major who enrolled in postsecondary institutions in 1989–1990, 42% of associate's degree seekers and 64% of those pursuing a certificate had achieved or exceeded their objectives by 1994 (*Statistical Snapshot*, 2000).

Lynch (2000) reports that secondary career and technical education today is rebounding in both image and enrollment. Educational reform efforts have led to program improvements; business and industry partnerships, organized as a result of the School-to-Work program initiatives, have expanded work-based program options; learner interest in computers and technology has led to the creation of new programs and courses that are attractive to more learners; and both learners and their parents have concluded that some form of job skills will be required in order to fund the increasing cost of postsecondary education. An increasing number of learners are opting to earn diplomas, which have both an academic and a career and technical education program seal.

Lynch states that secondary career and technical education is at a crossroads, with at least two major paths leading to different outcomes. One path features programs that are technologically current, are well equipped, are led by competent teachers, offer an integrated, rigorous academic and career and technical curriculum, and are guided by career plans that lead to immediate employment after graduation or to continuing education. The other path leads to schools and programs that have not been able to keep current in offering curriculum experiences that meet the demands of business and industry or in offering preparation for some form of postsecondary education. Enrollment in these schools and programs is largely composed of learners from special populations. Often career and technical teachers do not have the necessary training or equipment to serve these learners adequately. Furthermore, the curriculum has been diluted so that it neither prepares learners for satisfying employment or for further education.

Lynch reports that at least four schools of thought are evident in the literature and championed by different constituencies as to the direction that secondary career and technical education should take. The first school of thought is "education through occupations" where career and technical education is viewed as an instructional modality for teaching academic content. The integration of academic and career and technical content is critical for this type of education. Scholars in the educational community hold this view.

The second school of thought holds career and technical education as a means of imparting general work preparation skills as well as job skills for about one-third of high school learners who are not college bound after graduation. Instruction is organized and delivered around broad career clusters and learners not only develop knowledge of all aspects of an industry, but also develop some fairly specific job skills as well. Mostly educators of traditional career and technical education programs support this school of thought.

The third school is career and technical education that features concentrated preparation in specialized job skills and is targeted to alternative learners doing poorly in regular high school courses in order to keep them from dropping out and to approximately 8–12% of the educationally disadvantaged learners who are not likely to attend postsecondary education after graduation and need specific skill training in order to enter employment. This view is embraced by many academic subject educators as well as middle- and upper-class parents and some local policy makers.

The fourth school of thought is career and technical education offered largely through the tech-prep program format. This format features an articulated curricular agreement between high schools and postsecondary schools to provide a sequence of nonduplicative courses integrating academic and career and technical subjects and leading to graduation from high school followed by immediate enrollment in a postsecondary education institution where learners will eventually earn an associate's degree, diploma, certificate, and career placement. Members of Congress and business and industry leaders endorse this school of thought

Career and technical education has traditionally responded to the needs of business and industry, and business leaders have been very vocal about the changes that are needed in order to better prepare high school graduates for the workplace. More than ever before, these leaders are demanding a say in standards development, curriculum development, and assessment programs to ensure that learners receive the needed academic and workplace skills required for businesses to compete in the global market place. Business and industry leaders are forming partnerships with schools to get more formally involved in helping youth make the transition from school to work and continuing education.

Career and technical education in the United States is being transformed by becoming more academically rigorous and career relevant, which is the essence of "new" vocational education according to Lynch (2000). The curriculum now requires learners to demonstrate competence in meeting industry standards, high academic standards, and related general work preparation knowledge, as well as demonstrating skills and attitudes required for employment and continuing education. Instructional programs are becoming more contextual through authentic in-school learning experiences as well as learning experiences in the community and at worksites. Learners are demonstrating their knowledge and skills through a number of performance assessments such as performance projects, performance tests and portfolios. Schools are providing new equipment and educational technology to enable teachers to provide training and deliver instruction that is interesting and engaging to learners. Teachers are becoming more professional and competent as they seek opportunities to engage in professional development activities provided at the local, state, and national levels through their professional associations and business and industry partners.

Framework for Workforce Preparation Programs

Career and technical education encompasses a broad array of programs for the delivery of work preparation in the United States, which makes it difficult to define and communicate the meaning of career and technical education to learners, parents, and the general public. Over the years beginning in the 1970s with the career education clusters, the United States Department of Education has attempted to establish broad career clusters as a framework for workforce preparation programs. In 1998, seven major industry clusters were identified in a study by the U.S. Department of Education entitled *Toward a New Framework of Industry Programs for Vocational Education: Emerging Trends in Curriculum and Instruction*. These clusters were common to national initiatives and most state efforts (U.S. Department of Education, 1998).

In 2000 the U.S. Department of Education finalized its effort in establishing an industry classification system for education with 16 broad career clusters reflecting a new direction for education. These 16 clusters consist of all entry-level through professional-level occupations in a broad industry area and include both academic and the technical skills and knowledge needed for further education and careers. The clusters provide a framework for educators, counselors, and parents to help youth and adults identify their career interests and goals and to plan for their future. These 16 clusters are as follows:

• Agriculture and Natural Resources
• Business and Administration
• Education and Training
• Health Science
• Human Services
• Law and Public Safety
• Government and Public Administration
• Scientific Research/Engineering
• Arts, A/V Technology and Communication
• Architecture and Construction
• Finance
• Hospitality and Tourism
• Information Technology
• Manufacturing
• Retail/Wholesale Sales and Service
• Transportation, Distribution, and Logistics

The career clusters provide a way for educators to organize instruction and learner experiences around 16 broad categories that encompass nearly all occupations from entry-level through professional. The U.S. Department of Education has identified sample occupations for each cluster but many more occupations can be added to each.

CAREER AND TECHNICAL EDUCATION PROGRAMS

Career and technical education programs are commonly grouped into the following categories: agricultural education, business education, family and consumer sciences education, health occupations education, marketing education, technical education, technology education, and trade and industrial education, as well as career and technical special needs and career and technical teacher education. Each of these programs has evolved from occupational needs and addresses specific requirements of society today.

Agricultural Education

"Agriculture is the broad industry engaged in the production of plants and animals for food and fiber, the provision of agricultural supplies and services, and the processing, marketing, and distribution of agricultural products" (Herren & Donahue, 1991, p. 9). According to National FFA statistics, agriculture is the nation's largest employer with more than 22 million people working in some phase of it—from growing food and fiber to selling it at the supermarket.

Over the last decade the terms agriculture/agribusiness and renewable resources have evolved to more fully describe the activities that are associated with agriculture (Herren & Cooper, 2002). The U.S. Department of Education categories list agriculture as Agriculture and Natural Resources in its 16 broad career clusters.

According to the National Council for Agricultural Education (2001), "agricultural education is a systematic program of instruction available to learners desiring to learn about the science, business, and technology of plant and animal production and/or about the environmental and natural resources systems." As its mission "agricultural education prepares learners for successful careers and a lifetime of informed choices in the global agriculture, food, fiber, and natural resources systems." The vision of agricultural education includes the view of a "world where all people value and understand the vital role of agriculture, food, fiber, and natural resources systems in advancing personal and global well-being." Today more than 800,000 learners participate in formal agricultural education instructional programs offered in grades seven through adult throughout 50 states and three U.S. territories. The *Statistical Snapshot* (2000) reveals that 12% of career and technical education concentrators are enrolled in the agriculture program at the secondary level.

Agricultural education is an important program area of career and technical education designed to provide learners with the knowledge, skills, and personal attributes required to explore and prepare for careers in agriculture and natural resources. Learners are provided with opportunities to develop leadership skills, experience personal growth, and prepare for careers through a three-part instructional delivery program: (1) classroom/laboratory instruction (contextual learning), (2) supervised agriculture experience programs (work-based learning), and (3) learner leadership organizations (the FFA, The National Young Farmer Educational Association, and the National Postsecondary Agricultural Student organization). Many former agricultural education graduates are now in leadership positions in government agencies, education, and business and industry as a result of the leadership training they received in their career and technical student organization activities, which are an integral part of agricultural education programs.

Agricultural education instruction is provided at the local level through the nation's middle and high schools, community and technical colleges, and technical institutes. State leadership is provided through a number of agencies and institutions including state departments of education, state departments of agriculture, land grant universities, community colleges, and other agencies. The U.S. Department of Education and the Agricultural Education Division of the Association of career and technical education provide leadership for agricultural education at the national level. Agricultural education is supported by a number of organizations at the local, state, and national levels. The umbrella organization for agricultural education is the National Council for Agricultural Education (The Council).

Agricultural education has consistently changed its instructional programs to meet the needs of the dynamic, rapidly changing industry of agriculture, as well as aquaculture, which emphasizes how to select, culture, propagate, harvest, and market domesticated fish, shellfish, and marine plants (Georgia Department of Education, 2000). Agriculture is becoming highly scientific and technical in new frontiers such as biotechnology, which deals with genetic engineering and tissue culture. Agricultural education is responding with new programs like agriscience, which consist of a series of laboratory courses that emphasize the basic biological and physical science principles and practices associated with agriculture.

Agricultural programs are increasingly being planned to prepare learners for a wide range of career options. Like other areas of vocational and applied technology education, more attention is being given to integrating academic subjects such as communications, mathematics, and science with the applications of technology. Agricultural education is being offered in grades 7 through 14 in over 7,600 high schools and 570 postsecondary institutions in the U.S. According to the national FFA, more than 11,000 agricultural education teachers deliver a cutting-edge, innovative curriculum to learners with more than 92% of them offering agriscience, 71% offering advanced agriscience and biotechnology, 59% offering agricultural mechanics, 49% offering horticulture, 43% offering animal science, and 24% offering environment-related courses. Many learners begin career awareness and exploration programs in agriculture in the middle/junior high school years and continue in this area of interest in a high school agriculture program. Some learners continue their education for two or more years by enrolling in community colleges and four-year colleges or universities where they earn associate's degrees or baccalaureate degrees in agriculture or related areas (Lee, 1994).

The instructional program in agricultural education utilizes three major components: classroom and laboratory instruction, supervised experience, and FFA and PAS—the career and technical student organizations. Classroom and laboratory instruction involves teaching learners the underlying concepts and principles of agriculture and providing them with opportunities to apply what they have learned in a hands-on environment. A supervised agricultural experience (SAE) involves structured learning activities that build on what has been learned through classroom and laboratory instruction. Supervised agricultural experiences are applied outside the regular class time, providing an opportunity for learners to interact with a number of adults and to develop on-the-job skills. They may vary from traditional on-the-farm home projects to entrepreneurship, cooperative work experience in production agriculture or agribusiness, or projects conducted in land laboratories provided on or near the school's campuses. The FFA is the vocational student organization specifically for agricultural education learners and operates as an integral part of the total instructional program. Learners are provided with an opportunity to develop personal and leadership skills as well as to practice good citizenship and cooperation. In addition, FFA provides opportunities for learners to become involved in a variety of competitive events and professional development activities to expand their learning and to receive recognition for their accomplishments (Lee, 1994).

Postsecondary agricultural learners and young adult farmers also experience integrated curriculum activities in their instructional programs through the National Postsecondary Agricultural Student Organization (PAS) and the National Young Farmers Educational Association (NYFEA). PAS provides similar activities to postsecondary learners, as does the FFA for secondary learners. NYFEA provides opportunities for young adult farmers to develop leadership skills and enhance their knowledge and skills in agriculture after they have left formal education programs.

Agricultural education encompasses a wide variety of programs and courses offered in middle/junior high schools, high schools, and postsecondary institutions. These programs and courses range from traditional production agriculture to agriscience and technology to the emerging field of agricultural biotechnology, which involves working with genetically modified plants, feed supplements for animals, and innovative pharmaceuticals. Most states have developed curriculum guides that provide the basic curriculum framework for instructional programs at the local institution level. Basic agriculture programs/courses typically include (a) agricultural plants and animals, (b) agricultural mechanics, (c) agricultural sales and service, (d) forestry, (e) environmental horticulture, (f) agricultural products and processing, (g) natural resources, (h) specialty animals, (i) agribusiness, (j) agriscience, and other agricultural specialty areas. See Figure 2-3.

Agricultural education in this country has a long and rich history beginning with the land grant colleges created by the Morrill Act of 1862 and the Smith-Hughes Act of 1917 and continuing today under the provisions of the Carl D. Perkins Vocational and Technical Education Act of 1998. It has evolved from a tradition of preparing learners for farming (growing plants and raising animals) to a focus on agriculture as a science, to preparing learners for varying careers and a lifetime of choices in the global agriculture and natural resources systems. While the field has enjoyed tremendous success, there are a number of challenges facing agricultural education, such as integrating agricultural examples into academic courses like social science, English, math, history, communications and business. One of the most pressing challenges is how to attract more young people to enter teacher education programs and become agricultural education teachers.

The professional development of agricultural education teachers has always been a priority of the field. Agricultural education has developed a network of federal, state, and local school agencies in partnership with business and industry to provide leadership and deliver services to agricultural educators, including agricultural teachers, teacher educators, and supervisors of agricultural education at the local and state levels. Agricultural educators and supervisors can join and/or participate in the professional development activities of the Agricultural Education Division of the ACTE and the state level affiliates of this organization, the American Association for Agricultural Education (EAAA), the National Association of Agricultural Educators (NAAE), the National Council for Agricultural Education (NCAE), the National Association of Supervisors of Agricultural Education (NASAE), and the Career and Technical Student Organizations of the FFA, the National Postsecondary Agricultural Student Organization (PAS), and the National Young Farmer Educational Association (NYFEA).

Business Education

Business education is the career and technical education program that prepares learners for tomorrow's business community. It is not solely for those who are preparing to enter business occupations; rather, it is a program that serves the total school population through a cutting-edge, relevant curriculum that provides career direction, a sound foundation for further study, and the development of knowledge, employability skills and technical skills required for productive employment in business and for business roles in diverse occupations. In addition to preparing individuals for employment, business education provides learners with the knowledge, understanding, and fundamental skills needed to conduct personal business affairs and to effectively use the services of the business world as a consumer. Policy Statement No. 64 of the National Business Education Association (NBEA, 2001) describes the role of business education at all educational levels. This includes serving persons regardless of age, gender, and career aspirations in learning about business. The NBEA policy statement views business education as "a rigorous discipline that challenges learners to develop their creative thinking skills and become independent learners through analysis, synthesis, and evaluation as they apply their business knowledge and skills in other disciplines and in the real world."

Business education courses are offered at the middle/junior high school levels as well as secondary and postsecondary levels. It is the most popular career and technical education program at the secondary and postsecondary level, with over one-half of all learners who have taken one or more occupational education courses enrolled in business education. About 8% of high school graduates concentrated in business education and about 14% of subbaccalaureate postsecondary learners chose this major (NCES, 2000). The *Statistical Snapshot* (2000)

SAMPLE LISTING OF AGRICULTURAL EDUCATION PROGRAM/COURSE TOPICS

- Agricultural Plants and Animals
- Agricultural Mechanics
- Agricultural Sales and Service
- Forestry
- Environmental Horticulture
- Agricultural Products and Processing
- Natural Resources
- Specialty Animals
- Agribusiness
- Agriscience
- Agricultural Biotechnology
- Entrepreneurship
- Leadership Development

- Employability Skills
- Environmental Management
- Exploring Careers in Agriculture
- Conserving Natural Resources
- Agricultural Economics
- Forest Technology
- Animal and Dairy Science
- Agronomy
- Agricultural Communications
- Agricultural Engineering
- Agricultural Technology Management
- Animal Science

- Botany
- Crop Science
- Poultry Science
- Dairy Science
- Entomology
- Food Science
- Landscape and Ground Management
- Agricultural Ethics
- Plant Pathology
- Environmental Literacy
- Agricultural Diesel Machines
- Veterinary Technology

Figure 2-3. Examples of the variety of programs found in agricultural education.

reveals that 30% of career and technical concentrators enroll in the business education program.

Business education taught as general labor market preparation provides instruction to help learners develop basic literacy in business, economics, and informational technology. Business education taught as a specific labor market preparation program prepares learners for business occupations, which is the largest segment of the labor market. According to the Business Education Division of the ACTE, the skills taught in business education programs include (1) communications, (2) information systems/technology, (3) financial procedures, (4) economics, (5) entrepreneurship, (6) international business, (7) principles of management and law, (8) interpersonal and leadership skills, and (9) career development.

Business education, like other career and technical education programs, has had to continuously change curriculum and instructional practices to keep pace with changes in business, equipment, organization, policy, and market demands. Instruction focuses on skill development with word processors, computers, high-speed copiers, laser printers, fax machines, and e-business conducted over the Internet. Business principles and concepts have also changed focus from secretarial office procedures to management systems and entrepreneurship, from a local economic community to an international one, and from computer applications to information systems (Phillips, 1994).

Although the knowledge base of modern business has existed for decades, digital technology, including the Internet, is changing the way America does business. Computers, fax machines, and electronic mail are now commonplace, and new technologies, such as e-business, which involves the exchange of business information by digital transmission, are the new frontiers. More specifically, according to Policy Statement No. 66, e-business involves the exchange of products and services from business to business through digital technology (NBEA, 2001).

Business education instructional programs have made dramatic philosophical shifts in educational practices from single learning to multiple learning, rigidity to flexibility, isolated content to interrelated content, memorized responses to problem awareness and problem-solving, national dimensions to international proportions, one career to multiple career preparations, and job-specific skills to broad-based transferable skills. As technology continues to impact this field, new and innovative educational approaches must be established to provide business education learners with the enhanced skills and knowledge they will need to participate in the international marketplace (Georgia Department of Education, 1992).

To meet the rapid changes in the business world, the NBEA (2001) has developed standards in 12 business areas that are used as guidelines for schools in establishing a quality business education curriculum. These standards are used to identify expectations and as a basis for determining whether these expectations have been met for both teachers and learners. The standards do not mandate a curriculum for schools to follow, rather they state what learners should know and be able to do in business. It is up to states and local schools to develop a curriculum around these voluntary standards that will help learners meet their needs for self-sufficiency in personal business affairs as well as meeting the needs of the business world. These standards are made available to state education departments, educational institutions, associations, and individuals and can be obtained by contacting NBEA. The 12 curricular areas identified by NBEA under which standards are organized are as follows:

- Accounting
- Business Law
- Career Development
- Communications
- Computation
- Economic and Personal Finance
- Entrepreneurship
- Information Systems
- International Business
- Interrelationships of Business Education Standards
- Management
- Marketing

Using the business education standards as a guide, the business education instructional program consists of sequenced courses ranging from introductory to advanced. These courses are nearly always conducted in a laboratory environment since the use of office equipment is an integral part of most instructional topics. Business education teachers, using modern visual-presentation technology, can deliver instruction to an entire class of learners and observe individual performance on applied academic or business education assignments without moving away from the command center. Introductory courses acquaint learners with technological concepts and principles, application courses and experiences facilitate the learners' abilities to apply these concepts, and advanced courses emphasize transferability of knowledge and higher order skills such as problem solving and decision making. Business education learners are provided with opportunities to engage in participatory activities in school-based enterprises and in real-life situations in the business community through long-term projects, job shadowing, internships, cooperative business education, and youth apprenticeships. Like other career and technical education program areas, business education learners enhance their business skills and leadership skills by participating in Future Business Leaders of America (FBLA) or Business Professionals of America (BPA), which are the career and technical student organizations for secondary business education learners. Postsecondary business education learners can participate in Phi Beta Lambda (PBL), the postsecondary career and technical student organization (NBEA, 2001).

Business education courses, such as keyboarding, are offered in some elementary schools and in many middle/junior high schools as exploratory, pre-vocational courses and provide learners with a broad understanding of business education and career options. At the secondary school level, business education courses serves two purposes: as general labor market preparation and preparation for executing personal business transactions and as specific labor market preparation for careers in business. Business education courses for specific labor market preparation are also offered at the postsecondary level in community colleges, technical institutes/colleges, and four-year colleges and universities at less than baccalaureate degree programs. Business education programs offer a wide variety of courses or classes including: keyboarding, word processing, spreadsheets, database management, business graphics, and electronic publishing. See Figure 2-4.

Business educators are also establishing youth apprenticeship programs that link education with business through a partnership of school-based learning and work-based learning. In youth apprenticeships, learners have an opportunity to apply core-subject knowledge, develop workplace readiness skills, and experience significant relationships with skilled adults called mentors (Cassidy, 1994).

Business education programs provide secondary learners with opportunities to continue their education at the postsecondary level through articulated tech-prep programs. Business educators at the secondary and postsecondary levels are establishing tech-prep programs consisting of carefully sequenced courses in the last two years of high school and the first two years of postsecondary education. Tech-prep programs provide learners a way to obtain advanced placement in postsecondary programs leading to certificates, diplomas, associate's degree programs, and ultimately, to employment in highly skilled technical occupations in the business world.

Successful business education programs are dependent upon the professional development of business education teachers. Teachers have the responsibility for educating learners; therefore teachers must have the knowledge, expertise, and power to make decisions about the teaching-learning environment. Professional development of teachers is no longer an option, it is required for rapid changes in the business world, and educational practice compels business educators to commit themselves to continuing professional renewal. As discussed in Policy Statement No. 60, professional development requires teachers to become part of the professional community that places inquiry and excellence at its core and focuses on building capacity for continuous learning (NBEA, 2001). Business education teachers can become active members of the following professional organizations: the Business Education Division of the ACTE, the National Business Education Association (NBEA), and the National Association of

Classroom Educators of Business Education (NACBE). Teacher educators and supervisors of business education can join the professional organizations of the National Association of Teacher Educators for Business Education (NATEBE) and the National Association of Supervisors of Business Education (NASBE).

Family and Consumer Sciences Education

According to the Family and Consumer Sciences Education organization (2001), family and consumer sciences education is the career and technical education program that "empowers individuals and families across the life span to manage the challenges of living and working in a diverse, global society. The unique focus of the discipline is on families, work and their interrelationships." The Family and Consumer Sciences Division of the ACTE reports the mission of family and consumer sciences education as the program to "prepare learners for family life, work life and careers in Family and Consumer Sciences by providing opportunities to develop the knowledge and skills, attitudes and behaviors needed for:

- Strengthening the well-being of individuals and families across the life span.
- Becoming responsible citizens and leaders in family, community and work settings.
- Promoting optimal nutrition and wellness across the life span.
- Managing resources to meet the material needs of individuals and families.
- Balancing personal, home, family and work lives.
- Using critical and creative thinking skills to address problems in diverse family, community and work environments.
- Successful life management, employment and career development.
- Functioning effectively as providers and consumers of goods and services.
- Appreciating human growth and accepting responsibility for one's actions and success in family and work life."

Family and consumer sciences education today is vastly different than it was in 1899 when Ellen Richards, the founder and first president of the American Home Economics Association, now called the American Association of Family and Consumer Sciences (AAFCS), addressed the participants attending its Lake Placid conference. For one thing, the name of the discipline has changed from home economics education, vocational home economics education, and consumer and homemaking education, to family and consumer sciences education. This change of name to family and consumer sciences education occurred at the Scottsdale, Arizona Conference of 1993. At this conference, a new conceptual framework for the discipline was developed and accepted by the membership. This new conceptual framework included a tripartite mission of empowering individuals, strengthening families, and enabling communities (Stage & Vincent, 1997).

SAMPLE LISTING OF BUSINESS EDUCATION PROGRAM/COURSE TOPICS

- Business Communications
- Office Management
- Office Procedures and Technology
- Systems Analysis and Design
- Accounting
- Business Law
- Economics
- Computer Technology
- Speedwriting
- International Business Management
- Banking and Finance
- Keyboarding
- Database Management

- Desktop Publishing
- Computer Graphics
- Consumer Economics
- Technology, Life, and Careers
- Exploratory Business
- Leadership Development
- Personal Skill Development
- Cooperative Business Education
- Local Area Networks (LAN)
- Telecommunications/Teleconferencing
- Multimedia Presentations
- Information Systems

- Networking
- Electronic Mail
- Computer Programming
- Entrepreneurship
- Executive Secretarial
- Legal Secretarial
- Information and Office Technology
- Business Data Entry/Peripheral Equipment
- Voice-Reproduction Systems/Voice Activated Equipment
- Spreadsheets

Figure 2-4. Examples of courses in business education programs.

Today, under the leadership of the American Association of Family and Consumer Sciences, the discipline continues to evolve. Its primary focus is on an integrative approach to the reciprocal relationships among individuals, families, and communities and the environments in which they function. The nature of family and consumer sciences has evolved because of the changes in the family, changes in American culture and resources, new knowledge in the basic disciplines, and applied research.

From the early beginnings of home economics education until today, professionals have discussed and debated the content of what should comprise the body of knowledge of family and consumer sciences education. Reports of 10 Lake Placid conferences and many professional meetings have revealed differing points of view. In January of 2000, a group of 20 family and consumer sciences professionals met at the headquarters of AAFCS to develop a philosophical framework for the family and consumer sciences body of knowledge. A philosophical framework emerged from this conference in the form of threads of continuity that were viewed as central to the work of family and consumer sciences. Two categories of threads emerged—those that were integrated across disciplines (crosscutting threads) and those that identified specialization within the field (specialization threads). Crosscutting threads included (1) basic human needs (2) communication skills, (3) public policy, (4) critical thinking, (5) diversity, (6) global perspective, (7) professionalism, (8) independence, dependence, and interdependence of creative thinking. (9) community development, (10) technology, and (11) moral, ethical, and spiritual development. Specialization threads included (1) health, (2) food for basic nutrition and health and future scientific development in the creation of foods, (3) clothing and textiles, (4) shelter, (5) economics and management, (6) relationships and social leadership, and (7) wellness. A model was developed that presented family and community systems, resource acquisition and man-

agement, and human life span development as fundamental to the knowledge base. (American Association of Family and Consumer Sciences, 2001).

Family and consumer sciences education is both a general labor market program as well as a specific labor market program, which makes it difficult to determine current learner enrollment in the program at the secondary level. NCES' *Fast Facts* (2000) lists the average number of Carnegie units earned by all 1998 graduates in consumer and homemaking education as .51 but does not break out the number of credits earned by family and consumer sciences learners who are enrolled in specific labor market preparation. *The Statistical Snapshot* (2000) includes data for career and technical concentrators by program but does not use family and consumer sciences as a reporting category. It reports data in three areas: food service and hospitality, child care and education, and personal services that probably include most of the concentrators enrolled in family and consumer sciences at the secondary level. The report lists the following percent of concentrators enrolled in the three family and consumer science areas: 1.4% in food service and hospitality, 2% in childcare and education, and 4% in personal services. See Figure 2-5.

The curriculum for family and consumer sciences education is drawn from various disciplines, including the social sciences, physical sciences, biological sciences, economics, psychology, philosophy and the arts. Subject matter is identified to form an integrated curriculum that prepares learners for the practical problems of the home, family, community and the workplace. In 1997 a new curriculum framework was developed for the discipline in the form of the National Standards for Family and Consumer Sciences Education, and states and local school agencies are in the process of changing programs to implement these standards. According to the Family and Consumer Sciences Education organization (FACSE), the content standards are organized under the following 16 content areas:

- Career, Community and Family Connections
- Consumer and Family Resources
- Consumer Services
- Early Childhood, Education, and Services
- Facilities Management and Maintenance
- Family
- Family and Community Services
- Food Production and Services
- Food Science, Dietetics, and Nutrition
- Hospitality, Tourism, and Recreation
- Housing, Interiors and Furnishings
- Human Development
- Interpersonal Relationships
- Nutrition and Wellness
- Parenting
- Textiles and Apparel

Each major content area has a standard followed by several task statements. For example, under the content standard area of Career, Community, and Family Connections, the standard is "Integrate multiple life roles and responsibilities in family, career and community roles and responsibilities." One of the tasks needed to accomplish this standard is to analyze strategies for managing multiple individual, family, career, and community roles and responsibilities.

Family and consumer sciences education programs are found in middle/junior high school, high schools, and postsecondary institutions such as career centers, two-year academic and technical colleges, four-year colleges, and adult education centers. At the middle/junior high school level, family and consumer sciences education programs

are usually exploratory in nature and are designed to introduce learners to the knowledge, attitudes, and skills that will enable them to balance roles and responsibilities within the home, family, and workplace. In addition, middle/junior high school learners explore career opportunities in family and consumer sciences. The middle/junior high school curriculum focuses on the following:

- self-esteem
- self-concept
- physical development
- social development
- interpersonal relationships outside the family
- roles and responsibilities within the family
- freedom and responsibility
- values clarification
- decision making
- personal finance
- nutrition
- wellness
- conservation of natural resources
- consumer practices
- communication skills
- employability skills
- leadership skills

The family and consumer sciences curriculum at the high level is based on the National Standards for Consumer Sciences Education, which includes content in 16 areas that contain competencies required to manage the challenges of living and working in a diverse, global society. Learners are provided with opportunities to develop

SAMPLE LISTING OF FAMILY AND CONSUMER PROGRAM/COURSE TOPICS

- Housing and Living Environment
- Consumer and Resource Management
- Individual, Child, and Family Development
- Nutrition and Food
- Textiles and Clothing
- Personal Development
- Interpersonal and Communication Skills
- Families in Today's Society
- Parenting
- Nutrition, Health, and Wellness
- Consumer/Resources Management
- Decision Making
- Child Safety/Babysitting
- Indentity/Self-esteem, and Self-concept
- Values Clarification
- Consumerism

- Career Exploration/Career Development
- Child Care
- Elder Care
- Leadership Development
- Chef/Cook
- Child Development
- Dietetic Assisting
- Clothing/Textiles Management, Production, and Service
- Family/Individual Health
- Family Living and Parenthood
- Food Management, Production, and Service
- Home Management
- Hospitality (Travel and Travel Service)
- Housing, Home Furnishing, and Equipment
- Hotel/Motel Management

- Institutional Management
- Interior Decorating/Design
- Waiter/Waitress
- Culinary Arts
- Employability Skills
- Balancing Work and Family
- Entrepreneurship
- Careers in Family and Consumer Sciences
- Cultural Diversity
- Personal Relationships
- Prenatal/Postnatal Care
- Family Relationships
- Personal/Family Budgeting
- Food Science, Safety, and Nutrition
- Food Biotechnologies
- Food Microbiology
- Toxicology

Figure 2-5. Various disciplines of family and consumer sciences programs.

competencies in the following broad curricular areas: (1) career, community and family connections, (2) consumer and family resources, (3) consumer services, (4) early childhood, education and services, (5) facilities management and maintenance, (6) family, (7) family and community services, (8) food production and services, (9) food science, dietetics, and nutrition, (10) hospitality, tourism and recreation, (11) housing, interiors and furnishings, (12) human development, (13) interpersonal relationships, (14) nutrition and wellness, (15) parenting, and (16) textiles and apparel.

The instructional programs of family and consumer sciences education consist of classroom and laboratory instruction; supervised experiences in the home or in real-life situations through work-based program options like cooperative education, internships, or apprenticeships; and learning experiences provided through the integrated activities of the Family Career and Community Leaders of America (FCCLA), the career and technical student organization serving family and consumer sciences learners. Classroom instruction includes integration of academic skills with concepts and principles, which form the basis for subjects in family and consumer sciences. Laboratory instruction provides learners with opportunities to apply classroom learning in problem solving and to practice their skills in performing many diverse tasks related to family and consumer sciences, from nutrition to textiles and apparel. Supervised experiences are provided through long-term projects that can be completed at home or in real-life situations in the community through cooperative education, internships, or mentoring. Through involvement in FCCLA activities, learners are given expanded opportunities for knowledge application, leadership training, community involvement, and personal growth. At the center of the FCCLA is learner involvement in projects requiring them to plan, carry out, and evaluate themselves. The national FCCLA has developed a special program entitled Implementing the National Family and Consumer Sciences Standards through FCCLA that outlines how organization activities can help teachers integrate the national standards into the family and consumer sciences curriculum.

Family and consumer sciences education programs are taught by dedicated and professionally prepared educators who take advantage of the many opportunities for professional development made available through a cadre of organizations at the local, state, regional, and national levels. These professional organizations provide members with publications and offer a variety of services including meetings, seminars, and conferences where participants can learn and work together to improve their knowledge and skills and to help shape the discipline. The American Association of Family and Consumer Sciences (AAFCS) is one of the oldest professional societies in the United States. Professional development within the AAFCS encompasses a certification program for educators to document

their mastery of the knowledge and skills required to perform the services of the discipline. The accreditation program ensures that family and consumer sciences education at the college and university level meets professional standards. The AAFCS offers family and consumer sciences educators numerous opportunities to assume leadership roles, publish in professional journals, and enhance personal knowledge and skills through participation in meetings, seminars, and workshops at district, state, and national levels.

There are several other professional organizations that provide leadership and professional development services to family and consumer sciences educators. The Family and Consumer Sciences Education Division of ACTE operates at the national level to represent the interest of family and consumers sciences education, to provide information through publications, and to provide professional development activities such as meetings, conferences, and recognition programs. The ACTE also operates at the regional and state levels with each state having a division of family and consumer sciences education that provides similar services to those provided at the national level. The Family and Consumer Sciences Education Association (FCSEA) is a voluntary organization of family and consumer sciences educators and other interested individuals that promotes effective education programs, supplements existing services and resources available to family and consumer science educators, and cooperates with other associations in related fields. The National Association of Teacher Educators for Family and Consumer Sciences (NATEFACS) is the professional organization dedicated to improving and strengthening teacher education in family and consumer sciences. Professional development activities and services for family and consumer sciences educators are also provided through the FCCLA.

Health Occupations Education

Health Occupations is the career and technical education program that provides learners with opportunities to explore the many careers in the health care industry; it provides the knowledge, skills, and attitudes necessary to succeed in a chosen health services occupation. Health occupations consist of a wide range of job opportunities which are usually organized under the categories of professional specialty (physicians, registered nurses, physical and respiratory therapists, dentists, pharmacists, and others); service (nursing aids, psychiatric aids, personal care and home health aids, medical assistants, dental assistants, food preparation workers, and others); administrative support (general office clerks, receptionists and information clerks, medical secretaries, bookkeeping and accounting clerks, and others); technical and related support (licensed practical nurses, surgical technologists, clinical laboratory technologists and technicians, radiological technologists and technicians, dental hygienists, and others); executive, administrative, and managerial (health services managers, general managers, and top executives); and precision production, craft, repair (dental lab technician).

According to the *Occupational Outlook Handbook* from the U.S. Department of Labor, Bureau of Labor Statistics (2000), health services are one of the largest industries in the country, with about 11.3 million jobs including the self-employed. It is estimated that about 14% of all wage and salary jobs created between 1998 and 2008 will be in the health services. Twelve out of 30 occupations projected to grow the fastest are concentrated in health services. The health services industry is projected to increase 26% through 2008 as compared to an average of 15% for all other industries. Rapid growth in the health service industry will mainly result from an aging population, new medical technologies, and the subsequent increase in the demands for all types of health services. Industry growth will also occur as a result of the shift from inpatient to less expensive outpatient care, made possible by technological improvements and America's increasing emphasis on all aspects of health.

Most jobs require less than a four-year college degree, and preparation for these jobs are the business of secondary and postsecondary health occupations programs across the country. In fact, 56% of the workers in nursing and personal care facilities have a high school diploma or less, as do 24% of the workers in hospitals. A variety of postsecondary programs provide specialized training for jobs in the health services. Learners preparing for health careers enroll in postsecondary institutions where they can earn a certificate, diploma, associate's degree, baccalaureate degree, professional degree or graduate degree. While workers at all levels of education and training will be in demand, in many cases the job edge will go to those workers who have health-specific training. Specialized training and licensure is a requirement for many jobs in health services and is an asset even for those who aspire to many administrative jobs. Health service workers are often provided with on-the-job training or classroom training as well as continuing education through health services establishments.

More than 460,000 establishments make up the health services industry with two-thirds of them functioning as offices of doctors and dentists. Health services are provided in eight different segments: (1) hospitals, (2) nursing and personal care facilities, (3) offices and clinics of physicians, including osteopaths, (4) home health care services, (5) offices and clinics of dentists, (6) offices and clinics of other health practitioners, (7) health and allied health centers (kidney dialysis, rehabilitation centers, etc.), and (8) medical and dental laboratories (U.S. Department of Labor, Bureau of Labor Statistics, 2000).

Health occupations programs are found at the middle/ junior high school, high school, and postsecondary levels. The *Statistical Snapshot* (2000) indicates that 4% of all career and technical education concentrators enroll in health occupations programs at the secondary level, which is up from 2% in 1982. At the middle/junior high school level, learners are provided with a broad overview of the health care industry and are given opportunities to explore a number of health care careers. Secondary health occupations programs provide learners with opportunities to explore health occupation careers, gain an understanding of the basic concepts and principles of health care, and apply these concepts and principles in a health occupation laboratory in simulated life situations. Advanced secondary health occupation learners may also gain real job experience in a health care setting through an internship (practicum) or cooperative education option. Most health occupations programs in secondary schools are designed to prepare people to be nurse's aides/ assistants and patient care workers.

Postsecondary health occupation learners are usually enrolled in the following special health care programs: practical nursing, medical assisting, ophthalmic dispensing, respiratory therapy, physical therapy, dental assisting, dental hygiene, dental laboratory technician, surgical technology, radiological technology, emergency medical care, and patient care assistance. These programs range from less than one year for some certificates to two-year associate's degree programs. Postsecondary health occupations programs require admissions tests and other entrance requirements. Registered nursing programs range from two to four years in length, and bachelor degree programs are available to prepare people for leadership positions in the health care industry. According to the the *Statistical Snapshot* (2000), of all postsecondary career and technical education program majors, 22% enroll in health services programs. This is up from 20% in 1990. This increase is reflective of the demand for health services workers, particularly those with health-specific career preparation.

As the health care industry continues to expand, more demand will be made of education to provide skilled health care professionals. A major thrust of educational reform in the health field is to improve the relevancy of the health occupations curriculum. The National Consortium on Health Science and Technology Education (NCHSTE), a consortium of over 30 health related organizations, was instrumental in the development of the National Health Care Skill Standards. The consortium, along with a number of other organizations, worked with WestEd (formerly Far West Laboratory) to develop the standards in the form of the *National Health Care Skills Standards Project (NHCSSP)*, which was completed in 1996.

The National Health Care Skills Standards inform current and future educators, health care workers, and employers about what skills and knowledge workers need to succeed in a job and in lifelong learning. The standards consist of a set of core standards that apply to workers across the entire health care industry and sets of additional skill standards that apply to four specific clusters of services: therapeutic, diagnostic, informational, and environmental. In their current form, the standards indicate the knowledge and skills that are expected of health care workers. They are not performance standards, which specify a level of achievement. Each standard follows a specific format. The standard statement consists of three parts: (1) a brief title describing the skill area or topic covered by the standard, (2) a description of the knowledge and the skill which make up the standard, and (3) specific applications which consist of example points to clarify the standard statement. Health care core standards include the areas of (1) academic foundations, (2) communications, (3) systems, (4) employability skills, (5) legal responsibilities, (6) ethics, (7) safety practices, and (8) teamwork. Nine skills areas make up the therapeutic/diagnostic core standards ranging from health maintenance practices to client status evaluation. The diagnostic cluster standards consist of five areas including planning and reporting. Five skill areas make up the information services cluster standards, which include analysis and operations. Finally, the environmental services cluster standards consist of four areas: environmental operations, aseptic procedures, resource management, and aesthetics. Copies of the standards are available from the NHCSSP.

Recognizing the need to help educational leaders in health occupations to align their curriculum to the standards, the NCHSTE has developed the National Health Science Career Path Model based on the national standards, which is designed to help educators develop a curriculum that will result in learners being better prepared upon leaving high school and seeking immediate employment and/or further education. The model provides a structure for health occupations teachers to develop career awareness, exploration, orientation, and preparation opportunities for learners. It organizes learner goals and links them with postsecondary education and employment opportunities. It also includes information about establishing partnerships with health care employers, public secondary and postsecondary education, and professional organizations to help develop and maintain their career paths. Products that are available to help in developing curriculum include 160 validated, integrated instructional plans for K–12 and aligned assessment modalities.

States and local education agencies have either developed or obtained curriculum materials that are based on the national standards to support their instructional programs in health occupations. The instructional program at the high school level consists of integrated academic and health occupations classroom instruction that is delivered in sequenced courses and covers technical content of a variety of health care topics, including those that make up the national core skill standards and selected standards in cluster areas. Classroom instruction is followed by laboratory work that provides learners with opportunities to apply what they have learned in the classroom. See Figure 2-6.

Secondary health occupations learners often have the opportunity to further develop their knowledge and skills in a practical or real-life health care setting under the supervision of a clinical instructor. Health occupations learner can develop leadership skills and enhance their personal skills through participation in one of two career and technical organizations serving health occupations

SAMPLE LISTING OF HEALTH OCCUPATIONS PROGRAM/COURSE TOPICS

- Emergency Medical Care
- Medical Assisting
- Medical Laboratory Technology
- Medicine and Premedicine
- Respiratory Therapy
- Home Health Aids
- Licensed Practical Nursing
- Nurse Practitioner
- Nursing Assists
- Registered Nurses
- Personal Services
- Nursing Science
- Pharmacology
- Basic Nutrition
- Human Anatomy and Physiology
- Human Development
- General Psychology

- Chemistry
- Dental Assisting
- Dental Hygiene
- Dental Laboratory Technology
- Physical Therapy Assisting
- Recreational Therapy
- Surgical Technology
- Medical Research Aids
- Microbiology
- Radiological Technology
- Physician Assistant
- Clinical Practice
- Biomedical Equipment Technology
- Health Care Assisting
- Medical Secretary
- Occupational Therapy Assisting

- Medical Records Technology
- Optometric Technology
- Nurse Anesthetist
- Nurse-Midwife
- Exercise Psychologist
- Music/Art/Dance Therapist
- Dialysis Technician
- Nuclear Medical Technologist
- Hypnotherapist
- Psychiatric Technician
- Health Care Receptionists
- Sports Medicine
- Medical Terminology
- Veterinary Assisting
- Magnetic Resonance Imaging Technology

Figure 2-6. Examples of program and career opportunities in health occupations.

learners—Skills USA-VICA or Health Occupations Students of America (HOSA). These career and technical student organizations offer a number of activities that can be integrated into the health occupations program for leadership development, professional development and skill development.

Health programs are very popular at the postsecondary level with over 24% of all vocational learners enrolled in this growing program (*Statistical Snapshot,* 2000). Health occupations instructional programs at the postsecondary level consist of a number of sequenced academic and technical courses in a specialized health care field that are designed to provide a variety of necessary techniques and materials. These techniques and materials enable learners to acquire the essential knowledge and skills needed to give competent care. Examples of academic core courses include English, mathematics, and basic psychology. Fundamental occupational courses may include medical terminology, anatomy and physiology, and nursing fundamentals. Specific occupational courses may include medical surgical nursing I and medical surgical nursing II practicums. Classroom instruction is followed with laboratory practice and a variety of clinical experiences or practicums in health care settings that are organized so that theory and practice are integrated under the guidance of the clinical instructor.

Secondary and postsecondary health occupations teachers are almost always licensed health professionals but may or may not hold a baccalaureate degree. These teachers recognize the need to stay current in the rapidly changing health care industry and engage in a variety of professional development activities offered in their local institutions and at the state and national levels. They recognize the value of continuing their professional development by becoming members of professional organizations like the Health Occupations Division of the Association of Career and Technical Education, which provides professional development opportunities at the national and state levels through a state affiliate. The National Association of Health Occupations Teachers (NAHOT) is a national organization for all secondary and postsecondary classroom health occupations teachers that provides relevant, updated teaching techniques and curricula for its members. State and local school agency supervisors can join the National Association of Supervisors and Administrators of Health Occupations Education (NASAHOE). Teacher educators can engage in professional development activities and services offered by the Association of Health Occupations Teacher Educators (AHOTE). All health occupations educators can utilize the information and services provided by the NCHSTE. Health occupations teachers can also join one or both career and technical student organizations, SkillsUSA-VICA or HOSA, and participate in professional development activities.

Health occupations teachers and leaders are responding to the challenge of aligning their curriculum to meet the national standards and are changing their instructional and assessment practices to better prepare learners for employment in the health care field and for further education. They are involved in professional development activities to keep current and to become better prepared to help their learners meet the demands of a challenging career in the health care industry.

Marketing Education

Marketing education, as described by the Marketing Education Division of the ACTE, is the career and technical education program "designed to prepare learners to conduct the critical business functions associated with directing the flow of products and services from the producer to the consumer." Marketing, simply defined, is the selling of ideas, products, and services of all kinds to identified and qualified markets. Marketing is the process of determining consumer needs and then directing products and services to meet those needs. Marketers manage the massive system of traditional and electronic distribution that brings goods and services to industrial users and consumers worldwide. Marketing involves information gathering, recruiting, image building, promoting, training, campaigning, financing, lobbying, researching, communicating, packaging, buying and selling, transporting, storing, servicing, and insuring. It borrows heavily from the traditional disciplines of psychology, sociology, and economics and the new discipline of computer sciences. Marketing is a process that can be easily adapted to virtually every economic, social or public activity, and is an essential ingredient in making America's free enterprise system work (DECA, 2001).

A fundamental understanding of the marketing concept and the development of basic marketing skills are not only needed by learners preparing to enter marketing occupations but also by all workers. Futurists are predicting that economic survival in nearly every setting or profession will require individuals who have the ability to understand marketing functions and make wise marketing decisions. Marketing education provides learners with knowledge and skills that will be invaluable for a lifetime. The mission of marketing education as defined in the *National Marketing Education Standards* (2000) is "to enable students to understand and apply marketing, management, and entrepreneurial principles; to make rational economic decisions; and to exhibit social responsibility in a global economy." (p.3)

Marketing education is offered in more than 7,000 high schools, in most community/technical colleges, and in four-year colleges and universities with more than 15,000 teachers instructing in these programs. It is estimated that more than a million learners with diverse ability levels and career interests enroll in marketing education courses (*National Marketing Education Standards*, 2000). Learners may take marketing courses for career exploration and personal use, or they make take several courses in a sequence to prepare for a specific marketing career. The *Statistical Snapshot* (2000) reveals that in 1994, 8% of all secondary career and technical concentrators enroll in marketing education programs and in 1996, 1% of all career and technical majors enrolled in marketing and distribution programs at the postsecondary level. According to the marketing Education Division of the ACTE, marketing programs at the postsecondary level go by several different names such as mid-management, marketing and management, marketing and distribution, or simply, marketing. Marketing programs at the college and university level are often taught in colleges of business, but marketing education is most often taught in colleges of education in order to prepare individuals to become marketing education teachers.

Careers in marketing can be found in U.S. and international businesses, organizations, offices, and in a variety of both profit and nonprofit agencies. Individuals employed in marketing jobs may specialize in one marketing function, such as selling, performing market research, or advertising, or they may choose to obtain a broad understanding of all marketing functions as would be needed by a manager or owner of a business. The service industries employ nearly 80% of the nation's workforce, and marketing is one of these industries.

The U.S. Department of Labor, Bureau of Labor Statistics (2000) projects that occupations in marketing and sales will increase by 15% between 1998 and 2008, with the service industries accounting for the largest percentage of increase. Most workers are involved in marketing in one form or another. Examples of career applications that require marketing education as listed in the *National Marketing Education Standards* (2000) include (1) advertising, (2) customer service, (3) e-commerce, (4) entrepreneurship, (5) fashion merchandising, (6) financial services, (7) food marketing, (8) hospitality marketing, (9) importing/exporting, (10) international marketing, (11) marketing research, (12) product management, (13) professional sales, (14) public relations, (15) real estate, (16) restaurant management, (17) retail management, (18) sales management, (19) service management, (20) sports management, and (21) travel/tourism marketing.

The marketing education curriculum in secondary and postsecondary schools is based on the *National Marketing Education Standards*, which are divided into two major parts: foundations and functions. The standards which make up foundations are fundamental to understanding marketing and are essential to successful progress in the more specific standards listed in the functions areas. The *National Marketing Education Standards* (2000) lists the four foundations areas as (1) Business, Management, and Entrepreneurship, (2) Communication and Interpersonal Skills, (3) Economics, and (4) Professional Development. The seven functions address marketing in terms of how it is practiced and how it is applied in business operations. The seven functions are (1) Distribution, (2) Financing, (3) Marketing-Information Management, (4) Pricing, (5) Product/Service Management, (6) Promotion, and (7) Selling. The sequence of recommended marketing courses is career awareness and career exploration at the middle/junior high schools levels, marketing foundations and some course preparation in selected function areas at the high school level, and marketing specialization at the postsecondary school level. Marketing education integrates academic and technology applications throughout the curriculum.

Each of the foundations and functions are described by a standard statement and a number of performance indicators that are stated as learner expectations for each standard. For example, under the foundation area of economics, the standard reads, "Understand the economic principles and concepts fundamental to marketing." Some of the performance indicators listed include (1) explaining the concept of economic resources, (2) interpreting the impact of supply and demand on price, and (3) identifying factors affecting a business's profit. A similar system of listing standards and performance indicators is used for each of the seven functions. A complete listing of standards and performance indicators is contained in the *National Curriculum Planning Guide* available from the Marketing Education Resource Center, Columbus, Ohio.

Like other major career and technical education areas, marketing education can be taught as a general labor market preparation program or as a career and technical program for specific labor market preparation. Exploratory marketing programs are offered at the middle/junior high school level to provide learners with the basic foundations of marketing and to provide them with an opportunity to explore marketing occupations and careers through job shadowing, field trips, and short-time internships. Marketing programs at the secondary and postsecondary levels consist of sequenced courses such as advertising, sales promotion, job preparation, management, marketing research, sales, transportation and distribution, human relations, purchasing, and entrepreneurship. Some programs may include specialized courses in the areas of hotel/motel marketing, fashion marketing, or establishing small businesses. See Figure 2-7.

Marketing education provides learners with the foundation for careers that have a marketing, management, entrepreneurial, or service orientation. While specialization in one area is possible, most marketing education programs are designed to allow learners to choose a concentration from among a number of marketing industries and occupations. General workplace skill development is integrated into the marketing education curriculum to provide opportunities for learners to develop leadership, teamwork, participatory skills, applications of technology, and other important workplace skills. Marketing education, like other career and technical education fields, is participating in tech-prep programs that help learners make the transition from secondary schools to postsecondary schools and into high-paying careers in marketing.

SAMPLE LISTING OF MARKETING EDUCATION PROGRAM/COURSE TOPICS

- Entrepreneurship
- Distribution
- Market Research
- Fashion Merchandising
- Hotel Marketing
- International Marketing
- Real Estate
- Advertising and Visual Merchandising
- Product/Service Management
- Food Service Management
- Leadership Development

- Employability Skills
- Career in Marketing
- Marketing Information Management
- Web Page Design and Maintenance
- Banking and Finance
- Pricing
- Product/Service Planning
- Sales Promotion
- Purchasing/Buying
- Risk Management

- Sales
- Selling
- Management
- Transportation and Distribution
- Human Relations
- Small Business Management
- Insurance
- Organization Management
- Behavioral Theory and Marketing
- Computer Applications

Figure 2-7. Marketing, management, entrepreneurial, and service opportunities of marketing education programs.

Classroom instruction for marketing education is delivered through a number of modalities, including traditional lecture/discussion; cooperative group learning; self-paced instruction through learning activity packages (LAPs); presentation software using videos, CDs, and computer discs; and the Internet. For many years marketing educators have been using LAPs to provide self-paced or small group instruction in many subject areas, including basic areas like math, as well as with marketing functions like pricing and selling.

Instructional programs of marketing education are also likely to include a school-based enterprise such as a school store, an ongoing project related to marketing in the business community, or a marketing internship (cooperative education), which provides learners with an opportunity to experience supervised work in a real-life marketing environment with pay. Cooperative education, which is a combination of planned on-the-job training and classroom instruction, has been part of quality marketing education programs from the beginning. Marketing learners develop leadership skills and enhance marketing skills through participation in the DECA, the secondary career and technical student organization for marketing learners. DECA provides learners with a number of programs and activities such as leadership development, professional development, and competitive events to help them with personal development as well as to further their understanding of the civic and ethical responsibilities of business. Postsecondary learners can benefit from the activities of Delta Epsilon Chi, the postsecondary student organization for marketing education learners (DECA, 2001).

Marketing teachers at the secondary levels are professional educators who hold baccalaureate or higher degrees. To keep current in their field, they read the professional literature in marketing education and participate in local, state and national professional development activities. Marketing educators belong to and participate in the activities of several professional organizations. The Marketing Education Division of the ACTE provides leadership to the field at the national level, and each state has an affiliate organization of the ACTE that serves marketing educators at the state level. These organizations provide informative publications and hold meetings, seminars, and conferences to deal with issues facing the discipline and to share information that can lead to personal and program improvement. The Marketing Education Association (MEA) is the primary professional organization representing the specific interests and needs of marketing educators. This organization provides an ongoing program of information, communications, and professional development and support for its members. The American Marketing Association (AMA) is the largest association of marketing professionals and embodies a full range of marketing practitioners, educators, and learners. National DECA and Delta Epsilon Chi, the career and technical student organizations at the secondary and postsecondary levels for marketing education learners, provide instructional materials, publications, and meetings for marketing educators.

Technical Education

Technical education is the career and technical education program that prepares people for technical occupations, one of the fastest growing segments of the work force. Technical occupations are defined as occupations that require workers to use higher levels of math, science, and technology in decision-making than is normally required in skilled-trades occupations. Technical education is viewed both as a program and a level of education. Technical education, viewed as a level of education, is provided in other occupational areas, such as agricultural education or health occupations, and occupies a position in the occupational continuum between skilled workers and craftsmen and professionals such as physicians, engineers, researchers, and managers. One way to delineate between traditional vocational education, technical education, and professional education is to think about the major orientation of each. Vocational education is primarily practice oriented, technical education has a combined theory and practice orientation, and professional education is primarily theory oriented. See Figure 2-8.

Technical education prepares individuals for careers as technologists and technicians. According to the U.S. Department of Labor, Bureau of Labor Statistics (2000), employment for technicians and those in related support occupations is projected to grow 22% by 2008. Workers in this group provide technical assistance to engineers, scientists, physicians, and other professional specialty workers and operate and program technical equipment. Over half of the projected employment growth among technicians is among health technicians and technologists with strong growth in computer programmers and paralegals. The digital revolution is transforming the American economy, and technology is changing how Americans learn, work, and go about their daily lives. Most jobs are becoming more technical and require workers who can apply academic, thinking, reasoning, and teamwork skills, skills in using technology, and a cluster of special technical skills.

It is nearly impossible to determine the number of learners at the secondary and postsecondary levels who are enrolled in technical education programs because of the way enrollment is reported at the state and national levels. The *Statistical Snapshot* report for secondary career and technical education program concentrators does not list a program area for technical education; rather, it lists a Technology and Communications program that includes some technical programs besides the technology education program, which is a general workforce preparation program. The percentage of all secondary career and technical education concentrators enrolled in the Technology and Communications program was 3%. At the postsecondary level, the *Statistical Snapshot* report lists a career and technical education program area of Engineering/Sciences Technologies. This includes some technical

education programs, but most of the other program areas such as health and trade and industry have technical education emphases, especially at the associate's degree programs levels. The percentage of all postsecondary career and technical education program majors enrolled in engineering/science technologies is 12%.

Technical education, viewed as a program, prepares technicians and technical workers through a curriculum that emphasizes a field of technical specialization including practical skills, supporting sciences, and mathematics. Technicians and technical workers must have functional academic skills, a command of the theoretical principles related to the technology of the occupation, and the practical skills and abilities the specialization area requires. The Secretary's Commission on Achieving Necessary Skills (SCANS) report (1991) *What Work Requires of Schools* stated that a high-performance workplace requires workers who have a solid foundation in basic literacy and computational skills, in the thinking skills necessary to apply knowledge to solve work problems, and in the personal qualities that make workers dedicated and trustworthy. Technical workers who have the ability to manage resources, work amicably and productively with coworkers, acquire and use information, master complex systems, and work with a variety of technologies are the kinds of employees needed for the high-performance workforce called for in the SCANS report.

Kenneth Gray (1993) noted a 1980 study by the American Society for Training and Development that identified three types of technical workers: professionals, technicians, and blue-collar technical workers. Professional technicians usually are prepared in a baccalaureate degree program; technicians usually hold associate's degrees or two-year certificates; and blue-collar technical workers—the fastest growing technical area—are high school graduates who usually complete one or more years of postsecondary career and technical training. Examples of blue-collar technical workers include electricians, medical technicians, air

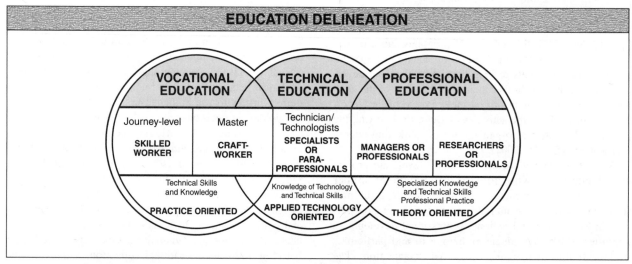

Figure 2-8. The major orientations of vocational, technical, and professional education.

conditioning and refrigeration technicians, and automotive service specialists.

All career and technical service areas can become involved in producing technical workers through the tech-prep program, which is designed to produce high skilled and technical workers through a two-year secondary vocational education program. These programs include courses in mathematics, sciences, and communications that are articulated with a two-year postsecondary experience in a community college, technical institute, or through apprenticeship. The *Statistical Snapshot* (2000) indicates that secondary health and technical programs are increasing, which reflects articulation efforts between secondary and postsecondary career and technical education programs.

The majority of technical education programs are offered at the postsecondary level in public and private postsecondary institutions including community colleges, technical colleges/institutes, technical centers, engineering schools, and four-year colleges offering technical programs of less than baccalaureate degree programs. Technical education constitutes 23% of all postsecondary Career and technical education learner enrollment and this percentage is expected to increase as technology continues to make the workplace more technical (Boesel & McFarland, 1994). See Figure 2-9.

Technical education programs are offered on a full-time or part-time basis and lead to certificates, diplomas, or associate's degrees. Technical education programs consist of sequenced courses containing a number of tasks/competencies that have been validated by technical committees to ensure that they are adequate, relevant, and current. The typical technical education program consists of general core courses, which include academic subjects that provide a foundation in the basic skills required in an occupation; fundamental occupational courses, which provide the knowledge base and foundation for more highly specialized courses in an occupational area; and specific occupational courses, which build upon fundamental occupational courses and provide the basic knowledge and skills required for individuals to function effectively in a chosen occupation. In addition, elective courses are often provided to accommodate the specialized interest of learners within the occupational area (Stonehouse, 1994).

Technical education instruction is delivered through classroom presentations that provide learners with the basic concepts and principles of an occupational area, followed by laboratory assignments that call for learners to apply what they have learned in real or simulated work tasks, projects, or situations. Some technical programs include internships or practicums, which require learners to continue their knowledge and technical skill development in a structured on-the-job training experience. Postsecondary technical learners can enhance their personal development through participation in one of the postsecondary career and technical student organizations such as SkillsUSA-VICA for trade, industrial, technical, and health occupations learners; Phi Beta Lambda (PBL) for business education learners; Delta Epsilon Chi (DEC) for marketing learners; and the National Postsecondary Agricultural Student Organization (PAS) and the National Young Farmers Student Education Association (NYSEA) for agricultural education learners.

Technical education teachers have various levels of education ranging from high diplomas and two-year degrees to

---

SAMPLE LISTING OF TECHNICAL EDUCATION PROGRAM/COURSE TOPICS

- Automatic Technology
- Aerospace Production Planning
- Aerospace Tool Design
- Aircraft Structural Technology
- Air Conditioning Technology
- Aviation Maintenance Technology
- Information and Office Technology
- Instrumentation Technology
- Advanced Machine Tool Design
- Marine Engine Technology
- Marketing Management
- Automated Manufacturing
- Biomedical Engineering Technology
- Biotechnology
- Mechanical Engineering Technology
- Medical Assisting

- Medical Laboratory Technology
- Microcomputer Specialist
- Paralegal Studies
- Commercial Plumbing Technology
- Business Equipment Technology
- Business and Office Technology
- Respiratory Therapy
- Computer Operations
- Printing/Graphics Technology
- Computer Programming
- Construction Management
- Dental Laboratory Technology
- Forest Technology
- Surgical Technology
- Veterinary Technology

- Electronic Engineering Technology
- Environmental Engineering
- Industrial Electricity Technology
- Telecommunication Technology
- Welding and Joining Technology
- Automotive Collision Technology
- Drafting and Design Technology
- Robotics Workcell Technology
- Radiological Technology
- Management and Supervision Development
- Research Laboratory Technology
- Visual Communications Technology
- Electrical Distribution Technology
- Civil Engineering Technology

Figure 2-9. Examples of technical education programs.

baccalaureate and graduate degrees. Nearly all of them, however, have extensive work experience and a growing number of them are industry certified. They recognize the value of continuous professional development, and most of them belong to one or more professional organizations. The primary professional organization for technical educators (teachers, supervisors, and teacher educators) is the Technical Division of the ACTE, which provides leadership to technical education at the national level and a wide range of services to its members. States have affiliate organizations of the ACTE for each major career and technical area including one for technical education. Teacher educators involved with technical education can join and benefit from the activities and services provided by the National Association of Industrial and Technical Teacher Educators (NAITTE). Technical educators can also join and receive the services of the American Association of Community Colleges (AACC). Technical education teachers can participate in professional development activities provided through SkillsUSA-VICA, the career and technical student organization for trade, technical, and health occupations learners at the secondary and postsecondary levels. Technical education teachers can also receive professional development activities and services through other national professional or technical field organizations.

Technology Education

Technology education (formerly industrial arts education) is the career and technical education program that focuses on the study of technology as a means of developing technological literacy. Technology as defined by the International Technology Education Association, is "human innovation in action." Technological literacy is "the ability to use, manage, and understand technology." (International Technology Education Association [ITEA], 1996, p.6)

Technology education learners learn about the technological world that inventors, engineers, scientists, and other innovators have developed. They study how energy is generated, distributed, and controlled; how manufacturing and materials-processing industries convert natural and man-made materials into useful products; how products are transported on the ground and in the air; how information processing has revolutionized our world; how medical technology has extended the life span of individuals and contributed to an improved quality of life, and much more. They study new technologies like genetic engineering and emerging technologies such as fusion power, which may provide solutions to some of the world's energy supply problems. Learners learn that technology can provide tools to solve problems but it can also generate new problems like toxic wastes, which are by-products of chemicals used in manufacturing processes. Learners study technology in three

contexts: informational, physical and biological (ITEA, 2000). See Figure 2-10.

A major thrust of technology education is to assist learners in developing technological literacy and an understanding of what technology is, how it is created, how it shapes society, and how society gives form to technology. Learners benefit in many ways from what they learn in technology education classes. They are provided with the knowledge of how to interpret information concerning technology, how to put that information in context, and how to form conclusions based on the information provided. Learners are provided with career exploration activities and basic knowledge of careers in one or more technological areas that can give them a head start in preparing for careers after high school. All learners can profit from the study of technology because it is a prevailing force in our economy and in nearly every aspect of modern life. Technological literacy can help learners make more informed decisions about the purchase and use of goods and services ranging from food and disposable diapers to cars and electronic devices. Finally, technological literacy can help young people make the tough decisions that will surely face them as our world continues to be affected by technology and problems like global warming, depletion of natural resources, and air pollution. Technological issues and problems have more than one solution and informed individuals will have to decide what, how, and when to use various technological systems (ITEA, 2000).

The International Technology Association (ITEA) lists the following basic beliefs about technology education. Technology education

- is an essential learning experience for all learners at all grade levels, abilities, and backgrounds, so that they may confidently use, manage, assess, and understand technology;
- provides the basic knowledge and technical skills needed to participate in society;
- enhances the opportunity for learners to develop career awareness or career path preparation;
- provides for academic, technical, and social growth;
- provides a wholesome change in learners by enhancing their understanding of how technology is changing the human-made world and the natural environment;
- develops self-evaluation of attitudes toward constructive work and how work can be used for health, recreation, or economic value; and
- requires competence, compassion, a desire for excellence, and a vision from its educators.

Technology education programs operate at the elementary, middle/junior high school, and high school levels and at the collegiate level for learners specializing in technological fields, as well as for those preparing to become teachers. The International Technology Education Association estimates that more than 40,000 technology educators provide instruction about technology in grades K–16. The *Statistical Snapshot* (2000) reveals that 3% of all high school career and technical education concentrators enroll in technology and communications, but there are many other high school learners who enroll in one or more courses in technology education without being classified as concentrators. It is nearly impossible to count the number of learners who receive technology education instruction at the elementary and middle school levels but this number is very large. Likewise, it is difficult to count the number of learners who are engaged in the study of technology at the postsecondary levels. The *Statistical Snapshot* (2000) also reports that 12% of all postsecondary career and technical education program majors enroll in engineering/science technologies, but there are many learners studying technology in other reporting categories such as health, business and office, marketing and distribution, and others.

Technology education at the elementary level is designed to help learners learn and achieve in order to meet the educational goals of the elementary curriculum. Learning experiences in technology education help develop perceptions and knowledge of technology, contribute toward psychomotor skills development, and help form values and attitudes toward the interrelationship of technology, society, and environment. Regular elementary teachers deliver technology education instruction as a result of preservice and in-service training they have received (ITEA, 1996).

At the middle/junior high school level, technology education programs are designed to provide active learning situations that enable learners to explore and develop a broader view of technology. Technology education should be integrated into the regular middle/junior high school curriculum. The middle school technology education curriculum assists learners in learning about the processes that apply to design, problem-solving, development, and use of products within the contexts of the three technological systems: informational, physical, and biological. Through action-oriented activities, middle/junior high school learners broaden their understanding of the nature and evolution of technology; develop a greater interest and capacity in academic subjects, such as science, mathematics, and social studies; engage in hands-on activities in the production of models and real technological products; and discover their personal interests, talents, and abilities related to a career in technology. A certified technology education teacher guides

SAMPLE LISTING OF TECHNOLOGY EDUCATION PROGRAM/COURSE TOPICS

INFORMATION AND COMMUNICATIONS TECHNOLOGIES

- Desktop Publishing
- Photography
- Computer-Aided Drafting & Design
- Radio and Television Broadcasting
- Telecommunications
- Acoustic Communications
- Light Communications
- Graphic Communications
- Electronic Communications

MANUFACTURING TECHNOLOGIES

- Robotics
- Mass Production
- Computer-Aided Manufacturing
- Plastics
- Synthetic Materials
- Manufacturing Inputs and Outputs
- Transformation Processes
- Managerial Processes
- Manufacturing Systems
- Manufacturing Materials
- Manufacturing Processes
- Manufacturing Enterprise
- Automatic Manufacturing Systems
- Manufacturing Technology

CONSTRUCTION TECHNOLOGIES

- Construction Managed Activities
- Construction Production Processes
- Construction Managerial Processes
- Preparing for Construction Projects
- Designing and Planning the Project
- Managing Construction Activities
- Building the Structure
- Installing Systems
- Finishing the Project
- Closing the Contract

TRANSPORTATION TECHNOLOGIES

- Technological Base
- Acts of Transporting
- Technical Systems
- Environmental Factors
- Internal Combustion Engines
- Electric Motors
- Careers in Transportation
- Land Transportation
- Water Transportation
- Air Transportation
- Space Transportation
- Pipeline Transportation
- Conveyor Transportation

Figure 2-10. Four divisions of technology education.

learning in middle/junior high school technology education programs through the use of modular instruction as well as through more traditional instructional practices.

Technology education at the high school level involves learners in problem-based learning activities that utilize math, science, and technological principles. Learners engage in designing, developing, and utilizing technological systems. They learn to apply design concepts, scientific principles, engineering concepts, and technological systems in the solution of everyday problems and situations. High school learners work individually as well as in teams to complete learning tasks through discussion, problem-solving, design research, and the development and application of technological devices needed to function in a technological laboratory. Technology education learners are also afforded an opportunity to develop leadership, social, and problem-solving skills as a result of participating in Technology Student Association (TSA) activities. The ultimate goal of high school technology education programs is for learners to become technologically literate. Graduates should be prepared with the foundation for a lifetime of learning about technology and equipped with information that will help them determine whether or not they want to pursue technological careers such as engineering, architecture, computer science, engineering technology, or teacher education. Certified technology education teachers employ a variety of cognitive, manipulative, and affective learning strategies to help learners with open-ended, problem-based learning activities including modular instruction (ITEA, 1996).

The study of technology at the postsecondary level is varied and multidimensional. At the community and technical college level, learners can choose from a variety of field-specific technology programs like design technology, electronic technology, information technology, radiological technology, surgical technology and many others. At the four-year college and university levels, learners who choose majors like engineering, architecture, health sciences, computer sciences, and biological sciences are directly involved in the study of technology. Learners who enroll in technology education programs do so in preparation to become teachers. Learners enrolled in technology education programs are prepared to teach in middle school or high school technology education programs. Technology education majors experience a curriculum that involves a mix of theory courses, thus enabling them to develop the knowledge and skills required for successful teaching. They are also afforded the opportunity to develop leadership, social, and problem-solving skills as a result of active participation in the Technology Education Collegiate Association (TECA), which is affiliated with the ITEA. The national competitive events for the TECA are held annually at the ITEA conference.

The United States has been transformed by technology and is dependent upon it, yet its citizens are largely ignorant of the fundamental nature of the technology that sustains them. With the growing importance of technology to the American society, it is vital that all learners receive an education that includes technological literacy. The International Technology Education Association has been a key leader in determining what learners should know and be able to do to be technologically literate and has developed a document entitled *Standards for Technological Literacy* that identifies the important content for the study of technology for grades K-12. The standards do not prescribe a curriculum for the study of technology; rather they identify the content of technology education that should be included in the curriculum, which is left for states, school districts and local schools to develop (ITEA, 2000).

These standards are organized into five major categories: (1) the nature of technology, (2) technology and society, (3) design, (4) abilities for a technological world, and (5) the designed world. There are 20 standards total with specific standards listed under each of the five major categories. For example, "the nature of technology" category includes standards 1–3 which are (1) the characteristics and scope of technology, (2) the core concepts of technology, and (3) the relationships among technologies and the connections between technology and other fields. The format for the standards includes (1) the standard statement, (2) a narrative describing what is included in the standard and why it is important, (3) the recommended grade level where content to meet the standard should be taught, (4) a narrative of the standard explaining the benchmarks by grade level or where and how this standard should be presented in the classroom and laboratory, (5) benchmarks that provide specific requirements or enablers of what the learner should know and be able to do to meet the standard, and (6) a vignette or situation that provides an example of how standards can be implemented in the classroom and laboratory (ITEA, 2000).

These standards for technology education are at the center of a massive effort nationwide by state departments of education, school districts, and technology teachers to develop curriculum guides and materials to implement the standards. In addition, colleges and universities are working with state's departments of education and local school leaders to provide both the preservice and in-service training necessary to prepare or upgrade teachers so that they will be able to develop a curriculum based on the standards and successfully deliver it to meet the goal of improving technological literacy for all learners.

Technology education has changed considerably since its early days when it emerged out of industrial arts education. It now has national standards to guide the selection of content for technology education programs at the elementary, middle/junior high school, and high school levels. These standards will undoubtedly have a very positive impact on helping learners become more technologically literate. As in other career and technical education programs, one of the critical need areas is the replacement of retiring technology teachers as well as the filling of new positions created by the expansion of technology education programs nationwide. In addition, the field recognizes the need to develop other standards such as assessment standards, program standards, and professional development standards for preservice and inservice teachers.

Technology education teachers and leaders recognize the importance of staying current since technological systems are constantly changing. Also, educational research and reform is changing what is known about how learners learn and educational practice. Technology educators have several important professional associations that they can join to receive member services including publications, opportunities to become actively involved, and professional development activities. The Technology Education Division of the ACTE provides leadership to the field at the national level, publications, and a number of services including professional development activities for technology education teachers. Each state has an affiliate of the ACTE that provides similar services at the state level. The premier professional organization for technology educators is the International Association of Technology Education (ITEA). This organization is the largest professional association for technology education and its principal voice, as well as an information clearinghouse devoted to enhancing technology education internationally. Teachers can also participate in professional development activities associated with TSA, the career and technical student organization for technology education learners. Teacher educators involved in preparing technology education teachers can participate in professional development opportunities provided by the NAITTE.

Trade and Industrial Education

Trade and industrial education, often called T&I and referred to in some states as vocational industrial education, is the career and technical education program area that prepares individuals for initial employment in a wide range of vocational industrial occupations, assists employed adults in advancing in their chosen occupations, and retrains those individuals displaced because of technological developments and organizational changes. The mission of T&I education is to prepare individuals at the secondary and postsecondary levels for skilled occupations and technical work in industrial occupations.

The major goal of T&I education for learners is the development of sufficient knowledge and skills to secure initial employment or advancement through experiences that (a) focus on performance skills required in an occupational field; (b) provide an understanding and use of functional technology related to a chosen occupational area; (c) prepare individuals to deal effectively with personal and group relationship problems; (d) assist individuals in developing desirable work habits, ideals, and attitudes essential to suc-

cessful job performance; and (e) provide relevant instruction to enable individuals to develop critical thinking and problem-solving skills, manipulative skills, safety judgments, technical knowledge and provide related occupational information to prepare individuals for meaningful, productive employment in vocational industrial pursuits (National Association of Trade and Industrial Education [NATIE], 1994).

Trade and industrial education programs prepare individuals for employment in the diverse industrial and service sectors of our nation's economy. Trade and industrial education includes training for apprenticeable trades, technical occupations, and other industrial and service occupations. Trade and industrial education is considered to be the broadest of all career and technical education fields, with training programs designed to prepare workers in a wide range of occupations that are classified on multiple levels of employment ranging from operatives to semi-skilled to skilled craftspersons to technicians with less than a baccalaureate degree.

Trade and industrial occupations are found in a variety of job categories such as manufacturing, construction, communications, printing, transportation, mining, protective services, visual arts, personal services, and building and grounds service. Areas in this career and technical education program involve but are not limited to layout, design, producing, processing, assembling, testing, maintaining, servicing or repairing; cooperative programs with industry, middle management and supervisory development; entrepreneurship and other special training for industrial programs that ensure growth and development in the industrial sector; and emergency industrial mobilization training programs and services.

Trade and industrial education programs provide secondary and postsecondary learners with specific labor market preparation in a number of technical areas. According to the *Statistical Snapshot* (2000), of all the secondary career and technical education program concentrators (learners who took three or more courses in a program area), more learners enroll in trade and industrial education courses than any other program area. In 1994, 34% of secondary career and technical education concentrators enrolled in trade and industry programs while 30% of concentrators enrolled in business, the second most popular program area. It is more difficult to determine the percentage of postsecondary learners enrolled in trade and industry programs since they are usually classified as technical. The *Statistical Snapshot* reveals that 6% of postsecondary career and technical education majors enroll in trade and industry programs with 12% enrolling in engineering/science technologies. Business and office and health are the programs that attract the largest enrollment of postsecondary career and technical education majors with 29% of learners enrolled in business and office courses and 22% enrolled in health.

Trade and industrial education programs reflect the current and projected trends in business and industry through the utilization of functional advisory committees and partnerships. The curricula for the many programs, such as electronics or automotive technology, are derived from occupational analysis and involve employability skills, technical knowledge, attitudes, job skills, and communication and leadership skills. In addition, the curriculum includes mastery of complementary technology; related mathematics and science; technical communication skills; drawing, art, or design; occupational safety and hygiene; labor, industrial relations, and management; and other directly related and supplementary experiences. Instruction may be full-time or part-time and may be provided in a school, technical college/institute, or community college setting or provided cooperatively at the worksite through internships, cooperative education, and youth apprenticeships.

Instructional programs in trade and industrial education are offered in some middle/junior high schools as exploratory courses, which introduce learners to the many diverse occupations and careers in the business and industrial sector of the economy and provide them with opportunities to engage in basic work tasks in a laboratory environment. These programs are usually delivered in one-hour instructional blocks for part of a quarter or semester, giving learners an opportunity to select or be scheduled for several different occupational program areas.

Trade and industrial education programs at the high school level are delivered through specific labor market preparation programs using the cluster approach or single-occupation approach. The State of Georgia delivers most trade and industrial instruction through the cluster approach, with one occupational program preparing learners for several jobs. For example, the construction program offers learners opportunities to experience instruction in carpentry, masonry, electrical, and plumbing trades. Other states deliver instruction in one occupational area such as a carpentry program. There are many occupational areas in trade and industrial education. See Figure 2-11.

Since trade and industrial education occupations are so diverse, the industrial cooperative education program is provided in many schools to allow learners the opportunity to receive work preparation in occupations that are not part of the regular school career and technical program or to develop job skills in a real work environment to enhance what they have learned in available trade and industrial education programs.

Secondary trade and industrial education programs, like other career and technical technology education programs, provide classroom instruction in applied academics and the basic concepts and principles of an occupation or job, followed by opportunities to apply this knowledge in laboratory projects and actual live-work projects, such as repairing other learners' cars in an automotive technology program. Advanced learners may have an opportunity to develop on-the-job experience through internships, cooperative education, or youth apprenticeship programs. Trade and industrial education learners as well as health occupations learners, develop leadership skills and enhance job skills through participation in the many activities of the SkillsUSA-VICA, which is the career and technical student organization for both of these vocational programs. SkillsUSA-VICA activities, such as chapter activities, professional development, and competitive events, are integrated into the instructional program to motivate learners to exert more effort in preparing for occupational careers. The awards associated with SkillsUSA-VICA activities provide learners with recognition for quality effort and work.

Nationwide trade and industrial programs at the secondary and postsecondary levels are becoming certified through business and industry certification programs like the one developed for automotive education by National Automotive Technicians Education Foundation, Inc. (NATEF). Industry certification of career and technical education programs represents a way of insuring the highest quality in an instructional program. Only those programs that have successfully undergone rigorous reviews by leaders from business and industry are recognized and awarded industry certification. Industry-certified programs convey to learners that the program is in compliance with current industry standards, thus ensuring that learners who complete the program will be able to obtain employment in a specific labor market field as well as possessing the preparation required for continuing education. Learners who complete industry certified programs can obtain a portable credential that is recognized and respected by employers to enhance their employment opportunities. Industry certification of trade and industrial programs represents to employers that program completers are adequately prepared to take their place as productive employees. Currently in the state of Georgia, there are 7 industry certification programs, including automotive education, construction, drafting, electronics, metalworking, printed/graphic arts, and welding (Georgia Department of Education, 2000).

Trade and industrial educators are becoming more involved in tech-prep programs, youth apprenticeship, and other types of work-based programs. Many years before the term tech-prep was introduced, many secondary trade and industrial education teachers had established articulated curriculum patterns with postsecondary instructors to encourage learners to continue their preparation for work. Tech-prep programs lead to an articulated curriculum between the last two years of high school and the first two years of postsecondary education or apprenticeship and encourages the integration of academic skills in mathematics, science, and communication into the curriculum.

Many occupations that use registered apprenticeship programs as a source of highly trained workers are in the trade and industrial areas, which makes the establishment of youth apprenticeship programs easier to accomplish. Apprenticeship is a program that provides comprehensive performance-based training in the theoretical and practical aspects of an occupation to entry-level workers. An apprenticeship contract is developed between the high school and an employer that identifies the practical on-the-job training to be provided by a journeyman with the related instruction to be provided by a competent trade and industrial education teacher who was a former journeyworker. Secondary learners attend classes in school part of the day and spend the balance of the day developing job skills at the workplace.

Trade and industrial teachers are employed on the basis of their occupational experience and are generally not required to have a bachelor's degree in order to teach. However, new teachers who do not have pedagogical preparation are required to complete a series of professional education courses in order to meet state certification requirements. The NAITTE has developed the *Standards of Quality for the Preparation and Certification of Trade and Industrial (T&I) Education Teachers*, designed to serve as benchmarks to education policymakers for improving teacher education programs and intended for use by state agencies in certifying candidates to teach T&I programs. The standards are of two types; the first type deals with the process or delivery of T&I teachers, while the second focuses on curriculum content and instructional aspects of preparation (National Association of Industrial and Technical Teacher Educators, 1995).

Trade and industrial educators, like other career and technical education professionals, recognize the need for continuing education and professional development. There are several national professional organizations that serve T&I educators by providing publications and professional development activities. The Trade and Industrial Education Division of the ACTE provides leadership for T&I education at the national level and provides services to its members through publications and professional development opportunities. Each state has an affiliate association of the ACTE with a T&I division to serve the needs of teachers at the state level. The National Association of Trade and Industrial Education is the only national voice dedicated solely to T&I education. It works to promote T&I, to influence national policy, to offer greater visibility to T&I, to involve labor and management in T&I, to promote SkillsUSA-VICA, and to provide professional development opportunities for its members. State supervisors charged with providing leadership for T&I at the state level can become members of the National Association of State Supervisors for Trade and Industrial Education. Teacher educators who prepare T&I teachers can join and participate in the professional development activities of the NAITTE.

Career and Technical Special Needs Programs

Before describing career and technical special needs programs, it might be helpful to take a brief historical journey covering how such programs were created. Beginning with the Vocational Education Act of 1963 (PL 88-210), federal

---

SAMPLE LISTING OF TRADE AND INDUSTRIAL EDUCATION PROGRAM/COURSE TOPICS

- Machine Trades
- Automotive Service Technology
- Collision Repair Technology
- Transportation Occupations Cluster
- Metal Fabrication Cluster
- Construction Occupations Cluster
- Electromechanical Cluster
- Electronics Cluster
- Drafting Technology
- Cosmetology
- Food Service
- Barbering
- Electronics
- Graphic Arts
- Carpentry
- Masonry Trades
- Electrical Trades
- Air Conditioning and Refrigeration
- Appliance Repair

- Air-Cooled Gasoline Engine Repair
- Sheet Metal Fabrication
- Residential and Commercial Plumbing
- Cabinetmaking
- Commercial Baking
- Commercial Photography
- Diesel Equipment Technology
- Fire Fighting
- Upholstering
- Marine Mechanics
- Architectural Drafting
- Industrial Maintenance Technology
- Technical Drafting
- Welding
- Electronic Products Servicing
- Culinary Arts
- Aviation Maintenance Technology
- Textile Technology
- Law Enforcement

- Television Production
- Motorcycle Service Technology
- Robotic Workcell Technology
- Custodial Services
- Brick Masonry
- Commercial Tile Setting
- Advertising Design
- Aircraft Structural Technology
- Automated Manufacturing
- Telecommunications Technology
- Heavy Equipment Mechanics
- Truck Repair Technology
- Precision Machine Technology
- Plastics Technology
- Painting and Decorating
- Tailoring
- Computer Maintenance Technology
- Computer Assisted Drafting and Design

Figure 2-11. Examples of the variety of programs found in trade and industrial education.

legislation began to respond to a number of pressing social issues and shifted its focus from maintaining strong occupational programs to programs that served different groups of people. The Vocational Act of 1963 was the first federal vocational act to specifically address programs for persons having academic, socioeconomic, or other handicaps preventing them from succeeding in regular vocational programs. By 1976 federal legislation was beginning to push even harder for programs that addressed social issues, such as meeting the needs of disabled and disadvantaged learners. In 1984, the Carl D. Perkins Vocational Act focused on improving vocational programs and serving special population learners. In 1990 the Carl D. Perkins Vocational and Applied Technology Education Act further strengthened the provisions related to providing educational services to disadvantaged, disabled, and other special population learners. The Individuals with Disabilities Education Act Amendments of 1997 (IDEA) introduced changes that were intended to better serve the special needs learners in regular education programs including vocational education. The Carl D. Perkins Vocational and Technical Education Act of 1998 streamlined many of the provisions of the 1990 Vocational Act and provided states with greater flexibility in delivering services to learners from special populations without imposing so many requirements that other provisions of the act would suffer. The new act places much greater accountability requirements on states but gives them greater flexibility for delivering programs that serve all learners well, including special populations.

In response to federal mandates, most states have established a number of programs that provide support services to learners from special populations so that they can prepare for and succeed in regular career and technical education programs. For example, in Georgia in the early 1970s, the Coordinated Vocational and Academic Education (CVAE) program was established to serve learners who were academically and/or economically disadvantaged and were limited in their ability to participate in regular career and technical education programs. CVAE programs were taught by special education teachers who delivered special support services to learners to help them improve their knowledge of career and technical education subjects as well as to improve their computational, communications, intrapersonal, interpersonal, and employability skills. This program was highly successful in helping learners from special populations to enter and succeed in regular career and technical programs. Similar programs were established throughout the United States (Georgia Department of Education/Technology Career Division, 2000).

Another example of a Georgia Career and Technical Education special needs program is "Project Success,"

Case Study . . . Trina

Trina is a postsecondary student with a physical disability. She is enrolled in a drafting and design technology program. She is a bright, capable student who has a strong desire to complete her program and enter competitive employment with an engineering firm in a nearby community. She is married, but her husband and family are not very supportive of her efforts to become employed. They continue to remind her that she will not be able to find employment easily because of her disability, even though it has only a minor effect on her ability to perform work tasks. Sometimes she hears other students talk about the difficulty in obtaining high-paying jobs in the drafting field, and she is beginning to have doubts about her employability because of her disability.

Joan, her instructor, sensed that something was troubling Trina and asked her to stay after class to discuss her plans for the future. Trina explained her fears of not being able to obtain a drafting job because of her limited mobility and the competition for drafting jobs in her area of the state.

Joan reminded her that there are new federal and state laws regarding the employment of individuals with disabilities and suggested she should investigate these laws so she would be more informed about her employment rights. Trina acknowledged that she knew little about these laws and indicated that she would conduct research into legislation for the disabled. Joan suggested that she start with the book entitled The Educators Guide to the Americans with Disabilities Act, *which was in the library, and ask the librarian for assistance in locating other information.*

Trina began her study of the rights of disabled individuals and was amazed at the number of laws that have been passed over the years pertaining to the hiring and training of individuals with disabilities like hers. She shared her findings with her husband and family and with her drafting instructor. Her instructor was impressed with the information she had compiled and asked if she would be willing to share this information with the class. Trina accepted the invitation and informed her classmates about laws guaranteeing the rights of all Americans, including the disabled.

Trina has regained her enthusiastic spirit thanks to more support from her family and improved interaction with her classmates. The entire class has become interested in employment for the disabled and are sharing newspaper clippings, magazine articles, and personal stories on successfully employed workers with disabilities.

Trina decided to share her findings in a school publication and was surprised at the number of individuals with disabilities that thanked her for her information. Trina has now formed a school support group for individuals with disabilities and has involved professionals from the employment service and vocational rehabilitation to meet with her group. The entire school is much more aware of the needs and rights of individuals with disabilities, thanks to the efforts of Trina and her group.

which assists 9th and 10th grade learners who have been identified as potential high school dropouts to remain in school. This successful innovative program uses a "school-within-a-school" approach, where a team of vocational and academic instructors are block-scheduled to teach and counsel a select group of participants. This program provides learners with the concentrated assistance they need to realize their self-worth and potential and to learn the basic work-related, employability, and life-coping skills needed to become productive, useful citizens (Georgia Department of Education, 1990).

Career and technical special needs personnel provide a wide variety of support services for individuals with special needs through individualized support provided in career and technical education classrooms and laboratories. For example, the Georgia Related Vocational Instruction (RVI) program supports the special needs of learners with disabilities by providing them with courses and counseling that enable them to acquire entry-level job skills. Learners are provided instruction in special courses that deliver content jointly planned by the RVI teacher and the vocational teacher, but they also receive special assistance from the RVI teachers during the time they are in the career and technical education classroom and laboratory.

Career and technical special needs personnel at the secondary and postsecondary levels provide a wide variety of support services ranging from coordinating the development of IEPs and ITPs to providing supplemental instruction. The services range from vocational assessment to vocational guidance and program placement; arranging for additional support from support personnel to obtaining support from community agency service providers; coordinating the learner's school instructional program to arranging for job shadowing and other work-based opportunities; and assisting individuals with special needs to obtain job placements to providing the follow-up and follow-through services necessary to help these individual adjust and advance in employment.

According to the Special Needs Division of the ACTE, career and technical and special education teachers, teacher educators, and administrators are dedicated professionals who work with individuals who have special learning needs. These individuals include youth and adults who face the following challenges:
- academic and/or economic disadvantages
- disabilities
- limited English proficiency
- current or past incarceration
- long-term unemployment or underemployment
- teenage pregnancy and parenthood
- lack of education (dropouts or dropout risks)
- nontraditional backgrounds.

Career and technical special needs personnel provide the training, support services, and special resources required for these individuals to gain equal access to the quality education and training needed to successfully compete for satisfying employment.

Professionals who work with learners from special populations, are involved in a number of professional organizations to help shape the field and to keep abreast of the many changes that occur as the nation's schools try to improve education for all learners. One of the professional organizations these educators can join is the Special Needs Division of the ACTE. This organization strives to develop professional attitudes and standards; offers services that will help members improve and extend the quality of career and technical education programs for learners from special populations; acts as a clearinghouse for the dissemination of new ideas and research; and promotes professional relationships with other agencies and organizations that provide services to learners with special needs. An affiliate organization to the Special Needs Division is the National Association of Vocational Education Special Needs Personnel (NAVESNP). This professional organization publishes *The Journal for Vocational Special Needs Personnel*, produces the NAVESNP newsletter, and provides regional conferences and meetings for special needs educators. State department of education leaders involved with special needs programs can join the National Association of Special Needs State Administrators (NASN). The National Association of Special Needs Teacher Educators (NASNTE) provides membership services and professional development for college and university professors who prepare teachers to work with learners from special populations.

SUMMARY

Career and technical education is the primary system in America through which youth and adults explore career areas and prepare to enter competitive employment and continue lifelong learning. It is delivered through the program services areas of agriculture, business, family and consumer sciences, health occupations, marketing, technical, technology, and trade and industrial education. Some of these programs provide exploratory courses at the middle school level and all of them offer instruction at the secondary and postsecondary levels. The curricula of career and technical education programs include materials that focus on the development of foundational skills, as well as common core workplace competencies and the specific competencies required for employment. Career and technical education utilizes real-life situations in classrooms and laboratories and supervised work experiences through several work-based programs such as youth apprenticeship, cooperative learning, and internships. Today the vast majority of secondary learners enroll in at least one career and technical education course in a program area and about half of the subbaccalaurate learners enrolled in postsecondary institutions take career and technical education courses.

The current system of career and technical education in the United States is the product of an extended period of experimentation and development through an evolutionary process spanning thousands of years. Formerly called vocational education, it has evolved from informal education provided by family members to their children to highly sophisticated educational programs using state-of-the-art equipment and processes. Career and technical education has been affected and continues to be affected by the technological, social, and economic changes that are transforming our world, and educators at every level are responding to these forces by changing their curricula and instructional practices to better prepare learners to compete in the job market and succeed in continuing education. Today some career and technical education programs are offered entirely through web-based courses, providing many benefits to both learners and educational institutions.

For over 80 years, Congress has responded to the forces impacting career and technical education by enacting legislation in a cooperative venture with states and local education agencies. The focus of early career and technical education was on the early programs of agriculture, home economics, and trade and industrial education, but beginning in the 1960s, the focus moved away from building and supporting programs to providing services to people. For nearly 40 years Congress has attempted to address the needs of individuals from special populations enrolled in career and technical education programs, and that focus has not diminished. The Carl D. Perkins Vocational and Technical Act of 1998 has provisions designed to improve and extend programs to better prepare individuals for the highly skilled workforce needed for global competition. The act further strengthens the provisions related to providing services to disadvantaged, disabled, and other special population learners. In addition to the Perkins Act, Congress enacted the Individuals with Disabilities Education Act Amendments of 1997, providing funding to help individuals with disabilities prepare for work and productive citizenship.

SELF-ASSESMENT

1. What is career and technical education and where are its programs found?
2. What are the purposes of career and technical education at the secondary and postsecondary levels and how are these two levels of programs alike and different?
3. What are tech-prep, cooperative education, and youth apprenticeship programs?
4. What will learners experience in job shadowing, internships, and practicums?
5. What is agricultural education, business education, family and consumer sciences education, health occupations education, marketing education, technology education, technical education and where and how are these programs delivered?
6. How did the work of European educational reformers affect American education?
7. What were the mechanics institute, American Lyceum, manual training, manual labor, sloyd, and arts and crafts movements?
8. How were youth educated and prepared for work in early American colonies?
9. How did universal education develop in America?
10. How did junior and comprehensive high schools develop and begin to offer career and technical education programs?
11. Why was their increasing interest on the part of the federal government and business and industry leaders in some form of career and technical education in the early 1900s?
12. How did the work of the Douglas Commission, the National Society for the Promotion of Industrial Education, and the Commission on Federal Aid to Vocational Education lead to the passage of the Smith-Hughes Act of 1917?
13. Why did the federal government become involved in career and technical education and why do they support it today?
14. What are the major provisions of the Carl D. Perkins Vocational and Technical Education Act of 1998 and how does this act impact career and technical education for learners from special populations?
15. What are the major provisions of the Individuals with Disabilities Education Act Amendments of 1998 and do the provisions of this act differ from earlier legislation for individuals with disabilities?
16. What are the major provisions of the Workforce Investment Act of 1998 and how will this act impact education for individuals from special populations?

ASSOCIATED ACTIVITIES

1. Contact your state department of education by mail, telephone, or through the Internet and obtain information about your state's plan for career and technical education.
2. Visit secondary schools and postsecondary institutions to obtain firsthand information about a program of interest, such as an articulated tech-prep program.
3. Collect historical publications pertaining to the development of career and technical education for faculty and learners to use.
4. Access the Internet and determine the offerings of a selected career and technical education postsecondary institution.
5. Involve career and technical student organizations in promoting career and technical education during the month of February (the month dedicated to promoting career and technical education nationwide).

REFERENCES

Adams, D. A. (1993). The organization and operation of vocational education. In C. Anderson & L. C. Rampp (Eds.). *Vocational education in the 1990s, II: A sourcebook for strategies, methods, and materials* (pp. 35-59). Ann Arbor, MI: Prakken Publications.

American Association of Family and Consumer Sciences. (2001). *Body of knowledge for family and consumer sciences* [On-line]. Available: http://www.aafcs.org/who/knowledge.html

American Society for Training and Development & U.S. Department of Labor (1988). *Workplace basics: The skills employers want.* Washington, DC: U.S. Government Printing Office.

American Vocational Association. (1998) *The official guide to the Perkins Act of 1998.* Alexandria, VA: Author.

Association for Career and Technical Education. (2001). [On-line] Available: http://www.acteonline.org

Barella, R. (1981). The vocational education movement: Its impact on the development of industrial arts. In T. Wright & R. Barella (Eds.), *An interpretative history of industrial arts: The relationship of society, education and industrial arts.* 30th Yearbook. American Council on Industrial Arts Teacher Education. Bloomington, IL: McKnight.

Barlow, M. L. (1976). 200 years of vocational education 1776-1976. *American Vocational Journal, 51* (5), 21-108.

Boesel, D., Hudson, L., Deich, S., & Masten, C. (1994). *National assessment of vocational education: Final report to Congress, volume II, participation in and quality of vocational education.* Washington, DC: U.S. Department of Education, Office of Educational Research and Improvement.

Boesel, D., & McFarland, L. (1994). *National assessment of vocational education: Final report to Congress, volume I, summary and recommendations.* Washington, DC: U.S. Department of Education, Office of Educational Research and Improvement.

Cassidy, W. H. (1994). Youth apprenticeship programs—business and school partnerships. In A. McEntree (Ed.), *Expanding Horizons in Business Education* (pp. 18-22). Reston, VA: National Business Association, National Business Education Yearbook, No. 32.

DECA. (2001). [On-line] Available: http://www.deca.org

Dykman, A. (1995). On the block. *Vocational Education Journal. 70* (6), 26-31, 56.

Edwards, N., & Richey, H. G. (1963). *The school in American social order* (2nd ed.). Boston: Houghton Mifflin.

Evanciew, C., & Rojewski, J. W. (1999). Skill and knowledge acquisition in the workplace: A case study of mentor-apprenticeship relationships in youth apprenticeship programs. *Journal of Industrial Teacher Education, 36* (2), 24-53.

Family and Consumer Sciences Education. (2001). *National Standards* [On-line]. Available: http://www.facse.org

Georgia Department of Adult and Technical Education. (2001). [On-line] Available: http://www.dtae.org

Georgia Department of Education. (1990). *Georgia secondary vocational education.* Atlanta GA: Author.

Georgia Department of Education (1992). *Business education computer applications volume IV: Electronic publishing curriculum guide (grades 10-12).* Ellijay, GA: Vocational Education Materials Center.

Georgia Department of Education. (1999). *Standards and guidelines for work-based learning programs in Georgia.* Atlanta, GA: Georgia Department of Education

Georgia Department of Education. (2000). *The technology/career education industry certification handbook.* Atlanta, GA: Georgia Department of Education.

Georgia Department of Education Technology/Career Division. (2000) *Creating a future for students.* Atlanta, GA: Author.

Gray, K. (1993). Challenging an uncertain future. *Vocational Education Journal, 68* (2), 35-38.

Gregson, J. A. (1995). The school-to-work movement and youth apprenticeship in the U.S.: Educational reform and democratic renewal? *Journal of Industrial Teacher Education, 32* (3), 7-29.

Herman, A. M. (1998). The workforce investment act of 1998: A vision for youth. Washington, DC: United States Department of Labor.

Herren, R. V., & Cooper, E. (2002). *Agricultural mechanics: Fundamentals and applications.* Albany, New York: Delmar Division of Thomson Publishing.

Herren, R. V., & Donahue, R. L. (1991). *The agriculture dictionary.* Albany, NY: Delmar Publishers.

Hettinger, J. (1999). The new Perkins...finally. *Techniques 74* (1), 40-42.

Hoachlander, G., & Klein S. (1999). Answering to Perkins. *Techniques 74* (2), 46-48.

International Technology Education Association. (1996). *Technology for all Americans: A rationale and structure for the study of technology.* Reston, VA: Author.

International Technology Education Association. (2000). *Standards for technological literacy: Content for the study of technology.* Reston, VA: Author.

Kaufman, B. E., & Wills, J.L. (1999). *User's guide to the Workforce Investment Act of 1998. A companion to the law and regulations* Alexandria, VA: Association for Career and Technical Education.

Kincheloe, J. L. (1999). *How do we tell the workers? The socioeconomic foundations of work and vocational education.* Boulder, CO: Westview Press.

Knoblauch, B., & McLane, K. (1999) Overview of the Individuals with Disabilities Education Act Amendments of 1997 (P.L. 105-17): Update 1999. *ERIC EC Digest # E576.* ED 433668)

Lee, J. S. (1994). *Program planning guide for agriscience and technology education.* Danville, IL: Interstate Publishers.

Levesque, K., Lauen, D., Teitelbaum, P., Alt, M., Liberia, S., and Nelson, D. (2000). *Vocational Education in the United States: Toward the Year 2000* Washington, DC: U.S. Department of Education, Office of Educational Research and Improvement.

Lynch, R. L. (2000). *New directions for high school career and technical education. Information Series No. 384.* (ERIC NO: ED 444037). Columbus, OH: ERIC Clearinghouse on Adult, Career, and Vocational Education, Center on Education and Work.

Martin, G. E. (1981). Industrial education in early America. In T. Wright & R. Barella (Eds.), *An interpretative history of industrial arts: The relationship of society, education and industrial arts.* 30th Yearbook. American Council on Industrial Arts Teacher Education. Bloomington, IL: McKnight.

National Association of Industrial and Technical Teacher Educators. (1995). *Standards of quality for the preparation and certification of trade and industrial (t&i) education teachers* [On-line]. Available: http://www.coe.uga.edu/naitte

National Association of Trade and Industrial Education (1994). *Workforce 2020: Action report school-to-work opportunities national voluntary skill standards.* Leesburg, VA: Author.

National Business Education Association. (2001). *Business Education Standards* [On-line]. Available: http://www.nbea.org/curfbes.html

National Business Education Association. (2001). *Policy Statements* [On-line]. Available: http://www.nbea.org/curriculum/policy.html

National Center for Educational Statistics. (2000). *NCES Fast Facts* [On-line]. Available: http://nces.gov/fastfacts

The National Council for Agricultural Education website at www.agehdq.org/aged.htm (2001)

National Marketing Education Standards: Executive Summary (2000). Columbus, OH: Marketing Education Organization.

The Office of Vocational & Adult Education. (2000). [On-line] Available: http://www.ed-gov/offices/OVAE/techprep.html

Ordover, E. L., & Annexstein, L. T. (1999). *Ensuring access, equity, and quality for students with disabilities in school-to-work systems: A guide to federal law and policies.* Washington, DC: Center for Law and Education.

Phillips, J. (1994). All business is global. In A. McEntree (Ed.), *Expanding horizons in business education* (pp. 35-45). Reston, VA: National Business Association. National Business Education Yearbook, No. 32.

Roberts, R. W. (1971). *Vocational and practical arts education* (3rd ed.). New York: Harper & Row.

Secretary's Commission on Achieving Necessary Skills (SCANS). (1991). *What work requires of schools: A SCANS report for America 2000.* Washington, DC: U.S. Department of Labor.

Secretary's Commission on Achieving Necessary Skills (SCANS) (1992). *Learning a living: A blueprint for high performance.* Washington, DC: U.S. Department of Labor.

Smith, D. F. (1981). Industrial arts founded. In T. Wright & R. Barella (Eds.), *An interpretative history of industrial arts: The relationship of society, education and industrial arts.* 30th Yearbook. American Council on Industrial Arts Teacher Education. Bloomington, IL: McKnight.

Spring, J. (1990). *The american school 1642-1990* (2nd ed.). New York: Longman.

Stage, S., & Vincent, V. B. (Eds.). (1997). *Rethinking home economics–women and history of a profession.* Ithaca, NY: Cornell University Press.

Statistical Snapshot. (2000, May). *Techniques: Connecting Education and Careers, 75* (5), 36-39.

Stonehouse, P. (1994). *Georgia department of technical and adult education standards and program guide development: A presentation.* Atlanta, GA: Georgia Department of Technical and Adult Education.

U.S. Department of Education. (1998). *Toward a New Framework of Industry Programs for Vocational Education* [On-line]. Available: www.ed.gov/pubs/FrameworkIndustry/bodytext3.html

U.S. Department of Labor, Bureau of Labor Statistics. (2000). *Occupational outlook handbook.* Washington, DC: Author

U.S. Department of Labor, Employment and Training Administration. (1998). Skills for a New Century: A Blueprint for Lifelong Learning *Vice President's National Summit on 21st Century Skills* [On-line]. Available: http://wdr.doleta.gov/research/pdf/blueprint.pdf

Walter, R. A. (1993). Development of vocational education. In C. Anderson and L. C. Rampp (Eds.), *Vocational education in the 1990s, II: A sourcebook for strategies, methods, and materials* (pp. 1-20). Ann Arbor, MI: Prakken Publications.

Wright, T. (1981). Manual training: Constructive activities enter the public schools. In T. Wright & R. Barella (Eds.), *An interpretative history of industrial arts: The relationship of society, education and industrial arts.* 30th Yearbook. American Council on Industrial Arts Teacher Education. Bloomington, IL: McKnight.

Learners with Disabilities

3

INTRODUCTION

There are a variety of challenges facing individuals with disabilities. As a result, legislation has been passed to protect their rights. The Individuals with Disabilities Education Act (IDEA) provided assurances for learners with disabilities ages 0 to 21 in public school settings. This act also identified specific categories for eligibility for special education programs. The long-term goal of the IDEA is a smooth progression into jobs and independent living; thus, it helps prepare learners for their future through improved transition programs.

Section 504 of the Rehabilitation Act focuses on nondiscrimination by requiring that federally funded programs provide people with disabilities the same access to the full range of their programs' activities as they provide to people who do not have disabilities. The act assures that "reasonable accommodations" will be made for learners who are identified as having a disability.

This chapter presents an overview of the nature and needs of learners with disabilities. It is intended to help instructors understand the learning problems of these learners so that appropriate modifications can be made and necessary support services can be provided to enable them to successfully participate in and complete career and technical education programs.

OUTLINE

LEARNERS WITH DISABILITIES—FACING THE CHALLENGE
THE INDIVIDUALS WITH DISABILITIES EDUCATION ACT
SECTION 504 OF THE REHABILITATION ACT
LEARNERS WITH AUTISM
LEARNERS WITH MENTAL RETARDATION
LEARNERS WITH SERIOUS EMOTIONAL DISTURBANCES (BEHAVIOR DISORDERS)
LEARNERS WITH VISUAL IMPAIRMENTS
LEARNERS WITH HEARING IMPAIRMENTS
LEARNERS WITH ORTHOPEDIC IMPAIRMENTS
LEARNERS WITH HEALTH IMPAIRMENTS
LEARNERS WITH SPEECH OR LANGUAGE IMPAIRMENTS
LEARNERS WITH SPECIFIC LEARNING DISABILITIES
LEARNERS WITH SEVERE AND/OR MULTIPLE DISABILITIES
THE SPECIAL EDUCATION PROCESS
INCLUSION
SUMMARY
SELF-ASSESSMENT
ASSOCIATED ACTIVITIES
REFERENCES

OBJECTIVES

After completing this module, the reader should be able to accomplish the following:

1. Identify the challenges facing learners with disabilities.
2. List the general characteristics of learners with mental retardation and the implications of these characteristics in career and technical education settings.
3. Identify strategies that would help educators to successfully work with learners with mental retardation.

4. List the general characteristics of learners with serious emotional disturbances (behavior disorders) and the implications of these characteristics in career and technical education settings.
5. Identify strategies that would help educators to successfully work with learners who have emotional disturbances.
6. List the general characteristics of learners with visual impairments and the implications of these characteristics in career and technical education settings.
7. Identify strategies that would help career and technical educators to successfully work with learners who have visual impairments.
8. List the general characteristics of learners with hearing impairments and the implications of these characteristics in career and technical education settings.
9. Identify strategies that would help career and technical educators to successfully work with learners who have hearing impairments.
10. Identify the categories of orthopedic impairments and list the general characteristics of learners with orthopedic impairments as well as the implications of these characteristics in career and technical education settings.
11. Identify strategies that would help career and technical educators to successfully work with learners who have orthopedic impairments.
12. Discuss the accessibility issues that must be addressed in order for learners with disabilities to be able to fully participate in career and technical education programs.
13. Identify the categories of health impairments and list the general characteristics of each category as well as the implications of these characteristics for career and technical education settings.
14. Identify strategies that would help career and technical educators to successfully work with learners who have health impairments.
15. List the general characteristics of learners who are speech or language impaired and the implications for these characteristics in career and technical education settings.
16. Identify strategies that would help career and technical educators to successfully work with learners who have speech impairments.
17. List the general characteristics of learners who have learning disabilities and the implications for these characteristics in career and technical education settings.
18. Identify strategies that would help career and technical educators to successfully work with learners who have learning disabilities.
19. Discuss the steps in referring learners for assessment to determine whether they have a disability and what support services they would need in order to successfully participate in a career and technical education program.

TERMS

accommodation
adaptive behavior   *impulsivity*
attention deficit/hyperactivity disorder
autism
blindness
deafness
disability
disabled
disorder

hard-of-hearing
health impairment
hearing impairment
inclusion
learning disability
mental retardation
mobility
orthopedically impaired

partially sighted
physical or mental impairment
reasonable accommodation
seriously emotionally disturbed
speech and language impairment
traumatic brain injury
visual impairment
workplace inclusion

pg 163

LEARNERS WITH DISABILITIES—FACING THE CHALLENGE

Individuals with disabilities face a number of challenges. To meet these challenges, social, workforce, and educational issues must be recognized and addressed. The following is a brief overview of the current state of affairs concerning individuals with disabilities.

Social Issues

Kaye (1998) reported the following on the socialization of individuals with disabilities:

- People with disabilities continue to live in relative social isolation. Among persons living in the community rather than in institutions, those with disabilities are twice as likely to live alone as those without disabilities (19.6% vs. 8.4%). Half (51%) of the respondents to the 1994 Harris poll of Americans with disabilities said that lack of a full social life was a problem for them.
- More than twice as many people with disabilities as those without (30% vs.14%) socialize with close friends, relatives or neighbors less often than once a week.
- Twice as many people with disabilities (58% vs. 29%) reported that they had not gone to see a movie in the previous year. Three-fourths hadn't attended a live music performance (76% compared to 51% of those without disabilities), and two-thirds had not attended a sporting event (71%, vs. 43% for those without disabilities).
- Two-thirds (65%) of people with disabilities go out to eat less often than once a week, compared to less than half (45%) of nondisabled people. Church attendance is lower for people with disabilities (49% attend at least once a month, compared to 59% for those with no disabilities). And, while almost all American adults without disabilities go food shopping at least once a week (85%), only just over half (56%) of those with disabilities do so.

Workforce Issues

Individuals with disabilities are often confronted by challenges at work and in the workplace. The following are workforce issues that affect these individuals:

- Over the next few decades, the largest percentage of new growth will be composed of women, ethnic minorities, and immigrants. The number of employees with disabilities will also increase (President's Committee on Employment of People with Disabilities, 2001).
- People with disabilities are the nation's largest minority and an individual stands about a 20% chance of becoming disabled at some point during the working years. People with disabilities cross all racial, gender, educational, socioeconomic and organizational lines (President's Committee on Employment of People with Disabilities, 2001).
- Workers with disabilities are more likely to have jobs; are more likely to work part-time (and are more likely to work part-time because they cannot find full-time work); are more likely to be self-employed; are more likely to earn less from their own incorporated businesses; are more likely to earn less per hour, month, and year; are less likely to belong to a union; are less likely to work in one of the white-collar occupational groups; and constitute an underutilized workforce and a potential resource to the US economy. If 1 million of the 54 million Americans with disabilities were employed, it is projected that the nation would save $286 million annually in food stamp use and $1.8 billion in Social Security income benefits (President's Committee on Employment of People with Disabilities, 2001).
- Four-fifths (81%) of employers responding to a 1995 Harris poll said that they had made accommodations for workers with disabilities, up from 51% in 1986. But if employers are making greater efforts to provide job opportunities for people with disabilities, national surveys still do not conclusively show increased levels of employment (Kaye, 1998).
- The labor force participations rate for people aged 18-64 limited in activity due to chronic health conditions or impairments, obtained from an analysis of the National Health Interview Survey (NHIS), remained more or less constant at about 52% between 1990 and 1994; this figure included those who were either working or actively looking for work. The employment rate of people ages 16–64 with work disabilities (a limitation in the ability to work associated with a chronic health condition or impairment) was also steady at 28% to 29% (Kaye, 1998).
- People ages 21–64 with severe functional limitations (such as an inability to climb a flight of stairs without resting, hear normal conversation, or see words and letters) had an employment rate of 27.6% in late 1991, but that rate had risen to 32.2% by late 1994. On the other hand, people with any degree of functional limitation had a 48.6% employment rate in both 1991 and 1994 (Kaye, 1998).
- Data show no improvement in the economic well being of Americans with disabilities. In 1989, 28.9% of working-age adults limited in their ability to work lived in poverty; in 1994, the poverty rate was more or less the same, at 30% (Kaye, 1998).
- People with disabilities are more likely to hold part-time jobs; their earnings are lower than those of their nondisabled peers. In 1995, working men with disabilities earned annually while working women with disabilities made 72.6% as much as those without disabilities (Kaye, 1998).
- Men with work disabilities who had steady, full-time jobs earned 85% of the amount their nondisabled counterparts earned in 1984, compared to only 80% in 1995. Women with work disabilities earned 85% in 1984, compared to 87% in 1995 (Kaye, 1998).

- Even among people employed full time during the entire year, earnings levels are significantly lower for workers with disabilities. Median monthly income for men with work disabilities averaged $1,880 in 1995— 20% less than the $2,356 earned by their counterparts without disabilities; women with disabilities earned $1,511 monthly, or 13% less than the $1,737 figure for nondisabled women (Kaye, 1998).

Educational Issues

The National Center for Education Statistics (1997) described a study it conducted called the National Education Longitudinal Study of 1988 (NELS:88). NELS: 88 began with a base-year survey of eighth grade learners in 1988, followed up at two-year intervals in 1990, 1992, and 1994. Because of its broad scope and longitudinal design, NELS:88 provides an important source of data by which to examine the status and experiences of learners as they progress from middle school through the high school years.

- Learners identified by teachers or parents as disabled in NELS:88 were more often male, had lower scores on locus of control psychological measures, and were slightly older than learners not so identified. Learners identified as disabled by teachers were more likely to come from households headed by single females, to have lower individual socioeconomic status (SES) and lower self-esteem, and to have parents with lower levels of education than nondisabled learners.
- Similar percentages of parent-identified disabled learners and learners in the nondisabled population were members of minority groups (23.7% and 26.9%, respectively). Among learners identified as learning disabled by parents and teachers, teacher-identified learners more likely to be African-American than were parent-identified learners (16.6% vs. 7.9%, respectively). African-American learners were actually underrepresented among those learners classified by parents as learning disabled.
- Compared to learners not identified as disabled in NELS:88, learners identified by teachers and parents as disabled took more remedial mathematics and English courses, had earned fewer units in core curriculum areas, had more often repeated a grade prior to the eighth grade, and were more likely to have participated in dropout prevention programs. However, these learners evidenced relatively low levels of participation in "special education programs for the educationally or physically handicapped" (between 2% and 11.2%). In addition, learners identified by teachers as disabled participated in extracurricular activities to a lesser extent than nondisabled learners.
- Learners identified by teachers and parents as disabled in NELS:88 earned lower high school grades in core courses, scored lower on mathematics and reading proficiency, and were more likely to drop out of school than their nondisabled counterparts. In addition, these learners reported lower educational expectation for themselves and lower expectations by their parents, and were less prepared for higher education than their nondisabled counterparts by virtue of not having taken the ACT or the SAT.
- Among the different disability categories, learners identified by their parents as having emotional problems recorded the lowest grades and the highest levels of school dropout.

Challenges of Educating Learners with Disabilities

Heward and Orlansky (1992) identified a number of areas that will pose as challenges as the educational system deals with greater numbers of learners with disabilities:

- reducing the number of learners with disabilities who drop out of school;
- applying advances in high technology to greatly reduce or eliminate the handicapping effects of physical and sensory disabilities;
- combating the pervasive effects of childhood poverty on development and success in school (one in five American children under the age of 5 is living in poverty);
- developing effective methods for providing education and related services to the growing numbers of children entering school whose development and learning are affected by prenatal exposure to drugs or alcohol;
- improving the behavior and attitudes of nondisabled people toward those with disabilities; and
- opening up more opportunities for individuals with disabilities to participate in the full range of residential, employment, and recreational options available to nondisabled persons. (p. 25)

THE INDIVIDUALS WITH DISABILITIES EDUCATION ACT

Since 1975, there has been federal legislation to provide assurances and protective measures for individuals with disabilities in education programs. As a result of these acts, services and programs are provided to meet the specific needs of each individual.

> On November 29, 1975, president Gerald Ford signed the Education for All Handicapped Children Act (EHA). It was the most significant legislative effort that had ever been made for the purpose of helping disabled children prepare for a self-reliant future. More than a quarter of a century later, the law, now recognized as the Individuals with Disabilities Education Act (IDEA), is still protecting the rights of nearly 6 million disabled American youths and their families. (Armstrong, 2001, p.29)

On June 4, 1997, President William J. Clinton signed the bill reauthorizing and amending the IDEA. The bill became Public Law 105-17, the Individuals with Disabilities Education Act Amendments 1997. The law is frequently referred to as IDEA '97. IDEA '97 defines "children with disabilities" as having any of the following types of disabilities:

* autism
* deaf-blindness
* hearing impairments (including deafness)
* mental retardation
* multiple disabilities
* orthopedic impairments
* other health impairments
* serious emotional disturbance
* specific learning disabilities
* speech or language impairments
* traumatic brain injury
* visual impairments (including blindness)

and who, by reason thereof, need special education and related services. See Figure 3-1.

DISABILITY CATEGORIES

INDIVIDUALS WITH DISABILITIES EDUCATION ACT (IDEA) AMENDMENTS OF 1997

* autism
* deaf-blindness
* hearing impairments (including deafness)
* mental retardation
* multiple disabilities
* orthopedic impairments
* other health impairments
* serious emotional disturbance
* specific learning disabilities
* speech or language impairments
* traumatic brain injury
* visual impairments (including blindness)

In addition to these IDEA categories . . .

SECTION 504, REHABILITATION ACT OF 1973

* drug and alcohol related disorders
* conduct behavior disorders
* attention deficit disorders/attention deficit hyperactivity disorder (ADD/ADHD)
* asthma
* dyslexia
* HIV/AIDS
* diabetes

Figure 3-1. An overview and comparison of the disability categories covered in the Individuals with Disabilities Education Act Amendments and Section 504 of the Rehabilitation Act of 1973.

Armstrong (p. 29) remarks that the four basic purposes of the new IDEA are "to assure that all children with disabilities have available to them...a free appropriate public education which emphasizes special education and related services designed to meet their unique needs; to assure that the rights of children with disabilities and their parents...are protected; to assist States and localities to provide for the education of all children with disabilities; to assist and assure the effectiveness of efforts to educate all children with disabilities."

PL 105-17 retains the major provisions of earlier federal laws in the area, including the assurance of having a free appropriate public education (FAPE) available to all children with disabilities, in the least restrictive environment (LRE), and the guarantee of due process procedure and procedural safeguards. It also includes modification to the law. Some of the changes that affect special education practices nationwide include

* the participation of children with disabilities in state and district-wide assessment programs, with appropriate accommodations where necessary;
* the development of guidelines, as appropriate, for participation of children with disabilities in alternative assessment (for those children who cannot participate in regular assessments with accommodations and modifications);
* the development and review of the individualized education program (IEP), including increased emphasis on participation of children and youth with disabilities in the general curriculum and the involvement of regular education teachers in developing, reviewing, and revising the IEP;
* enhanced parent participation in eligibility and placement decisions;
* streamlined evaluation and re-evaluation requirements;
* a statement of the transition service needs of the learner that focuses on the learner's courses of study (beginning at age 14 and updated annually);
* the availability of mediation as a means of more easily resolving parent-school differences (at a minimum, mediation must be available whenever a due-process hearing is requested); and
* disciplinary procedures for learner with disabilities, including placement of certain learners with disabilities in appropriate interim alternative educational settings for up to 45 days. See Figure 3-2.

> Being integrated into the public school curriculum is only half the battle for disabled children. The long-term goal of IDEA is a smooth progression into jobs and independent living, so it is helping prepare learners for job placement through improved transition programs. Beginning at age 14, for instance, each child's IEP is required to include transition plans and procedure for identifying appropriate employment. (Armstrong, 2001, p. 29)

THE INDIVIDUAL WITH DISABILITIES EDUCATION ACT AMENDMENTS (PL 105-17)

OUTCOMES AND STANDARDS

- Included students with disabilities in state- and district-wide testing programs, with appropriate accommodations when necessary
- Established performance goals and indicators for students with disabilities

EVALUATION AND CURRICULUM

- Required a statement of any type of individual accommodation or modification needed for the student to be able to participate in state- or district-wide assessments
- Required states to ensure that students with disabilities had access to the general curriculum
- Required at least one regular education teacher of the child to be a member of the IEP team if the student participated or might participate in the regular education environment
- Expressly required that the IEP address positive behavioral intervention strategies in the case of students whose behavior impeded progress
- Required that parents be informed about the educational progress of their child at least as often as parents of nondisabled children
- Specified that a statement of transition services needs relating to the student's course of study be included in the student's IEP
- Provided for instruction in braille or the use of braille for blind or visually impaired students

PROCEDURAL SAFEGUARDS

- Required that the language used to deliver information to parents about their child's right be easy to understand
- Required that parents be given access to all records relating to their child, not just those "relevant" records on the identification, evaluation, and educational placement of their child

DISCIPLINE

- Ensured that no student with a disability be denied continuing educational services due to behavior
- Gave schools the authority to remove students with disabilities to appropriate interim alternative educational settings (IAES) for behavior related to drugs, guns, and other dangerous weapons for up to 45 days
- Allowed schools to suspend students with disabilities for up to 10 school days to the extent that such alternatives were used to children without disabilities
- Required the IEP teams to conduct a "manifestation determination" once a disciplinary action for a student with a disability was contemplated
- Permitted school personnel to report crimes allegedly committed by the student with disabilities to law enforcement authorities

Source: Knoblauch, B., & McLane, K. (1999). *An Overview of the Individuals with Disabilities Education Act Amendments of 1997 (PL 105-17): Update 1999.* Arlington, VA: The ERIC Clearinghouse on Disabilities and Gifted Education. EC Digest #E576.

Figure 3-2. An overview of the Individuals with Disabilities Education Act Amendments of 1997.

SECTION 504 OF THE REHABILITATION ACT

Section 504 of the Rehabilitation Act of 1973 is a federal law that is a civil rights statute designed to protect qualified individuals with disabilities from discrimination in any program that receives federal funding. Although sometimes confused with the IDEA, the law is not an entitlement or funding statute. It does, however, provide certain procedural protection for individuals with disabilities to ensure that their needs are met as adequately as the needs of individuals who are not disabled.

Section 504 focuses on nondiscrimination by requiring that federally funded programs provide people with disabilities the same access to the full range of activities as they provide to people without disabilities. Because they receive federal funding, public schools cannot exclude a learner with a disability from participating in any part of a school activity because of that disability. In order to ensure that learners with disabilities have the same ac-

cess to education as nondisabled learners, school districts must provide necessary regular or special education and related aids and services to learners who qualify under Section 504. Congress did not provide any funding to schools to help them come into compliance with the nondiscrimination requirements of Section 504. Instead, it chose to require that public schools comply with Section 504 as a condition of receiving future federal funds for school programs (such as special education and bilingual education). Section 504 identified the criteria for learners as follows:

- *Disability* is a physical or mental impairment that substantially limits one or more of the major life activities of an individual, a record of such an impairment, or being regarded as having such as impairment.
- *Physical or mental impairment* is any physiological disorder or condition, cosmetic disfigurement, or anatomical loss affecting one or more of the following body systems: neurological, musculoskeletal, special sense

organs, respiratory (including speech organs), cardiovascular, reproductive, digestive, genito-urinary, hemic and lymphatic, skin and endocrine. It is any mental or psychological disorder, such as mental retardation, organic brain syndrome, emotional, or mental illness and specific learning disabilities.

- *Major life activities* refers to functions such as caring for oneself, performing manual tasks, walking, seeing, hearing, speaking, breathing, learning, and working.
- *Substantially limited* means unable to perform a major life activity that the average person in the general population can perform or significantly restricted as to the condition, manner, or duration under which an individual can perform a particular major life activity as compared to the condition, manner, or duration under which the average person in the general population can perform that same major life activity.
- *Reasonable accommodation* means educationally and fiscally appropriate modifications or adjustments made by classroom teachers or other school staff designed to provide a learner with a disability free appropriate public education. This accommodation will not fundamentally alter the nature of the service, program, or activity or result in undue financial or administrative burden for the district.

Reasonable accommodations, that is, methods by which learners with disabilities may be addressed in regular education and activities, may include but are not necessarily required or limited to the following:

- modifications of frequency and type of communication with parents (e.g., developing a daily/weekly journal, developing designated parent/learner/school contacts and resources, scheduling periodic parent/teacher meetings, communicating by regular phone calls or e-mails, and providing parents with duplicate sets of text or assignments)
- alternate methods of instruction (e.g., providing additional time for tests or oral exams, individualizing classroom/homework assignments, using technology such as computers or tape recorders, utilizing visual or tactile materials suited to the learner's learning style, using attention-getting strategies such as eye contact, voice signals or touch, breaking assignments into shorter segments, and providing additional time for completion of assignments)
- modifications of schedules (e.g., providing more appropriate class schedules, allowing learners more time to pass in hallways, providing flexibility for make-up work and tests when learner is absent for disability-related reasons, and approving early dismissal or late arrival for medical or agency appointments)
- reorganization of classroom and learners (e.g., seating learners closer to instructor, providing learners with a study carrel, moving learners away from disruptive learners, reducing stimuli, and establishing a peer tutoring system)
- appropriate behavior management strategies (e.g., establishing a written behavior management plan, using positive reinforcement of good behaviors and strengths, establishing clear and logical consequences for misbehavior, and giving instruction in study and social skills)
- environmental adaptations (e.g., creating study areas or partitions to reduce distraction, providing a stand-up desk or study corner to allow for movement and variety, scheduling classes in accessible areas, modifying restrooms, doorways, counters, and other physical facilities, using air purifiers, and controlling temperature)
- medical/health intervention (e.g., developing an appropriate school health care plan with school nurses and medical providers, administering medication, applying universal precautions, accommodating special dietary needs, and establishing a system of reporting that allows appropriate information to be shared between school staff, parents, and medical providers) (U.S. Department of Education, Office for Civil Rights, n.d.).

Hidden disabilities are physical or mental impairments that are not readily apparent to others. They include such conditions and diseases as specific learning disabilities, diabetes, epilepsy, and allergy. A disability such as a limp, paralysis, total blindness or deafness is usually obvious to others, but hidden disabilities such as a low vision, poor hearing, heart disease, or chronic illness may not be obvious. A chronic illness involves a recurring and long-term disability such as diabetes, heart disease, kidney and liver disease, high blood pressure, or ulcers.

Approximately four million learners with disabilities are enrolled in public elementary and secondary schools in the United States. Of these, 43% are classified as learning disabled, 8% as emotionally disturbed, and 1% as other health impaired. These hidden disabilities often cannot be known without the administration of appropriate diagnostic tests.

As a result of this broad definition, there are conditions that may qualify a learner as disabled under Section 504 but not under the IDEA. For instance, the Office for Civil Rights has determined that the following conditions may be Section 504 disabilities, although they are not necessarily included under the IDEA:

- lengthy psychiatric hospitalization due to depression, dysthymic disorder, or other emotional problems
- acquired immune deficiency syndrome (AIDS) (also recognized as a Section 504 disability by state and federal courts)
- behavioral disorders resulting in incarceration
- drug and alcohol addiction
- social maladjustment
- attention deficit/hyperactivity disorder (ADHD)
- exiting a special education program for reasons other than satisfactory academic performance
- Tourette's syndrome
- obesity
- hepatitis B
- juvenile diabetes.

Section 504 learners who do not meet the definition of "children with disabilities" under the IDEA are entitled to accommodations and services in the general school setting in order for them to benefit from all programs and activities available to nondisabled learners. Appropriate accommodations and services must be documented in a Section 504 individualized accommodation plan (IAP) and may include test accommodations and other adaptations.

The following examples illustrate how schools can address the needs of their learners with hidden disabilities under 504 regulations:

- A learner with a long-term, debilitating medical problem such as cancer, kidney disease, or diabetes may be given special consideration to accommodate the learner's needs. For example, a learner with cancer may need a class schedule that allows for rest and recuperation following chemotherapy.
- A learner with a learning disability that affects the ability to demonstrate knowledge on a standardized test or in certain testing situations may require modified test arrangements, such as oral testing or different testing formats.
- A learner with a learning disability or impaired vision that affects the ability to take notes in class may need a note taker or tape recorder.
- A learner with a chronic medical problem such as kidney or liver disease may have difficulty in walking distances or climbing stairs. Under Section 504, this learner may require special parking space, sufficient time between classes, or other considerations to conserve energy for academic pursuits.
- An emotionally or mentally ill learner may need an adjusted class schedule to allow time for regular counseling or therapy.
- A learner with epilepsy who has no control over seizures and whose seizures are stimulated by stress or tension may need accommodation for such stressful activities as lengthy academic testing or competitive endeavors in physical education.
- A learner with arthritis may have persistent pain, tenderness, or swelling in one or more joints. A learner experiencing arthritic pain may require a modified physical education program.

A school district discriminates in violation of 504 when it

- denies a person with disabilities the opportunity to participate in or benefit from an aid or service which is afforded learners without a disability (e.g., district practice of refusing to allow any learner with a disability the opportunity to be on the honor roll; denial of credit to a learner whose absenteeism is related to his/her disability; expelling a learner for behavior related to his/her disability; refusing to dispense medication to a learner who could not attend school otherwise);

- fails to afford the learner with disabilities an opportunity to participate in, or benefit from, the aid or service that is equal to that afforded others;
- fails to provide aids or services to the person with disabilities that are equally effective (i.e., affording an equal opportunity to achieve equal results) as those provided to nondisabled persons (e.g., placing a learner with a hearing impairment in the front row as opposed to providing an interpreter);
- provides different or separate aids or services unless such action is necessary to be effective as the aids, benefits, or services provided to other learners (e.g., segregating learners in separate classes, schools, or facilities unnecessarily);
- perpetuates discrimination by providing significant assistance to an agency, organization, or person that discriminates on the basis of a disability;
- denies a person with disabilities the opportunity to participate as a member of a planning or advisory board strictly because of a disability;
- limits the enjoyment of any right, privilege, advantage, or opportunity enjoyed by others (e.g., prohibiting a person with a physical disability from using a service dog at school); or
- makes selections in determining the site or location of a facility that effectively excludes persons with disabilities, denies them benefits, or otherwise subjects them to discrimination.

LEARNERS WITH AUTISM

Autism disorder is one of the disabilities specifically defined in the IDEA. The IDEA defines the disorder as "a developmental disability significantly affecting verbal and nonverbal communication and social interaction, usually evident before age three, that adversely affects a child's educational performance. Other characteristics often associated with autism are engagement in repetitive activities and stereotyped movements, resistance to environmental change or change in daily routines, and unusual responses to sensory experiences." These characteristics may be observed in mild to severe forms.

Children with autism vary widely in abilities, intelligence, and behaviors. Some children do not speak; others have limited language that often includes repeated phrases or conversations. Those with more advanced language skills tend to stay with a small range of topics and have difficulty with abstract concepts. Repetitive play skills, a limited range of interests, and impaired social skills are generally evident as well. Unusual responses to sensory information—loud noises, lights, certain textures of food or fabrics—are also common. See Figure 3-3.

Early diagnosis and appropriate educational programs are very important for children with autism. From the age of three, these children are eligible for an educational program appropriate to their individual needs. These programs focus on improving communication, social, academic, behavioral, and daily living skills. Behavior and communication problems that interfere with learning sometimes require the assistance of knowledgeable professionals in the autism field who can develop and help implement a plan to be carried out at home and in school.

The classroom environment should be structured so that the program is consistent and predictable. Learners with autism learn better and are less confused when information is presented visually as well as verbally. Interaction with nondisabled peers is also important as these learners provide models of appropriate language, social, and behavior skills. To overcome frequent problems in generalizing skills learned at school, it is very important to develop programs with parents so that learning activities, experiences, and approaches can be carried over into the home and community.

With educational programs designed to meet a learner's individual needs and specialized adult support services in employment and living arrangements, children and adults with autism can live and work in the community (National Information Center for Children and Youth with Disabilities, 2001).

The Autism Source (2001) proposed the following tips for teaching high-functioning people with autism:

- People with autism have trouble with organizational skills, regardless of their intelligence and/or age. Even a "straight A" student with autism who has a photographic memory can be incapable of remembering to bring a pencil to class or of remembering a deadline for an assignment. In such cases, aid should be provided in the least restrictive way possible. Strategies could include having a student put a picture of a pencil on the cover of his notebook or reminders at the end of the day of assignments to be completed at home. Always praise the student when he remembers something he has previously forgotten. Never denigrate or "harp" at him when he fails. A lecture on the subject will not only NOT help, it will often make the problem worse. He may begin to believe he can't remember to do or bring these things.

- People with autism have problems with abstract and conceptual thinking. Some may eventually acquire a few abstract skills, but others never will. Avoid abstract ideas when possible. When abstract concepts must be used, use visual cues, such as gestures, or written words to augment the abstract idea.

- An increase in unusual or difficult behaviors probably indicates an increase in stress. Sometimes stress is caused by feeling a loss of control. When this occurs, the "safe place" or "safe person" may come in handy, because many times the stress will only be alleviated when the student physically removes himself from the stressful event or situation. If this occurs, a program should be set up to assist the student in re-entering and/or staying in the stressful situation.

- Don't take misbehavior personally. The high-functioning person with autism is not a manipulative, scheming person who is trying to make life difficult. Usually misbehavior is the result of efforts to survive experiences, which may be confusing, disorienting, or frightening. People with autism are, by virtue of the handicap, egocentric and have extreme difficulty reading the reactions of others. They are incapable of being manipulative.

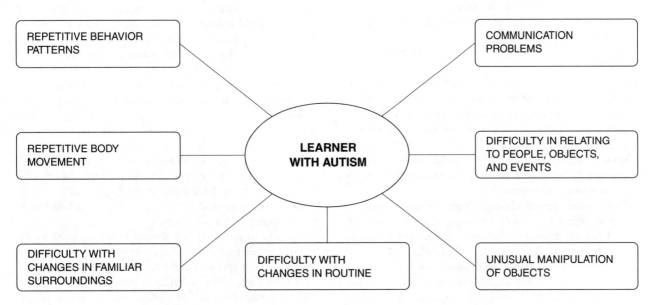

Figure 3-3. An overview of general characteristics that may be demonstrated by individuals with autism.

- Most high-functioning people with autism use and interpret speech literally. Until you know the capabilities of the individual, you should avoid idioms (save your breath, jump the gun, second thoughts, etc.); double meanings (most jokes have double meanings); sarcasm, such as saying, "Great!" after he has just spilled a bottle of ketchup on the table; nicknames; "cute" names, such as Pal, Buddy, Wise Guy, etc.
- Be as concrete as possible in all your interactions with these students. Remember that facial expression and other social cues may not work. Avoid asking questions such as, "Why did you do that?" Instead, say, "I didn't like the way you slammed your book down on the desk when I said it was time for gym. Please put your book down on the desk quietly and get up to leave for gym." In answering essay questions that require a synthesis of information, autistic individuals rarely know when they have said enough, or if they are properly addressing the core of the question.
- If the student doesn't seem to be able to learn a task, break it down into smaller steps or present the task in several different ways (e.g., visually, verbally, physically).
- Avoid verbal overload. Be clear. Use shorter sentences if you perceive that the student isn't fully understanding you. Although he probably has no hearing problem and may be paying attention, he may have a problem understanding your main point and identifying the important information.
- Prepare the student for all environmental and/or routine changes, such as assembly, substitute teacher, rescheduling, etc. Use his written or visual schedule to prepare for change.
- Behavior management works, but if incorrectly used, it can encourage robot-like behavior, provide only a short-term behavior change, or result in more aggression. Use positive and chronologically age-appropriate behavior procedures.
- Consistent treatment and expectations from everyone is vital.
- Be aware that normal levels of auditory and visual input can be perceived by the student as too much or too little. For example, the hum of fluorescent lighting is extremely distracting for some people with autism. Consider environmental changes such as removing some of the "visual clutter" from the room or seating changes if the student seems distracted or upset by his classroom environment.
- Since these individuals experience various communication difficulties, don't rely on the student with autism to relay important messages to their parents about school events, assignments, school rules, etc. unless you try it on an experimental basis with follow-up, or unless you are already certain that the student has mastered this skill. Even sending home a note for his parent may not work. The student may not remember to deliver the note or may lose it before reaching home. Phone calls to the parent work best until this skill can be developed. Frequent and accurate communication between the teacher and parent (or primary care-giver) is very important.
- If your class involves pairing off or choosing partners, either draw numbers or use some other arbitrary means of pairing. Or ask an especially kind student if he or she would agree to choose the individual with autism as a partner. This should be arranged before the pairing is done. The student with autism is most often the individual left with no partner. This is unfortunate since these students could benefit most from having a partner. (pp. 1-3)

LEARNERS WITH MENTAL RETARDATION

People with mental retardation are those who develop at a below average rate and experience difficulty in learning and social adjustment. The regulations for the IDEA provide the following technical definition for mental retardation: "Mental retardation means significantly subaverage general intellectual functioning existing concurrently with deficits in adaptive behavior and manifested during the developmental period, that adversely affects a child's educational performance."

General intellectual functioning is typically measured by an intelligence test. Persons with mental retardation usually score 70 or below on such tests. Intelligence tests sample only a small portion of the full range of a person's skills and abilities. The intelligence quotient (IQ) score is a derived score representing the individual's overall intelligence. A person's score on an intelligence test is compared to the statistical average of age-mates who have taken the same test. Performance on intelligence quotient (IQ) tests, cannot by itself accurately predict the social and vocational potential of a person. An IQ score merely predicts the potential academic ability level of the learner. Heward and Orlansky (1992) stated the following:

- The concept of intelligence is a hypothetical construct.
- There is nothing mysterious or all-powerful about an IQ test. It is simply a series of questions and problem-solving tasks.
- An IQ test measures only how a learner performs at one point in time on the items included in one test.
- IQ tests have proven to be the best single predictor of school achievement (i.e., verbal and academic tasks).
- Results from an IQ test are generally not useful in planning individualized educational objectives and teaching strategies for a learner.
- Results from an IQ test should never be used as the only criterion for labeling, classifying, or placing a learner in a special program.

In the past, many individuals who were classified as mentally retarded came from low socioeconomic or minority backgrounds. Factors such as poor health conditions, poor dietary habits, inadequate medical care, lack of exposure to common everyday experiences, cultural differences, and language barriers contribute to low scores on standardized intelligence tests. Because of these factors, caution must be observed when testing these individuals so that they are not unfairly labeled.

Many learners with mental retardation often have deficits in adaptive behavior. Defined by the American Association on Mental Deficiency, adaptive behavior represents significant limitations in a person's ability to meet standards of maturation, learning, personal, independence, and social responsibility that would be expected of another individual of comparable age level and cultural group (Grossman, 1983). Examples of these standards include appropriate personal-social behavior, adequate daily living skills, a foundation of basic academic skills, independent problem-solving abilities, and appropriate manipulative skills.

Adaptive behavior is usually measured by standardized adaptive behavior scales that use structured interviews or direct observations to obtain information. Adaptive behavior scales usually compare an individual to an established norm and measure the extent to which an individual takes care of personal needs, exhibits social competencies, and refrains from engaging in problem behaviors (Bruininks & McGrew, 1987).

In the American Association on Mental Retardation definition, the developmental period is stated as "the period of time between birth and the eighteenth birthday" (Grossman, 1983). This term is used within the definition of mental retardation to distinguish it from other conditions that may not originate until the adult years (e.g., strokes, head injuries).

Heward and Orlansky (1992) stated the following:

> Some children and adults are so clearly deficient in academic, social and self-care skills that it is obvious to anyone who interacts with them that they require special services and educational programming. For those individuals, how mental retardation is defined is not much of an issue; they experience substantial deficits in all or most areas of development. But this group comprises a small portion of the total population of persons identified as mentally retarded. The largest segment consists of school-age students with mild retardation. Thus, how mental retardation is defined determines what special educational services many thousands of students are eligible (or ineligible) to receive. (p. 88)

Learners who are classified as mentally retarded are usually placed in a special education program where they are assisted in developing academic, social, prevocational, and/or self-care skills. The development of these areas is important if they are to be successfully integrated into career and technical education programs. Individuals who have mental retardation have a learning capacity that is less than average. Generally, they can be expected to reach a sixth-grade level in academic areas (e.g., reading, math). These learners often have difficulty analyzing situations or tasks. Their skills in logical reasoning are limited or have not been fully developed. In some cases, this may be due to the limited number of appropriate experiences to which they have been exposed.

Case Study . . . Shawn

Shawn is a high school student who is enrolled in an industrial cooperative training (ICT) program. Shawn is mildly mentally retarded. Until he enrolled in the ICT program, school had been a frustrating and disappointing experience for him and his family. Shawn has a limited foundation of basic academic skills. His scores on achievement tests and intelligence tests have always been below average. Teachers he has had in the past have reported that Shawn has problems with math and reading, poor observation skills, and trouble retaining information. He has been in the special education program since the second grade.

In his sophomore year in high school, Shawn was involved in a career development activity that allowed him to explore the career and technical education programs offered at the school. He became interested in the ICT program after visiting several job sites in the community with Mrs. Willis, the ICT coordinator. When he initially enrolled in the program, Shawn had problems establishing a realistic career goal. Mrs. Willis met with Shawn, the special education teacher, Mr. Franks, and Shawn's parents to discuss job site opportunities in the community. After the discussion, Shawn expressed an interest in working at a large auto parts store in inventory control.

Mrs. Willis and Mr. Franks have worked as a team to help Shawn on the job as well as in his classes at school. A specific job analysis of Shawn's ICT job was completed with the help of his supervisor. Mrs. Willis visits the job site frequently to discuss effective training strategies and Shawn's work progress with the supervisor and to determine what needs to be done at school to assist Shawn. Mrs. Willis and Mr. Franks have coordinated efforts with Shawn's other instructors to concentrate on the development of his social skills and verbal communication skills. They are also focused on developing specific computer, reading, and math skills that relate to his inventory duties.

These learners often exhibit a short attention span. However, when appropriate instructional materials and teaching techniques are used, many of them are able to concentrate on tasks for long periods of time. A low frustration tolerance is frequently associated with this population. These individuals become easily frustrated when assignments or tasks are not appropriate for their ability level or when too much new material is presented at one time. Many learners with mental retardation have problems expressing themselves verbally to others and/or in comprehending what is being said to them. Their vocabulary is usually not as well developed as their peer group. Retention and recall of material is another problem. New concepts must be reinforced systematically so they can remember important points. See Figure 3-4.

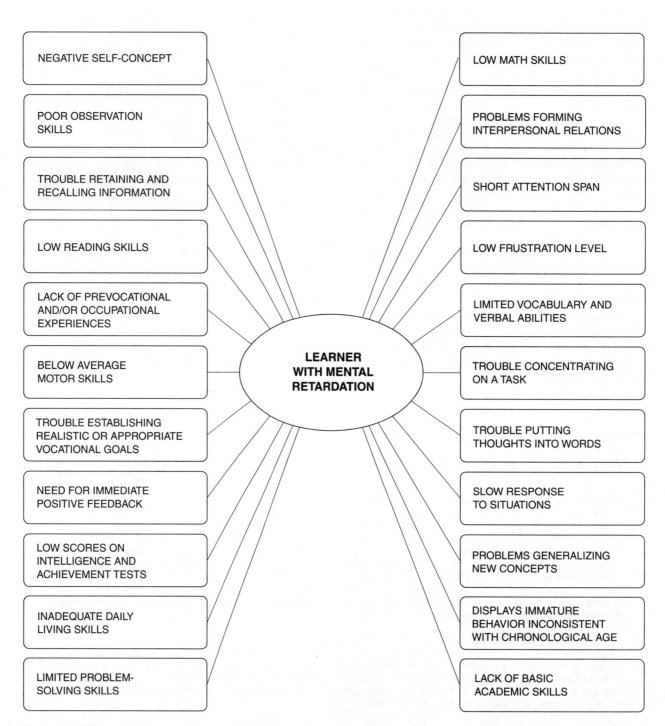

Figure 3-4. An overview of general characteristics that may be demonstrated by individuals with mental retardation.

Learners with Mild Mental Retardation

Learners with mild mental retardation usually receive some career development, community living skills and prevocational experiences in the elementary grades or in middle school. Functional academics are emphasized in their instructional program so that they can be integrated into regular class environments. Many learners with mild mental retardation can be successfully included in career and technical education programs at the secondary level. Special educators and/or other support personnel usually provide assistance when it is needed in the form of related academics and remedial assistance.

These learners usually function at a maximum of a sixth grade level in academic areas (e.g., reading, math). Their independent living skills are generally well developed so that they are able to learn job skills and support themselves independently or semi-independently in the community. They are able to communicate with others and react appropriately in work related and social situations. They can usually be prepared for employment at the low to medium level skilled jobs through participation in career and technical education programs or other related training programs. Most learners with mild mental retardation will not be recognized as mentally retarded after they leave the school environment.

Learners with Moderate Mental Retardation

Learners categorized as moderately mentally retarded do not have extensive formal reading or math skills. As they grow older, discrepancies generally grow wider between them and their age-mates in overall intellectual, social and motor development. These learners are generally taught in highly structured instructional programs where daily living skills and functional academics are emphasized. Many of these learners can develop skills that will enable them to be placed in supervised competitive employment settings. Productivity rates generally increase the longer the person performs the same task.

Learners with Severe and Profound Mental Retardation

People who have severe and profound mental retardation are usually identified in infancy. In the past, educational opportunities have been limited for individuals in these two categories. They were often institutionalized. However, recent advancements in instructional technology are making it possible for these individuals to learn skills previously thought to be beyond their capability so that semi-independence in working and living in the community is now an option. Learners with severe and profound mental retardation are extremely limited in the development of any academic skills. The emphasis of their instructional program is on developing basic self-care, socialization, communication and leisure skills.

Learners with Mental Retardation in Career and Technical Education Programs

Preparation for employment during the high school years should be a focal part of the educational program for individuals with mental retardation. Goals and objectives must be developed according to the demands of the employment opportunities in the geographic area and in conjunction with the functioning level of the individual. The focus should be on assisting the learner to learn and apply skills in a job setting while still receiving the necessary support services to succeed.

Research indicates that individuals with mental retardation, including those with moderate and severe differences, can work in a community employment situation if provided with adequate training and support. Hasazi, et al, (1989) presented the following guidelines that will help enable these learners to access and succeed in employment settings following school:

- The learner should receive employment training prior to graduation.
- Employment training should focus on work opportunities present in the local area where the individual currently lives.
- The focus of the employment training should be on specific job training as the learner approaches graduation.
- Collaboration between the school and adult service agencies must be part of the employment training program.

Competitive employment is an appropriate goal for many individuals with mental retardation. They are often able to function in the same jobs as other workers and are able to lead independent lives. In the past, the lack of vocational competence could be attributed, in part, to a lack of experience and inadequate training of teachers. Therefore, opportunities for these learners to enter career and technical education programs have been limited.

Career and technical education instructors can provide realistic educational opportunities for this population. With appropriate instructional materials and techniques, many of these individuals can identify a career goal and develop realistic skills that will help them to become economically independent upon leaving school. Support personnel and resources can also assist in this endeavor. Suggestions for career and technical education instructors who work with learners with mental retardation include the following:

- Introduce new material in small amounts and check to make sure that learners understand each step before continuing to the next step. A step-by-step approach to instruction can help eliminate frustration to the learners.
- Consider the reading level of learners before assigning a textbook, workbook, manual, or handout assignment.
- Use the demonstration approach for best comprehension.
- Allow the learners to take tests orally to minimize frustration and failure. In many cases, they will be able to correctly answer questions that are read aloud. If support personnel are administering a test orally, they may tape-record the responses for later evaluation.

- Develop a task analysis for each objective to allow learners to progress at their own learning pace. The task analysis can be broken down into smaller steps, depending on the rate at which each learner progresses.
- Establish instructional objectives that parallel the abilities of each learner. Work cooperatively with support personnel to determine these abilities and parallel them with the career and technical education curriculum.
- Provide for repetition and review for adequate comprehension of information.
- Allow extended time for learners to complete assignments and tasks.
- Provide positive reinforcement when learners successfully complete a task. This will help them to develop a feeling of accomplishment and thus motivate them to continue their efforts.
- Individualize instruction and use programmed learning methods when working with these learners.
- Allow sufficient time for overlearning. This concept is very important. Do not rush learners into new material until they have had sufficient time to grasp what has already been presented. Check their comprehension by asking them to explain and/or demonstrate.
- Use lists for written instructions or project directions. It is easier for learners to read this format as opposed to an entire page of writing.
- Use equivalent forms of the same directions so that learners understand that when you instruct them to "..." you want them to "...".
- Use nonverbal feedback to communicate with learners (e.g., pointing, guiding their hands through a process, blocking or stopping their actions when they begin to do something wrong).
- Videotape learner performance and graph or chart performance to provide realistic feedback.
- Use *chaining* when teaching a process or task that has multiple steps. Chaining involves going back to the first step and reviewing all previous steps each time a new step is introduced.
- Use visual aids, whenever possible (e.g., transparencies, charts, handouts, flipcharts, writing board).
- Provide learners with lecture outlines and structured overviews of what is to be covered in each class session/module/unit.
- Focus on developing problem-solving skills.
- Utilize peer tutoring.
- Develop a system of learner-teacher contracts that will allow learners to progress at their own pace through collaboratively establishing goals and criteria.

LEARNERS WITH SERIOUS EMOTIONAL DISTURBANCES (BEHAVIOR DISORDERS)

The IDEA defines a serious emotional disturbance as a condition exhibiting one or more of the following characteristics over a long period of time and to a marked degree that adversely affects educational performance:

- an inability to learn that cannot be explained by intellectual, sensory, or health factors
- an inability to build or maintain satisfactory interpersonal relationships with peers and teachers
- inappropriate types of behavior or feelings under normal circumstances
- a general pervasive mood of unhappiness or depression
- a tendency to develop physical symptoms or fears associated with personal or school problems

The term includes children who are schizophrenic or autistic. An individual with schizophrenia has a severe mental disorder characterized by losing touch with reality. An individual with autism has a severe communication disorder and is withdrawn and uninterested in others. The term does not include children who are socially maladjusted, unless it is determined that they are seriously disturbed.

Recently, committees and coalitions from a variety of professional health and educational organizations have proposed the following new definition and terminology for serious emotional disturbance for federal legislation:

Emotional or behavioral disorders (EBD) refer to conditions in which behavioral or emotional responses of an individual in school are so different from the generally accepted, age-appropriate, or cultural norms that they adversely affect educational performance in such areas as self-care, social relationships, personal adjustment, academic progress, classroom behavior, or work adjustment. The eligibility decision must be based on multiple sources of data about the individual's behavioral or emotional functioning. EBD must be exhibited in at least two different settings, at least one of which must be school related.

> Professionals have collaborated on a new definition because students with serious behavior disorders (e.g., eating disorders, depression, suicidal tendencies, social withdrawal) do not receive appropriate care and treatment because their academic achievement in school appears to be normal or above average, even gifted. Many clinicians believe that adoption of this new definition would lead to greater numbers of students with special needs being served. (Hardman, et al., 1993, p. 136)

A number of causes of emotional or behavioral problems have been determined, including the following:

- effects of minimal brain injury
- psychological stress
- problems in the central nervous system
- vitamin deficiencies
- allergies
- reaction to preservatives, chemicals, and dyes in processed foods
- a chemical imbalance within the body
- low blood sugar (hypoglycemia)
- a home environment that is too permissive and not conducive to developing self-control

Many learners in the public schools today have minor behavioral problems. Individuals classified in this category usually have long-standing problems. Their behavior is frequently inappropriate for the time and place in which it occurs. Another important distinction is that the rate of inappropriate behavior differs significantly from average learners. Learners with emotional or behavioral problems display disruptive or withdrawn behavior more frequently than their peers.

Although the behaviors exhibited by these learners vary from learner to learner, they generally lack the ability to control their own behavior. When they react to anxiety situations, their behavior is frequently inappropriate and not accepted by either peers or adults. See Figure 3-5.

Researchers have identified four distinct categories of behavior disorders in individuals of school age:

1. Conduct disorders–Involve such characteristics as overt aggression, both verbal and physical; disruptiveness; negativism; irresponsibility; and defiance of authority. All of these are at odds with the behavioral expectations of the school and other social institutions.
2. Anxiety-withdrawal–Involves overanxiety, social withdrawal, seclusiveness, shyness, sensitivity, and other behaviors implying a retreat from the environment rather than a hostile response to it.
3. Immaturity–Involves preoccupation, short attention span, passivity, daydreaming, sluggishness, and other behaviors not in accord with developmental expectations.
4. Socialized aggression–Involves gang activities, cooperative stealing, truancy, and other manifestations of participation in a delinquent subculture. (Von Isser, et al., 1980, pp. 272-73)

These learners are easily frustrated. They often resist authority and ignore discipline attempts. Many display immature behavior and are sometimes destructive to others or to themselves. When new tasks are assigned, many of these learners exhibit extreme anxiety and fears. Some of them may be on medication or special diets to control their excitable behavior. The career and technical education instructor must be aware of the effects of specific medication on the performance of the learner in a laboratory or working area.

Lack of self-confidence is a problem for most learners with emotional or behavioral problems. They doubt their ability to succeed in academic tasks, motor activities and social situations. Success in developing career and technical education skills can be an important key toward helping them cope with their fears and anxieties about failure. Doubts disappear as successful learning experiences are encountered. Therefore, participation in career and technical education programs can make a positive contribution toward their mental health as well as their employment potential.

Commonly Encountered Problems

There are a variety of behaviors that detract from a learner's ability to benefit from career and technical education and would certainly impede success in an employment situation. Learners with emotional and behavioral problems often evidence the following:

- Noncompliance–This can be characterized as failure to follow instructions properly or quickly enough. In school this is disruptive to the class routine and detracts from the learning experience. In an employment setting, this may be viewed as insubordination and be sufficient reason for dismissal.
- Bizarre and stereotypical behavior–These behaviors include a variety of actions that are easily identifiable by their atypical nature. Example behaviors include talking to oneself or imaginary others, excessive body rocking, and self-injurious actions such as chronic scratching. These behaviors may be so socially disruptive that maintenance in regular classroom situations and/or employment settings becomes difficult.
- Verbal aggression–This behavior includes obscene statements, threats, and other negative comments that may be directed toward teachers and/or fellow learners. Verbally aggressive statements are usually delivered in a loud and demonstrative manner. These behaviors are highly disruptive in the career and technical education classroom and laboratory and would pose significant problems in any employment setting. As a result, high priority must be given to strategies designed to reduce these problems.
- Physical aggression–Physical aggression toward teachers and/or fellow learners is probably the most severe behavior problem encountered in public school settings. Recently, several reports have suggested that these problems may be increasing.

> Expulsion and suspension policies have been widely criticized as being inappropriate for students with special needs. Furthermore, the use of corporal punishment and other aversive techniques has been restricted. As a result of these developments, instructors may be faced with more severe behavior problems and will need acceptable and effective means by which to manage these behaviors. (Bates, et al., 1982, p. 15)

Dealing with Disruptive Behavior

Career and technical education instructors are faced with the issue of maintaining appropriate behavior in their classrooms and laboratories. Learner misbehavior that is disruptive or annoying can be very dangerous, especially in a laboratory setting where the use of power tools and equipment requires close supervision. As the increase in behavior problems is becoming a reality in our nation's schools, it is imperative for instructors to become familiar with strategies that will assist them in creating a classroom environment where all learners can learn.

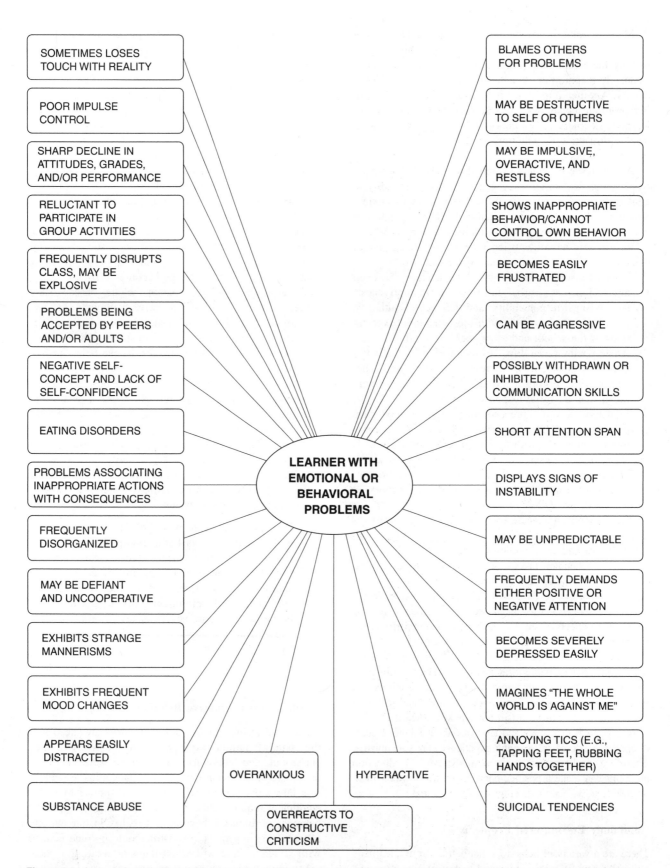

Figure 3-5. An overview of general characteristics that may be demonstrated by individuals with emotional or behavioral disorders.

Martin and Lauridsen (1974) identified some examples of techniques that may be useful:

- Use verbal reinforcers including teacher comments, praise, written and oral statements, engaging in a conversation about personal interests and experiences, acknowledging the learner outside of the classroom, offering help in a pleasant tone of voice, and sending home letters or notes with positive reinforcement.
- Use nonverbal reinforcers including eye contact when the learner desires it, a handshake or handclasp as a greeting or recognition of good performance, standing close to the learner during class or lab periods, and facial expressions which are positive.
- Use warning cues, preferably nonverbal. There should be only one warning and the less seen by the rest of the class, the better. Another term for these cues is "soft reprimands."

When learners with behavioral problems become aggressive or hostile during classroom or laboratory activities, the following strategies may be used to deal with outbursts of disruptive behavior:

- Remove the learner from the situation where the disruptive behavior occurred. A one-on-one discussion in the hall, in one corner of the classroom, or in an office is recommended. This is sometimes called a "time-out zone." It is important that there is no audience when trying to communicate with the learner.
- Calmly discuss the reason for the conference. Explain that the behavior was inappropriate for the classroom or laboratory and that it disrupted everyone in the class.

Do not show anger or hostility, which may excite the learner and make him or her more difficult to manage. If you are calm, the learner may begin to calm down also.

- Let the learner know that you are concerned about the situation and would like to help with any problem that exists. If learners feel that you care about them, it will make them feel more secure, which will foster communication rather than hostility.
- Allow the learner to explain what the problem is and provide a chance to release any frustrations and insecurities. In many cases, learners with emotional or behavioral problems will be disruptive if they are presented with tasks that are too difficult for them or if too much is expected of them at one time. These learners have difficulty working under pressure. The problems causing the inappropriate behavior may be directly related to classroom activities or assignments or to an incident that occurred elsewhere, such as a crisis in the home environment.
- Once the learner has had an opportunity to discuss any problems, cooperatively plan some solutions. For instance, if the learner is threatened by a task that was assigned, break the task into small steps or develop a teacher-learner contract collaboratively with the learner.
- Allow the learner to remain in the time-out zone for a short while in order to calm down and regain composure before returning to the classroom or laboratory.
- Stress that you are always willing to discuss problems with the learner. This will help to minimize feelings of inadequacy as well as to develop a sense of rapport.

Case Study . . . Sarah

Sarah is 17 years old and is enrolled in a high school metals class. Her records reveal that she has average intelligence but her grades in school show that she is failing in most classes. She displays frequent mood changes during the day. One minute her behavior is aggressive, and the next minute she becomes withdrawn and will not respond to others around her. When assigned a task in the class or laboratory, she is sometimes uncooperative and defiant. Sarah is reluctant to participate in any group activities because she is generally not accepted by her peers.

Sarah's continual demand for attention in class is beginning to irritate her career and technical education instructor. When he approached the guidance counselor to discuss the situation, he was told that Sarah has been experiencing some problems at home. Her father is an alcoholic and is frequently out of work. She spent several years in a foster home. Recently, her mother was involved in a serious car accident. Sarah is now responsible for managing the household and caring for her brothers and sisters. The career and technical education instructor and guidance counselor felt that Sarah could be helped through collaborative planning with the school social worker, psychologist, and special education teacher.

A team session was organized to discuss Sarah's problems and a plan of action was established. Sarah was introduced to a student mentor in the school who had received special training. The mentor meets informally several times a week with Sarah to talk about problems or pressures at home as well as challenges presented in school. In addition, Sarah meets periodically with the collaborative team at school where the counselor, the career and technical education instructor, the special education teacher and other personnel talk to her about her progress.

In the career and technical education program, Sarah and the instructor develop student-teacher contracts. Sarah has been assigned responsibilities in cooperative learning activities in the laboratory, and this has helped her to develop some positive relationships with her peers. As a result, she feels better about herself, and she has started to show some self-directed behavior in class.

The National Information Center for Children and Youth with Disabilities (1999) identified a number of approaches a school might take to make a difference in learner behavior:

- Classroom management and teaching strategies–Punishing, threatening, blaming, and criticizing learners as a way of influencing their behavior only works in the short-term. What research shows is that effective teachers rely instead on proactive strategies for preventing behavior problems. These strategies reinforce appropriate behavior and teach social problem solving. For learners demonstrating chronically disruptive behavior, teachers use point or token systems, time-out, contingent reinforcement, and response cost.

- Adapting instruction and curriculum–When instruction and curriculum are not adapted to meet the individual needs of learners, disruptive behavior can result. Any investigation of a learner's behavior needs to look closely at what adaptations can be made.

- Teaching social problem solving–The direct teaching of social problem solving is now a common feature of programs for preventing and resolving discipline problems, as well as for treating learners with the most serious antisocial behaviors. Although these interventions vary in the strategies emphasized, they share a common focus on teaching thinking skills that learners can use to avoid and resolve interpersonal conflicts, resist peer pressure, and cope with emotions and stress. The most effective are those that include a range of social competency skills that are delivered over a long period of time to continually reinforce skills.

- Schoolwide and districtwide programs–To build a climate that views appropriate behavior as an essential precondition for learning, certain programs have been implemented throughout the school or district. School rules are established, communicated clearly to staff and learners, and consistently enforced. Staff are trained to teach learners alternatives to vandalism and disruptive behavior. These programs have yielded promising results.

- Parent involvement–Research indicates that successful intervention programs almost always include a homeschool component. Parent management training and family therapy are two approaches that show considerable promise for affecting learner behavior. In parent management training, parents are taught such techniques as strategic use of praise, rewards, time-out, response cost, and contingency contracting. They have opportunities to discuss, practice, and review these techniques. Family therapy seeks to address family conflict. A primary goal is to empower parents with skills and resources necessary to solve their own family problems. This approach has been shown to be effective in reducing a range of delinquent behaviors. Although parent management training and/or family therapy may be a necessary component of programs for learners with a chronic history of antisocial behavior, less intensive interventions involving parents would be sufficient for most children.

- Alternative education programs and schools–Alternative education programs and schools are designed to create a more positive environment through low teacher-to-learner ratios, less structured classrooms, and individualized and self-paced instruction. The strongest and most consistent improvement for learners enrolled in such a program or school was their attitude toward school. Research results regarding their effectiveness, however, have been inconsistent and difficult to interpret, primarily because such programs tend to vary greatly in their interventions, learners served, structure, and program goals.

- Individual counseling–There are hundreds of different techniques used by counselors and therapists, the majority of which have not been evaluated through research. This makes it difficult to assess the impact of individual counseling as an intervention for chronic behavior problems. It would appear that, when used alone, (i.e., when not coupled with other interventions or strategies), programs that provide learners with individual counseling tend to be ineffective in decreasing antisocial behavior, especially when such behavior is chronic. The same is generally true of programs in which adults lead discussions with learners about their behavior, attitudes, and values.

- Peer involvement–There is no denying that peers can have a profound influence on a learner's behavior. Peer-oriented interventions are designed to capitalize on the potentially positive influence of peers in bringing about improvements in behavior. However, two such approaches (peer counseling and peer-led information groups) may actually be counterproductive in that the least disruptive learners in the group may be negatively influenced. Peer tutoring, cooperative learning, and peer collaboration tasks may be too demanding for many antisocial learners.

- Recreation and community activities–Many schools and communities offer recreational, enrichment, or leisure activities such as after-school sports or midnight basketball as alternatives to more dangerous activities. Evaluation results show that acts of delinquency and substance abuse decrease only while learners are directly supervised. These programs are more likely to be effective in reducing such behaviors if they are secondary components to programs that directly teach social competency skills.

- Fear arousal, moral appeal, and affective education–Programs that are designed to reduce substance abuse or improve behavior by disseminating information, arousing learners' fears, appealing to their concepts of right and wrong, or improving self-esteem generally have not been found to be effective. Approaches that include resistance-skills training (where learner learn about the social influences that can lead to substance use, as well as specific skills for resisting these pressures) have been shown to reduce substance use in the short-term. However, without continued instruction, positive effects of these programs are short-lived.

- Developing interim alternative educational settings– The 1997 Amendments to the IDEA balance the need for safe schools for all learners and protection of the rights of children with disabilities to a free appropriate public education (FAPE) and procedural safeguards. These amendments allow school personnel to order a change in placement to an interim alternative educational setting (IAES) for a learner with a disability under certain circumstances.

Multiple factors influence the behaviors of learners who are subject to disciplinary action, such as placement into an IAES. For example, three behaviors specifically targeted for IAESs—carrying a weapon to school or a school function, knowingly possessing or using illegal drugs or selling or soliciting the sale of a controlled substance at school or a school function, and the behavior determined by a hearing officer to be substantially likely to injure self or others—are typically influenced by a complex interaction of various personal and environmental factors, including a learner's thinking, emotions, social skills, family, teachers, school and community.

For interventions to be effective in both the short- and long-term, they must target as many of the factors mentioned above as feasible. That is, interventions should be comprehensive, broad-based, and enduring. It is unrealistic to expect most IAESs to deliver such interventions, especially since a learner's placement in an IAES is limited. It is realistic, however, to expect personnel at an IAES to begin interventions, while simultaneously working with the IEP team in planning and coordinating interventions that would continue after the learner leaves the IAES. Without continued services, it is very likely that behavior problems will recur, especially among learners with chronic patterns of antisocial behavior.

Clearly, there are a lot of approaches schools can use to prevent challenging behavior and to address it when it does occur. It's important to know that best practice indicates the following:

- Interventions must be developmentally appropriate and address strengths and weaknesses of the individual learner and his or her environment.
- Parent education and family therapy are critical components of effective programs for antisocial children and youth.
- Interventions are most effective when provided early in life. Devoting resources to prevention reduces the later need for more expensive treatment.
- Interventions should be guided by schoolwide and districtwide policies that emphasize positive interventions over punitive ones.
- Interventions should be fair, consistent, culturally and racially nondiscriminatory, and sensitive to cultural diversity.
- Interventions should be evaluated as to their short-term and long-term effectiveness in improving learner behavior. Both the process and outcome of each intervention should be evaluated.
- Teachers and support staff need to be well trained with respect to assessment and intervention. Staff working with learners who have behavior problems will require ongoing staff development and support services.
- Effective behavioral interventions require collaborative efforts from the school, home, and community agencies. (The National Information Center for Children and Youth with Disabilities, 1999).

Dealing with Depression and Suicide

By the time readers have finished this section, another teenager will have tried to commit suicide. In a federal survey, about 27% of high school learners questioned said they thought seriously about killing themselves in the preceding year, and 1 in 12 said they actually tried. What is worse, experts think the actual numbers are far higher than reported, because in some states a death is not classified as suicide unless a suicide note is found.

Teen suicide is the second leading cause of death in teens next to car accidents. The causes of teen suicide usually include drugs, sex, pressures at school, pressures at home, single parenthood environments, and latchkey environments. In addition, the following influences are often existent:

- early loss of a loved one, particularly a parent, through death, divorce, or separation
- long-term parental feuding or emotional distance from a parent
- repeated failures in communication so that an individual feels that he or she has no one to talk to who will understand
- serious psychiatric disorders in family settings (e.g., household characterized by aggression, hostility and little affection)
- series of life stresses (e.g., remarriage of a parent, frequent moves)
- lack of strong adult role models who can set limits and provide support
- feelings of hostility or anger usually directed toward a boyfriend, girlfriend, or parent;
- poor coping and problem-solving skills
- sense of powerlessness and despair
- intense academic pressure, competition with peers, and unrealistic expectations for success imposed by self or others
- child abuse, physical or sexual abuse, neglect, and psychological maltreatment.

Suicide seldom happens without warning, but instead is usually the culmination of a frustration or depression that was hardly a secret to those who observed the warning signs. Experts say 80% of those who take their lives warn people beforehand, often explicitly. About one-third to one-half of those who commit suicide have had a prior suicide attempt. The typical suicide victim has lost self-esteem and has a persistent sense of worthlessness. In 90% of cases, the suicide follows a devastating event, such as a scholastic failure or the breakup of a personal relationship. A family history of suicide or deep depression also increases the risk of suicide.

Adolescents are rarely subtle about suicidal intentions. Signs of trouble can include sudden changes in appetite and sleep habits, withdrawal, moodiness, excessive fatigue or agitation, alcohol or drug abuse and losing interest in hobbies and things that previously were pleasurable. Clues to watch for include the following:
- person talks about death in general
- preoccupation with death
- person talks about methods of dying
- person exhibits unexplained or unusually rebellious or disruptive behavior
- running away
- persistent boredom or difficulty concentrating
- failing grades
- unusual neglect of appearance
- radical personality change
- psychosomatic complaints about health
- joking around about death
- person begins to drop clues in conversation, assignments, etc., about death
- person begins to tie up loose ends (e.g., begins giving away prized possessions)

Following are specific tips for instructors working with individuals who evidence signs of depression:
- Listen to learners, watch their actions and observe their moods.
- Help learners to learn stress management techniques.
- Teach learners problem-solving skills, especially when major problems cannot be easily solved.
- Show learners that you think they are important and that you are concerned about their welfare.
- Help learners understand that seeking help is an acceptable way to cope with a problem.
- Share your own experiences and strategies to help learners overcome their feelings of depression.
- Let learners know that feelings are important and can be discussed.
- Give learners pride, recognition and increased responsibility to build self-esteem.
- Foster the idea of peer support.
- Find out about agencies in your community that can help individuals in a crisis situation.
- Don't pull away from learners if they have chosen to share problems with you, even if you feel overwhelmed. Suicidal adolescents rarely seek out professional help on their own. Find people in your school/district that can help.

- Trust your instincts if you sense that a learner is suicidal. Don't ignore the warning signs.
- Don't offer false reassurances (e.g., "Of course your family would understand and be supportive.").
- Let learners know that you want to help them but won't necessarily keep information confidential if they reveal something that might affect their safety.
- Don't offer simplistic solutions (e.g., "You're just having a bad day. Tomorrow everything will be alright.").
- Don't leave the learner alone if the situation is immediately life threatening. Stay with the learner while you send for help.
- Continue to provide support after a referral to a professional has been made.

Occasionally, outside help from the community will be necessary to assist learners with emotional or behavioral problems. Special needs personnel can help to identify these sources and work with them to make arrangements for services. These sources may include community mental health centers, counseling centers associated with local colleges or universities, psychiatric units located in local hospitals or clinics, and crisis centers.

Dealing with Challenges in the Workplace

Schelly et al. (1995) described the following obstacles the emotionally disturbed may face in finding and maintaining employment. Ineffective verbal and nonverbal communication and the avoidance of risk-taking present challenges. After obtaining a job, they may have difficulties following instructions, staying on task, accepting feedback, planning ahead, and demonstrating socially acceptable work behaviors. Many youths from this population are also multiply diagnosed with attention deficit disorder, attention deficit/hyperactivity disorder, and learning disabilities, all of which may make staying on task and following instructions even more of a challenge.
- Difficulty with verbal and nonverbal communication–Struggles with making phone calls and going through the interview process are common for youths with emotional disorders because they may have difficulties in verbal expression. Nonverbal communication skills may also be underdeveloped as evidenced through poor posture, limited eye contact, voice tone, facial expressions, and inappropriate dress, hairstyles, or jewelry. This nonconforming appearance combined with limited communication skills often creates a negative first impression for employers and thus becomes a barrier to obtaining employment.
- Avoidance of risk-taking situations–While youths with emotional disorders may have a desire to obtain employment, they may also have a desire to avoid a perceived risk-taking situation, as demonstrated by a lack of follow-through with job search activities and "cold feet" as they near possible employment. Further, the experience of success in any life area is often viewed as a risk-

taking situation because it may be unfamiliar territory with increased responsibilities and pressures. Because of this fear of the unknown, potentially successful opportunities are often sabotaged to avoid risky situations.

- Accepting feedback–A low sense of self-worth may contribute to an inability to deal with criticism and accept constructive feedback. In addition, many youths with emotional disorders have trouble managing their anger in a confrontational situation. As a result, confrontation on the job may lead to an explosion and end in job loss.
- Planning ahead–Reactive, impulsive behaviors often preclude planning ahead and anticipating undesirable consequences. On the job, these youths often act before they think, which may lead to negative consequences.
- General lack of socially acceptable work behaviors– The collective behaviors of youths with emotional disorders tend to indicate an overall lack of work ethic. Behaviors such as sticking with a job, taking initiative, coming to work on time, working to the best of one's ability, ending a job appropriately, or showing respect are often not apparent. One reason may be that many youths have not had role models that demonstrate effective work skills.

Schelly et al. also (1995) identified support strategies for individuals with emotional disorders:

- Functional community-referenced assessment–A community-based assessment process assists youths with emotional disorders in choosing and getting a job. This highly individualized process identifies strengths, interests, barriers, and support strategies in the work, school, community, recreational, home, and social-emotional domains. An ongoing approach, offering volunteer, short-term work trials to youth, uses community-based resources for constant learning opportunities. Hands-on experiences create a greater sense of personal confidence and lower the risk associated with acquiring a job. Assessment information targets specific behavior support needs for each youth, allowing for the immediate and ongoing implementation of functional behavioral support strategies.
- Modified supported employment–Many youths with emotional disorders need very little help with on-the-job acquisition and therefore typically will not benefit from a traditional job coach model. These youths need support with problem-solving, effective communication, and demonstration of appropriate behaviors in the workplace. Members of this population may be very concerned about fitting in with coworkers and peers and not being stigmatized in any way. Therefore a modified version of supported employment uses an employment consultant rather than a job coach. An employment consultant (1) helps to educate employers; (2) facilitates problem-solving and effective communication; and (3) provides behind the scenes support.
- Career skills preparation–Many youths with emotional disorders respond well to individualized support. There-

fore, the employment consultant works with youths individually to develop effective resumes, fill out applications, and practice interview skills. This support combined with an experiential, community-based career skills curriculum is effective in preparing youths with emotional disorders for the job search process.

- Problem-solving implementation–At the time of job placement, the youth, the employer, and the employment consultant sign a problem-solving agreement. This agreement helps to facilitate open communication between all parties and allows everyone to plan ahead for any future conflicts. If a problem arises, the agreement specifies a list of problem-solving steps. If the problem persists the agreement provides for implementation of a behavioral contract. This tool also helps employers recognize the needs of this population and helps them learn how to develop effective support strategies.
- Allowing natural consequences to occur–Many youths with emotional disorders are experiential learners. Some of the most meaningful learning opportunities occur as the result of natural consequences. For example, if youths continually act out on a job and refuse to take steps to correct their disruptive behavior, the best option may be to experience the natural consequences of losing their job. In this situation, the employment consultant can turn an unfortunate circumstance into a learning opportunity by helping youths process their experience and learn what to do differently in the future.
- Action planning–Youths with emotional disorders can be empowered to be in charge of every aspect of their lives through an action planning process. They look at each domain of their lives and decide what priority areas must be addressed to achieve successful employment outcomes. The employment consultant is available to help establish a timeline and set realistic goals and objectives. This action plan is reviewed repeatedly to guide support services, check progress, and adjust goals. In this way, service provision is youth driven.

Learners with Emotional or Behavioral Disorders in Career and Technical Education Programs

Some general suggestions for career and technical education instructors who work with learners with emotional or behavioral problems are as follows:

- Be consistent in standards and expectations regarding the learner's participation in a program. This is the key to dealing with this type of learner. The instructor should firmly establish any rules, regulations, or program standards, as well as the consequences if they are not met. The instructor must be firm and consistent by following through with established consequences as they become necessary.
- Contact special education personnel in the school or district to cooperatively develop and implement behavior management techniques. These techniques can also

be reinforced by special education teachers, support personnel, peer volunteers, industry mentors, and parents.

- Offer positive reinforcement for desirable behavior. Praise helps learners feel confident and successful.
- Provide a structured program with tasks and activities that do not require a great deal of decision making. Routine gives learners a feeling of security, which reduces impulsive behavior.
- Provide examples and tasks that are as concrete and as meaningful as possible. Abstract concepts can frustrate learners. Demonstrate the procedures for completing assigned tasks so that learners know exactly what do to.
- Develop and utilize learner-teacher contracts. A learner-teacher contract specifies the tasks that the learner will complete or the behavior that the learner will change within an established time limit. Rewards and consequences are agreed upon between the teacher and the learner.
- Do not overload or overstimulate these learners. This can cause a loss of concentration and make learners excitable. Instruction should contain only a few new steps or pieces of information. Always build on previously mastered tasks. Maintain a success-oriented environment as much as possible.
- Allow hyperactive learners opportunities to move around. This movement can be incorporated into the task or activity. The instructor can ask the learner to help organize the tool room, help supervise clean-up activities, or take a message to the office.
- Use programmed learning methods and individualized instruction. This allows learners to work successfully at their own pace without feeling threatened or pressured. Computer-assisted instruction and appropriate software can be extremely effective for some learners.
- Reduce the length of assignments. These learners may lose interest in a lengthy activity and become inattentive. Shortened assignments expose them to a variety of tasks, which stimulates attentiveness.
- Eliminate distractions by reducing excessive visual and auditory stimulation. Study carrels are very effective in doing this. If carrels are not available, seat the learner in the area where there is the least amount of distraction. Desks, tables and workstations should be kept free from unnecessary materials to prevent distractions.
- Praise learners for remaining on-task and for completing assigned work. Ignore as much of the negative behavior as possible. Attention paid to inappropriate behavior may only reinforce it. Use progress charts and other visible means of recording behavior improvements. Simply charting the improvement may serve as a reinforcer for some learners.
- Make certain that directions are very clear. When giving directions to the class, stand near these learners to help them to be attentive. Streamline instructions by using simple terms and phrases. After giving instructions to the class, check the comprehension of instructions by having the learner paraphrase the instructions back to you. Visual cues can be written on note cards and taped to the learner's desk or lab table. Prerecorded directions can also encourage learners to pay attention.
- Remember that different people have different standards for what constitutes inappropriate behavior. For example, some intructors are less tolerant of verbal activity in the classroom than others. You must take into consideration (a) your expectations for learners in your program, (b) your classroom rules and regulations, (c) the amount of inappropriate behavior you are willing to allow, and (d) your reaction to inappropriate behavior.
- Establish nonverbal cues for behavior that is unacceptable. For example, use eye contact and position yourself near the learner and use other signals that have been clearly established so that unacceptable behavior can be curbed as soon as possible.
- Never let learners operate equipment or machinery or work with tools when they are upset or appear out of control.
- Always get expert advice regarding effects of medication on learners prior to letting them work in a laboratory.
- Establish short-term goals for learners within the existing curriculum/sequence of tasks for the program.
- Provide a highly structured program for learners. Post and review schedules, procedures, rules, regulations and consequences for breaking the rules. Reinforce all of this information on a consistent basis.
- Establish a close and positive rapport with learners. This will enable a bond of trust to be established.
- Do not take the actions or words of learners with behavior disorders personally. Don't carry problems over from one day to another. This will only enhance a negative situation and make it worse for both the instructor and the learner.

LEARNERS WITH VISUAL IMPAIRMENTS

The terms *partially sighted, low vision, legally blind,* and *totally blind* are used in the educational context to describe learners with visual impairments. They are defined as follows:

- Partially sighted indicates that a need for special education has resulted from some type of visual problem.
- Low vision generally refers to a severe visual impairment, not necessarily limited to distance vision. Low vision applies to all individuals with sight who are unable to read the newspaper at a normal viewing distance, even with the aid of eyeglasses or contact lenses. They use a combination of vision and other senses to learn, although they may require adaptations in lighting or the size of print and sometimes, braille.
- Legally blind indicates that a person has less than 20/200 vision in the better eye or a very limited field of vision (20 degrees at its widest point).
- Totally blind learners learn via braille or another nonvisual media.

Learners with visual impairments may have problems achieving success in school. They may not be able to attain a level of academic achievement commensurate with their mental ability because of the visual problem. They require learning experiences and materials adapted to meet their needs. Many learners also have difficulties in motor coordination, mobility, speech and language development, and interpersonal relationships. Individuals classified as visually impaired are divided into two groups-blind and partially sighted. See Figure 3-6.

Learners Who Are Blind

Individuals who are blind become aware of their environment through smell, touch and hearing. The age at which individuals become blind greatly affects their specific educational needs. Those who have been blind since birth have difficulty understanding concepts such as depth, space, and relationships of one object to another. A person who becomes blind later in life will have problems adapting to blindness but can rely on experiences from the past. This memory of visual experience is helpful in adjusting to educational experiences.

Developing reading skills is difficult for learners who are blind. Braille is a system of reading that involves touching rather than seeing. Characters are made of combinations of six raised dots. In many ways, it is like shorthand. Abbreviations, which are called contractions, help save space and allow for faster reading and writing. By running their fingers over the characters, individuals who are blind learn to read the characters just as sighted people learn to recognize and read letters and words. Even though the braille system is over 150 years old it is the most efficient approach to reading by touch and is an essential skill for people who have too little vision to read print. However, reading braille is more time-consuming than reading regular print. Individuals who are visually impaired who use this method read at a slower rate than sighted learners who read regular print (about 70 words per minute as opposed to about 245 words).

Recent technological developments have made braille more efficient. This enables learners to function more independently in classroom settings. The VersaBraille II+ (Telesensory System, Incorporated) is a portable laptop computer on which learners with limited sight can take notes and tests in class and prepare assignments and papers at home. The keyboard has six keys that correspond to the dots in a braille cell, a numeric keypad, and a joystick. Students can check their work by reading a dynamic tactile display on the top of the VersaBraille II+ consisting of 20 braille cells, each made up of small pins that move up and down as the text progresses. Students store their work on a 3½-inch floppy disc that can be used with a talking word-processing program or to produce standard English print copies for teachers to read. (Heward and Orlansky, 1992, p. 340)

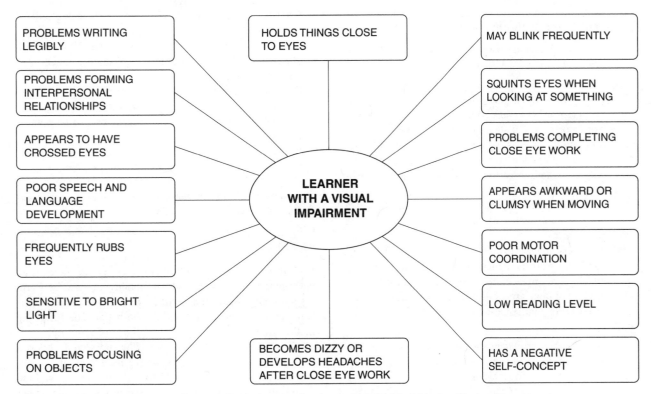

Figure 3-6. An overview of general characteristics that may be demonstrated by individuals with visual impairments.

Learners Who Are Partially Sighted

Individuals who have partial sight have limited vision even with corrections such as heavy lenses or surgery. Modifications to career and technical education education materials, equipment, or facilities may be necessary in order for them to succeed. Though they have some degree of sight, called residual vision, they rely heavily on other senses in the learning process.

Learners who have partial sight exhibit a variety of visual problems. They differ from individuals who are blind in that they have a limited ability to see print. Some have problems seeing clearly. Some cannot tell the difference between colors. Some are very sensitive to light, while others have a narrow field of vision that limits their ability to see. However, it is generally accepted that these learners should apply whatever visual ability they have to assigned tasks. Optical aids such as enlarged print and magnifiers, can be extremely useful in working with these learners. In addition, special lighting and prescription lenses may be required.

Following are some of the common visual problems experienced by learners with partial sight:
- Field of vision-A normal eye takes in a wide area, but an eye with limited field of vision sees only a very small part of the total picture.
- Color blindness-The individual cannot distinguish certain colors.
- Visual acuity-The individual may not see sharply or clearly or may have to get very close to objects.

Specialized Equipment, Materials, and Aids

The following equipment, materials, and aids may be used with learners who have a visual impairment:

Equipment
- Optical devices allow many learners with limited vision to perform better at certain tasks such as reading small print or seeing distant objects. Examples of these devices include glasses, contact lenses, handheld telescopes, magnifiers placed on top of printed pages and specially designed corrective lenses (e.g., prisms, fisheye lenses).
- Overhead projectors produce a larger image on a screen or a blank wall than information written on the writing board.
- Talking book machines are specially adapted record players. Talking books are recordings of books and other printed materials made for use with this machine.
- Talking calculators are available to help learners with tasks involving mathematics.

Materials
- Books and other printed materials with large type are helpful. Many materials are available from the American Printing House for the Blind. A catalog describing aids and appliances for individuals with visual impairments is published yearly. A section is devoted to vocational aids.
- Recording for the Blind, a national, nonprofit voluntary organization supported by contributions, provides recorded educational books free on loan to anyone who cannot read normal printed material because of visual, physical or perceptual disabilities. This organization records new books on request and retains Master Tapes of all titles recorded. Individual tape copies are made from these masters, as requested. The Library and Recording Services are fundamental aids to elementary, high school, college and graduate learners, as well as to those who require educational or specialized material in the pursuit of their occupations.
- The National Library Services for the Blind and Physically Handicapped, located at the Library of Congress in Washington, D.C., provides selected periodicals in braille, disc, cassette, large-type and open-reel tape editions. These materials are free of charge for individuals with disabilities. A descriptive listing of selected periodicals is available upon request.

Specialized Aids
- Magnifiers are useful for learners who have partial sight.
- Special contact lenses or glasses can assist learners who have partial sight.
- Peer or volunteer readers from the school and/or community can be an invaluable resource.
- Braille devices, tools and instruments such as braille rulers, micrometers, feed indicators, and control dials all have raised markings.
- Guards and templates can be specially designed for laboratory equipment and machinery.
- Attachments or auditory warning signals for machinery that produce an audible sound when a machine is on can be helpful.
- Special lighting to allow learners with partial vision to use their vision to the maximum extent possible.
- Control dials and switches on machines and equipment can be helpful.
- Instructors can make their own raised dots to form braille labels and instructions by using dots of glue.
- Diagrams using raised lines and three-dimensional models can help learners form a "mental blueprint" of what the instructor is explaining.

Mobility

Mobility refers to an individual's ability to move in an environment. Several methods of mobility are used by learners who are visually impaired. In general, the earlier a person can receive such instruction, the better. The following methods are the most frequent methods of mobility:
1. The sighted guide technique-The individual grasps a sighted person's arm just above the elbow and walks one-half step behind and to one side of the sighted guide. The guide does not have to change his or her

natural walking style. The individual will automatically feel changes and react accordingly.

2. The long cane-This technique usually is not begun until the early teens. Instruction is necessary and should be given by a qualified orientation and mobility specialist. The person with the visual impairment "sweeps" the cane back and forth while walking, lightly touching the ground ahead with it. In this way, travel is possible in a straight direction, identifying such obstacles as curbs, buildings, paths, and walls. The cane is painted white for added safety as it alerts drivers to the traveler at night.

3. Guide dogs-Guide dogs are usually not recommended for individuals under the age of 16 because they usually lack the physical strength and maturity to handle dogs properly. About 10% of individuals with visual impairments travel with the aid of guide dogs. These dogs are bred and trained by special agencies and both the person and the dog must take part in an intensive training period lasting several weeks. A person should be in good health, have a keen sense of direction, and be able to give verbal instructions to the dog in order to effectively use this mobility aid. The guide dog is most often used in situations where the user frequently travels through unfamiliar and complicated areas.

4. Independent travel-The most commonly used method is independent travel largely because this technique is taught at an early age. Many people who are visually impaired learn to use their senses of hearing and touch to detect obstacles in their path. Individuals with partial sight can learn to use their residual or remaining vision for traveling around.

Learners with Visual Impairments in Career and Technical Education Programs

Following are some general suggestions for career and technical education instructors who work with learners who have visual impairments:

- Learners should be oriented to the classroom and laboratory environment as soon as they are enrolled in the program so they can develop appropriate mobility, safety, and motor skills. It is crucial that they become familiar with the layout of the rooms as well as the specific tools, equipment and materials that will be used. A guided tour of the rooms is excellent, allowing them to feel where everything is located as the surroundings are described verbally. They can then form a "mental blueprint." Do not rearrange the environment without informing them.

- Do not become overprotective or try to restrict learners from moving around the classroom or laboratory. A variety of experiences helps them to become familiar with their surroundings.

- When addressing learners, specifically call them by their names so they know to whom you are speaking.

- Read words and figures out loud as you record them on the writing board. Learners can then keep up with the contents of the instruction.

- Allow learners to use cassette recorders during class discussions and lectures.

- Use raised lines and/or non-skid tape around safety areas in the laboratory to prevent accidents.

- When demonstrating a new task, procedure, piece of equipment, or tool allow learners to actively use their sense of touch so they will be able to understand the process. For example, take their hand and follow through with the process as you explain it verbally. This method is far more effective than merely telling them to "insert this part into this opening". Allowing learners to touch and feel a procedure in its successive stages will help develop their visualization skills. Hands-on examination combined with a verbal description will enable these learners to form a mental blueprint of an object or process.

- Peer tutors can help these learners succeed in laboratory assignments as opposed to completing the assignments for them.

- Have printed material converted to enlarged print, thermoform print (raised letters) or braille.

- Tape record lectures and demonstrations. Learners can borrow the tapes to review material covered in class.

- Learner note takers are helpful. Special pads are available that slip under a notebook page and record a carbon copy of notes taken. In this manner learners with visual impairments can either use a magnifier to read notes or have them transcribed on a cassette or typed on a braille typewriter.

- When making decisions about class seating arrangements, allow these learners to sit where they can hear and where the glare of the lights or sunlight will not bother them.

- Allow learners to type or use a computer to prepare assignments, reports and tests. Many of them can type much faster than they can write.

- Allow learners to tape record answers to tests or lengthy written assignments.

- Overhead projectors can help magnify a transparency even to the size of a wall, depending on the distance from the projector.

- The learner's desk or worktable should be well lighted with evenly distributed, glare-free light.

- Allow learners with partial sight to use felt-tipped markers or black ballpoint pens for completing written work. Also, these writing tools should be used to make large, bold lettering when they are grading written work so learners can read your comments.

- Try to keep the classroom and laboratory free of dangerous obstacles.

- Always keep doors fully open or closed. Half-open doors are a hazard for learners with visual impairments.

- Desks with adjustable tops are helpful since constant bending over a regular desk can be uncomfortable. The movable desk top often reduces glare and shadows if adjusted properly. Another suggestion is to place an easel on top of the desk for reading written work.

- Some learners with partial sight will use special low-vision aids in the classroom or laboratory. These may include contact lenses or special glasses, magnifiers, binoculars, or other devices. These aids should be used only when necessary and should be prescribed by a clinician with an expertise in low-vision problems.
- Allow learners with partial sight to use special writing paper with a dull finish and widely spaced green lines.
- Some learners with partial sight can read more easily with a bookmark just above the line being read or through a slot in a piece of dark paper that exposes only one or two lines of print at a time.
- Listening skills are very important. A learner sitting in a classroom does not develop effective listening skills automatically. These skills may have to be systematically developed and refined through practice.
- Sound helps learners identify and locate objects. Variations in sound can indicate successive stages of an operation. Make cassette tapes of the sounds in the laboratory environment so that learners can develop orientation skills.
- The learner should learn to use visualization to become familiar with and memorize sequential steps in using machinery or tools.
- Testing procedures should be modified for these learners. Some suggestions include extended time to take the test; reduction of the number of items on the test; administering the test orally; taping the test in advance; and sending the test to a support person or volunteer outside the class.
- In the classroom or laboratory you can help the learners locate something by giving verbal directions. The directions *left* and *right* should be in relationship to the learner's body.
- Make certain the learners know you are aware of their presence in the room.

LEARNERS WITH HEARING IMPAIRMENTS

Hearing impairment is defined by the IDEA as "an impairment in hearing, whether permanent or fluctuating, that adversely affects a child's educational performance." Deafness is defined as "a hearing impairment that is so severe that the child is impaired in processing linguistic information through hearing, with or without amplification." Thus, deafness may be viewed as a condition that prevents an individual from receiving sound in all or most of its forms. In contrast, a child with hearing loss can generally respond to auditory stimuli, including speech. See Figure 3-7.

The age at which an individual suffered a hearing loss is extremely important in determining the type and extent of interventions that will be needed to minimize the effect of the hearing impairment on the individual's life. Those who were born with a hearing loss (congenital) may have difficulty in developing regular speech patterns. They may also have problems developing reading skills. Learners who

suffer a hearing loss after birth (acquired) have had verbal instruction before suffering a hearing loss and can often rely on their auditory memory as an aid to learning.

The first three years of life are the most important for learning language and speech. The later in the individual's life the hearing loss occurs, the more capable that person is of understanding language. If the hearing loss occurs after the basics of language have been absorbed, the learner will have a language base. People with normal hearing capability acquire all the basic structures of language and a vocabulary of several hundred words by the age of three. A child with a hearing impairment who is five years old has a vocabulary of only about 50 basic words.

An individual's hearing impairment is usually described by the degree of impairment as follows:

1. Mild hearing loss–Individuals with a mild hearing loss can probably understand face-to-face conversation with little difficulty but might miss much of the discussion that goes on in the classroom, particularly if several people are speaking at once or if the learner cannot see the speaker clearly. Most peers will be unaware that the learner has a hearing impairment. Individuals in this category can often benefit from wearing a hearing aid and receiving occasional speech and language assistance from a speech-language pathologist.

2. Moderate hearing loss–Individuals with a moderate hearing loss probably cannot hear conversation without the use of a hearing aid unless the words are loud and clear. Individuals may have more difficulty with male or female voices depending on whether the hearing loss is in the higher or lower frequencies. Favorable seating in the classroom may have to be arranged for these learners, although most class discussions are impossible for them to follow. They must have assistance from speech and language professionals.

3. Severe hearing loss–Individuals with a severe hearing loss can probably hear voices only if they are very loud and about a foot or less from their ear. They must wear hearing aids. They can usually hear loud sounds (e.g., airplane flying overhead, vacuum cleaner). They will have to pay close attention to anyone speaking to them.

4. Profound hearing loss–Individuals with a profound hearing loss cannot hear conversational speech at all. Hearing aids may help them to be aware of certain loud sounds (e.g., fire alarm) but other sounds are unintelligible. Their speech patterns will often be extremely difficult to follow (Heward and Orlansky, 1992).

The degree of the hearing loss is determined by measuring the intensity of sound needed for the person to be able to hear. These tone and frequency levels are measured by an audiometer. Depending on the degree of impairment, learners may have problems learning the skills necessary to speak, read, and write in an age-appropriate manner. Learners with hearing impairments may require curriculum modification, appropriate learning materials, or supplementary aids in order to learn effectively.

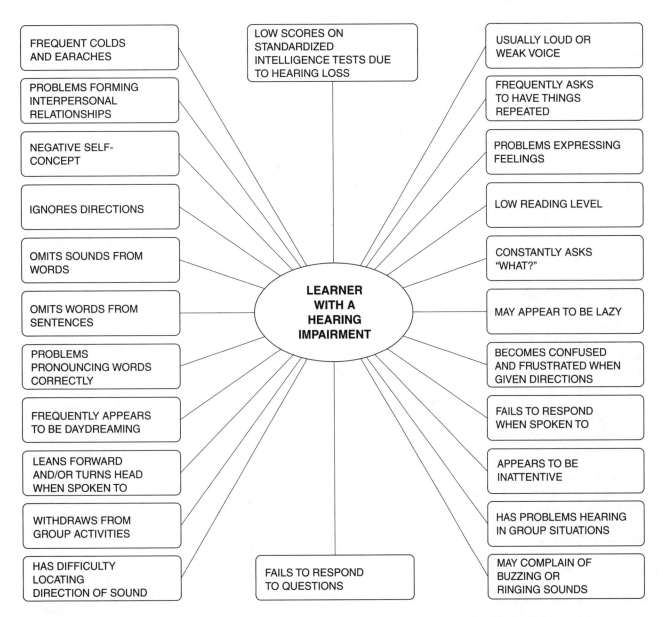

Figure 3-7. An overview of general characteristics that may be demonstrated by individuals with hearing impairments.

Learners Who Are Deaf

An individual who is deaf is unable to recognize sound or the meanings of sound pressure waves. The degree of hearing loss, measured on an audiometer, should not be the only reason for classifying someone as deaf. The diagnosis should be based on the individual's ability to comprehend spoken language auditorily. Individuals who are deaf have extreme or severe hearing losses and use touch, small and sight in the learning process. The education of individuals who are deaf has improved greatly in recent years, in large part because of the advances in technology. This population was formerly educated in separate, local or regional facilities. This situation is changing as a result of legislation mandating that these learners be included in regular classroom settings in the least restrictive environment.

> Many people who have hearing impairments can and do adjust successfully to life within their local communities. Unfortunately, others feel shunned by their own families and neighbors. Feeling like outsiders, they may deal with their stigma in a number of ways. Some may try to adjust as much as possible to the demands of the hearing world. Others may live a life of isolation, avoiding those who can hear. Still others may become part of organized groups whose members share the common bond of hearing impairment. (Hardman, et al., 1993, p. 278)

Learners Who Are Hard-of-Hearing

Hard-of-hearing means a hearing impairment, whether permanent or fluctuating, that adversely affects an individual's educational performance. The residual hearing, with the aid of a hearing aid, enables people to process linguistic information through the auditory mode. Individuals who are hard-of-hearing cannot hear the spoken word as clearly as someone with normal hearing. However, with a hearing aid or other supplemental aid, they can use their sense of hearing to some degree in the learning process.

Amplification instruments help individuals who are hard-of-hearing by making sounds louder. A hearing aid is probably the most widely used technological aid utilized by this population. There are many types of hearing aids. Learners can wear a hearing aid in one or both ears (monaural or biaural aids). The hearing aids produced today are smaller and lighter than models used in the past, although they are more powerful.

Hearing aids do not completely correct a hearing problem. Some distortion usually exists. These devices do not make words any clearer but only make what is being heard louder. Hearing aids essentially pick up a sound, magnify its energy and deliver this louder sound to the ear and brain of the user. Therefore, individuals who are hard-of-hearing never hear exactly what other learners hear. Also, the farther away the learner is from the source of the sound, the harder it will be to receive the sound adequately. Because of this, these learners should be seated close to the front of the classroom.

A study conducted by Blair, Peterson, and Viehweg (1985) found that the academic performance of learners with hearing impairments was positively correlated with the length of time they had worn their hearing aids. The earlier in life that these learners can be fitted with an appropriate hearing aid the more effectively they will learn to use hearing for communication purposes. It is the wearer of the hearing aid, not the aid itself, that does most of the work in interpreting conversation.

Communicating with Learners with Hearing Impairments

Most people who are hearing impaired have a communication problem to some degree, either in expressing ideas or in understanding language. Not all of these individuals use sign language, wear hearing aids, lip-read, or use understandable speech. Individuals who are hearing impaired use a variety of methods to communicate with others, including the manual alphabet, a sign language system, lipreading and total communication. Each method or combination of methods helps these individuals to understand what others are saying and to express their own ideas:

- Residual hearing–The degree of hearing ability an individual does have. Auditory training programs help individuals with hearing impairments to make the best use possible of residual hearing. Regardless of whether these learners prefer oral speech or manual sign language, they should participate in activities that help them improve their listening ability. Many of these learners have much more auditory capability than they actually use. Their residual hearing can be most effectively developed when they are actually involved in the context of actual communication within their daily experiences. The focus on auditory training is teaching the individual to "learn to listen" and "learn by listening" by concentrating on the comprehension of meaningful sounds (Ross, 1981).
- Cued speech–Cornett (1974) developed a system called cued speech. This is a method of supplementing oral communication. It seeks to supply a visual representation of spoken language by adding cues, in the form of hand signals near the chin, to assist the person with a hearing impairment in identifying sounds that cannot be distinguished through lipreading. Cued speech symbols must be used in conjunction with speechreading (lipreading). Cued speech symbols are neither signs nor manual alphabet letters and cannot be read alone. Eight different hand shapes are used to identify consonant sounds and four different locations identify vowel sounds. A hand shape coupled with a location gives a visual indication of a syllable. Reportedly this system can be learned in 10 to 20 hours of instruction.
- Manual alphabet (fingerspelling)–The manual alphabet is a procedure by which an individual uses different finger positions on one hand to represent the 26 letters of the alphabet. Also called fingerspelling, this technique enables the person to substitute the words formed by these visual letters for spoken language.
- Sign language–Sign language is a method of receiving and expressing language. Various hand and body movements have been formalized to convey words, concepts, and phrases. A person who uses sign language relies on fingerspelling to spell out proper names for which no sign exists and to clarify meanings. Three systems of sign language are the American Sign Language (AMESLAN), signed English (SIGLIGH) and Techsign.

American Sign Language (Ameslan or ASL) is a manual language system used by deaf individuals in the United States and Canada. It consists of signs formed by the hands to represent concepts. It is a shortcut to having each word completely spelled out. This system has its own vocabulary, syntax and rules of grammar and does not correspond exactly to spoken or written English. There are gaps that the person with a hearing impairment fills in. For instance, a learner using this system would sign "not understand" to mean "I do not understand."

Signed English (SIGLIGH) presents every word that is being said. It does not leave any gaps to be filled in. Using the previous example, the learner would sign the complete thought, "I do not understand," rather than an incomplete thought.

The Techsign project, developed at the Special Services Department of the Los Angeles Pierce College, has produced vocabulary materials to help learners with hearing impairments complete a variety of career and technical education programs. Many new occupations require highly technical skills. Individuals must understand and communicate technical language to enter into and survive in these occupations. Learners with hearing impairments would have difficulty in these fields if they did not know the necessary technical sign vocabulary. In the development of Techsign, words used in the career and technical education programs were collected from instructors and course materials. Definitions were written in nontechnical terms whenever possible and new signs were developed in accord with American Sign Language principles.

- Lipreading (speechreading)–An acquired skill, lipreading, or speechreading, is another technique used by individuals with hearing impairments to comprehend spoken language. This system is not always accurate and the individual gets only some of what is being said. Individuals who are hearing impaired have serious problems when attempting to lip-read because 40 to 60% of the sounds in the English language look just like some other sound on the lips. Many speech sounds look the same to the person who is lipreading (e.g., M, P, B). Some sounds cannot be seen at all (e.g., K, G). Vowels are usually the easiest sounds to lip-read. Therefore, individuals only pick up only between 30 to 50% of what the speaker is saying unless they are proficient lipreaders. They watch the speaker's facial expressions and rely on the previous content of the conversation, called "context clues," to piece together what the speaker is saying.
- Total communication–This is a means of receiving and expressing language by using a combination of residual hearing, fingerspelling, sign language, and speaking out loud.

Cooperative Planning with Interpreters

An interpreter is an individual who is certified and can transmit a verbal or written message to a person with a hearing impairment. An interpreter is sometimes provided for learners with hearing impairments who are not totally proficient at lipreading. This person interprets what the instructor is saying in class and repeats it to the learner through signing. This process involves a combination of fingerspelling, American sign language and mouthing the words.

The interpreter usually stands within several feet of the instructor during a lecture, demonstration, or discussion so that the learner can watch both interpreter and teacher. Learners should be seated away from any glaring light and in a spot that will enable them to see clearly. Teachers should check with the interpreter to determine whether they are talking too fast, especially when technical terms are being used. These terms must be completely spelled out and will take longer to interpret. There may also be times when the interpreter will ask to have information repeated.

It is often helpful for the interpreter to have a copy of lecture or class notes prior to the class session. Key concepts can be introduced to learners by the interpreter before they are presented in class. A list of relevant vocabulary and technical terms should also be provided for the interpreter, otherwise, learners with hearing impairments may become confused and frustrated when new material and unfamiliar terms are used in class.

The career and technical education instructor should establish a positive working relationship with the interpreter. Cooperative planning helps provide learners with the best possible means of communication in the classroom and laboratory. Both the interpreter and the learner should take part in the cooperative planning process so that realistic goals can be established and implemented.

Heward and Orlansky (1992) identified the following tips when working with an interpreter:

- The role of the interpreter is to facilitate communication between the instructor and the person with a hearing impairment. The interpreter should not be asked to give opinions, advice, or personal feelings.
- Maintain eye contact with learners and speak directly to them. They should not be made to take a back seat in the conversation. For example, say "How are you today?" instead of "Ask her how she is today."
- Remain face-to-face with the learner. The best place for the interpreter is behind and a little to the side of the instructor. Avoid strong or glaring light.
- Remember, it is the interpreter's job to communicate everything that the instructor and the learner say. Don't say anything that you don't want interpreted.

Case Study . . . Joyce

Joyce is enrolled in a cosmetology program. She has been deaf since she was five years old. Joyce has developed lipreading and sign language skills in the communication classes that she has attended. This is the second year that Joyce has been enrolled in the cosmetology program. Ms. Jones, her teacher, reports that Joyce has been doing very well in the program; however, her reading level is low and she requires some assistance from an interpreter at times. Joyce also works with the district communications specialist and a support person who assists her with reading. Ms. Jones and the other students in the class have learned to face Joyce when they are speaking to her so that she can read their lips. Ms. Jones has also modified her classroom instruction to meet Joyce's needs. When the time comes for Joyce to review for and take the state board exams, an interpreter will be provided for her.

Learners with Hearing Impairments in Career and Technical Education Programs

Some general suggestions for career and technical education instructors who work with learners with hearing impairments are as follows:

- Utilize appropriate specialized equipment and materials (e.g., lights can be installed on machinery and equipment to indicate when they are operating; visible warning signals can be attached to warning bells to ensure proper safety).
- Assess the learner's abilities in order to plan and implement instruction effectively. This includes the learner's intellectual potential, language development level, residual hearing ability (ability to hear after hearing loss) lipreading/speechreading ability, and manual communication ability.
- To get the attention of learners, call their name or gently tap their shoulder.
- Seat learners near the front of the room to make lipreading easier.
- Seat learners in the best lighting conditions possible. Try to have as much natural light as possible in the classroom or laboratory. Fluorescent lights tend to make lipreading much more difficult.
- If the classroom is darkened for videos or slides, make sure there is enough light on the face of the instructor for the learner to follow any discussion or questions.
- Seat interpreters next to the learner with a hearing impairment in classroom and laboratory settings.
- Present learners and/or interpreters with a copy of your class outline or lecture notes before you begin teaching so they can familiarize themselves with the content of the instruction and be better prepared to keep up in class. Also, they will have a chance to ask any questions in advance of the beginning of the class.
- Provide learners and/or interpreters with related vocabulary words and technical terms and their definitions so they may develop a basic understanding before instruction begins. List key terms on the board.
- Advise learners to turn the volume on their hearing aid down when they work in noisy areas.
- Consider the reading level of materials when assigning work. Learners often have reading levels below grade level.
- Use concrete examples whenever possible, with models, charts, diagrams and other visual representations.
- Ask learners to explain new material to you after you have introduced it. This will allow you to judge whether or not they comprehend material you have presented to them.
- Avoid multiple meanings of vocabulary words until learners understand the most commonly used meanings.
- Face learners when you are talking and make sure you have their attention before speaking.
- Use visual techniques whenever possible, including demonstrations, hands-on experiences, charts, and diagrams, as opposed to lecture and discussion techniques.
- Speak at a normal pace and at your usual volume. Learners who lip-read learn to do so with normal speech patterns and volumes. However, if your normal rate of speaking is extremely fast, try to slow down a bit.
- Let learners use a tape recorder if they can arrange to have someone transcribe the tape into written form.
- Encourage learners to ask to have statements repeated when they do not understand what has been said.
- Tell learners when they are speaking too loudly or too softly. Be honest and open with them.
- Vary classroom and laboratory activities to give them a break. Learners tire easily from the constant strain of trying to keep up with classroom discussions or lectures.

LEARNERS WITH ORTHOPEDIC IMPAIRMENTS

Orthopedic impairments may interfere with a person's mobility and coordination. An orthopedic impairment involves the skeletal system-bones, joints, limbs and associated muscles. A neurologic impairment involves the nervous system, which impacts on the ability to move, feel, use or control certain parts of the body.

An orthopedic impairment can adversely affect a learner's educational performance. See Figure 3-8. Learners in this category have a variety of unique characteristics. They differ as much from one another as other people. Often the specific statements made about them refer to the degree of the disability rather than to the disability itself. Examples are (a) traumatic brain injury, (b) cerebral palsy, (c) spinal cord injuries, (d) muscular dystrophy, and (e) amputations.

Learners who are orthopedically impaired represent a wide range of performance and ability levels. Some individuals have only mobility problems while others have trouble developing appropriate work tolerance levels. Therefore, such factors as physical strength, motor ability, muscular control and coordination must be considered for each learner when developing and/or modifying career and technical education instruction.

Learners with Traumatic Brain Injury

The IDEA defines traumatic brain injury in the following terms:

> An acquired injury to the brain caused by an external physical force, resulting in total or partial functional disability or psychosocial impairment, or both, that adversely affects a child's educational performance. The term applies to open or closed head injuries resulting in impairments in one or more areas, such as cognition; language; memory; attention; reasoning; abstract thinking; judgment; problem-solving; sensory, perceptual, and motor abilities; psycho-social behavior; physical functions; information processing; and speech. The term does not apply to brain injuries that are congenital or degenerative, or to brain injuries induced by birth trauma.

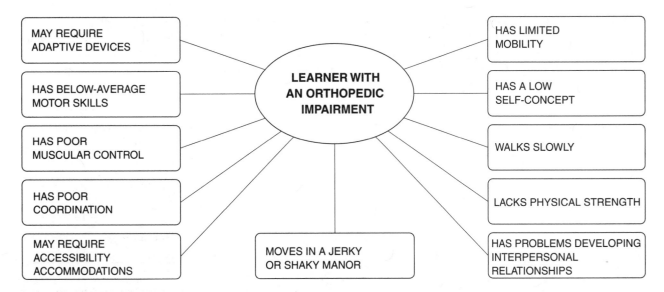

Figure 3-8. An overview of general characteristics that may be demonstrated by individuals with orthopedic impairments.

A traumatic brain injury (TBI) is an injury to the brain caused by the head being hit by something or shaken violently. This injury can change how the person acts, moves and thinks. A traumatic brain injury can also change how a learner learns and acts in school. See Figure 3-9. Individuals who sustain TBI may experience a complex array of problems, including the following:

- Cognitive impairments–The individual may suffer from short-and long-term memory deficits, impaired concentration, slowness of thinking and limited attention span, as well as impairments of perception, communication, reading and writing skills, planning, sequencing, and judgment.
- Psychosocial, behavioral, or emotional impairments–The individual may suffer from fatigue, mood swings, denial, self-centeredness, anxiety, depression, low self-esteem, sexual dysfunction, restlessness, lack of motivation, inability to self-monitor, difficulty with emotional control, inability to cope, agitation, excessive laughing or crying and difficulty relating to others.
- Physical impairments–The individual may suffer from speech, hearing and other sensory impairment, headaches, lack of fine motor coordination, plasticity of muscles, paresis or paralysis of one or both sides and seizure disorders, balance, and other gait impairments.

Any or all of the above impairments may occur to different degrees. The nature of the injury and its attendant problems can range from mild to severe, and the course of recovery is very difficult to predict for any given learner. It is important to note that, with early and ongoing therapeutic intervention, the severity of these symptoms may decrease, but in varying degrees. See Figure 3-10.

Despite its high incidence, many medical and education professionals are unaware of the consequences of childhood head injury. Learners with TBI are too often inappropriately classified as having learning disabilities, emotional disturbance, or mental retardation. As a result, the needed educational and related services may not be provided within the special education program. The designation of TBI as a separate category of disability signals that schools should provide children and youth with access to and funding for neuropsychological, speech and language, educational, and other evaluations necessary to provide the information needed for the development of an appropriate IEP.

Careful planning for school re-entry (including establishing linkages between the trauma center/rehabilitation hospital and the special education team at the school) is extremely important. It will be important to determine whether the learner needs to relearn material previously known. Supervision may be needed (i.e., between the classroom and restroom) as the learner may have difficulty with orientation. Teachers should also be aware that, because the short-term memory may be impaired, what appears to have been learned may be forgotten later in the day. To work constructively with learners with TBI, educators may need to

- provide repetition and consistency;
- demonstrate new tasks, state instructions, and provide examples to illustrate ideas and concepts;
- avoid figurative language;
- reinforce longer periods of attention to appropriate tasks;
- probe skills acquisition frequently and provide repeated practice;
- teach compensatory strategies for increasing memory;
- be prepared for learners' reduced stamina and increased fatigue and provide rest breaks as needed; and
- keep the environment as distraction-free as possible;
- find out as much as you can about the learner's injury and his or her present needs. find out more about TBI;
- give the learner more time to finish schoolwork and tests;
- give directions one-step at a time. For tasks with many steps, it helps to give the learner written directions;
- show the learner how to perform new tasks;

- let the learner know if the routine is going to change;
- check that the learner has actually learned the new skill and give the learner lots of opportunities to practice it;
- show the learner how to become organized by using an

assignment book and a daily schedule;
- keep in touch with the learner's parents and share information about how the learner is progressing; and
- be flexible about expectations.

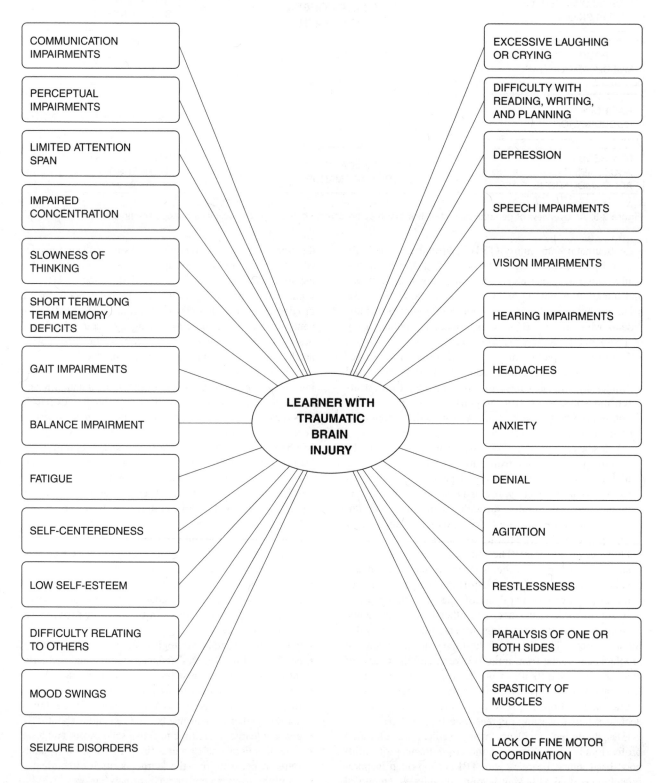

Figure 3-9. An overview of general characteristics that may be demonstrated by individuals with traumatic brain injury.

RANGE OF DISABILITIES RESULTING FROM ACQUIRED BRAIN INJURY

COGNITIVE PROBLEMS MAY INVOLVE

- Communication and language
- Memory, especially for learning new information
- Perception
- Attention and concentration
- Judgment, planning, and decision making
- Ability to adjust to change (flexibility)

SOCIAL AND BEHAVIORAL PROBLEMS MAY INVOLVE

- Self-esteem
- Self-control
- Awareness of self and others
- Awareness of social rules
- Interest and social involvement
- Sexuality
- Appearance and grooming
- Family relationships
- Age-appropriate behavior

NEUROMOTOR-PHYSICAL PROBLEMS MAY INVOLVE

- Vision and hearing
- Speed and coordination of movement
- Stamina and endurance
- Balance, strength, and equilibrium
- Motor function
- Speech
- Eye-hand coordination
- Spatial orientation

Source: Sitlington, Clark, & Kolstoe (2000). *Transition Education and Services for Adolescents with Disabilities* (3rd Ed). Needham Heights, MA: Allyn and Bacon, p. 89.

Figure 3-10. Range of disabilities resulting form acquired brain injury.

Learners with Cerebral Palsy

Cerebral palsy is a disability resulting from damage to the brain. It is caused by injuries, illnesses or accidents before birth (prenatal), at the time of birth (perinatal) or soon after birth (postnatal). The disability can range from mild to severe. It is one of the more prevalent physical disabilities of school-age learners. These individuals have disturbances of voluntary motor functions including extreme weakness, paralysis, involuntary convulsions and lack of coordination. Their arms, legs, vision, speech, and hearing can all be affected by this impairment.

Due to the fact that cerebral palsy is such a complex disability, it is most effectively managed through collaboration with physicians, physical therapists, occupational therapists, communication specialists, counselors, teachers, and others who work directly with these learners and their families. Regular exercise and appropriate placement in school settings help the individual to move to the maximum extent possible within the educational setting as well as to minimize progressive damage to muscles and limbs (Heward and Orlansky, 1992).

Learners with Spinal Cord Injuries

Spinal cord injuries occur when the spinal cord is traumatized or severed. These injuries can result from a number of causes including an automobile accident (responsible for about half of all spinal cord injuries), a sports injury or a fall. The specific impact of the spinal cord injury on the individual depends on the location and the severity of the injury.

In general, there is paralysis and loss of sensation below the level of the injury. The higher the injury on the spine and the more the injury cuts through the entire spinal cord, the greater the paralysis. Individuals who have spinal cord injuries often use wheelchairs for mobility. Rehabilitation programming generally consists of physical therapy, the use of adaptive devices, and psychological support.

Case Study . . . April

April is 30 years old and is enrolled in a graphic arts program at the postsecondary level. April was involved in an accident and suffered a spinal cord injury. She is paralyzed from the waist down. Since her accident she has received help from an orthopedic specialist, an occupational therapist, and a physical therapist. She has a motorized wheelchair for mobility. She has also had extensive training in self-care and community living skills.

April had a brief exploratory experience in the graphic arts area during high school, completing high school with a general diploma. Since she graduated, she has had a series of entry-level positions in the retail and fast food industries. She has now decided to return to school to become a draftsperson.

April has had a few difficulties since she entered the program. Mr. Lane, the drafting instructor, used a set of accessibility guidelines on the advice of the transition coordinator on campus to make certain that April would be able to fully participate in the program. After reviewing the guidelines, he decided that with a few minor changes in the classroom and laboratory setting, April would have no problem participating in the program. A few desks were rearranged to make the aisles wider. A lapboard was provided for April so that she could take notes in her chair during class lectures. A drafting table was lowered and adapted with an adjustable top. A hydraulic lift was installed on the wheelchair that enabled April to raise the chair to the level of the equipment in the lab.

Mr. Lane feels that April is performing very well in the program and has assured her that she should have no trouble finding a job when she completes the program.

Learners with Muscular Dystrophy

Muscular dystrophy is a chronic, inherited disorder characterized by progressive weakening and wasting of the voluntary skeletal muscles (U.S. Department of Health and Human Services, 1980). Individuals with muscular dystrophy progressively lose their ability to walk and the effective use of their arms and hands. The muscles of the hips, shoulders, arms, and legs are involved with this disability.

Individuals with muscular dystrophy focus on maintaining or improving their ambulatory independence for as long as possible. There is no known cure for most cases of muscular dystrophy. The disability is often fatal. A good deal of independence can be maintained by regular physical therapy, exercise, and the use of appropriate aids and appliances. As the disability becomes more serious, supportive devices are often prescribed (e.g., surgical corsets, walkers, braces). People with this condition may eventually be confined to a wheelchair.

Learners with Amputations

There are two general types of amputations. Congenital amputations are apparent at birth and can be triggered by a variety of substances that have adverse affects on the development of the fetus (e.g., Thalidomide). Acquired amputations are usually the result of a surgical procedure or an injury. (e.g., boating accident, crushed limbs).

> Prosthetic devices are often adapted for individuals who have experienced amputations. The first step in treatment is typically medical. An orthopedic surgeon is responsible for preparing the remainder of the arm or leg for use with a prosthetic device. Following surgery, the second phase of treatment begins, in which the individual is helped to cope with the feelings and self-perceptions that emerge from the loss of a limb. Rehabilitation is the third phase of treatment. During this stage, the orthopedic specialist, prosthetist, occupational therapist, physical therapist and rehabilitation personnel work together to help the individual adjust to his or her condition and prosthetic device. (Hardman, et al., 1993, p. 354)

The first and foremost objective in planning for learners with amputations is to provide access to the classroom, laboratory, machinery, equipment, and tools. Common architectural barriers that prevent learners with orthopedic impairments from participating in regular programs include doorways and aisles that are too narrow, worktables that are too high or too low, slippery floors, the absence of ramps and handrails, inadequate restroom facilities, lack of elevators, and the height and placement of controls on machinery and equipment.

Accessibility

The Rehabilitation Act of 1973, Section 502, and the Architectural Barrier Act of 1968 specifically stated that any institution receiving federal funds must make all reasonable efforts to eliminate architectural barriers and promote unrestricted accessibility. This includes public education facilities. Most institutions rely on information published by the American National Standards Institute (ANSI) to assist them in complying with barrier-free design. An Architectural Accessibility Checklist is provided at the end of this module directly after the Associated Activities.

Architectural accessibility is crucial if learners are to gain access to and succeed in career and technical education programs. According to Section 504 of the Rehabilitation Act of 1973, adaptations must be made to facilities, instructional procedures, and materials for individuals with orthopedic impairments as the need arises. Funds are available to make public facilities accessible.

In many cases existing facilities are adequate with slight modifications. For example, one learner may require a change in the way the classroom is arranged in order to maneuver a wheelchair around freely. Another learner with braces may require that the workspace be raised so that he or she may stand while working. Still another learner may require a nonskid floor surface for safe walking with crutches. Many learners require specific adaptive devices, such as wrist hold-downs for those with poor hand coordination and special pedals or hand controls for operating machinery.

Accessibility to the School. Before career and technical education programs can be made accessible, the building that houses the programs must be accessible. Therefore, the following modifications should be provided as necessary:
- adequate parking spaces
- curbcuts to the sidewalks
- walkways with appropriate slope and width
- appropriate ramps leading to the building entrance
- guide-rails in the hallways
- ramps or elevators leading from one floor to another
- doorways at least 32" wide
- nonskid floor surfaces.

Accessibility in the Classroom/Laboratory. Before learners can succeed in career and technical education programs, they must have access to classroom and laboratory facilities. Therefore, the following modifications should be made as necessary:
- doorways at least 32" wide
- aisle width sufficient for wheelchairs or individuals with crutches
- accessible work stations (e.g., enough room between the stations)
- worktables at appropriate height
- access to lockers and storage areas
- access to tool room
- access to controls for machinery and equipment (hand

and foot controls may be necessary)
- nonskid floor surfaces
- special guards for equipment, machinery and power tools
- specially adapted tools for specific disabilities
- access to sinks, faucets, outlets, and emergency power switches.

Learners with Orthopedic Impairments in Career and Technical Education Programs

The following are general suggestions for career and technical education teachers who work with these learners with orthopedic impairments:

- Seat learners where they will be most comfortable and have the greatest access to materials, equipment, lavatory facilities, restrooms and emergency exits.
- Contact the special education teacher and/or the district health office to identify any medical considerations for these learners including information about prescribed medication, possible side effects of medication, stamina limitations, physical limitations, and emergency procedures. The teacher should remember to monitor the effects of medication. Feedback should be provided about classroom and laboratory behavior after medication has been taken by the learner.
- Remember that some learners may have to be released from class periodically to use lavatory facilities, take medication, or go to the clinic for a short rest.
- Release learners who have wheelchairs, crutches, canes, or braces from class several minutes before the class ends so that they may get to their next class on time. A peer volunteer can help them travel from one class to another. This also fosters positive interpersonal relationships.
- If adaptations must be made in classroom and laboratory facilities or with equipment and machinery, ask learners

who will be using them to help determine exactly what changes must be made. They can often suggest modifications that are inexpensive and easy to create.

- Place materials and supplies to be used by learners using wheelchairs on lower shelves in storage areas.
- Allow learners with coordination problems longer periods of time to complete tasks, if necessary.
- Allow learners to tape assignments and tests if they are unable to write.
- Many learners have orthopedic appliances such as wheelchairs, canes, crutches, and braces. Consider these appliances in adapting the program and facilities and/or instruction.
- Provide special materials, such as large print books, oversized pencils, pencil grips, clipboards, and easy-to-grasp tools with larger handles as necessary.
- Use adaptive aids such as lapboards for wheelchairs, wrist harnesses to hold pens, and bookholders attached to wheelchairs. This helps some learners adapt to the classroom environment.
- Provide tutoring by a peer tutor, teacher's aide, parent volunteer, or homebound instructor if the learner is behind because of frequent absences.
- Inform nondisabled learners in the class of their peer's particular orthopedic impairment and advised as to how they can assist.

LEARNERS WITH HEALTH IMPAIRMENTS

Individuals with health impairments have limited strength, vitality or alertness, caused by chronic or acute health problems such as heart conditions, tuberculosis, rheumatic fever, nephritis, asthma, sickle cell anemia, hemophilia, epilepsy, lead poisoning, leukemia, or diabetes, which adversely affects a learner's educational performance. See Figure 3-11.

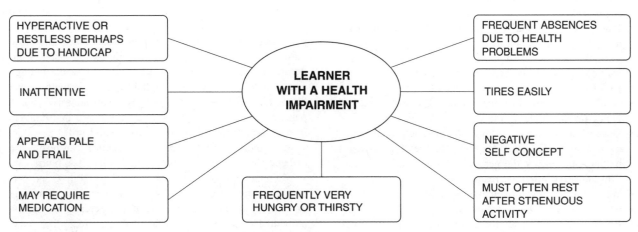

Figure 3-11. An overview of general characteristics that may be demonstrated by individuals with health impairments.

Learners with Epilepsy

The specific causes of epilepsy are not known. It is thought that when a particular area of the brain becomes electrically unstable, an individual becomes prone to having seizures. Epilepsy is a seizure disorder. A seizure is a cluster of behaviors that occur in response to abnormal neurochemical activity the brain. It typically has the effect of altering the individual's level of consciousness while at the same time resulting in certain characteristic motor patterns (Dreifuss, 1988).

The two types of seizures are tonic/clonic and absence seizures. A tonic/clonic seizure, formerly known as a grand mal seizure, affects the entire brain. The tonic phase of the seizure causes the body to stiffen. The clonic phase is characterized by repeated muscle contractions and relaxations. These seizures are usually preceded by an aura, or warning signal, in which the individual senses a unique physical sensation, odor or sound just before the onset of the seizure. In some cases, a cry or other sound signals the seizure.

These seizures usually last from one minute to as long as 20 minutes. After about five minutes the contractions slow down and the individual either goes to sleep or regains consciousness in a confused or drowsy state. These seizures may occur several times a day or as seldom as once a year. Potential danger from falling and striking objects in the environment should be a consideration. Characteristic aftereffects include drowsiness, nausea and headaches. A combination of rest and medication should be supplied for the learner.

The following are points to remember when an individual is experiencing a seizure:

- Reassure other individuals in the learning environment that the learner will be fine.
- Remain calm.
- Remember that you cannot stop the seizure (it has to run its course).
- Do not try to revive the learner and don't interfere with his or her movements.
- Ease the person to the floor, if possible.
- Remove any dangerous objects from the immediate area, if possible.
- Place a soft pad under the individual's head, if available (e.g., blanket, jacket).
- Turn the individual on his or her side to keep the airway clear and allow saliva to drain away.
- Don't try to force the person's mouth open.
- Don't try to hold on to the person's tongue.
- Don't put anything in the person's mouth.
- During the seizure, breathing may be shallow and may even stop briefly (in the event that breathing doesn't begin again, check the person's airway for an obstruction and give artificial respiration).
- When the jerking movements stop let the learner rest until consciousness is regained.
- Encourage the learner to remain in the classroom or return to the classroom as soon as possible.

- If seizures are a frequent occurrence, they may become a routine matter once the instructor and peers learn what to expect.
- Show the learners that they are accepted in the classroom and that you and the other learners are there to be supportive.

Absence seizures, formerly called petit mal seizures, occur during brief periods of time, from a few seconds to a minute. The learner experiences a brief loss of consciousness. Characteristics of these seizures include staring blankly, growing pale, dropping whatever the individual is holding, head twitching, inattention, and rapid eye blinking. These seizures can occur up to about 100 times a day. People who experience absence seizures are often mislabeled by instructors as daydreamers who do not pay attention and are not listening. Treatment and control of these seizures can be achieved through appropriate medication.

Learners with Diabetes

Diabetes is a hereditary or developmental disorder characterized by inadequate use or secretion of insulin. Insulin is produced by the pancreas to process carbohydrates. Without insulin, glucose accumulates in the blood and causes hyperglycemia, a condition which can cause severe problems for individuals with diabetes, causing them to lose consciousness or fall into a diabetic coma. People with glucose buildup in the blood will experience extreme hunger, thirst, and frequent urination. Diabetes can cause blindness, cardiovascular disease, and kidney disease.

Medical treatment revolves around the administration of insulin on a regular basis. Maintaining normal levels of insulin can now be achieved through the use of an insulin infusion pump. This device is powered by small batteries and operates continuously by delivering the prescribed dose of insulin. A diet and exercise program should be carefully followed along with the insulin.

Advances in medical technology make it easier for these learners to participate more fully in educational programs. For example, a "button infuser" is used by diabetics who need daily insulin injections. Instead of giving themselves numerous shots, diabetics can now wear this penny-sized plastic disk attached to a small needle that is inserted under the skin. The insulin is injected into the needle through a resealable cap. The device is held in place, usually above the beltline, for up to three days by a soft adhesive pad. A painless nasal spray has also been developed that delivers insulin as an alternative to injections and pills.

If an individual takes too much insulin it can result in a diabetic shock. The symptoms include dizziness, blurred vision, faintness, drowsiness and nausea, irritability, and personality change. A diabetic shock can be caused from missing or delaying a meal or from strenuous exercise. Giving the individual some form of concentrated sugar (e.g., fruit juice, candy bar) will end the insulin reaction within a few minutes.

A diabetic coma results when there is a lack of insulin in the person's body. It is more serious than a diabetic shock. The onset is gradual. The symptoms include thirst, dry, hot skin, excessive urination, fatigue, deep, labored breathing, and fruity-smelling breath. A health professional should be contacted immediately if an individual displays these characteristic symptoms.

Learners with Asthma

Asthma is a chronic lung disease. Individuals with asthma experience bouts of wheezing, coughing, and have difficulty breathing. Asthma is one of the most frequently cited reasons for learners missing school. Homebound instructional services may be necessary if the asthma is chronic.

An asthmatic attack can be triggered by a number of things including emotional stress, cigarette smoke, smog, pollens in the air, pets, and certain foods. Any of these irritants can result in a narrowing of the airways in the lungs. The severity of asthma varies. Individuals may only experience mild coughing or they may have extreme difficulty in breathing that requires emergency medical treatment.

Treatment of asthma involves analyzing the environment in which the individual works, plays and lives. The allergens or irritants that cause the most problems should be identified. Changes in temperature, humidity, or season may increase asthmatic attacks. A combination of medication and limited exposure to allergens that negatively affect the individual can help to control the asthma.

Learners with Cystic Fibrosis

Cystic fibrosis is an inherited disease, usually found among Caucasian children, that begins at conception. This disease involves the secretion glands that produce abnormal amounts of sweat, saliva, and mucus. Basically, the endocrine system excretes a thick mucus that can block the lungs and parts of the digestive system. Individuals have difficulty breathing. They may also have frequent and large bowel movements because food passes through the system after being only partially digested. People with cystic fibrosis are susceptible to respiratory infections. Characteristics of cystic fibrosis include chronic coughing, small stature, frequent gas pains, and delayed onset of puberty.

Medicine prescribed for people with cystic fibrosis include solutions to thin and loosen the mucus in the lungs and enzymes to help digest food. Vigorous physical exercise should be avoided. The lungs and air passages have to be cleared periodically. Treatment must continue throughout the individual's lifetime. Interventions include control of chest infections and adequate nutrition (high protein diet).

Learners with Hemophilia

Hemophilia is a hereditary disease where the blood does not clot as quickly as it should. Internal bleeding can cause permanent damage to tissues, internal organs and joints as well as overall swelling and pain. Blood transfusions may be necessary. Physical activity should be monitored carefully, although restrictions should not be any greater than necessary. During periods of high susceptibility individuals may need to use a wheelchair. Stress can intensify bleeding episodes.

Learners with Acquired Immune Deficiency Syndrome

Acquired immune deficiency syndrome (AIDS) is a fatal disease caused by a virus that cripples the immune system, the body's natural defense against disease-producing organisms. An individual with AIDS is vulnerable to various infections and certain types of cancer that take advantage of the body's inability to fight back.

It is believed that the AIDS virus is spread primarily through blood or semen contact during sexual intercourse, directly through the bloodstream (e.g., sharing contaminated needles with intravenous drug users, transfusion of blood or blood products contaminated with the virus) and from mother to child during pregnancy or shortly after birth through breast milk.

Human immunodeficiency virus (HIV) is a term for the virus that causes AIDS. It is estimated that between 30% and 50% of people infected with the virus will get AIDS. No one knows exactly how many teens are HIV-positive, but during the past three years, the cumulative number of 13-to-24-year-olds diagnosed with AIDS increased 77%. More than 5,000 children and young adults have died of AIDS, making it the sixth leading cause of death among 15-to-24-year-olds. By the end of 1991, the number of cases in that age group had been reported in almost every state and the District of Columbia. Nearly half of the afflicted teenagers come from just six places: New York, New Jersey, Texas, California, Florida, and Puerto Rico (Teenagers and AIDS, 1992).

Some educators doubt that significant numbers of teenagers participate in activities that would put them at risk of contracting AIDS. Unfortunately, there is plenty of evidence to the contrary. Recent surveys have been consistent in reporting numbers of teens that are sexually active. The highest rates of sexual activity among teenagers occur among out-of-school youth. Over 80% of male and female school dropouts report being sexually active. Teens living on the street had the highest rate (94%) (Tonks, 1993).

The AIDS virus lowers the ability of the body's natural immune system to fight infection and diseases. Common germs can, therefore, invade the body and cause serious medical problems. Some of the medical problems and infections associated with AIDS are listed below. These symptoms should become a concern if they are chronic and persistent. However, having one or more of these symptoms does not mean the AIDS virus is present. Likewise, not having one of these symptoms does not mean the AIDS virus is absent. It can take years for the virus to show up. An AIDS antibody test conducted by a qualified professional can help determine if these or other medical problems are symptoms of the AIDS virus:

- decreased awareness
- difficulty with breathing
- dramatic weight loss
- fever
- forgetfulness
- night sweat
- persistent cough
- poor concentration
- purplish blotches and bumps on the skin
- small blisters on the mucous membranes
- small blisters on the skin
- whitish sores in the mouth
- withdrawal
- loss of appetite
- skin rashes
- diarrhea
- fatigue
- infections
- swollen lymph nodes (William Gladden Foundation, 1989).

Byers (1989) suggests the following recommendations regarding individuals with AIDS in educational settings:

- We certainly must continue with an AIDS curriculum in grades K-12 in an effort to prevent the disease from further infiltrating the preadolescent and adolescent populations.
- Children harboring the virus cannot legally be excluded from schools unless they are deemed a direct health risk for other children (e.g., exhibit biting behavior, open sores). Consequently, chronic illness specialists, school psychologists, counselors and teachers will need to make AIDS a priority issue, and be active in facilitating school/peer acceptance and the social adjustment of a child with AIDS.
- Teachers, counselors, and other specialists will also need to be prepared to provide family therapy and broad-based support groups for parents and/or children within the school setting.
- Pediatric AIDS patients present a particular challenge for special education professionals, due to the erratic course of neurological deterioration. The child may be stable for a number of months and then deteriorate rapidly over a period of weeks and thus require regular monitoring of his or her educational needs.
- Specific educational treatments for children infected with HIV await further research and this appears to be the ultimate challenge for educators (p. 13).

Problems Associated with Learners with Health Impairments

Learners who are classified as health impaired have chronic health problems that affect their strength and vitality. These conditions also affect their ability to participate in regular classroom activities without some special considerations. These learners tire easily and often appear to be frail. Often they are described as inattentive. Some defense mechanisms that learners with health impairments may develop include denial, withdrawal, depression, high anxiety levels, hostility, living in their imaginations, and overdependency on parents, teachers, siblings, peers, or others.

These learners may have economic problems because the high cost of hospitalization, prescriptions, special diets, medical bills, and operations can become enormous. Transportation may be difficult in taking these learners in and out of school frequently for appointments with doctors, specialists, and at clinics. Interpersonal relationships are limited because of the amount of time learners spend out of school and apprehensions or misunderstandings from the peer group.

Learners who have health impairments frequently miss school because of health problems. In many school districts they are eligible for home instruction. Home instruction teachers act as a liaison between the home and the school. These personnel can help the regular classroom teacher in transferring work from the school to the learner and in providing remedial instruction. Many districts have one or more itinerant home instruction teachers who provide services to hospital/homebound learners in all the schools.

Two important specialists for many individuals with physical disabilities and health impairments are the physical therapist and the occupational therapist, each a licensed health professional who must complete specialized training and meet rigorous standards. A physical therapist (PT) uses specialized knowledge to plan and oversee a learner's program in making correct and useful movements. They may prescribe specific exercises to help the individual increase control of muscles and use specialized equipment effectively (e.g., braces). Physical therapy treatment may include exercise, massages, swimming, and heat treatments). These professionals encourage learners to be as independent as possible, helping them to develop muscular function. They also help to find strategies to reduce pain, discomfort or long-term physical damage. They may suggest dos and don'ts for sitting positions and activities in the classroom and laboratory.

> Occupational therapists (OTs) are concerned with the learner's participation in activities, especially those that will be useful in independent living, employment, communication and other aspects of everyday life. These professionals conduct specialized assessments and make recommendations to instructors regarding the effective use of materials, tools and other equipment in the learning environment. They also work with Vocational Rehabilitation specialists in helping students find opportunities for work after completion of an educational program (Heward & Orlansky, 1992, p. 402).

Case Study . . . Michelle

Michelle is a senior in high school. She is enrolled in the commercial food preparation program. Her goal is to establish her own catering business after graduation. Michelle is also an epileptic. Since she was born, she has experienced tonic-clonic seizures. Before she has a seizure, she experiences an aura, or warning signal, in the form of a ringing sensation in her ears. When the seizure begins, Michelle loses consciousness and has involuntary muscle contractions, violent shaking, irregular breathing, and severe perspiration. Her lips and face turn a slight blue color and she often loses bladder control during the seizure.

Five years ago, her physician prescribed a new medication with which Michelle has had success. She has only had one seizure since beginning this medication. Mr. Rhoades, her commercial foods instructor, knows about Michelle's health disorder. When she enrolled in the program, Mr. Rhoades discussed epilepsy with the health personnel in the district. He learned about what could be done in the classroom and laboratory if Michelle had a seizure. Information about epilepsy and seizures was shared with the class in a general orientation session on safety at the beginning of the semester.

Taking these preventive steps reassures Michelle that if she were to experience a seizure in class, her instructor and classmates would be able to identify the situation and act appropriately.

Learners with Health Impairments in Career and Technical Education Programs

The following are general suggestions for career and technical education instructors who work with these learners with health impairments:

- Work cooperatively with the health team in order to get to know more about the special needs of each learner.
- Use available community agencies and resource personnel (e.g., social workers and itinerant teachers for homebound learners). These resource people can deliver materials, assignments and handouts to learners and often provide remedial instruction.
- When learners do attend school, allow them sufficient time to rest during the day. Cooperative plans can be made with school health personnel. For example, arrangements can be made with the school nurse to allow learners to use the clinic's facilities, an empty classroom, or a vacant office during their study periods to rest.
- Arrange to seat learners in the most convenient place for easy access to necessary facilities (e.g., hall, restrooms, writing board, or laboratory work stations).
- Assess the health problems and abilities (physical, academic, and social) of each learner and relate this information to the exit points and entry-level competencies of the career and technical education program so that necessary modifications can be made. Career and technical education counseling with learners and parents may be needed at this time if severe difficulties arise.
- Identify special materials, equipment, or aids that will adequately meet the needs of each learner as well as local agencies and/or special funds that can help to provide them.
- Allow learners to work at their own pace.
- Individualized instruction and programmed instruction materials are very helpful in planning for learners.
- Tape lectures so that learners can listen to them at home. This helps them keep up with the instructional content of the program.

- Cooperatively assess the stamina and strength requirements involved in the program with support personnel to determine whether the limitations of the learners are too great to allow them to succeed in the program.

LEARNERS WITH SPEECH OR LANGUAGE IMPAIRMENTS

Speech and language disorders refer to problems in communication and related areas such as oral motor function. These delays and disorders range from simple substitutions to the inability to understand or use language or use the oral-motor mechanism for functional speech and feeding. Some causes of speech and language disorders include hearing loss, neurological disorders, brain injury, mental retardation, drug abuse, physical impairments such as cleft lip or palate, and vocal abuse or misuse. Frequently, the causes are unknown.

More than one million of the learners served in the public schools' special education programs in the 1998-99 school year were categorized as having a speech or language impairment. This estimate does not include children who have speech/language problems secondary to other conditions such as deafness. It is estimated that communication disorders (including speech, language, and hearing disorders) affect one of every 10 people in the United States.

Speech disorders refer to difficulties producing speech sounds or problems with voice quality. They might be characterized by an interruption in the flow or rhythm of speech, such as stuttering, which is called dysfluency. Speech disorders may entail problems with the way sounds are formed, called articulation or phonological disorders, or they may entail difficulties with the pitch, volume or quality of the voice. People with speech disorders have trouble using some speech sounds, which can also be a symptom of a delay. They may say, "see" when they mean, "ski" or they may have trouble using other sounds like "l" or "r". Listeners may have trouble understanding what someone with a speech disorder is trying to say. People with voice disorders may have trouble with the way their voices sound.

A language disorder is an impairment in the ability to understand and/or use words in context, both verbally and nonverbally. Some characteristics of language disorders include improper use of words and their meanings, inability to express ideas, inappropriate grammatical patterns, reduced vocabulary, and inability to follow directions. One or a combination of these characteristics may occur in children who are affected by language learning disabilities or developmental language delay. Children may hear or see a word but not be able to understand its meaning. They may have trouble getting others to understand what they are trying to communicate. (National Information Center for Children and Youth with Disabilities, 2001).

Communication Disorders

There are many recognized types of communication disorders and a variety of possible causes. Some speech impairments may be organic in nature. This means that they can be attributed to a specific physical cause such as cleft palate, cerebral palsy, hearing loss, absence of teeth, neurological impairments, and enlarged adenoids.

Most communication disorders are classified as functional. This means they cannot be attributed to a specific physical condition. Their origin is not clearly known. The individual has the physical capability of correctly producing sounds but does not. Two common functional causes are poor speech models (e.g., siblings or parents have articulation problems) or poor speech production habits (children may misarticulate sounds while they are very young and not outgrow their problems due to a "lazy tongue" or lack of motivation to change).

Communication disorders include the following:

1. Articulation disorders–An articulation disorder is an impairment of an individual's ability to produce speech sounds correctly. Articulation is the most common communication disorder among school age children. There are four types of articulation disorders:

- Omissions–The individual omits a sound in all or some words, phrases or sentences (e.g., omitting all "m" sounds from words, phrases, and sentences);
- Substitutions–The individual produces one sound in place of another sound (e.g., saying "punny" instead of "funny") even though they are often certain they have said the correct word and may resist correction;
- Distortion–The individual produces an approximation of the correct sound (e.g., lisping); and
- Omitting–Individuals may omit certain sounds (e.g., dropping consonants from the ends of words, leaving out sounds at times, "cool" for "school").

2. Voice disorders–A voice disorder is any pitch, intensity, or quality characteristic of the voice that is atypical or inappropriate (e.g., a loud voice used all the time.) Examples of voice disorders include the following:

- Problems of respiration–These voice disorders result from abnormal breathing patterns during speech;
- Problems of phonation–These voice disorders are symptoms of difficulty in the voice box that result in faulty sound production (e.g., breathiness, hoarseness, monotone); and
- Problems of resonance–These voice disorders occur in the oral and nasal cavities and are characterized by an impaired quality of sound (e.g., nasal voice).

3. Fluency disorders–Fluency disorders interrupt the natural flow of speech with inappropriate pauses, hesitations, or repetitions. Fluency disorders include the following:

- Stuttering–A communication disorder characterized by behaviors that interfere with forward-moving speech and are considered abnormal by the listener. Stuttering is situational in that it appears to be related to the setting or circumstances of speech. A learner is likely to stutter when talking to the people whose opinions matter most (e.g., parents and teachers) and in situations like being called on to speak in front of others. Most people who stutter are fluent about 95% of the time. A person with a fluency disorder may not stutter at all when singing, talking to a peer, or reciting information in unison with others. Clearly, the reactions and expectations of parents, teachers, and peers have a strong effect on any child's personal and communicative development (Heward & Orlansky, 1992).

4. Language disorders–Language is the set of verbal and nonverbal symbols understood by two or more people. Language disorders are usually classified as either receptive or expressive. A receptive language disorder occurs when an individual is unable to comprehend spoken sentences or to follow a sequence of directions. An expressive language disorder occurs when the individual has a very limited vocabulary, uses incorrect words and phrases, or may communicate only through gestures.

Learners with speech impairments are found in all schools and in all areas of the work force. They have no problems in developing the specific skills necessary for employment. Most people who have a speech impairment have normal intelligence and motor abilities. They may, however, need some help in personal adjustment to learn to cope with their communication problems. See Figure 3-12.

Individuals with speech impairments are usually identified through diagnostic testing by speech clinicians. After the evaluation, the speech specialist develops a plan for assisting the individual in the specific problem areas. Speech therapists and communications specialists are professionals trained to help individuals with their speech impairments. These personnel work with classroom teachers who have learners with speech impairments in their classes. Speech and hearing clinics are also available in many communities and are found in hospitals, clinics, and universities.

Communication specialists are often available in schools to help learners with academic problems associated with speech impairments. These support people can help learners with related academic work necessary to succeed in the career and technical education program.

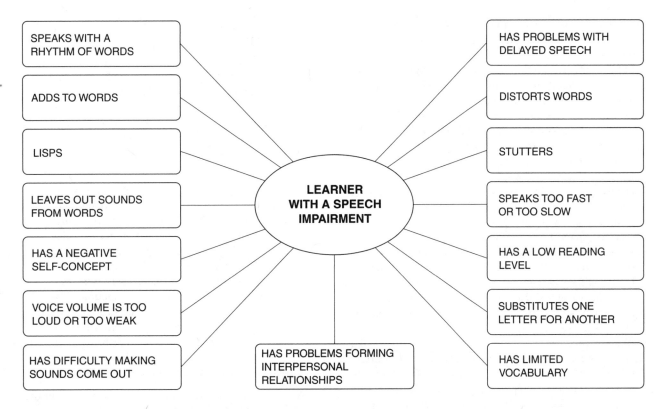

Figure 3-12. An overview of general characteristics that may be demonstrated by individuals with speech impairments.

Learners with Speech or Language Impairments in Career and Technical Education Programs

Following are general suggestions for career and technical education teachers who work with learners with speech impairments:

- Always maintain eye contact with learners when they are having difficulty communicating (e.g., stuttering, delayed speech). This will give them the confidence to complete their message.
- Work cooperatively with the speech therapist and/or communication specialist to determine which techniques are successful in assisting learners to communicate effectively.
- Encourage peer tutoring and small group activities that help to promote positive interpersonal relationships with other learners in the class. Acceptance and improved self-concept can help learners to improve their speech patterns.
- Develop a list of technical terms and vocabulary frequently used in the program. This list should be shared with the speech therapist and/or communication specialist to help these learners become familiar with the terms and feel more comfortable pronouncing them out loud.
- Always allow learners sufficient time to complete their sentences. Do not try to finish their thoughts for them when they have difficulty talking.
- Speech impairments are often associated with a hearing

impairment. Refer individuals who display the characteristics of a speech impairment for a hearing test.
- Speech impairments can often be the result of dental problems. A dental examination can determine whether a condition such as an extreme overbite is the cause of the speech impairment.
- Try not to act uncomfortable when learners are communicating with you. If you appear embarrassed it will make learners uncomfortable and the abnormal speech patterns may increase. For example, signals such as discontinuing eye contact, shifting your position, clearing your throat, or focusing on the floor while the individual is having difficulty delivering a message can be very discouraging.
- Do not force learners to prepare oral presentations or reports for the rest of the class until they are established and feel comfortable in the classroom environment. As learners begin to feel accepted in the class and begin to experience success, they will be able to assume more responsibilities. This will encourage them to speak more openly in class.
- Check reading levels of learners. Many individuals with speech impairments have low reading levels. Revise course materials accordingly and provide for remediation.
- Nod your head while learners are talking to give them support and confidence.
- Model correct sentence structure and grammar for learners so they can follow your example.

- Reinforce correct sound production. If the learner is having difficulty making the "i" sound, verbally reinforce the learner whenever the sound is correctly produced.
- Flash cards can be used to provide an opportunity to practice correct pronunciation of technical and other terms related to the curriculum.
- Data can be collected regarding the learner's speech problem. Successful therapy depends on a record of how often the learner is using language during the time spent in classroom and laboratory activities.
- Reinforce learners when they use their voice correctly.
- Devise a simple cuing system to help remind learners that the volume of their voice is inappropriate.
- Help learners with laryngitis by insuring that they observe complete vocal rest in class.
- Avoid behaviors that indicate discomfort with the learners' speech problem. These behaviors can include holding the breath, shifting position frequently, and clearing the throat while the learner exhibits speech problems. These increase the anxiety level of the learners and eventually contribute to increased dysfluent behavior.
- When particularly difficult activities are identified, the instructor can reduce speaking demands on the learner. For example, if the learner has a high rate of speech problems when speaking in front of the entire class, the instructor can decrease demands on the learner to speak in such large group situations. However, some expectations should be maintained for the learner's verbal participation in classroom activities. Over a period of time, as the pattern of speech problems decreases, the demands on the learner can be gradually increased.

Case Study . . . Bryan

Bryan is 17 years old and is enrolled in a heating, air conditioning and refrigeration program. Bryan was very shy and withdrawn when he first entered the program. Mr. Porter, the career and technical education instructor, knows that Bryan has a problem with stuttering and delayed speech. Because of his speech problem, Bryan is hesitant to talk to classmates or participate in group laboratory exercises and cooperative learning activities in the classroom.

Miss Larsen, the district communication specialist, works closely with Bryan and Mr. Porter to help make the placement in the program a successful one. She spends several hours a week with Bryan, both in individual speech therapy sessions and in the career and technical classroom. Miss Larsen also works with Mr. Porter to help him develop appropriate techniques to use with Bryan.

Mr. Porter now feels much more comfortable communicating with Bryan. Gradually, Bryan is gaining confidence in himself because he has successfully completed his assignments. This has helped his stuttering and delayed speech and prompted him to participate in several small group activities.

LEARNERS WITH SPECIFIC LEARNING DISABILITIES

The term *learning disability* (LD) describes a neurobiological disorder in which a person's brain works or is structured differently than the norm. These differences interfere with a person's ability to think and remember. Learning disabilities can affect a person's ability to speak, listen, read, write, spell, reason, recall, organize information, and do mathematics.

A specific learning disability is defined in the IDEA as follows:

> A disorder in one or more of the basic psychological processes involved in understanding or in using spoken or written language, which may manifest itself in an imperfect ability to listen, think, speak, read, write, spell or to do mathematical calculations...Learning disabilities include such conditions as perceptual disabilities, brain injury, minimal brain dysfunction, dyslexia, and developmental aphasia. Learning disabilities do not include learning problems that are primarily the result of visual, hearing, or motor disabilities; mental retardation; or environmental, cultural, or economic disadvantage.

According to the ERIC Clearinghouse on Disabilities and Gifted Education (1999)

- Fifteen percent of the U.S. population, or one in seven Americans, has some type of learning disability, according to the National Institutes of Health.
- Difficulty with basic reading and language skills is the most common learning disability. As many as 80% of learners with learning disabilities have reading problems.
- Learning disabilities often run in families.
- Learning disabilities should not be confused with other disabilities such as mental retardation, autism, deafness, blindness, and behavioral disorders. None of these conditions are learning disabilities. In addition, they should not be confused with lack of educational opportunities like frequent changes of schools or attendance problems. Also, children who are learning English do not necessarily have a learning disability. Attention disorders, such as attention deficit/hyperactivity disorder (ADHD) and learning disabilities often occur at the same time, but the two disorders are not the same.

Many different estimates of the number of children with learning disabilities have appeared in the literature (ranging from 1% to 30% of the general population). Differences in estimates perhaps reflect variations in the definition. In 1987, the Interagency Committee on Learning Disabilities concluded that 5% to 10% is a reasonable estimate of the percentage of persons affected by learning disabilities. The U.S. Department of Education (2000) reported that in the 1998-99 school year, over 2.8 million children with learning disabilities received special education and related services. Learning disabilities are characterized by a significant difference in the learner's achievement in some areas, as compared to overall intelligence. (National Information Center for Children and Youth with Disabilities, 2001).

Because learning disabilities cannot be seen, they often go undetected. Recognizing a learning disability is difficult because the severity and characteristics vary. A learning disability can't be cured or fixed; it is a lifelong issue. With the right support and intervention, however, learners with learning disabilities can succeed in school and go on to successful, often distinguished careers later in life. Parents can help learners with learning disabilities achieve success by encouraging their strengths, knowing their weaknesses, understanding the educational system, working with professionals and learning about strategies for dealing with specific difficulties.

Researchers have not been able to identify any one single cause that accounts for all learning disabilities. Some researchers believe that learning disabilities result from complications that occur before, during, or shortly after birth. Males are more likely to have a learning disability than females. The ratio of males to females may be as high as 10 to 1. Some researchers believe that the unborn or newborn male is more susceptible to injury, as is evident in the higher death rate among unborn and newborn males. Physicians, teachers, psychiatrists, and psychologists cannot agree on the exact cause of learning disabilities. They do agree that these individuals have slightly, moderately, or severely disorganized nervous systems.

With learning disabilities, a specific learning passage (e.g., auditory, visual, psychomotor) is partially blocked. This condition almost always affects academic performance in the areas of reading, writing, spelling, math, etc. Individuals with learning disabilities may have average or above-average intelligence but are often slower in achieving basic skills. These learners often have emotional and behavioral problems because they have so much potential but have suffered so many failures and frustrations in school.

Many learners with learning disabilities realize that they have difficulty performing tasks that other learners accomplish easily. See Figure 3-13. Many of these learners also experience failure at home, in school, among friends, and in other areas of life. These and other negative experiences can affect them and cause mental stress, emotional difficulties, personality problems, and can lead to overall feelings of worthlessness.

Many learners with learning disabilities:
- display learning problems in academic areas (although performance may vary from one subject to another);
- have poor coordination;
- display unpredictable behavior;
- seem lazy at times;
- have few or no study skills;
- do not know how to manage time;
- do not know how to organize school work;
- give up easily;

- explode when frustrated;
- panic if demanded to do something on the spot;
- volunteer information at their own pace, but do poorly on question and answer skills;
- are disorganized (e.g., often loses papers, books and other belongings);
- arrive at or leave classes late;
- tend to lose homework or hand it in late;
- do sloppy schoolwork;
- have trouble understanding and following directions;
- easily forget directions;
- work very slowly or rush without thinking;
- daydream and often lose focus on tasks;
- have perceptual problems such as visual, auditory, and psychomotor;
- are impulsive;
- display emotional insecurity;
- are hyperactive;
- have a short attention span; and
- display slow language development (William Gladden Foundation, 1989).

Overall, learners with learning disabilities have average or above average intelligence. They are usually capable of performing well, but their school records are usually poor. Many times their grades in one class differ greatly from their grades in another. These learners are often described as having a "hidden" disability because they may be able to cover up their deficiencies by emphasizing their strong points. They learn in different ways from their peers. Their main problem can be described as a great discrepancy between their ability level and their performance level. Gaps are usually most evident in reading and math. These learners often have low motivation and a general lack of interest in schoolwork. Problems associated with learning disabilities are found in the areas of behavior, perception, motor activities and language development.

Behavioral or Emotional Problems

Individuals with learning disabilities often have behavioral or emotional problems and are frustrated because their disability makes it difficult for them to succeed in school. Individuals with learning disabilities may exhibit the following characteristics:
- inappropriate reactions to frustrating situations
- inability to stay with one task or activity
- inability to develop positive peer relationships
- hyperactive (overly active) or hypoactive (slow to respond) behavior
- inability to shift from one task to another with ease
- difficulty developing appropriate problem-solving skills
- lack of emotional stability
- short attention span
- low self-concept
- insecurity
- overdependence on others

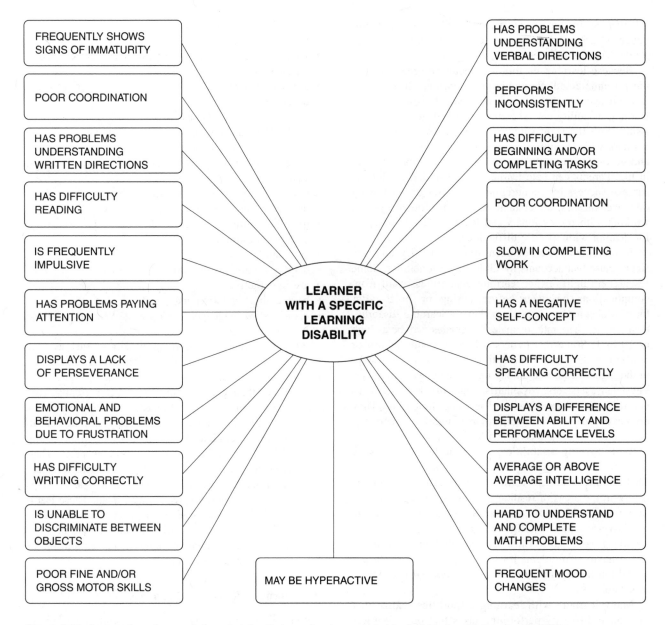

Figure 3-13. An overview of general characteristics that may be demonstrated by individuals with learning disabilities.

Perceptual Problems

In learning, the important senses are visual and auditory. Input does not refer to the physical condition of the eye or ear, but rather to how the brain processes what is heard or seen. The term used for this central process of perceiving the world is perception. Individuals with learning disabilities may have perceptual problems in which their central nervous system is affected. They have problems identifying, discriminating, and interpreting information. They also have definite weak and strong learning styles and must be taught through their strong learning mode in or-

der to profit from instruction. Problems in perception are usually visual and/or auditory. Learners with learning disabilities see and hear things in a distorted manner because their brain does not have accurate perceptions.

A learner with problems in visual perception may not be able to discriminate visual stimuli accurately (e.g., substitutes "m" for "w"), cannot discriminate between an object and its background (e.g., charts, words on a page), and may not be able to recall previously presented visual stimuli. Specific characteristics include the following:
• difficulty recognizing letters and figures
• problems with left-to-right progression

- reversing letters in words (e.g., "was" for "saw")
- difficulty reading and comprehending written directions
- difficulty interpreting words (for example, the word "engine" might appear to be "sncinc")
- difficulty remembering what was read
- difficulty judging distance or size
- looks up frequently when copying from the board
- avoids close desk work
- can follow verbal instructions but has difficulty with written instructions
- forgets things that have been seen (e.g., demonstrations in class, models)
- repeats or omits words when reading and confuses words that look alike

Learners with difficulty in auditory perception may not be able to discriminate between background noise and the main sound source. These learners may also have problems understanding spoken language because of difficulty discriminating between letters, words, and sentences. Auditory recall may also be poor. Specific characteristics include the following:
- difficulty recognizing sounds
- difficulty understanding verbal directions
- difficulty remembering what was heard
- difficulty comprehending a series of directions
- difficulty remembering what was discussed in class
- seems overly attentive when verbal instructions are given
- gives inappropriate or wrong answers to clear questions
- comprehends better on a one-to-one level
- cannot follow oral directions and frequently asks that instructions be repeated;
- cannot distinguish between similar sounding words or numbers (e.g., tired-tried, 689-986).

Individuals who have aphasia exhibit many of these characteristics. Aphasia is an auditory disability, usually the result of brain damage, that affects the ability either to send out or take in clear messages. Aphasia involves misinterpreting what is heard. Individuals with aphasia have no difficulty reading someone else's notes, but find it hard to take notes themselves because they cannot be sure that what they hear is correct.

Learners with Dyslexia

Dyslexia is a learning disorder which causes difficulties in reading, writing and spelling. The word "dyslexia" actually means "not good (dys) at language (lexis)." The problem is commonly seen in letter or word reversals, or mirror images in reading or writing. Dyslexia tends to be more common in males than in females, with a ratio of about three or four to one. About one child in 30 has dyslexia. Researchers have long been investigating a genetic link to this learning disability, experienced by 3% to up to 15% of the population.

A variety of characteristics is often displayed by learners with dyslexia:

- anxiety about testing
- behavioral problems in school due to frustration
- difficulty in recalling events (poor sequencing in time)
- difficulty learning to read and write (despite normal or above average intelligence)
- hyperactivity
- letter reversals (normal in young children, but not outgrown in individuals with dyslexia)
- mirror writing (e.g., "m" may be seen as "w"; letters, words or sentences may be reversed or backwards; whole words or sentences may be seen completely upside-down, as well as backwards as would be viewed if one held a mirror beneath a written sentence)
- other dyslexics in family
- poor handwriting
- poor left/right discrimination (spatial disorientation)
- poor spelling
- unusually fast speech

Parents, teachers, psychologists, and specialists should work together to assist learners with dyslexia by using the following strategies as they are appropriate:
- Allow time for questions and discussions. This technique helps to clarify and reinforces concepts.
- Allow the use of a tape recorder in class.
- Arrange for other learners to share their class notes, allowing the learner with dyslexia to concentrate on listening in class.
- Explain procedures in a step-by-step method.
- Highlight important words. This strategy allows learners to locate the main ideas in a jumble of writing and to memorize important concepts.
- Provide overviews of units of learning to help learners to organize information and materials.
- Read material out loud that is also presented visually for learners who have difficulty processing visual material.
- Use different colors to separate words or numbers. Colors may serve to separate and distinguish words or letters from each other.
- Verbally describe charts, graphs and diagrams. Symbolic representations can be as confusing as writing.
- Allow extra time to complete exams.
- Allow the use of a calculator so learners can deal with one digit at a time. Numbers or digits are just like writing and may be jumbled.
- Allow the use of a typewriter or computer as handwriting can be a struggle.
- Do not use computer-scored answer sheets in testing. The lines of squares, circles or dots can jump around on the page.
- Give partial credit for work completed.
- Permit the use of a dictionary for tests. Learners spend so much time trying to figure out how to spell a word that they cannot put full effort into answering questions.
- Put less emphasis on grammar and punctuation.
- Use oral instead of written exams (William Gladden Foundation, 1990).

Case Study . . . Jerry

Jerry is 16 years old and is enrolled in the building trades program. Mr. Grange, the career and technical education instructor, noticed that Jerry performed inconsistently in class. Some days he would be inattentive and uninterested in classroom activities. On those days Jerry would not listen to directions and would be unorganized when working on assignments. On other days, however, he would be attentive and work well. Jerry would frequently ask questions during class demonstrations and discussions and show leadership during small group verbal activities. He reads several grade levels below his grade placement in school. His spelling is poor and his handwriting is hard to read. He has problems reading, comprehending, and completing math problems. However, he easily understands concepts when they are presented verbally in class.

Recently, Mr. Grange met with Mrs. Powell, the special education teacher who works with learners with learning disabilities. Mr. Grange learned that Jerry has above average intelligence but has problems with visual perception. His most effective learning style is through auditory methods.

Mr. Grange, Mrs. Powell, and Jerry are now working cooperatively in planning his instructional program. Mr. Grange is using appropriate teaching and remediation methods to meet Jerry's learning style preference. Mrs. Powell is working with Jerry outside of class to help with related academics. Jerry has been asked to run for office in SkillsUSA-VICA, the career and technical student organization that Mr. Grange advises. This experience should help Jerry develop his natural leadership abilities and raise his self-confidence.

Motor Activity Problems

Individuals with learning disabilities may have problems with activities that involve hands-on or motor involvement. Specific characteristics include the following:

- lack of balance
- awkwardness when completing tasks
- lack of coordination
- poor gross and/or fine motor abilities
- difficulty telling the difference between left and right (orientation problems)
- saying or writing the same thing repeatedly
- poor tactile discrimination
- inaccuracy in reaching for and grasping objects
- writing or drawing
- slow to finish written work—the finished product is sloppy, with heavily drawn letters, either very small or very large
- inability to organize with no pattern in keeping a notebook or filing papers
- no definite hand preference but uses one hand and then the other

Language Development Problems

Individuals with learning disabilities may have problems in language development, expressing ideas, and putting words in correct sequential order. They may have limited verbal speech patterns, use poor grammar and poor sentence structure, have difficulty comprehending the concept of time (today, yesterday, tomorrow); and have difficulty putting concepts or thoughts into words.

Learning Styles

Individuals with learning disabilities have problems processing information during the learning process. Once received, information must be placed in the correct order (sequencing), understood in the context in which it is used (abstraction) and integrated with all other information being processed (organized). These problems may occur with either visual or auditory input. Therefore, instructors should be aware of the following difficulties that these learners often face during the learning process:

- Sequencing–Learners with learning disabilities might read or hear information and understand it. But, in retelling the same information, they may confuse the sequence of thoughts or events (e.g., starting in the middle, going to the beginning, and then to the end). Spelling errors in written work are common. All the letters may be in the words, but they are not in the proper sequence. Learners might be able to memorize a sequence of steps and repeat it in order, but may have difficulty using the sequence (e.g., they have to go all the way back to the beginning of the sequence every time you ask them a question about one of the elements or steps).
- Abstraction–Most people understand the meaning of some words or phrases based on how the words are used and can differentiate if a word has more than one meaning based on how the word is used (e.g., a "battery" in a car versus a "battery" of tests being administered). Learners with learning disabilities appear to follow the literal meaning of a word and may become very confused.
- Organization–Some learners can process separate pieces of information in isolation but have difficulty integrating the pieces into a whole picture. They might answer the questions at the end of the chapter but be unable to tell you what the chapter was about. Their lockers are a mess. Their notebooks are crammed with papers in the wrong place. Their lives are disorganized (Silver, 1989, p. 4).

Individuals with learning disabilities should be taught through their strongest learning modes. Although they are capable of learning, many have difficulty learning through traditional teaching methods. The strong learning style must be identified for each individual learner. Some learners learn best using a visual approach, others should have instruction delivered through auditory instruction. Still others need to become involved in the learning process through hands-on application. When appropriate teaching techniques are utilized learners will learn effectively.

Learners with Attention Deficit/Hyperactivity Disorder

Attention deficit/hyperactivity disorder (AD/HD) is a neuro-biological-based developmental disability estimated to affect between 3-5% of the school age population. The exact cause is unknown. Scientific evidence suggests that the disorder is genetically transmitted in many cases and results from a chemical imbalance or deficiency in certain neurotransmitters, chemicals that help the brain regulate behavior.

AD/HD is a condition that can make it hard for a person to sit still, control behavior, and pay attention. These difficulties usually begin before the person is seven years old. However, these behaviors may not be noticed until the child is older. See Figure 3-14.

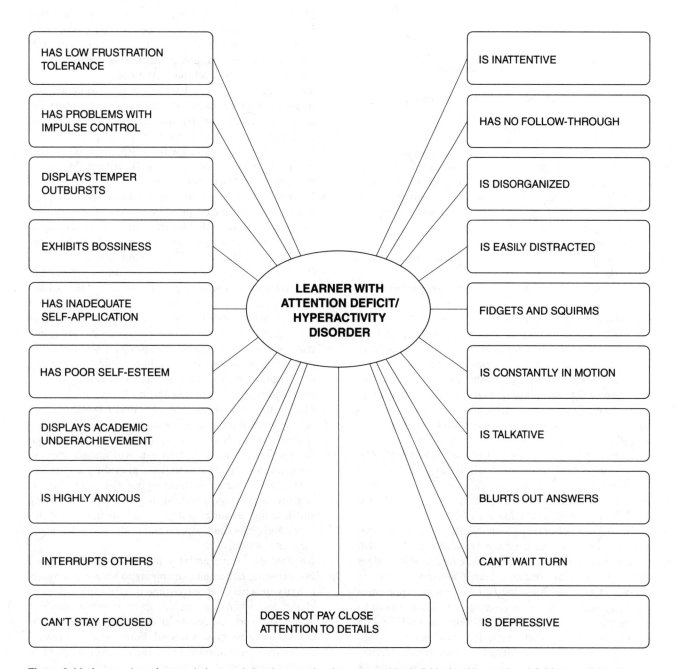

Figure 3-14. An overview of general characteristics that may be demonstrated by individuals with attention deficit/hyperactivity disorder.

Depending on the individual's age and developmental stage, parents and teachers may see low frustration tolerance, temper outbursts, bossiness, difficulty in following rules, disorganization, rejection, poor self-esteem, academic underachievement, and inadequate self-application.

Many learners with ADHD now may qualify for special education services under the "Other Health Impairment" category within the IDEA. The IDEA defines other health impairments as

> having limited strength, vitality or alertness, including a heightened alertness to environmental stimuli, that results in limited alertness with respect to the educational environment, that is due to chronic or acute health problems such as asthma, attention deficit disorder or attention deficit hyperactivity disorder, diabetes, epilepsy, a heart condition, hemophilia, lead poisoning, leukemia, nephritis, rheumatic fever, and sickle cells anemia, and adversely affects a child's educational performance.

The AD/HD diagnosis is made on the basis of observable behavioral symptoms in multiple settings. This means that the person doing the evaluation must use multiple sources to collect the information needed. A proper AD/HD diagnosis evaluation includes the following elements:
- a thorough medical and family history
- a physical examination
- interviews with the parents, the learner, and the learner's teacher(s)
- behavior rating scales completed by parents and teacher(s)
- observation of the learner
- a variety of psychological tests to measure IQ and social and emotional adjustment, as well as to indicate the presence of specific learning disabilities.

Generally, AD/HD will affect the learner in the performance areas of starting tasks, staying on task, completing tasks, making transitions, interacting with others, following through on directions, producing work at consistently normal levels, and organizing multistep tasks.

Researchers estimate that half of the learners with AD/HD will be able to perform to their ability levels without special educational services, provided the disorder is recognized, understood, and curriculum adjustments to the regular program of instruction are made.

The majority of children with AD/HD who require special education services (approximately 35% to 40%) will receive them through combined placements, which might include the regular education classroom with or without in-class support and the resource room. Support personnel are likely to be used as case managers and consultants to regular education teachers. Tips for educators working with learners who have AD/HD include the following:
- Figure out what specific things are hard for the learner. For example, one learner with AD/HD may have trouble starting a task, while another may have trouble ending one task and starting the next. Each learner needs different help.
- Post rules, schedules, and assignments. Clear rules and routines will help a learner with AD/HD. Have set times for specific tasks. Call attention to changes in schedules.
- Show the learner how to use an assignment book and a daily schedule. Also teach study skills and learning strategies, and reinforce these regularly.
- Help the learner channel his or her physical activity (e.g., let the learner do some work standing up or at the board). Provide regularly scheduled breaks.
- Make sure directions are given step by step and that the learner is following the directions. Give directions both verbally and in writing. Many learners with AD/HD also benefit from doing the steps as separate tasks.
- Let the learner do work on a computer.
- Work together with the learner's parents to create and implement an educational plan tailored to meet the learner's needs. Regularly share information about how the learner is doing at home and at school.
- Have high expectations for the learner, but be willing to try new ways of doing things. Be patient. Maximize the learner's chances for success.
- Place the learner with teachers who are positive, upbeat, highly organized problem-solvers. Teachers who use praise and rewards liberally and who are willing to go the extra mile to help learners succeed can be enormously beneficial to the learner with AD/HD.
- Provide the learner with a structured and predictable environment by displaying rules, posting daily schedules and assignments, calling attention to schedule changes, setting specific times for specific tasks, designing a quiet work space for use upon request, seating the child with positive peer models, planning academic subjects for morning hours, providing regularly scheduled and frequent breaks, and using attention-getting devices (e.g., secret signals, color codes, etc.).
- Modify the curriculum. In many cases, AD/HD learners benefit from the less is more maxim. If the learner can demonstrate proficiency in 10 problems, do not assign 20. Curriculum modification can also include mixing high and low interest activities, providing computerized learning materials, simplifying and increasing visual presentations, teaching organization and study skills, using learning strategies such as mnemonic devices and links, and using visual references for auditory instruction.
- Channel excessive activity into acceptable avenues. For example, rather than attempting to reduce a learner's activity, teachers can encourage directed movement in classrooms when it is not disruptive or allow standing during seatwork, especially at the end of a task. Teachers can use activity as a reward. For example, to reward a learner's appropriate behavior or improvement, a teacher might allow the learner to run an errand, clean

the board, organize the teachers' desk, or arrange the chairs in the room. Teachers can also use active responses in instruction. Teaching activities that encourage active responses such as talking, moving, organizing, or working at the board are helpful to many learners with AD/HD, as are activities such as writing in a diary or painting.

- Give the child substitute verbal or motor responses to make while waiting. This might include teaching the child how to continue on easier parts of a task (or a substitute task) while waiting for the teacher's help. When possible, allow daydreaming or planning while the child waits. For example, the child might be allowed to doodle or play with clay while waiting, or might be guided to underline or write directions or relevant information. When inability to wait becomes impatience or bossiness, encourage leadership. Do not assume that impulsive statements or behavior are aggressive in intent. Suggest alternative ways or behaviors (e.g., line reader, paper passer). It may be important to cue a learner when an upcoming task will be difficult and extra control will be needed.
- Decrease the length of the task or activity when failure to sustain attention to it is evident. There are many ways to do this, including breaking one task into smaller parts to be completed at different times or giving fewer spelling words or math problems. Make tasks interesting. Teachers can heighten interest in tasks by allowing learners to work with partners or in small groups, by using an overhead projector, and by alternating high and low interest activities. Make a game out of checking work, and use games to overlearn rote material.
- For noncompliance and failure to complete tasks, increase the choice and specific interest of tasks for the child. Teachers may allow the learner with AD/HD a

limited choice of tasks, topics, and activities. Teachers may also find it useful to determine which activities the learner prefers and to use these as incentives. Make sure tasks fit within the learner's learning abilities and preferred response style. Learners are more likely to complete tasks when they are allowed to respond in various ways (e.g., typewriter, computer, on tape) and when the difficulty of assignments varies (i.e., not all tasks are equally difficult). It is important to make sure that disorganization is not the reason the learner is failing to complete tasks.

- When difficulty at the beginning of tasks is evident, increase the structure of tasks and highlight important parts. This includes encouraging note-taking, giving directions in writing as well as orally, stating the standards of acceptable work as specifically as possible, and pointing out how tasks are structured (e.g., topic sentences, headers, table of contents).
- For completing assignments on time, increase the learner's use of lists and assignment organizers (notebooks, folders), write assignments on the board, and make sure that the learner has copied them. Establish routines to place and retrieve commonly used objects such as books, assignments, and clothes. Pocket folders are helpful here; new work can be placed on one side and completed work on the other. Parents can be encouraged to establish places for certain things (books, homework) at home. Learners can be encouraged to organize their desk or locker with the labels/places for certain items. Teach the learner that, upon leaving one place for another, the question "Do I have everything I need?" should be asked. (National Information Center for Children and Youth with Disabilities, 1999). See Figure 3-15. See Appendix.

ACCOMMODATIONS FOR DEALING WITH SPECIFIC BEHAVIORS OF STUDENTS WITH ATTENTION DEFICIT/HYPERACTIVITY DISORDER

The accommodations listed below are intended to be examples for schools to use in developing a plan to address a student's needs.

When You See This Behavior	Try This Accommodation
1. Difficulty following a plan (has high aspirations, but lacks follow through); sets out to get straight A's, but ends up with F's (sets unrealistic goals)	Assist student in setting long-range goals; break the goal into realistic parts. Use a questioning strategy with the student: Ask, "What do you need to be able to do this?" Keep asking that question until the student has reached an obtainable goal. Have student set clear time lines, and establish how much time he or she needs to accomplish each step. (Monitor student's progress frequently.)

Adapted from: Utah State Office of Education. (2002). *Section 504/ADA Guidelines for Educators.* Salt Lake City, UT: Author.

Figure 3-15. Accommodations for individuals with attention deficit/hyperactivity disorder.

Learners with Learning Disabilities in Career and Technical Education Programs

Some general suggestions for career and technical education teachers who work with learners with learning disabilities include:

- Identify the strong learning style preferences for each learner. Special education teachers and other support personnel can provide essential information about learner's styles and suggested instructional strategies.
- Use visuals and demonstrations as often as possible when explaining new concepts. This especially helps learners who are visual learners. Provide hands-on activities to reinforce classroom instruction and discussions.
- Use concrete examples when possible. Abstract concepts confuse and frustrate these learners.
- Provide learners with a lecture outline or advanced organizer of what you will be covering in class. They can review this material before and after it is presented and use it to take notes during class. It can also be an aid to teachers, parents, peers, and/or volunteers who reinforce program content with the learner outside of class.
- Allow learners to tape record assignments if they have visual perception problems.
- Allow learners to take tests orally. Having support personnel, peers or volunteer read test questions out loud and taping or writing the responses is a highly successful technique. Learners can also answer questions on a computer after they have been read out loud.
- Present new information in small amounts. Learners become confused and frustrated if confronted with too much new material at one time. Make sure they overlearn one concept before going on to the next.
- Make sure that writing assignments are relevant to the content of the program. Writing is often difficult for these learners and "busy work" overwhelms them and makes them react inappropriately.
- Allow learners longer time to complete assignments.
- List assignments in steps. Learners have a difficult time remembering a series of directions. They can follow directions more easily when given one at a time.
- Use task analysis to lower the frustration level of these learners. It allows them to progress at their own pace and offers immediate feedback after each step.
- Use learner-teacher contracts to identify specific tasks or assignments along with corresponding time limitations. In this manner, learners know exactly what is expected of them and how long they have to complete assigned work.
- Use programmed instruction materials and individualized instruction techniques. These formats can be delivered through computer-aided instruction.
- Alert support personnel to the basic academic skills the learner will need to succeed in the career and technical education program.
- Develop a list of technical terms and key words, along with definitions, the learner will need to know. Share this list with support personnel, peer tutors, and parents.

- Encourage learners to think their statements through before speaking.
- Perform tasks and talk through the steps while the learner observes. Then they can perform the same task under the direction of the instructor, volunteer or peer leader. Finally, they can demonstrate the task independently.
- Stress active participation in small group activities (e.g., cooperative learning).
- Make sure all safety signs, rules, labels and directions are clearly displayed.
- Use progress charts and provide immediate feedback.
- Involve as many senses as possible in planning instructional activities.
- Provide some visual clues to problem-solving tasks and problems.
- Use lists, not paragraphs, to provide written directions.
- Have learners paraphrase or repeat important information in their own words.
- Introduce vocabulary words before teaching. Underline key words and use a highlighter on important sections of written material.
- Modify evaluation techniques when necessary (e.g., open book tests, small group tests, oral reports, and videotaped activities).
- Be aware that many adolescents and adults with learning disabilities have a chance to develop coping strategies to compensate for their disability. They may be able to hide such problem areas as hyperactivity, memory and attention problems, and the inability to read. Do not be fooled by these compensation strategies. By the time these learners reach high school or postsecondary situations, they are likely to have a reduced self-image, poor self-concept, and lack of motivation.

LEARNERS WITH SEVERE AND/OR MULTIPLE DISABILITIES

People with severe disabilities are those who traditionally have been labeled as having severe to profound mental retardation. These people require ongoing, extensive support in more than one major life activity in order to participate in integrated community settings and enjoy the quality of life available to people with fewer or no disabilities. They frequently have additional disabilities, including movement difficulties, sensory losses, and behavioral problems.

In the 1998-99 school year, the states reported to the U.S. Department of Education that they were providing services to 107,591 learners with multiple disabilities (U.S. Department of Education, 2000). Children and youth with severe or multiple disabilities may exhibit a wide range of characteristics, depending on the combination and severity of disabilities and the person's age. Some of these characteristics may include

- limited speech or communication;
- difficulty in basic physical mobility;
- tendency to forget skills through disuse;

- trouble generalizing skills in different situations; and/or
- a need for support in major life activities (e.g., domestic, leisure, community, career and technical).

A variety of medical problems may accompany severe disabilities. Examples include seizures, sensory loss, hydrocephalus, and scoliosis. These conditions should be considered when establishing school services. A multidisciplinary team consisting of the learner's parents, educational specialists and medical specialists in the areas in which the individual demonstrates problems should work together to plan and coordinate necessary services.

Educational implications include the following:

- Early intervention programs, preschool, and educational programs with the appropriate support services are important to children with severe disabilities. Educators, physical therapists, occupational therapists, and speech-language pathologists are all members of the team that may provide services, along with others, as needed for each individual. Assistive technology, such as computers and augmentative/alternative communication devices and techniques, may provide valuable instructional assistance in the educational programs for learners with severe/multiple disabilities.
- In order to effectively address the considerable needs of individuals with severe and/or multiple disabilities, educational programs need to incorporate a variety of components, including language and social skill development. Related services are of great importance, and the appropriate therapists (such as speech and language, occupational, physical, behavioral and recreational) need to work closely with classroom teachers and parents. Best practices indicate that related services are best offered during the natural routine of the school and community, rather than by removing the learner from class for isolated therapy.
- Classroom arrangements must take into consideration learners' needs for medications, special diets, or special equipment. Adaptive aids and equipment enable learners to increase their range of functioning. The use of computers, augmentative/alternative communication systems, communication boards, head sticks, and adaptive switches are some of the technological advances that enable learners with severe disabilities to participate more fully in integrated settings.
- Integration/inclusion with nondisabled peers is another component of the educational setting. Research shows that attending the same school and participating in the same activities as their nondisabled peers is crucial to the development of social skills and friendships for children and youth with severe disabilities. Traditionally, children with severe disabilities have been educated in center-based, segregated schools. Recently, however, many schools are successfully educating children with severe disabilities in the neighborhood school within the regular classroom, making sure that appropriate support services and curriculum modifications are available.

The benefits to inclusion are being seen to benefit not only those with disabilities but also their nondisabled peers and the professionals who work with them.

- Modifications to the regular curriculum require collaboration on the part of the special educator, the regular educator, and other specialists involved in the learner's program. Community-based instruction is also an important characteristic of educational programming, particularly as learners grow older and where increasing time is spent in the community. School-to-work transition planning and working toward job placement in integrated, competitive settings are important to a learner's success and long-range quality of life.
- With the current vocational rehabilitation legislation and the practice of supported employment, schools are using school-to-work transition planning and working toward job placement in integrated, competitive settings rather than sheltered employment and day activity centers.

THE SPECIAL EDUCATION PROCESS

Special education is instruction designed for learners who require some degree of modification in their educational programs because of intellectual, emotional, sensory, or physical impairments. Modifications may include special curricular materials, specialized teaching strategies or behavior management techniques, and specially designed equipment or facilities. Learners with mild disabilities ranging from moderate to severe in nature require placement in special settings. All special learners, regardless of the type or degree of disability, share certain rights and needs, including

- the right to a free and appropriate public education;
- the right to an IEP specifying the learner's unique needs and the special education and related services the learner is to receive; and
- the need to have cognitive, linguistic, academic, and social/emotional characteristics considered and appropriate environmental modifications or adaptations made.

In any school, a portion of the learner body will experience learning and/or behavioral difficulties. However, not all of these learners are disabled and require special education services. The referral process is intended to define the learner's difficulties, document classroom modifications and/or other strategies attempted to correct the problem(s) and the success of those actions, and identify those learners for whom regular education interventions, modifications and/or other strategies have been unsuccessful. For these learners the learning and/or behavioral difficulty persists in spite of the interventions. These learners may require special education and related services.

A series of steps is typically necessary in order for the learner to receive special educational services. When such problems become evident, the parent or teacher can make a referral to the local school district's learner evaluation team and request an evaluation. An evaluation is performed to determine if the learner does indeed have a disability according to eligibility criteria set forth in state and federal law and if that disability is adversely affecting the learner's educational performance. If so, the learner may then be found eligible for special education services.

When a learner is found eligible for special education, the parents collaborate with school personnel to develop an IEP to address specific problems and unique learning needs, as well as strengths. Strategies to improve social and behavioral problems are also addressed in the IEP. After specifying the nature of the learner's special needs, the IEP team, including parents, determines what types of services are appropriate and whether these services will be delivered in the regular education classroom or elsewhere (such as the resource room or through individualized attention). See Figure 3-16.

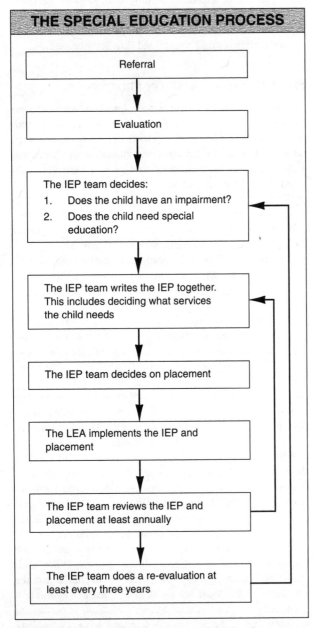

Figure 3-16. The referral process in special education.

Each state board of education has developed specific policies and procedures for referring, screening, assessing, and placing learners with disabilities according to the federal mandates established in the IDEA and Section 504 of the Rehabilitation Act. Similarly, each local education agency must follow the guidelines mandated by the state to evaluate and place learners with disabilities in educational programs to meet their needs. The following general steps should be followed:

1. Initial referral–A referral should be made to identify a learner, often in a regular education program, thought to have a learning problem resulting from a physical, mental, or emotional disability. The objective of this initial referral is to diagnose and evaluate the needs of the learner so that an appropriate educational program can be developed along with the necessary support services needed for success in school.

   The referral can be made from a number of sources, including teachers, counselors, administrators, judicial officers, social workers, parents/guardians, and physicians. The referring party should provide written documentation of the learner's strengths and limitations. Specific observations made while the learner is involved in classroom, laboratory, job, home or community activities should be made in writing for future reference.

   Teachers should keep a few important points in mind when preparing to refer a learner for assessment. A daily description of the learner's behavior can be helpful. Observation should continue for a period of time beyond one or two days to make certain that the behavior is not a result of a temporary problem. The teacher should note how the learner's behavior differs from that of other learners in the class. This information should be described accurately so that biases can be avoided. A positive attitude on the part of the teacher toward the learner should be maintained, since the expectations of the teacher usually significantly influence the outcomes of strategies that are prescribed for the learner in the program.

   In observing and recording learner behavior for referral and evaluation purposes, the following considerations should be addressed:
   - the severity of the behavior
   - the frequency of the behavior
   - the length of time that the behavior has been observed (e.g., one week, one month, several months)
   - the setting(s) where the behavior(s) occurs (e.g., classroom, laboratory, small group, large group, independent activities, social settings, a variety of settings)
   - how the behavior differs from the peer group and/or career and technical education program rules
   - how the behavior is interfering with the learning process.

2. Parent/guardian notification–Parents or guardians must be notified of the referral. The notification must be made in writing in the primary language spoken in the home.

The notification should include the following:

- reason for the referral
- explanation of the evaluation process
- statement of parent/guardian right to access all school records concerning the learner

The letter should encourage the parent/guardian to contact the school if there are any questions about the contents. Written permission is requested to allow the school to evaluate the learner to determine his/her unique needs. The parent/guardian has the right to attend the evaluation session(s). The letter should also ensure that the parent/guardian will be informed of the results of the evaluation process within a specified period of time. All signed parent/guardian permission forms should be kept on file.

3. Learner evaluation process–A comprehensive diagnostic evaluation is completed by a team of specialists. The general assessment areas for learner evaluation should include the following:

- educational information (initial referral forms, observation reports, intelligence tests, achievement tests, review of school records, aptitude scores, teacher reports and review of speech, language, and motor development)
- social history (information about the family background as well as the current home environment; usually provided by the social worker or a social agency)
- medical information (a comprehensive physical examination, vision test, hearing test, and review of past medical records and effects of any prescribed medication)

A decision about the educational placement and programming for a learner with a disability must be based on the results of several tests rather than on a single test. In this way, a thorough assessment is assured rather than a narrowly focused decision. When assessment procedures and specific instruments are selected, necessary adjustments must be made for learners who have different cultural or linguistic backgrounds. Testing situations, by law, cannot discriminate against such learners because of these differences. Finally, evaluation results must be current. Even after learners are placed in special programs, they must be reevaluated periodically to assure that the current placement is meeting their needs.

4. Committee review of evaluation results–A committee composed of professional personnel should review the results of the learner evaluation process. This team may include, among others, an administrator, counselor, special education teacher, social worker, referring party, psychologist, psychiatrist, career and technical education evaluator, health professional, speech or communications specialist, parent/guardian, and any other personnel who can contribute to the committee review and placement recommendations.

It is the responsibility of this committee to carefully review the results of all tests, reports, school records, medical history, social background, and referral information. Minimal data that should be available for this review include the following:

- vision screening test results
- hearing screening test results
- health records
- speech test results
- anecdotal observation information
- academic functioning levels (e.g., grades, results of standardized academic testing)
- psychological test results
- teacher comments and recommendations

The parent/guardian should be notified of the date and time of the screening conference and should be encouraged to participate. They can provide valuable insight into the review process.

5. Committee placement recommendation–Once the committee has reviewed the information from the comprehensive evaluation, a placement recommendation is made. The parent/guardian should be notified of the placement recommendation made by the committee. This notification must be made in writing and must describe the program or service that is being recommended. They must be informed of their right to review all records concerning their son/daughter. They have the right to challenge any of this information through an appeal process.

The parent/guardian must also be given an opportunity to present additional information that could affect a placement decision. Agencies in the community can often provide an independent evaluation for review by the committee. Finally, the parent/guardian must be informed of appeal procedures to which they can refer if they are dissatisfied with the committee recommendation.

INCLUSION

The term inclusion is used widely in educational circles and particularly in the disability field, but in truth there is no one definition for this word. It has been embraced by politicians, bilingual educators, people calling for systemic reform, and minority groups; in short, inclusion is not just a disability issue. See Figure 3-17. The National Information Center for Children and Youth with Disabilities (1995) defined inclusion as the process of educating learners with disabilities in the general education classrooms of their neighborhood schools.

The National Education Association (2001) published its policy statement on appropriate inclusion as follows:

> The National Education Association is committed to equal educational opportunity, the highest quality education, and a safe learning environment for all students. The Association supports and encourages appropriate inclusion. Appropriate inclusion is characterized by practices and programs, which provide for the following on a sustained basis:

- A full continuum of placement options and services within each option. Placement and services must be determined for each student by a team that includes all stakeholders and must be specified in the Individualized Education Program (IEP).
- Appropriate professional development, as part of normal work activity, of all educators and support staff associated with such programs. Appropriate training must also be provided for administrators, parents, and other stakeholders.
- Adequate time, as part of the normal school day, to engage in coordinated and collaborative planning on behalf of all students.
- Class sizes that are responsive to student needs.
- Staff and technical assistance that is specifically appropriate to student and teacher needs.

WHAT IS INCLUSION?	
Inclusion Is	**Inclusion Is Not**
Strong leadership by school principals and other administrators	Maintaining separate daily schedules for students with and without disabilities
Encouraging and implementing activities that promote the development of friendships and relationships between students with and without disabilities	Serving students with disabilities in age-inappropriate settings by placing older students in primary settings or younger students in secondary settings
Providing the planning, support, and services necessary for meaningful and successful participation of students with disabilities in regular programs	Denying students with disabilities services available to regular classrooms because the staff is not willing or hasn't been given direction in how to adapt instruction to meet the needs of diverse learners
Having a school and district mission that is comprehensive and sets high expectations for all students, including those with disabilities	Referring to special education students in stigmatizing terms such as "the handicapped class" or "the retarded kids"
Providing professional development and support for all personnel regarding effective practices for inclusion of students with disabilities	"Dumping" students with disabilities into regular programs without preparation or support
Scheduling classes for all school activities in a way that maximizes opportunities for participation by students with disabilities	Locating special education classes in separate wings at a school
Assuring that all schools and grade-level placements are age-appropriate	Exposing students to unnecessary hazards or risks
Having all people on the staff understand and support the notion that students with disabilities can be served appropriately in regular education classes, and that this sometimes requires the staff to meet learning needs that differ from those of most students	Placing unreasonable demands on teachers and administrators
	Ignoring parents' concerns
	Placing older students with disabilities at schools for younger children
Using "person first" language ("students with disabilities" instead of "disabled students") and teaching all students to understand and value human differences	Maintaining separate schedules for students in special education and regular education
Educating students with disabilities in the same school they would attend if they did not have disabilities	
Providing needs services within regular schools, regardless of the intensity or frequency	
Encouraging friendships and social relationships between students with disabilities and students without disabilities.	
Allowing students who are not able to fully participate in an activity to partially participate, rather than be excluded entirely	
Arranging for students with disabilities to receive their job training in regular community environments.	
Teaching all children to understand and accept individual differences	

Source: Maryland State Department of Education. Pices Full Inclusion Project. In Kochhar, C. & West, L. (1996). *Handbook of Successful Inclusion*. Gaithersburg, MD: Aspen Publishers, pp 7-8.

Figure 3-17. Characteristics of inclusion.

Stout (1996) provided an overview of the issue of inclusion as follows:

- Mainstreaming–Generally, mainstreaming has been used to refer to the selective placement of special education learners in one or more regular equation classes. Proponents of mainstreaming generally assume that a learner must earn the opportunity to be placed in regular classes by demonstrating an ability to keep up with the work assigned by the regular classroom teacher. This concept is closely linked to traditional forms of special education service delivery.

- Inclusion–Inclusion is a term that expresses a commitment to educate each learner, to the maximum extent appropriate, in the school and classroom the learner would otherwise attend. It involves bringing the support services to the learner (rather than moving the learner to the services) and requires only that the learner benefit from being in the class (rather than having to keep up with the other learners). Proponents of inclusion generally favor newer forms of education service delivery.

- Full inclusion–Full inclusion mean that all learners, regardless of handicapping condition of severity, will be in a regular classroom/program full time. All services must be taken to the learner in that setting.

- Regular education initiative–The three terms mentioned above relate to the way services are provided to learners. In contrast, regular education initiative refers to the merger of governance and funding for special education learners. The term was never intended to describe how children receive services. This concept was coined by a former official in the U.S. Department of Education (Madeline Will) and has generally been used to discuss either the merger of the governance of special and regular education or the merger of the funding streams of each.

  In addition to problems related to definition, it also should be understood that there is often a philosophical or conceptual distinction made between mainstreaming and inclusion. Those who support the IDEA of mainstreaming believe that a learner with disabilities first belongs in the special education environment. In contrast, those who support inclusion believe that the learner should always begin in the regular environment and be removed only when appropriate services cannot be provided in the regular classroom.

- The IDEA–The IDEA stipulates that each public agency must ensure that the placement of every learner with a handicapping condition be determined at least annually, be based on the learner's individualized education program, and be as close as possible to the learner's home. The various alternative placements included under the law are to be made available to the extent necessary to implement the individualized education program of each handicapped learner. Unless a handicapped learner's individualized education program requires some other arrangement, education should take place in the school the learner would attend if not handicapped. In selecting the least restrictive environment, consideration is given to any potential harmful effect on the learner or on the quality of services that the learner needs.

- Section 504 of the Rehabilitation Act of 1973–This legislation requires that a recipient of federal funds educate, or provide for the education of, each qualified handicapped person in its jurisdiction with persons who are not handicapped to the maximum extent appropriate to the needs of the handicapped person.

  A recipient is required to place a handicapped child in the regular educational environment operated by the recipient unless it can be demonstrated by the recipient that education in the regular environment with the use of supplementary aids and services cannot be achieved satisfactorily.

  The National Information Center for Children and Youth with Disabilities (1995) identified the components necessary for appropriate inclusion:

- Establish a philosophy that supports appropriate inclusionary practice–The philosophy will serve as both the foundation for and a stepping-stone to achieving inclusion. Best practice suggests that a philosophy supporting and affirming the education of all learners needs to be established at the state, district, and building levels, through discussion and agreement of major stakeholders. The responsibility for educating learners and for deciding how and where learners will be educated exists at each of these levels, and a clearly articulated philosophy at each level provides decision makers with a framework within which to weigh educational choices and alternatives. It also gives them the authority to commit resources to support the decisions that are made.

- Plan extensively for inclusion–Planning needs to include all those who will be involved in and affected by inclusion. If large-scale inclusion is anticipated (the state has determined that learners with disabilities will be educated within general education environments), then system-wide planning and capacity building must take place. If the inclusionary effort is limited to one school, then intensive planning and preparation needs to occur at that site. Teamwork and collaboration at the local school are always essential to addressing and answering (a) the many questions that come with inclusion and (b) the specific issues associated with the inclusion of each specific learner. It is also vital that there be someone clearly in charge of the inclusion effort. Among other things, this person (or persons) would have responsibility for calling meetings of those involved in planning; coordinating and overseeing IEP development and implementation for individual learners; ensuring that staff (including paraprofessionals) receive ongoing training; seeing that needed resources are made available; and monitoring the overall inclusion effort.

- Involve the principal as a change agent–The presence of a proactive, visible, and committed principal is often crucial to successful inclusion. If the principal is not already involved in the inclusion movement, then the support of that person must be enlisted. Through the principal's leadership, a model of accepting and welcoming learners with disabilities can be established, collaborative teaming encouraged, planning time for inclusion sanctioned, resources made available, parents involved, and progress made.

- Involve parents–By law, parents are entitled to be fully involved in planning the education of their child with a disability. Beyond the requirements of law, however, involving parents in efforts to plan for and implement the inclusion of the learner makes good sense. Parents possess expert, in-depth knowledge of their learner's personality, strengths, and needs. As primary stakeholders in inclusion, parents should be involved throughout the entire planning and implementation process: in the early information-gathering and planning meetings where decisions are made about the shape and scope of the inclusion program, in the IEP meeting where decisions are made about heir child's education, and when concerns or questions arise during the course of a school day or semester. Professional members of the team planning for inclusion can promote involvement of parent team members by appreciating and valuing the type of knowledge that parents bring to the planning table, by communicating openly and honestly with them, by respecting the family's cultural patterns and beliefs, and by listening carefully to the suggestions and concerns that parents have.

- Develop the disability awareness of staff and learners–Teachers, classroom aides, and other learners in the classroom and their parents need to have an understanding of disabilities and the special needs that having a disability can create. Teachers and aides need in-depth knowledge in order to understand and meet the learner's needs. This will also help teachers establish an atmosphere of acceptance and to plan activities that foster inclusion.

  Learners in general education classes also need information. A discussion of disability, what it means to have a disability and what it does not mean, can help learners understand and interact with their peers with disabilities. It is important, however, for the teacher (and other school staff) to know and observe the district's policies regarding confidentiality and to not reveal personal information about an individual learner, including the specific nature of the disability without the permission of the parents. Many teachers have found that the learner's parents are valuable partners in developing the awareness of other learners and school staff in regard to disability issues in general and their child's disability in particular. Depending on the nature of the learner's disability, classmates may also need information about classroom routines that might change, equipment that might be used by the learner, safety issues, and any additional individuals who may be in the class assisting the learner.

  Those involved in planning for and implementing inclusion should also recognize that developing the disability awareness of staff and learners needs to be an ongoing activity. Staff leave and new personnel are hired; learners leave and new ones arrive. Disability awareness training and activities, therefore, must be provided on a continual basis.

- Provide staff with training–It is unrealistic and unfair to expect general education teachers to creatively and productively educate and include learners with disabilities in their classrooms in the absence of adequate training. General educators must be provided with the training they need in order to meet the special learning and behavioral needs of learners. This training can come in many forms: seminars at local universities, in-service sessions provided by special educators, and materials specific to the nature of learners' disabilities. It is also vital that general education teachers have frequent opportunities for collaborative planning with other teachers, especially with special educators, and have ready access to the "disability" network and to inclusion specialists who can address their specific questions.

- Ensure that there is adequate support in the classroom–General education must not become a dumping ground where learners with disabilities are thrown without adequate support for them or their teachers. The IDEA states that when learners with disabilities are educated in regular classes, accommodation and supports must be provided as appropriate to each learner's special needs. Some supplementary aids and services that educators have used successfully include modifications to the regular class curriculum, assistance of an itinerant teacher with special education training, special education training for the regular teacher, use of computer-assisted devices, provision of note takers, and use of a resource room. The supports to be provided should be listed explicitly in the learner's IEP, which then documents the school's obligation and commitment to provide the supports.

  A primary means of support is the presence of additional staff, when necessary, to meet the learner's needs. Schools are increasingly relying upon the use of classroom aides and paraprofessionals to provide assistance. This person may work individually with the learner on adaptations to the curriculum suited to that learner's IEP goals and objectives and the content of the subject matter under study or may provide direct assistance in terms of positioning, note taking, interpreting, or facilitating communication or interaction with others.

  Another form of support is any assistive technology that helps the learner operate within the mainstream. Much information is available on the types of assistive technology available to learners with disabilities; it is the school's responsibility under IDEA to identify what assistive technology devices or services would allow the learner to benefit from the educational experience. These devices or services need to be listed specifically in the IEP. The school is then responsible for providing them to the learner and for providing training in their use.

- Provide structure and support for collaboration–Collaboration between stakeholders and participants is seen as the key to successful inclusion of all and involves a nonhierarchical relationship in which all team members are seen as equal contributors, each adding expertise or experience to the problem-solving process.

  Collaboration needs to occur all along the path of inclusion: during the initial planning stages, during implementation, between home and school, and during the course of the school day. It needs to occur between all members of the learner's individual planning team, between general and special educators, between teachers and administrators, and between learners. Indeed, the importance of collaboration cannot be overemphasized. It is especially important that time be built into teachers' schedules to allow for collaboration; the principal can be of great assistance in making this possible.

- Establish a planning team for each included learner–Each learner with disabilities included in the mainstream needs to have an individual planning team that meets on a regularly scheduled basis and collaboratively discusses and problem-solves the specific details of including that learner. This team may look similar to the IEP team and will probably include many of the same members, but its purpose is to maintain program quality throughout the year and provide a vehicle for creative problem solving, regular home-school communication, proactive rather than reactive planning, collaborative consultation, and program coordination. Again, collaboration between team members is essential; each member brings to the table expertise and creativity. Working together and pooling their knowledge, team members can do much to ensure that a learner's inclusion is successful.

- Make adaptations–One of the challenges of inclusion is adapting the general education curriculum and environment to meet the needs of learners with disabilities. Adaptations can be defined as any adjustments or modifications in the environment or instruction or materials used for learning that enhances the learner's performance or allows at least partial participation in an activity. For many learners with physical disabilities, many academic tasks pose unrealistic physical demands. Adaptations must be made because a learner should not be excluded from an activity due to the fact the learner can perform only a portion of the required skills. These modifications may mean (a) using materials and devices, (b) adapting skill sequences, (c) providing personal assistance, (d) adapting rules, and (e) adapting the physical environment.

- Establish policies and methods for evaluating learner progress–As general and special education become increasingly united within the context of general education classrooms, questions arise about how a teacher reasonably and fairly evaluates learners, particularly learners with disabilities who are not working with the same curriculum or for similar goals as their peers without disabilities. The IEP provides a benchmark against which to measure learner progress. Has the learner achieved the goals and objectives listed in the IEP? Other questions about evaluation exist as well, including how the performance of learners with disabilities will be counted within state reporting systems.

- Establish policies and methods for evaluating the inclusion program–One of the concerns that has been expressed about inclusion is the lack of empirical data on its effectiveness. On a national scale, research into effectiveness is certainly needed; at the local level, schools and communities will want information about how well their program in its various aspects is working. Are learners, those with disabilities and those without, achieving the outcomes projected? Are teachers getting the training they need and do they have adequate opportunities to collaborate with others? How effectively are the individual (and other) planning teams collaborating? How do parents feel about the program? What adjustments need to be made to the program to improve its operation?

One of the greatest challenges contributing to this debate about inclusion is the relative lack of similarity between the regular and special education systems in today's districts and schools. Successful inclusion practices depend on restructured schools that allow for flexible learning environments, with flexible curricula and instruction. Under ideal conditions, all learners work toward the same overall educational outcomes. What differs is the level at which these outcomes are achieved, the additional support that is needed by some learners and the degree of emphasis placed on various outcomes. See Figure 3-18.

A restructured system that merges special and regular education must also employ practices that focus on high expectation of all and rejects the prescriptive teaching, remedial approach that leads to lower achievement. It must also be acknowledged that diversity (ability, racial, etc.) is valuable.

When considering a move form traditional/regular special educational programming to a more inclusive approach, it is important that the entire school community be involved in a thoughtful, carefully researched transition. Dramatic top-down directives will polarize parents and teachers and will create environments that are hostile to any change. As is true in other areas of school restructuring, change must be based on research and broadly shared beliefs and philosophies.

THE MANY FACES OF CIVIL RIGHTS: EVOLUTION OF THE TERM INCLUSION

1900s through 1960s – Normalization. A philosophy imported from Scandinavia, based on the belief that individuals with disabilities should be viewed as being entitled to the same freedoms to choose life circumstances and opportunities as their nondisabled peers

1950 through 1960s – De-institutionalization and community integration. Two principles that gained wide acceptance after the Kennedy administration's leadership in promoting the movement of people with metal retardation out of large institutions and into their families or smaller facilities in their communities

1970s – Least restrictive environment (LRE). A principle embodies early special education law (PL 94-142), which required that students be educated in settings that were least restrictive of their freedom and most supportive of interaction with nondisabled peers

1980s – Mainstreaming. A term based on the LRE principle, which represented efforts to restructure school programs to permit students with disabilities to be served to the extent possible in their home schools and in classrooms with their nondisabled peers

1990s – Inclusion. A term similar to mainstreaming, but which specifically refers to integration of students with disabilities into regular academic classes with nondisabled peers

Mid-1990s – Full inclusion. A term that refers to the principle and practice of placing any and all students into regular classrooms with nondisabled peers, regardless of the type or severity of their disability, for the social benefits that may be gained

Source: Kochhar, C. & West, L. (1996). *Handbook for Successful Inclusion.* Gaithersburg, MD: Aspen Publishers, p. 10.

Figure 3-18. The evolution of the term inclusion.

The following recommendations can help districts or buildings in designing a positive transition to a more inclusive environment:

- A continuum of placements, supports, and services should be made available for all learners; however, it should be assumed that every learner's first placement is in regular education.
- All placement decisions should be based on a well-developed IEP with an emphasis on the needs of the learner, the learner's peers, and the reasonable provision of services.
- Top-down mandated full inclusion is inappropriate. Neither federal nor state law requires full inclusion.
- Before any new programs are developed, the building staff must agree on a clearly articulated philosophy of education (an education ethic). Teachers and support staff must be fully involved in the decision-making, planning, and evaluation processes for individual learners and building-wide programs.

- Extensive staff development must be made available as a part of every teacher's and paraprofessional's workday. Areas of emphasis include higher-order thinking skills, integrated curricula, interdisciplinary teaching, multicultural curricula, and life-centered curricula.
- The district should work toward unifying the special education and regular education systems. Separate evaluations and evaluation systems are counterproductive.
- In inclusive settings, reduced class sizes and/or increased numbers of teachers in the classroom are necessary. The district should ensure that sufficient licensed practitioners are employed to address the social, emotional, and cognitive needs of all learners. Appeal processes must be developed that allow teachers to challenge the implementation of IEPs and placements they determine inappropriate for the learner.
- Involve parents and learners as partners in the decision making process.
- When developing programs, the district should consider multiple teaching/learning approaches like team teaching, coteaching, peer partners, cooperative learning, heterogeneous grouping, study team planning, parallel teaching, and station teaching (Stout, 1996). See Figure 3-19.

Inclusion in the Workplace

Workplace inclusion is gaining a competitive advantage through workplace environments that accept, accommodate, and appreciate the talents of all employees and customers regardless of disability. People with disabilities are an important employment resource—a highly educated, newly enabled pool of potential employees. Inclusive businesses support workplace environments that accept and accommodate all employees and customers. The Inclusion Network (2001) identified a variety of ways that inclusive businesses can promote workplace inclusion:

- include employees with disabilities in inclusion promotion efforts
- narrowcast job openings to people with disabilities
- work with vocational rehabilitation agencies to identify qualified job candidates
- develop a mentoring program for new hires
- promote inclusion training at all levels
- convene focus groups of people with various disabilities
- establish employee inclusion networks
- offer career planning for employees with disabilities
- provide written information in multiple formats
- initiate a corporate self-study of inclusion practices
- retain disability consultants
- identify and remove physical barriers
- compensate and promote giving consideration to the furthering of inclusion
- profile inclusion efforts in company publications
- feature people with disabilities in corporate advertising
- hire a learner with a disability as company spokesperson

- hire people with disabilities as "mystery shoppers"
- establish a formal procedure for requesting and providing accommodations
- identify the individual responsible for corporate ADA compliance
- install a telephone device for the deaf (TDD)
- provide captioning and audio description for all corporate video productions
- offer special employee benefits for those who adopt children with special needs
- develop a text-only version of the company's web site
- join the Inclusion Network
- invite guest speakers on disabilities related topics
- purchase disability related resources for company library
- reserve a guide dog "relief area"
- install wind chimes over outdoor entrances
- have wheelchairs and electric scooters available on loan
- provide employee shuttles and carpooling
- commit that all company pubic gatherings will be IN-Vents (inclusive events)
- encourage employees to participate actively in disability related organizations
- match donations to disability related organizations
- provide support for disability related organizations

- set up an inclusion suggestion box
- sponsor inclusive sports events
- purchase tactile corporate art
- encourage suppliers to practice inclusion
- establish a support policy for vendors owned by people with disabilities
- provide "free days" to allow employee participation in disability related activities
- partner with an inclusive school or career and technical education program
- determine what functions can be performed by home-based employees
- give awards to company and community leaders in inclusion
- convene informal inclusion discussion groups
- provide bonuses for employees who recruit new workers with disabilities
- issue an annual "Inclusion Report" to employees, stockholders, and the public
- celebrate successful inclusion and accommodation practices
- circulate a corporate inclusion resource guide
- sponsor internships for learners with disabilities (*50 Things You Can Do*)

INCLUSION: A ROLE FOR EVERYONE

EDUCATIONAL NEEDS
- Student
- General education teacher
- Special education teacher
- Parent or guardian

SUPPORT SERVICES NEEDS
- Social and family service personnel
- Rehabilitation therapist
- Counselor and case manager
- Job coach
- Job placement specialist
- Occupational therapist
- Physical therapist
- Reading specialist
- Speech/language therapist

SOCIAL, PHYSICAL, AND RECREATIONAL NEEDS
- Classmates
- Physical education teachers
- Sports coaches
- Personal assistant
- Extracurricular, activity, and school club leaders
- Theater, chorus, and music program teachers

OTHER COMMUNITY MEMBERS WHO ARE NEEDED TO SUPPORT THE INCLUSION INITIATIVE
- Parents and advocates
- Educators and administrators
- Related and support services personnel
- Rehabilitation personnel
- Adult and community-based services personnel
- Public and private health services personnel
- Post-secondary institution personnel
- Employers, employment services, and private nonprofit agency personnel
- Job training program personnel
- Business-education liaisons
- School board members and other community decision makers
- Probation and parole workers
- Police
- Advocacy agency leaders
- Recreation and leisure service providers
- College and university personnel
- Civic and religious group leaders
- Local and state politicians
- Social services personnel
- Business-industry personnel

Kochhar, C., & West, L. (1996). *Handbook for Successful Inclusion.* Gaithersburg, MD: Aspen Publishers, p. 23.

Figure 3-19. Necessary elements of inclusion.

SUMMARY

Individuals with disabilities, as defined by the Carl D. Perkins Vocational and Applied Technology Education Act (PL 101-392), includes individuals who

- are identified as disabled under the Americans with Disabilities Act (PL 101-336), which includes any individual who has a physical or mental impairment that substantially limits one or more of the major life activities, has a record of impairment, or is regarded as having such an impairment; or
- are evaluated under the Individuals with Disabilities Education Act (PL 101-476) and deemed in need of special education and related services; and
- any individual considered disabled under the Rehabilitation Act of 1973.

In order for career and technical education instructors to work effectively with learners with disabilities, they must become familiar with the general characteristics and learning problems that these learners have. Instructors need to understand the learning problems of these learners so that appropriate modifications can be made and support services can be provided to enable these learners to successfully participate in and complete career and technical education programs.

SELF-ASSESSMENT

1. Describe why it is important to keep individual differences in mind when working with learners who have a disability.
2. Describe the general characteristics of learners who are mentally retarded.
3. Identify the levels of mental retardation.
4. List some of the strategies that instructors can use to assist learners with mental retardation in career and technical education programs.
5. Describe the general characteristics of learners with serious emotional disturbances (behavior disorders).
6. Identify some problems that are often encountered in working with learners with serious emotional disturbances?
7. Describe some strategies that will help instructors to deal with disruptive behavior.
8. Describe some strategies that will help instructors to deal with depression and suicide.
9. List some strategies that the instructor can use to assist learners with emotional or behavior disorders in career and technical education programs.
10. Identify the general characteristics of learners who have a visual impairment.
11. Identify specialized equipment, materials and aids that can be used to assist learners who are visually impaired in career and technical education programs.
12. Discuss methods of mobility that are used by individuals who have a visual impairment.
13. Identify strategies that instructors can use to assist learners with visual impairments in career and technical education programs.
14. Identify the general characteristics of learners who have a hearing impairment.
15. Identify several methods of communicating with learners with hearing impairments.
16. Describe methods of cooperative planning with interpreters who work with learners who are hearing impaired.
17. Identify strategies that instructors can use to assist learners with hearing impairments in career and technical education programs.
18. Identify the general characteristics of individuals with orthopedic impairments.
19. Discuss the importance of accessibility in order for learners with orthopedic impairments to participate in career and technical education programs.
20. Identify strategies that instructors can use to assist learners with orthopedic impairments in career and technical education programs.
21. Identify the general characteristics of individuals with health impairments.
22. Identify some of the problems associated with learners with health impairments.
23. Identify strategies that instructors can use to assist learners with health impairments in career and technical education programs.
24. Identify the general characteristics of individuals with speech or language impairments.
25. Describe what communication disorders are.
26. Identify strategies that instructors can use to assist learners with speech impairments in career and technical education programs.
27. Identify the general characteristics of individuals with specific learning disabilities.
28. Discuss the importance of learning styles information in working with learners with learning disabilities.
29. Identify strategies that instructors can use to assist learners with learning disabilities in career and technical education programs.
30. Describe the steps in the process to refer individuals for assessment.

ASSOCIATED ACTIVITIES

1. Contact a special education teacher, Section 504 coordinator, transition coordinator, and/or other personnel who work with secondary level learners with disabilities. Discuss the general characteristics of these learners as well as appropriate techniques that can be used to meet their needs. Explain your program goals, exit points, and competencies. Identify appropriate career goals for learners with disabilities who are enrolled in your program.

2. Contact a special education teacher, special needs coordinator, and/or support personnel to talk about program modifications for learners who are mentally retarded. Discuss your program goals, exit points, and competencies. Identify appropriate career goals for the individual learners in your program. Ask about strategies that would assist these learners to successfully participate in your program.

3. Contact a special education teacher, special needs coordinator, and/or support personnel to talk about program modifications for learners who are visually impaired. Discuss your program goals, exit points, and competencies. Identify appropriate career goals for individual learners in your program. Find out about specialized equipment, materials and aids that are available to assist these learners. Ask about strategies that would assist learners with visual impairments to successfully participate in your program.

4. Contact a special education teacher, special needs coordinator, interpreter, and/or support personnel to talk about program modifications for learners who are hearing impaired. Discuss your program goals, exit points, and competencies. Identify appropriate career goals for individual learners in your program. Collaboratively plan with interpreters if they are going to be in your classroom and laboratory. Make provisions to share lecture notes and other appropriate information. Ask about strategies that would assist learners with hearing impairments to successfully participate in your program.

5. Contact a counselor, social worker, or homebound teacher who works with learners who are health impaired. Discuss the general characteristics of these learners as well as appropriate techniques that can be used to meet their needs. Explain the nature of your program and discuss ways in which realistic career preparation opportunities can be delivered to these learners.

6. Contact personnel in your school or district who work with learners who have orthopedic impairments. Discuss the nature of your program as well as specific exit points and competencies. Discuss specific adaptations that could be made in your classroom, laboratory, and/or curriculum for learners enrolled in your program who have orthopedic impairments. Find out about community agencies that can provide assistance to these learners.

7. Contact the speech therapist or communication specialist who works with learners who are speech impaired. Discuss the general characteristics of these learners as well as appropriate techniques that can be used to meet their needs. Explain the nature of your program and discuss ways in which realistic career preparation opportunities can be developed for these learners.

8. Contact a special education teacher, Section 504 coordinator, transition coordinator, and/or other support personnel who work with learners who have a learning disability. Discuss your program, curriculum, exit points and competencies. Find out about the learning styles of the learners enrolled in your program. Discuss effective teaching techniques and compensation strategies that will assist these learners to succeed in your program.

9. Contact a special education teacher, Section 504 coordinator, transition coordinator, and/or other support personnel who work with learners who have emotional and behavior problems. Discuss your program, curriculum, exit points and competencies. Discuss appropriate behavior management techniques that can assist these learners to successfully participate in your program.

REFERENCES

Armstrong, R. (March, 2001). Is the new IDEA a good idea? *Techniques, 76*(3), p.29.

The Autism Source. (2001). Tips for teaching high functioning people with autism. [On-line]. Available: www.maapservices.org

Bates, P., Morrow, S., Anderson, J.,& Pancsofar, E. (1982). *Behavior management.* Normal, IL: Illinois State University.

Blair, J., Peterson, M., & Viehweg, S. (1985). The effects of mild hearing loss on academic performance of young school-age children. *Volta Review, 87,* 87-93.

Bruininks, R. & McGrew, K. (1987). *Exploring the structure of adaptive behavior.* Minneapolis, MN: University of Minnesota, University Affiliated Program on Developmental Disabilities.

Byers, J. (1989). AIDS in children: Effects on neurological development and implications for the future. *The Journal of Special Education, 23,* 5-16.

Cornett, A. (1974). What is cued speech? *Gallaudet Today, 5* (2), 3-5.

Dreifuss, F. (1988). What is epilepsy? In R. Behrman & V. Vaughan III (Eds.), *Nelson textbook of pediatrics* (13th ed.). Philadelphia: Saunders.

ERIC Clearinghouse on Disabilities and Gifted Education (1999). *Learning disabilities—Frequently asked questions.* Arlington, VA: Author.

Grossman, H. (Ed.). (1983). *Classification in mental retardation.* Washington, DC: American Association on Mental Retardation.

Hardman, M., Drew, C., Egan, M., & Wolf, B. (1993). *Human exceptionality* (4th ed.). Boston, MA: Allyn and Bacon.

Hasazi, S., Johnson, R., Hasazi, J., Gordon, L., & Hull, M. (1989). Employment of youth with and without handicaps following school: Outcomes and correlates. *Journal of Special Education, 23,* 243-45.

Heward, W., & Orlansky, M. (1992). *Exceptional children: An introductory survey of special_education.* (4th ed.). New York: Macmillan.

The Inclusion Network. (2001). *What is workplace inclusion?* [On-line]. Available: http://www.inclusion.org/consulting/workplace/index.html

Individuals with Disabilities Education Act of 1990, Pub. L. No. 101-476, United States Statutes at Large, (104), 1103. Washington, DC: U.S. Government Printing Office.

Individuals with Disabilities Education Act Amendments of 1997, Pub. L. No. 105-17, United States Statutes at Large, (111), 37. Washington, DC: U.S. Government Printing Office.

Kaye, S. (May, 1998). Is the status of people with disabilities improving? San Francisco, CA: University of California, Disability Status Center. Abstract 21.

Knoblauch, B. & McLane, K. (1999). *An overview of the Individuals with Disabilities Education Act Amendments of 1997 (PL 105-17): Update 1999.* Arlington, VA: The ERIC Clearinghouse on Disabilities and Gifted Education. ERIC Digest #E576.

Kochhar, C., & West, L. (1996). Handbook for successful inclusion. Gaithersburg, MD: Aspen Publishers.

Martin, R., & Lauridsen, D. (1974). *Developing student discipline and motivation.* Champaign, IL: Research Press.

Maryland State Department of Education. (1996). Pices full inclusion project. In Kochar, C., & West, L. *Handbook for successful inclusion.* Gaithersburg, MD: Aspen Publishers. pp. 7-8.

National Center for Education Statistics. (June, 1997). *Profiles of students with disabilities as identified in NELS:88.* [On-line]. Available:http://nces.ed.gov/pubsearch/pubsinfo.asp?pubid=97254

National Education Association. (2001). National education association policy statement on appropriate inclusion. Washington, DC: Author.

National Information Center for Children and Youth with Disabilities. (July, 1995). Planning for inclusion. *NICHCY News Digest, 5*(1).

National Information Center for Children and Youth with Disabilities (August, 1999). *General information about attention deficit hyperactivity disorder (AD/HD).* Fact Sheet 19. Washington, DC: Author.

National Information Center for Children and Youth with Disabilities. (October, 1999). *Interventions for chronic behavior problems.* Research Brief 1. Washington, DC: Author.

National Information Center for Children and Youth with Disabilities. (January 2001). *General information about autism and pervasive development disorders.* Fact Sheet 1. Washington, DC: Author.

National Information Center for Children and Youth with Disabilities. (January, 2001). *General information about learning disabilities.* Fact Sheet 7. Washington, DC: Author.

National Information Center for Children and Youth with Disabilities. (January, 2001). *General information about speech and language disorders.* Fact Sheet 11. Washington, DC: Author.

President's Committee on Employment of People with Disabilities. (2001). *I-CAN ONLINE.* Washington, DC: Author.

Rehabilitation Act of 1973, Pub. L. No. 93-112. United States Statutes at Large, (87), 355. Washington, DC: U.S. Government Printing Office.

Ross, M. (1981). Review, overview and other educational considerations. In M. Ross & L. W. Nober (Eds.), *Educating hard-of-hearing*. Reston, VA: Council for Exceptional Children.

Schelly, C., et al. (1995). *Vocational support strategies for students with emotional disorders*. ED 383152.

Silver, L. (1989). *Attention deficit-hyperactivity disorder and learning disabilities*. Summit, NJ: CIBA-GEIGY.

Sitlington, P., Clark, G., & Kolstoe, O. (2000). Transition education and services for adolescents with disabilities (3rd ed.). Needham Heights, MA: Allyn & Bacon.

Stout, K. (1996). *Special education inclusion*. [On-line]. Available: http://www.weac.org/resource/june96/speced.htm

Teenagers and AIDS. (1992, August 3). *Newsweek*. 45-50.

Tonks, D. (1993). Can you save your students' lives? Educating to prevent AIDS. *Educational Leadership, 50*(4), 48-54.

U.S. Department of Education. (2000). *Twenty-second annual report to Congress*. Washington, DC: Author.

U.S. Department of Education, Office for Civil Rights. (n.d.). *Section 504 students with accommodations*. Washington, DC: Author.

U.S. Department of Health and Human Services. (1980). *Muscular dystrophy and other neuromuscular disorders*. Bethesda, MD: National Institute of Health, National Institute of Neurological and Communicative Disorders and Stroke, Office of Scientific and Health Reports.

Utah State Office of Education. (2002). *Section 504/ADA guidelines for educators*. Salt Lake City, UT: Author.

Von Isser, A., Quay, H., & Love, C. (1980). Interrelationships among three measures of deviant behavior. *Exceptional Children, 46*, 272-276.

William Gladden Foundation. (1989). AIDS and children. Huntington, NY: Author.

William Gladden Foundation. (1990). *Children with dyslexia*. Huntington, NY: Author.

William Gladden Foundation. (1989). *Learning disabled children*. Huntington, NY: Author.

Additional Special Populations

INTRODUCTION

Individuals with disabilities have been discussed in the previous chapter. However, special populations also includes other learners who should be addressed when planning career and technical education. A large number of learners enrolled in these programs are identified as disadvantaged.

The Carl D. Perkins Vocational and Technical Education Act of 1998 (PL 105-332) defined individuals from special populations as
• individuals with disabilities;
• individuals from economically disadvantaged homes;
• individuals preparing for nontraditional training and employment;
• single parents; and
• individuals with other educational achievement barriers, such as a limited English proficiency.

Additional individuals from special populations that will be covered in this chapter include homeless individuals, displaced homemakers, individuals in correctional facilities, migrant populations, and gifted and talented learners.

There are a variety of societal issues that affect individuals from special populations outside the classroom. Issues that will be discussed in this chapter include substance abuse, child abuse, teen suicide, violence, and gang involvement.

This chapter presents an overview of the nature and needs of individuals from special populations. It is intended to help instructors better understand the learning problems of these individuals so that appropriate modifications can be made in career and technical education programs and necessary support services can be provided to enable them to successfully participate in and complete the curricula.

OUTLINE

OVERVIEW
ECONOMICALLY DISADVANTAGED LEARNERS
LEARNERS FROM NONTRADITIONAL FAMILIES
LEARNERS IN NONTRADITIONAL TRAINING AND EMPLOYMENT
LEARNERS WHO ARE SINGLE PARENTS
LEARNERS WITH EDUCATIONAL ACHIEVEMENT BARRIERS
OTHER DISADVANTAGED POPULATIONS
ISSUES THAT AFFECT LEARNERS FROM SPECIAL POPULATIONS
SAFE AND EQUALLY RESPONSIVE SCHOOLS
ASSESSING LEARNERS FROM SPECIAL POPULATIONS
SUMMARY
SELF-ASSESSMENT
ASSOCIATED ACTIVITIES
REFERENCES

OBJECTIVES

After completing this chapter the reader should be able to accomplish the following:
1. Identify the special populations, other than individuals with disabilities, identified in the Carl D. Perkins Vocational and Technical Education Act of 1998 (PL 105-332).
2. Discuss special needs of economically disadvantaged learners.
3. Identify strategies for instructors to help economically disadvantaged learners succeed in career and technical education programs.

4. Discuss special needs of learners from foster families.
5. Identify strategies for instructors to help learners from foster families succeed in career and technical education programs.
6. Discuss special needs of individuals preparing for nontraditional training and employment.
7. Identify strategies for instructors to prevent gender bias in career and technical education programs.
8. Discuss special needs of single parents.
9. Identify strategies for instructors to help single parents succeed in career and technical education programs.
10. Discuss special needs of learners who are educationally disadvantaged.
11. Identify strategies for instructors to help learners who are educationally disadvantaged succeed in career and technical education programs.
12. Discuss special needs of limited English-proficient learners.
13. Identify strategies for instructors to help limited English-proficient learners succeed in career and technical education programs.
14. Discuss special needs of homeless learners.
15. Identify strategies for instructors to help homeless learners succeed in career and technical education programs.
16. Discuss special needs of displaced homemakers.
17. Identify strategies for instructors to help displaced homemakers succeed in career and technical education programs.
18. Discuss special needs of learners in correctional facilities.
19. Identify essential components of an effective correctional education program.
20. Discuss special needs of learners from migrant populations.
21. Identify strategies for instructors to help learners from migrant populations succeed in career and technical education programs.
22. Discuss the special needs of gifted and talented learners.
23. Identify strategies for instructors to help gifted and talented learners succeed in career and technical education programs.
24. Identify characteristics of a school that is safe and responsive for all learners.
25. Describe the referral process for learners from special populations.

TERMS

at-risk
child abuse
correctional facility
disadvantaged
displaced homemaker
diversity
economically disadvantaged
educational achievement
educationally disadvantaged

foster children
gang involvement
gender bias
gender equity
gifted and talented individual
homeless individual
limited English-proficient learner
migrant

nontraditional training and
  employment
poverty
single parent
substance abuse
teen father
teen pregnancy
teen suicide

OVERVIEW

The next decade will usher in the beginnings of a steady and significant increase in the number of school-age children in the United States during the 21st century. By the year 2100, public and private institutions, from pre-kindergarten through college, will accommodate an estimated 94 million American children and young adults, an increase of more than 42 million from the current school population. These future generations of children will require many more public resources, including a major investment in the construction, modernization and renovation of school facilities, many of which are already overcrowded and in disrepair. Indeed, population growth is already well underway (Riley, 2000).

The consequences of an enrollment crescendo will not immediately overwhelm the education system. In fact, enrollment in elementary and secondary schools will briefly stabilize between 2005 and 2010 before a rise that is expected to continue for the remainder of the century. Unlike the 20th century, when enrollment rose and dipped repeatedly, growth in the 21st century will be constant. Between 2010 and 2020, the number of school-age children aged 5 to 17 years old will increase by 6%. In 2020, about 55 million children will be enrolled in the nation's schools and this number will rise to 60 million by 2030 (Riley, 2000).

By the year 2020, the majority of America's public school learners will be living under conditions that place them at risk of educational failure. This is a projection, of course, but the trend toward ever higher percentages of poorly housed, malnourished, abused, and neglected children is inarguable.

The Federal Interagency Forum on Child and Family Statistics (2000) presents a composite portrait of children in our country. In 1999, there were 70.2 million children in the United States, 0.3 million more than in 1998. This number is projected to increase to 77.2 million in 2020. The number of children under 18 has grown during the last half-century, increasing about half again in size since 1950. During the baby boom (1946 to 1964), the number of children grew rapidly. During the 1970s and 1980s, the number of children declined and then grew slowly. Beginning in 1990, the rate of growth in the number of children increased, although not as rapidly as during the baby boom. Children are projected to comprise 24% of the population in 2020.

In 1999, 65% of the U.S. children were white, 15% were African-American, 16% were Hispanic, 4% were Asian/Pacific Islander, and 1% were Native American/Alaska Native. The percentage of children who were white, non-Hispanic decreased from 74% in 1980 to 65% in 1999. The percentages of African-American, non-Hispanic and Native American/Alaska Native children have been fairly stable during the period from 1980 to 1999. The number of Hispanic children has increased faster than that of any other racial-ethnic group, growing from 9% of the child population in 1980 to 16% in 1999. By 2020, it is projected that more than one in five children in the U.S. will be of Hispanic origin. The percentage of Asian/Pacific Islander children doubled from 2% to 4% of all U.S. children between 1980 and 1999. Their percentage is projected to continue to increase to 6% in 2020 (Federal Interagency Forum on Child and Family Statistics, 2000).

The number of school-age children (ages 5 to 17) who spoke a language other than English at home and who had difficulty speaking English was 2.4 million in 1995, up from 1.3 million in 1979. This represented 5% of all school-age children in the U.S. Children of Hispanic or other (mostly Asian) origin are more likely than white, non-Hispanic and African-American, non-Hispanic children to have difficulty speaking English. Thirty-one percent of children of Hispanic origin and 14% of children of Asian or other origin had difficulty speaking English in 1995, compared with 1% of white, non-Hispanic or African-American, non-Hispanic children (Federal Interagency Forum on Child and Family Statistics, 2000).

In 1999, 68% of American children lived with two parents, down from 77% in 1980. In 1999, almost a quarter (23%) of children lived with only their mothers, 4% lived with only their fathers, and 4% lived with neither of their parents. Since 1996, the percentage of children living with only one parent has not changed significantly. Among the factors associated with change in the percentage of children living with just one parent is the percentage of births to unmarried mothers. White, non-Hispanic children are much more likely than African-American children and somewhat more likely than Hispanic children to live with two parents. In 1999, 77% of white, non-Hispanic children lived with two parents, compared with 35% of African-American children and 63% of children of Hispanic origin. The majority of children living with one parent lived with their single mother (Federal Interagency Forum on Child and Family Statistics, 2000).

Every day in America

- 2,377 babies are born to mothers who are not high school graduates;
- 2,658 public school learners are corporally punished;
- 3,356 high school learners drop out;
- 5,500 high school graduates do not go on to college;
- 5,702 children are arrested; and
- 17,152 public school learners are suspended (Thompson, 1999).

Since the 1970's general characteristics of learners who are at risk have been identified. These characteristics can be used to identify learners in need of assistance in school. Some at-risk indicators may represent persistent problems from early elementary school years for some learners. Other learners may overcome early difficulties but begin to experience related problems during middle school or high school. For others, some of these indicators may become noticeable only in early adolescence. To intervene effectively, parents and teachers can be aware of some common indicators of an adolescent at risk for school failure. See Figure 4-1.

GENERAL CHARACTERISTICS OF AT-RISK LEARNERS

CLASSROOM BEHAVIOR
- Attention problems
- Disruptive behavior
- Poor attitude
- Frequently disciplined
- Sudden change in school behavior
- Resents authority
- Immature
- Impulsive
- Inability to work in a team situation
- Withdraws from class discussions
- Absenteeism
- Tardiness

ACADEMIC ABILITY
- Multiple retentions in grade
- Poor grades; barely-average or below-average levels
- Poor reading skills
- Poor math skills
- Poor language skills
- Limited leadership skills
- History of failure
- Lack of involvement; sports, music, or other school-related extracurricular activities

SELF-CONCEPT
- Negative self-concept
- Lack of confidence
- Low motivation
- Low level of aspiration
- Belief that success is linked to natural intelligence rather than hard work
- Belief that own ability is insufficient, and situation cannot change
- Limited goals for the future
- Unaware of available career options
- Poor personal hygiene

OUTSIDE INFLUENCES
- Lack of parental guidance
- Problems with the law
- Drug/substance abuse
- Alcohol abuse
- Gang involvement
- No work experience

Source: Robertson, A. (1997). *If An Adolescent Begins to Fail in School, What Can Parents and Teachers Do?* Champaign, IL: ERIC Clearinghouse on Elementary and Early Childhood Education.

Figure 4-1. Characteristics demonstrated by at-risk learners.

In studies conducted on the base-year and first follow-up of the National Education Longitudinal Study (NELS) surveys (8th and 10th graders), many factors were identified as being associated with an increased probability of school failure and dropping out. These factors were often highly correlated with learners' demographic characteristics, especially gender, racial-ethnicity, and socioeconomic status (SES). However, after controlling for these demographic factors, there were five factors related to family background or early school experiences that still substantially increased the odds of dropping out of high school. These factors included being from a single parent household, having an older sibling who dropped out of high school, changing schools two or more times other than the normal progression (i.e., from elementary to middle school), having poorer than average grades, and repeating an earlier grade.

Learners were further identified according to their level of risk based on the number of risk factors they had accumulated. One risk factor was considered low risk, two risk factors constituted moderate risk, and learners with three or more risk factors were considered to be at high risk of dropping out. Learners who showed at least two risk factors had much higher odds of dropping out of school than learners who had no risk factors. In terms of odds, compared with learners with no risk factors, learners who had one risk factor were four times more likely to drop out of school, learners who had two risk factors were 13 times more likely to drop out, and learners who had three or more risk factors were 30 times more likely to drop out (*Toward Resiliency: At Risk Students Who Make It to College*, 1998).

The educational risks assessed in the 1983 report, *A Nation At Risk: The Imperative for Educational Reform*, were documented in the following testimony received by its 18-month commission:
- International comparisons of learner achievement, completed a decade previous to the findings, revealed that on 19 academic tests American learners were never first or second and, in comparison with other industrialized nations, were last seven times.
- Some 23 million American adults were functionally illiterate according to simple tests of reading, writing, and comprehension.
- About 13% of all 17-year-olds were considered functionally illiterate. Functional illiteracy among minority youth ran as high as 40%.
- Average achievement of high school learners on most standardized tests was lower than 26 years prior, when Sputnik was launched.
- Over half the population of gifted learners did not match their tested ability with comparable achievement in school.
- The College Board's Scholastic Aptitude Tests (SATs) demonstrated a virtually unbroken decline in scores from 1963 to 1980. Average verbal scores fell over 50 points and average mathematics scores dropped nearly 40 points.
- College Board achievement tests also revealed consistent declines in such subjects as physics and English.

- Both the number and proportion of learners demonstrating superior achievement on the SATs (i.e., those with scores of 650 or higher) dramatically declined.
- Many 17-year-olds did not possess higher order intellectual skills instructors should expect of them. Nearly 40% could not draw inferences from written material; only one-fifth could write a persuasive essay; and only one-third could solve a multistep mathematics problem.
- There was a steady decline in science achievement scores of American 17-year-olds as measured by national assessments of science in 1969, 1973, and 1977.
- Between 1975 and 1980, remedial mathematics courses in public four-year colleges increased by 72% and constituted one-quarter of all mathematics courses taught in those institutions in the early 1980s.
- Average tested achievement of learners graduating from college was also lower.
- Business and military leaders complained that they are required to spend millions of dollars on costly remedial education and training programs in such basic skills as reading, writing, spelling, and computation. The Department of the Navy, for example, reported to the commission that one-quarter of its recent recruits could not read at the ninth grade level, the minimum needed simply to understand written safety instructions. Without remedial work they could not even begin, much less complete, the sophisticated training essential in much of the military (The National Commission on Excellence in Education, 1983).

Fifteen years later, *A Nation Still At Risk—An Education Manifesto* was produced by the Center for Education Reform (1998). Among the interesting comparisons are the following:

- Observed high school seniors had not even started school when the Excellence Commission's 1983 report was released. A whole generation of young Americans passed through the education system in the years since, but many have passed through without learning what is needed. Since 1983, over 10 million Americans reached the 12th grade not even having learned to read at a basic level. Over 20 million reached their senior year unable to do basic math. Almost 25 million reached 12th grade not knowing the essentials of U.S. history. This reflects only those learners who completed their senior year. During the same time period, over six million Americans dropped out of high school altogether. The numbers were even more bleak in minority communities. In 1996, 13% of all African-Americans aged 16 to 24 were not in school and did not hold a diploma. Seventeen percent of first-generation Hispanics had dropped out of high school, including a tragic 44% of Hispanic immigrants in this age group.
- Academically, U.S. learners fall off a cliff somewhere in the middle and upper grades. Internationally, American youngsters hold their own at the elementary level but falter in the middle years and drop far behind in high school. The U.S. seems to be the only country in the world whose children fall farther behind the longer they stay in school. This is true of advanced learners and so-called good schools, as well as those in the middle. Remediation is rampant in college, with some 30% of entering freshmen in need of remedial courses in reading, writing, and mathematics after arriving on campus. Employers report difficulty finding people to hire who have the skills, knowledge, habits, and attitudes they require for technologically sophisticated positions. Silicon Valley entrepreneurs press for higher immigration levels so they can recruit the qualified personnel they need. Though the pay they offer is excellent, the supply of competent educated American workers is too meager to fill available jobs.
- In today's schools, many disadvantaged and minority learners are not being challenged. Many are left to fend for themselves when they need instruction and direction from highly qualified teachers. Many are passed from grade to grade, left to sink or swim. Many are advanced without even learning to read, though proven methods of teaching reading are now well known. When so little is expected and so little is done, such children are victims of failed public policy.
- Equal educational opportunity is the next great civil-rights issue. This refers to true equal opportunity that results from providing every child with a first-rate primary and secondary education and to the development of human potential that comes from meeting intellectual, social, and spiritual challenges. The educational gaps between advantaged and disadvantaged learners are huge, handicapping poor children in their pursuit of higher education, good jobs, and a better life.

It is also no longer sufficient for the United States to examine the achievement of its learners solely with internal comparisons. As competition stiffens with other countries, international comparisons provide perspective on America's ability to survive in a global economy.

Americans assume that the best U.S. learners can compete with the best learners anywhere. This is not true. International assessments have focused attention on the relatively poor standing of all American learners. These tests also show that our top-performing learners are undistinguished at best and poor at worst when compared with top learners in other countries.

International test data provide the best comparison of mathematics and science achievement. For a comparison of the humanities, a look at the curriculum and expectations as they are expressed on national exams reveals much about how American learners perform. The test data and exam questions clearly show that the best U.S. learners are not receiving as challenging an education as learners in other nations. For example, to gauge achievement of American high school learners in science, we can turn to a study comparing U.S. seniors taking advanced placement (AP) courses in science with top learners in 13 other countries.

The U.S. learners represented the top 1% of learners in the nation. The study found that American learners were 13th out of 13 in biology, 11th out of 13 in chemistry, and ninth out of 13 in physics. When controlled for selectivity (a higher percentage of the total school population in other countries takes advanced classes), American learners scored the lowest of the participating nationals in all three areas (U.S. Department of Labor, Women's Bureau, 2000).

The Perkins Act of 1998 defines special populations as

- individuals with disabilities;
- individuals from economically disadvantaged homes;
- individuals preparing for nontraditional training and employment;
- single parents; and
- individuals with other educational achievement barriers, such as a limited English proficiency.

A previous chapter focused on individuals with disabilities. The remainder of this chapter will provide information on the remaining populations defined by this act.

ECONOMICALLY DISADVANTAGED LEARNERS

Childhood poverty has both immediate and lasting negative effects. Children in low-income families fare less well than children in more affluent families. Economically disadvantaged learners from low-income families face many challenges. See Figure 4-2. Compared with children living in families above the poverty line, children living below the poverty line are more likely to have difficulty in school, to become teen parents, and, as adults, to earn less and be unemployed more frequently.

Lumsden and Coffey (2001) present the following information on poverty:

- The ranks of the poor in our nation have risen markedly in recent years. Every forty seconds, a child is born into poverty; 27 children die from poverty-related causes every day.
- The rate of child poverty in the U.S. is two to nine times higher than it is in every other industrialized country.
- Myths persist about who composes the poor in America. Contrary to what many people assume, the majority of poor children come from families with working parents. In fact, the working poor outnumber those on welfare by two to one. Also, most poor children live in rural and suburban areas, not in inner cities.
- For each year that children live in poverty, the likelihood that they will perform below their current grade level increases by 2%. If a child attends a school that enrolls a large percentage of low-income learners, the likelihood of failure in school rises dramatically. From the beginning, many poor children have several strikes against them. For example, poor mothers often receive little or no prenatal care and are more likely to have low-birthweight babies. In poor families, the diet and medical care of children are often inadequate, which impairs their ability to be attentive and responsive in school.
- Children in low-income families are also more likely to be ill in their early years and are more prone to sensory-motor deficits. In addition, children growing up in poverty often have fewer opportunities for socialization.

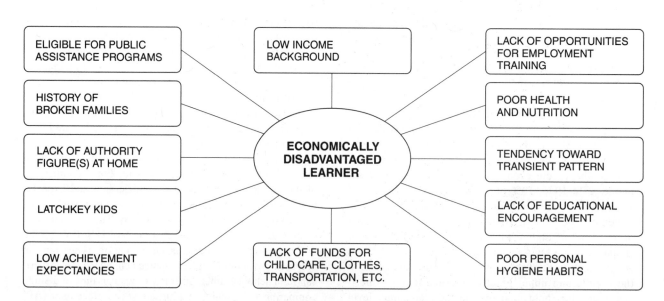

Figure 4-2. General characteristics demonstrated by economically disadvantaged learners.

- Poverty, not minority status, seems to be the most reliable predictor of below-average educational performance. A child who is a member of a minority group and whose parents are college graduates living in the suburbs tends to perform roughly the same academically as a white learner who is a child of parents with comparable socioeconomic status and educational levels. Therefore, if the proportion of minority learners living in poverty could be reduced, we would expect to see a corresponding increase in educational performance among minority learners.
- One reason children in poverty perform less well in school than learners in wealthier families is that some teachers expect less from learners living in poverty than from learners who come from more economically enriched backgrounds. Teachers are forced to lower their standards or reduce their expectations for learners living in families that are not financially well off. To expect less of such learners is to shortchange them and, in many cases, to cause them to lower their sights for themselves.

Case Study . . . Timothy

Timothy is a sophomore in high school. He is the oldest in a family of 6 children. His mother is a single mother who works two jobs in order to support her children. Timothy has two part-time jobs after school to help his mother. He also has the responsibility of looking after his brothers and sisters until his mother comes home from her second job at about ten o'clock in the evening.

If any of the children are sick, Timothy has to miss school and stay at home with them while his mother works. His frequent absences have caused his grades to gradually slip. He could do better in school if he had the time and privacy at home to concentrate on his schoolwork. Timothy has not been able to participate in any extracurricular activities at school, and he has few friends.

This year, Timothy enrolled in Retail Merchandising. For the first time, he feels that school has something to offer him. Mrs. Foster, the marketing education teacher, has worked closely with the counselor and is aware of the challenges of Timothy's life. She has found a volunteer group in the community to assist Timothy's mother with child care several afternoons a week. This will allow Timothy to become involved in some DECA student organization activities. His involvement will help him network with his peers and establish friendships. Mrs. Foster has also found Timothy a job in a retail store at the mall that will help him get some experience in the marketing field. There is also a possibility that Timothy's family may be adopted by a local church. If this happens, there will be assistance with food, clothing, child care, dental, and medical care.

Renchler (1993) provided examples of the challenges facing children from low socioeconomic status (SES) and its impact on their education:

- The statistics on children who live in poverty portray a picture of a nation struggling to keep up with the problem and perhaps not fully committed to solving it. The United States has a much higher incidence of child poverty than do other western nations, and the percentage of impoverished children in the population has continued to increase during the past two decades.
- The price these children pay for being born poor is enormous. Several sources indicate that low-SES children living in inner cities are much more likely to have educationally damaging circumstances as part of their life experiences than are high-SES children. The dangers low-SES children face include prenatal exposure to drugs and AIDS, low birthweight, poor nutrition, lead exposure, and personal injuries and accidents.
- Poor inner city youth are seven times more likely to be victims of child abuse or neglect than are high-SES children.
- Not unexpectedly, these circumstances lead low-SES learners to drop out of school far more frequently than their high-SES counterparts. As many as one million at-risk learners drop out every year.
- The costs of not acting to assist low-SES youths are enormous. According to one estimate, the lifetime personal income lost as a result of dropping out ranges from $20,000 to $200,000 per individual.
- The initial costs of programs focused on keeping economically disadvantaged youths in school are, according to most experts, well worth the investment, yielding a long-term savings of $4.75 for every dollar spent.

Some of the most frequently occurring problems career and technical education instructors encounter when working with economically disadvantaged learners are

- excessive absence or poor attendance;
- hygiene problems and poor personal appearance;
- lack of supplies, materials, and/or equipment to complete assigned projects;
- lack of basic preparation skills in reading and math;
- lack of a value system that is conducive to preparation for a career;
- lack of interest and motivation for education or work;
- lack of background information regarding learner's family, health records, and school records; and
- low self-esteem and/or lack of confidence.

Some services that educationally and economically disadvantaged learners may need include

- career-development activities;
- career and technical education assessment;
- curriculum and/or instructional modifications;
- placement in remedial class;
- special supplies;

- job-seeking and retention skills;
- employment skills development;
- career counseling;
- job placement assistance;
- transportation;
- child care;
- financial aid; and
- follow-up assistance.

LEARNERS FROM NONTRADITIONAL FAMILIES

Many learners in urban schools come from nontraditional families. These include multiracial couples, gay and lesbian couples, grandparents and relatives, and foster parents. Schwartz (1999a) identified these family types and how they affect learners in our nation's urban schools:

- Multiracial families–This family group comprises both children whose parents have different ethnic heritages and those who themselves are different ethnically from their parents. The development of a multiracial identity of such children, which extends through adolescence, is mediated by parental attitudes about personal classification and ethnicity in general. Society's attitudes, particularly racist attitudes, toward multiracial individuals also influence the identity of these children.
- Families with gay or lesbian parents–Children who live with gay or lesbian parents may be either adopted or the biological offspring of one parent. They have no more socioemotional problems and are no more likely to be homosexual than children raised by heterosexuals. However, some may suffer from the emotional consequences of a bitter legal custody battle that denigrated their gay parent, or be victimized by homophobic peer ridicule. Children in middle childhood (ages 7 to 11) are more likely to treat their home life matter-of-factly, while adolescents may be more critical of their home life.
- Families with grandparents and relatives as parents–A growing segment of foster parents consists of grandparents or other relatives of children. Frequently, they must assume responsibility for children with little notice and while they are all in the throes of grief. Grandparents may be concerned about having too little energy for parenting again, but they nevertheless usually thrive in their role and mitigate for children the negative consequences of moving into a new home situation.
- Foster families–Some foster children have developed crucial survival skills and exhibit minimal behavior and adjustment problems. Others, perhaps the majority, demonstrate the effects of past neglect and abuse, grief over separation from their biological family, and the trauma of frequent placement changes. Repeated school transfers force foster children to adjust to different learning environments. They may not have developed learning skills, may never have received educational support at home, and may be more concerned about meeting their survival needs than their educational needs. Because some foster

families include several children of different ages and parents' attention may be divided, schools need to design responsive programs to involve parents. New parents may need help in creating a home environment conducive to learning and, particularly, doing homework.

The National Clearinghouse on Child Abuse and Neglect Information (April 2001) defined foster care as 24-hour substitute care for children placed away from their parents or guardians and for whom the state agency has placement and care responsibility, whether or not the placement is licensed or payments are made. This clearinghouse reported the following facts about foster care in this country:

- As of September 30, 1999, there were 568,000 children in foster care.
- During 1999, 143,000 children entered foster care.
- During 1999, 122,000 children exited foster care.
- Of the 568,000 children in foster care on September 30, 1999, 36% were white non-Hispanic, 42% were African-American non-Hispanic, 15% were Hispanic, and 7% were other racial-ethnic origins.
- Of the 122,000 children who exited foster care during 1999, 45% were white non-Hispanic, 33% were African-American non-Hispanic, 13% were Hispanic, and 9% were other racial-ethnic origins.
- Of the 568,000 children in foster care in 1999, 52% were male and 48% were female.

More than half a million children live with foster families. Predominantly children of color and residents of urban areas, they are a rapidly increasing group. Nearly all have suffered traumatic experiences, and many have had multiple homes. Foster parents are challenged by their children's many needs and their own inadequate training, the demands of a social welfare system that enforces strict rules but allocates too little money and support, and the knowledge that the children may leave at any time. Despite all these difficulties that affect family functioning, schools must place, educate, and keep track of foster children, and also help parents promote their children's learning (Schwartz, 1999b).

Schools can help staff focus on the stability and quality of a learner's home environment rather than on its composition by providing in-service training that includes

- the great variety of lifestyles that promote children's ability to achieve academically and develop into personally satisfied and productive adults;
- ways to identify, understand, and overcome personal feelings of bias;
- legal issues related to family composition, including custody, consent, confidentiality, and the rights of non-custodial and non-related caregivers;
- ways to respond effectively and sensitively to learner misbehavior; and
- the characteristics of individual learners and their families, as the information relates to their education and to behavior and communication with their family (Schwartz, 1999a).

Schools can also employ the following strategies for promoting acceptance of diverse families:

- Provide library and classroom resources that reflect family diversity.
- Select and use inclusive terms for caregivers in all family communications.
- Use student and school contact forms that allow families to identify themselves in the way that they choose and to report all the information they believe is important.
- Give families the opportunity to provide relevant information, such as the way interracial children want to be identified, and the opportunity to express concerns and review the school's handling of diversity issues.
- Develop a curriculum strand to increase learner knowledge of the various types of families that exist both in their school and in general, and invite family input (Schwartz, 1999a).

LEARNERS IN NONTRADITIONAL TRAINING AND EMPLOYMENT

The Workforce Investment Act defined nontraditional training and employment as "occupations or fields of work for which individuals from one gender comprise less than 25% of the individuals employed in each such occupation or field of work." The Perkins Act of 1998 defined nontraditional training and employment in the same way and included the careers in computer science, technology, and other emerging high-skill occupations. See Figure 4-3.

Men experience being nontraditional learners when they enroll in occupational training programs where fewer than 25% of the learners in the program are men, such as

- accounting;
- fashion marketing;
- medical secretary;
- administrative assistant;
- paralegal;
- interior design;
- child care and development;
- dental hygienist;
- nursing-associate degree;
- medical laboratory technician;
- occupational therapy assistant;
- respiratory care practitioner;
- electroneurodiagnostic technology;
- radiography;
- health information technology;
- community developmental disabilities associate;
- farm business and production management;
- nursing assistant;
- dental assistant;
- health unit coordinator; and
- surgical technologist.

NONTRADITIONAL JOBS

NONTRADITIONAL JOBS FOR FEMALES

Accounting	Computer technology	Hotel and lodging management
Agricultural mechanics	Custodial services	Industrial first aid
Agricultural production	Diesel mechanics	Industrial technology
Agricultural supplies and services	Drafting	Law enforcement
Architectural technology	Electrical	Machine shop
Auto mechanics	Electrical technology	Maritime occupations
Automotive	Electronics	Renewable natural resources
Aviation	Electronic technology	Sheet metal
Body and fender repair	Emergency medical technician	Small engine repair
Carpentry	Environmental control technology	Stationary energy sources
Civil technology	Fire fighting	Welding and cutting
Commercial pilot training	Forestry	Woodworking occupations

NONTRADITIONAL JOBS FOR MALES

Apparel and accessories	Home furnishings	Optometric technician
Child care	Medical assistant	Practical nurse
Cosmetology	Medical laboratory technician	Rehabilitation
Dental assistant	Nurse	Stenographer/secretary
Dental hygiene	Nursing assistant	Typing and related occupations
Food distribution		

Figure 4-3. Examples of nontraditional jobs for men and women.

Although most teachers believe that they treat females and males the same, research indicates that they frequently do not. The teacher's gender seems to have little bearing on the outcome; it is the gender of the learner that makes the difference. Studies show that teachers often exhibit differential behavior even though circumstances do not warrant it, such as in the following examples:

- Male learners receive more of the teacher's attention (acceptance, praise, criticism, and remediation) and are given more time to talk in class from preschool through college.
- Although differences among subject matter areas have not been well examined, recent research has found student-teacher interaction in science classes to be biased toward boys.
- Gender is a factor in the assignment of learners to ability groups in mathematics, and males are more likely to be assigned to the high ability group.
- Males receive harsher punishment than females, even for the same or a similar offense.
- Teachers ask boys more higher-order questions than they ask girls.

At one level, schools have made much progress in eliminating gender discrimination from their policies, programs, and practices. However, vestiges of gender discrimination, gender bias, and gender stereotyping remain. These vestiges continue to have a powerful and often negative influence on many learners. For example, although a policy prohibiting females from enrolling in career and technical education courses historically nontraditional to their gender would be rare, girls and young women are not enrolling in large numbers in carpentry, auto mechanics, heating and air-conditioning installation, or other such courses.

The U.S. Department of Labor, Women's Bureau, (2000) released the following information:

- Most women work out of economic need.
- Nearly 58 million women were employed in 1995 with the largest part still working in technical, sales, and clerical jobs. Of these, 42 million worked full-time (35 or more hours per week), and 16 million worked part-time (less than 35 hour per week). Two-thirds of all part-time workers were women (68%).
- The average woman worker is 34 years old and can expect to spend the majority of years of her life in the workforce.
- The more education a woman has, the greater the likelihood that she will seek paid employment.
- Of the 14 million families maintained by women, 4.2 million were below the poverty level in 1994. This represents 34.6% of all single-parent families maintained by women.
- In 1995, 3.4 million women were self-employed in nonagricultural industries. A large number of these women worked in wholesale and retail trades and professional, personal, and social services.
- Labor force participation for women continues to be highest among those in the 35 to 44 year-old age group (77%).

- Of all labor force participants age 25 years and over in 1995, women were more likely than men to have completed high school.

Central to the Perkins Act of 1990 is the goal to ensure that all learners have equal access to all career and technical education programs. Providing access to career and technical education includes programs, services, career guidance and counseling, and activities to eliminate bias and discrimination. Historically, career and technical education had gender-segregated programs that may or may not have reflected the actual interest of the learner. The goal should be to strive to provide equity and fairness in a wide range of programs and experiences while maintaining high standards and high expectations for all learners.

Major gender equity issues include

- girls at risk of dropping out of school;
- gender bias in student-teacher interactions;
- the participation and achievement of girls in mathematics and science;
- learners enrolling in and completing career and technical education courses historically nontraditional to their gender;
- gender bias in standardized tests;
- gender differences in learning styles;
- teen pregnancy and parenting; and
- sexual harassment of learners by their peers.

The Mid-Atlantic Equity consortium and The NETWORK (1993) detail key issues involving gender equity that instructors must be conscious of and address in the classroom. Their article looks into some of the possible causes for gender inequality in education and particular professional careers.

> The possible causes for the persistent sex segregation in vocational programs are multiple and not always easily identified or remedied. Possible factors include isolation from friends by being in a separate school or separate part of a building; lack of female role models as teachers; absence or small number of other female students; hostile learning environment, especially because of sexual harassment; apparent lack of employment opportunities for women in a particular field; and strong societal traditions of sex-appropriate careers. Lack of awareness of programs, peer pressure not to enroll in any form of vocational training, and lack of support for students who wish to enroll in vocational education are also possible factors. In fact, the historical patterns have been so difficult to break that some policymakers now believe that pursuing pay equity in the workplace (increasing the pay in many traditionally female occupations to that of men in comparable occupations) is likely to have a greater pay off than attempting to increase the number of women in male-dominated fields. (pp. 8-9)

Their publication goes on to provide techniques for assessing and addressing gender equity issues in the classroom. See Figure 4-4.

ASSESSING AND ADDRESSING GENDER INEQUALITY

Ask the following questions to determine whether gender equity has been addressed:

- How many learners are currently enrolling in and completing courses nontraditional to their gender?
- Is there a policy to protect learners from sexual harassment and other forms of gender discrimination both at school and on their cooperative or work-study jobs? Is it effective?
- Does program recruitment involve both role models (either teachers or workers) and learners of a gender not traditionally associated with the field of study?
- Does the program schedule facilitate hands-on experience in the career and technical education shops or laboratories?
- Have common physical barriers or impediments based on gender been identified and eliminated?
- Are support programs such as nontraditional mentors, supplemental instruction, child care, and counseling available for all learners?
- Do career and technical education programs serve all learners, regardless of gender, well in terms of knowledge, skills, and employability?

Determine possible methods to address gender inequality such as the following:

- Revise the recruiting program to include learners, teachers, and workers who are not traditionally associated with the field of study. Ensure that the recruiting program has equal status and treatment as recruiting programs in other areas
- If the program is located at a separate facility, make sure that all learners have access to the site
- Redesign middle school career and technical education orientation programs to ensure all learners have access to hands-on exposure in areas both traditional and nontraditional to their gender
- Prohibit sexual harassment of learners by both faculty and other learners, and enforce it through a written policy. The policy should specifically prohibit a hostile and intimidating learning environment

---

Source: Mid-Atlantic Equity Consortium, Inc. & The NETWORK, Inc. (1993). *Beyond Title IX: Gender Equity Issues in Schools.* [On-line]. Available: http://www.maec.org/beyond.html

Figure 4-4. Techniques for assessing and addressing gender inequality in schools.

There are a number of classroom and laboratory strategies that will promote gender equity, such as the following:
- Prepare a list of examples that reflect the interests of experiences of both males and females.
- Observe the group dynamics and praise positive cross-gender interactions.

- Enforce equal interactions and expectations between the sexes, thereby providing the same opportunities for participation in all activities.
- Display classroom posters on the contributions of both males and females in career and technical fields.
- Incorporate the historical and contemporary contributions of female and male scientists in science (e.g., biographical readings about women in science).
- Look for, create, and use test banks and sets of examples that are gender neutral or somewhat emphasize the interests of the gender nontraditional to the area of study.
- Make sure instructional materials are appropriate with respect to gender presentation.
- Make use of a broader range of professional organizations for career motivational materials and appropriate role models.
- Invite both male and female role models who are inspirational to present or demonstrate to the class.
- Establish professional development programs in equity. Instructors may avoid bias by doing the following:
- Alternate questioning between males and females.
- Recall that assertive learners are not necessarily more capable than less assertive learners.
- Be alert to teasing. It discourages participation by female learners.
- Encourage ALL learners equally.
- Especially monitor achievement of female learners on a regular basis.
- Generally, females, unlike males, avoid tasks labeled difficult and don't return to difficult tasks if they experience failure. Encourage them to do so.
- Give females early and continuing exposure to hands-on learning experiences and cooperative problem solving.
- Have high expectation for all learners. Positive expectations tend to increase learner achievement.
- Learn as much about female learners as males.
- Especially, inform female learners that most jobs in the future will require strong math, computer, science and technology skills.
- Make sure that instructional strategies are appropriate for all learners.
- Monitor achievement on a regular basis, including participation in classroom discussions, experiments, etc., of all learners.
- Make task assignments random or use a list of learners' names and check them off after you ask a question.
- Offer help to any and all learners when the material is difficult. Suggest after-school help for everyone.
- Recognize effort as well as accomplishment, especially for female learners.
- Respond fully to the comments of all learners.

Cunanan and Maddy-Bernstein (1993) investigated strategies around the country that have helped nontraditional learners in career and technical education programs.

They presented the following suggestions for the successful recruitment and retention of learners in nontraditional occupational training programs:

- Develop orientation programs in which males participate in traditionally female programs and females participate in traditionally male occupational areas.
- Include representations of females in audiovisual, instructional, and orientation materials used during recruitment fairs and career days.
- Encourage parents to play a strong role in supporting their child's career goals and/or assist learners in identifying one person (relative, friend, instructor) who is supportive of their nontraditional career path.
- Arrange job-site visits, shadowing activities, and experimental work experiences to introduce learners to nontraditional careers.
- Establish a mentor network for men or women interested in entering nontraditional occupations.
- Eliminate any stereotypical instructional materials from the classroom.
- Enforce fair and consistent discipline, dress standards, safety regulations, achievement expectations, and grading procedures for all learners.
- Provide on-site child care, transportation, and assistance with textbooks and other required educational materials, tools, and uniforms.
- Sensitize teachers to the effects of bias, stereotyping, and discrimination of learners.
- Provide counseling for learners regarding strengths and limitations and how they relate to occupational choices, focusing on opportunities in nontraditional occupations.
- Provide information to learners in nontraditional programs about the support services available to them.
- Encourage the development of support groups so that nontraditional learners can meet and share problems, concerns, and successes.
- Encourage learner participation in related professional seminars and state and national career and technical organizations.
- Identify tutoring and mentoring volunteers for nontraditional learners from role models in the business sector.
- Develop and implement an effective placement process for nontraditional learners who complete a career and technical education program. A key component to the success of these learners is a variety of career and work opportunities.
- Provide an open-entry, open-exit policy that allows learners to enroll at any time.
- Provide internships with local employers for learners to gain practical, hands-on experience as well as for employers to see that nontraditional learners can work successfully in a work environment.

Appropriate classroom support for nontraditional learners in postsecondary programs also includes the following:

- Send introductory letters to learners in nontraditional programs to welcome them and inform them of available support services.
- Develop a buddy system where a graduating nontraditional learner acts as a big brother or big sister to an incoming nontraditional learner.
- Offer peer tutoring to help nontraditional learners gain confidence.
- Assist nontraditional learners in obtaining information on community resources.
- Plan an orientation session at the beginning of the school year to give nontraditional learners the opportunity to meet one another.
- Provide a support group for nontraditional learners.
- Seek advice and support from a career and technical advisory committee concerning activities that support gender equity.
- When talking about occupations or professions in class, use language that does not reinforce limited views of gender roles and career choices. Often, examples can be effectively cast into I and you form with the instructor taking the role of one party and the class the other (e.g., "Suppose I am the electrician/doctor/restaurant manager and you came to me.").
- Tell classes you expect both female and male learners to participate in class discussions.
- Make a specific effort to call directly on female as well as on male learners.
- In addressing the class, use terminology that includes both male and females in the group.
- Respond to female and to male learners in similar ways when they make comparable contributions to class discussion by crediting comments to their author "as Jeanne said…" and coaching for additional information.
- Notice whether the feminine or masculine style of a learner's command, question, or response affects your own perception of its importance.
- Ask female and male learners qualitatively similar questions.
- Give female and male learners an equal amount of time to respond after asking a question.
- Give female and male learners the same opportunity to ask for and receive detailed instructions about the requirements for an assignment.
- Use parallel terminology when referring to or addressing male and female learners.
- Avoid placing professional women in a special category. For example, woman (or worse, lady) accountant.
- Experiment with language that reverses expectations based on gender. One teacher, for example, used "she" as the generic term for one semester and asked her learners to evaluate its impact on their perceptions and feelings. Avoid using "he" as a generic term whenever possible.
- Use the same tone with both female and male learners.
- Consider female as well as male learners when choosing classroom, teaching, and research assistants.
- Make a special effort to consider females for teaching and research assistantships in traditionally masculine fields and vice-versa.

- Offer to write letters of recommendations for nontraditional learners.
- Consider female and male learners when asking nominations for fellowships, awards, and prizes (Wood, 1991; Stevens & Burt, n.d.).

LEARNERS WHO ARE SINGLE PARENTS

The Perkins Act of 1998 specifically identifies single pregnant women when dealing with the special population of single parents. Lumsden and Coffey (2001) report that teen pregnancy has a negative effect on both quality of education and educational completion rates among teens who are pregnant or who have given birth. Over the past 30 years, schools have been slow to respond to the crisis of teen pregnancy. Some problems that interfere with pregnant teens being served appropriately by the schools include failure of teachers and administrators to view teen pregnancy as a dropout issue, lack of effort to reach teen fathers, and lack of scheduling flexibility to accommodate pregnant teens' need to receive medical attention.

Although the rate of teenage pregnancy in the United States has been declining, it remains the highest in the developed world. Approximately 97 out of every 1,000 women ages 15 to 19 (one million American teenagers) become pregnant each year. The majority of these pregnancies (78%) are unintended. Moreover, because the average age of menarche has reached an all-time low of about 12 or 13 years, and because four out of five young people have sex as teenagers, a greater proportion of teenage girls are at risk of becoming pregnant than ever before (Lumsden & Coffey, 2001).

Childbearing by teens has become a pressing problem. Each year, approximately 500,000 U.S. teens give birth. According to the U.S. Department of Health and Human Services, the preliminary U.S. birthrate for teenagers in 1996 was 54.7 live births per 1,000 women aged 15 to 19 years, down 4% from 1995 and down 12% from 1991 when the rate was 62.1. Although current teen pregnancy rates reverse the 24% increase that occurred between 1986 and 1991, these rates are still higher than they were in the early to mid-1980s, when the teen birthrate was at an all-time low—between 50 and 53 births per 1,000 teens ages 15 to 19 (Lumsden & Coffey, 2001).

Most of the teens giving birth are unmarried and are not ready for the emotional, psychological, and financial responsibilities and challenges of parenthood. Teen mothers are much less likely than older women to receive timely prenatal care, are more likely to smoke, are less likely to gain the recommended weight during their pregnancy, and are more likely to have a low birthweight infant. Most teen mothers also live in poverty, have dropped out of school, and are unemployed. In addition, between half and two-thirds of all female dropouts cite pregnancy as their principal reason for leaving school. Nearly two-thirds of births to teenagers (65%) were unintended when they were conceived, compared with 31% of births to women overall.

Teenage wives face a much higher risk of separation and divorce than women who wait longer to marry. Forty-seven percent of women who married before age 18 saw their marriage dissolve within 10 years, compared with 19% of women who married at age 23 or older (Lumsden & Coffey, 2001).

Much has been written about the negative consequences of teen motherhood for both mother and child, but little attention has been paid to teenage fathers. For a teenager, fathering a child may be just one event on a continuum of deviant behaviors, but one with particularly far-reaching consequences for the father, the child, and society. Teen fathers are unlikely to be in a position to provide financial, emotional, or other parental support for their children, and in this regard can be considered poor role models. Their legacy to their children is likely to be one of socioeconomic disadvantage, poor health, and poor education, among other hardships. Factors associated with teen fathers include the following:

- Boys who become teenage fathers are also likely to engage in a constellation of other problem behaviors such as noncriminal misbehavior (status offending), disruptive school behavior, and drug use.
- Teenagers who engage in delinquent acts and other problem behaviors create immediate consequences for themselves and for those around them, but when they also father children, there may be serious repercussions for many years to come, even for generations.
- Teenage fatherhood has received very little scrutiny—far less than teenage pregnancy or motherhood. Yet, like teen motherhood, teen fatherhood has many negative educational, financial, social, health, and other developmental consequences for these young men and their children.
- National surveys have indicated that somewhere between 2% and 7% of male teenagers are fathers, with higher rates among inner-city and African-American youth.
- The rate of teen fatherhood grew substantially between 1986 and 1996 when, according to the National Center for Health Statistics, 23 of every 1,000 males between 15 and 19 years of age became fathers. This figure, however, probably undercounts the actual number of teenage fathers. Information on fathers is often missing from birth certificates, contributing to the difficulty in assessing the prevalence of teen fatherhood.
- Prior research has shown that African-American teenagers are more likely to be fathers than are white or Hispanic teenagers.
- Additionally, teen fatherhood has been empirically associated with boys who come from impoverished families and neighborhoods and with those who engage in delinquency and other problem behaviors (Thornberry et al., 2000).

Because teenage fathers almost never plan pregnancies, their initial reactions may be denial, fear, and a desire to escape. Young fathers frequently face family rejection, barriers to contact with child and mother, a lack of ways to contribute financially, and an inability to envision future achievements enabling them to function effectively as a father. They also may believe that they are simply unwelcome and inadequate as parents. Their emotional state is further complicated by the need to reconcile the contradictory roles of adolescent and father and assume the responsibilities of adulthood before they are sufficiently mature (Schwartz, March 1999).

Communities, frequently with government and school assistance, can implement programs that help young men develop into caring and responsible fathers. Father programs can be independent or components of programs designed for families, teen mothers, or young men generally. It is undisputed that a father's commitment benefits children, families, and society; therefore, it is worth the time and effort of schools and community organizations to implement programs for young fathers that will enable them to develop into responsible adults, meet their obligations, and create a generation of well-nurtured and effectively educated children.

Many schools have comprehensive programs for pregnant and parenting females, in which they encourage mothers to identify and involve fathers in their children's lives and to recruit them for father programs. They may invite fathers to some programs for mothers. Some schools also implement and contribute to programs for fathers. They enable fathers to continue their general education, offer them parenting courses, and facilitate their efforts to find part-time work and make career plans.

The following effective program components for teen fathers were identified by Schwartz (March 1999):

- Goals and perspectives–Successful programs help young fathers develop the behaviors and assume the responsibilities common to committed parents by providing them with emotional support and useful services. Reflecting the current position of the Federal government, program goals indicate a shift in the orientation of many agencies: from solely attempting to secure child support payments to helping youth acquire fatherhood skills and increase their earning ability. Programs now seek to demonstrate that there are benefits to accepting the responsibilities of fatherhood as well as obligations.
- Community outreach–Program recruiters assume that fathers want to be involved. To find prospective participants, they urge mothers to supply names, encourage the youth's parents to recruit him, and go to neighborhood places where youth congregate. Fathers already involved with their children are recruited at birthing centers, clinics, and preschools.

   To entice youth to enroll, recruiters talk about the benefits of the program, give fathers practical help at the outset, and arrange attractive, structured father-child activities. Promises of other services also help fathers to enroll: legal advice about paternity issues, empowering information about the birth process and meeting infant needs, sex education counseling and

personal medical care, and mediation that leads to successful co-parenting. Other recruitment strategies are offering new fathers a safe and supportive place to talk about their children and other concerns and suggesting that program participation may give them added credibility with their children's mothers.

Establishing trust in the program helps fathers overcome their possible fear of authority and legal responsibilities, and negative and fatalistic beliefs. Thus, recruiters are honest and clear about all the ways a child benefits from having an involved father and also about how hard, but uniquely satisfying, fathering is. It is beneficial for the outreach worker to share, or be familiar with, the recruit's cultural background. One effective strategy is for the first (if not all) contact to be made by another teen father who can speak from experience. Older men who have overcome the difficulties of early parenthood also recruit effectively.

- Service provision–Young father programs can offer many different services, ranging from on-site support to referrals (i.e., legal aid, GED courses, job training). Some offer only group activities; others, one-on-one mentoring. Some programs function as a liaison between fathers and government agencies to help men both meet their financial obligations and become eligible for public services under the 1996 Federal Act. The Institute for Responsible Fatherhood and Family Revitalization, however, is opposed to accepting public assistance and focuses on developing self-reliance. One local YWCA even produced a handbook for fathers to use, either with the program or as a stand-alone resource.
- Education–It is crucial to help fathers get as much education as possible; programs may need to act as advocates if school personnel encourage them to leave. If fathers want to drop out of school, counselors can foster persistence by building confidence that they can succeed, helping them get a job that will not interfere with schoolwork, and securing tutoring. Fathers who have already dropped out are referred to GED programs. High school graduates are encouraged to enroll in higher education as a way of increasing their long-term career and economic prospects and helping them model educational achievement for their children.
- Parenting education–As they explain why a father's involvement is crucial to a child's development, counselors also teach how fathers can help their children develop cognitively, socioemotionally, and physically. Equally important, they help fathers develop strategies for controlling their anger when their children misbehave and for constructively disciplining the children. Many audiovisual aids are available to demonstrate good fatherhood practices.
- Career development–Programs can help fathers find short-term employment to meet their child support obligations; make long-range career plans; and enroll in training programs, such as Federal Job Opportunities

and Basic Skills Training. It may be necessary to provide a crash course in job-seeking and job-training skills. African-American fathers may need help in overcoming negative attitudes which, while based on historical experience, impede their chance for employment success now.

- Counseling–Counselors help youth clarify their feelings about impending fatherhood and assuming adult responsibilities early. To help fathers feel less isolated, they provide a place for sharing feelings, asking questions, and identifying commonalities within the group. Counselors also help them develop a mature definition of masculinity so they can enjoy a healthy relationship with a woman and defer fathering additional children.

Strategies that should be employed to assist pregnant and parenting teens include

- taking intensive approaches to improve retention and graduation rates;
- recognizing the links between teen pregnancy, domestic violence, and substance abuse;
- improving teens' knowledge about nutrition, general health habits, and family planning;
- assuring pregnant teens' access to health care, including prenatal care that begins during the first trimester;
- helping pregnant teens quit smoking and substance abuse;
- expanding opportunities for education in alternative schools and programs;
- reaching pregnant and parenting teens early, while they are still attending school;
- facilitating a prompt return to school after childbirth;
- building mentoring relationships that help motivate teen parents to stay in school;
- implementing Title IX so that pregnant and parenting teens are not denied educational opportunities, including the choice of remaining in their home schools;
- incorporating asset-based approaches that strengthen identity and self-esteem in efforts to discourage childbearing by teens;
- offering supportive learning environments for pregnant and parenting teens in public schools and applying lessons learned from successful alternative schools;
- developing competency-based learning and other flexible programs of study in public high schools for pregnant and parenting teens and other at-risk learners;
- arranging for quality child care services in or near schools attended by teen parents;
- arranging for on-site health care, developmental screenings, and follow-up services for children of teen parents;
- strengthening the involvement of fathers in the care and support of their children;
- developing and implementing comprehensive, multigenerational approaches to providing education and supports to teen parent families;
- emphasizing the value of nurturing and stimulating environments for children beginning in infancy, helping teen parents to maintain such environments at home,

and guiding their searches for suitable child care; and
- developing effective and well-coordinated systems of case management in programs serving teen-parent families (Institute for Educational Leadership, 1997).

LEARNERS WITH EDUCATIONAL ACHIEVEMENT BARRIERS

Amid the social, political, and technological changes of the last 30 years, interest in the education of America's children has remained high. During the 1970s and 1980s, concern for educational achievement prompted a back-to-basics movement followed by a call for learning expectations beyond competency. In the 1990s, the desire that all learners attain high levels of academic achievement was expressed through the establishment of challenging national education goals and state academic standards.

Campbell, Hombo, and Mazzeo (2000) reported results of the 1999 National Assessment of Educational Progress. Generally, the trends in mathematics and science are characterized by declines in the 1970s, followed by increases during the 1980s and early 1990s and relatively stable performance since then. Overall improvement across the assessment years is most evident in mathematics. See Figure 4-5. However, many learners still struggle against barriers to achievement.

ASSESSMENT OF EDUCATIONAL PROGRESS

READING QUARTILES
- Among nine-year-olds, the average reading scores of learners in each quartile range in 1999 were higher than in 1971
- Among 13-year-olds, overall gains are evident mostly for learners in the upper quartile and, to a lesser extent, in the middle two quartiles
- Among 17-year-olds, overall improvement is evident only among learners in the lower quartile

MATHEMATICS QUARTILES
- The overall gains that were seen for each age group in the national average mathematics scores are also evident in each quartile range
- For nine-, 13-, and 17-year-olds, the 1999 average score in each quartile range was higher than in 1978

SCIENCE QUARTILES
- Among nine- and 13-year-olds, overall gains in science since 1977 are evident in each quartile range
- Among 17-year-olds, scores increased between 1977 and 1999 in the upper and middle two quartiles, but not in the lower quartile

Source: Campbell, J., Hombo, C., & Mazzeo, J. (2000, August). *NAEP 1999 Trends in Academic Progress: Three Decades of Student Performance.* Washington, DC: U.S. Department of Education, Office of Educational Research and Improvement, National Center for Education Statistics.

Figure 4-5. Results of the 1999 National Assessment of Educational Progress.

Educationally Disadvantaged Learners

Educationally disadvantaged learners have problems in general academic achievement. See Figure 4-6. They often have low motivation to succeed in school. As a result, these learners frequently have low scores on achievement tests and poor attendance records. Many are potential dropouts. Individuals who are educationally disadvantaged often have a poor foundation in the basic academic skills. They may have difficulty applying basic mathematical concepts to problem-solving situations or task-related activities in career and technical education programs.

A lack of vocabulary development often prevents them from reading or writing at the minimum level necessary for success in a career and technical education program. Often they read two or more years below grade level. They frequently have difficulty putting their thoughts into writing and following written directions to perform tasks.

This group of learners often has language problems. Characteristics include poor speech patterns, trouble comprehending vocabulary and technical terms, difficulty in pronouncing words, problems constructing a proper sentence, poor spelling, and difficulty in carrying on a conversation with others. Because of the difficulty they have with verbal communication, they appear to have a limited ability to learn.

Although all learners and learners from minority populations can excel when expectations for them are high and content is challenging, most schools don't teach all learners at the same high level. In fact, the educational system is so full of inequities that it actually exacerbates the challenges of race and poverty, rather than ameliorates them. Simply put, we take learners who have less to begin with and give them less in school, too. The fact that progress in minority achievement has stopped at a time when minorities comprise a growing portion of the learner population should sound a wake-up call to the whole country. While virtually all learners from minority populations master basic skills by age 17, disproportionately few master the higher-level skills they need to assume productive roles in society (Lumsden & Coffey, 2001).

Learners who are not educated will more than likely lack adequate skills to secure employment and become self-sufficient adults. In 1993 approximately 63% of high school dropouts were unemployed. When they are employed, high school dropouts are often on the low end of the pay scale without employee benefits or job security. Over their lifetimes, high school dropouts will earn significantly less than high school graduates and less than half of what college graduates are likely to make in their lifetimes. Similarly, dropouts experience more unemployment during

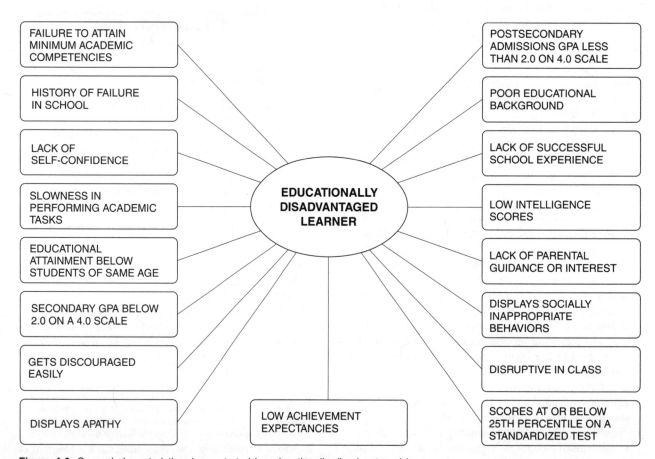

Figure 4-6. General characteristics demonstrated by educationally disadvantaged learners.

their work careers and are more likely to end up on welfare. Many dropouts struggle to maintain a minimum standard of living, often requiring welfare system support. Indeed, individuals who do not receive a basic education must overcome tremendous barriers to achieve financial success in life or even meet their basic needs (U.S. Department of Justice, 1997).

The National Center for Education Statistics (2001) reported the following:

- Five out of every 100 young adults enrolled in high school in October 1998 left school before October 1999 without successfully completing a high school program. This estimate was similar to the estimates reported over the last 10 years, but lower than those reported in the early 1970s.
- Hispanic learners were more likely than white learners to leave school before completing a high school program. In 1999, 7.8% of Hispanic learners were event dropouts, compared with 4% of white learners. However, the event dropout rate of white learners was not significantly different from those of African-American learners (6.5%) or Asian-American learners (5%).
- In 1999, young adults living in families with incomes in the lowest 20% of the income distribution were five times more likely to drop out of high school than their peers from families in the top 20% of the income distribution.
- Although dropout rates were highest among learners age 19 or older, about two-thirds (67.3%) of the current-year dropouts were ages 15 to 18. Moreover, about two-fifths (43.2%) of the 1999 dropouts were ages 15 to 17.
- In October 1999, five out of every 100 young adults enrolled in high school in October 1998 had left high school without successfully completing a high school program. In total, these dropouts accounted for approximately one-half million of the 10 million 15- to 24-year-olds enrolled in high school in the previous October. These numbers have not changed appreciably in recent years.
- The cumulative effect of hundreds of thousands of young adults leaving school each year short of finishing a high school program translates into several million young adults who are out of school, yet lacking a high school credential. In 1999, there were 3.8 million 16- to 24-year-olds who, although not enrolled in school, had not yet completed a high school program. Overall, 11.2% of the 34 million 16- through 24-year-olds in the U.S. were dropouts. Although there have been a number of year to year fluctuations in this rate, over the past 28 years, there has been a gradual pattern of decline that amounts to an average annual percentage change of .1 percentage point per year.
- The goal of reducing the dropout rate is to increase the percentage of young adults who complete a high school education. Despite the increased importance of a high school education, the high school completion rate has shown limited gains over the last quarter of a century and has been stable throughout most of the 1990s. In

1999, approximately three-quarters of the 18- to 24-year-olds who were not still in high school held regular diplomas (76.8%); another 9.2% of these youths were reported as having completed high school by an alternative route such as the GED.

- Over the last 10 years, the percentage of young adults completing high school has been relatively stable for whites and African-Americans. During the same period, the percentage of those completing high school through an alternative to a regular diploma has increased, with alternative completion rates of about 9% to 11% for white, African-American, and Hispanic young adults in 1999.
- Learners from low-income families are 2.4 times more likely to drop out of school than are learners from middle-income families, and 10.5 time more likely than learners from high-income families. In 1999, 11% of learners from families in the lowest 20% of the income distribution dropped out of high school. In comparison, 5% of learners from the middle 60% of the income distribution dropped out, as did 2.1% of learners from families with incomes in the top 20%.
- Data from 1995 show that more than half of the foreign-born Hispanic youths who were considered dropouts had never enrolled in a U.S. school, and 80% of these young adults who were never enrolled in U.S. schools were reported as either speaking English not well or not at all. Some of the young Hispanic immigrants who did not enroll in school in the U.S. may have entered the country beyond what is considered normal high school age, and some may have come to the U.S. in search of employment rather than education. However, the data also suggest that language may be a barrier to participation to the U.S. schools. Regardless of the reasons for the large proportion of Hispanic young adults without a high school credential the impact is the same. Whether they were born in the U.S. or elsewhere and whether or not they enrolled in U.S. schools, these young adults probably do not have the basic level of education thought to be essential in today's economy.
- Potential dropouts tend to be retained in the same grade, have poor academic grades, and feel disengaged from school. They are more likely to come from low socioeconomic status families where parents did not get very far in their schooling. These learners tend to be part of a large peer group, to be involved in more passive activities, to adhere frequently to deviant norms, to manifest behavior problems, to be arrested frequently by the police, and to exhibit psychological vulnerability.
- High school graduates, on the average, earn $6,415 more per year than high school dropouts.
- Each year's class of dropouts will cost the country over $200 billion during their lifetimes in lost earnings and unrealized tax revenue.

Case Study . . . Ryan

Ryan is in his junior year of high school. He failed several grades in elementary school and is already 18 years old. He is on the edge of failing again. His grades are very low in all his courses except for agribusiness management and marketing.

Ryan first developed an interest in agriculture education during an exploratory experience in ninth grade. After participating in Introduction to World Agricultural Science and Technology, he finally found a clear direction and decided that this was going to be his career path. His counselor helped to establish a coherent sequence of courses to support this career objective.

It became apparent that Ryan would need assistance in improving his academic foundation skills. This was accomplished by the integration of academic and vocational curricula in the district. Science, math, and language arts information was reinforced in the agricultural education curriculum. In addition, the academic teachers reinforced vocational concepts in their classrooms.

Ryan began to realize the importance of his academic courses. His instructor arranged for some peer tutoring in the classroom and laboratory. As Ryan started to achieve success and saw his grades improving, his motivation increased. He began to attend a remedial "breakfast club" class in the morning before school where volunteer students and parents helped him to improve his academic foundation skills. His agriculture education instructor has recently made arrangements for a local merchant who has a successful pesticide control business to mentor Ryan. The merchant visits Ryan at school for lunch once a month. In addition, Ryan has been given a part-time job with the pesticide company.

The National Dropout Prevention Network (2001) reported the following:

- A dropout will earn $250,000 less than a high school graduate over the course of a lifetime.
- Nationwide, about 25% of dropouts are unemployed at any point in time.
- Each year's new group of dropouts may cost the nation as much as $240 billion in crime, welfare, health care, and social services.
- For every dollar spend on education, it costs $9 to provide services to dropouts.
- People who drop out of school are six to 10 times more likely to turn to a life of crime than those who graduate.
- Eighty-two percent of prisoners in America are high school dropouts.
- It is cheaper to send someone to Yale than to jail, but jail is easier to get into.
- Each inmate costs the nation about $28,000 a year.

DeKalb (1999) states that absenteeism affects learner achievement. Truancy has been labeled one of the top 10 major problems of this country's schools, negatively affecting the future of American youth. In fact, absentee rates have reached as high as 30% in some cities. Learner nonattendance is a problem that extends much further than the school. It affects the learner, the family, and the community. Absenteeism is detrimental to learners' achievement, promotion, graduation, self-esteem, and employment potential. Clearly, learners who miss school fall behind their peers in the classroom. This, in turn, leads to low self-esteem and increases the likelihood that at-risk learners will drop out of school. Before determining the most effective means of controlling unexcused absences, the causes of truant behavior must be understood. Not only may the cause vary from learner to learner, but school staff and learners may disagree about the underlying causes. Although many teachers may be empathetic and willing to help learners, this difference in opinion may create a barrier of understanding between teacher and learners. In one survey, learners cited boredom and loss of interest in school, irrelevant courses, suspensions, and bad relationships with teachers as the major factors in their decision to skip school. On the other hand, most of the school staff believed truancy to be related primarily to learner problems with family and peers.

Learners with truancy problems often face problems with underachievement. Underachievement is tied intimately to self-concept development. Learners who come to see themselves in terms of failure eventually begin to place self-imposed limits on what is possible. Any academic successes are written off as flukes, while low grades serve to reinforce negative self-perceptions. This self-deprecating attitude often results in comments such as "Why should I even try? I'm just going to fail anyway," or "Even if I do succeed, people will say it's because I cheated." The end product is a low self-concept, with learners perceiving themselves as academically weak. Under this assumption, their initiative to change or to accept a challenge is limited. Specific strategies to address underachievement must be employed to motivate these learners. See Figure 4-7.

Two broad, common influences, (1) school and (2) community and home, underlie the reasons why youth end up outside the educational mainstream. Factors related to school include lack of motivation due to poor academic performance, low self-esteem resulting from classification as one who is verbally deficient or a slow learner, lack of personal and educational goals due to absence of stimulating academic challenges, and teacher neglect and lack of respect for learners. Factors related to the community and home include negative role models exemplified by friends who are chronically truant or absent from school, pressures related to family health or financial concerns, lack of family support and motivation for education in general, violence in or near the learner's home or school, and difficulty coping with teen pregnancy, marriage, or parenthood (U.S. Department of Justice, 1997).

STRATEGIES TO REVERSE PATTERNS OF UNDERACHIEVEMENT

SUPPORTIVE STRATEGIES
- Allow learners to feel they are part of a family, not a factory
- Hold class meetings to discuss learner concerns
- Design curriculum activities based on learners' needs and interests
- Allow learners to bypass assignments on subjects in which they are competent

INTRINSIC STRATEGIES
- Incorporate the idea that learners' self-concepts are tied closely to their desire to achieve academically
- Encourage attempts, not just successes
- Value learner input in creating classroom rules and responsibilities
- Allow learners to evaluate their own work before receiving a grade

REMEDIAL STRATEGIES
- Recognize that learners are not perfect; each learner has specific strengths and weaknesses as well as social, emotional, and intellectual needs
- Give learners chances to excel in their areas of strength and interest while providing opportunities in specific areas of learning deficiencies
- Create a safe environment in which mistakes are considered a part of learning for everyone, including the instructor

Source: Whitmore, J. (1980). *Giftedness, Conflict and Underachievement.* Boston: Allyn and Bacon.

Figure 4-7. Progress strategies that can be used to reverse patterns of underachievement.

Home experiences influence learner achievement at school. For example, exposure to reading in the home influences attitudes towards reading and reading ability. Consider that the number of different types of reading materials in the home has decreased between 1971 and 1999. A smaller percentage of 13- and 17-year-olds read for fun daily in 1999 than in 1984. There was no significant change in frequency of reading for fun among nine-year-olds. A smaller percentage of 17-year-olds saw adults reading in their homes in 1999 than in 1984. However, a greater percentage of 17-year-olds were watching three or more hours of television each day in 1999 than in 1978. A smaller percentage of 9- and 13-year-olds were watching six or more hours of television each day in 1999 than in 1978 (Campbell, Hombo & Mazzeo, 2000).

Some techniques for career and technical education instructors working with educationally and economically disadvantaged learners include the following:
- Collect and analyze all available information relating to the learner.
- Help the learner establish short-term and long-range goals that are realistic.

- Focus on learner abilities as they relate to your program, curriculum, exit points, and competencies.
- Select and create materials that will interest and challenge the learners and build in strategies for developing higher-order skills.
- Minimize lectures. Actively engage learners in activities to match learners' particular interests and needs. Use lots of small group learning and incorporate journal writing so learners develop habits of analysis and reflection.
- Do not label disadvantaged learners as low achievers because of their different learning styles.
- Identify the ability levels of the learner and develop an open system of individualized instruction documented in an individually prescribed program. Involve learners in the planning process.
- Modify teaching techniques to the style and rate of learning of each learner. Use practical experiences and explanations rather than abstract concepts.
- Use concrete, tangible demonstrations rather than verbal and abstract lessons.
- Use illustrations, audiovisual aids, field trips, and direct experiences whenever possible.
- Keep learners aware of progress at all times and give them reason to believe that they are succeeding.
- Encourage learner expression whenever possible, such as during teacher-student planning and group activities.
- Format instructional materials into shorter units of work.
- Provide for frequent evaluation of learner progress to identify and provide necessary remedial assistance.
- Work as closely and as frequently as possible with other school resources and agencies.
- Use simple, direct vocabulary to keep communication channels open.
- Recognize that the learner's vocabulary may be more limited and less precise than that of the peer group.
- Make directions simple, explicit, and precise.
- Provide written assignment sheets or have learners copy assignments in notebooks to develop organizational skills.
- Use hands-on activities whenever possible.
- Provide reading materials with appropriate vocabulary levels (e.g., sentence structure and content suited to the learner's reading level, interests, and experience).
- Allow learners to progress at their own pace.
- Provide for closure at the end of lessons and units.
- Present examples of successful workers from various cultural or minority groups to serve as role models for learners. Invite workers in the community from various cultural backgrounds to come and share their experiences.
- Identify learners' reading and math levels. Use this information to select or develop instructional materials.
- Encourage learners who are proficient in hands-on skills to become peer tutors for other learners. This situation can serve as a motivating activity, as a way for disadvantaged learners to increase their academic skills by reviewing related reading and math material, and as a reinforcement for positive peer relationships.

- Utilize field trips and shadowing experiences to provide exposure to people who hold jobs associated with the program. Many learners have no role model to follow in selecting or pursuing a career pathway.
- Work with support staff to develop and implement appropriate behavior management techniques for those learners who display apathetic, hostile, or defiant behavior. Occupationally accepted behavior should be stressed at all times.

Limited English-Proficient Learners

As the cultural makeup of society becomes more diverse, educators must become familiar with a variety of cultures and grasp both the advantages and challenges that accompany serving a more diverse learner population. Teachers and administrators must create multicultural environments in which learners from a wide array of backgrounds feel academically challenged as well as personally accepted and supported.

Along with increasing racial-ethnic diversity comes increasing linguistic diversity. Both the number and the percentage of children who have difficulty speaking English have risen in recent years. Immigrant children and the children of immigrants often do not speak English well.

The Perkins Act of 1998 defines limited English proficiency (LEP) as persons who were not born in the U.S., or whose native language is a language other than English, who came from environments where a language other than English is dominant, or who are Native Americans or Alaskan native learners and who come from environments where a language other than English has had a significant impact on their English proficiency.

The Urban Institute (2001) presented the following facts regarding immigrant teens:

- A growing share of all K–13th grade learners are immigrant teens–Children of immigrants (foreign-born or having a foreign-born parent) represent a sharply rising share of all learners in school, tripling from 6.3% in 1970 to nearly 20% in 1997.
- A larger share of secondary school learners are immigrant teens–Foreign-born children represent a substantially larger share of the total secondary school population (5.7%) than of the primary school population (3.5%).
- Immigrant teens are not fully fluent in English–As many as a quarter of all foreign-born children are not fully fluent in English; about 75% of these children are Hispanic and speak Spanish at home.
- Many lack LEP instruction resources–While more than three-quarters of LEP elementary school learners receive special English-language development instruction, fewer than half of secondary school LEP learners receive such instruction.
- They are experiencing sharp increases in poverty–Foreign-born children have experienced sharp increases in poverty, from 17% in 1970 to almost 44% in 1995.

- Immigrant teens are linguistically, ethnically, and economically isolated–Children of immigrants tend to be linguistically isolated in schools as well as economically and ethnically segregated. Almost one-half of all LEP children attend schools in which 30% or more of the learners are also LEP. Only 2% of non-LEP learners attend such schools.

Educational barriers for limited English-proficient learners include limited staff capacity, organizational rigidity, lack of accountability and standards, and knowledge gaps. The following list summarizes barriers and suggested remedies:

- Teachers of mainstream subjects, such as math or history, often lack training to work with LEP learners and often maintain that developing learners' basic literacy skills is not part of their core task. Principals and counselors frequently lack the language skills and cultural understanding needed to communicate effectively with these learners. A suggested remedy could be implementing professional development programs for veteran teachers focused on making mainstream subject classes more accessible to learners still learning English.
- The rigid organization of schools, including the division of secondary schools into departments along university lines, the isolation of language-development teachers, and the division of the day into 50-minute periods, hampers needed individualized instruction. For example, the time allotted for learning is too short for learners to master both the language and content needed to graduate. A suggested remedy could be restructuring the secondary school schedule so that language and subject teachers have the opportunity to collaborate and to reorganize their use of classroom time.
- Curriculum content standards for English-language development programs vary widely across states, schools, and even classrooms. Secondary schools also lag behind elementary schools in creating instructional strategies and curricula specially designed to help LEP learners meet new grade promotion and graduation standards. A suggested remedy could be expanded development of strong curricular and learner performance standards for English as a Second Language (ESL) and bilingual programs, which serve as gateways to secondary schools' mainstream curriculum.
- Reformers face wide knowledge gaps in how to simultaneously build both language and subject matter learning among LEP learners. Both types of learning are necessary for immigrant teens to graduate in the short time available to reach that goal. The lack of reliable assessment instruments for LEP learners is particularly troubling to teachers. Suggested remedies include more demonstration projects on promising curricular models and more research that addresses four broad areas: needs of understudied subpopulations; optimal ways to teach core subject material to LEP learners; educational and social effects of linguistic isolation on learners; and development of relevant assessment tools.

Case Study . . . Jarunee

Jarunee is a junior in high school. She has language difficulties in school because English is not her native language. Her family came to the USA from Thailand seven years ago. They settled in a town where there were a large number of Thai families, establishing a small Thai community. This provides cultural support for them. The family members speak Thai in the home and in the small ethnic community rather than English, which makes Jarunee's transition to school a difficult one.

Jarunee is enrolled in the culinary arts program at high school. Her instructor, Mrs. Gentry, has coordinated closely with the special needs coordinator at the school to identify resources to assist Jarunee. A volunteer from the Thai community comes to the school several times a week to work with teachers who have Jarunee in their class. This helps open communication with the home as well as preventing any miscommunication and/or misdirection that may occur with Jarunee in her classes due to language difficulties. In addition, the school has set up a peer-partnership program with Thai students working together for translation and collaboration. The peer-partnership group meets after school once a week. Flexibility is emphasized in the school philosophy so that students can attend class with their partner for short periods of time if difficulty arises and translation is needed. Teachers work together to facilitate this program.

Although Mrs. Gentry does not speak Thai, she is employing techniques in the classroom and laboratory that are helping Jarunee. Thai-English labels have been placed in the laboratory to identify equipment and supplies used in activities and projects. Jarunee has established a pictionary section in her notebook where English words are placed next to the picture of equipment, tools, and supplies used in the culinary arts program. When preparing written materials to be used by Jarunee, Mrs. Gentry turns narrative sections into lists, uses large clear print, and keeps sentences as short as possible. Mrs. Gentry has also attempted to learn about Jarunee's culture, and some Thai foods have been integrated into lab activities so that all of the students in the program experience a cross-cultural exchange.

Jarunee is given additional time when taking tests and Mrs. Gentry is available to discuss questions if there is any problem with comprehension. Jarunee has shown remarkable progress and feels very good about her accomplishments. Her social skills are improving as well as her English-speaking skills.

LEP persons—especially immigrants—often come not only from a different language background but also from a very different cultural background; English-language instruction must often provide cultural as well as linguistic orientation. Immigrants in particular may experience profound adjustment or transformation of their social identity—all those aspects of the self (family role, life skills, sense of community, etc.) that define how people understand themselves in relation to others. Four specific cultural factors that may affect learner-teacher interaction in the classroom include the following:

1. Roles of learners and teachers–Learners may expect more traditional, formal, authoritarian, ordered, and structured instructional styles and activities and may be put off by informal practices such as using first names and moving freely around the room. Likewise, teachers may expect learners, especially adult learners, to be self-reliant, expressive, and assertive—a potential conflict with learners who are carefully deferential and reserved.
2. Gender-related issues–Learners may expect different behavior from male and female instructors. Likewise, gender issues might affect group configurations or activities. Finally, different definitions of appropriate gender roles can prevent or discourage LEP women from pursuing training.
3. Appropriate topics for instruction–Topics that are innocuous to one person may violate social, dietary, or religious prohibitions for another. In addition, some recent immigrants may have great difficulty describing the homes they fled in fear or answering personal questions that might have a bearing on their unresolved immigration status.

4. Appropriate behavior at school–Different cultures define what is appropriate differently. Some learners may balk at moving classroom furniture or may expect a quiet, orderly classroom at all times. On the other hand, learners may expect to be able to eat, drink, smoke, or litter freely in the classroom (Wonacott, 2000).

High dropout rates among language-minority secondary school learners are one indication that many schools are failing to adequately support the needs of these learners. The belief that learner dropout is due to a lack of proficiency in English often leads educators to overlook the economic, cultural, academic, and personal issues that immigrant adolescents must confront on a daily basis. To be effective, programs must begin with a compassionate understanding of these learners and recognize and build on the identity, language, and knowledge they already possess. Instruction developed for native English-speaking learners may not be appropriate for learners who are still learning English. To engage immigrant adolescents in school, educators must provide them with avenues to explore and strengthen their ethnic identities and languages while developing their ability to study and work in this country. See Figure 4-8.

The Center for Law and Education (2001) provides information regarding federal education law and language minority learners. The federal laws protecting language minority learners do not specify particular services a school must provide, either to LEP learners in general or to individual learners, nor do they set out particular procedures for requesting or developing services for individual learners. State law, however, may require particular programs, services or procedures.

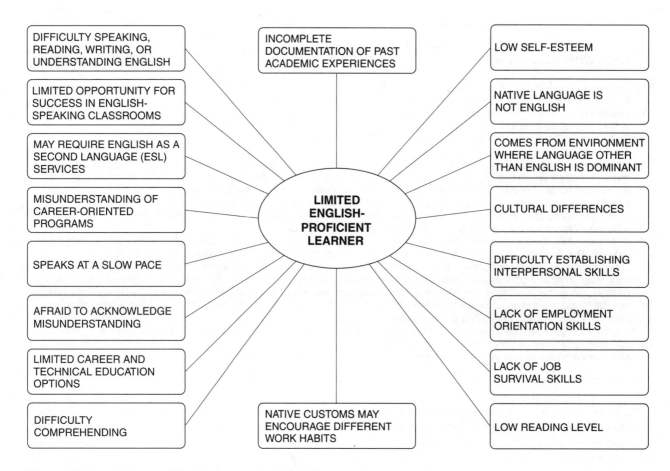

Figure 4-8. General characteristics demonstrated by limited English-proficient learners.

The Equal Educational Opportunities Act of 1974 requires states and school systems "to take appropriate steps to overcome language barriers that impede equal participation by its students in its instructional programs." To fulfill this duty, a school system first must (1) adopt an educational approach that experts believe is sound, or promising as a new strategy, and (2) actually put the approach into practice, including devoting the resources necessary to implement it effectively. Most importantly, the school system must obtain good results. A school system that stays with an ineffective approach illegally denies equal educational opportunity (The Center for Law and Education, 2001).

The lack of specific service requirements notwithstanding, courts and the U.S. Department of Education's Office for Civil Rights have recognized certain broad features as critical to an effective, legally sufficient program. School systems should have a comprehensive approach to educating LEP learners, including identification of youth not in school, identification of those with a home language other than English, adequate assessment to determine learners' ability to read, write and comprehend English, and adequate curriculum, texts and materials. Children must learn to read and write in English and must receive academic content instruction in a language they understand.

Schools must assess learners in their dominant language to determine whether they are falling behind academically while English skills are being stressed and to provide compensatory services as needed. Staff must have the skills and training necessary to implement the chosen program. Teachers in bilingual programs should be able to speak, read and write both languages, and be fully qualified to teach their subject. Learners must have access to all facets of the school's educational program, including Title I (formerly Chapter 1) services, career and technical education, and appropriate special education services when necessary (The Center for Law and Education, 2001).

Exit criteria for termination of LEP services must ensure that learners can read, write, and comprehend English well enough to learn successfully in an English-only program. Exit criteria that simply test a learner's oral skills are inadequate. In addition, a school's exit criteria should be suspect if, for example, former LEP learners cannot keep up with English-speaking peers, need simplified English materials in order to succeed in all aspects of the school's curriculum, or have higher grade retention or dropout rates than do other learners. Once exited, individual learners should be monitored for their ability to function in the mainstream (The Center for Law and Education, 2001).

Title I of the Elementary and Secondary Education Act (ESEA), the Carl D. Perkins Vocational and Technical Education Act, and the Individuals with Disabilities Education Act all speak to the needs of learners with LEP. Title I of the ESEA requires that any school that receives Title I money must be making adequate yearly progress toward getting all learners to meet state standards. Title I schools must provide an accelerated curriculum, effective instruction, timely and effective assistance when they begin to fall behind, and high-quality teaching staff with high-quality professional development. All of this must be provided in a program developed in partnership with parents. Title I provides that LEP learners are eligible for Title I services on the same basis as other learners selected to receive services. Further, LEP learners must be held to the same high content and performance standards required for all Title I learners, and assessed to determine how well they are progressing toward these standards. Assessments must provide for reasonable accommodations and LEP learners must be assessed, to the extent practicable, in the language and form most likely to yield accurate and reliable information on what such learners know and can do to determine such learners' mastery of skills in subjects other than English. Their parents, to the extent practicable, must be given the opportunity to be full participants in their children's education (The Center for Law and Education, 2001).

The Perkins Act prohibits discrimination against LEP learners and requires that they be afforded equal access to all programs. Perkins also mandates that states, local school systems, and individual schools plan their career and technical education programs to meet the needs of LEP learners and enable these learners to meet the standards set for all learners, and to prepare for further learning and high skill, high wage careers (The Center for Law and Education, 2001).

Learners with LEP who have disabilities are entitled to all of the services that learners with LEP are otherwise entitled to and all of the services to which learners with disabilities are otherwise entitled. These rights include the right to special education and related services provided in the learner's primary language as necessary in view of the learner's needs. While the Individuals with Disabilities Education Act has always protected learners with LEP, a 1997 amendment to the law emphasizes that language needs must be taken into account in designing the particular special education services a learner is to receive. Other provisions of the IDEA protect LEP learners in the special education evaluation process, require that parents be provided notices in their native language, and obligate schools to provide interpreters at meetings held to plan or review a learner's special education services (The Center for Law and Education, 2001).

Working with Limited English-Proficient Learners

Instructors should adapt the way that spoken English is used to deliver career and technical curriculum so LEP learners can learn effectively. Suggested strategies include
- avoiding unnecessary slang;
- keeping terminology constant by using simple terms learners may already know and by using generic terms;
- speaking at a slower pace;
- giving and receiving verbal confirmations to make certain learners understand and are being understood; and
- providing outlines of lectures.

Instructors may have to modify instructional materials for LEP learners enrolled in career and technical education programs. Strategies include
- determining the reading level of the material being used;
- determining the degree of difficulty of given vocabulary;
- illustrating technical material whenever possible using tables, graphs, prints, schematic diagrams, and illustrations;
- identifying the key points of a page of text or instructional material;
- using brightly colored markers to draw arrows and underlining or circling important words, statements, and illustrations in an instructional material;
- recording key passages or notes in English or in the native language of the learner to go along with written materials;
- using written materials on a variety of reading levels; and
- having important points underlined with accompanying vocabulary lists.

General strategies that are successful in working with LEP individuals in career and technical programs include the following:
1. Be aware of the student's cultural background and allow for individual differences.
2. Encourage students to bring dictionaries to class.
3. Use as many hands-on experiences and demonstrations as possible.
4. For the oral portion of instruction, speak slowly and use simple vocabulary and grammar.
5. Try not to simplify technical terms too much or learners will not learn them.
6. Use bright felt tip markers or highlighters to mark important words, passages, or illustrations.
7. Use a translator to translate important concepts and to share with you any problems that students are having.
8. Work closely with limited English-speaking and English-as-a-Second-Language (ESL) support personnel.
9. Adjust the length of assignments. It may require two or more hours for an LEP learner to accomplish what a native English speaker can accomplish in half that time.
10. To check for comprehension, ask students what you have said. Refrain from asking them if they understand. Individuals from some cultures will say "yes" even if they don't understand.

11. Use simple sentences in writing test items so learners can concentrate on responding to questions rather than deciphering them.

12. Give students more processing time to come up with a response to a question.

13. If learners have a correct and understandable answer, don't correct their grammar. Instead, repeat the answer in standard English form and let them know that you are pleased with their response.

14. Speak directly to students, emphasizing important nouns and verbs. Use as few extra words as possible.

15. Don't force reluctant students to speak. Instead, give them the opportunity to respond through nonverbal behavior and manipulating objects.

16. Support students' home language and culture. Ask them to share their customs and information about their culture, religion, and family life.

17. Help fluent English-speaking learners see the LEP students as knowledgeable people from a respected culture.

18. Pair or group LEP students with native speakers. Give students tasks to complete that require interaction of each member of the group, but arrange the tasks so that the LEP students have linguistically easier tasks at first.

19. Simplifying written English by turning narratives into lists; using large, clear print; replacing pronouns with nouns; keeping sentences as short as possible; and using illustrations and activities as a supplement.

20. Have students build their own bilingual technical dictionary from program material.

21. Individualize instruction as much as possible. Specially designed instruction sheets with illustrations and technical terms in both the learner's native language and English can be invaluable. Volunteer peers, parents, or others can help to develop these sheets.

22. Infuse employability skills into the curriculum for LEP students (e.g., appropriate social behavior, expected work habits, patterns in the American workforce, proper interviewing techniques, etc.).

23. Use a variety of labels, signs, and visual aids in the classroom and laboratory, both in the student's native language and in English.

24. Clearly state what is expected from students in terms of performance objectives. Follow these objectives when presenting material and evaluating learner performance.

25. Be conscious of your body language. Hand and body gestures vary in meaning from culture to culture.

26. Audio or videotape your lessons and make them available to students and ESL or bilingual personnel.

27. When taking attendance during the first few days of class, have students introduce themselves. This will provide an opportunity for teachers to hear the proper pronunciations of names and note them phonically in order to practice and remember them.

28. Present class information in small, discrete, and sequential steps.

29. Supplement texts with study guides, lists of key terms, extra visuals depicting concepts or procedures. These are helpful when translated into the student's native language.

30. Encourage pair or group projects so that peer modeling and tutoring can occur. Pair LEP students with bilingual students of their own language background if possible.

31. When testing LEP students, utilize these suggestions:
   - provide frequent check points prior to the test;
   - inform students of evaluation measures, especially as they relate to technical language;
   - provide exercises and reinforcement activities using test formats to teach test-taking skills;
   - allow the use of a bilingual dictionary;
   - eliminate time constraints; and
   - if extensive reading or essay writing is required, divide the test in two. LEP students need more time to read a test and to develop a written response. (Lopez-Valadez, 1982, p. 26)

Friedenberg (1995) identified the following five approaches to content-area instruction:

1. Bilingual/bicultural education provides content-area instruction to LEP learners (usually all with the same native language) in their native language; ESL instruction is also provided at the same time. Over time, use of the native language for instruction is decreased and the use of English is increased.

2. Multilingual/multicultural approaches provide limited content-area instruction in native languages when there are LEP learners with different native languages in a class or when bilingual or multilingual teachers or aides are not available. The instructor becomes more a facilitator than a provider of instruction. ESL instruction is also provided at the same time.

3. Sheltered-content instruction uses English to provide content-area instruction but begins by first developing appropriate vocabulary by extensive use of visual aids, gestures, graphic organizers, and cooperative hands-on activities. It is often used for classes with multiple language groups or multiple English proficiency levels or when bilingual teachers or aides are unavailable.

4. Immersion is an approach used frequently but inconsistently, ranging from carefully structured sheltered techniques with bilingual assistance to nothing more than submersion. In immersion, a LEP learner's native language is not used.

5. Submersion is an approach that provides no special services at all to LEP learners—it's either sink or swim.

Walqui (2000) provides 10 principles of effective instruction for LEP learners:

1. The culture of the classroom fosters the development of a community of learners, and all learners are part of that community–Limited English-proficient learners bring a variety of experiences to the classroom that, if tapped, can serve as a springboard for new explorations that enrich everyone's experience. In effective classrooms,

teachers and learners together construct a culture that values the strengths of all participants and respects their interests, abilities, languages, and dialects. Learners and teachers shift among the roles of expert, researcher, learner, and teacher, supporting themselves and each other.

2. Good language teaching involves conceptual and academic development–Effective ESL classes focus on themes and develop skills relevant to learners and their studies in mainstream academic classes. LEP learners need to learn not only new content, but also the language and discourse associated with the discipline; therefore, all subject matter classes must have a language focus.

   Effective teaching prepares learners for high-quality academic work by focusing their attention on key processes and ideas and allowing them to practice these processes and ideas. English as a second language teachers need to know the linguistic, cognitive, and academic demands they are preparing their learners for and help them develop the necessary proficiencies. Content-area teachers need to determine the core knowledge and skills learners need to master.

3. Learners' experiential backgrounds provide a point of departure and an anchor in the exploration of new ideas–Limited English-proficient learners know a great deal about the world, and this knowledge can provide the basis for understanding new concepts in a new language. Learners will learn new concepts and language only when they build on previous knowledge and understanding. Some learners have been socialized into lecture and recitation approaches to teaching, and they expect teachers to tell them what lessons are about. But by engaging in activities that involve predicting, inferring based on prior knowledge, and supporting conclusions with evidence, learners will realize that they can learn actively and that working in this way is fun and stimulating.

4. Teaching and learning focus on substantive ideas that are organized cyclically–To work effectively with English learners, teachers must select the themes and concepts that are central to their discipline and to the curriculum. The curriculum should be organized around the cyclical reintroduction of concepts at progressively higher levels of complexity and interrelatedness. Cyclical organization of subject matter leads to a natural growth in the understanding of ideas and to gradual correction of misunderstandings.

5. New ideas and tasks are contextualized–English-language learners often have problems trying to make sense of decontextualized language. This situation is especially acute in the reading of textbooks. Secondary school textbooks are usually linear, dry, and dense, with few illustrations. Embedding the language of textbooks in a meaningful context by using manipulative objects, pictures, a few minutes of a film, and other types of media can make language comprehensible to learners. Teachers may also provide context by creating analogies based on learners' experiences. However,

this requires that the teacher learn about learners' backgrounds because metaphors or analogies that may work well with native English speakers may not clarify meanings for English-language learners. In this sense, good teachers of immigrant learners continually search for metaphors and analogies that bring complex ideas closer to the learners' world experiences.

6. Academic strategies, sociocultural expectations, and academic norms are taught explicitly–Effective teachers develop learners' sense of autonomy through the explicit teaching of strategies that enable them to approach academic tasks successfully. The teaching of such metacognitive strategies is a way of scaffolding instruction; the goal is to gradually hand over responsibility to the learners as they acquire skills and knowledge.

   The discourse of power—the language used in this country to establish and maintain social control—should also be taught explicitly because it is not automatically acquired. Guidance and modeling can go a long way toward promoting awareness of and facility with this discourse. For example, preferred and accepted ways of talking, writing, and presenting are culture specific. Developing learner awareness of differences, modeling preferred language styles, and studying these differences and preferred styles are three steps in the development of proficiency and autonomy that needs to be included in the education of LEP learners.

7. Tasks are relevant, meaningful, engaging, and varied–Some research indicates that most classes for LEP learners are monotonous, teacher-fronted, and directed to the whole class; teacher monologues are the rule. If learners do not interact with each other, they do not have opportunities to construct their own understandings and often become disengaged. Because immigrant learners are usually well-behaved in class, teachers are not always aware that they are bored and not learning. Good classes for LEP learners not only provide them with access to important ideas and skills but also engage them in their own constructive development of understandings.

8. Complex and flexible forms of collaboration maximize learners' opportunities to interact while making sense of language and content–Collaboration is essential for second language learners. To develop language proficiency, they need opportunities to use the language in meaningful, purposeful, and enticing interactions. Collaborative work needs to provide every learner with substantial and equitable opportunities to participate in open exchange and elaborated discussions. It must move beyond simplistic conceptions that assign superficial roles, such as being the go-getter or the timekeeper for the group. In these collaborative groups, the teacher is no longer the authority figure. Learners work autonomously, taking responsibility for their own learning. The teacher provides a task that invites and requires each learner's participation and places the responsibility for accomplishing the task or solving the problem on the learners.

9. Learners are given multiple opportunities to extend their understandings and apply their knowledge–One of the goals of learning is to be able to apply acquired knowledge to novel situations. For English learners, these applications reinforce the development of new language, concepts, and academic skills as learners actively draw connections between pieces of knowledge and their contexts. Understanding a topic of study involves being able to carry out a variety of cognitively demanding tasks.

10. Authentic assessment is an integral part of teaching and learning–Assessment should be done not only by teachers but also by learners who assess themselves and each other. Considerable research supports the importance of self-monitoring of language learning. Authentic assessment activities engage LEP learners in self-directed learning, in the construction of knowledge through disciplined inquiry, and in the analysis of problems they encounter. See Figure 4-9.

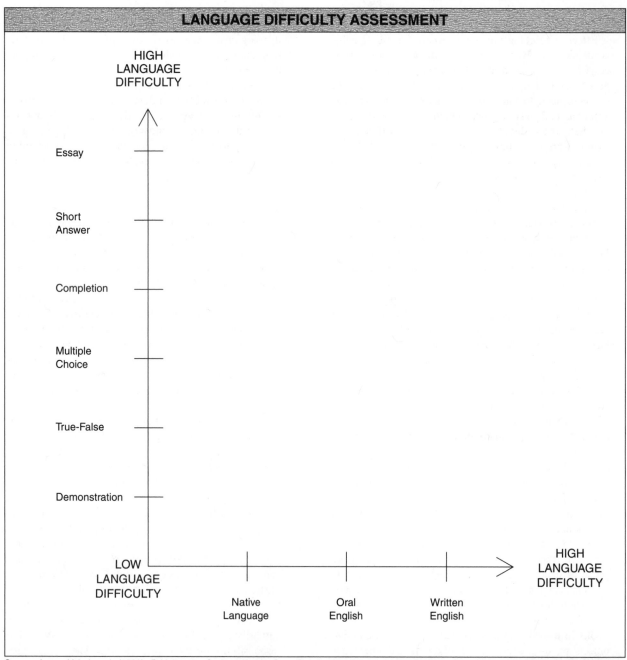

Source: Lopez-Valadez, J. (1982). Bridging the Communication Gap: Tips for Teaching the LEP Student. *The Journal of Vocational Special Needs Education, 5*(1), p. 27.

Figure 4-9. A graph for assessing the level of language difficulty of various testing methodologies for limited English-proficient learners.

Language proficiency in all four modalities (listening, speaking, reading, and writing) is key to academic achievement. The following provides some examples of how teachers can focus on developing learner competence in the language and literacy of the instruction across the curriculum:

- Listen to learners talk about familiar topics, such as home and community.
- Respond to learners' talk and questions, making on-the-spot changes that directly relate to their comments.
- Assist language development through modeling, eliciting, probing, restating, clarifying, questioning, and praising, as appropriate in purposeful conversation.
- Interact with learners in ways that respect their speaking style, which may be different from the teacher's, such as paying attention to wait-time, eye contact, turn-taking, and spotlighting.
- Connect language with literacy and content area knowledge through speaking, listening, reading, and writing activities.
- Encourage learners to use content vocabulary to express their understanding.
- Provide frequent opportunities for learners to interact with each other and with the teacher during instructional activities.
- Encourage learners to use their first and second languages in instructional activities.
- Present information in known contexts.
- Model appropriate language and vocabulary.
- Provide visuals and other materials that display language.
- Use familiar language from learners' funds of knowledge.
- Use sentence patterns and routines frequently.
- Adjust questioning to meet learners' needs.
- Ask learners to explain their reasoning.
- Invite learners to paraphrase often.
- Provide opportunities for parents to participate in classroom instructional activities.
- Vary activities to include learners' preferences, from collective and cooperative activities to individual and competitive ones.
- Vary styles of conversation and participation to include learners' cultural preferences, such as co-narration, and call-and-response (ERIC Clearinghouse on Languages and Linguistics, 1998).

OTHER DISADVANTAGED POPULATIONS

In addition to the specific populations identified by the Perkins Act of 1998, there are a number of other populations that are at risk in our nation's schools. These populations include the homeless, displaced homemakers, individuals in correctional facilities, migrant populations, and gifted and talented learners.

Individuals Who Are Homeless

For many Americans, the word homeless evokes a snapshot of a transient individual. In fact, the picture of homelessness in America is increasingly a family portrait: Children and families make up the fastest growing segment of the homeless population. Consider, for instance, that over half of all homeless children never have lived in their own home. Over 40% of these children have been homeless more than once. Most homeless mothers never completed high school or have never worked to support their families. Homeless children are three times more likely than non-homeless children to be placed in remedial education programs and four times more likely to drop out of school (U.S. Department of Education, Division of Adult Education and Literacy, 1998). According to Schwartz (1995), residence in a shelter is not conducive to good parenting, nutrition, or hygiene, provides no sense of stability, and offers little privacy for homework or family interaction. Further, shelter life may expose children to violence—as victims, witnesses, or even participants.

The Stewart B. McKinney Homeless Assistance Act of 1987 (PL 100-77), defines homeless individuals as those who lack a fixed, regular, and adequate nighttime residence or have a primary nighttime residence that is either a supervised, publicly or privately operated shelter designed to provide temporary living accommodations (including welfare hotels, congregate shelters, and transitional housing for the mentally ill); an institution that provides a temporary residence for individuals intended to be institutionalized; or a public or private place not designed for, or ordinarily used as, a regular sleeping accommodation for human beings.

Lumsden and Coffey (2001) described the homeless situation in this country as follows:

- In 1997, more than 750,000 school-age American children were homeless. Not surprisingly, the performance of the vast majority of these children is well below grade level. These children typically lag behind their peers developmentally as well as academically.
- Living at a shelter instead of in one's own home obviously places a strain on all family members. Being without a home creates instability, uncertainty, and stress. Residing at a shelter can create school-enrollment barriers for children. Although learners may legally be permitted to continue attending the school they attended before becoming homeless, logistically this may not be feasible. Families may be forced to choose between transporting their children long distances to a former school or transplanting their children to a new school that is closer to where they are staying.
- In addition to logistical barriers, a host of other factors impede homeless children's pursuit of education. According to Nunez and Collignon, homeless children are often left out of long-term class projects, they are subjected to ridicule by peers concerning their homeless status, and they are three times more likely than

their non-homeless peers to be recommended for special-education services. Once referred, many of these children never escape the special-education label and are maintained in special-education programs for the remainder of their public education.

- Parents of homeless children are most often single mothers with one or two children. The average homeless parent reads at or below a sixth grade level and has left school by the 10th grade. Many of these parents are not in a position to provide significant academic support and assistance to their children, particularly when faced with a multitude of immediate crises related to their homeless status.

Homeless children, like all children, have different levels of resilience. The length of time without a home, the reasons for homelessness, the availability of support systems, and the age, gender, and temperament of the child all contribute to a particular child's reaction to being homeless. For many children, the stress of homeless life frequently causes high levels of depression, anxiety, and low self-esteem. Many children deal with these emotional states by engaging in either aggressive or withdrawn behavior. Other more specific behaviors, such as truancy, hyperactivity, dependent behaviors, or underachievement, may become pronounced. Lack of nutrition and lack of sleep, the latter caused by the noise of the shelter or the child's stress level, often result in cognitive difficulties in reading and calculating and difficulties in concentrating. Suicidal feelings are common among children over five years old.

Some feelings suffered by homeless children can take a great toll on their academic success: Fatigue can destroy concentration, hopelessness can undermine initiative, and anger can cause bad behavior. Many children need comprehensive support for recovery. Some exhibit little evidence of the turmoil in their lives but can benefit from supports that help them achieve their full potential. Children who assume the role of family caregiver and function at a higher level than other homeless children need to be relieved of burdens not appropriate for a child to carry (Schwartz, 1995).

Feelings of shame or embarrassment usually accompany homelessness. Parents are often embarrassed about the child's homeless status, and children frequently fear that they may be stigmatized by their classmates if their homeless status becomes known. Because of the psychological and cognitive difficulties they face and the stresses of living in shelters, homeless children often need special counseling and other forms of assistance if they are to succeed in educational settings (Goins & Cesarone, 1993).

Homeless learners are also a growing concern in today's schools. In order to assist learners who are homeless, educators should establish connections with local shelter personnel and identify a primary person who can serve as a contact person with the school. Linehan (1992) identified the following four primary conditions that characterize the experience of children who are homeless:

1. Constant moving–Individuals have no sense of roots, personal space, or possessions. Because they lack control in other areas of their lives, they will fight for control in school. They tend to have problems with transitions, are easily frustrated, and have a poor attention span. Assist learners by
- breaking tasks into small segments;
- keeping checklists of completed work;
- contracting with them to finish assignments;
- giving them classroom jobs and responsibilities;
- encouraging them to make choices;
- teaching them appropriate ways of expressing frustration; and
- teaching them transition skills to help them move from one activity to another.

2. Frequent change of school–Individuals may lack structure and continuity. They may be unwilling to risk forming interpersonal relations and may become withdrawn or depressed. They may fall behind academically with changes in curricula and teachers. The lack of school records may cause learners to be placed inappropriately. Help learners by
- providing classroom structure by establishing and posting clear, concise rules;
- assigning peer assistants to arriving learners;
- involving them in cooperative learning situations; and
- identifying and obtaining necessary support services for them.

3. Overcrowded living quarters–Individuals who live in one room or in shared areas lack privacy and have little space of their own. They may be unable to do homework and may fall behind academically. Assist learners by
- helping them to attend to important information by providing them with highlighting, lecture outlines, writing notes on board, etc.; and
- arranging assignments so that learners can keep up without having to take things home.

4. Lack of access to basic resources–Individuals may be reluctant to attend school due to a lack of clothing. A lack of nutritious food can lead to health problems that can lead to learners feeling listless and weak. A lack of transportation can lead to tardiness or absenteeism. Assist learners by
- keeping living situations confidential;
- strengthening self-esteem;
- not penalizing learners for being late
- helping to ensure learners' participation in extracurricular activities; and
- having nutritional snacks available.

Vissing (1999) provided the following insight into implications of homelessness:

- A diversity of people with possible rights to elementary and secondary educational services comprise the homeless: young children, single teenagers on their own (e.g., pregnant teens, teen parents, runaways), and young adults. Failure to provide appropriate educational services for these people magnifies their misfortune and frustrates the growth of their intellectual capacities.

- Just enrolling homeless children in school and ensuring their attendance can be difficult. Residency requirements bar homeless children from attending school in 60% of the states. Other obstacles to admission include missing health and education records. Seventy percent of the states report difficulties getting records of homeless children who transfer to their schools. Often, homeless children need to be re-immunized. These obstacles are falling in many places, but the rural situation is unclear.

- Although many homeless rural children continue to do well in school, transience, uncertainty, and emotional turmoil strongly undermine success. Many, perhaps most, homeless learners will develop physical, behavioral, and emotional problems including posttraumatic stress disorders, depression, and anxiety.

- Existing health problems may go untreated, and the stressors of homelessness inevitably produce new health problems. Transience may disrupt the task of preparing and serving regular meals. Quantity and quality of food commonly suffer as well.

- Profound emotional troubles accompany homelessness. Some children feel guilty, as if they were the cause of their family's poverty. They may also resent their parents for not being better providers, and they may actively resent other learners, teachers, and administrators for not understanding homelessness. Self-destructive behaviors and psychic numbing are common. Homeless children may act out to get needed attention, but withdrawal is more common. Suicidal tendencies increase with homelessness, as do incidences of unplanned pregnancies and sexually transmitted diseases.

- Children usually hide their homelessness. Among all others who interact with children, teachers are in the best position to identify problems unobtrusively. They should observe their learners carefully from day to day.

It is important to keep in mind that homeless learners should be included in the educational setting. These learners need positive peer relationships and friendships. Teachers ought to be aware of the degree to which homeless children are accepted within the group and take measures to assure that homeless children are included in the culture of the classroom in positive ways. Teachers can use such strategies of inclusion as peer pairing, the use of cooperative learning groups, acceptance of diversity, and promotion of friendship development.

The McKinney Act of 1987 calls for every homeless child to have access to free education and provides funds for the provision of this education. The act, which was amended in 1988 and 1990, mandates that states review their school residency laws and revise any laws that prevent homeless children from receiving public education. If a child moves during the school year, the act mandates that the child either be allowed to remain in his or her first school, or move to a school in the new district, whichever is in the child's best interest. Parents' opinions are to be considered in the deciding of which school the child is to attend. Homeless children are to receive school services that are comparable to those other children receive. School districts must maintain homeless children's records and expedite their transfer as necessary. Schools are prohibited from delaying a homeless child's entry into school due to delays in obtaining school records. The act provides a grant for each state board of education to establish an Office of the Coordinator of Education of Homeless Children and Youth.

In response to the McKinney Act of 1987 and amendments, which mandated removal of barriers to homeless children's access to education and provided funding, schools revised their policies and developed a range of education and social service programs. Schwartz (1995) identified policies and procedures that lend support to homeless learners:

- Recruitment–Some schools leave brochures at local shelters to encourage children's attendance by providing parents with information about enrollment procedures and transportation. Some even send teams to shelters, consisting of staff and, perhaps, parents of homeless learners. Team members answer questions, help fill out forms, and generally support parents; they also check on frequently absent learners.

- Enrollment–Some schools have relaxed policies for enrolling homeless children, such as residency requirements and proof of immunization. They may also arrange for required pre-enrollment health examinations. By involving most of the staff, many schools have developed procedures to integrate new homeless learners quickly. They expedite learner and parent orientation, assessment and placement, acquisition of records, and transportation arrangements. In some places, state and local agency cooperation can further streamline enrollment; for example, the Texas Office of Assistance to Homeless Children maintains a database that enables school districts to get information on a child from a central source.

- Service coordination–Schools often coordinate the delivery of various social services among themselves, shelters, and other agencies and host regular staff meetings. While preserving the confidentiality rights of families, schools can share information about learners to maximize the value of each intervention. Since schools are in regular contact with parents, it can make sense for them to assume responsibility for providing information on community health and social services.

Since changing schools seriously compromises learners' academic performance, schools must help transport homeless children in order to retain them despite frequent moves. Some schools seek additional funds for buses.

- Instructional practices–Homeless learners may be more tired and have more concerns than their peers, so engaging their attention can be difficult. Teachers should explain the usefulness of mastering a task. They should encourage learners to ask questions because their families may not be able to prompt their inquisitiveness. Learners may respond particularly to one-on-one instruction and cooperative learning.

Since learners in difficult life circumstances and those who do not speak standard English may comprehend less than other learners, teachers should teach decoding strategies rather than use repetitious learning drills, guiding learners in discussing the meaning of what they read.

- Curriculum–One way to lessen the stigma that homeless learners feel (and to educate all learners about social and economic conditions) is to discuss the reasons for poverty and homelessness. For example, learners can research real estate trends to learn how low-income rental apartments were converted to higher priced cooperatives.
- Tutoring–A tutoring program can be administered by volunteers, possibly homeless parents. Tutors can be solicited from local colleges, high schools, corporations, and senior programs. Homeless learners can themselves be tutors, thus increasing their self-esteem as they help each other. After-school tutoring in school provides learners with more learning time in a safe place.
- Staff recruitment and training–Since reaching out to all learners is a school's obligation, schools need to train teachers, counselors, and other staff to work effectively with homeless families and service agencies. Administrators should establish an environment where it is assumed that homeless families will be treated equally and with dignity. When reviewing applicants, schools should consider candidates who have experience working with homeless learners and who have the ability to work as part of a case management team. They should also try to assemble a multicultural staff that reflects the composition of the student body.

Staff training should consist of sensitization to the situation of homeless families by providing facts, indicating similarities between the staff and the families, and visiting shelters; instruction in the use of customized education strategies; and training in ways to work effectively in case management teams. Program leaders should be adept at building coalitions with the school and service agencies.

- Ancillary services–A school can provide a special place where homeless learners can go for a chat with a counselor or another sympathetic person, or simply some quiet time between the chaos of a shelter and the start of the school day. It should also offer privacy so that learners can seek help without fear of being overheard. If possible, the room should remain available in the evening so learners have a safe place for homework. A school may also provide nutritious meals, including dinner for learners who participate in after-school activities, storage space for personal belongings, clothing (secondhand or new items solicited from apparel companies), personal hygiene items and bathing facilities, health services or clinic referrals, and information on public assistance and services.

Displaced Homemakers

A displaced homemaker is any person, male or female, who has spent a number of years as an unsalaried homemaker and by circumstance must find gainful employment. The circumstances causing a homemaker to be displaced include the death of a spouse, displacement of a spouse out of the paid labor force, disability of a spouse, divorce, separation, or abandonment. In many cases, a displaced homemaker will need comprehensive training to enter into the job market and be competitively employable. The Workforce Investment Act defined a displaced homemaker as

> an individual who has been providing unpaid services to family members in the home, and who (1) has been dependent on the income of another family member but is no longer supported by that income, and (2) is unemployed or underemployed and is experiencing difficulty in obtaining or upgrading employment.

The Perkins Act of 1998 defined a displaced homemaker as

> an individual who (1) has worked primarily in the home without remuneration to care for a home and family, and for that reason has diminished marketable skills; (2) has been dependent on the income of another family member but is no longer supported by that income; or (3) is a parent whose youngest dependent child will be ineligible to receive assistance under Temporary Assistance for Needy Families (TANF) not later than two years after the date on which the parent applies for career and technical education assistance; and (4) is unemployed or underemployed and is experiencing difficulty in obtaining or upgrading employment.

Specifically, a displaced homemaker is an individual who has worked in the home for 10 or more years providing unsalaried household services for family members on a full-time basis, is not gainfully employed, and needs assistance in securing gainful employment. Furthermore, a displaced homemaker must also have been dependent on the income of another family member but is no longer supported by that income, have been dependent on federal assistance but is no longer eligible for that assistance; or is supported as the parent of minor children by public assistance or spousal support, but whose youngest children are within two years of reaching 18 years of age.

There is an increasing number of people in this country who, having fulfilled a role as homemaker, find themselves displaced in middle age through divorce, death of spouse, disability of spouse, or other loss of family income of a spouse. As a consequence, displaced homemakers are

- very often left with little or no income;
- ineligible for categorical welfare assistance;

- subject to the highest rate of unemployment of any sector of the workforce;
- facing continuing discrimination in employment because of their age and lack of recent paid work experience;
- ineligible for unemployment insurance because they have been engaged in unpaid labor in the home;
- ineligible for social security benefits because they are too young and many never qualify because they have been divorced from the family wage earner;
- facing losing beneficiaries' rights under employer's pension and health plans through divorce or death of spouse; and
- often unacceptable to private health insurance plans because of their age.

Women Work! (1998) reported the following:

- The Women Work Network, which represents local programs serving displaced homemakers nationwide, indicates that although economic recovery has improved the lives of many Americans in the last few years, displaced homemakers continue to be left behind. Studies reveal that in 1997, there were 17 million displaced homemakers in the United States. This is virtually unchanged from the 1990 figure of 17.8 million. Of these 17 million displaced homemakers, 43% are age 64 or younger and 57% are age 65 or older.
- The studies also indicate that in 1997, 3.3 million displaced homemakers lived below the poverty threshold. In fact, approximately 83% of displace homemakers earned less than $20,000 in 1997. Of that 83%, 59% earned less than $10,000.
- An in-depth analysis of the 1997 Census Bureau data reveals that throughout the 1990s the economic status of displaced homemakers and single mothers became even more tenuous. Despite women's rising workforce participation, the number of displaced homemakers under age 65 in the U.S. has remained virtually unchanged in recent years—decreasing only .1 million to 7.3 million in 1997. The number of single-parent families maintained by women, however, rose significantly from 8.4 million in 1990 to 10.7 million in 1997.
- The economic status of displaced homemakers and single mothers is poor. Two in five single mothers and their families live in poverty. Three in five displaced homemakers under age 65 have personal incomes of less than $10,000 per year. In 14 states, more than half of displaced homemakers live in poverty. At a time when unemployment is low, employment rates are actually dropping for displaced homemakers with just 49% in 1990.

Services and assistance that many displaced homemakers may require should assist them to

- overcome personal barriers to education and employment;
- develop action plans by providing self-assessment activities, career exploration opportunities, and information concerning education and training options;
- develop job search skills through practice in identifying and exploring job opportunities, resume writing, and interviewing;
- gain access to training fields that offer economic self-sufficiency and potential for advancement;
- gain access to additional educational opportunities with support services such as counseling, support groups, and financial assistance for child care, transportation, tuition, and books; and
- gain access to basic education classes to improve basic skills or earn a GED.

Such services to assist displaced homemakers may include

- job counseling services that are specifically designed for displaced homemakers who may be entering the job market for the first time or who may be re-entering the job market after a number of years as a homemaker;
- job training and job placement services that shall be developed in conjunction with federal, state, and local government agencies and the private sector;
- assistance in gaining admission to existing public and private job training programs and opportunities;
- assistance in identifying community needs and in creating new jobs for displaced homemakers in the public and private sectors;
- health education and counseling services in cooperation with existing health programs with respect to general principles of preventive health care, family health care and nutrition, alcohol and drug addiction, and health care consumer education;
- financial management services that provide information and assistance with respect to insurance, taxes, estate and probate problems, mortgages, loans, and other related financial matters;
- educational services that shall include outreach and information about courses offering credit through secondary or postsecondary education programs and information about such other programs that are determined to be of interest and benefit to displaced homemakers by the chancellor;
- referral of displaced homemakers to the appropriate private and public agencies for advice and assistance on health care, financial matters, educational opportunities, public assistance, and legal problems and on such other matters as shall be determined to be of interest and benefit to displaced homemakers; and
- traditional and nontraditional occupational skill training.

Learners in Correctional Facilities

Cutshall (2001) provides important information about individuals in correctional facilities. The adult correctional population is primarily poor, unskilled, and unemployed or underemployed. Approximately 49% of the prison population does not have a high school diploma or a GED, compared to 24% of the general population. The incidence of learning disabilities among inmates has been estimated at between 30% and 50%, compared with 5% to 15% of the general adult population. Over half the offenders released from institutions each year will return within three years. Inmates who undergo correctional education average up to a 20% reduction in recidivism rates from that of the general prison population.

Most states have some type of correctional education programs in their prisons, which can include academic, career and technical, and life/job-skills training. Findings from a recent survey of prison inmates conducted by the National Institute of Justice indicated that approximately 400,000 inmates (57%) in state correctional facilities had participated in some type of education program. Nineteen percent of those had taken career and technical education courses, 45% had enrolled in basic academic education courses, and another 36% had enrolled in both career and technical and academic courses (Cutshall, 2001).

Growing concerns about crowding in secure juvenile correctional facilities, high rates of recidivism, and escalating costs of confinement have fueled renewed interest in bringing change and innovative programming to juvenile aftercare/parole philosophy and practice. Unfortunately, the juvenile corrections field has compiled a dismal record in its effort to reduce the repeat-offender rate of juveniles released from secure confinement. Research indicates that failure occurs disproportionately with a subgroup of released juvenile offenders who have established a long record of misconduct that began at an early age. Such high-risk youth not only exhibit a persistent pattern of justice system contact (e.g., arrests, adjudications, placements), but they also are plagued by a number of other need-related risk factors. Frequently these risk factors involve a combination of problems associated with family, negative peer influence, school difficulties, and substance abuse. In addition to these common need-related risk factors, high-risk youth often exhibit a variety of notable ancillary needs and problems. Although these factors are not generally predictive of repeat offenders, they must be addressed because these conditions are still present in some, and at times, many high-risk youngsters. For example, because there is widespread consensus that learning disabilities and emotional disturbance are linked to delinquency, these conditions should not be ignored when present. See Figure 4-10.

Also known as protective factors, assets are personal characteristics that protect youth from a host of high-risk antisocial behaviors, including substance abuse, dropping out of school, delinquency, and violence. While risk factors are key components in understanding and identifying potentially violent youth, it is just as important to recognize the factors that keep youth from becoming violent. These are the factors that keep the majority of youth from becoming involved in serious delinquency, despite living in poor and high-crime areas. See Figure 4-11.

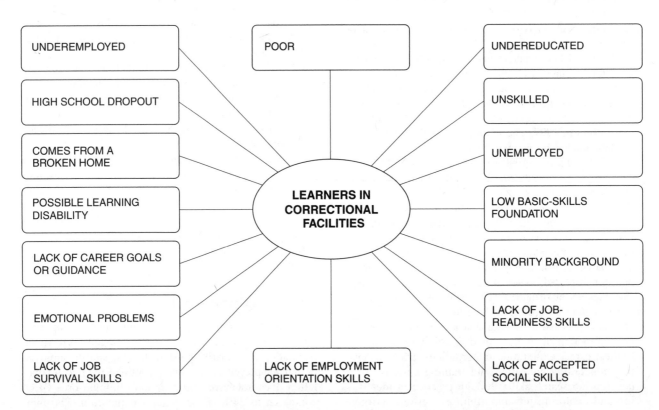

Figure 4-10. General characteristics demonstrated by individuals who are incarcerated in correctional facilities.

Case Study . . . Mario

Mario is a 17-year-old student who dropped out of high school a year ago. He comes from a single-parent family. His mother struggles on public assistance to raise Mario and his eight brothers and sisters. Mario's school records profile a learner who has always had problems. He has a history of failing grades. Mario found little relevance in what school had to offer him.

In middle school, he became associated with a group of learners who were notorious for problems inside and outside of school. This group became involved in a variety of crime throughout the high school years. They were caught vandalizing the school. Several members were caught breaking and entering a warehouse to steal merchandise that would have been sold to buy drugs.

After floundering in school, Mario finally dropped out. He had neither a career plan nor any entry-level skills to enter the labor market. After trying several jobs at local fast food restaurants, he became disgruntled and stopped working. His days consisted of hanging out with friends.

At one point, Mario tried to break away from this group of friends by becoming involved in a neighborhood community center. He even developed a mentoring relationship with the director of the program who found Mario a part-time job. However, his lack of basic skills and employment orientation skills led to his being fired. After this happened, Mario lost faith in the work ethic that was being preached at the community center and returned to his group of friends.

Finally, in a burglary attempt, Mario and two of his friends were caught with a weapon and jailed. After his release, his probation officer worked with the personnel at the high school to have Mario registered again and enrolled in a career and technical education program after appropriate vocational assessment and counseling activities.

Leone and others (1991) provided the following insight into juvenile corrections and individuals with disabilities:

- It has been estimated that 28% of incarcerated youths in the U.S. have been identified as having disabilities. There is some evidence that this estimate is low—studies have found that even higher numbers were identified as disabled by the youths' school districts prior to their incarceration. The most common disabling conditions among incarcerated youth are mild to moderate mental retardation, learning disabilities, and behavior disorders. There is no cause-and-effect relationship between these conditions and illegal behavior, but some of the social disadvantages and characteristics associated with them may lead to increased likelihood of contact with the criminal justice system.
- Poorly developed social skills and lack of ability to comprehend questions and warnings increase the likelihood that disabled offenders will be committed to correctional facilities and may make these youths vulnerable to inequitable treatment by the juvenile justice system. For example, youths with mental disabilities may not understand the rights read to them, may confess and say what they think another person wants to hear, may have difficulty communicating with lawyers and court personnel, and may not be recognized as mentally disabled. In addition, they are more likely to plead guilty, less likely to plea bargain for reduced sentences, more often convicted, and less likely to have their sentences appealed or placed on probation or parole. They serve longer sentences than nondisabled persons incarcerated for the same crimes. It has been recommended that, in addition to providing social skills instruction, secondary school curricula for youth with disabilities include law-related education that focuses on teaching adolescents their legal rights and helps them develop a sense of community.

- A successful transition from the institution to the community requires the coordinated efforts of institutional staff, families, probation and aftercare professional, and educators. Many youths do not adapt well to changes in their environments or to societal expectations for law-abiding behavior. Furthermore, many youths with disabilities do not return to school after leaving correctional institutions.

The National Center on Education, Disability and Juvenile Justice (2001) revealed the following about quality education in juvenile correctional facilities:

- More than 125,000 youth are in custody in nearly 3,500 public and private juvenile correctional facilities in the U.S. The majority of youth enter correctional facilities with a broad range of intense educational, mental health, medical, and social needs. A large number of incarcerated juveniles are marginally literate or illiterate and have experienced school failure and retention. These youth are also disproportionately male, poor, minority, and have significant learning and/or behavioral problems that entitle them to special education and related services.

- Because education is critical to rehabilitation for troubled youth, it is considered foundational in most juvenile institutions. Helping youth acquire educational skills is also one of the most effective approaches to the prevention of delinquency and the reduction of recidivism. Literacy skills are essential to meet the demands of a complex, high-tech world in school and at work. Higher levels of literacy are associated with lower rates of juvenile delinquency, re-arrest, and recidivism.

- While illiteracy and poor academic performance are not direct causes of delinquency, empirical studies consistently demonstrate a strong link between marginal literacy skills and the likelihood of involvement in the juvenile justice system. Most incarcerated youth lag two or more years behind their peers in basic academic skills, and have higher rates of grade retention, absenteeism, and suspension or expulsion. For example, a national study found that more than one-third of youth incarcerated at the median age of 15 and a half read below the fourth-grade level.

- The negative consequences of marginal literacy extend beyond the greatly heightened risk for incarceration among adolescents. The rate of poverty among those in the labor force without a high school diploma is approximately three times that of high school graduates. Eighteen to 23-year-olds least proficient in the basic skills of reading and mathematics are more likely to be unemployed, living in poverty, and not enrolled in any type of schooling.

PERSONAL ASSETS . . .

EXTERNAL ASSETS

Support
- Family support–Family life provides high levels of love and support
- Positive family communication–Young person and her/his parent(s) communicate positively, and young person is willing to seek advice and counsel from parent(s)
- Other adult relationships–Young person receives support from three or more nonparent adults
- Caring neighborhood–Young person experiences caring neighbors
- Caring school climate–School provides a caring, encouraging environment
- Parent involvement in schooling–Parent(s) actively involved in helping young person succeed in school

Empowerment
- Community values youth–Young person perceives that adults in the community value youth
- Youth as resources–Young people are given useful roles in the community
- Service to others–Young person serves in the community one hour or more per week
- Safety–Young person feels safe at home, at school, and in the neighborhood

Boundaries and Expectations
- Family boundaries–Family has clear rules and consequences and monitors youth's whereabouts
- School boundaries–School provides clear rules and consequences
- Neighborhood boundaries–Neighbors take responsibility for monitoring youth's behavior
- Adult role models–Parent(s) and other adults model positive, responsible behavior
- Positive peer influence–Young person's best friends model responsible behavior
- High expectations–Both parent(s) and teachers encourage the young person to do well

Constructive Use of Time
- Creative activities–Young person spends three or more hours per week in lessons or practice in music, theater, or other arts
- Youth programs–Young person spends three or more hours per week in sports, clubs, school organizations, and/or community organizations
- Religious community–Young person spends one hour or more per week in activities in a religious institution
- Time at home–Young person is out with friends with nothing special to do two or fewer nights per week

INTERNAL ASSETS

Commitment to Learning
- Achievement motivation–Young person is motivated to do well in school
- School engagement–Young person is actively engaged in learning
- Homework–Young person reports doing at least one hour of homework every school day
- Bonding to school–Young person cares about her/his school
- Reading for pleasure–Young person reads for pleasure three or more hours per week

Positive Values
- Caring–Young person places high value on helping other people
- Equality and social justice–Young person places high value on promoting equality and reducing hunger and poverty
- Integrity–Young person acts on convictions and stands up for her/his beliefs
- Honesty–Young person tells the truth even when it is not easy
- Responsibility–Young person accepts and takes personal responsibility
- Restraint–Young person believes it is important not to be sexually active or to use alcohol or other drugs

Additional Special Populations

... PERSONAL ASSETS

Social Competencies
- Planning and decision making–Young person knows how to plan ahead and make choices
- Interpersonal competence–Young person has empathy, sensitivity, and friendship skills
- Cultural competence–Young person has knowledge of and comfort with people of different cultural/racial/ethnic backgrounds
- Resistance skills–Young person can resist negative peer pressure and dangerous situations
- Peaceful conflict resolution–Young person seeks to resolve conflict nonviolently

Positive Identity
- Personal power–Young person feels he/she has control over things that happen to him/her
- Self-esteem–Young person reports having high self-esteem
- Sense of purpose–Young person reports that his or her life has a purpose
- Positive view of personal future–Young person is optimistic about her or his personal future

Source: National Institute of Justice. (1998, July). *Assets That Protect Youth from High-Risk Antisocial Behaviors.* Washington, DC: Author.

Figure 4-11. Assets that protect youth from high-risk antisocial behaviors.

Juvenile crime prevention efforts have been used in public school settings for a number of years. During that time, some practices have been successful in decreasing the rate of juvenile crime while other attempts have proven less than successful. See Figure 4-12.

Today's labor market demands a more comprehensive and advanced training curriculum in both academic and career and technical education. Incarcerated youths should be afforded the opportunity to develop their competitive skills and move forward to tackle increasingly complicated tasks. Successful juvenile correctional education programs include academic programs, special education, psychoeducational programming, employment training, and transitional services.

JUVENILE CRIME PREVENTION EFFORTS ...

WHAT WORKS
- For infants–Frequent home visits by nurses and other professionals
- For preschoolers–Classes with weekly home visits by preschool teachers
- For delinquent and at-risk preadolescents–Family therapy and parent training
- For schools–Organizational development for innovation, including use of school teams; communication and reinforcement of clear, consistent norms; teaching of social-competency skills; and coaching of high-risk youth in thinking skills
- For older male ex-offenders–Career and technical training reduces repeat offending
- For rental housing with drug dealing–Nuisance abatement action on landlords reduces drug problems in privately-owned rental housing
- For high-crime spots–Extra police patrols
- For high-risk repeat offenders–Monitoring by specialized police units and immediate incarceration upon reoffense reduces their crime
- For domestic abusers who are employed–On-scene arrests reduce repeat offenses
- Incarceration of offenders who will continue to commit crimes–Works with more active and serious offenders. Diminished returns with less serious/active offenders
- For convicted offenders–Rehabilitation programs with risk-focused treatments
- For drug-using offenders in prison–Therapeutic community treatment programs

WHAT DOESN'T WORK
- Gun buyback programs–Although reducing the number of guns on the street, programs operated without geographic limitations on eligibility of people selling guns back fail to reduce gun violence
- Community mobilization against crime in high-crime poverty areas–Fails to reduce crime in those areas
- Police counseling visits to homes of couples days after domestic violence incidents–Fails to reduce repeat violence after an arrest or warrant
- Counseling and peer counseling of learners in schools–Fails to reduce substance abuse or delinquency and can increase delinquency

. . . JUVENILE CRIME PREVENTION EFFORTS

- Drug Abuse Resistance Eduation (D.A.R.E.)–Fails to reduce drug abuse when the original D.A.R.E. curriculum is used
- Drug prevention classes focused on fear and other emotional appeals, including self-esteem–Fails to reduce substance abuse
- School-based leisure-time enrichment programs–Includes supervised homework and self-esteem exercises; fails to reduce delinquency risk factors or drug abuse
- Summer jobs or subsidized work programs for at-risk youth–Fails to reduce crime or arrests
- Short-term, nonresidential training programs (including Job Training Partnership Act and JOBSTART) for at-risk youth–Fails to reduce crime
- Diversion from court to job training as a condition of case dismissal–Fails to reduce adult offending, but increases offending in juvenile program
- Neighborhood watch programs organized with police–Fails to reduce burglary or other target crimes, especially in higher crime areas where voluntary participation often fails
- Arrest of juveniles for minor offenses–Causes them to become more delinquent in the future than policy exercise discretion or alternatives to formal charging
- Arrest of unemployed suspects for domestic assault–Causes higher rate of repeat offending versus nonarrest alternatives
- Increased arrests or raids on drug market location–Fails to reduce violent crime or disorder for more than a few days
- Storefront police officers–Fails to prevent crime in surrounding area
- Police newsletters with local crime information–Fails to reduce victimization rates
- Correctional boot camps using traditional military basic training–Fails to reduce repeat offending after release
- Scared Straight programs where minor juvenile offenders visit adult programs–Fails to reduce participant reoffending and may increase crime
- Shock probations, shock parole, and split sentences adding jail time to probation or parole–Fails to reduce repeat offending compared to similar offenders under community supervision. Increases crime rates for some groups
- Home detention with electronic monitoring–Fails to reduce offending for low-risk offenders in comparison to standard community supervision without electronic monitoring
- Intensive supervision on parole or probation (ISP)–Does not reduce repeat offending compared to normal levels of community supervision; varies by site, with some exceptions
- Rehabilitation programs using vague, unstructured counseling that does not specifically focus on each offender's risk factors–Fails to reduce repeat offending
- Residential programs for juvenile offenders using challenging experiences in rural settings–Fails to reduce repeat offending as compared to standard training schools

Source: National Institute of Justice. (Fall, 1998). *Preventing Crime: What Works, What Doesn't, What's Promising.* Washington, DC: Author.

Figure 4-12. Successful and unsuccessful practices in juvenile crime prevention.

Academic Programs. A fundamental assumption underlying academic curriculum in the past was that basic skills had to be mastered before learners could be given more advanced tasks, such as problem solving, cognitive reasoning, reading comprehension, and written communication. Current thinking challenges this concept. The new paradigm is based on the assumption that all learners can succeed and that educationally disadvantaged learners can profit from more challenging tasks (Gemignani, 1994).

Classrooms in correctional settings often reflect the old model, which emphasizes workbook exercises, remediation, drill, and practice in the basics. Under this model, educational assessments focused on what learners could not do in order to provide remedial instruction. Classroom management centered on discipline and control, with time-out periods in which unruly offenders were separated from other learners. A more effective model involves changes in educational philosophy, curriculum, and instructional techniques, as demonstrated by the following characteristics:

- The academic curriculum features comprehension and complex problem-solving tasks, allowing learners to develop their cognitive skills.
- The curriculum integrates basic skills into more challenging tasks that allow learners to apply these skills to real-life situations.
- The curriculum allows for a number of simple skills to be combined and applied to accomplish more complex tasks.
- Knowledge sharing is emphasized through cooperative learning, peer tutoring, and team problem solving.
- Teachers model cognitive processes through a variety of instructional strategies, including externalizing thought processes, encouraging multiple approaches to problem solving, and focusing on dialog and reciprocal learning.

- A variety of assessment and evaluation measures are used. Progress is based on mutually defined goals emphasizing competence.
- Instruction involves multiple strategies appropriate to each learner's interests and needs.
- Reading, writing, and oral expression are interrelated (Gemignani, 1994).

Special Education. As many as 40% of youth in correctional facilities may have some form of learning disability. Incarcerated youth with learning disabilities must be provided special education in full compliance with federal and state law. It is essential that correctional education employ trained and certified staff with the capacity and resources to provide a full spectrum of special education programs and services. Correctional staff should be trained to meet the mandates of the Americans With Disabilities Act. Essential components of an effective special education program include

- assessment of the deficits and learning needs;
- a curriculum that meets each learner's needs;
- career and technical education training opportunities;
- transitional services that link the correctional special education services to prior educational experiences and to the educational and human services needed after release;
- a comprehensive range of education and related services; and
- effective staff training.

Youth with learning disabilities should be included in regular academic programs, classrooms, and educational activities to the greatest extent possible. Independent living, social, and career and technical skills that prepare learners for adult living supplement the regular academic program. The special education program should help youth in their transition between public schools and corrections or between corrections and independent living and work (Gemignani, 1994).

Psychoeducational Programming. Delinquents are often deficient in cognitive problem-solving skills, moral reasoning, and communication and social skills essential for successful functioning in daily life. Sound juvenile correctional education programs enhance offenders' thinking and social skills while ameliorating their academic and career and technical education deficiencies.

Such programs include a social metacognitive skills curriculum focusing on such areas as social interactions and communications, moral and spiritual values, problem solving, and conflict resolution. The following factors are key to successful psychoeducational programming:

- Learners are assessed in social skills and cognitive reasoning.
- Social skills education is integrated into life at the facility.
- Opportunities are created for practicing and applying social skills in the community.

- Learners are afforded opportunities to participate in school and facility governance.
- Academic and career and technical education instructors are trained in such instructional techniques as modeling, small-group discussions, and cooperative learning (Gemignani, 1994).

Employment Training. The majority of delinquents age 16 and older do not return to school after release from a correctional setting or do not graduate from high school. While correctional educators must find better ways to motivate learners to return to school, they must also provide learners with the knowledge, skills, and attitudes needed in entry-level jobs. Education programs should afford learners the opportunity to develop competencies in basic skills such as reading, writing, and mathematics; thinking skills such as creative thinking, decision making, and problem solving; and personal qualities such as responsibility, sociability, and honesty.

Learners should develop the following workplace competencies:

- using resources and staff;
- working productively with others on teams;
- acquiring and using information;
- understanding and utilizing systems; and
- using technology.

Opportunities should be provided for learners to apply knowledge through on-the-job training, work experience, internships, apprenticeships, mentorships, or observing workers on the job. Learners should also develop a portfolio that includes credentials, work samples, work history, a resume, letters of recommendation, relevant community service, and extracurricular experiences. Partnerships are developed with employers to enhance current programs and provide post-release support for learners (Gemignani, 1994).

Transition Services. Expanded and improved transition services are needed to bridge the gap from community schools to correctional facilities and from correctional facilities to home or independent living. Lack of services may undo many of the benefits learners have received through their educational programs while incarcerated. Effective transition services will increase learners' rates of reenrollment in school, their high school graduation rates, and their success in independent living and employment and should include the following:

- Incarcerated youth are provided opportunities to acquire social skills, survival skills, independent living skills, preemployment training, and law-related education.
- Student records are transferred in a timely fashion between the releasing and the receiving institutions.
- Educational information is used to make prompt and appropriate placements.
- Learners are scheduled and preregistered prior to their reentry into community schools (Gemignani, 1994).

Migrant Populations

The extreme poverty that faces migrant families negatively affects their housing, nutrition, and health care. Serious health threats come to migrant families, especially expectant mothers, from working in fields where toxic substances are used in growing crops. Migrant families are often plagued with mental health problems as well as physical ailments. The problems of loss of school time, irregular attendance, movement among several schools, and resulting educational deficiencies have been studied for the past 50 years.

The children of migrant workers are especially disadvantaged due to the unusual characteristics of their lives. Learners from migrant populations move from one school district to another as their family seeks employment in agriculture or in an agriculture-related industry. The learners often leave school at a very early age to work in the fields in order to contribute to the economic survival of the family. Learners from migrant populations are disadvantaged in a variety of ways. Factors such as poverty, negative self-concept, health and nutrition problems, and trouble developing interpersonal relationships are characteristic of individuals from this population.

Martin (1994) reported the following based on the National Agricultural Worker Survey (NAWS):

- In the absence of a single federal definition for migrant farm workers, the NAWS study defined migrants as workers who travel 75 miles or more in search of crop work. About 42% of the 7,200 workers interviewed while holding crop farm jobs between 1989 and 1991 fit this definition of migrant workers. This suggests that approximately 840,000 of the nation's two million crop workers are migrants.
- Migrant and seasonal farm workers average about $5 hourly for 1,000 hours of work, for an average income of $5,000 annually.
- The NAWS study revealed that the migrant farm workers were primarily Hispanics (94%), born in Mexico (80%), married with children (52%), working on farms in the U.S. without their families (59%), mostly men (82%), and were unauthorized workers (67%).
- Migrant farm workers are probably the largest needy workforce in the United States. Evidence exists that migrant children's chances for success in the U.S. economy are hurt rather than helped by their parents' occupation.

Davis (1997) created the following profile of farm laborers and the hazards that confront their children:

- Farm worker families are overwhelmingly minorities. Seventy percent or more are Hispanic and others are African-American, Asian-American, Haitian, West Indian, and Native American. The median education level among farm workers is eighth grade, and many speak little or no English. Approximately 75% of all farm workers are U.S. citizens or have lawful resident status.

- Economic necessity is the cause of most child labor on farms. According to the Census Bureau, 46% of all farm workers live below the poverty line. With average annual earnings of $6,500, many farm workers do not earn enough money to keep a family of four out of poverty even when both parents work. Among migrant farm workers (i.e., those who travel more than 75 miles from their home to work), the median income is even lower, only $5,000 per year, and 57% live in poverty. Even worse, an estimated 73% of migrant farm workers' children under age 14 live in poverty.
- The health and well-being of children and adolescents who work in agriculture are jeopardized by long hours of labor and dangerous working conditions. Work takes place before, during, and after school hours. An estimated 27,000 children under age 20 who both live and work on farms suffer work-related injuries, and an additional 300 die from work-related accidents. These figures understate the extent of the problem because they exclude youngsters who work on farms but do not live there.
- Children on farms climb ladders to prune trees, use knives to harvest crops, carry heavy buckets full of produce, drive or ride on tractors, and care for animals. Many work for long hours from early in the morning to late in the night. Job-related injuries and fatalities are caused primarily by tractors, farm machinery, pesticides, farm animals, falls, and drowning. The lack of sanitary facilities in the fields also leads to dermatitis, third-world levels of parasitic and urinary tract infection, respiratory illness, eye disease, and heat-related illness.
- Economic pressures lead many farm workers' children to work when they should be in school. Many enter school at an older age and drop out before they can graduate from high school. Work schedules of parents and children also interfere with education, as some migrant children begin their school year in October or November and leave before the semester is finished. For children whose families return to Mexico during the year, the disruption may be even more severe, because school systems on both sides of the border generally have not recognized the progress learners make outside of their own systems. This may be changing, however, with the Migrant Education Binational Program, which now involves 32 Mexican and at least 10 U.S. states in information exchanges about individual learners.
- Even when farm workers' children attend school, they are often tired, irritable, or unable to concentrate due to hunger, illness, or fatigue. A 1991 California study, analyzing some of the factors that adversely affect migrant learners' educational achievement, found that 70% of migrant learners entering kindergarten had low English proficiency (which remained at 30% for migrant 12th graders); 49% of migrant learners were average for their grade level; and substantial numbers had poor attendance records.

Rasmussen (1988) identified the following special needs of learners from migrant populations in secondary schools:

- Affective needs are perceived by migrant school staff to be at the root of many learners' cognitive failures. Repeated experiences of frustration, failure, and lack of acceptance due to mobility, have produced low self-concept, feelings of isolation, and reduced motivation. Provision of a supportive, positive atmosphere can be highly productive and have great impact on acceptance, goal setting, and role model identification.
- Cognitive needs are specific, practical needs for academic success. They include remedial assistance in math, reading, ESL, etc.; study skills development; time management; and academic and career and technical guidance.
- Technical needs reflect problems that learners encounter with school systems and that affect them individually, but over which they have no control. This includes inappropriate age and/or grade placement (this is the highest predictor of dropout behavior, with a 99% dropout rate for learners more than one year over age); credit deficiencies due to frequent moves and no means for earning partial credits; and inadequate knowledge of graduation requirements that vary from district to district.

Migrant learners present a challenge to the educational system and, at the same time, they enrich it. Some of the enriching factors these learners bring are their cultural and ethnic heritage and their knowledge of more than one language. They also have extensive travel experiences and firsthand experience with agricultural, dairy, or fishing-related industries. It is important that educators build on the richness of migrant learners' experiences and culture to make learning more meaningful. Educators should present authentic real-life examples to learners, make content information culturally relevant, and use instructional strategies that promote cooperative learning and develop learners' metacognitive skills. When migrant learners can relate to the information being presented, they are more likely to understand academic concepts and experience success in school. See Figure 4-13.

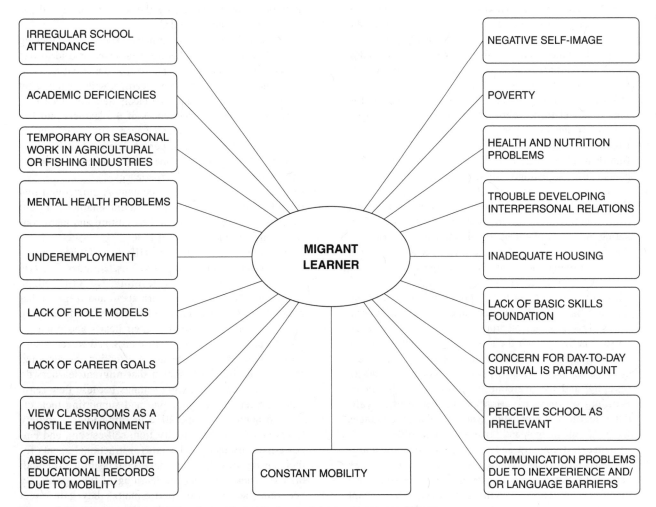

Figure 4-13. General characteristics demonstrated by learners from migrant populations.

Case Study ... Manuel

Manuel is 16 years old. He comes from a migrant family that travels from New York to Florida each year working in the fields harvesting crops. Manuel is one of 9 children. His parents speak no English. Neither of them has had an education other than what they learned in the fields.

Manuel and his family move frequently. As a result, there is little chance for him to establish roots in any school. Manuel has health problems. He is severely anemic, is underweight, and suffers from migraine headaches. He is frequently absent from school because his parents need his daily wages from working in the fields. There is little value placed on obtaining an education, with the day-to-day struggle to survive being the foremost goal for the family.

Manuel has problems communicating with his teachers and peers due to his restricted experiences as well as the language barriers that naturally occur when English is not spoken in the migrant camp. As a result, he has a negative self-image and great difficulties developing positive relationships with his peers at school. Manuel's teachers have a difficult time developing appropriate goals for him due to the lack of educational records.

Moving from school to school makes it difficult to establish and follow an individualized program for him. At Manuel's present school, the counselor has made a concerted effort to involve Manuel in some exploratory experiences in career and technical education programs as well as some vocational assessment activities to identify his interests, abilities, and special needs. With this information, the counselor and teachers plan to develop a portfolio that he can take with him when he leaves to present at the next school in which he enrolls.

Several factors associated with the migrant lifestyle predispose migrant learners to being at risk of dropping out of school early. Irregular school attendance, traveling from one temporary site to another, and LEP can limit the educational success rate of these learners, leading some to drop out of school as early as the upper elementary grades. As with all learners, migrant learners achieve best when the schools honor and value who they are.

Menchaca and Ruiz-Escalante (1995) identified the following strategies for teachers to help migrant learners overcome circumstances that may jeopardize their success:

- Create a positive environment–Migrant learners often find themselves in new and unfamiliar classrooms. The challenge of adjusting to strange, new living and learning environments often contributes to feelings of isolation and loneliness. Teachers can help learners overcome these feelings by modeling respect and eliminating any form of threat or ridicule. Teachers can further foster a sense of safety and trust by sharing some of their own experiences and by assigning older learners to act as mentors or buddies to new migrant learners.
- Build on migrant learners' strengths–Most migrant learners have lived, traveled, and studied in several states. Teachers can incorporate into lessons these diverse experiences and the richness of learners' cultures and languages. Examples include recognizing migrant children for their travel experiences, knowledge of geography, and for overcoming crises on the highway. Building on these experiences and capabilities validates learners' knowledge. Such validation enhances learners' self-images and sense of self-worth.
- Enhance self-concept and self-esteem–Migrant learners must have faith in their own abilities so that they can persist and succeed despite the many obstacles they encounter in school. Having a positive self-concept helps learners achieve, which then further enhances

self-esteem. When necessary, teachers should modify assignments to allow for real success in meaningful activities that are valued by the learner and by others, such as family and friends.

- Personalize lessons with learners' experiences–Drawing from life experiences helps learners understand ideas and transfer them to other content. To find out about learners' experiences, teachers can have learners write or tell about themselves. Later, teachers can incorporate both their own experiences and the experiences of the learners into lessons in content areas such as language arts, social studies, and science. Teachers can personalize content by using familiar places, familiar names, and analogies to connect new concepts to learners' experiences.
- Integrate culturally relevant content–A curriculum that includes culturally relevant content enables migrant learners' to develop pride in their culture and learn content from a familiar cultural base.
- Encourage positive ethnic affiliation–Doing so can influence the development of values, attitudes, lifestyle choices, and approaches to learning. Nurturing ethnic affiliation also helps all to learn about and respect other cultural groups' heritages and histories, while keeping their own culture instilled in their hearts and minds.
- Use cooperative learning–Both theory and research support cooperative learning as an effective instructional strategy. Studies have shown that migrant learners do well in cooperative learning settings because they sense other learners are encouraging and supporting their efforts to achieve. Cooperative learning lowers anxiety levels and strengthens motivation, self-esteem, and empowerment by using learners as instructional agents for their classmates. Learners take responsibility for both their own learning and the learning of their peers. By becoming active group participants, they gain equal access to learning opportunities.

In a study conducted by the U.S. Department of Education (1999) the following information was collected from a representative sample of Title I schools that had, as of the 1996–1997 school year, implemented the schoolwide program option and served migrant learners:

- Most of the school staff did not view the educational or support service needs of migrant learners as significantly different from the needs of other educationally disadvantaged learners in their schools. The only notable exception involved the greater need of migrant learners for English-language assistance.
- The primary educational needs of all learners were in reading and mathematics, and the majority of survey schools made supplemental instruction in these areas available to all of their learners.
- English as a second language was the area in which the highest percentage of schools (about 11%) offered supplemental instruction only to migrant learners. In addition, about 5% of the schools provided bilingual education to only migrant learners.
- Most of the survey schools made support services available to all learners and few believed their migrant learners had unique support service needs.
- Counseling and medical screening or treatment were considered the most pressing support service needs of all learners, closely followed by nutrition and social work.
- Some principals did identify unique support-service needs for migrant learners. These services included dental screening or treatment (12%), clothing (12%), medical screening or treatment (10%), and social work (10%).
- School staff may not have identified migrant learners particular needs because they did know which of their learners were migrants and because needs assessments did not focus on the needs of particular groups of learners.

Schoolwide programs can be particularly effective in serving migrant learners by

- providing an enrichment rather than a deficit model of instruction;
- validating migrant learners' language and culture, including their migrant experiences;
- supporting the aspirations of migrant learners;
- providing migrant learners with role models from the local community;
- implementing bilingual curricula and programs and employing bilingual staff;
- providing for the full involvement of the parents of migrant learners; and
- maintaining and transferring learners' education and health records.

Due to their at-risk status, migrant learners have a variety of basic educational needs including native language development and instruction, ESL instruction, self-concept enhancement, acculturation enhancement, and family and community involvement.

Salend, Michael, and Taylor (1984) conducted a study to identify the competencies that teachers should develop in working with learners from migrant populations. The most highly rated competencies identified were

- employing methods for enhancing self-concept;
- creating a positive social-emotional climate in the classroom;
- demonstrating a sensitivity to their language, geographical background, and cultural variations;
- developing individualized educational programs;
- implementing classroom strategies for behavior management;
- organizing the classroom environment in order to maximize learning including consideration for scheduling, seating arrangements, presentation of materials, and setting limits;
- creating an awareness of community agencies that provide services to learners and their families;
- maintaining records of learner performance; and
- developing and maintaining interpersonal communication skills with other professionals.

Gifted and Talented Learners

The Jacob K. Javits Gifted and Talented Students Education Act of 1988, under the Elementary and Secondary Education Act, Title IV, defined gifted and talented learners as children and youth who give evidence of high performance capability in areas such as intellectual creative, artistic or leadership capacity, or in specific academic fields, and who require services or activities not ordinarily provided by the school in order to fully develop such capabilities. See Figure 4-14.

A report by the U.S. Department of Education, Office of Educational Research and Improvement (1993) entitled *National Excellence: A Case for Developing America's Talent* (1993) proposed a revised definition of gifted and talented learners that eliminated the word "gifted" and utilized the terms "outstanding talent" and "exceptional talent." The proposed definition suggested that talent, or giftedness, occurs in all groups across all cultures and is not necessarily identified solely by a test score, but in "high performance capability" in the intellectual, in the creative, and in the artistic student. The report went on to state that the best way to find these learners is by providing opportunities and in observing their performance (pp. 54-55).

Schools must develop a system to identify gifted and talented learners that does the following:

- Seeks variety–It must look throughout a range of disciplines for learners with diverse talents.
- Uses many assessment measures–It must use a variety of appraisals so that schools can find learners in different talent areas and at different ages.
- Is free of bias–It must provide learners of all backgrounds with equal access to appropriate opportunities.

- Is fluid–It must use assessment procedures that can accommodate learners who develop at different rates and whose interests may change as they mature.
- Identifies potential–It must discover talents not readily apparent in learners as well as those that are obvious.
- Assesses motivation–It must take into account the drive and passion that play a key role in accomplishment (U.S. Department of Education, Office of Educational Research and Improvement, 1993).

Renzulli (2001) has suggested there are three interlocking clusters of ability that characterize gifted and talented learners. These clusters include general ability versus specific ability, task commitment, and creativity. See Figure 4-15.

Although parents and teachers may be concerned about academic planning for gifted and talented learners, they often assume that career planning will take care of itself.

Learners may have many choices available because of multiple gifts or a particular talent. A career choice in a particular area seems inevitable; therefore, there is no need for career planning. The learner is simply expected to make an occupational decision around the sophomore year of college and then follow through on the steps necessary to attain that goal.

Unfortunately, evidence is mounting that youthful brilliance in one or more areas does not always translate into adult satisfaction and accomplishment in working life. Studies with such diverse groups as National Merit Scholars, Presidential Scholars, and graduates of gifted education programs have shown that the path from education to career is not always smooth, and it may be complicated by social-emotional problems and needs of gifted learners that differ from those of more typical learners.

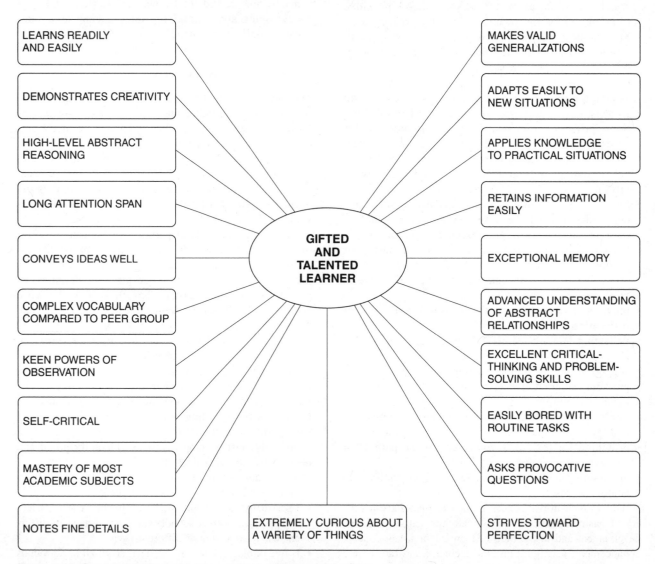

Figure 4-14. General characteristics demonstrated by gifted and talented learners.

CHARACTERISTICS OF GIFTED AND TALENTED LEARNERS

GENERAL ABILITY

- High levels of abstract thinking, verbal and numerical reasoning, spatial relations, memory, and word fluency
- Adaptation to the shaping of novel situations encountered in the external environment
- Automatization of information processing including rapid, accurate, and selective retrieval of information

SPECIFIC ABILITY

- The application of various combinations of general abilities to one or more specialized areas of knowledge or areas of human performance (e.g., the arts, leadership, administration)
- The capacity for acquiring and making appropriate use of advanced amounts of formal knowledge, tacit knowledge, technique, logistics, and strategy in the pursuit of particular problems or the manifestation of specialized areas of performance
- The capacity to sort out relevant and irrelevant information associated with a particular problem or areas of study or performance

TASK COMMITMENT

- The capacity for high levels of interest, enthusiasm, fascination, and involvement in a particular problem, area of study, or form of human expression
- The capacity for perseverance, endurance, determination, hard work, and dedicated practice
- The ability to identify significant problems within specialized reason, and to tune into major channels of communication and new developments within given fields
- Self-confidence, a strong ego, and belief in one's ability to carry out important work
- High standards for work, an openness to external and self-criticism, and an aesthetic sense of taste, quality, and excellence about their work and the work of others

CREATIVITY

- Fluency, flexibility, and originality of thought
- Openness to experiences and receptive to that which is new and different (even irrational) in thoughts, actions, and products of oneself and others
- Curious, speculative, adventurous, and mentally playful, and are willing to take risks in thought and action, even to the point of being uninhibited
- Sensitive to detail, aesthetic characteristics of ideas and things, and are willing to act on and react to external stimulation and their own ideas and feelings

Source: Renzulli, J. (2001). *A Practical System for Identifying Gifted and Talented Students.* The National Research Center on the Gifted and Talented. [On-line]. Available: http://www.sp.uconn.edu/~nrcgt/sem/semart04.html

Figure 4-15. Identifying gifted and talented learners.

Minority gifted learners have special career planning needs as well as needs related to multipotentiality or early emergence. Minority learners from African-American, Hispanic, and Native American backgrounds are less likely to have been selected for gifted education programs and less likely to perform well on standardized achievement tests than their nonminority peers. In addition, they may have lower career aspirations because of lower societal expectations. Nevertheless, the patterns of leadership and out-of-class accomplishments of gifted minority learners are very similar to those of nonminority gifted learners. Minority gifted learners are active leaders in other communities. Therefore, career counseling for these learners may be most effective when it focuses on raising career aspirations and emphasizes out-of-class accomplishments as indicators of possible career directions. Career planning must also go hand in hand with building a strong ethnic identity if later conflict between ethnic identity and achievement in majority society is to be avoided (Kerr, 1990).

Persisting gender stereotypes and the continued socializing of females into secondary roles means that, despite great gains in certain fields such as medicine and law, gifted females are less likely than gifted males to achieve their full potential. Although gifted females outperform gifted males in terms of grades, gifted males achieve higher scores on college admissions examinations. Compared to gifted males, gifted females are underprepared academically, having taken fewer mathematics and science courses and less challenging courses in social studies. As a result, they have fewer options for college majors and career goals. Bright females apparently let go of career aspirations gradually, first through underpreparation and later through decisions that may put the needs of spouses and families before their own. Gifted females fall behind gifted males in salary, status, and promotions throughout their working lives. In order to ensure that gifted females have the greatest possible chance to fulfill their potential, career planning should emphasize rigorous academic preparation (particularly in mathematics and science), maintain high career aspirations, and identify both internal and external barriers to the achievement of career goals (Kerr, 1990).

Sometimes problems arise in working with gifted and talented learners. Some of the anticipated problems and possible solutions include the following:

- Impatience–Because of their above-average abilities, gifted and talented learners will be eager to get on with it and will jump into the application of new material. Consequently, some learners will prefer to go over the theory very lightly. To make sure that both theory and tasks are mastered, encourage each learner to study the theory and demonstrate an appropriate knowledge base before applying it.
- Isolation–Some learners may feel set apart or singled out because of independent study and other appropriate methods designed to challenge them. To lessen this problem, emphasize to learners they are being given an opportunity to advance according to their ability, and/or encourage learners to attend demonstrations and work with other learners to help those learners with practice and performance of tasks.

• Impracticality–Some learners might be able to breeze through theory but will experience trouble with more practical concepts. If this happens, provide individual tutoring and coaching, encourage learners to work with some of their more proficient peers, attend group demonstrations or observe some pertinent live work projects, and provide some additional resources (e.g., films, tape or slide programs, video presentations of demonstrations, etc.) (Alabama State Department of Education, 1984).

Gifted and talented learners often excel in one area but may still be deficient in some other areas. Each learner should be assessed carefully so that no assumption is made that they are not gifted in all areas. Piirto (1994) summarizes some important principles in working with gifted and talented learners including the following:

1. Differentiation is necessary for academically talented children because of three of their learning characteristics:
   • they often have different interests than non-academically talented students;
   • they have the ability to learn faster; and
   • they have the ability to learn in greater depth.
2. The teacher should have an open attitude about adjusting the pace and depth of work for these learners.
3. The major technique for providing appropriate curriculum for academically talented students in regular classroom settings is "compacting," "telescoping," or "compressing" the required material. This involves pretesting. In compacting, the teacher pretests the students on the knowledge they are to acquire before beginning the unit, chapter or lessons to be taught. The teacher arranges for them to learn what they have not acquired and provides enrichment activities rather than have them drill and review what they already know.
4. Giving academically talented students more work instead of different work often results in having them try to hide their giftedness.
5. Certain practices by the teacher such as compacting, questioning, conducting discussions, and skilled lecturing can contribute to a successful education for academically talented learners.
6. There are quite a few out-of-school options for these learners including special Saturday and summer programs, internships in industry, mentorships, and exploration and shadowing activities in the workforce. (pp. 473-474)

Hearne and Maurer (2000) describe several basic models of service delivery for gifted learners, including self-contained classrooms, pullout classrooms, cluster groupings, cross-grade groupings, schoolwide enrichment models, resource teachers, adjunct programs, and special schools. See Figure 4-16.

SERVICE DELIVERY MODES . . .

SELF-CONTAINED CLASSROOMS
• Can be for all or part of a day and are appropriate at all levels
• Have curriculum and instruction designed to meet the needs of gifted learners
• Have staff trained in gifted strategies
• Provide resources above grade level
• Maintain heterogeneity within the identified gifted population
• Allow for individualized instruction
• Allow learners to be challenged to their full potential and to interact with others of like ability

PULLOUT MODEL
• Consists of learners leaving their regular classroom for a specified period of time for specialized instruction and then returning to spend the remaining time in the regular classroom
• Allows learners to work in areas of interest commensurate with their ability level
• Provides flexible delivery including seminars, field trips, special classes, resource rooms
• Does not necessarily provide individualized instruction to meet the needs of the gifted learner in the regular classroom
• Obligates learners to make up work they have missed in addition to their accelerated curriculum
• Requires teachers to work together closely to make this an advantageous experience for the gifted learners

PULLOUT MODEL COMBINED WITH CLUSTER GROUPING
• Occurs within the regular classroom
• Assigns identified learners to the same room where the teacher modifies the curriculum and instruction to meet their needs
• Allows learners to remain in the regular classroom, have access to others of like ability, and reduces the need for pullout
• Requires a teacher who has been trained in differentiation of curriculum and the needs of gifted learners

... SERVICE DELIVERY MODES

CROSS-GRADE GROUPING
- Combines several age-grade groups in one classroom
- Allows for a range of resources and pacing of instruction
- Reduces the lock step age placement
- Provides a viable alternative for instructional grouping of gifted learners when team teaching and looping are added to this model

RESOURCE ROOMS
- Allow learners to come and go from the regular classroom
- Enhance learning and provide options for teachers who are seeking to develop special talents or interests of learners
- Provide only minimal experience for the gifted learners
- Frequently provide only a minimal amount of time for learners' use, thus reducing the depth and breadth of study

SCHOOLWIDE ENRICHMENT MODEL
- Is generally attributed to Renzulli
- Impacts the education of all learners in the schools
- Benefits all learners by using resident experts in specific curriculum areas, both through schoolwide activities and classroom extensions
- Assembles learners who are identified as needing additional depth and breadth of learning in small study groups or ultimately with a mentor or advocate
- Assumes that giftedness can be developed and is directly connected to specific aspects of gifted behaviors
- Can be used in conjunction with any of the other models to best meet the needs of identified gifted learners, especially when the cirruiculum compacting component of this model is effectively used
- Allows the gifted learner to move ahead at a pace commensurate with his or her own ability

RESOURCE TEACHERS
- Provide additional support for highly capable learners
- Impact the entire classroom through demonstration, curriculum modification and the introduction of advanced or alternative materials
- Can influence the professional development of colleagues and serve as mentors and teammates for curriculum integration and accommodations

ADJUNCT PROGRAMS
- Can include mentors, tutors, internships, and independent study
- Focus on special interests of gifted learners
- Are generally used in conjunction with the regular classroom

SPECIAL SCHOOL MODEL
- Is recommended for highly capable/gifted learners
- Allows for interaction with others of high ability
- Focuses on both curriculum and instruction

Source: Hearne, J., & Maurer, B. (2000). *Gifted education: A primer (2000)*. Seattle, WA: New Horizons for Learning.

Figure 4-16. Several basic models of service delivery for gifted and talented learners.

Classroom climate is a major concern in any teaching situation because it has a direct influence on the learning styles and interests of the learners. Teachers need to develop an appropriate and positive attitude toward interacting with gifted and talented learners. It is the teacher's attitude that determines the classroom climate. An appropriate learning environment may include
- freedom of choice within a discipline;
- opportunities to practice creativity;
- group interaction;
- independence in learning;
- complexity of thought;
- openness to ideas;
- mobility of movement;
- acceptance of opinions; and
- extending learning beyond classroom walls.

By keeping these learning environment ideals in mind, the teacher will be able to make appropriate choices about what to teach, how to teach, what materials and resources to have available and how to assess learners' academic growth.

Curriculum Compacting. Curriculum compacting is one of the most common forms of curriculum modification for academically advanced learners. It is also the basic procedure upon which many other types of modification are founded. Compacting is based on the premise that learners who demonstrate they have mastered course content, or can master course content more quickly, can buy time to study material that they find more challenging and interesting.

Both basic skills and course content can be compacted. Although basic skills compacting is easier for teachers new to the process, the latter is probably more common in secondary schools. Basic skills compacting involves determining what basic skills learners have mastered and eliminating the practice or repetition of those skills. For example, beginning chemistry learners who have demonstrated mastery of the periodic table would have little need for further drill and practice in its use and would be better served by advancing to more complex course content.

Sometimes, academically advanced learners may not have mastered course content, but they are capable of doing so at an accelerated pace. They may have some understanding of the content and may require minimal time or instruction for mastery. In these cases, content compacting is useful. The compacting procedure is simple—determine what the learners already know and what they still need to learn and replace it with more challenging material that they would like to learn (Reis, Burns, & Renzulli, 1992).

Generally, two basic principles are recommended when compacting. First, grades should be based on the material compacted (what the learner has mastered) rather than the replacement material. Learners may be reluctant to tackle more challenging material if they risk receiving lower grades that may subsequently reduce their chances for academic scholarships. This is not to say that replacement activities should not be evaluated. Second, replacement material should be based on learner interests. Since replacement material will require greater effort from the learner, commitment to the task and the responsibility necessary to work independently (which is often, but not always, the learning situation) mandate that the learner have a vested interest in the content.

There are eight basic steps to curriculum compacting:
1. Determine the learning objectives for the material.
2. Find an appropriate way to assess those objectives.
3. Identify learners who may have already mastered the objectives (or could master them more quickly).
4. Assess those learners to determine their mastery level.
5. Streamline practice or instruction for learners who demonstrate mastery of the objectives.
6. Provide small group or individual instruction for learners who have not yet mastered all objectives, but are capable of doing so more quickly than their classmates.
7. Offer more challenging academic alternatives based on learner interest.
8. Maintain a record of the compacting process and instructional options provided.

Case Study . . . Alicia

Alicia is a senior in high school. For the past two years she has been enrolled in the electronics program. When Alicia first entered the program there were some problems. She is extremely curious and very outgoing. This turned out to be a combination that created some friction in the class.

Alicia is an eager learner who demonstrates keen powers of observation and has a long attention span. Her ability for abstract reasoning at high levels causes her to ask numerous questions out loud in class during lectures, discussions, and demonstrations. Mr. Young, her electronics instructor, became frustrated while trying to deliver the electronics curriculum to the rest of the class while still attempting to enrich Alicia by providing higher level content and extensive answers to her frequent questions. If he didn't answer her questions, Alicia often became persistent and continued to repeat them. He didn't always have time to meet with her individually during breaks, before class, or after class due to other tasks that came up.

Despite her frustration, Alicia continuously received the highest grades in the class and performed at levels from above average to excellent on laboratory projects and activities. At one point, Mr. Young assigned Alicia as a peer tutor to several learners in the class who were having difficulty grasping concepts or performing some tasks in the lab. The peer tutor situation worked for a while, but eventually Alicia resented being the one who had to continuously interrupt what she was doing to help other learners. Then Mr. Young began to give Alicia more work than others in the class were assigned, although the content remained at the same level and presented no challenge and no new learning for her. Alicia was resentful and refused to complete what she called "more of the same," even though she was told that she would receive extra credit.

At his wits end, Mr. Young went to the vocational counselor for help. The counselor called a meeting with the district's coordinator of gifted and talented programs, who then worked with Mr. Young to identify some strategies that would work with Alicia. First, Alicia was provided with an opportunity to complete assignments and tests at her own pace, which allows her to accelerate through the curriculum quickly although she still completes the same competencies required of all learners in the program. At the same time, Mr. Young provided her with enrichment assignments that required greater depth of content. They meet each Wednesday morning before school to discuss these assignments and work toward them through student-teacher contracts. Alicia has also been spending some time shadowing workers in the electronics industry. After shadowing and interviewing these individuals, she comes back and reports to the entire class. She has identified an industry mentor at one of the electronics companies in the community who will meet with her on a regular basis to discuss career plans and technical questions.

Through the counseling office, Mr. Young is also looking into the prospect of Alicia attending some classes in electronics at the local community college. Finally, Alicia has recently been elected as president of her district SkillsUSA-VICA student organization. This provides her with leadership development opportunities that are challenging. Under her leadership, the SkillsUSA-VICA chapter is planning several community service projects as well as two fund-raising activities to help members attend SkillsUSA-VICA district and state competitions.

Educators new to the process should consider the following recommendations:

- Start with one or two responsible learners.
- Select content with which they feel comfortable.
- Try a variety of methods to determine learner mastery of the material (a brief conversation with a learner may be just as effective as a written pretest).
- Compact by topic rather than time.
- Define proficiency based on a consensus with administrators and parents.
- Don't be afraid to request help from available sources such as community volunteers (Reis, Burns, & Renzulli, 1992).

Teaching Creative and Critical Thinking. It is easy to spot creative and critical thinkers among learners. Creative thinkers are more apt than other learners to draw well, write with fresh ideas, respond to questions with unusual answers, or develop unique solutions to problems. They generate ideas fluently, elaborate, think flexibly and produce original products. Learners with strong critical-thinking skills often see flaws in arguments, point out teachers' and other learners' mistakes, enjoy debate, quickly draw inductive conclusions from observations, or deduce solutions from previous inductions. Further, both creative and critical thinkers may unwittingly intimidate other learners and teachers by their special talents.

It is just as easy to spot those learners who have had their creativity and thinking squelched. These are the learners who claim they cannot draw, write, sing, act or come up with any kind of creative idea. These are the learners who claim they cannot do word problems in math, cannot follow the logic of a geometry proof, cannot counter an argument in debate, or cannot organize their thoughts while writing an essay or an outline for paper.

Creative problem solving encourages learners to generate solutions to problems by following a specific format. See Figure 4-17. The following steps illustrate a creative problem-solving format:

- Fact finding–List everything you know about the problem or challenge using *who, what, where, when, why,* and *how* questions.
- Problem findings–Generate a list of questions that capture the central core of the problem. Begin each question using the following stem: "In what ways might we…"
- Idea finding–Generate ideas to solve the problem. This is the divergent-thinking, brainstorming stage. Ideas should be listed without criticism or evaluation. Unusual and far-out ideas are to be encouraged.
- Solution finding–List criteria for evaluating the ideas, evaluate the ideas and select one or more of the best ideas. For example, the criteria for evaluating the various ideas might include these questions: "Will it work?" and "What is the possibility of success?"
- Acceptance finding–Incorporate the best ideas into an action plan. Use *who, what, where, when, why,* and *how* questions to help generate the plan.

CREATIVE PROBLEM SOLVING FORMAT

PROBLEM
- Students write graffiti on school buildings

FACT FINDING
- Why do students write graffiti on school buildings?

PROBLEM FINDING
- In what ways might students be provided with the opportunity to use graffiti in a constructive manner?

IDEA FINDING
- Allow students to create a mural on the west side of the school building

SOLUTION FINDING
- Will the idea work?
- What is the probability of success?
- Is the idea feasible?

ACCEPTANCE FINDING
- Who will oversee work on the mural?
- When will it occur?
- What is the time frame for completing the work?
- Who will be allowed to participate?

Figure 4-17. A format for generating solutions using creative problem-solving strategies.

Socratic questioning, often used by debate teams and lawyers, puts the responsibility for thinking and learning on the learner. The teacher acts as the facilitator for thinking about and discussing the topic at hand. Divergent thinking (thinking that generates different ideas) can be encouraged using the Socratic method when questions focus learners on thinking intuitively, generating hypotheses, and changing perspectives. The teacher must be careful not to pose only convergent questions (single-answer questions) or to ask manipulative questions that lead to a forgone conclusion. See Figure 4-18. The following are the six levels of Socratic questioning listed from easiest to hardest.

1. Clarification–The purpose of this type of question is to solicit information and help the questioner better understand the statement of the previous speaker. The questioner may be the teacher who is asking a learner to clarify a position or the use of a word or phrase. Or, the questioner may be a learner asking the teacher or another learner for clarification.
2. Probing assumptions–The purpose of these questions is to explore the beliefs, values, perspectives, and philosophies that led the speaker to make the statement that is in question.
3. Asking for reasons, evidence or causes–The purpose of these questions is to find additional support for the speaker's argument.
4. Probing perspectives–The purpose of these questions is to solicit other ways of looking at the topic under discussion.

5. Exploring implications and consequences–The purpose of these questions is to help the person being questioned focus on future results of holding to the current position.
6. Questions about the question–These questions are metacognitive in nature. They focus on whether a particular question is the right question for the current discussion, or they focus the question for better discussion.

SOCRATIC QUESTIONING

CLARIFICATION
- What did you mean by . . . ?
- What is your main point?

PROBING ASSUMPTIONS
- What are you assuming?
- Is that always the case?

ASKING FOR REASONS, EVIDENCE, OR CAUSES
- What would be an example of that?
- Is there evidence for believing that?

PROBING PERSPECTIVES
- What is an alternative?
- What would an opponent say?

EXPLORING IMPLICATIONS AND CONSEQUENCES
- What effect would that have?
- If this is the case, what else must be true?

QUESTIONS ABOUT THE QUESTION
- Do we all agree that this is the most essential question?
- How can we find out?

Figure 4-18. Examples of questions that apply to each of the six levels of Socratic questioning.

Working with Gifted and Talented Learners

Advanced placement (AP) and honors classes help meet the needs of academically gifted learners and other advanced learners; however, not all schools offer AP and honors classes, and some schools offer only a small number of such classes. Further, AP and honors classes typically do not address the needs of learners talented in the areas of creativity, leadership, and the visual and performing arts. With the limitations of AP and honors classes in mind, teaching gifted and talented high school learners in the regular classroom takes on added importance. Suggestions for teaching learners in the regular classroom include the following:
- Listen to the learners. Find out what interests them and incorporate those interests within the regular curriculum. Use examples that draw from learners' comments, hobbies, and interests. Allow assignments that meet objectives but also allow for learner choice. Include assessment questions or projects that appeal to learner interests.

- Invite outside speakers whose professions link the content area with a career, hobby or trade. Demonstrate to the learners the links between academic learning and the nonacademic world.
- Provide gifted and talented learners with the opportunity to display their knowledge by having them develop sophisticated products and performances (e.g., presentations, models and displays). Encourage learners to create unique products that challenge existing ideas and produce new ideas.
- Integrate critical- and creative-thinking skills into the curriculum. Include reasoning, logic, creative thinking and higher-level thinking skills. Gifted and talented learners need the opportunity to think abstractly and to be challenged.
- Develop and implement curriculum that is related to broad-based issues, themes, or problems. Include interdisciplinary studies that require the integration of both concepts and methodology from various disciplines. Thematic and interdisciplinary curriculum encourages gifted and talented learners to think more deeply about an issue and generalize to other fields of study.
- Encourage interested learners to purse a real-world problem. This may include applying specific knowledge and skills to identified community problems (e.g., reducing water pollution, creating a bicycle path).
- Encourage various types of research, including interviews, surveys, and the use of the Internet.

The following are techniques that can be used when working with gifted and talented learners in career and technical education programs:
- Accelerate learners through the curriculum at a more rapid rate than others to keep them challenged (individualized instruction format).
- Enrich the regular curriculum with greater depth of content and/or a wider range of experiences (emphasize more complex content) to challenge learners.
- Set up seminars for small groups of learners to meet regularly to study and discuss applications of career and technical education concepts and information taught in class.
- Promote independent study of a related topic with an in-depth report delivered to the class (the level of this assignment should be specifically designed to challenge the learner's level of functioning).
- Offer summer enrichment programs to provide further depth and application of content introduced in a career and technical education program. Special projects can also be planned at this time.
- Develop student-teacher contracts involving a project that applies the knowledge learned in the program (e.g., related problems could be identified and solutions proposed). These contracts could be with an individual learner or with a small group of learners.
- Design individual and/or group research reports (library-based research efforts with oral reports given to the entire class).

- Encourage participation in career and technical student organization activities (e.g., development of leadership capabilities).
- Promote articulation activities with postsecondary programs (e.g., joint enrollment, exploration sessions, contracts to complete accelerated projects).
- Allow for early completion of career and technical education program requirements so that learners can exit to further training and/or entry-level job placement.
- Design and monitor school and/or community projects related to concepts learned in the program where they would assume responsibility for planning, implementing, evaluating, and reporting results.
- Recognize the exemplary efforts and products of learners (e.g., honors day, certificates, plaques, media coverage, newspaper clips).
- Arrange for learners to spend time in a related job site to practice what they have learned.
- Have available in the classroom and/or laboratory materials that are written on a wide range of areas applicable to the content of the program.
- Design capstone experiences in the community where learners who have mastered the competencies in a program remain enrolled in that program while spending time learning advanced skills at a community-based work site.

ISSUES THAT AFFECT LEARNERS FROM SPECIAL POPULATIONS

There are a variety of issues that affect youth, including individuals from special populations. These issues cut across all special populations, impact day-to-day lives, and create great challenges. Some of these issues include substance abuse, child abuse, teen suicide, violence, and gang involvement.

Substance Abuse

Substance abuse is the taking into the body of any chemical substance that causes physical, mental, emotional, or social harm to an individual. Substance abuse is a problem faced by many young people today. It cuts across all ethnic and socioeconomic groups. All youth are vulnerable as they are confronted with the pressures of today's world. Research shows that millions of teenagers are abusing one or more substances and many more are threatened by the pressure to start using alcohol, tobacco, and other drugs.

Drugs are usually ingested or inhaled and cover a wide variety of natural and synthetic chemicals that may be legal or illegal to use. Commonly abused substances include prescription drugs (e.g., sedatives, diet pills, sleeping pills, tranquilizers), illegal drugs (e.g., narcotics, amphetamines, marijuana, cocaine, crack, PCP, LSD), and legal substances (e.g., cleaning fluids, paints, lighter fluid, glue, nonstick cooking spray, hair spray, nail polish remover, gasoline fumes).

Califano and Booth (1997) reported the following findings based on a national survey of teens, their parents, teachers and principals:

- The characteristics of a teen's school rival the characteristics of a teen's family as indicators of teen substance abuse risk.
- Learners who attend schools where drugs are kept, used, or sold are nearly four times likelier to try marijuana than are those who attend drug-free schools.
- Sixty-six percent (76% of high school learners and 46% of middle school learners) say their schools are not drug-free.
- Teens are more likely to encounter drugs on school grounds or in their schools than on their neighborhood streets; more high school learners have witnessed drug sales at school (41%) than in their neighborhoods (25%).
- Twenty-five percent of teachers say learners who appear to be drunk or high show up in their classes at least once a month.
- In the past year, one-fourth of middle school teachers and one-third of high school teachers have reported a learner for using illegal drugs.
- Forty-one percent of middle school teachers and 51% of principals and high school teachers think a learner can use marijuana every weekend and still do well in school.
- Eighty-three percent of schools where learners smoke and drink on school grounds are not drug-free. Schools where learners smoke and drink are three times likelier to be drug-plagued than schools with neither smoking or drinking on premises.
- High school learners estimate that on average 50% of their classmates use drugs at least once a month. In contrast, high school teachers estimate that only 24% of their learners use drugs at least monthly and principals estimate only 10%.
- While 41% of high school learners and 30% of middle and high school learners have seen drugs sold on school grounds, only 12% of high school teachers and 14% of middle and high school principals have seen such sales.
- Teens again tell us drugs are the most important problem they face (cited by 35%, versus 32% in 1995 and 31% in 1996). Parents, teachers and principals underestimate the extent of teen concern about drugs.
- Forty-one percent of teens report attending a party in the past six months where marijuana was available. Twenty-five percent of high school learners and 11% of middle school learners report attending a party in the past two years where parents provided alcohol.
- Exposure of teens to harder drugs such as acid, cocaine, or heroin is climbing. Most (56%) know a friend or classmate who uses these harder drugs.
- Teens who smoke are three times more at risk of using drugs than those who do not.
- Twenty-three percent of teachers are less than totally confident their school administration would back them up if they reported a learner suspected of drinking or

using drugs, and 56% of principals are less than totally confident that the parents of a learner suspected of drinking or using drugs in school would back them if that learner were disciplined.

- A large majority of teachers (61%) and principals (68%) support the drug testing of teachers.
- Teens, parents, teachers, and principals support firm steps to keep drugs out of schools, including random locker searches, zero-tolerance policies, and drug testing of athletes. Half of learners (52%) and principals (53%) support drug testing of all learners, compared with 42% of parents and 38% of teachers.
- While a narrow majority of teachers feel they are adequately trained to spot substance abuse (54%), less than half (46%) feel they have been adequately trained to teach learners about the dangers of substance abuse and how to deal with it.
- Sixty-two percent of middle school learners would report a drug dealer on school grounds to school officials, while only 36% of high school learners would.
- Most teachers (57%) believe that drugs have diminished the quality of education in the nation's schools.
- Large majorities of parents (82%), teachers (83%), principals (88%), and teens (66%) think that portraying the adverse effects of alcohol in movies and on TV would result in fewer teen drinkers. A majority believes that if fewer rock and rap stars used illegal drugs, fewer teens would use illegal drugs. Most parents and educators also think less smoking in movies would result in fewer teen smokers.
- Thirty-eight percent of teachers consider the typical parent to be in denial about drugs. Yet, half of parents know their teen's school is not drug free, and 34% expect their teen will try illegal drugs.
- Teachers and principals are less likely than the parents of their learners to have tried marijuana in their youth. Twenty-six percent of teachers and 23% of principals say they have tried marijuana, versus 50% of parents.
- Seven signs of trouble in school that greatly increase the risk of substance abuse are smoking, drinking, drugs, weapons, expulsion for drugs, death in drug or alcohol related incidents by a learner, and learners showing up in class drunk or stoned. Teens say only 24% of their middle schools and a mere 4% of their high schools are free of all of these signs of trouble.
- As the size of the school increases, as the commitment of the principal to create and maintain a drug-free school decreases, and as the confidence of teachers that their principals will back them up if they report a learner for drinking or using drugs decreases, the likelihood of more signs of trouble also goes up.
- The affluence of the community where the school is located; whether the school is in an urban, suburban, or rural community; and the percentage of minority learners in the student body bear little relation to the number of signs of trouble at school.

A combination of factors makes substance abuse a more serious problem than ever before in our history. Never have so many substances with the potential for abuse been so widely available to young teens. With such ready availability, it is not surprising that from 1992 to 1996 teen substance use involving nicotine, marijuana, amphetamines, and other illicit drugs like cocaine, heroin, acid, and inhalants has been rising. Binge drinking has also begun to increase, particularly among younger teens (National Center on Addiction and Substance Abuse, 1997).

Alcohol is the most abused drug among youth in this country. Alcohol is a drug that affects the nervous system after reaching the brain. About 90% of the alcohol is immediately absorbed into the blood while the remaining 10% is eliminated through the kidneys and lungs. Moderate amounts of alcohol usually do not harm the body organs, but abusive or prolonged drinking may seriously affect the heart, liver, stomach, and other body organs. Alcohol is a depressant that affects individuals in three stages, depending on the amount consumed. The first stage affects judgment and lowers restraint and inhibitions. The second stage is marked by memory loss, dulled thinking, slower reflexes, and slurred speech. The third stage can result in stupor, coma, and even death. Alcoholism is the nation's third largest health problem behind cancer and heart disease.

In the experimental stage, youth do not always exhibit behavioral signs of substance abuse. As individuals use more alcohol and drugs and use becomes abuse, one or more of the following behaviors may be observed:

- lack of interest in physical activities
- difficulty in thinking and concentrating
- impaired ability to work
- poor school performance
- truancy or absenteeism
- hostility
- aggressive behavior
- discipline problems
- withdrawal or inability to relate to people
- changes in friendship
- extreme mood swings, apathy and lethargy
- borrowing or stealing money
- secretiveness about friends and activities
- lack of interest in personal appearance and hygiene
- changes in eating and sleeping patterns
- physical symptoms (e.g., red eyes, sores on nose or mouth, fatigue, drowsiness, altered speech, marks on arm)
- wearing sunglasses
- long-sleeved shirt in hot weather
- association with known alcohol or drug users
- frequent trips to the rest room
- presence of drug paraphernalia
- a pattern of crime or delinquency

Some things that can be done by educators if substance abuse is suspected include the following:

- Provide an atmosphere of openness and trust so that learners will feel comfortable expressing themselves and in seeking advice from you.
- Listen seriously to what learners have to say.
- Give learners praise, recognition, and increased responsibility and let them know you value them. Learners who feel accepted are less likely to abuse substances.
- Encourage learners to set realistic goals that can be achieved. Some learners may be overachievers and need to be motivated to perform at a realistic level, rather than trying to please someone else.
- Teach learners stress management and assertiveness training techniques.
- Consult a counselor to become familiar with programs and agencies that can provide substance abusers with help (e.g., Alcoholics Anonymous, Al-Anon, Alateen, family therapy, area hot lines, area council on alcoholism and drug abuse, counseling centers).
- Working with a counselor and/or other support personnel, conduct a corrective interview with the learner when the documented record of unsatisfactory performance warrants it under the school/program policies and procedures. The parent could also be involved in this session.

Bosworth (1997) summarized research identifying that prevention programs need to be comprehensive and have sufficient intensity to reasonably expect that prevention skills can be taught. An effective prevention curriculum includes the following content areas:

- Normative education–This helps learners realize that use of alcohol, tobacco, and other drugs is not the norm for teenagers. Learners generally overestimate the proportion of their peers actively involved in abusive substances. Hence, it is easier to be pressured by the myth that everybody is doing it. Surveys and opinion polls are used to help learners understand actual use rates.
- Social skills–Improving verbal skills may help learners increase their ease in handling social situations. Decision making, communication skills, and assertiveness skills are particularly important during the late elementary and middle school years when puberty changes social dynamics between young people themselves as well as with the adults in their lives.
- Social influences–These help learners recognize external pressures (e.g., advertising, role models, peer attitudes) to use abusive substances and help them develop the cognitive skills to resist such pressures.
- Perceived harm–This helps learners understand both the risks and short- and long-term consequences of substance use. The message must come from a credible source and be reinforced in multiple settings.
- Protective factors–These support and encourage the development of positive aspects of life such as helping, caring, goal setting, and challenging learners to live up to their potential and facilitate affiliations with positive peers.
- Refusal skills–Learning ways to refuse abusive substances effectively and still maintain friendships was a strategy heavily relied on in many early curricula. Recent research indicates that it is most relevant in supporting teens who do not want to use drugs and in conjunction with other activities such as social influences and normative education.

Child Abuse

The National Clearinghouse on Child Abuse and Neglect Information (2001) defines a child as a person who has not attained the lesser of the age of 18 or, except in cases of sexual abuse, the age specified by the child protection law of the state in which the child resides. They further define child abuse and neglect as, at a minimum, any recent act or failure to act on the part of a parent or caretaker that results in death, serious physical or emotional harm, sexual abuse or exploitation of a child, or an act or failure to act that presents an imminent risk of serious harm to a child. They define sexual abuse as the employment, use, persuasion, inducement, enticement, or coercion of any child to engage in, or assist any other person to engage in, any sexually explicit conduct or simulation of such conduct for the purpose of producing a visual depiction of such conduct; or the rape, and in cases of caretaker or inter-familial relationships, statutory rape, molestation, prostitution, or other form of sexual exploitation of children, or incest with children.

Carter (2001) reported the following:

- Domestic violence and child abuse takes a devastating toll on children and society at large. Early childhood victimization, either through direct abuse, neglect, or witnessing parental domestic violence, has been shown to have demonstrable long-term consequences for youth violence, adult violent behaviors, and other forms of criminality.
- The U.S. Advisory Board on Child Abuse and Neglect suggests that domestic violence may be the single major precursor to child abuse and neglect fatalities in the U.S.
- Domestic violence perpetrators sometimes intentionally injure children in an effort to intimidate and control their adult partners. These assaults can include physical, emotional, and sexual abuse of the children.
- Children whose mothers are abused sometimes suffer at the hands of their mothers as well. One study found that the rate of child abuse by mothers who were beaten is at least double that of mothers whose husbands did not assault them.
- The impact of domestic violence and child abuse may continue through adolescence and adulthood. Adolescents who have grown up in violent homes are at risk for recreating the abusive relationships they have seen. They are more likely to attempt suicide, abuse drugs

and alcohol, run away from home, engage in teenage prostitution and other delinquent behavior, and commit sexual assault crimes. A study conducted by the Office of Juvenile Justice and Delinquency Prevention found that 70% of adolescents who lived in families with parental conflict self-reported violent delinquency, compared to 49% of adolescents from households without this conflict. This study also revealed that exposure to multiple forms of violence, including domestic violence, child abuse, and general family climate of hostility, doubles the risk of self-reported youth violence.

- Researchers have also found that men who as children witnessed their parents' domestic violence were twice as likely to abuse their own wives than were sons of nonviolent parents. A significant proportion of abusive husbands grew up in families where they witnessed their mothers being beaten. Clearly, domestic violence and child abuse are spawning grounds for the next generation of abusers, as well as for violent juveniles.

- The overlap between child abuse and domestic violence is not limited to their consequences or prevalence. Many of the risk factors that are highly associated with child maltreatment are the same factors that put women at risk for domestic violence and children at risk for juvenile violence. For example, child abuse risk factors include young age of parents, social isolation, the abuser's history of being a victim of child abuse or a witness to domestic violence as a child, and poverty, among others.

The National Clearinghouse on Child Abuse and Neglect Information (2001) stated that there are four major types of maltreatment: physical abuse, neglect, sexual abuse, and emotional abuse. While state definitions may vary, operational definitions can help identify these forms of maltreatment nationwide. Although any of the following forms of child maltreatment may be found separately, they often occur in combination. Emotional abuse is almost always present when other forms are identified.

- Physical abuse is characterized by the infliction of physical injury as a result of punching, beating, kicking, biting, burning, shaking or otherwise harming a child. The parent or caretaker may not have intended to hurt the child; rather, the injury may have resulted from overdiscipline or physical punishment.

- Child neglect is characterized by failure to provide for the child's basic needs. Neglect can be physical, educational, or emotional. Physical neglect includes refusal of or delay in seeking health care, abandonment, expulsion from the home or refusal to allow a runaway to return home, and inadequate supervision. Educational neglect includes the allowance of chronic truancy, failure to enroll a child of mandatory school age in school, and failure to attend to a special educational need. Emotional neglect includes such actions as marked inattention to the child's needs for affection, refusal of or failure to provide needed psychological care, spouse abuse in the child's presence, and permission for drug or alcohol use by the child. The assessment of child neglect requires consideration of cultural values and standards of care as well as recognition that the failure to provide the necessities of life may be related to poverty.

- Sexual abuse includes fondling a child's genitals, intercourse, incest, rape, sodomy, exhibitionism, and commercial exploitation through prostitution or the production of pornographic materials. Many experts believe that sexual abuse is the most underreported form of child maltreatment because of the secrecy or silence that so often characterizes these cases.

- Emotional abuse (psychological/verbal abuse/mental injury) includes acts or omissions by the parents or other caregivers that have caused, or could cause, serious behavioral, cognitive, emotional, or mental disorders. In some cases of emotional abuse, the acts of parents or other caregivers alone, without any harm evident in the child's behavior or condition, are sufficient to warrant child protective services (CPS) intervention. For example, the parents/caregivers may use extreme or bizarre forms of punishment, such as confinement of a child in a dark closet. Less severe acts, such as habitual scapegoating, belittling, or rejecting treatment, are often difficult to prove; therefore, CPS may not be able to intervene without evidence of harm to the child. See Figure 4-19.

Persons engaged in the following professions and activities are subject by law to report suspected child abuse:

- physicians, dentists, medical residents or interns, hospital personnel and administrators, nurses, health care practitioners, chiropractors, osteopaths, pharmacists, optometrists, podiatrists, emergency medical technicians, ambulance drivers, undertakers, coroners, medical examiners, alcohol or drug treatment personnel, and persons performing a healing role or practicing the healing arts

- psychologists, psychiatrists, mental health professionals, social workers, and licensed or unlicensed marriage, family, and individual counselors

- teachers, teacher's aides/assistants, school counselors and guidance personnel, and school officials/administrators

- child care workers and administrators

- law enforcement personnel, probation officers, criminal prosecutors, and juvenile rehabilitation or detention facility employees

- foster parents

- commercial film and photo processors

The law does not require the person reporting to be certain that a child is being abused or neglected before reporting, only to have reason for believing it. It is a good idea to talk to the child to see if there is a simple or plausible explanation for the appearance of injury or neglect. But a concerned adult should stop well short of trying to investigate or intervene in the suspected abuse. Reasonable suspicions of abuse must be reported to the appropriate authorities, and any time a child discloses abuse to an adult, the adult has reason to make a report. This is true even if the adult feels skeptical about what the child has said; the disclosure should be reported so that appropriate authorities can judge the need for investigation.

A person wishing to report suspected child abuse or neglect may call any state or local law enforcement agency or child protective services (CPS). In an acute case, when a child appears to be in immediate danger of serious harm, it is best to call 911 (where that service is available) or the nearest police or sheriff's department to ensure the fastest possible response time to protect the child.

The law offers protection for those who report abuse. The identity of the person making a report is confidential and may be disclosed only upon order of the court or to a law enforcement officer conducting a criminal investigation of the report. In addition, the person reporting is immune from civil or criminal liability as long as the report is made in good faith. Good faith means the person making the report took reasonable steps to learn facts that were readily available and at hand. The person reporting is also protected from liability if testifying or participating in judicial proceedings resulting from the report.

Child abuse prevention is a fundamental first step in crime prevention and violence reduction. Most abused and neglected children grow up to be peaceful and productive citizens, but within the criminal justice system, mistreated children are significantly overrepresented. In their report, *Preventing Crime: What Works, What Doesn't, What's Promising,* The National Institute of Justice (1998) found that child abuse victims are 40% more likely than nonabused children to become delinquents and adult criminals. Abused and neglected children are 53% more likely to be arrested as juveniles, 38% more likely to be arrested as adults, and 38% more likely to be arrested for violent crimes. Physically abused children are more likely to be aggressive toward their peers and adults and are more likely to have poor impulse control than nonabused children. The more frequent and serious the abuse, the greater the risk that the child will grow up to be troubled in these ways if no one intervenes.

INDICATORS OF CHILD ABUSE ...

PHYSICAL ABUSE

- Unexplained bruises (in various stages of healing), welts, or human bite marks
- Unexplained burns (especially cigarette burns)
- Unexplained fractures, lacerations, or abrasions
- Self-destructive behaviors
- Individual is uncomfortable with physical contact
- Learner arrives at school early or stays late as if afraid
- Chronic runaway (adolescents)
- Complains of soreness or moves uncomfortably
- Wears clothing inappropriate for the weather

EMOTIONAL MALTREATMENT

- Speech disorders
- Delayed physical development
- Substance abuse
- Ulcers, asthma, severe allergies
- Habit disorders (e.g., rocking)
- Antisocial, destructive behavior
- Neurotic trains (sleep disorders)
- Passive and aggressive behavioral extremes
- Delinquent behavior (especially adolescents)
- Developmental delay

PHYSICAL NEGLECT

- Abandonment
- Unattended medical needs
- Consistent lack of supervision
- Consistent hunger, inappropriate dress, poor hygiene
- Lice, distended stomach, emaciated
- Regular displays of fatigue or listlessness, falling asleep in class
- Stealing food, begging from peers
- Reporting that no caretaker is at home
- Frequent absences or tardiness
- Self-destructive behavior
- School dropout

. . . INDICATORS OF CHILD ABUSE

SEXUAL ABUSE

- Torn, stained, or bloodied underclothing
- Pain or itching in genital area
- Difficulty walking or sitting
- Bruises or bleeding in external genitalia
- Venereal disease
- Frequent urinary or yeast infections
- Chronic depression
- Excessive seductiveness
- Role reversal, overly concerned for siblings
- Poor self-esteem, self-devaluation, lack of confidence
- Peer problems, lack of involvement
- Massive weight change
- Suicide attempts (especially for adolescents)
- Hysteria, lack of emotional control
- Sudden school difficulties
- Premature understanding of sex
- Threatened by physical contact or closeness
- Promiscuity

Source: Broadhurst, D., Edmunds, M., & MacDicken, R. (1979). *Early Childhood Programs and the Prevention and Treatment of Child Abuse and Neglect—The User Manual Series.* Washington, DC: U.S. Department of Health, Education, and Welfare.

Figure 4-19. Examples of possible physical or behavioral child-abuse indicators.

Bear, Schenk, and Buckner (1992) suggested supportive techniques for teachers so that a safe classroom environment is established for learners who have been abused:

1. Establish high expectations–Emotionality may interfere with the students' thinking process. It is important that appropriate goals be established so that they feel confident in their abilities. Vocational and applied technology [career and technical] education classes can be a place where these learners rebuild their self-esteem, assert themselves, and experience success.

2. Provide structure–Abused students may feel powerless to control their environment. To cope, they may refuse to strive to manipulate everything around them (e.g., bossing peers, controlling belongings), express disproportionate feelings whenever they feel threatened (e.g., yell, scream, threaten), and refuse to even try to control what happens around them (e.g., can't make even the simplest decision, look to others for direction).

3. Help students feel a sense of control in a positive manner–Teachers should give students accurate information and build trust.

4. Establish opportunities for students to develop personal identity–Abused children have little sense of identity. Teachers can help by pointing out the learners' strengths, by asking questions that help them formulate a position on issues, and by promoting decision-making skills.

5. Build self esteem–Learners who have been abused have little self-esteem. Teachers can help by showing them that they are accepted, valued, and capable. With each successful completion of a task, their sense of competency will increase.

6. Establish a sense of belonging–Students who have been abused think they did something wrong and that they are bad. They assume that there is a reason for them to be isolated from others because they have been harboring a secret from everyone. Teachers should facilitate a sense of belonging by making a conscious attempt to include them in classroom activities, vocational student organizations, and laboratory assignments.

7. Establish social skills–The learners may have learned inappropriate behaviors and language through an abusive relationship. They may feel unworthy to interact on an equal basis with peers and may fear rejection. Teachers should establish a classroom environment of caring, appreciation for differences, consistent rules, and recognition of small successes. (pp. 46–47)

It is important that teachers learn communication techniques to use with abused learners. In a crisis situation, educators should remember to

- refrain from suggesting that learners' problems are small or that students are overreacting;
- avoid the tendency to moralize about students' feelings or behaviors (e.g., "You shouldn't be feeling that way.");

- never suggest that students were abused because they did something wrong;
- facilitate counseling immediately for students threatening to run away or take other drastic actions;
- resist the urge to take sides against family members because this can make students feel even more alone;
- do not validate feelings of hopelessness or helplessness but emphasize to students that they can take positive steps to regain control over their lives;
- communicate the view that the crisis is temporary, that help is available, and that you are willing to stand by the student; and
- realize your own limitations and do not be afraid to ask for assistance. (*Educating At-Risk Youth*, March 1992, p. 4)

Although teachers are not responsible for investigating whether child abuse is occurring, they are legally obligated to report suspected abuse. School staff should not call or visit the home when questions of abuse or neglect arise unless they have been directed to do so by protective agency staff. It is not the educator's responsibility to determine whether abuse was intentional or to identify the conditions surrounding an abusive situation. These questions should be conducted by professional case workers. Teachers should compare the learner's behavior with other educators if abuse is suggested. Also, contact with the counselor, the school district child abuse team, or the Department of Social Services is appropriate. The appropriate individuals and/or agencies will conduct the investigation and make decisions as to what should happen to keep the learner safe.

Teen Suicide

Statistics from the National Center for Injury Prevention and Control (2002) reveal the following information:

- Overall, suicide is the eighth leading cause of death for all Americans and is the third leading cause of death for young people aged 15 to 24.
- Although the age-adjusted suicide rate has remained constant since the 1940's, suicide rates shifted for some groups during the period between 1980 and 1992. For example, suicide rates increased among persons between the ages of 10 and 19, among young African-American males, and among elderly males.
- Nearly 60% of all suicides are committed with a firearm.
- In 1995, more than 90% of all suicides in this country were among whites, with males accounting for 73% and females 18% of all suicides. However, during the period from 1979 to 1992, suicide rates for Native Americans were about 1.5 times the national rates. There was a disproportionate number of suicides among young male Native Americans during this period, as males 15 to 24 accounted for 64% of all suicides by Native Americans.
- In 1980, the rate of African-American suicide for teens aged 15 to 19 more than doubled from 3.6 per 100,000 to 8.1 per 100,000. Although white teens still have a higher rate of suicide, the gap is narrowing.

Depression is also a very common illness among teenagers. The feelings of helplessness and worthlessness that can accompany it, along with disturbances in sleep or appetite, can fuel a downward spiral of health and grades, further clouding perspective and making even thought seem intolerably difficult. The warning signs of serious depression include

- social withdrawal;
- poor communication and sharing;
- reduced effort and involvement with others;
- changes in friends to a preference for those who are angry or negative;
- loss of interest in previous pursuits;
- sleep impairment, either increased or decreased;
- defiance;
- dishonesty;
- overt emergence of an I don't care attitude;
- morbid preoccupation in dress, color, poetry, music, peers or attitude;
- poor impulse control;
- increasing demands;
- reduced honest cooperation with authority figures; and
- overt discussions of lack of pleasure in life or reason to live.

The American Psychiatric Association (1988) revealed the following about young people and suicide:

- Young people who have attempted suicide in the past or who talk about suicide are at greater risk of future attempts. Listen for hints like "I'd be better off dead," or "I won't be problem for you much longer," or "Nothing matters; it's no use."
- Adolescents who consider suicide generally feel alone, hopeless, and rejected. They are more vulnerable to having these feelings if they have been abused, feel they have been recently humiliated in front of family or friends, have parents with alcohol or drug problems, or have a family life affected by parental discord, disruptions, separation, or divorce. However, a teenager may be depressed and/or suicidal without any of these.
- Some teens who abuse alcohol or drugs are more likely to consider, attempt, or succeed at suicide than are nonabusers.
- Teenagers who are planning to commit suicide might clean house by giving away favorite possessions, cleaning their rooms, or throwing things away. They may also become suddenly cheerful after a period of depression because they think they have found a solution by deciding to end their lives.
- One of the most dangerous times of a teen's life is after suffering a loss or humiliation of some kind, such as loss of self-esteem by doing poorly on a test, a breakup with a boyfriend or girlfriend, or the trauma of parents' divorce.
- Depression and the risk for suicide might have biological as well as psychological causes. Studies have found that some people who are depressed have altered levels

of certain brain chemicals. Other studies have shown that aggressive and impulsive people who make violent suicide attempts have reduced amounts of serotonin, a key brain chemical.

- A family history of suicide is a significant risk factor in a young person. The family link might be because young people often identify with those closest to them and are likely to repeat their actions. However, there may be a genetic link as well. Biological relatives of a suicidal person are six times more likely to attempt or succeed in suicide than are adoptive relatives.
- Suicide is the third leading cause of death among young people aged 15 to 24. More than 13 of every 100,000 people aged 15 to 24 committed suicide in 1990. Experts estimate that each year nearly 5,000 teenagers commit suicide.
- The ratio of male to female suicides is four to one. However, young women attempt suicide four times more frequently.
- Reports of suicide clusters, in which one suicide appears to trigger several others within a group, such as a school or community, have increased.

Tips on talking with a suicidal teen include the following:

- Be yourself. Having the right words are unimportant. If you are concerned, your voice and manner will show it.
- Listen. Let the person unload despair, ventilate anger. If given an opportunity to do this, the teen will feel better by the end of the conversation. No matter how negative the talk seems, the fact that it exists is a positive sign, a cry for help.
- Be sympathetic, nonjudgmental, patient, calm, accepting. The teen has done the right thing by getting in touch with another person.
- If the person is saying, "I'm so depressed, I can't go on," ask "Are you having thoughts of suicide?" This is not putting ideas in their head; it is doing a good thing for them. It is showing them that there is concern, they are being taken seriously, and it is OK for them to share their pain.
- If the answer is yes, begin asking a series of further questions: "Have you thought about how you would do it?" (plan), "Have you got what you need?" (means), "Have you thought about when you would do it?" (time set). Ninety-five percent of all suicidal people will answer "no" at some point in this series or indicate that the time is set for some date in the future. This will be a relief for both the learner and instructor.
- Simply talking about their problems for a length of time will give suicidal people relief from loneliness and pent-up feelings, awareness that another person cares, and a feeling of being understood. They also get tired—their body chemistry changes. These things take the edge off their agitated state.
- Avoid arguments, problem solving, advice giving, quick referrals, belittling, and making the person feel

the need to justify their suicidal feelings. It is not how bad the problem is; how badly it's hurting the person is what's important.

- If the person is ingesting drugs, get the details (what, how much, alcohol, other medications, last meal, general health) and call for help.
- Reassure the person that there is someone to turn to. Family, friends, school counselors, physicians, or teachers are probably very willing to listen. It's difficult for the teen to know how to ask to talk with other people about something as serious as personal emotions.

Violence

Juvenile crime in this country continues to be a problem. In 1999, U.S. law enforcement agencies made an estimated 14 million arrests. Of these, 17% involved juveniles under age 18. Another 28% involved youth between the ages of 18 and 24 (Butts, 2000).

In many schools, crime and fear of crime are interfering with the education process. Learners are concerned about crime in their neighborhoods and schools—with one in five African-American and Hispanic teens indicating that crime or the threat of crime was the cause of staying home from school or cutting class. The increase in disruptive and violent behaviors and weapons possession in schools has been accompanied by a proportionate increase in suspensions and expulsions (U.S. Department of Justice, 1997).

The Federal Interagency Forum on Child and Family Statistics (2000) defined serious violent crimes as those involving aggravated assault, rape, robbery, and homicide. Aggravated assault is an attack with a weapon, regardless of whether or not an injury occurred, or an attack without a weapon when serious injury resulted. Robbery is stealing by force or threat of force. They went on to reveal the following statistics on youth victims and perpetrators of serious crimes:

- In 1998, the rate at which youth were victims of serious violent crimes was 25 crimes per 1,000 juveniles aged 12 to 17, totaling about 570,000 such crimes.
- The serious violent crime victimization rate fluctuated between 34 and 43 per 1,000 from 1980 to 1990 and peaked at 44 per 1,000 in 1993. Since 1993, the rate of serious violent crime against youth decreased to 25 per 1,000 in 1998.
- Males are nearly twice as likely as females to be victims of serious violent crimes. In 1998, the serious violent crime victimization rate was 32 per 1,000 male youth, compared with 17 per 1,000 female youth.
- Younger teens (aged 12 to 14) are somewhat less likely than older teens (aged 15 to 17) to be victims of serious violent crimes. In 1998, the serious violent crime victimization rates were 20 per 1,000 for younger teens and 29 per 1,000 for older teens.
- In 1998, the serious violent juvenile crime offending rate was 27 crimes per 1,000 juveniles aged 12 to 17, totaling 616,000 such crimes involving juveniles. The rate

dropped by over half from the 1993 high and was the lowest level recorded since the national victimization survey began in 1973.

- Between 1980 and 1989, the serious violent juvenile crime offending rate fluctuated between 29 and 40 per 1,000 and then began to increase from 34 per 1,000 in 1989 to a high 52 per 1,000 in 1993. Since then, the rate steadily dropped to 27 per 1,000 in 1998.
- Between 1980 and 1998, the percentage of all serious violent crime involving juvenile offenders ranged from 19% in 1982 to 26% in 1993, the peak year for youth violence. In 1998, 22% of all such victimizations involved a juvenile offender.

Weiler (1999) reported the following about gender and violence:

- Violent crimes committed by females differ significantly from males' offenses. Males are two to three times more likely to carry weapons, and females are more likely to use knives than guns, males' weapon of choice. Females are more likely than males to murder someone as a result of a conflict rather than during a crime and to murder and fight with family members. Females remain less likely than males to be arrested in general, and far less likely to be arrested for violent crimes (homicide, forcible rape, aggravated assault) and serious property offenses (burglary, arson). The gender ratio of arrests has changed very little over the decade, since the recent increases in the arrest of females parallel increases in males' arrests, suggesting that the upward trend simply reflects an overall change in youth behavior.
- Most, but certainly not all, aggressive acts in school, such as physical fighting, bullying, and weapon carrying, are carried out by males and aimed at males. One study reported that while nearly 18% of males carry a weapon to school only 5% of females do so. Another showed, however, that in schools characterized by large numbers of males carrying weapons, there is a correspondingly high rate of females with weapons, although males may carry guns while females carry knives.
- In general, school failure increases young people's risk for violence and delinquency, although poor school performance appears to have a stronger effect on females than males. While high grades and positive self-esteem seem to depress females' involvement in violence and delinquency, males' high grades raise their self-esteem, creating favorable orientations to risk-taking and thus greater delinquency.
- Females jailed for crimes, compared with their male counterparts, are much more likely to report previous sexual or physical abuse, ranging from 40% to 70% of respondents in various surveys. Violent young females are more likely to come from troubled or violent families. Their home life, characterized by poverty, divorce, parental death, abandonment, alcoholism, and frequent abuse, leaves them quick to anger, distrust, and revenge.

- Females from poor families may seek recognition by adopting a bad girl image upon finding that their college aspirations will go unrealized, as they are unable to gain status through white middle-class means (i.e., schooling, careers). But they also embrace traditional gender role expectations for the future: marriage, support by a man, a large family, and employment in stereotypically female jobs. They think that males should be strong and assertive, and females should be passive and nonviolent. Such beliefs may hold young females in abusive romantic relationships and raise their risk of engaging in delinquent and violent acts.

Flannery (1998) explained that exposure to violence is not without consequence. Fifty percent of children exposed to trauma under age 10 develop psychiatric problems later in life, including increased rates of anxiety and depression. Children exposed to chronic violence are also more likely to form disorganized attachment (e.g., breech delivery, preeclampsia, oxygen deprivation due to long delivery duration) when accompanied by early maternal rejection, and a child temperament characterized by impulsivity, high activity levels, inflexibility, difficulty with transitions, and easy frustration and distraction. He describes the following consequences resulting from early exposure to violence:

- limited intelligence, particularly verbal intelligence; low school achievement and lack of attachment to school; poor problem-solving and social skills; and a tendency to have impaired social judgment
- the early onset and stability of aggressive, antisocial behavior, beginning even at the kindergarten level
- poor parenting, including maltreatment and abuse, neglect, rejection, frequent and harsh but inconsistent and ineffective punishment, parental criminal behavior, and living in a climate of hostility
- exposure to and victimization by violence in school, community, or home
- high exposure to violence in the media, which can cause acceptance and emulation of aggression, desensitization to violence and its consequences, and development of a mean world syndrome that increases fear of victimization and a need to protect oneself and mistrust others

Gang Involvement

Wilson (2000) reported the following:

> A federal study conducted in 1995 revealed 28 percent of adolescents between the ages of 12 to 19 reported street gang activity is happening in their schools. The idea of staying in school is extremely appealing for many gang members, but not for the sake of acquiring an education. Gang members perceive schools as a haven for conducting gang activity. Not only does school allow them to keep each other abreast of what is going on within the gang, but students are easy targets to recruit as new members, especially

when violence is threatened to students opposing gang involvement. Often students will succumb to the pressure and join for the sake of protection. (Gangs in Schools)

Psychological factors relating to gang membership include the following:

- The need for affiliation–Adolescents are in a stage of development in which fashioning a personal identity is a primary goal. This has been a problem for immigrant families whose children are caught between two cultures with opposing value systems and incompatible behavior standards. Often these adolescents seek an identity by joining gangs with similar backgrounds to their own. A gang member may appear to have more loyalty to the gang than to family.

- The need for achievement–The American dream has included the idea that achievement is the way out of the ghetto. Parents in these circumstances however, may be unable to be role models and help their children be successful in school. Many gang members have not been successful in school due to learning disabilities or special education needs that were not diagnosed. Once learners have failed in school and dropped out, their chances to be successful, productive citizens are small. At this point, the gang can offer a social network of friends, income, and a chance for dropouts to make a life for themselves that the larger culture does not offer.

- Lack of self-responsibility and an openness to outside influences–At many levels, adolescents question adult authority and the emotional dependence they have on their parents, whom they regard as controlling and lacking in understanding. During this turbulent and rapidly changing period of their life, many adolescents are unable or unwilling to turn to their parents for help. It is not surprising that their peers become important during this period.

- Learned helplessness–When adolescents fail in school and fail at getting a job, it creates a sense of helplessness. Teens develop an apathetic attitude that drains them of self-confidence, fosters depression, robs them of resourcefulness, and blinds them to opportunities. A gang may seem to be the only hope.

- Risk-taking behavior–Adolescents tend to believe they are invincible and that nothing can harm them. These beliefs make risks seem nonthreatening, and worse, a necessary part of their lives. Children raised in deprived environments are at risk for seeking high levels of stimulation. Seeking stimulation often involves breaking the law and incurring risks that may even be life-threatening.

- Low self-esteem–Adolescents whose self-esteem has been damaged by peer rejection, school failures, discrimination, or physical development that is too fast or too slow may find a new identity and sense of self-worth in a gang. When an adolescent has no activities that provide a sense of accomplishment or competence, gangs can provide acceptance, affiliation, a substitute family, a way to succeed, money, drugs, and power.

- Lack of positive role models–Power and fame are major factors in motivating kids to become gang members. Often, gang members believe that money and weapons can give them the power and fame they believe they deserve in a society that discriminates against them. They may view their struggling parents as powerless people unable to show their children how to achieve the good life, while they view a veteran gang member, who drives a flashy car, carries a beeper, and wears expensive clothes as a role model for success.

- Boredom–In many neighborhoods where gangs exist there are no recreational activities to meet teenagers' needs. Churches, schools, and private facilities are not open to youth because of fear of violence and destruction of property. School dropouts who are unemployed or young people with nothing to do after school are good candidates for chronic boredom. As soon as boredom sets in, hanging out with the neighborhood gang becomes an attractive alternative that adds some excitement to life (Lawson, 1994).

Researchers agree that most gangs share certain characteristics. Although there are exceptions, gangs tend to develop along racial and ethnic lines and are typically 90% male. Gang members often display their membership through distinctive styles of dress—their colors—and through specific patterns of behavior. In addition, gangs almost universally show strong loyalty to their neighborhood, often marking out their territory with graffiti. All of these representations can be visible in the schools.

The specifics of gang style and activity can vary tremendously from gang to gang and can even change rapidly within individual gangs. For instance, African-American gangs tend to confine their activities to their own communities; in contrast, Asian-American gangs often travel hundreds of miles from home in order to conduct their activities. In addition, African-American and Hispanic gangs are much more likely to display their colors than are Asian-American gangs. Anglo gangs are often made up of white supremacists. Gangs can also vary tremendously in numbers and age ranges of members (Burnett & Walz, 1994).

Characteristics of individuals who are involved in gang activities or who want to be a member of a gang include

- having gang tattoos;
- wearing gang garb that could include the color of clothing, types of clothing, head covering, or methods of grooming;
- displaying gang markings or slogans on personal property or clothing;
- possessing literature that indicates gang membership;
- admitting gang membership;
- attending functions sponsored by the gang or known gang members;
- exhibiting behavior fitting police profiles of gang-related drug dealing;
- loitering, riding, or meeting with a gang member;

- selling or distributing drugs for a known gang member; and
- helping a known gang member commit a crime. (*Educating At-Risk Youth*, February 1992, p. 6)

Cantrell (1992) identified some steps that educators can take in order to deal more effectively with gangs and learners associated with them:

- Become informed–Talk to local police or others about the names of gangs, their territories, gang signs, colors, and information about known gang members. Ask the straight kids about who is intimidating and recruiting.
- Use dress and discipline codes–Adopt dress codes that exclude gang identifiers. Consider adopting school uniforms to avoid learners' wearing gang colors or flaunting expensive clothing. School rules should prevent learners from representing gang affiliation in school. All recruiting should be reported. Beepers and headphones should be confiscated. School policies should develop clear assault and weapons policies and all weapons offenses should be reported.
- Declare and make the school a neutral zone for gangs–School policies should be publicly announced and repeated as often as possible. Graffiti should be searched for and destroyed, using volunteer-student efforts if possible. Schools should work toward establishing a school norm that supports a stand against violence.
- Curriculum initiatives–Schools should develop an anti-gang curriculum and utilize resources that help to de-glamorize the gang lifestyle and provide realistic alternatives and support. Components of a curriculum should include training in problem-solving and decision-making, pro-social skills training and values education, nonviolence conflict resolution methods, education in AIDS prevention and personal safety, self-esteem initiatives, substance abuse information, career development information, and incentives and support for academic performance.

Though strategies to counteract gang involvement offer no magical solution for eliminating gangs, they offer valuable interventions that may make gangs appear less attractive and prepare individual learners to more effectively resist pressure to join gangs. These strategies include the following:

- Target learners vulnerable to gang recruitment to receive special assistance, particularly through the use of peer counselors and support groups. Mentoring, conflict resolution programs, and tutoring can be particularly effective.
- Establish moral and ethical education, values clarification, and conflict resolution as important components of the school curriculum.
- Create an inviting school climate where every learner feels valued.
- Educate all school staff, including support staff, about how gangs develop and how to respond to them.

- Offer special programs for parents on gangs and how to deal with them as a parent. Present information in a culturally sensitive way, and in a variety of languages, to reflect the diversity of the community.
- Monitor youths who are not enrolled in school but hang out on or near school property. This can help school officials assess the existence of gangs in the neighborhood and anticipate and prevent their formation in the school.
- Offer educational programs for learners about gangs, their destructiveness, and how to avoid being drawn into them, preferably in small groups where they can express their feelings comfortably.
- Provide regular opportunities for learners individually and/or in small groups to discuss their experiences in school and make future plans that offer hope and personal rewards.

Chemers (1999) reported the following options to prevent violence in children and youth:

- Although there has been much focus on recent violent incidents in and around our schools, reliable data actually indicate that the real problem area is not the school itself but the world our children return to after the dismissal bell rings. The latest numbers from the FBI's National Incident-Based Reporting System show that juvenile violence increases in the after-school hours. On school days, the number of robberies, aggravated assaults, and sexual assaults by juveniles peak between 3 p.m. and 4 p.m. In fact, juveniles injure more victims in the hours around the close of school than any other time of day.
- In today's society, fewer and fewer children have a parent waiting for them at home when school lets out. Approximately 28 million school-age children have working parents; an estimated seven million of them receive no adult supervision after school. As a result, youth often supervise themselves and younger siblings after school with varying degrees of oversight by parents and guardians. Most juveniles are responsibly engaged in an array of positive activities after school, such as sports, clubs, or homework, or they hang out harmlessly with friends. However, for youth who have few activities available, whose friends are prone to negative behavior, or who experience other risk factors, the unsupervised hours between school and dinner time offer ample opportunity to go astray. Statistics show that serious violent crime committed by juveniles peaks in the hours immediately after the close of school.
- At the same time, we should not fail to recognize that during these after-school hours, juveniles are most likely to become victims of crime, including violent crimes such as robberies and aggravated assaults. In this unsupervised time, youth are more vulnerable and more likely to be exploited, injured, and even killed. Effective, well-supervised after-school programs have an added benefit in that they can provide protection to juveniles, who are also at highest risk of being victims

of violence at the end of the school day than any other time of the day. One in five of all violent crimes with juvenile victims occurs between 3 p.m. and 7 p.m. on school days.

- This information focuses on the need for schools and communities to develop strategies for youth during these after-school hours. This information also demonstrates the desirability of exploring policy changes, such as flexible work schedules so parents can provide more direct supervision during these crucial hours, and indicates that after-school programs have more crime reduction potential than juvenile curfews, since the rate of juvenile violence in the after-school period (between 3 p.m. and 7 p.m. during the school year) is four times the rate in the juvenile curfew period (between 10 p.m. to 6 a.m. every day).

- After-school programs contribute to the reduction of delinquency and violence. Research shows that after-school programs improve academic achievement, a protective factor for at-risk children. Learners in after-school programs show better achievement in math, reading, and other subjects. Research also shows that appropriate after-school programs for middle school children contribute to increasing rates of high school graduation. They also cut school absenteeism.

After-school programs keep youth safe. They keep youth out of the places where they are likely to get in trouble: in their unsupervised homes, in the malls, or on school grounds. They provide young people with positive alternatives to drugs, alcohol, tobacco use, and other high-risk behaviors. They also offer opportunities to gain self-confidence, to develop supportive relationships with adults and their peers, to learn how to handle conflict in a positive way. Mentored youth have been shown to get along better with family and friends and to be less likely to assault someone. Children who experience positive emotional climates in their after-school programs exhibit fewer behavioral problems at school.

SAFE AND EQUALLY RESPONSIVE SCHOOLS

Research has demonstrated repeatedly that school communities can do a great deal to prevent violence. Having in place a safe and responsive foundation helps all learners, and it enables school communities to provide more efficient and effective services to learners who need more support. The next step is to learn the early warning signs of troubled learners so that effective interventions can be provided.

Well-functioning schools foster learning, safety, and socially appropriate behaviors. They have a strong academic focus, support learners in achieving high standards, foster positive relationships between school staff and learners, and promote meaningful parental and community involvement. Most prevention programs in effective schools address multiple factors and recognize that safety and order are related to the learner's social, emotional, and academic development.

The Center for Effective Collaboration and Practice (2000) identified the following effective prevention, intervention, and crisis response strategies for school communities:

- Focus on academic achievement–Effective schools convey the attitude that all can achieve academically and behave appropriately, while at the same time appreciating individual differences. Adequate resources and programs help ensure that expectations are met. Expectations are communicated clearly, with the understanding that meeting such expectations is a responsibility of the learner, the school, and the home. Learners who do not receive the support they need are less likely to behave in socially desirable ways.

- Involve families in meaningful ways–Learners whose families are involved in their growth in and outside of school are more likely to experience school success and less likely to become involved in antisocial activities. School communities must make parents feel welcome in school, address barriers to their participation, and keep families positively engaged in their children's education. Effective schools also support families in expressing concerns about their children, and they support families in getting the help they need to address behaviors that cause concern.

- Develop links to the community–Everyone must be committed to improving schools. Schools that have close ties to families, support services, community police, the faith-based community, and the community at large can benefit from many valuable resources. When these links are weak, the risk of school violence is heightened and the opportunity to serve learners who are at risk for violence or who may be affected by it is decreased.

- Emphasize positive relationships among learners and staff–Research shows that a positive relationship with an adult who is available to provide support when needed is one of the most critical factors in preventing violence in school. Learners often look to adults in the school community for guidance, support, and direction. Some learners need help overcoming feelings of isolation, and they need support in developing connections to others. Effective schools make sure that opportunities exist for adults to spend quality, personal time with learners. Effective schools also foster positive interpersonal relations among learners; they encourage learners to help each other and to feel comfortable assisting others in getting help when needed.

- Discuss safety issues openly–Learners come to school with many different perceptions—and misconceptions—about death, violence, and the use of weapons. Schools can reduce the risk of violence by teaching learners about the dangers of firearms, as well as appropriate strategies for dealing with feelings, expressing anger in appropriate ways, and resolving conflicts. Schools also should teach learners that they are responsible for their actions and that the choices they make have consequences for which they will be held accountable.

- Treat learners with equal respect–A major source of conflict in many schools is the perceived or real problem of bias and unfair treatment of learners because of ethnicity, gender, race, social class, religion, disability, nationality, sexual orientation, physical appearance, or some other factor—both by staff and by peers. Learners who have been treated unfairly may become scapegoats and/or targets of violence. In some cases, victims may react in aggressive ways. Effective schools communicate to learners and the greater community that all are valued and respected. There is a deliberate and systematic effort (e.g., displaying learners' artwork, posting academic work prominently throughout the building, respecting learners' diversity) to establish a climate that demonstrates care and a sense of community.
- Create ways for learners to share their concerns–It has been found that peers often are the most likely group to know in advance about potential school violence. Schools must create ways for learners to safely report troubling behaviors that could lead to dangerous situations, and learners who report potential school violence must be protected. It is important for schools to support and foster positive relationships between learners and staff so learners will feel safe providing information about a potentially dangerous situation.
- Help learners feel safe expressing their feelings–It is very important that learners feel safe when expressing their needs, fears, and anxieties to school staff. When they do not have access to caring adults, feelings of isolation, rejection, and disappointment are more likely to occur, increasing the probability of acting-out behaviors.
- Have in place a system for referring learners who are suspected of being abused or neglected–The referral system must be appropriate and reflect federal and state guidelines.
- Offer extended day programs for children–School-based before- and after-school programs can be effective in reducing violence. Effective programs are well-supervised and provide learners with support and a range of options, such as counseling, tutoring, mentoring, cultural arts, community service, clubs, access to computers, and help with homework.
- Identify problems and assess progress toward solutions–Schools must openly and objectively examine circumstances that are potentially dangerous for learners and staff and situations where members of the school community feel threatened or intimidated. Safe schools continually assess progress by identifying problems and collecting information regarding progress toward solutions. Moreover, effective schools share this information with learners, their families, and the community at large.
- Support learners in making the transition to adult life and the workplace–Youth need assistance in planning their future and in developing skills that will result in success. For example, schools can provide learners with community service opportunities, work-study programs, and apprenticeships that help connect them to caring adults in the community. These relationships, when established early, foster in youth a sense of hope and security for the future.

ASSESSING LEARNERS FROM SPECIAL POPULATIONS

Learners enrolled in career technical education programs who are thought to have special needs should be referred for assessment. Teachers should carefully observe learners in their classes to determine those who

- are overage for grade level;
- have difficulty communicating in writing or speaking;
- lack basic academic skills;
- have a record of failing grades;
- have a reading level at least two grade levels below grade placement;
- have a math level at least two grade levels below grade placement;
- exhibit hostile or apathetic behavior on a consistent basis;
- need economic assistance to continue in school;
- are frequently tardy;
- are disorganized and have poor work and/or study skills;
- have difficulty with English;
- appear to have signs of abuse;
- are teen or single parents;
- appear to be involved in gang activities; and/or
- have a record of subject or course failure over repeated grading periods.

Precise referral and assessment procedures must be established and followed carefully if learners with special needs are to be provided with appropriate program modifications and support services. False labeling of learners should be avoided. Labeling is a practice that has often resulted in negative effects for both learners and teachers. By emphasizing the differences between learners from special populations and other learners, labels tend to obscure the fact that these individuals are more like their peers than they are unlike them. They have strengths and weaknesses, likes and dislikes, desires and fears similar to all learners. The majority of these individuals lack career development, prevocational, and vocational preparation backgrounds because they have not been provided with appropriate opportunities.

The specific referral process will differ from district to district. However, the information contained in the initial referral provided by the career and technical education instructor should contain

- background information (e.g., name, address, age, gender, birthday, grade placement, program placement, parent/guardian name);
- date of referral;
- reason for referral (description of learner behavior, limitations, strengths); and
- recommendations for services/program modifications.

Specific data should be reviewed before a determination is made about necessary modifications or services that should be provided for the learner for successful participation in and completion of the career and technical education program. This data should include

- anecdotal records;
- school records;
- social worker/social service agency report;
- comments and recommendations from counselors, administrators, and teachers;
- medical and health records;
- results of student and/or parent conference(s);
- results of diagnostic and psychological tests;
- language assessment information;
- information from parent/guardian;
- employment history and career goals;
- current and past services provided; and
- current instructional grade at which the special population learner is functioning.

If a career and technical education instructor notices that a learner seems to be having difficulty, the learner should be carefully observed. The teacher should note the specific behaviors. Details of the learner's behavior should be documented in writing over a period of time to provide crucial information for the assessment process.

The first step in the identification and placement process is an initial referral. The teacher who feels that a learner is in need of evaluation should contact the person in the school who handles the initial referral forms. This could be an administrator, guidance counselor, transition coordinator, or another professional.

Once the referral has been made, the parent/guardian should be notified in writing of the referral. The letter should request permission to evaluate the learner. When permission has been obtained, the review committee collects relevant information, test data, and records that will be used to determine the appropriate support services that will be required. After the comprehensive evaluation process is completed, the committee reviews all the information relative to the learner. The career and technical education instructor, as the person who submits the initial referral, usually contributes to the review committee by discussing the reason for the referral as well as the specific learning problems and behavioral characteristics that have been displayed in classroom and laboratory settings.

Finally, a decision should be made by the committee regarding the program modifications and support services that will be necessary for the learner to succeed in the educational program. An individualized career plan is sometimes developed to outline the direction that the learner will take in the educational program, specific courses that will be taken, support services that will be provided, and the ultimate transition objective for the learner (e.g., entry-level employment, postsecondary education, military).

SUMMARY

By the year 2020, the majority of America's public school learners will be living under conditions that place them at risk of educational failure. This is a projection, of course, but the trend toward ever-higher percentages of poorly housed, malnourished, abused, and neglected youth is inarguable. The Perkins Act of 1998 addressed these conditions and defines special populations as

- individuals with disabilities;
- individuals from economically disadvantaged homes;
- individuals preparing for nontraditional training and employment;
- single parents; and
- individuals with other educational achievement barriers, such as a limited English proficiency.

Additional individuals from special populations include homeless individuals, displaced homemakers, individuals in correctional facilities, migrant populations, and gifted and talented learners. Our goal must be to develop the talents of all to their fullest. Attaining that goal requires that we expect and assist all learners to work to the limits of their capabilities. We should expect schools to have genuinely high standards rather than minimum ones and parents to support and encourage their children to make the most of their talents and abilities.

There are a variety of issues that affect individuals from special populations. Variables such as substance abuse, gender bias and stereotyping, child abuse, teen pregnancy, gang involvement, violence, and homelessness touch the lives of many learners in today's educational system. These issues cut across all special population categories, impact on individuals' day-to-day struggles, and create great challenges for them. Educators must become aware of these issues and create a network of professionals and volunteers who can assist in providing support services to help these learners to succeed.

Career and technical education instructors must learn to identify the general characteristics of learners from these special populations as well as the curriculum modifications and support services that the learners will need in order to successfully enroll in and complete these programs. Specific strategies that will assist learners from special populations should be utilized in delivering the curriculum.

SELF-ASSESSMENT

1. Identify the special populations, other than individuals with disabilities, identified in the Perkins Act of 1998.
2. Describe the general characteristics of educationally disadvantaged learners.
3. Identify the problems or barriers that educationally disadvantaged learners may face in career and technical education programs.
4. Identify the general characteristics of economically disadvantaged learners.
5. Identify the problems or barriers that economically disadvantaged learners may face in career and technical education programs.
6. Identify some services that academically and economically disadvantaged learners may need in order to succeed in career and technical education programs.
7. Identify strategies that career and technical education instructors should use to assist educationally and economically disadvantaged learners enrolled in their programs.
8. Identify general characteristics of individuals in correctional facilities.
9. Describe several strategies that educators should use in collaboration with juvenile authorities in order to identify and develop appropriate long-range plans for minors who have been involved in crime.
10. Identify several key components of effective career and technical education programs in correctional institutions.
11. Identify the general characteristics of individuals from migrant populations.
12. Identify the problems or barriers that learners who are from migrant populations may face in career and technical education programs.
13. Identify strategies that career and technical education instructors should use to assist learners from migrant populations who are enrolled in their programs.
14. Identify the general characteristics of LEP learners.
15. Identify the problems or barriers that LEP learners may face in career and technical education programs.
16. Identify strategies that career and technical education instructors should use to assist LEP learners who are enrolled in their programs.
17. Identify the general characteristics of gifted and talented learners.
18. Identify the problems or barriers that gifted and talented learners may face in career and technical education programs.
19. Identify strategies that career and technical education instructors should use to assist gifted and talented learners who are enrolled in their programs.
20. Discuss the impact of substance abuse on learners from special populations.
21. Discuss the impact of child abuse on learners from special populations.
22. Discuss the impact of teen suicide on learners from special populations.
23. Discuss the impact of violence on learners from special populations.
24. Discuss the impact of gang involvement on learners from special populations.
25. Describe the referral process for learners from special populations.

ASSOCIATED ACTIVITIES

1. Investigate services in your school, district, and community that assist learners who are educationally and economically disadvantaged. Create a network with educators, agency representatives, business and industry volunteers, and others so that these learners can be provided with the assistance and services they need to succeed in your program.
2. Contact the Department of Corrections to determine the role and responsibilities of educators in working with juvenile offenders. Offer information about your program, exit points in the community, competencies, and support services available at the school that may help corrections officials to counsel juvenile offenders and develop long-range goals.
3. Identify what services are available for learners from migrant populations in your school, district, and community. Ask if there is a communication network available for finding current educational information about a specific migrant learner. Volunteer to assist in developing and maintaining student portfolios (e.g., career and technical education assessment results, competencies demonstrated) while learners are in your program so that they can take the portfolios with them when they move on.
4. Investigate services in your school, district, and community to assist LEP learners. Create a network with educators, agency representatives, business and industry volunteers, and others so these learners can be provided with the assistance and services they need to succeed in your program.
5. Identify individuals in your school or district who work with gifted and talented learners. Plan collaboratively with them in order to offer appropriate accelerated learning and enrichment activities in your curriculum. Work closely with business and industry to establish capstone programs for these learners once they have mastered the required competencies in your curriculum. Coordinate with area postsecondary institutions to determine whether joint enrollment opportunities can be arranged.

6. Work with counselors and other individuals in your school, district, and community to learn about substance abuse programs that are available. Learn about the warning signs of substance abuse and become familiar with the appropriate referral procedures for obtaining help.

7. Closely examine the recruitment policies for entrance into your program to check for any gender stereotyping or gender bias. Encourage nontraditional learners to enroll in your program. Examine your teaching materials to check for discriminatory language, examples, or role models. Provide examples of both successful men and women in your occupational area.

8. Talk to counselors and others in your school, district, and community to determine the services available to learners who are victims of child abuse. Become familiar with the referral process and the warning signs of child abuse.

9. Investigate services in your school, district, and community to assist learners who are teen parents. Create a network with educators, agency representatives, business and industry volunteers, and others so that these learners can be provided with the assistance and services they need to succeed in your program.

10. Learn about gang involvement and violence in your community. Talk with counselors, educators, community agencies, and other resources to determine warning signs of gang involvement as well as services that are available to assist individuals and families.

11. Investigate services in your school, district, and community to assist learners who are homeless. Create a network with educators, agency representatives, business and industry volunteers, and others so that these learners can be provided with the assistance and services they need to succeed in your program.

12. Locate the individuals in your school or district who are responsible for the initial referral forms for the identification and assessment procedure. Obtain a copy of the referral form and review it. Keep it in your files in case you observe a learner in your program whom you feel should be referred for evaluation.

REFERENCES

Alabama State Department of Education. (1984). *Implementation manual for accelerated vocational programs.* Montgomery, AL: Author.

American Psychiatric Association. (1988). *Teen suicide.* Washington, DC: APA Joint Commission on Public Affairs and the Division of Public Affairs. [On-line]. Available: http://www.psych.org/public_info/teenag~1.cfm

Bear, T., Schenk, S., & Buckner, L. (1992). Supporting victims of child abuse. *Educational Leadership, 50*(4), pp. 42-47.

Bosworth, K. (1997). *Drug abuse prevention: School-based strategies that work.* Washington, DC: ERIC Clearinghouse on Teaching and Teacher Education. ED 409316.

Broadhurst, D., Edmunds, M., & MacDicken, R. (1979). *Early childhood programs and the prevention and treatment of child abuse and neglect–The user manual series.* Washington, DC: U.S. Department of Health, Education and Welfare.

Burnett, G., & Walz, G. (1994). *Gangs in schools.* New York: ERIC Clearinghouse on Urban Education. ED 372175.

Butts, J. (2000, December). *Youth crime drop.* Washington, DC: Urban Institute, Justice Policy Center. [On-line]. Available: http://www.urban.org/UploadedPDF/youth-crime-drop.pdf

Califano, J. Jr., & Booth, A. (1997, September). *1997 CASA national survey of teens, their parents, teachers and principals.* New York: Columbia University, The National Center on Addiction and Substance Abuse.

Campbell, J., Hombo, C., & Mazzeo, J. (2000, August). *NAEP 1999 trends in academic progress: Three decades of student performance.* Washington, DC: U.S. Department of Education, Office of Educational Research and Improvement, National Center for Education Statistics.

Cantrell, M. (1992). What we can do about gangs. *Journal of Emotional and Behavioral Problems, 1*(1).

Carl D. Perkins Vocational and Applied Technology Act of 1990, Pub. L. No. 101-392, United States Statutes at Large, (104), 753. Washington, DC: U.S. Government Printing Office.

Carl D. Perkins Vocational and Technical Education Act of 1998, Pub. L. No. 105-332, United States Statutes at Large, (12), 3077. Washington, DC: U.S. Government Printing Office.

Carter, J. (2001). *Domestic violence, child abuse, and youth violence: Strategies for prevention and early intervention.* San Francisco, CA: Family Violence Prevention Fund.

The Center for Education Reform. (1998, April). *A nation still at risk: An education manifesto.* Washington, DC: Author. [On-line]. Available: http://edreform.com/pubs/ manifest.htm

Center for Effective Collaboration and Practice. (2000). *Early warning, timely response.* [On-line]. Available: http://cecp.air.org/guide/files/4.htm

Center for Law and Education. (2001). *Federal education law and language minority students.* Washington, DC: Author.

Chemers, B. (1999, October). *Impact of after-school programs on preventing violence in children and youth.* Washington, DC: U.S. House of Representatives, Congressional Children's Caucus.

Cunanan, E., & Maddy-Bernstein, C. (1993). Working together for sex equity: Nontraditional programs that make a difference. *TASPP Brief, 5*(1), pp. 1-6.

Cutshall, S. (2001, February). Teaching hope behind bars. *Techniques, 76*(2), pp. 22-25.

Davis, S. (1997, February). *Child labor in agriculture.* Charleston, WV: ERIC Clearinghouse on Rural Education and Small Schools. ED 405159.

DeKalb, J. (1999, April). *Student truancy.* Eugene, OR: ERIC Clearinghouse on Educational Management. ED 429334.

Educating At-Risk Youth. (1992, February). Austin, TX: Texas Education Agency, 4-6.

Educating At-Risk Youth. (1992, March). Austin, TX: Texas Education Agency, 4.

Elementary and Secondary Education Act of 1965, Pub. L. No. 89-10, United States Statues at Large, (79), 27. Washington, DC: U.S. Government Printing Office.

ERIC Clearinghouse on Languages and Linguistics. (1998). *Developing language proficiency and connecting school to students' lives: Two standards for effective teaching.* Washington, DC: Author. ED 424790.

Equal Educational Opportunities Act of 1974, Pub. L. No. 93-380, United States Statutes at Large, (88), 484. Washington, DC: U.S. Government Printing Office.

Federal Interagency Forum on Child and Family Statistics. (2000). Population and family statistics. In *America's children: Key national indicators of well-being, 2000.* [On-line]. Available: http://www.childstats.gov/ac2000/pdf/ac00pt1.pdf

Flannery, D. (1998). *Improving school violence prevention programs through meaningful evaluation.* New York: ERIC Clearinghouse on Urban Education. ED 417244.

Friedenberg, J. (1995). *The vocational and language development of limited English proficient adults.* Columbus, OH: ERIC Clearinghouse on Adult, Career, and Vocational Education. ED 391104.

Gemignani, R. (1994, October). Juvenile correctional education: A time for change. *Juvenile Justice Bulletin,* pp. 1-3.

Goins, B., & Cesarone, B. (1993). *Homeless children: Meeting the educational challenges.* Urbana, IL: ERIC Clearinghouse on Elementary and Early Childhood Education. ED 356099.

Hearne, J., & Maurer, B. (2000). *Gifted education: A primer.* Seattle, WA: New Horizons for Learning.

Individuals with Disabilities Education Act of 1990, Pub. L. No. 101-476, United States Statutes at Large, (104), 1103. Washington, DC: U.S. Government Printing Office.

Individuals with Disabilities Education Act Amendments of 1997, Pub. L. No. 105-17, United States Statutes at Large, (111), 37. Washington, DC: U.S. Government Printing Office.

Institute for Educational Leadership. (November, 1997). *School-based and school-linked programs for pregnant and parenting teens and their children.* [On-line]. Available: http://www.ed.gov/pubs/ParentingTeens/index.html

Jacob K Javits Gifted and Talented Students Education Act of 1988 (Title II, Subpart 6 of the No Child Left Behind Act of 2001), Pub. L. No. 100-297, 20 U.S.C. § 8031. Washington, DC: U.S. Government Printing Office.

Kerr, B. (1990). *Career planning for gifted and talented youth.* Reston, VA: ERIC Clearinghouse on Handicapped and Gifted Children. ED 321497.

Lawson, A. (1994). *Kids and gangs: What parents and educators need to know.* Minneapolis, MN: Johnson Institute.

Leone, P, and Others. (1991). *Juvenile corrections and the exceptional student.* Reston, VA: ERIC Clearinghouse on Handicapped and Gifted Children. ED 340153.

Lopez-Valadez, J. (1982). Bridging the communication gap: Tips for teaching the LEP student. *The Journal of Vocational Special Needs Education,* 5(1), pp. 25-27.

Lumsden, L., & Coffey, E. (Eds.). (2001). *Trends and issues: Social and economic context.* Eugene, OR: ERIC Clearinghouse on Educational Management. [On-line]. Available: http://eric.uoregon.edu/trends_issues/socecon/index.html

Martin, P. (1994). *Migrant farmworkers and their children.* Charleston, WV: ERIC Clearinghouse on Rural Education and Small Schools. ED 376997.

Menchaca, V., & Ruiz-Escalante, J. (1995). *Instructional strategies for migrant students.* Charleston, WV: ERIC Clearinghouse on Rural Education and Small Schools. ED 388491.

Mid-Atlantic Equity Consortium, Inc. & The NETWORK, Inc. (1993, September). *Beyond Title IX: Gender issues in schools.* http://www.maec.org/beyond.html

National Center for Education Statistics. (2001). *Dropout rates in the United States: 1999.* Washington, DC: Author.

National Center for Injury Prevention and Control. (2002). *Suicide in the United States.* [On-line]. Available: http://www.cdc.gov/ncipc/factsheets/suifacts.htm

National Center on Addiction and Substance Abuse. (1997, August). *Substance abuse and the American adolescent: A report by the Commission on Substance Abuse among America's Adolescents.* New York: Columbia University.

National Center on Education, Disability and Juvenile Justice. (2001). *Juvenile correctional education programs.* College Park, MD: University of Maryland.

National Clearinghouse on Child Abuse and Neglect Information. (2001). *What is child maltreatment?* [On-line]. Available: http://www.calib.com/nccanch/pubs/factsheets/ childmal.cfm

National Clearinghouse on Child Abuse and Neglect Information. (2001, April). *Foster care national statistics.* [On-line]. Available: http://www.calib.com/nccanch/pubs/factsheets/foster.cfm

The National Commission on Excellence in Education. (1983, April). *A nation at risk: The imperative for educational reform.* [On-line]. Available: http://www.ed.gov/pubs/NatAtRisk

The National Dropout Prevention Network. (2001). *Stats and Facts.* Clemson, SC: Clemson University.

National Institute of Justice. (1998, July). *Assets that protect youth from high-risk antisocial behaviors.* Washington DC: Author.

National Institute of Justice. (1998, July). *Preventing crime: What works, what doesn't, what's promising.* Washington, DC: Author.

Piirto, J. (1994). *Talented children and adults: Their development and education.* New York: Macmillan College.

Rasmussen, L. (1988). *Migrant students at the secondary level: Issues and opportunities for change.* Las Cruces, NM: ERIC Clearinghouse on Rural Education and Small Schools. ED 296814.

Reis, S., Burns, D., & Renzulli, J. (1992). *Curriculum compacting: The complete guide to modifying the regular curriculum for high ability students.* Mansfield Center, CT: Creative Learning Press.

Renchler, R. (1993, May). *Poverty and learning.* Eugene, OR: ERIC Clearinghouse on Educational Management. ED 357433.

Renzulli, J. (2001). *A practical system for identifying gifted and talented students.* Storrs, CT: The National Research Center on the Gifted and Talented. [On-line]. Available: http://www.sp.uconn.edu/~nrcgt/sem/semart04.html

Riley, R. (2000, July). *Growing pains: The challenge of overcrowded schools is here to stay.* Washington, DC: U.S. Department of Education.

Robertson, A. (1997). *If an adolescent begins to fail in school, what can parents and teachers do?* Champaign, IL: ERIC Clearinghouse on Elementary and Early Childhood Education. ED 415001.

Salend, S., Michael, R., & Taylor, M. (1984). Competencies necessary for instructing migrant handicapped students. *Exceptional Children, 51*(1), pp. 50-55.

Schwartz, W. (1995). *School programs and practices for homeless students.* New York: ERIC Clearinghouse on Urban Education. ED 383783.

Schwartz, W. (1999a). *Family diversity in urban schools.* New York: ERIC Clearinghouse on Urban Education. ED 434188.

Schwartz, W. (1999b). *School support for foster families.* New York: ERIC Clearinghouse on Urban Education. ED 434189.

Schwartz, W. (1999, March). *Young fathers: New support strategies.* New York: ERIC Clearinghouse on Urban Education. ED 429143.

Stevens, R., & Burt, P. (n.d.). *Nontraditional students.* Springfield, IL: IVSSN Project.

Stewart B. McKinney Homeless Assistance Act of 1987, Pub. L. No. 100-77, Title VII-B. 42 U.S.C. § 11431 et seq. Washington, DC: U.S. Government Printing Office.

Thompson, A. (1999). *Risky business: Building resources for at-risk youth.* Englewood, CO: Colorado School-to-Career Consortium.

Thornberry, T., Wei, E., Stouthamer-Loeber, M., & Van Dyke, J. (2000, January). Teenage fatherhood and delinquent behavior. *Juvenile Justice Bulletin.* [On-line]. Available: http://www.ncjrs.org/html/ojjdp/jjbul2000_1/contents.html

Toward resiliency: At risk students who make it to college. (1998, May). *Data, definitions, and methods.* Washington, DC: U.S. Department of Education, Office of Educational Research and Improvement. [On-line]. Available: http://www.ed.gov/pubs/Resiliency/index.html

The Urban Institute. (2001, January). *Most secondary schools overlook and underserve immigrant students, according to new Urban Institute report.* Washington, DC: Author.

U.S. Department of Education. (1999, February). Meeting the needs of migrant students in schoolwide programs. Washington, DC: Author

U.S. Department of Education, Division of Adult Education & Literacy. (1998, June). *Adult education for the homeless: A program in jeopardy.* Washington, DC: Author. [On-line]. Available: http://www.ed.gov/offices/OVAE/AdultEd/aehomeless/

U.S. Department of Education, Office of Educational Research and Improvement. (1993, October). *National excellence: A case for developing America's talent.* Washington, DC: Author.

U.S. Department of Justice. (1997, February). *Reaching out to youth out of the mainstream.* Washington, DC: Author.

U.S. Department of Labor, Women's Bureau. (2000). *Labor supply in a tight market.* Washington, DC: Author.

Vissing, Y. (1999). *Homeless children: Addressing the challenge in rural schools.* Charleston, WV: ERIC Clearinghouse on Rural Education and Small Schools. ED 425046.

Walqui, A. (2000, June). *Strategies for success: Engaging immigrant students in secondary schools.* Washington, DC: ERIC Clearinghouse on Languages and Linguistics. ED 442300.

Weiler, J. (1999). *Girls and violence.* New York: ERIC Clearinghouse on Urban Education. ED 430069.

Whitmore, J. (1980). *Giftedness, conflict and underachievement.* Boston: Allyn and Bacon.

Wilson, K. (2000). Gangs in Schools. *Gang involvement: Is your child at risk?* Olympia, WA: Parenting Today's Teen. [On-line]. Available: http://www.parentingteens.com/ prevention7.shtml

Women Work! (1998). *Women work, poverty still persists.* [On-line]. Available: http://www.womenwork.org/new_report.htm

Wonacott, M. (2000). *Preparing limited English proficient persons for the workplace.* Columbus, OH: ERIC Clearinghouse on Adult, Career, and Vocational Education. ED 440252.

Wood, M. (1991). *Teacher aide handbook.* Springfield, IL: Sangamon Area Vocational Education Region.

Workforce Investment Act of 1998, Pub. L. No. 105-220, United States Statutes at Large, (112), 937. Washington, DC: U.S. Government Printing Office.

Vocational Assessment

INTRODUCTION

It is particularly important that vocational assessment be conducted for those learners who are at risk of not succeeding in our educational institutions. Most effective vocational assessment processes include activities that collect information in the following areas: basic skills levels, vocational interests, vocational aptitudes and abilities, learning styles, and employability skills/work related skills.

There is no single instrument or assessment tool sufficient for all learners or all purposes. Due to language barriers, cultural differences, different learning styles, and/or academic deficiencies many learners from special populations have had difficulty with traditional assessment methods; therefore, a variety of techniques should be available in order to collect relevant information about each learner so that appropriate decisions can be made regarding realistic career goals. Some of the most widely used methods for collecting vocational assessment information include interviews, career and technical education program tryouts, situational assessments, checklists, and work samples.

An important component of the vocational assessment process is the collection and organization of relevant information about the learner. This information should be organized into a learner profile or portfolio. Each local district/campus should decide upon a format for a learner profile that should contain all of the relevant pieces of information about the learner, which are necessary in order to make appropriate placement and planning decisions.

Vocational assessment should be a cooperative process involving a variety of professionals and specialists who offer a continuum of services. Primary individuals involved in the assessment process include administrators, transition specialists, vocational evaluators, counselors, career and technical education instructors, special education personnel, bilingual teachers, parents, and learners. The number of people involved in the process and the extent of their involvement will depend on a number of factors, including the amount of time allotted for collecting assessment information, the availability of the people, and the nature or amount of relevant information required for the assessment process.

The primary focus of vocational assessment should be the development of instructional goals and objectives that are appropriate for a specific learner as well as the identification of optimal strategies that should be used in career and technical education programs to effectively deliver the curriculum to the learner. Among the most effective uses of assessment information for educational programming purposes are recommendations for prevocational skills, functional skills and/or life skills development, recommendations for career exploration activities, recommendations for specific placement in a career and technical education program, specific instructional goals and objectives for the career plan being developed, identification of learner learning style(s) and suggested teaching techniques, recommendations for necessary support services, recommendations for curriculum modifications, and recommendations for appropriate career goals for the learner.

OUTLINE

OVERVIEW OF VOCATIONAL ASSESSMENT
BENEFITS OF VOCATIONAL ASSESSMENT
COMPONENTS OF VOCATIONAL ASSESSMENT
TRANSITION ASSESSMENT FOR LEARNERS WITH DISABILITIES
APPROACHES TO VOCATIONAL ASSESSMENT
LEVELS OF VOCATIONAL ASSESSMENT
TECHNIQUES AND METHODS FOR COLLECTING VOCATIONAL ASSESSMENT INFORMATION
DEVELOPING A LEARNER PROFILE
COOPERATIVE PLANNING
CONSIDERATIONS IN CONDUCTING VOCATIONAL ASSESSMENT ACTIVITIES
COMMUNICATING VOCATIONAL ASSESSMENT INFORMATION
USE OF VOCATIONAL ASSESSMENT INFORMATION
SUMMARY

SELF-ASSESSMENT
ASSOCIATED ACTIVITIES
REFERENCES

OBJECTIVES

After completing this chapter, the reader should be able to accomplish the following:
1. Define vocational assessment.
2. Describe the benefits of vocational assessment.
3. Identify four essential components of the vocational assessment process.
4. Describe the procedures conducted during the Level I, Level II, and Level III vocational assessment phases.
5. Identify five commonly used techniques and methods for collecting vocational assessment information.
6. Discuss the components of an effective vocational assessment learner profile.
7. Identify the individuals who should participate in the vocational assessment process and what their responsibilities should be.
8. Identify four approaches to collecting vocational assessment information.
9. Describe the effective uses of vocational assessment information.
10. Discuss considerations that should be addressed in conducting vocational assessment activities.

TERMS

aptitude
aptitude test
basic skills information
career and technical program
  exploration tryout
career development
career pathway
community-based vocational
  assessment
community workforce survey
cooperative planning
curriculum-based assessment
curriculum-based vocational
  assessment
Dictionary of Occupational Titles (DOT)

employability skill
formal assessment
functional living skill
generalizable skills
*Guide for Occupational
  Exploration (GOE)*
informal assessment
interest inventory
interview
job analysis
learner profile
levels of vocational assessment (I, II, III)
National Skill Standards
*Occupational Outlook
  Handbook (OOH)*

O*NET
personality assessment
portfolio
Revised Handbook for Analyzing Jobs
situational assessment
SCANS
*Standard Occupational
  Classification Manual*
transition assessment
vocational assessment
vocational interest
work habits
work-related social skill
work sample

OVERVIEW OF VOCATIONAL ASSESSMENT

Vocational assessment is a comprehensive process conducted over a period of time, involving a multidisciplinary team, with the purpose of identifying individual characteristics, education, and training needs that provide educators with the basis for planning an individual's career pathway. Lehmann and Hartley (1991) stated that vocational assessment can provide valuable information to guidance counselors, special needs personnel, teachers, administrators, parents, and learners. Through a well-coordinated assessment process, learners can explore occupations, gain experience in different job tasks, identify career goals, improve self-concept, and better define career objectives. The primary objectives of vocational assessment in an educational setting are the development of instructional goals and objectives matched to the learner's needs, the identification of appropriate teaching strategies to promote learner competency, and necessary curriculum modification for learner success.

Individuals from special populations often need support services when participating in career and technical education programs. If the special needs of these learners are not identified and taken into consideration, there is a strong possibility that many of them will have difficulty succeeding in the programs in which they are enrolled. Placement decisions have often been made with little regard for learner abilities and interests and minimal attention paid to the demands and expectations of the career and technical education programs. Vocational assessment can provide information that will lead to appropriate placement and support services for each learner. See Figure 5-1.

A successful career in the twenty-first century will differ significantly from the model of career success that prevailed in the previous century. New ways of working and new technology already dictate the important of bringing new skills to the workplace, but other changes are even more fundamental. Lifelong employment with the same employer has virtually vanished. Initial career decisions are no longer seen as lifetime determinations but rather as first steps in a career that is likely to include work for several employers in a variety of roles.

Career preparation helps learners develop the ability to handle changes. In a world of work where being a "good worker" is no longer an assurance of continued employment, career preparation serves learners in several ways. It helps them acquire the basic skills and attitudes for successful entry to the world of work. It also teaches them to be effective career managers by being knowledgeable about their talents, acknowledging their strengths, and addressing their weaknesses. Career preparation enables learners to recognize that challenges present opportunities and that they must be prepared to acquire new skills and new knowledge to take advantage of those opportunities. As a part of career preparation, learners learn to see education, not as something to be completed in 13 or 17 years, but as a continuing process, available throughout their lives to assist in coping with a fast-changing world.

Vocational assessment activities represent an important component in the career development process. Information collected during this process should be used to provide appropriate career counseling for individuals. It is particularly important that vocational assessment be conducted for those learners who are at risk of not succeeding in our educational institutions.

The results of vocational assessment should not be used to screen individuals out of career and technical education programs. Instead, this information should be carefully analyzed and used to determine appropriate program placement and planning procedures for the learner according to established abilities, interests, and needs. If limitations are observed during the assessment process, they can usually be strengthened through a combined effort by various discipline areas in the school setting. Therefore, the vocational assessment process can identify specific areas that can be accommodated and/or remediated to allow the individual to profit from participation in a specific career and technical education program. In addition, support services that a learner may need in order to successfully participate in a specific program can be identified. A holistic understanding of an individual is required for appropriate decisions to be made from vocational assessment information.

Lombard (1991) outlined assumptions upon which a vocational assessment process can be developed and implemented:

1. Vocational assessment must occur within the context of a comprehensive K–12 career development curriculum.
2. Vocational assessment is not an isolated event. It is an integral component of educational programming and transition planning.
3. The responsibility for vocational assessment and utilization of results must be shared across and throughout educational programs.
4. The validity of vocational assessment should be judged according to its impact on educational programming and development of postsecondary options.
5. Vocational assessment should focus on learner strengths and complementary programming.
6. The vast majority of vocational assessment data is obtained via procedures already in place, which represents the best educational practices for all learners.

BENEFITS OF VOCATIONAL ASSESSMENT

The benefits of vocational assessment include the following:

- Vocational assessment can be initiated at any point during the middle/junior or senior high school years.
- Vocational assessment activities help learners to start thinking about the world of work.

- Actual simulations of real jobs can be set up in the classroom or laboratory and tried out without any pressure.
- The collection and evaluation of assessment information is of an ongoing developmental nature that considers the skills and behaviors prerequisite to career and technical education course work and cooperative work placements.
- Vocational assessment activities can be an appropriate substitution for, or an addition to, the more traditional verbal classroom activities.

- Vocational assessment activities can motivate learners to learn more about related academic material (e.g., reading, math, communication skills).
- Vocational assessment activities facilitate the integration of academic skills into the context of career and vocational curriculum areas.
- Vocational assessment activities can be used as a tool for setting up behavior modification techniques relating to work habits and interpersonal relationships.

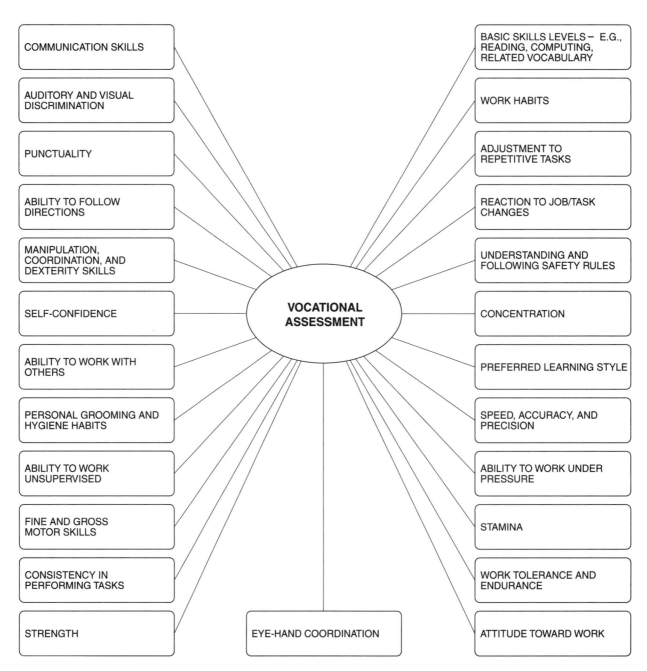

Figure 5-1. A variety of information obtained through the vocational assessment process and used to make career decisions for individuals from special populations.

- Vocational assessment results provide a means of comparing learner abilities with actual job competencies.
- Vocational assessment activities provide learners with a valid reason to learn material because they represent the real world.
- Vocational assessment results can identify specific vocational strengths and limitations.
- Vocational assessment experiences can build the self-confidence of learners.
- Vocational assessment can provide information suggesting modifications to curriculum, facilities, equipment, instructional delivery, and learner evaluation procedures.
- Data collected during the vocational assessment process are directly relevant to the career development process, career and technical education curriculum that the learner is going to be involved in, and the educators involved in delivering the curriculum.

COMPONENTS OF VOCATIONAL ASSESSMENT

Basic program considerations that many local districts follow in setting up a vocational assessment process include the following:

1. Vocational assessment activities should begin at the middle school level.
2. Vocational assessment should be an integral part of the delivery of career and vocational services for learners from special populations.
3. Vocational assessment information should contribute to ongoing career and technical education programming decisions.
4. Vocational assessment information should facilitate determination of the least restrictive learning environment for learners from special populations.
5. The validity of vocational assessment information should be judged by the extent to which it facilitates a match between requirements in the world of work and the skills and behaviors of learners from special populations.
6. Vocational assessment activities should be situational and should provide data that will contribute to efforts to increase the performance level of learners from special populations.
7. Vocational assessment information should contribute to school-to-work transitions or postsecondary experiences.
8. The most appropriate collectors of vocational assessment information are instructors who provide career and technical education instruction or supervision.
9. Vocational assessment should follow guidelines of current regulations governing service delivery to learners from special populations. (Dade County Public Schools, n.d., p. 6)

Basic Skills Information

Basic skills inventories measure achievement levels and competencies in the areas of reading, spelling, writing, math, and language development. These achievement tests measure the extent to which an individual has learned information. Standardized, norm-referenced achievement tests provide a grade-level or age-range score that allows educators to compare the achievement levels of learners who are in the same grade and who are the same age. This information often results in the identification of necessary remedial assistance or support services. Criterion-referenced and competency-based academic achievement tests focus on an individual's specific academic strengths and limitations rather than a comparison with a norm group. These tests present results in terms of what an individual does and does not know at the current time. This information should also be used to identify modifications and support services that will assist the learner.

The definition of interest, as used by inventory developers, researches, and counselors, typically reflects four components that may be characterized as determinants: personality, motivation or drive, expression of self-concept or identification, and environmental influences. One of the most popular theories for describing interests and their relationships to jobs, people, and environments is that of John Holland. Holland identified six vocational personality types or some combination of the six types: realistic (outdoors, mechanical), investigative (science, math), artistic (art, language, music), social (helping, teaching), enterprising (selling, business), and conventional (details, clerical). Holland's theory has had a tremendous impact on the fields of career counseling and interest assessment, and many interest inventories include scales that measure interests related to Holland's six types (Hansen, 1995).

The vocational interests that individuals have can be an important contribution to the vocational assessment process. Elksnin and Elksnin (1993) reported a number of advantages of assessing the interests of learners with special needs including (a) providing a focus for vocational evaluation and planning; (b) obtaining information that can be used to enable the learners to achieve vocational goals; and (c) identifying occupations that were not considered previously by the learner, teacher, or parent.

Vocational interests can be difficult to measure, particularly in an adolescent population where aspirations are often based on unrealistic perceptions, as well as being subject to constant change. It becomes even more of a challenge with individuals who have often had limited exposure to occupational information and few experiences upon which to base decisions. It is important that learners be provided with opportunities to learn about different types of work through career development activities (e.g., field trips, guest speakers, career-related classroom activities, job shadowing, worker interviews, media presentations, industry mentoring experiences, and career and technical education program exploration).

The following are basic methods of identifying vocational interests:

1. Expressed interests–Learners may have ideas about what occupations they may be interested in pursuing. However, some of these ideas may be based on inaccurate information of job duties and may change frequently. Interviewing learners about their occupational interests is still useful information to have as a part of the vocational assessment process. See Figure 5-2. If a learner does not express any occupational preferences, the vocational assessment process should be based on information and activities designed to allow for career development and vocational exploration.

2. Manifest interests–Manifest interests are expressed when a learner makes a choice of what to do when allowed to select from a variety of different types of activities. Information about manifest interests can also be obtained by asking questions about a learner's hobbies and extracurricular activities.

3. Measured interests–Interest inventories are designed to ask individuals to choose between different types of activities. There are no right or wrong answers. Individuals are usually asked to register their preferences on a scale ranging from most liked to least liked. The information gathered from interest inventories can easily be slanted due to a desire to appear interested in occupational areas that are perceived as being more acceptable or prestigious. Learners who are unaware of their abilities and limitations may express interest in unrealistic occupational areas. Some interest inventories are administered through a paper-pencil approach. See Figure 5-3.

VOCATIONAL INTEREST LEARNER INTERVIEW

Student's Name: _____   Date: _____

Parent/Guardian Name: _____

Address: _____   Phone: _____

1. What kind of high school program would you like to take?
   _____ Classes preparing for college
   _____ Classes in which basic reading, math, writing, and world of work skills are taught
   _____ ½ day classes and ½ day work for school credit

2. What kind of skills would you like to learn in school? (math, reading, writing, spelling, job-seeking skills, job-keeping skills, etc.)
   Please list: _____
   _____

3. If a ½ day class – ½ day work program was recommended for you during high school, would you consider such a program?
   YES _____   NO _____

4. What do you see yourself doing after high school?
   (circle one)

   College

   Junior College

   Military

   Trade School

   Skilled employment (mechanic, welder, carpenter, etc.)

   Semi-skilled employment (grocery store, restaurant, factory, construction labor, etc.)

   Others

5. List two jobs that you think you could succeed at and enjoy.
   _____
   _____

Source: Texas Education Agency. (1982). *Vocational Assessment of Students With Special Needs.* Austin, TX: Author.

Figure 5-2. A format for collecting information concerning career and technical education interests.

PAPER-PENCIL INVENTORY

Directions: Show how much you would like doing the activities by carefully drawing a circle around the D (Dislike), the ? (I don't know), or the L (Like) for each activity. Consider whether you would LIKE or DISLIKE an activity rather than your ability to do it. Try to answer LIKE or DISLIKE to as many activities as possible.

Take inventory in a store	D	?	L
Study the effects of vitamins on animals	D	?	L
Sort, count, and store supplies	D	?	L
Balance a checkbook	D	?	L
Measure chemicals in a test tube	D	?	L
Conduct business by phone	D	?	L
Sketch and draw pictures	D	?	L
Make out income tax returns	D	?	L
Use a microscope or other lab equipment	D	?	L
Figure shipping costs for catalog orders	D	?	L

Responses to items on this inventory produces a profile in the following areas:

Business Sales and Management Cluster
  promotion and direct contact sales
  management and planning
  retail sales and services
Business Operations Cluster
  clerical and secretarial work
  paying, receiving, and bookkeeping
  office machine operation
  storage, dispatching, and delivery
Technologies and Trades Cluster
  human services crafts
  repairing and servicing home and office equipment
  caring for plants/animals
  construction and maintenance
  transport equipment operator
  machine operating, servicing, and repairing
  engineering and other applied technologies

Natural, Social, and Medical Sciences Cluster
  natural sciences and mathematics
  medicine and medical technologies
  social sciences and legal services
Creative and Applied Arts Cluster
  creative arts
  applied arts (verbal)
  applied arts (visual)
  popular entertainment
Social, Health, and Personal Services Cluster
  educational and social services
  nursing and human care
  personal and household services
  law enforcement and protective services

Source: The American College Testing Program. (n.d.). *Vocational Interest, Experience, and Skill Assessment.* Boston: Houghton Mifflin.

Figure 5-3. An example interest inventory using a paper-pencil approach.

There are disadvantages in using paper-pencil interest inventories with some learners from special populations, especially those who may have problems with reading and comprehension. Elksnin and Elksnin (1998) reported that learner directions for many of these instruments are frequently written at high readability levels. In investigating the readability of directions of 17 inventories, they reported that the results ranged from first-grade level to college level, with most directions written at the high school level.

Other interest inventories provide the individual with pictures and information about workers and jobs. These pictures can be presented through photos, slides, or video shots. Learners respond to the pictures that generate the most interest to them as well as pictures that represent jobs to which they react negatively. In some inventories, individuals are asked to respond to items developed to measure job knowledge and job-seeking skills. Responses are analyzed and provide specific job titles or occupational clusters that the respondent has indicated an interest in. Further activities such as career counseling and exploratory experiences in career and technical education programs can be conducted to collect additional assessment information regarding vocational interest.

Vocational Aptitudes/Abilities

An aptitude is the capacity and capability to acquire competencies with a given amount of formal or informal training. Aptitudes are distinguished from achievement in that aptitudes represent potential or abilities while achievement represents accomplishments. Aptitude tests do not necessarily predict whether a person has the ability to learn; rather, they provide information about the level of difficulty an individual may have in performing certain tasks and learning accompanying procedures. Aptitudes are natural talents—special abilities for doing, or learning to do, certain kinds of things easily and quickly. They have little to do with knowledge or culture, or education, or even interests. Musical talent and artistic talent are examples of aptitudes.

Some people can paint beautifully but cannot carry a tune. Others are good at talking to people but slow at paperwork. Still others can easily repair a car but find writing difficult. These basic differences among people are important factors in making one person satisfied working as a banker, another as an engineer, and still another as an editor.

Every occupation, whether it is engineering, medicine, law, or management, uses certain aptitudes. The work you are most likely to enjoy and find satisfying is the work that uses your aptitudes. For example, if you are an engineer but possess aptitudes that are not used in engineering, your work might seem unrewarding, and if you lack the engineer's aptitudes, your work will be difficult. A person might develop the skills needed to be an engineer, but that doesn't mean that person has the aptitudes that would make the work easy and rewarding. Of course, knowledge is necessary in order to use aptitudes effectively. Aptitudes suggest the directions in which learning might best take place, but they are no substitute for the learning itself. Aptitude batteries or multiple ability tests measure and individual's general abilities and aptitudes. Some general areas measured by aptitude tests include the following:

- General intelligence–This is general learning ability, the ability to "catch on" or understand instruction and underlying principles and to reason and make judgments. It is closely related to doing well in school.
- Verbal–This is the ability to understand the meanings of words and to use them effectively, to comprehend language, relationships between words, and meanings of whole sentences and paragraphs.
- Numerical–This is the ability to perform arithmetic operations quickly and accurately.
- Spatial–This is the ability to think visually of geometric forms and to comprehend the two-dimensional representation of three-dimensional objects and the ability to recognize the relationships resulting from the movements of objects in space.
- Form perception–This is the ability to perceive pertinent detail in objects or in pictorial or graphic material, the ability to make visual comparisons and discriminations and see slight differences in shapes and shadings of figures and widths and lengths of lines.
- Clerical perception–This is the ability to perceive pertinent detail in verbal or tabular material, the ability to observe differences in copy, to proofread words and numbers, and to avoid perceptual errors in arithmetic computation. A measure of speed of perceptions is required in many industrial jobs even when the job does not have verbal or numerical contents.
- Motor coordination–This is the ability to coordinate eyes and hands or fingers rapidly and accurately in making precise movements with speed, to make movement response accurately and swiftly.
- Finger dexterity–This is the ability to move fingers and to manipulate small objects with fingers rapidly and accurately.
- Eye-hand-foot coordination–This is the ability to move the hand and foot coordinately with each other in accordance with visual stimuli.
- Color discrimination–This is the ability to match or discriminate between colors in terms of hue, saturation, and brilliance, to identify a particular color or color combinations from memory and be able to perceive harmonious or contrasting color combinations.
- Graphoria–This is clerical ability, or adeptness at paperwork and dealing with figures and symbols.
- Color perception–This is the ability to distinguish colors.
- Ideaphoria–This is the ability to produce a flow of ideas.
- Inductive reasoning–This is the ability to reason from the particular to the general, to form a logical conclusion from scattered facts.
- Analytical reasoning–This is the ability to organize concepts or to arrange ideas in logical sequence.
- Numerical aptitudes–This is the ability to use numerical information in solving problems and to perform arithmetic operations.
- Structural visualization–This is the ability to visualize the structure of three-dimensional forms.
- Music aptitudes–This is the ability to remember rhythms and tone sequences and to distinguish between fine differences in pitch.
- Memory aptitudes–This is the ability to remember design and numbers, learn new words, and spot changes or irregularities.

Some aptitude tests are specialized and measure specific aptitudes such as mechanical comprehension, clerical ability, color discrimination, and forms/spatial perception. Examples of instruments that measure specialized aptitudes include the following:
- Bennett Hand Tool Dexterity Test
- Crawford Small Parts Dexterity Test
- Talent Assessment Program
- Purdue Pegboard

Other aptitude tests measure general abilities or aptitudes in more than one area:
- APTICOM
- Armed Services Vocational Aptitude Battery (ASVAB)
- Career Ability Placement Survey (CAPS)
- Microcomputer Evaluation and Screening Assessment (MESA)
- Occupational Aptitude Survey and Interest Schedule (OASIS)

Aptitudes can be measured through several mediums:

- Paper-pencil aptitude tests–Since most paper-pencil aptitude tests can be administered in group settings and since few take more than two to four hours to administer, they are often the method used to collect aptitude information. In order to maximize the usefulness of paper-pencil ability and aptitude tests in the assessment of learners from special populations it may be necessary to break up the testing time into several sessions. For learners with limited reading skills, the use of performance-based aptitude instruments might be more appropriate than paper-pencil tests. See Figure 5-4.

- Performance-based aptitude tests–Some aptitude tests are administered through a hands-on approach. An example of a hands-on aptitude instrument is the Bennett Hand Tool Dexterity Test, which is designed to measure proficiency in using ordinary hand tools. The individual is given nuts, bolts, mechanic's tools, and a testing board and is allowed 15 minutes to complete the required task. A wooden frame is clamped to a table. There are three sizes of nuts and bolts together in the upper left quadrant. Ordinary hand tools are arranged in the center. The learner is to use the hand tools to remove the pieces from the left quadrant from large to small. After the individual removes the small and medium pieces, he or she begins reassembling the pieces in the lower right quadrant from small to large.

- Computerized aptitude tests–There are a variety of aptitude tests that are computerized. The Vocational Research Institute developed the APTICOM, a computerized desktop console that tests cognitive, manipulative, and perceptual aptitudes. The APTICOM is self-timed, self-scored, and produces an aptitude profile related to established occupational patterns. From start to finish, administration takes less than 70 minutes to provide an individualized assessment. This instrument has several separate tests. See Figure 5-5.

SEPARATE APTICOM TESTS	
Test Name	**Aptitude Measured**
Practice Object Identification	Form Perception (P)
Abstract Shape Matching	Form Perception (P)
Clerical Matching	Clerical Perception (P)
Eye-Hand-Foot Coordination	Eye-Hand-Foot Coordination
Pattern Visualization	Spatial (S) General Learning Ability (G)
Computation	Numerical (N)
Finger Dexterity	Finger Dexterity (F)
Numerical Reasoning	Numerical (N) General Learning Ability (G)
Manual Dexterity	Manual Dexterity
Word Meanings	Verbal (V) General Learning Ability (G)
Eye-Hand Coordination	Motor Coordination (K)

Figure 5-5. A breakdown of different APTICOM tests.

PAPER-PENCIL APTITUDE TEST

Directions: Look at the following names or numbers and decide whether they are exactly alike or different. If the item is exactly the same, darken the bubble (S) for same. If they are different, darken the bubble (D) for different.

1. James D. Lighter	James D. Lighter	(S)	(D)
2. Francis X. Gallahan	Frances X. Gallahan	(S)	(D)
3. Freindly Super Markets	Friendly Super Markets	(S)	(D)
4. Federal Surety Bank	Federal Security Bank	(S)	(D)
5. Michael P. Goldstein	Michael P. Goldstein	(S)	(D)
6. Dept. of Urban Affairs	Dept. of Urban Affairs	(S)	(D)
7. James H. Mathews & Co.	James H. Matthews & Co.	(S)	(D)
8. Mark-Albert Hair Stylists	Mark-Albert Hair Styles	(S)	(D)
9. Maison Restaurant	Maison Restaurant	(S)	(D)
10. Federal Enterprizes, Inc.	Federal Enterprises, Inc.	(S)	(D)
11. 74351	74315	(S)	(D)
12. 61757	61757	(S)	(D)
13. 8835437	8835347	(S)	(D)
14. 8215787252	8215787252	(S)	(D)
15. 53272	53722	(S)	(D)

Source: Prince George's County Board of Education. (1988). *Interest/Learning Style/Aptitude Vocational Assessment.* Upper Marlboro, MD: Author.

Figure 5-4. A paper-pencil aptitude test sample item.

The APTICOM automatically converts test scores and generates a printout of occupational aptitude patterns. Department of labor work groups are individualized for each test taker.

An advantage of using aptitude tests includes observation of how the learner works through a problem during the administration of the test. Information can be obtained about work-related behaviors, including ability to follow directions, frustration tolerance, and attention to task. There are several disadvantages in relying heavily on the results of aptitude tests. Learners with special needs often have had little work experience to bring to a testing situation. This can adversely affect job predictability. Paper-pencil tests are not always reliable because they require reading skills in order to respond to the test items. See Figure 5-6.

Aptitude tests provide information that helps the career decision-making process of individuals who score at the upper and middle ranges of ability. Because of problems involved in predicting aptitude of individuals who score in the lower range of ability, data from aptitude tests should be combined and compared with other vocational assessment information.

Employability Skills

Employability skills are those skills necessary to seek and keep a job. These are not technical skills learned in the vocational classroom, but rather those that deal with social and verbal interactions. They include such competencies as cooperating with coworkers, communicating effectively, following directions, and being punctual. The possession of these skills affects the performance of individuals in the classroom, on the job, and in everyday life situations. It is the teaching of these employability skills that is being recognized as the responsibility of the classroom teacher.

Examples of employability skills include the following:
- arriving on time
- asking questions

APTICOM REPORT

NAME: Jane   SCHOOL: GRADE: 11

APTITUDE SUMMARY:

Cognitive scores were in the average range while performance scores were in the average to above average range. Jane has the potential to succeed in a variety of occupational areas if she applies herself and works up to her ability.

Manual Dexterity, Motor Coordination, and Clerical Perception were all rated as above average and Finger Dexterity was not far behind.

INTEREST SUMMARY:

The clerical or business areas were rated as high-interest areas on three separate instruments; the MECCA Career Survey, the CPS Interest Sort, and the APTICOM.

An interest in the Artistic area and the Accommodating area were also indicated in a review of the assessment results.

SUMMARY RECOMMENDATIONS:

Jane has been out of school for several months and has expressed an interest in returning to school to work towards a high school diploma. Her high interest in the clerical/business area and her performance scores on the APTICOM indicate a high potential for success in a clerical career. In reviewing her academic record, it is clear that her reading level would need to improve for her to realistically pursue her many career areas and it is therefore recommended that she be enrolled in the C.A.L. (Computer Assisted Lab) for academic assistance, especially in the reading area.

OTHER RECOMMENDATIONS:

Enrollment in the Cashier Training course at GTI (Gateway Technical Institute).

Enrollment in the DAC Dropout Retrieval Work Study Program.

Enrollment in Typing in the DAC Business Lab.

Enrollment in an Art class and Record Keeping class at Horlick High School.

Scheduling for business classes at Horlick and further assistance from the C.A.L. next year.

Ongoing motivational counseling should be provided to enhance her chances for successfully completing high school.

Case management services should be provided as needed for at least one year.

Source: Damaschke, G., and Nielsen, D. (n.d.). *APTICOM Report*. Racine, WI: Racine Unified School District.

Figure 5-6. A sample APTICOM report that includes an overview of aptitude and interest information as well as recommendations for possible career directions.

- communicating and cooperating with authority
- communicating and cooperating with peers
- completing a questionnaire
- demonstrating good attendance
- using dictionary for spelling and meaning
- dressing properly
- following multiple oral or written directions
- gaining job-related information
- obtaining notes
- organizing work spaces
- participating in care of work area
- demonstrating personal grooming
- proofreading
- reading charts, graphs

- reading reference lists
- displaying appropriate social behavior
- showing respect for property
- speaking clearly
- writing legibly
- telling time
- using a calculator and calendar
- using an index and a table of contents
- working independently
- exercising safety

Employability skills affect the performance of learners in the classroom, on the job, and in everyday life situations. Instruction of these skills may be integrated into all subject areas. See Figure 5-7.

EMPLOYABILITY SKILLS/WORK RELATED SKILLS

WORK HABITS

	EXAMPLES
Complies with attendance policy	Maintains acceptable attendance record. Provides rationale for absence or requested release time. Follows proper notification procedure
Practices punctuality	Arrives on time for class/work and from breaks; is on time for appointments
Works cooperatively with coworkers	Performs as a member of a team. Interacts with co-workers to complete tasks
Works cooperatively with supervisor	Interacts with staff/supervisors in a businesslike manner. Shows respect for authority
Remains at work station/route	Requests permission to leave a task. Takes appropriate breaks at designated times
Communicates wants/needs/assistance	Appropriately seeks help and communicates necessary information to coworkers and supervisors
Converses appropriately	Communicates in ways acceptable to co-workers and supervisors
Follows directions	Exhibits willingness to perform task the way it is taught by employer/vocational trainer
Accepts criticism	Accepts realistic criticism from co-workers and staff/supervisors. Tries to improve on required tasks
Adapts to change	Accepts change without becoming upset or disruptive. Maintains work space
Attends to task	Focuses attention on own work

WORK SKILLS

Uses time card	Follows designated procedure to account for time spent on the job
Handles materials appropriately	Demonstrates ability to maintain and care for workstation, tools, and materials
Initiates work routine	Starts work without being told. Sees what needs to be done and does it
Follows work routine	Follows established sequence for performing tasks
Maintains work quality	Completes work of acceptable quality. Work does not have to be done over
Meets production standards (speed)	Works at an appropriate pace. Completes maximum amount of assigned work within a given time period
Recognizes and corrects errors	Realizes and corrects own errors
Retains work skills	Remembers methods for completing tasks from day to day and after vacations
Maintains work area	Cleans up after activity. Keeps activity/job task within own space and organized
Adapts work speed to situation	Recognizes need to adjust work pace

APPEARANCE/CONDUCT

Dresses appropriately	Dresses in a manner suitable for the job. Clothing is clean and well-fitted
Meets grooming standards	Displays adequate hygiene (clean body, face, hands, hair)
Uses unstructured time well	Displays appropriate behavior while waiting for job assignment, transportation, or while on break

Source: Intermediate District 287. (n.d.). *Employability Skills/Work Related Skills.* Plymouth, MN: Hennepin Technical College.

Figure 5-7. A listing of work habits and work skills to be developed and reinforced through the educational process.

These skills are usually assessed through observation of the learner in classroom and laboratory activities, both individual and group. They are documented on checklists and in portfolios. See Figure 5-8.

The advent of sophisticated technology has revolutionized the workplace and its skills requirements. For one thing, many kinds of routinized, repetitive work have been completely eliminated. For another, the faculty employees and office workers of today must be able to perform increasingly

sophisticated operations, such as operating computers and analyzing data. The reference to interpersonal skills points to yet another reason for the changes in employability skill needs of today's workplace: the increasingly multicultural nature of the workforce. The U.S. Department of Labor projected that by the year 2000, three-quarters of workers would be women and/or minorities and/or immigrants. Good interpersonal skills are more in demand the more multicultural the workforce becomes (Cotton, 1993).

EMPLOYABILITY SKILLS/WORK RELATED SKILLS CHECKLIST

Name _____

1. QUALITY OF WORK
Over 50% of work is unacceptable ( )
25-50% of work is unacceptable ( )
Less than 25% of work is acceptable ( )
Work usually meets minimum standards ( )
Work is of good quality ( )

2. QUANTITY OF WORK
Wastes time ( )
Production below staff expectations ( )
Meets minimum standards ( )
Produces more than required ( )
Very high output ( )

3. INITIATIVE
Needs constant reminding ( )
Works on own but needs frequent checks ( )
Needs average supervision ( )
Applies self to task ( )
Looks for things to do ( )

4. PERSISTENCE
Works with difficulty ( )
Stays on task but easily distracted ( )
Needs average supervision ( )
Diligent to most tasks ( )
Persistent regardless of circumstances ( )

5. ATTITUDE
Antagonistic to tasks ( )
Avoids tasks ( )
Performs tasks without enthusiasm ( )
Shows enthusiasm for some tasks ( )
Usually enthusiastic for tasks ( )

6. APPEARANCE: DRESS AND GROOMING
Not suitable to tasks ( )
Seldom suitable
Moderately suitable ( )
Usually suitable to task ( )
Always suitable ( )

7. ATTENDANCE
Absent 5-6 days per month ( )
Absent 3-4 days per month ( )
Absent 1 day per month ( )
Absent 1 day in each 60-90 days ( )
Absent 2-4 days per year ( )

8. ACCEPTANCE OF AUTHORITY
Antagonistic ( )
Violates rules occasionally ( )
Accepts but needs occasional reminder ( )
Knows and follows without reminder ( )
Follows rules consistently ( )

9. HUMAN RELATIONS WITH PEERS
Unable to work with peers ( )
Able to work with only 1-2 peers ( )
Usually no conflict with peers ( )
Effective worker in small group ( )
Works well in all peer groups ( )

10. COMPREHENDING TASKS
Does not understand directions ( )
Slowly catches on ( )
Usually understands ( )
Needs only brief explanations ( )
Grasps ideas quickly ( )

11. ABILITY TO REMEMBER INSTRUCTIONS
Almost never remembers ( )
Occasionally remembers simple instructions ( )
Usually remembers 1-2 steps ( )
Remembers 3 or more steps 75% of the time ( )
Remembers most instructions most of the time ( )

12. TEACHER OVERALL REACTION TO STUDENT
Not employable ( )
Employable in highly supervised work ( )
Employable in some entry-level jobs ( )
Employable at most nontechnical entry-level jobs ( )
Recommended without reservations ( )

Figure 5-8. A sample checklist of employability and work-related skills of learners.

One important reason for the increased interest in equipping young people with basic, higher order, and effective skills is the growing awareness of what happens when a great number of people lack these qualifications. Commentary on the necessity of equipping people with these skills follows:

- Employment and employability are not the same thing. Being employed means having a job. For a youth or adult who is not adequately prepared, having a job is likely to be a temporary condition. Being employable means possessing qualities needed to maintain employment and progress in the workplace.
- For most of our young people, the United States has a more or less do-it-yourself system for making the transition from school to work. What they learned in school is not adequately related to what they need to know to succeed after leaving school.
- The socioeconomically disadvantaged young—whether white, African-American, Hispanic, male or female—face almost impenetrable employability barriers.
- The employment picture for African-American and Hispanic young Americans who do not continue on to college is horrible—and it worsened in the 1980s. According to 1990 data, only 29% of African-American high school dropouts between the ages of 16 and 24 were working at any job, and only a little more than half of all African-American youths with high school diplomas were employed.

- Roughly one-third of all high school graduates, and somewhat more of high school dropouts, fail to find stable employment by the time they are thirty. For this group, the rather casual American system does not work very well.
- Work-related failure or even unsatisfactory work experience can have serious negative repercussions for the well-being of those individuals unfortunate enough to experience it.
- Employability skill development can be thought of as a civil rights issue. Those responsible for programs in this area have a moral obligation to provide the most complete education and training possible for learners and clients (Cotton, 1993).

Work-Related Social Skills

The need for socially competent workers, coupled with the fact that many learners are socially unskilled, make a strong case for occupational social skills instruction to be included in part of a learner's preparation to make the transition from school to work. See Figure 5-9. Many learners with special needs demonstrate social skills deficits. In fact, 29% of these learners leaving high school during the 1994–95 academic year were anticipated to have a primary need for social skills training beyond high school (Elksnin & Elksnin, 1998).

OCCUPATIONAL SOCIAL SKILLS IDENTIFIED BY EMPLOYMENT EXPERTS . . .		
Author(s)/Year	**Occupational Social Skills Identified**	**Information Source**
Bullis, Nishioka-Evans, Fredericks, & Davis (1992)	*Job-Related Social Problem Domains* 1. Accepting criticism or correction from a work supervisor 2. Requesting help from a work supervisor 3. Following instructions from a work supervisor 4. Quitting a job 5. Taking time off 6. Social problems created by not working as fast as coworker 7. Talking to a work supervisor about personal problems 8. Social problems created by working with a coworker 9. Dealing with teasing or provocation from coworkers 10. Managing personal concerns in the workplace 11. Making friends with coworkers 12. Talking with a coworker about his or her behavior 13. Accepting criticism or correction from a coworker 14. Job-related fighting 15. Stealing and lying 16. Job-related dating	Review of literature relating to students with behavior disorders (BD); adolescents with BD; service providers

... OCCUPATIONAL SOCIAL SKILLS IDENTIFIED BY EMPLOYMENT EXPERTS ...		
Author(s)/Year	**Occupational Social Skills Identified**	**Information Source**
Greenan (1983) Greenan & Smith (1981)	Generalizable Social Skills: *Work Behaviors* 1. Work efficiently under supervision 2. Work without need for close supervision 3. Work cooperatively as a member of a team 4. Get along and work effectively with people 5. Show up regularly and on time 6. Work effectively under pressure 7. See things from another's point of view 8. Engage appropriately in social interactions 9. Take responsibility for one's own judgments, decisions, and actions 10. Plan, carry out, and complete activities at one's own initiation *Instructor/Supervisor Conversation Skills* 11. Instruct/direct someone in performance of task 12. Follow instructions/directions 13. Demonstrate how to perform a task 14. Assign others to carry out specific tasks 15. Speak in a relaxed, confident manner 16. Compliment/provide constructive feedback 17. Handle criticism, disagreement, disappointment 18. Initiate and maintain conversations 19. Initiate, maintain, and draw others into group conversations 20. Join in group conversations	Vocational educators in two states
Elrod (1987)	1. Gets along with others 2. Takes criticism constructively 3. Follows directions 4. Works as a member of a team 5. Positive attitude 6. Dependable 7. Accepts responsibility 8. Works independently 9. Honesty 10. Obeys safety rules	270 vocational educators
Mathews, Whang, & Fawcett (1980, 1981, 1982)	1. Getting a job lead from a friend 2. Telephoning a potential employer to arrange a job interview (when there is a job opening) 3. Telephoning a potential employer to arrange a job interview (when there is not a job) 4. Participating in a job interview 5. Accepting a suggestion from an employer 6. Accepting criticism from an employer 7. Providing constructive criticism to a coworker 8. Explaining a problem to a supervisor 9. Complimenting a coworker on a job done well 10. Accepting a compliment from a coworker	Review of literature; survey of vocational counselors, university placement counselors, employers, personnel managers

...OCCUPATIONAL SOCIAL SKILLS IDENTIFIED BY EMPLOYMENT EXPERTS		
Author(s)/Year	**Occupational Social Skills Identified**	**Information Source**
Minskoff (1994)	*Domains* 1. Verbal communication (13 skills) 2. Nonverbal communication (4 skills) 3. Social problem solving (6 skills) 4. Social awareness (2 skills) 5. Compliance (3 skills) 6. Cooperation (3 skills) 7. Civility (2 skills)	100 educators from Virginia; validated by employers, job incumbents, vocational teachers
Montague (1988)	1. Ordering job responsibilities 2. Understanding instructions 3. Asking a question 4. Asking for help 5. Asking for assistance 6. Offering assistance 7. Giving instructions 8. Convincing others 9. Apologizing 10. Accepting criticism	Review of literature, interviews with employers
U.S. Department of Labor (1996)	*Interpersonal Competencies* 1. Participates as a member of a team 2. Teaches others new skills 3. Serves clients/customers 4. Exercises leadership 5. Negotiates 6. Works with diversity	National appointed panel (CEOs, presidents) in business, labor, education

Source: Elksnin & Elksnin. (1998). *Teaching Occupational Skills.* Austin TX: PRO-ED.

Figure 5-9. An overview of occupational social skills.

Most people realize that a college education or vocational training improves their career opportunities, but many are less aware that interpersonal skills may be the set of skills most important to their employability, productivity, and career success. Employers typically value verbal communications, responsibility, initiative, and interpersonal and decision-making skills. A question all employers have in mind when they interview a job applicant is, "Can this person get along with other people?" Having a high degree of technical competence is not enough to ensure a successful career. A person also has to have a high degree of interpersonal competence. (Johnson & Johnson, 1990, p. 32)

Occupational social skills are implicit in career and technical education programs. Therefore, they should be a part of the assessment process to identify which skills learners demonstrate and which skills they need to develop so as to be adequately prepared for the workforce. See Figure 5-10.

Personality Assessment

Personality assessment attempts to measure a whole host of personality factors that may affect an individual's behavior at work, attitude toward work, ability to operate effectively in particular environments, attitudes toward colleagues, capacity to cope with stress, etc. Individuals often require help in understanding the impact of personality factors on their career choice. This is particularly so when considering new opportunities. However, it can also be used in a development context to help individuals understand why they are finding some aspects of a job difficult or why they are not succeeding in a particular work situation.

There are very few jobs that rely solely on possession of particular personality attributes. Personality testing can provide extremely useful information but needs to be complementary to the results from an aptitude or ability assessment or evidence of educational attainment.

There are a number of well-recognized assessment tools that look at personality. These tools are used extensively in recruitment and selection. On the whole, personality

EXAMPLES OF SOCIAL SKILLS INCLUDED AS SKILL STANDARDS FOR SELECTED OCCUPATIONAL CLUSTERS

AGRICULTURAL BIOTECHNOLOGY TECHNICIAN
Interpersonal Skills
- Develop and use listening skills
- Develop objectivity
- Demonstrate understanding of team planning, problem solving, and how communications processes and individuals contribute to the group
- Develop conflict resolution and consensus-building techniques
- Explain the concepts of group trust and systems orientation, within and between teams
- Develop initiative-taking and observation skills
- Develop understanding of individual roles and responsibilities in groups
- Identify team expectations and service responsibilities
- Identify and explain diversity issues (i.e., values, work styles, cultures)

ELECTRONICS TECHNICIAN
Interpersonal Relationships
- Respond constructively to suggestions for improvement
- Provide praise and suggestions for improvement
- Channel/control emotional reactions constructively
- Recognize problems and work toward their solution
- Exhibit positive behavior
- Exhibit sensitivity to internal and external customer needs
- Treat people with respect
- Recognize nonverbal communication

GROCERY
Exhibiting Good Interpersonal Skills
- Use courtesy
- Show respect and empathy for others
- Cooperate with others
- Assist others
- Work productively with others
- Respond positively to criticsm
- Provide criticism constructively
- Provide praise
- Respond to praise
- Accept and follow directions
- Perform as a team member
- Respect cultural diversity
- Respect others in nontraditional jobs
- Respect physically and mentally challenged individuals

Source: Elksnin, N., & Elksnin, L. (1998). *Teaching Occupational Social Skills.* Austin TX: PRO-ED.

Figure 5-10. Social skills lists for several career clusters.

assessment is seen as a more complex and controversial area of psychometrics and a higher level of professional skill is required to administer and interpret test scores.

Alessandro and Hunsaker (1993) designed a personality style model that applies to communicating with others in work settings. See Figure 5-11. The model bases four different personality styles on two distinct dimensions of behavior:

- Indirectness versus directness: This dimension describes the person's observable behavior. Directness means the tendency to move forward or act outwardly by expressing thoughts, feelings, or expectations in order to influence others.
- Supporting versus controlling: This dimension explains the motivating goal behind our observable actions. People who are supporting tend to put relationships with others as their chief priority while the priority for people who are controlling is accomplishment of the task at hand. (p. 22)

> In order to better understand a person's style, we need to ask two simple questions: Is the person more direct or more indirect? Is the person more supporting or more controlling? Once we can answer those two questions, we will understand the dominant style of that person and we will know what style language to use in our communication. (Alessandro & Hunsaker, p. 22)

Generalizable Skills

The lack of job-related academic and interpersonal skills are two fundamental reasons why learners with special needs will (a) drop out of school, (b) become underemployed or unemployed after leaving school, or (c) be unable to maintain employment. If the primary objective of vocational education is to assist learners in developing employable skills and in providing for their successful transition from school to work, then basic or generalizable skills literally become vocational skills that should not be underestimated or overlooked by the career and technical educator or others working with learners with special needs.

A generalizable skill, operationally defined, is a cognitive, affective, or psychomotor skill or skill area that is basic to, necessary for success in, and transferable (or common) within and among career and technical education programs and occupations. See Appendix. These skills constitute an integral rather than an additional component in career and technical education programs.

Four generalizable skill areas have been identified through recent research:
1. mathematics
2. communications
3. interpersonal relations
4. reasoning

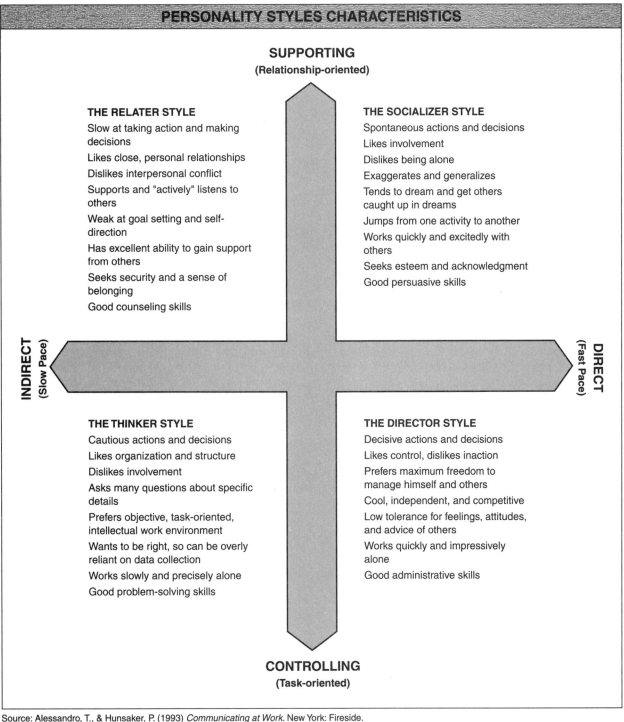

PERSONALITY STYLES CHARACTERISTICS

SUPPORTING
(Relationship-oriented)

THE RELATER STYLE

Slow at taking action and making decisions

Likes close, personal relationships

Dislikes interpersonal conflict

Supports and "actively" listens to others

Weak at goal setting and self-direction

Has excellent ability to gain support from others

Seeks security and a sense of belonging

Good counseling skills

THE SOCIALIZER STYLE

Spontaneous actions and decisions

Likes involvement

Dislikes being alone

Exaggerates and generalizes

Tends to dream and get others caught up in dreams

Jumps from one activity to another

Works quickly and excitedly with others

Seeks esteem and acknowledgment

Good persuasive skills

INDIRECT
(Slow Pace)

DIRECT
(Fast Pace)

THE THINKER STYLE

Cautious actions and decisions

Likes organization and structure

Dislikes involvement

Asks many questions about specific details

Prefers objective, task-oriented, intellectual work environment

Wants to be right, so can be overly reliant on data collection

Works slowly and precisely alone

Good problem-solving skills

THE DIRECTOR STYLE

Decisive actions and decisions

Likes control, dislikes inaction

Prefers maximum freedom to manage himself and others

Cool, independent, and competitive

Low tolerance for feelings, attitudes, and advice of others

Works quickly and impressively alone

Good administrative skills

CONTROLLING
(Task-oriented)

Source: Alessandro, T., & Hunsaker, P. (1993) *Communicating at Work.* New York: Fireside.

Figure 5-11. Personality styles characteristics.

These skill areas are generalizable within and across career and technical programs in agriculture, business, marketing, and management, in health, in home economics, and in industrial education. See Figure 5-12. They are also vital for general gainful employment. Following are sample key skills in the four skill areas:

Mathematics (28 skills)
- whole numbers (5 skills)
- fractions (4 skills)
- decimals (6 skills)
- percents (2 skills)
- mixed operations (4 skills)

- measurements and calculations (6 skills)
- estimates (1 skill)

Reasoning (40 skills)
- verbal reasoning (16 skills)
- problem solving (10 skills)
- planning (14 skills)

Communications (27 skills)
- words and meanings (9 skills)
- reading (8 skills)
- writing (3 skills)

- speaking (3 skills)
- listening (4 skills)

Interpersonal Relations (26 skills)
- work behaviors (10 skills)
- instructional and supervisory (6 skills)
- conversations (6 skills)
- social conversations (4 skills)

Career and technical education teachers can use generalizable skills to revise curricula. Further, these skills may be used in writing vocational program goals and behavioral objectives for individual learners. Activities such as

GENERALIZABLE MATH SKILLS: EXAMPLES OF APPLICATION IN CAREER AND TECHNICAL EDUCATION AREAS . . .

Math Concepts	Agriculture	Health Occupations	Home Economics
Whole numbers	Livestock inventory count Feed order Hay baled per acre	Patient liquid intake Chart Patient vital signs Dry supplies inventory	Tabulate customer's order Menu pricing Kindergarten coloring activity
Fractions	Compute food needed per livestock head Portion hay bales per head needed Divide pasture land per livestock grazing need	Patient height chart Syringe readings	Measuring liquid/dry ingredients Determine fabric required per pattern
Percent	Crop yield per growing season Profit margin on sales Carcass loss vs. saleable beef	Liquid intake vs. output chart Dietary needs - fat, carbohydrates, proteins in specialized diets	Nutritional values per food Family budgets Sales profits
Decimals	Balance ledger Quarterly statements of profit/loss	Patient statements Balance ledger	Balance checkbook Monthly budget Taxes
Measurements and calculations	Fencing materials needed to fence pasture Special feeding instructions/blends Products needed to fill customers orders	Determine distance for orthopedic therapy tract Distance for reading eye charts Time/medication dispensed per patient	Time cooking processes Weight food per recipe Portion food for special dietary needs
Mixed operations	Calculate employee payroll - hours, wages, taxes Order supplies for operations	Calculate employee payroll - hours, wages, taxes Order medical, dry supplies	Calculate employee payroll - hours, wages, taxes Order supplies
Estimation	Order feed per livestock based on previous usage Project new crop yield Estimate plan order for landscape	Estimate patients progress/hospital stay as per current rate of progress Estimate beds available on holiday weekend from previous year's report Estimate supply needs from rate of usage	Order food supplies as per banquet needs Determine fabric for drapery order Anticipate number of kindergarten students for next school year

Math Concept	Marketing/Business Occupations	Trade/Industrial Occupations
Whole numbers	Total daily sales receipts Inventory stock Bank transactions Balance ledger	Inventory control Computing bill of lading Filling supply order
Fractions	Compute window display footage requirements Calculate word processing paper setups	Order fabric for upholstery project Measure, mix hair color Cut hair per customer request
Percent	Compute interest, loan rates Determine quarterly profit/loss Balance ledger	Determine products for project - painting car Determine cost per class project - brick mailboxes Compute lumber for storage building
Decimals	Banking transactions - deposits, withdrawals Balance store ledger Make change to customers Operate cash register	Itemize total customer's bill Balance shop ledger Banking transactions Operate cash register
Measurements and calculations	Calculate carpet for office Determine glass shelving for store display	Compute volume of materials for roofing a specified house Determine amount of hair color for different types/lengths of customers' hair Calculate length of electrical wire for standard 2000 sq ft structure
Mixed operations	Calculate employee payroll - hours, wages, taxes Quarterly profit/loss statement Compute insurance premiums for varied situations Estimate time to print forms on computers Estimate product turnover rate	Calculate employee payroll - hours, wages, taxes Compute job costs - materials cost, time required Estimate inventory based on previous month's usage Determine product cost to consumer Estimate product completion time Estimate job completion vs. job cost

GENERALIZABLE MATH SKILLS: EXAMPLES OF APPLICATION IN CAREER AND TECHNICAL EDUCATION AREAS

Source: Pickard, S. (1990). Integrating Math Skills into Vocational Education Curricula. *The Journal for Vocational Special Needs Education, 1* (13), 11-12.

Figure 5-12. An example of practical application of generalizable math skills.

these provide an excellent opportunity for career and technical educators and special educators to work together. In addition, generalizable skills should also be addressed during all planning, support services, resources, teaching, personnel preparation, and program evaluation activities. If career and technical education is to meet the challenges facing it, generalizable skills must be part of all instructional components in its programs.

TRANSITION ASSESSMENT FOR LEARNERS WITH DISABILITIES

The 1997 amendments to the Individuals with Disabilities Education Act (IDEA) emphasized that learners with disabilities are to be prepared for employment and independent living and that specific attention is to be paid to the secondary education they receive. The law also requires coordinated and documented planning. Early and

meaningful transition planning, which actively involves learners and their families, has a positive influence on learners' postschool success and independence.

Section 300.29 of the IDEA regulations defines transition service as a coordinated set of activities for a learner with a disability that

- is designed within an outcome-oriented process that promotes movement from school to postschool activities, including postsecondary education, vocational training, integrated employment (including supported employment), continuing and adult education, adult services, independent living, or community participation;
- is based on the individual learner's needs, taking into account the learner's preferences and interests; and
- includes instruction, related services, community experiences, the development of employment and other postschool adult living objectives, and the acquisition of daily living skills and functional vocational evaluation.

Case Study . . . Mr. Garland

Mr. Garland is a career and technical instructor in a Commercial Foods program. He has several students who are interested in serving an internship as a Cook/Meal Manager. He has met with the Food Service Manager, to whom the intern will be responsible, at a large conference center in the community. During the meeting, the Food Service Manager identified the following qualifications for the internship experience:

- *training and experience in vegetarian cooking for large groups*
- *ability to work well with a team and meet daily deadlines*
- *ability to prepare foods for special needs groups (vegans, diabetics, etc.)*
- *knowledge of food preparation and service standards, health, safety, and sanitation procedures.*
- *ability to accept feedback and guidance*
- *good character, integrity, and adaptability*
- *enthusiasm, a sense of humor, patience, and self-discipline*
- *fluent in English*

Among the interested students are two learners with special needs. Mr. Garland had several planning sessions with the transition coordinator and other support personnel. During these sessions, it was decided that they would all participate in observing specific learners perform work tasks through situational assessment activities. A checklist was developed to record their observations. The checklist paralleled the essential functions and specific responsibilities of a Cook/Meal Manager.

The activities developed by Mr. Garland included work tasks that had to be performed in his career and technical education program. The tools, equipment, and materials used in the program were included in these tasks. It was decided that observations made during these activities would be used to evaluate basic skill levels. Mr. Garland divided the class into small groups. Each group had an opportunity to participate in the situational assessment activities. At the beginning of each activity, Mr. Garland introduced the tools, equipment, and materials to be used for the work task. He then explained the procedure for completing each work task.

While the groups performed the task, Mr. Garland and the other educators observed the performance of the learners with special needs. They recorded their observations on the situational assessment checklist. They paid particular attention to the interpersonal interactions that occurred in the small group setting during task completion. These observations enabled Mr. Garland and the support personnel to select the student for the internship.

Realistic transition activities must be outlined in the individualized education program (IEP). Developing skills for an unneeded labor market does not promote employment and obtaining a job without transportation options compromises the possibility of success. Roles and responsibilities should be written into the plan. Examples of transition activities include the following:

- assessing learner needs, interests, or preferences for future education, employment, and adult living and setting future goals in these areas
- identifying, exploring, and trying out transition placements that match the learner's assessment and vision and providing community experiences related to future goals
- instructing the learner in the academic, career, and adult living skills needed to achieve transition goals, including self-determination
- identifying and providing the accommodations, supports, or related services the learner needs
- coordinating with adult services organizations and helping families identify resources and natural support
- providing or planning follow-up or follow-along support once the learner graduates or develops independence in a transition activity

Generally, an IEP addresses services to be provided to the learner during one school year. But when it comes to transition requirements, the IEP team must think and plan several years ahead. The highest incidence of dropping out and of disciplinary actions such as suspension or expulsion occurs during the first two years of high school. To combat this pattern, the IDEA requires that the IEP team carefully consider postschool goals when the learner is about to enter high school at age 14. Beginning at age 16 (or younger, if appropriate) a statement of transition services needed by the learner must be included in the IEP.

High school experiences, both academic and social, greatly influence future options for all learners. For adolescents with disabilities, these experience are pivotal. Decisions about any transition service needs or a learner's course of study should be grounded in the answers to the following questions:

- What are the learner's dreams? What is the learner's vision for life as a young adult?
- What are the learner's strengths? How will the learner use them to build success during high school?
- Will the learner seek a regular high school diploma requiring a prescribed course of study with possible accompanying proficiency tests?

- Will the learner work toward a vocational completion certificate?
- Does the learner have a career interest now? If not, when and how can the team help the learner discover interests and preferences?
- Does this team believe that the learner will remain in public school through the maximum age of eligibility? If so, what age-appropriate experiences may be available after 18?
- What skills need to be developed or improved to help the learner make progress toward goals?
- Are there any at-risk behaviors that might interfere with the learner's success during high school?
- In what school and community activities will the learner participate?
- What does the team believe the learner's high school course of study will look like?
- What transition services, supports, and accommodations does the learner need for success in high school? (deFur, 2000).

Transition services encompass career education, vocational education, and other life skills development. Transition assessment is

> the ongoing process of collecting data on the individual's strength, needs, preferences and interests as they relate to the demands of current and future working, educational, living, and personal and social environments. Assessment data serve as the common thread in the transition process and form the basis for defining goals and services to be included in the Individualized Education Program (IEP). (Sitlington, Neubert, & Leconte, 1997, p. 71)

Sitlington, Clark, and Kolstoe (2000) related the following information relative to transition assessment:

- Transition assessment is the umbrella term that encompasses both career assessment and vocational assessment. It relates to all life roles and to the support needed before, during, and after the transition to adult life.
- Assessment data collected during the transition assessment process should be used to assist individuals with disabilities in making informed choices. Thus, assessment activities serve as the basis for determining an individual's strengths, needs, preferences, and interests related to career development, vocational training, postsecondary education goals, community functioning, health, and personal and social skills.
- Assessment should occur in a variety of environments that are natural to the individual's life. Special and general education personnel must be prepared to work cooperatively with individuals with disabilities, their families, related school personnel, and community service providers to determine what types of assessment data need to be collected and which methods will facilitate the career goals of the learner.

Clark (1998) identified areas that should be addressed in transition assessment:

- Interests–Interests are like preferences. They focus on what a person is curious about, likes to spend time doing, or sees as a possible benefit. When asked what interests them the most (or least) at school, at home, or in the community, children or youths will reveal a wide range of topics or activities that indicate their likes and dislikes, what they are or are not curious about, and what they consider important for their time and attention. Interests across age levels are typically based on cultural and cross-cultural influences. Preschoolers show interest in play and family activities; elementary and middle/junior high school learners show interest in group activities (i.e., with family, school groups, and community groups) as well as individual interests (e.g., collections, board games, television, reading, computer games, sports, hobbies); adolescents show peer-related interests (e.g. clothes, music, movies, dating, sexuality, group acceptance) and more advanced individual interests, including more selective occupational interests; and adults demonstrate peer-related interests (e.g., occupations, lifestyle, consumerism, parenting, and continuing education) and adult-related individual interests.
- Preferences–The concept of preferences for families and individuals with disabilities is the result of a value for decision making that is based on informed personal choices among interest-related options. The length of family involvement depends on the choice-making skills and preferences of the persons with disabilities. Certainly by the late teen years, most individuals with disabilities should be stating their own preferences about where they want to live, where they want to work, what they want to do with their free time, and other choices that most adults make.
- Physical health and fitness–The area of physical health and fitness covers the expected areas of general health status and physical condition, such as strength, stamina, endurance, range of motion, and mobility. Attention to physical health and fitness is also important for identifying physical or sensory impairments that affect a person's motor or sensory functioning and the consequences of the impairment(s), such as the need for medications, medical procedures, prosthetics, orthotics, or assistive technology.
- Motor skills–Motor skills across the age span vary. They are important for planning and conducting activities at school, at home, or in the community. Gross and fine motor skills, manual and finger dexterity, agility, and motor coordination are examples of motor skills that need to be developed and used in life activities at all ages.
- Speech and language–Assessment of speech and language development is a routine procedure for children with disabilities. Upon entering elementary school,

learners still experience some focus on speech and language development and any delays that need specialized attention, but they also encounter a shift toward the oral and written communication skills that are basic to elementary and middle school instruction: reading, writing, spelling, and grammar. Pragmatics refers to the use of language in social contexts for effective communication, such as appropriate slang or jargon, giving and taking directions, social conversation, telephone communication, and communicating personal interests and preferences.

- Cognitive development and performance–Cognitive development from birth through the preschool years is of high interest because of its importance as a foundation for all human performance areas throughout life. Perception, learning, memory, reasoning, and problem-solving skills are basic to success in school environments as well as in community living. Lack of cognitive development or low cognitive performance should never diminish the rights and opportunities of individuals, but assessment in these areas can be helpful in determining relative strengths and, when necessary, in establishing eligibility for programs and services.

- Adaptive behavior–Adaptive behavior is a general term encompassing a wide range of skills and human activity. In adolescence adaptive and daily living skills take the forms of more advanced dressing skills (e.g., colors, weather-appropriateness, comfort), personal hygiene skills (e.g. feminine hygiene, shaving, use of deodorants), basic food preparation, care and maintenance of clothing, driving or use of public transportation, and learning and complying with explicit rules and policies governing behavior at school and in the community. Adult adaptive behavior skills include all areas of daily living at home, community participation, and employment.

- Socialization skills–Socialization skills vary across age levels but comprise the basic interpersonal skills used in family, school, and community relationships. Skills include positive social behaviors such as sharing, cooperation and collaboration, respecting others' privacy and property, knowing socially appropriate and inappropriate behaviors, sensitivity to others' feelings and preferences, sensitivity to multicultural diversity, environment-special social behaviors and a basic understanding of how moral, ethical, legal, and religious values guide our individual social behavior and our communities' and government's public policies.

- Emotional development and mental health–Emotional development and mental health are concepts that are to some extent parts of a continuum, but they are also separate phenomena. Positive, healthy emotional development in children and adolescents contributes to good mental health in adulthood. Learning to deal with fear, anger, rejection, and grief are important for good mental health. On the other hand, children and adolescents can develop normally in these areas without any signs of lack of emotional control or poor mental health and yet have mental illness or poor mental health as adults. The converse can also be true. It is important in transitions assessment that attention be given to both the emotional development and the mental health of individuals of all ages. Few would argue against the importance of self-esteem, freedom from fear, and freedom from anger.

- Independent and interdependent living skills–Independent living skills are highly valued, and the majority of people with disabilities do achieve significant levels of independence. Adult indicators include mobility, employment, living in a preferred residential situation, and access to community resources (e.g., health care, legal assistance, and financial assistance). Interdependent living skills across all ages refers to (a) the ability of individuals with disabilities to understand their need for certain kinds of support, (b) the interdependent roles that characterize most families of people with disabilities, and (c) adults with disabilities living alone with personal attendants or other support persons.

- Leisure skills–Assessment of leisure skills may overlap to some extent with assessment of motor skills and community participation. As in community participation, the opportunity to be exposed to and learn leisure skills is important, and assessment of leisure skills should take that into consideration. Leisure skills assessment is a process that also may be important as an indication of self-awareness and leisure activity awareness of the person being assessed.

- Pre-employability, employability, and vocational skills–Elementary and middle/junior high school learners with disabilities can and should be learning pre-employability skills that undergird all types of later employment such as following directions, on-task behavior, concern for quality work, recognizing errors or problems, and ability to take instruction and criticism. Older learners in middle/junior high schools need to go beyond pre-employability skills to employability skills; speed, accuracy and precision, minimum waste of materials, adjustment to repetition and monotony, adjustment to frequent and unexpected changes, acceptance of authority and policies relative to work, conformity to schedules, dependability in attendance and punctuality, and ability to be self-directed. High schools learners and adults need to demonstrate the complete range of pre-employability and employability skills in addition to having one or more specific vocational skills. Vocational skills can result from training and/or experience.

- Choice-making and self-determination skills–The development of choice-making skills is natural for most young children. However, children with disabilities may not get the same opportunities as other children if their parents take charge of their lives and provide and advocate for them. Assessment of choice-making skills among preschool, elementary, and middle/junior high school learners should tap all possible areas where choices and decisions are allowed and determine to what extent the learners are able to look at options and make decisions based on information and knowledge of possible consequences of their decision. Self-determination skills should emerge beginning at the middle/junior high school levels. Learners should be assessed for self-awareness and self-knowledge abilities, needs, and rights, as well as their abilities to plan for short-term and long-term goals, to set short-term goals, and to realize their goals. Self-advocacy is another skill needed by high schools learners, postsecondary learners, and adults. Assessment should cover the learners' knowledge of their preferences, needs, and rights in life; their ability to speak for their interests; and their ability to act as their own advocates.

- Community participation–Like adaptive behavior, community participation takes a variety of forms across age levels. Assessment topics in this area should include the nature and extent of activities the learners engage in outside home and school settings. Some of these activities are going to the public library; eating out in restaurants; going to malls; playing in parks and playgrounds; participating in community parks and recreation activities; going shopping for items they can buy; going to movies, parades, festivals or sporting events; participating with family in religious worship or attending religious education activities; voting; volunteering; and belonging to community organizations.
- Needed skills or information for next vertical transition–Assessing needed skills or information for an individual's next vertical transition in life is not an assessment that focuses only on that individual. Rather, it must include an ecological assessment of the conditions, demands, or expectations for an individual as he or she plans and begins a new life transition. It is important to examine the skill demands, the conditions under which skill performance occurs, the anticipated barriers or problems in the transition, and any application forms, assessments, expenses, or formal procedures involved.
- Needed family or other supports–Assessment of the family or internal supports that a child, youth, or adult might need should be based on the assessment information from each of the areas previously discussed. Identifying family or other support systems in the areas of physical health, motor skills, communication, adaptive-life skills, socialization, emotional development and mental health, independent living, leisure skills, employment, and community participation should be tied systematically to assessment procedures in these areas.

- Needed linkages with support services–Identification of specially needed linkages with support services at school or in the community is a result of good ecological and situational assessments of individuals.

Effective transition programs and services depend on the collaboration of a number of professionals. Depending on the specific school system, a various professionals may participate in the assessment process at some level. These can include special education teachers, guidance counselors, vocational educators, vocational evaluators, rehabilitation professionals, vocational support service personnel, school psychologists, social workers; and employers. The roles of some of these professionals are discussed below:

- Special education teacher–As happens in other areas of planning for learners with disabilities, vocational assessment activities and other forms of career guidance frequently become the responsibility of the special education teacher. Special educators may gather information about the learner by observing the learner's academic strength, employability skills, interpersonal skills, and degree of career awareness. They frequently work closely with other teachers, the learner, and the learner's family in identifying an individual's needs and areas of interest and, in collaboration with the family, help to develop IEP goals for the learners. The insights and recommendations of the special education teacher can be invaluable to the vocational assessment process, particularly when supplemented by formal testing.
- Guidance counselors–Vocational assessment, in some schools, is an integral part of a guidance counselor's work with learners. This can include interviewing youth about their career goals and vocational plans and perhaps administering one or two paper-pencil or computer-based tests to identify interests and/or aptitude, work values, or temperaments or by helping youth use state occupational information databases.

Often, guidance counselors serve in a position that enables them to act as case managers for coordinating the collection of assessment information from teachers, parents, and others. There are occasions when other professionals may administer assessment activities, but counselors may interpret the results for the learners, parents, and teachers. To interpret results most effectively, counselors must have three bases of concrete information. The counselor should know the learner, should have a working knowledge of the assessment instruments and/or processes used, and should have current information about the requirements of in-school and outside vocational education programs.

- Career and technical educators–Career and technical educators, such as auto repair or data entry teachers, have expertise in vocational training and work requirements. They can assist in the vocational assessment process by providing career information, helping others design realistic assessment activities, and working with vocational evaluators to assess learners in the vocational classroom or work site.

- Vocational evaluators/vocational assessment specialists–These professionals are often responsible for conducting vocational assessments of the learner. Additionally, they may serve as consultants who provide vocational assessment information to others, or they may coordinate the assessment activities of others. Vocational evaluators are professionals who work within secondary or vocational school settings, community-based programs, industry, adult rehabilitative services, adult job training services, and community colleges or other postsecondary educational settings. Trained, certified vocational evaluators are the most qualified to oversee and administer vocational appraisal services and activities since they are required to meet national standards of certification (National Information Center for Children and Youth with Disabilities, 1990).

Assistive Technology

Technology is receiving the attention of families, advocates, and professionals due to its potential for enhancing the lives of individuals with disabilities. From computers to communication devices to environmental controls, the world of technology offers many children and adolescents with disabilities the tools necessary to be more successful in school, at work, and at achieving independence in daily living. Indeed, opportunities unthought of ten years ago are now becoming available to some children with disabilities with the assistance of new technology, and rumors of emerging technology are raising new hopes.

Assistive technology (AT) is defined by the Technology-Related Assistance for Individuals with Disabilities Act Amendments of 1994 (PL103-218). An assistive technology device is "any item, piece of equipment, or product system, whether acquired commercially off the shelf, modified, or customized, that is used to increase, maintain, or improve functional capacities of individuals with disabilities." Assistive technology service is "any service that directly assists an individual with a disability in the selection, acquisition, or use of an assistive technology device." An AT intervention can be as simple as placing blocks of wood under a desk or as involved as utilizing a voice-activated computer system. Recent federal legislative acts have mandated the provisions of appropriate technology to assist individuals with disabilities. Legislation has clearly stated that AT considerations should occur throughout the rehabilitative process and within services related to vocational evaluation, assessment, and work adjustment.

The use of assistive technology (also known as rehabilitation technology) in the assessment process is often required in order to reach effective outcomes. A fundamental goal of the field of assessment and vocational evaluation is to assist individuals with disabilities in reaching their maximum potential. For many individuals this potential will be severely restricted without the benefit of assistive technology. The use of this technology within vocational evaluation, assessment, and work adjustment in order to enhance the performance of individuals is essential in determining their functional capabilities.

The use of AT during vocational evaluation, assessment, and work adjustment is often critical to a valid appraisal of the individual's true capabilities. The application of assistive technology can take various forms including (1) site assessment to provide better accessibility, (2) modification of assessment tools and instruments, such as adaptation to work samples, (3) use of technologies such as visual aids and computer adaptations, and (4) assessment recommendations that specifically focus on AT issues. In all these cases, assessment personnel can and should play a major role on the AT team, coordinating access to technology-related services and contributing to team recommendations. Assistive technology resources and services should be integral components of all comprehensive vocational evaluation programs as well as vocational assessment and work adjustment services (Vocational Evaluation and Work Adjustment Association, 1997).

Transition Planning

It is important to remember than when vocational assessment is begun early in a learner's education, re-evaluation of the learner should be scheduled yearly to update the recommendations. Learners improve skills over time and mature in their understanding of and interaction with the world. Assessment information, when used to make decisions, should be as current as possible. If it is available, comprehensive, formal vocational assessment should begin approximately one year prior to placement in career and technical education, usually around the ninth or tenth grade. At this point, assessment is conducted for the specific purpose of career and transition planning. In many school systems, planning of transition is being incorporated into the established IEP process as learners reach about the age of 14. See Figure 5-13.

Results of all assessment activities should be shared with parents and learners. A vocational profile should be developed for the learner. This profile should not only detail assessment results but should also include recommendations for career and technical education placement, postsecondary training, or employment. As a vital part of career and transition planning, placement, and programming, the vocational profile also serves as a record and vehicle of communication between the learner, family, school, and community personnel.

The next step in the planning process, based upon the assessment results and the nature of the learner's disability, is to identify the support services (e.g. transportation, assistive technology) the learner will need to implement the voca-

USES OF VOCATIONAL ASSESSMENT DATA	
Category	**Description**
Determination of career development	To find out where the student stands in terms of career awareness, orientation, exploration, preparation, placement, or growth/maintenance. Appropriate for middle school/early junior high and beyond
Measurement	To identify abilities, interests, capabilities, strengths, needs, potentials, and behaviors within the areas of personal/social, functional/academic, community/independent, employment and employability areas. Initial testing appropriate for middle school; more involved analyses appropriate for high school and beyond
Prediction	To match an individual's interests and abilities with appropriate vocational training, community employment, or postsecondary training. Appropriate for high school
Prescription	To identify strengths and needs, and to recommend types of adaptive techniques and/or remedial strategies that will lead to improved career development and vocational preparation. Appropriate for high school and young adults and beyond
Exploration	To "try out" different work-related tasks or vocational activities and to determine how interests match abilities for vocational education programs, community jobs, postsecondary, or other adult activities. Appropriate for high school and young adults
Intervention	To implement the techniques or remedial strategies that will help a student explore vocational or work options. Appropriate for high school and beyond
Advocacy	To develop a vocational profile to help students, their families, and other identify concrete ways to assist students in achieving their goals. Appropriate for high school and beyond

Source: National Information Center for Children and Youth with Disabilities. (1990). *Vocational Assessment: A Guide for Parents and Professionals.* Washington, DC: Author.

Figure 5-13. Categories and descriptions of the uses of collected vocational assessment data.

tional plan. An analysis of the employment or training site identified for the learner should also be made. What skills are necessary for the learner to perform the training or be successfully placed in the program? Does the learner have these entry-level skills? This analysis will indicate any additional training the learner needs before or during placement.

APPROACHES TO VOCATIONAL ASSESSMENT

There are a number of approaches to the vocational assessment process ranging from informal to formal procedures. The following seven principles serve as guides to the best practices across settings in vocational assessment:

1. A variety of methods, tools, and approaches should be used to provide accurate vocational evaluation and assessments. A broad range of questions must be posed to determine what makes an individual (as well as higher abilities and needs) unique. Assessment is aided when and individual's attributes, such as interest, aptitude, or learning style preferences, are separated into categories.
2. Vocational evaluation and assessment information should be verified using different methods, tools and approaches. Using alternative methods or approaches to validate findings can usually be achieved by
   - observing an individual's demonstrated or manifested behaviors, such as performances on actual work;
   - using an individual's self-report or expressed statements; and/or

- administering some type of survey, inventory, structured interview or test.
3. Behavioral observation is essential in any vocational assessment process. Behavioral observation, such as observing physical performance, social characteristics, and interactions with people and other aspects of the environment, should occur throughout the assessment process. The observation process
   - may be informal or formal;
   - may occur in a variety of environments;
   - may be made by a variety of people; and
   - should be documented and presented in an objective, nonbiased manner.
4. Vocational evaluation and assessment may be an ongoing and developmental process in career development. However, individuals, especially those with disabilities, may need evaluations/assessments of varying degrees given at different junctures over their career life spans.
5. Vocational evaluation and assessment should be the basis for planning needed services, resources, and support. Therefore, it is an integral part of the total service delivery system. Vocational evaluation and assessment information should be interpreted and conveyed to the consumer as well as others within the system.
6. Vocational evaluation and assessment requires the collection of input from a variety of individuals and an understanding of how to use the results of the

assessment process. An interdisciplinary team approach allows for the effective use of information that can be translated into effective planning, implementation activities (e.g. placements, support service, counseling), and fulfilled vocational development for consumers.

7. Vocational evolution and assessment should be current, valid and relevant. Vocational evaluation and assessment is grounded in career, vocational, and work contexts (Smith et al.,1995).

Formal Assessment

Formal assessment usually refers to those instruments that have been norm-referenced and are available with detailed administrative and scoring information. Instruments that are used to obtain formal assessment information include achievement tests, aptitude tests, personality tests, interest inventories, intelligence tests, dexterity tests, formal work samples, and work evaluation systems. The characteristics of formal assessment instruments include norm populations to compare learner performance to, norm referenced instruments, validity and reliability data, and standardized directions for use in administering and scoring the instrument.

Personnel who administer and analyze information used during formal assessment procedures are usually trained. Results usually compare the learner to a much larger group of learners from a national pool, comparing ability and scores with different types of information that may or may not be appropriate for planning the learner's vocational education plan within the context of the local curriculum.

McCarty-Warren and Hess-Grabill (1988) identified the advantages of using formal assessment methods, particularly the use of standardized, norm-referenced tests. Among the advantages of these types of information are

- they can be given in group settings;
- they can be scored by machine, which makes them relatively quick, easy, and inexpensive to administer;
- they allow for a comparison of performance between learners of similar age and/or grade placement, which is often the type of information necessary to determine programming needs and/or eligibility for support services;
- criterion-referenced instruments compare learner performance to a set of established criteria; and
- instruments identify competencies and deficits in areas assessed and provide information in a form useful for making prescriptive recommendations. (p. 38)

Informal Assessment

Informal assessment usually refers to information and data that have not been developed on a norm-referenced, standardized basis. It is information that can be obtained from school records already on file, observation, interviews, and discussions with learners, parents, and teachers. Informal assessment activities reflect the learner's experiences in the local school curriculum and community based settings utilizing teacher made tests, behavior rating scales, self-report or subjective ratings, checklists, informal diagnostic basic skills tests, and locally developed questionnaires and inventories.

Characteristics of informal assessment tools include flexible timing, comparison of learner performance to specific program requirements rather than to a norm group, flexible administration procedures, and accommodations for special needs during the test. The results of informal assessment activities are often more valid than those from standardized tests because they are primarily designed to identify specific strengths and limitations in skill development relative to specific career and technical education programs rather than comparison of performance to norm group data.

McCarty-Warren and Hess-Grabill (1988) stated that the primary advantages of informal assessment methods are their ability to relate directly to instructional programs (e.g., teacher-made tests), the capacity to accommodate individual learning styles and needs, the ability to obtain information from a variety of sources and perspectives, and the ability to customize the assessment to answer questions specific to individual students. Their purpose is more directly related to the identification of strengths and weaknesses and the use of this information in the development of future instructional and career guidance objectives. (p. 37)

Informal assessment involves observation skills. Tindall and Gugerty (1991) suggested that instructors gather informal impressions of learners' behaviors through observation. These observations should divide the class into two groups by answering two basic questions—"Which learners stand out in some way as exhibiting unusual behaviors?" and "If language, perceptual, motor, social, or emotional problems of a given learner are serious enough to be seen through observation, what types of assistance should be provided to help the learner?" Teachers should not rely on prior information about learners, either from other teachers or past experience with siblings. Instead, during their classroom and laboratory observations they should look for learners

- who do not complete a reasonable quantity of work within the time allotted for independent work;
- who do not follow directions, resulting in work prepared inaccurately or at variance with verbal or written instructions;
- who request frequent teacher aid (for example, not beginning work upon oral directions but waiting for the teacher to demonstrate the task);
- who read orally with many word-recognition errors or demonstrate poor comprehension of what was read;
- whose approach to tasks is exceptionally slow, purposeless, or disorganized;
- who frequently cannot locate the place in the text, lose work papers, or do not move to the proper location with the group during instruction;

- who demonstrate a tremor when holding a pencil or other tool;
- who stare into space, engage in repetitive motor activity, or exhibit other competing activity during independent work periods;
- who overreact when a task becomes frustrating;
- whose language or speech give the impression of a chronologically younger student;
- who seem to master a concept today but forget it tomorrow; and/or
- who must be given a number of trials to complete a task. (pp. 459–60)

Curriculum-Based Vocational Assessment

Blankenship (1985) described curriculum-based assessment as the practice of obtaining direct and frequent measures of a learner's performance on a series of sequentially arranged objectives derived from the curriculum used in the classroom. Bigge (1988) defined curriculum-based assessment as a course of study that is specified, measurable, and supported by a system of ongoing measurement of learner progress in terms of expected outcomes. Curriculum-based assessment is an approach that directly relates assessment information to instructional objectives. This approach to assessment involves the standardized observation, measurement, and documentation of a learner's abilities on tasks that relate directly to the content of specific course curricula. See Figure 5-14.

General characteristics of curriculum-based assessment include the following:

1. Direct measures
   - learner is tested on classroom learning
   - what is taught is tested
2. Measurable
   - assessment through objectives
3. Brief
   - short and simple tests/reviews
   - specific behavioral skills tested
4. Ongoing and continuous
   - multiple assessments at frequent intervals
5. Local norms established
   - expectations are curriculum standards and competencies

CURRICULUM-BASED VOCATIONAL ASSESSMENT STAGES

Stage	Definition	Purpose	Questions
I. Assessment during program placement and planning	Activities that occur prior to and during first few weeks of student participation in a career and technical education program	Program selection	Which program is most appropriate for the student?
		Program placement	What are the special service needs of the student in this particular program?
		Program planning	What will be the criteria used to determine student success?
II. Assessment during program participation	Activities that take place as student progresses in a career and technical education program	Monitor student progress	How is the student performing in the vocational setting?
		Determine appropriateness of program and service delivery plan	What changes are needed in the student's program?
		Evaluate success of student's program	
III. Assessment during program exiting	Activities that occur near the end of student's program and following completion	Plan future service needs of student	What are the special services needed to help the student transition into employment and/or postsecondary education?
			Which adult service agencies need to be linked up to the student?

Source: Albright, L., & Cobb, R. (1988, Winter). Curriculum Based Vocational Assessment. *The Journal for Special Needs Education, 10*(2), p. 16.

Figure 5-14. The stages, definitions, purposes, and related questions of curriculum-based vocational assessment.

6. Focus on the product of effective teaching
- goal is for every learner to function successfully through a variety of delivery techniques
7. Experimental
- emphasis on charting and teacher-made competency checklists
8. Emphasis on discrepancy
- importance lies in the discrepancy between expectations of curriculum and learner's performance
- basis for provision of support services.

There is a growing interest in curriculum-based assessment because of the dissatisfaction among educators about the heavy dependency on and/or usefulness of standardized commercial tests. They often feel that there is little correlation between what is taught in the classroom and what is tested. They express frustration that standardized tests are not sensitive to subtle changes in learner learning and performance over time. In addition, standardized and commercial tests do not provide relevant information concerning learners' competence in specific academic, social, and vocational skill areas. The most important factor in curriculum-based assessment is the learner's performance or progress on curricular tasks. Learning difficulty is diagnosed in terms of the discrepancy between the learner's current level of functioning within the context of the curriculum and the desired level of functioning.

Integrating the curriculum-based philosophy into the vocational assessment process is called curriculum-based vocational assessment (CBVA). The CBVA process is defined as a rating procedure designed to determine the interests, aptitudes, instructional needs, and skill development of learners based upon their ongoing performance within a career/vocational curriculum sequence. It is characterized as a continuous, performance-based assessment process used to answer questions about the instruction and special service needs of learners from special populations as they enter and progress through a specific career and technical education program. It is an approach designed to assess the interests, abilities, and needs of learners through hands-on, simulated activities related to the specific career and technical education curriculum or workplace setting in which the learner will participate.

This informal approach to vocational assessment suggests the use of checklists, rating sheets, and other informal methods to identify pertinent information relative to learners as they become involved in classroom and laboratory activities in the career and technical education program. The information collected from this process describes learner awareness and interaction with the world of work, including the development of work-related behaviors and skills.

In CBVA, assessment is conducted in the same setting in which instruction is delivered using the tools, equipment, and materials within the actual career and technical education program. It allows for direct observation of learners performing job related tasks that are an intrinsic part of the curriculum. The assessment is done through a team approach involving the educational personnel who will be working with the learner, including the career and technical education instructor, academic teachers, counselors, school psychologists, special educators, and support personnel. Since CBVA utilizes existing vocational, academic, and special services personnel in the district, the start-up and operational costs are largely in personnel training and collaborative planning.

The assessment of learner interests and achievement in career and technical education programs must be an ongoing, continuous process. Albright and Cobb (1988) stated that CBVA information is needed during three different stages of a learner's program:

1. when the career and technical education program placement decision is in process;
2. during the learner's participation in the program; and
3. as the learner exits the program.

Data from CBVA should be used for such purposes as

- selecting realistic vocational goals;
- writing individualized education plan (IEP) and individualized transition plan (ITP) goals and objectives for learners with disabilities;
- developing goals and objectives for individualized career plans (ICPs) for learners from special populations;
- providing instructional suggestions;
- identifying necessary support services;
- developing a learner portfolio;
- determining transition service needs;
- determining linkages with other programs/agencies; and
- determining job placement opportunities or postsecondary program goals.

Steps in the Development of a Curriculum-Based Vocational Assessment Process

Establishing a CBVA process requires organization and commitment on the part of administrators, teachers, and support staff at the local district or campus level. Following are the steps involved in developing and implementing a CBVA process:

Step One. This requires communicating career and technical education program opportunities to learners and parents.

1. Conduct a school or campus-based assessment to identify the career and technical education programs and support services available.
2. Develop a communication mechanism to communicate career and technical education program opportunities to learners and parents (e.g., newsletters, program brochures, learner handbooks, newspaper releases, displays at public places, video presentations, TV and radio spots, learner assemblies, counselor meetings, open houses, parent conferences, and career days).

3. Include the following information about each specific career and technical education program:
- eligibility criteria
- admissions procedures
- basic skills, knowledge, and employability skills that employers expect from entry-level workers and how they are part of the program
- an estimate of the amount of time the learner will typically spend in doing course work
- job opportunities with completion of a career and technical education program or portion of the program (multiple exit points)
- examples of methods available to instructors to teach entry-level or transferable skills to learners (e.g., cooperative education, supervised occupational experiences, simulated work experiences, participation in career and technical student organization activities)
- special support services available to learners enrolled in the program

Step Two. This entails determining whether career and technical education is the most appropriate curriculum for the learner. See Figure 5-15.
1. Develop a system for analyzing cumulative records and other appropriate existing information (e.g., basic skills levels, interest inventory results, aptitude test results).
2. Schedule informational meetings for learners who have an interest in career and technical education.
3. Schedule a one-on-one interview to determine assessment information needs and interests in specific programs.
4. Develop a placement assistance plan to test out learner indicated interests and possible support service needs.
5. Develop techniques for preparing a learner profile to use in placement and program planning decisions:
- career and technical program exploratory tryouts
- direct observations with criterion referenced checklists
- competency-based portfolios
- community-based or program-based job shadowing and interviewing
- informal career and technical education program cognitive and/or performance-based tests to determine academic and skill levels (teacher developed)
- comparison of current learner skill levels with entry-level performance associated with the various career and technical education programs

Step Three. This places the learner in a specific career and technical education program.
1. Decide what type of career and technical education placement is most appropriate for the learner.
2. Develop a learner support plan (e.g., individualized education program (IEP), individualized transition plan (ITP), individualized career plan (ICP).

Step Four. This requires monitoring and reviewing learner performance in career and technical education programs.
1. Identify learner progress information to be collected.
2. Develop appropriate instrumentation and procedures to collect learner progress information. See Figure 5-16.
3. Interpret team review of adequacy of the assessment, planning, and service delivery strategies.

Step Five. This involves creating transition service programming. See Figure 5-17.
1. Develop and implement a working relationship with local adult service agencies and contact persons.
2. Establish a transition placement team for future assistance after graduation if efforts in the step two assessment indicate that all school-related efforts are not productive for an individual learner.
3. Determine the nature and extent of service needs of learners that can be provided through the development of a specific transition plan (Kingsbury, 1986).

Community-Based Vocational Assessment

Once vocational competencies have been developed through participation in a career and technical education program or a decision has been made to place an individual in a cooperative education program, the next step in the assessment process should be to complete a job analysis of the specific career goal or training site identified for the learner. Job analysis, although time-consuming, can be useful at this time because the conditions that exist in a career and technical education program may differ from the conditions that exist at the specific job site. Job analysis should be conducted enough in advance of actual placement so that additional training needed for the particular job site can be provided.

Community Workforce Survey

A survey of workforce needs in the community can be helpful in collecting job analysis information. The survey of local industries can provide information relating to the types and numbers of available jobs, specific skills required for each job, and working conditions.

A variety of methods can be used to collect community workforce information including personal interviews, sending survey forms by mail, and collecting information by telephone conversations. The survey method selected should take into consideration the size of the community, the number of firms and industries available, and the amount of time to be spent on the survey. The local business and industrial firms to be included in the survey can be obtained from such sources as the Chamber of Commerce, the telephone directory, advisory committees, and community retail merchant groups.

LEARNER ANALYSIS PROFILE . . .

Assessment/Appraisal Team:

Learner: _____   _____

School: _____   _____

Date: _____   _____

Special Need Indicators	Learning Difficulty		Learning Strength		Documentation/Observed Behavior
QUANTITATIVE/NUMERICAL SKILLS					
Count and record					
Add/subtract					
Multiply/divide					
Measure					
General number use					
Money					
Other quantitative/numerical skills:					
VERBAL SKILLS					
Read					
Spell					
Record information					
Verbal communication					
Written communication					
Other verbal skills:					
COGNITIVE SKILLS					
Retention					
Sequence					
Attentiveness					
Planning ability					
Mechanical aptitude					
Transfer					
Other cognitive skills:					
PERCEPTUAL SKILLS					
Auditory discrimination					
Form perception					
Form discrimination					

...LEARNER ANALYSIS PROFILE

Special Need Indicators	Learning Difficulty			Learning Strength		Documentation/Observed Behavior
Space perception						
Color perception						
Touch discrimination						
Other perceptual skills:						
LANGUAGE SKILLS						
Listening						
Nonverbal expression						
Technical vocabulary						
Grammatical expression						
Other language skills:						
PSYCHOMOTOR/PHYSICAL SKILLS						
Physical strength						
Hand-eye coordination						
Manual dexterity						
Mobility						
Other physical skills:						
SOCIAL SKILLS						
Sociability						
Cooperativeness						
Conformity						
Loyalty						
Safety						
Responsibility						
Sensitivity						
Other social skills:						
OCCUPATIONAL INTERESTS						
Agriculture/Natural resources						
Automotive and power services						
Construction/Manufacturing						
Graphics/Communications						
Food/Clothing/Child Care						
Health						
Office/Business						
Other or specific occupational interests:						

Source: Phelps, L., & Lutz, R. (1977). *Career Exploration and Preparation for the Special Needs Learner*. Boston: Allyn and Bacon.

Figure 5-15. An example of a learner analysis profile for recording learner information during the assessment process.

CURRICULUM-BASED VOCATIONAL ASSESSMENT RATING FORM

Name _____

ID # _____

Exceptionality _____

Home School _____

Shared-time School _____

ESE Dept. Chairperson _____

School Year(s) _____   Grade(s) _____

Course Name: ESE-Industrial Education/Applied Electronics

Course #:   798009008

Rater's Name _____

Rater's Signature _____

Scale
Y = Yes
N = No
DO NOT RATE ANY ITEM NOT OBSERVED

Scale
P = Proficient
M = Pro. w/ modification
N = Not Proficient
DO NOT RATE ANY ITEM NOT OBSERVED

WORK RELATED BEHAVIORS: Dates:

1. Complies with attendance .... Y N
2. Practices punctuality .... Y N
3. Interacts with teachers or supervisors .... Y N
4. Cooperates as a team member .... Y N
5. Seeks assistance appropriately .... Y N
6. Works unsupervised .... Y N
7. Completes task accurately & in timely manner .... Y N
8. Uses good judgement .... Y N
9. Accepts changes .... Y N
10. Accepts constructive criticism .... Y N

Displays:
11. Initiative .... Y N
12. Integrity .... Y N
13. Frustration tolerance .... Y N
14. Good manners and personal habits .... Y N
15. Appearance required by situation .... Y N
16. Safe use & proper care of materials/equipment .... Y N
17. .... Y N
18. .... Y N
19. .... Y N
20. .... Y N

GENERALIZED SKILL OUTCOMES: Dates:

21. Understands/follows oral directions .... Y N
22. Communicates orally .... Y N
23. Communicates in writing .... Y N
24. Understands/follows written directions .... Y N
25. Applies related terminology .... Y N
26. Applies related measurement .... Y N
27. Applies related math computation .... Y N
28. Demonstrates problem solving .... Y N
29. Demonstrates computer literacy .... Y N
30. Shows interest in occupational area .... Y N

SPECIFIC SKILL OUTCOMES: Dates:

Sets up and safely performs basic operations with:
31. Hand tools ....
32. Portable electric tools ....

List on back of form: the hand tools and portable electric tools with which student is proficient.
33. Uses basic computer applications programs ....

List on back of form: the program/applications with which the student is proficient.
34. Uses basic electricity/electronic measuring instruments ....

List on back: instruments with which student is proficient.
35. Demonstrated skills in wiring and soldering ....

Demonstrates an understanding of:
36. Diagnostic procedures ....
37. Wiring diagrams and schematics ....
38. AC/DC circuits ....
39. Ohms and Watts Laws ....
40. Induction ....
41. Capacitance ....
42. Resistance ....
43. _____ ....

MODIFICATIONS: List date, item #, and modification for each (M) rating.

DATE	ITEM	MODIFICATION

Use back of form to list additional modifications or make general comments.

Source: Dade County Public Schools. (n.d.). Curriculum-Based Vocational Assessment Handbook. Miami, FL: Office of Vocational, Adult, Career, and Community Education.

Figure 5-16. An example of a rating form for recording learner performance levels during the assessment process.

CURRICULUM-BASED VOCATIONAL ASSESSMENT IMPLEMENTATION GUIDE

Key to Personnel

VSNT = Vocational Special Needs Teacher
SSE = Secondary Special Educator
VI = Vocational Instructor

VC = Vocational Counselor
VA = Vocational Administrator
* Suggested Lead Person(s)

Purpose for Assessment	Timing of Assessments	Personnel Involved in Assessment Activities	Instruments/Procedures Used in Assessment Activities
Module 1 Part I: Establishing a CBVA Process	Ongoing	*VSNT SSE VI *VA	CBVA Action Plan
Part II: Communicating program information	Starts at least one year prior to when vocational education is routinely available in district	VSNT *VC VI SSE	Review process to assure identification of all students with handicaps in district and their parents are informed of options
Module 3 Placing students in vocational education program	Semester prior to when vocational programs begin	*VSNT VC SSE VI	Review of student records; interview with student and parents; assessments in vocational tryout program
Module 4 Planning a student's vocational education program	During annual IEP review and first month of vocational class	*VSNT *SSE VI	Direct observations of student performances; inventory of program environment and curriculum
Module 5 Monitoring student progress	Throughout duration of vocational program	*VSNT *VI *SSE VC	Develop a monitoring system for individual students; conduct process and product assessments of student performance
Module 6 Planning transitional services	During semester prior to graduation	*VSNT SSE VC *VI	Review of student performance; interview with student and parent
Module 7 Evaluating CBVA process	Ongoing–annually	*VSNT VC *VA VI	Annual review process to evaluate CBVA processes/activities

Source: Albright, L., & Cobb, R. (1988). *Assessment of Students with Handicaps in Vocational Education: A Curriculum-Based Approach.* Alexandria, VA: American Vocational Association.

Figure 5-17. An overview of the curriculum-based vocational assessment process including assessment components, time frame, personnel involved, and procedures.

The survey form should be developed to include information that will meet the specific needs of the community, the career and technical education program, and the learners to be served. See Figure 5-18.

Job Analysis

Job analysis is another aspect of the vocational assessment process. This procedure provides information concerning what a worker does, how the job is done, and why it is necessary. When conducting a job analysis, career and technical personnel should identify necessary performance requirements for the job. Performance requirements may include the following:

- major job functions or duties
- work tasks
- skills or competencies
- performance standards
- work-related knowledge
- physical abilities
- work experience requirements
- education requirements
- training requirements
- certification requirements
- work environment factors

Information obtained by a job analysis can be used to develop job samples or work samples for use in assessing vocational interest and potential. The same machinery, equipment, tools, materials, and aids used on the job should be incorporated in the work samples whenever possible. The tasks involved in the work samples as well as the performance standards should be the same as those expected on the job. It is very important that the tasks and performance standards used in the job sample be valid so that a realistic and appropriate assessment of a learner's strengths and limitations can be made. Following are several good sources of occupational information.

Dictionary of Occupational Titles (DOT). The *Dictionary of Occupational Titles (DOT)* classification system was developed by the United States Department of Labor. It is a compendium, or dictionary, of occupational titles in common usage in U.S. industries. The *DOT* is one of the fundamental career tools used to assist individuals in making occupational choices. It is divided into seven groups:

- professional, technical, and managerial occupations
- clerical and sales occupations
- service occupations
- agricultural, fishery, forestry, and related occupations
- processing occupations
- machine trades occupations
- bench work occupations
- structural work occupations
- miscellaneous occupations

O*NET. The U.S. Department of Labor (2001) has developed a computerized occupational information database.

O*NET is a unique, powerful source of continually updated occupational information and labor market research. By using a contemporary, interactive skills-based database and a common language to describe worker skills and attributes, O*NET transforms data into precise, focused, occupational intelligence. O*NET On-Line is an application that was created for the general public in order to provide broad access to the O*NET database of occupational information. The O*NET database includes information on skills, abilities, knowledge, work activities, and interests along with occupations. This information can be used to facilitate career exploration, career counseling, and a variety of human resources functions, such as developing job orders and position descriptions and aligning training with current workplace needs. Information in O*NET is available for over 950 occupations. Each occupational title and code is based on the current version (1999) of the Standard Occupational Classification (SOC) system.

O*NET replaces the task-driven *Dictionary of Occupational Titles (DOT)*. O*NET joins state on-line career information systems (CareerZone 2000; CIS for Windows 2000) as perhaps the cutting edge of systems to organize and provide information about work, workers, and the workplace based on the skills shared by occupational rather than on industry sectors—in others words, based on the same concept that is the foundation of career pathways. Features of O*Net and the *DOT* include the following:

- descriptions for all jobs (nearly 1,2000) included in the new O*Net database
- a nontechnical introduction to the new O*Net system and how to use the O*Net DOT book for business, career counseling, occupational coding, and other purposes
- O*Net jobs organized into useful clusters that encourage browsing of related jobs by job hunters and others

O*Net contains over 1,1000 job descriptions that include the following:

- O*Net "occupational unit" number and O*Net job title
- related job title from the *Occupational Outlook Handbook (OOH)*
- lead description and job-specific tasks
- typical training
- average pay
- skills and knowledge
- generalized work activities
- interpersonal relationships
- physical and structural work conditions
- classification of instructional programs (CIP)
- related *Guide for Occupational Exploration (GOE)* groups
- related *Dictionary of Occupational Titles (DOT)* jobs

The database used in O*NET On-Line is based largely on data supplied by occupational analysts using sources such as the SOC. All government agencies are moving toward the SOC as the one standard system. O*NET, as one of the first systems to align with the SOC, will serve as the model for other programs.

COMMUNITY WORKFORCE SURVEY GUIDELINES

1. Source of data information:

    a. Name of firm: _____

    b. Address: _____

    _____

    c. Phone number: ( ) _____

    d. Employer(s) providing information
       (include name and official title): _____

    _____

2. Overview of employer and business (including number of full-time and part-time
    employees hired each year): _____

    _____

3. Types and number of jobs relating to the vocational program which are available:

Job Title	Number of Available Openings

4. Job description information:

Job Title	Job Description

5. Specific skills required for each job:

Job Title	Specific Skills Required

6. List of job tasks, frequency of task performance, and performance level(s) required:

Job Title	Job Tasks	Frequency of Task Performance	Performance Level(s) Required

7. Working conditions and environment:

Job Title	Working Conditions/Environment

8. Does your company receive assistance through federal contracts?

    _____ Yes   _____ No

9. If yes, do you have an affirmative action program for the individuals with disabilities in compliance with Sections 503
    and 504 of the Rehabilitation Act of 1973?

    _____ Yes   _____ No

Figure 5-18. A format for documenting information regarding community workforce opportunities.

O*NET On-Line also provides extensive linkages to additional resources for more information on accommodations, disabilities, and workplace issues. O*NET On-Line has made efforts to accommodate the diverse needs of users, following the guidelines of the World Wide Web consortium (W3C).

O*NET On-Line offers users the opportunity to

- find occupations to explore;
- search for occupations that use their skills;
- look at related occupations;
- view occupation snapshots;
- view occupation details;
- use crosswalks to find corresponding occupations in other classification systems;
- connect to other on-line career information resources; and
- access on-line comprehensive help information.

Business and human resources professionals use O*NET to

- develop effective job descriptions quickly and easily;
- expand the pool of quality candidates for open positions;
- define employee and/or job-specific success factors;
- align organizational development with workplace needs;
- refine recruitment and training goals; and
- design competitive compensation and promotion systems.

Job seekers use O*NET to

- find out which jobs fit their interests, skills, and experience;
- explore growth career profiles using the latest available labor market data;
- research what it takes to get their desired job;
- maximize earning potential and job satisfaction; and
- discover what it takes to be successful in their field and in related occupations.

Occupational Outlook Handbook. The *Occupational Outlook Handbook* is a nationally recognized source of career information designed to provide valuable assistance to individuals making decisions about their future work. Revised every two years, the *Handbook* describes what workers do on the job, working conditions, training and education needed, earnings, and expected job prospects in a wide range of occupations.

The valuable reference describes 250 different jobs—jobs held by 87% of American workers. Each description covers the following:

- nature of work
- future employment outlook
- earnings
- related occupations
- training/advancement
- employment opportunities
- sources of additional information

The *Handbook*'s addendum includes summary data for 77 other occupations covering another 6% of the workforce. The *Handbook* is updated every two years and features the 250 most popular jobs, has over 500 pages of pictures and charts, and is written in an easy-to-read narrative.

Guide for Occupational Exploration (GOE). The *Complete Guide for Occupational Exploration* is often used to identify groups of occupations a learner may be interested in or curious about. The *GOE* breaks down over 20,000 occupations into 66 subgroups, with questions and answers pertaining to each group. The *GOE* provides a list of related occupations and also includes reference numbers for the *DOT* for each of these groups. The reference numbers enable the user to look up any occupations not recognized. In addition, the *GOE* provides codes for each occupation that indicate the math requirements, language requirements, length of vocational preparation, and the amount of physical lifting expected on each job.

Standard Occupational Classification (SOC) Manual. The SOC system was developed in response to the growing need for a universal occupational classification system. Such a classification system allows government agencies and private industry to produce comparable data. Users of occupational data include government program managers, industrial and labor relations practitioners, learners considering career training, job seekers, vocational training schools, and employers wishing to set salary scales or locate new plants. It can be used by all federal agencies collecting occupational data, providing a means to compare occupational data across agencies. It is designed to cover all occupations in which work is performed for pay or profit, reflecting the current occupational structure in the United States.

All workers are classified into one of over 820 occupations according to their occupational definition. To facilitate classification, occupations are combined to form 23 major groups, 96 minor groups, and 451 broad occupations. Each broad occupation includes detailed occupation(s) requiring similar job duties, skills, education, or experience.

Revised Handbook for Analyzing Jobs. The *Revised Handbook for Analyzing Jobs* begins with an in-depth description of job analysis and its uses and principles. It is filled with over 300 pages of career information. This fourth revision also includes chapters on worker function, work fields, aptitudes, temperaments, the *GOE*, and physical demands and environmental conditions. The reader is familiarized with such topics as writing job summaries, task descriptions, and job analysis reports. The *Handbook* may be used with the ADA job analysis worksheet. It also corresponds with the 1991 *DOT* and the revised list of 72 worker traits.

LEVELS OF VOCATIONAL ASSESSMENT

The vocational assessment process should be learner-centered with all aspects directed toward a thorough understanding of the unique interests, abilities, and special needs of each learner. Vocational assessment is often viewed from a three-level approach. See Figure 5-19.

Level I

Level I vocational assessment activities include reviewing and compiling all previously existing information related to a learner's abilities, level of functioning, and other pertinent facts into a format that can be utilized for preparing a career plan for a specific learner. This level of assessment involves learning as much as possible about the learner from interests and ability inventories, informal interviews, and perspectives obtained from the learner, parent, and teachers. The purpose of collecting this type of information is to facilitate career guidance, decisions regarding the placement of the learner in a specific career and technical education program, curriculum modifications, and support services that are necessary for the learner to succeed in the program. For most learners, the information compiled during Level I assessment is sufficient to make an appropriate career placement decision and to provide recommendations regarding necessary support services, remediation, and follow-up services.

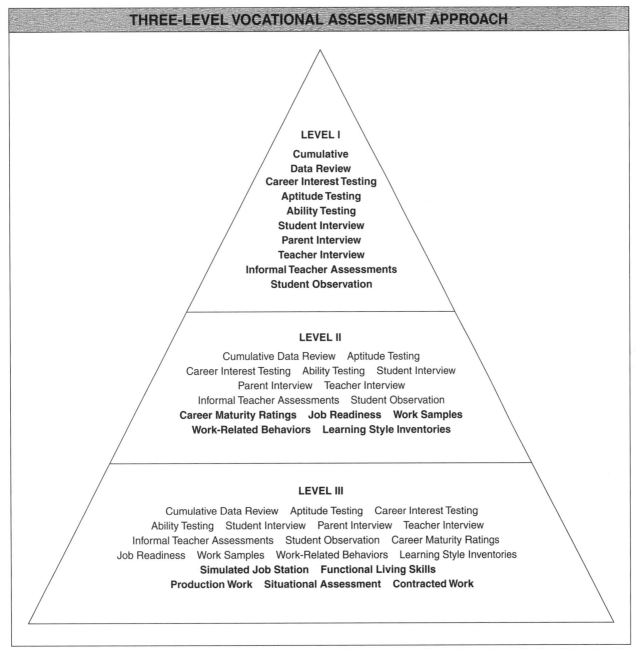

Source: McCarty-Warren, T., & Hess-Grabill, D. (1988). *Vocational Assessment of Secondary Special Needs Students.* Normal IL: Illinois State University, Office of Specialized Research.

Figure 5-19. Information about the learner appropriate for each level in a three-level assessment approach.

Personnel involved in Level I assessment include special needs and transition personnel, special education personnel, academic instructors, career and technical education personnel, bilingual personnel, guidance counselors, support personnel, parents/guardians, and learners.

Sources of information for Level I assessment include the following:
- attendance records
- anecdotal records/cumulative data review
- school academic records/transcripts
- psychological evaluations
- medical evaluations
- teacher observations (including information relative to the learner's functioning levels and learning styles in a classroom setting)
- informal teacher assessments
- personal interviews (including questions relative to the learner's level of occupational knowledge, possible career goals, interests, leisure activities, part-time or summer employment history, and other information that would help facilitate appropriate career planning)
- achievement profiles
- guidance counselor reports
- referral reports
- results of parent/guardian conferences (including questions relative to their perceptions of learner interests, abilities, limitations, educational needs, and possible career goals)
- career interest instruments (e.g., self-report inventories and checklists)
- aptitude tests
- interest inventories
- ability testing (e.g., reading, language, math, basic skills, motor coordination, manual/finger dexterity, tool usage)
- individualized education programs (for learners with disabilities in special education programs).

Level II

Level II vocational assessment activities are used to obtain more information about a learner who has difficulty identifying interests in a specific career and technical education program or demonstrating strengths on the paper-pencil inventories that indicate general interests and abilities. Sometimes there is conflicting information collected during Level I assessment and further clarification is necessary. Formal and/or informal inventories are identified specifically for this purpose.

Level II assessment activities include the use of informal work samples as well as formal work sample evaluations that allow the individual to become involved in a hands-on orientation to occupational areas. When formal, standardized work samples are utilized some individuals with special needs may need additional time

and/or modifications to the testing procedures. In addition, it is important that learning styles, maturity levels, and job readiness skills are assessed in order to facilitate appropriate career planning and placement decisions. These activities can help individuals identify their strengths and interests that have not surfaced through paper-pencil interest and aptitude inventories used in Level I assessment.

Personnel involved in Level II assessment include educational diagnosticians, special needs and transition personnel, career and technical education personnel, school psychologists, evaluators, counselors, and special education personnel. Sources of information for Level II assessment include the following:
- Career maturity inventories–These are instruments that measure a learner's values, attitudes, temperaments, personality style, and general occupational information base so that this information can be related to potential career paths.
- Work samples–These are samples of work, either real or simulated, that provide a learner with an opportunity to demonstrate abilities through hands-on experiences. Some work samples are purchased commercially. These work samples have norm groups, reliability, and validity. Other work samples are informal and developed through a curriculum-based approach by career and technical education instructors and support personnel at the local level.
- Learning style information–Sources of learning style information include one-on-one interviews with the learner, observations of learner performance in classroom and laboratory settings, and learning style inventories.
- Job readiness activities–These are competencies that will assist learners in seeking and obtaining employment (e.g., job applications, resume development, and job interview simulations).
- Work related behaviors/employability skills–These are the skills necessary to retain employment (e.g., observations, checklists, adaptive behavior scales, behavioral rating forms, and inventories).

Level III

Level III vocational assessment is necessary when school personnel cannot identify long-range goals or place a learner in a specific career and technical education program based on the information gathered from Levels I and II. Level III activities are generally conducted when more information is needed about a learner's cognitive abilities, physical abilities and limitations, and/or social-emotional behaviors. Many Level III activities are conducted outside the educational environment and are usually monitored by trained assessment specialists.

Personnel involved in Level III assessment include evaluators, trained vocational assessment specialists, special education personnel, job coaches, employment specialists, work supervisors, rehabilitation personnel, and agency personnel. Sources of information for Level III assessment include the following:

- Simulated job stations–These consist of simulated work activities that relate to specific jobs.
- Situational assessment–The learner's interests and abilities are assessed in an actual training or work setting. Structured criterion-based objectives should be used to evaluate the learner's performance.
- Contract work experiences–This is assessment through specific work tasks completed.

- Assessment of functional living skills–This is documentation of basic survival competencies necessary to function effectively in an independent living or community work setting It includes such areas as use of public transportation, money management, grooming and hygiene, health and safety skills, and survival reading and math skills.
- Production work–This consists of hands-on activities such as packaging, sorting, simple assembly, and collating and is used to identify such abilities as perceptual, discrimination, concentration, perseverance, and motor skills. See Figure 5-20.

VOCATIONAL ASSESSMENT REPORT - LEVELS I, II, AND III . . .

☐ Level I   ☐ Level II   ☐ Level III   Date: _____

I.   IDENTIFYING DATA:

Name: _____ School: _____ Grade: _____

Address: _____ Phone: _____ CA: _____

Referred By: _____ Assessed By: _____

II.   REFERRAL QUESTIONS:

_____

_____

_____

III. EDUCATIONAL RECORDS (vocationally significant):

Transcript

Related Courses	Grade	Teacher

Achievement/Aptitude Testing

Test/Subtest	Score	Below Aver.	Average	Above Aver.

... VOCATIONAL ASSESSMENT REPORT - LEVELS I, II, AND III ...

IV.   SPECIAL EDUCATION DATA (vocationally significant):

Reading-Grade Level: _____ Date: _____ Math-Grade Level: _____ Date: _____

WISC-R-Date: _____ Verbal IQ: _____ Performance IQ: _____ Full Scale IQ: _____

Significant Subtest Information: _____

_____

_____

Significant Affective Information: _____

_____

_____

Other Test Results: _____

_____

_____

Apparent Strengths (IEP): _____

_____

_____

_____

Apparent Weaknesses (IEP): _____

_____

_____

_____

Short Term Objectives (IEP): _____

_____

_____

_____

. . . VOCATIONAL ASSESSMENT REPORT - LEVELS I, II, AND III . . .

V.   INTERVIEW DATA (Synopsis of significant information):

Student: _____

_____

_____

_____

_____

_____

Parent: _____

_____

_____

_____

_____

_____

Teacher: _____

_____

_____

_____

_____

_____

Conclusions/Assessment Questions: _____

_____

_____

_____

_____

...VOCATIONAL ASSESSMENT REPORT - LEVELS I, II, AND III

VI.   INDEPENDENT LIVING SKILLS

	Much Improvement Needed	Some Improvement Needed	Acceptable	Very Good	Not Assessed
Food and Clothing					
Money and Finance					
Grooming and Hygiene					
Health and Safety					
Employability Skills					

VII.   LEARNING STYLE

	Insignificant	Minor	Major	Not Assessed
Visual Language				
Visual Numerical				
Auditory Language				
Auditory Numerical				
A/V Kinesthetic				
Social:				
Individual				
Group				
Expressive:				
Oral				
Written				

VIII.   CONCLUSIONS/RECOMMENDATIONS: _____

_____

_____

_____

_____

Source: Kennedy, T. (n.d.). *Vocational Assessment Report*. Port Huron, MI: Intermediate School District, St. Clair County.

Figure 5-20. A sample learner report using the Levels I, II, and III approach to vocational assessment.

TECHNIQUES AND METHODS FOR COLLECTING VOCATIONAL ASSESSMENT INFORMATION

Successful postschool planning must be linked to good vocational assessment. The question is, what type of assessment provides the informational needed to achieve these important outcomes? Formal psychometric approaches such as occupational interest inventories and vocational aptitude batteries are commonly used. But there are questions: Are these approaches appropriate for meeting the needs of learners who are members of special populations and can they provide sufficient data to achieve the outcomes characterized in the legislation? (Lombard, 1994).

Each local school district has a screening process designed to identify suspected physical, sensory, behavioral/emotional, or other problems that may significantly interfere with a learner's capability in achieving educational success. Prior to any evaluation, learners should be screened in the following seven areas:

- vision
- hearing
- health/motor
- cognitive (including adaptive behavior)
- academic achievement (pre-academic development for early childhood special education, transitions, and others)
- speech/language
- social/emotional/behavioral

In addition, information should be collected in the following areas to help create a more complete picture of the learners:

- Aptitude, achievement, and interest testing/inventories–Aptitude, achievement, and interest inventories can help the assessment team enroll learners in career and technical programs that suit their needs. Achievement testing assesses a learner's level of acquired academic skills gained from past education and vocational experiences. Aptitude testing assesses a learner's interests, preferences, and values related to occupations within career paths.
- Work readiness–Work readiness assessment refers to the assessment of a learner's job-seeking abilities as well as the learner's job-keeping abilities. For example, learners should be assessed on their ability to complete a job application, write a resume, and participate in an interview. Another work readiness skill is maintaining a professional appearance and attitude.
- Work-related behaviors–In addition to learner observation, behavior inventories can be administered in this phase. Objective behavior inventories facilitate a more systematic approach to vocational assessment. The study of work-related behaviors can identity problematic behaviors as well as those behaviors that indicate successful functioning in a vocational area.
- Learning style inventories–Information gathered about a learner's learning style is also beneficial in this phase. For example it may be helpful to discover whether a particular learner learns best through visual, audio, tactile,

kinesthetic, or integrated stimulation. Learners may be analytical, global, or integrated learners. By determining a learner's learning style, school districts can enroll learners in career and technical education programs that best suit their styles, needs, talents, and preferences.

- Functional living skills–Functional living skills are essential basic skills for independent living and/or independent working. Areas of basic life skills include basic math, basic communication (written and oral), proper hygiene, and appropriate attire. Learners should possess the ability to use public transportation, manage personal finance, and communicate effectively and respectfully.

West (1989) provided the following information about functional curriculum:

- Functional curriculum is one in which learners learn functional skills in the most appropriate setting for specific skills acquisition. It is one which prepares the learner for adult living and includes independent living skills, social skills, communication skills, vocational preparation and skill training, generalizable skills, study skills, etc. Also involved in functional curriculum is community involvement and specific planning for age-appropriate content.
- Functional curriculum enhances the outcome and is an essential component of the transition process. Emphasis is placed on the competencies and skills which a learner needs to acquire in order to be independent in our society. Tying together the learner's present curriculum and future plans requires interagency cooperation and community involvement. It is an ongoing process which changes as the learner's needs change.
- A functional curriculum should be adopted if the learner has significant difficulty learning new skills; has not kept pace with his or her peers in the total number of skills acquired; is actually engaged in instructional activities a very small portion of the day; or is approaching graduation.
- Functional curriculum can make a significant contribution to the learning experiences of learners with special needs. It provides the skill foundation for successful interaction with real-life environments. Functional skills' acquisition becomes more essential as learners get closer to graduation, but it is an approach to instruction that should begin in elementary grades.

One of the most widely used curricula for functional skills is the Life Centered Career Education (LCCE) Curriculum Program developed at the University of Missouri-Columbia under the direction of Donn E. Brolin, Professor, Department of Educational and Counseling Psychology. This K–12+ competency-based functional curriculum focuses on 22 major competencies and 97 subcompetencies arranged within three domain areas (daily living, personal-social, and occupational) that research has found to be critical for adult success in employment and independent living.

Daily Living Skills

1. managing family finances
2. selecting, managing and maintaining a home
3. caring for personal needs
4. raising children, family living
5. buying and preparing food
6. buying and caring for clothing
7. engaging in civic activities
8. utilizing recreation and leisure
9. getting around the community (mobility)

Personal-Social Skills

10. achieving self-awareness
11. acquiring self-confidence
12. achieving socially responsible behavior
13. maintaining good interpersonal skills
14. achieving independence
15. achieving problem-solving skills
16. communicating adequately with others

Occupational Guidance and Preparation

17. knowing and exploring occupational possibilities
18. selecting and planning occupational choices
19. exhibiting appropriate work habits and behavior
20. exhibiting sufficient physical-manual skills
21. obtaining a specific occupational skill
22. seeking, securing and maintaining employment (Brolin & Gysber, 1989)

These 22 competencies can be taught in both regular and special education classrooms by infusing them into the academic subject matter. The curriculum program includes (1) an LCCE curriculum guide for implementing the program and designing LCCE transitional curriculum plans, (2) an LCCE inventory consisting of knowledge and performance assessment batteries, and (3) 98 (secondary) LCCE subcompetency instructional units. The curriculum requires a substantial commitment to changing present practices in order to implement it on a comprehensive basis. This requires refocusing subject matter content and using many community resources and family involvement.

There is no single instrument or assessment tool that will be sufficient for all learners or all purposes. Due to language barriers, cultural differences, different learning styles, and/or academic deficiencies, many learners from special populations have had difficulty with traditional assessment methods. Therefore, a variety of techniques should be available in order to collect relevant information about each learner so that appropriate decisions can be made regarding realistic career goals. Some tools used for the vocational assessment process include the following:

- paper and pencil tests for interest and aptitude
- manual dexterity tests
- commercial assessment systems
- teacher-made performance samples (observations of process and product)
- anecdotal records (e.g., achievement results, medical and psychological data, teacher comments)
- learner interviews

- teacher-developed work samples and achievement tests
- entry level skills inventories for jobs and/or career and technical education programs
- exploration and shadowing activities
- direct observation checklists

McCarty-Warren and Hess-Grabill (1988) provided general guidelines for selecting instruments for use in the collection of assessment information. Careful selection of instruments is crucial in the assessment process. Duplication of existing information will only confuse the issue and using of instruments that do not provide realistic and relevant information about a learner who has special needs is a waste of valuable time. Therefore, in selecting those instruments to be used to assess a specific individual with special needs, the following guidelines should be utilized:

1. Review existing information to determine what is already known about a student and what questions still need to be answered. (e.g., age, grade level, limitations, current academic achievement level, native language proficiency of limited English-proficient learners, and strengths or limitations that may affect a student's test taking ability).
2. Identify specific questions to be answered and/or information to be obtained during the assessment process.
3. The intended purpose, target population, mode of instruction, content difficulty, and method of reporting scores of the instrument should be reviewed to determine if it has the capability to provide necessary student information.
4. Repeat assessment that will duplicate existing information only if further confirmation or documentation is necessary. If possible, attempt to use a different instrument designed to measure the same factor(s).
5. Failure to accurately interpret test results is a common problem associated with inadequate training. Be certain that instruments are within the capability of personnel to administer and interpret. If not, investigate the possibility of obtaining necessary training or select a different instrument.
6. If a norm-referenced test is considered, review the norming populations represented to determine whether they would be appropriate to use. Factors that should be considered include the ages, grade levels, gender, ethnic background, geographic area, socioeconomic class, and/or disability represented by members of the norm group.
7. If standardized instruments are used, it is important to know the purpose for which the test was intended and to use it only for that purpose. The test should not be changed nor should the instructions be modified in any way.
8. Try to select instruments that assess student abilities rather than limitations.
9. When there is more than one instrument capable of providing the information needed and several appear to have comparable validity and reliability, it is best to choose the one that appears easiest to administer and requires the least amount of time to complete. (pp. 40–41)

Case Study . . . Christina

Christina is a junior in high school. She is enrolled in an agribusiness program. She is interested in working in some area of agriculture or agribusiness, particularly in retail sales. Her manual dexterity is limited due to a birth defect affecting both her hands and her left forearm. Her reserved character and poor self-image are a result of her disability.

Christina realized her interest in agriculture and agribusiness as a result of an informal vocational assessment experience that she was involved in during her sophomore year. During this activity, she spent several days working in the agriculture laboratory completing informal work samples developed by the instructor. While she was occupied with these activities, the instructor observed and documented her progress on an observation checklist. When she completed these activities, she met with the instructor and the transition coordinator. They decided that the agriculture program would be a good placement for her during her junior and senior years.

In the meantime, the transition coordinator developed and shared learner assessment information with the agriculture instructor, including educational, academic, medical, social, and prevocational data. The results of paper-pencil interest and aptitude inventories were also reviewed. As a result, Christina was placed in the agribusiness program.

The agribusiness instructor is pleased with her performance in class. He feels comfortable working with her and appreciates the support they are receiving from academic and resource personnel. During her first year in the program, Christina demonstrated proficiency in turfgrass production management, sales, and service. During the spring quarter of her junior year, her instructor found Christina a short-term seasonal job with a local turf maintenance company. Her training in telephone sales techniques acquired in her agribusiness class began to pay off. Christina now works part-time year round. Afternoons are spent answering customer questions and concerns. Evenings are devoted to telephone sales. Intelligent, courteous answers to questions and recommendations for the customers' lawns have made Christina a star in this lawn care business.

Interviews

Interviews are an effective tool to collect important information about a learner's interests, abilities, goals, and history. Interviews can help to establish rapport between the learners and the educators who will be working with them. It is also an opportunity for learners from special populations to learn about the support services that are available to assist them in participating in career and technical education programs. Interviews can be conducted with a variety of people.

Informal Interview with Learner. The purpose of the learner interview is to determine the learner's interest in career and technical education and social competency or adaptive behavior related to performance in career and technical education programs. The school district may develop or use a structured interview form for this process. A teacher or counselor who has a good rapport with the learner may also conduct this part of the assessment.

Informal Conference with Teacher. The purpose of the teacher conference is to gather information about a learner's interests, abilities, and adaptive behaviors. Questions to the teacher should address general learning ability, general or specific interest, ability to follow directions, interpersonal skills, and communication skills. Inquiries about work-related behaviors are also relevant; examples include organizational skills, attention to detail, level of responsibility, and motivation.

Informal Conference with Parents. If the learner is under 18, parents should be interviewed. The purpose of this interview is to determine the parents' career expectations for the learner and to discuss their perceptions of the learner's social competence or adaptive behavior related to performance in career and technical education. Parents may be able to provide insight about the learner's aspirations that may not be evident through classroom observations.

Career and Technical Program Exploration Tryouts

Exploratory experiences in career and technical education programs can provide personnel with important assessment information through observing a learner's performance on tasks associated with exit points from the specific program. These curriculum-based experiences can provide valuable insight relative to appropriate program placement options for specific learners. Selection of specific career and technical education programs to be used for tryout experiences for each learner should be based on previous assessment activities, such as occupational exploration, interest inventories, and work samples. Tryouts are one method of providing some concrete information to be used for career and technical education program placement.

Hartley and Lehmann (1988) suggested the following guidelines for organizing a vocational [career and technical] education program tryout:

1. Ask the vocational instructor what skills are required for students entering the program.
2. Ask the instructor to choose one job/skill taught in the vocational program that is representative of the area. Skill must be hands-on, realistic, and related directly to curriculum. Tryouts should have a designated completion time (2-3 hours).
3. List entry level skills/competencies that the student will learn during the tryout. If the vocational program area requires academic and job related skills, include an assessment of both in the tryout.

4. Brainstorm with the vocational instructor some activities which would demonstrate the student's mastery of some of these skills. List the following assessment information: (a) setting; (b) materials/equipment needed; (c) tasks to be performed; and (d) evaluation standards.

5. Write an assessment plan which includes the following sections: (a) title; (b) materials/equipment needed; (c) materials/equipment identification sheet; (d) definitions of vocational vocabulary students should know in order to complete the assessment; (e) directions for performing the tryout (task analysis of the required steps); and (f) measures for evaluating student performance.

6. Additional considerations:
- Cover safety aspects of vocational area;
- Introduce student to instructor;
- Give student a tour of facility; explain rules;
- Supervise activities closely;
- Make sure assessment is hands-on;
- Observe student's tolerance, frustration, fatigue, and comfort levels. Make adjustments accordingly;
- Observer(s) must monitor student progress and give immediate feedback to the student; and
- Obtain student feedback on experience gained through the tryout (e.g., interest level, skills learned). (pp. 20–23)

Usually several career and technical education programs are selected for tryout experiences. Cooperative planning between career and technical education instructors and support personnel is essential when planning and implementing this assessment component. One advantage of this method is that the instructor has an opportunity to work directly with the learner being assessed. This helps the teacher plan appropriately for the learner in the event that final placement is made in the program. Another advantage is that the learner is better prepared to enter the program after establishing a rapport with the instructor, confirming a definite interest in the program, and building a level of self-confidence about participating. See Figure 5-21.

One of the most widely used vocational assessment approaches is situational assessment. This technique uses observation skills to record vocational behaviors and work habits that learners exhibit while performing specific work tasks. These work tasks can occur in a simulated environment or in an actual job situation. Learners are observed and evaluated while working in a group setting rather than on an individual basis. In this manner, the evaluator can observe the learner's hands-on skills as well as important interpersonal skills and social behavior. Rating scales and behavior checklists are normally used during situational assessment activities to record work performance.

Observation information gathered from situational assessment activities can be used to develop appropriate career and technical education program goals and objectives for learners from special populations. This technique can help to identify the specific hands-on skills that the learner can or cannot perform, work habits, social skills, and necessary remediation and/or support services. See Figure 5-22.

Brolin (1976) presented the following advantages of the situational assessment approach in the vocational assessment process:
- It simulates a real work situation.
- It allows the evaluator to observe social and interpersonal relationship behaviors as well as important hands-on skills necessary for the job.
- It is less time-consuming than formal or informal work samples.
- It is not expensive to develop related activities for this approach.
- It gives the individuals to be evaluated a chance to adjust to the activity in a more natural work environment than in a regular testing situation.
- It provides an opportunity for several professionals to observe and interpret behavior in a cooperative planning process. These personnel can include teachers, vocational assessment specialists, special needs and transition personnel, and others.
- It eliminates typical testing situations, and accompanying anxiety that standardized testing and work samples present.
- The evaluator can assess work behaviors that cannot be assessed with standardized vocational tests and work samples, such as interpersonal relationships, cooperation, response to work pressure, and response to orders from supervisors.
- Situational assessment is less expensive and less time consuming than work samples.
- It provides an opportunity to view and evaluate the individual in a setting where typical behaviors are more likely to be seen.
- It gives the individual an opportunity to be evaluated by several staff members in several work situations.
- An individual can be evaluated under various conditions, including different types of supervisors, co-workers, and circumstances. These can be varied systematically.

Checklists and Rating Scales

Checklists and rating scales are tools used to monitor learner progress in the career and technical education program or on the job. Progress is typically monitored through the administration of quizzes, performance checklists, observations of daily work, and supervisors' critique of a learners' progress on a job site. Criteria of learner success include attendance in class, knowledge of safety practices, quality of products developed, work habits demonstrated, and problem-solving ability (Albright & Cobb, 1988).

Tindall and Gugerty (1991) discussed the importance of checklists in the vocational assessment process. Vocational behavior checklists aid in careful assessment of individual

CAREER AND TECHNICAL EDUCATION PROGRAM TRYOUT CHECKLIST				

Instructor _____ Date _____

Student Name _____

Career and Technical Education Program   Business Education

Work Sample Area   Preparing Filing System

Materials Provided   Materials to be filed by subject, materials classified as to subject/name, set of numerically classified materials, manila folders, a typewriter, labels, file cards, A-Z file guides, and a file drawer.

	Completes Task Independently	Completes Task with Limited Supervision	Completes Task with Assistance	Cannot Complete Task
After being provided with specific directions (verbal, written, audio visual, demonstration, peer tutoring) the student will complete the following tasks:				
A. Alphabetical Filing System				
1. Assemble items to be filed.				
2. Review documents.				
3. Label manila folders as to subject name.				
4. Insert A-Z file guides in file drawer.				
B. Subject Filing System				
1. Determine categories into which materials will be filed.				
2. Sort materials into file categories.				
3. Label manila folders as to subject/categories.				
4. Place labeled folders in drawers.				
5. Type each subject/category onto a file card.				
6. List on each file card cross-references and associated subjects.				
7. File cards.				

Comments: _____

Recommendations: _____

Figure 5-21. A sample checklist for a career and technical education program tryout.

competencies. Their potential usefulness depends on an interaction of several factors–type of career and technical education program, learner's initial vocational behavior pattern, training setting, scope and objectivity of the checklist used, and the skill with which observers specify and record observations. See Figure 5-23.

SITUATIONAL ASSESSMENT OF WORK HABITS

Student _____ Date _____

Rater _____ School _____

On the basis of your knowledge of the student, assess him/her on the following continuum:

X	X APPLIES	INCLINED TO X	INCLINED TO Y	Y APPLIES	Y
1. INITIATIVE Student usually follows through on instructions.	←			→	Student fails to follow instructions.
2. QUALITY OF WORK Student's work is done correctly and carefully.	←			→	Student's work is not done correctly or carefully.
3. QUANTITY OF WORK Student's productivity is consistently high.	←			→	Student's productivity is low.
4. Student rarely wastes time.	←			→	Student often wastes time.
5. HUMAN RELATIONS Student relates well to peers.	←			→	Student does not relate well to peers.
6. Student works well on joint tasks.	←			→	Student does not work well on joint tasks.
7. ACCEPTANCE OF AUTHORITY Student accepts unpleasant tasks when assigned.	←			→	Student complains about unpleasant tasks when assigned.
8. ATTITUDE Student is neat, alert, and involved.	←			→	Student is sloppy, sluggish, and uninvolved.
9. ABILITY TO FOLLOW INSTRUCTIONS Student can understand most verbal directions.	←			→	Student cannot understand verbal directions.
10. Student can understand most written directions.	←			→	Student cannot understand written directions.
11. PERSISTENCE Student stays on difficult tasks.	←			→	Student does not stay on difficult tasks.
12. TEACHER'S OVERALL REACTION TO STUDENT Student should succeed in program of his/her interest.	←			→	Student will have difficulty succeeding in program without assistance.

Please recommend any support service that would benefit this student in realizing success in future career and technical education programs.

___ Remedial Math   ___ Remedial Reading   ___ Job seeking skills, i.e. forms   ___ Job survival skills, i.e. attitude

___ Curriculum Modification ___ Equipment Modification ___ Counseling by school counselor ___ Other

Source: Adapted from Esser, T. (Ed). (n.d.). *Client Rating Instruments for Use in Vocational Rehabilitation Agencies.* Stout, WI: University of Wisconsin, Stout Vocational Rehabilitation Institute.

Figure 5-22. A format for documenting learner performance relative to work habits demonstrated through situational assessment activities.

BEHAVIOR CHECKLIST

Student: _____

Date: _____

Observers: _____

_____

Job Task: _____

Observation	Rating		
	Excellent	Satisfactory	Needs Improvement
1. Work habits			
2. Punctuality			
3. Manipulation, coordination, dexterity			
4. Personal grooming/hygiene			
5. Ability to work unsupervised			
6. Ability to work under pressure			
7. Eye-hand coordination			
8. Speed, accuracy, and precision			
9. Strength			
10. Consistency in performing task(s)			
11. Work tolerance/endurance			
12. Understanding and following safety rules			
13. Fine motor skills			
14. Gross motor skills			
15. Ability to work with others			
16. Concentration			
17. Reaction to job/task changes			
18. Adjustment to repetitive tasks			
19. Ability to follow directions			
20. Quantity of work performance			
21. Quality of work performance			
22. Work attitude			
23. Initiative			
24. Motivation			
25. Accepts constructive criticism			
26. Accepts constructive authority			
27. Concentration			
28. Communication skills (speech)			
29. Completes assigned tasks			
30. Follows directions			
31. Remembers verbal directions			
32. Assumes responsibility			
33. Attention span			
34. Care of equipment and materials			
35. Frustration tolerance			
36. Perseverance			
37. Thoroughness			

Comments:

Recommendations:

Figure 5-23. An example of a checklist used to document learner behaviors.

Work Samples

Work samples simulate tasks that are closely associated with jobs in the labor market. The activities performed in work sample situations should be as realistic as possible. They incorporate the tools and standards associated with the actual job. An effective work sample parallels a specific or general work environment in its performance requirements, physical demands, decision-making requirements, tools, equipment, and machinery.

A basic function of work samples in almost any setting is to provide hands-on experiences for individuals who need exposure to a work environment. They can then make more realistic career choices about what they can do and would like to do after they have had an opportunity to try out representative tasks from actual occupational areas.

Work samples are a common component of the vocational assessment process because they emphasize performance skills and approximate work more closely than written activities and tests. These activities provide the observer with an opportunity to watch actual work behavior in a controlled setting. Results of observation and feedback lead to direct information rather than biased decisions based on little more than personal opinion.

Learners with special needs profit from work sample activities because they provide practical hands-on experiences. These experiences can assist learners in identifying their strengths and limitations, determining a realistic career goal, increasing self-esteem, and generating interest in the variety of career and technical education program alternatives available. At the same time, work sample activities provide the evaluator with observation information concerning the work habits, manipulative skills, physical abilities, interpersonal skills, and work capacity of the specific learner. This information is helpful in analyzing vocational potential, selecting appropriate training programs, and identifying necessary program modifications. The results of work sample evaluation can provide a useful tool in career counseling, program development, and job placement.

When selecting a commercial system to use with learners from special populations consideration should be given to the range of jobs available in the community compared to the range of jobs represented in the work sample system, validity and reliability data for special populations, and the specific objectives of the work sample battery compared to necessary information needed about the learners. Brolin (1976) identified a series of questions to ask when considering a commercial work sample system:

- Does the system take into account academic limitations?
- Does the system take into account verbal limitations?
- Does the system take into account experience limitations?
- Does the system take into account expectancy to fail?
- Does the system allow for more than one trial on tasks?
- Does the system allow for repeated instruction and check for comprehension?

- Does the system have face validity (i.e., is it an accurate assessment of the content presented)?
- Does the system allow for appropriate conditions for testing (i.e., does it offer pleasant surroundings, orderly administration, and considerations for fatigue of individuals)?
- Is the system adequately normed on learners with special needs?

There are several advantages of using commercial work samples in the vocational assessment process. Commercial work samples tend to motivate learners because they are more like real job tasks than paper and pencil activities. Although an individual's performance on work samples cannot predict success in actual job situations, it can provide the evaluator with important observational information about functional ability, work attitudes, and vocational interests. Work sample activities also provide experiences in following oral directions.

There are several disadvantages in using commercial work samples in the vocational assessment process. The systems are often expensive and time-consuming to administer. Some work samples that are supposed to represent various occupational areas are too simple and do not present a realistic view of the job. The norms provided for work sample performance may not relate to the learner being assessed.

Informal work samples such as locally developed work samples can represent an excellent means of assessment because they are more closely associated with the limitations and demands of the local labor market than commercially developed work samples. Work sample activities can be developed by career and technical personnel to evaluate the abilities of learners to perform specific work tasks. Informal work samples are generally not as expensive as commercial work sample systems. The tools, equipment, and supplies used in regular career and technical education programs are used in informal work sample experiences. These samples cannot always represent the total classroom curriculum, but they include tasks that suggest a potential for successful performance in the career and technical education program and help to point out potential areas for remediation and support services.

Informal work samples can be used to

- provide career exploration activities for learners with special needs;
- assess the work habits, coordination, physical capacity, and social skills of learners with special needs before they are enrolled in a specific career and technical education program;
- assess the abilities and limitations of learners with special needs after they have enrolled in a specific career and technical education program; and
- evaluate the skills that learners with special needs have developed in the career and technical education program before they exit the program and/or are placed in a job situation.

Career and technical education instructors should follow this sequence of basic steps when developing a work sample:

1. Survey the local career and technical education program curricula to determine programs that will be available to learners.

2. Based on the information collected, decide which courses are appropriate for work sample development.

3. Analyze the classroom environment and specific tasks to be simulated by the work sample. It is very important that the skills required for the class are the same as those represented in the work sample. If the skills are not the same, the work sample will not be valid.

4. Design the work sample by developing activities that simulate the tasks expected for a specific class. Keep in mind prerequisite skills that may be necessary, tools, equipment and materials used on the job, working conditions and the work environment associated with the career and technical education program, and criteria for successfully completing the work sample.

5. Determine how the work sample will be explained and/or demonstrated to learners with special needs. It is critical to have the sample reviewed by the career and technical education instructor who actually teaches the class before using it as an assessment tool.

6. Establish scoring criteria. The career and technical education instructor should identify what will be expected of learners who complete the work sample. Considerations in scoring may include: desirable work habits, quality of work produced, quantity of work produced, and time required to complete the work sample.

7. Pre-test the work sample with learners who have special needs before using it as an evaluation tool. This procedure will help to identify any problems that might arise while you are administering the work sample to the learner.

The recommended procedure for using informal work samples as an assessment tool includes the career and technical instructor first demonstrating the work sample and then asking the learner to perform it. If any reading is required, the material should be written at the fifth- or sixth-grade level. Tindall and Gugerty (1991) suggested that in evaluating learner performance during work sample activities, teachers should rate at least one factor from each of the following behavior groups:

<u>Group One</u>
- eye-hand coordination
- manual dexterity
- bi-manual dexterity
- use of hand tools
- measuring ability
- work pace

<u>Group Two</u>
- attention span
- ability to follow a model
- ability to follow verbal instruction
- performing a sequential task

<u>Group Three</u>
- persistence
- frustration toleration
- maturity

<u>Group Four</u>
- response to praise
- response to criticism
- reaction to assistance
- attitude toward work (p. 487)

It is often helpful to keep track of the vocational assessment activities that a specific learner has been involved in so that appropriate career planning decisions can be made. See Figure 5-24.

Case Study . . . Suzanne

Suzanne was referred to the transition coordinator in her school district for vocational assessment. After completing the basic Level I interest and aptitude inventories, Suzanne's career goal was still not clear. At that point, it was decided that she should try some work samples to experience the tasks involved in specific occupational areas. Her interest and aptitude results indicated that carpentry and drafting were two possible areas that might be appropriate for her.

The district had purchased a commercial work sample system for use in the vocational assessment process. The specific work samples selected were matched with the specific career and technical education programs available. The first work sample that Suzanne tried was the one involving carpentry skills. The evaluator seated her at the workstation. A variety of tools used in carpentry were on the worktable. A VCR was also mounted on the table. An audiovisual introduction was shown on the VCR. It provided Suzanne with information about work-related competencies involved in carpentry. The videotape went on to orient her to the proper use of the tools and equipment that were at the workstation. The next phase of the work sample activity took Suzanne through a step-by-step simulation in carpentry. The task was to make a product out of dowels, a board, and plywood. The task involved measuring, laying out, cutting, hammering, chiseling, and drilling the pieces for fabrication. The videotape instructed and illustrated each step of the task. Suzanne watched the screen, listened, and followed the directions given to her. She was allowed to stop the video presentation when she had trouble keeping up with the task.

While Suzanne was working on this task, the evaluator was observing her performance. She was rated on the speed and quality of her work. Her scores were compared to norm group scores to see how she performed compared to others. At the end of the task, the evaluator also asked Suzanne to rate herself for speed and quality of work.

VOCATIONAL ASSESSMENT CHECKLIST

Student: _____

Date of Referral: _____

Individual(s) Involved in Assessment Process: _____

_____

_____

Expressed Vocational Goal:

Assessed Vocational Interest:

Interest Summary:

Aptitude Summary:

_____ 1. Referral information (e.g., who made initial referral, eligibility for vocational evaluation):

_____ 2. Biographical information (e.g., student record information, academic information, social/family information, vocational/prevocational information, medical information):

_____ 3. Student orientation to vocational assessment process (e.g., orientation process, who explained the process, student reaction to orientation, possible problems):

_____ 4. Psychometric testing results (e.g., name, date and results of aptitude tests, dexterity tests, interest inventories):

_____ 5. Work sample results (e.g., description, date and results of student participation in commercial and/or information work sample activities):

_____ 6. Observation information (e.g., results of one-to-one conference with student after completion of vocational assessment components):

_____ 7. Student interview (e.g., results of one-to-one conference with student after completion of vocational assessment components):

_____ 8. Situational assessment information (e.g., student performance on job related tasks in a career and technical education program and/or performance on the job):

Summary and Recommendations:

Figure 5-24. An example of a checklist used to document information collected during the vocational assessment process.

DEVELOPING A LEARNER PROFILE

An important component of the vocational assessment process is the collection and organization of relevant information about the learner. This information should be organized into a learner profile. The profile should contain information in the following areas:

Educational/academic/psychological–The educational/ academic/psychological component of the learner profile should be compiled and used as a guide to the individual's achievement and potential in academic areas. Academic ability is certainly not the only consideration for vocational and employment placement. However, information compiled in this section of the learner profile can be beneficial in analyzing and applying the educational strengths and limitations of a specific individual as they relate to vocational development

and eventual employment opportunities. This information should also be used in identifying necessary program modifications. See Figure 5-25.

An important benefit of the vocational assessment process in middle/junior and high school years is the development of a vocational profile for the learner. The vocational profile is created by working together and drawing from assessment results, parents, professionals, and the learner. The profile begins with a summary of the assessment results. It goes on to describe a learner's personal and vocational attributes, as well as strengths and weaknesses. Recommendations regarding potential career direction and training programs suitable for the learner are also included. Instead of the learner simply entering a specific career and technical education program through default, as too often happens,

---

SUGGESTED BACKGROUND INFORMATION FOR LEARNER PROFILE-EDUCATIONAL/ACADEMIC/PSYCHOLOGICAL COMPONENT

The following educational, academic, and psychological information would be helpful in developing a learner profile to contribute to the vocational assessment process:

1. Overall performance levels (i.e., standardized achievement results):
   a. Reading level: _____
   b. Comprehension level: _____
   c. Mathematics level: _____
   d. Spelling level: _____
2. School achievement records (e.g., rate of learning = below average, average, above average): _____
3. Permanent record/Transcripts (i.e., grades): _____
4. Language development (speech or comprehension difficulty):
   a. listening skills: _____
   b. relating messages/information: _____
5. Psychological assessment:
   a. test used: _____
   b. date: _____
   c. test results: _____
6. Communication skills (e.g., conversation skills, writing skills): _____
7. Attendance records (i.e., attendance history, reasons for excessive absences): _____
8. Student's strong learning style:
   a. Visual (i.e., reading, demonstrations): _____
   b. Auditory (i.e. lecture, oral directions): _____
   c. Kinesthetic (i.e., motor or hands-on activities): _____
9. Appropriate instructional techniques: _____
10. Perceptual-motor kills development: _____
11. Specific problems that student is experiencing in academic areas: _____
12. Student's academic strengths: _____
13. Student's academic weaknesses: _____
14. Results of vocational interest batteries: _____
15. Specific teach observation reports: _____

Figure 5-25. Sample educational, academic, and psychological background information used in compiling a learner profile.

the assessment recommendations are based upon what the learner likes and dislikes, what skills the learner is capable of attaining or is good at, and where improvements need to be made. Following are the components of the learner profile:

- Physical/medical–The physical/medical component of the learner profile should be compiled and used as a guide to the individual's general health, physical capacities, and limitations as they relate to vocational development and eventual employment opportunities. This information should also be used in identifying necessary program or job modifications. See Figure 5-26.
- Social/interpersonal relations–The social/interpersonal relations component of the learner profile should be compiled and used as a guide to the individual learner's social skills and ability to get along with others. Important information in this area includes observation and data relating to maturity, work attitudes and habits, family background, and relationships with both peers and authority figures. See Figure 5-27.
- Prevocational/vocational–The prevocational/vocational component of the learner profile should be compiled and used as a guide to the individual's background preparation in prevocational skills, experiences in career and technical education programs, employment history, and expressed career goals. See Figure 5-28.

Each local district/campus should decide upon a format for a vocational assessment learner profile. This profile should contain all of the relevant pieces of information about the learner that are necessary in order to make appropriate career placement and planning decisions. See Figure 5-29.

SUGGESTED BACKGROUND INFORMATION FOR LEARNER PROFILE-PHYSICAL/MEDICAL COMPONENT

The following physical and medical information would be helpful in developing a learner profile to contribute to the vocational assessment process:

1. Condition of general health: _____
   a. Results of general medical examination: _____
   b. Date of general medical examination: _____
2. Physical capactites/limitation (i.e., strength, stamina, chronic illness, physical disabilities, etc.): _____
3. Sensory development: _____
4. Motor development: _____
   a. Fine motor skills: _____
   b. Gross motor skills: _____
5. Vision ability: _____
6. Hearing ability: _____
7. Manual and finger dexterity: _____
8. Eye-hand coordination: _____
9. Ability to cope physically in classroom/laboratory/job situations: _____
10. Modifications necessary in classroom/laboratory/job situations: _____
11. Modifications necessary in equipment/machinery/tools: _____
12. Is the student currently on medication? _____
13. If yes, what is the medication used for? _____
14. Possible side effects of the medication: _____
    a. Possible effect(s) of the medication on the social ability of the individual: _____
    b. Possible effect(s) of the medication on the emotional stability of the individual: _____
    c. Possible effect(s) of the medication on the academic ability of the individual: _____
    d. Possible effect(s) of the medication on the ability of the individual to perform/complete job assignments: _____

Figure 5-26. Sample physical and medical background information used in compiling a learner profile.

SUGGESTED BACKGROUND INFORMATION FOR LEARNER PROFILE- SOCIAL/INTERPERSONAL RELATIONS COMPONENT

The following social and interpersonal information would be helpful in developing a learner profile to contribute to the vocational assessment process:

1. Ability to cope socially in classroom/laboratory/job situation: _____
2. Ability to cope emotionally in classroom/laboratory/job situation:_____
3. Ability to cope in group activities: _____
4. Attitude:

   _____ defiant/hostile   _____ aggressive

   _____ antisocial   _____ withdrawn

   _____ passive   _____ other (specify)

   _____ moody

5. Motivation level: _____
6. Relationship with peers: _____
7. Relationship with teacher: _____
8. Personality characteristics:

   General attitude toward school: _____   Assumes responsibility: _____

   Accepts authority: _____   Maturity: _____

   Cooperation with adults: _____   Self-control: _____

   Cooperation with peers: _____   Reaction to criticism: _____

   Appropriate conduct: _____   Other (specify): _____

   Decision-making skills: _____

9. Grooming/Personal hygiene habits: _____
10. General family situation: _____

Figure 5-27. Sample social and interpersonal relations background used in compiling a learner profile.

SUGGESTED BACKGROUND INFORMATION FOR LEARNER PROFILE- PREVOCATIONAL/VOCATIONAL RELATIONS COMPONENT

The following prevocational and vocational information would be helpful in developing a learner profile to contribute to the vocational assessment process:

1. Results of formal vocational assessment (standardized tests, formal work sample, formal activities): _____
   _____
2. Results of aptitude tests: _____
3. Results of informal vocational assessment activities (exploration activities, job tryouts, situational assessment): _____
   _____
4. Results of interest surveys: _____
5. Results of student interview:

   Student interest: _____

   Career goal: _____
6. Prevocational background: _____
7. Work-study experience: _____
8. Work history (including employer's comments): _____
9. Career and technical information classes taken: _____
10. Student self-assessment (e.g., analysis of abilities, limitations, projected lifestyle): _____
11. Knowledge of tool usage: _____
12. Are work habits consistent with employment demands?_____
13. Vocational strengths: _____
14. Vocational weaknesses: _____

Figure 5-28. Sample prevocational and vocational background information used in compiling a learner profile.

VOCATIONAL ASSESSMENT LEARNER PROFILE ...

Student:_____

Assessed by:_____ Date:_____

I. Interests:

Measured

	Highest		Lowest	

Instrument _____ Date   Valid _____

Expressed   _____

_____

II. Aptitudes:

Cognitive Development	Low 1	2	3	High 4	Not Assessed
Reasoning					
Numerical					
Language					
Mechanical					

Perceptual/Motor Ability	Seriously Deficient 1	Deficient 2	Acceptable 3	Very Good 4	Not Assessed
Spatial Relations					
Form Perception					
Clerical Perception					
Motor Coordination					
Finger Dexterity					
Manual Dexterity					

...VOCATIONAL ASSESSMENT LEARNER PROFILE...

III.   **Commercial Work Sample Experiences:**

Work Sample	Summary of Performance

IV.   **Informal Work Sample Experiences:**

Vocational Program Area/Job Title	Work Sample Title/Description	Summary of Performance

V.   **Career and Technical Program Tryout Experiences:**

Career and Technical Program	Length of Time	Tasks Completed	Summary of Performance

VI.   **Situational Assessment:**

Assessment Activity (Name, description)	Learner Strengths	Learner Weaknesses

VII.   **Basic Skills Levels:**

Reading _____

Math _____

Language/Communication _____

Other _____

VIII.   **Student Preferred Learning Style(s):**

_____

_____

...VOCATIONAL ASSESSMENT LEARNER PROFILE

IX. Work Behaviors:

	Much Improvement Needed	Some Improvement Needed	Acceptable	Very Good	Not Assessed
	1	2	3	4	
Motivation					
Grooming/Hygiene					
Temperament					
Relationship with Co-workers					
Relationship with Authority					
Relationship with Self					
Relationship with Work Environment					

ANALYSIS OF INFORMATION

I. Learner Strengths or Assets _____

_____

II. Learner Weaknesses or Deficiencies _____

_____

III. Recommended Placement _____

    1. Postsecondary/Community College Program (specify) _____

    2. Regular career and technical program with minor modifications (specify) _____

    3. Work Experience/Coop Program (specify suggested job site area) _____

    4. Further career and technical exploration (specify program areas) _____

    5. Prevocational skills training _____

    6. Community worksite/job tryout (specify) _____

IV. Vocational Program Goals (if placement is recommended) _____

_____

V.

Specific Career and Technical Program Objectives	Suggested Strategies for Delivering Content (Match to Learning Style and Ability Levels)	Curriculum Modification	Support Services/ Assistance Necessary

Additional Comments _____

_____

Figure 5-29. A sample learner profile compiled through the vocational assessment process.

Portfolios

Authentic assessment (AA) is any type of assessment requiring learners to demonstrate skills and competencies that realistically represent problems and situations that may be encountered in daily life. Learners are required to produce ideas, to integrate knowledge, and to complete tasks that have real-world applications. Such approaches require the person making the assessment to use human judgment in the application of criterion-referenced standards. Authentic assessments stand in contrast to traditional educational testing and evaluation, which focuses on reproducing information such as memorized dates, terms, or formulas.

Assessments are authentic when they have meaning in themselves—when the learning they measure has value beyond the classroom and is meaningful to the learner. AAs address the skills and abilities needed to perform actual tasks. The following are tools used in authentic assessment: checklists (of learner goals, writing/reading progress, writing/reading fluency, learning contracts, etc.); simulations; essays and other writing samples; demonstrations or performances; intake and progress interviews; oral presentations; informal and formal observations by instructors, peers, and others; self-assessments; and constructed-response questions.

Authentic assessments must be carefully designed and evaluation criteria rigorously selected. Among the characteristics of good AA are the following:

- engaging, meaningful, worthy problems or tasks that match the content and outcomes of instruction
- real-life applicability
- multistaged-demonstrations of knowing, knowing why, and knowing how
- emphasis on product and process, conveying that both development and achievement matter
- rich, multidimensional, varied formats, both on-demand (in-class essays) and cumulative (portfolios)
- opportunities for learner self-evaluation
- cognitive complexity-reburying higher order thinking skills
- clear, concise, and openly communicated standards
- fairness in scoring procedures and their application

This process of assessment is potentially more equitable in accommodating learning styles and acknowledging multiple ways of demonstrating competence. AAs do not necessarily have to replace other forms of evaluation but can be used to augment and broaden the picture of learner progress. One of the most common forms of an AA is the development of a learner portfolio. Portfolios are collections of learners' work over time. A portfolio often documents a learner's best work and may include other types of process information, such as drafts of the learner's work, the learner's self-assessment of the work, and the parents' assessment. Portfolios may be used for evaluation of the learner's abilities and improvements.

Portfolio assessment is a multifaceted process characterized by the following recurrent qualities:

- It is continuous and ongoing, providing both formative (i.e., ongoing) and summative (i.e., culminating) opportunities for monitoring learners' progress toward achieving essential outcomes.
- It is multidimensional, covering a wide variety of artifacts and processes reflecting various aspects of a learner's learning process.
- It provides for collaborative reflection, including ways for learners to reflect about their own thinking processes and metcognitive introspection as they monitor their own comprehension, to reflect upon their approaches to problem-solving and decision-making, and to observe their emerging understanding of subjects and skills.

Although approaches to portfolio development may vary, all the major research and literature on portfolios reinforces the following characteristics:

- They clearly reflect stated learner outcomes identified in the core or essential curriculum that learners are expected to study.
- They focus upon learners' performance-based learning experiences as well as their acquisition of key knowledge, skills, and attitudes.
- They contain samples of work that stretch over time
- They contain a variety of work samples and evaluations of that work by the learner, peers, teachers, and possibly even parents.

There are several types of portfolios:

- Documentation portfolio–This type is also known as the working portfolio. Specifically, this approach involves a collection of work over time showing growth and improvement reflecting learners' learning of identified outcomes. The documentation portfolio can include everything from brainstorming activities to drafts to finished products. The collection becomes meaningful when specific items are selected to focus on particular educational experience or goals. It can include the best and weakest of learner work.
- Process portfolio–This approach documents all facets or phases of the learning process. It is particularly useful in documenting learners' overall learning process. It can show how learners integrate specific knowledge or skills and progress towards both basic and advanced mastery. Additionally, the process portfolio inevitably emphasizes learners' reflection upon their learning processes through the use of reflective journals, think logs, and related forms of metacognitive processing.
- Showcase portfolio–This type of portfolio is best used for summative evaluation of learners' mastery of key curriculum outcomes. It should include learners' very best work, determined through a combination of learner and teacher selection. Only completed work should be included. In addition, this type of portfolio is especially compatible with audio-visual artifact development, including photographs, videotapes, and

electronic records of learners' completed work. The showcase portfolio should also include written analysis and reflections by the learner upon the decision-making processes used to determine which works were included.

Moya and O'Malley (1994) identified five features typifying model portfolios that can be used as a systematic assessment tool in instructional planning and learner evaluation.

1. Comprehensive–The potential for determining the depth and breadth of a learner's capabilities can be realized through comprehensive data collection and analysis. A comprehensive approach (a) uses both formal and informal assessment techniques; (b) focuses on both the processes and products of learning; (c) seeks to understand learner language development in the linguistic, cognitive, metacognitive, and affective domains; (d) contains teacher, learner, and objective input; and (e) stresses both academic and informal language development.

   Although comprehensiveness is a critical component of a good portfolio procedure, a portfolio can too quickly become an aggregation of everything a learner produces. A screening procedure needs to be established that will include only selected, high-priority information in the portfolio. The degree of comprehensiveness should be tempered by practical limitations of the evaluation environment, such as teacher-learner ratios and workloads. Setting realistic goals for portfolio assessment increases the probability of sustained interest and use.

2. Predetermined and systematic–A sound portfolio procedure is planned prior to implementation. The purpose of using a portfolio, the contents of the portfolio, data collection schedule, and learner performance criteria are delineated as part of portfolio planning. Each entry in the portfolio has a purpose, and the purpose is clearly understood by all portfolio stakeholders.

3. Informative–The information in the portfolio must be meaningful to teachers, learners, staff, and parents. It also must be useable for assessment, instruction, and curriculum adaptation to the learner needs. A mechanism for timely feedback to the teachers and learners and a system for evaluating the utility and adequacy of the documented information are characteristics of a model portfolio procedure.

4. Tailored–An exemplary portfolio procedure is tailored to the assessment purpose for which it will be used, to classroom goals and objectives and to individual learner assessment needs. Assessment instruments and procedures are adapted to match information needs, to reflect learner characteristics, and to coincide with learner linguistic and developmental capabilities.

5. Authentic–A good portfolio procedure provides learner information based on assessment tasks that reflect authentic activities.

The following are the advantages of using portfolio assessment:

- It allows the evaluator to see the learner, group, or community as individual, each unique with its own characteristics, needs, and strengths.
- It serves as a cross-section lens, providing a basis for future analysis and planning. By viewing the total pattern of the community or of individual participants, the evaluator can identify areas of strengths and weaknesses, and barriers to success.
- It serves as a concrete vehicle for communication or exchanges of information among those involved.
- It promotes a shift in ownership; communities and participants can take an active role in examining where they have been and where they want to go.
- It offers the possibility of addressing shortcomings of traditional assessment and of assessing the more complex and important aspects of an area or topic.
- It covers a broad scope of knowledge and information from many different people who know the program or person in different contexts and environments (e.g., participants, parents, teachers or staff, peers, or community leaders).

COOPERATIVE PLANNING

Vocational assessment should be a cooperative process involving a variety of professionals and specialists who offer a continuum of services. Personnel who can provide relevant information and expertise for this process include the following:

- administrators (e.g., career and technical education, special education, general school/district administrators)
- evaluators
- special needs and transition personnel
- special education personnel
- guidance personnel
- career and technical education instructors
- academic teachers
- health personnel
- social workers
- hearing clinicians
- speech clinicians
- psychologists
- physical therapists
- occupational therapists
- rehabilitation personnel
- learners
- parents/guardians

Primary individuals involved in vocational assessment include the following:

- Administrators–Administrators help facilitate vocational assessment activities within the school-based curriculum. They can promote the establishment of a vocational assessment process that involves a variety of personnel.

- Special needs and transition personnel–These personnel are usually assigned the responsibility for facilitating vocational assessment at the local/campus level. These educators do not necessarily conduct all of the assessment activities but generally are responsible for overviewing the process and ensuring that all learners from special populations have access to the assessment process. They are often the people who coordinate the school-based team and organize the information collected through assessment in the learner profile. In addition, these individuals usually coordinate the provision of support services to learners with special needs who are enrolled in career and technical education programs.
- Vocational evaluators–Some states require evaluators to have certification prior to employing them. However, most states have not established minimum standards for evaluators and there is a great diversity regarding credentials, job requirements, roles, and responsibilities. Therefore, the approach to vocational assessment differs greatly from state to state, from district to district.
- Counselors–Counselors usually work with a variety of educational personnel to coordinate vocational assessment activities. Many counselors are actively involved in administering assessment instruments (e.g., interest inventories, aptitude tests, learning style inventories). They compile the information, interpret the results for learners, parents, other educators, and help learners to make decisions based on a realistic career goal. A working knowledge of the available career and technical education programs is essential for counselors. In addition, they need to be thoroughly familiar with the assessment instruments, administration guidelines, accommodations for learners with linguistic or cultural differences, and utilization of results in context to available career and technical education programs.
- Career and technical education instructors–These instructors may be involved in the initial referral for learners with special needs who require vocational assessment services. These instructors often become involved in developing, administering, interpreting, and relating informal curriculum-based vocational assessment activities to their classrooms and laboratories. Instructors must take vocational assessment information and relate it to their curriculum in order to identify areas for remediation and necessary support services that learners may require. They will be responsible for providing training to learners with special populations. Therefore, they must be provided with relevant information about learners as well as recommendations that might help them succeed in the program.
- Special education personnel–Formal and informal assessment is often conducted by special education personnel. Information from these assessments should be shared with counselors, vocational special needs coordinators, and career and technical education instructors so that appropriate career plans can be developed for learners with disabilities who are enrolled in career and technical education programs
- Bilingual teachers–Bilingual personnel assist in facilitating vocational assessment activities for limited English-proficient learners and interpret results to learners and parents.
- Parents–Parents can provide invaluable information about observations and perceptions from the home environment. They should be a part of the assessment process so that realistic career goals can be set for their son or daughter.
- Learners–Learners should be involved in the interpretation of assessment results and the planning of their career pathway. An awareness of their limitations and strengths will help them to make more realistic career decisions.

The number of people involved in the vocational assessment process and the extent of their involvement depend on a number of factors, including the amount of time allotted for collecting assessment information, the availability of the people, and the nature or amount of relevant information required for the assessment process.

CONSIDERATIONS IN CONDUCTING VOCATIONAL ASSESSMENT

A number of considerations should be addressed when developing and implementing a vocational assessment process. Several key considerations are addressed in the following sections.

Knowledge of Career and Technical Education Programs

A primary goal of vocational assessment is to provide effective career counseling to an individual so that an appropriate career and technical education program can be identified. It is important that individuals helping learners make career choices have a full understanding of each program available to the learner, including the competencies necessary for its successful completion as well as multiple exit points. An in-depth analysis of the curriculum and competencies can provide information about the skills, physical capacities, temperaments, and work environments involved in job titles intrinsic in each program. This information can be provided by the vocational instructors who teach the programs. Providing extensive information about the career and technical education programs in which learners from special populations will be entering will promote collaborative planning among educators and help to coordinate the resources and support services necessary for these learners to succeed in these programs.

Career Pathways

A career pathway is a coherent course of study that prepares an individual with the academic and career specific skills needed for entry into a broad cluster of related occupations and/or admission into postsecondary education.

All pathway groups, such as Engineering/Industrial, include entry-level, skilled, and professional occupations. See Figure 5-30. Job titles listed under the "Entry" column typically require a high school diploma and some orientation training. Job titles listed under the "Technical/Skilled" column typically require a postsecondary

ENGINEERING/INDUSTRIAL SYSTEMS CAREERS ...			
Pathway Ladders and Postsecondary Majors			
	Entry	**Technical/Skilled**	**Professional**
Automotive and Transportation	Auto Service Center Attendant Apprentice Technician Brake Technician Collision Repair Apprentice Detailer Porter	Aircraft Mechanic Auto Collision Technician Diagnostician Diesel Mechanic Estimator Parts Store Owner/Operator	Auto Dealership Owner/Manager Automotive Engineer Automotive Instructor Body Shop Owner/Manager Manufacturing Representative Service Manager
Communications Technology	Cable Installer Cellular Phone Installer Computer Hardware Installer Electrician's Helper	Design Technician Repair Technician Instrumentation Technician Sales and Service	Designer Engineer Radio Frequency Research/Design Specialist Station Manager Systems Design
Construction	Bricklayer Building Maintenance Worker Cabinetmaker's Helper Carpenter's Apprentice Electrician's Helper Journeyman Plumber Painter Roofer's Helper Welding Technician	Cabinetmaker Carpenter Heating and Air Conditioning Technician Licensed Electrician Licensed Plumber Pipefitter Quality Control Inspector Roofer	Architect Builder/Developer Construction Trades Teacher Construction Supervisor Engineer Master Plumber Master Electrician Welding Inspector
Industrial	Technician's Assistant Computer Operator Construction Worker Technician Drafter Trainer Mechanic's Assistant Machine Operator	Auto Technician Computer Maintenance Technician Construction Foreman Designer Drafter Electronic Technician Mechanical Technician	Architect Civil Engineer Construction Supervisor Construction Superintendent Electrical Engineer Mechanical Engineer Senior Draftsperson
Technology Manufacturing	Assembly/Solderer Fitter Machine Operator Materials Handler Welder	Finisher Machinist Quality Control Inspector Robotics/Automation Specialist Tools and Die Maker Welder Technician/Inspector	Business Owner Electrical Engineer Welding Engineer

Entry positions may require a high school diploma, GED, and/or on-the-job training
Technical/Skilled positions may require junior/technical/community college or apprenticeship.
Professional positions may require a bachelor's degree or advanced degree.

... ENGINEERING/INDUSTRIAL SYSTEMS CAREERS

Typical College Majors

Aerospace Engineering	Civil Engineering	Material/Metallurgical Engineering
Agricultural Engineering	Computer Engineering	Mechanical Engineering
Architectural Engineering	Electrical Engineering	Metallurgy
Bioengineering	Environmental Engineering	Nuclear Engineering
Biomedical Engineering	Industrial Engineering	Petroleum Engineering
Chemical Engineering	Marine Engineering	Textile Science and Engineering

Community College/Technical School Programs

Airframe and Power Plant Technology	Drafting	Machinist
Automotive Technology	Electrical/Electronic Technician	Plumber/Pipefitter
Computer Maintenance Technology	Electrician	Robotics
Construction Trades	Electronics	Welding
Diesel Engine Mechanic	Heating, Air Conditioning, and Refrigeration	

Figure 5-30. Sample of jobs for a given career pathway.

degree/certificate (e.g., associate's degree). Job titles listed under the "Professional" column typically require a baccalaureate degree. Flexibility is allowed horizontally as an individual increases the level of education and technical training.

Following are characteristics of career pathways:
• They are for all learners
• They organize each learner's course of study for the learner's entire learning experience in 11th and 12th grades.
• The course of study within a career pathway can be tailored to an individual learner's unique career and educational goals. Learners can work with their families, teachers, and counselors to select a course of study that includes career and technical courses in their career path, academic courses that are integrated into their career path, a structured work-based experience, and a capstone application project. To support informed choices by learners, schools are encouraged to offer a freshman orientation course on career investigation and a sophomore course for exploring each of the career pathways available during the learner's junior and senior years.
• Each pathway should offer courses of study designed for different anticipated job entry points—from high school, from an associate's degree or advanced technical training program, from a baccalaureate program—yet all must provide the rigorous academics essential for entry to postsecondary education. All learners within a career pathway, regardless of the planned job entry point, can enroll in courses focused on core skills common across the career pathway. This will prevent tracking.

• Each pathway offers seamless articulations with appropriate postsecondary programs
• Each pathway offers performance-based assessments and career portfolios that earn learners industry-recognized credentials that enhance employment opportunities through demonstrated skill accomplishment.
• Schools offering career pathways have more flexible scheduling and block scheduling to accommodate the different learning paths.

The career pathway approach enables all learners to pursue a career-related course of study that integrates academic and occupational content with work-based learning. Focus on a broad occupational theme and contextual learning can motivate learners and enrich classroom learning with practical experiences. The use of innovative instruction and integrated teaching methods enables all learners to apply skills and knowledge to solve problems typically encountered in the workplace. Within the career pathway organization, learners can begin to make informed decisions about their future. These decisions will be grounded in a more realistic understanding of workplace requirements and a greater appreciation for individual abilities, preferences, needs, and interests. In the end, all learners will be better prepared for their school-to-school and school-to-work transitions (Mooney, n.d.).

Selecting a career pathway provides an individual with an area of focus along with flexibility and a variety of careers to pursue. Although people change jobs many times, they seldom change from one pathway to another. The career pathway system offers
• a career development plan for all learners, regardless of their interests, abilities, talents or desired level of education;

- basic skills for all learners, regardless of the level of education or training they choose to attain;
- a variety of specific occupational choices, each requiring a different level of education and training;
- maximum flexibility in the career decision-making process, allowing learners to move between pathways at any time without a gap or penalty;
- a way for learners to discover the relevance of their selected school courses to actual occupations and careers; and
- an opportunity for learners to assess their own performances, improve where necessary, and attain personal and career goals.

Before selecting a pathway, learners are exposed to a wide variety of occupations in introductory career exploration courses. Each pathway offers occupation-related course work and training in transferable work-related skills. Career pathways provide an efficient way for learners to move from skill acquisition to skill application, from observation to hands-on activities, and from school-based learning to successful workplace performance.

Career pathways can encompass a variety of occupations so that all learners can fully participate. Occupations included in career pathways range from requiring highly skilled to moderately skilled backgrounds and include broad areas such as business and finance, health and human services, agriculture and natural resources, and communication technology, to name a few. Career pathways are often determined by local economic needs, teacher expertise, and labor market trends. Learners can join the workforce immediately after completing high school, or they can continue their career pathway as part of their postsecondary education. Several school systems, in fact, have organized pathways that lead into local postsecondary programs and/or link with technical preparation programs. Career paths that are linked to business, industry, labor, governments, and the community lead to further education and employment.

The use of career pathways moves away from training learners only for specific occupations. Instead, a broad-based approach is taken in which learners not only learn skills for a specific occupational area but also acquire concepts and skills that can be transferred to any occupation. For example a learner may need additional training in interpersonal communication. Rather than narrowly focusing instruction on job-specific procedures and processes, the career pathway approach provides much needed application and relevance. This approach prepares learners for a labor market in which change and mobility are standard. In addition, career pathways provide many opportunities for contextualized instruction in school and at the workplace (Mooney, n.d.).

- Arts/Communications/Humanities–Occupations in this career pathway are related to the creative, visual, craft, and performing arts. These include architecture, graphic design, interior design, fashion design, writing, film, fine arts, journalism, languages, media, advertising, public relations, and music.
- Business–Occupations in this career pathway are related to business occupations, administration, management, marketing, and sales. These include entrepreneurship, sales, marketing, computer/information systems, finance, accounting, personnel, economics, and management.
- Health services–Occupations in this career pathway are related to the promotion of health and treatment of disease. These include research, prevention, treatment, and related health technologies.
- Human services–Occupations in this career pathway are related to economic, political, and social systems. These include education, government, law and law enforcement, leisure and recreation, military, religion, child care, social services and personal services.
- Engineering/Industrial systems–Occupations in this career pathway are related to technologies necessary to design, develop, install, and maintain physical systems. These include engineering, manufacturing, construction, service, and technologies.
- Natural resources/Agriculture–Occupations in this career pathway are related to agriculture, the environment, and natural resources. These include agricultural sciences, earth sciences, environmental sciences, fisheries, forestry, horticulture, and wildlife.

SCANS

The Secretary's Commission on Achieving Necessary Skills (SCANS) was appointed by the Secretary of Labor to determine the skills our young people need to succeed in the world of work. The commission's fundamental purpose is to encourage a high-performance economy characterized by high-skills, high-wage employment. The primary objective is to help teachers understand how curriculum and instruction must change to enable learners to develop those high-performance skills needed to succeed in the high-performance workplace. See Figure 5-31.

SCANS has focused on one important aspect of schooling: what they called the "learning a living" system. In 1991, they issued their initial report, *What Work Requires of Schools*. As outlined in that report, a high-performance workplace requires workers who have a solid foundation in the basic literacy and computational skills, in the thinking skills necessary to put knowledge to work, and in the personal qualities that make workers dedicated and trustworthy.

High-performance workplaces also require other competencies: the ability to manage resources, work amicably and productively with others, acquire and use information, master complex systems, and work with a variety of technologies.

These foundation skills and workplace competencies should be assessed so that individuals are prepared to enter the global workforce of the future. The SCANS Commission suggested that each learner be provided with a certificate of initial mastery (CIM) that records the level of mastery demonstrated by the learner in the SCANS foundation skills and competencies. See Figure 5-32.

SCANS COMPONENTS

FOUNDATION SKILLS

1. Basic Skills – Reading, writing, arithmetic and mathematics, listening, and speaking
2. Thinking Skills – Creative thinking, decision making, problem solving, seeing things in the mind's eye, knowing how to learn, reasoning
3. Personal Qualities – Responsibility, self-esteem, sociability, self-management, integrity/honesty

WORKPLACE COMPETENCIES

1. Resources – Identifies, organizes, plans, and allocates time, money, materials, facilities and human resources
2. Information – Acquires and uses information, acquires and evaluates data, organizes and maintains files, interprets and communicates, uses computers
3. Systems – Understands complex interrelationships, understands systems, monitors and corrects performance, improves or designs systems
4. Technology – Works with a variety of technologies, selects, applies, maintains, and troubleshoots equipment
5. Interpersonal – Works with others
   a. Participates as a member of a team, contributes to group effort
   b. Teaches others new skills
   c. Services clients/customers (works to satisfy customer expectations)
   d. Exercises leadership, communicates ideas to justify position, persuades and convinces others, responsibly challenges existing procedures and policies
   e. Negotiates, works toward agreements involving exchange of resources, resolves divergent interests
   f. Works with diversity, works well with men and women from diverse backgrounds

Source: U.S. Department of Labor. (1992). *Learning a Living: A Blueprint for High Performance – A SCANS Report for America*. Washington, DC: Author.

Figure 5-31. Outline of SCANS components with necessary skills and competencies.

National Skill Standards Board

The National Skill Standards Board (NSSB) is an unprecedented coalition of leaders from business, labor, employee, education, community, and civil rights organizations created in 1994 to build a voluntary national system of skill standards, assessment, and certification systems to enhance the ability of the United States workforce to compete effectively in a global economy. These skills are being identified by industry in full partnership with labor, civil rights, and community-based organizations. The standards are based on high-performance work and are portable across industry sectors.

The NSSB has categorized the workforce into the following 15 industry sectors that, under the guidance of the NSSB, are assembling skill standards, assessment and certification for their respective industries.

- agriculture, forestry, and fishing
- business and administration services
- construction
- education and training
- finance and insurance
- health and human services
- manufacturing, installation and repair
- mining
- public administration, legal and protective services
- restaurants, lodging, hospitality and tourism, and amusement and recreation
- retail trade, wholesale trade, real estate and personal services
- scientific and technical services
- telecommunications, computers, arts and entertainment, and information
- transportation
- utilities and environmental and waste management

In 1992 and 1993, the U.S. Departments of Labor and Education entered into cooperative agreements, called demonstration projects, with 22 organizations that represented a wide range of industries. Each project demonstrated an approach to setting voluntary skill standards. Building on these activities, in June 1996, the National Skill Standards Board sponsored nine one-year grants to 12 industry and research groups. These projects served as living laboratories of a national voluntary skill standards system.

The following industries have developed national skill standards through the National Skill Standards Board:
- advanced high-performance manufacturing
- agricultural biotechnology
- air conditioning, heating, and refrigeration
- automobile, auto body, medium/heavy truck
- bioscience
- chemical process industries
- computer-aided drafting and design
- electrical construction
- electronics/consumer electronics
- electronics/high-tech
- grocery
- hazardous materials management technology
- health care
- heavy highway/construction and environmental remediation
- hospitality and tourism
- human services

SCANS CERTIFICATE OF INITIAL MASTERY

Jane Smith 119 Main Street Anytown Home Phone: (817) 555-7373	Date of Report: 5/1/92 Soc. Sec.: 000-00-0000 Date of Birth: 3/7/73 Age: 19

SCANS Workplace Competency	Date	Proficiency Level
Resources	10/91	1
Interpersonal Skills	12/91	2
Information	11/92	3
Technology	1/92	2
Systems	4/92	3

Core Academic and Elective Courses	Date	Proficiency Level
English	11/91	3
Mathematics	12/91	3
Science	2/91	3
History	4/91	2
Geography	8/91	1
Fine Arts	11/91	4
Vocational/Industrial Education	4/92	2

SCANS Personal Qualities	Average Rating	No. of Ratings
Responsibility	Excellent	10
Self-esteem	Excellent	10
Sociability	Excellent	8
Self-management	Excellent	7
Integrity/Honesty	Good	6

Portfolio and Other Materials Available	Reference	
1. Report on grounds keeping (chemistry)	Mr. Kent	
2. Video on architectural styles (social studies)	Ms. Jones	
3. Newspaper article written	Ms. French	

Extracurricular Activities	Role	Date	Reference
Newspaper	Reporter	9/89 - 1/90	Frank Jones (advisor)
Basketball varsity	Center	9/90 - 6/91	Dean Smith (coach)

Awards and Honors	Date	Source	Reference
Teen Volunteer of the Year	6/91	Rotary Club	John Grove
Class secretary	9/91 - 1/92	Lincoln High	Emma Rice

Points Toward Certificate of Initial Mastery	Earned	Required
	300	500

(Supplied by student) Work Experience	Date	Place	Reference
Volunteer work	6/88 - 6/89	St. Joseph homeless shelter	Father John O'Connell (508)555-3304
Summer camp counselor	6/81 - 8/87	Camp Kiowa	Susan Miller (508) 555-5128
Office (word processor)	1/90- 5/92	PDQ secretarial help	Myrna Copper (508) 555-0202

Source: U.S. Department of Labor. (1992). *Learning a Living: A Blueprint for High Performance – A SCANS Report for America.* Washington, DC: Author.

Figure 5-32. A sample certificate of initial mastery.

- industrial laundry
- metalworking
- photonics
- printing
- retail trade
- welding

One of the primary goals of the National Skill Standards Board is to create an environment where people can easily communicate messages about work and what it takes to be competitive in the current and future workplace.

Benefits to Employers. A national system of skill standards increases competitiveness by boosting workforce quality; streamlines and reduces costs for employee recruitment, hiring, retention, and promotion; and encourages a high-performance workplace, improving the way work is organized and human resources are used.

Benefits to Educators and Trainers. The development of a national system of voluntary skill standards requires the assistance and expertise of educators and trainers. No one else plays a more important role in helping current and future workers achieve the necessary skills for success in the workplace. Skill standards benefit educators and trainers by assisting them in developing criteria, providing the context for learning, improving assessment, building partnerships, and demonstrating performance.

Benefits to Current and Future Employers. The clear requirements set out by skill standards help raise wages by raising competencies and business productivity; create long-term security by providing a personal, portable portfolio of skill and certifications; and improve opportunities by offering more complete learning options tied to real-world career information.

Benefits to Organized Labor. The development of fair and equitable skill standards processes helps unions achieve their broad societal goals of improving employment opportunities for workers. It also encourages a greater focus on continuing skill upgrading, providing clear guidelines for assessing workers' skills and aptitudes, and enhancing the capacity of works to actively contribute to workplace change and economic prosperity.

Benefits to Communities. Everyone benefits from improved employment opportunities, higher standards of living, and economic security. Labor unions, educators, job training programs, and other community organizations are all vital partners in skill standards development.

Knowledge and Appropriate Use of Vocational Assessment Instruments

Educators involved in developing a vocational plan for a learner with special needs must become familiar with standardized test administration, reliability, validity, and normative information for each formal vocational assessment instrument. Without this background these instruments can be misused and the information misinterpreted.

The use of formal assessment instruments, with their standardized directions for administration and scoring, makes it difficult, if not impossible, to make appropriate accommodations and modifications for learners from special populations. Norm referenced tests, for example, allow no deviation from standard administration and compare each individual to the performance of the norm population. Group testing procedures, often required in standardized testing procedures, make it difficult for some learners who have special needs. For example, some learners may have difficulty comprehending information, reading written test items due to perceptual problems or problems concentrating. If these problems are not accommodated, the results of standardized instruments cannot be considered valid.

Aids for Vocational Assessment Interpretation

There are a number of helpful tips that should be kept in mind when interpreting vocational assessment information:

- Before administering a test or inventory, it is necessary to state the nature and purpose of the activity. Sample questions that can be covered include "Why was the test given?" "What can the test do? What can the test not do?" "Who will receive the test results?" "What will the test results cover and how they will be used?"
- In interpreting the results, strengths should be emphasized and weaknesses discussed objectively.
- Recall of test results appears to be highest when the learner has been involved in the interpretations interview.
- Graphic presentations or auditory presentations should be selected based on the learner's style.
- Type of language required in test interpretation should be related to the capacities of the learner.
- Test-taking disposition of the learner is of considerable importance. An individual's motivations can affect the validity of the test results in different ways.
- It is necessary to see if the group on which an instrument was normed is similar to the group being assessed (Silvestri, n.d.).

Legal Issues in Vocational Assessment

There are legal implications involved in conducting vocational assessment activities that educators should be aware of. The reality of lawsuits based on issues of discrimination, inaccurate or misinterpreted test results, and unqualified evaluators should be addressed while planning, implementing, and monitoring assessment activities. Barrett (1987) made the following suggestions for individuals administering assessments regarding legal considerations:

- The purpose of the assessment should be clear.
- There should be a written analysis of the specific training program or job the assessment is designed to measure.
- The validity and reliability studies of all the instruments used should be known.

- Those administering assessments should be able to cite evidence that the instruments used were free from bias and discrimination.
- The evaluator and others involved in the assessment process should hold state certifications to perform their part in the process.
- The assessment findings should be correctly interpreted and used in the decision-making process.
- Professionals who administer assessments should understand normative data and be certain that publishers have representative norm groups.
- The professional interpreting the assessment findings should be aware of his or her cultural and gender biases and be especially careful to provide all possible options to learners.
- Oral and written career assessments for people with limited English proficiency should be in their native language.
- Professionals must keep abreast of new procedures and instruments as the field of career assessment of special populations advances.

Ethics in Vocational Assessment

The American Association for Counseling and Development's (AACD) Ethical Standards for Measurement and Evaluation were reported by Flanagan, et al. (n.d.) as follows:

The primary purpose of educational and psychological testing is to provide descriptive measures that are objective and interpretable in either comparative or absolute terms. The examiner must recognize the need to interpret the statements that follow as applying to the whole range of appraisal techniques including test and nontest data. Test results constitute only one of a variety of pertinent sources of information for counseling decisions.

- The examiner must provide specific orientation or information to the examinee(s) prior to and following the test administration so that the results of testing may be placed in proper perspective with other relevant factors.
- When making any statements to the public about tests and testing, the examiner must give accurate information and avoid false claims or misconceptions. Special efforts are often required to avoid unwarranted connotations of such terms as IQ and grade equivalent scores.
- Different tests demand different levels of competence for administration, scoring, and interpretation. Examiners must recognize the limits of their competence and perform only those functions for which they are prepared.
- The purpose of testing and the explicit use of the results must be made known to the examinee before testing.
- The examiner must proceed with caution when attempting to evaluate and interpret the performance of minority group members or other persons who are not represented in the norm group on which the instrument was standardized.

Confidentiality in Vocational Assessment

As a team begins the vocational assessment of a learner, it is essential for the team to obtain parental/guardian permission. The Family Educational Rights and Privacy Act (The Buckley Amendment) addressed the confidentiality of school records. This law allows for the following learner/parental rights:

1. Parents have the right to inspect and review education records within a reasonable period of time, but in no case more than 45 days after the request has been made.
2. Parents have the right to reasonable requests for explanations and interpretations of the records and the right to obtain copies of the records from the educational agency or institution.
3. Postsecondary institutions must exercise limitations on the right to inspect and/or review educational records. Whenever a learner has attained 18 years of age, or is attending an institution of postsecondary education, the rights and privileges previously belonging to the parents are transferred to the 18 year old.

The Elementary and Secondary Education Amendments of 1967 also addressed parental rights as follows:

1. No federal funds will be made available to schools that deny parents "the right to inspect and review any and all official records, files, and data directly related to their children."
2. Such data specifically include scores on standardized intelligence, aptitude, and psychological tests, interest inventory results, and teacher or counselor ratings and observations.

Confidentiality is a very important factor that must be considered when collecting, organizing, interpreting, and applying vocational assessment data. Parents have a legal right to access all records, including the results of standardized tests, aptitudes, interest inventories, personality inventories, and observation and rating checklists. The consent of the parent/guardian must be obtained before records and information can be released for learners under the age of 18.

Diversity Considerations in Vocational Assessment

Maddy-Bernstein (1991) stated that the issue of race and cultural bias in assessment instruments has received much press due to criticism by those who contend that most assessment instruments penalize minorities. Assessment findings for those persons who have limited English proficiency have also been suspect because of both culturally biased instruments and the group's inability to clearly understand written and/or oral English. Lopez-Valadez (1988) noted that people who have limited English proficiency are being assessed with inappropriate instruments, if at all. There have also been complaints of sex biases in many assessment instruments. Another problem with some standardized assessment tools has to do with the exclusion of special needs populations from norm groups. Barrett (1987) suggested that interest surveys are the most inaccurate and biased of all the assessment instruments and yet many profound decisions are based on their findings. See Figure 5-33.

Assessing Limited English-Proficient Learners

Limited English-proficient (LEP) learners need special considerations during the vocational assessment process. McCarty-Warren and Hess-Grabill (1988) stated that although the language demands vary across occupations,

---

CULTURAL APPROPRIATENESS RATING CRITERIA

DIRECTIONS

In this category, the rater should assess the cultural appropriateness of the test directions administered to the child. Concepts reflected in the directions should be comprehensible and clear. A rating will be given based on the following system:

0 = No manual

1 = Incorrect, major mistakes in translation

2 = Incorrect, several instances where this is need for retranslation

3 = Acceptable, but still likely to have questions from child

4 = Very acceptable, no problems anticipated

ITEM CONTENT

Evaluation within this category centers on the cultural appropriateness of the test items. of critical concern is whether the conceptual and behavioral elements expressed in each item are compatible with the cultural background of students for whom the instrument was assigned. A rating will be applied based on the following:

1 = Inappropriate, major mistakes in concepts

2 = Acceptable, but several items require elimination or revision

3 = Acceptable, almost no items require elimination or revision

4 = Very acceptable, no changes required

VOCABULARY

The cultural appropriateness of semantic content in test items is also to be assessed. Rater should check to see that the language used is neither too formal nor too informal and that regional differences in language don't discriminate unfairly between one subgroup and another of a given language. A rating will be based on the following:

0 = Not utilized

1 = Incorrect, consistently poor choice of words throughout items

2 = Acceptable, but several items should be revised

3 = Acceptable, alternatives might be chosen but otherwise OK

4 = Very acceptable, no changes required

ILLUSTRATIONS

In this category, the rater is asked to judge the cultural implications of pictorial and graphic elements of the instrument. Items should be easily identifiable by children of the culture for whom the instrument was designed. The follow scale will be used:

1 = Inappropriate, most illustrations reflect one culture

2 = Acceptable, some illustrations need to be eliminated or changed

3 = Acceptable, almost no illustrations require change

4 = Very acceptable, no illustrations require change

FORMAT

Attention should be given to the cultural appropriateness of an instrument's visual design. This means taking into consideration the positioning of test items and the spacing allowed between test items in both the test booklet and the answer sheet. Here, care should be taken to distinguish between weak layouts that would penalize all children equally and culturally biased layouts that would penalize children of a specific culture. The following scale will be used:

1 = Inappropriate, requires major changes in layout design

2 = Acceptable, some changes are required

3 = Acceptable, a few changes are needed

4 = Very acceptable, no changes are necessary

Source: McCarty-Warren, T., & Hess-Grabill, D. (1988). *Vocational Assessment of Secondary Special Needs Students.* Normal, IL: Illinois State University, Office of Specialized Vocational Research.

Figure 5-33. Guidelines for assessing the level of cultural appropriateness of a test.

it is advisable to assess all four language skill areas: listening, speaking, reading, and writing. Since some support services as well as instructional and testing materials may be provided in the learner's native language, it is also important to determine how proficient or literate a learner is in the language spoken in the home.

Unfortunately, formal instruments are not available for all languages. In this case, informal strategies such as structured interviews, writing, samples, Cloze exercises, and short reading comprehension tests can yield basic information. It may be necessary to recruit the assistance of an adult or older learner who is proficient in the target language and can communicate in English. It is not recommended that relatives conduct the assessment as their evaluations are often too subjective.

Answers to the following questions yield some clues as to native language proficiency:

- How many years of formalized schooling has the learner completed in the native language?
- What is the level of educational attainment of the learner's parents?
- Does the learner read materials written in the learner's native language? What type?
- Does the learner have any training or work experience in the native language?

When testing limited English-proficient learners, the time constraints should be adjusted to adapt for the language barrier or the test instructions should be translated into the learner's native language. Bilingual or bicultural personnel should assist with test selection, modification, administration, and interpretation. When testing for the interests, aptitudes, and abilities of these learners instruments or methods should be identified that are in the learner's native language, do not rely on extensive aural or reading skills in English, and are adaptable or adapted to second language learners.

For the language minority learner who may benefit from career and technical education, accurate measurement can assure equal access to the full range of vocational opportunities and services mandated by law. The use of appropriate techniques and strategies can provide appropriate assessment information that will allow educators to make appropriate plans for the learner. The following general modifications should be considered during the vocational assessment process for LEP learners:

1. Use multiple techniques and tools, especially those that do not rely heavily on English reading skills (e.g., multisensory instruments, performance activities).
2. Pause frequently when speaking, speak slowly and clearly, use active verbs instead of passive ones, use body language, and use visual aids. This facilitates communication during the assessment process.
3. Use translated instruments in the native language of the learner whenever possible. Be sensitive to dialectical variances and cultural biases that may be present in a translated instrument.
4. Use shadowing to determine whether or not the course/job requirements are within the learner's ability level and/or scope of interest.
5. When using paper and pencil tests to assess the LEP learner, allow extra time, dictionaries, and aides to provide additional assistance in clarifying directions and to help the learner understand slang or expressions with which they are unfamiliar.
6. Use graphic ratings (combining few words with space on a continuum) and numerical rating sheets during observation activities.
7. Use self-rating exercises. They can be very valuable because they bypass translations and allow learners to develop thoughts and criteria within their own language structures.
8. Conduct learner interviews to determine
   - vocational interests and goals;
   - career/job awareness skills;
   - functional skills and acculturation;
   - educational levels and background in the learner's native language and/or country;
   - learning styles/preferences;
   - oral communication ability level; and
   - potential barriers to participation (e.g., financial or personal).
9. Develop portfolios. Portfolios present an ongoing selection of a learner's work. There is a growing consensus in the field of education that doing a portfolio presents the most appropriate assessment of achievement for LEP learners. In developing portfolios
   - emphasize that learners are not only preparing work for a teacher to read and grade, but rather to be better prepared for the world of work (e.g., future employers, community organizations, school committees);
   - promote teamwork (English often evolves out of a consensus approach); and
   - have learners illustrate their accomplishments and vocational competencies through photographs, graphs, graphics, designs, and constructed models.
10. Use project evaluation to assess the learner. Projects are a short-range approach of assessing a learner's ongoing progress. Assessment through project evaluation retains the factor of actively demonstrating performance, which is beneficial in assessing LEP learners (Todd, Fiske, & Dopico, 1994).

Assessing Culturally and Linguistically Diverse Learners

The National Information Center for Children and Youth with Disabilities (n.d.) reported the following:

- There is a great deal of research and numerous court decisions to support the fact that standardized tests (particularly intelligence and achievement tests) are often culturally and linguistically biased against learners from backgrounds different from the majority culture. On many tests, being able to answer questions correctly often depends upon having specific cultural-based information or knowledge. If learners have not been exposed to that information through their culture or have not had the experiences that led to gaining specific knowledge, then they will not be able to answer certain questions at all or will answer them in a way that is considered "incorrect" to the majority culture. This can lead to inappropriate conclusions about learners' ability to function within the school setting.

- When learners come from a nondominant culture or speak a language other than English, care must be taken in how they are evaluated. All professionals involved in the assessment process need to be aware that their beliefs and perceptions may not match those of the population they serve. Because most cognitive, language, and academic measures are developed using the standards of the majority English-speaking culture, their use with learners who are not from that culture may be inappropriate. Therefore, it is imperative that the evaluation team collect the majority of their information about the learner in other ways, such as through interviews, observations, and approaches like dynamic assessment, which has shown promise for use with minority learners.

- It may be particularly useful to gather information from the home environment, which will help the assessment team develop an understanding of the learner within his or her own culture. To facilitate this, parents need to communicate openly with the school and share their insight into their child's behaviors, attitudes, successes, and needs, and when appropriate, information about the minority culture.

- Before conducting any formal testing of a learner who is a non-native speaker of English, it is vital to determine the learner's preferred language and to conduct a comprehensive language assessment in both English and that native language. Examiners need to be aware that it is highly inappropriate to evaluate learners in English when that is not their dominant language (unless the purpose of the testing is to assess the learner's English language proficiency).

- Translating tests from English is not an acceptable practice either; the IDEA states that the tests and other evaluation materials must be provided and administered in the learner's primary language or mode of communication unless it is clearly not feasible to do so. If possible, the evaluator in any testing situation or interview should be familiar to the learner and speak the learner's language.

- When tests or evaluation materials are not available in the learner's native language, examiners may find it necessary to use English-language instruments. Because this is a practice fraught with the possibility of misinterpretation, examiners need to be cautious in how they administer the test and interpret the results. Alterations may need to be made to the standardized procedures used to administer tests. These alterations may include paraphrasing instruction; providing a demonstration of how test tasks are to be performed; reading test items to the learner rather than having the learner read them; allowing the learner to respond verbally rather than in writing; or allowing the learner to use a dictionary.

- However, if any such alterations are made, it is important to recognize that standardization has been broken, limiting the usefulness and applicability of the test norms. Results should be cautiously interpreted, and all alterations made to the testing procedures should be fully detailed in the report describing these learner's test performance. As mentioned earlier, it is also essential that other assessment approaches be an integral part of collecting information about the learner.

Testing Guidelines

Specific modifications and accommodations may need to be implemented when facilitating the vocational assessment process for learners from special populations. The following guidelines suggest possible accommodations that can be used during assessment:

1. When testing students, determine the level of reading comprehension necessary to understand the test questions and/or to follow the written directions. Consider putting the questions/directions on tape, have them read aloud, or use an informal instrument where questions/directions can be explained in simple, concrete language and practice time can be built into the process.

2. Students who have developed a negative attitude toward school due to a history of failure experiences or academic deficiencies should be assessed through hands-on performance-based assessment activities.

3. When testing students who have difficulty concentrating and attending to task, administer lengthy tests over several sessions rather than all at once. It may also help to administer the test(s) individually as opposed to large group or small group settings.

4. Students with physical disabilities may need assistance in recording answers on score sheets on paper-pencil instruments. Adaptive devices or modifications may be necessary during performance-based activities.

5. Determine the extent of hearing loss when testing hearing impaired learners so that accommodations can be made in the method of instruction. Interpreters should assist in delivering instructions to students who are deaf.

6. Written information on paper-pencil tests can be converted into a large print format for students with visual impairments. Some tests can be converted into braille for students who are blind. (McCarty-Warren & Hess-Grabill, 1988, pp. 41–43)

COMMUNICATING VOCATIONAL ASSESSMENT INFORMATION

Vocational assessment information should be shared with the variety of individuals who work as the collaborative team developing a realistic career and/or transition plan that mirrors the learners' abilities, interests, and special needs. See Figure 5-34.

USES OF VOCATIONAL ASSESSMENT INFORMATION

When vocational assessment is not a crucial part of the instructional process learners are frequently placed incorrectly. In order for appropriate placement in a career and technical education program to take place, as well as effective monitoring and follow-up procedures, the results of the vocational assessment activities must be a part of ongoing counseling and planning for the learner. Information obtained from vocational assessment activities should not be viewed in isolation. Rather, the results should be interpreted as they relate to other pertinent information.

The primary focus of vocational assessment should be the development of instructional goals and objectives that are appropriate for a specific learner as well as the identification of optimal strategies that should be used in career and technical education programs to effectively deliver the curriculum to the learner.

Assessment information should be used by educators to plan appropriate career preparation experiences for a specific learner. Among the most effective uses of assessment information for educational programming purposes are

- recommendations for prevocational skills, functional skills, and/or life skills that the learner should develop;
- recommendations for career exploration activities (e.g., career and technical education classroom/laboratory tryouts);
- recommendations for specific career and technical education program and/or academic course placement;
- specific instructional goals and objectives for the career plan being developed;
- identification of learning style(s) and suggested teaching techniques;
- recommendations for support services necessary for the career plan developed for the learner;
- recommendations for curriculum modifications in the specific career and technical education program; and
- recommendations for appropriate career goal(s) for learner.

ASSESSMENT INFORMATION DISSEMINATION					
	Learner	**Parents**	**Teachers**	**Counselor**	**Community Representative**
Interests	X	X	X	X	*
Current Strengths/Abilities	X	X	X	X	*
Achievement Levels/Compensatory Methods	X	X	X	X	*
Work Behaviors	X	X	X	X	*
Learning Styles	X	X	X	X	*
Aptitudes	X	X	X	X	*
Occupational Options	X	X	X	X	*
Weaknesses/Models of Remediation	X	X	X	X	*
Special Needs	X	X	X	X	*
Support Systems	X	X	X	X	*
Statistical Test Results	**				
Written Evaluation Summary	X (if 18 or older)	X	X	X	*

* Information should be given if requested or needed by the individual in order to provide services to the student

** Release of information is necessary

Source: Flanagan, M., Boyer-Stephens, A., Maxam, S., Hughey, J., & Alff, M. (n.d.). *Career Assessment Instrument Resource Guide.* Columbia, MO: University of Missouri-Columbia, Department of Special Education and Department of Practical Arts and Vocational-Technical Education.

Figure 5-34. Suggested dissemination of vocational assessment results to the individuals involved in educational planning.

Vocational assessment information should also focus on the environmental climate of a specific career and technical education program that may affect the ability of a learner to succeed. Lehmann and Hartley (1991) suggested that the following factors should be examined prior to matching a student with a particular career and technical education program to determine whether they can be modified or altered according to individual learner needs:

- Instructor Attitudes–What attitudes are expressed or demonstrated toward the learner?
- Physical Location and Layout of the Class–Is the setting accessible, can it be modified?
- Instructional Materials–Are instructional materials available that are appropriate for people with varying skill levels?
- Environment–How can lighting, sound, or seating be arranged to accommodate students?
- Equipment–Are tools and equipment functional for the student, or do they need to be adapted?
- Teaching Methods–Do instructional methods address the needs of learners with various learning styles? (p. 229)

Albright and Cobb (1988) identified the following questions to ask when reviewing vocational assessment information:

Placement
- Is career and technical education the most appropriate curriculum for the learner?
- Which career and technical education program is best suited to the learner?
- Responsible personnel–guidance counselors, special needs and transition personnel, special education teachers, parents, and learners
- Timing–semester prior to entrance into career and technical education program

Planning
- What type(s) of support services is the learner or the instructor going to need?
- How much support is necessary?
- Responsible personnel–career and technical education teachers, employers, learners, special needs and transition personnel, special education teachers, and parents
- Timing–prior to entrance into career and technical education program, during the first month of instruction, throughout the learner's participation in the career and technical education program

Monitoring
- How well is the learner progressing in the career and technical education program?
- Are any alterations in serving the learner called for based upon the learner's progress?
- Responsible personnel–employers, work supervisors, coworkers, learners, career and technical instructors, and special needs and transition personnel
- Timing–Throughout the duration of the career and technical education program

Transition
- What are the learner's expectations for the future?
- What information or support does the learner need to achieve desired goals?
- Responsible personnel–learners, career and technical instructor, career counselor, and special needs and transition personnel.
- Timing–planning begins upon the learner's entrance into career and technical education programming, specific services designed to assist the learner may be offered at the latest during the semester prior to completing the career and technical education program.

Tindall and Gugerty (1991) identified questions that vocational assessment can answer:

1. Is this student at the vocational awareness, exploration, or preparation stage and how was this determined?
2. In which occupational area is this student most interested and how was this determined?
3. For which occupational area(s) does this student have aptitude and ability and how was this determined?
4. What particular learning requirements will need to be met if this student is to succeed in a specific vocational and applied technology [career and technical] education program and how was this determined?
5. What particular employment outcome or post-school goal has been tentatively identified for this student? (pp. 454–6)

Using Vocational Assessment Results for Curriculum Modification

Lombard (1994) examined the type and extent of formal vocational assessments being conducted by educators within secondary schools in Wisconsin. Also investigated was the degree to which school staff utilized assessment information to carry out activities associated with the Perkins Act of 1990. The use of the MAGIC model was suggested as an alternative assessment approach for making curriculum or instruction modifications.

It appears that data drawn from traditional interests, aptitudes, and learning styles instruments are considered to be appropriate curricular and instruction modifications within career and technical education programs, the researchers suggest the use of alternative assessment approaches such as the MAGIC model. This assessment model incorporates both formal and informal vocational assessment strategies. It is designed to provide the information needed to increase access and successful completion of career and technical education programs for learners who are members of special populations. The five essential steps of the model include the following:

1. Make a predication–School personnel encourage learners to make tentative predictions regarding future career and technical education programs of study by using information from the formal assessment. Educators assist learners in examining the relationship between their interests and aptitudes to identify realistic program options.

2. Assess entry-level skills and learner outcomes–After appropriate career and technical education courses of study have been predicted, school personnel employ curriculum-based vocational assessment (CBVA) strategies to determine the type of curricular and/or instructional modifications needed. Informal CBVA strategies provide answers to the following curricular questions:

- What are the essential entry-level academic, career, and social skills required?
- What are the instructional preferences of the teachers?
- What evaluation approaches are employed by the instructor?
- What instructional and/or curricular modifications are needed?
- What are the learner outcomes associated with the course of study?

3. Guide learner acquisition of discrepant skills–After both formal and CBVA information has been collected, school personnel conduct a discrepancy analysis to determine which skills are required within a predicted course of study and which skills the learners already possess. The discrepant skills should then be defined as goals on IEP's and as a plan for learners to acquire these skills prior to entering the predicted course of study.

4. Instruct learner on generalization strategies–There is evidence that many learners with special learning needs have difficulty transferring skills from one environment to another. School personnel assist learners in acquiring independent behaviors that promote skill generalization. Generalization strategies that educators can use with learners include the following:

- teacher modeling followed by learner simulations
- use of verbal rehearsal techniques
- use of visual rehearsal techniques
- orientation of learners to settings where newly acquires skills can transfer
- application of newly acquired skills in multiple school and community settings

5. Coordinate maintenance checks following program placement–Following placement in career and technical education courses, school personnel must monitor the learner's progress toward exit level competencies. By evaluating learner performance, school staff determine if additional curricula and/or instructional modifications are required. See Figure 5-35.

The assurance of equal access to career and technical education courses for learners from special populations is only one of the issues related to meaningful vocational assessment approaches. Educators need to share the responsibility for implementing curriculum-based assessment methods in order to provide meaningful curriculum and instructional modifications. These modifications can increase the chances for learners with special needs to complete their chosen courses of study and subsequently enter the world of work with the skills and motivation they will need to be successful.

MAGIC VOCATIONAL ASSESSMENT PROGRAM

Make a Prediction for Student's Future
- Gather informal student data
  - Needs
  - Preferences
  - Interests
- Gather formal student data
  - Occupational interest
  - Vocational aptitude
  - Academic skills
  - Learning style
- Map career and technical congruence (direct connection between assessment results and career and technical education programs)

Assess Entry Level Skills
- Implement curriculum-based vocational assessment (CBVA)
- Conduct career and technical program inventory
  - Entry level skills
  - Applied academics
  - Vocational competencies
- Determine learner outcomes

Guide Skill Acquisition to Skill Mastery
- Coordinate discrepancy analysis
- Identify goals and objectives
  - Prioritize needs
- Instructional support
  - Direct
  - Indirect

Instruct for Generalization
- Skill rehearsal
- Orientation to applied work setting
- Activate skills in multiple settings

Conduct Maintenance Checks
- Ongoing assessment
  - Monitor student performance
- Modifications
  - Curricular
  - Instructional
- Evaluations
  - Student
  - Program

Source: Lombard, R., Larson, K., & Westphal, S. (1993). Validation of Vocational Assessment Services for the Special Populations in Tech Prep: A Model for Translating the Perkins Assurances. *The Journal for Vocational Special Needs Education, 1*(16), pp. 14-22.

Figure 5-35. The MAGIC model of vocational assessment.

SUMMARY

Individuals from special populations often need support services when participating in career and technical education programs. If the special needs of these learners are not identified and taken into consideration, there is a strong possibility that many of them will have difficulty succeeding in the programs in which they are enrolled. Placement decisions have often been made with little regard for learner abilities and interests and minimal attention paid to the demands and expectations of the career and technical education programs. Vocational assessment can provide information that will lead to appropriate placement and support services for each learner.

Vocational assessment is a comprehensive process conducted over a period of time, involving a multidisciplinary team with the purpose of identifying individual characteristics, education, training, and placement needs, which provides educators with the basis for planning an individual's career pathway. The primary objectives of vocational assessment in an educational setting are the development of instructional goals and objectives matched to a learner's needs, the identification of appropriate teaching strategies to promote learner competency, and the modification of curricula as necessary for learner success.

There is no single instrument or assessment tool sufficient for all learners or all purposes. Due to language barriers, cultural differences, different learning styles, and/or academic deficiencies, many learners from special populations have had difficulty with traditional assessment methods. Therefore, a variety of techniques should be available in order to collect relevant information about each learner so that appropriate decisions can be made regarding realistic career goals. Some of the most widely used methods for collecting vocational assessment information include interviews, vocational program tryouts, situational assessment, checklists, and work samples.

Assessment information should be used to plan appropriate career preparation experiences for a specific learner. Among the effective uses of assessment information for educational programming purposes are (a) recommendations for prevocational skills, functional skills, and/or life skills development; (b) recommendations for vocational exploration activities; (c) recommendations for specific career and technical education programs and/or academic course placement; (d) specific instructional goals and objectives for the career plan being developed; (e) identification of learner learning style(s) and suggested teaching techniques; (f) recommendations for support services for the learner's career plan; (g) recommendations for curriculum modifications in the specific career and technical education program; and (h) recommendations for appropriate career goal(s) for the learner.

SELF-ASSESSMENT

1. What is vocational assessment?
2. Why is vocational assessment process important?
3. What are the benefits of vocational assessment?
4. Discuss the importance of basic skills information in the vocational assessment process.
5. Discuss the importance of vocational interest information in the vocational assessment process.
6. Discuss the importance of vocational aptitudes and abilities in the vocational assessment process.
7. Discuss the importance of employability/work related skills in the vocational assessment process.
8. Describe the activities conducted during the Level I phase of vocational assessment.
9. Identify information collected and personnel involved in the Level I phase of vocational assessment.
10. Describe the activities conducted during the Level II phase of vocational assessment.
11. Identify information collected and personnel involved in the Level II phase of vocational assessment.
12. Describe the activities conducted during the Level III phase of vocational assessment.
13. Identify information collected and personnel involved in the Level III phase of vocational assessment.
14. Discuss the process of using interviews in collecting vocational assessment information.
15. Discuss the process of using career and technical education program tryouts in collecting vocational assessment information.
16. Discuss the process of using situational assessment in collecting vocational assessment information.
17. Discuss the process of using checklists in collecting vocational assessment information.
18. Discuss the process of using work samples in collecting vocational assessment information.
19. Why is the development of a learner profile and/or portfolio necessary for effective utilization of vocational assessment information?
20. Who should be involved in the vocational assessment process?
21. What are some formal vocational assessment measures?
22. What are some informal vocational assessment measures?
23. What is curriculum-based vocational assessment? What are some curriculum-based vocational assessment techniques?
24. What is community based assessment? What are some community-based assessment techniques?

25. How should vocational assessment information be used once it is collected?
26. Why is it important for personnel conducting vocational assessment information to have a knowledge of appropriate uses of vocational assessment instruments?
27. What legal issues should be considered when conducting vocational assessment?
28. What ethical standards should be considered when conducting vocational assessment?
29. What confidentiality issues should be considered when conducting, interpreting, and utilizing vocational assessment?
30. Why is it essential for individuals involved in vocational assessment to know the requirements of career and technical education.
31. How do racial and cultural biases affect the vocational assessment process?
32. What issues should be considered when assessing learners who have limited English proficiency?
33. Identify some effective testing guidelines for assessing individuals from special populations.

ASSOCIATED ACTIVITIES

1. Contact personnel in your district/campus who are in charge of vocational assessment for learners from special populations. These contacts may include special needs and transition personnel, special education personnel, career counselors, vocational rehabilitation personnel, and career and technical instructors. Discuss the initial referral process. Also ask to see a learner profile form. If none exists, suggest that a form be developed for use in the future.
2. Check with vocational assessment personnel to determine what commercial work sample batteries are used with learners who have special needs. Are these samples relevant to your program? Have these work samples been normed on the population(s) with which they will be used?
3. Work cooperatively with other staff members to develop informal work samples that can be used to assess learners with special needs. What specific information is necessary for successful participation in your program? How will vocational assessment information help you to better plan for these learners?
4. Develop a situational assessment checklist to use in observing learners with special needs participating in work tasks. This checklist should involve other personnel who may also be observing these learners.
5. Develop a job analysis information sheet that can be used to collect important information for use in your program.

REFERENCES

Albright, L., & Cobb, R. (1988). *Assessment of students with handicaps in vocational education: A curriculum-based approach.* Alexandria. VA: American Vocational Association.

Albright, L., & Cobb, R. (1988, Winter). Curriculum based vocational assessment. *The Journal for Vocational Special Needs Education, 10*(2), p.16.

Alessandro, T., & Hunsaker, P. (1993). *Communicating at work.* New York: Fireside.

The American College Testing Program. *Vocational interest, experience, and skill assessment.* Boston: Houghton Mifflin.

Barrett, S. (1987). The legal implications of testing. In P. LeConte (Ed.), *Using vocational assessment results for effective planning* (pp.105-110). Stevens Point, WI: The Department of Public Instruction.

Bigge, J. (1988). *Curriculum-based instruction for special education students.* Mountain View, CA: Mayfield.

Blankenship, C. (1985). Using curriculum-based assessment data to make instructional decisions. *Exceptional Children, 52*(3), 233-38.

Brolin, D. (1976). *Vocational preparation for retarded citizens.* Columbus, OH: Charles E. Merrill.

Brolin, D., & Gysber, N. (1989). Career education for students with disabilities. *Journal of Counseling and Development, 68,* 155-159.

Clark, G. (1998). *Assessment for transition planning.* Austin, TX: PRO-ED.

Cotton, K. (1993, November). *Developing employability skills.* Portland, OR: Northwest Regional Educational Laboratory.

Dade County Public Schools. (n.d.). *Curriculum-based vocational assessment handbook.* Miami, FL: Office of Vocational, Adult, Career, and Community Education.

Damaschke, G., & Nielsen, D. (n.d.). *APTICOM Report.* Racine, WI: Racine Unified School District.

deFur, S. (2000, November). *Designing individualized education program (IEP) transition plans.* Arlington, VA: ERIC Clearinghouse on Disabilities and Gifted Education.

Elementary and Secondary Education Amendments of 1967, Pub. L. 90-247, United States Statutes at Large, (81), 81. Washington, DC: U.S. Government Printing Office.

Elksnin, L., & Elksnin, N. (1993). A review of picture interest inventories: Implications for vocational assessment of students with disabilities. *Journal of Psychoeducational Assessment, 11,* 323-36.

Elksnin, N., & Elksnin, L. (1998). *Teaching occupational social skills.* Austin, TX: PRO-ED.

Esser, T. (Ed.). (n.d.). *Client rating instruments for use in occupational rehabilitation agencies.* Stout, WI: University of Wisconsin, Stout Vocational Rehabilitation Institute.

The Family Educational Rights and Privacy Act. (1974). Part 99 of Title 34 of the Code of Federal Regulations. 20 U.S.C. § 1232g; 34 CFR Part 99.

Flanagan, M., Boyer-Stephens, A., Maxam, S., Hughey, J., & Alff, M. (n.d.). *Career assessment instrument resource guide.* Columbia, MO: University of Missouri-Columbia, Department of Special Education and Department of Practical Arts and Vocational-Technical Education.

Hansen, J. (1995). *Interest assessment.* Greensboro, NC: ERIC Clearinghouse on Counseling and Student Services.

Hartley, N., & Lehmann, J. (1988). *Vocational assessment: Supplemental services manual.* Greeley, CO: University of Northern Colorado, Vocational Teacher Education Department.

Intermediate District 287. (n.d.). *Employability skills/work related skills.* Plymouth, MN: Hennepin Technical College.

Johnson, D., & Johnson, R. (1990). Social skills for successful group work. *Educational Leadership, 47,* 29-33.

Kennedy, T. (n.d.). *Vocational assessment report.* Port Huron, MI: Intermediate School District, St. Clair County.

Kingsbury, D. (1986). *Vocational assessment: A guide for improving vocational programming for special needs youth.* Bemidji, MN: Bemidji State University.

Lehmann, J., & Hartley, N. (1991). Effective assessment practices in vocational education. In Fry, R. *Fifth national forum on issues in vocational assessment: The issues papers.* Menomonie, WI: Materials Development Center, University of Wisconsin-Stout.

Lombard, R. (1991). Vocational assessment: A prevention vs. treatment model. In *Designated vocational instruction handbook.* Madison, WI: Wisconsin Department of Public Instruction.

Lombard, R. (1994, December). Vocational assessment practices: What works. *Office of Special Populations Brief, 6*(2). [Online]. Available: http://vocserve.berkeley.edu/Briefs/Brief62.html

Lombard, R., Larson, K., & Westphal, S. (1993). Validation of vocational assessment services for special populations in tech prep: A model for translating the Perkins assurances. *The Journal for Vocational Special Needs Education, 1*(16), 14-22.

Lopez-Valadez, J. (April, 1998). *Vocational education act: LEP position paper.* Unpublished manuscript, National Coalition for Vocational Education for Limited English Speakers.

Maddy-Bernstein, C. (1991). Special considerations regarding career assessment for special groups. *Career Planning and Adult Development Journal, 6*(4), 37-40.

McCarty-Warren, T., & Hess-Grabill, D. (1988). *Vocational assessment of secondary special needs students.* Normal, IL: Illinois State University, Office of Specialized Vocational Research.

Mooney, M. (n.d.) Career pathways. *Alliance Newsletter, 2*(1), 1-2.

Moya, S., & O'Malley, M. (1994, Spring). A portfolio assessment model for ESL. *The Journal of Educational Issues of Language Minority Students,* (13), 13-16.

National Information Center for Children and Youth with Disabilities. (1990). *Vocational assessment: A guide for parents and professionals.* Washington, DC: Author.

National Information Center for Children and Youth with Disabilities. (n.d.). *Assessing students who are culturally and linguistically diverse.* [Online]. Available: http://www.Kidsource.com/NICHCY/assessing.4.html

Phelps, L., & Lutz, R. (1977). *Career exploration and preparation for the special needs learner.* Boston: Allyn and Bacon.

Pickard, S. (1990). Integrating math skills into vocational education curricula. *The Journal for Vocational Special Needs Education, 1*(13), 9-13.

Prince George's County Board of Education. (1988). *Interest/learning style/aptitude vocational assessment.* Upper Marlboro, MD: Author.

Silverstri, R. (n.d.). *Diagnostic vocational assessment procedures for learning disabled individuals.* Sudbury, Ontario: YMCA Employment and Career Centers.

Sitlington, P., Clark, G., & Kolstoe, O. (2000). *Transition education and services for adolescents with disabilities.* Boston: Allyn and Bacon.

Sitlington, P., Neubert, D., & Leconte, P. (1997). Transition assessment: The position of the Division on Career Development and Transition. *Career Development for Exceptional Individuals, 20*(1), 69-79.

Smith, F., Lombard, R., Mewbert, D., Leconte, P., Rothernbacker, C., & Sitlington, P. (1995, October). Position paper on the interdisciplinary Council on Vocational Evaluation and Assessment. Arlington, VA: Council for Exceptional Children–Division on Career Development.

Technology-Related Assistance for Individuals with Disabilities Act Amendments of 1994, Pub. L. 103-218, United States Statutes at Large, (108), 50. Washington, DC: U.S. Government Printing Office.

Texas Education Agency. (1982). *Vocational assessment of students with special needs.* Austin, TX: Author.

Tindall, L., & Gugerty, J. (1991). *Still puzzled about educating students with disabilities?* Madison, WI: University of Wisconsin-Madison. The Vocational Studies Center.

Todd, S., Fiske, K., & Dopico, H. (1994). Vocational assessment for LEP students. *The Journal for Vocational and Special Needs Education, 16*(2), 16-28.

U.S. Department of Labor. (1992). *Learning a living: A blueprint for high performance – A SCANS report for America.* Washington, DC: Author.

U.S. Department of Labor. (2001). *Welcome to O*NET on-line.* Washington, DC: Author.

Vocational Evaluation and Work Adjustment Association. (1997). VEWAA position paper on the role of assistive technology in assessment and vocational evaluation. Colorado Springs, CO: Author.

What work requires of schools–A SCANS report for America 2000. (1991). Washington, DC: Department of Labor.

West, L. (1989). *Functional curriculum for transition: A resource guide.* Columbia, MO: University of Missouri-Columbia, Missouri Linc.

Individualized Education Programs

INTRODUCTION

One of the most important processes in which career and technical education personnel should be involved is the preparation, implementation, and evaluation of individual education programs (IEPs) for learners from special populations. When learners from special populations are integrated into career and technical education programs, it is important that the instructor and other school- and community-based personnel engage in a team effort to develop individual plans that will enable learners to succeed in meeting their career goals. The basic purposes of these plans include identifying realistic educational goals for learners with special needs, developing a system of accountability for providing specific educational services to these learners, and providing an open channel of communication among all personnel working with them.

Planning and implementing appropriate individual plans through a team effort is extremely important, and the success of the process is often determined by the effort expended in implementing the program contents. The vehicle for developing an individual education plan is based on a multidisciplinary assessment and is designed to meet the individual needs of each learner. This vehicle provides an opportunity for parents and educators to join together in establishing an appropriate educational experience for the learner. The result should be more continuity in the delivery of educational services.

A variety of individuals in a school-based setting should be involved in the development, implementation, and evaluation of these plans. They include transition coordinators, counselors, career and technical education instructors, administrators, special education personnel, support personnel, and parents. This chapter presents information about the development, use, and evaluation of IEPs for learners from special populations who are enrolled in career and technical education programs. Samples are provided to illustrate the component parts of an IEP as well as strategies to implement the plans and evaluate their success.

OUTLINE

THE INDIVIDUALIZED EDUCATION PROGRAM
COMPONENTS OF THE INDIVIDUALIZED EDUCATION PROGRAM
ROLE OF ASSESSMENT IN THE INDIVIDUALIZED EDUCATION PROGRAM
INDIVIDUALIZED TRANSITION PROGRAMS
SELF-DETERMINATION AND THE SELF-DIRECTED INDIVIDUALIZED EDUCATION PROGRAM
INDIVIDUALIZED EDUCATION PROGRAM TEAMS
REVIEWING AND REVISING THE INDIVIDUALIZED EDUCATION PROGRAM
USING THE INDIVIDUALIZED EDUCATION PROGRAM TO PLAN INSTRUCTIONAL DELIVERY
LEARNERS WITH A SECTION 504 ELIGIBLE DISABILITY
SECTION 504 ACCOMMODATION PLAN
INDIVIDUALIZED WRITTEN REHABILITATION PLANS
IMPLEMENTING THE INDIVIDUALIZED EDUCATION PROGRAM
SUMMARY
SELF-ASSESSMENT
ASSOCIATED ACTIVITIES
REFERENCES

OBJECTIVES

After completing this chapter the reader should be able to accomplishing the following:
1. Identify the essential components of an IEP.
2. Define what an IEP is for learners with disabilities.
3. Discuss the reason for developing IEPs for learners from special populations.

4. Describe the present level of educational performance mandated in the IEP.
5. Discuss the role of career and technical education personnel in determining the present level of educational performance.
6. Describe the annual goals and short-term objectives mandated in IEP.
7. Discuss the role of career and technical education personnel in determining annual goals and short-term objectives.
8. Discuss the specific educational services mandated in the IEP.
9. Discuss the role of career and technical education personnel in determining necessary educational services for a specific learner.
10. Discuss the extent of participation in regular education program activities mandated in the IEP.
11. Discuss the criteria for evaluating objectives and schedule for review mandated in the IEP.
12. Discuss the role of career and technical education personnel in establishing criteria for evaluating objectives of a learner's IEP.
13. Discuss the statement of transition services mandated in the IEP.
14. Discuss the career and technical education component of the IEP.
15. Identify the roles and responsibilities of members of the IEP team.
16. Describe the role of assessment in the development of the IEP.
17. Discuss methods of using the IEP to plan instructional delivery.
18. Discuss the ITP.
19. Discuss the IWRP for learners with disabilities.
20. Discuss the Section 504 accommodation plan.
21. List the benefits for career and technical education personnel participating in the IEP process.

TERMS

annual goal
assistive technology device
assistive technology service
career and technical education
   component of the IEP
individualized education
   program (IEP)

individualized transition program (ITP)
individualized written rehabilitation
   plan (IWRP)
major life activity
physical or mental impairment
present level of performance

related services
Section 504 accommodation plan
short-term objective
special education
special education teacher
transition services

THE INDIVIDUALIZED EDUCATION PROGRAM

The Individuals with Disabilities Education Act (IDEA), PL 101-476, passed in 1990, is the federal law that guarantees a free appropriate public education (FAPE) for eligible children and youth with disabilities. This law is one of several amendments to PL 94-142, the Education of the Handicapped Act (EHA), and is used by school systems around the country to guide the way in which special education and related services are determined and provided to eligible children and youth with disabilities. Passed in 1975, the EHA required that an individualized education program (IEP) be developed by a multidisciplinary team for each child or youth with a disability who was eligible for special education and related services. Among other things, the IEP was intended to set forth a plan for the services that would be provided to the learner.

The IEP is defined as a written statement for each child with a disability that describes the learner's educational program and is developed, reviewed, and revised in accordance with the IDEA. The IEP is a vital document, for it spells out, among other things, the special education and related services each learner will receive. An IEP is developed by a team that includes parents and school professionals and, when appropriate, the learner. The IEP should be developed with careful consideration of the learner's capabilities, strengths, needs, and interests. The IEP should direct the learner toward high expectations and toward becoming a successful member of the community and the workforce. It should function as the tool that directs and guides the development of meaningful educational goals. In short, it should assist the learner in meeting the goals of our educational system.

One important purpose of the IEP is to plan an educational program that is individually prescribed. The IEP is a general guide by which personnel can determine the most realistic direction to take. Goals and objectives help determine instructional activities to facilitate learner progress.

Another important purpose of the IEP is to provide a system of accountability for providing educational services to learners with disabilities. This accountability can be assured for a number of reasons. First, the IEP identifies specific personnel who will be responsible for implementing IEP contents. Second, a system for continuously monitoring learner progress is provided through the short-term instructional objectives and the criterion levels identified for each one. Third, the IEP provides for an open channel of communication among all personnel working with the learner. In this manner, a comprehensive, coordinated, and organized plan of action can be developed to meet the needs of the learner. The degree to which this coordinated effort is planned, implemented, and monitored greatly affects the level of success that the learner will experience in achieving the annual goals and short-term objectives. The IEP process also provides an opportunity for resolving any differences between the parents and the local educational agency concerning a learner's special education needs.

Developing an IEP for a learner comes as part of the special education process. The learner is first identified as having a disability, and then needed special education and related services are identified. An IEP is written after these determinations have been made. See Figure 6-1.

Generally, the IEP addresses services to be provided to the learner during one school year. But when it comes to transition requirements, the IEP team must think and plan several years ahead. The highest incidence of dropping out and of disciplinary action such as suspension or expulsion occurs during the first two years of high school. To combat this pattern, the IDEA requires that the IEP team carefully consider postschool goals when the learner is about to enter high school at age 14. Beginning at age 16 (or younger, if appropriate), a statement of the transition services needed by the learner must be included in the IEP.

There are two main parts of the IEP requirement: (1) the IEP meeting(s), where parents and school personnel jointly make decisions about an educational program for a learner with a disability, and (2) the IEP document itself, that is, a written record of the decisions reached at the meeting. The overall IEP requirement, comprised of these two parts, has a number of purposes and functions:

- The IEP meeting serves as a communication vehicle between parents and school personnel, and enables them, as equal participants, to jointly decide what the learner's needs are, what services will be provided to meet those needs, and what the anticipated outcomes may be.
- The IEP process provides an opportunity for resolving any differences between the parents and the agency concerning the special education needs of a learner with a disability—first, through the IEP meeting, and second, if necessary, through the procedural protections that are available to the parents.
- The IEP sets forth in writing a commitment of resources necessary to enable a learner with a disability to receive needed special education and related services.
- The IEP is a management tool that is used to ensure that each learner with a disability receives special education and related services appropriate to the learner's special learning needs.
- The IEP is a compliance/monitoring document that may be used by authorized monitoring personnel from each governmental level to determine whether a learner with a disability is actually receiving the free and appropriate public education agreed to by the parents and the school.
- The IEP serves as an evaluation device for use in determining the extent of the learner's progress toward meeting the projected outcomes.
- Teachers or other school personnel are not held accountable if a learner with a disability does not achieve the goals and objectives set forth in the IEP.

In addition to this, Heumann and Hehir (1997) state the following:
- IDEA '97 emphasizes the responsibility of parents and school personnel to work together and enhance the

effectiveness of the IEP. It also stresses the importance of linking a learner's IEP to all parts of the school day. In all states, parents must now be included in groups making eligibility and placement decisions about their children with disabilities. Previously, in some states, parents only had a right to be included in IEP meetings.

- Research tells us that IEP meetings have tended to focus on access to special education rather than on access to overall high-quality education. Indeed, they have rarely included the general education teacher. IDEA strengthens the IEP by requiring it to address critical areas of education planning associated with improved results as well as requiring a general education teacher to be part of the IEP team.

- Research also shows that although the integration of learners with disabilities into general education classrooms is associated with improved results, learners integrated without support and modifications have higher dropout rates. IDEA '97 explicitly requires that the IEP not only describe the extent to which a learner will be integrated, but also detail the aids, supports, and ac-

commodations the learner will receive within the inclusionary classroom.

- Recognizing the diversity of learners with disabilities, the law also requires that specific considerations be made for certain groups of disabled learners. IEP teams must consider, for example, communication needs of learners and the use of assistive technology for those who require it. In addition, the IEP team must also consider the use of behavior interventions, strategies, and supports in the case of behavior that impedes the learner's or others' learning processes.

- On the local government level, IDEA '97 underscores the fundamental idea that learners with disabilities should be learning what other learners are learning in school. Schools will be required to assume greater responsibility for assuring that learners with disabilities have access to the general education curriculum. School officials and parents must be jointly involved in placement decisions. Teachers and related services personnel will be required to keep parents regularly informed on the learner's progress.

THE BASIC SPECIAL EDUCATION PROCESS UNDER THE IDEA . . .

1. The child is identified as possibly needing special education and related services	Child Find. Each state must identify, locate, and evaluate all children with disabilities in the state who need special education and related services. To do so, they conduct Child Find activities. a child may be identified by Child Find, and parents may be asked if the Child Find system can evaluate their child. Parents can also call the Child Find system and ask that their child be evaluated. OR Referral of request for evaluation. A school professional may ask that a child be evaluated to see if he or she has a disability. Parents may also contact the child's teacher or other school professional to ask that their child be evaluated. This request may be verbal or in writing. Parental consent is needed before the child may be evaluated. Evaluation needs to be completed within a reasonable time after the parent gives consent.
2. The child is evaluated	The evaluation must assess the child in all areas related to the suspected disability. The evaluation results will be used to decide the child's eligibility for special education and related services and to make decisions about an appropriate educational program. If the parents disagree with the evaluation, they have the right to take their child for an independent educational evaluation (IEE). They can ask that the school system pay for this IEE.
3. Eligibility is decided	A group of qualified professionals and the parents look at the evaluation results. Together they decide if the child is a "child with a disability," as defined by the IDEA. parents may ask for a hearing to challenge the eligibility decision.
4. The child is found eligible for services	If the child is found to be a "child with a disability," as defined by the IDEA, he or she is eligible for special education and related services. Within 30 calendar days after the child is determined eligible, the IEP team must meet to write an IEP for the child.

Once the student has been found eligible for services, the IEP must be written. The two steps below summarize what is involved in writing the IEP.

5. IEP meeting is scheduled	The school system schedules and conducts the IEP meeting. School staff must • Contact the participants, including the parents; • Notify parents early enough to make sure they have an opportunity to attend; • Schedule the meeting at a time and place agreeable to parents and the school; • Tell the parents the purpose, time, and location of the meeting; • Tell the parents who will be attending; and • Tell the parents that they may invite people to the meeting who have knowledge or special expertise about the child.

. . . THE BASIC SPECIAL EDUCATION PROCESS UNDER THE IDEA

6. IEP meeting is held and the IEP is written	The IEP team gathers to talk about the child's needs and write the IEP. Parents and the student (when appropriate) are part of the team. If the child's placement is decided by a different group, the parents must be part of that group as well.
	Before the school system may provide special education and related services for the first time, the parents must give consent. The child begins to receive services as soon as possible after the meeting.
	If the parents do not agree with the IEP and placement, they may discuss their concerns with other members of the IEP team and try to work out an agreement. If they still disagree, parents can ask for mediation, or the school may offer mediation. Parents may file a complaint with the state education agency and may request a due process hearing, at which time mediation must be available.
7. Services are provided	The school makes sure that the IEP is being carried out as it was written. Parents are given a copy of the IEP. Each of the child's teachers and service providers has access to the IEP and knows his or her specific responsibilities for carrying out the IEP. This includes the accommodations, modifications, and supports that must be provided in keeping with the IEP.
8. Progress is measured and reported to parents	The child's progress toward the annual goals is measured, as stated in the IEP. His or her parents are regularly informed of their child's progress and whether that progress is enough for the child to achieve the goals by the end of the year. These progress reports must be given to parents at least as often as parents are informed of their nondisabled children's progress.
9. IEP is reviewed	The child's IEP is reviewed by the IEP team at least once a year, or more often if the parents or school ask for a review. If necessary, the IEP is revised. Parents, as team members, must be invited to attend these meetings. Parents can make suggestions for changes, agree or disagree with the IEP goals, and agree or disagree with the placement.
	If parents do not agree with the IEP and placement, they may discuss their concerns with other members of the IEP team and try to work out an agreement. There are several options, including additional testing, an independent evaluation, or asking for mediation (if available) or a due process hearing. They may also file a complaint with the state education agency.
10. Child is re-evaluated	At least every three years the child must be reevaluated. This evaluation is often called a "triennial." Its purpose is to find out if the child continues to be a "child with a disability," as defined by the IDEA, and what the child's educational needs are. However, the child must be reevaluated more often if conditions warrant or if the child's parent or teacher asks for the reevaluation.

Source: U.S. Department of Education. (2000, July). *A Guide to the Individualized Education Program.* Washington, DC: Office of Special Education and Rehabilitative Services. pp 2-4.

Figure 6-1. The steps in the special education process for identifying learners and needed services.

The Nebraska Department of Education (1998) developed a set of six foundations and indicators that can be helpful in developing and implementing an effective IEP:

1. The IEP is a process and a product that documents that the learner is receiving a free appropriate public education consistent with all federal and state requirements–The IEP is responsible for defining how to deliver a free appropriate public education to a learner requiring special education services. It reflects the vision and defines the educational services, activities, and linkages necessary for the learner to reach the vision. It also describes the services the learner needs to receive educational benefit. The IEP is a working document that must meet legal requirements and provide guidance for day-to-day instruction. The IEP team must ensure that all components of the specially designed plan are linked and implemented as described.

   - The IEP document is written in language understandable to all team members.
   - Services are implemented as outlined on the IEP.
   - The state IEP prototype meets all federal requirements.
   - The IEP is reviewed (and revised, if necessary) at least annually.

2. The IEP reflects the learner's and family's vision for the future–Each learner's IEP is based on the hopes, dreams, insights, and expectations of the learner and family with input from educators. A vision helps the IEP team focus on the learner's strengths and needs. It provides common ground for dialogue to occur among the learner, family, and educators. It guides the learner's plan and the standard used to prioritize needs. It is also used to design a program to meet the learner's unique needs and prepare the learner for the future. The development of the vision is achieved through ongoing discussion.

- As part of the IEP meeting, the family and the learner (as appropriate) are provided with an opportunity to dialogue about their hopes, dreams, insights, and expectations for the learner.
- The IEP process begins with the teams' dialogue about the vision.
- The vision is written on the IEP document.
- The vision is reviewed yearly.
- The vision is reflected throughout the IEP process.

3. To the maximum extent appropriate, learners requiring special education services are educated with individuals who do not require special education–Schools are responsible for providing an appropriate educational environment for each learner. For learners who require special education, the determination of the appropriate educational environment is based on the individual needs of the learner and must address the legal requirements described as the "least restrictive environment." Planning educational services for learners with disabilities begins with the assumption that the general education environment is the appropriate place to educate all learners. The general education environment also encompasses the locations where all learners participate in nonacademic and extracurricular activities.

- Learners are educated with nondisabled peers to the maximum extent possible.
- Learners are not taken from the general education environment for special services without justification.
- Learners with disabilities are neither unnecessarily nor inappropriately separated from their nondisabled peers for school experiences.
- Schools provide supplementary aids and services, accommodations and modifications, and supports, allowing learners with disabilities to be educated with their nondisabled peers whenever possible.
- Schools provide a continuum of service locations including special education classes and separate facilities.
- The preferred location for special education services is the school a learner with a disability would attend if not for the disability.
- The IEP team determines, on an individual basis, the appropriate educational setting for each learner. The team also considers the unique needs of the learner, the goals they have established for the learner, and the services required to achieve those goals.

4. The development of the IEP is a collaborative process–Collaboration among IEP team members is essential to ensuring that each learner's educational experience is a success. All members of the IEP team are equal partners. The opinions of all team members are valued and encouraged. Participants offer suggestions, listen carefully, encourage others, and ask questions. Equality and respect are extended to all team members. Because of their long-term perspective and unique relationship with the learners, parents and other family members bring a valuable understanding of the learner to the table. Learners also can express their own needs, strengths, and interests. With this in mind, educators must continue to recognize their responsibility to maintain and enhance partnerships throughout the school year with parents and learners in order to create a collaborative environment at the meeting.

- The learner participates as a self-advocate at the earliest age possible.
- The participation of the learner in the process reflects the learner's self-advocacy instruction.
- The parents and learner know and understand their rights (parental rights have been clearly communicated).
- The IEP meeting notice includes the name or title of all persons that will attend and have been invited to attend the meeting.
- The parents understand that they many bring "other individuals who have knowledge or special expertise regarding their child" with them to the IEP meeting.
- The IEP meeting is scheduled for a mutually agreeable time.
- All participants are focused on a common outcome.
- Community service agency representatives are invited and encouraged to participate in the IEP development as appropriate.
- The collaborative IEP process in made more efficient and effective using a group facilitation process.

5. The IEP team develops a learner's IEP in relationship to the general curriculum–Learners have greater success when they have access to the general curriculum, when they are provided the assistance necessary to progress in the general curriculum, and when educators hold high expectation for them. IEP teams must hold high expectation for all learners. They are also responsible for ensuring access to the general curriculum to the maximum extent appropriate. In doing this, the IEP team must identify the special education and related services, supplementary aids and services, assistive technology, modifications, and assistance for educators that are needed to ensure the learner's involvement and progress in the general curriculum.

- General education teachers actively participate on IEP teams.
- Individuals who are knowledgeable about the general curriculum are members of the IEP team.
- The learner's performance in relationship to the general curriculum is documented in the IEP's present levels of educational performance statement.
- Goals are selected from the general curriculum when appropriate.
- When possible, curriculum standards or benchmarks are used to assess a learner's progress.
- The IEP specifies the services and supports needed to ensure progress in the general curriculum.

6. The IEP process involves ongoing progress monitoring and decision making–Decision making is solution

focused, based on the learner's needs, and used to improve learner results. The IEP represents a plan for specially designed instruction and services for the learner. This instruction is most effective when guided by feedback that involves continuous progress monitoring. Progress monitoring is needed to provide objective information and to make instructional decisions. The decision-making process is focused on improved results for the learner and relates to progress in the general curriculum. Decisions should be based upon the ongoing collection of data and analysis of learner performance over time. Decisions should also respond to the results of educational interventions. The data collected from progress monitoring should serve as a communication tool for all members of the IEP team.

- Goals are meaningful, measurable, can be monitored, and are used to make decisions.
- A decision-making process is developed.
- There is evidence of a measurement strategy, an ongoing method of data collection, and data analysis that drives the decision-making process.
- All members of the IEP team, including parents, the learner, and others, as appropriate, receive information about progress on the goals.
- Progress is reported as often as in general education.

The IEP can be more than an outline and management tool for the learner's special education program. It can be an opportunity for parents and educators to work together as equal participants to identify the learner's needs. It is a document that is revised as the needs of the learner change. The IEP is a commitment in writing of the resources the school agrees to provide. Also, the periodic review of the IEP serves as an evaluation of the learner's progress toward meeting the educational goals and objectives. Finally, the IEP serves as the focal point for clarifying issues and for cooperative decision making by parents, the learner, and school personnel. For all of these reasons, the IEP is the cornerstone of special education.

Prior to the IEP meeting the school district should

- take steps to ensure one or both parents of the child with a disability are present at each meeting or offered the opportunity to participate;
- decide which general education teacher(s) should attend;
- gather information from other general education teachers;
- discuss the benefit of having the learner attend and then make the decision regarding his or her participation;
- establish a mutually agreeable date, time, and location;
- send meeting notice;
- inform participants of their roles and responsibilities;
- select people to fill roles such as facilitator or recorder;
- prepare the agenda;
- set standard ground rules;
- send worksheets and information to all team members so they can prepare for the meeting;
- prepare the meeting place (i.e., arrange furniture in a manner reflecting equality of team members);

- encourage learner-led meetings when appropriate;
- assure that the meeting is accessible to people with disabilities; and
- arrange for a qualified sign language interpreter for parents or learners who are deaf; and assistive listening device for parents or learners who are hard-of-hearing.

Bateman (1995) stated the following concerning IEPs:

- The core of educational utility is that the IEP spells out precisely how the school district will address each and every unique need and how it will determine whether and when a change in strategy or service is required. The IEP process must determine which needs or characteristics of the learner require special education (i.e., individualization of services); precisely how the district will address each need (i.e., what special education related services or modifications it will provide); and how and when the efficacy of those services will be evaluated.
- The only legitimate focus of an IEP meeting is on the special needs of the learner and how those needs are to be addressed. There may be a temptation for district personnel to sidestep into policy explanations or justifications or into what the parents have or have not done. If the learner is not present at the IEP meeting, a strategically placed photo can serve to help all participants stay focused on the needs of that learner. Many IEP meetings lose this essential focus and wander, becoming inefficient and frustrating for all.
- The single most important principle of the IEP process is that the school must appropriately address all the learner's unique needs without regard to the availability of needed services. Prior to the passage of the IDEA (PL 94-142) in 1975, schools were legally free to offer only the programs or services, if any, they had available. The primary purpose of the law was to turn that around and entitle the learner who has a disability to an individually designed free and appropriate public education.
- All members of the IEP team should remember the enormous power and responsibility that is theirs. When the IEP specifies a service is needed, the district must provide it. Too often parents are given a different impression: that only what is already available can be provided and often in smaller than needed amounts. This critical difference between the law and practice is typified by the following common situation: The parent believes the learner with a learning disability needs intensive, individual, daily language therapy, but is told that since the therapist is only in the building on Mondays and Wednesdays the learners will be included in an ongoing 20 minute speech therapy group for those two days only.

COMPONENTS OF THE INDIVIDUALIZED EDUCATION PROGRAM

The IDEA requires that certain information be included in each learner's IEP. It is useful to know, however, that states and local school systems often include additional information in IEPs in order to document that they have met certain aspects of federal or state law. The flexibility that states and school systems have in designing their own IEP forms is one reason why IEP forms look different from school system to school system or from state to state.

Specific Requirements

By law, the IEP must include the following information about the learner and the educational program designed to meet the learner's unique needs:

- Current performance–The IEP must state how the learner is currently performing in school (known as present levels of educational performance). This information usually comes from evaluation results such as classroom tests and assignments; individual tests given to decide eligibility for services or during reevaluation; and observation made by parents, teachers, related service providers, and other school staff. The statement about current performance includes how the learner's disability affects involvement and progress in the general curriculum.
- Annual goals–These are goals that the learner can reasonably accomplish in a year. The goals are broken down into short-term objectives or benchmarks. Goals may be academic, address social or behavioral needs, relate to physical needs, or address other education needs. The goals must be measurable, meaning that it must be possible to measure if the learner has achieved the goals.
- Special education and related services–The IEP must list the special education and related services to be provided to the learner. This includes supplementary aids and services. It also includes modifications to the program or supports for school personnel—such as training or professional development provided to assist the learner.
- Participation with nondisabled learners–The IEP must explain the extent (if any) to which the learner will not participate with nondisabled peers in the general education classes and social activities.
- Participation in statewide and districtwide tests–Most states and districts give achievement tests to learners in certain grades or age groups. The IEP must state what modifications in the administration of these tests the learner will need. If a test is not appropriate, the IEP must state why the test is not appropriate and how the learner will be tested instead.
- Dates and places–The IEP must state when services will begin, how often they will be provided, where they will be provided, and how long they will last.
- Transition services–Beginning when the learner is age 14 (or younger, if appropriate), the IEP must address (within the applicable parts of the IEP) the courses the learner needs to take to reach postschool goals. A statement of transition services needs must also be included in each of the learner's subsequent IEPs.
- Needed transition services–Beginning when the learner is age 16 (or younger if appropriate), the IEP must state

what transition services are needed to help the learner prepare for leaving school.

- Age of majority–Beginning at least one year before the learner reaches the age of majority, the IEP must include a statement that the learner has been told of any rights that will transfer to the learner at the age of majority. (This statement is needed only in states that transfer rights at this age.)
- Measuring progress–The IEP must state how the learner's progress will be measured and how parents will be informed of that progress.

In defining the IEP and making these requirements, the intent of Congress was to bring together teachers, parents, and learners to develop an educational program that would be tailored to the learner's needs and would provide documentation of a quality education based on those individual needs. Planning and implementing a procedurally sound IEP will always be a challenge. The developers of IEPs must deliver a high-quality framework to help teachers perform at their best in providing specially designed instruction for learners with disabilities.

Special Factors

In addition, there are special factors for consideration that may apply to an individual learner. These items also must be considered when the IEP is reviewed and revised. If, in considering these factors, the IEP team determines that a learner needs a particular device or service (including an intervention, accommodation, or other program modification) in order to receive a free appropriate public education, the IEP team must include a statement to that effect in the learner's IEP. Depending on the needs of the learner, the IEP team needs to consider what the law calls special factors, such as the need for assistive technology.

Learners Who May Need Assistive Technology. Some learners may require assistive technology devices and services to benefit from a free appropriate public education. The IEP must describe any specialized equipment and adaptive devices needed for the learner to benefit from education. The IDEA requires each school district to ensure that assistive technology devices and/or services are made available to a preschool or school-age learner with a disability as part of the learner's special education, related services, or supplementary aids or services as described in the IEP.

Assistive technology device, as defined by the IDEA, means any item, piece of equipment, or product system, whether acquired commercially off the shelf, modified, or customized, that is used to increase, maintain, or improve the functional capabilities of a learner with a disability.

Assistive technology service, as defined by the IDEA, means any service that directly assists a learner with a disability in the selection, acquisition, or use of an assistive technology device. This term includes

- the evaluation of the needs of a learner with a disability, including a functional evaluation of the learner in the learner's customary environment;

- purchasing, leasing, or otherwise providing for the acquisition of assistive technology devices by learners with disabilities;
- selecting, designing, fitting, customizing, adapting, applying, maintaining, repairing, or replacing assistive technology devices;
- coordinating and using other therapies, interventions, or services with assistive technology devices, such as those associated with existing education and rehabilitation plans and programs;
- training or technical assistance for a learner with a disability or, if appropriate, the learner's family; and
- training or technical assistance for professionals (including individuals providing education or rehabilitation services), employers, or other individuals who provide services to, employ, or are otherwise substantially involved in the major life functions of that learner.

Assistive technology devices or services shall be made available to learners with disabilities either as supplementary aids and services that enable the learner with a disability to be educated in the general education classes or as special education, related services. The following questions should be considered:

- What can the learner do now with and without assistive technology devices and services?
- What does the learner need to be able to do?
- Can assistive technology devices and services facilitate learner success in a less restrictive environment?
- Does the learner need assistive technology devices and services to access the general curriculum or to participate in nonacademic and extracurricular activities?
- What assistive technology services would help the learner access the general curriculum or classes?
- Does the learner need assistive technology devices and services to benefit from educational/printed materials?
- Does the learner need assistive technology devices and services to access auditory information?
- Does the learner need assistive technology devices and services for written communication/computer access?
- Does the learner need assistive technology devices and services for augmentative communication technology?
- Does the learner need assistive technology devices to participate in statewide and districtwide testing?
- Will the learner and/or staff need training to facilitate the learner's use of the assistive technology devices?
- How can assistive technology devices and services be integrated into the learner's program across settings such as work placements and for homework?

Facts about assistive technology and the IEP include the following:

- Assistive technology needs must be considered along with the learner's other educational needs.
- Technology needs must be identified on an individual basis.
- Identification of technology needs must involve family members and a multidisciplinary team.

- Parents or IEP members can ask for additional evaluation or an independent evaluation to determine assistive technology needs.
- When an evaluation is being conducted, fine motor skills, communication, and alternatives to traditional learning approaches must be considered.
- Lack of availability of equipment or cost alone cannot be used as an excuse for denying an assistive technology service.
- If included in the IEP, assistive technology services and devices must be provided at no cost to the family and, if so indicated, devices must be allowed to go home with the learner.
- Parents always have the right to appeal if assistive technology devices are denied.

Learners Who Are Blind or Visually Impaired. If a learner is blind or visually impaired, IDEA '97 requires the IEP team to consider provision of instruction in braille or the use of braille—unless the IEP team determines that instruction in braille or the use of braille is not appropriate for the learner. The IEP team is expected to evaluate the following:
- the learner's reading and math skills
- the learner's needs
- appropriate reading and writing media for the learner
- the learner's future needs for instruction in braille or the use of braille

The following questions should be considered:
- Does the learner have a disability in addition to blindness that would make the use of the hands difficult?
- Does the learner have residual vision?
- Does the learner use or need to learn to use assistive technology for reading and writing?
- Is the learner's academic progress impeded by the current method of reading?
- Does the learner use braille, large print, or regular print?
- Will the learner need to use braille in the future?
- Have provisions been made to obtain in braille the printed materials used by sighted learners?
- Does the learner need instruction in orientation and mobility?
- Does the learner have appropriate listening skills?
- Does the learner have age-appropriate social skills?
- What skills does the learner need in order to learn effectively?
- What accommodations are necessary for instruction and testing?

If the IEP team determines that the learner requires instruction in braille and the use of braille, team members must develop a statement of the learner's present level of educational performance, annual goals, and benchmarks or short-term objectives in the appropriate areas.

Learners with Limited English Proficiency. A learner may not be identified as disabled solely because English is his or her second language. However, limited English proficiency may have special learning needs related to that status. If a learner has limited English proficiency, the language needs of the learner as they relate to the IEP must be considered. For all learners with limited English proficiency, the IEP team must consider how the learner's language needs relate to the IEP. The following questions should be considered:

• Has the learner been assessed in the native language?
• Is the disability present when the learner is assessed in the native language?
• Does the disability impact on the learner's involvement and progress in the bilingual education or English as a Second Language (ESL) program of the general curriculum?
• What language will be used for this learner's instruction?
• What language or mode of communication will be used to address parents or family members of the learner?
• What accommodations are necessary for instruction and testing?

Learners Who Are Deaf or Hearing Impaired. The IEP team must consider the learner's communication needs. Also, if a learner is deaf or hard-of-hearing, the IEP team must consider language and communication needs. This includes opportunities for direct instruction in the learner's language and communication mode. For learners who are deaf or hearing impaired, the IEP team must explain the communication and language needs of the learner and the learner's opportunities for direct interaction with peers and educational personnel in the learner's own language and communication mode. Opportunities for direct interaction (without needing an interpreter) in the learner's own language and communication mode must be described.

The following questions should be considered:
• Does the learner use American Sign Language?
• What mode of communication does the learner use?
• What mode of communication does the family prefer?
• Is an interpreter or translator needed for the learner to participate in and benefit from classroom instruction and/or interaction with peers and educational personnel?
• Does the learner require assistive devices to facilitate the development and use of meaningful language and/or a mode of communication?
• Are there opportunities for the learner to communicate directly with peers and educational personnel?
• What opportunities exist for direct instruction (without an interpreter) in the learner's language and/or mode of communication?
• Does the learner use or need to learn to use assistive technology to help in developing social skills?
• What accommodations are necessary for instruction and testing?

If the IEP team determines that the learner has communications needs, team members must develop a present level of educational performance, annual goals, and benchmarks or short-term objectives in the appropriate areas.

Learners Who Demonstrate Behaviors That Impede Learning. When a learner's behavior impedes learning, the IEP team must consider strategies, including positive behavioral interventions and supports, to address those behaviors. The following questions should be considered:

• What behaviors does the learner exhibit that are different from those of same-age peers?
• When is the learner most likely to engage in inappropriate behavior?
• What specific events appear to be contributing to the learner's problem behavior?
• What function(s) does the problem behavior serve for the learner?
• What might the learner be communicating through problem behavior?
• When is the learner less likely to engage in the problem behavior?
• Does the learner's behavior persist despite consistently implemented behavioral management strategies?
• Does the learner's behavior place anyone (including the learner) at risk of harm or injury?
• Have the learner's cultural norms been considered relative to the behavior(s) in question?
• Do medication or other interventions affect the behavior?
• Does the learner's disability affect the ability to control the behavior?
• Does the learner's disability affect the understanding of the consequences of the behavior?
• What accommodations are necessary for instruction and testing?

A functional behavioral assessment should be conducted for all learners with behaviors that may impede learning. Functional behavioral assessments provide information on why a learner engages in a behavior, when the learner is most likely to demonstrate the behavior, and situations in which the behavior is least likely to occur. Behavioral needs should be integrated throughout the IEP as an integral part of planning for the learner.

It is important to note that whenever a learner's behavior impedes the learning process or the learning process of others, and whenever discipline occurs beyond 10 days of suspension, functional assessment of behavior must be conducted and a behavioral plan developed. If this has previously been done and included in the IEP, then the team must reevaluate and/or revise the plan. Beyond 10 days of suspensions, educational services must be provided to the learner. If the learner possesses a gun or illegal drugs at school, the learner may be placed in an alternative setting for the same amount of time that a learner without a disability would be subject to discipline.

Present Level of Educational Performance

The IEP starts by stating how the learner with a disability is currently doing at school. This is called the learner's present levels of educational performance. What are the learner's strengths and weaknesses? What areas or skills need to be addressed? This information is drawn from recent evaluations, observations, and input from parents and school personnel. See Figure 6-2. A new area of emphasis in IDEA '97 covers how the learner's disability affects involvement and progress in the general curriculum. This statement includes performance levels in a variety of educational content areas including academic achievement, personal-social skills, psychomotor skills, self-help skills, and prevocational and vocational skills.

The present level of performance should indicate how the learner functions in all applicable educational areas. The following is a list of educational areas in which assessments of learner functioning may be needed:

- academic (including reading, writing, mathematics, and career development)
- intellectual (including intelligence, learning potential, learning process, and learning styles)
- sensory (including hearing and vision)
- communication (including language development, speech production, and articulation)
- social/emotional (including distractibility, impulsivity, attention span, and aggressive behavior)
- adaptive behaviors (including history of developmental milestones and personal hygiene)
- motor (including fine motor skills, gross motor skills, sensory-motor integration, mobility, and muscular control)
- prevocational (including entry-level work skills, occupational interests, work attitudes, and job-keeping skills)
- vocational/career (including information specific to career and technical education program curriculum and criterion-referenced and informal skill assessment results)

- other (including medical considerations) (Midwest Regional Resource Center, 1983)

The information necessary to determine the present level of performance for a particular learner is gathered from a variety of sources. These sources include the following:

- consultations with school personnel, parents, and/or community agencies
- interviews with the learner
- rating scales, checklists, and inventories
- standardized tests
- criterion-referenced tests
- vision and hearing tests
- performance tests
- basic skills results
- work sample batteries
- aptitude tests
- interest inventories
- evaluation results available from learner records
- evaluations by teachers, counselors, psychologists, psychometricians, and work sample evaluators

Tests should be nondiscriminatory. Learners with limited English proficiency should be tested in the language spoken at home so the results will better predict the learner's abilities and interests. Modifications may have to be made in the testing procedure for various disabilities. Individuals who are deaf may need an interpreter to assist with questions. Learners who have visual impairments may need extended time for testing or require oral testing procedures.

PRESENT LEVEL OF PERFORMANCE CHECKLIST

	Yes	No
1. Does the present level statement list strengths of the student in each problem area?	_____	_____
2. Does it list weaknesses of the student in each problem area?	_____	_____
3. Does it include statements on what the student needs to learn to do next in those problem areas?	_____	_____
4. Is it based on information gathered from a combination of diagnostic procedures?		
a. Formal	_____	_____
b. Informal testing	_____	_____
c. Observation	_____	_____
d. Case history	_____	_____
5. Are the instruments or processes used in the evaluation identified?	_____	_____
6. Does it contain statements on		
a. instructional methods?	_____	_____
b. motivational factors?	_____	_____
c. style of learning?	_____	_____
d. instructional materials that have been used successfully or unsuccessfully with the student?	_____	_____
7. Is the information instructionally relevant?	_____	_____
8. Is it written in understandable language?	_____	_____
9. If there are any unresolved assessment questions, are they mentioned?	_____	_____

Source: Midwest Resources, Inc. (1981). *Writing Quality Individualized Education Programs: A Workshop.* Des Moines, IA: Author.

Figure 6-2. A sample checklist used to develop or critique the present level of performance information in an IEP.

Information obtained from tests should be recent in order to be helpful in assessing the present level of performance. Learners must be re-evaluated periodically so that current performance levels are known to personnel developing the IEP. The present levels of educational performance should (a) accurately describe the effect of the learner's disability on performance in any area of education that is affected, academic and nonacademic; (b) be written in objective measurable terms; and (c) create a direct relationship between the present levels of educational performance and the other components of the IEP.

The career and technical instructor should identify information about the learner that is helpful in developing realistic goals, objectives, and necessary services. Examples of pertinent information relating to the learner's present level of educational performance include the following:

- basic skills levels (e.g., reading, spelling, mathematics, written communication skills)
- vocational interest inventory results
- vocational aptitude test results
- previous career and technical courses taken
- gross and fine motor skills
- interpersonal relationship skills
- medication that affects physical or behavioral performance
- overt behavior problems
- strong learning style
- ability to work in groups
- work experiences
- prevocational background
- ability to follow safety rules

Special education can help to provide this information or arrange for appropriate testing to provide the information. This will assist the career and technical instructor in planning an appropriate program for the learner.

Role of Career and Technical Education Personnel. Career and technical education personnel who will be working with learners with disabilities can positively contribute to developing a learner profile through the identification and establishment of the present level of educational performance. See Figure 6-3. Following are examples of responsibilities assumed by these personnel to foster cooperative working relationships with special education personnel and ensure that this portion of the IEP is realistic:

- Analyze the prevocational and vocational background of the learner to determine the most appropriate program goals.
- Determine any architectural or equipment modifications needed for physical access to the classroom and laboratory.
- Identify academic, prevocational, and/or skill prerequisites that will help to determine whether the learner is prepared to enroll in the program and/or identify necessary services to assist the learner in succeeding (e.g., reading a ruler, following safety rules, recognizing specific career vocabulary terms essential to program success).
- Identify important career and technical program information that will help to determine appropriate goals and objectives relating to the abilities of the learner (e.g.,

proficiency skills necessary for entry-level employment, appropriate instructional areas/units in the program, specific safety standards that must be observed).
- Assist in providing career exploration activities for learners to assist them in identifying interests (e.g., informal hands-on activities, job information that can be obtained after completion of program/course requirements).

Annual Goals and Short-term Objectives

Having identified how the learner is performing in school, and in particular, where the learner is having difficulty, the IEP team now focuses on determining what educational goals are appropriate for the learner. See Figure 6-4. The goals must be annual—what can the learner reasonably accomplish in a year? They must be measurable and include benchmarks, or short-term objectives. They must relate to helping the learner progress in the general curriculum, and they must address other educational needs that arise due to the disability.

An annual goal is a statement of what a learner with a disability can reasonably be expected to accomplish in a year's time in a specific area. It is written to address an area of weakness identified in the present level of educational performance. There must be a direct correlation between the annual goal and the present level of educational performance.

The goal must reflect knowledge of the learner's current functioning in each skill area, the next sequence of skills in that area, and an estimate of the rate of leaning. If the learning rate is underestimated and the learner achieves the annual goal earlier, then new goals can be added. Priorities are established in choosing goals based upon the learner's physical limitations, age, time left in school, and expectations for the future. Thus the annual goals in the IEP are

- stated in terms of measurable, observable behaviors;
- inclusive of the major deficit areas identified in the present level of educational performance;
- based on the learner's present level of functioning;
- realistic in terms of the learner's physical and cognitive abilities;
- prioritized on the basis of the learner's age and amount of time left in school; and
- prioritized to meet the learner's need and to help the learner live independently. See Figure 6-5.

Sample goal statements that might be included in an IEP include an improvement in the following:

- math skills
- math reasoning
- written expression
- reading skills
- reading comprehension
- listening skills
- language/communication skills
- classroom behavior
- ability to follow directions
- employability skills

INDIVIDUALIZED EDUCATION PROGRAM (IEP)

SCHOOL SYSTEM: Stoneville County

Student Name Michelle London

Student's Address 380 Woodland Dr., Waterbury, GA

Birthdate/Age January 10

Dominant Language English

Health Conditions Diabetic (home insulin injections)

School Waterbury School District

Grade/Program 10th/Learning Disability/Auto Technology

Teacher(s) Mrs. Waters and Mr. Stone

IEP Coordinator Mrs. Waters

Date Written 6/5   Annual Review Date 6/3

Dates of IEP Meetings June 7; June 3

Placement(s)	Initiated	Duration
Learning Disab. Program	8/28	6/7
Automotive Technology Program	8/28	School year 6/7

Strong Learning Mode Visual. Hands on performance

Special Media and/or Materials

Vocational Applied Math - Auto Body

Bergwall and Prentice - Hall Auto Body Materials

IEP Team Members:

Name	Title
Mrs. Waters	Special Education Teacher
Mr. Stone	High School Principal
Mr. and Mrs. London	Parents
Mr. Brooks	Auto Technology
Ms. Michelle London	Student

Present Level of Education Performance (Academic, Psychomotor, Personal-Social, Self-Help Prevocational/Vocational):

Academic Skills: Michelle performed at the following levels on recently administered achievement tests. Reading 3.5 (greatest problem word attack skills). Math 4.0 (deficiency in the areas of measurement, fractions, and long division). She earned "C" grades in all courses taken last year.

Psychomotor Skills: Michelle demonstrated good psychomotor skill with a slight problem in fine finger dexterity.

Personal-Social Skills: Michelle is shy, withdrawn, and perfers working by herself. She communicates poorly with other students in group situations.

Self-Help Skills: No significant problems in this area.

Prevocational/Vocational Skills: Michelle satisfactorily completed career exploritory experiences at the junior high school level and a course in career development at the 9th grade level. She has indicated an interest in the automotive technology program.

Extent of Participation in Regular Educational Programs/Activities: Michelle will participate in the automotive technology program one hour per day, five days per week, during the academic year.

Special Services/Frequency:	Person/Agency Responsible:	Date Initiated:	Duration Date:
Remedial Reading (one period per day)	Reading Specialist	Sept. 15	June 7
Social Work (one home visit per month)	School Social Worker	Oct. 2	June 7
Remedial Math (one period per day)	Remedial Math Specialist	Sept. 15	June 7

Parent(s)/Guardian(s) Signature _____

Figure 6-3. A sample IEP with information on background and present level of educational performance.

- achievement/basic skills levels
- self-help skills
- physical mobility
- motor skills
- prevocational skills
- on-the-job performance
- involvement in student organization activities
- self-concept
- motivation
- attitude toward school and/or work

AUTOMOTIVE TECHNOLOGY—IEP ANNUAL GOAL STATEMENT AND SHORT-TERM OBJECTIVES

Student Name Katie Lane

Date IEP was Written June 5

IEP Coordinator Mr. Roberts

Program(s) Automotive Technology, Special Education

Annual Goal(s) Identify, Remove, and Replace Automobile Body and Frame Components   Review Date(s) 6/3

Quarter/Semester Goals _____

Review Date(s) 1/4

Instructional Task(s) Selected tasks listed in curriculum guide for body and frame component replacement

Short-Term Instructional Objectives	Instructional Strategies Methods and Materials	Evaluation of Instructional Objectives		
		Performance Criteria	Tests/Evaluation Procedures	Evaluation Date/Results*
1. Demonstrate an understanding of auto body structures and auto body safety procedures	Read textbook assignments Observe demonstrations Observe filmstrip (Bergwall, "Safety in the Auto Body Shop") Identify different metal configurations and frame construction on a car	Must describe metal configurations and their purpose. Must explain frame shapes and their construction Must explain low center of gravity (All explanations with 70% accuracy. Must score 100% on safety test.)	Written or oral tests on metal configurations and frame shapes Written or oral safety test worksheet assignments	Oct. 27-M
2. Name the parts of a vehicle and describe their functions	Read textbook assignments Observe demonstrations on body parts and panels Complete worksheet activities	Must explain inner construction differences between separate frame and body and unitized MacPherson strut system at 70% accuracy Must identify parts at 90% accuracy	Identification test on actual car Oral quiz on body and frame component functions Worksheet assignments	Nov. 10-M
3. Remove, replace, and align front and rear doors	Read textbook assignments Observe demonstration on door removal and replacement Observe Prentice-Hall, "Auto Body Repair: Metal Work" (Filmstrip #5) Practice door removal and replacement	Must follow correct procedures at 90% accuracy without missing any safety steps Door must align with no more than 1/4" gap on all sides and be flush with the body	Observation of actual performance using checklist for this task Oral quiz Worksheet assignment	
4. Remove and replace grills and gravel deflectors	Read textbook assignments Observe demonstration on wire connections and grill replacement Observe filmstrip #1 (Bergwall, "Auto Body Tools Explained")	Must follow correct procedures at 90% accuracy without missing a safety step Finished product must be correctly aligned and free from scratches	Observation of actual performance using a checklist for this task Oral quiz on procedures	

*M=Mastery, I=Incomplete

Figure 6-4. An example of an annual goal statement and short-term instructional objectives in a small engine repair program.

ANNUAL GOALS CHECKLIST		
	Yes	**No**
1. Are the goals clear and understandable?		
a. Not overly vague	_____	_____
b. Containing jargon	_____	_____
c. Too specific	_____	_____
2. Are the goals positively stated?	_____	_____
3. Is there at least one goal for each area of need stated in the "level of performance"?	_____	_____
4. Are there goals that cannot be justified on the basis of information contained in the present level of performance statements?	_____	_____
5. Are the goals practical/relevant to the student's academic, social, and vocational needs?	_____	_____
6. Are the goals practical/relevant when the student's age and remaining school years are considered?	_____	_____
7. Are the goals prioritized correctly based on assessment findings?	_____	_____
8. Do the goals reflect anticipated growth within the categories of instructional area?	_____	_____
9. Can the goals be accomplished within one year?	_____	_____

Source: Midwest Resources, Inc. (1981). *Writing Quality Individualized Education Programs: A Workshop.* Des Moines, IA: Author.

Figure 6-5. A sample checklist used to develop or critique the annual goals in an IEP.

Once the direction for a learner's educational program has been described in the annual goal statement, short-term instructional objectives are developed. These objectives represent intermediate steps between the learner's present level of performance and the annual goal. The objectives, written in behavioral terms, act as specific guidelines for accomplishing the established goals and specify for the learner what will be required for successful completion of the goal. Thus, the learner can follow a sequential pattern leading to satisfactory completion of established goals.

Role of Career and Technical Education Personnel. Annual goals developed for the learner enrolled in a career and technical education program should be general and comprehensive, should take into consideration the learner's present level of educational performance, and should be a realistic estimate of what he/she can accomplish in the specific program during the year. Short-term instructional objectives should be sequential steps that help the learner to progress from the present level of educational performance to the desired achievements stated in the established goals for the career and technical education program. See Figure 6-6.

Sources that can help career and technical education personnel in developing annual goal statements and accompanying objectives include curriculum guides, job-related employability skills lists, current employment prerequisite information obtained from industry, and competency-based checklists.

Career and technical education personnel should obtain, organize, and take the following materials to an IEP meeting in order to assist in the development of annual goals and short-term objectives:

- program/course descriptions
- admission requirements/prerequisites
- program/course outlines
- lesson plan notebook
- individualized learning packages
- tests and evaluation materials
- career and technical student organization materials
- textbooks and manuals used in the program
- transferable/generalizable skills needed for successful participation in the program
- information on career and technical education program facilities and equipment
- information on methods used to teach course content (e.g., classroom teaching, laboratory activities, cooperative education, career and technical student organization participation).

Some examples of responsibilities that can be assumed by career and technical education personnel to foster a cooperative working relationship with special education personnel and to ensure that this portion of the IEP is realistic are

- developing appropriate annual goal statement(s) for the career and technical education program based on the learner's abilities, interests, and occupational goal;
- developing a sequence of short-term instructional objectives for each annual goal;
- identifying appropriate criterion levels to determine whether each short-term objective has been met; and
- revising annual goals and short-term objectives as necessary during the year as a result of observing and evaluating learner progress.

SHORT-TERM OBJECTIVES EVALUATION CHECKLIST

	Yes	No
1. Does each objective answer the following:		
a. What must be done?	_____	_____
b. Who will do it?	_____	_____
c. When student progress will be measured?	_____	_____
2. Is each objective understandable?		
a. Not overly vague	_____	_____
b. Free of jargon	_____	_____
c. Not too specific	_____	_____
3. Does each objective relate to only one goal?	_____	_____
4. Are there two or more short term objectives written for each annual goal?	_____	_____
5. Are the objectives measurable?	_____	_____
6. Are the objectives sequenced logically?	_____	_____
7. Does the sequence of the objectives lead to the mastery of skills at a functional level?	_____	_____
8. Are all the objectives that the student must accomplish to meet the goal included? (This does not mean that objectives the student has already mastered must be included.)	_____	_____
9. Are the individual needs of your student reflected in the objective?	_____	_____

Source: Midwest Resources, Inc. (1981). *Writing Quality Individualized Education Programs: A Workshop.* Des Moines, IA: Author.

Figure 6-6. A sample checklist used to develop or critique the short-term objectives in an IEP.

Evaluation of Criteria

This component includes appropriate objective criteria to be used at least once a year to evaluate the extent to which the annual goals and short-term objectives have been met. This evaluation should be considered as an opportunity to determine to what extent the IEP is meeting the specific needs of the learner. One method of effectively evaluating learner progress during the year is to establish behavioral statements for each short-term instructional objective. These statements describe criterion levels or specific conditions necessary for mastering that objective. A system of record keeping and a schedule for evaluation should be developed by all personnel working with learners with disabilities so that progress can be monitored. The criterion levels established for each objective help to determine the method of recording and evaluating learner progress. Some examples include recording specific behaviors during observation and teacher-prepared skill checklists. If short-term objectives have not been met, the reason(s) for the failure should be discussed by all the participants at the IEP annual review meeting. This annual process assists the IEP team in planning future goals and objectives that are realistic.

Specific educational services provided in the IEP must also be evaluated. Each service should be addressed periodically during the year to determine whether the service is assisting the learner to achieve success and whether the service is still necessary. Again, evaluation of educational services should be documented in written form so that progress can be discussed and the IEP can be revised as needed. In cases where necessary services were not provided, justification must be documented.

An evaluation criterion is the level of performance necessary for mastery of a given objective. This can be expressed in percentage of accuracy required, number of times a certain performance is required, etc. Evaluation frequency is the schedule upon which a learner is evaluated. It tells how often a learner will be evaluated on a given objective. Objectives may be assessed daily, weekly, monthly, or by a specific date. The frequency of evaluation for each objective will vary based upon the nature of the specific objective, the developmental level of the learner, and/or the learner's anticipated rate of growth.

An evaluation procedure is the manner in which the skill will be assessed. Procedures may include specific tests, teacher-made tests, curriculum materials, interviews, anecdotal records, observations, and portfolios (academic and career/technical). The following are examples of methods for evaluating goals, objectives, and benchmarks:

- Baseline data–This is the documented number of times any given behavior is observed in the learner within any given period of time.
- Daily performance–This refers to formal or informal daily assessment (including daily teacher-made tests) of academic achievement or behavior.
- Individual achievement testing–This can be a standardized instrument or the district-developed assessments available at all grade levels.

- Class participation–This refers to an informal process of documenting some infrequent behaviors of severely disabled learners.
- Report card–This is documentation of a passing or specific grade for subject areas. When using these evaluation criteria, it is important to document any classroom or grading modifications on the IEP.
- Informal testing–This is any ongoing testing and observation data collection.

Role for Career and Technical Education Personnel. In order to positively contribute to the annual IEP review procedure, the career and technical education instructor should develop a system to evaluate and record learner progress during the year. This can be accomplished by monitoring the specific criteria developed for the short-term objectives. Some form of written data should be maintained. Examples include learner competency profiles, portfolios, and competency checklists.

The following are some examples of responsibilities that can be assumed by career and technical education personnel to ensure that this portion of the IEP is realistic:

- analyzing and recording learner performance according to specific criteria as it relates to short-term objectives
- establishing continuous evaluation procedures to provide feedback relative to learner progress (e.g., proficiency profiles, performance checklists)
- actively participating in and contributing to IEP conferences on learner progress and the adequacy and effectiveness of support services and programs
- assisting special education and support personnel in developing a profile of the learner's strengths and limitations so that remediation can be provided
- utilizing evaluation feedback as a management tool to revise goals, objectives, and services to meet the needs of the learner

The following are several examples of statements describing criteria specifications that can be used by career and technical education instructors to evaluate learner progress in meeting short-term instructional objectives and, ultimately, annual goals:

- The learner will score a minimum of 85% correct answers on a written review test.
- The learner will score a minimum of 90% correct answers on an oral review test.
- The learner will remain on task for a minimum of 90% of the time spent in the career and technical education classroom/laboratory.
- The learner will demonstrate proficiency on the stated task according to the criterion specifications established by the manufacturer.
- The learner will perform the assigned laboratory task with a minimum accuracy level of 95% as evaluated by the daily observation of the instructor.
- The learner will demonstrate each safety standard necessary for independent work in the laboratory with 100% accuracy.

Related Services

This component of the IEP identifies specific educational and related services that should be provided to assist learners in attaining annual goals. The determination of these services is based upon the IEP goals and objectives that correlate to the learner's present level of educational performance and can be categorized from among the following:

1. Direct special education services–Direct services are specialized instructional services provided directly to the learner. Instruction may be provided in the general education classroom, the special education classroom, community or other appropriate settings.
2. Indirect special education services–Indirect services include consultation services, in which the special educator is not responsible for direct services, but rather consults with the special education teacher and other service providers (e.g., school psychologist, career and technical education counselor, guidance counselor) to assist them in developing programs appropriate for the learner. The special educator may meet with the learner for monitoring purposes. The general education teacher of all mainstreamed learners should be provided with consultation services as needed.
3. Accommodations–Any accommodation, including supplementary aids and services needed by the learner to assist in both special and general (regular, career and technical) education, should be clearly listed and described in the IEP. This may include instructional modifications, assessment modifications, adaptive equipment, and/or assistive technology devices. The term assistive technology devices means any item, piece of equipment, or product system, whether acquired commercially, off the shelf, modified, or customized, that is used to increase, maintain, or improve functional capabilities of individuals with disabilities. Example accommodations in the form of supplementary aids and services include a note taker, written materials in braille, extra time to move between classes, modification of curriculum, and special seating arrangements.
4. Related services–Related services means transportation, and such developmental, corrective, and other supportive services (including speech pathology and audiology, psychological services, physical and occupational therapy, recreation, including therapeutic recreation, social work services, counseling services, including rehabilitation counseling, and medical services, except that such medical services shall be for diagnostic and evaluation purposes only) as may be required to assist a learner with a disability to benefit from special education.
5. Transition services–The IEP for learners beginning not later than the age of 16 and annually thereafter (and at a younger age, if determined appropriate) must contain a statement of needed transitional services, This includes, when appropriate, a statement of the interagency responsibilities or linkages (or both) before the learner leaves the school setting.

Transition services are a coordinated set of activities for a learner that are designed with an outcome-oriented process, which promotes movement from school to postschool activities including

- postsecondary education;
- career and technical training;
- integrated employment (including supported employment);
- continuing and adult education;
- adult services;
- independent living; and
- community participation.

The coordinated set of activities shall be based on the individual learner's needs, taking into account preferences and interests, and shall include

- development of employment and other postschool adult living objectives;
- instruction;
- community experiences; and when appropriate,
- acquisition of daily living skills and functional vocational evaluation.

For each of the services required by the learner, the following information must be included based upon the learner's needs:

- the total number of minutes and/or hours per day for each service that is provided for the learner
- the total number of times per week that each service is provided for the learner
- the date that the service is expected to begin and the date that the service is anticipated to end

Dates, frequency, location, and duration of services–Each learner's IEP must be very clear about when that learner's special education and related services (including modifications) will begin, how long they will go on (duration), how often they will be provided (frequency), and where (location) he or she will receive those services. Stating the "location" of services in a new requirement in the IDEA '97.

Although confidentially must be ensured, the contents of the learner's IEP should be shared with all instructional staff serving the learner. The individual managing the learner's IEP should review the IEP's goals and objectives, including accommodations, with all of the learner's general (regular, career and technical) education teachers. These individuals have a legitimate educational interest in the learner and should have access to all confidential information.

Services provided for learners enrolled in career and technical programs might include supplementary personnel, special equipment/devices/materials, and services from outside agencies. Examples of educational services that may be requested in the IEP include the following:

- psychologist or psychometrician to administer psychological tests, interpret results, and/or provide counseling
- audiologist to administer and interpret hearing tests and/or provide auditory training
- social worker
- support personnel to assist the learner in regular class settings

- speech therapist
- occupational therapist
- physical therapist
- interpreter/reader
- vocational/career counseling
- career and technical education exploration
- career development activities
- teacher aide/tutor
- remedial instruction (e.g., math, reading)
- curriculum specialist
- medical consultant (e.g., neurologist, orthopedist, psychiatrist)
- prosthetic devices
- equipment modification
- curriculum modification
- special instructional materials (e.g., captioned films, large print books, recordings of books)
- classroom/laboratory modifications to assure accessibility
- transportation services (e.g., revised time schedules, attendants for physically disabled individuals, assistance for learners who are visually impaired)
- special equipment
- vocational rehabilitation services
- community services (e.g., mental health services, special clinics)
- employment service
- family and child services
- department of human resources
- advocacy organizations

Once the specific educational services have been selected, the team developing the IEP projects will determine when each service will begin and when it will terminate. These dates are not binding, but merely help the team to plan for the services that a particular learner will require. The IEP can be modified whenever the committee deems necessary as long as the parent/guardian is notified.

Role of Career and Technical Education Personnel. Career and technical education personnel working with learners with disabilities should assume the same responsibilities that are associated with other learners enrolled in their programs. Specifically, career and technical education should assume responsibility for specific instruction in their program, provide relevant classroom and hands-on laboratory experiences, and encourage and assist learners to become actively involved in career and technical student organizations.

Following are examples of responsibilities that can be assumed by career and technical education instructors to foster a cooperative working relationship with special education and support personnel and to ensure that this position of the IEP is realistic:

- identifying and securing instructional materials for use in the career and technical education program in cooperation with special education and support personnel

- developing and/or modifying instructional materials for use in the career and technical education program in co-operation with special education and support personnel
- identifying and utilizing appropriate instructional techniques in cooperation with special education and support personnel
- arranging for extended time in the career and technical education program for learners who require it
- identifying necessary remedial assistance
- identifying necessary specific equipment or devices

Extent of Participation in Regular Education Program Activities

The IEP, in meeting the requirements of this component, must include information regarding the type of regular education program or activity that the learner will be involved in, justification for this type of placement, and the amount of time the learner is expected to participate. As the progress of the learner is reviewed throughout the year, the extent of participation can be increased or decreased as necessary.

Once a learner's IEP has been developed, the next step is to determine where the learner will receive the services outlined in the IEP. This decision is made only after the annual goals and short-term objectives have been agreed to. The learner's placement must be based upon the learner's goals and short-term objectives.

The placement of the learner must be in the least restrictive environment (LRE) appropriate for that learner. When determining this, consider the following:
- The learner should have the opportunity, to the maximum extent appropriate, to participate with nondisabled age-appropriate learners in academic, nonacademic, and extracurricular activities.
- The learner should be served in a setting as close as possible to the setting to which the learner would be assigned if the learner did not have a disability.
- The amount of time and the distance the learner must be transported from home should be factored in.
- The learner should be removed from the regular educational environment only when the nature and severity of the disability is such that education in regular classes using supplementary aids and services cannot be achieved.
- Any potential harmful effects the placement may have on the learner should be taken into account.
- The placement should provide the quality of services the learner requires.
- The program/service, as specified in the learner's IEP, should be appropriate to meet the learner's needs.

To assist in determining the placement, the IEP committee should consider a continuum of services. Once chosen, a justification statement is needed to explain why the option was chosen. The continuum service options include the following:
- direct instruction and/or consultative services within regular/career and technical education
- direct instruction and/or consultative services within regular/career and technical education, with content instruction in a resource room
- direct instruction and/or consultative services within regular/career and technical education, with content instruction in special education classes
- self-contained in a special education classroom with integration as appropriate
- self-contained in a special education classroom with no integration in regular public school
- separate public day school for learners with disabilities
- separate private day school for learners with disabilities
- public and/or residential facilities
- homebound or hospital

The IDEA has always preferred that learners with disabilities be educated with their nondisabled peers. This preference is manifested in IDEA '97 in this new IEP requirement: The IEP must now include an explanation of the extent, if any, to which the learner will not be participating with nondisabled learners in the regular class, in the general curriculum, and in extracurricular and nonacademic activities.

Role of Career and Technical Education Personnel. Learners with disabilities have the right to participate in career and technical education programs and activities to the maximum extent possible. This does not mean that all learners with disabilities automatically will be enrolled in a career and technical education program. A range of options should be available. Career and technical educators should work cooperatively with special education and support personnel to plan the extent to which each learner will participate in a program.

This range of placement options is in response to the "least restrictive environment" (LRE) requirement of the Individuals with Disabilities Education Act. This legislation assures that all learners have the right to learn in an environment consistent with their academic, social, and physical needs. Learners with disabilities are to receive their education with nondisabled peers to the maximum extent appropriate.

For example, some learners will be placed in a regular classroom environment and will receive no additional support services. Adaptations necessary for a given learner will be handled by the classroom teacher in many cases. In other cases, a learner is placed in a regular classroom setting with consultative services available to both the teacher and the learner. These services may be provided by a variety of professionals including special educators, speech and language specialists, behavior specialists, physical education specialists, occupational therapists, physical therapists, school psychologists, and social workers. Services may range from assisting a teacher in the use of tests or modification of curriculum to direct instruction with learners in the classroom setting.

Still other students may be placed in a regular class setting for the majority of the school day but also attend a resource room for specialized instruction in deficit areas. A resource room program is under the direction of a qualified special educator. The amount of time a student spends there varies according to his or her needs. Instruction in a resource room is intended to reinforce or supplement the student's work in the regular classroom. The student receives necessary assistance to ensure his or her keeping pace with regular education peers. (Hardman, et al., 1993, pp. 26-7)

The placement option selected should depend on the abilities and interests of the learner as well as the nature and severity of the disability. The following are examples of responsibilities that can be assumed by career and technical education instructors to ensure that this portion of the IEP is realistic:

- working with special education and support personnel to match the abilities and interests of the learner with an appropriate placement option
- reviewing pupil progress periodically to determine whether the placement is still appropriate
- revising the placement option based on learner progress

The following are examples of statements describing the extent to which a learner with a disability is to participate in a career and technical education program:

- The learner will participate in the horticulture program for a period of one hour a day, five days a week during this academic year.
- The learner will participate in the cosmetology program for a two-hour period of classroom instruction and a one-hour period of related laboratory instruction three times a week for the first semester of this academic year.
- The learner will participate in the family and consumer science program and related laboratory activities for a period of one hour, three times a week during this academic year.

Transition Services

The 1997 amendments to the IDEA emphasized that learners with disabilities are to be prepared for employment and independent living and that specific attention is to be paid to the secondary education they receive. The law also requires coordinated and documented planning. Early and meaningful transition planning, which actively involves learners and their families, has a positive influence on learners' postschool success and independence.

Section 300.29 of the IDEA defines transition service as a coordinated set of activities for a learner with a disability that

- is designed within an outcome-oriented process, that promotes movement from school to postschool activities, including postsecondary education, career and technical education training, integrated employment (including supported employment), continuing and adult education, adult services, independent living, or community participation;
- is based on the individual learner's needs, taking into account the learner's preferences and interests;
- includes instruction, related services, community experiences, the development of employment and other postschool adult living objectives, and, if appropriate, acquisition of daily living skills and functional vocational evaluation.

Realistic transition activities must be outlined in the IEP. Developing skills for an unneeded labor market does not promote employment, and obtaining a job without transportation options compromises the possibility of success. Roles and responsibilities should be written into the plan. Examples of transition activities include

- assessing learner needs, interests, or preferences for future education, employment, and adult living and setting future goals in these areas;
- identifying, exploring, and trying out transition placements that match the learner's assessment and vision and providing community experiences related to future goals;
- instructing the learner in the academic, vocational, and adult living skills needed to achieve transition goals, including self-determination;
- identifying and providing the accommodations, supports, or related services the learner needs;
- coordinating with adult services organizations and helping families identify resources and natural supports; and
- providing or planning follow-up or follow-along support once the learner develops independence in a transition activity or graduates (deFur, 2000).

For learners age 14 and older, the IEP, as a whole, must demonstrate the use of a coordinated set of activities as the means by which the learner can achieve the long-term adult outcomes. Beginning at age 14, the focus of activity is on instruction. At age 15 and older, the coordinated set of activities must address instruction, related services, community experiences, and the development of employment or other postschool adult living objectives. Examples of the coordinated set of activities include the following:

- Instruction–This is educational instruction that will be provided to the learner to achieve the stated outcome (e.g., general and/or special education course instruction, career and technical education, and advanced placement courses).
- Related services–These are specific related services such as rehabilitation counseling services, which will support the learner in attaining the stated outcome.
- Employment and other postschool adult living objectives–These are educational services that will be provided to the learner to prepare for employment or other postschool activities. Postschool activities will determine what other skills or supports will be necessary for the learner to suc-

ceed independently. Examples include participation in a work experience program, information about colleges in which the learner has an interest, and travel training.

- Community experiences–These are community-based experiences that will be offered, or community resources that will be utilized as part of the learner's school program, whether utilized during school or after school, to achieve the stated outcome (e.g., local employers, public library, local stores).
- Activities of daily living skills (ADL) (if appropriate)– This consists of ADL skills to be worked on to achieve the stated outcome (e.g., dressing, hygiene, self-care skills, self-medication).
- Functional vocational assessment (if appropriate)–If the vocational assessment has not provided enough information to make a career and technical program decision, additional assessment activities can be performed to obtain more information about the learner's needs, preferences and interests.

If one of these activities is not included in the IEP in a particular year, then the IEP must explain why that activity is not reflected in any part of the learner's program. Activities of daily living and functional assessment activities should also be included when appropriate to the learner's needs. The coordinated set of activities, in conjunction with the special education programs and services, should incrementally provide the learner with skills and experiences in preparation of long-term adult outcomes. See Figure 6-7.

When transition services and planning are being considered at an IEP meeting, the learner and the adult service agency must be invited to participate in the IEP development. If the learner chooses not to attend the IEP meeting, it is required that the learner be given alternative opportunities to have input into the transition program and service decisions. The committee must document that the learner's preferences and interests have been obtained and considered.

TRANSITION SERVICES MENU

CASE MANAGEMENT
- Transition planning
- IEP management
- Person-centered planning
- Transition curriculum
- Crisis management
- Work with at-risk coordinators

POSTSECONDARY AND CONTINUED EDUCATION
- Orientation and assessments related to college
- Financial aid related to college
- Orientation to disabled resources or services
- Completion of the ASSET/SAT/PSAT
- Assistance and referral for scheduling college courses
- High school completion
- Adult basic education/GED/etc.
- Explore adult/private education option like church outreach

VOCATIONAL TRAINING AND EMPLOYMENT
- Career guidance activities interests/aptitudes inventory job fair
- Resume development, applications, interviews
- School-based enterprise
- Work experience DECA/TSA program
- Military linkages/recruiter contact
- Apprenticeship linkages
- Vocational/trade schools for continued training
- On-the-job training from adult services

COMMUNITY PARTICIPATION
- Mobility training
- Driver's license/permit
- Community recreation and leisure
- Programs at church
- Anger management
- Parenting classes
- Special Olympics
- Hobbies/social skills/personal network development

INDEPENDENT LIVING
- Apartment search and rental contracts, "first time buyer"
- Meal perparation/cooperative shopping
- Budgeting and paying bills/ATM card use
- Loan application
- Income taxes
- Employment related paperwork/I-9 form, W-2, etc.
- Explore independent living programs
- Explore group homes/semi-independent living
- Guardianship/conservatorship issues and assistance

AGENCY ELIGIBILITY DETERMINATION
- VR referral/set up with a VR counselor
- Food stamps, housing, job services
- Religious affiliated support groups/programs
- Investigate support groups/diabetes/ADD/etc.
- Explore SSA supports and funding
- Private funding exploration/trust fund issue resolution/etc.

Adapted from: Peoria Unified School District #11. (n.d.). *Transition Services.* Peoria, AZ: Special Education Department.

Figure 6-7. Sample transition activities and programs that help the learner gain skills and experiences.

If an agency is likely to be providing or paying for a transition service for the learner, then a representative of that agency must be invited to attend the IEP meeting. If no representative can physically participate, then the committee must seek alternative ways of obtaining their input. For example, individual communication or telephone conference calling can be used to meet this requirement. Also, at all IEP meetings, the school division must ensure that the parents understand the proceedings. This includes the arrangements for an interpreter for parents who are deaf or whose native language is other than English.

In order to be effective, transition plans are best developed through the collaboration of many people—special educators, career and technical educators, parents, learners, adult service system providers, and possibly employers. All involved need to recognize and stress the importance of employment as a goal for young people with disabilities. In transition planning, as in all education planning and programming, parents must assume the role of both advocate and collaborator. It is the parent who must make sure that transition planning is an ongoing part of the learner's career development plans. See Figure 6-8. Most importantly, the learner should be involved in transition planning. Making the learner part of the planning team can help by motivating the learner in school and by helping the learner develop self-advocacy skills and self-reliance. In the end, transition planning should ensure that the curriculum of each learner include information about career options and where the leaner stands in terms of career options based on vocational assessment.

Through the assessment process, parents and professionals learn about the learners and the learner becomes self-aware. See Figure 6-9. Learners generally emerge from the vocational assessment process with a better understanding of their skills. When learners are being assessed, a number of changes can be observed. Learners often

- want to discuss their career futures;
- are able to say things they can do;
- show excitement about activities they are working on;
- enthusiastically talk with their families and friends about what they are doing in school;
- develop new, realistic career interests;
- show more self-confidence and/or self-esteem; and
- show more interest in their academic performances.

The transition component of the IEP is just that, a part of the learner's regular IEP. It is not a parallel document or a "transition IEP." All the IEP development requirements and procedures discussed earlier also apply to the transition component. Although only one aspect of the IEP process, the legal significance of transition is substantial. A learner is entitled to those transition services, which for that learner are either special education or related services necessary to enable the learner to benefit from special education. The period of the "benefit" to be considered has arguably been lengthened beyond school and into adult life, but the substantive entitlement is still to special education and related services, not to those plus transition services.

One logical beginning point for the transition component starts with the team reaching agreement about the individual learner's needs with regard to the three mandated areas: (a) instruction, (b) community experiences, and (c) employment and other postschool living objectives. See Figure 6-10. See Appendix. If the team deems it inappropriate to address an area, presumably because the learner presents no unique needs, the IEP must include the basis for that determination. The learner's needs, taking into account interest and preferences, can be explored prior to the meeting, and substantial input can also be gleaned from the questionnaires given to the parents.

When the purpose of the IEP includes developing a transition plan, families must be advised of this purpose. Prior to the meeting many schools send materials to families to encourage them to think about the learner's future. At the meeting, the staff asks family members to describe their vision for the learner. The IEP team uses the family's knowledge in planning and identifying resources the family can use during the transition process. Effective transition planning is sensitive to the culture and context of the family, thus empowering the family for its role in guiding the learner.

Transition planning should help learners and families connect with the adult service system. Adult service organizations that may provide or pay for transition services must be represented at the meeting. If representatives are unable to attend, then the school must find alternative ways of involving them in planning any transition services. Each transition activity should include someone who consents to monitor the provision of that service as outlined in the IEP. See Figure 6-11.

Career and Technical Education

The career and technical education component of the IEP provides a process for educational personnel and community agencies to successfully plan for career and technical education training for learners with disabilities. Local education agencies should assume responsibility for ensuring that the IEPs of learners enrolled in these programs contain a career and technical education component designed to modify the curriculum to meet the needs of the learner.

The following are suggested "pieces" of the IEP for a learner with a disability:

- career interest areas
- types of vocational assessment information (including interviews, observations, and hands-on experiences)
- vocational assessment results (including learner abilities, learner priorities, learner immediate needs, and learner occupational choice)
- career and technical education program in which the learner will be enrolled (including name, site, and instructor)
- career and technical education assistance requirements (including curriculum/competencies adaptations, specially designed instruction, instructional adaptations, equipment for classroom/laboratory modifications, and support personnel assistance or other service needs)

LEARNER PROFILE SHEET—PARENT FORM

Child's Name _____   Date of Birth _____

School _____   Phone _____

Grade Level _____   Date Completed _____

1. What my child is interested in:

2. Things my child is ready to learn:

3. My child is best at:

4. My child needs most help with:

5. Help my child has received in the past:

6. Problems with my child's current program:

7. Possible alternatives and/or additions to my child's current program:

8. Services that my child needs:

9. Special concerns I have about my child:

10. Suggestions I have about working with my child:

11. Strengths my child has in the area of:

    Academics:

    Speech:

    Motor:

    Social/behavior:

    Vocational/prevocational:

    Self-help:

    Self-advocacy skills:

12. Concerns I have for my child in the following areas:

    Academics:

    Speech:

    Motor:

    Social/behavior:

    Vocational/prevocational:

    Self-help:

    Self-advocacy skills:

13. When my child leaves high school as a young adult, I expect:

Source: Bateman, B. (1995). *Writing Individualized Education Programs (IEPs) for Success.* Learning Disabilities Association. [On-line]. Available: http://www.ldonline.org

Figure 6-8. A sample profile sheet for the learner–parent form.

LEARNER PROFILE SHEET—STUDENT FORM

Name _____   Date of Birth _____

School _____   Phone _____

Grade Level _____   Date Completed _____

1. I am interested in:

2. Things I want to learn:

3. I am best at:

4. I need most help with:

5. Help I have received in the past:

6. Problems with my current program:

7. Possible alternatives and/or additions to my current program:

8. Services that I need:

9. Special concerns I have:

10. Suggestions I have about working with me:

11. My strengths in the area of:

    Academics:

    Speech:

    Motor:

    Social/behavior:

    Vocational/prevocational

    Self-help:

    Self-advocacy skills:

12. Concerns I have in the following areas:

    Academics:

    Speech:

    Motor:

    Social/behavior:

    Vocational/prevocational:

    Self-help:

    Self-advocacy skills:

13. When I leave high school as a young adult, I expect:

Source: Bateman, B. (1995). *Writing Individualized Education Programs (IEPs) for Success*. Learning Disabilities Association. [On-line]. Available: http://www.ldonline.org

Figure 6-9. A sample profile sheet for the learner–student form.

TRANSITION PLANNING INTERVIEW

Name _____ Date _____ D.O.B. _____ Graduation Date _____

Please check each box Yes, No, ? if uncertain, or NA if an item does not apply.

A. Employment Career Awareness and Vocational Training

Yes	No	?	NA	
☐	☐	☐	☐	1. Name the top 3 careers you want 1) _____ 2) _____ 3) _____
☐	☐	☐	☐	2. Do you understand employment options: (full time, part time, etc.)
☐	☐	☐	☐	3. Do you want to be employed?
☐	☐	☐	☐	4. Do you need support to remain employed?
☐	☐	☐	☐	a. Can the support be arranged with the employer or employees?
☐	☐	☐	☐	b. Does the support require an outside agency?
☐	☐	☐	☐	5. Do you need sheltered industry? (Goodwill Center)
☐	☐	☐	☐	6. Do you want to be self-employed? If yes, doing what? _____
☐	☐	☐	☐	7. Would you like career exploration help to expand your career options?
☐	☐	☐	☐	a. Do you want or need help to obtain a career?
☐	☐	☐	☐	b. Do you want or need help to maintain a career?

Source: Peoria Unified School District #11. (n.d.). *Transition Services.* Peoria, AZ: Special Education Department.

Figure 6-10. A sample questionnaire to determine learner needs.

TRANSITION SERVICES PLAN . . .

Name: _____ Birthdate: _____ IEP Date: _____

Long Term Goal: _____

ANNUAL GOALS & SHORT TERM OBJECTIVES

Employment Skills

A.   Develop/improve employment skills   Completion Date

_____	1. Participate in a transition orientation	1. _____
_____	2. Complete a vocational assessment	2. _____
_____	a. ___ Level I b. ___ Level II c. ___ Level III	
_____	3. Participate in career counseling	3. _____
_____	4. Explore options	4. _____
_____	5. Participate in a career and technical education class	5. _____
_____	6. Demonstrate job seeking & retention skills	6. _____
_____	7. Complete a career and technical program referral	7. _____
_____	8. Participate in a school-related work experience	8. _____
_____	9. Explore summer job placement opportunities	9. _____
_____	10. Explore community college/4 year college opportunities	10. _____
_____	11. Explore vocational school opportunities	11. _____
_____	12. Explore armed services options	12. _____
_____	13. Explore supported employment options	13. _____
_____	14. Explore competitive employment opportunities	14. _____
_____	15. Explore sheltered employment opportunities	15. _____
_____	16. _____	16. _____
_____	17. _____	17. _____
_____	18. NA (Explain) _____	

Action to Meet Goals & Objectives	Responsible Person(s)	Begin	Review	End

. . . TRANSITION SERVICES PLAN

Daily Living Skills

B.   Develop/increase daily living skills   Completion Date

_____ 1. Acquire personal documents   1. _____
_____ 2. Perform applications of money management   2. _____
_____ 3. Develop mobility skills as appropriate   3. _____
_____ 4. Knowledge of living arrangement options   4. _____
_____ 5. Practice time skills   5. _____
_____ 6. Develop self-advocacy skills   6. _____
_____ 7. Use specialized/alternative equipment for school/work   7. _____
_____ 8. _____ 8. _____
_____ 9. _____ 9. _____
_____ 10. NA (Explain) _____ 10. _____

Action to Meet Goals & Objectives	Responsible Person(s)	Begin	Review	End

Community Living Skills

C.   Gain knowledge of community and service providers   Completion Date

_____ 1. Identify/define fuction of community facilities   1. _____
_____ 2. Use community services to locate employment appropriate to own abilities and disabilities   2. _____
_____ 3. _____ 3. _____
_____ 4. _____ 4. _____
_____ 5. NA (Explain) _____

Action to Meet Goals & Objectives	Responsible Person(s)	Begin	Review	End

Recreation/leisure

D.   Develop recreational/leisure skills   Completion Date

_____ 1. Identify leisure and recreational activities appropriate for ability and interest   1. _____
_____ 2. Initiate leisure and recreational activities individually and in a group   2. _____
_____ 3. _____ 3. _____
_____ 4. _____ 4. _____
_____ 5. NA (Explain) _____

Action to Meet Goals & Objectives	Responsible Person(s)	Begin	Review	End

E.   Additional Comments

_____
_____
_____
_____

Figure 6-11. A sample transition services plan delineating goals and responsible persons.

- transition and employment goals and objectives
- postsecondary education goals and objectives
- anticipated assistance needed in the future
- adaptations needed on the job site
- adaptations needed for seeking and maintaining employment (Pennsylvania Bureau of Vocational-Technical Education, 1993)

The following resources are helpful in developing the career and technical education component of the IEP:

- vocational assessment information (e.g., aptitudes, interests, exploratory experiences, employability skills)
- career and technical educators' ideas for possible goals and objectives
- basic skills information (strengths and limitations)
- learning style information
- realistic career goals/exit points from career and technical education programs
- potential employment opportunities in the community
- resources for transition services
- strategies and/or resources available to assist learners in career and technical education programs See Figure 6-12.

CAREER AND TECHNICAL COMPONENT OF THE INDIVIDUALIZED EDUCATION PROGRAM

SAMPLE PARTS

PRESENT EDUCATION LEVELS

STUDENT STRENGTHS:

ANNUAL GOAL(S)

-
-
-
-

OBJECTIVES

-
-
-

(Student criteria, evaluation procedures, accomplishments, and schedule for determining if objectives are being met.)

CAREER AND TECHNICAL INTEREST AREAS

1.   2.

VOCATIONAL ASSESMENT

DATES GIVEN _____   TYPES _____

VOCATIONAL ASSESSMENT RESULTS

1. ABILITIES/CAPABILITIES
2. PRIORITIES/IMMEDIATE NEEDS
3. OTHER RELATED INFORMATION
4. CAREER AND TECHNICAL CHOICE _____
CAREER AND TECHNICAL PROGRAM TITLE _____
PROGRAM SITE_____

TYPES OF SERVICES/ASSISTANCE REQUIRED AND LEVEL OF INTERVENTION NEEDED BY STUDENT

1. CURRICULUM/VOCATIONAL COMPETENCIES ADAPTATIONS:

2. SPECIFICALLY DESIGNED INSTRUCTION OR INSTRUCTIONAL ADAPTATIONS:

3. EQUIPMENT OR CLASSROOM/LAB MODIFICATIONS/ ASSISTIVE DEVICES:

4. SUPPORTIVE PERSONNEL ASSISTANCE/OTHER SERVICES:

TRANSITION/EMPLOYMENT/POSTSECONDARY

GOALS   OBJECTIVES

-
-
-

ANTICIPATED ASSISTANCE NEEDED IN THE FUTURE:

ADAPTATIONS NEEDED ON THE JOB SITE:

ADAPTATIONS NEEDED FOR SEEKING/MAINTAINING EMPLOYMENT:

IEP PARTICIPANTS:

SIGNATURE	NAME	TITLE
_____	_____	_____
_____	_____	_____
_____	_____	_____
_____	_____	_____

NOTE: A career and technical education representative must be included among the signatures to indicate involvement in IEP planning.

Figure 6-12. An overview of suggested information that should be included in the career and technical education component of an IEP.

ROLE OF ASSESSMENT IN THE INDIVIDUALIZED EDUCATION PROGRAM

Vocational assessment is a comprehensive process conducted over a period of time, involving a multidisciplinary team, with the purpose of identifying individual characteristics, education, and training needs to provide educators with the basis for planning an individual's career pathway. The primary objectives of vocational assessment in an educational setting are the development of instructional goals and objectives matched to a learner's needs, the identification of appropriate teaching strategies to promote learner competency, and the modification of curricula as necessary.

The IEP serves as a primary programming instrument for learners with disabilities. It should guide instructional decision-making as well as identify necessary support services that the learner will need to succeed. For learners with disabilities who are enrolled in career and technical education programs, it is imperative that vocational assessment information be incorporated into the IEP.

In making decisions about the programming elements to be included in the IEP, teachers are expected to summarize learners' strengths and weaknesses as measured by formal and informal assessment, generate statements of present level of functioning, and identify specific annual goals and objectives based on this information. If vocational assessment information is not used in the decision-making process, the IEP will not reflect learners' career and technical education programming needs and will have no systematic guidance for these needs (Cobb & Phelps, 1983).

The following questions should be examined:
- How does vocational assessment information impact the number of IEP career and technical education goals and objectives, i.e., how many IEP career and technical education goals and objectives were written prior to, and how many following, the collection of vocational assessment information?
- How does vocational assessment information impact the kinds of IEP items written, i.e., were the IEP career and technical education goals and objectives directly related to the type of vocational assessment information collected?
- How does the vocational assessment information collected impact the number of IEP career and technical education goals and objectives at each level of severity, i.e., did the number of IEP career and technical education goals and objectives vary depending upon whether a learner was mildly, moderately, or severely disabled?

Existing vocational assessment information about relevant learner strengths and limitations should be obtained in a timely fashion and directed to individuals involved in developing the learner's IEP. In addition, procedures should be developed to translate this information into realistic career and technical education goals and objectives.

INDIVIDUALIZED TRANSITION PROGRAMS

The successful movement from school to employment and community living is a desirable and appropriate outcome for all learners. Persons with disabilities must often cope with significant issues that result in the creation of additional barriers to overcome and hurdles to clear during this critical period. The individualized transition program (ITP) is a two- to four-year written plan identifying the progressive steps a learner will take to meet postgraduation goals. Included in the ITP are the goals and benchmarks needed to achieve identified outcomes. The ITP may include related instruction in life and employability skills designed to maintain actual employment. Evaluations and assessments may be identified to assist the learner in achieving stated outcomes. The objective of an ITP is to provide all essential resources, supports and experiences needed for adult daily living and for full community participation. See Figure 6-13.

Some states require an ITP, which is a separate document from the IEP, as the principal vehicle for guiding transition activities. Other states simply include transition goals within the existing IEP under a section typically entitled "Statement of Transition Services." Both the ITP and the statement of transition services tend to include linkage types of goals.

Regardless of whether or not an ITP is used, the critical issue is that both knowledge/skills and linkage goal statements are generated for all areas of need. The actual individual planning phase is predicated on appropriate assessment procedures. The planning is easy if the assessment phase provides useful information across a range of transition planning areas. For adequate plans to be developed, it is essential that a comprehensive needs assessment be conducted using a variety of sources and instrumentation. Equally important is the involvement of the learner and the parents in the development of transition plans.

Frequently, parents and learners are not sure where to begin when thinking about transition activities, and each learner is different and will need an individualized array of experiences and services to meet their interests, skills, and talents. The list that follows offers some general components of transition that families, school personnel, and learners can consider as they look toward the future. Learners and families can determine which of the components are important to them and which they already have in place and work toward including the important ones in their own life plans.
- School curriculum–The curriculum should include participation in general education classes and involvement in extracurricular activities. Learners should have opportunities to learn about different careers, develop employability skills and social skills, and participate in career and technical training experiences.

- Employment experience–Learners with disabilities can develop a resume of volunteer activities, career and technical education training, and part-time or summer work in the community.
- Self-advocacy skills–When learners have the opportunity to practice decision-making from early on in life, they increase their ability to make choices for themselves and to know what works best for them.
- Support network–A network of family and friends can offer support as the learner moves into the role of community member and worker.

- Coordinated transition–Coordination among the agencies and family is vital to ensure the needed transition services are in place and occur.
- Consideration of learner's interests, preferences, skills–Informal or formalized assessments can provide valuable information about the learner's interests, preferences, and need for support in living arrangements, work, and learning opportunities. These assessments can assist the learner in making decisions about work and living arrangements and provide educational experiences that will meet individual needs.

INDIVIDUALIZED TRANSITION PROGRAM . . .

1. Student information	2. Student's Vision for the Future Graduation Date:
Last name *Student* First name *Annie*	Employment: The student is interested in the following three career options: *Annie sees herself in the medical field, working with children, or helping animals.*
Rights Transfer Date: *10/02* Learner's initials: *AS*	Living Situation: The student sees him/herself living in the following setting(s): *Annie wants to live on her own in an apartment, then in a home married and with children*
Social Security Number *555-55-5555* High School Choice: NA (Elementary only)	Postsecondary Education/Training: The student is willing to continue training in: (Circle all that apply) (A four-year college) (a community college) (a vocational/trade school,) an apprenticeship, the military, on-the-job training only, other_____

3. Specific Student Preferences for Postschool Activities: (Complete all that apply and list specifics only.)

[X] Postsecondary Education *ASU, NAU, GCC*	[X] Employment Sites/Industry *St. Josephs w/dad, PUSD*	[X] Independent Living *Explore independent living skills training as a senior*	[X] Community Participation *Needs to get her driver's license*
[X] Vocational/ Trade Schools *Apollo College, Bryman, or Long Medical Institution*	[ ] Continuing/Adult Education *Not at this time*	[X] Adult Services *Explore RSA and SSI*	[X] Functional Evaluation *Possibly SAGE, RSA Vocational Evaluation, ACT, PSAT, SAT*

4. Statement of Services Needs: (Write a statement to describe how the service relates to the student's vision statement.)

Instruction not included on SP22D & SP22H (Statement of how instruction is different from that of a typical student; i.e., location; types of supports; modifications, etc.)
    [ ] Needed   [X] Not Needed: *No additional instructional assistance needed*

Employment (Describe/list courses, supports, and exploration the student will need in order to accomplish vision.)
    [X] Needed   [ ] Not Needed: *Medical, children, and animals*

Independent Living/Community Participation (Experiences to prepare students for independent living and/or community participation.)
    [X] Needed   [ ] Not Needed: *Will explore with parents how to obtain her driver's permit and license*

Related/Transportation Services (Related services the learner needs to move to adult life. List transportation issues.)
    [X] Needed   [ ] Not Needed: *Transition services, speech*

... INDIVIDUALIZED TRANSITION PROGRAM

Learner's Name Annie Student   Date of Meeting 10/15   Month this Plan is Written October

5. Projected Course of Study for Graduation or Program Completion
Beginning at age 14, project the events/activities/classes needed to transition to postschool activities.

	School Year 99 to 00		School Year 00 to 01		School Year 01 to 02		School Year 02 to 03
#	Course/Activity	#	Course/Activity	#	Course/Activity	#	Course/Activity
1.	Enroll in Discovery class at PHS	1.	Begin medical science program if selected	1.	Meet with the transition coordinator to identify post-graduation assistance. Explore RSA eligibility	1.	Complete COOP experience
2.	Complete the SAGE evaluation by contacting 486-6357 with teacher assistance	2.	Participate in Life FACS class	2.	Complete the PSAT	2.	Participate in the transition program for career exploration and job development
3.	Identify with the counselor when to take medical science and put into IGP	3.	Continue to improve attendance and tardiness	3.	Complete the ASSET placement assessment	3.	Complete the SAT or ACT for college
4.	Improve attendance and tardiness	4.	Investigate getting a driver's license	4.	Complete Health Care Tech Lab	4.	Identify two colleges to investigate with the counselor
		5.	Enroll in driver's education	5.	Complete Patient Care Tech Lab	5.	Continue with Health Care Tech Lab
				6.	Complete Child Psychology	6.	Continue Patient Care Tech Lab
						7.	Explore the use of an independent living skills program with RSA, if appropriate

Source: Peoria Unified School District #11. (n.d.). *Transition Services*. Peoria, AZ: Special Education Department.

Figure 6-13. A sample ITP.

The actual format of an ITP is not important, as long as goal statements for all areas needing instruction or linkages are listed. However, some ITP forms are better designed and organized than others. Most transition professionals will have to work with the forms their school districts have adopted. Although great variation exists regarding ITP formats, every goal statement within the ITP should be accompanied by the following components:
- present level of performance
- specific activities needed to be performed to accomplish the goal
- anticipated date of completion of activities
- person(s) responsible

Most ITPs include sections in addition to the goal statement section. Also, a section for a listing of any persons participating in the IEP meetings is important. Using the data collected from 17 states, Patton (2001) identified the transition planning domains used by more than half of these states:
- community participation
- daily living
- employment
- financial/income management
- health
- independent living (includes living arrangements)
- leisure/recreation
- postsecondary education
- relationships/social skills
- transportation/mobility
- career and technical education training

Resources available to the ITP team to develop relevant goals and associated experiences/activities include the following:
- professional associations (meetings, journals, networking)
- instructional materials
- interagency networking
- transition guidelines
- assessment and evaluation services
- school-to-work linkages
- parent training materials
- workshops and seminars
- conferences
- curriculum development

The curriculum should be tied very closely to the issues surrounding transition. The fact that one of the goals of education is to prepare learners to become contributing citizens implies that the content taught in school should have adult outcome competencies. Furthermore, a major goal of the actual transition planning process is to determine needs, some of which will require instruction. Elements of transition education should be part of the educational programs of all learners with special needs.

A number of models exist that are helpful for providing instruction on topics closely related to adult outcomes. The similarities across the programs are numerous, as reflected in their materials, content taught, and types of suggested classroom activities. However, differences can typically be found, primarily in the way the curriculum is designed. Every curriculum design establishes a somewhat different set of priorities and provides for a program developed to respond to a particular set of needs that are considered important by any number of individuals. Most curricular models designed to prepare learners for adult roles focus primarily on the introduction to and the acquisition of adult skills. Coverage of important life skills can be accomplished through either the establishment of course work that is life skills/transition education oriented or the integration of life skills topics into existing content.

Three themes seem to weave through the actual transition planning process:

1. The more that is known about the receiving settings and the learner's competence in dealing with these settings, the more likely are the learner's chances for success.
2. The more comprehensive the assessment of transition needs, the easier is the task of developing useful and appropriate transition plans.
3. The more the entire array of school-based professionals is involved in the transition process, the more likely they are to understand and be able to address a learner's needs.

Patton (2001) identified certain principles that are essential to guiding the transition process for learners with special needs. The 12 guiding principles discussed below have been gleaned from the professional literature on transition and from actual practice. They should serve as a frame of reference for the implementation of transition services.

1. Transition efforts should start early–Without question, it is preferable to consider the transition process from a proactive rather than a reactive perspective. Certain precursors of the knowledge and skills needed in adulthood can be started at the preschool level. Most can be addressed before transition needs are assessed prior to age 14. What is needed is a systematic K-12 transition education program that has a strong base at the elementary level. Families should be informed of the transition process early on. They can be provided information that they need to be considering as the learner moves through school. Some transition-related activities must be started early to ensure a seamless transition to postschool settings.
2. Planning must be comprehensive–The main point is that a range of adult outcome areas should be evaluated when a needs assessment is conducted. If a strong proactive

transition education program is in place, then fewer areas of need are likely to be identified. Nevertheless, a comprehensive look at each learner must be performed and dismissal of some transition planning areas should not be done as a function of the learner's disability. For instance, the transition needs of certain learners may be overlooked because of the misconception that these learners do not have needs in some areas (e.g., daily living).
3. Planning process must balance what is ideal with what is possible–Although this recommendation is sound and the accompanying suggestions warranted, the realities of serving large numbers of learners must be taken into consideration. The practices associated with sound transition planning must be acceptable to those who have to carry them out. This concept, known as treatment acceptability, is an important one to understand and keep in mind when developing transition services.

Recommended practices need to be immediately useful to school-based staff and cannot be time demanding. Some transition specialists have extremely large caseloads and are unable to conduct in-depth assessment of every learner. Techniques and methodologies are needed that provide as much information as possible within a reasonable amount of time and with a reasonable amount of effort.

4. Learner participation is essential–The literature of transition regularly stresses the importance of preparing learners to be active, contributing participants in the transition planning process. The physical presence of learners at the transition meeting is not sufficient; they should be the driving force behind this process and the meeting. Of course, this will not always be possible, as some learners are not capable of directing their transition planning process. However, far too few learners who are capable are active participants.
5. Family involvement is crucial–Families play a key role in the shared responsibility for preparing the learner for dealing successfully with the challenges of life. Moreover, for most young adults with disabilities, it is their parents or guardians who become their service coordinators, or transition specialists once school ends. For these reasons, it is imperative that parents and guardians become informed, skilled, and active in the transition process. In addition to determining the preferences and interests of learners, it is valuable to do likewise with families.

Transition professionals must not become disillusioned by the fact that a substantial number of parents and guardians either will choose not to assume the important role discussed above, or will be ineffective in this role. During the time the learner is still in school, it is possible and necessary for school-based personnel to take responsibility for certain activities for which the family should be responsible. After learners exit from the school system, they and their families must realize that they will be on their own without the supports they have previously had available.

Transition personnel must respect family values. It is important to recognize that families will base their requests, opinions, and comments on their own community or cultural values, practices, and traditions. Their perspectives must be respected, even when in conflict with those of school-based personnel.

6. The transition planning process must be sensitive to diversity–There is no question that the transition process is affected by the changing demography in this country. Heightened awareness of cultural diversity has emerged in recent years. Although sensitivity to specific cultural distinctions must be instituted, cultural diversity is only one type of diversity that must be addressed. Other dimensions that should be considered include racial, behavioral, ethnic, physical/sensory, religious, intellectual/cognitive, sexual orientation, and gender. Although all of these elements are worthy of attention, some are less obvious than others. For instance, the implications of gender in the transition process may be so subtle that they are overlooked. Female learners, for example, should not be limited in their consideration of career options; they should be afforded a wide range of choices.

7. Everyone uses supports and services–We are all interdependent beings, but it is very natural for us to use supports that exist in our everyday environments. With this in mind, it is essential that professionals convey to learners with special needs that the use of supports and services is acceptable. These individuals need to be taught when and how to use the array of natural supports and services available to them in the settings in which they live and work.

8. Community-based activities are important–Most learners with disabilities will prosper from experiences that are provided in real-life contexts. These learners are more likely to acquire the knowledge and skills they will need to function in community settings if they have opportunities to learn and practice in these settings.

Community-based assessment and instruction are strongly recommended for determining needs and providing meaningful learning. One of the strongest reasons for delivering instruction in community settings is that many individuals with disabilities have difficulty generalizing the skills they have learned in the classroom to community settings.

9. Interagency commitment, cooperation, and coordination must be improved–Adult service providers are key players in the transition process. Most adult service agencies, whether public or private, are responsible for a wide range of services, but transition is not one of their major charges. However, to enhance the overall effectiveness of the transition planning process, adult service providers must be involved. As a result, efforts must be ongoing to improve the coordination of various agencies and school-based transition services.

10. Timing is crucial if certain linkages are to be made and a seamless transition to life after high school is to be achieved–Changes associated with the reauthorization of the IDEA provide a strong message that the timing involved with the transition planning process in critical. A statement of transition needs is now required by age 14 for all identified learners. This requirement improves the chances that appropriate plans will be developed, needed services will be identified, and requisite activities will be performed. The overall goal is to move the learner from school to various subsequent settings without difficulty and without the interruption of needed services. Only when the timing is right can this goal be accomplished.

11. The transition planning process should be considered a capacity-building activity–Considering a learner's transition needs is by definition a deficit-oriented process. Although deficits cannot be totally ignored, this process should promote the recognition of the learner's strengths as well. A thorough needs assessment should determine both areas of concern and areas in which the individual shows competence and proficiency. Transition staffs need to consider both aspects of the learner's profile.

12. Ranking of transition needs must occur–Some youth will display an extensive list of needs. It is important not only to identify these needs, but also to determine which should be addressed first. If the learner is likely to exit school in the near future, a ranking of needs must be done. This ranking can be based on a number of factors, such as which areas are most critical for successful adult functioning or which areas the individual will encounter first. The priority ranking should be determined by the learner when appropriate.

Role of Career and Technical Education Personnel

Once transition goals and objectives have been developed for a learner in an IEP, school personnel then design activities to help the learner achieve each objective. Many employment-related transition goals can be realized through participation in career and technical education programs.

If employment is the postschool option for the learner, the following questions should be answered so that appropriate career planning can occur:

1. In what type of work is the student interested?
2. Considering the nature and severity of the student's disability and the nature of his or her job interests, is it realistic for the student to be involved in competitive employment?
3. If the student has chosen a particular occupational field, does he or she have the skills and abilities needed to succeed in that field? What specific work skills does the student not have?
4. Does the student know what employee behaviors are considered important for successful employment, and does he or she demonstrate these behaviors?

5. What school activities are needed in order for the student to acquire these work-related skills and behaviors?
6. What type of academic, social, and/or vocational and applied technology [career and technical] education program is needed to help the student acquire relevant work skills and behaviors before he or she exits high school? Is there such a program available within the school system or community? If not, what individuals and organizations (school, businesses, paraprofessionals, job coaches) can collaborate to develop a personalized program to address the student's needs?
7. What types of accommodations might the student need on the job? Is the student informed as to his or her rights under federal law to receive accommodations? Does he or she have the self-advocacy skills necessary to request and obtain these accommodations? (National Information Center for Children and Youth with Disabilities, 1993, p. 10)

If postsecondary education or training is the postschool direction for the learner, the following needs should be addressed so that appropriate career planning can occur:
- whether the student intends to pursue an academic or technically-oriented education after high school
- the nature and severity of the student's disability and how it affects pursuing postsecondary education
- the level of effective study habits that the student has developed
- accommodations needed during admissions tests for postsecondary institutions (e.g., test in braille, oral presentation of questions, untimed testing)
- identification of postsecondary institutions that offer appropriate training or education that meets the student's needs
- identification of the types of accommodations and support services the student would need after enrolling in a postsecondary institution (National Information Center for Children and Youth with Disabilities, 1993, p. 11)

A Framework for Implementing Transition Programs

The following sequential steps in strategic planning for transition services produce high quality results when utilized by a team of committed individuals drawn from a variety of disciplines:
1. Define the vision with a broad-based mission statement that incorporates the beliefs and values of the team and identifies a clear direction for the future. This focus may lead to a description of successful postsecondary learner performance and functioning.
2. Scan the environment and evaluate and determine the status of primary aspects associated with transition planning. This evaluation may be building-based or districtwide in scope. Include a review of curriculum, career and technical education, work-study, assessment, parent/learner involvement, forms/procedures, etc.

3. Select priority outcome by asking "What is most important? What's achievable? What needs to be accomplished?" Be selective since the probability of doing it all successfully might be quite low.
4. Identify barriers and opportunities by determining the present and future issues, people, and policies that may help to promote the vision or attainment of priority outcomes or may act to discourage or interfere with developing effective and innovative transition-planning practices.
5. Identify strategies by developing a list or menu covering a variety of possible ways of removing barriers and enhancing opportunities. Engage in constructive problem solving with the team and identify what may or may not work.
6. Identify supports and secure needed essential resources. Administrative support should be secured. Assess what will be needed in order to fully provide the support. Be careful not to underestimate.
7. Develop an implementation plan. Make it a clear, well-defined plan of action. Build in time lines and accountability and make sure that all team members are involved and invested. Keep it coherent, concise and simple. It should relate to the priority outcomes previously established.
8. Implement the plan by putting its activities and components in motion. Evaluate the ongoing plan to identify if more help is needed in certain areas or if an adjustment is needed based upon new information. Team meetings are critical at this stage.
9. Monitor outcomes by evaluating the products or outcomes associated with the teams efforts and activities. Measure what changes occurred and decide what still needs to be done.

Successful transition practices for learners with disabilities include the following:
- Learner development–Research indicates that work quality, attitude, social skills, and academic skills are related to postschool employment. On-the-job training that includes work-based and school-based learning enhances employment rates.
- Interagency and interdisciplinary collaboration–the IDEA requires collaboration on both the individual planning and community planning levels. Interagency collaboration focuses on programs, systems, and service delivery. Interagency coordinating bodies should include all stakeholders, including consumers, family members, service providers, and employers.
- Family involvement–Research indicates that parents and family members should be involved in transition planning. Because many families are involved in transition activities, practitioners should capitalize on their strengths and abilities.
- Program structure and attributes–To implement transition programs that reflect the above categories, schools and programs should be organized accordingly. Educational

programs must be based upon postschool goals and a variety of curricular options must be available to learners.

• Learner-focused planning–The IEP is the planning vehicle for implementing the transition requirements specified in the IDEA. Learner participation in the process is essential, and self-determination skills are considered to be fundamental for participation. The IEP should include identification of valued and attainable postschool goals (Kohler, 2000).

Practitioners should begin early to assist and guide learners in developing appropriate education programs based on individual transition goals such as the following:

• How to choose goals–Provide experiences so learners identify their interests, skills, and limits across transition areas.

• How to participate in and lead their IEP meetings–Teach learners self-determination, self-advocacy, and meeting skills.

• How to accomplish goals–Teach learners how to develop a plan to attain their goals, take action on the plan, and evaluate and adjust their plan of action (deFur, 2000).

With sufficient preparation and support, learners can participate in their IEP process in various ways. The extent of participation will depend on their abilities and interests. For example, some learners direct their own meetings, while others direct a specific part. Teachers experienced in involving their learners in the IEP process have made the following suggestions:

• Begin instruction as early as possible. Some areas of study, such as self-determination, can begin in the elementary school.

• Be prepared to support learners with sensitive issues. Some learners may never have seen their IEP and some may not even know what it means. Even if a learner knows about IEPs, reading about one's disability can be unsettling. Teachers need to work through all issues and questions with learners. It may help to talk individually with learners before sharing the IEP.

• Ensure that learners understand what their disability means. It is important that learners know about their disability and can talk about it to others. Encourage learners to become comfortable stating what they need and what they do not need.

• Make sure you feel comfortable with the process. Learners will know if adults are uncomfortable talking about a topic or allowing the learner to lead the IEP.

• Schedule time for learner to develop skills related to IEP participation on a regular basis. It is very easy to let other subjects—particularly academics—take priority. Teachers must believe that self-determination, planning, and self-advocacy skills are priorities.

• Teach IEP participation skills as a semester course. Learners need sufficient time to master the skills. Although learners can be taught skills once a week or in a daylong course, they must be allowed sufficient time in order to take an active role.

• Use motivational techniques to interest learners. Before you begin training, invite an individual with a disability to talk to learners. It helps to have role models as speakers (e.g., an individual who is a college graduate, an individual who has gone to a career and technical education center, an individual who works in supported employment, a person who owns a business).

• Communicate with families. Let parents know your intentions. It helps to invite families to a meeting where you can explain the approach and answer their questions (deFur, 2000).

SELF-DETERMINATION AND THE SELF-DIRECTED INDIVIDUALIZED EDUCATION PROGRAM

Learners with disabilities often confront numerous challenges as they transition from high school to adult life, including employment and independent living barriers, social isolation, discrimination, and difficulty in accessing and coordinating services. It is generally agreed that comprehensive transition planning is essential if youth with disabilities are to assume adult roles that reflect full and equal participation in society. It is also clear that planning efforts must promote the participation of youth, families, school staff, and representatives from community agencies whose mission is to assist learners to achieve transition objectives. Unfortunately, the active participation of youth in transition efforts has traditionally been overlooked. As a result, many learners with disabilities are excluded from opportunities to successfully shape the direction of their transition planning and to develop the requisite skills for their assumption of control over their lives following graduation. It is essential that the capacity of local school and state educational agencies to promote youth involvement in transition planning be bolstered. Learners must be able to exercise choice, control, and responsibility in the transition planning process.

IDEA '97 clearly supports learners' independence, self-management, and self-determination. The amendments require that learners be involved in the development of their IEPs as members of their own IEP teams and that they attend their IEP meetings as active participants. IDEA '97 also states that learners' education programs must be based on their preferences and interests. One year before the learner reaches the age of majority, learners must also be informed of the rights that will transfer to them when reaching their majority. These requirements put considerable responsibility on learners. To fulfill these requirements, we must support learners in learning new self-management and self-determination skills that foster independence.

In addition, the amendments state that the federal government has an ongoing obligation to support programs, projects, and activities that help learners acquire skills that will empower them to lead productive and independent adult lives. The amendments also state that "an essential element of our national policy [is] ensuring equality of opportunity, full

participation, independent living, and economic self-sufficiency for individuals with disabilities." Educational personnel are required to ensure that learners "have the skills
and knowledge . . . to be prepared to lead productive, independent, adult lives, to the maximum extent possible."

Self-determination is believing you can control your own
destiny. Self-determination is a combination of attitudes and
abilities that lead people to set goals for themselves and to
take the initiative to reach those goals. It means making
choices, learning to effectively solve problems, and taking
control and responsibility. Practicing self-determination
also means experiencing the consequences of making
choices. The development of self-determination skills is
a process that begins in childhood and continues throughout life. Self-determination involves many attitudes and
abilities including self-awareness, assertiveness, creativity,
pride, and problem-solving and self-advocacy skills. Self-
determination includes setting goals, evaluating options,
making choices, and then working to achieve those goals.

Self-determination is important for all people, but it is
especially important, and often more difficult to learn, for
learners with disabilities. Well-meaning individuals sometimes "protect" learners with disabilities by making all
their decisions for them, and sometimes people assume
that those with disabilities can't think for themselves.

Since self-determination skills are most effectively
learned and developed by practicing them, learners with
disabilities should be given ample opportunity to use their
self-advocacy, decision-making and socialization skills well
before they leave high school in order to prepare for working and living in their community. See Figure 6-14.

The synthesis team at the National Leadership Summit
on Self-Determination and Consumer-Direction and Control (1999) consolidated the following statements regarding self-determination:

- We must recognize that advancing and enhancing self-
determination is a lifelong issue that should not be
compartmentalized as a concern of one particular age
or disability group. While there are distinct issues faced
by these groups, they also share some common needs,
such as personal assistance services, affordable accessible housing, transportation, education, and other resources to support them in their decision making and
in their quality of life.
- Learners with disabilities and their families must have
a voice in planning and implementing the services and
supports that will assist them in their everyday lives.
- We should create partnerships/linkages between organizations (including government agencies at the federal and state levels), initiatives, and demonstration
projects focusing on self-determination and consumer
direction. This should include collaborative agendas
addressing commons issues. Special efforts should be
made by those affiliated with self-determination funding, quality of life, and skills initiatives to work together and integrate their efforts.

SELF-DETERMINATION		
	Methods That You Currently Use	**Areas To Develop or Improve**
Know Yourself What's your dream? Know your strengths, weaknesses, needs and performances; know the options; decide what is important.		
Value Yourself Accept and value your-self; admire strengths that come from unique-ness; recognize and respect rights and re-sponsibilities; take care of yourself.		
Plan Set goals; plan actions to meet goals; anticipate results; be creative; vis-ually rehearse.		
Act Take risks; communi-cate: access resources and support; negotiate; deal with conflict and criticism; be persistent.		
Experience Outcomes and Learn Compare outcome to expected outcome; compare performance to expected perform-ance: realize success; make adjustments.		

Source: Office of Superintendent of Public Instruction. (2001). *Self-Determination*. Olympia, WA: Special Education.

Figure 6-14. A chart to help determine strengths and weaknesses of self-determination skills.

- Schools should incorporate instruction in and opportunities for self-determination in integrated settings as
part of the general curriculum.
- Adults and children with disabilities may have different "pathways" to achieve self-determination. Children
may require skills training and capacity building before having the opportunity to exercise choice and make
decisions. For adults, the reverse may be true—training
and capacity building may follow choice.
- There is often great tension between individuals' preference for autonomy and independence their families'
desire for safety and protection for them.

- More research is needed in various areas related to personal, family, and community strategies to support self-determination. Some possible areas include fostering self-determination among younger children and persons with moderate to severe cognitive disabilities; ways in which families and home environments affect the development of self-determination; the effectiveness of peer support and training for older adults in consumer-directed services; and identifying innovative models of exercising choice and self-determination. Wherever possible, this research should be participatory action research involving input from individuals with disabilities and their families and examining issues from their unique perspectives.
- One of the biggest barriers to self-determination among persons with mental health disabilities is the culturally transmitted stigma attached to having a mental illness. Often this stigma may then be internalized by the person with the mental illness, which leads to a loss of self-esteem and an expectation of discrimination.
- It is necessary for individuals with disabilities and their families to explore and identify their own preferences, needs, values, abilities, capacities and desire for self-direction and their own vision of quality of life before they can truly exercise choice.
- Individuals with disabilities and family members acting on behalf of relatives with disabilities must possess good problem solving and communication skills in order to exercise self-determination.
- Families are a crucial component in the movement toward self-determination. They serve as role models for exercising choice and control and provide support, encouragement, feedback, and a "safe" place to take risks and make decisions.
- Peer support, as well as family support, can play an important role in the socialization of individuals of all ages with disabilities to the "culture" of self-determination.
- It is important to recognize and accommodate cultural diversity in creating programs and resources for people with disabilities and their families. This includes acknowledging that different cultures place differing value and importance on the concept of self-determination.
- Programs and supports for persons with disabilities need to be highly individualized in order to accommodate their distinct needs, preferences, and capabilities for self-determination.
- There must be opportunities for people with disabilities to receive services and support in the most integrated and inclusive settings possible (i.e., schools, workplaces, and home – as opposed to institutions).
- Communities (including schools, workplaces, and other environments) must be physically, cognitively, and attitudinally accessible in order for individuals to have real choice.
- There is a great need for affordable and accessible housing and transportation, as well as meaningful work and other activities for people with disabilities.

Learner involvement with the IEP maximizes self-determination. The IEP process must consider learner needs, preferences, and wishes. Self-management of the IEP offers the opportunity for learning self-determination skills. The central focus is to prepare the learner to plan the IEP staffing, lead the IEP meeting, and implement the IEP. The behaviors learned while managing the IEP are the same self-determination skills needed for success after school.

A basic component of self-awareness is identification of interests. Through situational experiences learners identify school, employment, post–high school education, personal, residential, and community interests. Once known, learners will present their interests in their IEP meeting and the subsequent plan will be based upon their interests. It is vital that educational systems, parents, and other service providers do everything they can to facilitate the development of each learner's self-determination skills. The IEP meeting is one critically important, and appropriate, place for the learner to have an active, self-determining role.

To facilitate the learner's participation in the transition process, however, many learners may need to be informed about the nature of their role in the IEP meeting and afterwards—specifically, what their participation entails. Expressing personal preferences and desires and advocating for themselves, particularly in the presence of authority figures such as administrators, teachers, and parents, may be a new role for learners. Parents can help prepare the learner to participate in IEP meetings by talking about its purpose, describing what goes on and who typically attends, and discussing transition issues with the learner before and after the meetings occur. Some learners may benefit from rehearsing certain aspects of meetings, such as greetings and appropriate ways to express preferences or suggest alternatives. If the learner requires any accommodation, such as an interpreter or an augmentative communication device, this should be arranged (by the learner, parents, or teacher) in advance of the meeting. Ultimately, the goal is for learners to assume control (with appropriate levels of support) over the transition program and identify and manage its various components.

Principles underlying self-determination include the following:
- Self-determination is essential to personal freedom, citizenship, self-sufficiency, and full participation in family and society.
- Access to information, the physical environment, employment, and other typical life opportunities are critical to the expression of self-determination.
- Self-determination should be promoted across the life span within the culture and ethnicity of the individual, family, and community.
- Implementation of self-determination practices requires society to support the capacities of all individuals to speak and care for themselves.

Special education demonstration projects were analyzed to identify the skills necessary for self-determination. These activities were placed into the following four categories:

1. Self-determination curriculum and instruction–In many projects, courses to teach self-determination skills were developed and offered either on an elective or required basis. Through such a course, learners typically identified their strengths and weaknesses, identified their ideal self and dreams, got feedback from others, learned decision making, and set personally meaningful goals. Some projects employed learners to choose their own topics related to self-determination. The format and strategies utilized to deliver the self-determination curricula varied as greatly as the projects themselves. In general, format consisted of individual or small group activities, and curricula were delivered in both school-based and community-based settings.

   All projects included in the analysis developed curricula that focused on developing specific skills associated with self-determination. Skill content across projects was diverse, but generally addressed one of three areas: problem solving, self-development, and self-advocacy and life skills. Content related to problem solving included individual and group decision making, clarification of stakeholders and their roles in decision making, and decision evaluation and team building. Self-development content included activities to enrich the individual and develop self-determination. Projects focused on interpersonal skills, assertiveness training, communication, and listening skills. On a more personal level, projects addressed such issues as self-talk, coping, self-management, and self-esteem and included activities to draw upon and activate creative potential.

2. Mentoring and modeling–Mentoring and modeling activities were used to deliver instruction and to provide learners with role models who have successfully acquired self-determination skills. Mentors served as role models and as advocates in order to promote self-determination skill development. Mentors received training relevant to their roles, responsibilities, and goals related to developing self-determination skills in learners.

3. Community-based learning and generalization across environments–Most projects conducted activities in community settings, offered opportunities to learn by doing, and provided support to learners in actualizing their dreams. Examples of community settings include employment sites, postsecondary institutions, independent living centers, and public agencies. Learners often participated directly in activities designed to let them learn by doing. Projects also structured activities to provide increased opportunities for learners to practice their newly learned skills in different environments.

4. Futures planning and learner involvement in planning–The ability and opportunity to plan for one's future are central to self-determination. Thus, most of the projects focused on developing skills related to goal setting and decision making and provided learners opportunities to practice these skills to plan for the future. Some projects developed curricula that focused on planning in general, while others focused specifically on transition planning and IEP development and then provided the opportunity for learners to participate formally in the IEP process.

In some projects, learners participated in specific curricular activities through which they identified goals, identified and selected options for achieving their goals, and then took action toward their goals through in-school and/or community-based activities. Learners also planned, made decisions, and took action with support from significant others. In projects that focused on the IEP process, learners identified their interests, life dreams, and their vision for the future through structured activities. Then they matched their preferences to available opportunities through activities that supported the discovery of conclusion about themselves and their environment. Through one project, learners utilized self-evaluation and evaluation by significant others to identify their skills and limits and participated in curricular activities that would help them direct their IEP planning (Ward, 1999).

Following are the nine propositions for self-directed transition planning:

1. Learners must be taught how to do transition planning.
2. Learners are not naturally motivated to do transition planning, which creates a potential barrier to getting them involved in the process.
3. Self-evaluation is an essential foundation for engaging successfully in transition planning. Learners must gain an understanding of who they are before they can explore meaningfully who they might become.
4. There are four important areas that learners should explore when they do transition planning: (1) personal life, (2) jobs, (3) education and training, and (4) living on your own.
5. To the extent possible, learners should develop and direct their own transition planning and meetings. For high school learners with disabilities, this often means directing the transition portion of their IEP meetings.
6. Learners must learn how to implement their transition plans. Simply developing a plan is not enough.
7. Wherever possible, parents should participate in a curriculum that focuses on self-directed transition planning.
8. A curriculum embedded within an existing instructional program is the best way to provide instruction in self-directed transition planning.
9. Since transition planning represents a type of problem solving that learners will need throughout their lives, it is more important for learners to learn a transition planning process than to select and work on the very best transition goals that are possible during the time that they are experiencing instruction on how to do transition planning (University of Colorado, n.d.).

INDIVIDUALIZED EDUCATION PROGRAM TEAMS

The IEP requires a cooperative planning effort. A team of individuals is responsible for developing the IEP. See Figure 6-15. The term "individualized education program team" or "IEP team" means a group of individuals composed of

- the parents of a learner with a disability;
- at least one regular education teacher of the learner (if the learner is, or may be, participating in the regular education setting);
- at least one special education teacher, or where appropriate, at least one special education provider of the learner;
- a representative of the local educational agency who is qualified to provide or supervise the provision of specially designed instruction to meet the unique needs of learners with disabilities and who is knowledgeable about the general curriculum and the availability of resources of the local educational agency;
- an individual who can interpret the instructional implications of evaluation results;
- other individuals (at the discretion of the parent or the agency) who have knowledge or special expertise regarding the learner, including related services personnel as appropriate; and
- the learner with a disability (whenever appropriate). See Figure 6-16.

RESPONSIBILITIES OF IEP TEAM MEMBERS							
Responsibility	Career and Technical Education Teacher	Special Education Teacher	Guidance/ Vocational Counselor	Administrator (Vocational Supervisor, Special Education, Local/ School Administrator)	Rep from Community Agency	Parent/ Guardian	Learner
Gather background information concerning a particular learner	X	X	X	X	X	X	X
Develop appropriate annual goals for participation in the career and technical education program	X	X		X	X	X	X
Develop realistic short term instructional objectives to accompany the IEP	X	X				X	
Develop specific criterion levels for successful achievements of short-term objectives	X	X					
Identify support services that will be necessary to aid the learner	X	X		X	X	X	
Provide the necessary support services		X		X	X		
Develop appropriate lesson plans that will implement the content of the IEP	X	X					
Utilize the appropriate teaching techniques	X	X					
Supply remedial assistance		X			X	X	
Periodically assess learner progress in achieving the goals and objectives	X	X					
Document learner progress for use in evaluating the IEP	X	X					
Participate in the annual review of the IEP	X	X		X	X	X	X

Figure 6-15. An overview of responsibilities of team members in the development and implementation of the IEP.

	Activities and Input for Special Education Personnel	**Activities and Input for Career and Technical Educators**
	RESPONSIBILITIES OF SPECIAL EDUCATORS AND CAREER AND TECHNICAL EDUCATORS IN THE IEP PROCESS	
Referral of students	Review and analyze referral information Disseminate referral procedure	Identify students encountering learning difficulties Refer students requiring special services to succeed
Informal data collection	Disseminate information describing available special education and related services	Provide requested information regarding career and technical education program and/or referred learner
Evaluation	Obtain consent for evaluation of learner from parents Collect additional information	
Eligible for services	Complete a comprehensive evaluation by psychologist and other special education personnel Determined by special education personnel	
Sharing assessment information	Contact parents Arrange meeting	Coordinate the determination of learner's vocational interest and aptitude
Placement decision	Appoint LEA representatives Conduct meeting(s) Identify the least restrictive environment placement	Review assessment information on the basic skills (e.g., reading) Assist in determining least restrictive environment Identify goals and objectives for the career and technical education program Select goals and objectives for the learner
Developing and writing the IEP	Develop annual educational goals and objectives	Design instructional plans and materials Specify support services and special materials needed Identify needed equipment and facility modifications
Implementing and monitoring the IEP	Provide specialized instructions Provide support and teacher consultation services	Develop cooperative arrangements for implementing and evaluating the IEP Compile and report learner progress information
IEP evaluation	Manage the monitoring and evaluation of the IEP	Assess learner attainment of goals and objectives Recommend changes in IEP Evaluate support services and assistance received

Adapted from: Kentucky Department of Education. (n.d.). *Procedures for Identification, Evaluation, and Placement of Exceptional Children.* Frankfort, KY: Bureau of Education for Exceptional Children.

Figure 6-16. An overview of suggested activities and inputs for special education and career and technical education personnel involved in the IEP process.

The law makes it clear that the learner is the most important member of the team. In fact, according to the IDEA regulations, the learner must be invited to participate in the IEP meeting (after reaching age 14) whenever the purpose of the meeting is related to transition. If the learner does not attend the meeting, then IDEA regulations expect schools to take other steps to ensure the learner's preferences and interests are considered.

The new legislation also increases the role of the regular education teacher on the IEP team to include, when appropriate, helping to determine (1) positive behavioral strategies and interventions and (2) supplementary aids and services, program modifications, and support for school personnel. The supplementary aids and support for school personnel are to be provided so that the learner can advance appropriately toward attaining the annual goals, be involved in and progress in the general curriculum and other activities, and be educated and participate with other learners with disabilities and nondisabled learners.

While a regular education teacher must be a member of the IEP team if the child is, or may be, participating in the regular education environment, the teacher need not (depending upon the learners needs and the purpose of the specific IEP team meeting) be required to participate in all decisions made as part of the meeting, be present throughout the entire meeting, or attend every meeting. For example, the regular education teacher who is a member of the IEP team must participate in discussions and decisions about how to modify the general curriculum in the regular classroom to ensure the learners involvement and progress in the general curriculum and participation in the regular classroom environment.

In determining the extent of the regular education teacher's participation at IEP meetings, public agencies and parents should discuss and try to reach agreement on whether the learner's regular education should be present at a particular IEP meeting and, if so, for what period of time. The extent to which it would be appropriate for the regular education teacher member of the IEP team to participate in IEP meetings must be decided on a case-by-case basis.

Other school and community personnel who may be involved in planning and implementing the IEP include the following:
- transition specialists
- counselors
- career and technical instructors
- academic teachers
- school psychologists
- diagnosticians
- vocational rehabilitation counselors
- school social workers
- therapists (e.g., occupational, physical)
- curriculum specialists
- media specialists
- physical therapists
- medical personnel (e.g., school nurse)
- vocational evaluators
- employers
- agency representatives for transitional services. See Figure 6-17.

When learners with disabilities are enrolled in career and technical education programs, career and technical education personnel should be represented on the IEP team. Special education personnel often do not have the background and preparation required to develop realistic career goals and instructional objectives for these learners. Therefore, it is essential that career and technical educators be involved in the IEP process. Career and technical education representatives can include
- career and technical education administrator/supervisor;
- career and technical education counselor; and/or
- career and technical education instructor responsible for working with the learner.

Career and technical educators should be participating members of the IEP team for a number of reasons:
- They will be able to receive important information regarding the learner's assessment data, past performance, and special training recommendations.

SUGGESTED CONTRIBUTIONS FROM THE IEP TEAM

TRANSITION SPECIALIST
- Entry level skill information
- Exit level competencies
- Available support services
- Employment information
  ~ related jobs
  ~ career ladder opportunities
- Information regarding transition
  ~ community agencies
  ~ state agencies
  ~ postsecondary training

COUNSELOR/EDUCATOR
- Knowledge of student's aptitudes and interests
- Background information contained in the permanent record
- Strengths and weaknesses of the student
- Information regarding transition resources

STUDENT
- Self-knowledge of personal interests, aptitudes, and needs
- Personal goals
- Likes and dislikes
- Motivation

SPECIAL EDUCATOR
- Strengths and weaknesses of the student (academic and behavioral)
- Learning style of the student
- Successful compensatory techniques
- Delineation of special needs/accommodations
- Informal assessment data on interests and aptitudes

PARENTS
- Personal goals and aspirations for their child
- Knowledge of home-related behaviors and patterns
- Knowledge of their child's demonstrated interests and abilities

VOCATIONAL EVALUATOR
- Knowledge of the student's strengths and weaknesses relative to vocational training and job placement
- Knowledge of tested interests and aptitudes
- Observations regarding motivation of the student
- Recommendations for improvement of skills and behaviors

Source: Center for Innovations in Special Education (formerly Missouri LINC). (n.d.). [Workshop handout]. Columbia, MO: University of Missouri, Department of Special Education and Department of Vocational Technical Education

Figure 6-17. An overview of IEP team member contributions.

- They will be responsible for providing the appropriate learning environment and carrying out the career and technical education component of the IEP.
- The IEP planning meeting will be the career and technical educator's first and perhaps last opportunity to ask questions about the learner prior to meeting the learner in class.
- Exploring the career and technical educator's program can be an extremely valuable tool for making a final decision regarding the learner's placement.

REVIEWING AND REVISING THE INDIVIDUALIZED EDUCATION PROGRAM

The IDEA '97 emphasizes periodic review of the IEP (at least annually) as previously required and revision as needed. A new, separate requirement exists as well: Schools must report to parents on the progress of the learner with disabilities at least as frequently as progress of nondisabled learners is reported. If it becomes evident that a learner is not making expected progress toward the annual goals and in the general curriculum, the IEP team must meet and revise the IEP. The insertion of this new language seems likely to affect how often IEPs are reviewed and, as appropriate, revised. See Figure 6-18.

IEP DEVELOPMENT CHECKLIST

Be sure the IEP for each learner includes the following:

___ A statement of progress the learner has made on previous IEP objectives

___ Information about current educational performance and how the disability affects a learner's involvement and progress in the general curriculum

___ Measurable annual goals

___ Short-term objectives or benchmarks for each annual goal

___ Method for measuring progress toward goals and objectives and how progress will be reported to the parent/guardian

___ Special education and related services to be provided

Figure 6-18. A checklist to aid in revising the IEP.

The new legislation specifically lists a variety of other circumstances under which the IEP team would also need to review and, as appropriate, revise the IEP, including revising the document to address the learner's anticipated needs, the results of any re-evaluation conducted, and information provided by the parents.

Revisions in the IEP may be needed during the school year for which the IEP is written. These revisions may include changes in the special education and/or related services; changes or additions of goals and objectives; addition or termination of related services; changes or additions of accommodations; and changes in the participation in general (regular, career and technical) education activities.

To make these revisions an IEP committee must be convened, which requires prior notice to the parent/legal guardian or surrogate parent. If the revised IEP results in the partial termination of special education and related services, then written parental consent is required before the partial termination occurs.

In keeping with the new emphasis upon the general curriculum and general education classroom, IDEA '97 expects the regular education teacher, as a member of the IEP team, to the extent appropriate, to participate in the review and revision of the IEP. See Figures 6-19. See Appendix.

USING THE INDIVIDUALIZED EDUCATION PROGRAM TO PLAN INSTRUCTIONAL DELIVERY

Once the IEP is written, it is time to carry it out—in other words, to provide the learner with the special education and related services as listed in the IEP. This includes all supplementary aids and services and program modifications that the IEP team has identified as necessary for the learner to advance appropriately toward the IEP goals, to be involved in and progress in the general curriculum, and to participate in other school activities.

The IEP can be a dynamic process where professionals, parents, and learners can plan for an instructional future that is truly responsive to the learner's unique individual needs. When professionals understand the necessity of the IEP and the opportunity it provides for collaboration, dynamic planning, and successful implementation, the lawful intent of specially designed instruction will be fulfilled. When professionals do not understand the IEP process, the following problems may stem from their differing roles and perspectives:

- General education teachers may feel untrained to handle the academic and behavioral needs for special education learners. They may feel that the input from specialists is too unrealistic for implementation in the regular classroom, or they may feel that IEP goals and objectives are only for the special education teacher and not relevant in their day-to-day instruction. Because of these attitudes, special educators may feel that they lack cooperation from regular education teachers, particularly in facilitating the mainstreaming of learners with special needs.
- Parents may be concerned about including their children in regular classes and whether they will be provided with the support services required for success.
- The IEP may be perceived as a document that is prepared by individuals who are not involved in the daily activities of the learner. Similarly, the IEP may be viewed as unnecessary paperwork that must be completed, with the special education teacher mostly responsible for its development. Another problem is that developing an IEP is often seen as cumbersome and time-consuming (Smith, 2000).

As schools explore educational options, many educators are being cast in unfamiliar roles and are acquiring new responsibilities. In the past, special educators provided classroom instruction to learners with disabilities. More recently, their responsibilities, like those of their colleagues in general education, have enlarged to include professional collaboration to support the participation of learners with disabilities in the general education curriculum.

Under the reauthorized IDEA, there is an increased emphasis upon not only teaching learners with disabilities in the general education curriculum but also assessing their progress by means of appropriate instruments and procedures. As members of IEP teams, general educators play an ever increasing role in collaboratively developing comprehensive management and instructional plans for learners with disabilities.

Many issues are involved in implementing a learner's IEP:

• Every individual involved in providing services to the learner should know and understand their individual responsibilities for carrying out the IEP. This will help ensure that the learner receives the services that have been planned, including the specific modifications and accommodations the IEP team has identified as necessary.

• Teamwork plays an important part in carrying out the IEP. Many professionals are likely to be involved in providing services and supports to the learner. Sharing expertise and insights can help make everyone's job a lot easier and can certainly improve results for learners with disabilities. Schools can encourage teamwork by giving teachers, support staff, and/or paraprofessionals time to plan or work together on such matters as adapting the general curriculum to address the

INDIVIDUALIZED EDUCATION PROGRAM CHECKLIST

Referral and Compilation of Information for Staffing

_____ Have you obtained copies of the IEP referral forms and procedures?
_____ Have you attended informational meetings to become familiar with your district's referral procedures and special education resources?
_____ Have you attended in-service training sessions on procedures and techniques for identifying special needs learners?
_____ Are you familiar with the individual(s) in your district responsible for collecting informal data on handicapped learners?

What types of information or data can you compile on the student?
___ Standardized test scores (achievement and aptitude)   ___ Results from diagnostic testing done on learners
___ Work evaluation results   ___ Behavioral observation data
___ Attendance record   ___ Interest inventory result
___ Progress evaluation reports

_____ Have all pertinent data on the student been collected and forwarded to the person responsible?

If additional information about career and technical education programs/classes is desired, can you make available any or all of the following?
___ Exit level skills   ___ Admission requirements
___ Course description   ___ Desirable vocational aptitudes and interests
___ Course outline   ___ Instructional materials used by learners
___ Instructional goals and objectives   ___ Information regarding opportunities for job placement

_____ Have you reviewed the learner's cumulative folders for the following types of information?
___ Reading and math achievement scores
___ Previous vocational or prevocational classes taken
___ Work or vocational evaluation results
___ Vocational interest inventory results
___ Information regarding special needs of the learner
___ Other pertinent information _____

_____ Have you met with the student's teachers (present or former) to discuss his/her progress?
_____ Have you met with other resource personnel who can provide additional information about the learner?
___ Parent(s) or guardian(s)   ___ Principals
___ Guidance counselors   ___ Referring teachers
___ School psychologist   ___ School social workers
___ School nurse   ___ Other specialists _____

_____ Have you identified organizations or agencies in the community (e.g., sheltered workshops, community colleges) where vocational testing and evaluations could be conducted?
_____ Have you identified organizations and agencies necessary for transitional needs?
_____ Do you have sufficient learning style information on the learner?

Adapted from: Center for Innovations in Special Education (formerly Missouri LINC). (n.d.). [Workshop handout]. Columbia, MO: University of Missouri, Department of Special Education and Department of Vocational Technical Education

Figure 6-19. A checklist to aid in period review of the IEP.

learner's unique needs. Teachers, support staff, and others providing services for learners with disabilities may request training and staff development.

- Communication between home and school is also important. Parents can share information about what is happening at home and build upon what the learner is learning at school. If the learner is having difficulty at school, parents may be able to offer insight or help the school explore possible reasons as well as possible solutions.
- It is helpful to have someone in charge of coordinating and monitoring the services the learner receives. In addition to special education, the learner may be receiving any number of related services. Many people may be involved in delivering those services. Having a person in charge of overseeing that services are being delivered as planned can help ensure that the IEP is being carried out appropriately.
- The regular progress reports that the law requires will help parents and schools monitor the learner's progress toward annual goals. It is important to know if the learner is not making the progress expected—or if the learner has progressed much faster than expected.

The IEP serves as a flexible master plan to guide and manage the overall educational process for learners with disabilities. It is not intended to be detailed enough to be used as an instructional plan. However, it should serve as the basis for developing a detailed instructional plan for the learner. See Figure 6-20. The annual goals and short-term instructional objectives provide general direction for the career and technical education instructor in delivering the curriculum to the learner. Information from the IEP can also be utilized to develop an individualized instruction format to deliver the career and technical education curriculum to the learner.

The self-paced lesson utilizes a one-page flow sheet to guide the learning process. See Figure 6-21. The learner and program identification data are presented at the top of the sheet, followed by a number of pointed blocks that indicate the flow of reading assignments, audio-visuals, practical applications, and checkpoints. The learner follows the sequence of directions at his or her own pace and is provided with periodic feedback from the instructor. To accompany the suggested strategies to deliver the IEP content, a competency-based checklist can be developed to evaluate the learner's mastery on the short-term instructional objectives. See Figure 6-22.

LEARNERS WITH A SECTION 504 ELIGIBLE DISABILITY

504 is a section of the Rehabilitation Act of 1973, an equal rights law for people with disabilities. Section 504 pertains to public institutions that receive federal funding, such as public school systems. The eligibility criterion for Section 504 is less stringent than under the IDEA. To qualify for services under section 504, an individual must have a disability that interferes with one or more major

life function such as caring for oneself, performing manual tasks, walking, seeing, hearing, speaking, breathing, learning, and working. Therefore many learners who do not qualify for services under the IDEA may qualify for services under Section 504.

Section 504 of the Rehabilitation Act of 1973 is Congress's directive to schools receiving any federal funding to eliminate discrimination based on disability from all aspects of school operation. It states "No otherwise qualified individual with a disability shall solely by reason of her or his disability, be excluded from the participation in, be denied the benefits of, or be subjected to discrimination under any program or activity receiving Federal financial assistance."

Section 504 is a civil rights statue and not a special education statute. Therefore, it is the responsibility of regular education staff and administration to implement those practices and procedures necessary for a school to fulfill this law's requirements. It is also important to understand that schools receive no additional funding to implement Section 504 accommodations. At each school, the responsibility for insuring Section 504 compliance rests with the building principal or principal's designee. When working with disabled learners, Section 504 serves the same propose as the ADA (Americans with Disabilities Act).

Like other learners, those learners with a 504 eligible disability are entitled to a free appropriate public education. An appropriate education for a Section 504 disabled learner may require the provision of specific accommodations and related services in order to meet the needs of the learner. Section 504 focuses on assuring access to educational services and the learning process that is equal to that given learners who do not have disabilities.

To qualify for Section 504 protection, the learner must meet three criteria: (1) a mental or physical impairment (or has a record of an impairment or is regarded as having an impairment), (2) which substantially limits, (3) one or more major life activities. It is important to understand that all three criteria must apply to a learner before that learner is eligible for Section 504 protection. In addition, this disability must be why the learner cannot equally access or receive benefit from the school's programs and services.

Mental or Physical Impairment

This might include any physiological disorder or condition, cosmetic disfigurement, or anatomical loss affecting one or more body systems. Additionally, this can include any mental or psychological disorder. This criterion does not limit eligibility to specific diseases or categories of medical conditions. The law was intentionally written this way so that the range of diseases or medical conditions that might be considered for Section 504 eligibility is not limited.

LESSON PLAN BASED ON AN IEP

Student's Name Amy Sloan

Disability Speech Impaired

Annual Goal(s) Improve Language Communication Skills

IEP Objective(s) Present a sales talk on a product or service

Performance Criteria Demonstrated talk and/or script, must meet the checklist criteria of 80% or higher for task

Materials and Supplies Fundamentals of Selling, pp. 282-289, Selling Principles and Practices, pp. 203-221, AVs on selling

Program/Grade Marketing Education

Course/Unit General Marketing/Personal Selling

Instructional Task(s) Presenting a sales talk on a product or service

Teacher(s) Mr. Sanders (MDE), Mrs. Lane (Communications Specialist)

Support Services Lesson Concepts

Lesson concepts Sales Talk	Instructional Steps	Special Provision for Amy Sloan
1. Definition and objectives of a sales talk/ presentation 2. Qualities of an effective sales talk 3. Types of sales talk/ presentations 4. Preparation for sales talk/presentation 5. Evaluation of a sales talk/presentation	a. Introduce sales talk topic and communicate lesson objective b. Relate a short story about personal selling c. Present each concept with words, pictures, and overhead transparencies d. Ask questions or pose situations during the presentation to involve students e. Summarize key points of lesson f. Ask for a student volunteer to play the role of a potential customer g. Demonstrate a simulated sales talk h. Assign students the task of preparing a script for a sales talk i. Randomly select students to present a talk and have peers evaluate the talk using a checklist	a. Provide Amy with an outline of the lesson (copy to communications teacher) b. Provide a model for Amy by speaking clearly and distinctly c. Provide a list of new words with their pronunciations to Amy and her communications teacher d. Encourage Amy and another student to work together in developing the script for the sales talk e. Encourage Amy to practice her talk before her family at home f. Work with the communications teacher to develop joint instructional experiences related to this lesson g. Videotape Amy's practice talk and review it with her before she presents to the class

Evaluation Strategies: Have Amy select a product or service and develop a talk to a potential customer. Ask Amy to deliver the talk to another student who evaluates her performance using a checklist. Ask Amy to present her talk to the entire class and let them evaluate her performance against checklist criteria.

Figure 6-20. An example of how information from an IEP can be used in lesson plan development.

IEP SELF-PACED LESSON

Student's Name	Jerry Lee
Disability	Speech Impaired
Support Services	Communication
Specialists	
Special Provisions	Jerry received instruction in communication skills two days per week from the communications specialist. Instructional tasks involving oral communication such as talking with customers and new word pronunciations should be jointly presented by vocational teacher and communications specialist

Program/Grade	Transportation/11
Course/Block	Steering and Suspension
Unit	401
Instructional Task(s)	
IEP Objective	Given tools, equipment and instructions, prepare vehicle, and balance tires using the static and dynamic processes
Performance Criteria	Student performance on worksheets, written test and performance test must meet 80% criterion. All work should follow accepted procedures and be to manufacturer's specifications

SEQUENCE OF ACTIVITIES

R-1 > C-1 > R-2 > P-1 > C-2 > R-3 > C-3 > P-2

C-4 > C-5 > P-3 > C-6 > > > >

> > > > > > >

READING ASSIGNMENTS

R-1　Assignment 401-8

R-2　Assignment 401-9

R-3　Assignment 401-11

R-4

AUDIO-VISUALS

A-1

A-2

A-3

A-4

PRACTICAL APPLICATIONS

P-1　Assignment 401-10

P-2　Assignment 401-12

P-3　Assignment 401-13

P-4

P-5

CHECKPOINTS

C-1　Information from instructor

C-2　Progress check (assignment 401-10)

C-3　Test (written)

C-4　Instructor demonstration

C-5　Performance observation

C-6　Progress check (assignment 401-13)

NOTE: (see assignments for texts, materials, and information)

Figure 6-21. An example of a self-paced lesson developed from an objective developed for an IEP.

IEP LESSON PLAN EVALUATION

Student's Name	Amy Sloan	Program/Grade	Marketing Education
Disability	Speech Impaired	Course/Block	General Marketing/Personal Selling
Evaluation Date(s)		Unit	201
Evaluation Summary		Instructional Task(s)	Present a sales talk on a product or service
		IEP Objective	Given a product or service to sell, present a sales talk to a prospective customer
		Performance Criteria	Talk must include at least 80% of the criteria on the talk presentation checklist

WRITTEN TEST

1. Administer and score a 25 item post-test on a sales talk.

OBSERVATION

Observe Amy and her peer developing the script for her talk. Review the videotape of Amy's presentation with her in private.

PERFORMANCE TEST

Evaluate Amy's talk script and/or Amy's talk to a peer student in a role playing situation by using the following checklist.

	Yes	No
1. Exhibited a friendly welcome		
2. Showed a sincere interest in helping the customer		
3. Used an appropriate opening statement		
4. Questioned the customer to determine customer interest		
5. Described the product/service with word pictures		
6. Used dramatic actions to enhance the presentation		
7. Exhibited enthusiasm for the product or service		
8. Involved the customer through questioning and application		
9. Handled customer interruptions and objections well		
10. Used an appropriate closing statement		

Figure 6-22. Examples of how to evaluate an instructional task in a marketing education program aligned with an objective from an IEP.

"Has a record of such an impairment" means that a person has a history of, or has been misclassified (by a recipient of federal funding) as having a mental or physical impairment that substantially limits one or more major life activities.

"Is regarded as having an impairment" means that an individual has a physical or mental impairment that does not substantially limit major life activities but that is treated by a recipient (of federal funds) as constituting such a limitation or has a physical or mental impairment that substantially limits major life activities only as a result of the attitudes of others toward such an impairment.

Thus, in the case of "has a record of" and "is regarded as having," individuals receive Section 504 protection, not necessarily because they have a qualifying disability, but to protect them from being injured by the prejudice or stereotypical attitudes of others. Schools have no obligation to identify these learners or provide them with a Section 504 plan. However, schools are prohibited from discriminating against them in all programs and activities.

Substantial Limitations

Section 504 does not specifically define "substantially limits." The basis for evaluating substantial limitation is the impact a disability has on one or more of a learner's major life activities. It is vital to understand that for a learner to qualify the impairment must impose an important and material limitation to one or more major life activities at the current time. The eligibility team will consider the nature and severity of the disability as well as how long the disability is expected to last. Simply having a condition or a disability does not automatically qualify a learner for Section 504 protection. The condition must present a barrier to the learner's ability to access the same educational opportunities as those afforded a nondisabled learner or a substantial limitation does not exist. The team may consider the manner, conditions, and duration in which a learner performs the task in comparison to how nondisabled learners perform the same task.

School personnel, after reviewing relevant learner information, must use their collective professional judgment in determining if an impairment (or disability) substantially limits one or more of a learner' major life activities. Making this determination will often challenge school staff, especially if this is their first opportunity to participate in the Section 504 eligibility process. When a learner is substantially limited by an impairment, the learner is

- unable to perform a major life activity that the average person in the general school population can perform; or
- the learner is significantly restricted as to the condition, manner, or duration under which an individual can perform a particular major life activity as compared to the condition, manner, or duration under which the average person in the general school population can perform that same major life activity.

The following three factors and related questions should be used by staff when determining if the substantially limits requirement is met:

- Nature and severity of the impairment–Is the impairment mild or severe? Does the impairment result in the learner not achieving near expected levels? Does the impairment impact on a major life activity? If so, how?
- Duration or expected duration of the impairment–Will the impairment be of such short duration as to not cause significant problems? Will the impairment cease impacting on the learner without any intervention?
- Permanent or long-term impact resulting from the impairment–Will the impairment be short or long in duration? If the impairment is of short duration, will it have a significant impact without intervention? If the impact will be long term, will the impact negatively affect the learners's status, academically, socially, emotionally, or behaviorally?

Major Life Activities

Major life activities include, but are not limited to, caring for oneself, performing manual tasks, walking, hearing, seeing, speaking, breathing, learning, and working.

A student study team (or similar group) should be designated to investigate the needs of learners who demonstrate a pattern of academic failure or other significant needs. The student study team (SST) conducts a preliminary review to determine the nature of the learner's needs. If it is determined that the learner should go through a 504 eligibility meeting then appropriate staff meet and conduct the meeting. A properly convened eligibility team will include individuals knowledgeable about the needs of the learner, the data being reviewed, and appropriate accommodation options. The eligibility team can include parents/guardians, teachers, SST members, counselors, related service providers, other school staff and administrators, and staff from community agencies. Parents/guardians should be included in this process whenever possible. This team's role is to review the nature of the learner's impairment and determine how it affects educational access. If the team determines that the impairment does limit a major life function then the team will construct a Section 504 plan that outlines the necessary learner accommodations.

Section 504 eligibility meetings are not intended to be as comprehensive as a special education evaluation. However, in every case the eligibility team needs to investigate the specific concern that triggered the learner review request. Information that might be considered includes (but is not limited to) grades, attendance reports, behavior plans, review requests, cumulative file information, psychological evaluation, medical information observations, and standardized testing information. The eligibility team may administer and use other formal and informal measures as deemed necessary.

Eligibility for 504 is always decided by evaluation and determining that all three criteria are present. The learner must have a mental or physical impairment. The mental or physical impairment must be substantially limiting. The impairment must substantially limit one of more major life activities. If any of the three criteria is missing or if there is no impact on the learner's access to school programs or services because of the disability, a 504 plan should not be created for the learner. Keep in mind that while a 504 plan might not be appropriate, other kinds of accommodation plans may be appropriate. Following are some of the common misuses of the 504 review request process:

- A parent and/or doctor presents the school with a disability diagnosis and a 504 plan is written without first determining if the disability causes significant impairment of a major life activity.
- A learner is placed on a 504 plan solely because the parent wants the learner to have additional time on college qualifying examinations (e.g., ACT, SAT).
- A learner fails to qualify for special education support and is automatically signed up for a 504 accommodation plan without first qualifying them based of Section 504 criteria.

- A learner is automatically placed on a 504 plan when the learner no longer qualifies for special education services without first qualifying for them based on Section 504 criteria, which are different.
- A learner is placed on a 504 plan as an alternative way to receive special education services because the parent refuses to label a learner by including the learner in a special education program.

SECTION 504 ACCOMMODATION PLAN

Section 504 requires that a learner with a disability be educated with nondisabled learners to the maximum extent appropriate. As with the IDEA, this is considered educating the learner in the least restrictive environment. Implementation of most Section 504 learner accommodations occurs within the regular classroom. See Figure 6-23.

TIPS FOR DEVELOPING 504 ACCOMMODATION PLANS

PHYSICAL

Provide Structured Environment
- post schedules on board
- post classroom rules
- use preferential seating (near teacher, between well-focused students, away from distractions)
- organize workspace
- use color codes

Provide Private Work Space
- quiet area for study
- extra seat or table
- standing work station
- "time out" spot

Provide Learning Centers
- reading corner
- listening center
- hands-on area

INSTRUCTIONAL

Repeat and Simplify Directions
- keep oral directions clear and simple
- give examples
- ask learner to repeat back directions when possible
- make eye contact
- demonstrate

Provide Directions in Written Form
- on board
- on worksheet
- copied in assignment book by learner and initialed by teacher

Individualize Homework Assignments
- reduce volume of work
- break long-term assignments into manageable tasks
- allow specified extended time without penalty for lateness
- offer alternative assignments
- provide extra set of texts at home

Use Technological Learning Aids
- tape recorders
- computers
- multi-sensory manipulatives

Modified Testing
- distraction-free area
- extended time

BEHAVIORAL

Use Positive Reinforcement
- positive verbal or written feedback
- reward systems and incentives
- tasks that can be completed
- private signals
- role-play situations
- weekly individual times
- conference opportunities

Be Consistent
- with rewards and consequences
- with posted rules

Promote Leadership and Accountability
- assign jobs that can be performed well
- start "student of the week/month"
- provide responsibilities

Specify Goals and Reinforce with Incentives
- state tangible goals and timetables
- use reward system
- use incentives chart for work and behavior
- use student contracts

Communicate with Parents, Teachers, etc.
- letters
- meetings
- phone calls
- help of school staff

Adapted from: Blazer, B. (1999, December). Developing 504 Classroom Accommodation Plans—A Collaborative Systematic Parent-Student-Teacher Approach. *Teaching Exceptional Children, 32*(2).

Figure 6-23. Examples of accommodations for a Section 504 eligible learner.

Accommodations generally are those minor adjustments to seating arrangements, lesson presentation, and assignments that provide the learner with equal access. An example could be moving the learner to a position in the room that best supports the learner's ability to attend to schoolwork. Accommodations might involve the use of special visual aids, large print, or video recordings. Allowing a learner additional time to complete a specific task is also an accommodation. Countless accommodations exist that can support a learner's equal access to educational opportunities. It is the job of the 504 eligibility team to identify those accommodations that best support the needs of a 504 eligible learner.

If the eligibility team determines that a learner has a Section 504 disability, the team's second responsibility is to identify learner needs and the services and/or accommodations the learner will receive. Documentation of the plan's details is in the Section 504 accommodation plan. This plan provides a summary of accommodations that a learner needs in order to have equal access to the learning process or to other programs, activities, and services. The eligibility team should review active Section 504 accommodation plans yearly, with more frequent reviews occurring when needed. The purpose of a review is to add, subtract, and/or modify learner accommodations as needed. See Figure 6-24.

The purpose of 504 plans is to accommodate individuals with disabilities and provide them equal access to the opportunities available to their nondisabled peers. Learners who need accommodations for nonacademic activities involving a school-related or sponsored function must be provided accommodations under Section 504.

For example, learners who use wheelchairs may need accommodations on field trips. The learner may need accessible transportation. The school must ensure that the place being visited (job shadowing site, cooperative education worksite, etc.) is accessible when the learner gets there. The school may be obligated to request accommodations on a learner's behalf. Learners with asthma may need the accommodation of bringing an inhaler on the field trip in case of an attack. Learners who are hard-of-hearing may need assistive listening devices. Learners with visual impairments may need enlarged written materials or written materials in braille or on tape, when going to a job site, etc.

Accommodations will vary depending on the learner's disability and limitations. Each accommodation should be specific to the learner's needs and ability level. Some learners may require physical access to buildings, classrooms, and equipment, while others may require accommodations to allow access to programs, activities, and school-related functions. Programmatic accommodations may be necessary as well. For example, learners with mild learning disabilities may need accommodations for written materials, reduced workloads, note-takers, and use of computers/assistive technology for written work and homework.

SECTION 504/ADA ACCOMMODATION PLAN

Student: <u>John Doe</u>   School: <u>Jefferson</u>

Date of Birth: <u>10/15</u>   Grade: _____

1. Describe the nature of the concern(s):

   John does not return his homework assignments. John has difficulty with organization of his work and pacing of assignments. He's easily distracted by extraneous stimuli, and he has difficulty listening to the lecture and taking notes at the same time.

2. Describe the basis for the determination of the disability:

   John was diagnosed three years ago as having attention deficit/hyperactivity disorder.

3. Describe how the disability affects a major life activity:

   John's mulidisciplinary team indicated that he daydreams and has difficulty staying on tasks at school. He is failing two classes because he has not turned in his homework.

4. Describe the services and/or accommodations that are necessary:

   John's teacher will provide a weekly schedule of his assignments one week in advance. John will be given one copy, and one copy will be mailed to his parents. John will be seated near the front of the room in close proximity to the teacher. John's parents will provide NCR (carbonless copy) paper so that a classmate can take notes and immediately give John a copy of the notes—or the teacher will provide a copy of the lecture notes.

Review/Reassessment Date:

Participants and Title:

John Doe
Student

Kristy Long
English Teacher

Jim Johnson
Assitant Principal/504 Coordinator

Connie Murphy
School Counselor

Sara Peters
Social Studies Teacher

Jane Doe
Mother

Adapted from: Jefferson County Public Schools (2000, July). *Section 504 Resource Guide*. Golden, CO: Author.

Figure 6-24. A sample accommodation plan for a Section 504/ADA eligible learner.

Behavior plans can and should be included in 504 plans when the learner has a behavior that prevents full participation in school-related activities. Health plans are another component that may be included. A health plan is typically written for a learner with a chronic medical condition. A health plan may include things such as identifying school staff who will execute the plan, provisions for dispensing medication at school or carrying medication to class, and identifying who will train staff if necessary.

INDIVIDUALIZED WRITTEN REHABILITATION PLANS

An individualized written rehabilitation plan (IWRP) is a document used by personnel from vocational rehabilitation services to plan for clients with disabilities. The career rehabilitation counselor develops this plan. If a learner with a disability has an IEP and is also a client receiving vocational rehabilitation services, the IWRP should be developed in coordination with the IEP. In both cases, career and technical education personnel should be involved in this process if the learner is involved in career preparation training, either by enrollment in a career and technical education program or a cooperative education program. The IWRP can become a vehicle to provide for the transfer of learners leaving high school so that they can transition into employment, postsecondary education, apprenticeship training, or other areas. See Figure 6-25. The IWRP contains the following:

- background information (e.g., name, case number)
- type of program (e.g., extended evaluation, occupational training)
- career objective (projected completion date)
- intermediate objectives such as contributing services (e.g., funding source, type of service necessary), projected initiation and completion dates, and evaluation criteria
- client and/or family participation and other resources (responsibilities and conditions)

There should be collaboration in the development of the IEP and the IWRP. An IEP/IWRP joint planning sheet can be used in reviewing an IWRP to see whether it coordinates with the IEP developed for the learner at the school. This joint planning sheet can also be used to transfer pertinent information from the learner's IEP to the IWRP. See Figure 6-26.

Case Study—Jeremy

Jeremy Bartlett is a student at Dunkirk High School and has a history of behavior problems. Last year Jeremy participated in a series of career exploration activities, including a variety of hands-on activities in the areas of masonry, carpentry, and plumbing. Jeremy had performed very well despite several instances of inappropriate behavior. After completing the career exploration activities, Jeremy expressed a desire to enroll in the construction program at his school.

Mrs. Proper, the special education teacher, asked Mr. Anderson, the construction teacher, to attend an IEP team meeting to discuss the possibility of Jeremy enrolling in the construction program. The team would consist of the school district's special education supervisor, the district's transition coordinator, Mrs. Proper, Mr. Anderson, Jeremy's parents, and Jeremy. Mrs. Proper told Mr. Anderson that his expertise was needed to help plan realistic goals and objectives for Jeremy in relationship to the construction program. She also emphasized that she was very eager to plan cooperatively in order to provide both Mr. Anderson and Jeremy with appropriate support help.

When the team met, they first examined school records, test data, attendance records, and vocational assessment reports to determine Jeremy's present level of educational performance. Jeremy has been in a special education program for learners with behavior problems for the past three years. During this time, he has been receiving assistance from Mrs. Proper, and she feels that he has made great strides. The team also discussed the efforts made during the previous year, especially the progress Jeremy made in the two regular classes (programs) he attended.

The next step was to determine the general scope of Jeremy's educational programs for the year and to develop appropriate annual goals to give direction to his program. Jeremy and his parents actively participated in this discussion by providing information about his interests and personal goals. Emphasis was placed on his desire to participate in the construction program. The vocational assessment information was reviewed along with the observations Mr. Anderson made during the exploration activities. Both sources indicated that Jeremy possessed the general work habits, attitudes, vocational aptitude, and personal interests that would benefit him in the construction program. It was decided that Jeremy should be enrolled.

Mr. Anderson then had an opportunity to tell the team members about the goals and objectives of his program. He was instrumental in developing the annual goals and short-term instructional objectives appropriate for Jeremy's IEP. Criterion levels for successful mastery of goals and objectives were also discussed. Finally, Mr. Anderson identified the student services and instructional materials he would need to help Jeremy succeed. Mrs. Proper assures him that cooperative planning will follow throughout the year. They agreed to establish and maintain an open system of communication and sharing as well as a process of periodic evaluation to determine whether the IEP is meeting Jeremy's needs. The IEP team plans to meet again in a year to discuss what benefit, if any, the IEP has had on Jeremy's education.

SAMPLE INDIVIDUALIZED WRITTEN REHABILITATION PLAN

Individualized Written Rehabilitation Program Office

_____

Initial Program _____

Amended Program # _____

Supplemental Program # _____

Date _____

SS # _____

PA # _____

SSDI _____

SSI _____

1. In accordance with Regulation 1361.37 of PL 93-112 as amended, the above named individual:
    _____ Meets the basic eligibility requirement for Vocational Rehabilitation Services specified in Regulation 1361.33b.
    _____ Does not meet the eligibility requirements for Vocational Rehabilitation Services specified in Regulation 1361.33b.
    _____ Meets the requirements specified in Regulation 1361.36a for a period of Extended Evaluation.

2. The basis for the decision checked in Item 1 is as follows:

3. Objective: (Only one of these items to be completed. Indicate projected completion date.)

    A. Tentative or None: (Extended Evaluation only)

    B. Occupational Grouping: _____   _____
                                                        Mo.   Yr.

    C. Specific Occupation: _____   _____
                                                      Mo.   Yr.

4. Intermediate Objectives, Contributing Services, and Evaluation Criteria:

	Funding Source	Initiation Date Mo. Yr.	Completion Date Projected Mo. Yr.
OBJECTIVE ONE:			
SERVICES:			
EVALUATION CRITERIA:			
OBJECTIVE TWO:			
SERVICES:			
EVALUATION CRITERIA:			

5. Schedule of Review and Evaluation of Progress:

6. Basis for closure: _____ Rehabilitated   _____ Other

7. Post-employment services planned with client.   _____ Yes   _____ Not Applicable

8. Annual review explained to client.   _____ Yes   _____ Not Applicable

_____   _____
              Supervisor   Counselor

Note: A copy of this program is to be furnished to the client, parent, or guardian.

> I have participated in the development of my "Individualized Written Rehabilitation Program."
> I accept it and understand that it is subject to change or termination on the basis of changing circumstances and new information. I acknowledge receipt of information regarding my rights in the event of any dissatisfaction.

_____
              Client, Parent, or Guardian

Figure 6-25. An example of an IWRP.

IEP/IWRP JOINT PLANNING SHEET

Individualized Education Program

Component	Information Available	Information Needed – Source	Does Information Coordinate with IWRP? (yes, no)
Present level of educational performance			
Annual goal			
Short-term objectives (criterion level for each)			
Services (specific service, projected dates of initiation, and termination)			
Amount of time in regular (vocational) class activities			
Date for review and evaluation of IEP (minimum–once a year)			

Individualized Written Rehabilitation Plan

Component	Information Available	Information Needed – Source	Does Information Coordinate with IEP? (yes, no)
Background information			
Type of program (extended evaluation, occupational cluster, specific occupation)			
Objective			
Intermediate objective (contributing services, projected initiation and completion dates, evaluation criteria)			
Client and/or family participation and other resources (responsibilities and conditions)			
Views of client regarding program			

Figure 6-26. Guidelines for the collaborative planning of an IEP and an IWRP.

IMPLEMENTING THE INDIVIDUALIZED EDUCATION PROGRAM

Implementing IEPs involves cooperative planning and instructional coordination, curriculum modification and development, personalized instructional delivery, and continuous monitoring and evaluation of the progress of each learner. In order to implement these programs, career and technical education personnel should employ the following activities:

- Obtain information about (a) referral, screening, evaluation, and placement procedures for learners with special needs, (b) requirements concerning the development and implementation of IEPs, (c) selection and adaptation of materials and equipment, (d) resources and services offered within the school and by community agencies, (e) record keeping and data collection for evaluating learner progress, (f) career and technical education program placement, (g) curriculum materials and curriculum development, and (h) complying with the school's career and technical education program requirements.
- Become contributing members on committees for placement, planning, and implementing programs and services for learners with special needs.
- Encourage and assist learners with special needs in becoming independent, capable learners and workers by: (a) helping them to develop the skills, knowledge, and attitudes required to become a productive worker, (b) promoting participation in career and technical student organization activities and other school activities, and (c) providing them with the attention and help needed for them to become competitive for jobs.
- Provide the direction for planning and implementing the career and technical education component of the IEP with the academic courses the learner is enrolled in (curricular alignment).
- Coordinate classroom activities, in-school training stations, and training stations in the community.
- Evaluate learner progress in all areas and adjust educational plans as needed.
- Provide direction for support personnel assigned to assist learners.
- Work cooperatively with counselors, teachers, and other school-based personnel and appropriate community agency representatives regarding (a) learner performance, (b) need for reassessment and/or placement in another program, and (c) need for additional support services.
- Develop teaching strategies, methods, and techniques to meet the unique learning styles of learners with special needs including (a) individualized, self-paced instruction, (b) modification of learning experiences as needed, (c) modification of instructional materials, (d) multimedia instructional delivery, and (e) utilization of the community as a learning site.
- Make extensive use of school system, community, governmental and private industry resources for learners with special needs.
- Develop effective interpersonal relations in dealing with learners, parents, teachers, and other professionals who are providing assistance to learners with special needs (Phelps, 1980).

Successfully implementing the individualized education programs for learners from special populations requires a constant effort in monitoring and evaluating activities to assess learner progress and to determine the need to modify the instructional program and services to enhance the learning process. Career and technical education instructors and other personnel must communicate regularly and meet as a group to discuss progress, problems, and other factors affecting the learner's performance. Time is a critical factor for all teachers and every effort should be made to use it in the most efficient manner. Informal contracts with teachers can often satisfy a need for information sharing, thereby eliminating the need for a formal meeting.

Perhaps the most critical implementation factor is commitment. Career and technical education instructors must be committed to the extra time and effort often required to meet the unique needs of learners from special populations. Participating in the IEP process requires effort. Assisting a learner with special needs to develop the competencies required for transition into postschool opportunities is often the best reward.

Benefits of Participation

Participating in the IEP process can be beneficial to career and technical education instructors in a variety of ways. The contents of these plans can assist instructors in organizing, teaching, monitoring, and evaluating ongoing program content and activities for learners. In addition, these plans can

- assist the instructor in understanding the strengths, abilities, interests, and needs of the specific learner;
- encourage the instructor to analyze specific program content in relation to the strengths, abilities, interests, and needs of the learner;
- assist the instructor to work as a team member with special education and support personnel to analyze the learner's present level of educational performance, abilities, and interests in order to identify a realistic career goal;
- assist the instructor in identifying appropriate and realistic annual goals that can be achieved by the learner during the year;
- aid the instructor in developing short-term instructional objectives that will lead to successful completion of the annual goals established for the learner;
- enable the instructor to use specific criterion levels and short-term instructional objectives in making continuous revisions and improvements in the program;

- enable the instructor to develop appropriate lesson plans for use with the learner;
- assist the instructor in selecting appropriate teaching procedures and materials to meet learner needs;
- provide the instructor with an opportunity to communicate the career and technical education program goals and objectives to administrators, parents, and special education personnel during the IEP process; and
- enable the instructor to work cooperatively with other school personnel to meet the needs of the learner.

SUMMARY

A written IEP is a management tool that relates the learning experiences, abilities, interests, and specific needs of learners from special populations to realistic educational goals and objectives. One of the most important processes in which career and technical education personnel should be involved is the preparation, implementation, and evaluation of IEPs for learners from special populations. When learners from special populations are integrated into career and technical education programs, it is important that the instructor and other school- and community-based personnel engage in a team effort to develop the IEPs that will enable them to succeed in meeting their career goals.

The vehicle for developing an IEP is based on a multidisciplinary assessment and is designed to meet the individual needs of each learner. This vehicle provides an opportunity for parents and educators to join together in establishing an appropriate educational experience for the learner. The result should be more continuity in the delivery of educational services.

The following individuals should be involved, in a school-based setting, in the development, implementation and evaluation of these plans:
- transition coordinators
- counselors
- career and technical education instructors
- administrators
- special education and support personnel
- parents

The most challenging and important phase of the IEP process is implementing the programs to enable learners with special needs to accomplish identified goals and objectives. Implementing these plans involves cooperative planning and instructional coordination, curriculum modification and development, personalized instructional delivery, and continuous monitoring and evaluation of each learner's progress.

SELF-ASSESSMENT

1. What are the primary reasons for developing IEPs for learners from special populations?
2. What is an IEP for learners with disabilities?
3. What are the essential components of the IEP?
4. What is the present level of educational performance mandated in the IEP?
5. What is the role of career and technical education personnel in determining the present level of educational performance in an IEP?
6. What are the annual goals and short-term objectives mandated in the IEP?
7. What is the role of career and technical education personnel in determining the annual goals and short-term objectives in an IEP?
8. What is the reason for the specific educational services mandated in the IEP?
9. What is the role of career and technical education personnel in determining necessary educational services for a specific learner?
10. What is the reason for the extent of participation in regular education program activities mandated in the IEP?
11. Why are criteria for evaluating objectives and schedule for review mandated in the IEP?
12. What is the role of career and technical education personnel in establishing criteria for evaluating objectives for a learner's IEP?
13. Why is a statement of transition services mandated in the IEP?
14. What is the importance of the career and technical education component of the IEP?
15. What are the roles and responsibilities of IEP teams?
16. What is the role of assessment in the development of the IEP?
17. What are some methods of using the IEP to plan instructional delivery?
18. What is the IWRP for learners with disabilities?
19. What is the Section 504 accommodation plan?

20. What is the ITP?
21. What is the role of career and technical education personnel in the development, utilization, and evaluation of the IEP?
22. What are some strategies for implementing IEPs?
23. What are some of the benefits for career and technical education personnel participating in the IEP process?

ASSOCIATED ACTIVITIES

1. Work cooperatively with special education and support personnel to establish some informal hands-on assessment activities for use in determining the learner's present level of educational performance in psychomotor skills and/or vocational skills.
2. Prepare a list of prerequisite skills and/or knowledge that would be useful for a learner with special needs to have prior to enrolling in your program. Use this list as a basis for discussion and decision making during the team meeting to develop the IEP.
3. Identify, in cooperation with special needs personnel, the support services and supplementary aids that are available in your school/district to meet the identified needs of learners from special populations. You can use this information to determine the specific educational services that a learner with special needs will need when enrolled in your program. This should be documented in the learner's IEP.
4. If you are currently working with learners with special needs in your program, contact the transition coordinator and request to see a copy of each learner's IEP. If you were not included in the initial development phase, check the goals, objectives, and services as they relate to learner participation in your career and technical education program as well as student organization activities. Cooperatively plan any necessary modifications or revisions with support personnel. Request that you be included in future team meetings to assure that the career and technical education component of the IEP is realistic and relevant.
5. Establish a file to keep copies of current IEPs, or at a minimum, the career and technical education component of these plans, so that you can refer to them for assistance in organizing the curriculum, developing instruction, and monitoring learner progress.

REFERENCES

Bateman, B. (1995). *Writing individualized education programs (IEPs) for success.* Learning Disabilities Association. [On-line]. Available: http://www.ldonline.org/ld_indepth/iep/success_ieps.html

Blazer, B. (1999, December). Developing 504 classroom accommodation plans—A collaborative systematic parent-student-teacher approach. *Teaching Exceptional Children, 32*(2).

Center for Innovations in Special Education (formerly Missouri LINC). (n.d.). [Workshop handout]. Columbia, MO: University of Missouri, Departments of Special Education and Vocational-Technical Education.

Cobb, R & Phelps, L. (1983). Analyzing individualized education programs for vocational components: An exploratory study. *Exceptional Children, 50*, 62-63.

deFur, S. (November, 2000). *Designing individualized education program (IEP) transition plans.* Arlington, VA: ERIC Clearinghouse on Disabilities and Gifted Education.

Education for All Handicapped Children Act of 1975, Pub. L. 94-142, United States Statutes at Large, (89), 773. Washington, DC: U.S. Government Printing Office.

Hardman, M., Drew, C., Egan, M., & Wolf, B. (1993). *Human exceptionality.* Boston, MA: Allyn and Bacon.

Heumann, J. & Hehir, T. (1997, September). Believing in children – A great IDEA for the future. *Exceptional Parent.*

Individuals with Disabilities Education Act of 1990, Pub. L. 101-476, United States Statutes at Large, (104), 1103. Washington, DC: U.S. Government Printing Office.

Individuals with Disabilities Education Act Amendments of 1997, Pub. L. 105-17, United Statutes at Large, (111), 37. Washington, DC: U.S. Government Printing Office.

Jefferson County Public School. (2000, July). *Section 504 resource guide.* Golden, CO: Author.

Kentucky Department of Education. (n.d.). *Procedures for identification, evaluation, and placement of exceptional children.* Frankfort, KY: Bureau of Education for Exceptional Children.

Kohler, P. (2000, Spring). New ideas for planning transitions to the adult world. *Research Connections in Special Edcuation.* [On-line]. Available: http://www.cec.sped.org/osep/recon6/rc6cov.html

Midwest Regional Resource Center. (1983). *Preparing quality IEP's.* Des Moines, IA: Author.

Midwest Resources, Inc. (1981). *Writing quality individualized education programs: A workshop.* Des Moines, IA: Author.

National Information Center for Children and Youth with Disabilities. (1993, March). *Transition summary.* Washington, DC: Author.

National Leadership Summit on Self-Determination and Consumer-Direction and Control. (1999, October). Synthesis of invited papers. [On-line]. Available: http://cdrc.ohsu.edu/selfdetermination/enhance.html

The Nebraska Dept of Education. (1998, August). *Guiding principles behind the IEP.* Lincoln, NE: Special Populations Office.

Office of Superintendent of Public Instruction. (2001). *Self-determination.* Olympia, WA: Special Education.

Patton, J. (2001). *Transition assessment and planning.* Austin, TX: Pro-Ed.

Pennsylvania Bureau of Vocational-Technical Education. (1993). *Vocational education component of the IEP.* Harrisburg, PA: Special Populations and Career Guidance Section.

Peoria Unified School District #11. (2001). *Transition services.* Peoria, AZ: Special Education Department.

Phelps, L. (1980). *Integrating secondary students into vocational and general education curriculums.* Des Moines, IA: Drake University, Midwest Regional Resource Center.

Rehabilitation Act of 1973 (Public Law 93-112). United States Statutes at Large, (87), 355. Washington, DC: U.S. Government Printing Office.

Smith, S. (December, 2000). *Creating useful individualized education programs (IEPs).* Arlington, VA: ERIC Clearinghouse on Disabilities and Gifted Education.

University of Colorado. (n.d.). *Self-directed IEP* (teacher's manual, student workbooks, and videotapes). Colorado Springs, CO: Center for Educational Research.

U.S. Department of Education. (2000, July). *A guide to the individualized education program.* Washington, DC: Office of Special Education and Rehabilitative Services. pp. 2-4.

Ward, M. (October, 1999). *The special education, self-determination initiative.* National Leadership Summit on Self-Determination and Consumer-Direction and Control. [On-line]. Available: http://cdrc.ohsu.edu/selfdetermination/mward.html

Curriculum Modification

INTRODUCTION

Career and technical education curriculum is the organized content of a program structured as a series of intended outcomes or competencies that a learner must master to attain an occupational goal. It involves the sum total of all experiences and learning activities encountered in the classroom and laboratory and encompasses what is to be taught and learned.

Curriculum modification is tailoring all the experiences and activities in pursuit of occupational preparation to meet the unique needs of the individual learner. Curriculum modification does not mean lowering or altering program standards. The basic objective of a program and the standards established for its completion remain constant. Curriculum modifications involve changes made in specific elements of the teaching-learning process such as instructional pace; classroom management strategies; classroom and laboratory environment accommodations; extended time in the program; adaptation of tools, equipment, and machinery; reinforcement techniques; blending learning styles and teaching strategies; identifying instructional materials; providing support services; and/or modifying evaluation procedures in the career and technical education program.

This chapter provides information and strategies for effectively modifying curricula in career and technical education programs for learners from special populations.

OUTLINE

RATIONALE FOR CURRICULUM MODIFICATION
ENVIRONMENTAL MODIFICATIONS
ESTABLISHING REALISTIC GOALS WITHIN CAREER AND TECHNICAL EDUCATION PROGRAMS
ESTABLISHING A FAVORABLE LEARNING ENVIRONMENT
SAFETY CONSIDERATIONS
CLASSROOM ORGANIZATION AND MANAGEMENT
UNIVERSAL DESIGN FOR LEARING
LEARNING STYLE MODALITIES
BRAIN-BASED LEARNING
LEARNING STYLE INVENTORIES
ANALYZING TEACHING STYLES
ADAPTING TEACHING STRATEGIES
INSTRUCTIONAL MATERIALS
COMPUTER SOFTWARE
ASSISTIVE TECHNOLOGY
EVALUATION STRATEGIES
SUMMARY
SELF-ASSESSMENT
ASSOCIATED ACTIVITIES
REFERENCES

OBJECTIVES

After completing this chapter, the reader should be able to accomplish the following:
1. Define curriculum modification.
2. Discuss reasons for modifying the career and technical education program for learners from special populations.
3. Discuss the principles of competency-based career and technical education programs.
4. Identify specific elements of the teaching-learning process that can be involved in curriculum modification.

5. List strategies that can help boost the self-concept and confidence of learners from special populations.
6. Identify behavior management strategies that are effective in working with learners from special populations.
7. Discuss the role of learning style information in the curriculum modification process.
8. Identify methods of modifying existing instructional materials for individuals from special populations.
9. List effective evaluation strategies to determine the progress of learners from special populations.

TERMS

accessibility
analytic learner
assistive technology
basic reading skills
behavior management
brain-based learning
career and technical education
   curriculum
competency-based curriculum

curriculum modification
curriculum softening
entry-level skill
environmental modification
exit skill
frustration reading level
global learner
independent reading level
individual option plan (IOP)

instructional reading level
learning style inventory
learning style modalities
modification
motivation
proximity control
readability formula
universal design for learning

RATIONALE FOR CURRICULUM MODIFICATION

Career and technical education curriculum is the organized content of a program structured as a series of intended outcomes or competencies that a learner must master to attain an occupational goal. It involves the sum total of all experiences and learning activities encountered in the classroom and laboratory and encompasses what is to be taught and what is to be learned. It is concerned with results (Stern-Otazo, 1980).

An assumption that will be made prior to discussing modification strategies for career and technical curricula is that all curricula is competency-based. In this manner, "curriculum softening" can be avoided. White (1987) described curriculum softening as the tendency among educators to provide access for learners by reducing the requirements for a program. This practice may have some merit when applied to traditional academic courses but has little merit when applied to career and technical education programs. Curriculum softening does not include practices that enable learners to participate (e.g., taped lectures, transferable physical modifications, use of oral rather than written exams) but instead removes instructional content and units from the learner's educational plan. This practice provides administrators, instructors, parents, and learners with a false impression of adult opportunities available following graduation and may, in many cases, leave a learner totally unprepared, without the entry-level competencies employers will expect for a specific occupation or career field.

The competency-based approach has emerged as an effective way to deliver career and technical curricula. This approach has two basic philosophies. First is the notion that "human competence" is the ability to actually perform. Knowledge, attitudes, and effort are of little value without results. The second philosophy holds that almost anyone can learn almost anything if given quality instruction and sufficient time. This philosophy has also been called mastery learning, performance-based instruction, and criterion-referenced instruction.

The following principles represent the foundation of competency-based programs:

1. Programs are based solely on specific, precisely stated learner outcomes, usually called competencies or tasks, that have been recently verified as being essential for successful employment in the occupation that the learner is being prepared for. These competencies are made available to all concerned and describe exactly what the learner will be able to do upon completing the career and technical education program.
2. Learners are provided with high quality, carefully designed, student-centered learning activities, media, and materials designed to help them master each competency or task. Materials are organized so that each individual learner can stop, slow down, speed up, or repeat instruction as needed to learn effectively. An essential part of this instruction is periodic feedback throughout the learning process with opportunities to correct their performance as they proceed through the curriculum.
3. Each learner is provided with enough time, within reason, to fully master one competency or task before being allowed or forced to move on to the next.
4. Each learner is required to perform each competency or task to a high level of proficiency in a joblike setting before receiving credit for attaining it. Performance is compared to an established, fixed standard based on business and industry requirements for employment and retention.

Curriculum modification is the tailoring of the experiences and activities in pursuit of career and technical preparation to meet the unique needs of the individual learner. Curriculum modification does not mean lowering or altering program standards. The basic objective of a program and the standards or competencies established for its completion remain constant. The changes made are in specific elements of the teaching-learning process, such as

- instructional pace;
- classroom management strategies;
- classroom and laboratory environment accommodations;
- extended time in the program;
- tools, equipment, and machinery;
- reinforcement techniques;
- blending learning styles and teaching strategies;
- identifying appropriate instructional materials;
- modifying existing instructional materials;
- providing appropriate support services; and/or
- modifying evaluation procedures in the career and technical education program.

When curriculum modification is effectively executed, the needs of the individual and essential proficiency levels necessary for employment are both served. See Figure 7-1. Stern-Otazo (1980) provided the following considerations that should be made when examining the specific career and technical education curriculum and the learner for whom the modification will be made:

1. Needs of the career and technical education program
- Content is based on selected tasks of a given job or cluster of jobs whose commonalities are critical for successful employment.
- Critical tasks are verified through local, state, or regional research matched against national task listings. These can be obtained from national curriculum centers.
- The jobs/occupations selected for analysis must have a long-range forecasted existence.
- The resulting employment after vocational technical preparation will sustain the individual above a poverty wage level.
- There are sufficient placement opportunities within a geographic region.
- The occupations or jobs require initial education and training of not less than six weeks and not more than two years for the average learner.

EXAMPLES OF SPECIFIC SKILL OUTCOMES WITH SAMPLE MODIFICATIONS PROVIDED TO FACILITATE PROFICIENCY

Specific Skill Outcome	Modification Provided
Safely performs basic operations with power tools	Safety checklist Adaptive operative device
Plans a balanced meal	Chart of basic food groups
Prepares sandwiches with garnishes	Model sandwich
Sews on a straight line	Machine edge guide
Threads sewing machine	Cue cards of task sequence
Uses repair manuals	Reading assistance Review of terminology
Prepares personal data form	Pocket resume
Performs assembly operations	Peer pairing (support)

Listing of Sample Modifications That Will Facilitate Proficiency

(1) Instructional Modifications
- Extra reading time
- Simplified directions
- Reduced vocabulary level
- Oral directions
- Step-by-step directions
- Demonstration
- Repetition
- Cooperative learning
- Cue cards
- Media reinforcement
- Frequent comprehension checks

(2) Materials or Equipment Modifications
- Digital or talking watch
- Adaptive operative devices on machines:
  - guard rails
  - hand or foot controls
  - warning lights or noises
  - Jigs or Fixtures
  - Illustrations vs. written directions
  - Taped, audio/video directions
  - Large-print materials

(3) Task Modifications
- Simplified task steps
- Additional performance time
- 3D model

(4) Environmental Modifications
- Adjusted height of furniture/equipment
- Individual work space
- Labeled equipment and work spaces
- Color coded equipment controls
- Minimized distractions

Source: Dade County Public Schools. (n.d.). *Curriculum-Based Vocational Assessment Handbook*. Miami, FL: Office of Vocational, Adult, Career, and Community Education.

Figure 7-1. Some examples of specific career and technical education modifications to facilitate specific learner outcomes.

- There is evidence of community support for the program.
- There is evidence that the curriculum will be supported financially.
- There is evidence that qualified personnel can be hired to facilitate the teaching-learning process.
2. Needs of the learner
- When working with learners from special populations, the curriculum may need to be modified or adjusted to take into account the specific needs of an individual learner. When making decisions to modify the curriculum, the vocational assessment information should be carefully reviewed. This information should include learner abilities, interests, and limitations. Curriculum modification occurs when realistic goals and competencies are identified for a learner and a variety of appropriate methods and strategies are used to meet those goals and competencies.

- Content can be organized in terms of tasks and performance objectives and programmed as units to help the individual reach milestone objectives.
- Content selected should relate to the specific needs of the individual such as need for occupational competencies, level of general education development, and need for personal interest, growth, and development. (p. 140)

ENVIRONMENTAL MODIFICATIONS

Without barrier-free access to career and technical education programs, many learners with disabilities cannot participate in these programs and develop their career and technical potential. Modifications may need to be made to physical facilities, equipment, and work stations. The most important concerns associated with accessibility are safety, efficiency, and convenience. A barrier occurs when the physical demands of a situation are difficult to cope with or cannot be overcome by a learner with a disability.

Architectural accessibility is a legal right of individuals with disabilities. The Architectural Barriers Act of 1968 (PL 90-480), amended in 1976 by PL 94-541, requires that public facilities built or renovated substantially since 1968 that receive federal support must be accessible. Section 504 of the Rehabilitation Act of 1973 (PL 93-112) specifies that individuals with disabilities cannot be excluded from participating in any program or activity receiving federal support because its facilities are inaccessible. See Figure 7-2.

The following are three major areas in most career and technical education facilities that may present barriers to individuals with disabilities:

1. Getting to and entering the building–This includes getting to the grounds from public or private transportation; parking, negotiating parking lot pavement; curbs, walkways, ramps and stairways; and entering exterior doors.
2. Moving about inside a building–This includes moving through corridors and hallways; moving from floor to floor; identifying and entering classrooms, laboratories, and auxiliary areas; moving through aisles and traffic lanes inside classrooms and laboratories.
3. Using school fixtures, appliances, and study/work station area equipment–This includes using restrooms, drinking fountains, audiovisual machines, vending machines, telephones, controls, tools, machines, equipment, and work station area equipment.

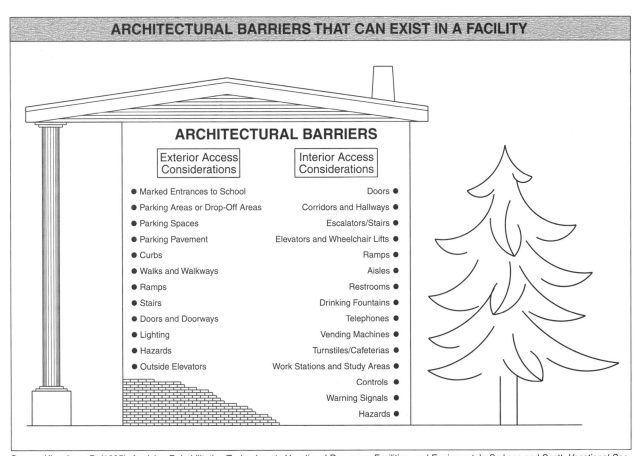

Source: Kingsbury, D. (1985). Applying Rehabilitation Technology to Vocational Programs, Facilities, and Equipment. In Sarkees and Scott. *Vocational Special Needs* (2nd Ed.). Homewood, IL: American Technical Publishers, p. 226.

Figure 7-2. Some exterior and interior architectural barriers that can exist in a career and technical facility.

The use of resources within a school district to modify environmental barriers depends upon the severity of the disability and the nature of the assistance and/or modifications required in the career and technical education program. See Figure 7-3. The following are general rules to observe in the modification process:

1. Make modifications based on the needs of the individual learner. The career and technical education instructor should remember that disabilities vary greatly even among people who have the same type of disability.
2. Avoid placing expectations of success or failure upon the learner's ability to perform a vocational task. Instructors may have difficulty in seeing how a learner with a disability can perform a task, but they fail to realize how individuals can compensate for disabilities. The learner is one of the most valuable sources of input leading to solutions for problems involving access.
3. Make modifications only to the extent that permits the learner to engage in a meaningful and productive educational experience.
4. Use conventional tools, equipment, and materials whenever possible.
5. Make sure that the problem is not the result of a policy barrier. Time limits and established procedures may work against some learners and serve no legitimate purpose.
6. Keep the environment flexible enough to accommodate the differences and preferences of individual learners.

7. Consider the practical cost factors involved in a technological intervention (modification). Solutions in terms of priority of cost usually follow a pattern of:
 • standard unmodified equipment
 • standard equipment with modifications
 • specially designed equipment, commercially available
 • adapted, commercially available, special equipment.
8. Remember that change often creates anxiety, insecurity, and resistance. Learners with disabilities will be more open to change if they have meaningful input into the design, development, and evaluation of the modification process. (Kingsbury, 1985, pp. 237-238)

ESTABLISHING REALISTIC GOALS WITHIN CAREER AND TECHNICAL EDUCATION PROGRAMS

One of the most important steps in curriculum modification is to make certain that goals established for learners from special populations who are enrolled in career and technical education programs are realistic. An effective method to establish appropriate goals for a specific learner is to have the career and technical education instructor identify pertinent information about what will be taught in the program, necessary requirements for program completion, multiple exit points, and entry-level competencies expected by employers for each of the exit points. This information provides direction for

---

SAMPLE PROBLEM SOLVING QUESTIONS WITH POSSIBLE SOLUTIONS FOR CURRICULUM MODIFICATION

Questions	Possible Solution
Is there a problem with:	
Access	Remove barriers (change doorknobs to levers)
Movement	Rearrange materials for freedom of movement (use flexible work table with lifts)
Safety	Eliminate danger (use jigs or fixtures to hold hot materials in welding)
Mobility	Reposition job site (provide ramps to classroom lab or move class setting)
Difficult procedure	Simplify approach (use a digital volt-ohm meter to measure electrical forces)
Judgment	Reduce the need (present measuring cups in lab activities)
Counting	Change procedures (use check sheets for tasks or visible samples in labs)
Measurement	Provide a standard (use colored lines on a precut board)
Reading materials	Provide tape recording of material (use devices such as voice emulators)
Strength	Provide a tool or assist (use a hoist or holder)
Touch or feeling	Texture surface (use sandpaper textures glued to switches and colored guides)
Vision	Improve lighting or develop orientation guides (use VCR equipment to magnify reading material)
Hearing	Develop alternative teaching methods (use visual models or examples to illustrate material)

Source: Kingsbury, D. (1985). Applying Rehabilitation Technology to Vocational Programs, Facilities, and Equipment. In Sarkees and Scott. *Vocational Special Needs* (2nd ed.). Homewood, IL: American Technical Publishers, p. 237.

Figure 7-3. Some suggested questions and solutions used to determine necessary modifications for learners from special populations.

the development of an individualized education plan for the learner as well as the identification of teaching strategies and support services that will be necessary for successful completion of the plan. School-based personnel should be aware of the specific skills that learners need to successfully participate in a particular career and technical education program. Interviews with individual instructors represent an accurate way of gathering specific program information. This information should include the following:

- physical skills
- academic skills (reading, mathematics, science)
- basic/generalizable skills
- safety proficiencies
- employability skills
- learning skills (study skills)

A copy of a specific course syllabus can be helpful in identifying information. See Figure 7-4. See Appendix.

SAMPLE COURSE SYLLABUS

DEPARTMENT: CAREER AND TECHNICAL EDUCATION
COURSE TITLE: BUILDING TRADES I
COURSE NUMBER: 12879
COURSE DESCRIPTION: This course will teach the basics of carpentry, from foundations through roof framing. Other topics include masonry, tools and equipment; plumbing instruction in systems, materials, tools and methods of installation; house wiring instruction in electrical terms, symbols, tool and steps of installation.

I.   GENERAL COMPETENCIES - The learner will be able to:
   1. Comprehend information received and apply information in a variety of everyday situations.
   2. Use a variety of information resources to obtain assistance and information.
   3. Know appropriate emergency responses to accidents and demonstrate preventive actions for health/safety hazards.
   4. Demonstrate skills necessary to obtain employment.

II. PERFORMANCE OBJECTIVES:
   Items listed below include the objectives and their indicators for this course:
   A. Carpentry
      1. The learner will safely utilize and operate all tools and equipment.
         (a) List safety rules for each machine.
         (b) Demonstrate safety of machines and tools.
      2. The student will perform tasks using knowledge of blueprint reading, foundations, and basic framing procedures of a residential building.
         (a) Utilize knowledge of signs and symbols.
         (b) Prepare batter boards.
         (c) Identify parts of floor system.
         (d) Identify parts of wall and ceiling systems.
         (e) Identify parts of a roof system.
   B. Plumbing
      1. The learner will safely perform the installation of the sewer and supply system of a residential home.
         (a) List safety rules.
         (b) Identify parts of sewer system.
         (c) Identify parts of supply system.
   C. Masonry
      1. The learner will safely perform the operation of tools and equipment used in the basic skills of masonry.
         (a) List safety rules.
         (b) Demonstrate skills of handling trowel.
         (c) Demonstrate ability to lay brick to the line.
   D. House Wiring
      1. The student will safely utilize and operate all tools and equipment according to the proper electrical code.
         (a) List safety rules.
         (b) Demonstrate safe wiring practices.

Figure 7-4. An example of a Building Trades course syllabus.

Specific entry-level skills should be identified for career and technical education programs. They provide an overview of the competencies necessary to participate in a specific program. This does not mean that learners must be able to demonstrate every entry-level skill at the time that they enroll in a program. However, there should be a reasonable assurance that learners will be able to develop them with assistance from appropriate support personnel and/or supplementary resources. See Figure 7-5.

In addition to entry-level skills necessary for participation in a career and technical education program, it is also helpful to have a list of exit skills associated with the program. These skills represent competencies that employers would expect learners to have when they apply for a job. See Figure 7-6.

Using the resources previously described, realistic career goals can be developed for learners from special populations by comparing learner profile information (e.g., strengths, limitations, interests, aptitudes, academic levels, career and technical experiences) with the data on career and technical education program content, entry-level skills and exit-level employment skills, multiple exit points, and associated competencies. At this point, an individualized education plan should be developed for the learner. Support services, instructional materials, teaching strategies, evaluation techniques, and timelines can then be established to complete an effective curriculum modification process.

ESTABLISHING A FAVORABLE LEARNING ENVIRONMENT

Several areas should be taken into consideration in order to establish a favorable learning environment that will allow learners from special populations to be successful. These areas include learner self-concept and self-esteem, motivation, and positive peer relationships.

Learner Self-Concept and Self-Esteem

Self-concept and self-esteem are important factors in learner performance and teacher effectiveness. Self-concept is a basic component of personality and has a major impact on interpersonal relationships. An expectation for success and the motivation for success can be difficult for many learners from special populations because of their lack of self-esteem. What learners think and how they perform are determined largely by their self-esteem. Often the self-fulfilling prophecy interferes with their ability to succeed. The self-fulfilling prophecy is a situation where low expectations of learners will influence their performance, and they start acting as expected without using all of their potential.

A direct relationship exists between self-concept and academic achievement. Successful learners have a relatively high opinion of themselves and are optimistic about their future and their ability to meet expected performance standards. They excel in their feelings of worth as positive, contributing individuals. The majority of unsuccessful learners see themselves as inadequate, incapable, and less reliable than their peers.

The following techniques can be used to help boost the self-concept and confidence of learners from special populations:

- Genuinely care about all of your learners.
- Let learners know you believe in them.
- Encourage learners to believe in themselves and in their own abilities.
- Provide a positive, caring, and supportive classroom environment.
- Remain open and responsive to the feelings and reactions of learners.
- Examine your expectations of each learner (e.g., underestimation may result in the self-fulfilling prophecy, overestimation may result in frustration and hopelessness).
- Provide immediate, specific feedback relative to learner performance and accomplishments.
- Be generous in offering praise, compliments, and congratulations whenever possible and appropriate.
- Assign activities that you know will result in success.
- Promote positive interaction with peers in small groups.
- Interact with learners on a one-to-one basis.
- Relate to learners and their lives outside of class. The more you know about them, the easier it will be to establish rapport with them.
- Let learners know you value their opinions and ideas.
- Post sayings and posters to create a positive atmosphere.
- Have learners help to establish the rules of the class and laboratory. This will provide ownership and promote empowerment and teamwork.
- Find something positive about each learner's work, behavior, and/or attitude.
- Let learners know who you are as a person, aside from being a teacher. Your "human side" will help to establish rapport with them.
- Be willing to learn from the learners.
- Involve learners in establishing their own personal goals. Assist them in reaching these goals. Ask them why they have chosen the goals they have established.
- Avoid calling on learners when there is a possibility or probability of failure.
- Display learner work and encourage learners to share their accomplishments with others (e.g., parents, siblings, relatives, peers, other teachers, neighbors, clergy).
- Allow learners to make corrections on assignments until the criterion level has been met.
- Focus on the process of learning, not the product of grades.
- Stop using red markers to highlight mistakes. Instead use them to point out things the learner does right.
- Accept all efforts and contributions without judging them.
- Accept the fact that changing self-concept is a slow process and takes time. See Figure 7-7.

SUGGESTED ENTRY LEVEL SKILLS FOR BUILDING TRADES PROGRAM

I. Behavioral Skills
   1. Attend to tasks
   2. Attend to task for 30 minutes
   3. Attend to class/work
   4. Follow through on commands
   5. Be on time
   6. Develop positive attitudes
   7. Show respect for authority
   8. Dress neatly
   9. Wear safety gear

II. Communication Skills
   1. Develop alternative strategy to obtain information
   2. Follow five step written direction
   3. Read work order
   4. Read blueprints
   5. Read directions on a package of wall paper paste
   6. Read directions on paint cans
   7. Read directions on storm doors
   8. Read directions on garage doors
   9. Read mixing instructions
   10. Read scale drawings and tell dimensions of house
   11. Listen/develop strategy to obtain information
   12. Follow four step oral direction
   13. Communicate on telephone with an unknown person
   14. Write legibly/develop strategy to report information
   15. Write specifications for building
   16. Estimate amounts of building materials required

III. Math Skills
   1. Calculate problems using the basic four operations
   2. Multiply two digit numbers
   3. Calculate square feet and yards
   4. Calculate cubic feet and yards
   5. Calculate board feet
   6. Add, subtract, multiply, and divide whole numbers and two column numbers
   7. Add, subtract, multiply, and divide fractions with common denominators

   8. Measure accurately
   9. Read rule to ¼th of an inch
   10. Read rule to ⅛th of an inch
   11. Tell time

IV. Physical Skills
   1. Possess manual dexterity
   2. Demonstrate eye-hand coordination
   3. Possess a sense of balance when working at heights
   4. Use hand arm movements effectively
   5. Perform specific motions
   6. Determine approximate sizes by visual inspection

V. Equipment Skills
   1. Identify common hand tools
   2. Identify a hammer
   3. Identify a tape measure
   4. Distinguish between a standard and a Phillips screwdriver
   5. Identify various types of shovels
   6. Identify a hand saw
   7. Identify pliers
   8. Identify nail sets
   9. Identify common power tools
   10. Identify a radial arm saw
   11. Identify a circular saw
   12. Use common power tools
   13. Use a radial arm saw
   14. Use an electric circular saw
   15. Identify materials commonly used
   16. Identify screws
   17. Identify nails
   18. Identify plywood
   19. Identify lumber
   20. Identify bricks
   21. Identify blocks
   22. Identify paint

Source: Cameron, C. & Johnson, J. (1983). *Entry Level Skills Criteria*. Columbia, MO: University of Missouri-Columbia, Center for Innovations in Special Education (formerly Missouri LINC), pp. 35-37.

Figure 7-5. An overview of suggested entry level skills for a Building Trades program.

EXIT SKILLS FOR BUILDING TRADES PROGRAM

I. Behavioral Skills
    1.   Work effectively with coworkers

II. Communication Skills
    1.   Read and interpret blueprints
    2.   Follow multi-step directions – a minimum of four
    3.   Define platform framing
    4.   Know vocabulary terms of building trades
    5.   State uses of devices such as nails, screws, and glue
    6.   Use telephone to order materials
    7.   State uses of paint, varnish, and stains
    8.   State space and structural requirements for plumbing fixtures
    9.   State space for structural requirements for heating and air conditioning system
   10. State use of plumbing fixtures

III. Math Skills
    1.   Calculate safe loads for girders
    2.   Calculate board feet of materials
    3.   Calculate square feet of materials
    4.   Abide by area building codes
    5.   Calculate load requirements on roads
    6.   Prepare bill of materials
    7.   Read a ruler to the $\frac{1}{16}$ of an inch
    8.   Calculate measurements of rafters

IV. Physical Skills
    1.   Balance on a 2×4 above ground
    2.   Nail floor joist
    3.   Nail subflooring
    4.   Nail wall sheathing
    5.   Drive a nail effectively
    6.   Use a ladder safely
    7.   Safely maneuver on skeleton of house

V. Equipment Skills
    1.   Demonstrate safe use of hand tools
    2.   Demonstrate safe use of chisels
    3.   Demonstrate safe use of knives
    4.   Demonstrate safe use of planes
    5.   Demonstrate safe use of power tools
    6.   Demonstrate safe use of drills
    7.   Demonstrate safe use of circular saw
    8.   Demonstrate safe use of router
    9.   Check power hand tools for electrical shorts
   10. Recognize electrical hazards
   11. Identify various types of wall and ceiling insulation
   12. Identify characteristics of types of lumber
   13. Identify types and grades of plywood
   14. Identify copper tubing and fittings
   15. Identify plastic pipes and fittings
   16. Work off ladders and scaffolds safely
   17. Use a combination square
   18. Lay out top and bottom plates and studs
   19. Lay out the floor joist

20. Build headers for windows and door openings
21. Cut and install bridging
22. Lay subflooring
23. Install wall sheathing and ceiling joists
24. Apply exterior siding
25. Install metal flashing
26. Construct built-up girders
27. Apply shingles
28. Install exterior windows and doors
29. Apply roof sheathing
30. Install various types of wall and ceiling insulation
31. Relate PSI, building strength in concrete to requirements
32. Build stairs
33. Build concrete forms for flat work
34. Finish concrete
35. Lay out interior wall partitions
36. Lay out ceiling joists
37. Use rafter tables on framing squares to cut rafters
38. Cut common rafters
39. Install interior doors
40. Install baseboard trim
41. Install window casings
42. Build cornice
43. Paint appropriately using brush and rollers
44. Install cornice boards
45. Install factory-built cabinets and counter tops
46. Sweat copper tubing
47. Install and finish gypsum drywall
48. Identify members of a wood truss
49. Hang wallpaper
50. Install internal wiring
51. Install roof and soffit vents
52. Install meter base and main breaker box
53. Install roofing metal flashing and edging
54. Install internal air conditioner ducts
55. Install guttering
56. Install panelling
57. Finish concrete driveways, porches, and sidewalks
58. Install heating and air conditioning equipment
59. Lay out roofing building paper
60. Select building site
61. Select building to fit site
62. Install bathtub complete
63. Select proper and appropriate building materials
64. Waterproof foundation
65. Install rough-in plumbing drains
66. Install outlets
67. Install plumbing fixtures
68. Install rough-in water supply lines
69. Install soffits

Source: Cameron, C. & Johnson, J. (1983). *Entry Level Skills Criteria*. Columbia, MO: University of Missouri-Columbia, Center for Innovations in Special Education (formerly Missouri LINC), pp. 93-96.

Figure 7-6. An overview of suggested exit skills from a Building Trades program.

SELF-RATING QUESTIONNAIRE

Directions: Answer "yes" or "no".

1. Do I really care and let my students know?
2. Do I really listen to my students and hear what they say?
3. Do students bring their personal problems to me?
4. Do I try to make each student feel important?
5. Can I tell when a student is uptight and respond appropriately?
6. Do I get my students to think instead of just responding to a question?
7. Do all my students participate in the class?
8. Can I admit my own mistakes openly?
9. Do my students and I feel a sense of accomplishment at the end of the year rather than merely a feeling of relief?
10. Do my students learn from my tests, instead of memorizing and then forgetting?
11. Do I keep my students from getting bored or going to sleep in my class?
12. Do I let my students know they are missed when they are absent from class?
13. Is there an orderly climate for learning in my classroom?
14. Do I emphasize learning more than discipline?

If you can answer "yes" to eight or more questions, pat yourself on the back. If you answer "no" to eight or more questions, your own self-esteem might need some attention.

Source: Huitt, F. & Pattison, P. (1980). *Self Esteem and the Handicapped.* Des Moines, IA: Midwest Regional Resource Center.

Figure 7-7. A questionnaire for instructors who want to create a positive learning environment to reinforce self-esteem in students.

Motivation

Motivation combines the needs and desires that move an individual to do something that will satisfy those needs and desires. Motivation is within an individual, although outside variables can affect it. For example, external things can be manipulated to help individuals develop their own motivation (e.g., contracts, rewards). Generally, the more highly motivated an individual is, the greater the learning that will take place. A key factor in learner motivation is teacher attitude. Once learners from special populations realize that an instructor respects their abilities, accepts them as individuals, and is willing to make adjustments and modifications in the instructional program to allow for individual differences, then insecurity and low motivation are often replaced by a strong desire to succeed.

Many problems in motivating learners result from their background of failure in school. Their reluctance to exhibit enthusiasm and effort often stems from negative experiences from the past. It is to be expected that learners who never have had successful experiences in school will be negative or apathetic toward new situations. The career and technical education instructor can promote learner motivation by providing classroom and laboratory experiences that will lead to success for each learner.

This objective can often be accomplished through individualized instruction and cooperative working relationships with other professionals involved in planning the educational program for learners from special populations. Once the instructor identifies the strengths and limitations, learners from special populations will begin to incorporate this information into individualized planning, and success will result. As an added bonus, the learner's self-concept will be positively affected and enthusiasm, determination, and motivation will replace inappropriate behavior. See Figure 7-8.

Brophy (1987) presented a synthesis of conclusions drawn from a review of the literature on motivation to identify principles suitable for use by teachers. This synthesis showed that no motivational strategies can succeed with learners if the following preconditions are not in effect:

1. Supportive environment–If the classroom is chaotic or if the learners are anxious or alienated, then learners are unlikely to be motivated to learn. Thus, the teacher must organize and manage the learning environment including encouraging learners, patiently supporting their learning efforts, and allowing them to feel comfortable taking risks without fear of being criticized for making mistakes.

HIGHLIGHTS OF RESEARCH ON STRATEGIES FOR MOTIVATING LEARNERS

Research on student motivation to learn indicates promising principles suitable for application in classrooms, summarized here for quick reference.

ESSENTIAL PRECONDITIONS

1. Supportive environment
2. Appropriate level of challenge/difficulty
3. Meaningful learning objectives
4. Moderation/optimal use

MOTIVATING BY MAINTAINING SUCCESS EXPECTATIONS

5. Program for success
6. Teach goal setting, performance appraisal, and self-reinforcement
7. Help students to recognize linkages between effort and outcome
8. Provide remedial socialization

MOTIVATING BY SUPPLYING EXTRINSIC INCENTIVES

9. Offer rewards for good (or improved) performance
10. Structure appropriate competition
11. Call attention to instrumental value of academic activities

MOTIVATING BY CAPITALIZING ON INTRINSIC MOTIVATION

12. Adapt tasks to students' interests
13. Include novelty/variety elements
14. Allow opportunities to make choices or autonomous decisions
15. Provide opportunities for students to respond actively

16. Provide immediate feedback to student responses
17. Allow students to create finished products
18. Include fantasy or simulation elements
19. Incorporate game-like features
20. Include higher-level objectives and divergent questions
21. Provide opportunities to interact with peers

STIMULATING STUDENT MOTIVATION TO LEARN

22. Communicate desirable expectations and attributions about students' motivation to learn
23. Minimize students' performance anxiety during learning activities
24. Model interest in learning and motivation to learn
25. Project intensity
26. Project enthusiasm
27. Induce task interest or appreciation
28. Induce curiosity or suspense
29. Induce dissonance or cognitive conflict
30. Make abstract content more personal, concrete, or familiar
31. Induce students to generate their own motivation to learn
32. State learning objectives and provide advance organizers
33. Model task-related thinking and problem solving

Source: Brophy, J. (1987). Synthesis of Research on Strategies for Motivating Students to Learn. *Educational Leadership, 45* (2).

Figure 7-8. Principles from research that are suitable for application in classrooms to motivate student learners.

2. Appropriate level of challenge or difficulty–Learners will be bored if tasks are too easy and frustrated if tasks are too difficult. Tasks should allow them to achieve high levels of success when they apply reasonable effort.

3. Meaningful learning objectives–Teachers should select activities that teach some knowledge or skill that is worth learning, either in its own right or as a step toward a higher objective. It is not reasonable to expect learners to be motivated to learn if they are continually expected to practice skills already thoroughly mastered, memorize lists for no good reason, copy terms that are never used in readings or assignments, or read material not meaningful to them because it is too vague, abstract, or foreign to their experience.

4. Moderation/optimal use–Motivational attempts can be overdone, and any particular strategy can lose its effectiveness if it is used too often or too routinely.

5. Program for success–Ensure that these elements are present in the educational program planned for the learner:
   - teach goal setting, performance appraisal, and self-reinforcement skills
   - help learners to recognize linkages between effort and outcome
   - offer rewards for good or improved performance
   - structure appropriate competition
   - call attention to instrumental value of academic activities
   - adapt tasks to learner interests
   - include novelty and variety in planning instruction
   - provide opportunities for learners to respond actively
   - allow learners to create finished products to help develop integrity and satisfaction
   - include simulation elements that engage learner emotions or allow them to experience events vicariously

- incorporate game-like features into exercises
- include higher-level objectives and divergent questions
- model interest in learning and motivation to learn
- minimize learner performance anxiety during learning activities
- project intensity that tells learners that the material deserves close attention either by saying so or by using rhetorical devices such as slow pacing, step-by-step presentation with emphasis on key words
- project enthusiasm
- induce curiosity or suspense
- model task-related thinking and problem solving (pp. 75-81)

Sullivan and Wircenski (1998) provided the following suggestions for motivating learners:

- Know the learners and use their names as often as possible.
- Plan for every class; never try to wing it.
- Pay attention to the strengths and limitations of each of the learners. Reward the strengths and strengthen the weak spots.
- Set up the room in a U-shape to encourage interaction among the learners.
- Send lots of positive messages with posters, bulletin boards, and pictures.
- Be sure that the classroom is comfortable; check the air circulation, temperature, lighting, and humidity.
- Keep the laboratory well organized and efficient.
- Vary instructional strategies; use illustrated lectures, demonstrations, discussions, computers, tutoring, coaching, and more.
- Review the class objective each day. Be sure the learners see how the entire program moves along.
- Make instruction relevant. Be sure the learners see how the content relates to them and the world of work.
- Open each presentation with an introduction that captures the interest of the learners.
- Move around the room when teaching; walk energetically and purposefully.
- Be facially expressive–smile!
- Put excitement into speech; vary pitch, volume, and rate.
- Use demonstrative movements of the head, arms, and hands; keep hands out of pockets.
- Use words that are highly descriptive; give lots of examples.
- Accept learners' ideas and comments, even if they are wrong; correct in a positive manner.
- Maintain eye contact and move toward the learners when interacting with them; be sure to nod your head to show that you are hearing what they say.
- Give lots of positive feedback when learners respond, offer their ideas, perform a task correctly, come to class on time, bring their materials to class.
- Foster an active career and technical student organization.
- Use appropriate humor in teaching and in tests to relieve anxiety.
- Post program-related cartoons, and use them on overheads and in handouts.
- Provide opportunities for the learners to speak in the class.
- Be available before class starts, during break, and after class to visit with learners.
- Return assignments and tests to learners ASAP. Be sure to make positive comments and suggestions.
- Teach by asking lots of questions during introductions, presentations, demonstrations, and laboratory work.
- Plan laboratory activities so that all of the necessary tools, equipment, and materials are available when the learners are ready to use them.
- Give the learners an opportunity to participate in the organization and management of the laboratory.
- Be aware of those learners requiring assistance, and then see that they get it.
- Maximize the use of time so that the learners keep busy with productive, relevant activities.
- Be a model of the work ethic in dress, language, support of the school, and respect for the profession.
- Be consistent in treatment of learners.
- Make sure that tests are current, valid, and reliable. They must be based on curriculum objectives.
- Organize a "learner of the month" award.
- Invite parents, advisory committee members, and school administrators to visit the program for special activities.
- Plan relevant study tips out of the school.
- Bring dynamic subject matter experts into the program.
- Recognize appropriate behavior and reward it on a continuing basis.
- Use a surprise–an interesting film, special break, or similar activity–to reward the class for good behavior.
- Use games and simulations to spark interest, provide a break in the routine, and to supplement a unit in the curriculum.
- Praise learners in front of the class; reprimand them in private.
- Explain why rules are used, why activities are important, and why some requests must be denied.
- Involve all of the learners in the lesson.
- Provide clear directions for program activities and assignments.
- Plan around 15-30 minute cycles–learners have difficulty maintaining attention after a longer period of time.
- Provide opportunities for the learners to read alone and in a group.
- Make home visits (in the summer) for new learners entering the program.
- Send "happy-grams" home to parents periodically.
- Use task and job sheets to help learners remember the steps to perform skills.
- Be enthusiastic about yourself, the learners, and the profession.

Positive Peer Relationships

Career and technical education instructors can use a variety of techniques to promote peer acceptance of learners from special populations. For example, the instructor and/or transition coordinator can conduct an informal orientation session for the class before the learner is enrolled to create a general awareness of the nature and needs of the learner and encourage acceptance. Once a learner with special needs enters the class, several strategies may be used to ensure a smooth transition. One is peer tutoring, or the buddy system, where a learner is paired with one or more classmates for support, aid, or assistance. An advantage of peer tutoring is that it promotes positive interpersonal relationships with classmates in addition to providing a source of remediation when necessary.

Grouping arrangements for activities, projects, and laboratory assignments should be flexible to provide learners from special populations with different interpersonal experiences. Flexible groups give them opportunities to interact with different people in various situations. They also learn to apply appropriate skills and attitudes to education, social, and work-related situations.

One of the most widely used techniques to promote positive peer relationships is to develop and use cooperative learning activities in the curriculum. In promoting positive peer relationships, Johnson and Johnson (1982) suggested the following:

- Ensure physical proximity between special needs learners and their peers.
- Structure cooperative interdependence and promoting activities that encourage learners to work together.
- Emphasize joint rather than individual products whenever feasible.
- Directly teach the interpersonal and small group skills needed to build and maintain collaborative relationships with peers (e.g., learners can be helped to learn how to be effective leaders).
- Give learners meaningful responsibility for the well-being and success of their peers.
- Encourage feelings of support, acceptance, concern, and commitment that are part of collaborative situations.

SAFETY CONSIDERATIONS

Basic principles of accident prevention are essential to the operation of any career and technical education program. Learners from special populations can be taught the proper use of machinery, equipment, and tools as effectively as their peers. It is natural to assume that every career and technical education instructor is concerned with the general safety environment and welfare of all the learners enrolled in the program. It is also understandable that because of the lack of training and experience in working with learners with special needs, these instructors are apprehensive about safety and liability considerations.

Learners with special needs should receive the same safety instruction and reinforcement that is provided for all learners. Each learner must recognize potential safety hazards and learn safety procedures that will reduce or eliminate potentially dangerous situations. They need to develop a positive attitude toward safety and learn safety habits essential for maintaining an accident-free environment.

Generally, the same safety precautions and techniques required for other learners can be successfully taught to learners from special populations. It is true that specific modifications may have to be made for some of these learners. For example, additional time for learning may be required before the learner can demonstrate a safety technique. The modifications needed to teach appropriate safety procedures should be made according to the individual needs of each learner.

A primary cause of accidents in a laboratory setting results from a lack of understanding of safety rules, confusion, and inattentiveness on the part of learners. These circumstances can occur with any learner if precautions are not taken before independent work is allowed in the lab area. A good procedure to follow with all learners enrolled in a career and technical education program is to develop and implement a comprehensive safety orientation program. This program should include general information on safety rules and practices, protective equipment, proper use of tools and equipment, and proper operation of machinery in the laboratory setting. As each learner demonstrates appropriate safety habits when using equipment and machinery, a safety profile should be developed. Using this method, career and technical education instructors can be certain that learners are able to operate machinery and equipment safely before they are allowed to work independently in the laboratory.

Individuals such as special needs personnel, special education teachers, and support staff can help learners with special needs in safety orientation instruction. The rules covered in the career and technical education program can be reinforced and reviewed by this support personnel. Cooperative planning between career and technical education and support staff will help learners successfully demonstrate appropriate safety habits.

Developing a Safety Profile

The student safety profile is an organized method of documenting progress in the safety orientation of a career and technical education program. For example, a safety profile form designed for a machine shop lists components commonly found in a comprehensive safety orientation program. See Figure 7-9. The form must be altered for other instructional programs, particularly in the area of tools and equipment. The form is arranged by specific objectives of the orientation program and provides a method of

STUDENT SAFETY PROFILE

Student: _____   Date: _____

Trade and Industrial
Program: _____   Date of Entry: _____

                                       Date of Safety
Instructor: _____ Orientation: _____

Date Student Completes Specific Objectives of Safety Orientation: _____

Specific Objectives	Date Accopmlished
Develops awareness of hazard and becomes more safety conscious	_____
Develops a serious attitude toward safety	_____
Prepares for safety before entering work area	_____
Prepares for safety at work stations	_____
Understands color coding	_____
Practices safety procedures	_____
Prepares for safety on leaving shop	_____

Develops awareness of hazards and becomes more safety conscious. Successfully responds to the following:

Date Competency Demonstrated

1.   Why provide safety for yourself and others?   _____
2.   How does shop safety help production?   _____
3.   What laws and agencies regulate shop safety?   _____
4.   What are the causes of shop accidents?   _____

Develops a serious attitude toward safety

1.   Gives serious thought to work safety   _____
2.   Remains alert in the shop area   _____
3.   Works carefully   _____
4.   Remains calm and holds temper   _____
5.   Focuses attention on what is being done   _____
6.   Assumes responsibility for own safety and safety of others   _____

Prepares for safety before entering shop

1.   Demonstrates knowledge of the characteristics of a training program   _____
    a.   Determines what tools, machines, and materials are required   _____
    b.   Determines what hazards are involved   _____
    c.   Determines what skills are needed   _____
2.   Demonstrates knowledge of clothing and safety equipment to wear
    a.   Recognizes types of clothing suitable for shop area   _____
    b.   Recognizes types of foot and leg covering   _____
    c.   Recognizes types of head covering   _____
    d.   Recognizes types of eye and face protection   _____
    e.   Recognizes types of hearing protection   _____
    f.   Recognizes types of hand and arm protection   _____
    g.   Recognizes types of lung and breathing protection   _____

Figure 7-9. A sample student safety profile for safety practices in a laboratory.

documenting when a learner has accomplished each. In addition, specific behaviors involved in accomplishing each major objective are listed and space is provided for documenting each.

Another approach in assuring a safe work environment in the laboratory is to develop a brief safety checklist. An instructor can check the crucial areas of safety performance as the learner demonstrates appropriate safety techniques. Safety checklists can be used in addition to the general laboratory safety demonstration profile or as a separate method of evaluating a learner's ability to work safely in the laboratory. See Figure 7-10.

SAFETY CHECKLIST		

Student: _____   Instructor: _____

Program: _____

Criterion: _____

_____

Safety Area	Date	Instructor Initials
1. Fire extinguishers		
2. Emergency exit charts		
3. Emergency exit procedures		
4. Emergency electrical circuit breakers		
5. General safety rules		
6. Hand tools		
7. Engine lathe		
8. Turret lathe		
9. Vertical milling machine		
10. Horizontal milling machine		
11. Drill press		
12. Radial drill press		
13. Horizontal band saw		
14. Vertical band saw		
15. Pedestal grinder		
16. Surface grinder		
17. Heat treating equipment		
Comments		

_____
Instructor Signature

Figure 7-10. A sample safety checklist for learner safety performance.

CLASSROOM ORGANIZATION AND MANAGEMENT

No other aspect of teaching is so often identified as a major concern by instructors as classroom management. Classroom management is the set of activities by which an instructor establishes and maintains effective classroom organization. Managing classroom behavior is a constant concern of all teachers. If an inappropriate behavior is permitted in the classroom and/or laboratory on a regular basis it can seriously affect the learning process. Instructors are often concerned that learners from special populations will exhibit inappropriate behavior that will be difficult to modify or control.

Effective classroom management is an important aspect of the teaching-learning process because effective management is a prerequisite to effective instruction. If the goal of instruction is to foster learner achievement, this goal cannot be realized in the absence of effective classroom management. A growing body of teacher effectiveness research suggests that there is a positive relationship between effective teacher classroom management behaviors and desirable learner outcomes. Effective classroom management is highly dependent on the teacher's ability to identify classroom problems correctly as instructional or managerial in nature and to act accordingly (Cooper et al., 1977).

A good learning environment is created when teachers use techniques that allow learners to experience security and confidence. One method of achieving this is to identify realistic objectives for the learners. Learners may be disruptive and behave inappropriately if they feel threatened by a new situation or by a goal they perceive as impossible to reach. Instructors should identify and sequence realistic objectives for learners with special needs so they can experience success on a regular basis. These successful experiences will help learners develop a high degree of motivation and self-direction.

A model of classroom management based on interactions and adaptations of four basic elements (content, instructional strategies, instructional settings, and learner behaviors) is helpful. The crucial point to remember is that adaptations in one element are likely to have an effect on the other elements (e.g., changes in the size of the group and the composition of learners may affect the instructor's choice of instructional strategies and management of learner behavior). See Figure 7-11.

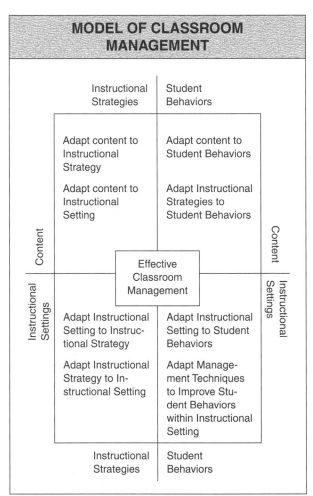

Source: Hoover, J. & Collier C. (1986). *Classroom Management Through Curricular Adaptations*. Lindale, TX: Hamilton Publications.

Figure 7-11. Effective classroom management strategies utilized by instructors through the adaptation of instructional content, instructional settings, instructional strategies, and learner behaviors.

Guidelines for positive classroom management include the following:

- Always be prepared (e.g., have materials ready).
- Control the learning experience from the beginning.
- Stress the positive.
- Be consistent.
- Learn to judge attention span of learners in the class.
- Determine the appropriate work level that matches the ability of the learner.
- Keep all learners occupied to help control behavior, especially if individualized activities are used.
- State learning objectives and provide advance organizers.
- Break down the task into components that are manageable by the learners.
- Teach in steps small enough to allow learner success.
- Reinforce learners after correct responses (continuous reinforcement), especially when teaching something new.
- Reinforce appropriate behaviors to prevent inappropriate behaviors.
- Provide appropriate reinforcement immediately after learners respond to a question.
- Rather than wait for a perfect performance, reinforce positive attempts in the right direction in the beginning.
- Gradually increase the number of correct responses needed before learners are given reinforcement (intermittent reinforcement).
- Move from outside or extrinsic reinforcements (points, grades) to internal or intrinsic reinforcements (pride, self satisfaction) whenever possible.
- Avoid too little reinforcement (deprivation) so that learners do not become frustrated and give up.
- Avoid too much reinforcement (satisfaction) so that learners do not become complacent and unchallenged.
- Always end the learning experience with a positive note.
- Facilitate and encourage creative thinking in class discussions, on outside assignment, on tests, and in career and technical student organization activities.
- Be flexible so that it is possible to take advantage of high-potential teaching moments.
- Let learners help to determine the room arrangement.
- Let learners evaluate others and themselves using a form developed by the instructor and the learners.
- Make time during class for individual learner conferences about assignments, tests, portfolios, and laboratory activities.
- Establish the philosophy that there is "no such thing as a dumb question" to encourage learners to be open and comfortable when they are having problems.
- Create a team atmosphere in class and facilitate learners working together.
- Be sure that every learner realizes that he or she has a contribution to make to the class and knows how important that contribution is.

Behavior Management

Behavior management is founded on the assumption that all behavior, both appropriate and inappropriate, is learned. Learning is controlled largely by events in the learning environment. The basic premise is that the acquisition of a particular behavior is contingent upon learning that its performance will be rewarded. The performance of that behavior will produce a form of reinforcement. Reinforcement is viewed as an event that enhances the possibility that a behavior will be repeated. The behavior strengthened by reinforcement may be either appropriate or inappropriate. However, if either type of behavior is rewarded, it is likely to continue.

Reinforcement may take different forms. It is seen as a reward given to a learner who displays appropriate behavior in the hope that the behavior will continue. Giving a reward for the purpose of maintaining an already acquired behavior is called positive reinforcement. The strengthening of a behavior through the removal of an unpleasant stimulus is called negative reinforcement.

Career and technical education instructors can use some specialized techniques to manage behavior in the classroom or laboratory setting. Before a behavior can be modified it must first be identified as inappropriate. Next, the instructor must decide what the target behavior is, then observe the target behavior to see how frequently it occurs and how it affects other learners in the class. Finally, an incentive must be identified to create and reinforce the desired behavior.

Dreikurs and Cassel (1972) identified four types of inappropriate behavior that may be displayed when an individual is frustrated in developing a feeling of belonging and a sense of self-worth through socially acceptable means:

1. Attention-getting behaviors–A learner who is not able to gain status in a socially-acceptable manner often seeks it through active or passive attention-getting behaviors. The active form is found in the show-off, the class clown, and the incessant questioner. The passive form of negative attention-getting is seen in the lazy learners who try to get others to pay attention to them by requiring constant help.
2. Power-seeking behaviors–A learner who is a power-seeker often lies, argues, contradicts, and refuses to do what is expected.
3. Revenge-seeking behaviors–A learner who is deeply frustrated and confused may seek success through hurting others. Openly defiant behavior, physical attacks, and sullen behavior characterize these learners.
4. Displays of inadequacy–A learner who displays inadequacy becomes so deeply discouraged in attempting to achieve a feeling of belonging that he or she has given up any hope of succeeding and expects only continued failure. These feelings of hopelessness are usually seen through withdrawal or dropout behavior.

Ginott (1972) provided a series of recommendations for teachers to effectively communicate with learners who are having problems managing their behavior:

- Address the learner's situation. Do not judge his or her character and personality, because this can be demeaning.
- Describe the situation, express feelings about the situation, and clarify expectations concerning the situation.
- Express authentic and genuine feelings that promote learner understanding.
- Diminish hostility by inviting cooperation and providing learners with opportunities to experience independence.
- Decrease defiance by avoiding commands and demands that provoke defensive responses.
- Recognize, accept, and respect the learner's ideas and feelings in ways that increase feelings of self-worth.
- Avoid diagnosis and prognosis, which result in labeling the learner, because this may be disabling.
- Describe processes and do not judge products or persons. Provide guidance, not criticism.
- Avoid questions and comments that are likely to incite resentment and invite resistance.
- Avoid the use of sarcasm, because this may diminish the learner's self-esteem.
- Resist the temptation to provide the learner with hastily offered solutions. Take the time to give the learner the guidance needed to solve his or her own problem. Encourage autonomy.
- Attempt to be brief. Avoid preaching and nagging, which is not motivating.
- Monitor and be aware of the impact one's words are having on learners.
- Use appreciative praise, because it is productive. Avoid judgmental praise, because it is destructive.
- Listen to learners and encourage them to express their ideas and feelings.

Examples of strategies that can be used for behavior management include the following:
- Utilize time-out–The time-out technique is frequently used with learners who are aggressive or hostile. If such negative behavior is occurring more and more frequently, it could mean that the learner is competing with the teacher for the attention of the class. This interferes with the progress of the other learners in the class.

In the time-out technique, the learner is removed from the classroom or laboratory to an area in the hall, in a corner of the class or laboratory, to the instructor's office, or anywhere that can provide a private, neutral space. Once the learner has been removed from the classroom or laboratory, the instructor can have an informal conversation on a one-to-one basis with the learner. This is not a time to reprimand, threaten, or lecture. It is important that this situation is a one-on-one between the instructor and the learner. The instructor explains that the behavior makes it difficult for other learners to learn or complete their work. It is a time to let the learner know why the behavior is inappropriate and what the consequences are. Once the learner begins to display appropriate behavior, the learner may be allowed to join the class again.

By using time-out, the instructor can eliminate the disruptive behavior from the class environment while at the same time, counsel the learner to find out what might have caused the behavior. The one-to-one instructor-learner relationship should help the learner to feel that the instructor cares. This can help to develop a positive self-concept.

- Ignore negative behavior–Learners who behave inappropriately or negatively are often looking for attention. When instructors respond to this behavior by reprimanding or threatening, they have accomplished the learner's objective of attracting attention both from the teacher and the entire class.

  One useful technique to avoid giving learners this attention is to ignore the inappropriate or negative behavior whenever possible. This technique is most effective if teachers begin reinforcing appropriate behavior with compliments and approval. Once this pattern has been established, learners begin to realize that they can gain attention when they behave in accordance with the rules and regulations of the class.

- Reward appropriate behavior–Giving attention, praise, and approval when appropriate behavior is displayed can be very effective. In this manner, learners receive positive reinforcement while at the same time improving their self-concept. Providing learners with activities and experiences that will lead to success in the career and technical education program can enhance this emphasis on appropriate behavior. As learners from special populations begin to feel competent and successful, positive behavior often replaces negative behavior. If instructors give attention when appropriate behavior is displayed, it will usually occur more often.

- Record specific behavior through a progress profile–If specific negative behaviors occur frequently, instructors should document the behavior. A progress profile can help to identify a pattern of behavior for a specific learner. Then appropriate techniques can be identified to modify the behavior. Instructors should document only objective statements in this record and not opinions of why the behavior occurred. The information recorded in the progress profile should include specific information about what happened and under what conditions the incident occurred. Information placed in learner records should always be signed and dated. Teachers should remember that parents of the learner have the right to inspect all records concerning the learner and may challenge any statements that they disagree with.

  Teachers and support personnel can use the profile to review the behavioral records of a particular learner and to determine the most effective method of behavior management. Many support personnel are trained in behavior management and can help the career and technical education instructor design and implement the most appropriate techniques for modifying negative behaviors. When the behavior management has been established in the career and technical education classroom and/or laboratory, it can be reinforced by the support staff when the learner is not in class.

  Learners can develop the habit of recording the frequency of their own behavior. In keeping track of a specific behavior, they become more aware of it. A peer can also be selected to keep track of the number of times a behavior occurs within a certain amount of time. Teacher-learner conferences should be scheduled regularly to discuss changes in behavior.

- Develop student-teacher contracts–Contracts can be effective in behavior management. The contract individualizes the tasks or responsibilities according to a learner's specific learning rate. The tasks to be completed are identified. The terms of the contract are then stated, such as the behavior changes that are expected and/or responsibilities that the learner is to assume. The specific time allowed for behavior change or for completing the assigned responsibility is established. Finally, the rewards or privileges are stated. These should be granted to the learner upon satisfactory completion of the contract requirements.

  An initial conference should be held between the learner, the career and technical education instructor, and any support personnel who work with the learner to discuss possible tasks and responsibilities to be included. A second conference is then held to review the contract after it has been developed. The contract is reviewed and evaluated as the learner completes the tasks.

- Initiate individual conferences–Conferences provide an opportunity for the career and technical education instructor to meet with the learner who is displaying inappropriate behavior. At this conference the teacher should explain his or her concern about the learner's unique problems, and emphasize that this behavior will not be tolerated in the classroom or laboratory. The teacher can follow up the conference by maintaining a positive relationship with the learner in class and combining this with positive reinforcement of appropriate behavior.

- Use proximity control–Proximity control is strategic positioning of the instructor in the classroom while inappropriate behavior is being displayed by learners. The theory is that the closer the instructor comes to the learner who is involved in disruptive behavior, the more the behavior will decrease. The theory also advocates touch control such as tapping a learner on the shoulder or touching the arm to diminish inappropriate behavior.

Hernandez (1989) summarized the philosophy of Hoover and Collier regarding the use of these techniques:

> They caution that proximity and touch control, while widely used and often effective, are culturally sensitive forms of nonverbal communication.

Instructors must keep in mind that personal space is defined differently across cultures. Standing behind learners to monitor behavior or within a certain distance can send very different messages from those intended. Likewise, a gentle tap on the shoulder or head could violate accepted norms of interpersonal contact for some learners. Teachers can decide to ignore certain behaviors to reduce the likelihood of confrontations over minor instances of misbehavior. (pp. 60-61)

UNIVERSAL DESIGN FOR LEARNING

The ERIC Clearinghouse on Disabilities and Gifted Education (1998) described the need for curriculum access for all learners. In every classroom there is a large number of learners who, to a greater or lesser degree, are not "getting" the curriculum. This group is not limited only to those learners who have been identified as having disabilities and who are provided with individualized education programs (IEPs), but it also includes those who are linguistically or culturally diverse, those who may be low achievers, and an amorphous number of unidentified learners who may understand some of the subject matter but not enough to become competent in it. The exact number of learners in this group may be impossible to determine, but these learners are there nonetheless, and they need to learn. As classrooms continue to become more inclusive and more diverse, the number of learners needing special attention increases, as do the pressures on their teachers to provide for their needs. Each learner, regardless of disability, difference, or diversity, needs access to the curriculum that is meaningful and that allows the learner to use his or her strengths.

The foundation of curriculum access for all learners is the design of educational materials, which are the primary tools used to teach curricular content. For instance, how can textbooks and other instructional materials in any medium meet the learning needs of learners with or without disabilities? Can they be readily adapted to accommodate the instructional needs of the many diverse learners in any classroom? The greater the flexibility built into the materials, the greater the number of learners who can be reached with a single curriculum. An important question to ask is how teachers can obtain curricular materials that allow them to customize challenges and supports for learners so they will receive just as much help as they need. This built-in flexibility of use is the premise of universal design for learning.

In terms of learning, universal design means the design of instructional materials and activities that allow the learning goals to be achievable by learners with wide differences in their abilities to see, hear, speak, move, read, write, understand English, attend, organize, engage, and remember. Universal design for learning is achieved by means of flexible curricular materials and activities that provide alternatives for learners with disparities in abilities and backgrounds. These alternatives should be built into the instructional design and operating systems of educational materials—they should not have to be added after the fact.

By using universal design principles, curriculum developers can create classroom tools that are successful for learners who have disabilities, who have no identified disabilities, or who have extraordinary abilities. When developers consider the needs of the full range of possible users during the design phase, the resulting products are more useful for everyone.

Universal design does not mean that the instructional materials and activities accommodate learners by lowering the standards. Universal design is not dumbing down the curriculum. It does not mean that the range of curriculum activity must be narrowed, or that teachers find the least common denominator that appeals to the broadest number of learners and teach the same thing in the same way to everyone. In fact, universal design is not ordinarily achieved by uniformity of any kind but is rather achieved by flexibility; universally designed instruction provides alternatives. It is helpful to remember that when we use the term universal design for learning we are speaking of an instructional resource, a means for diversifying instruction to deliver the general education curriculum to every learner, regardless of his or her abilities, and a means for diversifying the ways a learner can respond to the curriculum.

To accommodate learners' individual needs and to give them the opportunity to progress in content areas, educators traditionally have adapted or altered the textbook or tests. Typical accommodations include Braille or recorded texts for visually impaired learners, captioned materials for hearing-impaired learners, and customized supplementary materials or alternative texts that address cognitive disabilities. In most classrooms, these accommodations are added to the standardized curriculum much as a wheelchair ramp is added to a building where stairs formerly provided the only access.

Learning Styles

As classroom demographics continue to change and the need for adapted materials continues to grow, curriculum developers, particularly those who produce instructional software, are considering the advantages of universal design. With the federal government and states pushing for schools to incorporate more technology-based teaching tools in the classroom, understanding the foundations of universal design for curriculum access can help guide teachers towards implementation.

One of the most vital developments in American education today is the concept of individual learners' preferences. Teachers, school boards, and parents across the nation have become cognizant of various aspects of learning styles, and it is incumbent upon those who would be educational leaders to become knowledgeable about current research in learning styles.

Increasingly, educational leaders are recognizing that the process of learning is critically important and understanding the way individuals learn is the key to educational improvement. The challenge for schools today is to assess the learning style characteristics of each learner and to provide teaching and counseling interventions that are compatible with those characteristics.

Everyone has a learning style. Accommodating individual learning styles can result in improved attitudes toward learning and increased productivity, academic achievement, and creativity. To realize their intellectual capacity, learners must become engaged in learning stimulated by information that is presented in personally meaningful ways. Learning style research identifies a broad range of preferences that learners have for the way they assimilate information and the implications of those preferences for instructional design and delivery.

Most instructors do not have to be told that learners are very different from each other. They see these differences every day as they teach. Some learners sit quietly for long periods of time with long attention spans. Others squirm, daydream, or talk with others. Most educators recognize that learners in the same class seem to learn in different ways and through different approaches or materials. This is simply due to the fact that learners have different biological and environmental backgrounds and these contribute to the development of each learner's unique and individual learning style. The way in which new information or skills should be introduced and reinforced for certain learners can be determined by learning style. Teaching through individual learning styles is more effective than teaching each learner in the same way. Well-designed research verifies that learners learn more, more easily, and remember better when the instructional methods or materials used match their learning style characteristics (Dunn & Dunn, 1978).

> Educators know that learning styles exist. They know it's possible to apply them to all areas of education-curriculum and instruction, leadership, staff development, and counseling. They know there are different ways to apply the theories, and are beginning to know some things about the kinds of learners we have in schools and about which learners traditionally do better than others. Research indicates that people have different styles and intelligence; people who have different styles can be equally intelligent. It also indicates that there are many diverse styles in any culture, but cultural values do impact a learner's style. It's the nature/nurture relationship. Some approaches for accommodating learning styles can produce impressive gains in achievement. Attention to learning styles can impact school climate and staff and learner morale. (Guild, 1994, p. 11)

Basic theoretical assumptions of learning styles include the following:

- Individuals differ in their preference for taking in information and interpreting it.
- It is possible to match an individual's preference for learning to an instructional format.
- It is possible to determine and measure an individual's preference for learning styles.
- When a person's learning styles are matched with appropriate instructional methods, that person can usually achieve a 90% success level.
- When learning styles are converted to personalized instruction for a group, 90% of the group should achieve 90% success 90% of the time.

Dunn and Dunn Learning Style Method

Perhaps one of the earliest teams of research practitioners in the field of learning styles is that of Dr. Kenneth Dunn and Dr. Rita Dunn. Their model of learning styles can be classified as multidimensional.

The Dunn and Dunn learning styles model identifies several main principles or theoretical assumptions. In the use of the model, teachers, administrators and staff must be committed to the following principles:

- Most individuals can learn.
- Instructional environments, resources, and approaches respond to diversified learning style strengths.
- Everyone has strengths, but different people have very different strengths.
- Individual instructional preferences exist and can be measured reliably.
- Given responsive environments, resources, and approaches, learners attain statistically higher achievement and attitude test scores in matched, rather than mismatched treatments.
- Most teachers can learn to use learning styles as a cornerstone of their instruction.
- Many learners can learn to capitalize on their learning style strengths when concentrating on new or difficult academic material.

The learning styles model as developed by Dunn and Dunn is built on the theory that each individual has a unique set of biological and developmental characteristics. These unique characteristics impact substantially on how a person learns new information and skills. The Dunn and Dunn learning styles model has been developed for use across grade levels to improve the academic performance of all learners, and in particular, low achieving learners. The general goal of the model is to improve the effectiveness of instruction through the identification and matching of individual learning styles with appropriate learning opportunities.

The use of the Dunn and Dunn learning styles model involves two main types of activities, (1) the identification of individual learning styles, and (2) the planning and implementation of instruction to accommodate individual learning style strengths. Underlying both of these sets of activities is a series of 21 learning style elements as defined by Dunn and Dunn. The 21 elements are grouped across the following five stimuli categories: environmental preferences, emotional preferences, sociological preferences, physiological preferences, and psychological (cognitive processing) preferences. See Figure 7-12.

DUNN AND DUNN'S LEARNING STYLE ELEMENTS

Stimuli Categories	Learning Style Elements
Environmental stimuli preferences	Sound Light Temperature Design element
Emotional stimuli preferences	Motivation Persistence Responsibility Structure
Sociological stimuli preferences	Self Pair Peers Team Adult Varied
Physiological stimuli preferences	Perceptual Intake Time Mobility
Psychological stimuli preferences	Global-analytic Hemisphericity Impulsive-reflective

Figure 7-12. Examples of learning styles.

The following describes each of the 21 elements in the five stimuli categories defined by Dunn and Dunn:

Environmental Stimuli

- Sound element–This element refers to a learners' preference for background sound while learning. To what extent do they prefer silence, or background noise or music while concentrating or studying?
- Light element–The light element refers to the level of light that is preferred while studying and learning. This element explores the extent to which a learner prefers soft, dim or bright light while concentrating and studying.
- Temperature element–What level of temperature do learners prefer while involved in studying and/or other learning activities? Preferences on this element may vary from a cool room to a warm room while studying or engaged in various learning activities.

- Design element–The design element is associated with the room and furniture arrangements that the learner prefers while learning. Do they prefer to study sitting in a traditional desk and chair? Or, do they like a more informal arrangement with different types of furniture such as a couch, a reclining chair, or pillows and carpet on the floor?

Emotional Stimuli

- Motivation element–This element deals with the level and/or type of motivation the learners have for academic learning. That is, the extent to which learners are interested in school learning. Are they self-motivated (intrinsic), motivated through interest in, and contact with peers, or are they primarily motivated by adult feedback and reinforcement?
- Persistence element–This element relates to the learners' persistence on a learning or instructional task. The persistence preference relates to the learners' attention span and ability to, or interest in, staying on one task at a time. Do they have a preference for working on one task until it is finished or do they prefer to work on a variety of tasks simultaneously?
- Responsibility element–To what extent do learners prefer to take responsibility for their own academic learning? This element involves the preference to work independently on assignments with little supervision, guidance or feedback. Do they prefer to work independently without being told how to proceed? Or, do they prefer to have frequent feedback and guidance?
- Structure element–This element focuses on the learner's preference, or lack of preference, for structured learning activities and tasks. Do they prefer being told exactly what the learning task is, how they should proceed and what is expected of them? Or do they prefer to be given an objective and then be left alone to decide what procedures or options they will use to obtain the objective?

Sociological Stimuli

- Self element–The self element relates to the learners' preferences for working on a learning task by themselves. When working on an assignment do they prefer to work alone or do they prefer working as member of a group? Some learners prefer working on a learning task by themselves. Others may prefer working with someone else. With other learners, it may depend on the type of learning task.
- Pair element–This element relates to a learner working together with one other learner. Do they prefer working together with one other person as opposed to working as a member of a group? Some learners may prefer working with one other learner but not with a small group of learners or alone.
- Peers element–The peers element relates to the learners' preference to work on a task with their peers. How do learners react to working with peers?
- Team element–This element helps determine a learner's preference for working in a small group of learners with a lot of interaction, discussion, and teamwork. Some learners, however, have a preference to work alone.

- Adult element–This element relates to a learner's preference for interactions and guidance from an adult. How do learners react to working with an authority figure? Do they like to work together with an adult or instructor or do they react negatively to adult or instructor interaction during a task?
- Varied element–This element refers to a learner's preference for involvement in a variety of tasks while learning. Do learners like routines or patterns or do they prefer a variety of procedures or activities while learning?

Physiological Stimuli

- Perceptual element–Learning by listening, viewing, or touching is the focus of this element. Do learners prefer instruction and retain more information when the activities involve visual materials (viewing pictures, maps, or reading), auditory activities (listening to tapes, lectures, or music), or tactual and kinesthetic involvement, such as note taking or working on projects that involve making things (science projects, storybooks, diaries, or model building)?
- Intake element–The intake element is concerned with the need to eat, drink, or chew while engaged in learning activities. Do learners prefer to drink something while studying, such as a soft drink or coffee? Do they prefer to chew gum? Does munching on snacks help them to concentrate?
- Time element–This element is related to a learner's energy level at different times during the day. Do learners prefer to work on a task that needs concentration in the early morning, late morning, early afternoon, late afternoon, or evening?
- Mobility element–Can learners sit still for a long period of time as long as they are interested in what they are doing, or do they prefer to move constantly (standing, walking, changing body positions)? The mobility element is concerned with the extent to which learners prefer to be moving their bodies, perhaps even unconsciously, while involved in a learning task.

Psychological Stimuli

- Global-analytic element–This element relates to determining whether a learner learns best when considering the total topic of study, or when approaching the task sequentially (one aspect at a time). Learners that have a preference for global learning are concerned with the whole meaning and the end results. They need to start with an overview of the big picture before they deal with elements of the whole. Learners who prefer an analytic style of learning prefer to learn one detail at a time in a meaningful sequence. Once they know all the parts, they put the parts together and comprehend the big picture.
- Hemisphericity element–The hemisphericity element is associated with left- or right-brain dominance. Left-brain dominance tends to be associated with more analytic or sequential learners, while right-brain dominance tends to be associated with simultaneous or global learners. This preference element overlaps the global-analytic element.

- Impulsive-reflective element–This element relates to the tempo of a learner's thinking. Do learners prefer to draw conclusions and make decisions quickly or do they prefer to take time to think about the various alternatives and evaluate each of them before making a decision?

A personal learning plan can be developed for each learner in relation to the elements of the Dunn and Dunn learning style model. See Figure 7-13.

PERSONAL LEARNING PLAN

- What are my strengths?
- What am I challenged to do?
- How can I boost my learning power (natural tendencies of the styles opposite mine)?
- How do I stay motivated and energized?
- How do I create a feeling of success for myself?
- What is my best independent study environment?
  - ~ Workspace organization (orderly or non-linear)
  - ~ Food intake (while working or during breaks)
  - ~ Best time of day to work (morning or evening)
  - ~ Room temperature (cool or warm)
  - ~ Lighting level (bright or dim)
- How do study partners fit into my learning plan?
  - ~ When do I work with others? (up front and at the end, all along, or does it vary?)
- How do I make maximum use of my time in class?

Figure 7-13. A personal learning plan can be developed in relation to the Dunn and Dunn learning-style model.

Identifying Individual Learning Styles

For many learners from special populations learning problems become more acute at the secondary level. The instructional delivery system and the perceptual learning styles of learners may not match. At the secondary level, the majority of learners seem to be more visual in their learning style preferences or they may have mixed modalities. However, many teachers at this level tend to be more auditory in their presentation styles and often use the lecture or discussion methods for delivering content. Learners who have special needs often cannot compensate for a mismatch of their personal learning style preferences and their instructor's teaching style. In addition, they may not request assistance to compensate for their perceptual problems by asking the instructor to repeat, slow down, or present more visual cues (Texas Education Agency, 1989).

O'Neil (1990) stated that the unwillingness of schools to adapt to varying learning styles becomes more pronounced as learners work their way from elementary through high school. Many learners from special populations learn best through direct actual experience, cooperation and collaboration, and high levels of interaction. As they go up the grade levels, school becomes more competitive, more independent, more abstract in a system that ultimately works directly against them.

As dropout and learner disengagement rates persist at alarmingly high levels, attending to preferred learning styles is being viewed as one way to expand teaching methods and curricula to reach more learners. One of the keys to successful educational planning and instruction for learners from special populations is to build on their abilities and strengths rather than focusing on their limitations. This includes selecting the teaching strategies that will be used to introduce, reinforce, and review program material.

Marshall (1990) stated that teaching to identified learning styles represents a mutual challenge of accountability:

> If students don't learn the way we teach them, then we will teach them the way they learn. Students learn to understand and value themselves and others. They learn that they have power to contribute to their own learning success. Teachers learn that classrooms in which learning styles direct the methods of instruction are psychologically safe environments that promote active learning, mutual understanding, and respect. These classrooms promote the development of healthy self-concepts and social relationships along with increased academic skills. (p. 62)

There are several methods used to identify the positive learning style of a learner. One source of information concerning particular learning style is other teachers who have worked with the learner. Special education teachers, support personnel, special needs and transition coordinators, and other teachers can share ideas and experiences regarding successful teaching techniques and aids. This would prevent having to reinvent the wheel and would help assure successful experiences for the learner.

The planning team should not overlook the possibility of obtaining helpful information concerning preferred learning style from learners with special needs themselves. The learners can describe their preferences about various learning situations and learning modes. Parents of these learners can offer valuable insight into behaviors and learning characteristics exhibited in the home environment. Peers who have worked with these learners can also volunteer suggestions that will help in planning effective teaching strategies.

Another method is informal observation. By designing a series of activities for the learner to complete, the instructor and/or planning team can watch the way in which the individual negotiates the task. Some learners, for example, will perform better with verbal instructions while others will learn more effectively while doing something.

In analyzing an individual's learning style the following information may be helpful:

- the time of day when the learner is most alert (peak learning time)
- the environment where the learner is most comfortable when learning (e.g., classroom, laboratory, worksite)
- the perceptual strengths and weaknesses of the learner
- the personality style of the learner (e.g., an outgoing or an introverted personality) and the effect on the learner's learning pattern
- how much pressure the learner can tolerate while learning (e.g., does the learner work better under pressure or in a pressure-free situation)
- the type of task the learner prefers (e.g., written assignment, hands-on activity)
- the attention span of the learner (e.g., distractible, attentive)
- the type of learning environment the learner prefers (e.g., formal, casual)
- auditory aids or materials that help the learner to learn (e.g., verbal directions, lectures, cassettes)
- audiovisual aids or materials that help the learner to learn (e.g., films, videotapes)
- printed aids or materials that help the learner to learn (e.g., textbooks, workbooks, handouts, checksheets, lecture notes)
- psychomotor activities that help the learner to learn (e.g., laboratory activities, modeling activities)
- visual aids or materials that help the learner to learn (e.g., charts, diagrams, illustrations)
- the amount of formality the learner feels most comfortable with in a learning situation
- the amount of structure the learner feels most comfortable with in a learning situation (e.g., highly structured, flexible)
- the grouping pattern that the learner feels most comfortable with in a learning situation (e.g., working alone, in a team arrangement, in a small group, or in a large group)
- the physical conditions that provide for the best learning environment for the learner (e.g., lighting, noise level, ventilation)
- the amount and type of reinforcement the learner requires during the learning process (e.g., attention, praise, tokens)
- the response method preferred by the learner during the learning process (e.g., oral, written, typed, taped)
- the pace or rate that the learner feels most comfortable with during the learning process (e.g., individualized, accelerated)

LEARNING STYLE MODALTIES

Learning style modalities describe how learners learn through the senses of sight, sound and touch. Different learning style modalities include visual learners, auditory learners, and tactile/kinesthetic learners. See Figure 7-14.

COMPARISON OF LEARNING STYLE CHARACTERISTICS — VISUAL, AUDITORY, AND KINESTHETIC MODES OF LEARNING			
Area Observed	**Visual**	**Auditory**	**Kinesthetic**
Learning Style	Learns by seeing; watching demonstrations	Learns through verbal instructions from others or self	Leans by doing; direct involvement
Reading	Likes description; sometimes stops reading to stare into space and imagine scene; intense concentration	Enjoys dialogue, plays, avoids lengthy description; unaware of illustrations; moves lips or subvocalizes	Prefers stories where action occurs early; fidgets when reading, handling books; not an avid reader
Spelling	Recognizes words by sight; relies on configuration of words	Uses a phonics approach; has auditory word attack skills	Often is a poor speller; writes words to determine if they feel right
Handwriting	Tends to be good, particularly when young; spacing and size are good; appearance is important	Has more difficulty learning in initial stages; tends to write lightly; says strokes when writing	Good initially, deteriorates when space becomes smaller; pushes harder on writing instrument
Memory	Remembers faces, forgets names; writes things down, takes notes	Remembers names, forgets faces; remembers by auditory repetition	Remembers best what was done, not what was seen or talked about
Imagery	Vivid imagination; thinks in pictures, visualizes in detail	Subvocalizes, thinks in sounds; details less important	Imagery not important; images that do occur are accompanied by movement
Distractibility	Generally unaware of sounds; distracted by visual disorder or movement	Easily distracted by sounds	Not attentive to visual, auditory presentation; seems distractable
Problem Solving	Deliberate; plans in advance; organizes thoughts by writing them; lists problems	Talks problems out, tries solutions verbally, subvocally; talks self through problem	Attacks problems physically; impulsive; often selects solutions involving greatest activity
Response to Periods of Inactivity	Stares; doodles; finds something to watch	Hums; talks to self or to others	Fidgets; finds reason to move; holds up hand
Response to New Situations	Looks around; examines structure	Talks about situation pros and cons, what to do	Tries things out; touches; feels; manipulates
Emotionally	Somewhat repressed; stares when angry; cries easily, beams when happy; facial expression is a good index of emotion	Shouts with joy or anger; blows up verbally but soon calms down; expresses emotion verbally and through changes in tone, volume, pitch of voice	Jumps for joy; hugs, tugs, and pulls when happy; stamps, jumps, and pounds when angry, stomps off; general body tone is a good index of emotion
Communication	Quiet; does not talk at length; becomes impatient when extensive listening is required; may use words clumsily; describes without embellishment; uses words such as see, look, etc.	Enjoys listening but cannot wait to talk; descriptions are long but repetitive; likes hearing self and others talk; uses words such as listen, hear, etc.	Gestures when speaking; does not listen well; stands close when speaking or listening; quickly loses interest in detailed verbal discourse; uses words such as get, take, etc.
General Appearance	Neat, meticulous, likes order; may choose not to vary appearance	Matching clothes not so important, can explain choices of clothes	Neat but soon becomes wrinkled through activity

Source: Barbe, W., Swassing, R., and Milone, M. (1979). *Teaching Through Modality Strengths: Concepts and Practice.* Columbus, OH: Zaner-Bloser.

Figure 7-14. A comparison of learning style characteristics for individuals who have visual, auditory, and kinesthetic modes of learning.

Visual Learners

Visual learners learn through seeing. Characteristics of a visual learner include the following:

- asks for verbal instructions to be repeated
- watches speakers' facial expressions and body language
- likes to take notes to review later
- remembers best by writing things down several times or drawing pictures and diagrams
- is a good speller
- turns the radio or TV up really loud
- gets lost with verbal directions
- prefers information to be presented visually, (e.g. flipcharts or chalk board)
- is skillful at making graphs, charts, and other visual displays
- can understand and follow directions on maps
- feels the best way to remember something is to picture it in his or her head
- follows written instructions better than oral ones
- is good at solving jigsaw puzzles
- gets the words to a song wrong
- is good at visual arts

These learners need to see the instructor's body language and facial expressions to fully understand the content of a lesson. They tend to prefer sitting at the front of the classroom to avoid visual obstructions. They may think in pictures and learn best from visual displays including diagrams, illustrated textbooks, overhead transparencies, videos, flipcharts, and handouts. During a lecture or classroom discussion, visual learners often prefer to take detailed notes to absorb the information.

Auditory Learners

Auditory learners learn through hearing. Characteristics of an auditory learner include the following:

- follows oral directions better than verbal ones
- would rather listen to a lecture than read the material in a textbook
- understands better when he or she reads aloud
- struggles to keep notebooks neat
- prefers to listen to the radio rather than read a newspaper
- frequently sings, hums, or whistles to self
- dislikes reading from a computer screen, especially when the background is fuzzy
- can tell if sounds are the same or different when presented with two similar sounds
- requires explanations of diagrams, graphs, or maps
- enjoys talking to others
- talks to self
- uses musical jingles to learn things
- would rather listen to music than view a piece of artwork
- uses a finger as a pointer when reading
- likes to tell jokes, stories, and makes verbal analogies to demonstrate a point

These learners learn best through verbal lectures, discussions, talking things through, and listening to what others have to say. Auditory learners interpret the underlying meanings of speech by listening to tone of voice, pitch, speech, and other nuances. Written information may have little meaning to them until it is heard. These learners often benefit from reading text aloud and using a tape recorder.

Kinesthetic Learners

Kinesthetic learners learn through moving, doing, and touching. Characteristics of a kinesthetic learner include the following:

- reaches out to touch things
- collects things
- talks fast using hands to communicate what is wanted to be said
- constantly fidgets (e.g. tapping pen, playing with keys in pocket)
- is good at sports
- takes things apart and puts things together
- prefers to stand while working
- likes to have music in the background while working
- enjoys working with hands and making things
- likes to chew gum or eat in class
- learns through movement and exploring the surrounding environment
- may be considered hyperactive
- is good at finding his or her way around
- comfortable touching others as a show of friendship (e.g. hugging)
- prefers to do things rather than watch a demonstration or read about it in a book

Kinesthetic learners learn best through a hands-on approach, actively exploring the physical world around them. They may find it hard to sit still for long periods and may become distracted by their need for activity and exploration.

Knowing a learner's learning style modality can help an instructor plan the delivery or content of a specific program. A modality learning style inventory is one tool used to assess the preferred learning style modality of a particular learner. See Figure 7-15.

BRAIN-BASED LEARNING

In recent years, mountains of data have been gathered to help educators more conclusively understand how learners learn. One of the most interesting efforts, commonly referred to as brain-based research, seeks to understand learning from the perspective of where and how certain types of information are processed. It suggests there are two major types of learners–those in whom the right brain is dominant, and those with a dominant left brain.

MODALITY LEARNING STYLE INVENTORY

LIST A

_____ 1. People say you have terrible handwriting

_____ 2. You don't like silent filmstrips, pantomimes, or charades

_____ 3. You would rather perform (or listen to) music than do (or view) art, and you would rather listen to a tape than look at the filmstrip

_____ 4. You sometimes leave out words when writing, or sometimes you get words or letters backwards

_____ 5. You can spell out loud better than when you have to write it down

_____ 6. You remember things you talk about in class much better than things you have to read

_____ 7. You dislike copying material from the blackboard or bulletin board

_____ 8. You like jokes or riddles better than cartoons or crossword puzzles

_____ 9. You like games with lots of action or noise better than checkers or most other board games

_____ 10. You understand better when you read aloud

_____ 11. Sometimes you make math mistakes because you didn't notice the sign or because you read the numbers or directions wrong

_____ 12. It seems like you are the last one to notice something new, e.g., that the classroom was painted or that there is a new bulletin board display

_____ 13. Map activities are just not your thing

_____ 14. You must struggle to keep neat notes and records

_____ 15. You use your fingers as a pointer when you read

_____ 16. You frequently hum or whistle to yourself when you are working

_____ 17. Sometimes your eyes bother you, but your eye test comes out all right, or you have glasses which your eye doctor says are just right for you

_____ 18. You hate to read from photocopies, especially blotty ones

_____ 19. Matching test questions are a problem to sort out (over and above not knowing some of the answers)

_____ 20. Sometimes when you read you mix up words that look similar (e.g., pill-pull, bale-hale)

LIST B

_____ 1. It seems like you always have to ask somebody to repeat what he or she just said

_____ 2. Sometimes you may find yourself tuned out—staring out the window maybe when you were really trying to pay attention to something

_____ 3. Often you know what you want to say, but you just can't think of the words

_____ 4. Sometimes you may even be accused of "talking with your hands," or calling something a "thingamajig" or a "whatyacallit"

_____ 5. You have been in speech therapy at some time previously

_____ 6. You may have trouble understanding a person who is talking to you when you cannot see the person's face

_____ 7. You would rather review directions in a demonstration format than in spoken form

_____ 8. When you watch TV or listen to the radio, someone is always asking you to turn it down

_____ 9. Your family says that you say "huh?" way too much

_____ 10. You would rather demonstrate how to do something than give a speech

_____ 11. Spoken words that sound similar (bell, bill, pen or pin) give you trouble. Sometimes you can't tell them apart

_____ 12. You have trouble remembering things unless you write them down

_____ 13. You like board games such as checkers better than listening games

_____ 14. Sometimes you make mistakes in speaking (e.g., saying "He got expended from school")

_____ 15. You like artwork better than music

_____ 16. You have to go over most of the alphabet to remember whether, e.g., m comes before r

_____ 17. You like it better when someone shows you what to do rather than just telling you

_____ 18. You can do a lot of things that are hard to explain with words like fixing machines or doing macramé

_____ 19. You usually answer questions with "yes" or "no" rather than with complete sentences

_____ 20. You are always drawing little pictures on the edges of your papers, or doodling on scratch paper

_____ SCORE   Determine the number answered "yes" on each list. A higher "yes" score on List A indicates an auditory learner. A higher "yes" score on List B indicates a visual learner. A similar high "yes" score on both lists indicates a kinesthetic learner

Adapted from: Hayes, M. (1974). *The Tuned-In, Turned-On Book About Learning Problems.* Novato, CA: Academic Therapy Publications.

Figure 7-15. A modality learning style inventory.

Prior to the beginning of the twentieth century, little was actually known about the brain. In the late 1950s and early 1960s some significant research was conducted by Roger Sperry. Sperry's work, which later earned him the Nobel Prize for medicine in 1981, clearly showed that the brain is divided into two major parts or hemispheres—the right brain and the left brain. His research also identified that each of the parts of the brain specializes in its own style of thinking and has different capabilities. Experimentation has shown that the two different sides, or hemispheres, of the brain are responsible for different manners of thinking. See Figure 7-16.

Left-Brain/Analytic Learners

The left brain is associated with verbal, logical, and analytical thinking. It excels in naming and categorizing things, symbolic abstraction, speech, reading, writing, and arithmetic. The left brain is very linear; it places things in sequential order—first thing first and then second thing second, etc. As a rule of thumb, the left brain is mainly used to process languages and numbers and to deduce logic, which is very much emphasized for academic learning capabilities. The analytic learner is likely to say the following:
- Does spelling count?
- Should I skip lines?
- What are you looking for?
- What comes first? Second?
- Please check my work before I turn it in.
- Will this be on the test? (Center for Success in Learning, 1992).

Right-Brain/Global Learners

The right brain functions in a non-verbal manner and excels in visual, spatial, perceptual, and intuitive information. The right brain processes information differently than the left brain. For the right brain, processing happens very quickly and the style of processing is nonlinear and nonsequential. The right brain looks at the whole picture and quickly seeks to determine the spatial relationships of all the parts as they relate to the whole. This component of the brain is not concerned with things falling into patterns

TYPICAL BRAIN BEHAVIORS

Take a few minutes to look at the following descriptors which research shows relate to left and right hemispheric styles.

Analytic (left) brain behaviors respond to the following:	Global (right) brain behaviors respond to the following:
• Recognizing and remembering names	• Recognizing and remembering faces
• Verbal instructions	• Visual and kinesthetic instructions
• Emotional inhibitions	• Emotional responses (strong)
• Word for meaning	• Interpreting body language
• Producing logical thoughts/ideas	• Producing humorous thoughts/ideas
• Processing information sequentially	• Processing information subjectively and in patterns
• Serious, systematic problem-solving	• Playful problem solving
• Logical appeals	• Emotional appeals
• Critical analytical reading/listening	• Creative synthesizing, associating, applications in reading and listening
• Problem-solving through logic	• Problem solving through intuition
• Verbal instructions/information	• Demonstrational instructions/information
• Remembering through language	• Remembering through images/pictures
• Reading for details and facts	• Reading for main ideas/overviews
• Realistic stories	• Fantasy, poetry, myths
• Improving existing things/ways	• Inventing new things/ways
• Learning through systematic plans	• Learning through explorations
• Outlining rather than summarizing	• Summarizing, rather than outlining
• Intellectuality, then creativity	• Creativity, then intellectuality
• Avoiding hypnotism	• Remembering tonal qualities
• Remembering verbal qualities	• Open-ended assignments
• Well-structured assignments	

Source: Dunn, R., Cavanaugh, D., Eberle, B. & Zernhausern, R. (May, 1982). Hemispheric Preferences: The Newest Element of Learning Style. *The American Biology Teacher, 44* (5), pp. 292-94.

Figure 7-16. An overview of typical brain behaviors.

because of prescribed rules. On the contrary, the right brain seems to flourish dealing with complexity, ambiguity, and paradox. At times, right-brain thinking is difficult to put into words because of its complexity, its ability to process information quickly, and its non-verbal nature. The right brain has been associated with the realm of creativity. The global learner is likely to say the following:

- What are we doing this for?
- Not now—I'll do it later.
- I need a break!
- Don't touch the piles on my desk!
- I know where everything is.
- Why does it really matter?
- Let's start this project...and that one, too.

- Why can't I skip around in the book?
- I remember what he looked like... but not his name.
- I'll come back to this later. (Center for Success in Learning, 1992). See Figure 7-17.

The Center for Success in Learning (1992) provided the following examples of how analytic and global learners approach situations:

- Research paper–Analytic learners will approach a research paper by creating the outline first, while global learners would prefer to write the research paper first and create the outline last. If the learner created the outline last, it was because the learner could not tell what to put in the outline until the learner knew what the whole paper would say.

BRAIN-BASED LEARNING	
Left-Brain Analytical Learners	**Right-Brain Global Learners**

What does the analytic learner look like in the classroom?
1. Is independent
   • works alone
   • likes individual competition
   • becomes deeply involved in what he or she is doing
   • not concerned with personal experiences of instructor
2. Works step-by-step
   • one task at a time
   • one job at a time
3. Thinks logically
   • learns through systematic plans
   • thinks sequentially
   • serious, systematic problem solving
   • critical, analytic reading/listening
   • outlines rather than summarizes
4. Is verbal
   • responds to verbal instruction
   • recognizes and remembers names
   • uses words for meaning (rather than tone)
   • remembers through language
   • thinks in words or symbols
5. Concentrates on tasks at hand
   • remembers details
   • not easily distracted
6. Consistent with rules and assignments
   • likes to organize assignments
   • prefers options
   • analyzes a problem, then makes a decision
7. Prefers specific grading criteria
   • does not mind criticism
   • wants to know exactly what he or she did wrong
   • does not like vague questions
	What does the global learner look like in the classroom?
	1. Needs whole ideas before step-by-step
	   • reads the overall idea, skipping the details
	   • can work on several things at the same time
	   • writes the whole paper before the outline
	   • skips details
	   • often answers "It depends"
	   • summarizes rather than outlines
	   • reads for main ideas and overviews
	2. Is interested in team competition
	   • lets someone else go first
	   • likes working with others
	3. Sees relationships
	   • understands things in context
	   • motivated by having fun learning
	4. Remembers images, pictures
	   • good at interpreting body language
	   • remembers faces, not names
	   • likes fantasy, poetry, myths
	5. Thrives on humor
	   • playful problem-solving
	   • motivated by having fun learning
	6. Relates what is being taught to personal experiences
	   • needs praise
	   • distracted by facial expressions
	   • hard to take criticism, even constructive criticism
	   • feels better about accomplishments if rewarded, praised
	   • has strong emotional responses

Source: Center for Success in Learning (1992). *How Does Hemisphericity Relate to Learning?* Workshop handout. Dallas, TX.

Figure 7-17. Characteristics of left-brain/analytic learners and right-brain/global learners.

- Organization–An analytic learner tends to organize information into files, while a global learner will group information into piles. Most global learners can go to any pile and pull out exactly what they need. What appears to be disorganization may be different, spatial organization.
- Words or pictures–An analytic learner will prefer words, while a global learner will prefer pictures. If learners see pictures and patterns it does not mean they have trouble reading words or symbols, but it does mean they are more likely to remember words, dates or facts if they are connected to pictures and patterns.
- Project management–An analytic learner tends to work on one project at a time, while a global learner will be comfortable with many ongoing projects. If learners juggle many projects at once, it is not procrastination, but a way of thinking that allows them to pull ideas or concepts from one project to use in another. It can stimulate creativity for globals.
- Punctuality–Analytic learners tend to be punctual, while global learners are often running late. If learners have a tendency to run late, it may be that they have a holistic, polychronic sense of time, (they relate to chunks of time such as morning, day, week, month, year), rather than a linear, monochromic sense of time, (hour by hour, minute by minute).
- Names or faces–Analytic learners tend to remember names, while faces are remembered by global learners. Globals not only remember faces, but probably also remember the clothes, the expression on faces, the occasion, or the setting of a meeting. Analytics will remember not only the name, but the title and the company of the acquaintance.
- Word meaning or tone–An analytic learner will focus on the meaning of a conversation, while global learners will pay attention to the tone. Globals read additional meaning into conversation from the tone and inflection of the voice rather than relying on word meanings only.
- Logic or emotion–An analytic learner will rely on logic for problem-solving or decision-making, while a global learner will rely on emotion. Globals are often perceived as being intuitive. While an analytic may make a logical decision, a global may say things such as, "It doesn't feel right," or "It doesn't look right."

Both sides of the brain are involved in every human activity. The more connected the two halves are, the greater potential the brain has for learning. Most individuals have a distinct preference for one of these styles of thinking. The ultimate goal is to approach life and work using a whole-brain approach. Don't make the mistake of thinking that the left and right brains are two totally separate entities. They are connected and have areas of overlap. An integrated whole-brain approach begins to maximize the untapped potential of the human brain. The theory of brain-based learning supports the proposition that teachers must expand their repertoire of techniques for accommodating the learners' diverse learning styles.

LEARNING STYLE INVENTORIES

A learning style inventory is a formal tool used to ask learners how they feel they learn best. It is a direct attempt to identify the instructional strategies that access the best learner response to the learning environment. Learning style inventories are instruments that indicate the ways in which learners learn best, the qualities important to people in interacting with others, and the kinds of thinking patterns learners use to solve problems and make decisions. They do not show how much learners know or how intelligent they are. There are no right or wrong answers to the questions. Learners respond to each item exactly the way they feel about it.

The C.I.T.E. Learning Styles Instrument (Babich, Burdine, Albright, and Randol, n.d.) includes the statements that the learners are asked to respond to and the scoring sheet. This instrument can be used to develop a learning style profile for a learner. Specific areas of information that are reported by this instrument include the following:

- Auditory language–This is the way a learner hears words and processes spoken language.
- Visual language–This is the way a learner sees words and processes written language.
- Auditory numerical–This is the way a learner hears numbers and processes spoken numerical values.
- Visual numerical–This is the way a learner sees numbers and processes written numerical values.
- Auditory/visual/kinesthetic–This is the way a person learns by doing and involvement, emphasizing the experiencing/manipulative learning style, almost always accompanied by either auditory or visual stimuli, or a combination of both.
- Group learner–This is a learner who likes to work with at least one other person when there is important work to be completed.
- Individual learner–This is a learner who works and thinks best alone, usually a self-starter who frequently finds working with others distracting.
- Oral expressive–This describes learners who prefer to say what they know, utilize explanations; however, some learners may indicate this preference simply because they are too lazy to write things down.
- Written expressive–This is a learner who prefers to write down answers or explanations; learners who exhibit a reflective cognitive learning style may prefer this method.

When the profile has been developed as a result of learner responses to the C.I.T.E. Learning Styles Instrument, the information can be used by educators to plan for the delivery of curricular content. The profile shows the major and minor areas of strength of the individual's learning style.

A learning style/teaching style profile may be divided into two sections. One section measures the behaviors displayed in classroom situations that reflect a particular learning style. The other section represents a teaching style profile that allows instructors to assess the strategies that they use to deliver content in their program. This contrast should help teachers to select and use appropriate techniques to meet the needs of all learners. See Appendix.

Learners should be made aware of their learning styles. Hand (1990) identified a number of benefits for learners becoming aware of their own styles:

> They are more likely to develop strategies for dealing with the diverse demands of school and of life in general if they are aware of how they process information and learn. Information about learning style also helps them to understand many of the conflicts that arise in groups by showing students that different individuals will use a variety of strategies in completing a task. Students can also explore the impact of style on skills like organization and test-taking. They might brainstorm and experiment with strategies for note-taking or applying study skills. Students can also consider their styles in relation to their study environments at home by realizing that the ultimate test of an environment is the quality of thinking and work that the individual does there. By focusing on learning styles, students gain confidence in their strengths and develop diverse strategies for coping with the challenging situations that arise. Students begin to see how they learn most effectively and efficiently; therefore, they are better able to take responsibility for their own learning. Most important, they learn that their ways are not better or worse than those of their peers. They are simply different. (pp. 13-14)

ANALYZING TEACHING STYLES

In order to identify appropriate teaching strategies to meet the needs of learners from special populations, instructors should analyze the teaching styles they use most frequently. They should then match their particular teaching style with the learning styles of the learners. Evidence exists that teachers tend to teach learners in a style that matches the individual teacher's learning style. This can be very frustrating for those learners who do not have the same learning style as the teacher.

As educators analyze their teaching styles, they should address the following considerations:
- their educational philosophies
- the way the classroom and laboratory are designed and organized
- the type of teaching environment that is provided (e.g., flexible, rigid)
- the way learners are grouped (e.g., large groups, small groups, peer teams, flexible grouping, grouping by ability)

- the environment in which the instructor feels most comfortable when teaching (e.g., classroom, laboratory, supervising a learner on a job site)
- the amount and frequency of auditory strategies used in teaching (e.g., lectures, verbal directions, discussions, cassettes, questioning)
- the amount and frequency of visual strategies used in teaching (e.g., transparencies, charts, illustrations, flipcharts, writing board)
- the amount and frequency of audiovisual aids used in teaching (e.g., films, videotapes)
- the amount and frequency of printed materials used in teaching (e.g., workbooks, textbooks, manuals, handouts)
- the amount and frequency of psychomotor activities used in teaching (e.g., demonstrations, observations, laboratory activities)
- the amount of direction and supervision provided to learners
- the amount of learner interaction allowed or encouraged in the instructional process
- the working conditions that are important during the instructional process (e.g., lighting, noise level, ventilation;
- the level of formality the teacher feels most comfortable with during the instructional process (e.g., formal, casual)
- the level of structure the teacher feels most comfortable with during the instructional process (e.g., highly structured, flexible)
- the level of stress for learners that is incorporated into the instructional process
- the types and intensity of learner reinforcement that is incorporated into the instructional process (e.g., praise, attention, reinforcement)
- the amount of attention paid to the attention span of learners in the class

A teacher learning style and teaching style inventory provides an instrument to measure a teacher's learning style and teaching style that will allow the instructor to match it with the preferred learning style preferences of learners in the classroom. Once teachers have analyzed their own teaching and the preferred learning styles of their learners, they must plan appropriate teaching techniques in their instructional program. See Figure 7-18.

Teachers must know their own learning style and related teaching style strengths. Teaching style, after all, is a critical factor in communicating expectations of school learning styles. The assessment instruments noted in the previous paragraph are valuable tool for identifying both learning and teaching style tendencies. Above all, teachers must be warm demanders, adults who balance humanistic concerns with high expectations for achievement. They must communicate an attitude of understanding and caring while at the same time demand high performance.

MATCHING INSTRUCTIONAL TECHNIQUES WITH LEARNING STYLES			
Method or Resource	Learning Style Characteristics to Which It Responds	Learning Style Characteristics to Which It Does Not Respond	Learning Style Characteristics to Which It Can Be Accommodated
1. Programmed learning	Motivation, persistence, responsibility, and a need for structure; a need to work alone, a visually-oriented student	A lack of motivation, persistence or responsibility; a need for flexibility or creativity; a need to work with peers or adults; auditory, tactual, or kinesthetic perceptual strengths	Sound, light, temperature, and design; a need for intake, appropriate time of day, and a need for mobility
Note: When programmed learning sequences are accompanied by tapes, they will appeal to auditory learners; when they include films or filmstrips, they will reinforce the visually-oriented student; when teachers design small-group techniques such as team learning, circle of knowledge, or brainstorming, peer-oriented students may develop an ability to use programs more effectively than if they use them exclusively as individual learners.			
2. Contract activity package	A need for sound and an informal design; motivation, persistence, and responsibility; a need to work either alone, with a friend or two, or with an adult, all perceptual strengths and weaknesses and the need for mobility	None	Sound, light, temperature and design; motivation, persistence, responsibility; sociological needs; perceptual strengths, intakes, time of day, and the need for mobility
Note: Contract activity packages respond to all learning style characteristics provided that (1) they are used correctly, and (2) multisensory resources are developed as part of them.			
3. Instructional package	A need for sound or structure; a need to work alone; all perceptual strengths	A lack of responsibility; a need for peer or adult interactions	Light, temperature, and design; motivation, persistence; intake, time of day, and mobility
Note: Because of their multisensory activities, instructional packages are very effective with slow learners. Unless the curriculum is extremely challenging, they may be boring to high achievers.			
4. Task cards and learning circles	Motivation, persistence, responsibility, and the need for structure; visual or tactual strengths	A lack of motivation, persistence, responsibility, or a need for structure; auditory or kinesthetic strengths; a need for mobility	Sound, light, temperature, and design; the need to work alone, with peers, or an adult; intake and time of day
5. Tapes, audiocassettes	A need for sound; motivation, persistence, responsibility, and a need for structure; a need to work alone; auditory strengths	A need for silence; a need to work with peers or an adult; visual, tactual, or kinesthetic strengths, and a need for mobility	Light, temperature, and design; intake and time of day

Source: Dunn, R. and Dunn, K. (1978). *Teaching Students Through Their Individual Learning Styles: A Practical Approach.* Reston, VA: Reston Publishing Co., p. 3.

Figure 7-18. A variety of suggested instructional strategies used to respond to the learning style elements identified by Dunn and Dunn.

Some of the questions pertinent to instructor teaching style include the following:
- Where does the instructor teach best (e.g., classroom, laboratory, job site)?
- Does the instructor feel more comfortable teaching on a one-to-one arrangement, with pairs of learners, with small groups, or with large groups?
- What specific working conditions are important to an instructor (e.g., lighting, noise level, ventilation)?
- Does the instructor feel more comfortable with a formal or informal teaching format?
- Does the instructor teach more effectively when utilizing audiovisual materials (e.g., filmstrips, videotapes, films)?
- Does the instructor teach more effectively when utilizing auditory techniques (e.g., lectures, verbal directions, cassettes)?
- Does the instructor teach more effectively when utilizing visual materials (e.g., charts, diagrams, illustrations)?
- Does the instructor teach more effectively when utilizing hands-on techniques (e.g., demonstrations, observations, laboratory activities)?

- Does the instructor feel more comfortable with a lot of learner interaction?
- Does the instructor feel more comfortable using a highly structured or a flexible routine?
- Does the instructor feel more comfortable teaching in a formal or casual manner?
- Does the instructor utilize methods that reach both the introverted and extraverted learners?
- Does the instructor allow for the attention span of the learner (e.g., task analysis, short modules, units)?
- Does the instructor develop learning activities that parallel the learner's ability to handle stress?
- Does the instructor require the learners to complete learning activities at a predetermined pace or allow the learners to work at their own rates of performance?
- Does the instructor integrate a sufficient amount of attention, praise, and reinforcement to meet the needs of the learner?

As educators, our challenge is to draw classroom implications from all available sources in order to help students become better learners. Extensive data verify the existence of individual differences among learners—differences so extreme that a single teaching method, resource, or grouping procedure can prevent or block learning for many learners. Using teaching methods that take into consideration the learner's learning styles can increase achievement. Evidence supports the fact that traditional methods of instruction are no longer sufficient to meet the needs of today's learners. In addition, research reports that positive effects abound when instruction based on learning styles is used with special education, underachieving, and at-risk learners.

Culture and Learning Styles

The culture in which learners live or the culture they descend from affects their preferred learning style. Researchers report that generalizations about a group of people often lead to naive inferences about individual members of that group.

Guild (1994) identified some accepted conclusions about culture and learning styles:
- Students of any particular age will differ in their ways of learning.
- Learning styles are a function of nature and nurture.
- Learning styles are neutral. Every learning style approach can be used successfully, but can become a stumbling block if applied inappropriately or overused.
- Within a group, the variations among individuals are as great as their commonalities.
- There is a cultural conflict between some students and the typical learning experiences in schools.
- Evidence suggests that students with particular learning style traits are underachievers in school, irrespective of their cultural group. Students with such dominant learning style patterns have limited opportunities to use their style strengths in the classroom.

- Ideas about culture and learning styles can be of great help to instructors as they identify with instructional diversity. An instructor who truly understands culture and learning styles and who believes that all students can learn, one way or another, can offer opportunities for success to all students.
- If instructional decisions were based on an understanding of each learner's culture and ways of learning, educators would never assume that uniform practices would be effective for all. They would recognize that the only way to meet diverse learning needs would be to intentionally apply diverse strategies. (pp. 19-21)

In order to analyze individual learning styles instructors should do the following:
- Get to know the norms and values of the community the learner comes from.
- Be aware of learners' background knowledge and experiences.
- Discuss learners' learning styles with them; help them understand why they do what they do in learning situations.
- When planning activities, be aware that the time framework may be rigid and inflexible.
- Be aware of how questions are asked; think about the learners' communication styles.
- Remember, some learners do not like to be spotlighted in front of a group.
- Provide time for observation and practice before performance; let learners save face, but communicate that it is okay to make mistakes.
- Be aware of proximity preferences; find out how close is comfortable.
- Organize the classroom to meet the interactional needs of the learners; provide activities that encourage both independence and cooperation.
- Provide feedback that is immediate, consistent, and private, if necessary; give praise that is specific.
- Consider the whole person when organizing and planning for learning experiences; consider a whole-language, thematic approach.
- Be flexible and realize that while the goals remain constant, there are alternative ways for learners to reach the goals.

ADAPTING TEACHING STRATEGIES

Crenshaw (2000) conducted research regarding learning needs and effective instruction for at-risk learners. Elements that complement the learning needs of these individuals include the following:
- Clear, consistent, flexible classroom management and structure–Learner ownership avenues such as input or participation in the development of rules, incentives, and consequences are worthwhile components to include. Research further supports that one success factor of effective alternative and nontraditional schools

is clearly communicated and enforced rules and consequences, ideally, with a minimal number of rules so as to eliminate rigidity and provide flexibility. Succinctly stated, classroom (and school) management must be simple, fair, and consistent so that learners clearly recognize that rules and consequences are consistently and equitably applied so as to detract from learning and instruction as little as possible and so as to also maintain pleasant class climate.

- A responsive, supportive learning environment that allows for learner input and involvement in learning–Such an environment positively affects achievement. The classroom becomes a community that allows learners to actively explore ideas and experiences together. The classroom environment maintains or increases learners' critical-thinking and problem-solving skills. The learning environment affects learner performance. The learning environment should be flexibly structured to meet varying learner needs, to allow learners to have some responsibility for their own learning, and to have opportunities to develop skill as independent learners. High expectations for learners and a belief in their capabilities are both necessary ingredients for a responsive environment.

- Relationships with instructors and role models–Activities and interaction with adult role models and positive, supportive, nonauthoritative teachers who value and respect learner capabilities and ideas and who treat learners with respect provide needed support and contribute to improved achievement. A major factor appears to be a supportive environment.

- Variety and diversity of instructional activities and materials–Activities should include learner choices or options, activities in learner interest areas, engaging, participatory, hands-on learning, variety and novelty activities, shared responsibility of learning, nontraditional instruction, and challenging activities. Relevancy and real world application of learning must be clear in order to maximize learner interest. Since learning occurs differently for each person, presentation and delivery must be multidimensional and must accommodate varied learning styles.

- Activities and avenues for social interaction with peers–Learning activities that provide options to work in pairs, groups, or alone are beneficial to the learner, both in the classroom and on campus. Research on cooperative learning methodology is impressive–rewards for group success ensure the individual learning and contribution of each member. Cooperative learning activities must be designed not to limit or place a ceiling on learning and accomplishment potential, but rather, to encourage and nurture group and individual creativity and learning possibilities. Such activities offer a sense of belonging, social support, and bonding beyond the very traditional classroom setting.

- Flexibility with environmental/learning conditions– Matched teacher and learner preferences in lighting, seating, noise level, and scheduling is one method schools have implemented to improve achievement. Opportunities and experiences for success in academics, social arenas, and school in general must be numerous, regular, and varied. Teachers and activities that recognize learner motivation, attempts, and genuine desire to succeed tend to perpetuate a cycle of success. Encouragement should honestly recognize learner effort, desire, involvement, process versus product, and improvement. Evaluation should focus on the learner and the process of learning rather than just the content. Consistent, continued inclusion of opportunities for learner success and achievement ultimately change learner expectation for failure into an expectation for success.

- Information about and exposure to ideas, options, activities–Information regarding career, academic options, social issues (alcohol, drugs, sex), and emotional issues (getting along with others, counseling support, resiliency) provide support in areas important to learners. This might include opportunities for self-exploration and development (goals, plans, strengths, weaknesses, study skills, strategies to help learners succeed in school, problem-solving skills, decision-making skills) that aid in learner achievement and yield improved resiliency and coping skills.

By tailoring learning environments and instructional methods to meet the needs of learners, instructors can expect improved results in attitudes toward learning, learning skills, content mastery, and positive self-perception of learners. See Figure 7-19.

A goal of teaching is to create a learning environment for learners where learning is intrinsically rewarding and is based on teacher modeling of desired behaviors and attitudes. The following are teaching strategies that recognize the individualities of learners and promote learning:

- Utilize a flexible eclectic teaching approach; incorporate multimedia and multimodality instructional activities.
- Utilize instructional methods that demonstrate an understanding of the cross-cultural, gender, and age differences in style preferences.
- Assess learners' preferred ways of learning, ways of receiving instruction, and ways in which learner behaviors change from situation to situation. With this knowledge provide a collaborative learning environment that promotes success.
- Implement learning experiences that incorporate the learners' preferred ways of learning, using teaching methods, incentives, materials, and situations that are planned according to learner preferences.
- Allow learners to recognize their individual learning styles and reward them for their special strengths. Help them understand why they do what they do in learning situations.

FEATURES OF CLASSROOM LEARNING ENVIRONMENTS & EXPECTED OUTCOMES...

Features of Effective Classroom Learning Environments	Development of Positive Attitudes Towards Learning				Acquisition of a Variety of Learning Skills		
Expected Student Outcome →	Enjoyment in taking part in learning activities	Viewing help-giving and help receiving as positive experiences	Special interest in certain learning areas	Motivation for continuing learning	Ability to study and learn independently	Ability to plan and monitor learning activities	Ability to obtain assistance from others
Instructional content that is							
• essential to further learning			X				
• useful for effective functioning in school and society			X	X			
• clearly specified					X	X	
• organized to facilitate efficient learning				X	X	X	
Assessment and diagnosis that							
• provides appropriate placement in the curricula				X	X		
• provides frequent and systematic assessment of progress and feedback				X	X	X	X
Learning experience in which							
• ample time and instructional support are provided for each student to acquire essential content	X		X	X			
• disruptiveness is minimized	X				X	X	
• students use effective learning strategies/study skills				X	X	X	X
• each student is expected to succeed, and actually succeed in achieving mastery of curriculum content, and accomplishments are reinforced	X		X	X			
• alternative instructional strategies, student assignments, and activities are used	X			X	X	X	
Management of instruction that							
• permits students to master many lessons through independent study				X	X	X	
• permits students to plan their own learning activities	X			X	X	X	
• provides for students' self-monitoring of their progress with most lessons	X		X	X	X	X	
• permits students to play a part in selecting some learning goals and activities	X		X	X	X	X	
Collaboration among students that							
• enables students to obtain necessary help from peers	X	X				X	X
• encourages students to provide help	X	X	X				X
• provides for collaboration in group activities	X	X	X			X	X

The X indicates that extant findings from studies on effective teaching and learning suggest relationships between the implementation of specific features and the achievement of particular student outcomes.

FEATURES OF CLASSROOM LEARNING ENVIRONMENTS & EXPECTED OUTCOMES

Expected Student Outcome →	Mastery of Subject Matter Content		Development of Positive Self-Perceptions			
Features of Effective Classroom Learning Environments	Mastery of content and skills for effective functioning	Mastery of content and skills for further learning	Confidence in one's ability as a learner	Confidence in oneself as a contributing member of the school or community	Confidence in one's ability to take self-responsibility for learning and behavior	Perceptions of internal locus of control
Instructional content that is						
• essential to further learning	X	X	X			
• useful for effective functioning in school and society	X	X				
• clearly specified	X	X				
• organized to facilitate efficient learning	X	X		X		
Assessment and diagnosis that						
• provides appropriate placement in the curricula	X	X	X			
• provides frequent and systematic assessment of progress and feedback	X	X				
Learning experience in which						
• ample time and instructional support are provided for each student to acquire essential content	X	X				X
• disruptiveness is minimized	X	X	X			
• students use effective learning strategies/study skills	X	X	X		X	
• each student is expected to succeed, and actually succeed in achieving mastery of curriculum content, and accomplishments are reinforced	X	X		X	X	
• alternative instructional strategies, student assignments, and activities are used	X	X				
Management of instruction that						
• permits students to master many lessons through independent study	X	X			X	X
• permits students to plan their own learning activities	X	X			X	X
• provides for students' self-monitoring of their progress with most lessons	X	X			X	X
• permits students to play a part in selecting some learning goals and activities	X	X			X	X
Collaboration among students that						
• enables students to obtain necessary help from peers	X	X			X	X
• encourages students to provide help	X	X		X	X	X
• provides for collaboration in group activities	X	X		X	X	X

Figure 7-19. Learning environments and outcome correlations.

Source: Wang, M., Reynolds, M., & Walberg, H. (1986). Rethinking Special Education. *Educational Leadership, 44*, pp. 28–29.

- As tasks permit, provide learners the opportunity to choose how to receive instruction and how to demonstrate knowledge. Offer opinions in task types, times, and completion dates.
- Utilize questions and explorations of all types to stimulate various levels of thinking, from recalling factual information to drawing implications and forming analysis.
- Set clear purposes prior to all instructional experiences with a general overview of materials to be learned (i.e., structured overviews, advanced organizers, mapping, etc.) to facilitate associating learners' past experiences with new ideas.
- Utilize combinations of cooperative learning, individualized instruction, and group instruction, as well as teacher-directed and self-directed learning activities.
- Allow sufficient time for information to be processed and experienced. Pattern-seeking and program-building task time cannot be rushed.
- Utilize multisensory means for processing, practicing, and retrieving information.
- Repeat seemingly difficult learning tasks using different instructional methods.
- Utilize a variety of review and reflection strategies to bring closure to learning.
- Provide immediate, consistent, and descriptive feedback.
- Evaluate the learning experiences in terms of attainments of goals, observed learner behaviors, and involvement.
- As the year progresses, plan and implement learner participation in learning experiences that require behaviors that learners have previously avoided.
- Continue to provide familiar, comfortable, successful experiences, and gradually introduce the learners to learning in new ways.
- Assess learners through a variety of procedures and activities.
- Utilize assessments that are aligned with instruction.

In order for an instructor to determine what strategies will best meet the needs of the learners receiving the instruction, information should be collected about them. Learning style information should be reviewed to create as close a match as possible between the preferred learning styles of learners and the teaching techniques used by the instructor in the classroom. A student inventory can be used to collect pertinent information to identify areas in which modifications should be made in classroom and laboratory activities. Once information about learner needs is identified, appropriate modifications should be matched to these needs.

Instructors may want to make appropriate modifications to their curriculum for learners from special populations but may have difficulty due to a lack of planning time, absence of support personnel or lack of ideas about how to modify a lesson/unit. A form can be used for curriculum customization within a class lesson format. See Figure 7-20.

The Missouri Department of Elementary and Secondary Education (1999) provided the following examples of ways for instructors of learners with special needs to modify curricula:

Instructional Methods
- Provide frequent learner comprehension checks throughout lectures, demonstrations, or instructions.
- Emphasize key points; repeat or summarize them.
- Prepare a few questions to help gauge the extent of the learner's subject knowledge.
- Maintain eye contact.
- Present lengthy material in short segments, allowing for breaks.
- Use audiovisual aids to illustrate and clarify.
- Actively involve the learners; ask them questions and seek their help for demonstrations.
- Vary methods of presentations.
- Give feedback often.
- Use concrete examples.
- Use demonstrations.
- Break down tasks sequentially; provide step-by-step instruction.
- Minimize irrelevant information.
- Provide private workspace for a learner who is easily distracted.

Equipment Modifications
- Have a digital or talking watch.
- Install guard rails on machines.
- Modify hand or foot controls.
- Use warning lights or noises.
- Provide illustrated (not written) instructions.
- Provide tapes or audio-visualized instructions.
- Provide large-print materials.

Curriculum Modifications
- Administer oral testing.
- Use taped textbooks.
- Allow calculators.
- Do not grade for spelling.
- Allow note-taker use.
- Use cue cards for steps of task.
- Use assistive devices.
- Use study guides.
- Provide study skills instruction.
- List formulas for tests.
- Provide computer-assisted learning.
- Allow extended time for testing.
- Allow extended time for writing assignments.
- Provide more time for practice of certain tasks.
- Provide computers for writing tasks.
- Use readers.
- Highlight important facts in text.
- Give written rather than oral directions.
- Hold test review sessions.
- Provide conversion tables.
- List vocabulary for tests.
- Tape record lectures.

ADAPTING TEACHING STRATEGIES ...

Student Inventory

Directions Place a "+" next to items that are easiest for you to do.
Place a "-" next to items that are the most difficult for you to do.

A. GATHERING INFORMATION

_____ College level textbooks
_____ Course lectures
_____ Group discussion
_____ Audiovisual materials
_____ Audiotapes
_____ Concrete experience (e.g., by doing something)
_____ Observation of others
_____ Asking questions
_____ Role playing
_____ Other_____

_____ Map/charts/graphs
_____ Internships/practicums
_____ Other_____

B. LEARNING ENVIRONMENT

_____ Working independently
_____ Working with a peer tutor
_____ Participating in a small group/classroom
_____ Participating in a large group/classroom
_____ Listening to audiotapes
_____ Other_____

C. ASSIGNMENT

_____ Worksheets
_____ Short papers (2-3 pp.)
_____ Term papers (10-20 pp.)
_____ Demo/lab projects
_____ Art/media projects
_____ Oral reports
_____ Group discussions
_____ Word problems/math

D. TEST FORMATS

_____ Short answer
_____ Essay
_____ Multiple choice
_____ True-false
_____ Matching
_____ Computation/math
_____ Oral examinations
_____ Other_____

Directions Check the areas that give you the most trouble.

_____ Going to class on time
_____ Going to class prepared (e.g., pens, paper, etc.)
_____ Becoming motivated to start work
_____ Budgeting time
_____ Sticking with an assignment until completion
_____ Following oral directions
_____ Following written directions
_____ Organizing ideas and information
_____ Drawing conclusions, making inferences
_____ Understanding abstract concepts
_____ Finding the right word to describe something orally
_____ Expressing ideas precisely in writing

_____ Reading comprehension
_____ Reading rate
_____ Sounding out unfamiliar words
_____ Mathematical reasoning and word problems
_____ Mathematical computation
_____ Remembering specific course vocabulary
_____ Test-taking anxiety
_____ Lack of self-confidence
_____ Making new friends
_____ Understanding humor and sarcasm
_____ Making small talk

Directions Check the areas in which you would like additional information.

_____ General information on learning disabilities
_____ An assessment of basic skills
_____ Arranging for a hearing test
_____ Arranging for a vision test
_____ Counseling services
_____ TUTORIAL INSTRUCTION

_____ Notetaking in lectures
_____ Outlining a textbook
_____ Writing a term paper
_____ Spelling
_____ Basic grammar skills (e.g., punctuation, sentence construction, etc.)

_____ Basic math skills
_____ Basic reading skills
_____ Test taking skills
_____ Locating information in the library
_____ Special tutorial help in _____
_____ Other_____

... ADAPTING TEACHING STRATEGIES ...

Directions   *Describe your greatest academic/vocatonal strengths.*

_____

_____

_____

_____

_____

_____

Student _____   Grade_____   Date_____

_____ Assignment notebook monitored by teacher and parent, signed off weekly

_____ Study sheets provided by the teacher

_____ Repeated review and drill by the teacher

_____ Peer tutoring

_____ Cooperative learning (teaming)

_____ Preferential seating

_____ Concrete reinforcers

_____ Positive reinforcers, minimal punishment

_____ Targeted behaviors addressed one at a time and reinforced with improved self control

_____ Increased monitoring by the teacher/walking around the classroom–attending regularly

_____ Increased structure surrounding the student; daily routines and rules

_____ Reduction of visual and auditory stimuli in the classroom and at home during study time

_____ Increased intrinsic interest in a subject area by one-on-one teacher/student communication-weekly

_____ Organizational plan for class preparation and home activities with increased consistency

_____ Gain the student's attention before giving instruction (stand beside student, hand on shoulder, predesigned signals)

_____ Require work that has been completed rapidly to be proofed at least twice for errors

_____ Have student repeat instructions privately to the teacher before beginning the task

_____ Administer a learning styles inventory; involve the student in creating activities to tap individual modalities

_____ Assign individual projects to reveal mastery of content

_____ Regularly scheduled parent/teacher/student meetings

_____ Home/school behavioral contracts

_____ Suggested in-district resources (for parents or student)

_____ Provide additional study aids

_____ Provide tutorial time

_____ Break difficult tasks into smaller parts; teach each part separately if needed

_____ Provide student with optional quiet spot (possibly isolated) to do academic work or to avoid punishment

_____ Provide frequent teacher/student contacts to help student start and remain on task

_____ Give much encouragement and praise

_____ Limit criticism, especially before other students

_____ Develop legitimate ways for student to have movement in class, limiting confinement

_____ Pace the work (e.g., twelve 5-minute assignments achieve more than one 45-minute assignment)

_____ Make allowances for inconsistent performance; build rapport; increase personal respect (students work harder when there is a personal relationship with the teacher)

_____ Private instruction or use of a predesigned signal directing student to take a deep breath and get back on task when attention is lost

_____ Develop alternative assignments for more active learning, allowing the student to show mastery (in addition to or in place of traditional task)

_____ Assign alternative assignments to tap the student's learning style

_____ Establish contracts (student-teacher, student-administrator, student-parent, parent-teacher)

☐ **Regular Discipline Plan** (No modifications)

☐ **Regular Discipline Plan** (Minor modifications)

_____
Describe

☐ **Behavior Management Plan**

_____
Describe

Source: Brinckerhoff, L. (n.d.). *Student Inventory.* Madison, WI: University of Wisconsin-Madison, McBurney Resource Center.

... ADAPTING TEACHING STRATEGIES ...

Classroom Modifications

TO: _____   RE: _____
　　　　　Teacher(s) Responsible　　　　　　　　　　　　　　　Student

ADAPTATION OF MATERIALS:
Provide

_____ Reading materials at _____ grade level
_____ Peer to read materials
_____ Peer to take notes
_____ Peer or small group discussion of materials
_____ Tape recording of required readings
_____ Highlighted materials for emphasis
_____ Altered format of materials:_____
_____ Study aids/manipulatives:_____
_____ Outlines and study guides
_____ Other:_____

MODIFICATIONS OF INSTRUCTION:
Provide

_____ Shortened, simplified instructions
_____ Repeated instructions
_____ Opportunity to repeat instructions
_____ Opportunity to write instructions
_____ Written instructions
_____ Visual aids (pictures, flash cards, etc.):_____
_____ Auditory aids (cues, tapes, etc.):_____
_____ Instructional aids:_____
_____ Multisensory information:_____
_____ Extra time for oral response
_____ Extra time for written response
_____ Over learning
_____ Exams of reduced length
_____ Oral exams
_____ Open book exams
_____ Tests to be given by Content Mastery teacher
_____ Written review for exams
_____ Preview of test questions
_____ Study carrel for independent work
_____ Frequent feedback
_____ Immediate feedback
_____ Checks for understanding
_____ Minimize auditory distractions
_____ Encourage participation
_____ Extended "wait time"
_____ Other:_____

BEHAVIOR MANAGEMENT:
Provide

_____ Clearly defined limits
_____ Frequent reminders of rules
_____ Frequent eye contact
_____ Private discussion regarding behavior
_____ Seating near the teacher
_____ Opportunity to help teacher
_____ Supervision during transition
_____ Ignoring of minor infractions
_____ Implementation of behavior contract
_____ Positive reinforcement
_____ Emphasis on student's special talents
_____ Secret signal between teacher and student
_____ Other:_____

ALTERATIONS OF ASSIGNMENTS:
Provide

_____ Simplified homework assignments
_____ Reduced assignments
_____ Taped assignments
_____ Prioritize assignments
_____ Extra time for assignments
_____ Opportunity to respond orally
_____ Individual contracts
_____ Emphasis on major points
_____ Exemption from reading before peers
_____ Assistance in class discussions
_____ Special projects in lieu of assignments
_____ Other:_____

GENERAL MODIFICATIONS:
Provide

_____ Structured learning environment
_____ Computer-aided instruction
_____ Other:_____
_____
_____
_____
_____

Source: Grantham, J. (1993). Modifying Subject Matter and Curriculum for Secondary 504 Students: Can They Still Master the Essential Elements? Presentation at Texas Association of Section 504 Coordinators and Hearing Officers. Dallas, TX.

... ADAPTING TEACHING STRATEGIES ...

Curriculum Customization for Special Needs Learners

TASK: Tools and equipment used in tree surgery

Performance Objectives: When given the hand tools used in tree surgery, identify them with 95% accuracy on written test and use each in the field properly observing all safety precautions.

Criterion Reference Measure: Provided with an OSHA manual and pruning tools – identify each tool.

Learning Activities	Group Instruction Plans	I. Charlie	II. John

1. Identify and give uses for all tools (hand) in tree surgery
 	
2. Demonstrate proper use of each tool according to OSHA standards
  a. Chainsaw – cuts branches and tree trunks.
  b. Pruning saw – cuts branches 3″ in diameter or larger.
  c. Pole pruner and saw – used to cut high branches.
  d. Pruning shears
    (1) lopping – cuts branches 2″ to 3″ in diameter. (Also cuts ½″ to 1″)
    (2) Hand – cuts twigs ½″ diameter or less.
	1. Use overhead projector to display transparencies for tool identification; also display actual tools
	
	2. Review use of pruning tools with slide series
	
	3. Demonstrate use of each pruning tool
	
	4. Show a movie on pruning tool safety
	
	5. Provide hands-on experience pruning
		1. Resource teacher reviews slide series of tools and gives a name sign to each. This process is reinforced daily
		
		2. Chainsaw modification: On a safe location of the frame, spray bright yellow fluorescent paint. He will be able to feel vibration to determine if machine is on or off
			1. Have student review his set of flashcards picturing hand tools
			
			2. Using highlighting, have related instructor assist student in reading OSHA standards for operating a chainsaw

Materials and Resources	I. Charlie	II. John
	1. Interpretor 2. Resource teacher (MH deaf) 3. Flashcards 4. Videotape system 5. Related instructor	1. Related instructor 2. Vocational instructor 3. Flashcards

Group Evaluation Procedure/Techniques	I. Charlie	II. John
1. Oral quiz on tool identification 2. Student demonstration of correct use of pruning tools.	Student gives correct sign for each hand tool.	Give an oral quiz with no other students present or have student answer using flashcards.

Source: Johnson, C. (1980). Curriculum Customization for Special Needs Learners. *Journal for Vocational Special Needs Education*, April. pp. 3 - 6.

. . . ADAPTING TEACHING STRATEGIES			
Instruction Format for Curriculum Customization for Special Needs Learners			

Task:

Performance Objectives:

Criterion Reference Measure:

Learning Activities (Steps in Lesson)	Group Instruction Plans	Student A	Student B
1.	1.		
2.	2.		
3.	3.		

Materials and Resources	Student A	Student B
1. 2.		

Group Evaluation Procedure/Techniques	Student A	Student B
1. 2.		

Figure 7-20. A student inventory to identify learner needs, strategies for making classroom modifications, an example of curriculum customization, and a format for recording personalized program notes.

If the modifications/accommodations allow the learner to achieve the competencies other learners will achieve in class, the modifications are considered to be minimal.

Classroom Modifications

Classroom modifications generally fall into low-tech solutions such as adjustable tables, tilted monitors, one-handed keyboards, rolling chairs, and creating enough space for a learner who uses a wheelchair or crutches to easily access tools, equipment, and books. These might be considered architectural solutions. Classroom modifications can also be programmatic and applied to assist with individual learner needs or general classroom management. See Figure 7-21. The following are common modifications for the classroom and reasons for their use:
- Arranging desks or tables in a U-formation facilitates classroom discussion.
- Arranging desks or tables in a traditional line helps keep learners from distracting others.
- Seating assignments separate those who distract each other, but also encourages a fast learner to help a slower peer.

- A seating assignment in front of the class helps a learner with visual or hearing impairments or a learner with Attention Deficit Disorder (ADD).
- Cooperative learning assists group learners and tactile/kinesthetic learners.
- Videotaped demonstrations help learners who have been absent or reinforce a procedure.

- A buddy system helps learners assist each other, especially in shop areas.
- Developing behavior contracts assists learners in defining appropriate behaviors and consequences for inappropriate behaviors.
- Individual conferences assist all learners in understanding how their behavior helps or hinders their learning.

REGULAR CLASSROOM MODIFICATIONS

INSTRUCTION
- Simplified curriculum
- Individualize curriculum
- Extra practice on lessons
- Peer tutoring
- Academic skills grouping
- Computer-assisted instruction
- Small group instruction
- Remedial instruction
- Discrete; sequential units of instruction

TESTING
- Prior notice of test content
- Prior notice of test questions
- Study guide for tests
- Open-book tests
- Extra time for tests
- Untimed tests
- Simplified tests
- Shortened tests
- Oral testing
- Retake tests
- Tests taken in resource room
- Extra credit options
- Hands-on projects instead of tests

MATERIALS
- Alternative texts
- Copies of texts at home
- Consumable workbooks
- Modified worksheets
- Audio-visual aids
- High-interest reading materials
- Manipulatives
- Tape recorder
- Large-print books
- Calculator for math
- Computer for work processing

GRADING
- Grades based on effort and participation
- Grades based on effort and work
- Modified grades
- No spelling penalty on written work
- No handwriting penalty on written work

ORGANIZATION
- Give simple, clearly-stated instructions
- Repeat instructions
- Review instructions
- Provide lecture notes
- Provide story outlines
- Breaks between periods of instruction
- Desktop list of assignments
- Extra time to complete assignments
- Present one assignment at a time
- Shorter assignments
- Reduced assignments
- Weekly assignments
- Weekly assignment sheets
- Use notebook to organize assignments
- Preferential seating
- Study carrel

BEHAVIOR MANAGEMENT
- Positive reinforcement and encouragement
- Incentive program
- Assistive discipline program
- Corrective behavior plan
- Written behavior contract
- Support group
- Review/post school and classroom rules
- Immediate consequences for misbehavior
- Consistent enforcement of school rules
- Point reinforcement system
- Chart behavioral changes
- Progress reports sent to parents

Additional modifications: _____

_____

Figure 7-21. Regular classroom modifications that may need to be considered for a specific learner enrolled in a career and technical education program.

Classroom modifications may need to be considered for a specific learner enrolled in a career and technical education program. An individual option plan (IOP) identifies learner problems (classroom management, instruction, evaluation) and suggests teaching options for the instructor. See Figure 7-22. Curricular adaptations can be incorporated into an IOP.

Assignments

According to data collected from learners, a good assignment

- is different from other assignments;
- has an understood purpose;
- has clear and well-organized directions;
- allows for interpersonal or social interactions;
- is personally relevant for learners;
- provides opportunities for creative expression;
- allows for feedback;
- lists available resources;
- meets criteria for optimal challenge;
- includes learner choices;
- is considerate in relation to time demands; and
- lists evaluation criteria.

As career and technical education instructors develop and utilize learner assignments, careful attention should be paid to ensure that enough detail is provided to meet the needs of learners. A quality assignment planning chart provides guidelines for instructors. A quality assignment planning worksheet assists instructors as they prepare assignments. See Figure 7-23. An assignment handout is given to learners for a particular assignment.

INSTRUCTIONAL MATERIALS

Instructional materials should stimulate learner interest, motivate individuals to learn, and help them achieve realistic objectives. A variety of instructional materials is often critical to the successes of learners from special populations enrolled in career and technical education programs. These materials require careful analysis before being selected.

The format and content of the instructional material should undergo close scrutiny by the instructor. This analysis should focus on such elements as technical clarity of presentation, content, appropriate uses of the material (e.g., learner use, teacher use), interest level, and types and number of illustrations. When technical terms are used often, the materials must be clear and expressive. For some learners, it will be helpful or necessary to use numerous illustrations, examples, and analogies. Other effective devices used to emphasize content include drawings, cartoons, arrows, underscoring, and setting important points off in boxes. Most companies are cooperative and will send literature and/or representatives to illustrate their products.

SAMPLE INDIVIDUAL OPTION PLAN (IOP)

Name _____   Teacher _____   Date _____

District _____   School _____

Subject _____   Grade _____   Period _____

Directions: List the problems the student has in each assessment area. Then list teaching options to meet those needs

Areas	Student Problems	Teaching Options
Classroom Management	Needs a planned system of rules Has difficulty asking for help in class Needs an individual reward system	
Instruction	Has difficulty listening to lectures Has difficulty taking notes Needs hands-on experience	
Evaluation	Has difficulty with written tests Has difficulty answering complete questions Needs alternative grading procedures	

Source: Allegheny Intermediate Unit (1989). *Adapt – A Developmental Activity Program for Teachers.* Pittsburgh, PA.

Figure 7-22. An example of an individual option plan (IOP) that identifies learner problems and suggests teaching options for the instructor.

QUALITY ASSIGNMENT PLANNING CHART

Plan the Purpose of the Assignment

1. Answer the question, "What will students accomplish" by determining the knowledge or skills students should be able to demonstrate by completing the assignment

2. Answer the question, "How will they do this?" by determining how students will demonstrate their knowledge. To do this, select a verb and an assignment idea from the assignment ideas sheet

3. Answer the question, "Why is this important?" by stating how the knowledge and/or skills they acquire by completing the assignment will be of benefit in the future

Link Assignment to Student Needs and Interests

1. To make the assignment personally relevant for students, consider the physical, intellectual, social, emotional, and cultural characteristics and interests of students

   Consider offering assignments based on the following:
   - current events
   - TV
   - heroes/heroines
   - fantasy
   - social interaction
   - futurism
   - community involvement

2. Consider ways to produce a final product without boring or frustrating students

   Consider variations according to the following:
   - Format (match modality strengths – oral, written demonstration, etc.)
   - Organization (lists, diagrams, outlines)
   - Content (topics, task selection)
   - Purpose (practice, prepare, extend, create)
   - Location (library, home, study hall)
   - Social interaction (partner, group)
   - Resources (books, film strips, etc.)

3. Consider the following pitfalls that might prevent successful completion of the assignment:
   - Confusing vocabulary words
   - Unavailability of equipment
   - Unfamiliarity with equipment
   - Lack of particular academic skill
   - Low access to resources
   - Low motivation

4. Offer solutions to such problems

Arrange Clear Student Directions

To arrange clear student directions, jot down information that is complete and easy to follow. This includes the following:

ACTION STEP
The task broken into its component parts

SUPPLIES/RESOURCE
The human and material resources (text books, dictionaries, magazines, computers, people) needed to complete the work

GRADING CRITERIA
The way grades will be determined

DUE DATE(S)
The day on which the work is to be handed in; show time consideration

POINTS
The total points assignment is worth

Note Evaluation Date and Results

Specify a date for reviewing the appropriateness and outcomes of the assignment. This includes the following:

ASSIGNMENT REVIEW DATE
Note the date when the assignment results will be ready and an assignment discussion can be conducted

RESULTS
Record necessary changes in the assignment to ensure better performance the next time it is used or the course is taught

Source: University of Kansas Center for Research on Learning (July 1998). *Quality Assignment Routine – Trainer's Guide.* Lawrence, KS.

Figure 7-23. A quality assignment planning chart that provides guidelines for instructors.

A teacher's checklist of text selection criteria can be used when identifying and selecting textbooks for use in career and technical education programs. See Appendix. Instructors should keep these points in mind while reviewing materials they are considering using in their program.

Ideal characteristics of instructional materials include a practical presentation of content rather than a highly theoretical presentation using clear, unambiguous language. There should be opportunities to build an appropriate technical vocabulary. The most successful materials are flexible in their use, from individualized settings to group settings. Frequent diagnostic checkpoints for feedback and appropriate remediation (e.g., drill and practice exercises) should be given. Involvement in follow-up, hands-on activities is also preferable.

In evaluating and selecting instructional materials, Hoellein, Feichtner, and O'Brien (1979) identified that the materials should
- be written at a level that the learner can comprehend;
- include statements explaining the relevance and importance of the subject matter to the learner;

- include objectives stated in behavior terms and make them known to the learner;
- include appropriate pre-assessment materials to identify the learner's previously mastered skills;
- be designed in a sequential structure that is logical in its sequence of content and level of difficulty;
- include instructional objectives that provide a variety of learning activities; and
- include short term post-assessment activities to measure mastery of content skills.

Specific considerations that should be addressed when reviewing instructional materials that will be used by learners from special populations include the following:
- learning style
- amount of content covered in any given interval (e.g., chapter, unit, section)
- technical accuracy of the content
- clarity and complexity of directions
- organization of content (e.g., well-planned, sequenced)
- technical terminology (presented in bold print, glossary of technical terms provided)
- amount of reading material per written page or slide frame

- type and size of print and drawings
- margin spacing
- reading level of printed material
- attention requirements (e.g., length of time per lesson, level of difficulty of material)
- opportunities for learners to practice what they have learned from the material
- material that can be broken into subtasks, if necessary
- material that provides periodic reinforcement

An instructional material analysis sheet can either be followed explicitly when seriously considering a specific material or referred to as an overview of important considerations to keep in mind when reviewing materials for use with learners from special populations. See Figure 7-24.

The characteristics of the material should be compared with the abilities of individual learners who will be using them. The level of difficulty of the materials should be consistent with the current functioning level of the learner. Often information about the learner's functioning levels can be obtained from student files or from support personnel. See Figure 7-25.

INSTRUCTIONAL MATERIAL ANALYSIS SHEET . . .

Name of Material _____

Author _____ Copyright Date _____

Vendor Address _____

Cost _____

Type of material:

_____ textbook	_____ computer software	_____ model
_____ workbook	_____ slidetape	_____ other (specify)
_____ filmstrip	_____ videotape	

Format of printed materials:

_____ hardbound	_____ loose leaf notebook	_____ cassette accompanies printed material
_____ paperback	_____ diskette	_____ number of pages (if applicable)

Readability:

_____ readability level	_____ interest level (high, medium, low)	_____ print format (large, medium, small)

Intended use of material:

_____ student resource	_____ individual instruction	_____ reinforcement material
_____ teacher resource	_____ group instruction	_____ combination (specify)

Layout:

_____ empty or free space on printed page or screen (ample, sparse)	_____ paragraph spacing (excellent, good, poor)	_____ illustrations (frequently used, sparingly used)

Supplementary information:

_____ prerequisite materials necessary	_____ demand for math skills (high, moderate, low)	_____ basic skill requirments (specify)

... INSTRUCTIONAL MATERIAL ANALYSIS SHEET				
Items Under Consideration	**Yes**	**No**	**N/A**	**Notes**
1. The content of the material relates to the instructional program				
2. The material reinforces concepts covered in the classroom instruction (supplementary aid)				
3. The content is current and in line with recent technology				
4. The material is interesting				
5. Technical terms are defined and used in the material				
6. Technical terms are reinforced by explanation (illustrations, examples, activities)				
7. Technical terms are highlighted (bold letters, framed, repeated)				
8. The reading level of the material matches the reading ability of a particular learner or group				
9. Level of complexity and rate of speed at which information is presented is appropriate				
10. The concepts are presented clearly and simply and are easy to understand				
11. All directions can be clearly understood				
12. Important ideas are highlighted				
13. There is adequate space for learners to provide written responses				
14. The organization of information is clear and easy to follow				
15. There is a subject index provided				
16. A glossary of terms is presented				
17. Performance objectives are presented				
18. The instruction is or can be broken into reinforcing small steps				
19. The material is self-paced				
20. Text is reinforced with illustrations, graphs, charts, and diagrams				
21. The material provides a variety of periodic self-checks to reinforce learners				
22. Review questions and answer keys are provided				
23. Student activities and worksheets are provided				
24. Hands-on learning activities are provided				
25. A teacher's handbook or manual is provided				
26. The material provides for follow-up activities to reinforce concepts				
27. The material can be used for (a) individualized instruction, (b) small group instruction, and/or (c) large group instruction				
28. The amount of time required to prepare, administer, and evaluate learner progress on the material is reasonable				
29. Prerequisite materials are needed prior to using the material				
30. Equipment is needed to use the material				
31. Necessary equipment is available and accessible				
32. Adequate space is available in the classroom or laboratory to store the material				
33. Adequate work space is available in the classroom or laboratory so that materials can be used properly				
34. The cost of the material is compatible with the total budget				
35. Parts of the material can be purchased separately from the overall package				
36. The materials will be used often enough to justify the cost				
37. The material is well made and likely to withstand repeated use				
38. The material can be reproduced at a minimum cost				
39. The material is not difficult or expensive to reorder				
40. The material is presentable as it is or can be easily adapted				

Decision:

_____ purchase material for student use   _____ purchase material for reference

_____ order material for school/district   _____ do not purchase material
              curriculum library

Figure 7-24. A sample analysis sheet to use when reviewing instructional materials for learners from special populations.

LEARNER PROFILE FOR USE IN SELECTING INSTRUCTIONAL MATERIALS

The following information should be recorded and used when selecting instructional materials:

1. Channel of learning through which the learner can best acquire and retain information through instructional materials:

    _____ visual

    _____ auditory

    _____ kinesthetic/psychomotor

    _____ blend (specify)

2. Learner preference of grouping arrangement during the learner process:

    _____ independently

    _____ one-to-one with teacher

    _____ buddy arrangement with a peer

    _____ small group

    _____ large group

    _____ blend (specify)

    _____ other (specify)

3. Psychomotor problems that might interfere with learner's ability to manipulate materials (e.g., motor coordination, vision problems, hearing problems, speech problems).

4. Learner's English proficiency:

    _____ needs no assistance

    _____ requires some supplementary assistance

    _____ has little proficiency

5. Learner's reading level: _____

6. The pace at which the learner can receive information:

    _____

7. The ability of the learner to retain information (e.g., how much reinforcement is usually required):

    _____

8. Level of distractibility of learner: _____

9. Type of instructional material preferred by learner:

    _____ printed

    _____ audio

    _____ manipulative

    _____ audiovisual

    _____ blend (specify)

Figure 7-25. A learner profile used when selecting instructional materials for a specific student.

Readability Levels and Formulas

Basic reading skills include the ability to read words and comprehend their meaning. The lack of basic reading skills is a problem that many learners from special populations have. It has been well documented that reading deficiencies limit employment and educational opportunities for individuals. There is a definite relationship between inadequate reading skills and feelings of alienation and disenchantment about school.

Every learner has three reading levels. The independent reading level is the level at which an individual can read and comprehend information without assistance. The instructional reading level is the level at which an individual requires some assistance in identifying new words and/or in comprehending new content. The frustration reading level is the level at which an individual cannot read or comprehend material even with assistance.

Reading is an essential task in most career and technical education programs. Therefore, the type of reading deficiency the learner has should be identified and reviewed in relationship to successful participation in the program. The three general types of reading deficiencies are individuals who are nonreaders, individuals who can read words by sounding them out but are unable to comprehend what has been read, and individuals who are unable to read and comprehend at the level at which instructional materials are written.

As learners develop reading skills beyond the basic level, they become more ready to focus on technical content. Different career and technical education programs have different technical reading requirements. Each has its own vocabulary, distinctive requirements for comprehension, and unique materials. Both academic and career and technical education instructors need to be involved in selecting written materials for instruction that are appropriate for the occupational area. The career and technical course competencies and the occupational task analyses from which these course competencies are derived should be examined to identify technical reading aspects of each task. Of the many important technical reading skills, three are emphasized as essential to learners in career and technical education programs:

- Vocabulary–In developing vocabulary exercises attention should be focused on context clues, analysis of structure, and clues from previous knowledge. Analysis of written material can be facilitated by a vocabulary analysis chart.
- Comprehension–Reading for main ideas, reading for organization, and recognition of patterns must be taken into consideration when planning for comprehension of technical content.
- Interpretation of graphics–Most materials in career and technical education programs make extensive use of graphic material to reinforce and clarify concepts and to make the materials more interesting and attractive. In addition, students will encounter certain types of graphics on the job in manuals, reports, and trade journals in the form of charts and illustrations (National Center for Research in Vocational Education, 1987, chapter M-2).

A readability formula is used to help determine the reading level of instructional material. Career and technical and support personnel can use a readability formula to
- identify technical vocabulary skills;
- select appropriate textbooks;
- analyze teacher-prepared materials;
- modify texts and other instructional materials;
- plan reading assignments for an entire class, a small group, or an individual learner; and
- analyze worksheets.

There are a number of limitations of readability formulas. Most formulas only estimate the readability of text on the page or pages that content is extracted from to test for a readability level. They do not account for the amount of new information presented within the material or the escalating readability level within the material. Formulas are often not helpful in determining the difficulty level of diagrams and illustrations that accompany the text in a material. In addition, most formulas do not take into account the technical terminology that is an integral part of the text. These terms can escalate the readability of the material quickly.

Readability formulas can be used to determine the reading level of instructional materials. The Cloze Procedure is an example of a tool used in determining readability of materials and the reading level of learners. See Appendix.

Matching the reading demands of instructional materials to the reading abilities of the learners from special populations often involves assessment and adjustments. Learners whose general level of reading falls below the level of the material must be provided with modifications such as rewriting the material or recording the information on a tape so they can listen as they read. Once the readability of an instructional material has been determined and compared with the reading level of a learner, the career and technical education instructor and support personnel should identify any difficulties and decide how to overcome them (e.g., select instructional materials written at a lower reading level, adapt existing materials, assist the learner in remediation sessions). A variety of techniques can be used to help learners with reading deficiencies, including the following:
- Determine the readability level of the material and the reading level of the learner.
- Determine how well learners can read the textbook using readability formulas or the Cloze procedure.
- Utilize a format and content analysis to determine the appropriateness of a material. Reading material used in a career and technical education program should be compatible with the interest and ability levels of the learners enrolled.
- Use several books or materials at various levels of reading difficulty that cover the same content.
- Rewrite important passages or selections to lower reading levels by simplifying vocabulary and shortening sentences without deleting necessary technical terms.

- Tape important information from the text to a cassette.
- Introduce and reinforce background concepts needed to understand the material in the reading (e.g., films, videotapes, slides, models).
- Cover all unfamiliar technical terms and words that may present difficulty in the reading material.
- Review previously introduced terminology frequently used in the career and technical education program and assist learners in analyzing the meaning. Comprehension and reading can suffer if a learner has to pause too often to address unfamiliar words.
- Develop questions for learners before silent or oral reading assignments and follow up the activity by discussing the questions.
- Make certain that printed pages have enough blank space so that the learner will not be confused when reading, especially when there are pictures or diagrams involved.
- Technical terms should be in bold print and defined on the same page they are used or at the beginning or end of the chapter.
- A glossary should provide a guide to pronunciation of terms in reading materials.
- Important subject headings should be presented in bold print.
- Double-column pages provide for easier eye movement when reading content.
- Underline pertinent information and specific directions.
- Use a highlight pen to identify main ideas, important lists, technical terms, and important facts.
- Provide extra help for learners with reading problems.
- Once learners read and comprehend content, related activities with hands-on experience will help to complete the learning process.
- Modify test questions for easier comprehension.

Modifying Existing Instructional Materials

Many times career and technical education instructors do not have an opportunity to order materials that have been developed for learners with special needs. In this case, modifying existing materials may be necessary. Specific modifications may have to be made for certain learning problems. For example, hearing impaired learners may need simplified written versions of cassette tapes and other audio materials, an interpreter or tutor to relate verbal information, captioned materials, charts, and/or visuals. Visually impaired learners may need to have printed material converted into large type, frequently used material put on cassette tapes, support services such as readers and interpreters, or special equipment such as electronic scanning devices or extra lighting equipment. Individuals with learning disabilities or academic deficiencies may need to have information kept at an appropriate reading level, written and spoken material kept brief and simple, and visuals and audiovisuals or verbal responses to questions and tasks asked in print.

Kay (1980) provided these tips for rewriting materials:

1. Read the article or textbook passage and jot down the main ideas. This will help keep the written version short and to the point. If every word and idea is translated, the written version will be even longer than the original and more grueling for the learner to read.
2. Look over the main ideas, checking those especially that the learners should get from reading the information. This will help focus on why this information should be read and will help identify related assignments that can reinforce these main ideas.
3. Make a list of specialized vocabulary and important concepts that are difficult. Include this information in a study guide or cassette presentation and present it to the learners before giving them the revised reading materials.
4. Follow some of the following rules:
- use simple words, avoid multisyllabic words
- use words that are easily sounded out
- use common nouns
- underline proper names, alert learners to these names before they read the material
5. When rewriting materials, simplify length and complexity of paragraphs, format, and placement of page.
6. After the material has been written, type it with the largest type available. Leave wide margins. Encourage learners to use this space for notes or questions.

Adaptation takes less time than rewriting. Techniques that help modify instructional materials include the following:

- Prepare a vocabulary list of essential technical terms and provide meanings written at a basic reading level. A glossary can be used by support personnel to reinforce the career and technical vocabulary development. A technical terms tabulation sheet can be used by the career and technical education instructor and support personnel to teach necessary technical terms to learners from special populations. See Figure 7-26.

TECHNICAL TERMS TABULATION SHEET

Name _____ Text/Reference _____
Date _____ Chapter/Section _____ Pages _____

Vocabulary Terms	Application in Text					Teaching Strategies						Comments
	Defined in text content	Illustrated	Included in index	Included in glossary	Included in review questions	Teacher lecture	Teacher demonstration	Word lists	Puzzle or game	Written assignment	Computer exercise	
Wheel alignment						X	X					Demonstrate
Stability	X					X		X				Illustrate with transparencies
Ball joint	X	X				X	X	X				Show actuall ball joints
Spindle						X	X	X				Show actual spindle
Toe-in	X	X	X		X	X	X	X				Show with transparencies
Toe-out	X	X	X		X	X	X	X				Show with transparencies
Caster	X	X	X		X	X	X	X				Show with transparencies
Camber	X	X	X		X	X	X	X				Show with transparencies
Steering axis inclination angle	X	X	X		X	X	X	X				Chalkboard drawing
Steering knuckle	X		X			X	X	X				Show actual knuckle
Elongated holes	X	X	X			X	X					Chalkboard illustration
Control arms	X	X	X			X	X	X				Show actual control arms
Shims	X	X	X			X	X	X				Show shims
Visualiner	X	X	X			X	X					Audiovisual presentation
Lite-a-line	X	X	X			X	X					Audiovisual presentation
Tie-rods	X		X			X	X	X				

Figure 7-26. A format used to teach and reinforce terms for a specific program through written materials and teaching strategies.

- Develop smaller units of instruction so that success will occur within a reasonable length of time. This improves learner self-concept and motivation.
- Break essential tasks down into a step-by-step progression of instructions.
- Reorganize and sequence unit or chapter tasks into a logical order by chaining them together.
- Translate important information into graphic aids by representing the printed words in charts, graphs, maps, illustrations, mock-ups, and models.
- Create taped versions of written materials.
- Convert printed information to audiotape.
- Develop written versions of taped materials.
- Develop a cut-and-paste revision of existing material by cutting out only the necessary portions and pasting them on separate sheets of paper. In this manner, sequential units can be arranged, additional headings can be inserted to help in organizing and retaining ideas,

and distractions that are not essential can be removed (e.g., complicated charts, illustrations).
- Main ideas on the printed page can be highlighted or underlined.
- Nonessential information can be deleted from the printed page with a dark magic marker.
- Make large print versions of regular materials.
- Prepare organization aids for learners to use as they review instructional materials (pretests; performance objectives; outlines; key questions or study guides; chapter, unit, or section summaries; posttests). They can assist in putting content in a logical sequence for learning and retaining relevant information.

A text review evaluation sheet can be used when reading a unit, chapter, or manual to assist learners from special populations in learning key concepts. See Figure 7-27. General guidelines may be used for adapting instructional materials. See Figure 7-28.

TEXT REVIEW EVALUATION SHEET

Program _____ Course _____
Teacher _____ Text/Reference _____
Date _____ _____
Chapter/Section _____
Pages _____

MAJOR POINTS/CONCEPTS
Basic parts of two-stroke engines
Operation of two-stroke engines
NEW TERMS
Bypass port
Loop-scavenged
Reed valve
Rotary valve
Transfer port
Two-stroke-cycle engine
Transfer port
PICTURES AND ILLUSTRATIONS
Picture of two-stroke engine, p. 52
Illustration of two-stroke engine operation, pp. 52-54
Picture of cutaway of a two-stroke engine, p. 54
Picture of reed plate with four reed valves, p. 55
Picture of two-stroke main bearings, p. 55
Picture of crankcase for a two-stroke-cycle engine, p. 55
Picture of exhaust ports, p. 55
Picture of cylinder head, p. 56
Picture of pistons, rods, rings, pp. 56-57
Picture of crankshaft, p. 56
Picture of connection rods, p. 58
Drawings of loop-scavenged engine, p. 58

COURSE OUTLINE (Topics, sections)
I. Basic parts
  A. Exhaust part
  B. Intake part
II. How it works
III. Two-stroke-cycle engine parts
  A. Reed valve
  B. Crankcase and main bearing
  C. Cylinder and block
  D. Cylinder head
  E. Crankshaft
  F. Piston
  G. Piston ring
  H. Connecting rod and piston pin
IV. Loop-scavenged two-stroke engines
V. New terms
VI. Self check
VII. Discussion
LEARNER REQUIREMENTS (Study skills, abilities)
7th grade reading skills
Ability to understand drawings and pictures
Ability to take notes

Figure 7-27. A format used to outline and organize important information in a chapter of a textbook.

ADAPTING INSTRUCTIONAL MATERIALS	
Problem	**Adaptations/Strategies**
Visual perception, visual skills for reading behavior	**Enlarge Print** • Retype materials on primary typewriter • Utilize individual magnifying glasses • Project material on wall using opaque projector
Visual perception, visual skills in reading, spelling, computation, behavior, arithmetic readiness, problem solving	**Reduce Distraction on Page** • Reduce problems or items on page • Frame specific items on page • Cover area on page to reduce items
Visual perception, handwriting, motor, behavior	**Enlarge Space in Which Student Responds** • Provide separate answer sheet with space for response • Provide blackboard for written response
Visual skills in reading, reading comprehension, spelling, memory, perception, problem solving, computation, behavior	**Color Code Material** • Color code topic sentence in reading test and supporting sentences in another color • Color code directions, examples, and problems in different colors • Color code math symbols (=, +, −, ×) for easy recognition
Visual perception, visual skills in reading, spelling, handwriting, motor, perception, arithmetic readiness, computation, behavior	**Utilize Arrows for Directionality** • Provide arrows as cues for following an obstacle course • Provide arrows at top of worksheet or tape on desk as a reminder of left to right progression in reading or writing • Utilize arrows to indicate direction of math operations on number line
Reading comprehension, inner language, receptive language, problem solving, behavior	**Modify Vocabulary** • Rewrite directions in workbook • Provide vocabulary list with synonyms or simplified definitions • Instructor gives information or directions in simplified terms
Reading comprehension, auditory skills in reading, auditory perception, receptive language, memory, problem solving, behavior, arithmetic readiness, computation	**Tape Record Material** • Record directions for learner to refer • Record test; learner response verbally or written • Record passage; learner follows written text

Source: Center for Innovations in Special Education (formerly Missouri LINC). Columbia, MO: College of Education.

Figure 7-28. Suggested guidelines and procedures for adapting instructional materials for learners from special populations.

COMPUTER SOFTWARE

With the growing number of learners from special populations in career and technical education programs, instructors should develop varied teaching techniques to reach every learner in the classroom. The computer can be a valuable tool for many learners if appropriate software is used. In this high-technology and information-oriented society, knowledge and use of the computer is becoming extremely important for employment. However, learners cannot learn anything from the computer if good software is not available. A variety of items should be considered when selecting software:
• capacity to incorporate software into the curriculum
• concise presentation of content
• matching of program with individual learning styles

• quality and quantity of interaction
• technical content of the career and technical education program

The technical information presented in the software package should be accurate and up-to-date. Inaccurate or outdated information will confuse rather then enlighten learners. The information should also be applicable to actual working situations. Concrete examples of abstract concepts should be provided to make the learning more meaningful.

An instructor should never acquire a software package just to have something for learners to use on the computer. The software should fit into the curriculum and be relevant to the topics discussed in the classroom. The package should have a long life in a classroom where it can be used repeatedly. The program should actively involve the learner in the learning process and allow ample opportunity for learner response. It should not be a totally passive experience for the learner. The text should be clear and easy to read. This includes the number of lines on the screen at one time and the number of characters in each line. Some learners, especially visually-impaired learners, may need text written in large print. Graphic displays within the program should be easy to understand and used at appropriate times.

The appropriate use of a software program with an individual's learning style is important. The presentation of text should be near or at the level of the user, and the program should be able to operate at different difficulty levels, depending on the learner. Programs with numerous graphics and small print may not be appropriate for learners with low reading levels or visual perception problems. A software analysis form can be used in selecting computer software for use with learners from special populations in career and technical education programs. See Figure 7-29.

ASSISTIVE TECHNOLOGY

The Technology-Related Assistance for Individuals with Disabilities Act of 1988 (Tech Act) was designed to enhance the availability and quality of assistive technology (AT) devices and services to all individuals and their families throughout the United States. This legislation defines AT devices as any item, piece of equipment, or product system (whether acquired off the shelf, modified, or customized) that is used to increase, maintain, or improve functional capabilities of individuals with disabilities. AT devices may be categorized as high-technology and low-technology. Many low-tech devices can be purchased at a hardware store, selected from a catalog, or fabricated using tools and materials found in home workshops. Examples might be note-taking cassette recorders, pencil grips, NCR paper/copy machine, simple switches, head pointers, picture boards, taped instructions, or workbooks. High-tech devices frequently incorporate some type of computer chip, such as a hand-held calculator or a talking clock. Examples might be optical character recognition (OCR) calculators, word processors with spelling and grammar checking, word prediction, voice recognition, speech synthesizers, augmentative communication devices, alternative keyboards, or instructional software.

Areas where AT could assist learners with mild disabilities include organization, note taking, writing assistance, productivity, access to reference materials, cognitive assistance, and materials modification. A number of approaches are available to assist learners with mild disabilities in the following areas of instruction:

- Organization–Low-tech solutions include teaching learners to organize their thoughts or work using flowcharts, task analysis, webbing or networking ideas, and outlining. These strategies can be accomplished using graphic organizers to visually assist learners in developing and structuring ideas. A high-tech solution might be the outline function of word processing software, which lets learners set out major ideas or topics and then add subcategories of information.
- Note taking–A simple approach is for the teacher to provide copies of structured outlines for learners to use in filling in information. A high-tech approach might include optical character recognition, which is software that can transform typewritten material into computer-readable text using a scanner.

A teacher's typewritten notes can be duplicated using either NCR paper (carbonless copies) or a copy machine. A slightly more high-tech method is to use micro cassette recorders, or notes can be read by a voice synthesizer allowing learners with reading difficulty to review the notes much the same as reviewing a tape recording. Recorders are beneficial for learners with auditory receptive strength, but they may be less useful for those needing visual input. Videotaping class sessions may be helpful for visual learners who pick up on images or body language, or for learners who are unable to attend class for extended periods of time.

Laptop or notebook computers can provide high-tech note taking for many learners with disabilities. An inexpensive alternative to a full-function portable computer is the portable keyboard. The limitations of these keyboards are in formatting information and a screen display limited to four lines of text.

- Writing assistance–Word processing may be the most important application of assistive technology for learners with mild disabilities. Many of these learners have been identified as needing assistance in the language arts, specifically in writing. Computers and word processing software enable learners to put ideas on paper without the barriers imposed by paper and pencil. Writing barriers for learners with mild disabilities include mechanics (spelling, grammar, and punctuation errors), process (generating ideas, organizing, drafting, editing, and revising), and motivation (clarity and neatness of final copy, reading ability, and interest in writing). Grammar spell checkers, dictionaries, and thesaurus programs assist in the mechanics of writing.

Motivation is often increased through the desktop publishing and multimedia capabilities of newer computers. A variety of fonts and styles are available, allowing learners to customize their writing and highlight important features. Graphic images, drawings, and even video and audio can be added to the project to provide interest or highlight ideas. Multimedia often gives the learner the means and the motivation to generate new and more complex ideas.

- Cognitive assistance–A vast array of application program software is available for instructing learners through tutorials, drill and practice, problem solving, and simulations. Many of the assistive technologies described previously can be combined with instructional programs to develop and improve cognitive and problem-solving skills.

SOFTWARE ANALYSIS FORM

Evaluator _____   Date _____

I.   PROGRAM INFORMATION

Name of Program _____   Catalog Number (if applicable) _____

Cost _____   Copyright Date _____   Vendor Name _____

Vendor Address _____   Vendor Phone _____

Preview Policy _____

Hardware Required (brand, model of computer) _____   Memory Required _____

Reading Level _____   Math Level _____

Minimum Time to Use Program (length of operation) _____

Content Area _____   Target Population _____

Brief Description of Purpose and Content _____

Use of Program

_____ Instructional Purposes   _____ Drill/Practice   _____ Tutorial   _____ Instructional Game

_____ Problem Solving   _____ Simulation   _____ Diagnostic/Prescriptive   _____ Other_____

Instructional Grouping

_____ Individual Use   _____ Small Group Use   _____ Large Group Use

	Yes	No	N/A	Notes
II. TECHNICAL QUALITY				
1. Program is compatible with available hardware				
2. Individual can operate program independently (with demonstration, as needed)				
3. Program will continue running to completion regardless of learner response				
4. The initial cost is reasonable for the intended use of the program				
5. The pace of presentation is relevant to student's individual learning style(s)				
6. Program allows for repeated and/or prolonged use in the curriculum				
7. Teacher's instructions are concise and well-organized				
III. INSTRUCTIONAL DESIGN				
1. Goals and objectives of the program are specified				
2. Content is accurate and technically correct				
3. Information is presented in an up-to-date sequential format				
4. Information relates to the vocational curriculum				
5. Graphics are used appropriately				
6. Graphics, color, and sound are effective				
7. Size of print and spacing are appropriate				
8. Rate of presentation can be controlled by learner or teacher				
9. Reading and math levels are appropriate for learners using the program				
10. Technical terms are identified, defined, and reinforced				
11. Program format and operation relate to student learning styles				
12. Amount of information presented at one time is adequate				
13. Learner interaction is built into the program				
14. Learner response is reinforced appropriately				
15. Feedback to learners is motivating				
16. Program content promotes equity (gender, racial, cultural)				
17. Evaluation of learner				

IV.   ANALYSIS

1. Program strengths _____

2. Program limitations _____

3. Recommendation

_____ Use program as it is   _____ Program inappropriate   _____ Use program with modifications (specify) _____

4. Potential use _____

Figure 7-29. A sample format for analyzing software to use with learners from special populations.

Multimedia CD-ROM-based application programs offer another tool for assisted reading. Similar to talking word processors, CD-based books include high-interest stories that use the power of multimedia to motivate learners to read. These books read each page of the story, highlighting the words as they are read. Additional clicks of the mouse result in pronunciation of syllables and a definition of the word. When the learner clicks on a picture, a label appears. A verbal pronunciation of the label is offered when the learner clicks the mouse again. These books are available in both English and Spanish so learners can read in their native language while being exposed to a second language.

- Materials modification–Special educators are familiar with the need to create instructional materials or customize materials to meet the varied needs of learners with disabilities. Today there are powerful multimedia authoring and presentation tools that educators can use to develop and modify computer-based instructional materials for learners with mild disabilities, providing a learning tool that these learners can access and use to balance their weak areas of learning with their strong areas.

  Authoring software allows teachers and learners to develop instructional software that can incorporate video, pictures, animation, and text into hypermedia-based instruction (Berhmann, 1995).

EVALUATION STRATEGIES

Instructors in career and technical education programs may have to use alternative evaluation strategies when evaluating learners from special populations. The abilities, special needs, and preferred learning style of the learner should be taken into consideration when selecting an evaluation strategy that will adequately assess the learner's progress. Alternative assessment techniques include the following:
- verbal tests
- shortened tests
- frequency of tests
- types of responses on tests (e.g., short answer, multiple choice)
- length of time for product completion
- auditory modes of assessment (e.g., cassette tape)
- checklists/observation instruments

Stern-Otazo (1980) identified strategies that can be used to modify the evaluation procedure for learners from special populations:
- On written work, lightly correct errors in pencil or erase the incorrect answer and allow the student to correct.
- Grade when written work is handed in the second time.
- Grade all corrected parts with one-half the credits rather than no credit.
- Do not permit a third student, who may not be flexible, to grade; Either the instructor or the student who took the test or completed the assignment should grade.
- Grade as quickly as possible, preferably with the student present.
- If the submitted work seems hopeless, throw the work out and reteach the student or have a replay with a videotape of your first presentation.
- At times, analyze what seems to have been missed and attack only that aspect (a rerun may only take a few

minutes). Check out your perception of what was not understood with the student.
- As a standard technique, have separate tests for each student with individual names written on the test so that you can individualize and make the tests of more capable students longer.
- Involve the students in making up tests.
- Input tests so that there is plenty of empty space around the questions so that they stand out.
- Make sure that directions are repeated each time there is a new section of the test, a new page, or more than ten questions.
- Underline important verbs in directions (e.g., choose, list).
- Give a number of small tests instead of one long one at the end of the grading period, semester, or year.
- Do not introduce new materials on the day of the test.
- Use clear and simple language that reflects vocabulary learned during the unit.
- Grade notebooks, folders, and portfolios rather than give occasional exams.
- Test for affective skills as well as cognitive skills (i.e., important skills that go with a job, like being on time).
- Review before the test. Give a specific outline of concepts and terms to be tested.
- Give the test, or have it given, orally to students with low reading levels. Make sure that students understand exactly what the test questions are asking.
- Allow students to be responsible for only a portion of the test or allow them extended time.
- Make the choices short so that the reading problems don't hinder the student (multiple choice or matching may be easier than essay; recognition is easier than recall).
- Try to have tests that can be used later in an instructional manner.
- Make the first questions easier so that the student is not quickly discouraged.
- Discuss the area of test taking with the students. Allow them to tape the answers if that is their choice.
- Use clear, understandable language that makes each section's direction very clear and specific.
- Give grades for long term projects, like notebooks, that students can seek help to improve on (grades can be a motivational factor, but they can also be scary).
- Give open notebook exams. These might approximate the real life ability to locate information in a manual.
- Use contracts and independent assignments.
- To help the marginal student, contract for gradual improvements; ask for some low performance activity first, and use positive reinforcement. (pp. 150-52)

Reetz, Ring and Jacobs (1999) identified questions for teachers to determine how test modifications might be used for learners with special needs in the general education classroom:
- Can the learner do the same test at the same level as peers? In some instances no modifications may be needed because the area of assessment is not one in which the learner's disability has a detrimental effect.

• Can the learner do the same test with altered or more simple directions? Learners may be able to do the same test if the teacher underlines the key words of the directions, has the learner paraphrase back the directions before beginning the test, or provides directions in an alternative form such as reading them orally. Teachers may also allow the learner to ask clarifying questions regarding the exam.

• Can the learner respond appropriately with an example provided? On many tests, it may be possible to provide an example of how the learner should respond to the questions by answering the first item or providing a sample.

• Can the learner do the same test with adapted expectations? Particularly when learners have lower cognitive functioning, it may be appropriate for the learner to know some of the concepts presented but not others. In such instances, the examiner might alter the grading scale to accommodate limited cognitive functioning.

• Can the learners do the same test with a different delivery system? Having the test read to learners, using the voice synthesizer on a computer to say the question, or using an alternative administration setting may all impact the learners' ability to demonstrate a more accurate picture of their skills. For learners with visual or hearing impairments, the appropriate delivery is often in braille, large print, or sign language.

• Can the learner do the same test with different time constraints? A common option in this area is extended test time, such as double or one-and-a-half as much time to complete the exam. The IEP team should determine what is appropriate for the individual learner.

• Can the learner do the same test with flexible scheduling? Learners with difficulties such as attention deficits and health or physical needs may be allowed to complete one section of the test at a time and receive instructions on each section individually. This allows learners to address physical needs or accommodate limited ability to attend to task for extended periods of time. In addition, the test may be divided into parts that cover multiple days so the learner can study for part of the exam and be tested the following day, rather than having the full test in one day.

• Can the learner be held to the same course content if the type of assessment is varied to suit the individual learner's needs? There are multiple options for assessment. Perhaps the most common classroom tests are written objective tests with their various forms of multiple choice, matching, true-and-false, and completion items. There are also written essay tests and oral tests that allow learners to explain the necessary information in their own words. In addition, some content areas are adaptable for more of a performance or portfolio-based assessment in which the learner and instructor decide on documentation to demonstrate skill development.

• Can the learner complete objective tests if the multiple choice items are adapted? Limit the number of choices by crossing off some of the possible answers and presenting only an obvious right and wrong answer. Arrangement of items vertically allows learners to circle correct responses and avoid errors from copying letters incorrectly.

• Can the learner complete the matching items on objective exams if appropriate adaptations are made? Limiting the matching list to 5 to 10 items per set and keeping all matching items and answers on the same page and in a logical order may assist learners with memory deficits. If words in matching items are beyond the language level of the learner, the examiner can pencil in a synonym or short definition above the word provided, if the test is not specifically on vocabulary.

• Can the learner complete the objective test if the true-and-false items are adapted? Evaluate the syntax and vocabulary of test statements and rewrite them in less confusing syntactical forms with simpler vocabulary. Permitting learners to circle true and false rather then T or F will reduce the impact of letter confusion problems.

• Can the learner complete the objective test if the completion items are adapted? To avoid problems with memory of specific words, a word bank may be given to the learner, or the examiner can include a choice of words below the blank, like a multiple choice item. In addition, it is important to include hints as to the type of word required in the blank by indicating the category below the blank or the numerical units, as in a math problem.

• Can the learner respond to essay questions if appropriate adaptations are made? Allow the learner to outline answers rather than write complete paragraphs or sentences, verbalize the answers into a tape recorder, or use a peer secretary to transcribe the answers. Additional prompting cues beyond the main question may help the learner recall necessary content. Providing a writing frame for the answer to assist the learner in paragraph formation and recall may allow the learner to demonstrate knowledge (e.g., "The three primary reasons for the war were…").

• Can the learner complete part of or specific items of the same exam? Select questions that cover main points and mark these items by circling the number or adding an asterisk. Learners can respond on the same exam as the other learners but only to the items that have been marked.

• Can the learner do the same test with additional math learning tools? This could include such items as a calculator, a math fact table, or a cue card with arithmetic formulas or sample problems. A number line, counters, or geometric shapes the learner can manipulate can also assist with math.

• Can the learner do the same test with additional written language learning tools? In the area of written expression, tools might include a computer program such as a word processor, a spell check, or a grammar check. A dictionary or spelling machine may also be of assistance.

• Can the learner do the same test with additional memory tools? In the content areas, learners can be assisted during tests by a study guide, a self-prepared note card of key ideas, a textbook, or the learner's notes. In addition, where learners have developed mnemonic devices to remember lists, a copy of these mnemonic words may be allowed.

Case Study . . . Edward

Edward Pierce has a learning disability and is enrolled in a carpentry and cabinetmaking program. He has above average intelligence as indicated on his current psychological examination results. However, because of a visual perception problem he has trouble in reading and math.

Edward is enthusiastic at the start of every task or assignment but easily becomes frustrated and gives up. This habit is probably due to the many failures he has had in the past. He has made several close friends in the program and works very well in small cooperative learning groups.

The instructor has been working closely with the transition coordinator. They have both actively participated in the development of Edward's IEP. In order to facilitate the annual goals and short-term instructional objectives, a form was used to plan for Edward's participation in the carpentry and cabinetmaking program.

Edward's career goal is to work either in a custom cabinet shop or in a furniture manufacturing operation. With the combined assistance of both the instructor and transition coordinator, Edward has successfully completed units in printreading, use of hand and power tools, machine tool operation, and frame and form construction. He has required additional assistance in several areas that have taken him longer to complete, including related mathematics, door hanging, and window setting. The special education program has helped to modify these sections of the curriculum. The written materials have been reinforced verbally, and a variety of hands-on activities has been developed to allow for direct application of skills demonstrated in class. The program instructor has allowed for modification of assignments and activities to allow Edward to learn through his strongest learning style.

ANNUAL GOALS AND SHORT-TERM INSTRUCTIONAL OBJECTIVES

STUDENT NAME: Edward Pierce

CAREER AND TECHNICAL EDUCATION PROGRAM: Carpentry and Cabinetmaking

CAREER GOAL: Custom Cabinet Shop/Furniture Manufacturer Employee

ANNUAL GOAL(S) IN IEP: At the end of the year Edward will be able to read blueprints, demonstrate safe and effective use of power tools, demonstrate safe and effective use of machine tool operations, and demonstrate frame and form construction.

CURRICULUM MODIFICATION	SPECIFIC SERVICES TO BE PROVIDED	PERSONNEL INVOLVED
Cooperative Planning	Coordinated planning, assistance in related academics	Coordinator
School-Based Team	Extended time on some lab tasks	
Environmental Changes		
Classroom Management/ Behavior Management	Verbal reinforcement to increase self concept, cooperative learning activities to develop interpersonal skills	
Motivation Strategies	Involve parents for reinforcement from home, peer reinforcement through cooperative learning and small peer groups, industry mentorship with volunteer	
Learning Style Information	Auditory reinforcement, works well in groups, perfers to respond to questions orally	
Instructional Material Modifications	Use verbal reinforcement with instructional materials	
Teaching Techniques	Discussion, peer tutoring, taped cassettes, problem solving strategies	

- Can the learner do the same test if the language level is varied? Reduce the vocabulary or sentence complexity of a question by rewriting it. Another option is to provide a word bank or glossary to be used during the test to assist the learner in understanding the questions. For learners whose oral language exceeds their reading language levels, reading the test aloud may accommodate their needs. Another option may be to have someone sit beside the learner and clarify confusing language during the exam.
- Does the learner demonstrate emotional reactions to test-taking that need to be considered? The lack of success some learners with disabilities have experienced

on exams may lead those learners to increased test anxiety based on fear of humiliation or failure. All these issues may adversely affect performance. To alleviate some of this anxiety, instructors can weight learner performance on exams at a lower percentage compared to daily work, provide frequent review and more frequent exams, use practice tests, and assure learners that there are options for retaking the tests when needed.

• Does the learner need an alternative assessment? Learners whose goals and objectives are not to acquire content information from a specific class, but rather to develop other behaviors such as social skills, may need different documentation and assessment means to measure gains. Assessment of learners' entrance skills into a class through use of a pretest may also assist in determining the need for alternative assessment methods.

SUMMARY

Career and technical education curriculum is the organized content of a program structured as a series of intended outcomes or competencies that a learner must master to attain a career goal. It involves the sum total of all experiences and learning activities encountered in the classroom and laboratory and encompasses what is to be taught and what is to be learned. Curriculum modification is the tailoring of all the experiences and activities in pursuit of occupational preparation to meet the unique needs of the individual learner.

The identification, selection, and sequencing of concepts and skills to be taught in a career and technical education program must be considered as well as the methods used to teach them. Consideration should be given to the order, rate, and method of presentation and the amount to present at one time. In order for an instructor to determine what strategies will best meet the needs of the learners receiving the instruction, information should be collected about them.

Instructors in career and technical education programs may have to use alternative evaluation strategies when evaluating learners from special populations. The abilities, special needs, and preferred learning style of the learner should be taken into consideration when selecting an evaluation strategy that will adequately assess the learner's progress.

SELF-ASSESSMENT

1. What is curriculum modification?
2. Why is it necessary to modify the career and technical education program for learners from special populations?
3. What are the principles of competency-based career and technical education programs?
4. What are the specific elements of the teaching-learning process that can be involved in curriculum modification?
5. What strategies can be used to help boost self-concept and confidence of learners from special populations?
6. What are some effective behavior management strategies that can be used with learners from special populations?
7. What is the role of learning style information in the curriculum modification process?
8. Identify methods of modifying existing instructional materials for learners from special populations.
9. What evaluation strategies can be used to effectively determine the progress of learners from special populations in career and technical education programs?

ASSOCIATED ACTIVITIES

1. Identify the entry-level skills necessary for learners to successfully participate in your program.
2. Identify the multiple exit points for your program. For each exit point, identify the competencies necessary for learners to be prepared for that job. Share this information with learners, parents, support personnel, and other teachers.
3. Contact support personnel in your school or district to establish classroom management techniques that are appropriate for learners from special populations enrolled in your program.
4. Develop a safety profile to be used in your program.
5. Analyze your classroom and laboratory to determine barriers that may interfere with physical accessibility. Work cooperatively with others in your school or district to help overcome these barriers.
6. Have learners enrolled in your program complete a learning styles inventory. Analyze results and use the information to organize classroom and laboratory activities.
7. Use appropriate techniques to determine your teaching style and match it with identified learner styles.
8. Determine the reading level of materials used in your curriculum with an appropriate readability formula. Identify the reading level of learners enrolled in your program. Match this information accordingly and make appropriate modifications.
9. Analyze your instructional materials using an appropriate set of guidelines to determine what modifications may be needed to meet the needs of learners from special populations.
10. Review the methods used in your program to evaluate learner progress and make appropriate modifications for specific learners from special populations.

REFERENCES

Babich, A., Burdine, P., Albright, L., & Randol, R. (n.d.). *C.I.T.E. learning styles instrument.* Wichita, KS: Wichita Public Schools, Murdock Teachers Center.

Barbe, W., Swassing, R., & Milone, M. (1979). *Teaching through modality strengths: Concepts and practices.* Columbus, OH: Zaner-Bloser.

Behrmann, M. (1995). *Assistive technology for students with mild disabilities.* Arlington, VA: ERIC Clearinghouse on Disabilities and Gifted Education.

Brinckerhoff, L. (n.d.). *Student inventory.* Madison, WI: University of Wisconsin-Madison, McBurney Resource Center.

Brophy, J. (1987). Synthesis of research on strategies for motivating students to learn. *Educational Leadership, 45*(2), 40-48.

Cameron, C., & Johnson, J. (1983). *Entry level skills criteria.* Columbia, MO: University of Missouri-Columbia, Center for Innovations in Special Education (formerly Missouri LINC).

Center for Innovations in Special Education (formerly Missouri LINC). (1989). *Building self-esteem for students at risk.* Columbia, MO: College of Education.

Center for Success in Learning. (1992). *How does hemisphericity relate to learning?* Workshop handout. Dallas, TX: Author.

Cooper, J., Hansen, J., Martorella, P., Morine-Dershimer, G., Sadker, D., Sadker, M., Shostak, R., Sokolove, S., Tenbrink, T., & Weber, W. (Eds.). (1977). *Classroom teaching skills: A handbook.* Lexington, MA: DC Heath and Company.

Crenshaw, D. (2000, Fall). Reversing secondary underachievement. *Texas Study Magazine.*

Dade County Public Schools. (n.d.). *Curriculum-based vocational assessment handbook.* Miami, FL: Office of Vocational, Adult, Career and Community Education.

Dreikurs, R., & Cassel, P. (1972). *Discipline without tears.* NY: Hawthorn Books.

Dunn, R., Cavanaugh, D., Eberle, B., & Lernhausern, R. (1982, May). Hemispheric preferences: The newest elements of learning style. *The American Biology Teacher,* 292-94.

Dunn, R., & Dunn, K. (1978). *Teaching students through their individual learning styles: A practical approach.* Reston, VA: Reston Publishing.

ERIC Clearinghouse on Disabilities and Gifted Education. (1998, Fall). A curriculum every student can use: Design principles for student access. *ERIC/OSEP Topical Brief.* [On-Line]. Available: www.cec.sped.org/osep/ud-sec1.html

Grantham, J. (1993). *Modifying subject matter and curriculum for secondary 504 students: Can they still master the essential elements.* Presentation at Texas Association of Section 504 Coordinators and Hearing Officers. Dallas, TX.

Guild, P. (1994). The culture/learning style connection. *Educational Leadership, 51*(8), 16-21.

Hand, K. (1990, October). Style is a tool for students, too! *Educational Leadership, 48,* 13-14.

Hayes, M. (1974). *The tuned-in, turned-on book about learning problems.* Novato, CA: Academic Therapy Publications.

Hernandez, H. (1989). *Multiculture education.* New York: Macmillan.

Hoellein, T., Feichtner, S., & O'Brien, T. (1979). *Pennsylvania vocational administrator's guidebook.* Indiana, PA: Indiana University.

Hoover, J., & Collier, C. (1986). *Classroom management through curricular adaptations.* Lindale, TX: Hamilton Publications.

Huitt, F., & Pattison, R. (1980). *Self esteem and the handicapped.* Des Moines, IA: Midwest Regional Resource Center.

Johnson, C. (1980, April). Curriculum customization of special needs learners. *Journal for Vocational Special Needs Education,* 3-6.

Johnson, D., & Johnson, R. (1982). *Healthy peer relationships: A necessity not a luxury.* Minneapolis, MN: University of Minnesota.

Kay, C. (1980). *Improving the curriculum.* Columbia, MO: University of Missouri-Columbia, Center for Innovations in Special Education (formerly Missouri LINC).

Kingsbury, D. (1985). Applying rehabilitation technology to vocational programs, facilities, and equipment. In Sarkees and Scott. *Vocational special needs.* Homewood, IL: American Technical Publishers.

Marshall, C. (1990, October). The power of the learning styles philosophy. *Educational Leadership, 48,* 62.

Missouri Department of Elementary and Secondary Education. (1999, January). Transition: School to post-school activities. *Technical Assistance Bulletin.*

National Center for Research in Vocational Education. (1987). *Roadsigns from research: Dropouts.* Columbus, OH: The Ohio State University.

O'Neil, J. (1990, October). Making sense of style. *Educational Leadership, 48,* 4-9.

Reetz, L., Ring, M., & Jacobs, G. (1999, November). 20 ways to examine test modifications. *Intervention in School and Clinic, 35*(2), 17-18.

Stern-Otazo, K. (1980). Curriculum modification and instructional practices. In Meets, G. (Ed.). *Handbook of special vocational needs education.* Rockville, MD: Aspen Systems Corporation.

Sullivan, R., & Wircenski, J. (1988). 50 tips on motivating students. *Vocational Education Journal, 63*(5), 39-40.

Texas Education Agency. (1989). *Learning styles of at-risk youth: A school wide study skills program.* Austin, TX: Texas Dropout Information Clearinghouse.

University of Kansas Center of Research on Learning. (1998, July). *Quality assignment routine: Trainer's guide.* Lawrence, KS: Author.

Wang, M., Reynolds, M., & Walberg, H. (1986). Rethinking special education. *Educational Leadership, 44*, 28-29.

White, S. (1987). The modification of curriculum and instruction: Catalysts for equity. In G. Meets (Ed.). *Handbook of vocational special needs education* (2nd ed). Rockville, MD: Aspen Publishers.

Instructional Delivery

INTRODUCTION

Individuals from special populations represent a diverse group of learners that possesses a variety of different learning styles. They do not learn at the same rate or through the same instructional strategies as learners from other populations. The characteristics, abilities, interests, learning styles, and needs of each learner must be taken into consideration when planning career and technical classroom and laboratory instruction.

The instructional strategies selected by career and technical education instructors may make the difference between success and failure for many learners from special populations. One instructional strategy will not meet the unique needs of every learner. Therefore, a variety of techniques should be considered in designing the instructional delivery of a career and technical education program.

Research has shown that educators are in need of more information, training, and assistance with instructional strategies to successfully integrate learners from special populations into their programs. Strategies provided to these instructors should assist them in establishing appropriate learning environments for these learners. Successful instructors use a variety of techniques to assist learners from special populations to start learning on a positive note.

This chapter presents information on a variety on instructional techniques that can be used by career and technical educators to accommodate the learning styles and abilities of learners from special populations.

OUTLINE

THE TEACHING-LEARNING PROCESS
THE FOUR-PHASE LEARNING CYCLE
MULTIPLE INTELLIGENCES
DELIVERY OF INSTRUCTION
DIFFERENTIATED CLASSROOMS
CELEBRATING AND ACCOMMODATING LEARNER DIVERSITY
SELECTED INSTRUCTIONAL STRATEGIES
COMPUTERS AND TECHNOLOGY
COOPERATIVE TEACHING
STUDY SKILLS
CRITICAL-THINKING AND PROBLEM-SOLVING SKILLS
ASSISTANCE FOR LEARNERS WITH READING DEFICIENCIES
ASSISTANCE FOR LEARNERS WITH MATH DEFICIENCIES
ASSISTANCE FOR LEARNERS WITH DEFICIENCIES IN ORAL AND WRITTEN COMMUNICATION
EFFECTIVE INSTRUCTOR TOOLBOX
STRATEGIES FOR CULTURALLY DIVERSE LEARNERS
SUMMARY
SELF-ASSESSMENT
ASSOCIATED ACTIVITIES
REFERENCES

OBJECTIVES

After reading this chapter, the learner should be able to accomplish the following:
1. Discuss reasons why career and technical instructors should use a variety of teaching strategies to deliver their curriculum to learners from special populations.
2. Identify the steps in utilizing direct instruction with learners in a classroom environment.

3. Discuss the process of individualized instruction as an instructional strategy.
4. Discuss the philosophy of mastery learning and identify the steps involved in utilizing this technique in a classroom environment.
5. Identify effective study skills that learners can utilize to succeed in career and technical education programs.
6. Identify methods to teach critical-thinking/problem-solving skills in career and technical education programs.
7. List strategies to assist learners with reading deficiencies.
8. List strategies to assist learners with math deficiencies.
9. List strategies to assist learners who have problems with oral and written communications skills.

TERMS

cooperative learning
cooperative teaching
critical thinking
demonstration
differentiated classroom
direct instruction
discussion
field trip
flexible grouping

graphic organizer
individualized instruction
job shadowing
mastery learning
metacognition
multiple intelligences
peer and cross-age tutoring
problem solving

project
project-based learning (PBL)
role-playing
simulation
skeletal outline
student-teacher contract
study skill
task analysis

THE TEACHING-LEARNING PROCESS

It is important to focus on the teaching-learning process in general before addressing instructional practices that have proven to be successful with learners from special populations.

The following are a number of universal assumptions about learning:

1. Persons at all ages have the potential to learn, and some learn faster than others. Age may or may not affect a person's speed of learning, and individuals vary in the way they like to learn.

2. The learner experiencing a change process, such as a new learning situation, is likely to feel stress and confusion. Some anxiety often causes increased motivation to learn, but too much anxiety may cause fatigue, inability to concentrate, resentment, and other barriers to learning. Learning is more comfortable and effective when the environmental conditions support open exchange, sharing of opinions, and problem-solving strategies. The atmosphere should foster trust and acceptance of different ideas and values.

3. In the classroom, the instructor facilitates learning by incorporating learners' experiences, observations of others, and personal ideas and feelings. Exposure to varied behavior models and attitudes helps learners to clarify actions and beliefs that will aid in meeting their own learning needs.

4. The depth of long-term learning may depend on the extent to which learners try to analyze, clarify, or articulate their experiences to others in their family, work, or social groups. The depth of learning increases with new concepts, and skills are useful in meeting current needs or problems. This allows for immediate application of the theory to a practical situation.

5. Learning improves when the learner is an active participant in the educational process. When selecting from several teaching methods, it is best to choose the method that allows the learner to become most involved. Using varied methods of teaching helps the learner maintain interest and may help to reinforce concepts without being repetitious.

As instructors develop curriculum and plan lessons, it is important to consider some of the research on learning. Research shows learners learn at the following rates based on the way they receive information:

- 10% of what they read
- 20% of what they hear
- 30% of what they see
- 50% of what they see and hear
- 70% of what they discuss with others
- 80% of what they experience personally
- 95% of what they teach others (Walker, 1998)

The percentage of information retained by learners over a period of time differs depending on the delivery strategy used to relay the information. Higher retention rates are achieved when learners have more active participation in the learning process. See Figure 8-1.

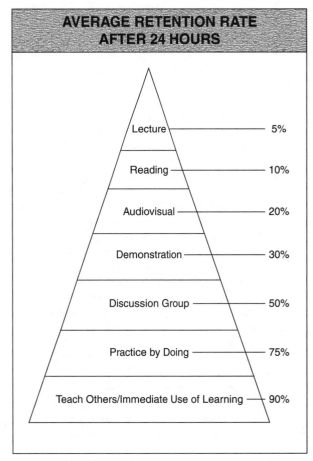

Figure 8-1. Learning retention rates for various forms of instructional delivery after 24 hours.

Successful instructors demonstrate principles of effective instruction. The Massachusetts Department of Education (2001) suggests that effective instruction involves focusing on many factors including the following:

- Curriculum–Successful instructors are effective in dealing with curriculum content. This includes demonstrating a working knowledge of core curriculum; framing curriculum around essential questions that provide opportunities for reasoning, analysis, and synthesis; keeping current in the field and applying new knowledge to the instructional program; and contributing to the ongoing evaluation of the curriculum.

- Planning and assessment–Successful instructors effectively plan curriculum and instruction. This includes having a personal vision of committed, confident learners and using that vision to guide learning goals, expectations, and standards; setting short-term and long-term goals for curricular units; identifying individual and group needs and planning appropriate strategies; using materials and resources appropriate to curricular goals and individual learning styles; framing curriculum around learners' prior knowledge and experience; and identifying prerequisite skills, concepts, and vocabulary.

They also collaborate with school-based specialists and resource personnel to better design curricula or make instructional modifications; plan engaging ways to introduce each unit of study; and design curriculum experiences in which learners take increasing responsibility for their own learning.

Successful instructors plan learning assessment effectively. This includes determining specific challenging learning standards, developing and using authentic assessment that describes a learner's achievements, and incorporating time for individual and interactive reflection.

Successful instructors monitor understanding of the curriculum and adjust instruction, materials, or assessments when appropriate. This includes regularly using a variety of formal and informal authentic assessments to determine instructional revision, implementing evaluation procedures that appropriately assess the objectives taught, and communicating learner progress to parents, learners, and staff members in a timely fashion using a range of information. They also prepare and maintain accurate and efficient record-keeping systems that document quality and quantity of learner work, use individual and group data appropriately, and maintain confidentiality concerning individual learner data and achievement.

- Classroom management–Successful instructors will exhibit effective management of the classroom environment. A successful instructor creates a positive environment for learning and learner involvement. This includes implementing instructional opportunities where learners are interacting with ideas, materials, instructors, and one another; implementing curriculum experiences in which learners take increasing responsibility for their own learning; and demonstrating openness to learner challenges about information and ideas.

They also use classroom time and classroom space to promote optimal learning, use their knowledge of principles and patterns of adolescent growth and development when working with learners, and establish classroom procedures that keep learners on task and ensure smooth transitions from one activity to another.

Successful instructors will maintain an appropriate standard of behavior, mutual respect, and safety. This includes establishing and administering a consistent and fair set of rules, regularly checking for understanding of content and concepts and documenting their progress, and identifying confusions and misconceptions as indicated by learner responses and regular assessment strategies. They also remediate, reteach, or extend teaching to meet individual and/or group needs; communicate clearly in writing and speaking; and show learners the relevance of the subject to lifelong learning.

Successful instructors will use appropriate instructional techniques. This includes using a variety of teaching strategies, including cooperative, peer- and project-based learning, audio-visual presentations, lecture, discussions and inquiry, practice and applications, and the teaching of others. They also provide options for learners to demonstrate competency and mastery of new material; use a variety of appropriate materials in order to reinforce and extend skills, accommodate learning styles, and match instructional objectives; help learners to become active in summarizing important lessons and integrating them with prior knowledge; and demonstrate a working knowledge of current research within a particular discipline.

Successful instructors will use appropriate questioning techniques in the classroom. This includes using a variety of questioning techniques, presenting information that recognizes multiple points of view, and encouraging learners to assess the accuracy of information presented.

Successful instructors evaluate teaching methods, try innovative approaches, and refine instructional strategies. They use technology effectively to increase learning and learner confidence. This includes regularly trying innovative approaches to improve instructional practices, continually evaluating these approaches, and assessing instructional strategies by comparing intended and actual learning outcomes.

- Learner achievement–Successful instructors promote high standards and expectations for learner achievement. They communicate learning goals and expectations of high standards to learners. This includes regularly communicating objectives or learning outcomes to learners and regularly providing feedback to learners on their progress. They also communicate standards, expectations, and guidelines to learners and parents regarding the quality and quantity of work, work procedures, and interpersonal behavior of the learner; and respond to learners' questions and work to keep them open, thinking, and willing to take risks and persevere with challenging tasks.

Successful instructors promote confidence and perseverance in the learner, which stimulates increased personal learner responsibility for achieving curriculum goals. This includes using prompt feedback and encouraging goal setting in order to increase learner motivation and ownership of learning; developing and supporting learners' awareness of themselves as learners and their ability to overcome the self-doubts associated with learning and taking risks; nurturing learners' eagerness to do challenging work; and providing incentive, interest, and support.

They also act on the belief that all learners can learn, and that virtually all learners can master a challenging core curriculum with appropriate instruction modifications. They encourage learners to believe that effort is a key to high achievement; regularly identify learners needing extra help, secure learner cooperation and participation in extra help sessions, identify learners who are not meeting expectations, and develop a plan that designates the instructor's and the learner's responsibilities regarding learning. They should demonstrate attitudes of fairness, courtesy, and respect, which encourages active participation and commitment to learning; build positive relationships with learners and parents; and recognize and respond appropriately when a learner is having social and/or emotional difficulty that interferes with learning and/or participation in class.

- Equity and diversity–Successful instructors promote equity and appreciation of diversity. They strive to ensure equitable opportunities for learning by including all learners in the full range of academic programs and activities and extracurricular activities, and they address the needs of diverse learner populations by applying and adapting constitutional and statutory laws, state regulations, and Board of Education policies and guidelines.

The instructor demonstrates appreciation for diversity among individuals by being sensitive to differences in abilities, modes of contribution, and social and cultural backgrounds and by developing and implementing educational and organizational strategies that are effective in meeting the needs of a diverse student body.

- Professional responsibilities–Successful instructors fulfill professional responsibilities. They are constructive and cooperative in interactions with parents and receptive to parent contributions. This includes keeping parents informed of the learner's progress and working with them, in culturally appropriate ways, to aid in the total development of the learner.

Successful instructors share responsibility for accomplishing the goals and priorities of their grade, team, department, building, and school district by maintaining professional boundaries with colleagues, working constructively with others to identify school problems and possible solutions, participating in student or school activities, cooperating with other instructors concerning learners' overall workload, and working collaboratively with other staff to plan and implement interdisciplinary curriculum, instruction, and other school programs and share expertise and new ideas with colleagues.

Successful instructors are reflective and continuous learners. This includes thinking about and acting on what learners need to know and be able to do, participating in activities that demonstrate a commitment to the teaching profession, seeking out information in order to grow and improve as professionals, being receptive to suggestions for professional growth and development, and using available resources (professional organizations, academic course work, school-based staff, administrative and community resources, and other colleagues) to analyze, expand, and refine professional knowledge and skills (Massachusetts Department of Education, 2001).

THE FOUR-PHASE LEARNING CYCLE

All human learning can be thought of as having four components or phases. The first phase is preparation, or the arousal of interest. The second phase is presentation, or the initial encounter of new knowledge or skill. The third phase is practice, or the integration of the new knowledge or skill. The fourth and final phase is performance, or the application of the new knowledge and skill to real-world situations. Unless all four components are present in one form or another, no real learning occurs. See Figure 8-2. Meier (2000) described activities that the instructor should plan for in each phase of the learning cycle.

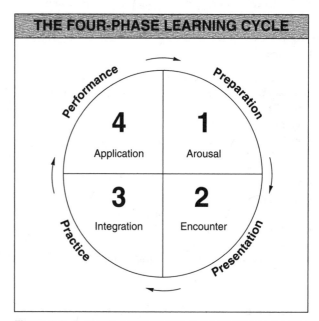

Figure 8-2. A graphic representation of the four-phase learning cycle in practice.

Preparation

The goal of the preparation phase is to arouse learners' interest, give them positive feelings about the forthcoming learning experience, and put them into an optimal state for learning. This is done through

- positive suggestions;
- learner benefit statements;
- clear, meaningful goals;
- curiosity raising;
- creating a positive physical environment;
- creating a positive emotional environment;
- creating a positive social environment;
- calming people's fears;
- removing learning barriers;
- raising questions and posing problems;
- arousing people's curiosity; and
- getting people fully involved from the start.

Presentation

The goal of the presentation phase is to help the learners encounter the new learning materials in ways that are interesting, enjoyable, relevant, multisensory, and appeal to all learning styles. This is done through

- collaborative pretests and knowledge sharing;
- observations of real-world phenomenon;
- whole-brain, whole-body involvement;
- interactive presentations;
- colorful presentation graphics and props;
- variety to appeal to all learning styles;
- partner- and team-based learning projects;
- discovery exercises (personal, partnered, or team-based);
- real-world, contextual learning experiences; and
- problem-solving exercises.

Practice

The goal of the practice phase is to help learners integrate and incorporate the new knowledge or skill in a variety of ways. This is done through

- learner processing activities;
- hands-on trial/feedback/reflection/retrial;
- real-world simulations;
- learning games;
- action learning exercises;
- problem-solving activities;
- individual reflection and articulation;
- partner- and team-based dialogue;
- collaborative teaching and review;
- skill-building practice activities; and
- teachbacks.

Performance

The goal of the performance phase is to help learners apply and extend their new knowledge or skill to the job so that the learning sticks and performance continually improves. This is done through

- immediate real-world application;
- creating and executing action plans;
- follow-through reinforcement activities;
- post-session reinforcement materials;
- ongoing coaching;
- performance evaluation and feedback;
- peer support activities; and
- supportive organizational and environmental changes.

MULTIPLE INTELLIGENCES

When considering the question "What makes a person intelligent?" the most common responses will often note a person's ability to solve problems, utilize logic, and think critically. These typical traits of intelligence are sometimes lumped together under the label of raw intelligence.

Intelligence, traditionally speaking, is contained in the general intellect—in other words, how each and every person comprehends, examines, and responds to outside stimuli, whether it be to solve a math problem correctly or to anticipate an opponent's next move in a game of tennis. Intelligence, therefore, is a singular, collective ability to act and react in an ever-changing world.

Psychologist Howard Gardner of Harvard advanced the theory of multiple intelligences (MI) in the 1980s, and that theory has attracted widespread interest among educators. The basic idea is straightforward; each individual has several intellectual potentials and diverse talents. In some respects, MI runs counter to Western societies' emphasis on standardized multiple-choice tests for assessing academic skills by noting that intellectual and creative abilities can be expressed in many ways. In fact, most standardized tests are useful only as predictors of performance in school. They do a remarkably poor job of predicating success in a job or profession. The multiple intelligence theory provides information for reconsideration of the educational practice of the last century. See Figure 8-3.

GARDNER'S THEORY OF MULTIPLE INTELLIGENCES	
Traditional View of Intelligence	**Multiple Intelligences Theory**
People are born with a fixed amount of intelligence	Human beings have all of the intelligences, but each person has a unique combination, or profile
Intelligence level does not change over a lifetime	Each person can improve each of the intelligences, though some people will improve more readily in one intelligence area than in others
Intelligence consists of ability in logic and language	M.I. pedagogy implies that teachers teach and assess differently based on individual intellectual strengths and weaknesses
Teachers teach a topic or subject	Teachers structure learning activities around an issue or questions and connect subjects. Teachers develop strategies that allow for learners to demonstrate multiple ways of understanding and value their uniqueness

Figure 8-3. A comparison of traditional views on intelligence and Gardner's theory of multiple intelligences.

Gardner (1993) stated that all human beings have multiple intelligences. These multiple intelligences can be nurtured and strengthened, or ignored and weakened, and they each respond to different types of stimuli. See Figure 8-4.

GARDNER'S EIGHT INTELLIGENCES

VISUAL/SPATIAL

Images, graphics, drawings, sketches, maps, charts, doodles, pictures, spatial, orientation, puzzles, designs, looks, appeal, mind's eye, imagination, visualization, dreams, films, and videos

LOGICAL/MATHEMATICAL

Reasoning, deductive and inductive logic, facts, data, information, spreadsheets, databases, sequencing, ranking, organizing, analyzing, proofs, conclusions, judging, evaluations, and assessments

VERBAL/LINGUISTIC

Words, speaking, writing, listening, reading, papers, essays, poems, plays, narratives, lyrics, spelling, grammar, foreign languages, memos, bulletins, newsletters, newspapers, E-mail, faxes, speeches, talks, dialogues, and debates

MUSICAL/RHYTHMIC

Music, rhythm, beat, melody, tunes, allegro, pacing, timbre, tenor, soprano, opera, baritone, symphony, choir, chorus, madrigals, rap, rock, rhythm and blues, jazz, classical, folk, and jingles

BODILY/KINESTHETIC

Art, activity, action, experimental, hands-on experiments, try to do, perform, play, drama, sports, throw, toss, catch, jump, twist, twirl, assemble, disassemble, form, re-form, manipulate, touch, feel, immerse, and participate

INTERPERSONAL/SOCIAL

Interact, communicate, converse, share, understand, empathize, sympathize, reach out, care, talk, whisper, laugh, cry, shudder, socialize, meet, greet, lead, follow, gangs, clubs, charisma, crowds, gatherings, and twosomes

INTRAPERSONAL/INTROSPECTIVE

Self solitude, meditate, think, create, brood, reflect, envision, journal, self-assess, set goals, plot, plan, dream, write, fiction, nonfiction, poetry, affirmations, lyrics, songs, screenplays, commentaries, introspection, and inspection

NATURALIST

Nature, natural, environment, listen, watch, observe, classify, categorize, discern patterns, appreciate, hike, climb, fish, hunt, snorkel, dive, photograph, trees, leaves, animals, living things, flora, fauna, ecosystem, sky, grass, mountains, lakes, and rivers

Source: Fogarty, R. (1997). *Multiple Intelligences Classroom*. Arlington Heights, IL: Skylight Training and Publishing.

Figure 8-4. Characteristics of Gardner's eight intelligences.

Gardner believes each individual has eight intelligences:

1. Visual/spatial intelligence–This is the capacity to think in images and pictures and to visualize accurately and abstractly.
2. Logical/mathematical intelligence–This is the ability to think conceptually and abstractly and the capacity to discern logical or numerical patterns.
3. Verbal/linguistic intelligence–This includes well-developed verbal skills and sensitivity to the sounds, meanings, and rhythms of words.
4. Musical/rhythmic intelligence–This is the ability to produce and appreciate rhythm, pitch, and timber.
5. Bodily/kinesthetic intelligence–This is the ability to control body movement and to handle objects skillfully.
6. Interpersonal/social intelligence–This is the capacity to detect and respond appropriately to the moods, motivations, and desires of others.
7. Intrapersonal/introspective intelligence–This is the capacity to be self-aware and in tune with inner feelings, values, beliefs, and thinking processes.
8. Naturalist intelligence–This is the ability to recognize and categorize plants, animals, and other objects in nature.

According to Gardner, all human beings possess all intelligences in varying amounts, each person has a different intellectual composition, we can improve education by addressing the multiple intelligences of our learners, and these intelligences are located in different areas of the brain and can either work independently or together. In Gardner's view, learning is both a social and psychological process. When learners understand the balance of their own multiple intelligences they begin to manage their own learning and to value their individual strengths.

Lazear (1999) identified the following indicators that learners of multiple intelligences demonstrate:

- doodling during a lecturer or discussion
- having an irresistible urge to discuss work with friends
- humming quietly to self while working or while walking down the hall
- having precision in language and thought
- having difficulty sitting still or staying in seat
- having recognition of and delight in abstract patterns
- being very quiet and self-reflective
- using quick problem solving
- having creative ideas, suggestions, and answers
- using body gestures and physical movements to express self
- tapping pencil, foot, or finger while working
- remembering thinking formulas and problem-solving strategies
- relentlessly asking questions; avid curiosity
- being good at listening to and communicating with others
- being helped by visuals; likes drawing, coloring, or painting
- liking hands-on (manipulative) assignments
- being highly intuitive (flies by the seat of the pants)
- being good in sports, well-coordinated physically
- having a strong curiosity about or attraction to animals and insects
- wanting to grow things; loving plants and flowers

Accepting Gardner's theory of multiple intelligences has several implications for teachers in terms of classroom instruction. The theory states that all intelligences are needed to productively function in society. Instructors, therefore, should think of all intelligences as equally important. This is in great contrast to traditional education systems that typically place a strong emphasis on the development and use of verbal and mathematical intelligences. Educators should recognize this and emphasize a broader range of talents and skills.

Another implication is that instructors should structure the presentation of material in a style that engages most or all of the intelligences. For example, if you're teaching or learning about the law of supply and demand in economics, you might read about it (linguistic), study mathematical formulas that express it (logical-mathematical), examine a graphic chart that illustrates the principle (spatial), observe the law in the natural world (naturalist) or in the human world of commerce (interpersonal); examine the laws in terms of food supply and the body's demand for food (bodily-kinesthetic and intrapersonal); and/or use a song that demonstrates the law (musical).

Everyone is born possessing all of these intelligences. Nevertheless, all learners will come into the classroom with different sets of developed intelligences. This means that each learner will have a unique set of intellectual strengths and weaknesses. These sets determine how easy (or difficult) it is for an individual to learn information when it is presented in a particular manner. This is commonly referred to as a learning style.

Many learning styles can be found within one classroom. Therefore, it is impossible, as well as impractical, for an instructor to adapt every lesson to all of the learning styles found within the classroom. Nevertheless, the instructor can show learners how to use their more developed intelligences to assist in the understanding of a subject that normally employs their weaker intelligences.

DELIVERY OF INSTRUCTION

As educators prepare to deliver instruction, there are four components of the teaching process that have to be addressed. These components are planning, managing, delivering, and evaluating instruction. Addressing each of these components when preparing to deliver instruction makes teaching more effective. See Figure 8-5.

A comparison of traditional classroom and contemporary work environments shows how the traditional classroom does not address the challenges learners will face in their careers. The contemporary work environment has created pressure for traditional classroom practices to change. Contemporary classroom practices can better prepare learners to function in the environments they will face outside of the classroom. See Figure 8-6.

TEACHING PROCESS COMPONENTS	
Components	**Principles**
Planning instruction	Decide what to teach Decide how to teach Communicate realistic expectations
Managing instruction	Prepare for instruction Use time productively Establish a positive classroom environment
Delivering instruction	Present instruction Teach thinking skills Motivate students Provide feedback Provide relevant practice Keep students actively involved Modify instruction
Evaluating instruction	Monitor student understanding Monitor engaged time Maintain records of learner progress Use data to make decisions Make judgments about learner performance

Figure 8-5. Principles to adhere to for each component of the teaching process.

DIFFERENTIATED CLASSROOMS

A differentiated classroom offers a variety of learning options designed to tap into different readiness levels, interests, and learning profiles. In a differentiated class, the teacher uses (1) a variety of ways for learners to explore curriculum content, (2) a variety of sense-making activities or processes through which learners can come to understand and master information and ideas, and (3) a variety of options through which learners can demonstrate or exhibit what they have learned.

A class is not differentiated when assignments are the same for all learners and the adjustments consists of varying the level of difficulty of questions for certain learners, grading some learners harder than others, or letting learners who finish early play games for enrichment. It is not appropriate to have more advanced learners do extra math problems, extra book reports, or extension assignments after completing their regular work. Asking learners to do more of what they already know is hollow. Assigning them their regular work plus more work inevitably seems like punishment to them.

Four characteristics shape teaching and learning in an effective differentiated classroom: concept-focused, principle-driven instruction; ongoing learner assessment; flexible grouping; and instructor-guided active exploration.

COMPARING TRADITIONAL CLASSROOMS TO CONTEMPORARY WORK ENVIRONMENTS

Traditional Classroom Environment	Contemporary Work Environment
Instructor provides information and direction	Employees need to solicit information and resources from supervisors and peers
Students follow instructions and do only as they are instructed	Projects are self-initiated and managed
Individual students follow procedures and processes to arrive at the one correct answer or solution	Employees work in groups to solve problems
There is one recognized way to do things—the instructor's way	Rational justifications for methods are acceptable
Students use books as their primary source for information	Coworkers and managers are primary resources
Students complete assignments as instructed, with timelines determined by the instructor	Timelines are negotiated and set by employees and managers together
Grades are determined by the instructor	Assessments are qualitative and include input from individual employees, peers, and supervisors
Students are expected to listen and take notes in class. Questions are acceptable only to clarify what has been said	Personal interest, participation, experimentation, and active questioning are major job components
Group work is considered to be unfair	Cooperative group skills are essential to getting things done

Source: Yamashiro, K. (n.d.). *The Traditional Classroom and the Contemporary Work Environment.* Honolulu, HI: Office of the Chancellor for Community Colleges.

Figure 8-6. Similarities and differences between traditional classrooms and contemporary work environments.

The first characteristic of an effective differentiated classroom is that instruction is concept-focused and principle-driven. All learners have the opportunity to explore and apply the key concepts of the subject being studied. All learners come to understand the key principles on which their study is based. Such instruction enables struggling learners to grasp and use powerful ideas and at the same time encourages advanced learners to expand their understanding and application of the key concepts and principles. Such instruction also stresses understanding or sense making rather than retention and regurgitation of fragmented bits of information. Concept-based and principle-driven instruction invites teachers to provide varied learning options. A coverage-based curriculum may cause a teacher to feel compelled to see that all learners do the same work. However, in concept-focused and principle-driven curriculum, all learners have the opportunity to explore meaningful ideas through a variety of avenues and approaches.

An effective differentiated classroom has ongoing assessment of learner readiness and growth built into the curriculum. Teachers do not assume that all learners need a given task or segment of study, but continuously assess learner readiness and interest, provide support when learners need additional instruction and guidance, and extend learner exploration when there are indications that a learner or group of learners is ready to move ahead.

In an effective differentiated classroom, flexible grouping is consistently used. Learners work in many patterns in a differentiated class. Sometimes they work alone, sometimes in pairs, sometimes in groups. Sometimes tasks are readiness-based, sometimes interest-based, sometimes constructed to match learning style, and sometimes a combination of these. In a differentiated classroom, whole-group instruction may also be used for introducing new ideas, planning, and sharing learning outcomes.

Learners are active explorers and teachers guide the exploration in an effective differentiated classroom. Because varied activities often occur simultaneously, the teacher works more as a guide or learning facilitator than as an information dispenser. Learners must be responsible for their own work. Not only does such learner-centeredness give learners more ownership of their learning, but it also facilitates the important adolescent learning goal of growing independence in thought, planning, and evaluation. Implicit in such instruction is (1) goal-setting shared by teachers and learners based on learner readiness, interest, and learning profile, and (2) assessment predicated on learner growth and goal attainment.

Adjustments based on learning profiles encourage learners to understand their own learning preferences. For example, some learners need a longer period to reflect on ideas before beginning to apply them, while others prefer quick action. Some learners need to talk with others as they learn, while others need a quiet workspace. Some learn best as they tell stories about ideas being explored, others as they create mind maps, and still others as they construct three-dimensional representations. Some learners may learn best through a practical application of ideas, others through a more analytical approach.

Effective teachers have been differentiating instruction for as long as teaching has been a profession. It has to do with being sensitive to the needs of learners and finding ways to help learners make the necessary connections for learning to occur in the best possible way. In this day and age, we have extensive research available to us to assist in creating instructional environments that will maximize the learning opportunities of all.

Among instructional strategies that can help teachers manage differentiation and help learners find a good learning fit are the following:
- Concrete to abstract–Learners advanced in a subject often benefit from tasks that involve more abstract materials, representations, ideas, or applications than less advanced peers.
- Simple to complex–Learners advanced in a subject often benefit from tasks that are more complex in resources, research, issues, problems, skills, or goals than less advanced peers.
- Basic to transformational–Learners advanced in a subject often benefit from tasks that require greater manipulation of information, ideas, materials, or applications than less advanced peers.
- Few facets to multi-facets–Learners advanced in a subject often benefit from tasks that have more facets or parts than less advanced peers.
- Smaller leaps to greater leaps–Learners advanced in a subject often benefit from tasks that require greater mental leaps in insight, application, or transfer than less advanced peers.
- More structured to more open–Learners advanced in a subject often benefit from tasks that are more open in regard to solutions, decisions, and approaches than less advanced peers.
- Less independence to greater independence–Learners advanced in a subject often benefit from greater independence in planning, designing, and self-monitoring than less advanced peers.
- Quicker to slower–Learners advanced in a subject will sometimes benefit from rapid movement through prescribed materials and tasks. At other times, they may require a greater amount of time with a given study than less advanced peers so that they may explore the topic in greater depth.

Steps to planning effective differentiated instruction include the following:
1. Determine the ability level of your learners. This can be done by surveying past records of learner performance to determine capabilities, prior learning, past experiences with learning, etc.

2. Survey learner interest. It is also important to get to know learners informally. This can be done by an interest inventory, an interview/conference, or asking learners to respond to an open-ended questionnaire with key questions about their perceptions regarding how they learn.
3. Realize the importance of having a repertoire of teaching strategies. Because one size does not fit all, it is imperative that a variety of teaching strategies be used in a differentiated classroom. There are many teaching strategies that can be considered—direct instruction, inquiry-based learning, cooperative learning, information processing strategies, and more.

Teaching strategies may include the following:
- Direct instruction–This is the most widely used and most traditional teaching strategy. It is teacher-centered and can be used to cover a great amount of material in the amount of time teachers have to cover what learners need to learn. It is structured and based on mastery learning. Direct instruction involves (1) clearly communicating goals for learning, (2) structuring academic tasks for learners, (3) demonstrating the steps necessary to accomplish a particular academic task, (4) monitoring learner progress, (5) providing learner practice and teacher feedback to ensure success, (6) over-learning of skills, and (7) holding learners accountable for their work through frequent teacher review.
- Inquiry-based learning–Inquiry-based learning has become very popular in teaching today. It is based on the scientific method and works very well in developing critical-thinking and problem-solving skills. It is learner-centered and requires learners to conduct investigations and discoveries independent of the teacher.
- Cooperative learning–Probably one of the most misunderstood strategies for teaching is cooperative learning. Yet, if employed properly, cooperative learning can produce extraordinary results in learning outcomes. It is based on grouping small teams of learners heterogeneously according to ability, interest, background, etc. However, one of the most important features of cooperative learning is to pick the best strategy that will be used to assign the task for learners to accomplish.
- Information processing strategies–Teaching learners how to process information is a key factor in teaching learners how to strategically organize, store, retrieve, and apply information presented. Such strategies include, but are not limited to, memorization, reciprocal teaching, graphic organizing, scaffolding, or webbing.
- Identifying a variety of instructional activities–Engaging learners in the learning process using activities that motivate and challenge them to remain on task is probably one of the most meaningful events in the teaching-learning process. In a differentiated classroom,

activities are suited to the needs of learners according to their mixed ability levels, interests, backgrounds, etc. Good activities require learners to develop and apply knowledge in ways that make sense to them and that they find meaningful and relevant.

- Identifying ways to assess or evaluate learner progress–Varying methods of learner assessment is necessary if learners are to be given every opportunity to demonstrate authentic learning. Authentic assessment has been around for a long time and is now taking the limelight as we attempt to measure learners' progress in a fair and equitable way. A variety of assessment techniques can include portfolios, rubrics, performance-based assessment and knowledge mapping.

Differentiated instruction is using teaching strategies that connect with an individual learner's learning strategies. The ultimate goal is to provide a learning environment that will maximize the potential for learner success. The important thing to remember is to hold on to the effective teaching strategies that lead learners to positive learning outcomes and to make adjustments when necessary. Successful instructors are flexible and open to change. They are open to taking risks and trying teaching and learning strategies that they would have otherwise ignored. They manage instructional time in a way that meets the standards and also provides motivating, challenging, and meaningful experiences. These are very exciting times for the teaching profession. Instructors are faced with a generation of learners who are challenging them to think about how they deliver instruction.

CELEBRATING AND ACCOMMODATING LEARNER DIVERSITY

Celebrating and accommodating learner diversity rather than striving for uniformity in learner attitudes and achievements demands a different perspective of the instructor's role. The instructor is viewed as the facilitator of learning in the classroom. Curriculum is viewed as something to be manipulated and modified by the instructor. Independence, freedom to make important decisions regarding adaptations, support for experimentation with all facets of instruction, encouragement to break away from traditional approaches to learning and instructing, and collaboration with colleagues should all be encouraged through administrative support that recognizes instructors as both knowledgeable and capable education professionals.

A recognition of learner differences and the need to accommodate these differences is not new to the educational community. Increasing diversity in learner populations combined with a shift in philosophical, psychological, and pedagogical perspectives in education in recent years has resulted in significant changes in the way instructors are expected to accommodate the diverse needs of learners.

Adapting instruction refers to the selection of appropriate instructional strategies, methods, and skills for all learners. See Figure 8-7. This does not mean that instructors must instruct every learner in the class differently. Rather, intstructors plan instructional practice with every learner in mind so that every learner has an equal opportunity to learn.

INSTRUCTIONAL STRATEGIES, METHODS, AND SKILLS . . .

Instructional Methods and Techniques

- Analyzing life experiences
- Apprenticeship
- Behavior modification
- Challenge activity
- Demonstration
- Discovery learning
- Drill and practice
- Experience
- Failure
- Field trip
- Homework
- Illustration
- Independent study
- Individualized instruction
- Inquiry
- Internship
- Integrated examples—career pathways

- Laboratory report
- Language laboratory
- Large and small group instruction
- Learning packages and workstations
- Lecture
- Making assignments
- Mental rehearsal
- Metaphor (verbal pictures, symbols)
- Oral report
- Problem solving
- Programmed instruction
- Project method
- Questioning
- Quiz
- Reading
- Recitation

- Reflection
- Research
- Self-paced and self-directed learning
- Simulation games and practice
- Socratic method
- Supervised study
- Team teaching
- Testing (as a method of teaching)
- Textbook
- Trial and error
- Visualization and guided imagery
- Written report
- Workbook

...INSTRUCTIONAL STRATEGIES, METHODS, AND SKILLS

Group Methods and Techniques

- Brainstorming
- Buzz sessions
- Case study
- Classroom meetings
- Coaching
- Committee meeting
- Cooperative learning
- Debate
- Directed discussion

- Games
- Group discussion
- Interviewing experts
- Mentoring
- One-on-one tutorial
- Panel discussion
- Peer tutoring
- Question and answer sessions
- Resource people and guest speakers

- Review sessions by and for students
- Role playing
- Sociodrama
- Story telling
- Symposiums and forums
- Teaching others

Material-Oriented Methods and Techniques

- Bulletin board
- Cartoon
- Chalk or dry erase board
- Chart
- Computer-assisted instruction
- Diagram
- Exhibit
- Film/Video

- Filmstrip
- Graph
- Map
- Model
- Multimedia presentation
- News article
- Overhead transparency

- Poster
- Picture
- Radio or audio presentation
- Recording
- Satellite presentation
- Slide
- Television/Video

Source: Lenger, S., & Lenger, W. (1977). *57 Ways to Teach.* Los Angeles, CA: Crescent Publications.

Figure 8-7. Categories of various instructional strategies, methods, and skills.

The teacher has options when making instructional decisions regarding the approved curriculum. For example, the teacher may choose from the following, depending on the situation:

- The teacher may decide it is appropriate to instruct the whole class in the same matter. This can be accomplished through direct instruction, through heterogeneous group work, or through any instructional method the teacher deems appropriate for the task.
- The teacher may decide to adapt instruction for a small group of learners with similar needs, interests, or abilities. This could be for the purpose of enrichment, extension, reinforcement, or differential teaching.
- The teacher may decide that a learner requires adaptive instruction for any number of reasons, including enrichment, extension, or reinforcement. The adaptation could range from one-to-one instruction to independent study.

The teacher is the facilitator of learning. First, the strengths, interests, and the needs of the learners are assessed. Then, the teacher makes the adaptations that are deemed necessary in order to maximize the learning potential of each learner. The professional judgment of the teacher is the critical factor in decision making with respect to accommodations. Decisions regarding these choices are based on ongoing assessment and evaluation and are always dynamic and changing. Instructional decisions recognize that learners' needs may vary from subject to subject, as well as over time.

Networking, consultation, and collaboration with parents/guardians and professional colleagues are important ways to enhance the teacher's decision-making effectiveness. Shared responsibility for decision-making and delivery of appropriate programming invites classroom teachers, school administrators, other professionals, and support staff to contribute to the formulation of an effective adaptation plan. Once the classroom teacher has accumulated sufficient information about the learners' abilities, aptitudes, interests, and performance baseline, the appropriate consultation and collaboration with parents/guardians, colleagues and others can occur. With input from others, the teacher can then exercise professional judgment in determining the best course of action. See Figure 8-8.

Schlecty (2001) set forth 10 qualities or attributes that teachers might focus on to create work that is more engaging for learners. The following qualities could serve as a framework for ongoing professional development:

1. Product focus–This is work that engages learners by almost always focusing on a product of importance or significance to them.
2. Clear and compelling standards–Learners prefer knowing exactly what is expected of them and how those expectations relate to something they care about. Standards are only relevant when those to whom they apply care about them.
3. Protection from adverse consequences for initial failures–Learners are more engaged when they can try tasks without fear of embarrassment, punishment, or implications for failure. Unfortunately, current school structures and grading practices often make this difficult to achieve.

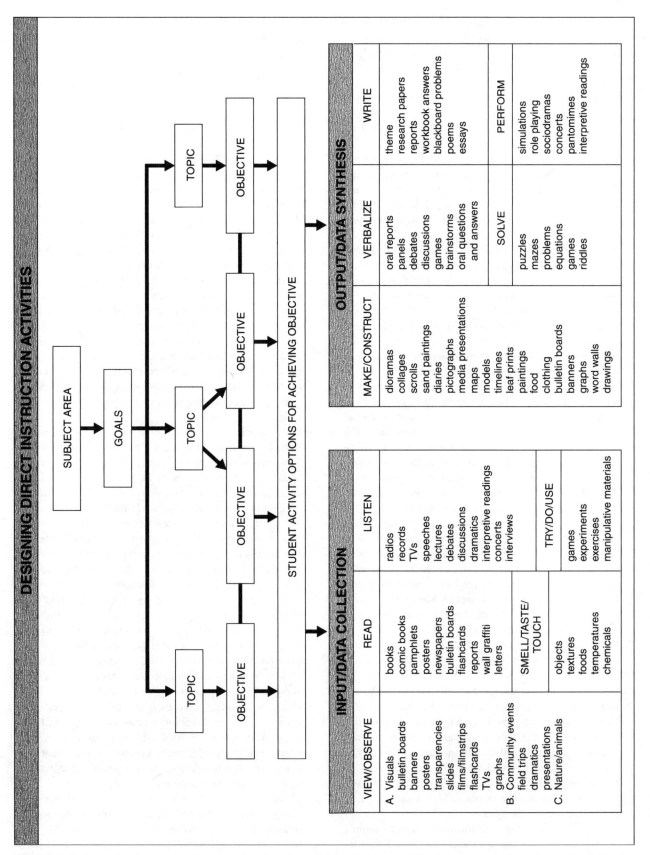

Figure 8-8. An instructional management system that slows for a variety of student activities in order to achieve an instructional objective.

4. Affirmation of the significance of the performance–Learners are more highly motivated when their parents, teachers, fellow learners, and significant others make it known that they think the learner's work is important. Portfolio assessments, which collect learner work for scrutiny by people other than the teacher, can play a significant role in making learner work more visible.

5. Affiliation–Learners are more likely to be engaged by work that permits, encourages, and supports opportunities for them to work interdependently with others. Those who advocate cooperative learning understand this well and also recognize the critical difference between learners working together and learners working independently on a common task, which may look like group work, but isn't.

6. Novelty and variety–Learners are more likely to engage in the work assigned to them if they are continually exposed to new and different ways of doing things. The introduction of computers in writing classes, for example, might motivate learners who otherwise would not write. New technology and techniques, however, shouldn't be used to create new ways to do the same old work. New forms of work, and new products to produce, are equally important?

7. Choice–When learners have some degree of control over what they are doing, they are more likely to feel committed to doing it. This doesn't mean learners should dictate school curriculum, however. Schools must distinguish between giving learners choices in learning activities and letting them choose what they will learn.

8. Authenticity–Clearly, when learners are given tasks that are meaningless, contrived, and inconsequential, they are less likely to take them seriously and be engaged by them. If the task carries real consequences, on the other hand, it's likely that engagement will increase. What teacher, for example, hasn't noticed that learners who produce a documentary video on a topic are likely to be engaged in a more authentic learning experience than those who listen to a series of lectures on the topic, with the sole goal of passing a test later to assure they were listening?

9. Organization of knowledge–Learners are more likely to be engaged when information and knowledge are arranged in clear, accessible ways, and in ways that let learners use the knowledge and information to address tasks that are important to them. This doesn't mean that all content must be inherently interesting or relevant to learners; they will learn many important things in school that they may not care about at the time. The content should be organized, however, so that access to the material is clear and relatively easy, and that the learners' work has enough attractive qualities to keep them engaged.

10. Content and substance–Educators should commit themselves to inventing work that engages all learners and helps them attain rich and profound knowledge.

Learning to read and to write complete sentences, for example, is not the same as learning to write persuasively and to read critically, thoughtfully, and well. If such profound mastery is limited to learners who are more socially or economically advantaged—or otherwise already capable of high-quality intellectual work without as much teacher effort—then the dream of democracy cannot truly be realized.

Fulk (2000) stated that three explosions are simultaneously vibrating through our schools and classrooms. The first is an explosion of content information to be taught. The second is an increased emphasis on learning outcomes. The third is the growing number of learners with learning and attention difficulties who struggle with grasping new concepts and retaining information over time. The following instructional strategies are designed to maintain learner interest, maximize learner engagement, and optimize the retention of content information over time:

• Grab their attention–Employ a variety of introductory activities or attention grabbers to stimulate learner interest in the learning task. Stress strategies that are meaningful or applicable to learners' lives and outside interests.

• Make it relevant–State a clear purpose and objective for each lesson. Tell learners exactly what is expected of them in order to follow each teaching segment. Stress goal attainment so that learners recognize and take pride in their own progress.

• Do it together–Stress the active engagement of learners in their own learning process. Encourage them to correct their own mistakes and to learn from them. Use any mistakes made by the instructor as teachable moments. Encourage cooperation rather than competition so learners seek ways to be coaches and study buddies for each other.

• Try teams–Utilize the social needs of your learners for added motivation. Many learners will work harder for the success of a peer group than they would when working alone. Use learning teams whose members are rotated regularly. Learners can practice the interpersonal skills required to work effectively with different individuals as they achieve essential learning outcomes.

• Keep it visual–Teach learners to monitor and graph their progress toward the goals that they select. Simple graphs provide excellent visual displays and documentation of learner progress. As an added benefit, these graphs are good learning activities in themselves.

• Create a schemata–Take time to explore learners' prior knowledge before teaching a new concept or skill. Become an expert in creating bridges from learners' past experience to new learning. Emphasize ways that new content relates to learners' prior knowledge as well as to content that was presented in class.

• Think big–Stress the relationship and use graphics to visually display the link between global concepts and related ideas. Less skilled learners, in particular, may fail to see the relationship between topics unless these are stated explicitly.

- Take aim–Teach goal setting and encourage learners to set their own realistic goals. Instructors can help learners by providing a realistic range. These short-term goals are easily met, yet are stepping-stones to larger achievements.
- Draw it out–Employ a variety of graphic organizers. Charts, diagrams, maps, and semantic webs are examples of visual displays that are useful for facilitating learning and comprehension. Generic templates can be easily modified for use across content areas.
- Show them how–Provide numerous examples, models, and illustrations of the new concept or skill. Be sure to include more complex problems as well as some straightforward examples. Ask learners to create additional examples for each other and for the class.
- Stimulate process thinking–Think-aloud when demonstrating the steps to a new process or procedure. Tell learners exactly what is being thought and why as each step is employed. The key is to verbalize explicitly those self-regulating cues that the instructor would normally perform automatically. Consider the needs of skill novices and try to prevent areas of difficultly with specific instruction.
- Teach a trick–Stress the use of mnemonic techniques for improved retention of facts. (e.g. ROYGBV for colors of the rainbow: red, orange, yellow, green, blue, violet).
- Talk out loud–Coach learners to elaborate as they reason through topics that follow logical sequences or action-reaction formats. Encourage learners to problem solve by asking probing questions (e.g. "Why does it make sense that...").
- Build on what they know–Use scaffold learning by providing very detailed instruction and materials during early learning. Offer less scaffolding as learners become more skillful with the content. Once you have molded a procedure on numerous occasions, you can prompt learners to become more independent in their use of this technique.
- Keep the action going–Employ a variety of methods for actively involving learners in practicing their new skills. Small dry-erase boards and individual chalk or game boards provide and require increased levels of learner input.
- Make a note–Teach learners to take lecture notes using a series of guided steps. For the earliest lessons in note-taking, provide a structured outline that requires learners to fill in the blanks. In subsequent lessons, gradually decrease the amount of information provided and require increased levels of learner input.
- Think ahead–Encourage learners to make predictions, to summarize, and to monitor their comprehension as they read independently. After direct instruction of these reading strategies, learners can be promoted to use and practice comprehension skills across content areas.
- Practice, practice, practice–Provide lots of opportunities for learners to practice a new skill. These can take the form of coaching activities (e.g., "Tell your buddy," "Show the person on the left," or "Read to your partner.") or other relevant practice methods.

- Provide closure–Use specific closure activities to complete a learning segment or lesson (e.g., "Tell two important things you have learned today," "Summarize in one sentence what you learned about...," or "Before the class ends we have just enough time to name the steps we learned today.").
- Refresh their memories–Provide a systematic review for content taught. Even the most motivating instruction will not be remembered unless it is reviewed. Devise a schedule of weekly review sessions and be sure to include games or other activity-based formats.

SELECTED INSTRUCTIONAL STRATEGIES

Individuals from special populations represent a diverse group of learners who possess a variety of different learning styles. They do not all learn at the same rate or through the same instructional strategies. The instructional strategies selected by career and technical education instructors may make the difference between success and failure for these learners. One instructional strategy will not meet the unique needs of every learner with special needs. Therefore, a variety of techniques should be considered when designing the instructional delivery of a career and technical education program.

Research has shown that career and technical educators are in need of more information, training, and assistance with instructional strategies to successfully integrate learners from special populations in their programs. A study conducted by the Furman University Center of Excellence looked at the necessary skills to teach learners with special needs. The following results show a profile of an instructor who will be able to successfully work with all learners within a classroom environment:

1. Personal Skills/Competencies–Instructors should be:
- accepting of each student as an individual of worth
- caring, concerned, empathetic, loving, respecting, humanistic
- enthusiastic and energetic
- humorous
- patient
- effective communicators with students and parents
- creative
- flexible
2. Professional Skills/Competencies–Instructors should:
- be professional (reliable, punctual, dedicated)
- utilize resources from other educators as well as the community at large
3. Materials–Instructors need to:
- adapt materials to appropriate levels
- develop and utilize manipulatives
- utilize a wide range and variety of materials
4. Methods–Instructors need to:
- possess organizational skills (planning, time management, record keeping)
- set realistic goals and objectives for students (high expectations)

- diagnose, prescribe, and evaluate students (formally and informally)
- make learning relevant
- individualize instruction
- utilize small group instruction
- utilize a variety of techniques and methods
- reteach and give students time to practice the skill or concept
5. Learning Environment–Instructors need to:
- be a "cheerleader" (be positive, use motivational strategies, reward, enhance self-concepts, and ensure successful experiences)
- create a warm, inviting learning environment
- be firm, consistent, and fair in classroom management (establish rules and penalties, make them clear to all students, enforce them with consistency, do not make idle and frequent threats, listen to both sides of a disagreement, and make decisions fairly)
- consider the total learner (mental, physical, and emotional elements) (Lehr and Harris, 1988, pp. 56-61)

The characteristics, abilities, interests, learning styles, and needs of each learner must be taken into consideration when planning classroom and laboratory instruction. Some initial considerations should be addressed by career and technical education personnel when selecting instructional delivery strategies. These considerations include such important elements as

- the pace at which the learner learns most effectively;
- the ability level of the learner (e.g., reading level, math level, vocational assessment results);
- the objectives identified for the learner in the individualized education program (IEP) for participation in a career and technical education program;
- the preferred learning style of the learner;
- difficulty of subject matter to be covered (e.g., readability of books and materials, related terminology, level of math involved in the instructional program); and
- the evaluation procedures established to determine learner proficiency on competencies taught.

Successful instructors use a variety of techniques to assist learners with special needs to start learning on a positive note. Examples of effective strategies include

- teaching essential study skills;
- training learners in self-monitoring techniques (e.g., providing a card with a checklist of assignments so that learners can monitor their own progress);
- assisting learners in setting and completing realistic goals;
- utilizing an attention getter when beginning a lesson;
- giving clear directions, modeling expected behaviors, and having selected learners model these behaviors;
- having learners select a peer to work with when they need help;
- monitoring independent and laboratory work carefully;
- asking learners with special needs in a nonjudgmental way to repeat instructions;
- having learners use help cards at their seats to signal

when they need assistance;
- specifying the amount of work and delineating time limits for its completion; and
- utilizing pre-tests to know the appropriate place to begin instruction (Lehr & Harris, 1988).

Instructors should analyze the way that they deliver their curricula. Questionnaires may be used by instructors to determine the extent to which they are examining their delivery style and selecting effective instructional strategies to meet the needs of all learners in the class. It helps to take a few minutes to answer questions about instructional practices in the classroom and laboratory and review possible methods of meeting the specific needs of learners.

Even when curriculum is standardized, if four instructors are teaching the exact career and technical education program, there will be four different ways to deliver the curriculum. The delivery style will differ depending on the learning style and teaching style of the individual instructor. In order to make the most appropriate match between a learner with special needs and an instructor, information should be reviewed to make the most appropriate decision regarding placement for each learner. An example of information that could be helpful in this process is the Career and Technical Program Inventory. See Figure 8-9. An instructor should complete this information. Then, using specific information about a specific learner with special needs, a comparison can be made. This should help to determine areas in which the learner may need assistance and support services during participation in the program.

Not every instructional technique presented here will be successful with every learner. It will require a degree of flexibility and experimentation on the part of instructors to determine what techniques best meet the needs of individual learners. Cooperative planning with personnel who are familiar with the learner will be very helpful in selecting and utilizing appropriate instructional techniques. Following are a number of instructional strategies that can be used effectively when instructing learners from special populations.

Direct Instruction

Direct instruction assumes that, by manipulating the presentation of concepts and items, anything can be taught to anyone. Research has supported the direct instruction model as effective, especially in classroom settings where there is a wide range of abilities among learners. Direct instruction stresses the importance of the instructor as a critical manager of learner behavior and instructional time. This approach to teaching is implemented through teacher-directed, rather than learner-initiated, activities. Information is presented with practice in sequential steps, with immediate corrective feedback, and the opportunity for a high degree of success.

CAREER AND TECHNICAL PROGRAM INVENTORY ...

_____ Program Title

_____ Instructor

_____ Textbook Title/Author

_____ Reading Level

1 = Used Often   **2 = Used Less Frequently**

INFORMATION INPUT
(Instructional Methods)

INFORMATION OUTPUT
(Types of Assignments)

Information Sources

_____ Textbook
_____ Worksheets
_____ Lecture
_____ Discussion
_____ Audio-visual material
_____ Audiotape
_____ Concrete experience
_____ Other

Test Format

_____ Short answer
_____ Essay
_____ Multiple choice
_____ True-false
_____ Matching
_____ Computation
_____ Word problems/math
_____ Other

Structure

_____ Directed
_____ Independent
_____ Peer tutor
_____ One on one adult
_____ Small group
_____ Large group/class
_____ Other

Assignments

_____ Worksheets
_____ Short papers
_____ Term papers
_____ Demo/lab projects
_____ Oral reports
_____ Group discussion
_____ Computation
_____ Word problems/math
_____ Maps, charts, graphs
_____ Other

Grading Criteria _____

_____

_____

_____

Extra Credit _____

_____

_____

_____

. . . CAREER AND TECHNICAL PROGRAM INVENTORY

OTHER PROGRAM REQUIREMENTS
(Check only high-priority requirements)

ACADEMIC SKILLS NEEDED

_____ Becoming interested
_____ Paying attention to the spoken word
_____ Paying attention to the printed word
_____ Following directions
_____ Keeping track of materials, assignments
_____ Staying on task
_____ Completing tasks on time
_____ Working in groups
_____ Working independently
_____ Learning by listening
_____ Expressing him/herself verbally
_____ Reading textbooks
_____ Reading study sheet or tests
_____ Understanding what is read
_____ Writing legibly
_____ Expressing him/herself in writing
_____ Spelling
_____ Seeing relationships
_____ Understanding cause and effect; anticipating consequences
_____ Drawing conclusions/making inferences
_____ Remembering
_____ Notetaking
_____ Outlining
_____ Independent researching
_____ Measuring
_____ Other

BEHAVIORAL SKILLS NEEDED

_____ Coming to class on time
_____ Coming to class prepared
_____ Following directions
_____ Staying in seat
_____ Staying on task
_____ Completing tasks on time
_____ Understanding/following safety rules
_____ Asking questions or for help when needed
_____ Working in groups
_____ Working independently
_____ Other

OTHER PREREQUISITES _____

HOMEWORK POLICY _____

MAKE-UP WORK POLICY _____

ATTENDANCE POLICY _____

OTHER PROGRAM RULES _____

Source: Adapted from Model Resource Room Project, Plymouth, MI. (1981). In Albright, L., & Cobb, R. (1988). *Assessment of Students with Handicaps in Vocational Education: A Curriculum-Based Approach.* Alexandria, VA: American Vocational Association.

Figure 8-9. A sample inventory that can be filled out by a specific instructor so that learners entering the program are aware of expectations and necessary support services can be planned.

White (1987) identified the following principles of direct instruction:

1. Teach one thing at a time.
2. Provide students with multiple opportunities to respond to each lesson.
3. Reinforce students for correct responses throughout the lesson.
4. Correct errors immediately by reteaching through one of the response paradigms. See Figure 8-10.
5. Review each lesson at the beginning, middle, and end.
6. Keep the pace of interaction quick and "rhythmic."
7. Signal clearly (let students know when lessons begin and when they are expected to respond).
8. Give students opportunities to respond verbally and physically.
9. Keep the process interactive. (p. 153)

Direct instruction should occur several times during each class session. Teaching one thing at a time is the best practice for making certain that learners understand what the instructor is teaching. The following are the three basic phases to direct instruction:

1. Structuring phase–During the structuring phase, the instructor prepares learners for instruction by stating the lesson objectives and describing activities that will occur during the instruction. A review of previous instruction is a component of this phase so that new material can be linked to what has previously been learned.

2. Demonstration phase–During the demonstration phase, the instructor presents a variety of examples of a concept that is being presented. Learners talk about the concept as they perform an assigned task. They are expected to explain the processes they are using and why they are using them as they work through the assignment. Questioning is a very important component of this phase. The use of questions and prompting or clueing help learners to focus attention on the task to be accomplished. This provides an opportunity for repeated practice with the concepts involved in the lesson and serves to discourage guessing, which may deter learning.

3. Consolidation phase–During the consolidation phase, the instructor closely monitors learner errors, helps learners to correct their errors, and provides a variety of opportunities for practice with immediate feedback after learner performance. This feedback prevents repetition of incorrect practices or responses. Repeated practice of correct responses leads to consolidation of skills and mastery of concepts.

A summary of research has shown the following:

- Direct instruction methods show positive correlation with learner achievement of lower order cognitive objectives.
- Fewer behavior problems occur in classes where direct instruction is practiced.

		Paradigm		
	Presentation	Rule	Comparison	Sequence
Type	Description			
Model:	Instructor demonstrates (models) the task or states the concept	X	X	X
Lead:	Instructor and learners perform task together while repeating concept	X		
Test:	Instructor asks students to perform tasks independently	X		
Alternating test:	Instructor juxtaposes examples in such a way as to require students to attend to relevant features of an item. Instructor presents vastly different examples of correct possibilities and incorrect items that are minimally different from correct item. This rules out features that may lead to misinterpretation of meaning		X	
Delayed test:	A test of a skill is presented later in the lesson, providing opportunity to separate skill from cycle and require students to perform skill out of context		X	
Guided practice:	Students participate in performing sequence while instructor provides minimal verbal and/or physical support required for students to perform skill in fluid, timely fashion			X
Solo practice:	Students perform sequence unassisted, while instructor provides immediate feedback following task			X

DIRECT INSTRUCTION RESPONSE PARADIGMS

Figure 8-10. A variety of strategies used to teach and reinforce rules/principles, the process of comparison, and/or the process of sequencing.

• Higher rates of learner response and on-task behavior occur in classes utilizing direct instruction.
• A greater possibility of moving expeditiously through learning activities exists when teachers engage in direct instruction (Greene, et al., 1987).

Direct instruction is an effective instructional technique for learners from special populations. Peryon (1978) stated that the strength of direct instruction lies in the structure it provides for teaching a specific set of concepts and skills. This structure creates a framework for learners with special needs to develop the necessary skills to master specific learning tasks. This instructional strategy also provides more modeling of correct responses and thinking than other forms of teaching. It emphasizes the importance of an instructor's role in the learning process and increases instructor clarity and enthusiasm during instruction.

Individualized Instruction

Individualized instruction is tailored to meet the particular needs of each learner and allows the career and technical education instructor a variety of alternatives in delivering program instruction. This method is particularly effective because it allows learners to work at their own pace using resources, media, and materials that will assist them in the learning process. Individualized instruction can be an effective method of instructing learners from special populations because it actively involves the learner in the learning process, identifies instructional objectives and criteria for the learner, divides the learning task into an appropriate number of specially designed instructional activities, and allows the learner to complete activities within a range of assessment activities (e.g., hands-on projects, pretests, posttests, checklists, observations, and self-checks).

Individualized instruction does not require that instructors water down course objectives or competencies necessary for program completion. It does, however, mean that career and technical education instructors should work closely with other school personnel to gain as much relevant information about each learner with special needs so that an appropriate individualized instruction format can be established and implemented. This information should include such details as the learner's reading level, math level, interests, career goals, and preferred learning style. Individual differences among learners must be taken into consideration in planning individualized instruction.

This instructional strategy can assist the career and technical education instructor in helping more learners in the class. By working at their own pace and ability level, learners can successfully progress through the task or assignment with a minimum amount of help from the instructor. Many of the reading and writing assignments can be self-checked by the learner. Spot checks, pretests, and posttests can be administered by the teacher, peer evaluator, and/or support person to help assess learner progress.

There are various techniques involved in the individualized instruction approach. Examples of these techniques include units, chapters, learning activity packets, learning center activities, self-paced and programmed instructional materials, and independent and supervised study activities.

In designing a program of individualized instruction for use with learners from special populations, the following considerations should be addressed by career and technical education instructors:

• Individualized instruction experiences can be developed specifically for one learner or for a small group whose members have similar abilities and interests. See Figure 8-11.
• Even if it takes some learners longer to complete required tasks or assignments, they should be given the same credit as other learners who complete the work in less time as long as the quality of the completed work meets the standards of the instructor.
• Specific objectives should be developed and carefully explained to learners before they begin the activity or assignment and should be stated in performance terms so that learners clearly understand exactly what they are to do.
• Instructors should determine what previous knowledge and/or skills are necessary for completion of the individualized assignment and make certain that learners possess the prerequisite information, terminology, and skills.
• Learners should be aware of the tools, equipment, materials, resources, media, and aids that will be provided to assist them in completing the activity or assignment.
• Routine and periodic supervision should be provided by instructors while learners are working on individualized instruction activities.
• Criteria for evaluation should be clearly defined and understood before the activity or assignment is started.
• The learning environment where individualized instruction is to take place should be flexible and allow for a variety of activities and experiences according to the specific needs of the learners.
• Individualized instruction materials, chapters, units, or packets have been developed for many career and technical education programs. Instructors should contact the Department of Education, curriculum centers, other instructors, companies producing commercial materials, and other sources to obtain readily available materials that can meet the specific needs of learners with special needs as well as maintain the standards of the career and technical education program. See Figure 8-12.

INDIVIDUALIZED INSTRUCTION ASSIGNMENT SHEET

MAJOR BLOCK Basic engine tune-up   **NAME** _____

TASK Cleaning or replacing spark plugs

UNIT 223-9   **TIME (est.)** 2 hrs.   **(act)** _____

OBJECTIVE(S) To remove and diagnose condition of spark plugs, analyze spark plug deposits, clean plugs, file electrodes, and set plug gap to specifications; plug gap to be within .001 of recommended setting. Ground electrode must be at right angle to center electrode. Install and torque to specifications. Correctly answer 16 of 20 test questions on spark plug types, applications, and service procedures.

START ➡ W-1 ▷ W-2 ▷ A-1 ▷ L-1 ▷ C-1 ▷ L-2 ▷ L-3 ▷

C-2 ▷ L-4 ▷ C-3 ▷ ▷ ▷ ▷ ▷ ▷ ▷

▷ ▷ ▷ ▷ ▷ ▷ ▷ ▷ ▷

WRITTEN

W-1 Assignment sheet 223-9
W-2 Assignment sheet 223-9-1
W-3 _____
W-4 _____
W-5 _____
W-6 _____
W-7 _____

AUDIO-VISUALS

A-1 Slide set 223-9
A-2 _____
A-3 _____
A-4 _____
A-5 _____
A-6 _____
A-7 _____

LABORATORY

L-1 Assignment sheet 223-9-2
L-2 Install spark plugs
L-3 Performance test plugs
L-4 Secure work station
L-5 _____
L-6 _____
L-7 _____
L-8 _____
L-9 _____

CHECKPOINT

C-1 Instructor check
C-2 Instructor check
C-3 Give test, evaluate, and make next assignment
C-4 _____
C-5 _____
C-6 _____
C-7 _____
C-8 _____
C-9 _____

Figure 8-11. An example of an individualized assignment that can be used for a specific learner.

Mastery Learning

Mastery learning involves the identification of segments of learning and then the mastery of them by individual learners. It is based on the philosophy that all learners can learn, but it will take some longer than others. The expectation is that learners will all succeed. This is an excellent strategy for use with learners from special populations.

The strategies associated with mastery learning pull together much of what is known about effective instruction as well as what is known about individual learning styles of learners. Based on the original work of Dr. Benjamin Bloom at the University of Chicago, the premise of mastery learning is that by following a set of sequenced instructional activities, instructors can provide a higher quality of teaching for a larger portion of learners.

STEPS TO FACILITATE INDIVIDUALIZED INSTRUCTION ACTIVITIES

Sequence	Component	Individual(s) Involved
1	Goals and objectives selected	Special needs learner Parent/guardian Career and technical education teacher Support personnel Peer tutor
2	Pre-assessment is administered and recorded	Special needs learner Career and technical education teacher Support personnel
3	Appropriate activities, methods, and materials are identified for each specified goal or objective	Career and technical education teacher Support personnel
4	Component assigned activities are completed by special needs learner	Special needs learner Career and technical education teacher Support personnel Peer tutor
5	Post-assessment is administered	Career and technical education teacher Support personnel Peer tutor
6	Analysis of posttest results is recorded and used to determine next step a. if performance criteria is met, the learner moves on to the next objective and associated activity b. if performance criteria is not met, further instruction and remediation is provided	Career and technical education teacher Support personnel

Figure 8-12. A sequence for individualizing instruction for a learner through a team effort.

Bloom (1971) stated that most learners can master what is taught. The basic instructional task is to define what is meant by mastery of a subject and to discover methods and materials to help the largest proportion of learners reach it. The philosophy behind the mastery learning concept includes the following points:

- Individual differences exist between learners. A fundamental task in education is to develop strategies that will take into account individual differences in such a way as to promote, rather than inhibit, the fullest development of each learner.
- The quality of instruction must be developed with respect to the needs and characteristics of individual learners, rather than groups of learners.
- The ability to understand instruction is defined as the ability of learners to understand the nature of the task they are to learn and the procedures they are to follow in learning it. If learners can understand the instructor's communications and the instructional materials, they will have little difficulty learning the subject.

- There are many instructional strategies that, given help and various types of aids, instructors can use to fit their instruction to the differing needs of all their learners, including small group study sessions, tutorial help, alternative textbook explanations, workbook and programmed instruction units, audiovisual materials, and games and simulations. The use of alternative methods of instruction and instructional materials is an attempt to improve the quality of instruction in relation to the ability of each learner to understand that instruction.
- Perseverance is the time the learner is willing to spend in learning. Perseverance is not fixed. It can be increased by increasing the frequency of reward and evidence of learning success. The need for perseverance can be decreased by high quality instruction. There seems to be little reason to make learning so difficult that only a small proportion of learners can persevere to mastery. The emphasis should be on learning, not on endurance and discipline.

- Most learners can achieve mastery if they are allowed to spend the necessary amount of time on a learning task. The learning time needed will be affected by the learner's aptitudes, ability to understand the instruction, and the quality of instruction provided in class and outside of class.

Guskey (1980) described the following steps in the mastery learning approach:

1. An instructor analyzes the content of a specific curriculum for a specific course that is to be delivered to learners over a predetermined length of time (e.g., semester, academic year).
2. The content is organized into units depending on the level and difficulty of the content. Learning units in mastery learning usually consist of material that could be covered by the instructor in a week or two of instructional time.
3. The units are divided into learning objectives. Learners are aware of the learning objectives for each unit.
4. Tests are developed to measure acquisition of objectives.
5. Learners receive instruction and study the content. This is typically done through a unit format.
6. The first test is given over this content. The criterion for acceptable performance is established by the instructor. Instead of signifying the end of instruction on that unit, the test represents a check on learning progress to that point. Each question or problem on the test is designed to include a particular concept that has been identified as important to learning the subject material. The test is not counted as part of a learner's grade, but is designed to provide precise feedback to both the instructor and the learner regarding what concepts have been mastered and what have not. The test also includes specific suggestions to the learner as to what might be done to help correct any learning difficulties. The learner then works on only those concepts that have not as yet been mastered. The correctives may point out where in the text a specific concept was discussed so that those pages might be reread, or an alternate learning resource such as a different text, cassette tape, or video. The correctives may also indicate sources of additional practice such as study guides or worksheets. As a result of this formative test, the learner has a very individualized prescription of what else needs to be done to master the material in that unit.
7. Learners who pass the test receive enrichment activities. Learners who do not pass receive corrective feedback (e.g., reteaching using alternate materials, tutoring, use of learning centers, computer-assisted instruction).
8. After additional study and use of correctives, learners take a parallel test covering the content.

One positive attribute of using mastery learning is the flexibility it provides for the instructor. The instructor serves as an instructional leader and facilitator. Learners work at their own pace and take responsibility for their own learning.

Task Analysis

Task analysis is a technique that can be extremely effective with learners from special populations. This technique involves analyzing a job and the tasks required to successfully complete the job. The task should have a major goal or objective associated with it, which should be clearly described at the beginning of the task analysis so that the career and technical education instructor, the learners, and/or support personnel will have a clear understanding of what is expected at the completion of the task.

Skills and competencies associated with the task should be identified. This includes prerequisite skills that are necessary to perform the task as well as skills that will be necessary to complete the specific steps of the task analysis. Identification of skills and competencies can be facilitated by consulting industry standards, curriculum guides, other career and technical education personnel, and specific program requirements.

The steps of the task analysis should be written in performance terms so that the learner knows exactly what has to be done to complete each step. The directions for completing each step should be short, clear, and specific. The steps should be listed in order so that when all of the sequential steps have been successfully completed, the task will be mastered. The number of steps that the task is broken into depends upon the abilities and needs of the learner.

Use the following steps as a guideline for planning material according to the task analysis method:

1. Start with one item or task at a time.
2. Know the materials (technical update of current operating procedures, equipment, terminology, etc.).
3. Determine the objective of the task.
4. Identify the component steps of the objective.
5. Analyze the steps and eliminate repetitive or unnecessary steps.
6. Sequence the steps in a logical order.
7. Identify prerequisite skills or knowledge needed for the task.
8. Establish criteria for successful completion of the task.
9. Alter the tasks and sequences as needed.
10. Make sure the learner repeats the task enough for overlearning to take place.

For learners from special populations who learn more slowly than other learners, the job task should be broken down into more specific steps. See Figure 8-13.

The task analysis procedure is an effective technique to use with many learners with special needs because only one step of the task is introduced at a time. Learners work at their own pace and can practice each step as many times as necessary until success is experienced. A new step is not introduced until all previous steps in the task analysis have been mastered. Therefore, this procedure is effective in allowing these learners to master the task at their own pace while at the same time motivating them from one step to another.

APPLIED TASK ANALYSIS LEARNING OBJECTIVES

Changing Oil in a Vehicle

I. Get tools and materials
   A. Get out materials
      1. Wrenches
      2. Drain container
      3. Oil spout
   B. Remove from trunk of car
      1. New oil
      2. New oil filter
II. Prepare car
   A. Drive vehicle over pit
   B. Check position of vehicle over pit
      1. If front tires are not in the track along sides of pit
         a. Then drive vehicle forward
         b. Drive vehicle backward if necessary
      2. Check position of vehicle over pit
   C. Turn off engine
III. Change oil
   A. Remove old oil
      1. Place drain container under the oil pan plug
      2. Remove oil pan plug
      3. Drain used oil into container
      4. Replace oil pan plug
   B. Remove old oil filter
      1. Place drain container under the old filter
      2. Loosen old filter with filter wrench
      3. Take off filter with hands
      4. Drain old oil filter into the drain container
   C. Put on new oil filter
      1. Wipe groove on engine where oil filter fits with rag
      2. Put a little oil on the gasket of the oil filter
      3. Put new oil filter in place and tighten with hands until snug

D. Add new oil
      1. Lift engine hood
      2. Take off oil cap
      3. Pour four quarts of 10W-40 weight oil into engine
      4. Replace oil cap
      5. Shut engine hood
IV. Finalize Procedures
   A. Run new oil through engine
      1. Start engine
      2. Idle engine for one minute
      3. Stop engine
   B. Check for oil leakage around oil plug
   C. If there is an oil drip from around the oil plug:
      1. Tighten plug
      2. Wipe area clean with a rag
      3. Check for oil leakage
   D. Check for oil leakage around oil filter
   E. If there is an oil drip from around oil filter:
      1. Tighten oil filter with hands
      2. Wipe area clean with a rag
      3. Check for oil leakage
   F. Clean up
      1. Drain oil bottles and used oil filter of all remaining oil
      2. Place discarded oil in proper container.
      3. Wipe drain container clean and discard oil rags in proper container
      4. Place empty oil botles and old filter in the garbage can
      5. Put away tools in the garage
      6. Clean hands
      7. Take discarded oil in proper container to the proper recycling facility

Figure 8-13. An example of breaking down a task into elements and subelements for a learner who may need additional information, examples, or practice.

Demonstrations

The demonstration method is a very effective technique to introduce a new skill to learners from special populations. By showing learners how to perform a task while explaining the procedure, the learners use more than one sense and learning mode. They can listen to the instructor while observing the proper performance steps of the task or skill being demonstrated. Usually an activity or laboratory assignment will follow that allows learners to practice what they have seen and heard.

In preparing a demonstration, the career and technical education instructor should identify the sequence of steps that will be necessary to fully display the specific skill, task, or procedure. Tasks should be broken down into small steps to avoid confusing or frustrating learners. Sufficient time should be set aside for the demonstration without attempting to present too much new material at one time. A demonstration can be organized into several sessions, if necessary.

Tips that may be useful to career and technical education instructors in preparing a demonstration include the following:
- Arrange all supplies, materials, tools, and equipment that will be needed during the demonstration.
- Introduce the demonstration by reviewing previously taught information and/or skills relevant to demonstration.
- Introduce and discuss any technical terms that are relevant to the demonstration.
- Emphasize relevant safety practices during demonstration.
- Demonstrate the manipulative skill or task in a way that closely resembles the actual work environment where the skill or task will be performed.
- Use visual materials whenever possible to reinforce the performance steps being demonstrated (e.g., charts, diagrams, and models).
- Question learners periodically during the demonstration to be certain that they are able to follow and understand the performance steps being demonstrated.

- The demonstration may have to be repeated for learners who did not fully grasp all of the details, and in some cases, broken down into smaller steps and presented more slowly. A videotape of the demonstration can be helpful for learners who need to review the steps involved in a process being demonstrated.
- Assign a related activity following the demonstration (The National Center for Research in Vocational Education, 1977a).

Some specific considerations regarding learners with disabilities to keep in mind when preparing a demonstration include the following:

- Visually impaired learners may need to stand close to the instructor while the demonstration is taking place and/or be allowed to feel the various performance steps as they are shown.
- Hearing impaired learners may need to stand close to the instructor while the demonstration is taking place and in some cases may need to be provided with the services of an interpreter.
- Special considerations may have to be made for specific physical disabilities during the demonstration and/or related application activities.
- Learning disabled, mentally retarded, and/or emotionally disturbed learners may profit from hearing and seeing the demonstration more than once if the instructor will tape record and/or videotape the session.
- Focus the learners on what they are to learn to do. Make certain that they understand the objective before beginning the demonstration.
- Present the demonstration in small steps. Don't assume that learners understand what you are doing simply because they do not ask questions during the demonstration.
- Periodically ask questions, summarize, and have learners state what has taken place in the demonstration to make certain that you are not going too fast for comprehension to occur.
- Avoid digressions during a demonstration. They will confuse learners. Stick to the simple steps of the demonstration.

Project-Based Learning

Project-based learning (PBL) is a model for classroom activity that shifts away from the classroom practices of short, isolated, teacher-centered lessons and instead emphasizes learning activities that are long-term, interdisciplinary, learner-centered, and integrated with real-world issues and practices. One immediate benefit of practicing PBL is the unique way that it can motivate learners by engaging them in their own learning. PBL provides opportunities for learners to pursue their own interests and questions and make decisions about how they will find answers and solve problems.

This technique helps make learning relevant and useful to learners by establishing connections to life outside the classroom, addressing real-world concerns, and developing real-world skills. Many of the skills learned through PBL are those desired by today's employers, including the ability to work well with others, make thoughtful decisions, take initiative, and solve complex problems.

In the classroom, PBL provides many unique opportunities for teachers to build relationships with learners. Teachers may fill the varied roles of coach, facilitator, and co-learner. Finished products, plans, drafts, and prototypes all make excellent conversation pieces around which teachers and learners can discuss the learning that is taking place.

In the school and beyond, PBL also provides opportunities for teachers to build relationships with other teachers and with those in the larger community. Learner work, which includes documentation of the learning process as well as the final project, can be shared with other teachers, parents, mentors, and the business community, who all have a stake in the learners' education.

Project-based learning typically begins with an end product in mind, the production of which requires specific content knowledge or skills and typically raises one or more problems that learners must solve. Projects vary widely in scope and time frame, and end products vary widely in level of technology used and sophistication. The project-based learning approach uses a production model. First, learners define the purpose of creating the end product and identify their audience. They research their topic, design their product, and create a plan for project management. Learners then begin the project, resolve problems and issues that arise in production, and finish their product. Learners may use or present the product they have created and ideally are given time to reflect on and evaluate their work. The entire process is meant to be authentic, mirroring real-world production activities and utilizing learners' own ideas and approaches to accomplish the tasks at hand. Though the end product is the driving force in project-based learning, it is the content knowledge and skills acquired during the production process that are important. See Figure 8-14.

Project learning is organized around the creation, execution, and production of something. The project usually occurs within a reasonable timeframe, ranging from a week to a semester depending on the nature of the project. In addition, it often has well-defined parameters and published guidelines, such as a list of required materials, performance specifications, and definite deadlines that must be adhered to. For example, book reports, research papers, multimedia presentations, and mechanical inventions are all projects that are strong organizers for tailoring the curriculum to learners' interests, talents, and resourcefulness. Project learning encourages industry collaboration, creativity, and experiential learning through the completion of the final product.

Fogarty (1997) described the following types of projects:

- Structured projects–Structured projects have specific limitations. Certain criteria are predetermined, which usually include project specifications in terms of size, materials, and functions. Structured projects also tend to fall into a typical time frame, such as a semester, a quarter, or even a week.

PROJECT-BASED LEARNING

CURRICULUM ISSUES
- What is the goal of your group (e.g., main point or concept)?

TIME FRAME
- What did you do as you planned your project (e.g., selecting topics, finding resources, using storyboards, outlines)?
- What changes did you make while you were planning it (e.g., changes in content, organization, media, language)?
- In what ways did your classmates and teacher give you suggestions on how to improve your project?
- How long did you work on this project? How much time did you spend on planning, gathering and selecting information, editing, and putting it all together?
- Do you wish that you had been given more time to work on this project?
- What else would you have done?

STUDENT DIRECTION
- How did you select the information to include?
- What resources did you use?
- Why did you leave some information out?

MULTIMEDIA
- Which types of media did you include (e.g., graphs, photos, movies)?
- How did you decide which media you would use to make your information clear?
- How did your teacher help?

AUDIENCE
- Who is your audience?
- How did you choose information and media to capture your audience's attention?
- How would you change your project for a different audience?

COLLABORATION
- How did the whole team contribute to this project?
- How did your team make choices during the project?

ASSESSMENT
- What did you learn during this project (e.g., about concepts, media, teamwork)?
- What will you do differently during your next project?

Source: San Mateo County Office of Education. (2001). *Project-Based Learning with Multimedia*. Redwood City, CA: Author.

Figure 8-14. Guidelines for planning a project-based learning lesson.

- Topic-related projects–Topic-related projects evolve from a unit of study and often incorporate individual or small group assignments. Learners choose a topic of interest from a list of options provided by the teacher or brainstormed by the class or a group of learners. These are typical, traditional kinds of school-related projects.

- Open-ended projects–Open-ended projects give minimal guidelines, few criteria, and little structure to encourage risk-taking and innovative thinking. Open-ended projects promote discovery, insight, and invention. Learners seek new ideas in open-ended projects and often find themselves in uncharted waters, which allows them to find unique solutions.

Activities often utilized in project learning include
- brainstorming ideas;
- analyzing data;
- charting information;
- drawing and sketching models;
- drafting ideas;
- developing prototypes;
- filling in missing information;
- visualizing the big picture;
- reconciling conflicting data;
- finding a focus;
- assigning a theme;
- creating a metaphor;
- looking for patterns;
- seeking connections;
- playing with ideas;
- finding materials;
- reading for background information;
- researching and taking notes;
- building a reference list;
- interviewing experts;
- viewing films and videos;
- developing an outline;
- talking with peers;
- surfing the Internet;
- checking and double-checking sources;
- visiting sites; and
- gathering charts, maps, illustrations.

Projects can be a useful technique in providing learners with special needs an opportunity to develop independent and interpersonal skills. They can also provide career and technical education instructors with a method of observing and evaluating learner progress. Projects can be done individually or in small groups. Specific projects can be assigned, or they can be selected or developed by the learners.

Work on the project can take place in the classroom, in the laboratory, in other areas of the school, at home, in a community environment, or in a combination of these settings. When assigning a project, instructors should make certain that the objectives are clearly stated and understood, as well as the general tasks involved in the project and the specific criteria for evaluation. Advantages of using such projects to assist learners with special needs include the following:
- They can act as motivating experiences for learners to demonstrate the competencies and skills they have learned in the career and technical education program.
- They can help learners relate the knowledge and skills of the instructional program to practical experiences.

- They can help learners to develop responsibility in selecting an appropriate project area and/or in actively participating in the planning and completion stages.
- They allow learners to practice the proper use of machinery, tools, equipment, and raw materials associated with the career and technical education program.
- They allow supervision of learners as they progress at their own pace.
- They allow instructors to evaluate the level and degree of proficiency that learners demonstrate while working on the project as well as the quality of the finished product.

Field Trips, Job Site Visitations, and Shadowing Activities

Many learners from special populations have had little or no exposure to specific occupations that are available in the job market. Field trips or job site visitations can provide learners with an opportunity to observe workers on the job, become familiar with specific duties involved in jobs related to the career and technical education program, and provide information about possible career opportunities.

Field trips and job site visitations can be arranged for the entire class, small groups of learners, or on an individual basis. See Figure 8-15. Field trips and job site visitations can be used as

- career exploration activities;
- incentives or rewards for completion of program assignments and units;
- individual, group, or class projects;
- class reports;
- industry mentoring activities; and/or
- preplacement exposure experiences.

One particular method that allows learners to experience field trips and job site observations is called shadowing. This experience involves making arrangements for an individual learner or small group of learners to spend time on the job with a worker in a particular occupational area. By acting as a shadow, learners gain insight into the actual work environment and work tasks associated with the job. For learners who have never before observed workers on the job, this experience offers a realistic look into the working world and can assist them in making appropriate career decisions. Sources of workers that can be contacted for shadowing experiences include employers who have hired former graduates and career and technical education advisory committee members.

TIPS FOR FACILITATING FIELD TRIPS		
Before the trip, the teacher	**YES**	**NO**
1. Identified an object that lends itself to the use of a group field trip	_____	_____
2. Identified community resources that would help to attain the objective	_____	_____
3. Explained to students how the trip would help attain the objective	_____	_____
4. Planned an agenda that was feasible and convenient to carry out	_____	_____
5. Involved students in planning specific on-site activities	_____	_____
6. Explained student individual responsibilities during the trip	_____	_____
7. Provided background information on experiences that prepared students for the trip	_____	_____
8. Advised students about clothing, grooming, money, and other personal needs	_____	_____
9. Explained rules of conduct for the trip to students	_____	_____
10. Provided information to assist students during the trip	_____	_____
11. Prepared a written request for parental consent	_____	_____
12. Made provisions for the special needs that students might have (e.g., accessibility consideration for visually impaired or physically handicapped students)	_____	_____
During the trip, the teacher		
1. Checked attendance against the trip roster	_____	_____
2. Was available when students needed information or assistance	_____	_____
3. Directed student attention to the objective(s) of the trip	_____	_____
4. Expressed and/or helped students express thanks to all those who made the trip possible	_____	_____
After the trip, the teacher		
1. Helped students summarize what they learned during the trip	_____	_____
2. Helped students evaluate the trip in terms of their progress toward the objectives	_____	_____
3. Provided follow-up activities to clarify, reinforce, or extend what students learned during the trip	_____	_____

Source: The National Center for Research in Vocational Education. (1977b). *Direct Field Trips*. Columbus, OH: The Ohio State University.

Figure 8-15. Tips for facilitating a successful field trip for learners.

A form may be provided for learners to use to collect and record information during shadowing experiences. This information can later be shared with the entire class. In this manner, career development can be facilitated for all learners in the program. Instructors can use this instructional strategy to develop leadership skills and evoke a sense of responsibility in learners from special populations by including them in the various stages of planning field trips, job site vitiations, and shadowing experiences. They can be given responsibility for contacting the business or industry, making arrangements with the employer and/or coworkers, planning for appropriate transportation services, obtaining permission from school officials, and taking responsibility for preparing class reports, group discussions, and follow-up activities.

Student-Teacher Contracts

Student-teacher contracts developed between learners from special populations and career and technical education instructors can be an effective method in assisting learners to succeed in meeting program requirements. See Figure 8-16. The contract should be honest, fair, and positive. The terms of the contract should be developed cooperatively. It should contain terms and conditions that are clearly understood by all parties involved. The contract payoff or reward should be identified as well as the consequences to be accepted by the learner if contract terms are not met. The following are guidelines for developing and implementing student-teacher contracts:

- Decide on the task or project.
- Specifically state the requirements.
- Determine the minimum acceptable accuracy.
- Set a time limit. Initially, short assignments and short time periods are best.
- Identify consequences. Both positive and negative consequences should be mutually agreed upon. Suggestions for positive rewards should be provided by the learner to ensure motivation.
- Discuss the contract in detail with the learner and, if appropriate, with support personnel and/or parents.
- Have all parties sign the contract.
- Have the learner work toward completion of the requirements in the contract.
- Provide directed teaching and positive reinforcement.
- Provide positive reinforcement to the learner if the terms of the contract are satisfactorily met.
- Analyze uncompleted student-teacher contracts to determine the barriers and problem areas.
- Develop new contracts cooperatively with the learner and support personnel.

STUDENT-TEACHER CONTRACT

Date _____ Career and Technical Program _____

Student _____ Career and Technical Education Instructor _____

Support Personnel (if appropriate) _____

Description of Task	Criteria for Competition	Instructor Initials When Completed

I _____ agree to complete the task(s) identified above. I will complete the task(s) by _____
(student name)   (date)

and understand that the established criteria for the task(s) must be met. After I have successfully completed this task, I may

_____.
(reward)

_____	_____
Student Signature	Date
_____	_____
Career and Technical Education Instructor Signature	Date
_____	_____
Support Personnel Signature(s)	Date

Figure 8-16. A sample student-teacher contract that can be used to individualize instruction.

The basis of a performance contract is an agreement of tasks to be completed. These tasks should be clearly understood and listed so that the learner and the instructor can keep track of progress. As each task or assignment is satisfactorily completed, the instructor dates the performance contract. This serves as a progress report as well as an immediate reinforcement for the learner. Performance contracts include the learner in the planning process and place the responsibility of completing program requirements on the learner. The learning then becomes self-managed and individually paced. See Figure 8-17.

Career and technical education instructors should address the following concerns to effectively evaluate student-teacher contracts:

- Does the learner with special needs understand the contracting process?
- Do the support personnel working with the learner understand the contracting process?
- Was the assigned task realistic for the learner?
- Was the specified time period appropriate in relationship to the learner's abilities and limitations?
- Did the learner enter into the contract voluntarily?
- Did the learner begin the contract within a reasonable amount of time?
- Did the learner organize essential materials, supplies, tools, and equipment in a way that makes the best use of time?
- Did the learner organize overall project time wisely?
- Did the instructor provide positive reinforcement when the learner was working to complete the contract requirements?
- Were the requirements for successful completion of the contract reasonable?

PERFORMANCE CONTRACT

Student _____ Date _____
Program _____
Instructor _____
Unit/Module _____
Approximate Time for Completion _____

Task/Assignment	Criteria	Date Completed	Comments
1. Install 110V light controlled by a special switch			
2. Install two 110V lights in parallel			
3. Install 110V lights and duplex receptacle in parallel with light controlled by special switch			
4. Install one 110V light controlled by two 3-way switches			
5. Install one 110V light controlled by two 3-way switches and one 4-way switch			
6. Install one 110V light controlled by two 3-way and two 4-way switches			
7. Install a circuit with four receptacles and one special switch so it controls one receptacle while others remain hot			
8. Install a light dimming system			

Remarks: (Include pertinent comments and suggestions about special needs from the student and support personnel.)

_____ Date — Student Signature
_____ Date — Instructor Signature
_____ Date — Support Teacher Signature

Results of Performance Contract: _____

Figure 8-17. A sample performance contract used to monitor a learner's progress.

- Was the reward something that motivated the learner to work toward successful completion of the contract?
- Would a system of self-checks have been beneficial to the learner (e.g., self-correcting exercises or programmed instructional materials)?

Peer and Cross-Age Tutoring

Peer and cross-age tutoring is a system of instruction in which one learner helps another to learn the curriculum for a specific course. Tutors can be very effective in working with learners from special populations. This method of instruction can be beneficial in a number of ways. The learner with special needs is given an opportunity to develop interpersonal relations with others. It also relieves the career and technical education instructor from spending the majority of class time with only one or two learners. Tutoring enables learners progressing slower than others to develop the proficiencies needed for success in the program. Tutors can assist the instructor in the following ways:

- teach/reteach content
- assist with remedial academics
- perform presentations and demonstrations
- assist with one-to-one or small group activities in the laboratory
- aid on completing assignments and projects
- help review for tests
- administer and evaluate tests

Some advantages of initiating tutoring situations for learners from special populations include the following:

- The learner remains in the career and technical education program and also receives assistance.
- The tutor acts as a good peer model for the learner.
- Tutors can help the learner develop interpersonal skills.
- Tutors can help the learner to increase self-concept and motivation levels.
- Tutors allow the career and technical education instructor to work with others in the class.

Tutors can be recruited from a variety of sources. The following are examples of the types of volunteer tutors available to career and technical education instructors:

1. Instructors–Tutoring can be done by the career and technical education instructor, career and technical education support staff, academic teachers, or others within the educational facility. Tutoring can be done on a one-to-one basis or in small groups, depending on the number of individuals with special needs who require assistance.
2. Peers–Tutoring done by peers employs what is commonly referred to as the buddy system. This method pairs a learner with special needs with another learner in the class. In many cases, both the peer tutor and the learner improve through reinforcement of program content. The peer tutor feels competent and useful by being selected to tutor. The learner with special needs can progress at an individualized pace without pressure from others in the class.

Peer tutors can be recruited from learners in the same class, learners enrolled in advanced courses, and learner volunteers interested in pursuing a career in teaching (e.g., members of the Future Teachers of America). Extra credit can be offered as an incentive. Schedules will have to be arranged cooperatively with learners and other teachers. Peer tutoring relationships frequently foster enthusiasm, motivation, confidence, increased attendance, improved performance, and positive attitudes toward school.

Different learners should be involved in the tutoring process so that the learner with special needs is not always the one being tutored. The instructor should assess the competencies of all learners in the class and utilize their abilities to the greatest degree possible. Learners with special needs also have strengths that can be used to assist other learners. Pairing of learners must be given careful consideration so that appropriate behaviors will result from the tutoring process.

Ervin (1980) identified the following qualities and characteristics necessary for learners selected to be tutors. Tutors must

- make a commitment to help learners that are different from them;
- have skills and knowledge in the career and technical education area they will be tutoring in;
- be mature and emotionally stable;
- have leadership ability;
- understand the necessity and repetitions of operations and procedures;
- be able to make decisions when necessary;
- be able to plan and evaluate work done by learners;
- be able to determine if quality and quantity of work is acceptable;
- be able to communicate with and relate to others;
- be able to give constructive criticism that will motivate other learners to do better;
- be able to rectify problems that may arise; and
- be able to handle emergencies.

Steps that are very important to the success of a peer tutoring situation include carefully selecting the peer volunteer, assuring that confidentiality of information will be respected, preparing the tutor with the necessary skills through an appropriate training session, matching the tutor with the learner with special needs, supervising the tutor-learner situation, providing communication and support to the tutor, and evaluating the effectiveness of the learning arrangement.

3. Senior citizens–This valuable resource should not be overlooked. Retirees have many years of occupational experience from which to draw. They have a need to feel useful and contributive. They can share their experience and expertise with learners from special populations. In return, they receive a sense of dignity and

respect, a chance for social interaction, and a sense of commitment to share their knowledge with others. In addition to tutoring learners in skills development and remedial academics, they can offer career guidance and job-seeking information. Retirees have an understanding of the requirements, performance skills, and social skills necessary for employment in specific career areas. They may also have contacts in the community who would be willing to mentor and/or hire learners.

4. College students–If these individuals are in teacher preparation programs, they may wish to work with learners and gain some practical teaching experience.

5. Workers in the community–These individuals can provide tutoring services as well as relevant career development information and mentoring. The schedules of the learner must be modified in some cases to meet the schedules of the tutors.

6. Parents–The career and technical education instructor can enlist the services of parents regarding program objectives and specific services they can provide through tutoring.

There are a number of considerations that should be addressed when developing a tutor assistance program. These considerations include

- developing program policies and philosophy;
- selecting tutors;
- providing orientation and training for tutors;
- purchasing and ordering materials;
- developing instructional materials;
- planning facilities;
- developing forms;
- establishing and maintaining student files;
- providing public relations and recruitment information for tutors and learners who will receive tutoring;
- coordinating faculty participation; and
- evaluating the tutoring assistance program.

The role of a tutor should be clearly defined. Orientation and training sessions should provide the following information to tutors:

- philosophy and goals of the tutoring program
- criteria for selecting tutors
- criteria for selecting learners who will receive tutoring
- how the program will operate (hours involved—before school, during school hours, after school)
- who will supervise tutoring sessions
- forms to be filled out by tutors
- incentives for tutors (e.g., money, academic credit, recognition, awards provided by parent organization, industry, school)
- dates for program related activities
- who will supervise tutors
- tips for tutoring
- methods of providing feedback to learners
- methods for motivating learners
- revising instructional materials
- information about learning styles

- information about teaching study skills
- materials needed by tutors (e.g., course outlines, syllabi, sample tests, textbooks, workbooks, manuals used in career and technical education programs)
- the concept that it is alright to ask for assistance
- awareness that the tutoring program is designed to help strengthen the academic abilities of the learner rather than to emphasize limitations
- sample schedules showing the amount of time commitment involved in the tutoring process
- a video showing an actual tutoring session
- sample forms that must be completed by learners who participate in the tutoring program
- methods of evaluating learners who will receive tutoring services

An evaluation form may be provided to be completed by the learner who has received tutoring. This form should provide valuable feedback about the tutoring experience.

Asselin (1986) stated that career and technical education instructors who are going to use tutors in their classrooms and laboratories need to recognize the roles and responsibilities of tutors as well as the benefits of using tutors to assist learners with special needs. A familiarity with the specific skills and abilities the tutors will possess after their training program is helpful. With information about the benefits, roles, and skills of tutors, both the teacher and tutor hold similar expectations. This permits the teacher to maximize the skills of the tutor as progress is monitored and evaluated. Teachers should have a role in the development of criteria for selecting tutors and matching them with learners who need assistance.

Flexible Grouping Strategies

Flexible grouping can be an effective way for career and technical education instructors to individualize classroom instruction and laboratory activities for learners from special populations. This method consists of organizing learners into various-sized groups according to the objective of the lesson or the nature of the activity. Matthews (1992) stressed that if we group learners heterogeneously at all times, the only one providing assistance will probably be the highest-achieving learner. Flexible grouping gives the low achievers the opportunity to realize the positive effects of being the explainer, and provides all learners with opportunities to get to know and work with a wide range of learners.

Flexible grouping allows the instructor to arrange classroom and laboratory experiences so that learners with special needs are integrated and participate with their peers. It can also be used as a strategy to provide remedial assistance by forming small groups of learners in need of academic, technical, or socialization assistance.

Instructors using this technique form different types of grouping arrangements in different situations so that all learners in the class learn to work together in a variety of situations. Learners can be grouped according to interests and experiences. They can be grouped according to progress made on a particular activity. They can also be organized arbitrarily according to number.

Flexible grouping has several advantages for both the instructor and the learner, such as the following:

- It allows the instructor more time to work among learners in the class rather than having to spend a great deal of time with one or two learners.
- It allows the instructor to individualize instruction, tasks, and assignments to meet the needs of learners in a specific group.
- It provides learners from special populations with an opportunity to work with peers and to establish positive interpersonal and working relationships with them.
- It serves as a motivating factor for learners with special needs because the individualized nature of group work does not threaten or frustrate them and allows them to work at their own pace through their strongest learning style.
- It allows another effective instructional technique, peer tutoring, to develop between learners from special populations and their peers.
- It allows instructors to arrange for instruction for the entire class, small group discussions, project groups, and small remedial sessions so that instruction will be diversified and more meaningful for all learners enrolled in the career and technical education program.
- It allows the instructor to meet the learning needs of specific learners in a small group through the use of media, supplementary services, and instructional resources.
- It allows the instructor to modify the task or assignment for a small group of learners with specific needs.

Acceleration Strategies

Getting the best performance from every learner is a challenging task, especially in classrooms where they are many different levels of ability. Often, learners who are gifted are not challenged to perform to their full capacity because they seem to be doing just fine. Unfortunately, these learners may never achieve their potential because they have not had complex tasks and have never learned to really work.

It is little wonder that academically advanced learners often report feeling bored and unchallenged. Instead of completing work quickly that they know they have already mastered, they sometimes become disenchanted, mentally drop out, and fail to finish even the simplest of assignments. Five to 15% of secondary learners could benefit from some form of curricular acceleration.

Developing curriculum that is sufficiently rigorous, challenging, and coherent for learners who are gifted is a challenging task. Strategies for differentiating the curriculum include the following:

- Activities must be restructured to be more intellectually demanding. For example, learners need to be challenged by questions that require a higher level of response or by open-ended questions that stimulate inquiry, active exploration, and discovery. Although instructional strategies depend on the age of the learners and the nature of the disciplines involved, the goal is always to encourage learners to think about subjects in more abstract and complex ways. Activities should be used in ways that encourage self-directed learning.
- Gifted learners learn best in a receptive, nonjudgmental, learner-centered environment that encourages inquiry and independence, includes a wide variety of materials, provides some physical movements, is generally complex, and connects the school experience with the greater world. Although all learners might appreciate such an environment, for learners who are gifted it is essential that the teacher establishes a climate that encourages them to question, exercise independence, and use their creativity.

Curriculum compacting is one of the most common forms of curriculum modification for academically advanced learners. It is also the basic procedure upon which many other types of modification are founded. Compacting is based on the premise that learners who demonstrate that they have mastered course content, or can master course content more quickly, can be given time to study material that they find more challenging and interesting.

The following are eight basic steps to curriculum compacting:

1. Determine the learning objectives for the material.
2. Find appropriate ways to assess those objectives.
3. Identify learners who may have already mastered the objectives (or could master them more quickly).
4. Assess those learners to determine their mastery level.
5. Streamline practice or instruction for learners who demonstrate mastery of the objectives.
6. Provide small group or individual instruction for learners who have not yet mastered all of the objectives but are capable of doing so more quickly than their classmates.
7. Offer more challenging academic alternatives based on learner interest.
8. Maintain a record of the compacting process and the instructional options provided.

The following guidelines are useful for curricular areas where learners move between an instructional group and extension or accelerated activities:

- At the beginning of a unit, provide opportunities for interested learners to demonstrate mastery in some way.
- Learners who achieve a specified competency level or grade attend class only on the days when instruction includes concepts they have not mastered. On those occasions, they become part of the regular class and participate in assigned activities.
- For each learner who achieves a specified competency level on the pre-assessment activity, prepare a contract listing required concepts, enrichment options, and specified guidelines. Check only the topics learners have not mastered so they know when to join the larger group.

Case Study . . . Miguel

Miguel is enrolled in the Health Science Technology Education (HSTE) program at the Centerville Community College, an area postsecondary institution. He has always wanted to be a pediatric nurse. His academic record has not been a total success due to the fact that Miguel has visual perception problems that have created a barrier to his learning. From test scores, personal comments, and instructor observation, it appears that Miguel is an auditory learner. When questioned in class and during clinical activities, he seems to have no problem understanding the material. However, this understanding does not come through on his written tests. During the last midterm evaluation, he gave many obvious clues to his problem. Miguel feels that he remembers material best when he repeats it to himself or to a peer. Also, he seems to understand more after hearing a lecture than after reading the material.

Miguel has learned to cope fairly well. He did well in high school primarily because many of his instructors taught using the lecture technique, but at Centerville Community College, he saw getting the individualized instruction he needed as an obstacle that he could not overcome. The program involved a great deal of technical reading. Miguel is a quiet man and is hesitant to approach the instructor with his problems. This shyness, along with his reading comprehension problems, has caused his test scores to drop. However, Miguel's interpersonal skills are well developed. He relates well to his peers and his patients and is very personable.

Appropriate instructional strategies have been selected to meet his needs, helping him to change his performance in the HSTE program. The first strategy was to give him more time to review material that he did not understand during the first and second quarters. Review sessions consisted of discussing the material with the instructor, watching audiovisuals, and listening to tapes. After the review, Miguel completed a test on each unit. Additional strategies that were successful included taping all lectures, including more audiovisuals, and involving him in more hands-on learning activities in the clinical portion of the program. The exit criteria for the program were not changed, but adaptations in the way the material was presented helped Miguel to succeed.

Using the information provided about Miguel, complete the following activity. Select a unit that is taught in your career and technical education program. Identify a lesson that would be taught within that unit. Complete the individualized instruction planning form to teach this lesson to Miguel.

INDIVIDUALIZED INSTRUCTION PLANNING FORM

Career and Technical Education Program: _____

Unit Title: _____

Lesson Title: _____

INTRODUCING THE LESSON

Lesson objective(s):

Introduction strategies (i.e., How would you introduce this lesson to the entire class?) List strategies or steps in order:

Special consideration(s) in introducing the lesson to Miguel:

Anticipated problem(s)   Suggested strateg(ies)

TEACHING THE LESSON

Steps in presenting the lesson to the entire class   Special considerations for Miguel

Specific steps in order: (e.g., additional assistance needed)

EVALUATION TECHNIQUES

Methods of evaluating learner progress on lesson objectives: Evaluation techniques for Miguel

Cooperative Learning

Cooperative learning is a term applied to any type of instructional strategy in which learners work in teams to accomplish instructional objectives while maintaining individual accountability and group responsibility. It involves grouping learners of different backgrounds, academic achievement levels, and social skills together.

> There is a crucial difference between putting students into groups to learn and in structuring cooperative interdependence among students. Cooperation is NOT having students sit side-by-side at the same table to talk with each other as they do their individual assignments. Cooperation is NOT having students do a task with instructions that those who finish first are to help the slower students. Cooperation is NOT assigning a report to a group of students wherein one student does all the work and the others put their names on the product as well. Cooperation is much more than being physically near other students, discussing material with other students, although each of these is important in cooperative learning. (Johnson, et al., 1984, p. 8)

There are four elements that need to be included for small group learning to be cooperative: positive interdependence, individual accountability, collaborative skills, and group processing. The following describes each of the elements:

1. Positive interdependence–Learners must feel that they need each other in order to complete the group's task, that they sink or swim together. Some ways to create this feeling are (a) establishing mutual goals (learners must learn the material and make certain group members learn the material); (b) joint rewards (if all group members achieve a certain percentage on the test, each will receive bonus points.); (c) shared materials and information (one paper for each group or each member receives only part of the information needed to do the assignment); and (d) assigned roles (summarizer, encourager of participation, elaborator). No magic exists in positive interdependence in and of itself. Beneficial education outcomes are due to the interaction patterns and verbal exchanges that take place among learners in carefully structured cooperative learning groups. Oral summarizing, giving and receiving explanations, and elaborating (relating what is being learned to previous learning) are types of verbal interchanges.

2. Individual accountability–Cooperative learning groups are not successful until every member has learned the material or has helped with and understood the assignment. Thus, it is important to frequently stress and assess individual learning so that group members can appropriately support and help each other. Some ways of structuring individual accountability include giving each group member an individual exam and randomly selecting one member to give an answer for the entire group.

3. Collaborative skills–Not all learners come to school with the social skills they need to collaborate effectively with others. Cooperative learning activities provide learners with opportunities to develop the communication skills, leadership, trust, decision-making, and conflict management skills that allow groups to function effectively.

4. Group processing–Processing means giving learners the time and procedures to analyze how well their groups are functioning and how well they are using necessary skills. This processing helps all group members achieve while maintaining effective working relationships among members. Feedback from the teacher and/or student observers may help the group to improve their group processing effectiveness.

Cameron (1991) summarized different domains of cooperative learning as identified by Kagan. See Appendix. The following domains describe competencies that learners who participate in cooperative learning will develop:

1. Team building
 * expressing ideas and opinions
 * participating equally
2. Class building
 * meeting classmates/getting acquainted
 * identifying alternative hypotheses
 * clarifying values
 * Identifying problem-solving approaches
3. Communication building
 * knowing and respecting different points of view
 * developing vocabulary
4. Communication mastery
 * role taking
 * reviewing
 * checking for knowledge
 * comprehending
 * memorizing facts
 * practicing skills
 * tutoring
 * helping others
5. Concept development
 * praising
 * sharing personal information and developing reactions
 * forming conclusions
 * generating and revising
 * reasoning inductively
 * reasoning deductively
 * applying concepts
 * analyzing concepts
 * understanding multiple relationships
 * differentiating concepts
6. Multifunctional skills
 * applying combination of these examples (p. 136).

The following are benefits of small-group learning:

* Celebration of diversity–Learners learn to work with all types of people. During small-group interactions, they find many opportunities to reflect upon and reply to the

diverse responses fellow learners bring to the questions raised. Small groups also allow learners to add unique cultural perspectives to an issue. This exchange inevitably helps learners to better understand other cultures and points of view.

- Acknowledgement of individual differences–When questions are raised, different learners will have a variety of responses. Each of these can help the group create a product that reflects a wide range of perspectives and is thus more complete and comprehensive.
- Interpersonal development–Learners learn to relate to their peers and other learners as they work together in group enterprises. This can be especially helpful for learners who have difficulty with social skills. They can benefit from structured interactions with others.
- Actively involving learners in learning–Each member has opportunities to contribute in small groups. Learners are apt to take more ownership of their material and to think critically about related issues when they work as a team.
- More opportunities for personal feedback–Because there are more exchanges among members in small groups, learners receive more personal feedback about their ideas and responses. This feedback is often not possible in large-group instruction, in which one or two learners exchange ideas and the rest of the members listen.

In small groups, learners can share strengths and also develop their weaker skills. They develop their interpersonal skills and learn to deal with conflict. When cooperative groups are guided by clear objectives, learners engage in numerous activities that improve their understanding of subjects explored.

In cooperative learning, small groups provide a place where

- learners actively participate;
- teachers become learners at times, and learners sometimes teach;
- respect is given to every member;
- projects and questions interest and challenge learners;
- diversity is celebrated, and all contributions are valued;
- learners learn skills for resolving conflicts when they arise;
- members draw upon their past experience and knowledge;
- goals are clearly identified and used as a guide; and
- learners are invested in their own learning.

In order to create an environment in which cooperative learning can take place, three things are necessary. First, learners need to feel safe but also challenged. Second, groups need to be small enough that everyone can contribute. Third, the task learners work together on must be clearly defined.

There is always a danger that some learners will hitchhike, although those determined to get a free ride will usually find a way whether the assignments are done individually or in groups. In fact, cooperative learning that includes provisions to assure individual accountability—such as individual tests on the group assignment material—cuts down on hitchhiking. Learners who don't actually participate will generally fail the test, especially if the tests truly reflect the skills involved in the

assignments. If group work only counts for small fraction of the overall course grade (say, 20%), hitchhikers can get high marks on the group work and still fail the course.

One way to detect and discourage hitchhiking is to have team members individually or collectively distribute the total points for an assignment among themselves in proportion to the effort each one puts in. Learners want to be nice to one another and so may agree to put names on assignments of teammates who barely participated, but are less likely to credit them with high levels of participation. Another technique is to call randomly on individual team members to present sections of project reports or partial solutions to problems, with everyone in the group getting a grade based on the selected learner's response. The best learners will then make it their business to see that their teammates all understand the complete solutions, and they will also be less inclined to put a hitchhiker's name on the written product and risk having that learner be the designated presenter.

Persuading learners that group work is in their interest is only the first step in making this instructional approach work effectively. The instructor must also structure group exercises to promote positive interdependence among team members, assure individual accountability for all work done, facilitate development of teamwork skills, and provide for periodic self-assessment of group functioning.

Instructors may also give teams the last-resort option of firing uncooperative members after giving them at least two warnings, and instructors may give individuals carrying most of the workload the option of joining another group after giving their uncooperative teammates at least two warnings. Teams almost invariably find ways of working things out themselves before these options have to be exercised.

Johnson, et al. (1984) described the following steps that should be taken to implement cooperative learning activities in a classroom:

1. Specifying instructional objectives–At the beginning of the lesson, the instructor should specify the academic objective that relates directly to the curriculum and the collaborative skills objective that details what collaboration skills will be emphasized.
2. Determining the size of the cooperative learning groups–Group size ranges from two to six members. Cooperative learning groups need to be small enough for everyone to be involved in mutual discussion while achieving the group's goal. Factors that influence the size of a group include:

- as the size of the group increases, the range of abilities, expertise, skills, and number of minds available for acquiring and processing information increase;
- the more individuals in a group, the greater the chance to have someone who has special knowledge helpful to the assignment and the more talent is available to complete the task;
- the larger the group, the more skillful members must be in coordinating the actions of group members so that everyone participates;

- the number of materials available for groups to use may influence the size of the groups;
- the shorter the period of time available, the smaller the learning groups should be;
- beginning instructors may want to start with pairs or groups of three for easier management; and
- groups of six may be the limit for cooperative learning so that no student is left out of the process.

3. Assigning students to groups–There are a variety of methods to use in assigning groups. Self-selected groups don't often work because students who are high achievers tend to choose others like themselves. Teacher-assigned groups often have the best mix since instructors can put together optimal combinations of students.

   Groups should stay together long enough to accomplish the group goal. Groups should change often enough that they do not become too comfortable and predictable. There is merit in having learners work with everyone in their class during a semester or year.

4. Arranging the room—The room should be organized so that group members can effectively work together. Eye contact is very important in a group situation. Thus, an arrangement in a circle is very effective. Group members should be seated close together for maximum collaboration. Materials to be utilized for the cooperative learning assignment should be visible and accessible to all groups. Groups should be far enough apart so as not to disturb one another.

5. Structuring instructional materials–Depending on the level of collaboration skills of the groups, instructional materials needed to reach the group goal should be structured. Groups that have little experience in working together may receive one copy of the materials so that they are in a "sink or swim" situation and have to collaborate. Group members may each be given one of the materials necessary to complete the task so that they have to share.

6. Assigning roles to group members–Assigning each group member a specific role is helpful so that the group can function as a whole. Suggestions of roles include:

- Facilitator–makes certain that everyone gets what they need to complete the task within the group;
- Checker–makes sure everyone has finished with their portion of the work to reach the group goal;
- Observer–watches to keep track of how well the group is functioning;
- Encourager–reinforces the contributions that individual group members make;
- Recorder–writes down the group's decisions and edits the group report;
- Summarizer–stops the group at intervals to summarize progress and make certain that all members understand what has been accomplished and how it has been done;
- Runner–makes certain that the group has all materials needed to complete the group goal; and
- Reporter–tells what the group found out or produced during the large group wrap-up.

7. Structuring positive goal interdependence–The instructor should communicate with group members that they have to work together and count on each other in order to accomplish the goal. Group members are responsible for learning the assigned material, making sure that all other group members learn the assigned material, and making sure that all other group members successfully complete the assignments. This can be done by asking the group to produce a single product or report and providing group rewards.

8. Structuring individual accountability–Instructors need to frequently assess the level of performance of individual group members. This can be accomplished by giving practice quizzes, randomly selecting members to explain answers, having learners edit each other's work, or randomly selecting one paper from the group to grade.

9. Structuring intergroup cooperation–Cooperation among groups can be facilitated by offering the class a bonus if all members in the class reach a preset criterion of excellence on a task or assignment.

10. Explaining criteria for success–At the beginning of the lesson the instructor should carefully explain the criteria by which the completed assignments will be evaluated. The criteria should be structured so that each group can reach it without penalizing another group.

11. Identifying desired behaviors–Instructors should specifically define the concept of cooperation. Examples of expected behaviors to occur during the cooperative learning activity include listening, encouraging others, asking questions, critiquing ideas, and reaching consensus.

12. Monitoring student behaviors–The instructor's role in cooperative learning is to observe groups as they work. A formal observation sheet can be very helpful in accomplishing this. Assigned observers can also participate in this task. Observation should help to identify skills that groups are developing in the collaboration process as well as the problems they are having in completing the assignment and in working together. These observations should be brought out during the large group wrap-up.

13. Providing task assistance–Instructors should help to clarify instructions, review important procedures and strategies for completing the assignment, answer questions, and teach task skills as necessary.

14. Intervening to teach collaborative skills–Instructors may decide to intervene after observing students or groups that do not have the necessary skills to collaborate effectively. Suggestions can be made regarding effective teaming skills that might help the group to move forward. The best time to teach collaboration skills is when they are needed. Intervention can also take place to reinforce particularly effective and skillful behaviors as they are noticed.

15. Providing closure to the lesson–Students should be able to summarize what they have learned and to understand where they will use it in future lessons. Instructors may wish to summarize the major points in the lesson, ask learners to recall ideas or give samples, and answer any final questions the class may have.

16. Evaluating the quality and quantity of student learning–Aside from the product developed by the group, the learning needs of the students in the class should be assessed using a criteria-referenced system.

17. Assessing how well the group functioned–Periodically the instructor should facilitate an assessment of how well the group functioned with the group members. If no processing is done, teachers may find the group's functioning level decreasing, and important relationships left undiscussed. Processing the functioning of the needs of the group needs to be taken as seriously as accomplishing the task. Group processing should focus both on the contributions of the members to each other's learning and to the maintenance of effective working relationships among group members. (pp. 26-40)

When developing cooperative learning projects, a number of assignments can be designed for use with groups of learners who work toward a common goal. This can result in a variety of products including

- videotapes;
- slide presentations;
- oral presentations;
- audio cassette reports;
- maps, graphs, and charts;
- overhead projections;
- posters and drawings;
- simulations and role-playing situations;
- polls, surveys, and questionnaires;
- games;
- debates and panel discussions;
- bulletin board displays;
- interviews;
- projects;
- dioramas and scale models;
- collages; and
- displays.

An instructor's planning guide for cooperative learning activities is an effective planning tool. See Figure 8-18.

Cooperative learning may occur in or out of class. In-class exercises, which may take anywhere from 30 seconds to an entire class period, may involve answering or generating questions, explaining observations, working through derivations, solving problems, summarizing lecture material, troubleshooting, and brainstorming. Out-of-class activities include carrying out experiments or research studies, completing problem sets or design projects, writing reports, and preparing class presentations.

INSTRUCTOR'S PLANNING GUIDE FOR COOPERATIVE LEARNING ACTIVITIES

OBJECTIVES:

Academic: Students will discuss the origin of organized labor

Collaborative: Students will help the group and other team members

Task: Students will research information about the American labor movement

Group size: 4

How much time will the group have? Group will meet in class for three days and present report in one week (e.g., Monday, Thursday, Friday—Report Monday)

Room arrangement: Desks arranged in groups of four. On the day of presentation, standard classroom arrangement with podium in front of class

Roles	Name	Assignment
Leader	_____	Will decide topics of individuals' assignment. Will lead planning meetings, make assignments
Recorder	_____	Will keep attendance of meetings and write report with input. Will keep record of decisions, meetings
Presenter	_____	Will aid recorder in writing report. Will present report to the class
Encourager	_____	Will make certain all members participate. Will be in contact with teacher if problem arises

Group Goal: Present a report to the class on the history of the labor movement in America

Team Evaluation Criteria: Team will be evaluated by how completely the report meets group goals

Adapted from: Huck, R., Myers, R., & Wilson, J. (1989). *ADAPT – A Developmental Activity Program for Teachers* (2nd ed.). Pittsburgh, PA: Allegheny Intermediate Unit.

Figure 8-18. A sample planning guide for an instructor using cooperative learning activities.

Several examples of specific cooperative learning activities include the following:

- KWLH technique–The KWLH teaching technique is a good method to help learners activate prior knowledge. It is a group instruction activity that serves as a model for active thinking. K stands for helping learners recall what they *know* about the subject. W stands for helping learners determine what they *want* to learn. L stands for helping learners identify what they *learn* as they participate in the class. H stands for *how* learners can learn more (other sources where additional information on the topic can be found). See Figure 8-19.

THE KWLH TECHNIQUE			
K (Know)	W (Want to learn)	L (Learn)	H (How to find more)

Figure 8-19. A table for planning material with the KWLH technique.

- Think-pair-share–This is another cooperative learning technique that helps learners give meaning to the information they receive. First, learners listen while the teacher poses a question. Next, learners are given time to think of (or write) a response. Then, learners turn to a partner and discuss their responses. Finally, learners share their responses with the class.
- Pairs to squares–Learners discuss problems, write answers to questions, and work on problems in pairs. Pairs turn to another pair (forming a square) to check their answers. If the two sets of answers are not the same, the square must discuss until one answer is agreed on.
- Bookends–In this learning activity, learners focus on the teacher. The teacher gives information to the class for 15 minutes or less. Next, learners discuss the information in pairs. Then, the teacher gives learners additional information for 15 minutes or less. Learners discuss the new information. Finally, the teacher assigns a task to the class. Following are the procedures for using this tool:
  1. Before the lesson, the teacher uses direct questioning to determine what learners know about the content from prior instruction and personal experience. The teacher may guide the learners to categorize the information they have generated. This is an opportunity to correct misconceptions learners may have about the information to be studied. This technique may also be used to build interest in the topic.
  2. Next, the learners think about they want to learn. They fill in questions they have about what they are about to study. Teachers may want to take the list from each group and combine them into a class list. The list should be displayed so that the class may refer to it throughout the lesson.
  3. After the lesson, the learners evaluate what they have learned. This is also an opportunity for the teacher to evaluate whether the lesson has answered learner questions and misconceptions.

- Jigsaw–The jigsaw technique is very simple to use. First, divide learners into five- or six-person jigsaw groups. The groups should be diverse in terms of gender, ethnicity, race, and ability. Next, appoint one learner from each group as the leader. Divide the unit or lesson into five or six segments. Assign each learner to a segment, making sure learners have direct access only to their own segment. Give learners time to review and learn their segments at least twice and become familiar with them. Next, form temporary expert groups by having one learner from each jigsaw group join other learners assigned to the same segment. Give learners in these expert groups time to discuss the main points of their segment and to rehearse the presentations they will make to each of their own jigsaw groups. Then, bring the learners back into their jigsaw groups. Ask learners to present their segments to the group. Encourage others in the group to ask questions for clarification. Float from group to group, observing the process. If any group is having trouble (e.g., a member is dominating or disruptive), make an appropriate intervention. Eventually, it's best for the group leader to handle this task. At the end of the session, give a quiz on the material so learners quickly come to realize the importance of these sessions. See Figure 8-20.
- Student team learning–Student team learning is a cooperative learning strategy that stimulates engagement in learning through small group activities involving learner cooperation and group competition. Although two types of team learning have been developed and tested in classrooms, the basic elements of each are the same.

  Teachers using the learner team method first present information to the entire classroom using traditional instructional methods such as lecture or audiovisual presentation. Learners are told that the information being presented is important because it serves as a basis for work they will do in teams. Learners are then placed in small teams of four to five. Each team is balanced in terms of race, ethnicity, or other variables characterizing the learner population. In their teams, learners work on materials provided by the teacher, discussing problems, comparing answers, and correcting mistakes made by individual members. Learners cooperate to help each other learn.

While the focus is on cooperation in the learning process, learners know that they as a team are competing against other teams engaged in the same types of activities. Their effectiveness as individual learners and as learners helping each other is determined in one of two ways. Quizzes may be given to each learner to determine how well they have learned the material, to determine an improvement score based on their individual perfor-

mance on past quizzes of a similar nature, and to derive a team score that represents the improvement made by the team as a whole. Alternatively, academic team tournaments may be held where learners from different teams compete with learners from other teams who are similar to them in past academic performance.

The following are some suggestions to make cooperative learning activities effective:

• Give assignments to teams of three or four learners. When learners work in pairs, one of them tends to dominate, there is usually no good mechanism for resolving disputes, and in teams of five or more it becomes difficult to keep everyone involved in the process. Collect one assignment per group.

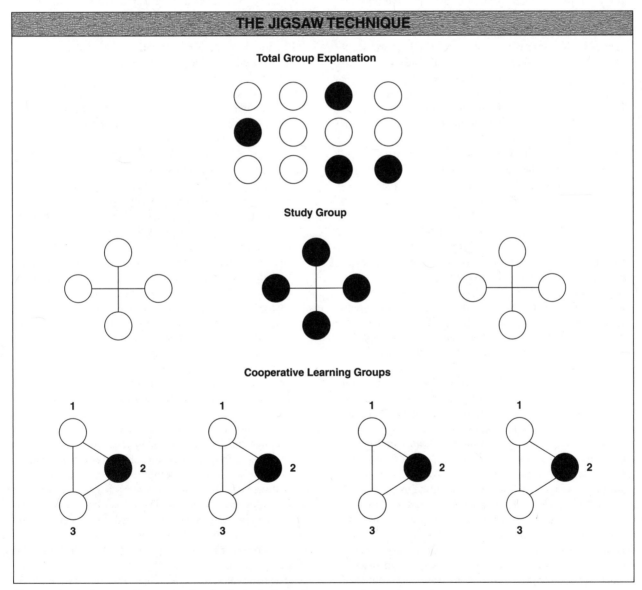

Figure 8-20. A diagram of learners using the jigsaw technique.

- Try to form groups that are heterogeneous in ability level. The drawbacks of a group with only weak learners are obvious, but having only strong learners in a group is equally undesirable. First, the strong groups have an unfair advantage over other groups in the class. Second, the team members tend to divide up the homework and communicate only with one another, omitting the dynamic interactions that lead to most of the proven benefits of cooperative learning. In mixed ability groups, on the other hand, the weaker learners gain from seeing how better learners study and approach problems, and the stronger learners gain a deeper understanding of the subject by teaching it to others.

- Assign team roles that rotate with each assignment. Example roles could be, for example, (1) the coordinator (organizes assignments into subtasks, allocates responsibilities, keeps group on task), (2) the checker (monitors both the solutions and every team member's comprehension of them), (3) the recorder (checks for consensus, writes the final group solution) and (4) the skeptic (plays devil's advocate, suggests alternative possibilities, keeps group from leaping to premature conclusions). Only the names of the learners who actually participated should appear on the final product, with their team roles for that assignment identified.

- Promote positive interdependence. All team members should feel that they have unique roles to play within the group and that the task can only be completed successfully if all members do their part. Strategies to achieve this objective include the following: (1) Require a single group product. (2) Assign rotating group roles. (3) Give each member different critical resources, as in the jigsaw technique. (4) Select one member of each group to explain (in an oral report or a written test) both the team's results and the methods used to achieve them, and give every team member the grade earned by that individual. Avoid selecting the strongest learners. (5) Give bonuses on tests to groups for which the lowest team grade or the average team grade exceeds a specified minimum.

- Promote individual accountability. The most common way to achieve this goal is to give primarily individual tests; another is the technique of selecting an individual team member to present or explain the team's results. Some instructors suggest having each team member rate everyone's effort as a percentage of the total team effort on an assignment and using the results to identify those who do not contribute (and possibly to adjust individual assignment grades). Others recommend against this procedure on the grounds that it moves the team away from cooperation and back toward competition.

- Have groups regularly assess their performance. Especially in early assignments, require learners to discuss what worked well, what difficulties arose, and what each member could do to make things work better the next time. The conclusions should be handed in with the final group report or solution set, a requirement that motivates the learners to take the exercise more seriously than they otherwise might.

- Provide assistance to teams having difficulty working together. Teams with problems should be invited or required to meet with the instructor to discuss solutions. The instructor should facilitate the discussion and may suggest alternatives but should not impose solutions.

- Allow teams to fire uncooperative team members if every other option has failed. Also allow individuals to quit if they are doing most or all of the work and team counseling has failed to yield improvements. Fired team members or members who quit must then find other teams willing to accept them.

- Don't reconstitute groups too often. A major goal of cooperative learning is to help learners expand their repertoire of problem-solving approaches, and a second goal is to help them develop collaborative skills—leadership, decision-making, communication, etc. These goals can only be achieved if learners have enough time to develop a group dynamic, encountering and overcoming difficulties in working together. Cooperative groups should remain together for at least a month for the dynamics to have a chance of developing (Felder and Brent, 1996).

The role of the instructor in implementing cooperative learning in classroom environments was described by Slavin (1990) by the following:

1. Selecting appropriate instructional goals and objectives–Objectives from the curriculum should be selected as well as objectives from the cooperative learning foundation such as team building or communication-skills building.

2. Selecting team members–A variety of factors should be taken into consideration when putting teams together, including verbal abilities, leadership skills, and interests. The size of a cooperative learning group will vary according to the teaming skills of group members, the number of resources necessary for the task, and the nature of the task.

3. Structuring the cooperative learning environment–Cooperative learning teams should be clustered so that all team members can see and utilize relevant instructional materials and collaborate with other team members.

4. Explaining the rules of cooperative learning to learners–The concepts of positive interdependence, face-to-face interaction, individual accountability, group processing, and social skills development must be carefully overviewed with learners before cooperative learning activities are conducted. The steps of the cooperative learning process should be reviewed. These steps include

- the goal of the activity or task;
- the process that the group will go through during the activity or task;
- the materials, tools, equipment that will be used during the activity or task;

- the criteria for evaluation of the product that the group produces as a result of the cooperative learning activity; and
- the reward for successful completion of the activity or task, according to identified criteria.

5. Developing and/or providing appropriate instructional materials–Materials necessary for successful completion of the cooperative learning activity must be accessible to all groups. Finding and using appropriate materials should not be a competitive situation among groups (e.g., there is only one set of materials and only one group will have a chance to use them). These materials may require that groups operate outside the confines of the classroom (e.g., laboratory, library, community, industrial site).

6. Monitoring group activities–The role of the instructor is to monitor cooperative learning activities as groups progress toward their goal. The process that the group experiences is as important as the product that the group produces. The instructor should become involved in group activities only when it is obvious that no further

progress can take place without intervention. Otherwise, groups should be left alone, even when disagreements occur or an impasse is imminent. When an intervention is necessary, the instructor should work with the group to point out the skills that should be used so that the team members can arrive at a decision as to what direction they will take next.

7. Observing performance levels of individual learners in cooperative learning groups–Instructors and group members should observe the individual contributions of each member of a cooperative learning group. This information will be important for the feedback phase of the cooperative learning process.

8. Evaluation of the progress of individual members of cooperative learning groups–Each learner should be evaluated individually on his or her contribution to the assigned activity. This is necessary in order to satisfy the condition of individual accountability that asserts that progress of each learner will be measured as the group progresses toward the identified criterion. See Figure 8-21.

EVALUATING LEARNER PERFORMANCE	
Answer a random oral quiz	Pick one person from the group to answer the question
Take a post-activity quiz	Have all learners take a quiz at the end of the lecture or activity Instead of grading the quizzes, have learners compare and discuss their work
Write a paper	Have all learners write an essay, letter, or memo to summarize the lesson
Sign on the line	Have learners sign the idea they contributed or the problem they solved
Explain to a neighbor	Select one half of the class to explain why an answer was correct or incorrect to the other half of the class
Get signatures from all	Have everyone in the group sign the statement: "I made my best contribution."
Hold a tournament	Teams that raise the quiz scores of all its members earn points
Use a group evaluator	Give one learner in the group a checklist with which to observe and give feedback on participation, idea sharing, and other social skills
Make a test	Have each group make a test on a topic Rotate groups
Give round-robin answers	Use a round-robin (also called forced response and wraparound) with different lead-ins to check skills
Share group products	Have each group present its product to the class All members have a role in their presentation
Explain the answers	After one student gives an answer, select another to explain why it is or is not correct
Coach a partner	Instruct groups that finish a task first to coach groups still working
Create individual applications	Have each learner brainstorm a way to apply or transfer a concept
Make log entries	At the end of each lesson, have learners complete the stem "I learned. . ." in their logs Randomly check their entries
Use a teacher-observer	Tell the class which participation skills will be observed Wander through class, make notes and give feedback
Make a team ad	Have students list the positive contributions of each team member on a team ad

Source: Bellanca, J., & Fogarty, F. (1991). *Blueprints for Thinking in the Cooperative Classroom.* Arlington Heights, IL: Skylight Training and Publishing.

Figure 8-21. Suggestions for evaluating learner performance through cooperative learning activities.

9. Evaluation of group products–The individual performance of each learner in a cooperative learning activity will collectively produce a team product. The philosophy of cooperative learning asserts that, in order for a team to successfully complete a cooperative learning assignment, each learner must demonstrate successful completion at a minimal level of competence (individual accountability) and the team must share knowledge with others (interdependence).

10. Identifying and utilizing a criterion-referenced evaluation system–Individual learners and team performance should both be based on a criterion-referenced standard. Each team should be afforded the opportunity to be successful at meeting this standard. Appropriate rewards should be provided for all teams that reach the standard.

11. Reinforcing group performance/products–Each group that meets the criterion-referenced standard should receive an appropriate reward. Group members should recognize that the collective efforts of all group members achieved the established goal. Each team member should recognize personal efforts in assisting and supporting other group members to achieve the group goal.

COMPUTERS AND TECHNOLOGY

Despite the popular inclination to equate computers and other high-tech electronic tools with the term *technology*, the definition includes two components: a product—the tool that embodies the technology—and a process—the information base of the technology. Both technological products and their systematic processes have a great deal to offer schools. The following are primary reasons for using technology in educational environments:

1. Graduates must be proficient at assessing, evaluating, and communicating information. Educational technologies can, by design, provoke students to raise searching questions, enter debates, formulate opinions, engage in problem solving and critical thinking, and test their views of reality. The communication process used by students involved in technology may require reading, thinking, and writing; creating charts, graphs, and other images; or the organization and production of information using spreadsheets and databases.

2. Students learn and develop at different rates. Technology can individualize instruction. Through computer networks called integrated learning systems, instructors can prescribe individual learning paths for students.

3. Technology can foster an increase in the quantity and quality of students' thinking and writing. One of the best documented successes with computers in education is in developing students' writing. Features of word processors seem to reduce the phobia often associated with writing.

4. Graduates must solve complex problems. Higher level process skills cannot be taught in the traditional sense. They cannot be transferred directly from the teacher to the learner. Students need to develop these skills for themselves, with appropriate guidance.

5. Technology can nurture artistic expression. Modern technology-based art forms (video production, digital photography, computer-based animation) have great appeal, encouraging artistic expression among our diverse student population.

6. Graduates must be globally aware and able to use resources outside the school. With few exceptions, students' domains of discovery during the school day are limited to the classroom and the school. Technological tools allow students to inexpensively and instantly reach the world.

7. Technology creates opportunities for students to do meaningful work. Students need to produce products that have value outside school, receive feedback on their work, and experience the rewards of exhibiting their work to others. Computers link students to the world outside of school and can become an instant link to parents, relatives, mentors, business, and industry.

8. All students need access to high-level and high-interest courses. Electronic media can bring experiences and information previously unimagined by students into the classroom. Laser discs and CD-ROMs put thousands of images and topics at students' fingertips. Distance education technologies can bring important learning experiences to learners.

9. Students must feel comfortable with the tools of the Information Age. Computers and other technologies are an increasingly important part of the world in which students live and will have to work.

10. Schools must increase their productivity and efficiency. Technology can supplement the instructor. Technologies can support students and assume many of the routine tasks done by teachers, thus elevating the role of the teacher. (Peck & Dorricott, 1994, pp. 12-13)

Computer technology is an important component of most current instructional programs. Meier (2000) provided some suggestions for more effectively using computer technology as an adjunct to learning. Computers serve learners best when they help create learning environments that are the following:

- Collaborative–All good learning is social. Peer teaching, according to a Stanford University study, far outperformed computer tutorials and every other form of instruction. By creating learning programs for teams of two or more people (rather than just for an individual), learners can tap into the power of dialogue and peer teaching, which has proven to enhance the quantity and quality of learning for everyone.
- Relaxed experimental–Playing around with something is the best way to start learning about it. Good learning programs should not try to over control the learning

process, but allow the learner time to play, to explore, and to experiment. Research has indicated that people learn better by experimenting, asking others for help, and following menu prompts than they do from highly-controlled computer-based tutorials, lecture-driven seminars, or videotaped presentations.

- Option-rich–The computer should never be thought of as the master teacher and the sole delivery system for learning, but just one component in a whole suite of resources. Instructors should create an option-rich learning environment, making the computer not a one-dish meal, but simply one item in a complete learning smorgasbord.
- Activity-based–People generally learn more from activities and real-world experiences than they learn from presentations (whether delivered by lecturers or computers).
- Problem-centered–Rather than using the computer as a know-it-all information source, have the computer pose problems for the learners to solve. Problem-posing rather than answer-giving gets learners totally involved and teaches them how to think, how to search for information, and how to turn information into actionable knowledge—valuable skills in today's world.
- Creative–Knowledge is not something learners absorb but is something learners create. Computers are used most wisely when they don't simply provide information but help learners create their own meaning, knowledge, and applications.

Instructors can successfully translate traditional text-based, lecture-recitation-seatwork instructional approaches to new electronic medium. Whole-group instruction can decrease as individual learners work at assignments at their own pace. The instructor becomes a facilitator in this environment rather than the primary person delivering content. Learner enthusiasm and attendance usually increase with the use of computer technology in the learning environment. In addition, learner attitude toward self and learning increase steadily. See Figure 8-22.

> Apple Classrooms of Tomorrow found that the role of technology in the advancement of instruction has a very positive effect. Personal computers, printers, laser disc players, VCRs, scanners, and general-purpose tool software like word processors provide a nurturing environment for students to collect information in multiple formats and then organize, visualize, link, and discover relationships among facts and events. Students can then use the same technologies to communicate their ideas to others, to argue and critique their beliefs, to persuade and teach others, and to add greater levels of understanding to their own growing knowledge. (Dwyer, 1994, p. 9)

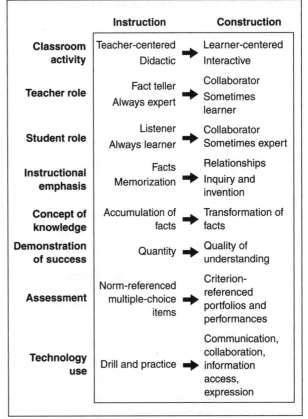

NEW LEARNER COMPETENCIES WHERE TECHNOLOGY IS INCORPORATED IN THE LEARNING PROCESS

	Instruction	Construction
Classroom activity	Teacher-centered Didactic	Learner-centered Interactive
Teacher role	Fact teller Always expert	Collaborator Sometimes learner
Student role	Listener Always learner	Collaborator Sometimes expert
Instructional emphasis	Facts Memorization	Relationships Inquiry and invention
Concept of knowledge	Accumulation of facts	Transformation of facts
Demonstration of success	Quantity	Quality of understanding
Assessment	Norm-referenced multiple-choice items	Criterion-referenced portfolios and performances
Technology use	Drill and practice	Communication, collaboration, information access, expression

Source: Dwyer, D. (1994). Apple Classrooms of Tomorrow: What We've Learned. *Educational Leadership, 51*(7), p. 9.

Figure 8-22. The shift in the instructional process and specific roles of learners and teachers in classrooms using technology.

Technology, combined with effective practices, can help learners with disabilities to be more productive in the learning environment. Examples of applications of technology with learners from this population include the following:

1. Word prediction and abbreviation expansion can help students with motor or speech impairments to circumvent the fine-motor and spelling demands of writing. With word prediction, as each letter in a word is typed, a list of words beginning with those letters appears in a window. The target word can be chosen from this window and inserted with a single keystroke. With abbreviation expansion, entire messages can be encoded and retrieved with a simple keystroke combination. For students with severe speech impairment, speech feedback with word processing can significantly bolster writing development by supporting their attempts to reread as they compose and edit their written messages.

2. By easing the physical burdens of writing, computers with word processing help students with learning disabilities to express themselves, monitor their writing and participate in the processes essential to good writing. Strategy instruction allows teachers to provide explicit direction in planning, writing, and revising on the computer.

3. Students with significant hearing loss have not had full access to oral language in order to translate what they have heard into written words. Researchers are currently exploring ways in which technology can help students who use American Sign Language to write. By using E-mail, these learners have the opportunity to practice reading and writing as part of meaningful and purposeful learning.

4. Technology can assist learners with visual impairments by offering them alternative means of text input, helping them monitor the text while writing, and providing ready access to written products in either print or braille format. While some of these learners use the traditional keyboard, others use a braille keyboard or a nine-key device that enables them to input braille text. Small electronic devices enable learners to make notes in braille, which can subsequently be listened to by synthesized speech, downloaded to a computer file, or ultimately printed out in braille or text. (Zorfass, Corley & Remz, 1994, pp. 62-65)

Computer-assisted instruction (CAI) can provide a positive contribution to the learning process. Tindall and Gugerty (1982) suggested that CAI instruction can contribute to career and technical education programs by
- providing a supplement to the regular curriculum;
- providing improved achievement;
- providing an informal interaction at a low anxiety level;
- reducing instructional time;
- operating at the learner's individual learning pace;
- not talking down to or embarrass learners;
- giving learners instant feedback;
- providing tutoring, drill, and practice;
- assisting in problem solving;
- providing surprise, imagination, challenge, and curiosity; and
- testing and questioning.

Computers can help learners from special populations by tailoring instruction to meet their individual needs. Computer instruction is self-paced and allows learners to focus on one task at a time. Mistakes can be made privately and the positive reinforcement provided by the computer motivates them to continue learning. Feichtner (1989) stated that, with appropriate software, computers can empower learning through
- word processing programs, which ease the physical burden of writing and revising, helping learners to write better;

- instructional programs that train students to break down problems into component parts and set strategies for their solution, by promoting the development of higher-order thinking skills;
- simulations that help students understand abstract concepts in vocationally specific content areas; and
- database programs that help students manipulate data, and so understand relationships among ideas. (p. 36)

Warren-Sams (2001) writes that instructors may be guilty of perpetuating inequities in the classroom through unconscious stereotyping. This is evident in research suggesting different groups of learners, such as ethnic minorities, lower-income learners, learners with different abilites, and female learners, use computer technology in different ways. A self-evaluation of how computer technology is used in the classroom may help instructors challenge learners equally. See Figure 8-23.

COOPERATIVE TEACHING

Cooperative teaching involves co-teaching by two or more teachers in order to meet the special needs of a single learner or small group of learners in the classroom. In one type of cooperative teaching, two teachers work together on the same curriculum content. One teacher instructs in advance those learners who need assistance with such things as vocabulary, concepts, study skills, and research skills that will be required in the lessons to be delivered by the other teacher in the upcoming days or weeks. In another type of cooperative teaching, one teacher provides instruction in the curriculum content while the other teacher provides instruction in such things as reading, writing, and organizational skills.

Vaughn, Schumm and Arguelles (1997) described a number of models of co-teaching including the following:
- Teaching on purpose–In teaching on purpose, teachers provide 60 second, 2 minute, or 5 minute lessons to individual learners, pairs of learners, or even a small group of learners. Teaching on purpose often involves a follow-up to a previous lesson or a check and extension of what is presently being taught. Teachers who implement teaching on purpose keep a written log of information for each special needs learner who needs follow-up. Sometimes this follow-up work is related to key ideas, concepts, or vocabulary from the lesson or unit. Teachers may realize that selected learners are still unsure of critical information; during teaching on purpose lessons they approach the learner, check for understanding, and then follow up with a mini-lesson.
- Two teachers teach same content–In this situation, the learners in the class form two heterogeneous groups and each teacher works with one of the groups. The purpose of using two smaller groups is to provide additional opportunities for the learners in each

group to interact, provide answers, and to have their responses and knowledge evaluated by the teacher. Because small-group discussions and teacher instruction always result in somewhat different material being addressed in each group, teachers may want to pull the groups together to do a wrap-up. The purpose of the wrap-up is to summarize the key points that were addressed in each group, therefore familiarizing the whole class with the same material. A wrap-up also assists learners in learning to critically summarize key information.

• One teacher re-teaches, one teacher teaches alternative information–In this situation, teachers assign learners to one of two groups based on their levels of knowledge and skills for the designated topic. Although learners with special needs are often in the group that requires re-teaching, this is not always true. The criterion for group assignment is not ability but skill level on the designated topic. Though ability and skill level for the designated topic are often related, they are not the same. This is often referred to as flexible grouping

because the group to which learners are assigned is temporary and relates solely to their knowledge and skills for the designated topic. As the topic and skill change, so does group composition.

• Two teachers monitor/teach–This situation is much like using learning centers or cooperative learning groups. Teaching content may vary. Activities related to the topic or lessons are arranged in designated areas throughout the classroom. (One area may have computers; another may have audio equipment, etc.) Groups of learners either alternate working in each of the designated areas or are assigned to work in a particular area that responds to their specific needs. Teachers can perform one of several roles such as monitoring learner progress, providing mini-lessons to individual learners or small groups of learners, or working with one group of learners during the entire period while the other teacher monitors the remaining learners and activities. This multiple-group format allows all or most learners to work in heterogeneous groups, with selected learners pulled for specific instruction.

ASSESSING TECHNOLOGY ACCESS AND USE

Questions	Always	Usually	Rarely	Never
1. Do students from low-income and minority backgrounds have an opportunity to use computers in the same way as higher income white students?				
2. Do all students, regardless of academic ability, income level, race, gender, English-speaking ability, and physical condition, have an opportunity to use computers for higher-level cognitive activities? In other words, do low-income, low-achieving, and ethnic minority students use the computer for high- as well as low-level cognitive tasks (drill and practice)? Do low-achieving students use the computer to solve problems and learn applications as well as to learn basic skills?				
3. Are females and students of color proportionally represented in elective and advanced programming classes? Have unnecessary prerequisites been eliminated?				
4. Are females and males equally represented in application (word processing) classes?				
5. Do all groups have equitable access to the computer laboratory before and after school and during other free times?				
6. Are the most competent and experienced teachers assigned to teach low-achievers as well as high-achievers and the gifted?				
7. Are younger students made aware of technology careers and technology education classes available in high school?				
8. Do high school students not enrolled in technology programs have sufficient flexibility to allow them to consider taking technology courses as electives?				
9. Are all parents or guardians educated about the importance of technology skills for their children?				
10. Are all groups of students represented in computer clubs?				

Source: Warren-Sams, B. (2001). Assessing Technology Access and Use: A Checklist for Equity. *Closing the Equity Gap in Technology Access and Use: A Practical Guide for K-12 Educators.* Portland, OR: Northwest Regional Educational Laboratory.

Figure 8-23. A checklist for assessing equity in computer technology access and use in school.

Team teaching, as in the case of cooperative planning, is an excellent way to combine the knowledge and expertise of several professionals in a common effort to help learners from special populations to succeed in career and technical education programs. The team can be composed of two or more individuals who use various skills to meet the specific needs of these learners. Team membership can include representation from other career and technical education instructors, support personnel, special education personnel, paraprofessionals, parents, and community volunteers.

Team teaching requires planning and coordination among the team members in order to clarify goals, objectives, content, instructional techniques, and evaluation methods for a specific unit, chapter, lesson, or activity. This method of instruction works particularly well when combined with flexible grouping. In this manner, team members can work with a small group of learners and use a variety of teaching strategies, media, and remedial strategies to meet the needs of the learners.

Members of the team should contribute and lead in areas where their strength and expertise lie. Cooperative team teaching arrangements for learners from special populations should incorporate a schedule and a list of responsibilities so individuals can prepare their contributions to the team effort. Planning should also take into consideration

- use of media;
- amount of time required for each session or activity;
- necessary facilities, supplies, equipment, and tools; and
- appropriate assessment methods. See Figure 8-24.

Planning can be organized for large group sessions, small group sessions, and individualized one-on-one sessions. This allows for one team member to work with learners with special needs who may need remedial assistance with technical terms, reading assignments, related math, preparing for a test quiz, or practicing hands-on skills. A checklist may be helpful in planning team teaching activities. See Figure 8-25.

STUDY SKILLS

Efficient learners develop methods that enable them to acquire and use information successfully in a systematic way. To develop these abilities, learners should be taught techniques, principles, and rules that will result in acquisition, storage, and retrieval. Study skills are a group of skills that are used to promote learning the content of any

---

COOPERATIVE TEACHING PLANNING FORM

Co-Teachers _____ Class/Subject(s) _____ Date _____

Teaching Session No. _____ Day(s) Mon. Tues. Wed. Thurs. Fri. Week(s) of _____

Next Planning Session Day _____ Time _____ Loc _____ Date _____

Goal(s)

1. _____
2. _____
3. _____
4. _____
5. _____

Time	Location/Person Responsible	Activity Format/Media	Student Activity	Teacher Responsibilities	Accommodation Strategies/Materials	Assessment Methods

Comments _____
_____
_____

Figure 8-24. A sample format for planning cooperative team teaching assignments.

course of study. This includes classroom skills such as note taking, time management, test taking, listening, organization, and memorization.

TEAM TEACHING PREPARATION CHECKLIST

I. PLANNING

_____ Did team members share their opinions on matters related to the instructional program?

_____ Did team members share ideas in their area of specialty?

_____ Were team members actively cooperative (willing to compromise, patient, willing to learn from others)?

_____ Did members act as both leaders and followers?

_____ Did members share the total responsibility equally?

_____ Did members communicate openly?

_____ Did members constructively evaluate ideas?

II. IMPLEMENTING

_____ Were options for student independent study provided?

_____ Did the plan include a variety of available media and educational technology?

_____ Were the instructional tools selected relevant to the subject to be learned?

_____ Did the team make plans for using small-group discussion?

_____ Did the team make plans for using large-group instruction?

_____ Were members assigned to groups of students varying in size and composition?

_____ Were plans made for self-diagnosis?

_____ Did plans call for members to share diagnostic and evaluation responsibility?

_____ Were the group sizes selected based on group purpose?

_____ Was the group composition selected based on group purpose?

_____ Was the time allotted to each group based on group purpose?

_____ Was the physical environment selected based on group activities involved?

_____ Were tasks assigned to each team member based on individual talents?

_____ Was the nature of supervision provided for each group based on group purpose?

_____ Did subject matter content include provisions for individual differences?

Source: The National Center for Research in Vocational Education. (1977c). *Employ the Team Teaching Approach.* Columbus, OH: The Ohio State University.

Figure 8-25. A sample checklist for planning and facilitating team teaching.

Many learners from special populations are disorganized and lack effective strategies that would enable them to use their abilities to their advantage in educational settings. Many learners with special needs experience difficulties in classrooms because they cannot take notes, use their time well, use available resources to find answers, or complete assigned tasks within a given time period. Instructors have a responsibility to teach effective strategies to learners so that they will be able to effectively learn.

Metacognition was defined by Costa (1981) as an individual's ability to regulate cognitive behavior. Metacognition represents the strategies used in learning how to learn. If instructors wish to develop intelligent behavior as a significant outcome of education, instructional strategies purposefully intended to develop learners' metacognitive abilities must be infused into teaching methods, staff development, and supervisory processes. To develop metacognition, learners must develop skills in concentrating, organizing, questioning, reflecting, rehearsing, summarizing, and generalizing.

Costa (1984) identified a variety of strategies to enhance metacognition, independent of grade level and subject area, including the following:

1. Planning strategy–Prior to any learning activity, instructors should point out strategies and steps for attacking problems, rules to remember, and directions to follow. Time constraints, purposes, and ground rules under which students must operate should be identified and internalized.

2. Generating questions–It is useful for learners to pose study questions for themselves prior to and during their reading of textual material. This facilitates comprehension and encourages students to pause frequently and think about whether they are grasping the concept, if they can relate it to what they already know, if they can give other examples, and whether they can use the main idea to explain other ideas or predict what may come next.

3. Choosing consciously–Students should learn to explore the consequences of their choices and decisions prior to and during the act of making a decision. Providing nonjudgmental feedback to students about the effects of their behaviors and decisions on others and on their environment helps them become aware of their own behaviors.

4. Evaluating with multiple criteria–Instructors can enhance metacognition by causing students to reflect upon and categorize their actions according to two or more sets of evaluative criteria (e.g., what the student did that worked and didn't work, or what were positive and negative features about the assignment).

5. Taking credit–Students are asked to identify what they have done well and must seek feedback from their peers. They will then become more conscious of their own behavior and apply a set of internal criteria for those behaviors that they consider good.

6. Outlawing "I can't"–Students should be asked to identify what information is required, what materials are needed, or what skills are lacking in their ability to perform the desired behavior. This helps them identify the boundaries between what they know and what they need to know.

7. Paraphrasing or reflecting back students' ideas–Inviting students to restate, translate, compare, and paraphrase each other's ideas causes them to become not only better listeners of others' thinking but better listeners of their own thinking.

8. Labeling students' behaviors–When teachers place labels on students' cognitive processes, they become conscious of their own actions.

9. Clarifying students' terminology–Asking students to clarify what they have said causes them to operationally define their terminology and to examine the premise on which their thinking is based.

10. Role playing and simulations–Role playing can promote metacognition because when students assume the roles of other persons they consciously maintain the attributes and characteristics of that person. Taking on another role contributes to the reduction of ego-centered perceptions.

11. Journal keeping–Writing and illustrating a personal log or a diary throughout an experience causes students to synthesize thoughts and actions and to translate them to symbolic form.

12. Modeling–Since students learn best by imitating the adults around them, the instructor who publicly demonstrates metacognition will undoubtedly produce learners who will be able to practice these skills. (pp. 123-125)

Some important aids to study include note taking, graphic organizers, mind maps, fishbone diagrams, textbooks, and organizational skills.

Note Taking

Learners should be taught the following tips that will help them take notes:

- Number and date all notebook pages.
- Develop a personal system of note taking that is comfortable but effective.
- Use margins to note topics, main ideas, and key words.
- Record more important information closer to the margin.
- Indent subordinate ideas.
- Write as much as needed to understand the content later.
- Include main ideas, definitions, examples, important details, repeated points, and board or transparency notations.
- Review notes within 24 hours to clarify, complete, and reorder notes.
- Get notes from any classes missed.

An example of a teacher-prepared note-taking system is a skeletal outline. See Figure 8-26. A skeletal outline helps to organize information from a lecture or discussion into a partial outline to be completed by the learner. It provides a format for recording important information and a guide for taking notes. The outline can serve as an aid for studying and reviewing for tests. Steps to take to develop a skeletal outline include the following:

1. Develop a completed outline to follow a textbook, manual, specific lecture, or discussion.
2. Use the same numbering system and include letter, word, or phrase clues.
3. Provide a copy of the outline for each learner to complete during the oral presentation.
4. Have learners copy the skeletal outline from an overhead projector or writing board.

SKELETAL OUTLINE – COSMETOLOGY

I. Facials
  A. Definitions of facials are
    1. <u>The scientific method of manipulating all structures of the face for a certain purpose.</u>
    2. <u>To preserve and beautify the skin.</u>
  B. The benefits of a facial include the following:
    1. breaks down   <u>fatty tissue</u>
    2. tones and   <u>strengthens weak muscles</u>
    3. activates   <u>oil glands</u>
    4. nourishes   <u>skin</u>
    5. relaxes and   <u>soothes nerves</u>
    6. may   <u>relieve pain</u>
    7. increases   <u>blood circulation</u>
    8. makes skin   <u>soft and pliable</u>
  C. Types of creams include the following:
    1. cleansing cream   <u>replaces soap, cleans the face</u>
      other names   <u>cold cream, vanishing cream</u>
    2. massage cream   <u>lubricates the skin</u>
      makes it easier to   <u>slide and glide over the skin</u>
      other names   <u>texture, emollient, lubricating</u>
  D. Massage movements include the following:
    1. petrissage   <u>kneading, knuckling movement</u>
    2. effleurage   <u>stroking movement</u>
    3. tapotement   <u>digital tapping movement</u>
    4. hacking   <u>chopping movement</u>

Source: Huck, R., Myers, R., & Wilson, J. (1989). *ADAPT–A Developmental Activity Program for Teachers* (2nd ed.). Pittsburgh, PA: Allegheny Intermediate Unit.

Figure 8-26. An example of an outline for learner use.

Graphic Organizers

A graphic organizer is a visual representation of knowledge that structures information by arranging important aspects of a concept or topic into a pattern using labels. There are a variety of graphic organizers including semantic map, concept map, visual organizer, structured overview, story web, main idea table, and sequencing chain. Graphic organizers are wonderful tools to get learners actively involved in their learning. Because graphic organizers include both words and visual images, they are effective with a wide variety of learners. Graphic organizers such as concept maps present information in concise ways that highlight the organization and relationships of concepts. See Figure 8-27. They can be used with any subject matter at any level.

Bromley, DeVitis and Modlo (1999) listed a number of reasons for using graphic organizers including the following:

- Graphic organizers help learners focus on what is important because they highlight key concepts, vocabulary, and the relationships among them, thus providing the tools for critical thinking.
- The human mind organizes and stores information in a series of networks. Graphic organizers are visual depictions that remember networks and allow learners to add

or modify their background knowledge by seeing the connections and contradictions between existing knowledge and new information.

- Graphic organizers serve as mental tools to help the learner remember. The information in a graphic organizer is visual as well as verbal, highlights the relationships between ideas, and focuses on the most important information. Thus, the learner is better able to understand and retain the material.
- Constructing or evaluating graphic organizers requires the learner to be actively involved with the information. Both when working independently and working with others, the dialogues and decision making required to construct graphic organizers promote interaction with the material.
- The negotiation and construction of meaning that is integral to the creation of graphic organizers allows learners to build on one another's knowledge.
- Graphic organizers are effective with diverse learners in a variety of settings. Graphic organizers can be particularly beneficial for learners who have difficulty with composing. They provide an optional way of depicting knowledge and understanding.
- Learners who use graphic organizers in the classroom develop their ability to use them independently as study tools for note taking, planning, presentation, and review.

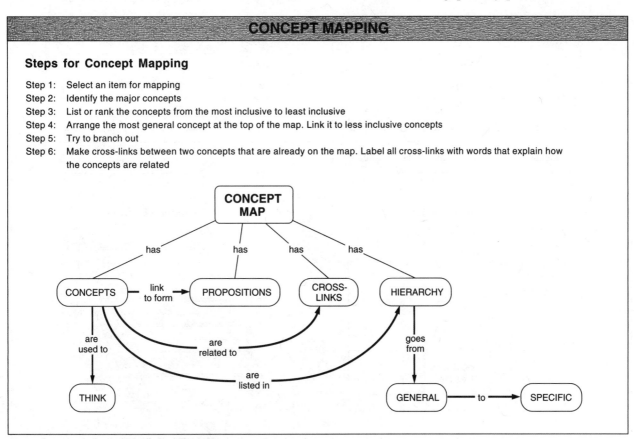

CONCEPT MAPPING

Steps for Concept Mapping

Step 1: Select an item for mapping
Step 2: Identify the major concepts
Step 3: List or rank the concepts from the most inclusive to least inclusive
Step 4: Arrange the most general concept at the top of the map. Link it to less inclusive concepts
Step 5: Try to branch out
Step 6: Make cross-links between two concepts that are already on the map. Label all cross-links with words that explain how the concepts are related

Figure 8-27. The steps for concept mapping and an example.

- Graphic organizers are used more and more often in business and industry and in print and electronic media. The ability to interpret, critique, and create these organizers is part of visual literacy now considered basic to education.
- Graphic organizers are visible alternatives to more traditional assessments. Instructors have successfully used graphic organizers to monitor learning by having learners construct them before a topic or unit of study, and then add or modify them as knowledge is gained through learning and research. Using organizers for the final assessment focuses both learners and teachers on key concepts and their interrelationships. Remember, when using graphic organizers for assessment, learners should have the option to explain their organizers and defend their reasoning. This combination of oral or written explanation and the visual depiction of the knowledge provides powerful insights into learners' learning and provides valuable feedback on instructional design and implementation.
- More and more often, textbooks are using graphic organizers. Learners and instructors need to be able to evaluate the organizers and use them as models and learning aids. See Figure 8-28.

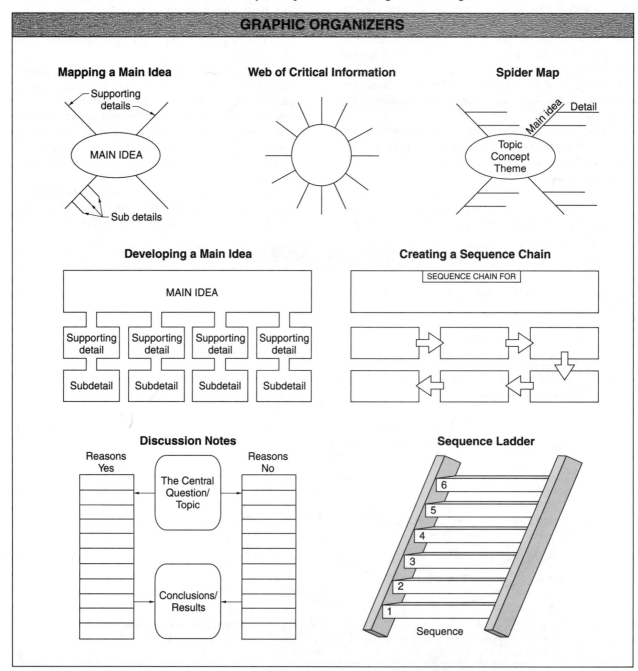

GRAPHIC ORGANIZERS

Mapping a Main Idea

Supporting details

MAIN IDEA

Sub details

Web of Critical Information

Spider Map

Main idea   Detail

Topic Concept Theme

Developing a Main Idea

MAIN IDEA

Supporting detail | Supporting detail | Supporting detail | Supporting detail

Subdetail | Subdetail | Subdetail | Subdetail

Creating a Sequence Chain

SEQUENCE CHAIN FOR

Discussion Notes

Reasons Yes

The Central Question/ Topic

Reasons No

Conclusions/ Results

Sequence Ladder

6
5
4
3
2
1

Sequence

Figure 8-28. Various examples of the different kinds of graphic organizers.

Mind Maps

A mind map is a brainstorming tool that uses colors and pictures to symbolize key concepts. The combination of colors and pictures produces more association than words do. It is particularly effective for visual and nontraditional learners. Steps to creating a mind map include the following:

1. Write the name or description of the object or problem in the center of a piece of paper and draw a circle around it.
2. Brainstorm each major facet of that object or problem, placing your thoughts on lines drawn outward from the central thought like roads leaving a city.
3. Add branches to the lines as necessary.

4. Use additional visual techniques. For example, using different colors for major lines of thought, circling words or thoughts that appear more than once, and connecting lines between similar thoughts are all techniques that can be employed. See Figure 8-29.

Fishbone Diagrams

The Fishbone diagram is primarily a group problem identification technique, but it can be used by individuals as well. This process is called the fishbone diagram because of the unique way in which the information gathered is arranged visually. When a problem and its causes are

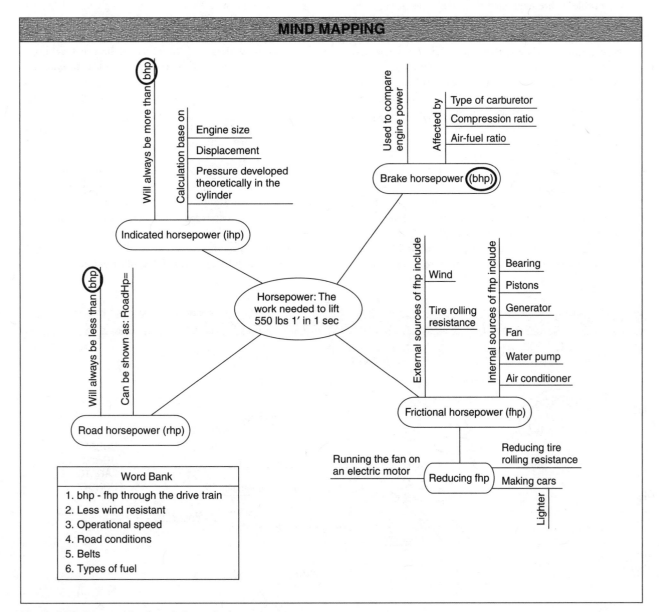

Figure 8-29. An example of a mind map for horsepower.

recorded, they form a diagram that resembles the skeleton of a fish. The problem is written down and enclosed in a semicircle on the right side of a sheet of paper. A straight line is drawn to the left and appears much like the backbone of a fish. The next step involves drawing stems at a 45° angle to the backbone line. At the end of each of these stems are listed all of the causes of the problem. Branches can be placed on each stem for further breakdowns of each cause. The causes should be listed with the least complicated nearest the head of the fish and the most complicated at the tail, with those in between listed on a continuum from least to most complicated. See Figure 8-30.

When the diagram is completed, the individual or group begins to analyze the stems and the branches to determine the real problem or problems that need to be solved. If simpler problems are examined first, they can be removed from consideration before more complicated problems are tackled. If the problem solvers decide that certain causes are more significant than others, these will be given more attention in the generation of possible solutions.

The fishbone diagram is extremely useful for identifying problems for several reasons including the following:
- It encourages problems solvers to study all parts of a problem before making a decision.
- It helps show the relationship between causes and the relative importance of those causes.
- It helps start the creative process because it focuses the problem solvers on the problem.
- It helps start a logical sequence for solving a problem.
- It helps problems solvers see the total problem as opposed to focusing on a narrow part of it.
- It offers a way to reduce the scope of the problems and solve less complex issues rather than more complex ones.

Textbooks

Learners should be taught how to read a textbook or manual as well as skills to appropriately mark a textbook so that important information can be addressed. Suggestions for learners to follow when reading a textbook or manual include the following:
- Plan sufficient time to read assigned material carefully, allowing for the possible need to reread, look up new terms, and reflect.
- Preview the selection. Spend two or three minutes noting titles, introductory material, headings, and subheadings. Be alert to note italicized print, pictures, and charts. Mentally connect major topics to determine their relationship.
- Question before reading. Turn headings into questions and read to find the answers. Actively extract main points and important details.
- Be sure to understand the material before marking it up. If the information is new or difficult, rereading a couple of paragraphs may be necessary. Going ahead a short distance may help. Reading troublesome passages aloud may help to improve concentration. Exaggerated expression enhances comprehension. If unknown terms are blocking understanding, pause to look them up.

A helpful tool for learners to use when reading textbooks, manuals, or units is a structured study guide. See Figure 8-31. This guide provides structure and location clues to help learners read for understanding and information. Steps to take in developing a structured study guide include the following:

1. Identify key ideas and related information.

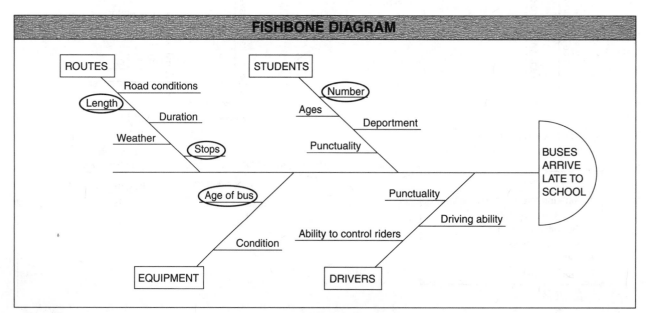

Figure 8-30. A fishbone diagram identifying causes of buses arriving late to school.

STRUCTURED STUDY GUIDE

Chapter 2 – Introducing Proofs (pp. 41-54)

Directions: Use your book to complete the statements below.

Three Theorems

(p. 42)   1. Complementary angles are two angles whose _____ total _____.

(p. 25)   2. A statement that is accepted without proof is a _____.

(p. 42)   3. A _____ is a statement which has been proven.

(p. 43)   4. _____ angles are two angles whose _____ total 180˚.

(p. 42)   5. If two angles are complements of equal angles (or of the same angle), then the _____ are equal.

(p. 43)   6. Vertical angles are _____. (Theorem 1 – Memorize!)

(p. 43)   7. If two angles are supplements of _____ (or the same angle), then the two angles are _____.

"If . . . then" Statements

(p. 46)   8. In the statement "If A, then B,"

   A is called _____, then

   B is called _____.

(p. 46)   9. The converse of "If A, then B" is "If _____, then _____."

(p. 47)   10. Some true statements have _____ that are false.

(p. 47)   11. The _____ of a statement is formed by exchanging the _____ and the _____ of the statement.

(p. 46)   12. In the statement, "If X is a sparrow, then X is a bird," "X is a bird" is called the _____.

Writing Proofs

(p. 54)   13. A geometric _____ consists of steps that show how a _____ follows logically from other statements.

(p. 54)   14. There are _____ kinds of reasons which can be used to _____ a step in a proof.

(p. 54)   15. The reasons used in a proof are:

   A. _____ information

   B. *D*_____

   C. *P*_____ (These are statements accepted without _____.)

   D. *T*_____ (These are statements accepted without _____.)

Source: Huck, R., Myers, R., & Wilson, J. (1989). *ADAPT - A Devleopmental Activity Program for Teachers* (2nd ed.). Pittsburgh, PA: Allegheny Intermediate Unit.

Figure 8-31. An example of a study guide used by a learner to review pertinent information.

2. Write open-ended statements using exact words in text.

3. Include the important points from the section to be read.

4. Provide sufficient space for the learners to write on the paper that the structured study guide is written on.

5. Provide page clues to the left of the text statements so that learners can find the section.

6. Organize the structured study guide according to the subheadings or sections that are in the text.

Suggestions for learners to use when marking a textbook or manual include the following:

- Mark information that will be needed later for test preparation. Be selective. Do not over mark or the purpose of shrinking a large amount of material to a manageable amount is defeated.
- Underline a portion at a time. Read a paragraph to the end before deciding what is important enough to mark.
- Be sure to understand the material before marking it. It may be necessary to read an entire section before you are ready to mark the paragraphs in it.
- Mark what you know is important. Set off main points, definitions, examples, and primary supporting details.
- Use a system for marking. For example, underline main points and definitions. In the margin, write EX beside helpful examples. Write DET beside primary details. Number items in a series, within text. Write key words or ideas in margin. Star anything that is obviously important.

Organizational Skills

Learners need organizational skills to store papers, retrieve necessary materials, and to transport materials from class to class and from home to school. Whatever the system, the instructor must introduce it, demonstrate its use, and provide practice in storing and retrieving materials. The instructor should check the system, provide positive and negative consequences for use of the system, provide a time for cleaning out the system, and remind learners to use the system (Center for Innovations in Special Education, formerly Missouri LINC, 1991). Suggestions to assist learners in developing organization skills include

- having a spiral bound notebook or a section of a loose-leaf notebook for each class;
- having a color-coded folder with holes to fit into a notebook to hold papers for each class;
- having a paper calendar that fits into the loose-leaf notebook, and place it at the front of the notebook;
- developing a code for the calendar as a reminder to indicate when an assignment is due and another for a week before it is due;
- marking the calendar immediately after receiving an assignment or test date; and
- reviewing the calendar daily.

CRITICAL-THINKING AND PROBLEM-SOLVING SKILLS

It is becoming very clear that all learners leaving high school will need a solid foundation of critical-thinking and problem-solving skills. Employers of workers at all levels stress their need for employees who not only have strong basic skills but who can apply them in a reasoned, thoughtful way to make decisions. The term critical thinking means the mental processes, strategies, and representations used to solve problems, make decisions, and learn new concepts.

Developing a learner's ability to think critically is a primary responsibility of all instructors. All educators should be concerned with helping learners develop the knowledge, skills, and attitudes they will need to live and work in society. One of the most crucial of these abilities is the ability to solve problems on their own and apply problem-solving techniques to the great variety of situations they will face in life. Among other skills, the basics of tomorrow will include

- evaluation and analysis skills;
- critical-thinking skills;
- problem-solving strategies;
- organization and reference skills;
- synthesis;
- application;
- creativity; and
- decision making when given incomplete information.

If instructors tell learners the answer to every question, or the best solution to every problem, they will not be giving learners an opportunity to learn how to apply problem-solving techniques. Every course that learners take presents opportunities to elicit and expand these skills. The instruction will be most relevant if performance evaluation is based not only on how well learners complete a task, but on how well they apply processes, justify decisions, and respond to questions. Higher-order thinking skills should be developed in context of the subject matter in which they are involved. Providing learners with examples of different critical-thinking strategies will aid them in developing their own critical-thinking and problem-solving skills. See Figure 8-32.

In order to develop a comprehensive program for increased emphasis on the development of thinking skills in career and technical education programs, it is important to identify assumptions that will guide planning and implementation. The Maryland State Department of Education (n.d.) identified a series of assumptions that would lead to improved instruction in thinking skills, including the following:

- One of the primary objectives of career and technical education is to provide skills that are transferable to the work world. The abilities to think and to solve problems are important skills for the future work force in order to ensure the nation's productivity and economic growth.
- Certain thinking skills are inherent in career and technical education programs. Teaching them more explicitly will enhance learning.
- Thinking and basic skills development are interdependent processes. Helping learners to become better thinkers will help them become better learners and future employees.
- Benefits from instruction in the area of critical thinking transfer from one instructional area to another. Career and technical education can make a contribution to the development of thinking skills as a part of the comprehensive educational program.
- Mental abilities, particularly skills of creative problem solving, can be developed and improved through direct instruction, practice, and exercise.

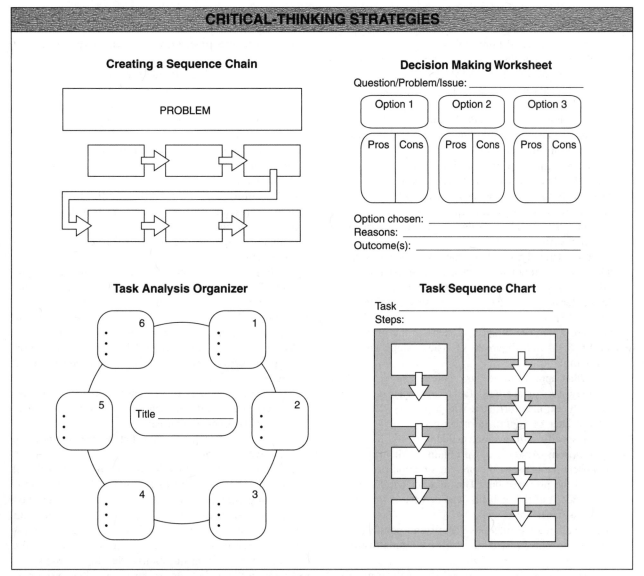

Figure 8-32. Various examples of critical-thinking strategies for problem solving.

- Team problem solving and competition produce a motivation vehicle for developing creativity, cooperation, and planning skills. Career and technical student organization activities included as an integral part of instruction can enhance learners' thinking skills.
- Teachers of career and technical education are professionally and occupationally competent. They must work cooperatively with academic and support personnel to plan for increased emphasis on teaching for thinking. Staff development programs should reflect this assumption.

Norris (1985) reported the following highlights from research on critical thinking:

1. Critical thinking is a complex of many considerations. It requires individuals to assess their own and others' views, to seek alternatives, make inferences, and to have the disposition to think critically.

2. Critical thinking is an educational ideal. It is not an educational option. Students have a moral right to be taught how to think critically.

3. Critical-thinking ability is not widespread. Most students do not score well on tests that measure ability to recognize assumptions, evaluate arguments, and appraise inferences.

4. Critical thinking is sensitive to context. Students' background knowledge and assumptions can strongly affect their ability to make correct inferences. Inferences are more likely to be correct when the context relates to the individual's personal experience and when performance is not associated with threats or promises.

5. Teachers should look for the reasoning behind students' conclusions. Coming up with a correct answer may not be the result of critical thinking. Essay tests are more likely to reveal the student's thought

processes than are objective tests. And the tests themselves must be evaluated critically to make sure they require critical-thinking skills.

6. Simple errors may signal errors in thinking at a deeper level. In trying to solve complex problems, for example, students may err not only by making a miscalculation, but also by using an incorrect approach to the problem. They should be encouraged to take time before solving a problem to decide how to go about finding the solution.

7. Having a critical spirit is as important as thinking critically. The critical spirit requires one to think critically about all aspects of life, to think critically about one's own thinking, and to act on the basis of what one has considered when using critical-thinking skills.

8. To think critically, one must have knowledge. Critical thinking cannot occur in a vacuum. It requires individuals to apply what they know about the subject matter as well as their common sense and experience. (p. 27)

There are a number of specific steps to the problem-solving process. See Figure 8-33. These steps include the following:

1. State what appears to be the problem–The real problem may not surface until facts have been gathered and analyzed; therefore, start with a primary statement that can later be confirmed or corrected.

2. Gather specific information, including facts, feelings, and opinions–Analyze the problem by determining the difference between the present situation or condition and the preferred one. This may include identifying the scope of the problem, who or what is involved, and what forces are at work.

3. Identify alternative solutions–Identify all possible solutions through individual or group brainstorming session(s).

4. Analyze alternative solutions–What solution will provide the optimum solution? Identify the risks and resources needed as well as the resources that will be needed to implement the solution.

5. Rate each solution–Place solutions in order of preference according to the practicality of alternatives.

6. Select the best solution–Choose the alternative that seems to be the best solution to the stated problem, considering issues of practicality and resources available.

7. Develop an action plan–This involves making a commitment to the plan, identifying specific steps to carry out, determining what resources are needed, identifying who will be involved in implementing the plan, providing for potential barriers, and planning for the evaluation of the action plan.

8. Evaluate the action plan/alternative solution(s) used–The alternative outlined in the action plan should be evaluated as to the level of success in solving the stated problem.

Strategies to extend learner thinking include the following:

- Remember wait time. Provide at least three seconds of thinking time after a question and after a response.
- Play devil's advocate. Require learners to defend their reasoning against different points of view.
- Call on learners randomly. Avoid the pattern of only calling on those learners with raised hands.
- Survey the class. Ask how many learners agree with the author's point, the possible solution, or the opinion of the group by raising their hands or indicating a thumbs-up.
- Utilize think-pair-share. Allow individual thinking time, discussion with a partner, and then open up for the class discussion.
- Withhold judgment. Respond to learner answers in a non-evaluative fashion.
- Ask follow-ups. Use such phrases as "Why?", "Do you agree?", "Can you elaborate?", "Tell me more.", and "Can you give me an example?"
- Allow for learner calling (e.g., "Eva, will you please call on someone else to respond to this question?").
- Ask learners to unpack their thinking. Ask the learners to describe how they arrived at the answer (i.e., "Think aloud.").
- Cue learner responses (e.g., "There is not just one correct response to this question. I want you to consider as many alternatives as you can.").
- Encourage learner questioning. Let the learners develop their own questions.
- Set up questions on 3 x 5 index cards. Use different colored cards to write different levels of questions regarding content that is to be delivered to the class (e.g., yellow cards for recall questions, blue cards for analysis questions, pink cards for comparison questions, green cards for inference questions, and white cards for evaluation questions). See Figure 8-34.
- Avoid questions that can be answered with a yes or no response. If they are used, call for an explanation of the response from the learner.
- Whenever possible during oral questioning, use all the component categories from lower to higher order to advantage. Begin with recall and proceed step by step to evaluation, making all the stops along the way.
- Ask one learner to paraphrase or explain what another learner has said.
- Keep the whole class involved by calling on those who do not volunteer regularly.
- Frequently have the learners consider questions in small groups.
- If learners are working in groups, be sure they are aware of all sources they can use to gather information. Then help them to develop a list of where they can go for information.
- Assign learners to serve as discussion leaders, moderators, or critics.

THE PROBLEM-SOLVING PROCESS

This format can be utilized to involve learners in problem-solving situations that arise through participation in career and technical education program settings.

Career and Technical Education Program: Electronics

Individuals Involved in Problem Solving Situation: Rick Sullivan, electronics instructor

Electronics Lab Team Members: Emily Johnson, Natasha Sorenson, Chang Lee, Mike Clifford

DESCRIPTION OF THE PROBLEM:

Emily Johnson has been assigned to a project team in her electronics class. Mr. Sullivan has noticed that Emily has refused to do her part of the experiments and to work effectively as a team member. Several members of her team have complained that Emily has been late in turning in her part of the team project, and on other occasions she has refused to do her assigned work.

BRAINSTORM SESSION WITH TEAM MEMBERS:

Mr. Sullivan bet with the team members except for Emily to brainstorm possible solutions to this problem. The team members collectively came up with a number of possible solutions.

Possible Solutions:	Poor	Good	Excellent
1. Meet with Emily to discuss situation	1	2	3
2. Meet with team to discuss situation	1	2	3
3. Meet with Emily and team members to discuss situation	1	2	3
4. Assign Emily to another team	1	2	3
5. Assist team in developing daily written assignments of roles for each team member	1	2	3

PRIORITIZE SOLUTIONS:

Once a list of solutions was organized, the team members prioritized the solutions and developed a plan of action based on the solution that they felt would be the most effective.

SELECT SOLUTION TO BE FOLLOWED THROUGH A PLAN OF ACTION:

The group consensus was that the most appropriate solution to the problem was the following:

Mr. Sullivan will meet with Emily and team members to discuss the situation, allow each person on the team to present his or her viewpoint, and assist the team in reaching a compromise. The next time a team project is assigned in the electronics program, the team will employ the following action steps:

ACTION PLAN STEPS:

Action Plan Step	Person Responsible	Date
1. Ask each member of the team to prepare a brief description of their contribution to the overall team project	Team members	_____
2. Set up a time for a team meeting	Mr. Sullivan	_____
3. Brief each team member as to the nature of the meeting	Mr. Sullivan	_____
4. Conduct team meeting	Team members	_____
5. Team members will discuss their assigned roles	Team members	_____
6. Team members will brainstorm possible solutions	Team members	_____
7. Assign a new team leader each day	Team members	_____
8. Team assignment will be written and distributed to each team member each day	Team members	_____
9. Monitor team project	Mr. Sullivan	_____

MEASUREMENT OF PROPOSED SOLUTION:

Team leader assigns daily duties to each team member. In addition, each member of the team has an opportunity to serve as a team leader.

Figure 8-33. An example of a team approach to problem solving.

- Utilize a technique where a large group is broken into several small groups. Each small group responds to a different question or problem. After deliberation, the small group appoints a representative to report back to the large group.

- Utilize the nominal group technique where group members work individually on a specific task and then report their ideas to the group for discussions. Suggested ideas or solutions are ranked individually by group members and then presented for summary rank ordering.

SUMMARY OF THINKING SKILLS		
Level	**Definition**	**Relation to Bloom's Taxonomy**
Recall	Most tasks require that students recognize or remember key facts, definitions, concepts, rules, and principles. Recall questions require students to repeat verbatim or to para-phrase given information. To recall information, students need most often to rehearse or practice it, and then to associate it with other related concepts. The Bloom Taxonomy levels of knowledge and comprehension are subsumed here, since verbatim repetition and translation into the student's own words represent acceptable evidence of learning and understanding	Recall Comparison
Analysis	In this operation, students divide a whole into component elements. Generally the part/whole relationships and the cause/effect relationships that characterize knowledge within subject domains are essential components of more complex tasks. The compo-nents can be the distinctive characteristics of objects or ideas, or the basic actions of procedures or events. This definition of analysis is the same as that in the Bloom Taxonomy	Analysis
Comparison	These tasks require students to recognize or explain similarities and differences. Simple comparisons require attention to one or a few very obvious attributes or component processes, while complex comparisons require identification of and differentiation among many attributes or component actions. This category relates to some of the skills in the Bloom level of analysis. The separate comparison category emphasizes the dis-tinct information processing required when students go beyond breaking the whole into parts in order to compare similarities and differences	Analysis
Inference	Both deductive and inductive reasoning fall in this category. In deductive tasks, students are given a generalization and are required to recognize or explain the evidence that re-lates to it. Applications of rules and if-then relationships require inference. In inductive tasks, students are given the evidence or details and are required to come up with the generalization. Hypothesizing, predicting, concluding, and synthesizing all require stu-dents to relate and integrate information. Inductive and deductive reasoning relate to Bloom levels of application and synthesis. Application of a rule is one kind of deductive reasoning; synthesis, or putting parts together to form a generalization, occurs in both inductive and deductive reasons	Application Synthesis
Evaluation	These tasks require students to judge quality, credibility, worth, or practicality. Generally, we expect students to use established criteria and explain how these criteria are or are not met. The criteria might be established rules of evidence, logic, or shared values. Bloom's levels of synthesis and evaluation are involved in this category. To evaluate, stu-dents must assemble and explain the interrelationship of evidence and reasons in sup-port of their conclusion (synthesis). Explanation of criteria for reaching a conclusion is unique to evaluate reasoning	Synthesis Evaluation

Source: Stiggins, R., Rubel, E., & Quellmalz, E. (1988). *Measuring Thinking Skills in the Classroom*. Washington, DC: National Education Association.

Figure 8-34. An overview of the levels of thinking skills in the classroom in relationship to Bloom's taxonomy.

- Set criteria for grades that reflect the importance of moving beyond recall. Extra points might be given for higher-order skills.
- Present learners with an answer and have them ask a set of questions that would allow them to arrive at the cor-rect question for that answer.
- Have learners list questions about what they will need to find out before they can begin an activity in the laboratory.
- Utilize focus groups where a small group of individuals are selected to discuss a particular topic, issue, person, organization, or consumer product to help the group leader better understand how individuals perceive the topic.
- Utilize quality circles where a small group participates in decision making by meeting on a regular basis for

the purpose of improving productivity and work qual-ity using brainstorming and other group problem-solving methods.

ASSISTANCE FOR LEARNERS WITH READING DEFICIENCIES

It has been well documented that inadequate reading skills limit educational opportunities and, in many cases, em-ployment possibilities. A strong relationship exists be-tween reading disabilities and the syndrome of alienation concerning the school experience. Numerous research ac-tivities have reported the high proportion of nonreaders among school dropouts. Therefore, there is an urgent need to help learners remain in school and develop career and technical skills. Reading means comprehending written or printed symbols. Because learners are reluctant to read does not mean that they are reluctant to learn. Teaching reading skills in a career and technical setting means teaching a process, not teaching more content material.

Among the important points to remember about reading are that: (a) learners will need help in learning to read materials before they can use those materials to learn concepts, (b) career and technical materials are often written to accommodate the technical needs and not the learner needs, and (c) career and technical content areas have specialized vocabulary that should be brought to the learner's attention (Stern-Otazo & D'Oronzio, 1980).

Each learner has the following three reading levels:

1. Independent reading level–Learner can read and comprehend information independently and requires no assistance.
2. Instructional reading level–Learner will probably require some assistance in identifying new words and in comprehending new content.
3. Frustration reading level–Learner is unable to read or comprehend material.

The problems that learners with reading deficiencies have can be categorized into three areas that identify the type of reading problem the learner has in relationship to participating in the career and technical education program. A few learners may be identified as nonreaders because of their inability to read anything at all. Other learners who have reading deficiencies will be able to read the written words but will be unable to comprehend what they have read. Still others are able to read and comprehend written material, but not at the level at which assigned instructional materials are written.

In any classroom, the instructor will have learners reading at many different grade levels. Their differing abilities should be matched with instructional materials and techniques if these learners are going to be successful. Cooperative planning among educators can prove to be very helpful. A compilation of tips and techniques that can assist educators in meeting the needs of learners who have reading deficiencies include the following:

- Make a tape recording of written passages. Allow learners to listen and read materials at the same time. Volunteer learners, paraprofessionals, parents, or peer tutors can also make these tapes.
- Label all tools and equipment in the laboratory.
- Graphically illustrate procedures performed in the class.
- Use transparencies when lecturing.
- Construct written directions. Number each task. Use short sentences and put them in sequential order.
- Construct a dictionary of technical and common words frequently used in your program.
- Demonstrate procedures. Use a flip chart to illustrate the term that identifies the procedure.
- Read written content information out loud.
- Request easier-to-read materials from publishers.

- Have recordings of texts available. These may be obtained commercially or learners can record them for extra credit.
- Evaluate the readability level of all chapters of a text, manual, pamphlet, or handout. Match these results with the reading level of specific learners.
- Make sure alternate instructional techniques use the same content, terms, and sequence used in printed materials (e.g., slides, video, cassettes).
- Encourage note taking by peer volunteers to allow learners with special needs to listen and concentrate on content being presented.
- Use posters and bulletin boards to create a reading atmosphere.
- Teach learners to break words into syllables.
- Have learners construct vocabulary games to use in class.
- While watching a film or video, ask learners to write down the main idea of specific portions. Details can be added by providing learners with a guided outline.
- Create a picture dictionary of tools and equipment used in the laboratory.
- Prepare group reading activities so that learners can learn from one another.
- Do not use one unfamiliar term to explain another.
- Have learners repeat unfamiliar terms and write them on the board so they can both hear them and see them.
- Have materials available at many reading levels. Preview all materials before purchasing so that the content, terms, and sequence are in line with the instructional objectives.
- Record lectures so that learners can review the content auditorily.
- Develop worksheets rather than textbook reading assignments by copying specific pages from a book or manual. With this method the learner does not have to deal with an entire text.
- Present as many hands-on experiences as possible to offset the learner's inability to read.
- Develop key concept worksheets to be completed prior to reading assignments.
- Preteach the special technical vocabulary or trade talk terms that your learners must know in order to understand reading material, as well as those important illustrations that they often ignore.
- Use structured overview diagrams showing the relationship of words to each other. See Figure 8-35.

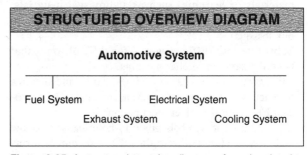

Figure 8-35. A structured overview diagram of words related to the topic automotive system.

- Use a vocabulary scan where the learner looks for unfamiliar words in an assigned reading, looks words up in the glossary, and gains a general understanding of their definitions by reading sentences in which they are placed.
- Create a vocabulary workbook of survival vocabulary for the career and technical education program. The definitions should not be seen as complete, but rather as a first step in understanding a word (e.g., Electrical Survival Vocabulary—circuit, current, resistance, flowing, amperage, meter, ammeter).
- Have the learner create a glossary of terms as instruction progresses. Use of appropriate glossaries is important in building the learner's vocabulary. Definitions of terms should be self-explanatory. Only use words that have been defined previously.
- Review the definitions given in the glossaries of the textbook or manual being used in a course. If the definitions are too difficult, instructors may have to write their own or direct the learner to other glossaries or dictionaries that pertain to the subject (pictures, diagrams, and sketches are extremely useful).
- Work on comprehension skills (e.g., recalling facts/details, choosing main ideas and concepts, drawing conclusions, making inferences/judgments, placing events/items in order, observing cause-and-effect, developing critical-thinking skills, perceiving relationships).
- Tab books and pamphlets to indicate what topics are available from them.
- Use a wall chart to indicate what materials the learner may consult when looking for alternatives to a topic.
- Cut up texts and arrange in folders with extraneous parts deleted and teacher explanations added for important or confusing sections.
- Explore the organization of each chapter before the learner reads the material independently (e.g., subheadings, analyzing illustrations, reading introductory paragraphs, highlighting important sentences, reading the concluding paragraphs/summary, and glancing at questions and/or exercises).
- Provide study guides (i.e., outline main points, define important terms, note important sections/directions/visuals/activities, provide questions that lead to various parts of the text, and guide learners to other related materials or activities such as audiovisual materials, alternate written materials, specific projects, and previous lessons).
- Substitute less difficult words for difficult ones that have the same or similar meaning.
- Utilize vocabulary chapters (slides, cards, and pictures to teach a learner how to use and recognize basic vocabulary within a given occupation).
- Develop a basic symbols guide to help learners follow task sheets and/or develop a related technical terms sight vocabulary for a specific career and technical education program. See Figure 8-36.

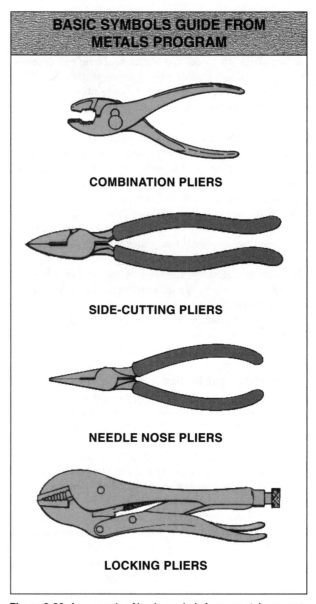

BASIC SYMBOLS GUIDE FROM METALS PROGRAM

COMBINATION PLIERS

SIDE-CUTTING PLIERS

NEEDLE NOSE PLIERS

LOCKING PLIERS

Figure 8-36. An example of basic symbols from a metals program to help learners follow a task sheet and/or develop a technical terms sight vocabulary.

ASSISTANCE FOR LEARNERS WITH MATH DEFICIENCIES

Some learners from special populations will have math deficiencies. Some may have problems with basic computation (addition, subtraction, multiplication, division). Others may have difficulty with reading numbers on objects (rulers, thermometers), measurement, telling time, converting fractions, determining numerical place value, or making estimations. Often these learners will have difficulty reading math problems and communicating an answer in writing, even though mental calculation is possible.

The math abilities of a learner can be determined by referring to learner records, asking support teachers, or utilizing teacher-made or standardized checks of critical basic operations and measurement prior to regular instruction. Nothing about a learner's abilities should be taken for granted. Find out from support personnel who work with the learner exactly what math deficiencies the learner has.

Stern-Otazo (1980) and Kok (1982) suggested some tips that would assist educators in working with learners who have math deficiencies including the following:

- If learners are unable to complete an entire assignment, offer a choice of doing any 10 out of 20 problems or the top or bottom half of a page.
- Have a timed daily quiz (two to three minutes) at the beginning of a class. Each day, have the learners correct the quizzes themselves. Make the time allotment for the quiz not quite long enough for most learners to complete. Give the same quiz four days in a row or give the same problem and only change the numbers. Grade on the last day.
- Concentrate on what the learner is ready for.
- By the eleventh grade, bypass what the learner is having trouble with by using calculators, tables, pocket charts, etc.
- Develop worksheets on shortcuts, such as one depicting number values (e.g., tens, ones) and multiplication charts.
- Learners might have trouble keeping track of numbers in their heads. When learners must count out several measures (such as for a feed mixture or a large recipe), teach them to use a computer to keep track.
- Check for the basics such as telling time, reading numbers up to six places, reading whole numbers and decimals to .001″, knowing basic geometric shapes, reading and using the ruler to $\frac{1}{32}$″, measuring temperature, and estimating time.
- Check for understanding of the math vocabulary. List the vocabulary and define at the beginning of class.
- Present materials in an organized, step-by-step way. List and number the steps.
- Make the symbols clear and understandable.
- If learners reverse numbers or mislay them during operations, have them use graph paper or work the operation in a tic-tac-toe configuration.
- Never require learners to perform concurrent math operations unless you are sure they can perform all the operations required.
- Remember, the product is the most important aspect of your math objectives for learners as opposed to the process.
- Increase the use of visual aids, particularly in the area of measurement in the classroom and laboratory.
- Have the learner say the math problem out loud and verbally indicate the steps.
- If the emphasis is on process and accuracy, allow extra time and the use of the calculator.

- Use oral tests in which learners can explain process and pinpoint problems.
- Talk through word problems and draw a chart to show the reasoning.
- Practice with formulas and make them understandable by putting them into common terms.
- Bring in a math specialist to the classroom to teach a specific area such as linear or square measurement and conversion of fractions to decimals.
- An important point in teaching math skills will be the instructional sequence (i.e., simple to complex) rather than trying to teach math skills as a whole.
- Only teach those math skills that are essential to the completion of a performance task. Do not waste time teaching concepts that are not directly related to what the learner is being asked to do.
- If the task requires a number of steps, give only one step at a time. For some learners, smaller steps will have to be identified, and even for that smaller step your instructions will have to be more complete.
- Let learners learn the last step in a series first and work back to being able to do the entire series.
- Set aside an hour a week to work on math-related skills.
- Gather math-related materials that correspond to the interest area of the career and technical education program of the learner.
- Use visual and tactile materials to demonstrate math concepts (e.g., measure the floor of the classroom to figure footage; use charts, graphs, diagrams, and prints to develop math problems).
- Mark a clear plastic bottle with the required amounts of ingredients for solutions, rather than having them count out capfuls or measuring ingredients.
- Some learners find decimals easier to work with than fractions. Convert recipes, formulas, or measurements from fractions to decimals.
- Spell out all words, rather than using abbreviations (e.g., tablespoon for "tbs").

ASSISTANCE FOR LEARNERS WITH DEFICIENCIES IN ORAL AND WRITTEN COMMUNICATION

Many learners from special populations have problems with communication skills. This includes writing skills such as spelling, capitalization, correct grammar, punctuation, appropriate wording, and appropriate form and style of writing. Writing skills are essential for many jobs. Both career and technical instructors and academic instructors should inform learners of the writing tasks they will have in the work world and help them to develop appropriate skills.

Learners will also have to demonstrate appropriate oral communication skills in order to be employable. They will be expected to communicate with customers, peers, and supervisors on a day-to-day basis. They will have to give clear instructions to others. In addition to speaking, learners will also have to practice effective listening skills, as listening is equally important in the workplace. They will have to follow verbal instructions given to them by others.

A compilation of tips and techniques that can assist career and technical educators in meeting the needs of learners who have reading deficiencies include the following:

- Identify career requirements by reviewing occupational and task analyses from which course competencies are derived to determine writing aspects of a job. (e.g., one task of a medical assistant is to receive and record laboratory test results).
- Identify the writing needs of each learner. Language arts and English teachers can be very beneficial in this process. Strengths and limitations should be shared with all teachers working with the learner.
- Provide career-relevant writing models to be used in both English and career and technical education programs (e.g., memos).
- If the career and technical education instructor and the English teacher have worked out a systematic cross-correlation of their course tasks, it is particularly effective to schedule related work in each course at the same time, or close to the same time.
- Individualize writing instruction in order to meet individual needs.
- Learners improve more quickly with feedback on how they have improved and what areas still need work. Feedback from both career and technical instructors and English teachers will help them to improve their writing and will reinforce the integrated nature of educational planning.
- Plan and critique oral presentations in career and technical education programs and in English classes. It is possible to ask other learners in the classes to offer feedback both on the basis of content and of presentation skills.
- Utilize role-playing, simulations, and real-life situations to encourage learners to practice oral skills in a situation as close to the actual work world as possible (The National Center for Research in Vocational Education, 1989).

EFFECTIVE INSTRUCTOR TOOLBOX

No matter how many strategies are in an instructor's "toolbox," there is always room in it for new ideas. Instructors have found the following list of suggestions effective in delivering instruction:

- Provide learners with booklists, course outlines, and a schedule of assignments. A list of pertinent study skills for the subject matter would also be very helpful.
- Make provisions for key course text and materials to be audio taped or scanned to disk.
- Announce reading assignments well in advance for those learners who are using audio-taped materials or have to arrange for readers.

- Provide information about any changes in the lecture/tutorial schedule, assignments, or examinations both orally and in writing.
- Provide guides that help learners with practical tasks (e.g., a guide to essay or paper writing).
- Always present an outline of the structure of a lecture, lab activity or tutorial session.
- Allow audio taping of lectures.
- Make copies of lecture summaries, outlines of lecture content, and overheads available to supplement the learners' own lecture notes.
- Use demonstrations and concrete examples where appropriate. Relate new or abstract concepts to everyday life.
- Provide learners with study guides that direct them to key points in their reading.
- Explain complex ideas as clearly and simply as possible by repeating and rephrasing explanations and information.
- Be sensitive about learners with identified learning problems being self-conscious in lectures and tutorials.
- Where appropriate, use diagrams or charts to disseminate information and provide copies for learners. Information presented in this manner may stay longer in short-term memory than information that is only heard.
- Encourage learners to form cooperative learning groups in which to discuss and review class material.
- Encourage learners who are experiencing learning difficulties to consult counseling, language, and learning support personnel.
- Allow the use of FM transmitters and receivers. This is especially helpful for learners with auditory language processing difficulties.
- Allow for alternative assignment formats (e.g. oral reports, demonstrations, use of video, tape recorder, or word processor).
- Permit time extensions for written assignments when appropriate.
- Consider alternative or supplementary assignments (e.g., taped interviews, slide presentations, photographic essays or handmade models).
- Provide feedback on completed work in appropriate formats (e.g., oral, typed, or on tape).
- Let learners know as early as possible if they are not reaching required standards.
- Allow for the use of alternative modes of assessment (e.g., allow learners to demonstrate knowledge and understanding in oral or audio-taped examinations or class presentations).
- Permit time extension of examinations and tests when appropriate.
- Allow the use of aids and equipment such as dictionaries, word processors with spelling and grammar check programs, scribes, and talking calculators.
- Tolerate deficiencies in handwriting and spelling in some learners. It must be reiterated that while learners with learning disabilities should receive appropriate

accommodations and support, it is not suggested that core elements or inherent requirements of a course be diminished in any way. Educators will need to carefully consider the value and relevance of core elements in each course they offer.

STRATEGIES FOR CULTURALLY DIVERSE LEARNERS

There are several educational factors that affect the success of culturally diverse learners—the school's atmosphere and overall attitude toward diversity, involvement of the community, and culturally responsive curriculum. Of all these factors, the personal and academic relationships between teachers and their learners may be the most influential. This relationship has been referred to as the core relationship of learning.

Burnette (1999) identified certain behaviors and instructional strategies that enable teachers to build a stronger teaching/learning relationship with their culturally diverse learners. Many of these behaviors and strategies exemplify standard practices of good teaching, and others are specific to working with learners from diverse cultures. They include the following:

- Appreciate and accommodate the similarities and differences among the learners' cultures. Effective teachers of culturally diverse learners acknowledge both individual and cultural differences enthusiastically and identify these differences in a positive manner. This positive identification creates a basis for the development of effective communication and instructional strategies. Social skills such as respect and cross-cultural understanding can be modeled, taught, prompted and reinforced by the teacher.

- Build relationships with your learners. African-American high school learners who presented behavior challenges for staff revealed that they wanted their teachers to discover what their lives were like outside of school and that they wanted an opportunity to benefit from the school's reward system. Developing an understanding of learners' lives also enables the teacher to increase the relevance of lessons and make examples more meaningful.

- Teach learners to match their behaviors to the setting. Everyone behaves differently in different settings. For example, people generally behave more formally at official ceremonies. Teaching learners the differences between home, school, and community settings can help them switch to appropriate behavior for each context. A teacher may talk about the differences between conversation with friends in the community and conversation with adults at school and discuss how each behavior is valued and useful in that setting. While some learners adjust their behavior automatically, others must be taught and provided ample opportunities to practice. Involving families and the community can help learners learn to adjust their behavior in each of the settings in which they interact.

- Use a variety of instructional strategies and learning activities. Offering variety provides the learners with opportunities to learn in ways that are responsive to their own communication styles, cognitive styles, and aptitudes. In addition, variety helps them develop and strengthen other approaches to learning.

- Consider learners' cultures and language skills when developing learning objectives and instructional activities. Facilitate comparable learning opportunities for learners with differing characteristics. For example, consider opportunities for learners who differ in appearance, race, sex, disability, ethnicity, religion, socioeconomic status, or ability.

- Incorporate objectives for effective personal development–Provide increased opportunities for high- and low-achievers to boost their self-esteem, develop positive self-attributes, and enhance their strengths and talents. Such opportunities can enhance their motivation to learn and achieve.

- Communicate expectations. Let learners know the classroom rules about talking, verbal participation in lessons, and moving about the room. Tell them how long a task will take to complete or how long it will take to learn a skill or strategy. For example, it may be necessary to encourage learners who expect to achieve mastery but are struggling to do so. They may need to know that they have the ability to achieve mastery, but must work through the difficulty.

- Provide rationales. Explain the benefit of learning a concept, skill, or task. Ask learners to tell you the rationale for learning and explain how the concept or skill applies to their lives at school, home, and work.

- Use advance- and post-organizers. At the beginning of lessons, give the learners an overview and tell them the purpose or goal. If applicable, tell them the order that the lessons will follow and relate it to previous lessons. At the end of the lesson, summarize the main points.

- Provide frequent review of the content learned. Provide a brief review of the previous lesson before continuing on to a new and related lesson.

- Facilitate independence in thinking and action. There are many ways to facilitate learners' independence. For example, when learners begin their work without specific instructions from the teacher, they are displaying independence. When learners ask questions, the teacher can encourage independence by responding in a way that lets them know how to find the answer for him- or herself. When teachers ask learners to evaluate their own work or progress, they are also facilitating independence.

- Promote learner on-task behavior. Keeping learners on-task maintains a high level of intensity of instruction. By starting lessons promptly and minimizing transition time between lessons, teachers can help learners stay on-task. Keeping learners actively involved in lessons (e.g., asking learners questions) also helps them stay focused and increases the instruction's intensity.

- Monitor learners' academic progress during lessons and independent work. Check with learners to see if they need assistance before they have to ask for help. Ask if they have any questions about what they are doing. Also make the learners aware of the various situations in which a skill or strategy can be used as well as adaptations that will broaden its applicability to additional situations.
- Provide frequent feedback. Feedback at multiple levels is preferred. The teacher may give positive feedback by stating the appropriate aspects of a learner's performance. Finally, the teacher may give positive corrective feedback by making learners aware of specific aspects of their performance that need work by reviewing concepts and asking questions, making suggestions for improvement, and having the learners correct their work.
- Require mastery. Require learners to master one task before going on to the next. When tasks are assigned, tell the learners the criteria that define mastery and the different ways mastery can be obtained. Give learners corrective feedback to let them know what aspects they have mastered and what aspects still need work. When the task is complete, let learners know that mastery was reached.

Culturally responsive schools and classes exhibit the following traits:

- The curriculum content is inclusive, meaning it reflects the cultural, ethnic, and gender diversity of society and the world.
- Instructional and assessment practices build on the learners' prior knowledge, culture, and language.
- Classroom practices stimulate learners to construct knowledge, make meaning, and examine cultural biases and assumptions.
- Schoolwide beliefs and practices foster understanding and respect for cultural diversity and celebrate the contributions of diverse groups.
- School programs and instructional practices draw from and integrate community and family language and culture and help families and communities to support the learners' academic success.

Davis (1999) described the following general strategies to work effectively with a diverse range of learners in a classroom:

- Recognize any biases or stereotypes that may have been absorbed. Do instructors undervalue comments made by speakers whose English is accented differently than their own?
- Treat each learner as an individual and respect learners for who they are. Everyone has some characteristics in common with others of their gender, race, place of origin, and socio-cultural group, but these are outweighed by the many differences among members of any group. Individuals tend to recognize this point about groups they belong to but sometimes fail to recognize it about other individuals. However, any group label involves a wide variety of individuals—people of different social and economic background, historical and generational experience, and levels of consciousness. Instructors should try not to project their experiences with, feelings about, or expectations of an entire group onto any one learner. Keep in mind, though, that group identity can be very important for some learners.
- Rectify any language patterns or case examples that exclude or demean any groups. Do instructors use both "he" and "she" during lectures, discussions, and in writing? Do instructors recognize that their learners may come from diverse socioeconomic backgrounds? Do instructors refrain from remarks that make assumptions about their learners' experiences? Finally, do instructors try to draw case studies, examples, and anecdotes from a variety of cultural and social contents?
- Be sensitive to terminology. Terminology changes over time, as ethnic and cultural groups continue to define their identity, their history, and their relationship to the dominant culture.
- Emphasize the importance of considering different approaches and viewpoints. Some of the primary goals of education are to show learners different points of view and to encourage them to evaluate their own beliefs. Help learners begin to appreciate the number of situations that can be understood only by comparing several interpretations, and help them appreciate how one's premises, observations, and interpretations are influenced by social identity and background.
- Make it clear that all comments are valued. Learners need to feel free to voice an opinion and empowered to defend it. Instructors must not allow their own differences of opinion prevent communication and debate. Step in if some learners seem to be ignoring the viewpoints of others.
- Encourage all learners to participate in class discussion. Instructors can prevent any one group of learners from monopolizing the discussion through active solicitation of alternative viewpoints. Encourage learners to listen to and value comments made from perspectives other than their own. Instructors may want to have learners work in small groups early in the term so that all learners can participate in nonthreatening circumstances. This may make it easier for learners to speak up in a larger setting.
- Speak up promptly if a learner makes a distasteful remark even jokingly. Don't let disparaging comments pass unnoticed. Explain why a comment is offensive or insensitive. Let learners know that racist, sexist, and other types of discriminatory remarks are unacceptable in class.
- Avoid singling out a learner as spokesperson. It is unfair to ask a learner to speak for an entire race, culture, or nationality.
- Be sensitive to learners whose first language is not English. Ask an English as a second language (ESL) specialist for advice about how to grade papers and for information about typical patterns of errors related to your learners' native languages.

- Suggest that learners form study teams that meet outside of class. By arranging for times and rooms where groups can meet, you can encourage learners to study together. Peer support is an important factor in learner persistence in school.
- Assign group work and collaborative learning activities. Learners report having their best encounters and achieving their greatest understandings of diversity as side effects of naturally occurring meaningful educational or community service experiences. Consider increasing learners' opportunities for group projects in which three to five learners complete a specific task, for small group work during class, or for collaborative research efforts among two or three learners to develop instructional materials or carry out a piece of research study. Collaborative learning can be as simple as randomly grouping (by counting off) two or three learners in class to solve a particular problem or to answer a specific question.

SUMMARY

Individuals from special populations represent a diverse population of learners who posses a variety of different learning styles. They cannot all learn at the same rate or through the same instructional techniques. The characteristics, abilities, interests, learning styles, and needs of each learner must be taken into consideration when planning classroom and laboratory instruction. Methods used by career and technical education instructors to present program content may make the difference between success and failure. One instructional technique will not meet the unique needs of every learner who has special needs. It will require a degree of flexibility and experimentation on the part of the instructor to determine what techniques best meet the needs of every learner who has special needs. Therefore, a variety of techniques should be used to address individual differences of these learners. It is often helpful for career and technical education instructors to work cooperatively with other personnel who may be familiar with appropriate instructional techniques.

SELF-ASSESSMENT

1. Why should career and technical education instructors use a variety of teaching strategies to deliver their curriculum to learners from special populations?
2. What are the steps in utilizing direct instruction with learners in a classroom environment?
3. What is the process of individualized instruction as an instructional strategy?
4. What is the philosophy of mastery learning and what are the steps involved in utilizing this technique in a classroom environment?
5. What are some effective study skills that learners can utilize to succeed in career and technical education programs?
6. What are some effective methods to teach critical-thinking and problem-solving skills in career and technical education programs?
7. What are some effective strategies to assist learners with reading deficiencies?
8. What are some effective strategies to assist learners with math deficiencies?
9. What are some effective strategies to assist learners who have problems with oral and written communication skills?

ASSOCIATED ACTIVITIES

1. Make a list of all the learners from special populations enrolled in your program. Contact support personnel and other instructors to discuss the learners' ability levels, strong learning styles, and specific needs. Discuss what instructional techniques would be most effective in planning for each learner.
2. Plan a demonstration to be incorporated into a lesson or unit that you will be teaching. Be sure to keep in mind the considerations mentioned in this chapter.
3. Plan job site visitations and shadowing experiences for the entire class or a small group of learners with special needs. Allow these learners to participate in planning and implementing these experiences.
4. Study your class list and develop some flexible grouping patterns that would help learners with special needs to succeed in classroom or laboratory activities, projects, and program assignments.
5. Talk to other career and technical education instructors, support personnel, career and technical education administrators, and state department contacts to determine whether there are commercial or teacher-prepared individualized instructional materials available for use by learners from special populations.
6. If there are no individualized instruction materials readily available to you, inquire about the existence of funds to purchase some of these materials. If you still receive a negative response, work cooperatively with other personnel to develop individualized materials and activities for your program.
7. Develop a format for student-teacher contracts to be used with learners with special needs in your program. Plan contract format, guidelines, and evaluation criteria in coordination with learners and support staff.

8. Design a peer and cross-age tutoring system for your program. Plan elements of this tutoring system with colleagues on campus to make it a campus-wide effort.

9. Incorporate cooperative learning activities into your curriculum. Involve learners in determining the roles they will play in the cooperative learning groups. Change the group composition periodically so that learners have an opportunity to work with as many peers as possible.

10. Collaborate with your colleagues to plan some team teaching sessions where several instructors can parallel their curriculum. Share course competencies and decide where there is material to team teach.

11. Emphasize the importance of study skills to learners in your program. Work collaboratively with other colleagues to reinforce the development of these study skills in your program.

12. Plan activities in your curriculum to assist learners in developing critical-thinking and problem-solving skills. Make certain that learners are familiar with and feel comfortable in utilizing the steps in problem solving.

13. Utilize strategies to assist learners who have deficiencies in math, reading, and communication skills whenever possible.

REFERENCES

Asselin, S. (1986, Winter). Peer tutors: An idea that works. *Journal for Vocational Special Needs Education,* 31-24.

Bellanca, J., & Fogarty, F. (1991). *Blueprints for thinking in the cooperative classroom.* Arlington Heights, IL: Skylight Training and Publishing.

Bloom, B. (1971). Mastery learning. In J. Block (Ed.), *Mastery learning: Theory and practice.* New York: Holt, Rinehart and Winston.

Bromley, DeVitis, & Modlo. (1999). *50 graphic organizers for reading, writing & more.* New York: Scholastic Books.

Burnette, J. (1999, November). *Critical behaviors and strategies for teaching culturally diverse students.* Arlington, VA: ERIC Clearinghouse on Disabilities and Gifted Education.

Cameron, C. (1991). Cooperative learning. In L. West (Ed.), *Effective strategies for dropout prevention of at-risk youth.* Gaithersburg, MD: Aspen Publishers.

Center for Innovations in Special Education (formerly Missouri LINC). (1991). Study skills. *Linefact,* 27.

Costa, A. (1981). Teaching for intelligent behavior. *Educational Leadership, 39*(1), 29-32.

Costa, A. (1984). Mediating the metacognitive. *Educational Leadership, 42,* 57-62.

Davis, B. (1999, September). Diversity and complexity in the classroom. *Tools for Teaching.* San Francisco: Jossey-Bass.

Dwyer, D. (1994). Apple classrooms of tomorrow: What we've learned. *Educational Leadership, 51*(7), 4-10.

Feichtner, S. (1989, March). Computers for special populations. *Vocational Education Journal,* 36-37, 51.

Fogarty, R. (1997). *Multiple intelligences classroom.* Arlington Heights, IL: Skylight Training and Publishing.

Fulk, B. (2000, January). 20 ways to make instruction more memorable. *Intervention in School and Clinic, 35*(3), 183-84.

Gardner, H. (1993). *Frames of mind: The theory of multiple intelligences.* Boulder, CO: Basic Books/Perseus Books Group.

Greene, G., Albright, L., Kokaska, C., & Becham-Greene, C. (1987). *Strategies for provision of regular vocational education for special education students: A handbook.* Sacramento, CA: California State Department of Education: Special Education Division.

Guskey, T. (1980, October). What is mastery learning? And why do educators have such hopes for it? *Instructor,* 80-86.

Huck, R., Myers, R., & Wilson, J. (1989). *ADAPT-A developmental activity program for teachers* (2nd ed.). Pittsburgh, PA: Allegheny Intermediate Unit.

Johnson, D., Johnson, R., Holubee, E., & Roy, P. (1984). *Circles of learning.* Washington, DC: Association for Supervision and Curriculum Development.

Kok, M. (1982). *Three options for placement.* College Station, TX: Texas A&M University, Industrial Education Department.

Lazear, D. (1999). *Eight ways of teaching.* Arlington Heights, IL: Skylight Professional Development.

Lehr, J. & Harris, H. (1988). *At-risk, low-achieving students in the classroom.* Washington, DC: National Education Association.

Lenger, S., & Lenger, W. (1977). *57 ways to teach.* Los Angeles, CA: Crescent Publications.

Maryland State Department of Education. (n.d.). *Enhancing thinking in vocational programs.* Baltimore, MD: Division of Vocational-Technical Education and Division of Instruction.

Massachusetts Department of Education. (2001). *Principles of effective teaching and examples of descriptors.* [On-line]. Available: http://www.doe.mass.edu/lawsregs/603cmr35/603cmr35_3.html

Meier, D. (2000). *The accelerated learning handbook.* New York: McGraw-Hill.

Model Resource Room Project, Plymouth, MI. (1981). In L. Albright & R. Cobb, *Assessment of students with handicaps in vocational education: A curriculum-based approach.* Alexandria, VA: American Vocational Association.

The National Center for Research in Vocational Education. (1977a). *Demonstrate a manipulative skill.* Columbus, OH: The Ohio State University.

The National Center for Research in Vocational Education. (1977b). *Direct field trips.* Columbus, OH: The Ohio State University.

The National Center for Research in Vocational Education. (1977c). *Employ the team teaching approach.* Columbus, OH: The Ohio State University.

The National Center for Research in Vocational Education. (1989). *Basics: Bridging vocational and academic skills.* Columbus, OH: The Ohio State University.

Norris, S. (1985). Synthesis of research on critical thinking. *Educational Leadership, 42,* 40-45.

Peck, K., & Dorricott, D. (1994). Why use technology? *Educational Leadership, 51*(7), 11-14.

Peryon, C. (1978). *Direct instruction: Don't I instruct directly?* Agana, Guam: International Reading Association Annual Conference.

San Mateo County Office of Education. (2001). *Project-based learning with multimedia.* Redwood City, CA: Author.

Schlechty, P. (2001). *10 critical qualities of student work: Phil Schlecty on student work.* [On-line]. Available: http://www.middleweb.com/schlechty.html

Slavin, R. (1990). Here to stay—or gone tomorrow. *Educational Leadership, 47*(4), 1.

Stern-Otazo, K. (1980). Curriculum modification and instructional practices. In G. Meers (Ed.), *Handbook of special vocational needs education.* Rockville, MD: Aspen System Corporation.

Stern-Otazo, K., & D'Oronzio, A. (1980). Helping vocational students improve reading skills. *Journal for Vocational Special Needs Personnel, 2*(3), 7-12.

Stiggins, R., Rubel, E., & Quellmalz, E. (1988). *Measuring thinking skills in the classroom.* Washington, DC: National Education Association.

Tindall, L., & Gugerty, J. (1982, December). *Microcomputers for the vocational education of special needs students.* St. Louis, MO: Presentation at the 1982 American Vocational Association Convention, Special Needs Division.

Vaughn, S., Schumm, J., & Arguelles, M. (1997, November/December). The ABCDEs of co-teaching. *Teaching Exceptional Children, 39*(2).

Walker, D. (1998). *Strategies for teaching differently.* Thousand Oaks, CA: Corwin Press.

Warren-Sams, B. (2001). Assessing technology access and use: A checklist for equity. *Closing the equity gap in technology access and use: A practical guide for K-12 educators.* Portland, OR: Northwest Regional Educational Laboratory.

White, S. (1987). The modification of curriculum and instruction: Catalyst for equity. In G. Meers (Ed.), *Handbook of vocational special needs education.* Gaithersburg, MD: Aspen Publishers.

Yamashiro, K. (n.d.). *The traditional classroom and the contemporary work environment.* Honolulu, HI: Office of the Chancellor for Community Colleges.

Zorfass, J., Corley, P., & Remz, A. (1994). Helping students with disabilities become writers. *Educational Leadership, 51*(7), 62-66.

Evaluation Strategies

INTRODUCTION

Assessing learner progress is an important component of the learning process. Traditionally, instructors viewed assessment as the process of determining learner achievement after instruction had been delivered. Assessment was primarily used to arrive at grades or symbols representing what learners knew and to a lesser extent, what they could do. Educational reform in the 1980s and 1990s ushered in the standards movement and accountability became more important than ever. Educators were asked to develop new models of schooling with assessment directed not on what learners could memorize to pass traditional tests, but on what they needed to know and be able to do in real life.

States and local schools have made considerable progress in developing new educational standards and developing new assessment formats to measure learner progress in light of these standards. Today, instructors at every level are updating their knowledge and skills of traditional assessment and new assessment methods to improve the way they assess learner achievement in relation to performance standards. New assessment strategies and techniques such as portfolios, writing scenarios, learning logs and journals, performance events and projects, and graphic organizers are being used to make assessment an integral part of instruction rather than something occurring at the end of instruction for grading purposes. These new assessment tools are particularly suited for use with learners from special populations because of their flexibility, allowing learners to maximize their strengths.

The information contained in this chapter should be very useful in helping teachers and support personnel improve how they assess learners from special populations. The chapter contains information on the status of assessment used with learners from special populations, how to modify traditional assessment strategies, how to use new alternative assessment tools to improve learning, and how to arrive at a more fair and accurate assessment of learner progress in relation to identified learning outcomes.

OUTLINE

CURRENT STATE OF ASSESSMENT
NATIONAL SKILL STANDARDS: BASIS FOR ASSESSMENT
ALTERNATIVE ASSESSMENTS
TRADITIONAL ASSESSMENT AND EDUCATIONAL REFORM
GENERAL ASSESSMENT CONSIDERATIONS
BENEFITS PROVIDED BY EVALUATION
PROTECTING CONFIDENTIALITY OF INFORMATION
PROSPECTIVE ON ASSESSMENT
IEP AND ITP AS GUIDES FOR ASSESSMENT
ESTABLISHING EVALUATION SYSTEMS
EVALUATION TOPICS
EVALUATION METHODS AND TECHNIQUES
GRADING AND REPORTING SYSTEMS
MARKING SYSTEMS
SUMMARY
SELF-ASSESSMENT
ASSOCIATED ACTIVITIES
REFERENCES

OBJECTIVES

After completing this chapter, the reader should be able to accomplish the following:

1. Define what a national skill standard is and describe why a system of voluntary, national skill standards should be developed and used to guide instruction and assessment.
2. Identify and describe the four recent legislative enactments that promote the development of work transition programs, performance standards, and performance measures.
3. Explain why proponents for alternative assessments argue for their use in assessing learner progress and growth.
4. Describe how assessment should be viewed in terms of the educational process.
5. Discuss why teachers and schools have been slow to use alternative assessments.
6. List some design criteria for alternative assessments.
7. Describe why traditional assessment practices are insufficient for performance-based education approaches.
8. Discuss the general assessment considerations for evaluating learners from special populations.
9. Describe why a cooperative team approach should be used in developing the assessment components of a learner's IEP or ITP.
10. Identify and briefly describe the components that should be considered in establishing an evaluation system for learners with special needs.
11. Describe the common item formats for cognitive achievement tests.
12. Describe how cognitive achievement test directions and items can be modified to make them more suitable for learners with special needs.
13. List some of the feedback techniques teachers can employ to improve learning.
14. Describe why learners should be encouraged to reflect on their learning and how learners can record and assess their reflective thinking.
15. Describe why teachers need to emphasize the connections between past, present, and future learning and how teachers can assess a learner's ability to establish connections.
16. Describe why learners need to be encouraged to assess their work and how teachers can facilitate this process.
17. Describe some of the practices teachers can follow to modify the way tests are formatted and administered to learners with special needs.
18. Describe the different types of rubrics and how to construct and use them to assess learner performance.
19. Discuss the learner project method of assessment and how the C-TAP project is assessed.
20. Discuss the written scenario assessment method used in the C-TAP project.
21. Describe how the portfolio can be used to assess achievement of learners from special populations.
22. Discuss how observational techniques can be used to evaluate learner behaviors on a daily basis.
23. Discuss how the peer evaluation technique can be used with learners from special populations.
24. Discuss some of the problems with grades and current reporting systems and how to overcome them.

TERMS

alternative assessments	measurement	portfolio
assessment	metacognitive assessment	reflection
authentic assessments	multiple intelligences	rubrics
benchmark	peer assessment	self-assessment
evaluation	performance assessment	specific feedback
grading	performance event	test
graphic organizer	performance project	testing
learning logs and journals	performance standards	

CURRENT STATE OF ASSESSMENT

Education reform in the 1980s and 1990s placed considerable emphasis on making schools more accountable and forced educators and policy makers at all levels to rethink what schools should teach and what learners should learn. Report after report called for a new model of schooling with assessment directed not on what learners can memorize but on what they need to know and be able to do. Numerous reports such as the SCANS (*Secretary's Commission of Achieving Necessary Skills*) have identified competencies that individuals must possess to successfully participate in the modern workplace. *America's Choice: High Skills or Low Wages*, a landmark 1990 report, called for the United States to create a single comprehensive system for general, professional, and technical education that meets the needs of everyone from high school learners to dislocated workers, from the hard-core unemployed to working adults who want to update and expand their skills. Four major pieces of legislation, the Perkins Amendments of 1990, the 1994 Goals 2000: Educate America Act, the 1994 School-to-Work Opportunities Act, and the Carl D. Perkins Vocational and Technical Education Act of 1998, encouraged the development and use of performance standards and measures and promoted the development of programs to help individuals make the transition from school to work more effectively. As a result of legislative enactments at the federal and state levels, there is a strong nationwide movement to develop national skill standards and a system of performance-based assessments to measure and document what learners know and are able to do in authentic situations.

Many states have made considerable progress in identifying and adopting educational standards and performance outcomes and developing new measurement formats to assess them. The National Center on Education and the Economy has developed a workforce skills program to implement the recommendations of the Commission on the Skills of the American Workforce and the New Standards Project. This voluntary partnership of states and school districts is committed to developing new assessments based upon recognized standards that can change the way teaching and learning occur in schools and how learner progress is measured and reported.

Teaching to the national skill standards level will involve the identification of educational outcomes and the use of both traditional and new assessments to ensure that our nation's learners graduate with more than basic skills. They need the ability to develop understanding and apply knowledge and skills to real-life situations. Career and technical education teachers will need to update their knowledge and skills of traditional and new assessment methods if they are to be ready to demonstrate how their learners' performances measures up against the specific outcomes that will be derived from voluntary national skill standards.

Wiggins (1997) states that the implications of the standards movement require wholesale changes in the way courses are designed and in our curriculum frameworks. He recommends that courses be designed backwards from worthy and authentic tasks and their particular demands, which meet high standards for work design, not from a logic based simply on the arrangement of textbook content or an analytical adult view of subject matter, which is the case in traditional curriculum frameworks. Wiggins states that curriculum must be developed from authentic tasks related to important standards and that these standards provide the rationale for content selection, skills, and modes of instruction. Wiggins maintains that three different types of standards are being offered in educational reform: content standards, or what learners should know and be able to do; performance standards, or how well learners must perform their work; and work-design standards, or what is worthy and rigorous work or what essential performance tasks learners should be able to do. He argues that standards must be set for the daily work teachers expect of learners and that teachers must design assessment strategies that will determine how well learners are meeting these standards.

A study of vocational learner assessment practices by Todd, et al. (1994) identified two major problem areas in present assessment practices: (1) They are often incomplete in that they do not cover all learning outcomes which should be assessed and/or they do not allow for full expression of the capabilities and needs of the learner, and (2) they are inappropriate in that they do not measure what is really needed or what is relevant to the learner. These authors included a statement from the California Assessment Collaborative (1991) that stated "The present form of assessing student performance does not assess the skills that students need to succeed in the field of work. Current assessment practices often do not adequately determine the students' ability to use their knowledge to solve real world problems," (p. 16). Ideally, what is needed is an assessment system that allows for a comprehensive, multifaceted look at a learner's personal attributes, capabilities, growth, and educational achievement. A cadre of alternative assessment practices promise to improve the way learners are assessed and to make assessment an ongoing part of instruction.

New assessment techniques such as portfolios, written scenarios, performance events, projects, interpretive events, demonstrations, computer simulations, and graphic organizers provide a means for making assessment an integral part of instruction that guides the learning process for all learners. These assessment practices are often labeled as authentic assessments because they are valuable learning activities in themselves and involve the performance of tasks that are directly related to real-life problems. These new performance-based assessment methods are particularly suited for use with learners from special populations because of their flexibility, allowing learners to emphasize their strengths. They provide opportunities for learners to plan, organize, and take responsibility for completing an assigned learning activity and for assessing their own progress. Additional benefits of performance-based assessments that make them attractive for use with learners from special populations include the following: (a) They focus on what learners can do, rather than on what they cannot do, (b) they accommodate a variety of learning styles, (c) they can assess a wide range of learning tasks, (d) they are open-ended, allowing learners to show extended knowledge and skills, (f) they require learners to take a more active, responsible role in their education, which enhances self-determination, and (g) they provide an opportunity for teachers and learners with special needs to collaborate about learning and assessments, which not only provides a clearer picture of learner achievement, but also allows learners to see how the quality of their work has evolved over time. New assessments as well as traditional assessments can be modified in a variety of ways to make them more meaningful to learners, teachers, and parents.

Traditional assessments commonly used in career and technical education programs often need to be modified to make them more effective and meaningful for evaluating learners from special populations. These modifications need to be made on an individual basis so that a more accurate and complete picture of the learner's strengths and needs can be obtained. Modifications can be made to test items, test item directions, the way tests are constructed, and the way they are administered and scored. In addition, modifications can be made in the way scores are summarized and reported to learner, parents, and others.

The evaluation system for measuring, assessing, and reporting the progress and growth of learners from special populations should be based on their needs and abilities related to specific competencies that are identified in each learner's individualized education program (IEP) or individualized transition program (ITP). The system should be comprehensive in scope, assessing a variety of important learning outcomes and using a variety of measurement and evaluation techniques. The system should not be designed and viewed as an add-on to instruction, but rather as an ongoing part of instruction. The challenge for career and technical education teachers is to design an evaluation and reporting system that identifies which forms of assessments are most appropriate for which educational purpose and to fold assessment into the instructional program so that learners are actively involved.

In general, career and technical education teachers need help in performing the role of evaluating learner progress and development—particularly in light of the development and use of alternative assessments. Effective evaluation is an ongoing, daily activity that consumes a considerable amount of a teacher's time. Stiggins (1988) indicated that about 30% of a teacher's time is directly involved in assessment activities, such as checking daily assignments, observing learning, monitoring learner progress, checking learner understanding through quizzes and oral discussion,

and critiquing learner written or computer work. He stated that about 90% of evaluation takes place in the classroom. He summarized the importance of teacher proficiency in their evaluation role with the statement "The assessments that count—the assessments that most strongly influence student learning and academic self-concept—are those developed and used by teachers in the classroom," (p. 368).

Ryan and Miyasaka (1995) describe the current state of testing and assessment as "in progress" with a growing body of new concepts, principles, methods, procedures, techniques, and policies. A review of literature reveals major changes in how we assess learners' abilities and achievements. There are many factors driving the current assessment reform movement, including a change of educational goals for American education; a changing global community that requires new knowledge and abilities; findings from cognitive psychology on the nature of meaningful, engaged learning; development of higher standards for learner learning in every state of the nation; the implementation of Howard Gardner's theory of multiple intelligences; limitations of standardized and teacher-made tests; the phenomena of teaching to the test; a shift from psychometrics to the assessment of learning (Stiggins, 1999); tests that sort and label learners and force them into molds that often create or reinforce barriers to equal opportunity (Zappardino, 1995); gross inequities resulting from inferences based solely on standardized and teacher-made tests; the applications of technology for instruction and assessment; and the realization that changes in assessment practices directly influence changes in the classroom.

Proponents for change in assessment maintain that what we assess and how we assess it affects both what is taught and the way it is taught. They argue that when curriculum, instruction, and assessment are integrated in a meaningful way, assessment becomes a valuable learning experience in itself. In the past few years, critics of the current assessment practices have called for dramatic changes in how we test and assess what learners know and are able to do. The proposition expressed by Resnick and Resnick, (1991) "you get what you assess" and "you don't get what you do not assess," is being widely embraced as a fundamental concept in the movement toward performance-based assessments (p. 59).

It should be noted that while there has been an overemphasis on assessment of elements of subject matter and a widespread use of objective test items that can be quickly scored by many teachers, skillful and effective teachers have been utilizing a cadre of meaningful tasks and good assessment techniques that require learners to analyze and synthesize information, apply what they have learned, and perform or demonstrate their understanding of the material according to specific criteria. These teachers have developed learning and assessment experiences that engage learners and teach them how to produce knowledge, not simply reproduce it (Burke, 1992).

Newman (1991) states the following:

> We must recognize the unfortunate record of traditional efforts to teach a virtually limitless list of fragmented pieces of declarative knowledge and commit ourselves to finding a better way to teach the current curriculum to students that involves the challenge of producing, rather than reproducing knowledge. (p. 459)

Steven Ferrara and Jay McTighe (1992) report that "many teachers are seeking to involve their students in the meaningful applications of knowledge and skills. These teachers seek to create a thoughtful classroom in which students assume a greater responsibility for constructing meaning for themselves," (p. 337). They argue such a classroom emphasizes active learning where learners work together to examine information and issues, solve problems, and communicate ideas in the form of completed projects and assignments. Teachers assume a more facilitative role, guiding learners in individual and group work, rather than dispensing subject matter content and then using traditional paper-pencil tests to measure cognitive knowledge. Thoughtful classrooms also place more emphasis on assessments that involve learners in authentic tasks, measure a variety of abilities and outcomes, and involve learners in self-assessment and reflection.

D. Monty Neill (1997), associate director of the National Center for Fair and Open Testing, describes his vision of a new assessment system in which

> teachers have a wide repertoire of classroom-based, culturally sensitive assessment practices and tools to use in helping each and every student learn to high standards; in which educators collaboratively use assessment information to continuously improve schools; in which important decisions about a student, such as readiness to graduate from high school, were based on the work done over the years by the student; in which schools in networks hold one another accountable for student learning; and in which public evidence of student achievement consists primarily of samples from student's actual schoolwork rather than just reports of results from one-shot examinations. (p. 34)

These ideas are at the core of *Principles and Indicators for Student Assessment Systems*, developed by the National Forum on Assessment. This forum advocates a radical reconstruction of assessment practices, with learning made central to assessment reform.

NATIONAL SKILL STANDARDS: BASIS FOR ASSESSMENT

The demands of the American workplace have been changing drastically in the last few years requiring workers at every level who can think, reason, question, understand, and contribute to delivering quality services and products to global customers. Today's workers need to provide leadership and function well in teams. They need to challenge the existing goals and ways of doing things and determine what is worth doing and how to do it better. They need to have broad-based, high-level technical and employability skills to adjust quickly to the changing demands of the work environment.

The American public has observed the American educational system and found it wanting. It has come to realize that only a small number of learners exiting American high schools have the skills employers say they want. At the forefront of educational reform is performance-based education and assessment with voluntary standards as the cornerstone. One of the major proposals to affect real change in America's schools is to abandon the system of credentialing learners based on seat time and courses taken in favor of one based on meeting high standards of achievement. Instead of a system that holds time constant and lets the standard of achievement vary among learners, the new system would hold the standard constant and let the time taken to reach it vary. New educational thought claims that all learners can learn at high levels given an interesting curriculum that is intellectually demanding and a compelling reason to work hard in school. Educational reformers who support the development and utilization of national standards would require that learners acquire a deep mastery of the core academic subjects as well as the capacity to apply what they know to the complex problems that characterize modern life and work (Workforce Skills Program, 1994).

Any new educational reform, like the national standards system, has its critics. Some would argue that adoption of national standards would eliminate local autonomy and lead to a rigid learning environment that could prevent access for some learners. Ravitch (1992) disagreed and said that

> far from standardizing and homogenizing American education and culture, these voluntary standards will offer a vision of excellence that can be reached through many approaches. And far from creating new barriers for minority children, the new standards will provide new hope by raising expectations and by establishing a vision of what is possible for all children. (p. 13)

What are national education standards? They are defined as what every learner should know and be able to do with their knowledge. They are statements of behavior requiring high-level mastery and they require that learners use their minds to think, to solve problems, and to reason. They are sometimes called world-class because they meet or exceed the standards established by our nation's strongest competitors (*The National Education Goals Report,* 1993).

Standards refer to both content and level of performance. Content standards describe the areas of knowledge and skill that all learners should master in order to be the productive workers and fully educated citizens of tomorrow. Although the subject matter standards are being developed separately, content standards should ultimately enhance efforts to combine ideas and skills from different subjects in meaningful ways to solve problems in the workplace and in everyday life. Performance standards are needed to serve as the basis of assessment to determine how well learners have mastered content standards. Basically, performance standards are statements describing how good is good enough. Learners will be assessed using measuring strategies that are based on content standards and scored against performance standards. Content and performance standards set high expectations for learners, but they also challenge teachers and parents to expect high levels of learner achievement (*National Education Goals Report,* 1993).

Congress has been actively involved in the educational reform movement and has passed several important enactments that have the potential to improve the quality of American education in general and particularly the way career and technical education programs deliver and assess the knowledge and skills of individuals preparing for postsecondary technical education and work.

On March 31, 1994 President Clinton signed the Goals 2000: Educate America Act into law and because it was made law before April 1st, Congress was able to take advantage of $100,000,000 appropriations for the new program in 1994, allowing the Department of Education to initiate planning grants to states after July 1 of that year. There are five major titles of this law; two are of primary interest here. The act created a National Education Goals Panel and the National Education Standards and Improvement Council. This Council is to certify voluntary national education content standards in core academic subjects and certify voluntary national opportunity-to-learn standards. The act also created the National Skill Standards Board, which will make grants to coalitions of education, business, and labor to develop voluntary national skill standards in a number of individual occupations. The National Skill Standards Board is charged with identifying broad clusters of major occupations in the United States and encouraging and facilitating the development of skill standards within those clusters with an initial set of skill standards developed by December of 1995. This board will then certify these voluntary standards. The reader should contact the National Skills Standards Board for the latest information on standards they have been developed top guide assessment. (*Vocational Education Weekly,* April 4, 1994).

The Goals 2000: Educate America Act defined eight national education goals that each state must work to achieve. See Figure 9-1. It also provided for the development of national education performance and content standards, and encouraged voluntary adoption of these standards by states or, if they wish, states may develop their own standards using the national standards as a model (Brustein & Mahler 1994).

On Monday, May 4, 1994 President Clinton signed the School-to-Work Opportunities Act (STWOA) into law. This act established a program to integrate work-based learning and school-based learning, integrate academic and occupational learning, and build effective linkages between secondary and postsecondary education. Section 102 of this act called for evaluations involving ongoing consultation with learners and dropouts to identify academic strengths and weaknesses, academic progress, workplace knowledge, goals, and the need for opportunities to master core academic and vocational skills (*Vocational Education Weekly,* May 2, 1994).

NATIONAL EDUCATION GOALS

1. All children in America will start school ready to learn.

2. The high school graduation rate will increase to at least 90%.

3. All students will leave grades 4, 8, and 12 having demonstrated competency over challenging subject matter including English, mathematics, science, foreign languages, civics and government, economics, arts, history and geography, and every school in America will ensure that all students learn to use their minds well, so they may be prepared for responsible citizenship, further learning and productive employment in our nation's modern economy.

4. The nation's teaching force will have access to programs for the continued professional development activities that will provide such teachers with the knowledge and skills needed to teach an increasingly diverse student population with a variety of educational, social, and health needs.

5. United States students will be first in the world in mathematics and science achievement.

6. Every adult American will be literate and will possess the knowledge and skills necessary to compete in a global economy and exercise the rights and responsibilities of citizenship.

7. Every school in the United States will be free of drugs, violence, and the unauthorized presence of firearms and alcohol and will offer a disciplined environment conducive to learning.

8. Every school will promote partnerships that will increase parental involvement and participation in promoting the social, emotional, and academic growth of children.

Source: Brustein, M., & Mahler, M. (1994). *AVA Guide to the School-to-Work Opportunities Act.* Alexandria, VA: American Vocational Association.

Figure 9-1. A listing of the National Education Goals defined by the Goals 2000: Educate America Act of 1994.

The STWOA required states to develop their own skill standards using the following criteria:

1. They must be benchmarked to high quality standards, to ensure that learners receiving portable skill certificates under the school-to-work system will have the ability to enter high-skill, high-wage employment.
2. They must be built upon available standards and assessments, which might be composed of a comprehensive set of broad-based workplace skills.
3. They must be developed to meet the requirements of broad clusters of related occupations and industries, rather than those of individual jobs or occupations, which would not provide the flexibility for learners or employees to move from one job to another.

These skill standards are expected to lead to nationally recognized skill certificates. Skill certificates are portable credentials certifying that a learner has mastered the skills of an industry that are at least as challenging as those developed by the National Skill Standards Board (Brustein & Mahler, 1994).

The Carl Perkins Vocational and Applied Technology Education Act of 1990 required states to develop and implement a state-wide system of performance standards and measures for vocational education programs. Local educational institutions were to implement these performance standards and measures with approved modifications. Performance standards and measures were to assess learning and competency attainment including basic academic skills, job skill or work skill attainment, retention in schools, and placement in additional training and or work after leaving the school (*The AVA Guide to the Carl D. Perkins Vocational and Applied Technology Education Act of 1990*, 1990).

The Carl D. Perkins Vocational and Technical Education Act of 1998 called on states to set expected performance levels for four categories: (1) learner attainment of academic as well as career and technical education proficiencies; (2) acquisition of secondary or postsecondary degrees or credentials; (3) placement and retention in postsecondary education or employment; and (4) completion of career and technical education programs that lead to nontraditional training and employment. The act requires that performance levels for these four indicators be expressed in percentages or numbers that make them objective, quantifiable, and measurable. The Perkins act requires states and local schools to provide programs for special populations and to evaluate these programs and assess how special populations are being served. Increased accountability is a cornerstone of the new Perkins Act and states will have to make adjustments in how data is collected and reported. States and local schools will have to assess and report learner achievement in a way they never have before. Career and technical education teachers need to develop and use a variety of assessments in order to present the most fair and accurate picture of achievement for all learners (American Vocational Association, 1998).

All four of these legislative enactments encouraged the development and use of performance standards and measures. Career and technical educators and selected industry groups are responding to this legislation and are now heavily involved in the development of national voluntary skill standards and learner assessment strategies that are closely linked to the four federal acts previously mentioned.

The Goals 2000: Educate America Act (PL 102-227) included Title V, which is known as the National Skill Standards Act. This act established the National Skill Standards Board (NSSB) composed of a coalition of leaders from business, labor, employee, education, civil rights, and community organizations, including career and technical student organizations, working together to build a voluntary national system of skills standards, assessment and certification systems to enhance the ability of the United States workforce to compete effectively in the global economy. The driving force for their efforts is the belief that standards are necessary because of the lack of connection between the skills needed in the modern workplace (characterized by advancing technology) and those imparted through education and training programs (*VICA Professional*, May, 1994). The NSSB has categorized the workforce into 15 industry sectors ranging from Agriculture, Forestry and Fishing to Utilities and Environmental and Waste Management. Each of these sectors is assembling skill standards, assessments, and certification for their respective industries. The U.S Department of Education and the U.S. Department of Labor jointly funded 13 demonstration projects that have served as models for the development of many others (National Skill Standards Board, 2001).

The NSSB has provided grants to several national organizations that are committed to the development of national skill standards like the Sales & Service Voluntary Partnership Inc., a national body serving as the catalyst for skill standards development for the retail, wholesale, real estate, and personal services industries; the Education and Training Partnership, a coalition of organizations developing a national system of voluntary standards, assessments, and certification systems for the education and training industry; and the Manufacturing Skill Standards Council, developing national skills standards systems for the manufacturing industry.

Another national organization, the National Center on Education and the Economy, is working to create a workforce development system that provides all Americans—from high school learners to dislocated workers to working adults who want to improve their skills—with the kind of education, training, information and guidance they need to pursue rewarding careers. This organization has developed the Workforce Development Program to carry out the mission first outlined in their 1990 report, *America's Choice: High Skills or Low Wages*. This workforce development program has played a key role in the National Skill Standards Board, whose goals include boosting the competitiveness of American firms, increasing the skills of the workforce, connecting skilled workers to better jobs, opening new opportunities for all workers, and reducing training and retraining costs for business. In addition to focusing on skill standards for the workforce, the center is organized to provide resources to schools, districts, and states interested in standards-based reform. One of the center's major products is the development of the New Standards Program, which represents the nation's most comprehensive and integrated internationally benchmarked performance standards for schools. Part of the program is the development of performance assessments that are matched to standards with assessments available now for mathematics and English language arts with development of assessments underway in science and applied learning (National Center on Education and the Economy, 1990).

Many states have followed the lead of the NSSB and the National Center on Education and the Economy, identifying and adopting educational standards and performance outcomes and developing new measurement formats to assess them. Under state leadership, school districts and local schools are developing new assessments based on recognized standards, which changes the way teaching and learning occurs and how learner achievement is measured and reported.

Benefits of Skill Standards

Skill standards are being designed to help employers, workers, and educators. Educators should benefit because skill standards will help them
- develop a better understanding of skills workers need;
- develop more relevant programs and curriculum;
- improve facilities and equipment;
- improve learner entry-level skills and abilities;
- improve the technical skills of instructors;
- provide work site mentors;
- understand the work-readiness skills that high school graduates need for competitive employment in high-skill, high-wage jobs;
- develop partnerships with industry and reach a common understanding about education needs.
- strengthen their relationships with local business;
- provide learners with career information and advice;
- market their programs more effectively because they will be recognized as being based on industry needs;
- communicate more effectively with parents about changes needed in education; and
- improve the image of career and technical education (*Vocational Education Weekly*, March 7, 1994; Piper, Smith, & Wiblin, 1994).

Advocates for skill standards claim the following further benefits:
- greater worker mobility and portability of credentials
- more job opportunities for workers, higher wages, and greater job security

- more efficient recruitment, screening, and placement for employers
- clearer goals and directions for learners
- more consistent, targeted instruction and curriculum
- greater accountability for educational institutions, programs, teachers, and learners
- improved quality products and services
- higher consumer confidence and satisfaction (Hoachlander & Rahn, 1994).

The National Advisory Commission on Work-Based Learning (1990) included the following benefits that might result from a national occupational standards system:
- Workers can safeguard their employment security through accredited, portable skills that enable continued employment independent of economic conditions affecting any one industry. Employees would be able to choose to obtain certification of their skills to protect against dislocation, to pursue career advancement, and to enhance their ability to re-enter the workforce through a work portfolio based on training directly related to industry standards.
- Employers can reduce the cost of recruiting, increase the return of training investments, and improve the accountability of training providers through adoption of industry-based standards. They could also use attainment of skill certification to reduce the costs and legal risks associated with assessment of job candidates and make more objective employment decisions.
- Federal, state, and local governments can protect public expenditure integrity by tying competency-based, employment-related training directly to industry standards.
- Trainers and educators can use skill standards and certificates to design and deliver relevant training to employers, employees, and government clients.
- Labor unions can assist their members in choosing training options related to specific industries and wider labor market needs. Skill standards could be used to increase their members' employment security through access to competency-based training and certification.
- Industry can use skill standards as a vehicle for information, training the providers and prospective employees of skills required for employment (*Workforce 2020*, 1994).

Challenges of Skill Standards

The national skill standards initiative is well on its way, but some challenges need to be overcome before a national system can be put in place. Hoachlander and Rahn (1994) identified four major tasks that need to be accomplished to establish an effective system of national skill standards. These tasks are (1) reaching consensus on what constitutes an industry and the occupations within it, (2) settling in on how specific and detailed our lists of skills will be and how we will determine them, (3) determining how to set standards and who will decide them, and (4) figuring out how best to assess learners and what certification signifies.

The developers of academic and skill standards have already indicated that they expect to use a variety of assessment tools, including the use of authentic assessment measures like portfolios and performance-based tests. Many career and technical education teachers are ill-prepared to employ the variety of assessment alternatives that will be needed as the profession implements these voluntary national skill standards. Certainly, most teachers have been engaged in at least two forms of alternative assessments being advocated today, the performance test and the learner project. There are, however, a number of other alternative assessment techniques that teachers seldom use or have not used at all.

ALTERNATIVE ASSESSMENTS

Perhaps at no time in American education has there been so much attention given to reforming traditional testing and assessment practices that focus largely on measuring learner retention of facts and small procedures using objective test items like multiple choice in favor of assessment strategies and methods that emphasize complex knowledge and performances and that require learners to engage in self-assessment and reflection.

Isolated concepts, facts, definitions, and names have their place in education and knowledge of them should be assessed, but our current assessment practices place far too much emphasis on assessing subject content items like those mentioned above and far too little attention to the skills and knowledge required to perform real-life tasks. Traditional assessment practices emphasize whether or not a learner has memorized a set of facts and can recognize them on a written test. These assessments tend to stress compartmentalized academic knowledge rather than effective application of knowledge and skills as applied to technical or social problems (Hoachlander, 1998). They stress what learners know at a given point in time and not what they can do. Shephard (1989) states the following:

> The notion that learning comes about by the accretion of little bits is outmoded learning theory. Current models of learning based on cognitive psychology contend that learners gain understanding when they construct their own knowledge and develop their own cognitive maps of the interconnections among concepts and facts. Thus, real learning cannot be spoon-fed one skill at a time. (pp. 5-6)

Authentic assessments, on the other hand, emphasize high-level thinking and more complex learning and measure how well learners use knowledge in a variety of contexts. These assessments are designed to measure and promote the complex thinking and learning outcomes that are known to be essential to academic success in school, to continuing success in lifelong educational endeavors, to productive and satisfying work, and to effective participation in communities. Lauren and Dan Resnick, leading researchers at the University of Pittsburgh, state the following:

> The idea is to construct assessments that are *worth teaching for* because they embody the standards we hold for student performance. We purposely use assessments to communicate both a vision and the reality of what's expected of students, to illustrate models for teaching and learning practice, to provide useful feedback to support improvement and to motivate performance. (Herman, *The State of Performance Assessments*, 1998, p. 1)

The new assessment reform movement is replete with educational buzzwords like authentic assessment, alternative assessment, performance-based assessment, direct assessment and others. Regardless of the terms used, these types of assessments have two common features. First, all are viewed as alternatives to traditional multiple-choice achievement tests. Second, all refer to direct observation and evaluation of learner performance on important tasks that are relevant to real-life out of school (Worthen, 1993).

Proponents of these new assessment strategies claim a number of positive benefits for both teachers and learners. Proponents of alternative assessments maintain that learning can best be assessed by examining and judging a learner's actual or simulated performance on significant and relevant tasks encountered in life. They argue that such assessments can focus on the learning processes revealed through self-assessment checklists or rubrics, oral reports, graphic organizers, learning logs and metacognitive reflections; products such as learner projects, journals, portfolios, and exhibits; and performances like manipulative performance tests, oral debates, interviews, knowledge bowls, and simulated events. (Worthen, 1993).

Many of the forms of so-called alternative assessments have been used by thoughtful teachers for years, so why the current interest? According to Guskey (1994), two major factors have intensified the interest in alternative assessment. First, advances in cognitive science have provided insights into how complex learning is and how important it is to use diverse means to assess learning fully and fairly. Second, many educators have come to recognize the limitations of traditional assessment measures that use the multiple choice and short answer format to measure desirable higher-order skills.

Worthen identified four reasons for the current interest in alternative assessments. These are (1) public demand for accountability in American schools, (2) use if high-stakes testing, (3) negative consequences of high-stakes testing, and (4) increasing criticisms of standardized tests.

One common argument for the increased use of performance assessment tools is that they provide information about learners' understanding of knowledge they have learned and their abilities to analyze and apply information to authentic situations, whereas more traditional forms of assessment that employ forced-choice response formats are often limited to assessing learners' recall or recognition of information.

Proponents of performance assessment advance the following arguments for performance assessments: (1) They focus on learners' ability to apply skills and knowledge to real world problems, (2) learners are provided with clear guidelines about teacher expectations, (3) effective use is made of teacher judgment, (4) they reflect real-life challenges, (5) they allow for learner differences in style and interests, and (6) they are more engaging of learners and teachers than other forms of assessment (Marzano, 1994).

Today, many educators are interested in other forms of assessment besides the traditional pencil-paper tests. There is a lot to think about when considering alternatives to multiple choice test items. There is the concern of validity and reliability of these new assessment measures. There are also the problems of content sampling, fairness, and consideration of transfer or generalization. Finally, there is the very real concern of the amount of time and money required to develop, administer, and score performance-based assessments (Bracey, 1993).

Among the most active professionals who are trying to evaluate various forms of authentic assessment are the researchers at the Center for Research on Evaluation, Standards, and Student Testing (CRESST) coheadquartered at UCLA and the University of Colorado. Recently these researchers have developed a set of criteria that they feel should be applied to all authentic assessments. It is already clear that few present forms of authentic assessments will meet these criteria since these assessments are relatively young and undeveloped (Bracey, 1993).

The Center for Research on Evaluation, Standards, and Student Testing (CRESST/UCLA) has completed a study into the methodologies for the assessment of competencies needed for the workforce. In their report entitled *Measurement of Workforce Readiness Competencies: Design of Prototype Measures*, CRESST researchers presented a 14-step methodology for the assessment of workforce readiness using the work of the SCANS. The SCANS is the commission charged by the U.S. Secretary of Labor to investigate what is required in today's and tomorrow's workplace and to determine the extent to which high school learners are able to meet those requirements. The CRESST report contained approaches to the assessment of the information and interpersonal competencies, which are two of the five major SCANS competencies (O'Neil, Allred, & Baker, 1993).

Far West Laboratory for Educational Research and Development has produced the Career-Technical Assessment Program (C-TAP) for the California Department of Education. This program is described in two 1994 publications, *The Career-Technical Assessment Program Teacher Guidebook* and *The Career-Technical Assessment Program Student Guidebook*. The C-TAP assessment program incorporates the California Model Curriculum Standards for each career-technical area into an assessment process leading into a certification process. The California Career Preparation Standards include (1) personal skills, (2) interpersonal skills, (3) thinking and problem solving skills, (4) communication skills, (5) occupational safety, (6) employment literacy, and (7) technology literacy.

The assessment system to measure learner achievement relative to these standards features cumulative assessments and on-demand assessments. Three major assessment components comprise the system, (1) an assessment project, (2) written scenario, and (3) a portfolio. Each of these assessment components has several elements that help learners build the knowledge and skills required for employment and successful living. Performance criteria in the form of summary requirements and rating instruments are employed to improve scoring so that the best measure of the learner's absolute achievement can be obtained. This is one of the most comprehensive systems involving alternative assessment of learners enrolled in career and technical programs today and can serve as a model for other states as they develop and refine their own alternative assessment systems.

Teaching to national skill standards will involve the identification of educational outcomes and the use of both traditional and new assessment techniques to ensure that our nation's learners graduate with more than basic skills–with abilities to develop understanding and to apply skills and knowledge to real-life situation which occur in the family, workplace, and community.

The March 1994 issue of *Phi Delta Kappan* contained an interview with Howard Gardner, a Harvard University professor who is widely known for his research and views on intelligence. Gardner's greatest concern about American education was learner lack of understanding of what they have learned—the inability of learners to take knowledge, skills, and other attainments and apply them successfully to new situations. He attributed this problem in part to our American fixation on the mastery of facts and the administration of short-answer instruments of assessment. He believes that one important component of any educational effort to increase learner understanding is to build directly into the regular curriculum many opportunities for assessment, so that assessment becomes a "habit of mind." He favors some kind of national system of assessment in which learners will take performance-based examinations and will also present their own exhibitions and portfolios for assessment (Siegel & Shaughnessy, 1994).

While classroom and laboratory use of assessment is undoubtedly the most important to career and technical education teachers, performance assessment is being marketed for system monitoring, accountability, and program evaluation as part of state-wide assessment systems. For example, the Kentucky Instructional Results Information System (KIRIS) is a high-stakes assessment program because the results will be used to grant financial rewards to schools that improve significantly and to levee sanctions against schools that fail to show progress (Guskey, 1994).

Regardless of the purposes for alternative assessments, career and technical education teachers need to update their knowledge and skills of traditional and new assessment methods and techniques if they are going to be ready to demonstrate how their learners' performance measures up against the specific outcomes that will be derived from national skill standards. The most important reason for teachers to develop competence in performance assessment is not to meet the demands of coming skill standards, but to explore questions at the very heart of the purposes and processes of schooling (Jamentz, 1994).

Assessment needs to be viewed not as an add-on to instruction, but as an ongoing part of instruction. New assessment techniques such as essays, demonstrations, interpretive events, scenarios, computer simulations, open-ended questions and problems, exhibitions, learner projects, performance events, and portfolios provide a means for making assessment an integral part of instruction that guides the learning process. These assessment practices are often collectively labeled as "authentic" assessments because they are valuable activities in themselves and involve the performance of tasks that are directly related to real-world problems (Guskey, 1994).

Many leaders of outcome-based education argue that performance-based assessments—not standardized, multiple choice tests—are necessary to measure learner attainment of outcomes, but are learner assessments currently available up to the task? Most experts agree that designing performance assessments linked to high-level and broadly written outcomes—ones that will probably characterize national skill standard outcomes—presents enormous technical challenges (O'Neil, 1994).

Since teachers usually regard performance assessments as better measures of learning than traditional tests, why have many teachers been reluctant to use more performance-based assessments? In 1993, G. J. Vitali, conducted a study of selected Kentucky teachers in which he found the vast majority of teachers to be dedicated, hard-working individuals who want their learners to do well. He also found that, in general, teachers were ill-prepared to adapt their instructional practices to the demands of the authentic, performance-based assessment program mandated in their state. Most teachers had limited knowledge, personal experience, or formal training with the various types of performance-based assessments or ways to use them as instructional tools. If teachers did receive training, it was in the form of one-day staff development workshops scattered throughout the school year (Guskey, 1994).

The Vitali study also uncovered teacher-perceived issues that may be limiting the conversion of their instructional programs toward authentic assessment and authentic classroom and laboratory practice. These include (1) be-

ing required to do more and teach more, without any increase in time allowed for planning or instruction, (2) the belief that performance-based assessments would require a lot more time to administer and score, and (3) the lack of appropriate teaching and assessment material. The combined effect of these perceptions of too little time and lots of extra work, with inadequate experience, training, and materials are keeping teachers from making the changes in their instructional programs to accommodate the new assessment system (Guskey, 1994).

New Assessment Strategies

The 1990s and the beginning of the new millennium marked a period of experimentation with a variety of assessment techniques as assessment researchers and classroom teachers sought better means for measuring learning (Mabry, 1999). The professional literature on assessment began to emphasize terms like *authentic assessment*, *performance assessment*, *direct assessment*, and *alternative assessment*. These are umbrella terms that have some differences and similarities, but one thing they do have in common is the requirement that learners construct responses rather than simply select responses from those included as alternatives to test items. Through understanding assessment terms, principles, and options, classroom teachers and assessment professionals can develop assessment instruments and practices and communicate their knowledge and experiences to other professionals.

Assessment Defined

Gronlund and Linn (1995) define assessment as "a general term that includes the full range of procedures used to gain information about student learning (observations, ratings of performance or projects, paper and pencil tests) and the formation of value judgments concerning learning progress," (p. 5). They state assessment is sometimes used in a limited way to describe information-obtaining procedures, but assessment is much more comprehensive than measurement; it always involves making judgments about the desirability of the behavior being measured. Assessment answers the question "How well does the individual perform in relation to established criteria?"

Wiggins (1993, p. 13) defines assessment as "a comprehensive, multifaceted analysis of performance; it must be judgment-based and personal." He further states that "at the very least, assessment requires that we come to know the student in action," (p. 17). He presents the challenge of assessment, which is to develop a picture of the whole person using a variety of evidence, including tests, and to do so in the most feasible and helpful way for the learner. Wiggins cautions educators that every test and every grade affects the learner. "Every dull test—no matter how technically sound—affects the learner's future initiative and engagement," (p. 24). Assessment is serious business: if done correctly it has the power to promote learning; if done poorly it has the power to discourage learners and give them an inaccurate sense of failure and hopelessness.

Neill (1997) offers the following seven principles for new assessments. These principles have received widespread support among educators and civil rights leaders. The seven principles endorsed by the forum are (1) the primary purpose of assessment is to improve learning, (2) assessment for other purposes supports learning, (3) assessment systems are fair to all learners, (4) professional collaboration and development support assessment, (5) the broad community participates in assessment development, (6) communication about assessment is regular and clear, and (7) assessment systems are regularly reviewed and improved.

Stecher, et al. (1997) report three broad uses of educational assessment: to improve learning and instruction, to certify individual mastery, and to evaluate program success. Career and technical educators use the results of tests and other assessments to monitor learner progress, diagnose learner needs, and make adjustments to instructional programs. Upon completion of courses, career and technical education programs use assessments to certify that learners have achieved a required level of mastery or have met industry standards. Finally, information obtained over time regarding learner progress (acquired knowledge and skills, success in courses, etc.) is used to judge the quality of the instructional program. The most common reason for assessing learners is to measure their individual progress toward expected learning outcomes as a means of improving learning and instruction. Assessments used by career and technical educators needs to be sensitive to the unique contexts of career and technical programs.

Alternative Assessment Defined

Interest in alternative assessments (assessment other than pencil-paper selected response) has grown since the 1990s as a result of dissatisfaction with selected response tests and a renewed desire to improve learner learning. Conventional assessments are made up of tests and essays that tend to be skewed in favor of learners who can reproduce the same themes and content presented to them in class. These assessments tend to be artificial and controlled in terms of their timing, format, and lack of interaction and emphasize only one type of intelligence (Butts, 1997). Assessments that require learners to construct their own responses or produce things have been labeled *alternative assessments*, but as Hoachlander (1998) says, the term *alternative* is unfortunate because most advocates of these types of assessment practices never intended alternative assessments to become substitutes for conventional assessments, rather they were to be used as supplements with the potential to provide a more complete picture of what learners know and can do. Alternative assessment requires that assessment activities be varied and numerous.

There are many different definitions offered for alternative assessment and no single definition prevails. According to Hamayan (1995) "alternative assessment refers to procedures and techniques which can be used within the context of instruction and can be easily incorporated into the daily activities of the school or classroom," (p. 212).

Huerta-Macias (1995) contrasts alternative assessments with traditional testing by stating "students are evaluated on what they integrate and produce rather than on what they are able to recall and reproduce," (p. 8) The author also notes that the main goal of alternative assessments is to "gather evidence about how students are approaching, processing, and completing real-life tasks in a particular domain." (p. 10) Alternative assessment provides an umbrella for a variety of nontraditional assessment methods and techniques such as direct assessment, authentic assessment, and performance assessment (Butts, 1997). A key factor in alternative assessments is the development of worthwhile tasks that enable learners to use and demonstrate a wide range of abilities and intelligences. These tasks must be real or interesting enough to engage learners in real thinking and performances, openended enough to encourage different approaches and tap learner creativity, but sufficiently constrained to permit learner self-assessment and reliable scoring (*Alternative Assessment and Technology*, ERIC Digest, 1999). A wide range of options is available to teachers who wish to improve learner assessment including performance portfolios, journal or learning logs, interviews, observations, attitude inventories, performance events, performance projects, writing samples, supervised practical experiences, and more.

Authentic Assessment

Newman (1991) states the following:

> The kinds of skills required to earn school credits, good grades, and high scores on typical tests are often considered trivial, meaningless, and contrived—by both students and parents. In contrast, a restructured vision of the goals of education seeks to evaluate performance activities that are worthwhile, significant, and meaningful; in short, activities that are authentic. (p. 459)

Grant Wiggins, president and director of the Center on Learning, Assessment, and School Structure (CLASS) is a widely known advocate and sought-after consultant for authentic assessment in education. Wiggins (1993) describes authentic assessment as tasks and procedures in which learners are engaged in applying skills and knowledge to solve real-world problems, giving the tasks a sense of authenticity. Wiggins (1989) states "we have lost sight of what a true test of intellectual ability requires; the performance of exemplary tasks," (p. 703). He believes that authentic assessments must replicate the challenges and standards of performance that typically face writers, business people, scientists, community leaders, designers, and technical workers. These tasks include writing essays and reports, conducting individual and group research, designing proposals or mockups, developing cost estimates, developing building or product plans, assembling portfolios, and so on. To design an authentic test, teachers must first decide what actual performances they want learners to be good at and then they must decide how to frame learning experiences in a context that provides the connections between real-world experiences and school-based ideas (Lund, 1997).

Lund (1997) identified the following characteristics of authentic assessment:

- Authentic assessment requires the presentation of worthwhile and/or meaningful tasks that are designed to be representative of performance in the field. These tasks are considered important in their own right and approximate something the person would actually be required to do in a given setting.
- Authentic assessments emphasize high-level thinking and more complex learning. They are intended to determine how well a learner can use knowledge, rather than whether or not a learner has memorized a set of facts and can recognize them on a written test.
- The criteria used in authentic assessment are articulated in advance so that learners know how they will be evaluated. Authentic assessments evaluate the essentials of performance against well-articulated performance standards often expressed as rubrics. Because learners know the criteria, they are expected to self-evaluate as they complete the learning task.
- Assessments are so firmly embedded in the curriculum that they are practically indistinguishable from instruction. Assessment can be continuous/formative rather than summative. Because the task is so central to instruction, it is repeatedly done because it is an important component of the curriculum. Teachers can actually teach to the test, a concept generally looked on with disfavor, but if the task/assessment is meaningful and important, it is worth teaching.
- Authentic assessment changes the role of the teacher from adversary to ally. With an authentic assessment, because of the formative nature of the assessment, learners have many chances to prove that they have achieved mastery, thus working in concert with teachers. The assessment also gives feedback for future performance and allows learners an opportunity to practice and improve. Teachers can adjust instruction, based on continuous feedback information, to help learners reach the criteria.
- Learners are expected to present their work publicly. This lets learners know the work is significant and important. Accountability is stronger when learners know their material will be publicly presented.

- Assessment must involve the examination of the process as well as the products of learning. The process of creating the product for assessment is equal to or even more important than the product itself.
- Authentic assessment requires learners to demonstrate skills and knowledge by engaging in a complex performance set in a given context, creating a significant product, or accomplishing a complex task using higher order thinking, problem solving, and often creativity. Authentic assessment requires real-world applications of skills and knowledge that have meaning beyond the assessment activity (Archbald & Newman, 1988).

Performance Assessment

Performance assessment is defined by the U.S. Congress, Office of Technology Assessment, (1992) as "testing methods that require students to create an answer or product that demonstrates their knowledge and skills." Performance assessments are best understood as a continuum of assessment formats ranging from the simplest learner-constructed responses, like writing samples, to comprehensive demonstrations or collections of work over time as found in portfolios (Elliott, 1995). Common features of performance assessment involve (1) learners constructing responses rather than selecting them, (2) direct observation of learner behavior on tasks resembling those commonly required for successful adult functioning in the world outside of school, (3) illumination of learners' learning and thinking processes along with their products of the learning process, and (4) learner self-assessment and teacher assessment using rubrics that contain the essential criteria for both process and product quality (Elliott, 1995).

Performance assessments are common to disciplines that already focus on performance, such as the arts, athletics, and career and technical education. They can be used for any objective that is skills-based or behavioral. Performance assessment basically involves asking learners to do something and then observing and rating the process and the finished product against predetermined criteria or a standard. Much of career and technical education relates to skill development (affective, cognitive, and psychomotor), which means that performance assessment can be adapted and implemented easily.

Joan Herman (1998), associate director of the National Center for Research on Evaluation Standards and Student Testing, states that the "essence of performance assessments—whether in the form of open-ended questions, essays, experiments or portfolios—is that they ask students to create something of meaning," (p. 2). She argues good performance assessment involves complex thinking and/or problem solving, addresses important disciplinary content, invokes authentic or real-world applications, and uses tasks that are instructionally meaningful. In addition, because learners must construct responses, performance assessments typically are scored by humans exercising judgment, rather than by machines (although there are now computer programs that allow scoring of essays, the oldest known form of performance assessment).

What's the difference between authentic and performance assessment? Carol Meyer (1992) says that performance assessment and authentic assessment are often used interchangeably. While they do share many of the same characteristics they are not automatically the same. The difference surfaces in the context in which the performance occurs. For example, technology education learners in Mr. Jackson's class are assigned a paper on critical technologies that requires them to complete their work in two 45-minute class periods. On the first day, they are expected to develop an outline and write an introduction section. One day two, they must complete the paper using the outline. This is a performance assessment. Learners are asked to produce a product that provides evidence that they can write. In another example, Mr. Jackson conducts a direct writing assessment in May, at about the same time that he used to set aside for the traditional two-day performance test. Instead of requiring the learner to write under contrived conditions, Mr. Jackson meets with each learner to help the learner determine which paper on critical technologies to submit for assessment purposes. These portfolio papers were not generated under controlled conditions but rather represented the ongoing work of learners for the year. All the papers in the learners' portfolios were generated using as much or as little time as they needed. This is a performance test. Learners were required to produce a product. This is also an authentic test. Learners complete the paper in a context more like real life, where they can spend as much or as little time as needed to complete their paper. The context in which the performance occurs determines its authenticity. The question that must be asked is "authentic to what?" The assessor must specify in what respects the assessment is authentic. Also, it should be noted that authentic assessment is multidimensional, with some assessment more authentic than others.

In developing performance assessments there are some key factors to consider. Amy Brualdi (1998) identifies the following basic steps in developing performance assessments:

1. Define the purpose of the performance assessment by asking questions such as the following: What concept, skill, or knowledge am I trying to assess? What should my learner know and be able to do? At what level should my learners be performing? What type of knowledge is being assessed, reasoning, memory, or process?

2. Choose the activity after taking into account time constraints, availability of resources, and the amount of data needed in order to make an informed decision about the quality of a learner's work. The two major forms of performance assessment activities teachers can choose from are informal and formal. In informal assessment, the learner does not know the assessment is taking place. In formal assessment the learner knows

that he or she is being evaluated. Typically the learner is required to perform a task or complete a project while the teacher observes and rates behavior and the completed tasks or project.

3. After determining the activity, teachers must decide which elements of the tasks or project will be used to determine the quality of the learner's performance. In other words, teachers must determine the criteria that will be used to assess the process of completing the activity and the quality of the completed activity. Teachers can sometimes obtain criteria for tasks from curriculum guides and other published materials or they can generate their own criteria based on a careful analysis of what it takes to complete an activity.

4. Once the criteria for an activity is identified, a rubric or scoring device must be developed that can be used to determine the varying degrees to which a person is successful or unsuccessful. A rubric is a rating instrument by which teachers can determine the level of proficiency a learner is able to perform at when completing a task or project. There are an increasing number of resources available to help teachers create and use rubrics. Learners can assist in developing rubrics for some tasks and projects, which can give them a better understanding of expected criteria and levels of performance to better self-assess their own performance.

5. The final step in performance assessment is to use the rubric to assess learner task or project performance. Learners should be expected to use rubrics to assess their own performances, which provides them with opportunities to develop evaluation skills, to reflect upon the quality of their own work, and to learn from their successes and errors. Teachers should structure an interview with the learner following the performance to share observations and to identify areas where performance can improve.

Claims and Shortcomings of Alternative Assessments

Alternative assessments, like standardized and teacher-made tests, have their advantages and shortcomings. One important contribution of authentic assessments is their focus on engaging learners in real-life tasks necessary for learning and life (Burke, 1992). Authentic assessments allows learners to practice and to perform meaningful tasks that are representative of life outside the classroom such as writing, giving speeches, performing tasks, creating projects, developing products, solving problems, making decisions, and using criteria to self-evaluate their own work. Authentic assessments are more in line with findings from cognitive psychology on the nature of meaningful, engaged learning. They also provide a way to assess the multiple intelligences of learners. Alternative assessments consist of a wide variety of assessment strategies. They provide opportunities for learners to be active in the assessment process, including using rubrics to self-assess their own performance. Many alternative assessments sample learner work over an extended period of time, providing a more valid picture of what a learner knows and can do. Alternative assessments are having a profound affect on curriculum and instructional practice. They provide teachers with a means of assessing how learners approach problems as well as how effective they are in applying what they have learned to solve them. Alternative assessments provide a means of holistic evaluation rather than basing assessment on the accretion of little bits of information. They are openly communicated to learners and invite their participation. Finally, alternative assessments communicate clearly what learners are to learn and what is important in a discipline.

Alternative assessments also have some shortcomings. First, alternative assessments require more teacher time in development and implementation than is required for conventional testing. Time demands is perhaps the biggest problem with alternative assessment practices—time for the teachers to become familiar with new assessments and their administration, to understand how to develop meaningful learning and assessment tasks, to identify criteria and standards for learner performance, and to develop rating instruments (rubrics) that learners can use to self-assess their work and that teachers can use to score the work and areas needing improvement.

Another limitation of alternative assessments is the selection and design of assessment tasks. Research has shown that learners can do well on some tasks but not so well on others. Attention will have to be paid to designing and using a number of assessment tasks in order to obtain a reliable estimate of learner performance in a content area. Teachers must identify challenging, interesting, and worthwhile tasks that include the essential knowledge and skills in a discipline, while structuring curriculum and assessment activities so that curriculum, instruction, and assessment come together.

Another potential barrier to implementing alternative assessments is the lack of teacher knowledge about and preparation to adopt, adapt, and create these assessments. Teachers are usually not adequately prepared for their role as assessor of learning, particularly when it comes to assessing higher order learning outcomes that require demonstrated performance. This is alarming when one considers that teachers may spend as much as a third of their available professional time involved in assessment related activities. Stiggins, (1999) states "teacher training programs have been notorious over the decades for their lack of relevant assessment training at both the graduate and undergraduate levels," (p. 25). Moreover, teachers must make a special effort to become knowledgeable about alternative assessments. They need staff development experiences and time to work with other teachers and support personnel to identify worthwhile tasks and to develop criteria and rubrics to score learner performances. The professional

literature on alternative assessments has grown significantly in the last ten years and excellent resources are available to help teachers prepare to implement alternative assessments in their classrooms.

Alternative assessments require teachers to make judgments about the degree to which learners perform expected tasks in relation to benchmarks, models, and established criteria rather than to simply score learner responses as right or wrong answers on pencil-paper tests. Teachers must accumulate benchmarks or models of exceptional performance that will enable both them and their learners to compare and score learner performance. They will also have to develop easy-to-use scoring rubrics to guide learner performance and to assess it. As is the case with conventional testing methods, teachers who develop and use alternative assessment methods and techniques will have to pay special attention to validity and reliability issues when scoring learner work. They will also have to become more skilled at observing and rating learner performance, otherwise the scores learners earn will become more of a measure of who does the scoring rather than the quality of the work.

Alternative assessments also require learners to construct responses, usually in the form of completing a task or producing a product. In career and technical education, many assessment tasks will involve the use of a facility along with machines, tools, equipment and supplies. Teachers will have to carefully schedule performance assessments so that the facility and equipment will be available when needed. Alternative assessments often require that adequate supplies be made available to support the assessment process. They usually cost more per learner than conventional testing practices and this cost difference will have to be addressed.

Connecting, Reflecting, Self-Assessment, and Feedback

There are four important aspects of any type of alternative assessment: connecting, reflecting, self-assessment and feedback. As previously mentioned, there is considerable attention now being paid to the reform of testing. An effort is being made to go beyond selected response tests, which tend to emphasize fragments of information, in favor of developing methods for assessing complex knowledge and materials that require connecting facts, concepts, and principles together to solve problems or produce a product. New learning theory holds that learners gain understanding when they retrieve previously learned knowledge, construct new knowledge, and develop their own cognitive maps of the interconnection among facts, concepts, and principles. Thus, learning that is spoon-fed one fact or skill at a time and tested in that manner will not lead to the depth of understanding needed to function in our modern society. Robert Glaser (1988) describes a number of different types of evidence collected through assessment with coherence of knowledge being an important one. "Beginners' knowledge is spotty and superficial, but as learning progresses, understanding becomes integrated and structured. Thus assessment should tap the connectedness of concepts and the student ability to access interrelated chunks," (p. 4).

Connecting

Alternative assessments are almost always framed in the form of learning tasks. These tasks must be arranged in sequence from simple to complex and build on each other. They must be connected by teacher orientation so learners will see how knowledge and skills learned in previous tasks can be used to complete a related or more complex task. Transfer of knowledge and skills is enhanced when learners can recognize the connectedness of learning. A number of alternative assessments such as graphic organizers, writing samples, and portfolios require learners to connect what they have learned to produce a finished product. In writing samples learners must connect writing skill mechanics to content ideas and coherence of expression to produce an acceptable paper. Many technical tasks presented in career and technical programs require learners to connect their previous knowledge of mathematics, science, social studies, and English to solve problems and complete tasks and projects. In fact, one of the terms used in education today is *articulation*, another word for connection.

Reflection and Self-Assessment

Unfortunately, many teachers assume that knowledge and skills are the only viable factors to measure learner outcomes in education. This situation may be a result of some school systems reporting only achievement scores involving knowledge and skills to parents, with attitudes and affective behaviors sometimes reported separately or not at all. It may also be a result of lack of teacher preparation in the area of measurement in the affective domain. In order to obtain a holistic picture of learner achievement and growth, it is essential that the assessment system include measurement of attitudes and behaviors (Parnell, 1990; Terenzi, 1989). Cohen and Brawer (1969) go so far as to suggest that behavior change in learners is the ultimate criterion for measuring learner learning. Traditional achievement and skill performance tests are very limited in ascertaining learner attitudes and behavior change. Stiggins (1994) notes that learner motivation can be influenced significantly by specific attitudes; however, the consistent use of attitude inventories in the classroom is not common. As long as we continue to use conventional measurement techniques, we will have an incomplete picture of learner achievement and growth.

A wide range of assessment options are available to teachers who wish to improve learner assessment that go beyond cognitive achievement and psychomotor skills to include assessment of attitudes and other affective behaviors. These assessments offer learners the opportunity to recognize their progress by becoming actively involved

in self-assessment, to reflect on their progress and discover what steps they can take to improve performance. A key component of many of these alternative assessments, such as portfolios, is the opportunity for learners to reflect on their thinking, their practices, and their learning. Han (1995) indicates that researchers generally define reflection as a natural process that facilitates the development of future action from the contemplation of past and/or current events. Han reports that John Dewey believed that reflectivity involves active, persistent, and careful consideration of any belief or practice in light of its supporting grounds and its eventual consequences. Han attributes much of the writing on the topic of reflection in teacher education to Dewey, who believed that two important, distinct components are involved in reflective thinking: process and content. Knowles, Cole and Presswood (1994) define reflection for teachers as an ongoing process of critically examining and refining practices, taking into account the personal, pedagogical, societal, and ethical contexts associated with schools, classrooms, and the multiple roles of teachers. This definition includes the important factor of context for reflective thinking. A common method for obtaining learner reflections is to ask learners to make comments on their performances after rating themselves using a rubric. There are a number of other ways to involve learners in reflection that are not task specific like journal writing, autobiographical writing, and metacognitive reflection.

Robin Fogarty (1994) offers a working definition of metacognition as a sense of awareness—knowing what you know and what you don't know. Metacognitive thinking is the process of assessing what one knows, how it is known, and why it is known. Barell (1992) extends this definition to include feelings, attitudes, and dispositions because thinking involves not only cognitive operations but also the dispositions to engage in them when and where appropriate. Kay Burke (1994) notes that metacognitive reflections provide learners with the opportunity to manage and assess their own thinking strategies. "Metacognition involves the monitoring and control of attitudes such as students' beliefs about themselves, the value of persistence, the nature of work, and their personal responsibilities in accomplishing a goal," (p.96). She states that these attitudes are inherent in all tasks, both academic and nonacademic. Teachers need to provide opportunities for learners to step out of assessment tasks long enough to reflect on "what we did well, what we would do differently next time, and whether or not we need help," (p. 96).

Researchers (Perkins and Salomon, 1992; Fogarty, Perkins, and Barell, 1992; and Barell, 1992) describe the critical relationship between metacognition and learning transfer. Barell (1992) states that "in order to transfer knowledge of skills from one situation to another, we must be aware of them; metacognitive strategies are designed to help students become more aware," (p. 259). Fogarty, Perkins and Barell (1992) define transfer as "learning something in one context and applying it in another," (p. ix). For example, suppose you learn how to operate a drill press to drill holes in materials and you reflect on what you did in the laboratory to accomplish this task. Then you are faced with the challenge of drilling holes in materials out on a job site with a portable power drill that you have never learned to operate. Through reflection of what was done to drill holes with the drill press you will be able to recall specific procedural steps that are similar in drilling holes using a portable drill in a job site context.

In the constructivist's view of learning, individuals take in information and make sense of that information through metacognitive reflection. Reflection allows individuals to recognize the gaps that exist in their understanding of some phenomenon. If the ultimate goal of classroom learning is to transfer what learners learn and use that learning in other places, then fostering meaningful application through reflection is paramount.

Kay Burke (1994) and Robin Fogarty (1994) present many metacognitive strategies that can be used by classroom teachers. These include Mrs. Potter's Questions, KWL charts, PMI charts, transfer journals, wrap-around, reflection pages, learning logs, seesaw thinking, pie in the face, stem sentences and many others. For example, Mrs. Potter's Questions include "What were you expected to do in this assignment?" "What did you do well?" "If you had to do this task over, what would you do differently?" "What help do you need from me?" The KWL strategy, created by Donna Ogle (1986), consists of a three-column chart in which the first column (K) is devoted to what I know, the second (W) to what I want to know, and the third (L) to what I learned after finishing this lesson or assignment. See Figure 9-2. The PMI strategy, created by Edward de Bono

(1983), is similar to the KWL chart except the first column (P) is devoted to the plus or favorable things found in a learning experience, the second (M) focuses on the minuses or unfavorable findings, and the third (I) is devoted to what the learner found interesting about the learning experience.

Self-Assessment and Rubrics

In the adult world individuals are faced almost daily with assessing or evaluating a situation, then making judgments and decisions. In the workplace, self-evaluation is a very important skill as most workers are responsible for monitoring their own performance and making judgments as to the quality of their work in light of established standards or criteria. Brookhart (1997) states that self-assessment and peer assessment are always happening informally in classrooms and formally in good classrooms. Learners are always asking themselves the question "What kind of learner am I?" The judgments learners form about themselves as learners inform future study, effort, and ultimately the rest of their educational future. While a few teachers are using formal self-assessment strategies, formal self-assessment is rare in most schools and even in colleges. In most schools, learners have little opportunity to evaluate their own performances because teachers have assumed the assessment role and are only too willing to tell learners what they don't know or what they cannot do well, that they are not doing as well as their peers, or in some unfortunate cases, that they don't deserve the opportunities provided in this program or school. Teachers often lament learner apathy, lack of personal investment in their own educations, willingness to only do what is necessary to pass courses, and even learner willingness to cheat on

KWL CHART		
KWL Chart Name _____ Topic: _____		
K	W	L
What do I know?	What do I want to know?	What have I learned?

Source: Ogle, D. (1986). K-W-L group instruction strategy. In A. Palinscar, D. Ogle, B. Jones, & E. Carr (Eds.), *Teaching Techniques as Thinking (Teleconference Resource Guide)*. Alexandria, VA: Association for Supervision and Curriculum Development.

Figure 9-2. A sample graphic organizer.

tests or submit work that has been copied from other learners. A common response witnessed by parents when they ask their children "What did you learn today?" is "Nothing." Is it any wonder that learners assume a mostly passive role when we deny them personal responsibility for exercising judgment and making choices? This situation can be redressed by resisting the temptation to be the sole assessor and to maintain all control, by sharing authority, by letting learners have a real voice in the curriculum, and by getting them involved in the self-assessment process.

Learners who are given the opportunity to become more engaged in the learning process and in assessing their own progress respond with intelligence, responsibility, and determination after a learning period in which they develop assessment skills (Mabry, 1999). D'Urso (1996) reports the results of a second grade study of learners involved in their own assessment. She concludes that learners' sense of self improves, their work becomes more meaningful to them, they become protective of the knowledge they have learned, they start reflecting on what they know and on what they still need to discover, and they discover their own voices and a deeper sense of themselves.

One of the exciting dimensions of alternative assessments is learner self-assessment. Many learners want to know how they are doing while in the process of performing a task, and they want to know how well they did when the task is completed. In traditional assessment, learners generally have to wait until they receive feedback in the form of a scored test or performance from their teachers. In classrooms in which alternative assessments are used, learners are required to engage in self-assessment and to collaborate with teachers to review performance and decide the next steps in learning. Learners need to be able to assess their own performances according to their own references and in relation to criteria or standards. In self-referenced assessment, learners evaluate performance in light of their goals, desires, and previous attainments and thus become more aware of present performance and what needs to be done to further learning. In this type of self-assessment, standards come from the learner's work, not just from outside sources. In standards referenced self-assessment, learners compare their own characteristics of performance against established standards, or criteria and indicators of performance that are usually contained in a scoring tool called a rubric. An ultimate goal of education is for learners to be able to learn without relying on teachers. As learners become engaged in developing and using rubrics to evaluate their work, they learn more deeply what quality work looks like and can more clearly understand their own learning process (Neill, 1997).

Rubrics

The most common method for learner self-assessment of a performance is a scoring rubric, which is defined by Marzano, Pickering, and McTighe (1993) as "a fixed scale and list of characteristics describing performance for each of the points on the scale," (p. 29). They say rubrics are simply scoring devices (or tools) that are designed to assist in the process of clarifying, communicating, and assessing expected performance. Since teachers do not have a scoring key available for a performance event like they would with a multiple-choice test, some form of rating instrument is needed to facilitate the subjective judgment about the quality of the learner's work. Rose (1999) presents the view that rubrics differ from traditional methods of assessment in that they can be used to examine learners engaged in the actual process of learning, clearly showing them how their work is being evaluated. Scoring rubrics provide a way for both learners and teachers to make more fair and sound judgments regarding a performance. Moskal (2000) states that rubrics provide at least two benefits to the evaluation process. First, they provide a means for both learners and teachers to examine how well performances comply with specified criteria. Second, they provide specific feedback to learners regarding their performance, and if followed up with a learner/teacher reflection session, they provide specific feedback information necessary for improving future performance.

There are many advantages that well-developed rubrics provide for both learners and teachers. They (1) enable assessment to be more objective and consistent, (2) focus attention of the assessor on the important outcomes with an assigned value for each, (3) demystify the expectations for the learner by assigning values for expected outcomes, (4) allow learners to identify strengths and to focus on weak areas while providing an opportunity to revisit them, (5) force teachers to identify critical behaviors required for task completion and to establish the criteria for performance in specific terms, (6) encourage learners to develop a consciousness about the necessary criteria of their performances as well as the criteria they can use to assess their own abilities and performances, (7) promote an emphasis on formative as well as summative evaluation, (8) provide benchmarks against which to measure and document progress, (9) lower learner anxiety about what is expected of them, (10) assure that learners' work is judged by the same standards, and (11) lead learners toward quality performance.

There are a few disadvantages associated with the use of rubrics. Rubrics can consume considerable time and effort in development and use. It is sometimes challenging to identify desirable criteria and performance indicators. Rubrics can be challenging to format and type. It takes a fair amount of time for both learners and teachers to learn how to use rubrics effectively. Popham (1997) reminds us that well-constructed rubrics have enormous potential for improving the assessment of learner performance, but first, corrections will have to be made to eliminate the flaws that render many teacher-developed rubrics almost worthless. He identifies the following four flaws that are all too common in commercial and teacher-made rubrics. First, some rubrics contain too many specific evaluative criteria rather than the essential ingredients of the skill being measured. Second, some rubrics employ excessively general evaluative criteria using such words as *beginning* or *advanced* without the inclusion of any cues as to what is genuinely significant in the learner's response. Third, some rubrics are too lengthy and contain too much detail, resulting in busy teachers disregarding them. Rubrics need to be somewhat abbreviated and designed to capture the key evaluative criteria needed to judge the learner's response. Finally, some rubrics are used in a manner that make the test more important than the skill being tested. Teachers can be more focused on whether or not the learner arrived at the correct solution or developed a quality product instead of how well the learner performed the skills required for successful task completion.

Rubrics are grading tools that contain specific information about what is expected of learners based on selected criteria that are often complex and subjective. Rubrics enable both learners and teachers to evaluate performances that more closely replicate the challenges of life than do isolated traditional written tests. Rubrics typically contain two important features: (1) They identify and clarify specific performance expectations and criteria, and (2) they specify the various levels of learner performance. Rubrics in their simplest form are check-off lists requiring a yes or no response. More complex rubrics include a written standard of expected learner performance with different levels of performance indicators. All rubrics (1) are focused on measuring a stated or identified performance objective, performance, behavior, or quality; (2) include some form of scale used to rate learner characteristics of performance; and (3) contain some specific and identifiable performance characteristics arranged in levels and indicating the degree to which a standard has been met. Rubrics should also have logistical information such as the learner's name, date, performance task title, and score; directions for completing the rubric; and a comments section that allows both learner and teacher to record significant information resulting from a reflection session regarding the performance.

Advocates of alternative assessments maintain that authentic tasks that resemble the context in which adults do their work need to be selected and refined for instruction, and learners need to be provided with adequate time to plan, complete their work, self-assess, revise, and consult with others. Authentic assessments must include standards and criteria that are similar to what is used to judge adult performance on similar tasks (Meyer, 1992). Alternative or performance assessments must have rubrics with criteria and performance indicators for two important reasons: (1) The criteria and performance indicators define for learners and others the type of behavior or attributes of a process or products which are expected, and (2) a well-defined scoring rubric allows the teacher, the learner, and

others to evaluate a performance or product as objectively as possible while providing a means of identifying areas of performance that need more work. If performance criteria are well-defined, learners, teachers, and others acting independently will award essentially the same score for a given performance or performance product. Stiggins (1991) notes that teachers need to develop rubrics that include the full dimensions of performance in a continuum from poor or unacceptable to exemplary in order to teach learners to perform at the highest levels and to help them evaluate their own performances more objectively. For example, learners asked to submit a technical writing sample are provided with a rubric in which writing mechanics is one of the criteria and is defined as "student correctly uses proper grammar, punctuation, and spelling with a performance dimension ranging from high quality (well-organized, good transition with few errors) to low quality (errors so numerous that the paper is difficult to read and understand).

There are as many different types of rubrics as there are rubric designers. Most rubrics fall into one of two categories: holistic or analytical. Holistic rubrics consider performance as a whole with the primary purpose being to determine overall performance or competency on some task or project. One advantage of using this type of rubric is rapid assessment and ease of scoring. A major disadvantage is that holistic rubrics provide less specific feedback and are usually better for summative assessments.

A rubric with two or more separate scales is called an analytical rubric. An analytical rubric considers performance by breaking it down into its component parts. Its purpose is to provide considerable feedback on the level of performance on each major part. It has the advantage of providing a detailed analysis of behavior that detects strengths and weaknesses and identifies areas for refinement. The major disadvantage of analytical rubrics is that they involve a lengthy process in comparison to holistic rubrics.

There is no single best type of rubric that can be used for all purposes. Many different rubrics can be used to assess a performance task. The Chicago Public School System (2001) in its web site *Instructional Intranet* presents the following criteria for evaluating scoring rubrics:

- Is the rubric related to the outcome(s) being measured? Does it measure important outcomes that have been taught while being free from anything extraneous?
- Do the rubric criteria reflect current conceptions of excellence in the field? For example, does the highest point scale truly represent an exemplary performance or product?
- Are dimensions of rubric scales clearly defined so they are easily understood by everyone?
- Is there a clear basis for assigning scores at each scale point so that learners and teachers know exactly what action is needed to receive a score?

- Can the rubric be scored consistently by different raters?
- Can the rubric be understood by learners and parents?
- Is the rubric content appropriate for the developmental level of learners?
- Can the rubric be applied to a variety of tasks?
- Is the rubric fair and free from bias?
- Is the rubric useful, feasible, manageable, and practical?

Rubrics are powerful communication tools when they are shared among learners, teachers, and parents. Rubrics shared with learners prior to a performance serve as a guide to expected behavior. They also provide a means for learners to self-assess their own performances. Rubrics help teachers communicate what is expected of learners in a course and provide a means of sharing how learner performance is graded. Rubrics shared with parents provide concrete information for parents to understand expected behaviors of their children and how their achievement will be assessed and graded.

Constructing rubrics is a time-intensive task when teachers develop them from scratch. Many teachers find it easier to adopt or modify existing rubrics. Rubrics can be revised by (1) modifying or combining two or more rubrics, (2) rewording parts of a rubric, (3) dropping or changing scales of an analytical rubric, (4) omitting criteria not appropriate to the task to be measured, and (5) mixing and matching scales from other rubrics. Existing rubrics can be found on the Internet and in educational journals and other publications. Teachers can also involve learners in the constructing of scoring rubrics. Assisting in constructing rubrics provides learners with an opportunity to see firsthand what constitutes good and poor performance and how performance can be scored fairly.

Following are some general guidelines for instructors offered by Heidi Goodrich (1997) for involving learners in the construction and use of rubrics:

- Begin by looking at models. Show learners examples of good and poor work. Identify the characteristics that make the good models good and the bad ones bad.
- List the critical criteria for the performance. A good guide is to think about what you would need to include if you had to give feedback to a learner who did poorly on a task. Learners can be involved in discussing the models. This will help in beginning a list of what counts in quality work.
- Articulate graduations of quality or determine the quality continuum. Describe the best and worst levels of quality, then fill in the middle based on knowledge of common problems associated with the performance. Use descriptive terms like *not yet, O.K.,* and *awesome* instead of *failure, average, and excellent.*
- Engage learners in using the rubrics created to evaluate the models given them in step one as practice in self-assessment and to test the rubrics.
- Give learners their tasks. As they work, stop them occasionally for self- and peer assessment using the rubrics provided.

- Give learners time to revise their work based on the feedback they received in step 5.
- Use the same rubric learners used to assess their work. This is made possible by including a scoring column for learners, peers, and teachers.
- Schedule a debriefing time with learners to compare their rubric scoring with those completed by the teacher. Require learners to reflect on the next steps in the learning process.

Feedback

One of the expected outcomes of using alternative assessment methods is specific feedback that provides learners with direct, usable insights into current performance in relation to desired performance. Wiggins (1993) notes that many teachers erroneously believe they are providing feedback with test scores and a few coded comments like *good work, vague, awkward,* and so forth. We have all experienced such comments on our work at some time and did not know what to do to avoid such comments in future work. Wiggins states that coded praise and blame words are not feedback. "What is wanted and needed by learners is user-friendly information on how one is doing and how one specifically might improve what is being done," (p. 182). He argues learners need information that will help them self-assess and self-correct so that assessment itself becomes a learning experience.

Mannie (2000) states that feedback is becoming an increasingly critical constituent of learning. He points out that feedback offers three important functions in the learning process: positive reinforcement (positive statements about specific behaviors demonstrated), specific feedback information (statements that describe what is good and what needs improvement), and motivation (statements that encourage and provide incentives for learners to expend more effort and improve performance levels). While all three of these functions are important, the most important is providing specific feedback that includes the learner recognizing performance flaws, verbalizing this information to the teacher or coach, and receiving specific information required to correct errors and improve performance. Teachers must give precise, meaningful and useful information to learners in an easy-to-understand format, keeping in mind that most individuals have limited capacity to acquire, store, and recall detailed information on a specific task.

Wiggins (1993) makes a distinction between guidance and feedback. Guidance gives direction while feedback indicates whether or not a learner is on course. For example, written directions indicate how to use a power tool safely, but sights and sounds in performing work with a power tool tell the operator how well they are using the tool to do quality work. To clarify the notion of including signs and landmarks to help learners along the performance road, think of how useful directions to a friend's house are when they include information on structures like churches, painted mailboxes, and barns that supplement the map. Feedback, like road signs, needs to be continuous, but the typical classroom lacks adequate performance feedback. This is evident by the continuous barrage of learner questions like "Am I on the right track?" "Is this what you want?" "How am I doing?" Test and project scores do provide learners with a sense of being on the right track and may give learners a sense of being adequately prepared for performance without knowing specifically what the performance entails.

Wiggins (1993) states that "we are locked in a mindset that education is teaching and assessment is testing but we must develop the mindset that successful performance of complex tasks are possible only when students learn through effective use of built-in, more timely, and helpful feedback," (p. 187). He warns that feedback is commentary, not measurement. Real feedback is descriptive of behavior and free from value communication. Feedback tells learners whether or not they are on the right track without labeling or judging effort or performance. Wiggins states that most teachers operate on the premise that every performance must be measured and that the most important response to performance is to measure it. What learners need more of are descriptions of their behavior in relation to standards and criteria rather than evaluation of errors made. Feedback should occur often while the performance is taking place, not after it is evaluated. If feedback is given only after a performance is evaluated, learners must wait until the next performance to make adjustment in their approaches to and performance of tasks. Thorndike's law of effect, a very old law of learning, states that learning is enhanced when people see the effects of their work while they are doing it and receive external feedback as soon after completing a performance as possible.

All complex performances require many practice runs and thus the correcting of many errors through feedback. For example, it is rare for a professional actor to do a scene that is done so well it is labeled a "wrap" on the first attempt. More often than not, an actor receives feedback and adjusts the performance accordingly until it meets the standards of performance expected by the director. Unlike professional acting, teachers seldom have time to intently observe a learner's performance, give one-on-one specific feedback, and allow the learner to perform in many trials until expectations are met. What is needed is to develop a feedback system that minimizes human intervention and that is rich with built-in road signs to provide learners with the feedback required to refine the performance.

Wiggins (1993) describes a feedback system that emphasizes concurrent feedback (feedback while the performance is underway) as a system that provides learners with a learning goal or destination, that has a plan mapping out the exemplary route, and that has numerous indicators or landmarks guiding learner performance toward a successful conclusion. He emphasizes that feedback must occur during performance as well as after a task is performed. This concurrent feedback is information that comes to us as we perform. Concurrent feedback serves as the basis for readjusting the approach taken to tasks and specific procedural steps. Mastery of complex learning tasks does not involve simply responding to probing questions following performance but solving complex problems by responding to the feedback provided within the complex task itself. Successful performance requires concurrent feedback inherent in the context in which the task is performed that enables learners to self-assess and self-correct as accurately as possible.

Teachers must prepare learners to self-assess and to recognize the road signs of performance inherent in the context so that they will know that they are on the right track. This is not unlike many life situations in which we get some feedback either from the environment or from family members, friends, coworkers, supervisors, or other persons. In world-class manufacturing environments, workers are provided with performance aids and exemplary models of what their work should look like so they can self-assess and self-regulate and maintain quality control at every workstation along the road to producing a quality product or delivering a service. In career and technical education classes, teachers need to provide exemplary models of desired products, make performance tests self-sustaining and complete with rubrics for self-assessment, provide for reflection along the way and at the end of performance, provide trouble-shooting guides, provide performance aids, and provide time for self-assessment and peer assessment supported by scoring rubrics if concurrent feedback is to occur.

Effective feedback is the key to improved learner performance, yet many teachers are reluctant to spend the time required to develop and exhibit exemplary models of learner performances, to develop scoring rubrics, to teach learners how to self-assess and self-regulate their performances, or to provide specific feedback to learners as needed. Some teachers believe that providing models will simply lead to learners reproducing the models shown, which will stifle creativity. Others believe that showing models will discourage some learners because they cannot see how they will ever do work that approaches the quality shown in the models. Some teachers also avoid placing any feedback statements on learner work to avoid negativity. Teachers must realize that effective feedback may well be the one thing that helps learners improve. Time and effort need to be given to the development of feedback systems that utilize models, criteria, and standards and to preparing learners to self-assess and self-correct their learning.

Alternative Assessment Strategies

One of the important premises that should guide thoughtful teachers is that authentic assessments are real-life tools that reflect the knowledge, skills, and attitudes necessary for learning and for life. Authentic assessments should provide opportunities for learners to practice and perform meaningful tasks that are reflective of life outside the four walls of the classroom, such as preparing and giving speeches, developing resumes, filling out job applications, writing letters, engaging in problem-solving activities, making decisions and choices, and using criteria to self-assess their work. Teachers must expand their repertoire of teaching and assessment strategies to attract and hold the interest of learners, cause them to be actively engaged in both learning and assessment, and provide them with opportunities to learn and work together in a collaborative, thoughtful classroom. Authentic assessment starts with the selection of meaningful learning tasks and these tasks need to be organized and structured so that they are contextualized, integrative, metacognitive, related to the curriculum taught, flexible (requiring multiple applications of knowledge and skills), open to self-assessment and peer assessment, ongoing, and informative, and have specified standards and criteria (Weber, 1999).

Linda Mabry (1999) notes that we must match purpose or outcome expectations with assessment strategies. She says that teachers need to ask and seek answers to the following questions: "What do we want to assess—and do we really need to assess it?" "Why do we want to assess it—what will we do with the results?" "How should we assess—how can we get the information we need?" "How can we assess without harmful side effects?" Answers to these questions should help teachers choose assessment methods and techniques.

Assessment is all about measuring what one knows and can do and what one does not know and cannot do at a given time. But assessment must be more than just gathering and storing information about learners, it must foster growth and development. Authentic assessments must become valuable learning experiences in themselves. Learners should be able to recognize the changes and development within themselves as they learn, grow, and progress. Robin Fogarty (1998) says what is needed is a combination and balance of assessment practices.

Stecher et al. (1997) identified four categories of alternative assessment that are widely used in career and technical education. These are (1) written assessments (selected response, like multiple choice, and constructed response, like essay items or writing samples), (2) performance tasks, (3) senior projects (research paper, performance project, oral presentation), and (4) portfolios. For many years, effective career and technical education teachers have been using a number of assessment strategies similar to the four mentioned above, such as traditional written tests, performance tests, performance projects, and notebooks resembling a portfolio containing samples of learner work. However, much has been learned in recent years about how to make these assessment strategies more efficient and effective. In addition, the application of computers in designing and delivering assessment strategies has made it possible to increase their use.

There are as many different formats (tasks) for learner work and for assessments as there are teachers who create them. See Figure 9-3. The alternative assessment methods and techniques presented in this chapter can help teachers transform their assessment programs from teacher-directed and summative in focus to learner-centered and more formative in focus.

TRADITIONAL ASSESSMENT AND EDUCATIONAL REFORM

Educational reform is being driven by the realization that the American economy depends on an educational system capable of producing workers who can think, solve problems, work in teams, adapt to changing work environments, and utilize technology. State after state has passed legislation requiring learners to demonstrate mastery of a core body of knowledge at certain grade levels and some have made satisfactorily passing these exams a condition of graduation. The National Commission of Testing and Public Policy noted in its 1990 report, *From Gatekeeper to Gateway: Transforming Testing in America*, that learners take 127,000,000 separate tests in a year which averages about three tests per learner. Many of these exams are standardized tests that utilize the multiple choice or "bubble" test items that are easily machined scored, but other forms of performance-based assessments are being developed and used to overcome the deficiencies of forced-choice tests. For example, the California Department of Education has developed the Career-Technical Assessment Program (C-TAP). It requires learners to complete three components: the portfolio, the project, and the written scenario which, when taken together, form a rich, comprehensive system of measuring learners' knowledge and skills. Performance-based assessments have become one of the most hotly debated topics in education today.

Career and technical educators have long taken pride in their performance-based instructional system. For the most part, career and technical education program curricula are derived from ongoing analyses of work roles and tasks in specific occupations and verified by current practitioners in the field, usually through advisory or technical committees. The focus of instruction is on assisting learners to develop acceptable levels of competence on important work tasks and to develop applied academic and general employability skills. Career and technical educators deliver instruction through a performance-based education curriculum which includes defining what learners should know and be able to do, planning ways for them to learn to do it, teaching them in simulated or in some cases realistic work environments, and assessing their performance as part of instruction. Teachers inform learners of the factors that count toward their final grade—so many points for quizzes, tests, projects, and reports. Measurement practices usually include objective tests (multiple choice, true-false, completion) and performance tests (product/project checklists, task element rating forms). Teachers convert learner scores on tests and observational ratings into grades according to school system guidelines and learners and parents/guardians are notified as to the level of achievement usually reported by letter grades of A, B, etc. The assumption of an A letter grade is that the learner has mastered 90% or more of the course content. Grades are used to communicate the achievement of learners to parents and others, to provide incentives to learn, and to provide information that learners can use for reflection and self-evaluation.

The problem with the traditional evaluation and reporting system just described is that it lacks a context: compared to what? Is the learner's performance based on high uniform occupational standards? Is learner performance measured against teacher expectations? Is the learner making satisfactory progress toward graduation? Does the letter grade involve judgments about growth, effort, and

ALTERNATIVE ASSESSMENT FORMATS

- Concept maps
- Editorials
- Data tables or charts
- Cause and effect diagrams
- Run control charts
- Pareto diagrams
- Check sheets/check lists
- Job applications
- Interviews
- Journals/graphics
- Management plans
- Geometry problems
- Observation reports
- Posters
- Workplace scrapbooks
- Time line graphic organizers
- Event chains/graphics
- Team reports
- Human graphs
- Portfolios
- Big idea generation
- Story time/anecdotes
- Life-coping skills reports
- Games/quiz bowls
- Consumer reports
- Training plans
- Ballads
- Book reviews
- Constitutions/bylaws
- Demonstrations
- Displays
- Booklets
- Models
- Patterns
- Proposals
- Sale notices
- Home projects
- Technical repairs

- Business letters
- Displays
- Cause and effect essays
- Graphs (pictorial, bar, & line)
- Essays on some topic
- Histograms
- Surveys
- VITAs/Resumes
- Inventions
- Lab reports
- Geographic maps
- Models
- Logs/reflective journals
- Research reports
- Workplace skits
- Venn diagrams
- Computer slide shows
- PMI strategy reports
- Mrs. Potter's questions
- Performance projects
- Job skills demonstrations
- Prepared speeches
- Job searches
- Cartoons or comics
- Student-led conferences
- Exhibits
- Announcements
- Bulletins
- Critiques
- Designs
- Fashion articles
- Invitations
- Newscasts
- Plays-TV/radio scripts
- Recipes
- Signs
- Action research
- Tune-ups

- Autobiographies
- Drawings or illustrations
- Experiments
- Performance events
- Flow charts on some process
- Correlation/scatter diagrams
- Storyboard reports
- Idea webs/graphic organizers
- Issues/controversies
- Information seeking letters
- Math problems
- Learning progress reports
- Pamphlets
- Career fair displays
- Slide shows/videos
- Bulletin board displays
- Grant applications
- Problem solving events
- Career plans
- Connecting elephants
- Writing samples
- Extemporaneous speeches
- Shadowing reports
- Collages
- Video yearbook
- Ranking ladders
- Biographies
- Commercials
- Crossword puzzles
- Directories
- Handbooks
- Menus
- Questionnaires
- Requisitions
- Edit manuscripts
- Mind mapping

Figure 9-3. A listing of commonly used alternative assessment formats.

attitude? What abilities does the letter grade represent? Are letter grades good indicators of what learners can do or are they indicative of the learners' ability to memorize facts and take tests? Are scores awarded on the basis of absolute achievement or are they grades that are influenced by the teacher's knowledge of the personal characteristics of their learners such as attitudes, self-esteem, motivation, physical and mental characteristics, and family situation?

The evaluation portion of an instructional program is more than preparing, administering and scoring tests, and reporting grades. A comprehensive evaluation component continuously measures and assesses learner accomplishments of a variety of specified performance outcomes believed to be important for success in productive employment, future learning opportunities, and independent living. It involves learners in meaningful learning and evaluation processes and provides information to them about their areas of strength and areas that need more attention. Teachers are provided with valuable feedback information on what instructional methods and strategies work well and where there is need for improvement. Parents/guardians become partners in the learner's educational progress when they are provided with input into how learners were evaluated and on what basis grades were assigned. The evaluation process requires considerable time and effort to develop worthwhile learning/assessment activities, measuring instruments, and strategies for fairly scoring and interpreting results for several different purposes. It also requires teachers to develop an effective record keeping and grade reporting system that provides a means of communicating learner achievement to parents and others.

Without question, one of the challenging, daily roles of the career and technical education teacher is to measure and evaluate learner achievement in reference to specified learning goals and objectives based on occupational performance standards. Many teachers feel uncomfortable in their evaluation role with "regular" career and technical education learners but sometimes express even more concern when they are asked to test, evaluate, and report the grades of learners from special populations. Teachers are concerned about how to make evaluation and grading practices fair to both learners from special populations and other learners without lowering program standards. Many teachers are convinced of the need to modify their measurement and evaluation methods and techniques to make them more authentic learning experiences in themselves and to increase their accuracy in assessing the achievement of learners from special populations, but are unsure as to how to make the modifications acceptable in light of school grading policies.

Teachers also fear the impact of minimum competency tests that are used in some school systems as one factor in faculty retention decisions. No teacher wants to defend why a learner earned a passing grade in a course only to have the same learner fail in a minimum competency test. The problem of evaluating learners from special populations enrolled in career and technical education subjects is made even more acute in that many career and technical education teachers perceive themselves as having inadequate preparation in traditional and alternative measuring, evaluating, and reporting strategies for learners from special populations.

The practice of grading learners and reporting their progress to parents is a long-standing tradition in the nation's public education system, but it is not without controversy. Despite the primary role of grading in improving learner learning by providing specific feedback to learners and parents, limited agreement exists as to the best way to grade learners and report learner progress. Grading and reporting systems come under increased scrutiny and debate when grading practices are associated with mainstreamed learners from special populations. Teachers are faced with finding defensible answers to the following and many other questions.

- Should special needs learners be graded by the same standards as other learners?
- Should effort, progress, and attitude be used in combination with achievement in relation to established performance standards to determine grades for learners from special populations?
- Should there be two different grading systems, one for regular learners and another for mainstreamed learners from special populations?
- If one grading systems is used for all learners, is it fair to grade learners the same when special needs learners are disadvantaged by a unique set of individual differences that affect learning and achievement?

Issues surrounding grades and grading practices of learners from special populations are complex and important and need to be resolved by teachers and school leaders. Rojewski, Pollard, and Meers (1990), in a review of the professional literature on grading learners from special populations, reported on a number of different views held by educators regarding grading and reporting learner progress for mainstreamed special needs learners. Some professionals believe that the traditional grading system penalizes learners from special populations. One reported that the dilemma of grading mainstreamed learners is exasperated by the difference between the way learners are typically evaluated in career and technical education and how learners are evaluated in special education programs. Other professionals reported that often teachers fail to communicate clearly and accurately the meaning of grades issued to learners. Still other professionals reported great inconsistencies among states regarding graduation requirements for learners from special populations.

Grading learner achievement is demanding for all teachers in terms of time and professional knowledge, but Rojewski, Pollard, and Meers (1990) concluded from their research into grading practices for mainstreamed learners from special populations that this important role has received relatively little professional discussion. Teacher educators have apparently given little attention to the issues involved in grading learner achievement of mainstreamed learners. The professional literature offers only a cursory treatment of evaluation methods and grading. While there are a number of articles available that describe current grading practices for learners from special populations or offer information on alternative grading methods, few authors offer a grading system that is based on a philosophy, theory, or unified procedure with regard to grading these mainstreamed learners. Likewise the grading practices of career and technical educators regarding mainstreamed learners from special populations have also been given inadequate treatment.

Motivated by the lack of information regarding how career and technical educators evaluate and grade mainstreamed learners from special populations in their classes, Rojewski, Pollard, and Meers (1990) conducted a qualitative study into the practices and attitudes of secondary career and technical educators in grading these learners. Four major themes emerged from this study:

1. current grading practices used by career and technical education teachers with emphasis on successful grading practices and concerns when grading learners from special populations,
2. perceptions of career and technical educators regarding the intended messages they believe grades communicate to learners, parents, and others,
3. the degree of initial preparation and ongoing training and support teachers received on the topic of grading learner progress, and
4. a common developmental process (evolution) in grading practices learned through experience and the application of common sense.

The current grading practices included the traditional norm-referenced grading system in which all learners are evaluated by the same standards. Also included was a criterion-referenced or competency-based grading system in which learners are evaluated in terms of their individual performance in light of an established performance standard rather than by comparing individual performance against the performance of other learners. A most commonly used system was a combination of norm-referenced and criterion-referenced grading system that combined the most favorable elements of both. Career and technical education teachers were divided in terms of how learners from special populations should be held to performance standards. Some advocated the inclusion of other grading factors like attitude and effort in making grading decisions with performance in relation to standards paramount. The six successful grading techniques identified were

1. individualization and modification of instructional techniques and evaluation based on the learner's abilities,
2. flexibility of teaching and evaluation methods,
3. successful collaboration with special education and support staff,
4. use of pre-stated objectives, competencies, and standards,
5. multiple evaluation methods, and
6. emphasis placed on positive aspects of performance with learners and parents.

Rojewski, Pollard, and Meers also found that most career and technical educators had concerns over the messages and meaning grades communicate to learners and others. They found that the meaning of grades appears to be generalized for learners and parents in contrast to the specific interpretations of other teachers and administrators. Administrators were more concerned with the distribution of grades than their meanings. Most career and technical educators believe that grades should convey the degree of success learners had within a class with respect to the quality of work performed by the learner in light of pre-established performance standards. Some career and technical educators presented the idea that college bound learners and their parents are more concerned with grades than are mainstreamed learners and their parents who are more concerned with learning and improved performance than they are with letter grades.

The Rojewski, Pollard, and Meers study revealed that career and technical educators overwhelmingly felt that their preparation and training in grading learner progress, especially grading special needs learners, was woefully inadequate. Teachers reported that they learned how to grade through trial and error and through duplicating the practices of other teachers. Because there are so many different grading practices used by different teachers and school systems, the grading practices adopted and/or developed by teachers really result from other teachers' practices, from experience, and from the application of common sense.

Finally the theme of a developmental process revealed in the study confirmed that career and technical education teachers do indeed change their grading practices over a period of time, moving from being quite rigid and unyielding at first toward becoming more flexible and more learner-oriented as time passes. Teachers reported that changes occurred in their grading practices through a developmental process as they became more comfortable with their roles as teachers and as they became more knowledgeable about evaluation and grading practices primarily learned from colleagues and other professionals.

The evaluation system for measuring and reporting the progress of learners from special populations should be based on their needs and abilities related to specified performance outcomes or competencies rather than how well these learners perform as compared to other learners. The educational needs and abilities of disabled learners are identified and listed in the individualized education plan with a transition component (IEP/ITP), while the needs and abilities of other learners should be identified and specified in the individualized transition plan (ITP). These two individualized plans serve as a basic guide for each learner's instructional program and evaluation component, and the cooperative effort of IEP and ITP planning team members can result in an evaluation system that is fair and reasonable for all learners. The evaluation system must be comprehensive in scope and employ a variety of measurement and evaluation techniques to provide information that is useful to the learner and the teacher. The evaluation system must be communicated to learners and their parents to minimize fear and anxiety as well as to gain their acceptance and participation. The evaluation system must also be consistent with the testing, evaluation, and grading policies of the school system.

GENERAL ASSESSMENT CONSIDERATIONS

The evaluation and grading system used by career and technical education teachers in working with learners from special populations should emphasize individual-to-individual accomplishments and be criterion-referenced. It should be based on the learner's capabilities and needs rather than on a system that compares learners with other learners. It should be criterion-referenced, which means that testing should render information concerning what tasks a learner can or cannot perform to a predetermined standard in a clearly defined area independent of the performance of other learners. In other words, the evaluation system should be based on the amount of progress made by learners toward prescribed outcomes and the quality of work produced as compared to the assessed abilities, interests, and needs of each learner.

Fairness requires that work of learners with special needs not be compared with their more able peers. But honesty requires that these learners be assessed on how they are doing against predetermined standards. Wiggins stated that learners are robbed of the chance of a successful future if they are not provided with honest feedback about their absolute performance. He also indicated parents and others are deceived when low-performing but highly motivated and hard-working learners are given a single, high letter grade in which growth and effort are combined (Wiggins, 1994).

Career and technical education teachers realize that grades are taken seriously by learners, parents, and school administrators and that poor grades often have negative consequences such as reduction of learner interest and effort. Grades are sometimes used to make decisions on retention, promotion, and placement in special programs and on admission to postsecondary education institutions. They are also used in some states to regulate participation in extracurricular activities. This does not mean, however, that career and technical education teachers should lower program standards for learners from special populations so they can earn passing grades. If individuals from special populations are to be successful in postsecondary options and to be employable upon completion of the program, they must meet postsecondary education standards and employability standards of business and industry. Rather than lowering program standards, career and technical education teachers need to design flexibility into instructional programs and provide training for a variety of

jobs that require different sets of competencies and different levels of achievement. In addition, they need to employ a variety of assessment methods and techniques to measure a variety of learning outcomes.

Multiple exit points leading to a variety of jobs in business and industry can be identified for each career and technical education program. For example, in the occupational area of auto mechanics, a learner may receive instruction in an educational program that has identified certain tasks which, when completed, lead to employment in a number of job titles such as a service station attendant, front end alignment specialist, parts clerk, automobile engine overhaul mechanic, and others. This approach can provide career and technical education teachers with a way to match the abilities and proficiencies of learners with realistic employment opportunities and improve the chances for learners to successfully complete portions of the total program leading to productive employment.

Flexibility in planning career and technical education programs involves more than providing multiple exit points. It also entails providing learners with extended time, when necessary, to successfully complete individual education programs. If the final goal is for learners to master a specified set of competencies at set employment standards, then it makes sense to allow learners from special populations more time to develop these competencies when necessary. This procedure is certainly better than failing these learners because they cannot keep up with the regularly established achievement pace.

Flexibility in planning programs in which learners from special populations can experience success should also involve support personnel. These individuals can assist in identifying learning problems and can offer remedial instruction to learners who are not able to keep up with other learners in assigned work activities. This additional instruction can often mean the difference between success and failure for individuals from special populations enrolled in career and technical education programs.

BENEFITS PROVIDED BY EVALUATION

The measurement and evaluation component of career and technical education programs for learners from special populations must be designed for more than the function of providing an administrative grade at the end of a specified marking period. It should provide a number of benefits to learners, teachers, parents, and employers. See Figure 9-4.

Benefits to Learners

There are four major benefits that learners from special populations can derive from an effective evaluation effort. First, learner motivation is enhanced. Tests can encourage learners to study assigned materials and to practice skills if they are designed to be authentic, interesting, rewarding, and within the learner's ability level. Tests often evoke varied responses from learners ranging from an increased desire to succeed in a course and to compete with other learners to a renewal of the fear of failure and the frustration of not being able to perform up to perceived ability level because of imposed testing and evaluation methods.

Obviously, the testing and evaluation component for learners from special populations should be designed to reduce the negative responses and emphasize positive ones that lead to motivated learners. For example, testing and grading practices can be modified so they are more flexible in time, cover a more narrow scope of content, and include the factor of the degree of learner effort put forth. Evaluation techniques such as using graphic stickers, tokens, special privileges, and certificates can be used to encourage learners to achieve at higher levels. Learners from special populations are seldom motivated internally and usually are initially motivated by secondary or external rewards. Teachers can help these learners become motivated by providing prompt feedback and by using appropriate feedback and reward techniques. Teachers can also help learners with special needs become more motivated by assigning them to a cooperative learning team where the efforts and contributions of each member are important and recognized as essential to completing the team's assignment.

A second major benefit of the evaluation system for learners from special populations is the opportunity to learn self-evaluation skills. Mitchell (1992) noted that the ultimate aim of an educational evaluation system must be to empower learners to assess their own progress and products and advocate appropriate assessment methods that can serve as models so that learners can learn self-assessment from the practices they encounter in schools. Blake (1998) points out that if teachers fail to require learners to assess their own work—a process based on internal factors and criteria—they are likely to become dependent on external rewards from others, not knowing how to begin to assess their own performances.

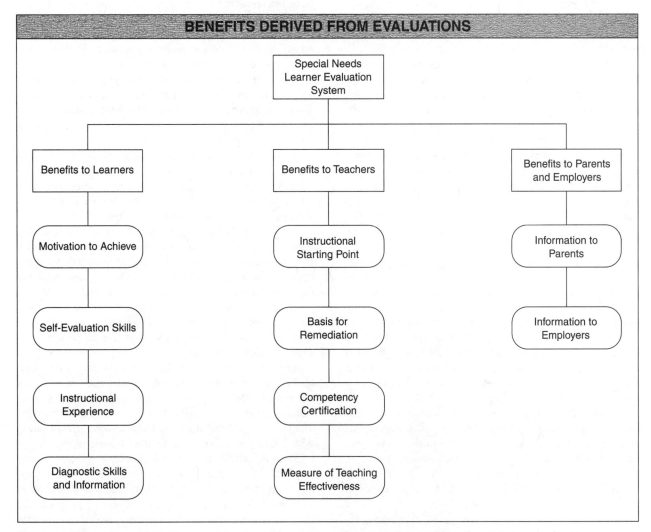

Figure 9-4. An example of benefits to learners, teachers, parents, and employers derived from the student evaluation process.

She concludes that if teachers don't ask for learner self-assessment, they aren't likely to get it. Individuals from special populations can learn how to evaluate their own performance on tests and assignments through teacher feedback and evaluative assignments. Seely (1994) noted that classrooms are moving from a testing culture–where teachers exercise absolute authority, learners work alone, and learning is focused on preparing for tests–to an assessment culture–where teachers and learners are collaborative about learning, assessment takes many forms for multiple audiences, and the lines between learning and assessment are blurred. For example, portfolio assessments include some form of self-assessment so that learners can see how the quality of their work has evolved through effort. Mitchell (1992) noted that portfolio development and assessment provides an opportunity for learners to take responsibility for their own learning, to work at developing self-critical capacity, and to trust their judgment, which are important skills in the workplace as well as in the pursuit of a satisfying life as a citizen and a lifelong learner. Stephen Covey (1989) recognized the importance of self-directedness, which he called "proactivity," and included it as one of his seven habits of highly effective individuals.

In the California C-TAP program, the project requires learners to present three pieces of evidence that show their progress toward developing the final product and an oral presentation in which learners describe the project, explain what skills were applied, and evaluate their work. Individuals can learn what minimum performance is and what it takes to move through the satisfactory level to a higher standard of achievement if they are provided with established rubrics or descriptions of performance for each assessment criteria. As learners develop self-evaluation skills they usually begin to develop a more positive self-concept, which is essential for success in most jobs.

Career and technical education teachers can encourage learners from special populations to develop self-evaluation skills through utilization of portfolios, projects, writing scenarios, graphic organizers and by designing learning and assessment experiences that require learner self-evaluation before teacher evaluation occurs. For example, a teacher could design a checklist for the learner to use in evaluating a product constructed from an instructional experience such as the creation of a dress in an industrial sewing class. The checklist could have two rating columns, one for the learner to use and one for the instructor to complete after the learner has responded. After the learner and teacher evaluate the product, a friendly, supportive discussion should occur in which evaluation points and ratings are discussed. By following this procedure, learners can develop and polish their self-evaluation skills.

A third benefit to learners from special populations resulting from the evaluation system is that evaluation ac-

tivities are important learning experiences in themselves. Announced test and evaluation activities can encourage learners to review and perhaps study material for the first time, which helps them to organize and understand concepts and principles essential in completing occupational tasks. As learners prepare for tests, they are often able to identify the important content of a lesson or learning unit and relate newly learned materials to previous learning in order to form a bigger picture of an instructional area. Learning occurs in taking tests as concepts are reinforced and the application of learned material is provided. Career and technical education teachers can promote learning through evaluation activities by emphasizing that they are learning experiences and by making them authentic, fun, and rewarding when possible. Teachers can help learners improve their performance on tests by teaching them how to prepare for and take examinations.

The fourth benefit is the one learners derive from a well-designed evaluation system in which they can diagnose or recognize and judge what concepts and tasks they have mastered and which ones need more work. Learners from special populations, with initial help from teachers and other school support professionals, can identify commonly made errors and make adjustments in their study habits and the way they view content.

Career and technical education teachers can make evaluation activities diagnostic for learners by providing them with descriptive scoring rubrics and prompt, specific feedback and by requiring learners to review their test results, look up concepts they missed on test items, and describe their thinking for selecting the incorrect response. One way teachers can encourage learner involvement in the diagnostic function is to award points toward the final course or individual learner program grade for learner effort in reviewing test results and correcting errors.

Guskey (1994) described three categories of learning criteria that can help diagnose what learners have learned: product criteria, process criteria, and progress criteria. Supporters of using process criteria for grading and reporting focus on measuring what learners know and can do at a given point of time. They usually base learner grades exclusively on final exam scores, overall assessments, or other culminating demonstrations of learner performance such as course projects.

Teachers who favor process criteria emphasize how learners arrive at the final course results and not solely on the results. They include measurements on such dimensions as effort, work habits, attendance, homework assignments, class participation, and classroom quizzes along with final exam scores to determine learner progress.

Progress criteria refers to improvement in learning over a specified time span. It is also called "improvement scoring" and "learning gain." Teachers and learners look at benchmark information early in a course or program and look for evidence of how far learners have come individually rather than where they are at present. In actual practice, most teachers use a combination of these three criteria types to report learning progress. Researchers and measurement specialists caution teachers on using process and progress criteria because of the inherent bias and subjectivity of these two criteria and recommend that if these criteria are used at all, they be reported separately.

Involving learners from special populations in assessing their own learning places the responsibility for learning on them and gives them a way of monitoring their own progress as they strive to meet learning objectives and goals. After all, in real life adults are expected to constantly assess and evaluate their performances in family, work, and leisure and to make whatever adjustments are needed to improve their performances and capabilities. When learners from special populations are significantly involved in helping structure a multidimensional evaluation system, they improve their performances and develop self-direction and personal efficacy.

Benefits to Teachers and Support Personnel

Career and technical education teachers and other school support personnel involved in working with learners from special populations also receive benefits from a well-designed evaluation component. The first major benefit is that teachers can identify an instructional starting point. Teachers can prepare appropriate pretests and other initial measurement instruments to determine the approximate benchmark in an instructional area. For example, the career and technical education teacher can choose the first learning objective or goal from a learner's ITP and construct and administer a quiz or test covering the major concepts of the unit dealing with the objective. The quiz or test results can be reviewed by both teacher and learner and a joint determination made concerning a tentative starting point for instruction.

A second benefit resulting from the evaluation system is that teachers are provided with information that can be used as the basis for remedial instruction. By studying the results of a given test, career and technical education teachers and support personnel can spot the gaps in learner knowledge and skills and determine what needs to be done in the remediation process. Learners from special populations need to be involved in reviewing their test results and in determining what course of action is needed to correct deficiencies.

A third benefit career and technical education teachers derive from the evaluation component is a form of learner competency certification. Once instruction inherent in the IEP or ITP has taken place, teachers can design and administer a competency test to verify the level of learner competence on specified goals and objectives for each learner from special populations associated with their career choice. These test results can be recorded on a competency record and can be used as a type of certification that learners can use in seeking employment.

The fourth benefit career and technical education teachers receive from the evaluation effort is feedback information about teaching effectiveness and new insights in how learners learn. Not only are learners provided with a valuable learning experience in the form of tests, but teachers are provided with an effective teaching tool if used appropriately. By reviewing learner test results, career and technical teachers can determine what instructional strategies, methods, and techniques worked with learners from special populations and what did not. Teachers can determine how well they covered instructional material, what needs to be improved or reinforced, and how they can make their instructional activities more interesting and effective for learners from special populations as well as other career and technical education learners. When learners are required to reflect on their work in writing or orally as in the case of portfolios, projects, and scenarios, teachers are given new pictures of learner understanding and thinking patterns. In addition, the use of portfolios encourages collaboration between learners and teachers, changing the view of assessment from something done to another to establishing a partnership in learning (Far West Laboratory, 1992).

A final benefit to teachers is described by Mitchell (1992). She noted that professional development is one of the major benefits of portfolio assessments. Portfolio group grading meetings provide an opportunity for teachers to see a wide range of learner work other than the work of their own learners and to debate standards, scoring criteria, and exemplary work. They also are provided with an opportunity to exchange curriculum and teaching ideas and to reflect more deeply on learner work and how they learn. Teachers who participate in developing scoring rubrics and using these devices to evaluate learner progress are more likely to evaluate learner achievement like others who teach similar subjects in the school system or region. Participation in assessment brings out fundamental questions about teaching and learning. For example: What do we value? Are we teaching toward what we value? Is what we value the most important part of the subject? A recognized outcome of teacher involvement in new assessment strategies is that they tend to monitor learner achievement more closely, refine their own teaching techniques, and experiment more with efficient record-keeping systems (Sperling, 1994).

Career and technical education teachers will undoubtedly continue to change the way they assess and evaluate all their learners, Many teachers will use a blend of traditional and nontraditional measures. As career and technical educators become more informed and experiment with alternative assessment tools and practices, they will begin to feel more comfortable with their role of helping learners improve their learning through meaningful and fair assessments. They will discover that their curriculum and teaching practices will change and their learning environments will improve, resulting in improved learning for all learners.

Benefits to Parents

Parents of learners from special populations can receive benefits from the evaluation effort. Parents can be assured that the testing, evaluation, and grading system is appropriate for their son or daughter because they have direct input into its formation if they become involved in planning the IEP or ITP. Career and technical education teachers can actively involve parents in the evaluation process by encouraging them to help their sons or daughters study for tests and complete homework assignments. Learner test results can be shared with parents so they can assist in correcting deficiencies and in improving the study habits of their children. Parents can be instrumental in the motivation of their children toward higher achievement through appropriate words of encouragement and understanding if career and technical education teachers communicate with them regarding the curriculum, performance expectations, and how learner performance is to be evaluated. If parents understand and support the curriculum and assessment practices, and hold high expectations for their children, the chances of the learner completing school and entering postsecondary education or productive employment is vastly improved.

Benefits to Prospective Employers

Prospective employers of individuals from special populations also benefit from an effective learner evaluation component. When career and technical education teachers use a variety of measurement and evaluation activities and report learner achievement in terms of competency attainment in addition to grades, prospective employers have a better idea of what the applicant can do. Many employers feel uneasy in making employment decisions when they are provided with a learner's grade transcript without other achievement indicators. Employers are very much involved in the development of national occupational standards and certificates of initial mastery. They are also involved in decisions about the assessment system used to grant the certificate. One picture of the assessment system is a portfolio that contains the work of learners accumulated over several years that include the results of projects, reports, papers, scenarios, work samples, career and technical student organizations (CTSOs) competition results, documented work experience, and test results.

PROTECTING CONFIDENTIALITY OF INFORMATION

It is important to note that learner achievement information must be cleared by the parents before it is forwarded to a prospective employer. The transfer of personal information about learners is a topic not well understood by many. The irresponsible transfer of personal information about individuals has led to the passage of federal, state, and local laws to regulate the dissemination of information gathered on individuals. There are several notable pieces of legislation that regulate the flow of information about people. The Family Educational Rights and Privacy Act of 1974 (PL 93-380) (FERPA), commonly known as the Buckley amendment, is one of these laws that applies to all learners. The Individuals with Disabilities Education Act (PL 101-476) also contains sections regulating the flow of information of learners with disabilities in special education programs.

Section 504 of The Rehabilitation Act of 1973 protects the confidentially of information concerning individuals with disabilities. In general, these pieces of legislation prohibit the transfer of learner information without the consent of learners who are over 18 years of age or without the consent of the learner's parents or guardians when learners are under the age of 18. Under PL 101-142, learner information gathered specifically to develop the IEP may be disseminated only if the parents or learner give their consent.

Under the provisions of FERPA, secondary learner information may be transferred to postsecondary schools to which the learner has applied without the consent of either the learner or parents when certain conditions are met. Readers should review Sections 99.31 and 99.34 of FERPA for a discussion of these conditions. Under FERPA, individuals working with a learner are granted the right to access information concerning that learner, however that individual cannot transfer information gained to a third party whether it be a teacher, employer, or agency representative.

Title I Section 102 of the Americans with Disabilities Act (ADA) prohibits making inquiries about disabilities or conducting medical examinations before a job offer is made. Mandates of the act also directly affect what questions educators can ask on applications, medical questionnaires, and during interviews. No questions can be asked on applications or during interviews that either directly or indirectly relate to a disability (Maoris, 1993). The ADA allows individuals with disabilities to be tested for ability to do job-related functions at any point in the employment relationship.

As a result of the impetus of legislation, many states and localities have drafted interagency agreements that outline the roles and responsibilities of career and technical education, special education, and rehabilitation services in providing comprehensive career and technical education services for individuals. These agreements do assure that the rights of disabled persons will be protected in compliance with the mandates mentioned above. However, most of these agreements provide for the exchange of pertinent information to individuals working directly with the disabled person.

Career and technical education teachers should consult with the special education teacher, guidance counselor, or school administrator if there is any question regarding the confidentially of information concerning learners with disabilities. Some school systems include information on this topic in their faculty and staff handbooks.

PROSPECTIVE ON ASSESSMENT

While testing, evaluation, and grading methods specifically developed for learners from special populations can render more accurate information about learner achievement, caution should be exercised in thinking that this information is unquestionable. Tests and other measurement devices cannot be used to measure everything of importance and what they do measure is usually limited to a sampling of expected behavior. For over 20 years, standardized tests have been accepted as the best measure of achievement. Now, more than ever before, influential decision makers and educators are beginning to raise serious questions about the limitations of these tests. For example, how useful for accountability purposes are data from norm-referenced multiple choice tests when the test compares learners with one another instead of established performance standards and when they emphasize skills out of context rather than through thoughtful application?

While educators have been vocal about the misuse of standardized tests, they also realize that the bulk of tests learners take are teacher developed and some of them are even worse than the published ones (Brandt, 1994). It is estimated that over 90% of evaluation takes place in the classroom in the form of teacher observations, teacher responses to written work and oral presentations, informal discussion with learners about their work, and quizzes and tests developed by teachers or copied from curriculum materials. Stiggin's research findings on teacher-designed tests, as reported in Mitchell (1992), confirmed that multiple choice tests place too much emphasis on memorizing and recall of facts and teachers' essay tests show a clear lack of training in evaluation techniques. He concluded that teacher training programs provide little, if any, preparation in evaluation which results in teachers having to learn how to develop, score, and administer tests on the job from other teachers and through trial and error teaching experience.

Tests are better perceived as teaching tools. They provide a good deal of useful information for learners, teachers, parents, and prospective employers. Test results, however, should be viewed as only one type of systematically obtained information upon which to make judgments about learners. This point of view was expressed by the National Commission on Secondary Vocational Education in its report entitled *The Unfinished Agenda* (1984):

Achievement testing dominates measurement of learner performance in basic academic subjects. Knowledge is subdivided into discrete units, delivered in curriculum chapters, and monitored at regular intervals through standardized tests. We urge that such tests not be the sole criterion of school and program effectiveness. There is more to teaching and learning than high achievement scores. Schools and career and technical education programs help young people achieve personal intellectual, social, and career goals. Achievement tests measure learner success in only one small area of one of these goals: they should be only one small part of the learner's performance assessment. (p. 16)

Most people agree that standardized tests do not measure everything of importance, but the challenge is finding true alternatives that provide additional evaluation data that can enhance learning. Mitchell (1992) noted that there should be no single replacement for standardized, multiple choice tests but that a multi-indicator system that makes use of teacher observations, portfolios (collections of learner work over time), group learning tasks, timed examinations, authentic performance assessments (work samples, projects, written scenarios), and cognitive and performance tests is needed to represent the complexity of what teachers need to know about the learners' intellectual, emotional, and social development and how school programs affect these developments. Equally controversial is the practice of using a number of alternative assessments to guide instruction and monitor learner progress only to condense multiple measurements into a single grade that becomes part of the learner report card. The issue is compounded further when one considers how grades are interpreted by different audiences.

The search is on for performance assessments that are more closely aligned to classroom instruction and assess learner outcomes more fully and more accurately than teacher developed or standardized multiple choice tests. According to the Far West Laboratories, *C-TAP Teacher Guidebook*, performance assessments are defined as "criterion-referenced measures—measures that are judged against an established set of criteria or standards—that show progress toward instructional goals." Performance assessments include performance events such as projects or written scenarios to a collection of learners' work over time such as portfolio assessments. Cumulative assessment tasks such as long-term projects and portfolio collections provide opportunities for learners to recognize their achievement through self-evaluation and to voice their successes to others. The many forms of alternative assessments being developed and tested in our nation's schools promise a new cadre of measurement and evaluation strategies that are flexible enough to provide information teachers need to enhance the learning of an increasingly diverse learner population.

One of the promising features of alternative assessments, particularly performance assessments such as learner portfolios and learner projects, is their flexibility, which allows learners with special needs to work over a longer time period than most other measures, and provides them with an opportunity to emphasize their strengths. In addition, performance-based assessments tend to be accessible to learners from special populations, emphasize functional skills, and allow for assistance from teachers, classmates, parents, and others. These assessments can be modified to accommodate learners with special needs. Career and technical education teachers need to present performance-based assessments to other members of the IEP and ITP planning team in order to make the most appropriate accommodations for learners from special populations.

IEP AND ITP AS GUIDES FOR ASSESSMENT

The overall guide for evaluating learners with disabilities enrolled in career and technical education programs should be the career and technical education component of the individualized education program (IEP). Likewise, the guide for evaluating other learners from special populations is the individualized transition plan (ITP). The IEP and ITP contain a list of goals and short-term objectives that relate to the needs and abilities of learners in relation to the instructional program and a predetermined job or career. Evaluation should be based on the progress or achievement that these learners have demonstrated in successfully accomplishing the content specified in the IEP or ITP.

The rules and regulations of PL 101-476 specify that the short-term objectives of the IEP be evaluated at least once annually. This is a minimal standard, however, for it is inconceivable that teachers would allow a year to pass before evaluating learner progress toward accomplishing the objectives specified in the IEP. If teachers only evaluated learner progress on the IEP annually, they would not be able to recognize problem areas and make appropriate adjustments in the objectives of the IEP, teaching techniques, instructional materials, classroom and laboratory environment, and support services which are often required to help learners achieve their maximum potential. Evaluation must become an integral part of the daily teaching-learning progress and not simply an exercise that occurs at the end of a specified grading period.

The Individuals with Disabilities Education Act (IDEA) Amendments of 1997 (PL 105-17) reaffirm the need for annual development of IEPs that contain detailed requirements for planning the education of individual learners, but it also includes a requirement that each individual learner must be provided with a comprehensive evaluation of individual educational needs at least once every three years. The IDEA amendments also mandate that transition planning begin by age 14 for learners with disabilities and that IEPs must include transition service needs. One additional provision of the IDEA amendments is the participation of learners with disabilities in state and district-wide assessment programs (including alternative assessments) with appropriate accommodation when necessary (Ordover & Annexsteine, 1999).

ESTABLISHING EVALUATION SYSTEMS

Career and technical education teachers will need to plan which factors they will consider in evaluating each learner from special populations. The IEP and ITP can be useful tools for planning and implementing the evaluation system. During the preparation of the IEP and ITP, the teacher should discuss evaluation and grading practices used in the instructional program with other team members or support professionals. This discussion should include factors to be evaluated, the criteria for each factor, the methods that will be used to evaluate each factor, and the way grades will be determined. Special education teachers, support personnel, and other IEP or lTP team members can provide information about how they believe the learner will respond to the tentative evaluation system and what problems might occur in assessing each evaluation factor.

There are a number of advantages in using the cooperative planning team approach to establishing an evaluation and grading system. First, career and technical education teachers can receive input from others in determining which factors should be included, which standards of performance will be used, and what rubrics will be used to determine the learners score and grade. Second, career and technical education teachers can receive some idea of what assistance or support services they can receive from support personnel in preparing learners for evaluation. Third, support personnel can provide valuable tips on evaluation methods and techniques that may be needed to enable the learner to more accurately demonstrate achievement. For example, it may be necessary to print tests in large type to aid visually impaired persons, to allow more time for mentally disabled learners to take a test or demonstrate a competency, or provide remedial assistance and reinforcement for educationally disadvantaged learners in preparing for a test. Finally, the team approach provides an extra stimulus to base evaluation and grading practices on specified proficiencies in the IEP and ITP, which assures that the evaluation system will assess each learner's performance against predetermined standards rather than assessing against other learners.

EVALUATION TOPICS

There are many factors regarding learner progress that should be considered when designing and implementing testing and evaluation as an integral part of the instructional program:
• task or competency performance
• work habit development
• attendance

- attitude and personal growth
- daily class participation
- quality of homework and outside assignments
- performance on tests measuring cognitive achievement
- safety practices
- completed projects or products
- ability to work in groups/teams
- learning how to learn processes

Cognitive Achievement

The learner's knowledge and level of understanding of the technical information necessary to perform an occupational job is an important evaluation factor. Knowledge about something is more than simply being able to recognize or recall a concept or principle. Gardner (1994) suggested that knowledge take the form of deep understanding–the ability of learners to take knowledge, skills, and other apparent attainments and apply them in new situations. Wiggins and McTighe (1998) define understanding to mean that learners possess more than simply textbook knowledge and skill—that they have developed insights and abilities that are reflected in varied performances and contexts. Knowledge itself is of little value unless it can be combined with other knowledge and skills

to make decisions, solve problems, and meet the daily challenges of work and life. Teachers need to consider the taxonomy of learning for the cognitive domain developed by Benjamin Bloom that includes the following levels:

1. knowledge (recognize and recall facts, concepts, ideas)
2. comprehension (demonstrate understanding of knowledge and relate to previous learning)
3. application (use learned knowledge in new situations)
4. analysis (break down learned knowledge into parts and relate them to each other)
5. synthesis (assimilate learned knowledge for use in solving problems and performing tasks)
6. evaluation (make decisions or judgments on the value of material or some endeavor)

The usual method of measuring this factor out of context is through written or oral tests composed of different types of items. Examples of test items to measure cognitive achievement include multiple choice, sentence completion, listing, true-false, matching, essay, and modified forms of each type. Contextual measurements include performance events, projects, written scenarios, portfolio assignments, group problem-solving events, and competitive events. Regardless of the types of items used, they should measure important concepts and ideas that relate to performance standards expected in the workplace and in life.

Case Study . . . Karen

Karen is an educationally disadvantaged learner enrolled in a 10th grade child care program in a comprehensive high school. She is the oldest sister in a large family where the father is deceased. Her mother works long hours to provide for the family. This has forced Karen into the role of caring for her younger sisters and brothers. Karen has missed many days of school this year and she is falling further behind. She is a slow learner with very low basic skills. Karen scored in the 49th percentile on a standardized achievement test and is presently earning a 1.9 on a 4.0 grading scale in her classes. Her reading and math scores are measured at the 5th grade level.

Since Karen has always been a low achiever in school, she lacks confidence in her ability to improve her grades. She usually does better on performance tests in her child care classes than she does on written tests. Her daily classroom and laboratory grades are average.

Karen's child care instructor has met with the school system's special populations coordinator and has developed a tentative ITP to use as a guide for Karen's instructional program. This guide is designed to prepare her for employment in the child care field. The coordinator is providing instruction in basic reading and math skills and is reinforcing the academic skills associated with child care learning tasks.

Karen is also receiving help from a peer tutor so she can keep up with her classmates. She is beginning to improve in the instructional program but is still having difficulty with written tests. Although Karen requires extra time to complete performance tests, she continues to earn slightly above average grades on these tests. With each new successful experience on performance tests, Karen's self-confidence increases.

After Karen's instructor and the special populations coordinator met, it was determined that an evaluation component that was better suited to Karen's ability and needs should be developed. The career and technical instructor is preparing more skill performance tests to administer to Karen. In addition, plans are being made to begin the development of a portfolio, allowing Karen to become more involved in the learning and assessment process over time. Karen and her instructor have discussed Karen's limitations in taking written tests and have explored methods that may lead to improvement. One accommodation has been for Karen's instructor to modify written tests, using items that are shorter in length and that cover less content in a single testing. Also, Karen's teacher has prepared study guides similar in format and content to major tests and is providing more time for review before the test is administered. Karen has been given more time to take the shortened versions of tests. She is also permitted to take the test during a regular class study period rather than in a group testing situation and, in some cases, to use notes and references. One final accommodation provided is allowing Karen to correct her errors and rewarding her with a portion of points added in relation to errors made.

Psychomotor or Manipulative Performance

The ability to apply cognitive learning with learned skills to perform an actual or simulated work task is an important achievement factor to evaluate. The usual methods of measuring skill performance include (a) observing learner performance in following specific work procedures and rate performance with a rubric (checklist or other rating device), (b) assessing the quality of the completed job, project, or work assignment using a rubric (product rating scales), and (c) assessing both the step-by-step process of performance as well as the quality of the completed product.

Work Habit Development

One of the most important areas of learner development is work habits. Employers place high value on the demonstration of work behaviors like planning for work, following directions, giving an honest day's work, arriving to work and leaving work at the appropriate time, showing initiative, accepting criticism, etc. Work habits are usually measured by observation using a rating form that identifies the level of behavior for each desired work habit. Learning logs or journals and selected graphic organizers can also be used to help learners assess their own work habit development.

Interest

A learner's interest in education and preparation for a chosen occupational field or career is also an important factor to be assessed. Interests are formally evaluated using self-report pencil-paper inventories or can be identified through computerized job search programs. An informal way to assess a learner's interest is to have the learner record a verbal statement of choice or a statement promoting the program to others. Volunteering for work-related tasks, wanting to stay after school to work in the laboratory, and participating in competitive events associated with career and technical student organizations (CTSOs) is also indicative of interest.

Attitude

A factor closely related to interest is the learner's attitude or feeling toward the instructional program or chosen occupational area. Attitudes are formally measured by paper-pencil self-report inventories or they can be measured through direct questions such as those posed in a structured interview. Like interest, attitude can be measured informally through observation and the use of recording devices. Experienced teachers can be quite adept at sensing a learner's attitude through facial expression as well as initiative.

Amount of Work Completed

The amount of work that a learner completes in a specified time period relative to assessed ability should also be evaluated in a career and technical education program. The usual method of measuring this factor is by observing and recording information on a progress chart or individual competency records that list the learner's coded number, expected behaviors, and time-lines. Learners should keep record of their progress as they complete each work task or project. Most career and technical education teachers use progress charts to monitor required learning activities.

Time Required to Complete Instructional or Work Tasks

Employers expect workers to complete tasks in a standard window of time. Therefore, teachers should evaluate the time required for learners to complete learning tasks. The usual method is to time tasks according to an established timetable for each one. Advisory committee members or incumbent workers can assist in determining time specifications for occupational tasks. Learners should be required to keep track of the beginning and ending time for each assigned learning activity on the project sheet provided to guide instruction.

Creativity

Another important area for evaluation is the learner's ability to solve problems in unique ways or to come up with new ideas or approaches to perform tasks. According to Torrance (1994), creative persons demonstrate a high degree of the abilities of fluency, flexibility, originality, and ability to sense deficiencies, elaborate, and redefine. To encourage creativity, teachers can show one way to perform a work task but challenge learners to come up with a better way if they can.

Cramond (1994) described the work of Torrance in creativity testing in which one of the purposes of measuring creativity is to point out potentialities that might otherwise go unnoticed—especially in children from culturally diverse and lower socioeconomic backgrounds. Cramond reported from her own research that using creativity tests can highlight strengths in children who have previously been viewed as school problems.

The usual method teachers use to measure creativity is to observe learner behavior and record notes on a record keeping device. Creativity can also be measured through the completion of assigned projects such as creating a solution to a problem or inventing some new product. Products should be judged for creativity by the collective opinion of experts in the field if possible (Baer, 1994).

Safety

A learner's attitude, understanding, and practice of safety are other important factors to be evaluated. Measurement methods include performance tests, paper-pencil tests, and observational techniques supported by rating devices.

Leadership Development

Employers are constantly looking for individuals with leadership ability, and career and technical education programs can assist learners in developing and assessing leadership skills. One of the best ways to test leadership abilities is through the leadership contests that are part of every CTSO program. For example, the SkillsUSA-VICA Championships have several leadership contests such as extemporaneous speaking, club business procedures, and the job interview contest, each containing rating devices that can be used to measure and assess learner leadership skills. In addition, VICA has a professional development program which has assessment activities included that measure learner leadership development. Teachers can also develop their own rating and recording forms with stated criteria to measure learner leadership skills.

Quality of Homework and Outside Assignments

Career and technical education teachers, like other teachers, assign learners homework and other out-of-school assignments and these should be assessed like other achievement factors. To measure the quality of learner homework, teachers need to determine assessment criteria in advance of scoring and use performance criteria in the form of scoring rubrics or models of excellent work to guide evaluation. Learners should also be required to write a short summary of what they learned from doing the homework assignment and how they felt about their work.

Daily Class Participation

Some teachers measure learner participation in classroom and laboratory activities as a way of helping learners develop good work habits and keeping learning productivity high. One way to view this factor is to consider it as effort, but awarding learners low scores for effort seldom improves their enthusiasm for learning and awarding learners high scores for effort with low performance results can cause learners to think that even when they work hard, they are just too dumb to complete tasks correctly. A better way to view class participation is to focus attention on the growth of the learner. Clarridge and Whitaker (1994) have developed a system of awarding scores based on learner qualities that include the factors of self-directed learner, collaborative worker, problem-solver, responsible citizen, and quality producer. See Figure 9-5.

SCORING RUBRIC FOR SELF-DIRECTED LEARNER

4. Learner regularly sets achievable goals, considers risks and makes choices about what to do and in what order to do them, reviews progress, and takes responsibility for own actions

3. Learner often sets achievable goals, considers risks and makes choices about what to do and in what order to do them, usually reviews the progress being made, and often takes responsibility for own actions

2. Learner rarely sets achievable goals, has difficulty making choices about what to do and in what order to do them, needs help to review progress, and seldom takes responsibility for own actions

1. Learner requires help setting goals, completing tasks, and making choices; does not yet take responsibility for own actions

Source: Clarridge, P. B. & Whitaker, E. M. (1994). Implementing a New Elementary Progress Report. *Educational Leadership, 52* (2), 7-9.

Figure 9-5. An example of guidelines for assessing the learning outcome of a self-directed learner.

Ability to Work in Groups and Teams

An important skill required by an increasing number of workers is the ability to work effectively in teams. Kohl (1998) includes the skill of "the ability to understand how people function in groups" as one of his six basic skills that people want learners to acquire. Teachers are preparing learners for participation in work teams by implementing cooperative learning events. Johnson, Johnson, and Holubec (1990) described cooperative learning as "the instructional use of small groups so that learners work together to maximize their own and each other's learning," (p.4). In cooperative learning, learners have two major responsibilities: learn the required material and ensure that all members of the group participate and learn the material. Two other important outcomes of cooperative learning are development of interpersonal and small group skills and group-processing skills. Interpersonal and small group skills are demonstrated when learners (1) get to know and trust each other, (2) communicate accurately and unambiguously, (3) accept and support each other, and (4) resolve conflicts constructively. Group processing is defined as reflecting on a group session to describe what member actions were helpful and unhelpful and making decisions about what behaviors to continue or change. Interpersonal and small group skills and group-processing behaviors can be measured by observation supported by rating forms or can be evaluated in the form of written reports submitted by learners describing their group process.

Learning How to Learn Processes

All learners need to develop the ability to continue life-long learning. The competencies identified by the Secretary's Commission on Achieving Necessary Skills (SCANS) in their report *Learning a Living: A Blueprint for High Performance* (1992) include three types of foundation skills. The skill areas are basic skills—writing, arithmetic, mathematics, speaking, and listening; thinking skills—ability to learn, reason, think creatively, make decisions, and solve problems; and personal qualities—individual responsibility, self-esteem and self-management, sociability, and integrity. Teachers need to consider these important learning outcomes as they develop assessment strategies. A variety of alternative assessment strategies such as performance projects, writing scenarios, and portfolios can be used to assess the development of learning how to learn.

Many career and technical education teachers make use of multiple factors in their evaluation and grading systems. They have found that including a variety of factors provides an incentive for learners to develop proficiencies in the three major areas that concern employers: (1) skill performance, (2) theory or understanding required to perform work tasks effectively, and (3) work attitude, work habits, and team work skills required to become a productive employee.

The practice of using multiple factors in the evaluation and grading system provides several advantages for learners from special populations. First, it provides learners with a guide to the type of behaviors expected in the program. If learners are aware that their grades will be based on daily work performance, demonstration of good work habits, and a positive attitude, quizzes and written tests, and performance of required tasks or competencies, they may direct more attention to these areas.

The second advantage is that it provides some components that can be covered through remedial instruction provided by support personnel to improve learner performance. A third advantage is that it provides a way of earning a passing grade in a class even though a learner may do poorly on one factor, such as quizzes or tests. Finally, using a variety of evaluation factors makes it possible to provide more specific feedback to the learner about areas of strength and weakness in preparing for employment. It also provides direction to the teacher for altering the instructional approach or learning environment.

EVALUATION METHODS AND TECHNIQUES

The primary purpose of evaluation is the improvement of learning and instruction. This purpose suggests that learning occurs during a test and improves as a result of receiving feedback on test results. It implies that teachers and their instructional programs will also improve as teachers discover what works best in helping learners.

Other purposes and outcomes of cognitive achievement evaluation are as follows:

- Learner motivation–Learners are usually more attentive and apply themselves better when they know they will be tested and evaluated. They may become motivated to study for exams because of: (a) competition with other learners, (b) a desire to improve their knowledge and skills, (c) feelings of guilt and anxiety or the fear of failure, and (d) a need to see how successful they are in applying learned content.

- Diagnosis of learner capabilities–Teachers who use pretests can provide information to their learners and themselves about basic prerequisite knowledge and skills believed to be essential for learning in an occupational program. They also are able to use pretest results to determine the current level of knowledge and skills learners possess in order to sequence instruction better.

- Improving teacher and instructional effectiveness–Teachers who analyze test results are able to modify their assessment instruments and techniques as well as their instructional program to meet all or certain learners' special needs because they know what methods or learning activities produced desirable outcomes.

- Test taking as an important instructional experience–Preparing for tests causes both teachers and learners to review key concepts, principles, and points that can be used in solving educational and occupational problems. When learners actually take a test, they are provided with an overall review of lesson or unit content and important learning outcomes.

- Test results as important self-evaluative information–When learners receive their test results and teachers take time to go over items missed, learners learn how others view their performance and begin to develop the skills of self-evaluation.

The appropriate selection of measurement and evaluation methods and techniques is essential to determine what the learner really knows, understands, and can apply to function in school, the workplace, and in the family and community. There are a variety of measurement, evaluation, and reporting methods and techniques from which career and technical education teachers can select to measure the progress of learners from special populations.

Individualized Instruction and Competency Assessment

The first method involves the use of a sequenced series of individualized units that contain specific competencies. As the learner demonstrates each competency, the career and technical education teacher evaluates performance through performance tests and records it on progress charts, individual competency records, and proficiency profiles. See Figure 9-6.

PROFICIENCY/COMPETENCY PROFILE

Student: Isabelle Anderson   Date: 1-24

Instructor: June Sullivan   Program/Course: Food Service

Module: Short Order Cooking-Breakfast Preparation

Competency/Skill	Date Completed	Instructor Initials	Evaluation		
			Needs Assistance	Adequate	Very Good
Prepares juices	2-1	J.S.	5	6, 7	1, 2, 3, 4
Prepares hot cereals	2-14	J.S.	6, 7	1, 5	2, 3, 4
Prepares cold cereals	2-16	J.S.		4, 6, 7	1, 2, 3, 5
Prepares eggs	3-2	J.S.	6, 7	4, 5	1, 2, 3
Prepares omelets					
Prepares breakfast meats					
Prepares breakfast fruits					
Prepares breakfast breads/ baked goods					
Prepares coffee					
Prepares tea					

General Criteria for Evaluation Tasks

1 – Planned work

2 – Followed directions

3 – Followed safety rules

4 – Followed correct procedures

5 – Used kitchen equipment correctly

6 – Quality of work/product

7 – Rate of work

Comments:

Figure 9-6. An example of a profile used to record a learner's performance level on identified competencies.

Progress charts have been used by career and technical education teachers for years to record learner progress on assigned learning activities. Progress charts are forms that are arranged as a matrix with the learner's names listed down the left side of the form and learning outcomes such as tasks, competencies, assignments, projects, etc. listed across the top. See Figure 9-7.

According to Eschenmann (1993), progress charts have been used over the years for many purposes including (a) assessing learner performance, (b) preparing for job interviews, (c) making tests, (d) job enrichments, (e) preparing for CTSO contests, (f) meeting state and local standards, (g) motivating learners, (h) resume building, (i) identifying class projects, (j) assigning learner jobs, (k) counseling, (l) scheduling live work, (m) writing learner recommendations, and (n) planning for peer teaching. Progress charts can be modified to serve a variety of purposes and to meet the needs of learners and teachers. The most common purposes for using progress charts include the following:

- Learner motivation–Learners can see their progress in relation to course requirements and progress of others.
- Teacher picture of learner progress–Teachers can quickly determine what tasks learners are currently working on and which tasks have been completed.
- A means of sequencing instruction–Progress charts provide a way to organize learning activities according to some sequencing pattern (prerequisite skills, simple to complex, logical order, etc.).

- Monitoring learner achievement–Teachers can constantly check learner progress and counsel learners as well as record a general indicator of performance without placing scores on the chart (Eschenmann, 1993).

Progress charts are mainly used to show the progress of all learners for a class on one form and are frequently displayed for all to see. They are not designed to include performance ratings or scores because this information is personal and should be kept private. The individualized competency record serves the purpose of recording the learner's level of performance in relation to the competencies (skills, work habits, attitudes) required for entry-level employment. The individual competency record (ICR) is a summary recording device. See Figure 9-8.

The summative ratings to be placed in the individualized competency record should be based on ratings taken from instruments such as performance tests, checklists, work habit rating scales, and descriptive attitudinal behavior rating scales. Individual competency records can be modified to include a method of assigning grades based on the summative information included in them. Their best use, however, is to show summative information that learners, parents, and employers can use to verify what competencies were included in the career and technical program and the learner proficiency level for each. Individualized competency records are also sometimes referred to as competency profiles, competency check sheets, and individualized competency plans.

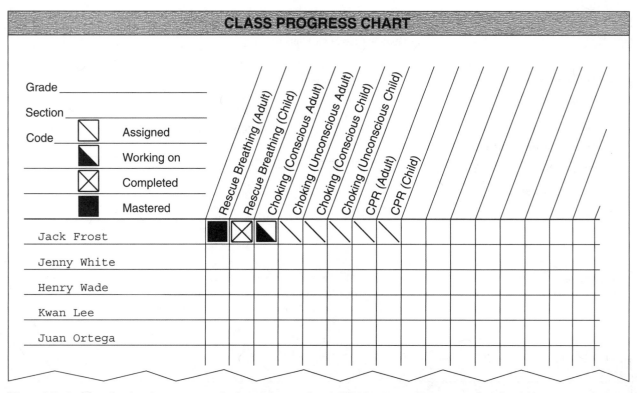

Figure 9-7. An example of a class progress chart used to record and show learner progress on assigned activities.

INDIVIDUALIZED COMPETENCY RECORD

Student _____ Date_____

Grade Period_____to_____

		Competencies									Work Habits				
		Rescue Breathing (Adult)	Rescue Breathing (Child)	Choking (Conscious Adult)	Choking (Unconscious Adult)	Choking (Conscious Child)	Choking (Unconscious Child)	CPR (Adult)	CPR (Child)		Dependability	Respects authority	Cooperates with others	Follows directions	
Directions: Record the appropriate letter or code for the factors in the left column under each competency or work habit. Record attendance in the space provided to the right of each factor.															
Competency Code															
1. Skilled, needs no supervision		1	1		1	1									
2. Moderately skilled, needs limited supervision				2			2								
3. Limited skills, needs close supervision								3							
4. No experience									4						
Attendance Record															
1. Total days on roll															
2. Total days tardy															
3. Total days absent															
4. Days made up															
Work Habit Code															
A. Outstanding											A				
B. Exceeds Minimum												B	B		
C. Minimum														C	

Figure 9-8. An example of an abbreviated individualized competency record summarizing learner progress.

Learner-Teacher Contracts

A learner-teacher contract is a performance conract developed by the career and technical teacher with input from the learner and resource personnel. It describes the tasks to be performed, the minimum acceptable performance levels, and the amount of time required to complete the contract. See Figure 9-9. The learner and teacher discuss the contract before signing it. As the learner completes each component of the contract, the learner's performance is evaluated according to specified criteria included in the contract. At the end of the contract period, the teacher and learner jointly evaluate progress using rating forms and arrive at a fair grade. Performances that have not been completed successfully can be included in the contract for the next grading period. See Figure 9-10.

PERFORMANCE CONTRACT

Student: Francis Joseph   Date: 9-12

Program: Residential Wiring

Instructor: Joe Smith

Unit/Module: Switching Circuits

Approximate Time for Completion: Six weeks

Criteria: Must meet performance checklist criteria for each task

Task/Assignment	Date Completed
1. Install 110 V lamp controlled by a special switch.	
2. Install 2 – 110 V lights in parallel.	
3. Install 110 V lights and duplex receptacle in parallel with light controlled by special switch.	
4. Install 1 – 110 V light controlled by two 3-way switches.	
5. Install 1 – 110 V light controlled by two 3-way switches and one 4-way switch.	
6. Install 1 – 110 V light controlled by two 3-way and two 4-way switches.	
7. Install a circuit with 4 receptacles and 1 special switch so it controls 1 receptacle while others remain hot.	
8. Install a light dimming system.	

Comments: (Include pertinent comments and suggestions about handicap from the student and support personnel.)

Francis has limited use of his left arm. He cannot use this arm for any tasks requiring strength and power. He has exceptional strength in his right arm and can perform most tasks using it. Adaptations may be required for tasks requiring two arms.

_____   _____
Date   Student Signature

_____   _____
Date   Instructor Signature

Figure 9-9. An example of a performance contract outlining what is to be learned, how it is to be learned, how it is to be assessed, and timelines for completion of the work.

TASK PERFORMANCE/PRODUCT RATING CHECKLIST

Task or Competency Install a Single Switch/Single Light Circuit   Unit _____

Student _____   Date _____

Directions: Rate the student's level of performance on each indicator by placing an "I" in the upper diagonal portion of the box if you are the instructor and an "S" in the lower diagonal portion of the box if you are a student.

Level of Performance

Performance Indicators	0 N	1 P	2 F	3 G	4 E
1. Prepared and used schematic					
2. Selected correct tools, equipment, & materials				I/S	
3. Wore protective clothing & equipment					I/S
4. Followed proper sequence of steps				I/	/S
5. Technique in using tools & equipment					
6. Installed components properly					
7. Checked work with instructor before energizing					
8. Light and switch work properly					
9. Time taken for completing job					

Level of Performance
All items must receive Good or Excellent responses. If any items received a None, Poor, or Fair response, the learning or part of it must be repeated. Discuss this with your teacher.

0	1	2	3	4
U	D	C	B	A

Student Signature _____   Teacher Initials _____

Figure 9-10. An example of a performance/product rating checklist used by learners and teachers to evaluate learner performance or the performance outcome.

Cognitive Achievement Tests

Cognitive achievement is usually measured through teacher developed paper-pencil tests. However, an increasing number of textbook publishers are providing written items or computer disks containing test items for each chapter that teachers can use to make appropriate cognitive tests. Career and technical education teachers need to identify an appropriate unit of instruction or block of content from the IEP or ITP for a learner from a special population and develop or adopt a pool or bank of test items. These items can be written on 3 × 5 index cards and placed in an organized, mechanical test file, or they can be coded and placed on a microcomputer diskette for later test preparation. It is probably best to use recognition items such as matching or multiple choice to reduce learner requirements for written responses in early tests and gradually move to completion/short answer, interpretive, and essay items as learners develop reading and writing skills and instructional tasks that call for higher order cognitive behaviors.

Test preparation is relatively easy provided teachers have an adequate bank or pool of test items covering content taught in their instructional areas. If the items are stored mechanically in a test file, the teacher need only select the appropriate items for a specific test and have them typed, duplicated, and prepared for administration. It is even easier to prepare a test if the teacher has stored test items on microcomputer diskettes. The career and technical education teacher simply needs to insert a test generation program along with their data disk containing items into a microcomputer and follow the prompts to generate an appropriate test for a given learner from special populations.

Paper-pencil tests are by far the most common form of tests administered in career and technical education with performance tests in second place. Paper-pencil tests are fairly easy to construct and administer. Most learners can perform at the satisfactory level or above on them, but they do have limitations. The results of a pencil-paper test can only tell us if learners know how to do a task and not whether they can actually perform it satisfactorily. Also, written test results give us a distorted picture of a learner's level of achievement if the learner has reading deficiencies, a poor vocabulary, or difficulty following directions.

Paper-pencil tests usually are made up of a number of different types of test item formats. The two major divisions of item formats are (a) supply type items that require learners to generate their own responses or answers and (b) selection type items that require learners to select from among several possible responses or answers. These item formats are also labeled "recall versus recognition" and "constructed response versus the objective item." Objective items include multiple choice, true-false, matching, and short answer/completion. The essay item is the only example of a subjective item.

The most common item formats used in paper-pencil tests are completion, matching, multiple choice, true-false, and essay. Each of these items has advantages and limitations. The completion item is fairly easy to develop but requires learners to generate a written response. Because learners respond differently to a given item and are required to write the answer, scoring completion items fairly is difficult. Matching items involve two columns of related information that require learners to associate content in Column I with responses in Column II. They are somewhat difficult to write and can be difficult for learners to complete. The multiple choice format is usually considered the most desirable to measure a wide range of content, different types of learning, and at different learning levels. Multiple choice items provide learners with a stem, usually expressed as an incomplete sentence or as a question, followed by 3 to 5 responses, one of which is correct; the balance of responses are plausible but incorrect. These items are somewhat difficult to write but easy to score and are relatively easy to computerize (Scott, 1993).

The true-false or alternate response item is limited to factual information and single-concept information. Since learners either respond true or false to the item, the chance of guessing the correct response without knowing the answer is high. Some teachers feel these items are easy to write, but effective true-false items are really quite difficult to write. Some of the limitations of true-false items can be eliminated by the teacher modifying the forms as follows:

- Require learners to decide if a statement is true or false; then if it is false, the learner must indicate what changes are needed to make it a true statement by underlining the appropriate word(s) or phrase(s). If the statement is true learners are to underline the key word(s) or phrase(s) that make it true.

- Require learners to decide if a statement is true or false. If the statement is true, no further action is needed. However, if the statement is false, the learner must insert in a special blank space lettered A the word or phrase that makes the statement false. Then the learner is required to insert the correct word or phrase in a special blank space lettered B that will make the statement true.

- Require learners to read an incomplete statement followed by several items that will make it either true of false, then require them to circle T or F for each item that completes the stem as a false or true statement.

Essay test items are easy to write but hard to score. They usually require learners to write sentences and paragraphs that require writing skills and high-level cognitive skills in addition to recalling content. They also take considerable time to score and are difficult to score objectively.

A rather new item type format that can be written to require learners to recognize correct responses or to supply them is the interpretive item. Learners are provided with information in the form of a scenario, picture, or table of information that they are directed to read, and specific questions are given for them to respond to that can be presented either in true-false, completion, multiple-choice, or essay format. This type of item is becoming more popular because it authentic and calls for learners to consider a block of information and demonstrate an understanding of it in order to respond correctly to a number of items about the information.

Modifying Test Items and Test Directions

The modified measurement technique of reducing the reading requirements in written tests for learners from special populations deserves special attention. Some learners with special needs have difficulty understanding test item formats, following directions, and reading test items that involve unnecessary words or phrases. Therefore, it is desirable to keep the directions and test items as short and concise as possible. Directions can be shortened by focusing only on how you want learners to respond to items and clarified by underlining key words like *choose* or *circle* in a phrase such as "choose the correct alternative that answers the item."

Directions should contain information about the content of the items that follow. For example, a common practice is to simply write directions that call for the learner to circle the letter of the response that correctly answers the question or completes the sentence. A better practice is to inform the learners as to the content area of the items in the directions. For example, directions for a series of multiple-choice items on wood products should read, "For each item below concerning wood products, circle the letter of the response that correctly completes the sentence or answers the question." Whenever possible, examples of completed items should be constructed so the learner can see how to respond to the items as directed. Also, point values for items should be included in test item directions. See Appendix.

The reading level of test items can be reduced by putting only necessary information in the item stem and keeping the alternatives as brief as possible. When possible, use drawings or graphic illustrations on test items calling for learners to identify things such as tools or equipment. See Figure 9-11.

Reducing Fear of Cognitive Achievement Tests and Providing Feedback

Modifying test items and techniques for measuring the achievement of learners from special populations will result in more accurate evaluation information and increased learner performance. There are two other important practices that can lead to improved learner achievement. These are minimizing fear of testing and providing frequent and continuous positive feedback on performance. Many learners become fearful when the words "test time tomorrow" are spoken by the teacher. The moments preceding the actual test administration are anxious ones, as evidenced by facial expressions, the biting of nails, and other nervous actions. While the fear learners experience in the testing situation may not be entirely eliminated, there are some techniques that career and technical teachers can use to minimize the fear of testing:

- Review the scope of the test the day before the test is scheduled to be administered.
- Explain testing procedures adequately and emphasize how test results can be helpful to learners.
- Explain minimum performance standards and their importance to learners.
- Use words of encouragement and reinforcement.
- Provide practice quizzes and tests for learners when it is appropriate.
- Establish a supportive atmosphere during the test administration by friendly smiles and the skillful use of humor.
- Encourage learners to self-evaluate their performance.

The second teacher practice that can result in improved learner performance on tests and other measurement activities is the skillful use of prompt feedback. Career and technical education teachers should try to score tests for learners from special populations as well as all other learners as quickly as possible, preferably with the learners present so immediate feedback is made possible. Other feedback techniques include

- asking learners to describe their performance and to indicate areas that need more work;
- providing feedback to learners in a constructive, friendly manner;
- providing continuous feedback information to learners such as informing them about recorded observations on classroom and laboratory behaviors, safety behaviors, and other rated behaviors;
- using appropriate media to provide visual and auditory feedback such as transparencies, charts, videotapes, and audiotapes;
- summarizing all appropriate progress data at least weekly and presenting the summary to learners from special populations and IEP or ITP team members;
- communicating to learners that it is important to correct errors and to learn from them; and
- using PC software packages to administer quizzes and tests that provide immediate feedback regarding correctness of response.

Learners must be encouraged to assess their own performances in relation to exemplary models using objective scoring rubrics. Teachers must take the time to meet with learners to critique performance and must encourage learners to identify areas that need more work. They must also share with them specific information that can lead to improved performance. Teachers need to guard against being overprescriptive and simply directing learners on what to do to get a task done. A better practice is to help learners identify areas that need more work and present some alternatives that they can use to improve performance.

MODIFIED WRITTEN TEST ITEMS

Family and Consumer Services

Written Test Items

Directions

For each item below, circle the letter of the response that correctly completes the sentence or answers the question.

1. Which of the following cooking implements would be best to use with teflon coated pans?

    a. Stainless steel utensils

    b. Table utensils

    c. Wooden utensils

    d. Nylon utensils

Modified Test Items

Directions

Read each item below and circle the letter of the correct answer.

1. The best cooking implements to use with teflon coated pans are

    a. stainless steel utensils

    b. table utensils

    c. wooden utensils

    d. nylon untensils

Trade and Industrial

Written Test Items

Directions

Choose the hammer that is used to install rivets and circle its letter.

    a. Ball peen

    b. Rawhide faced

    c. Brass

    d. Plastic tipped

Modified Test Items

Directions

Circle the letter of the hammer used to install rivets.

    a.   ball peen

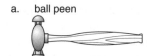

    b.   plastic tipped

    c.   brass

Figure 9-11. An example of how test directions and items can be modified to accommodate learners from special populations.

Constructing Cognitive Achievement Tests

Constructing good tests requires careful planning. Career and technical education teachers must develop and select a sufficient number of test items to adequately sample learning outcomes taught in an instructional time period. It is impossible to include all the test items covering important content in any one test, so teachers must carefully select an adequate sample of items to measure each essential learning outcome. Teachers should also select test items to measure the different levels of learning outcomes in the cognitive domain. The practice of teachers developing unit tests by going through their lesson plans, reading assignments and other assigned resources, and choosing content that is important to them without much thought about levels of learning or the make up of the test should be avoided.

Tests constructed without adequate planning are poor measuring devices. They frequently contain trivial items with few that measure higher order learning outcomes like the ability to analyze a situation or apply knowledge to solve realistic occupational problems. Tests constructed in this manner often contain content in one area and few or no items measuring other important learning outcomes.

Teacher-made tests can be improved significantly if teachers use this six-step planning process:

1. Develop test specifications–Some general guidelines or specifications should be developed that address basic questions such as the following: What is the purpose of the test? What performance objectives will be measured? What is the time limit of the test? What type of measures should be used (paper-pencil, performance test, or both)? What type of items formats would work best? How many items and what will be the point value of the test? What equipment and materials are available (computer, test generation software, scantron, duplicating machines) to produce and score the test? What should be included in test directions?

2. Determine performance objectives–The most appropriate basis for selecting test items are the performance objectives that have been taught during an instructional time period. These objectives should be listed on a test objectives planning sheet along with the percentage value or degree of emphasis each of these objectives should receive in the test. See Figure 9-12. This listing of objectives and their degree of emphasis during instruction can serve as a rough guide for selecting items from a test bank or for developing new items to include in a test.

3. Analyze performance objectives–Carefully analyze the measurable behaviors described in the performance objectives but be aware that some performance objectives are not written specifically enough to identify all the content which should be measured with test items. In most occupational programs, the measurable behavior component of a performance objective is an occupational task. Analyzing the tasks taught in an instructional unit to determine what steps; key points of information; tools, equipment, and materials needed; and safety precautions and work habits using a task analysis recording sheet will provide a rich source of possible test items topics. See Figure 9-13.

4. Develop a content outline–Analyze task elements to identify the content topics to include in a test. To organize these topics, it is helpful to construct a content outline for each unit to be measured on the test. The amount of detail to be included in the outline is up to each teacher but it is essential to identify important information that will provide a solid source of test item content required to adequately sample subject matter taught.

5. Construct test items–Using the performance objectives, task analysis recording sheets and content outline as guides, construct test items of different types and at different learning levels to measure the subject-matter content. Test items can be written on index cards, sheets of paper, or they can be entered directly into a computer test development program or word processing program for later use. The traditional practice is to use a test file card system using different color cards to separate categories. The first card to construct is a course card that

---

PERFORMANCE OBJECTIVES FOR A TEST

STEM: Given a paper-pencil test, students will be able to:

OBJECTIVES	EMPHASIS
1. Demonstrate knowledge and understanding of how iron is made including the raw materials, the smelting and remelting processes, and the types of iron produced. The performance expectation for this objective is at the 80% criterion level.	15%
2. Demonstrate knowledge and understanding of how iron is converted into steel including the ingredients, steel production methods, and types of steel produced. The performance expectation for this objective is at the 80% criterion level.	15%
3. Demonstrate a knowledge and understanding of the properties of metals and why these properties are important to know. The performance level for this objective is at the 90% criterion level.	20%
4. Demonstrate a knowledge and understanding of the basic methods of identifying steel and identify types of steel provided by spark testing. The performance level for this objective is at the 90% criterion level.	30%
5. Demonstrate a knowledge of nonferrous metals and the properties and typical application of each. The performance expectation for this objective is at the 90% criterion level.	20%

Figure 9-12. An example of a test planning sheet showing performance objectives and the degree of emphasis placed on each.

displays the name of the course in large print and may contain information on how the course fits into other courses in the instructional program. The second type of card contains several different types of general test directions. This card can be followed by other cards that contain specific directions for each type of test item format. The next cards in the system should be header cards with large type indicating the type of test item format such as completion. The final cards in the system are the actual item cards arranged in numerical order for easy retrieval.

The test item cards should be preprinted with appropriate information so that the amount of time needed to compete cards is kept to a minimum. A sample test item card showing information printed on the front and back contains the file code and test item code used to organize and retrieve cards. See Figure 9-14. A file code is necessary to store and retrieve the item from a file cabinet or box. For example, a completion item on a test card could be coded as follows:

- Course = BGM (file B, General Metals) ITEM CODE BGM2222104.
- Unit = 2 (second unit)
- Lesson = 2 (second lesson)
- Item = 2 (completion)
- Learning type = 2 (understanding)
- Item No. = 10 (item number in bank or system)
- Source = 4 (reference code number 4)

Another method, which is increasing in popularity, is to build test item banks using the computer and test generation software. A number of test generation programs are available that are menu-driven and very user friendly, even for teachers whose computer skills are very limited.

6. Construct a table of specifications–In order to ensure that the appropriate number and types of items measuring different learning behaviors are selected for each performance objective, a table of specifications should be constructed. A table of specifications is simply a matrix with two different categories of information: one listed across the top of a form and the other listed down the left side, forming a table or chart. There are two different types of specification tables used: one for performance objectives and types and levels of learning and a second that charts test items based on course unit content. The first type lists the performance objectives down the left side of the form with the types and levels of learning across the top. See Figure 9-15. The cells for each objective and learning type contain (a) numbers representing the degree of emphasis expressed as a percentage and (b) the number of items to be written for each type of learning outcome. The bottom of the table contains a listing of the total number of items to be written in order to measure all of the performance objectives.

The second type of test specification table can be developed based on the subject matter content and performance objectives. In this type of table, instructional content expressed in outline form for each performance objective is listed down the left side of the form with learning types listed across the top. Again, the cells for each content outline of a performance objective and each learning type contain (a) numbers representing the degree of emphasis expressed as a percentage and (b) the number of items to be written for each type of learning outcome. See Figure 9-16.

TASK ANALYSIS RECORDING SHEET

PROGRAM: _____ COURSE NO.: _____

UNIT/NO.: _____ LESSON NO.: _____

PERFORMANCE OBJECTIVE: _____

Sequenced Steps	Tools, Equipment, Materials	Key Information Points	Supporting Resources	Safety Precautions Work Habits

Figure 9-13. An example of a task analysis recording sheet used to identify content for constructing tests.

TEST ITEM CARD

FRONT

Completion: FILE CODE: _____

ITEM CODE: _____

ITEM:

ANSWER:

BACK

COURSE NO./TITLE:

UNIT NO./TITLE:

LESSON NO./TITLE:

SUBJECT:

LEARNING TYPE(S):

SOURCE OF ITEM/PAGE NO.:

DATE WRITTEN/AUTHOR:

DATE REVISED/AUTHOR:

REMARKS:

DIFFICULTY INDEX: _____   DISCRIMINATION INDEX: _____

Figure 9-14. An example of a test item card format used for writing test items and for storage in test item banks.

PERFORMANCE OBJECTIVES AND LEARNING TYPES

Objectives	Emphasis	Types & Levels of Learning				
		Knowing	Understanding	Applying	Feeling	Total
1. Demonstrate knowledge and understanding of how iron is made, including the raw material used, the smelting and remelting process, and the types of iron produced. The minimum performance level is 80%.	10%	8	12	0	0	20
2. Demonstrate knowledge and understanding of how steel is made, including the ingredients, steel production methods, and types of steel produced. The minimum performance level is 80%.	20%	9	14	0	2	25
3. ...						
4. ...						
5. ...						
Total % and Items	100%	17	26	0	2	45

Figure 9-15. An example table of specifications used to identify the number of items needed to measure the different types of learning outcomes for each objective covered in a test.

INSTRUCTIONAL CONTENT AND TYPES OF LEARNING

Content Outline	Emphasis	Types & Levels of Learning				
		Knowing	Understanding	Applying	Feeling	Total
I. History and Importance of Iron	10%				1	1
A. Early Iron Production		1	1			2
B. Sources of Iron Ore		1				1
II. Ingredient of Iron						
A. Ore			1			1
B. Coal		1	1			2
C. Limestone			1			1
III. Blast Furnace						
A. Parts of Furnace		1	1			2
B. Furnace Operation			1			1
IV. Types of Iron						
A. Pig Iron						
B. Cast Iron		1	1			2
C. Malleable Cast Iron			1			1
D. Wrought Iron			1			1
V. Uses of Iron						
A. Castings		1	1			2
B. Stoves and Furnaces						
C. Ornamental Structures		1				1
D. Making Steel		1	1			2
VI. ...						
Total % and Items	100%	8	11	0	1	20

Figure 9-16. An example table of specifications using learning types to identify the number of test items needed to measure instructional content for each objective.

Cognitive Test Construction and Administration Modifications for Special Learners

The Americans with Disabilities Act (ADA) requires educators to provide reasonable accommodations when testing disabled individuals (Maoris, 1993). Some of the accommodations described by Maoris include the following:

- changing the method and making modifications to the type of test and the way it is administered
- adjusting the time limit of the test or changing the test location
- accepting the work samples developed instead of administering tests
- using a computer or allowing a disabled person to take tests on a personal computer
- adjusting the furniture or allowing a learner to take tests in a comfortable chair using a lap board
- using interpreters or readers or allowing support persons to assist with testing
- making other adjustments, such as modifying examinations, employing other assessments, and modifying scoring procedures

The following are techniques for constructing modified tests for evaluating learners from special populations:

- constructing an individual test for each learner from a special population and placing the learner's name on it to make it more personal
- involving learners in making up a test when possible
- typing tests using large typefaces and leaving adequate spacing to make each item stand out on the page
- placing easier test items at the beginning of the test to reduce anxiety
- grouping similar items together on the test
- repeating the item format directions on subsequent pages of the test
- providing lined paper for tests when long responses are required.
- underlining the key words in the directions and providing an example item as part of the directions
- following sound principles of writing test items contained in testing and evaluation references
- administering taped tests
- involving learners in generating test items
- administering practice tests to reduce test anxiety
- providing alternative projects and assignments to demonstrate knowledge and understanding of a topic or subject
- videotaping learner performances and comparing them with a model videotaped performance
- using an overhead projector to increase type size of test items and having learners respond orally
- using a panel of judges, possibly advisory committee members, to evaluate performance
- decreasing the number of items on a test and administering more tests with fewer items to measure complex performances

- recording comments made in class discussion and including them in measurement decisions.
- giving the study guide as the test

Jones, et al. (1990) compiled a list of suggestions for designing tests for learners with special needs that includes the following:

- Construct the test in a logical, sequential order—from simple to complex problems.
- Use test items that reflect the technique used to teach the material. For example, if learners were taught primarily recall of facts, essay questions would not be appropriate.
- Type or print test using large letters and black ink.
- Prepare a study guide for the test that closely resembles the design of the actual test.
- Construct test items that directly relate to the performance objectives of the course.
- For learners who need more time to complete tests, administer an adapted or shortened version of the test. This can be done by circling either odd or even numbers and having learners complete these one day and the encircled ones another day. A second technique could be to administer half the test one day and the remainder another day.
- Make the general format of a modified test for a learner with special needs the same as the one used for other learners and administer it at the same time dealing it from the bottom of your stack discretely.
- Design the test to measure desirable learning outcomes rather than the learner's ability to read and follow directions, act with speed, or use an elaborate vocabulary.
- Keep readability level of the test at learner's level.
- Prepare the test with item formats written in short groups so that the test can be administered separately if necessary and learner frustration in answering any one type of item will be reduced.
- Place one type or group of item per page, particularly matching items and essay items.
- Prior to the actual test, review for the exam individually with the learner or allow the peer tutor or resource person to conduct the review.
- After consultation with the learner's special education teacher regarding personal testing preference, design the test to meet the learner's unique needs.
- Avoid using the chalkboard for tests, but if you must, erase all other material and print or write in large letters.
- For learners with copying difficulties, keep tests short in length.
- Use oral tests and quizzes only when special situations demand them.
- Allow disabled learner to take the test in the special education classroom if necessary.
- Avoid using purple ditto duplicated tests with all learners, but if necessary, place the test under a yellow sheet of acetate for learners with visual impairments.

Administering Cognitive Achievement Tests

Career and technical education teachers sometimes make mistakes in assuming that (a) all learners know how to take tests, (b) that they will understand and follow rules of behavior during the test, and (c) that they can read and understand the general and specific test directions. Another common teacher error is failing to prepare test materials or organize seating and the facility for a testing session in advance. Also, teachers sometimes fail to prepare the learners for the learning experience of taking a test. In short, there are a number of factors involved in preparing learners for and administering tests.

First of all, teachers need to prepare all learners for the positive experience of taking tests. Teachers should avoid making light of test-taking or making jokes that place test in the light of punishment. Instead, teachers should use words of encouragement and communicate to learners that test are important learning experiences that will yield information that will help them provide better instructions as well as help learners improve their learning and preparation for employment. Learners should be given adequate notice regarding the date, time, performance objectives, content covered, and the types of items that will be included in the test. Test days should be announced well in advance and daily reminders should be given to learners in a positive manner so that learners will view the test as an opportunity to showcase what they have learned. Avoid scheduling examinations on Mondays, the day before and day after holidays, and on days when major school events such as "homecoming" are planned.

Teachers should review test-taking tips with learners, particularly on tests that count heavily in the grading system. Some of the information that should be shared with learners includes the following:

• How to study for tests–Here, remind them of the PQRST method of studying, which involves (a) previewing materials, (b) questioning, (c) reading, (d) studying, and (e) testing themselves by generating possible test items.

• How to respond after reading test items–Remind them of the steps to follow, which include (a) selecting or providing the response or answer believed to be correct, (b) finding the number and item on the answer sheet, and (c) use a pencil rather than a pen to respond according to the directions provided that may call for circling, blackening in, marking through, or writing a word, phrase, or sentence in the space provided.

• How to read and follow directions–Here, inform the learners that following directions is an important work habit emphasized by educators and employers and go over examples of test directions with sample items so they will have practice in following directions.

• How to make the best possible score–Here, learners should be reminded of the following tips: (a) do not spend too much time on any one item, (b) answer items that are known first; then go back and try to answer remaining ones, and (c) review responses to items if time permits but use caution in changing responses unless a marking error was made or the item was misread.

Teachers need to prepare the exact number of test booklets and answer sheets for distribution to protect test integrity, as well as support materials needed for the examination such as extra pencils, lap boards, answer keys, and folders in which to place completed examinations. Arrange seating for maximum spacing between learners and regulate the lighting and temperature of the room for optimal conditions.

At the beginning of the testing session, assign seats or regulate seating, and request that learners remove all materials from desks or tables. Remind them to sharpen pencils and obtain any other instruments such as protractors, rules, and calculators required for the test. Inform learners about the time they have to complete the test, the procedures for asking questions, and the procedure for turning in completed examinations. Use a positive, friendly, supportive tone of voice when preparing learners for exams rather than one that is threatening or communicates "payback" time for the teacher. Distribute papers face down and ask learners to leave them so until all have received a copy. Read the general test directions to learners, then signal to start.

During the test, try to stay in one general location where all learners are in a line of sight and move quietly about the room if learners need a question answered. General test directions should state that only questions dealing with equipment failure or problems with the test instrument should be asked during the exam and not content-related questions. If questions arise, answer them in a quiet manner. When learners turn in their test materials, be sure that names are on the answer sheets and that they have completed all items. Place all completed test materials in a file folder and place them in a secure place.

At the earliest possible time, score the exams and particularly before the next class day if possible. Immediate feedback to learners about their performance enhances learning. At the next class session, review the test results with learners in an encouraging manner. Point out common errors made on the test and discuss how to correct them in future exams. Encourage learners to find the answers to items they missed if time permits and remind them that learning from mistakes is an important part of improvement in any endeavor. A growing number of teachers provide incentives for learners to correct errors in unit tests and quizzes by awarding a percentage of points for correcting items that were missed. This is made possible when teachers provide the sources and page locations for test items, which helps learners find information that can be used to correct errors. Learners should be encouraged to develop the habit of learning from mistakes and correcting them, as this is an important adult behavior.

Scoring Cognitive Achievement Tests

It is important to score tests as soon as possible after they are administered so that feedback can be given to learners to enhance learning. Scoring is the process of (a) checking completed tests to determine whether or not each item is correct and (b) assigning a numerical score, which is usually the raw score or number of items a learner answered correctly. Scoring procedures for cognitive achievement tests usually involve hand scoring test booklets or answer sheets, but an increasing number of schools have available optical test scanning machines that can score test items quickly and provide analysis information on test items. Most career and technical education teachers prefer to use simple scoring procedures that provide raw scores, but scoring can be made more complex if teachers elect to assign weights to different item types or employ correction from guessing formulas.

Answer keys, or a listing of correct or acceptable responses with coded resources, must be prepared for each item of the test. One common method for developing a master key is to take one of the test booklets or answer sheets and record the correct responses in colored pen or pencil for ease of reading. Scoring is performed by comparing learner responses with the key response and placing a check or X beside the incorrect numbered or lettered item and mark through the correct response or write it in above the learner's response.

A second method, which is much faster, is to prepare and use a scoring key in the form of heavy paper or card stock for each page of the exam. This scoring device is called a strip key because correct responses are placed on the strip key corresponding to spaces in the test booklet. Scoring is done by laying the strip key alongside of the test booklet and marking in the same manner as when using the master key. One suggestion for preparing strip keys is to simply copy the answer sheet or page of the test booklet and paste it on the card stock. Strip keys save time because teachers do not need to turn pages of a master key.

When separate answer sheets are used, it is desirable to construct a scoring stencil. This device is simply a copy of the answer sheet pasted on heavy paper of card stock with holes punched out or response lines cut out which allows the correct response to appear when laid over a learners answer sheet. When using the scoring stencil, teachers must be careful to register the stencil correctly, then mark through the correct response with a colored pen or pencil. After scoring is complete, check to be sure learners responded only once to items, then place a check or X beside each numbered or lettered test item that is incorrect or has two marked responses. The correct response should be written in colored pen or pencil above incorrect learner responses for completion or short answer items. Pro-

viding correct responses facilitates test review and helps the learner to correct errors quickly. Regardless of the type of scoring key used, it is important to have the sources of items included to facilitate learner correction of errors.

Essay items or written materials, such as homework assignments, reports, and sections of a portfolio, present unique scoring problems because each learner response is somewhat different. Subjectivity becomes a real problem unless teachers carefully analyze each item and write down the specific segments of each accompanied by a recommended point value. Decisions have to be made as to whether or not points will be assigned to essay items on such factors as grammar, spelling, and punctuation. Teachers should also follow the practice of scoring each learner's identical numbered items in succession before advancing to different essay items.

Developing model responses to essay items and other written assignments can be extremely helpful in scoring learners' work. Scoring rubrics can help to reduce subjectivity and increase consistency of evaluation. Simply defined, a rubric is a set of guidelines for assigning scores to learner work. Rubrics can be used to answer the questions "What do mastery or high level work look like?" and "What does varying levels of learner performance on assigned work look like?" Rubrics usually contain a listing of traits or factors to be evaluated along with a scale of possible scoring points. They also contain a range of typical performance on sample traits to help both teachers and learners determine where one's performance falls. (Far West Laboratory, Knowledge Brief, 1992). The amount of detail given to rubrics is up to the school guidelines or individual teacher choice. A holistic scoring rubric for a written assignment in which writing skills are the desired performance was developed by Clarridge and Whitaker (1994). See Figure 9-17. A sample analytic scale or rubric for problem solving was developed by Szetela and Nicol (1992). See Figure 9-18.

Developing and using rubrics is a challenging task. Teachers have to come to grips with what good performance is. For what kinds of errors will points be deducted and to what degree? How will performance factors be weighted relative to other factors? For example, how will the importance of neatness or the number of paragraphs in an essay be weighted? Then, decisions need to be made as to whether analytic or holistic scoring, or both, are best for learner work. Analytic scoring involves looking at specific dimensions such as reading a learner's report for syntax, then reading it again for rhetorical effectiveness, using separate rubrics for each factor. Holistic scoring involves developing a rubric and using it to make an overall judgment of the completed report or product that doesn't rely on specific traits or factors (Far West Laboratory, 1992).

SAMPLE RUBRIC FOR SCORING WRITING SKILLS DEVELOPMENT

4. Learner writes in a clear, well written, meaningful way; uses appropriate detail, description, grammar, and spelling; follows a logical order; and chooses the appropriate format.

3. Learner writes in a clear, well written way that may have minor interruptions; often uses appropriate detail, description, grammar, and spelling; and sometimes follows logical order.

2. Learner writes with some organizational flaws, seldom writes in an appropriate or logical way, provides few details or descriptions, and uses inappropriate grammar and spelling.

1. Learner does not yet understand how to communicate through writing and needs to attempt to write more often with supervised help.

Source: Clarridge, P. B. & Whitaker, E. M. (1994). Implementing a New Elementary Progress Report. *Educational Leadership*, *52*(2), 7-9.

Figure 9-17. An example holistic rubric for scoring writing skills development.

ANALYTIC RUBRIC FOR SCORING PROBLEM SOLVING

Understanding the problem
0. No attempt
1. Completely misinterprets the problem
2. Misinterprets major parts of the problem
3. Misinterprets minor parts of the problem
4. Completely understands the problem

Solving the problem
0. No attempt
1. Totally inappropriate plan
2. Partially correct procedure but with major fault
3. Substantially correct procedure with minor omission or procedural errors
4. A plan that could lead to a correct solution with no arithmetic errors

Answering the problem
0. No answer or wrong answer based upon an inappropriate plan
1. Copying error: computational error; partial answer for problem with multiple answers; answer statement; answer labeled incorrectly
2. Correct solution based on an appropriate plan

Source: Szetela, W. & Nicol, C. (1992). Evaluating Problem Solving in Math. *Educational Leadership*, *49*(8), 42-48.

Figure 9-18. An example analytic rubric for scoring problem solving.

Performance Tests

Most career and technical education instructors are concerned with measuring the learner's ability to complete tasks which are similar to those performed daily by workers. Many of these work tasks involve hands on performance or the application of motor skills and interpersonal skills. For example, if a learner from a special population enrolled in a marketing education program were to perform the task of transacting a sale with a customer, the best way to determine whether the learner can perform the task is to administer a performance test in a simulated or real work situation. Performance tests can be administered to measure either a complete, simulated task, or a work sample that is actually a segment of the task. Ideally, performance tests should evaluate learner performance on actual work tasks using actual equipment under realistic work conditions and standards.

The use of performance tests in career and technical programs ensures that instruction is consistent with job requirements and serves as the link between learning objectives and job tasks. Campbell (1993) offered the following benefits of using performance tests:

1. They provide a more objective, valid, and reliable measure of each learner's ability to perform a manipulative task than can be obtained by other methods of assessment. Performance tests make bluffing impossible, eliminate the guessing factor, and reveal who can and cannot do the task at acceptable performance standards.

2. They identify specific deficiencies in knowledge and skills so that prescriptive remediation can be provided to bring learner task performance up to standards.

3. They provide opportunities for determining whether learners can handle the pressure of actual task performance under working conditions and whether they can transfer previous learning to successfully complete a manipulative task.

4. They serve as a benchmark for controlling the quality of the instructional program and the level of learner learning. Learners who pass these tests are certifiable as being job ready and the teaching effort can be considered successful.

5. They serve as a way to ensure proper placement in the instructional program when learners change schools or transfer from or into a related program.

6. They document learner proficiency in occupational tasks for purposes of advanced standing or participation in work-based programs such as apprenticeship.

7. They provide behaviorally written performance objectives and a source of information for developing job sheets.

Worker tasks usually involve carrying out a number of performance steps in order to complete a job or produce a product. Therefore, performance tests need to consider whether the process of performing the task should be measured, the end product alone, or both. For example, in a business education class the teacher may be interested only in the product—a keyboarding assignment. A career and technical education teacher assessing a health occupations learner who is administering CPR will be interested in both the process and the end product. Many career and technical education tasks or competencies will require both process and product evaluation.

There are some general guidelines that can be used to determine whether process or product evaluations are most appropriate for a learning experience. Process evaluation is most appropriate when (a) the usage of tools, machines, and equipment is most appropriate, (b) health and safety hazards are involved, (c) time on task is a primary consideration, and (d) interior operations or parts are hidden in the final product. Product evaluation is most appropriate when (a) the end product or result of task performance is more critical than the procedure, (b) several possible alternative procedures or processes could be used to produce the final product, and (c) the process is difficult to observe and measure.

Performance tests are perhaps the strongest measure of learner achievement since there are no intermediate tasks between what learners are taught to perform and how they are evaluated. However, performance tests are time consuming to administer and usually require a one-to-one teacher-learner focus. In addition, they require adequate equipment and a large inventory of consumable supplies. Because of these limitations, career and technical education teachers may choose to use performance tests primarily for those tasks that are difficult to assess by other measurement techniques or those that consume a limited amount of materials. A suggested time to administer a comprehensive performance test may be at the completion of each objective in a learner's IEP or ITP. This practice usually involves assessing a broader competency or job involving a number of learning tasks. Administering performance tests provides a form of competency certification for learners and gives them a sense of worthwhile accomplishment.

Many learning tasks in career and technical education involve considerable manipulative performance, although other types of learning are involved as well. The learner must be able to recall and apply knowledge of tools, materials, and processes in order to complete tasks. Learners must also be able to demonstrate good work habits and safety practices such as following directions, organizing their work, and observing safety rules in order to complete tasks in a safe manner according to predetermined standards.

There are a number of formats for developing manipulative tests described in the literature. Campbell (1993) provided a recommended format in the form of a worksheet that can assist teachers in developing a manipulative performance test. Key information from Campbell's worksheet with modifications that should be included in performance tests follow:

- logistical information, including performance test title, course, unit, task, learner's name, exam date, score, grade, and date of test review (placed on a cover page or on the first page of a performance test)
- introduction that includes a rationale or description of the expected performance and an explanation of why this task performance is important in the workplace
- objectives written as a terminal objective with a listing of more specific enabling objectives
- skill listing or a list of the specific skills that should be demonstrated in the test
- standards or a listing of specific criteria that must be met at a certain performance level
- performance conditions that include information on the setting, equipment, materials, and time limit
- administrative directions that include information as to what must be done before the test, during the test, and following the test
- learner directions that include information as to what learners are to do before the test, during the test, and after the test is completed
- performance scenario that provides a cue to initiate performance, such as a customer complaint or a behavioral situation
- performance specifications (usually in the form of a task or job sheet) that direct the learner to perform task elements
- scoring rubrics that can be product or process rating scales, checklists, and other formats to measure performance; rubrics should contain logistical information, rating capability for examinee and examiner, a comments section, and a place to record that a reflection session to review the test performance had occurred between examinee and examiner.

Campbell (1993) also recommended that teachers consider the following procedural steps in developing a performance test for a work task:

1. determine testing constraints (money, facilities, equipment, time, personnel, safety)
2. determine if product, process, or both should be measured
3. determine performance condition and simulate realistic conditions and standards of the workplace:
- the actual setting in which performance will occur
- tools, equipment, furniture, materials, and supplies
- references, special instructions, and job performance aids
- special physical demands
- safety and possible use of support personnel
4. determine scenario and initiating cue (customer complaint, noise of some kind, sensory recognition)
5. determine attainment standards (categories for measuring proficiency):
- quality
- accuracy
- number of allowable variations or errors
- quantity
- time limits
- amount of supervision provided
- other established standards or criteria in references

6. determine if all parts of the task will be assessed
7. develop scoring rubric(s) and procedures for administering the test
8. validate or verify the test (analyze information over a number of tryouts and revise test)

In evaluating the performance of learners from special populations on required tasks and competencies, career and technical teachers must develop performance-rating devices if they are not already available.

Performance tests require learners to actively accomplish complex tasks while bringing to bear prior knowledge, recent learning, and relevant skills to solve realistic or real-world problems (Herman, et al., 1992). Effective measurement of the skills involved in completing a performance test requires the development of some form of rating instrument, such as a performance rating sheet, checklist, or other rubric format. Rubrics were presented in a previous section of this chapter but additional information may be useful in helping teachers construct performance test instruments. In order to develop performance rating sheets, checklists, and other forms of scoring rubrics for each selected tasks or competency, career and technical teachers should review the following procedures:

1. Select the task or competency to be evaluated.
2. Select the criteria to be used to determine successful performance of the task. These criteria should accurately reflect industry standards. They consist of task steps, points, items, and concepts representing successful performance of the task according to industry standards. See Figure 9-19. For example, in the figure the criteria of "tested battery for full state of charge" stands for the task of charging the battery. Notice that the criteria in the example address both the *process* of charging the battery and the end *product* of a fully charged battery. Eventual success of graduates depends upon how tasks are performed as well as the quality of the end product or service.
3. Validate the criteria for each task or competency. Although career and technical education teachers are competent in their occupational field and are knowledgeable about industry standards for task performance, it is good practice to have task criteria validated by appropriate members of a craft advisory committee, practitioners in the field, or by other teachers in a similar program.
4. Establish a system for determining the level of performance for learners from special populations, either in descriptive or symbolic form. For example, in the figure only symbolic performance indicators are established for levels of performance ranging from unsatisfactory to excellent with point values for objective scoring. Descriptive indicators could have been established for each performance level, such as for the first criteria or performance component of "all protective clothing and eye protection was worn properly"

for the excellent rating followed by descriptions of behavior characterizing each other level of the rating scale. Some learners may be able to self-assess with qualitative rubric scale points expressed in the forms of words like *not yet, developing, achieving* or *novice, apprentice, proficient,* and *distinguished.* Some learners from special populations will need more descriptive information for each point scale that actually describes the expected behavior for each performance level. For example instead of *not yet,* the scale may include the description of *begins work but fails to solve the problem.* Some learners from special populations will need each point on the scale clearly labeled and defined. Rubrics that contain specific descriptions are harder to construct and take more time for both learners and teachers to complete, but they do provide detailed feedback information to use in correcting errors. The level of performance must also consider the total number of criteria as an indicator of successful performance of the task.

5. Construct the task performance-rating instrument. In constructing the rating instrument, the career and technical teacher simply writes the directions and includes the criteria and level of performance developed in steps 2 through 4 of this procedure. If desired, the teacher can include an additional step in the rating instrument—a conversion table for translating numbered criteria into letters for the grading system.

The development of performance rubrics for performance events and projects makes it possible to implement a more objective performance-based instructional program. Either (1) the learner from a special population develops the competency and performs the task at the established level of performance and is allowed to continue on to the next task, or (2) the learner cannot meet the acceptable level of performance and must engage in additional activities in order to meet the predetermined standard. Performance tests can be altered in format to the degree of support needed to assist learners with special needs to complete the test and with accommodations to reduce the effect of a learner's disability.

Performance Events

The performance event is similar to what career and technical education teachers have been doing for many years in the form of the performance test. A performance event is an actual or simulated event that allows learners to apply knowledge, skills, and experience to solve some problem or complete a hands-on demonstration of some real or simulated tasks or problem situation encountered in the workplace. Learners are required to (1) gather information, (2) interpret information and link it to what is known, (3) diagnose problem situations, (4) develop possible alternatives or solutions to the problem or task, (5) implement a course of action, and (6) follow-up their work.

Performance events are valued because

- learners have the opportunity to apply their knowledge and skills to complete real or simulated workplace tasks;
- they can be used for selection, development, training, placement, and certification and licensing purposes;
- they have good face validity and appear to measure what they are supposed to measure;
- they provide an opportunity to observe and evaluate learners actually performing a task or problem-solving procedure in a testing environment approximating reality;
- they have a variety of applications such as work samples, assessment centers, and a series of discrete situations;
- evaluation can be conducted directly or indirectly;
- they provide abundant, behavioral data for evaluation and feedback to learners and teachers;
- they engage learners in higher order learning behaviors, including motivating, structuring, applying, searching, and experimenting;
- assessment is based on actual curriculum outcomes;
- they allow learners to evaluate their own work;
- they increase learners' understanding of requirements; and
- they reinforce importance of organization and sequence.

PERFORMANCE RATING SHEET

Rubric for Charging an Automotive Battery

Name_____ Date _____ Reflection date_____ Score_____

Directions: Rate the level of performance on each of the following performance components involved in charging a lead-acid automotive storage battery that has been discharged. Examinees place an X in the appropriate rating column under the level of performance, and examiners place a checkmark in the appropriate column. When the exam is over, schedule a reflection session between examiner and examinee.

	Level of Performance				
Perfomance Components	Not done	Poor	Fair	Good	Excellent
The worker:	0 U	1 D	2 C	3 B	4 A
1. Put on safety goggles and clothing					
2. Cleaned the battery case and terminals					
3. Tested the battery following correct procedures					
4. Placed charger cable clamps correctly					
5. Regulated the charger correctly					
6. Cleaned and returned all tools and equipment					
7. Tested battery for a full state of charge					
8. Battery was fully charged					

Level of Performance

All items in the scoring rubric must receive a fair, good, or excellent response. Failure to earn this rating will require additional learning and a retest. Discuss your level of performance with your examiner.

Figure 9-19. An example of a performance rubric for the performance test of recharging an automotive battery.

Performance events also have some important considerations and problems to address. These include (a) developing a detailed job and task analysis; (b) determining performance event logistical requirements; (c) devoting additional time for planning and conducting performance events; (d) developing rubrics for scoring performance to ensure fairness and reliability; and (e) budgeting for the additional expense required for some performance events.

Learner Projects

Learner projects have always been a part of the public school curriculum at all levels. They are especially useful in career and technical education and have a long history of widespread use in most programs. Learner projects are planned, long-term learning experiences that are designed by learners to present a real-life project through which learners can demonstrate a number of skills believed to be important in work, family and community life. While it is likely that projects were used as a method of instruction since the beginning of time, William H. Kilpatrick of Teachers College, Columbia University, was one of the earliest American educators to launch the project method of instruction around 1918. He was searching for an instructional method that would unify a number of important related aspects of the educational process and hoped for one concept that would serve this end (Bickel, 1994).

Bickel (1994) notes a connection between the project method as conceptualized by Kilpatrick and the increasing focus on alternative assessment in education today. He sees today's focus on learner-centered activities as a 1990s version of Kilpatrick's project method. It is interesting to note that the Southern Regional Educational Board has published a guide to preparing a syllabus for its High Schools That Work program that includes a major focus on projects as the centerpiece of curriculum, instruction, and evaluation. This guide, *Designing Challenging Vocational Courses,* authored by Bottoms, Pucel, and Phillips (1997), describes the procedures required to select and sequence major course projects, develop project outlines, decide on an instructional delivery plan, and develop an assessment plan.

Several states, notably California and Kentucky, have made successful completion of a learner-initiated culminating project (senior project) a part of their learner assessment system. The project is a major piece of hands-on work designed and completed by learners. The project becomes an instructional and assessment tool that allows learners to demonstrate the skills and knowledge learned in a sequenced instructional program. Completing the project shows the learners' abilities to plan, organize, and create a product or event. In carrying out the long-term process of completing a project, learners are provided with opportunity to pursue their own interests, meet professionals in the field who can offer advice and instruction related to their project, work cooperatively with others in certain parts of the project, and apply the knowledge and skills they have learned in other school subjects. Each learner's project must be related to the career-technical program in which they are enrolled and can take as little as a few weeks or several months to complete. Learners are allowed to work on the project themselves or in small groups.

There are four major sections of the California C-TAP project: (1) Plan–a process that helps the learner design the project, (2) Evidence of Progress–three pieces that show the learner's progress toward developing the final product, (3) Final Product–a final product that is the result of the learner's work, and (4) Oral Presentation–an oral presentation in which the learner describes the project, explains what skills were applied, and evaluates the work. See Figure 9-20.

The C-TAP project is evaluated in two ways and learners receive two separate scores. The project is rated using a rubric that has the three main evaluation dimensions of content, communication, and responsibility. Content pertains to career-technical knowledge and skills, communication relates to the overall presentation of work, and responsibility pertains to the learner's ability to complete work on his or her own. A separate project presentation rating rubric with the evaluation dimensions of public speaking skills, content knowledge, and analysis is used to award an oral presentation score. The final project and presentation are rated using a three-part rubric as follows:

- Basic–Performance is unsatisfactory and does not meet requirements.
- Proficient–Performance is very good and meets all requirements, demonstrating important skills and abilities relating to one or more model curriculum standards.
- Advanced–Performance is outstanding and goes beyond what is required, demonstrating important skills and abilities relating to one of more model curriculum standards (Far West Laboratory, 1994).

There are many different types of projects that can be developed to challenge learners to produce something rather than reproduce knowledge on traditional tests. The topics for projects are extensive, and it is fairly easy for career and technical educators to select projects that will allow learners to demonstrate a variety of skills including communication, technical, interpersonal, organizational, problem-solving, and decision-making—all of which are important outcomes (Burke, 1994). A number of the formats for learner work and assessment presented earlier can be adopted as meaningful and authentic projects, such as exhibits, pamphlets, models, and videos.

Projects provide learners with opportunities to establish criteria for determining the quality of the planning process, the construction process, and the completed project. Learners can analyze different types of completed projects and determine what are the good and poor characteristics. It is important for learners to generate their own criteria so they know the standards of a good project and so they can use these standards as a guide through project activities. It is important for learners to use rubrics to assess their own projects before the project is assessed by teachers. Teachers can provide input into the construction of the learner-generated rubrics, develop one of their own, or adapt one that has been used by other teachers. It is recommended that learners present their projects to selected audiences and that their presentations be assessed with rubrics similar to the way presentations are assessed in the C-TAP project.

The advantages provided by using the learner project alternative assessment include

- a wide variety of projects in which learners are interested can be used as the end product of learning experiences;
- the learner project can be undertaken by all learners provided they are given appropriate encouragement and support;
- the project is learner generated, requiring creative thinking, careful planning, and long-term commitment;
- learners are encouraged to interact with other learners, parents/guardians, teachers, and appropriate individuals from the community;
- the project focuses on real-world tasks requiring planning, problem-solving; troubleshooting, and other skills frequently performed under changing conditions;
- the project approach raises expectations of both learners and teachers;
- the learner project changes the role of teachers from information-givers to mentors, advisors, and coaches;
- learner projects emphasize basic skills of researching, writing, applying knowledge, and speaking;
- learner projects provide the means for some learners to shine because they can choose an area in which they have some knowledge, skills, and previous experience;
- learners experience writing and following contracts that include what they are going to do, how, and when, to guide their learning;
- learner projects provide a means for involving other teachers (academic and career and technical) in assessment processes;
- learners experience a sense of support through interaction with other learner and teachers; and
- learner projects provide a means for learners to self-assess the process they used in completing the project as well as the finished product.

SUMMARY OF REQUIREMENTS FOR PROJECT	
Entry	**Requirements**
OVERALL	relates to one or more career-technical standards
	involves "hands-on" application of skills
PROJECT	
Planner	completeness, including
	- aim
	- description of activities
	- time estimates for each step
	- resources required
	- evidence of progress to be evaluated
	- final product to be evaluated
Evidence of Progress	documents major steps necessary to complete the project
	includes at least 3 pieces of evidence
	represents student's own work
	neatness and organization
Final Product	documents mastery of skills specified in career-technical standard(s)
	represents student's own work
	if final product is not included, documentation must be provided (photo must be accompanied by caption)
	neatness and organization
PRESENTATION	completeness, including steps completed, career-technical knowledge and skills applied, and what might have been done differently
	visual aid(s)
	minimum of 3 minutes
	organization and coherence (adequate detail for others to understand what was done)

Source: Far West Laboratory (1994). *Career-Technical Assessment Program: Teacher Guidebook and Career-Technical Assessment Program: Student Guidebook.* Sacramento, CA: California Department of Education, Career-Vocational Division and Far West Laboratory.

Figure 9-20. An example of project requirements from the C-TAP project.

While there are many advantages provided by the learner project assessment technique, there are also some issues or problems that need to be considered and resolved. These include the following:

- There are ever-present technical issues of ensuring validity and reliability.
- There is the challenge of ensuring that learners have actually done the work.
- There are logistical concerns such as securing judges to assist in evaluating learner projects and storing completed projects.
- There is the challenge of how to lessen the performance gap between high-achieving and low-achieving learners.
- There is the demanding task of developing rubrics to ensure fair and accurate judging and scoring of the learner projects. Rubrics often consist of a fixed scale and characteristics describing performance for each point of the scale. Usually, several rubrics must be developed to assess each section, and another one is developed for the overall project.
- Teachers must be taught how to change instructional and assessment methods to accommodate learner projects.
- There is the challenge of dealing with other common assessment concerns such as fairness, equity, and consistency in applying standards.

Written Scenario

A specific type of performance event developed as part of the C-TAP project is the written scenario that presents a real-life problem or situation to solve on demand. See Figure 9-21. Learners are required to read the scenario, think about possible solutions, organize their thoughts, and propose a solution in writing. The scenario provides learners with the opportunity to demonstrate their ability to apply knowledge, interpret information, think critically, and explain ideas clearly. The scenario is administered in a single class period, usually near the end of the instructional program, but learners are given a practice scenario to prepare for the real one. Learner performance is rated on the three criteria of basic, proficient, and advanced.

Portfolio Assessment

One of the alternative assessment methods gaining popularity across the country that is particularly useful for learners from special populations is portfolios. Portfolios are collections of learners' work gathered over time. In this assessment strategy, portfolios are created by learners who examine a larger collection of materials and choose some for inclusion in their portfolios according to established criteria. Portfolios are then assessed by learners and the teacher for effort and progress, examining both the process of learning as well as the products (Fingered, 1993).

In education, portfolios mean many things. Some teachers describe portfolios as folders (also computer discs) in which they maintain records of learners' test scores and other achievements. Other teachers refer to portfolios as an instructional and assessment process through which learners analyze their work and present a sample that illustrates particular criteria or judgments about their learning, often in relation to established goals. Another definition of portfolios is a collection of learner work over a period of time that demonstrates selected skills, abilities, and ambitions. For career and technical education, it can be an innovative approach to instruction and assessment that enables learners to discover, document, and develop their employability skills (Fingered, 1993). Paulson, Paulson, and Meyer (1991) defined portfolios as a "purposeful collection of student work that exhibits the student's effort, progress, and achievement in one or more areas. The collection must include student participation in selecting contents, the criteria for selection, the criteria for judging merit, and evidence of student reflection" (p. 60).

Benefits of Using Portfolios. Portfolio assessment offers many benefits, but Frazier and Paulson (1992) note that the "primary worth of portfolios is that they allow students the opportunity to evaluate their own work." Further, "...portfolio assessment offers students a way to take charge of their learning; it also encourages ownership, pride, and high self-esteem" (p. 65). They state portfolios can be kept several years and can be used as "passports" as learners transition from one level of education to another. They can be used as valuable tools for obtaining employment in business and industry.

The use of portfolios in education is rapidly growing in popularity as an alternative to traditional assessment for the following reasons:

- Portfolios can be used in a wide range of subjects.
- Portfolios are a valuable teaching tool, providing learners ownership, motivation, a sense of accomplishment and active participation in the learning process.
- They result in more reliable evaluation by using multiple samples of learner performance.
- They serve as an end-of-the-year or culminating activity.
- Portfolios can be used to help learners better represent themselves to postsecondary institution admission personnel and prospective employers.
- They result in a more thorough evaluation by allowing comparisons of learners' work over time.
- Portfolios provide valuable information to facilitate effective instruction and learning.
- Portfolios allow both teachers and learners to recognize important tasks to be learned and applied in real life.
- Portfolios provide a means for teachers and learners to jointly set goals and objectives for personalized instruction.
- Portfolios make learners more aware of the process of learning.
- They can increase learners' knowledge about the scope of what they have learned.

- Portfolios provide a means for learners to self-evaluate their work in order to see the progress they are making.
- They provide a connection to the contents and personal histories of teaching and make it possible to document the unfolding of both teaching and learning over time (Wolf, 1991).
- Portfolios can be used as one component of a state-wide assessment system.
- Portfolios support the integration of academic and occupational skills.
- Portfolios allow learners to take charge and assume ownership of their own learning.
- Portfolio assessment has the potential to reveal information about a learner's current values through review of content choices.

- Portfolios provide a window for teachers to understand the educational process from a learner point of view.
- Portfolios provide opportunities for learners to write.
- Portfolios provide a connection between reading, writing, thinking, and applying.
- Portfolios can be used for teacher/parent conferences.
- Portfolios reinforce the value of daily writing.
- Portfolios foster professionalism and collaboration among teachers.
- Portfolio assessment provide opportunities for the professional development of teachers.
- Portfolio assessment provides an alternative to standardized testing.
- Portfolios provide documented research on how learners think, value, and learn.

C-TAP WRITTEN SCENARIO RATING GUIDE

	Basic	Proficient	Advanced
CONTENT			
Knowledge of major ideas and concepts in career-technical standards	Shows gaps in knowledge; misunderstands major ideas and concepts; may fail to include relevant information	Shows knowledge of major ideas and concepts; covers required content	Shows clear understanding of major ideas and concepts; fully covers required content, explaining how ideas and concepts apply to the scenario
Supporting arguments	Fails to justify response or provides weak arguments	Justifies response with adequate detail	Convincingly justifies response with well-developed reasoning and detail
ANALYSIS			
Address scenario requirements	Does not address scenario requirements	Addresses all scenario requirements	Addresses all scenario requirements in detail
Evaluation of evidence	Ignores evidence or demonstrates incomplete understanding of the problem	Links response to evidence presented	Links response to all evidence presented
COMMUNICATION			
Organization and clarity	Ideas are presented in a disorganized way	Ideas are presented in an organized way	Writing is clear and well organized throughout the response
Language mechanics	Writing style or mechanics interfere with communication of ideas	Ideas are understandable; language errors do not interfere with communication	Ideas are presented effectively and are easy to understand

Source: Far West Laboratory (1994). *Career-Technical Assessment Program: Teacher Guidebook and Career-Technical Assessment Program: Student Guidebook.* Sacramento, CA: California Department of Education, Career-Vocational Division and Far West Laboratory.

Figure 9-21. An example of a rating guide for the C-TAP written scenario.

Teacher Findings in Using Portfolios. Schools and teachers that have used portfolios report a number of encouraging findings:

- Portfolios can be designed to serve as a teaching tool and an assessment medium at the same time.
- Portfolios empower learners and teachers; teachers rediscover the important role they play in challenging learners to learn and learners develop capacity to examine their own learning strategies and communicate their thinking to others.
- Portfolios convey to learners that development is equally important to achievement. They allow learners and teachers to see patterns of success and failure over time and reflect on the reasons behind them.
- Portfolios encourage collaboration between learners and teachers. The view that both parties have of assessment as something done to them gives way to a realization that assessment is something they do together for mutual benefit.
- Portfolios help validate different learning approaches. While writing remains the major instructional activity involved in portfolios, learners can experiment with other ways of learning that makes sense to them such as artwork, mediated productions, and the like.
- Portfolios prepare learners for adult life. They provide learners with the opportunity to take responsibility for their own learning, to develop ability to monitor their own learning progress, and to trust their own judgments–capabilities that are central to functioning as an adult in our society.
- Portfolios help train learners to assess themselves. Through collaborative activities, learners see how teachers use criteria to evaluate their work and model this behavior in identifying criteria and using strategies to critique their own work.
- Portfolios foster professional development. They provide teachers with new insights into their own work and with others. Teachers meeting to discuss the contents and methods of assessing portfolios become professional development sessions of the highest order as teachers debate standards and teaching ideas—key elements in effective teaching and assessment.
- Portfolios promote action research. Teachers who experiment with portfolios are developing new insights and are contributing to the knowledge base of the teaching/learning process (*Knowledge Brief*, 1992).

Contents of Portfolios. The range of works that go into portfolios is deliberately diverse due to individual learner differences and course/program requirements. The contents of portfolios are limited only by the theme and the developer's imagination and creativity. Some of the common items that appear in portfolios include (a) learner narratives about how they developed the contents and about what they have learned; (b) classroom and laboratory assignments; (c) works learners develop to show their interests and abilities; (d) self-reflections; (e) observations and comments from teachers, parents, and significant others;

(d) rough drafts, finished papers, and reports; (e) best and worst tests; (f) records of books and magazine articles read; (g) samples of homework completed; (h) physical accomplishments; (i) artistic achievements; (j) career development plan including resumes, completed application forms, letters of recommendation, cover letters for applications, letters from past and present employers, and future oriented career plans; (k) documentation of employability skills; (l) recognition awards and honors; (m) performance appraisals from teachers; (n) transcripts with class descriptions and grades for related classes; (o) photographs or videotapes of completed projects and other events; (p) learner published materials; (q) project reports; (r) selected daily work; (s) copies of important documents such as driver licenses, first aid training cards, insurance cards and the like; (t) daily schedule of classes; (u) selected excerpts from personal diaries; (v) record of participation in learner and community organizations; and (w) cooperative education training programs and agreements.

California's C-TAP Portfolio. The C-TAP project includes portfolios as the third major component of its assessment program. A portfolio, as defined in the teacher guide published by Far West Laboratory (1994), is "a major piece of hands-on work designed and completed by each student." Development of the portfolio provides learners with (a) an opportunity to master important skills valued by employers and postsecondary institutions; (b) an opportunity to showcase their best works to potential employers; and (c) an opportunity to take responsibility for planning and documenting their accomplishments, as well as to identify areas needing improvement. Through the portfolio, learners can demonstrate their ability to plan, organize, create, and evaluate a product or event.

The C-TAP portfolio has the following five components:
- Presenting Your Portfolio–This consists of a table of contents and a letter of introduction presenting the learner's work to an external reviewer.
- Career Development Package–This consists of an application for employment or for a postsecondary institution, a letter of recommendation, and a resume preparing learners for job searching, advanced training, or postsecondary education.
- Writing Sample–This consists of four examples and descriptions of work, demonstrating mastery of important career-technical skills.
- Writing Sample–This is a sample of writing, demonstrating investigative, analytical, and writing abilities.
- Supervised Practical Experience Evaluation–This is documentation of a learner's practical or work experience, demonstrating workplace readiness.

The C-TAP portfolio evaluation system is a two-step process: (1) the evaluation of each potential portfolio entry as the learner completes it, and (2) reviewing and rating the completed portfolio. Teachers evaluate each entry using a summary of requirements for portfolios and make a decision to accept it or to return it to the learner for revisions. See Figure 9-22.

Entry	Requirements
REQUIREMENTS FOR PORTFOLIO ENTRIES	
Entry	Requirements
PRESENTATION	
Table of Contents	organization
	accuracy and completeness
	neatness
	correct spelling
Letter of Introduction	an original letter containing three parts:
	- description of self (personal or career goals with plans for achieving them, strengths and qualities, and/or important achievements)
	- description of best work sample (why work sample was selected as "best" and what special abilities the work sample highlights)
	- explanation of what portfolio means to the student (how the pieces relate to personal or career goals, what was achieved by completing the portfolio, and/or how work has improved)
	effective writing (neat, organized, clear, and correct grammar and spelling)
CAREER DEVELOPMENT PACKAGE	
Application	neatness, a good overall appearance (typed or written in ink)
	completeness, no blanks
	correct grammar and spelling
	accuracy
Letter of Recommendation	letter of recommendation from an appropriate person who gives a good picture of career-related strengths and skills
Resume	accuracy
	completeness; must include:
	- contact information
	- career and educational plans
	- education
	- paid/unpaid work experiences
	- at least one of the following: activities, achievements, skills, strengths, abilities, references, and special interests
	neatness, good overall appearance
	correct grammar and spelling
WORK SAMPLES	
	coverage of all required standards
	completeness, including appropriate documentation and summaries for four work samples. Summaries must include:
	- a description of the work sample and the steps taken to complete it
	- the standards or skills covered
	- what was learned by doing the work sample
WRITING SAMPLE	
	coverage of at least one content standard
	effective writing (neat, organized, clear, and correct grammar and spelling)
	final draft (at least 3 pages in length, typed double spaced with 1 or 1½-inch margins on 8½ × 11 paper, single-sided)
	bibliography including at least three different sources of information
SPE EVALUATION	
	completed SPE evaluation form, signed by supervisor

Source: Far West Laboratory (1994). *Career-Technical Assessment Program: Teacher Guidebook and Career-Technical Assessment Program: Student Guidebook*. Sacramento, CA: California Department of Education, Career-Vocational Division and Far West Laboratory.

Figure 9-22. An example of the requirements for portfolio entries from the C-TAP project.

The second step in evaluating the C-TAP portfolio is to rate completed portfolios as basic, proficient, or advanced. Basic means the performance is unsatisfactory and does not meet requirements for each section. Proficient means the performance is very good and meets all of the requirements for each section, demonstrating important skills and abilities. Advanced means the performance is outstanding and goes beyond what is required, demonstrating important skills and abilities. The holistic ratings of basic, proficient, and advanced are based on the four dimensions of content, career preparation, analysis, and communication. These dimensions are described as follows:

- Content–This is breadth, depth, and application of knowledge and skills related to the career-technical model curriculum standards.
- Career preparation–This is an understanding of career preparation and personal employability attributes.
- Analysis–This is the ability to apply analytical skills to the gathering of information and evaluation of own work.
- Communication–This is effective use of communication skills.

A scoring rubric with basic, proficient, and advanced performance criteria for the content, career preparation, analysis, and communication dimensions was developed in the form of the C-TAP portfolio-rating guide. See Figure 9-23.

Problems with Using Portfolios. While portfolios provide many benefits to learners and teachers, they also have problems of their own. Following are some issues that must be considered and resolved:

- There are decisions that must be made regarding what should be included in portfolio guidelines—what type of content and who should be involved in the selecting process. Should only the best work be included or should representative work of effort and accomplishment covering the spectrum be included?
- There is the problem of determining the main purpose for using portfolios—to improve instruction, to assess learner work, or both.
- There is the issue of who should be involved in assessing and scoring learner portfolios.
- There are a number of challenges involved in evaluating portfolios, such as developing scoring rubrics, evaluation procedures, etc.
- There is the issue as to how to communicate learner achievement determined through portfolio assessment to parents.
- Teachers often lack knowledge of how to develop and implement portfolio assessment.
- There is the challenge of helping learners gear up for portfolio assessment, which requires that they be brought into a process of continuous planning, implementing, assessing, and revising (Fingered, 1993).
- Portfolio assessment often requires subjective discussions with learners, which can be frightening.
- There is the challenge of making portfolio assessment an integral part of the instructional program rather than an add-on evaluation technique.
- Implementing portfolio assessment requires careful planning, much work to help learners learn how to assess themselves instead of being assessed, and constant monitoring of learner progress to help them become responsible so they do not loose their portfolio materials.
- There is the problem of where portfolios should be stored and how they will be accessed.

Characteristics of Effective Portfolios. Paulson, Paulson, and Meyer described the essential characteristics of effective portfolios and offer eight guidelines for developing portfolios. First they give the following three major descriptors of portfolios. Portfolios are effective when (1) they provide a complex and comprehensive view of learner performance in context, (2) learners are participants in, rather than the object of, assessment, and (3) they provide a forum that encourages learners to develop the abilities needed to become independent, self-directed learners. Second, the authors offer the following guidelines for capturing the power of portfolio assessment:

- Portfolios offer learners an opportunity to learn about learning, therefore, it is important that information that shows learner self-reflection be included.
- The portfolio is something that is done by the learner, not to the learner. Portfolio assessment provides a meaningful way for learners to learn how to value their own work and to value themselves as capable learners. For these outcomes to happen, learners must be involved in selecting the pieces to be included in the portfolio.
- The portfolio is separate and different from the learner's cumulative folder. Documents and information contained in learners' cumulative folders should only be included in portfolios when this data takes on new meaning within the context of other exhibits in the portfolio.
- Portfolios must convey explicitly or implicitly the learner's major activities under the headings of (a) rationale—purpose for forming the portfolio, (b) intents—its goals or purposes, (c) contents—actual displays and exhibits, (d) standards—what is good and what is poor performance, and (e) judgments—what the contents tell the reader.
- The purpose served by the portfolio throughout the year may differ from the purpose it serves at the end. Learners may include developmental materials in the portfolio because it is instructional at a given period of time but may elect to remove this material before it is made public at the end of the assessment period.
- Portfolios have multiple purposes, but these should remain in harmony. Learners' personal goals and interests are reflected in their selection of materials, but information included may also reflect the interests of teachers, parents and the district. A common purpose of most portfolios is to show learner progress on goals, objectives, and outcomes represented in the instructional program.

C-TAP PORTFOLIO RATING GUIDE

	Basic	Proficient	Advanced
CONTENT			
Knowledge of major ideas and concepts in career-technical standards	Shows gaps in know ledge; misunderstands major ideas and concepts	Shows knowledge of major ideas and concepts; covers the content of important career-technical standards	Shows clear under- standing of major ideas and concepts; explains how ideas and concepts relate to each other
Knowledge of how skills in career-technical standards are applied	Hands-on work demonstrates minimal knowledge or skill	Hands-on work demonstrates a variety of skills	Hands-on work demonstrates superior skill
CAREER PREPARATION			
Career planning	Shows little or no evidence of planning for a career	Shows evidence of planning and developing a career	Shows excellent under- standing of career planning; describes a realistic plan that leads to clear career goals
Personal qualities needed for employment	Does not identify own personal qualities needed to be success- fully employed	Identifies own per- sonal qualities needed to be suc- cessfully employed	Highlights own personal qualities needed to be successfully employed throughout the portfolio
ANALYSIS			
Evaluation of own skills and work	Gives incomplete or sketchy evaluation of own work	Gives accurate evaluation of own work	Shows understanding and insight in evaluating own work
Investigation and information gathering	Does not gather information from several sources	Shows ability to find and use information from several sources	Demonstrates superior ability to gather and combine information from various sources
COMMUNICATION			
Attention to audience	Shows little or no awareness of the audience	Effectively presents self and ideas to outside reviewer	Self and ideas "come alive" to outside reviewer
Using own ideas	Writing is not original; copies the ideas of others	Writing is original	Writing is original and may be creative
Organization and clarity	Ideas are presented in a disorganized way	Writing is clear and organized	Writing is clear and well organized throughout portfolio
Accuracy, neatness, and completeness	Work lacks accuracy and completeness; appearance interferes with communication of ideas	Work is accurate, neat, and complete	Work is accurate and complete; appearance helps the communica- tion of ideas
Language mechanics, sentence structure, and vocabulary	Writing contains errors in language use that makes ideas difficult to understand	Writing contains few language errors; ideas are not difficult to understand	Writing is almost free of language errors and is easy to understand

Source: Far West Laboratory (1994). *Career-Technical Assessment Program: Teacher Guidebook and Career-Technical Assessment Program: Student Guidebook.* Sacramento, CA: California Department of Education, Career-Vocational Division and Far West Laboratory.

Figure 9-23. An example of a portfolio rating guide from the C-TAP project.

- Portfolios should include information that shows effort and growth. There are many ways to demonstrate effort and growth. One common way is to include a series of samples of actual school performance that show how learners' skills have improved as a result of effort. Changes observed on interest inventories, records of out-of-school activities such as reading logs, or on attitude measures are other ways to determine learner growth.
- Finally, the skills and knowledge required of both teachers and learners to produce effective portfolios do not just happen by themselves. Teacher and learners need models of portfolios, as well as examples of how others develop and reflect upon portfolios. There is a rapidly growing body of information on the use of portfolios available in the professional literature as well as commercially available material to support implementation of portfolio assessment.

Few will question that portfolios consume more time and demand more from teachers than traditional assessment activities. Some would question if they are really worth the effort. There is enough evidence to support the view that the problems they present are greatly outweighed by improved teaching and learning. Teachers need to adopt the view that portfolios can create real change in classroom instruction and learning. They are manageable, they can improve communications with parents and administrators, and they will be viewed favorably by the community when marketed successfully (Far West Laboratory, 1992).

Portfolio Development Decisions. Portfolio assessment requires careful thought and preparation on the part of both teachers and learners. There are a number of decisions that have to be made in establishing a portfolio assessment system. Vavrus (1990) offers the following decisions and recommendations to consider when developing such a system.

- What will it look like? Portfolios have to have both a physical structure (binder as well as the arrangement of documents within the portfolio) and a conceptual structure (underlying goals for learner learning).
- What goes in? To answer this question other questions will have to be addressed: Who is the intended audience for the portfolios? What will this audience want to know? How will the audience be involved in portfolio development? Will selected documents of the portfolio show aspects of learning that traditional test results don't show? What kinds of evidence will best show learner progress toward expected learning outcomes? Will the portfolio contain only best works, a progressive record of learner growth, or both? Will the portfolio include more than finished pieces (notes, ideas, sketches, drafts, and revisions)?
- How will learner working files and portfolios be kept secure? When will learners select documents to include in their portfolios? Will some portfolio documents be taken out to specialize the portfolio? What criteria or

assistance will be provided to learners so that they can reflect on their work, monitor their own progress, and select pieces for inclusion in the portfolio? Will learners be required to provide a rationale or explanation for work selected for inclusion in the portfolio?
- How will portfolios be evaluated and who will be involved? It is critical that learners be actively involved in assessing their own work. To facilitate learner self-assessment, teachers will have to answer the following questions: Will factors such as achievement in relation to standards, learner growth along a continuum, or both be evaluated? What models, standards, criteria and instruments will have to be developed to guide assessment? When will portfolio entrees be evaluated? Will other teachers be involved in assessing portfolio pieces? Will parents or guardians be involved in assessing the portfolio? If so, how?
- What will happen to the portfolio at the end of the semester or school year? Will it be turned over to learners at the end of the course or school year to keep and use as they see fit? Will learners be encouraged to keep their portfolios over an extended period of time and use them as passports for entry into other levels of education or into the workforce?

Observation Techniques

Observation techniques are also widely used in evaluating behaviors that are common to most career and technical education programs, such as classroom and laboratory behavior, work habit development, and safety procedures. Teachers make observations of these on-going behaviors and record them on rating devices. Each safety behavior is evaluated by written test as well as by performance ratings involving observational techniques. See Figure 9-24.

Observation rating sheets should contain necessary administrative information such as the learner's name and subject or behavior to be rated. The columns on the rating sheet should indicate behaviors to be observed, a scale of scoring options, a place for both learners and teachers to rate behaviors, a comment section, and a place for learners and teachers to sign their names. See Figure 9-25.

Observation rating sheets that contain descriptions of behavior for each performance level can increase the objectivity of both teacher and learner rating of important work behaviors. See Figure 9-26.

Peer Evaluation Techniques

Career and technical education teachers often do not have the time to evaluate the progress of each learner when it is needed. This is particularly true for teachers who administer large numbers of performance tests in laboratory settings. One of the best evaluation methods for learners from special populations is the performance test, which requires a great deal of teacher time because these learners often progress more slowly than other learners. A good solution to this problem is to use learners who have mastered specific learning tasks and performance tests to evaluate the task performance of learners from special populations using performance-rating instruments.

The practice of using learner or peer evaluators is instructionally sound. Both peer learner evaluators and learners from special populations being evaluated receive reinforcement of program content through the evaluation experience. The peer evaluator feels competent and useful by being selected as an evaluator and is provided with an opportunity to build self-esteem. The peer evaluator is provided with an additional opportunity to learn and practice evaluation skills. Learners from special populations often perform better under the observation of peer evaluators because they feel less threatened and more at ease. Learners from special populations are provided with an additional opportunity to develop closer relationships with other learners. The peer evaluation relationship frequently fosters enthusiasm, motivation to achieve, confidence, improved performance, and a more positive attitude toward school.

SAFETY CHECKLIST

Student: _____

Instructor: _____

Program: Machine Shop

Criterion: The student will demonstrate appropriate safety techniques in each of the following areas with 100% accuracy prior to working independently in the laboratory.

Safety Area	Date	Instructor Initials	Student Initials
1. General Safety Rules			
2. Hand Tools			
3. Engine Lathe			
4. Turret Lathe			
5. Vertical Milling Machine			
6. Horizontal Milling Machine			
7. Drill Press			
8. Radial Drill Press			
9. Horizontal Band Saw			
10. Vertical Band Saw			
11. Pedestal Grinder			
12. Surface Grinder			
13. Numerical Control Machine			
14. Heat Treating Equipment			
15. Fire Extinguishers			
16. Emergency Exit Charts			
17. Emergency Exit Procedures			
18. Emergency Electrical Circuit Breakers			

Comments:

_____

Instructor Signature

Figure 9-24. An example of a safety checklist for recording observed learner safety behaviors.

Peer evaluators can be selected from learners in the same class or can be recruited from advanced classes or from volunteer learners who have expressed an interest in teaching as a career. When peer evaluators are selected from outside the regular career and technical class, schedules will have to be arranged cooperatively with other teachers and cleared by the administration.

Career and technical education teachers must prepare peer evaluators before scheduling performance evaluations. Peer evaluators should be trained in observation techniques, performance tests, and performance rating instruments that address common methods and techniques for measuring and evaluating the behavior and performance of all career and technical education learners. Frequently, however, these methods and techniques need to be altered to meet the evaluation needs of learners from special populations.

Learning Logs and Journals

There are many things happening with alternative assessments, including affording learners opportunity to reflect on what they have learned or are learning, providing a means of self-assessment, and providing a means whereby they can keep track of their learning in portfolios, learning logs, and journals. While journals have been used in English classes for years, they are becoming widely used by other teachers to provide an opportunity for learners to make connections, examine complex ideas, and think about ways to apply what they have learned over an extended period of time. Herman, Aschbacher, and Winters (1992) suggest that the fundamental purpose of learning logs and journals is that they provide teachers with the learner's account of learning progress, particular concerns about learning, and metacognitive reflection of that learning.

CLASSROOM AND LABORATORY BEHAVIOR CHECKLIST

Student: _____   Date: _____

Scale: 5 - Excellent   Directions:
        3 - Adequate   Student circles rating.
        1 - Poor   Teacher underlines rating.

Behavior/Indicators	Comments					
1. Participates in class discussions	_____	5	4	3	2	1
2. Completes class assignments on time	_____	5	4	3	2	1
3. Respects rights of others	_____	5	4	3	2	1
4. Listens attentively	_____	5	4	3	2	1
5. Values time/time on task	_____	5	4	3	2	1
6. Takes pride in work	_____	5	4	3	2	1
7. Takes care of equipment	_____	5	4	3	2	1
8. Neat and orderly	_____	5	4	3	2	1
9. Attendance - on time	_____	5	4	3	2	1
10. Works well with others	_____	5	4	3	2	1
11. Has a positive attitude about service or training area	_____	5	4	3	2	1
12. Works safely	_____	5	4	3	2	1
13. Follows directions	_____	5	4	3	2	1
14. Asks for help when needed	_____	5	4	3	2	1

Student Totals

Instructor Totals

Student Signature_____   Instructor Signature_____

Figure 9-25. An example of a generic classroom and laboratory behavior checklist for recording observed learner behaviors.

DESCRIPTIVE WORK HABITS RATING SCALE

STUDENT: _____ DATE: _____

SCALE: 4 = Outstanding   3 = Good   2 = Satisfactory   1 = Poor

DIRECTIONS: Place the number corresponding to the level of performance demonstrated in the blank space provided for each criteria.

SCALE	TRAITS	DEMONSTRATED PERFORMANCE			
		4	3	2	1
_____	Quality of Work	Superior	Very good	Average	Poor
_____	Knowledge of Work	Excellent	Good	Adequate	Insufficient
_____	Work Attitude	Very enthusiastic	Shows great interest	Shows interest	Normally indifferent; uninterested
_____	Attendance	Attends daily	Infrequently absent	Warned for absence	Frequently absent
_____	Punctuality	Always on time	Infrequently late	Warned for tardiness	Frequently late
_____	Decision-Making Ability	Makes effective decisions	Needs occa-sional assistance	Often needs assistance	Cannot make decisions
_____	Industry	Industrious; works hard	Works steadily; good effort	Persistent in effort	Avoids work
_____	Work Initiative	Seeks more work; highly motivated	Alert to opportunities	Regular work performed	Needs explan-ation of routine tasks
_____	Organizational Ability	Highly capable of organizing	Fairly well organized	Sometimes disorganized	Often disorganized
_____	Attitude Toward Others	Positive; takes interest in others	Pleasant, polite	Sometimes difficult	Inclined to be un-cooperative to work with
_____	Acceptance of Responsibility	Welcomes responsibility	Accepts without protest	Accepts with protest	Avoids when possible
_____	Follows Directions	Always follows directions	Usually follows directions	Occasionally follows directions	Seldom follows directions

Source: Moses, M. (1991). How to Create a Performance Assessment. *Vocational Education Journal, 66*(6), 26.

Figure 9-26. An example of a descriptive work habits rating scale for recording observed learner behaviors.

Kay Burke (1994) makes a distinction between learning logs and journals. Learning logs usually consist of short, objective entries under specific headings such as problem solving, observations, questions about content, lists of outside readings, homework assignments, or anything than lends itself to record keeping. Learner responses are usually brief, factual, and impersonal. Fogarty and Bellanca (1987) recommend that teachers provide lead-ins or stem statements to encourage learner responses that are analytical (breaking something down into its parts), synthetic (putting something together into a whole), and evaluative (forming judgment about the worth of something). Example log stems include the following:

- One thing I learned yesterday was . . .
- One question I still have is . . .
- One thing I found interesting was . . .
- One application for this is . . .
- I need help with . . .

Journals, in contrast to logs, which are usually brief, factual, and impersonal, tend to include information written in narrative form, are more subjective, and deal more with feelings, reflections, opinions, and personal experiences. Journal entries are more descriptive, longer, and more spontaneous then logs. They are often used to respond to situations, describe events, reflect on personal experiences and feelings, connect what is being learned with past learning, and predict how what is being learned can be used in real life (Burke, 1994). Like in learning logs, learners usually need stem statements or lead-ins to help them target responses. Example lead-ins include the following:

- My way of thinking about this is . . .
- My initial observation is . . .
- Upon reflection I . . .
- The best part of this . . .
- I wonder what would happen if . . .
- A similar or connecting idea is . . .

Teachers need to create some original stem statements or lead-ins that will motivate learners to record responses in their learning logs and journals. They need to select the format to record responses, which usually includes titles like "Reflective Lesson Log" or "Double-Entry Journal"; logistical information such as a place for the learner's name, topic, and date; and spaces for their entries under stem statements or columns headed by lead-in or stems. If the content of the learning logs or journals is going to be used as part of the formal assessment system, then scoring rubrics that contain criteria and indicators with point values will have to be constructed. Remember, learners should be asked to assess their learning logs and journals before teachers assess them.

Kay Burke (1994) reports the work of a number of researchers who have identified ways that learning logs and journals can be used on a regular basis to promote reflection and provide feedback that can improve learning. Learning logs and journals can be used to

- record key ideas from a lecture, video, presentation, field trip, or reading assignment;
- make predictions about what will happen next in a story, video, experiment, event, situation, process, or lesson;
- record questions;
- summarize main ideas of a lesson, article, paper, video, or speech;
- reflect on the information presented;
- connect the ideas presented to previous learning or to other subjects or events in a learner's life;
- monitor change in an experiment or event over time;
- respond to questions from the teacher or other learners;
- brainstorm ideas about potential projects, papers, presentation, assignments, and problems;
- help identify problems;
- record problem solving techniques; and
- keep track of progress in solving problems, readings, homework assignments, projects, and experiences.

Learning logs and journals can be effective instructional tools to help learners sharpen their thinking and communication skills. They give learners the opportunity to interact with the teacher, lesson content, textbook, and each other. They afford learner opportunities to think about material, clarify confusing issues, discuss key ideas with others, connect with previous learning and experiences, and reflect on the personal meaning of materials and experiences. They provide a record over time of what has been presented and learned. They also reflect another dimension of the achievement and growth of learners and should be used primarily as a type of formative assessment, although they can also be structured to provide summative assessment information.

Graphic Organizers

Graphic organizers are visual renderings, worksheets, charts, or mental maps that represent important skills like sequencing, comparing and contrasting, and classifying. They involve learners in active thinking about relationships and associations and help learners make their thinking visible. Learners of today are faced with an overwhelming amount of written and graphic information from which they must synthesize, interpret, and construct meaning. Many learners have trouble connecting or relating new information to prior knowledge. Graphic organizers help learner memory by making abstract ideas visible and concrete, thus helping the learner organize thoughts. This is particularly true for visual learners, who need graphic organizers to help them organize information and remember key concepts.

Hyerle (1996) states that visual tools like graphic organizers are becoming increasingly more popular in the teaching, learning, and assessing process. Burke (1999) states that they have been used by some teachers for many years, particularly in the elementary grades to facilitate learning. Bellanca (1992) states that graphic organizers can empower learners to become self-directed in what and how they learn. He also advocates the use of graphic organizers to facilitate cooperative learning and creative thinking.

Innovative teachers have used visual tools like graphic organizers to introduce topics and provide worksheets for learners to record their responses to assignments or to organize their notes. Visual materials, like graphic organizers, are increasingly being used as assessment tools as they provide an organized way for learners to demonstrate what they have learned and are easily assessed using scoring rubrics. Graphic organizers used as tools to assess learner learning will provide learners with a creative way to express what they know and are able to do. Teachers who assign graphic organizers need to develop exemplary models that can be used for assessment. Criteria describing the content and relationships that should be visually demonstrated in a learner's work on graphic organizers need to be developed and used in a rubric (scoring) form for a more objective assessment. Just as essay questions require written expression in a connected manner, graphic organizers require learners to present important information in a connected manner using a visual form.

Burke (1999) provides the following suggestions to teachers for using graphic organizers as assessment tools:

- Include graphic organizers as part of paper-pencil quizzes and tests, providing learners with opportunity to respond to authentic situations in a creative and holistic manner.
- Require learners to complete or create a graphic organizer to show their understanding of some assignment. Score the completed product with a rubric and a presentation of the product with another rubric.
- Assign learners to select one graphic organizer to analyze a problem situation, such as troubleshooting a defective appliance, to show their thinking on possible causes and effects of a malfunction. Grade the completed product with a rubric with appropriate rating criteria.
- Allow learners to select one or more of their completed graphic organizers and include it in their portfolio.
- Assign cooperative learning groups the tasks of organizing their thinking on an assigned topic using a graphic organizer of their choice.
- Require learners to include a graphic organizer as part of their assigned project.
- Require learners to develop a graphic organizer to show their metacognitive thinking on some class related topic.

Graphic organizers are first and foremost learning tools, but they can also be used as authentic assessments. Graphic organizers used as assessment tools are best used for formative evaluation in that they provide both learners and teachers information for improving learning throughout a course. Learners may respond better to graphic organizers if they recognize them more as learning tools rather than

assessment instruments that result in scores entered into the grading system. Perhaps the most valuable type of assessment is the daily class work that provides specific evidence of what learners are learning and a means for teachers to provide specific feedback to learners that results in correcting errors.

Teachers can help learners understand how to use graphic organizers by modeling how to use the organizer with a topic that can be easily understood. For example, teachers may want to use the brainstorming technique to complete a total class Venn diagram on how two phenomena are alike and different, such as country and western music and rock and roll. A good starting point is to introduce learners to a note-taking graphic organizer and get them started in taking notes in graphic form. Learners can develop understanding and skill in creating graphic organizers if they are allowed to work first in small groups and can select a topic of their choice related to the lesson content.

One of the oldest and most often used graphic organizers is the note-taking form. Some learners have trouble taking class notes during class presentations. Effective teachers provide a note-taking graphic organizer to assist learners in recording important information for future use. See Figure 9-27.

Career and technical education teachers, with assistance from other school support personnel, must identify appropriate assessment techniques for each learner from special populations. In formulating the evaluation component for learners from special populations, the team should identify special needs that would present problems in assessing learner knowledge and performance. If some are identified, consideration should be given to modifying evaluation methods, techniques, and materials to better fit learner's level of physical, cognitive, emotional, and sensory functioning.

GRADING AND REPORTING SYSTEMS

There is a nationwide movement toward performance-based education, which includes defining what learners should know and be able to do, planning ways for them to learn how to perform, assessing their performance, and recording and reporting learner performance to parents and others. More than half the states now require some type of performance-based assessments with portfolios leading the way (Far West Laboratory, 1992). Most school leaders are encouraging teachers to use a number of alternative assessments to guide instruction and monitor learner achievement, progress, and growth, but how can all this new assessment information be recorded and reported into the single letter grade that characterizes most school report cards? Cizek (1996) reports that despite all the changes in the ways students are being assessed, a student's educational performance is still primarily reported using grades. He considers grades the final frontier in assessment reform.

SAMPLE GRAPHIC ORGANIZER	
Note-Taking Form Topic _____	Student _____
DIRECTIONS: Record notes or information about each content item in the notes space to the right opposite each item included in the form.	NOTES: Print or write important concepts and information.
Floor Framing	**Notes**

1. Terms and Definitions
    A. Sill plates
 	
    B. Girders
 	
    C. Joists
 	
    D. Headers and Bands
 	
    E. Bridging
 	
    F. Framing Hangers
 	
    G. Floor Openings	

Figure 9-27. Sample note-taking graphic organizer.

Wiggins (1994) argued against the use of a single grade to represent achievement, progress, and growth because it leads to difficulty in grading fairly. He notes that "fairness demands that less skilled students not have their work compared to their more talented peers, but honesty demands that teachers report how all students are doing against high, uniform standards," (p. 28). Bailey and McTighe (1996) offer a similar view to Wiggins regarding reporting one grade for all performance factors, maintaining that grades often reflect a combination of achievement, progress, and other factors and the tendency to collapse several independent elements into one single grade may blur their meaning. Consider the fact that the cut-off between grade categories is arbitrary and difficult to justify. If learner scores for a B grade range from 80 to 89, all learners in this nine point spread receive the same letter grade while a learner who scores 79, one point away from the B cut-off receives a letter grade of C.

Austin and McCann (1992) noted that policy makers are beginning to question the various use of grades and the messages they sent to parents and others. Kohn (1994) questioned why we grade at all and argued that most of the commonly offered reasons for grading are questionable at best. Hunt (1996) reports on one school system that offers the option to parents of not having grades reported to them or to anyone. She points out that grades may be more harmful than good in that grades are often notoriously subjective and can become a barrier for learning by destroying learners' motivation and belief in their own worth and abilities. She maintains that even good grades give learners an undesirable message that extrinsic rewards are more important than the intrinsic value of learning.

Bellanca (1992) reports that grades, especially those based on a competitive curve, create anxiety for both learners and teachers. Competitive curve grading results in branding learners as either winners or losers and works against the goal of successful learning. Traditional grading practice presents a never-ending challenge for teachers as they try to sum up a learner's performance over time into one numerical or letter grade. Teachers react in many ways to this grading dilemma, some by ignoring all assessments, others by developing complex accounting procedures to justify their grading systems, and still others by teaching only what is easily measured by conventional assessment practices rather than the important tasks and outcomes that require alternative assessments.

Teachers face a real dilemma in grading learners fairly, reporting learner progress and growth clearly to parents while fulfilling their obligations to the school system. Few school systems provide teachers with adequate instruction and guidance in grading and reporting to ensure adequacy and consistency (Austin & McCann, 1992).

The debate over grading and reporting is a hot topic in education as evidenced by the October, 1994 issue of *Educational Leadership* dedicated to reporting what learners are learning. Guskey (1994) noted that the issue of grading and reporting has perplexed educators for the better part of this century. He noted that one method won't adequately serve all purposes. Schools must identify their primary purpose for grading and select or develop the most appropriate approach. Teachers and administrators are in general agreement that a letter grade does not provide sufficient information about learners' achievement, progress, and growth. An increasing number of schools are engaging administrators, teachers, and parents in designing new ways to grade and report learner achievement and growth.

Functions of Grades

Grades are often dreaded by learners and teachers alike. However, they do serve an important role in the instructional process. They can serve as a source of motivation and provide an incentive to learn. Grades provide learners with information they can use for self-evaluation so they can determine their progress in learning or lack of it. Grades can serve a guidance function in that they can be used to decide whether a learner is interested in or prepared for a chosen job or career. Grades also provide a means of communicating the level of learner achievement to other teachers, parents, school administrators, and eventually to employers and postsecondary institution admission personnel. Schools use grades to identify or group learners for particular educational programs and to evaluate a program's effectiveness. School systems use learner grades as one source information to make decisions on retention, promotion, and placement in special programs; participation in extra curricular activities; and admission to postsecondary institutions.

Teachers recognize the importance attached to grades by learners, parents, and school administrators and they recognize that poor grades sometimes have undesirable consequences for learners. They want to challenge learners to take on more performance-based tasks and communicate more effectively, but they recognize the adverse effect that low grades have on these more challenging learning experiences. When learners are asked to stretch into more demanding learning tasks, teachers realize that they need to support their effort over longer periods of time than traditional grading periods allow. As a result, teachers who are familiar with the personal characteristics of their learners often use value judgments and ethical reasoning in determining learner grades. Instead of grades representing true learner growth and achievement, they often reflect justice tempered with mercy (Seely, 1994).

Teachers' perceptions of learners' behavior and capabilities can also significantly influence their judgments of achievement and, therefore, affect grades earned (Hills, 1991). Behavior disorder learners often have little chance of earning a favorable grade because their infractions overshadow their true performance. Grades must be determined carefully and uniformly so that they provide an accurate picture of learner progress in relation to specified objectives and occupational standards that lead to preparation for productive employment. To be meaningful, grades must be reflective of accurate judgments of learner (a) demonstrated performance in relation to standards, (b) progress in relation to expectations, and (c) demonstrated effort in relation to assessed capabilities. To be fair, they must be interpreted by learners, teachers, administrators, parents, and others in the same way.

Problems of Grades and Reporting Systems

According to Wiggins (1994) the giving of a grade is always an ugly compromise that teachers must make in which they summarize their view of learner performance measured against their expectations for that learner, yet somehow related to classroom, school district, and even regional and national standards. And, as already discussed, teachers factor in judgments based on the learner's personal characteristics as well as effort and attitude.

Assessment reform has become a centerpiece of efforts to improve learning in America's schools. Cizek (1996) states that it is reasonable to conclude that assessment reform efforts are making great strides toward improving the range and quality of information about a learner's performance to the learner, parents, administrators and the public, but this conclusion may be premature. Despite all the changes in assessment practice, a learner's educational performance is still primarily reported using the age-old grade, or more precisely, a mark on a report card.

Current report cards provide little information about the specific learning tasks that learners have mastered or their performance levels. They also say little about learner progress toward exit-level standards. In addition, grades seldom represent what parents believe they represent—true measures of learner achievement. Wiggins does not advocate the demise of letter grades but argues against the continuing use of a single letter grade with no clear, consistent meaning to summarize all aspects of a learner's performance. He argues for more, not fewer grades, and different kinds of grades with comments if parents and others are to understand what grades are intended to communicate. He recommends that reporting systems include a set of background materials such as samples of learner performances, scoring rubrics, descriptions of how grades were determined, and teacher commentaries so learners and parents will know how the grade was derived. Above all, he recommends the reporting system be easy to comprehend.

Wiggins (1994), proposed six new approaches for teachers that can lead to better report cards:

1. Indicate a clear distinction between standard-referenced and norm-referenced achievement in reports.
2. Develop a system with two types of teacher judgments: one involving progress toward uniform standards for each grade level and a second focusing on growth–progress measured against teacher expectations for each learner. Progress is defined as an objective measure of performance made over time on a standard-referenced, longitudinal scale. It is measured backward from a desirable performance standard. Growth, on the other hand, represents a judgment about whether current performance falls short of, meets, or exceeds a teacher's expectations at a given time period. Measuring growth requires teachers to look back to past performance as the basis for making judgments regarding change in learners.
3. Develop a longitudinal reporting system that charts achievement against exit-level standards for the range of grade levels.
4. Include many more "subgrades" of performance in reports such as strengths and weaknesses in the diverse priority areas, topics, skills, and understandings that comprise subjects.
5. Make accurate distinctions between the quality of a learner's work and the sophistication or degree of difficulty and complexity of the work.
6. Make evaluations of the learner's intellectual character—habits of mind and work based on performance and products. These include the cadre of work and study habits that are essential for success in higher education and work.

Grades, in themselves, are not inherently bad; it is the misuse of them that causes problems. For example, grades are sometimes used to "whip a learner into line." Research indicates that awarding a learner a low grade as punishment in hopes that he or she will try harder usually causes learners to withdraw from learning (Guskey, 1994). Grades are also misused when they result in sorting individuals into segregated groups and teaching them separately (Kohn, 1994). Grades are also misused when they become the major motivation for learner learning instead of learning for its own sake. Letter grades that attempt to summarize all the learner's performance, as well as intellectual character, fall far short of the mark. They are not good predictors of what learners know and are able to do. Wiggins (1994) summed up the problem of grades when he noted, "Our urge to reduce things to one number and our overuse of norm-referenced testing and grading are the culprits, not the letter grades themselves," (p. 29).

Guskey (1994), in his article "Making the grade: What benefits students?" summarized points of agreement of researchers on the topic of grading and reporting:

- Grading and reporting aren't essential to instruction but checking learner progress is.
- There is no one single method of grading and reporting that serves all purposes well.
- Grading and reporting remain inherently subjective regardless of methods used, but informed subjectivity may yield very accurate descriptions of what learners have learned.
- Grades have some value as rewards, but no value as punishments.
- Grading and reporting should always be done in reference to learning criteria, never on the curve.

The grading and marking system for learners from special populations should be based upon assessment of multiple factors in the two dimensions of demonstrated performance or progress made toward specified objectives and growth toward the teacher's expectations for each learner in a specified grading period. It should be fair and should reflect the competencies developed by each learner rather than how well the learner did compared to other learners. It should be based on multiple factors and take into consideration learner ability, effort, and achievement. It should also report learner progress in relation to the degree of difficulty and complexity of learning content. The grading system should provide for learner involvement in determining progress and growth, and should be planned by the career and technical education teacher with input from support personnel whenever possible.

The grading system must be manageable, must be easily understood by learners, parents, and others, and must be consistent with school grading and reporting guidelines to have the support of school administrators. If possible, the reporting system should feature more than one single grade summarizing all achievement. It should contain a number of "subgrades" which describe the many faces of performance and intellectual character required to function in today's workplace and in daily life. It should also contain different materials and formats to serve the various instructional, informational, guidance, and administrative functions of different audiences.

Characteristics of Grading Systems

Following are some characteristics of an effective grading system for learners from special populations. The grading system should

- be fair to each learner, i.e., based on each learner's capabilities and achievement level;
- accurately reflect the performance of identified competencies against standards;
- be designed to enhance the learner's self-concept;
- include the multiple grading factors of learner effort, growth, and achievement;
- address both quality and quantity of work performed;
- be easily understood by learners, parents/guardians, other teachers, and support personnel;

- provide for learner involvement in evaluating work and determining grades;
- be flexible to accommodate changing needs of learners;
- be individualized in order to reduce anxiety and competition over grades;
- be designed to encourage learners to accept more responsibility for their own earning and accomplishments;
- be simplified to ease the teacher's burden in determining grades;
- be designed to assist in cooperative planning activities;
- be continuous so learners can assess their progress in relation to predetermined goals, objectives, and standards
- be consistent with school system grading policy; and
- take into account the degree of difficulty and complexity of learning tasks.

Grading Techniques

Career and technical education teachers must develop a fair and impartial system for arriving at grades for learners from special populations. In few situations can the teacher simply award a grade of pass or fail and, even if this is the case, there must ultimately be a way to arrive at the decision. In most schools, Career and technical teachers are expected to grade learners on a five-factor scale. This scale may be communicated either as grades or points that stand for levels of performance. The translation of such a reporting system is usually as follows:

Letter Points Status
A–4 Excellent
B–3 Good
C–2 Fair
D–1 Poor
F–0 Failure

There are a number of techniques that career and technical education teachers can use in determining grades for learners from special populations. One of these is to grade learner work as either satisfactory or unsatisfactory. This system works best when specific performance standards have been established for a learning experience. For example, a floriculture learner may be required to take cuttings from plants which are to be 3″ to 5″ in length and free from disease, broken stems, or otherwise undamaged. Learner work is either satisfactory or unsatisfactory and activities rated as unsatisfactory must be repeated after the learner has received appropriate remedial instruction. Satisfactory/unsatisfactory grades often need to be converted into another set of grades such as the A, B, C, D, and F system.

When making this conversion, career and technical education teachers should consider many factors such as the quality of the work performed in relation to the degree of difficulty of the task, relative importance of the work, quantity of work performed, and possibly the time factor.

The pass/fail grading system is similar to the satisfactory/unsatisfactory system. The criteria for arriving at a learner grade may be the same as in the satisfactory/unsatisfactory grading system or it may be set on another basis. For example, learners working at the D level or above are passing and those working below a D are failing.

Another system for grading is the use of a continuum of performances for describing learner progress such as the system reported by Sperling (1994). Her continuum features four levels of performance: (a) not yet, (b) developing, (c) achieving, and (d) extending. Learner performance is described in each of these levels so that both learners and parents know what learners can do.

Another grading technique is to use written comments in conjunction with another grading system. This technique is especially useful with learners from special populations in that it provides the details and specific information that give a more complete explanation of learner performance. Few learners, parents, or employers question a learner grade of A, but they often wonder about B and C grades. ("Why wasn't the grade an A instead of a B?") Career and technical education teachers who take the extra time to write comments to accompany letter grades of learners from special populations will make available information that not only better describes the learner's performance but gives suggestions for improvement. For example: "Susan's work in our food service program is acceptable and has been awarded a grade of C. She has mastered the tasks of personal hygiene and sanitation, safety, and tools and equipment. However, she is still experiencing difficulty in weights, measures, and recipes. School support teachers are working with her in these areas and she is beginning to make some progress. Susan works slowly and probably would not be able to meet the production demands in the industry at this time, but given enough time and reinforcement, she may develop entry level abilities."

In writing learner comments, begin with positive accomplishments and then indicate areas of weakness. Make the comments specific enough to reflect the learner's progress toward performance standards, yet broad enough to offer an overall assessment of the learner's achievement. Likewise, make comments about the learner's growth in relation to expectations based on past performance and assessment data. Finally, make comments about the learner's intellectual character, including learning and study skills, work habits and attitudes toward learning, and other important attributes such as initiative, creativity, intelligent questioning, independent research, decision making, and self-determination (Alff & Kearns, 1988).

Another grading technique is to include scoring rubrics, skill reports, or competency checklists along with the school's official report card. Skill reports, along with competency checklists, are especially valuable to prospective employers who want to know what a learner can or cannot do. See Figure 9-28.

BUSINESS EDUCATION

SkillReport: Processing U.S. Mail

Name: _____   Teacher: _____

Skill \ Rating	1			2			3		
	Above Average	Average	Below Average	Above Average	Average	Below Average	Above Average	Average	Below Average
Process outgoing mail	X			X			X		
Process outgoing bulk mail		X			X		X		
Process incoming mail		X		X			X		
Forward mail			X		X			X	
Handle special mail			X		X		X		
Keep postage meter records		X			X		X		
Prepare parcels for mailing		X			X		X		

Grade Conversion:

Excellent	A	90 - 100
Above Average	B	80 - 89
Average	C	70 - 79
Below Average	D	60 - 69

Figure 9-28. An example of a skill report for a business education program.

A highly recommended grading technique is to have learners self-evaluate their work against models or excellent examples of completed work using scoring rubrics, rating scales, or specification checklists. For example, a secretarial learner's performance on the task of answering the telephone could be self-evaluated against a checklist which contains behaviors under the headings of Beginning the Call, Developing the Call, Taking Messages, Closing the Call, and Voice Personality. After learners have evaluated their performance against correct models or approved checklists, they should be required to explain orally or in writing why they evaluated themselves as they did. Having learners critique and summarize their work gives them valuable practice in self-evaluation as well as practice in oral and written communication skills, which are so important in further education, work, and family and community living.

A grading technique similar to self-evaluation is to form peer grading groups to evaluate each other on a weekly basis against models and scoring rubrics. (Alff & Kearns, 1988). Note that peer grading allows learners to become self-evaluators, to develop observations skills, and to learn from reviewing each other. Weekly grading that takes into account such factors as quantity and quality of work, initiative, and social and behavioral skills provides support and recognition of the progress and growth of learners as well as providing corrective feedback and a sharing of learning approaches among learners.

The practice of using multiple grades for learners from special populations to reflect the diversity of learning outcomes and their unique capabilities is another grading technique used by many career and technical education teachers. This technique provides rewards for the overall progress a learner makes even if some areas of achievement and growth are below the satisfactory level. One type of multiple grading system involves the three areas of pretest achievement level, present achievement level, and growth (includes effort expended). See Figure 9-29. A sample multiple-grading record from a teacher's grade book is shown. Grades are recorded under each content area assessed during the grading period using a letter grade representing present achievement and two numerals indicating pretest level and growth. The sample multiple-grading record shows that Marci Hughes has earned a grade of A in vocational math with a very high pretest achievement level and with only moderate growth. The multiple grading factors could be different from the ones applied in this example. For instance, B42 could represent a letter grade of B on some subject or competency area with the first numeral representing reading level or math level and the second numeral representing growth or some other factor. The multiple-grading system provides additional information to the learner, parent, and teacher and can be used to alter instruction for a learner with special needs to make it more relevant.

Another grading technique is coded grading, suggested by Huck, et al. (1989). A coded grading system uses numerals representing specific information along with the letter grade that usually represents achievement or progress. For example, a coded grade for a learner enrolled in a masonry program of B23 could represent a B level grade representing performance achievement in a given reporting period, with the first numeral 2 representing a measure of growth in terms of realistic expectations for the learner and the second numeral 3 representing functioning above grade level. Other numerals could be added. See Figure 9-30.

Another grading technique that can be used with learners from special populations is shared grading. Shared grading is the practice of involving two or more teachers in determining a learner grade for a marking period. This system works well when resource or support teachers are working with learners from special populations who are mainstreamed into career and technical education classes.

Performance contracts are developed jointly between the career and technical teacher and the learner with special needs with input from support staff. The contract is based on information contained in the learner's IEP or ITP and identifies specific activities to be completed by the learner at set performance criteria. The career and technical education teacher should consider the learner's abilities, achievement level, and other factors of the IEP and ITP in planning the grading contract. Recommended elements of the performance contract include the following:
- type of work—project, portfolio, work sample, invention—to be completed by the learner
- the quantity and quality of work to be completed
- time lines for the completion of the work
- period written progress reports accompanied by

samples of work in progress
- identification of persons and resources to be used in completing contract work
- signatures of the learner, teacher, and parent/guardian when appropriate

Another grading technique is to encourage learners to correct their work by awarding up to one-half of the points originally deducted for corrected work. This practice is facilitated if adequate space is provided between test items for corrections on test instruments. In addition, points can be awarded if learners can show their thinking on required work and test items they missed. When learners are required to look up the correct answers for the test items they missed and describe their thinking, learners are provided with a learning reinforcement experience and teachers gain new insights into how a learner with special needs thinks.

Alff and Kearnes (1988) described one other method of grading offered by Stevens called the adjusted scoring system. In this system, the score a learner with a disability earns in an assessment activity is adjusted to accommodate the learner's limitations. For example, a learner who has difficulty in spelling and writing because of a disability can have his or her scores on this assessment activity normalized by reducing the point requirements for this task. If the writing assignment was worth 100 points for a perfect score, an adjustment can be made to reduce the points to 80 to factor in the learner's disability which means he or she would only need to earn 80 points instead of the 100 to have a perfect paper. The adjusted points for an assessment activity become the denominator or bottom of a scoring fraction. For example, suppose Marla earned a score of 60 points on a written scenario and her point total was adjusted to 80. Her adjusted score would be computed by placing the 60 (points she earned) over 80 (adjusted point total) yielding a fraction of 60/80 and a score of 75, which would be entered in the multi-factor grading system.

MULTIPLE GRADING RECORD (MODIFIED TEACHER'S GRADE BOOK)							
Name	Subject	Voc Math		Unit I Safety		Unit II Hand Tools	
1. Erin Porter		B		A		B	
		3	3	4	4	3	4
2. Marci Hughes		A		B		B	
		5	3	3	4	2	4
Code: Letter = Achievement grade (A - F) 1st Numeral = Pretest level (1 - 5) – 1 = lowest 2nd Numeral = Effort (1 - 5) – 1 = lowest							

Figure 9-29. An example of a grading report with multiple grades recorded.

Huck, et al. (1989) described another type of alternative grading procedure which they label "incentive grading." Incentive grading provides a way for learners from special populations to improve the final grade for a reporting period. Several different strategies can be used as incentives and the learner can practice decision making by selecting one or more of these incentive strategies that follow:

- Floating point value in the A range–The learner is given an extra point value representing an A which can be used to replace the lowest score grade earned which will improve the learner overall grade average.
- Elimination grade–The learner is given a chance to eliminate the lowest grade earned in a reporting period in order to improve the grade average.

- Alternative credit grade–The learner is allowed to do an alternative assignment to improve a grade.

The development of an accommodation checklist is another alternative grading procedure offered by Huck, et al. (1989). An accommodation checklist provides a summary of the accommodations provided to a learner with disabilities in order for them to achieve success in a program. Accommodation checklists included with other reporting information can help parents and others better understand the learning environment that affects learner performance. See Figure 9-31. A checklist may include the following:

- language interpreter assistance
- test items read orally for learner
- test previewed in the form of a study guide

CODED GRADE REPORTING SYSTEM

The information contained in this coded grade reporting system is designed to provide more information to the reader than is provided with a single letter grade. Numerals are added to provide additional information on student progress and growth in relation to performance standards, teachers expectations based on the student's past performance and assessed capabilities, and grade level functioning.

The codes are explained as follows:

Letters represent judgments of overall performance in relation to established standards.

The first numeral represents a judgment of progress in terms of teacher expectations determined from past performance and assessed capability.

The second numeral represents a judgment of the degree of growth that has occurred in the program.

The third numeral represents the student's present performance in terms of longitudinal grade levels.

KEY

Grades Overall Progress	First Numeral Expectations	Second Numeral Degree of Growth	Third Numeral Grade Level
A–Excellent	1–Working on expectation level	1–Getting started	1–Working on grade level
B–Above average	2–Working below expectation level	2–Making progress	2–Working below grade level
C–Average	3–Working above expectation level	3–Achieving	3–Working above grade level
D–Below average			
F–Failing (Needs immediate attention)			

	REPORTING PERIOD			
SUBJECT	1	2	3	4
Masonry Construction	B111			
Applied Math				
Applied Communications				

Bill, a tenth grade masonry student has been awarded a coded grade of B111 for the first marking period. He is achieving above average as determined by multiple grading factors. He is working on the expectation level determined for him as indicated by the numeral "1." Bill is just getting started in terms of growth (numeral 1) and is working at grade level (numeral 1).

Figure 9-30. An example of a coded grade reporting system.

- test administered as an open-book exam, allowing use of notes and other resources
- individual instruction given at times
- peer grading used to reinforce learning and provide corrective feedback

- coordinated instruction provided by career and technical education and special education teachers
- modified assignments and tests
- self-assessment made part of the evaluation system
- performance evaluated with school-wide scoring rubrics

ACCOMMODATION CHECKLIST

Student: _____   Teacher: _____

Program: _____   Subject: _____

Career Goal: _____   Date: _____

This special report is a supplement to other reporting information provided to help you understand the special accommodations being provided to help your child learn and to assess achievement and growth. Accommodations are provided when they are needed based on assessment information, the judgment of professionals, and the request of the student or parents. Some of these accommodations are identified in the IEP or ITP for your child.

Modifications have been made in the following areas:

Grading Periods   **Accommodations**

1	2	3	4	
				Instruction planned and delivered according to IEP or ITP
				Only parts of the program/course were changed
				Individual assistance is provided daily
				Student is assigned to a learning team
				Student performance contract was used
				Tests were modified (items, length, scoring)
				Peer-evaluation is used to enhance learning
				A multi-factor adjusted grading system is used
				Other:

Teacher's Signature: Grade: Comments:

1st
Reporting period_____   _____   _____

2nd
Reporting period_____   _____   _____

3rd
Reporting period_____   _____   _____

4th
Reporting period_____   _____   _____

FINAL _____

Source: Adapted from Huck, et al. (1989). *Adapt: A Developmental Activity Program for Teachers* (2nd ed.). Pittsburgh, PA: Allegheny Intermediate Unit.

Figure 9-31. An example of an accommodations checklist used to inform parents and others of special accommodations.

A grading technique used in some elementary schools but with utility at any grade level is the use of different rubber stamps or stickers to summarize learner progress. Grading stamps are available with different characters and messages to indicate performance levels. The use of these graphic stamps or stickers often has the same motivational effect as attendance stars do for the elementary grade school learner.

A final grading technique offered here is the use of a grading system that allows learners to select the weights given to different performance factors within ranges set by the teacher. For example, technology education teachers usually include learning modules, projects, quizzes, unit tests, final test, work habits, portfolio, and other performances in their grading and marking systems. Teachers can assign a weight range for each factor based on past learner performances, such as from 15% to 25% for module work, quizzes from 3% to 5%, and unit tests from 15% to 20%. Learners can choose weights according to their best performances or capabilities. This makes them feel like they have input into how their grades are determined. See Figure 9-32.

The primary purpose of calculating grades and reporting them to learners, parents, administrators, and appropriate others is to communicate learner achievement as accurately as possible. While there are many criticisms that can be leveled against issuing grades (and there are those who advocate a system of assessment without grades), the practice of grading and reporting is likely to continue for the foreseeable future. Reedy (1995) states that the public demands secondary schools evaluate learners and report learner achievement in ways that they understand. State organizations also require accountability for learner achievement of course objectives and acceptable performance on national achievement tests. Colleges and universities request grade point averages and class standings to make admission decisions. Parents need and are entitled to regular reports on learner progress and most are familiar with the traditional report cards. Considering the expectations for accurate grading of different audiences, teachers and schools must do everything possible to create a learner assessment mechanism that culminates in reporting each learner's achievement of learning goals for each course as accurately as possible. Traditional grading practices need to change so that assessment and grading align with and support current research into the way learners learn and achieve (O'Conner, 1999).

MARKING SYSTEMS

There are many marking systems in use today, but they generally fall into two categories: the point system and the averaging system.

Point System

In the point system, each evaluation factor is awarded a certain number of points. The sum of these point values represents the total number of points that a learner can earn in a given marking period. See Figure 9-33.

Points earned for different evaluation factors can also be weighted to reflect the value, importance, and difficulty of each type of performance. For example, performance on tasks or competencies is usually given more weight in the grading system than other factors. See Figure 9-34.

WEIGHTED GRADING COURSE ASSESSMENT SYSTEM			
Criteria	Weight Range %	Chosen Weight %	Points
Article Reports	02 to 05		
Unit Test Development Project	10 to 30		
Performance Test Project	05 to 15		
Authentic Assessment Project	10 to 20		
Cooperative Learning Project	10 to 20		
Mid-term Exam	05 to 15		
Final Exam	10 to 20		
Portfolio	05 to 10		
Class Participation	02 to 04		
	Total: 100	Total: 100	Total: 100

Grade Conversion:

90-100 = A, 80-89 = B, 70-79 = C, 69 or below = No person's land

Grade =

Figure 9-32. An example of a weighted grading system.

POINT SYSTEM FOR DETERMINING GRADES

Evaluation Factor	Points	Points Earned
Task Performance (10 tests @ 30 points each)	300	___
Written Exams (3 exams @ 100 points each)	300	___
Work Habit Development (10 observations @ 20 points each)	200	___
Attitude and Effort (10 observations @ 10 points each)	100	___
Outside Assignments (5 evaluations @ 20 points each)	100	___
TOTAL	1000	___

Point Conversion Chart

Points	Grade
800–1000	A
600–799	B
400–599	C
200–399	D
0–199	F

Figure 9-33. An example of a point system for determining grades.

WEIGHTED POINT SYSTEM FOR DETERMINING GRADES

Evaluation Factor	Points	Weight	Weighted Points	Percentage of total Weighted Points
Task Performance (10 tests @ 30 points each)	300	.20	60	60%
Written Exams (3 exams @ 100 points each)	300	.05	15	15%
Work Habit Development (10 observations @ 20 points each)	200	.05	10	10%
Attitude and Effort (10 observations @ 10 points each)	100	.05	5	5%
Outside Assignments (5 evaluations @ 20 points each)	100	.10	10	10%
TOTAL	1000		100	100%

NOTE: Weights can be arbitrarily assigned or they can be assigned on the basis of percentage of total weighted points. This can be calculated by converting weighted points on a 100-point scale, which reflects the desired percentage value. The weights can then be determined by dividing the weighted points by the total points assigned to each factor. For example, task performance was given a percentage weight of 60% in the chart above or a weighted point value of 60. The weight value was calculated by dividing 60 by 300, which gives a weights of .20. To determine a given student's weighted point value for any factor, multiply the total points earned by the assigned weight. To avoid small numbers, multiply by a value of 2 to convert the 100-point scale to 200.

Weighted Point Scale

Points	Grade
90–100	A
80–89	B
70–79	C
60–69	D
50–59	F

200 Point Conversion Chart

Points	Grade
180–200	A
160–179	B
140–159	C
120–139	D
0–119	F

Figure 9-34. An example of a weighted point system for determining grades.

In establishing a point system, career and technical educators, with input from support personnel, should review each learner's IEP or ITP and decide what evaluation factors should be included. They should assign realistic point values to each evaluative factor after determining which factors are most important. They should also determine the point limits for letter grades. The career and technical education teacher can use past experiences with other learners in determining the upper and lower limits of the point system as a general guideline. However, it is important to consider the abilities of learners from special populations as well as their IEPs and ITPs in establishing the point value system.

There are several methods that can be used to determine point spreads for letter grades. One way is to establish the lower limits of the A and D levels of performance based on experience. Then, establish the lower limits of the B and C levels by subtracting the lower limit of the D level from the lower limit of the A level and dividing by three. For example, the point conversion table in figure 9-34 shows that the lower limit of the weighted point value for the A grade is 90 and the lower limit of the D grade is 60. To establish the lower limits of the B and C levels, simply subtract 60 from 90 (90-60=30) and divide 30 by 3. This yields a point spread of 10 between each grade level. It is necessary to establish the upper limits of the B, C, and D levels one point less than the lower limit of the next higher grade to separate grade levels. Reading the conversion chart, the lower limit of the B level would then be set at 80 since 10 subtracted from the lower limit of the A level of 90 yields 80. The lower limit of the C level would be established in a similar fashion. Some learners like to see larger points in a grading system. Teachers can multiply the standard 100 point conversion table by 2 or other numbers. Figure 9-34 shows a conversion chart using a 200 point scale.

The second method for determining point limits for grades is similar to the first but uses a different math procedure. A point conversion chart calculated by this method is shown in Figure 9-33. The first step is to use the maximum number of points that can be earned as a starting point. In the example, this value was 1000 points for the upper limits of the A grade level. In order to establish the lower limits for each grade level, divide the upper limit of the A level or the maximum point value of 1000 in the example by 5, which yields a value of 200 points.

Averaging System

The second major system that is used to determine grades for learners from special populations in a given marking period is the averaging system. Each evaluation factor and activity, such as task performance and performance test, is evaluated against a common base (highest achievement as 100% or an adjusted base) and given a relative weight in relation to other activities and factors. The total is averaged and final grade determined by comparing it against school's marking system. For example, the school may follow the limits of 90-100% equals an A grade. See Figure 9-35.

The career and technical education teacher, in cooperation with support personnel, will need to decide which grading system is the most appropriate for meeting school requirements as well as the capabilities and needs of the learner. Regardless of which system is used, a clear understanding of it should be communicated to the learner and other appropriate school personnel at the beginning of the grading period.

Grade Reports and Competency Records

Learner achievement is reported in as many ways as there are school systems. However, most schools use the traditional learner report card with grades, percentages, pass/fail, and satisfactory/unsatisfactory ratings of learner progress in relation to identified subjects or competencies.

Some states and local school systems are including additional information to report learner achievement of occupational competencies. The State of Florida has implemented a form of competency record keeping entitled The Career Merit Achievement Plan (Career Map). The Career Map lists major categories of the instructional program corresponding to major divisions of an occupation followed by coded competencies which the learners must master in order to perform the work associated with the category. See Figure 9-36. Each learner competency must be verified by the teacher or some other authority and must be rated with a 1, 2, or 3 in the boxes provided for each competency to indicate conditions of competency performance. A rating of 1 corresponds to the learner performing the competency satisfactorily with supervision. A rating of 2 indicates satisfactory competency performance with only periodic supervision. A rating of 3 indicates that the learner performed the competency satisfactorily without supervision. Each competency is also coded as either primarily cognitive (C) or primarily performance based (P) in learning type.

The State of Georgia has included a certificate of competency in their curriculum guides that lists the tasks that the learner can satisfactorily demonstrate in an occupation or job on the back. A certificate is included in the guide for each job or exit point from the career and technical instructional program.

Competency certificates, competency checklists, and other forms of competency records provide learners, parents, and potential employers with more detailed information about what learners can and cannot do. It is important to remember that competency records and other learner information must be cleared for release to potential employers so that confidentiality is maintained according to established laws. They are valuable supplements to the traditional report card and high school transcript. Competency records can be modified for use with disabled learners to indicate not only their record of competency achievement but also to indicate what modifications, accommodations or support services are needed.

AVERAGING SYSTEM FOR DETERMINING GRADES

Evaluation Factor	Relative Weight	Maximum Points
Task Performance (10 tests @ 30 points each)	50%	300
Written Exams (3 exams @ 100 points each)	20	300
Work Habits (10 observations @ 20 points each)	15	200
Attitude and Effort (10 observations @ 10 points each)	5	100
Outside Assignments (5 evaluations @ 20 points each)	10	100

STUDENT EXAMPLE

Example of How to Calculate a Factor

Three Unit Written Exams

Exam 1 - 24 out of 30 points converted to 100% scale (24 ÷ 30 = .80)

Exam 2 - 45 out of 50 points converted to 100% scale (45 ÷ 50 = .90)

Exam 3 - 38 out of 40 points converted to 100% scale (38 ÷ 40 = .95)

                                                    2.65

Total = 2.65   2.65 ÷ 3 = .88 or 88%

To arrive at final weighted grade for exams, multiply 88 × 20 (assigned weight) = 176.

Summary of Other Student Factors

Factor	Weighted Value	Grading Scale		Example Grade
Performance Tests	282	880 - 1000 points	= A	Individual earned 835 points
Written Exams	176	780 - 879 points	= B	resulting in a grade of B.
Work Habits	192	680 - 779 points	= C	
Attitude and Effort	97	600 - 679 points	= D	
Outside Assignments	88	Below 600 points	= F	
Total	835			

Figure 9-35. An example of an averaging system for determining grades.

FLORIDA CAREER MERIT ACHIEVEMENT PLAN

Industrial Electronics
IN 47.010500
Electronic Technology
(IN 15.030300)

Name _____   Date Started _____
Address _____
Institution _____   Instructor _____

Categories

A → A → DC Circuits

B → B → AC Circuits

A 001 (P) Solve Basic Algebraic Problems as Applicable to Electronics	1 ☐ 2 ☐ 3 ☐	A 002 (C) Related Electricity to the Nature of Matter	1 ☐ 2 ☐ 3 ☐
_____ Authentication		_____ Authentication	
B 001 (P) Solve Basic Trigonometric Problems as Applicable to Electronics (Prerequisite to AC)	1 ☐ 2 ☐ 3 ☐	B 002 (C) Identify Properties of an AC Signal	1 ☐ 2 ☐ 3 ☐
_____ Authentication		_____ Authentication	

Source: Florida Career Merit Achievement Program. (1988). Tallahassee, FL: Florida Department of Education.

Figure 9-36. An example of the Florida Career Merit Achievement Program competency record.

SUMMARY

Over the past decade, the nation's public has observed our educational system and found it wanting. The 1990 landmark report of the Commission on the Skills of the American Workforce, *America's Choice: High Skills or Low Wages*, called for the United States to create a single comprehensive system for general, professional, and technical education that meets the needs of everyone from high school learners to dislocated workers, from the hard-core unemployed to working adults who want to improve their skills. Employers have been demanding a new type of worker, one who can think, reason, question, and contribute to company goals. The complexity of living in America also requires a better educated citizen, one who can understand democratic responsibilities, take advantage of economic opportunities, take advantage of higher education and training opportunities, and provide leadership to the American family and the community.

There is a nationwide effort to develop educational programs that will assist individuals in making the transition from school-to-work or continuing education. Three major pieces of federal legislation have been passed: the Perkins Amendments of 1990, the 1994 Goals 2000: Educate America Act, and the 1994 School-to-Work Opportunities Act . . . all with a focus on improving the quality of education and preparation for work. At the forefront of this effort are performance-based education and the establishment of voluntary national performance standards for academic and occupational education programs. There is an equally important movement to develop a performance assessment system to measure learner progress and growth toward these standards using authentic assessment measures like portfolios, learner projects, and performance-based tests.

There are many factors that are driving assessment reform in this country including a disenchantment with standardized and teacher constructed selection tests; findings from cognitive psychology that have shed new light on meaningful, engaged learning with a focus on producing knowledge rather than reproducing it; the development of higher standards for learner performance in every state in the country; the implementation of Howard Gardner's theory of multiple intelligences; the application of technology to assessment; and the focus on the application of knowledge rather than the storage of knowledge only long enough to reproduce it on conventional tests. Organizations that specialize in assessment such as the Far West Laboratory and the Center for Research on Evaluation, Standards, and Student Testing are working with school systems to develop and test alternative assessments, and the results are promising in terms of reform in curriculum and instructional practice as well as in increased learner engagement in the learning and assessment process. Many prominent researchers like Grant Wiggins, Lauren and Dan Resnic, Dennie Palmer Wolf and others have provided leadership to the alternative assessment movement. As a result, teachers now have a large body of research they can draw on to change the way they assess learners to include alternative assessments along with their traditional assessments.

The current push for alternative assessments is an outgrowth of concern among educators that standardized tests and other conventional tests seldom measure how well learners can think, solve problems, apply knowledge and skills in real-life or simulated situations, and take charge of their own learning. Alternative assessments are also being proposed as a way to shift the place of assessment from the end result of instruction to an integral component of the learning process.

Proponents of alternative assessment maintain that learning can best be assessed by examining and judging a learner's actual or simulated performance on significant tasks that are often encountered in real life. They argue that such assessments can focus on the learning processes as revealed through self-assessment checklists, graphic organizers, oral reports, and learning logs; products such as learner projects, diaries, written scenarios, portfolios, and exhibits; and performances like manipulative performance tests, oral debates, knowledge bowls, and simulated events.

Alternative assessments can be especially valuable in assessing learning development and outcomes for learners from special populations. Alternative assessments are very flexible, allowing learners with special needs to emphasize their strengths. They also provide the following benefits, which are well-suited to assessing the progress and growth of special needs learners: (a) They focus on what learners can do, rather than what they cannot do, (b) they accommodate a variety of learning styles, (c) they assess a wide range of learning tasks, (d) they are open-ended, allowing learners to show extended knowledge and skills, (e) they require learners to take a more active, responsible role in their education, which enhances self-determination, and (f) they provide an opportunity for teachers and learners with special needs to collaborate about learning and assessments that will not only provide a clearer picture of learner achievement, but will also allow learners to see how the quality of their work has evolved over time.

What is desired is an assessment system like the one described by D. Monty Neill, in which teachers have a wide repertoire of classroom-based, culturally sensitive assessment practices and tools to use in helping every learner achieve high standards; teachers and administrators collaboratively use assessment information to continuously improve schools; important decisions about a learner, such as readiness to graduate from high school, are based on work done over the years by the learner; schools in networks hold one another accountable for learning; and public evidence of learner achievement consists primarily of samples from learners' actual schoolwork rather than just reports of results.

Career and technical education teachers and support personnel will need to update their knowledge and skills to modify traditional assessments and use new assessment tools if they are going to be ready to demonstrate how their learners' performance measures up against the specific outcomes that will be derived from national skill standards.

SELF-ASSESSMENT

1. Why is it important not to compromise task performance standards in order to help learners from special populations improve their grades in a career and technical education program?
2. Explain why the evaluation systems for assessing the achievement of learners from special populations should be based on the IEP or ITP rather than on a comparison of the learner's achievement with the achievement of others.
3. Identify and describe some evaluation factors that should be considered in an evaluation system for learners from special populations.
4. Describe the steps involved in developing performance tests to measure learner performance on tasks and competencies.
5. Describe the steps involved in constructing paper-pencil cognitive achievement tests for learners from special populations.
6. Describe some of the modifications that can be made to paper-pencil test items and directions and give an example for each item format.
7. List some of the traditional and alternative methods and techniques that can be used to evaluate the progress and growth of learners from special populations.
8. Describe the procedures for developing and using portfolio assessment for learners from special populations.
9. Describe the procedures of using the project method for assessing learner performance.
10. Explain why the considerations of minimizing the fear of tests and providing continuous feedback are important to evaluating the progress of learners from special populations.
11. Describe how to construct and use portfolios to assess learner progress and achievement.
12. List some of the characteristics of an effective grading system for learners from special populations.
13. List and explain different grading practices that can be used with learners from special populations.
14. What are some benefits of using alternative assessments with learners with special needs?
15. Describe how teachers can assist learners in assessing their work.
16. Describe how teachers can assist learners in reflective thinking and in assessing the level of their thinking through graphic organizers.
17. Describe rubrics, their applications, advantages, disadvantages, and how to construct and use them.

ASSOCIATED ACTIVITIES

1. Contact academic and career and technical education teachers in your school district and state to inquire what assessment strategies they use with learners from special populations.
2. Contact your state's department of education and identify information pertaining to the state's program of testing and guidelines recommended for assessment.
3. Contact a college or university in your area and inquire about testing measurement and evaluation courses in which you could enroll to update your knowledge and skills of assessment.
4. Form an assessment team composed of special needs professionals, other career and technical education teachers, and interested academic teachers to develop/adopt performance standards and performance criteria (rubrics) to ensure assessment is performance-based.
5. Contact other career and technical education teachers in your region and state to see if they would be willing to share test item banks and performance tests that they have developed and are presently using to test the technical knowledge and skills of the learners.
6. Secure and use a microcomputer test generator program to create and store test items and construct tests for learners from special populations.
7. Write an article for publication in an educational magazine or journal on the topic of evaluation of learners from special populations.
8. Develop a new overall grading and reporting system for your course and present it to the administration as a model to consider for changing the system presently in use.

REFERENCES

Alff, M. & Kearns. (1988). Teacher feature: Alternative grading. *Journal of Vocational Special Needs Education, 10*(2), 36-39.

Alternative assessment and technology (1999). Syracuse, NY: Eric Clearinghouse on Information and Technology. ED 365312.

American Vocational Association. (1998). *The official guide to the Perkins Act of 1998.* Alexandria. VA: Author.

Archbald, D. A., & Newmann, F. M. (1988). *Beyond standardized testing: Assessing authentic achievement in secondary school.* Madison, WI: University of Wisconsin, National Association of Secondary School Principals.

Austin, S., & McCann, R. (1992). *Here's another arbitrary grade for your collection: A statewide survey of grading policies.* Paper presented at the annual meeting of the American Educational Research Association, San Francisco, CA.

The AVA guide to the Carl D. Perkins Vocational and Applied Technology Education Act of 1990. (1990). Alexandria, VA: American Vocational Association.

Baer, J. (1994). Why you still shouldn't trust creativity tests. *Educational Leadership, 52*(2), 72-73.

Bailey. J., & Mighe, J. (1996). Reporting achievement at the secondary level: What and how. In T.R. Guskey (Ed.), *Communicating student learning: ASCD yearbook 1996.* Alexandria, VA: Association for Supervision and Curriculum Development.

Barell. J. (1992). Like an incredibly hard algebra problem: Teaching for metacognition. In A. L. Costa, J. A. Bellanca, & R. Fogarty (Eds.), *If minds matter: A forward to the future, Volume I* (pp. 257-266). Palatine, IL: IRI/Skylight Publishing.

Bellanca, J. (1992). *The cooperative think tank II.* Arlington Heights, IL: Skylight Training and Publishing Company.

Bellanca, J. (1992). How to grade if you must. In A. L. Costa, J. Bellanca, & R. Fogarty (Eds.), *If minds matter: A foreword to the future.* (pp. 297-310). Palatine, IL: IRI/Skylight Publishing.

Bickel, F. (1994). Student assessment: The project method revisited. *Clearing House, 68,* 40-42.

Blake (1998). Reflection, self-assessment and learning. *Clearing House, 72*(1), 13-17.

Bottoms, G., Pucel, D. J., & Phillips, I. (1997). *Designing challenging vocational courses.* Atlanta, GA: Southern Regional Education Board.

Bracey, G. W. (1993). Assessing the new assessments. *Principal, 72*(3), 34-36.

Brandt, R. (1994). We can do better. *Educational Leadership, 52*(2), 3.

Brookhart, S. M. (1997). Classroom assessment: Pervasive, pivotal, and primary. *National Forum: Phi Kappa Phi Journal 77*(4), 3, 5.

Brualdi, A. (1998). *Implementing performance assessment in the classroom.* ERIC/AE Digest Series EDO-TM. [On-line]. Available: http://www.ericae.net/digests/tm9807.htm

Brustein, M., & Mahler, M. (1994). *AVA guide to the school-to-work opportunities act.* Alexandria, VA: American Vocational Association.

Burke, K. (1999). *The mindful school: How to assess authentic learning* (3rd ed.). Arlington Heights, IL: Skylight Professional Development.

Burke, K. A. (Ed.) (1992). *Authentic assessment: A collection.* Palatine, IL: IRI/Skylight Publishing.

Burke, K. A. (1994). *The mindful school: How to assess authentic learning.* Palatine, IL: IRI/Skylight Publishing.

Butts, P. (1997). Finding alternative assessment resources on the web. *Technology Connection, 4*(7), 10-14.

California Assessment Collaborative. (1991). An introduction to the California assessment collaborative. *Performance Counts.* San Francisco, CA: Author.

Campbell, C. P. (1993). Manipulative performance tests. In L. G. Duenk (Ed.), *Improving vocational instruction.* South Holland, IL: The Goodheart-Willcox Company.

Chicago Public School System. (2001). *Instructional Intranet.* [On-line]. Available: http://intranet.cps.k12.il.us/

Cizek, G. J. (1996). Grades: The final frontier in assessment reform. *NASSP Bulletin 80*(584), 103-110.

Clarridge, P. B., & Whitaker, E. M. (1994). Implementing a new elementary progress report. *Educational Leadership, 52*(2), 7-9.

Cohen, A. M., & Brawer, F. B. (1969). *Measuring faculty performance.* Washington, DC: American Association of Junior Colleges.

Covey, S. R. (1989). *The seven habits of highly effective people: Restoring the character ethic.* New York: Simon & Shuster.

Cramond, B. (1994). We can trust creativity tests. *Educational Leadership, 52*(2), 70-71.

de Bono, E. (1983). The direct teaching of thinking as a skill. *Phi Delta Kappan, 64*(1). 703-708.

D'Urso, J. H. (1996). What happens when students take part in their own assessment. *Teaching and Change, 4*(1), 5-19.

Elliot, S. N. (1995). *Creating meaningful performance assessments.* Reston, VA: ERIC Clearinghouse on Disabilities and Gifted Education. ED 381985.

Eschermann, K. K. (1993). The individualized competency record. In L. G. Duenk (Ed.), *Improving vocational instruction.* South Holland, IL: The Goodheart-Willcox Company.

Far West Laboratory (1992). *Knowledge Brief* (Number 9). San Francisco, CA: Far West Laboratory for Educational Research and Development.

Far West Laboratory (1994). *Career-technical assessment program: Teacher guidebook* and *Career-technical assessment program: Student guidebook.* Sacramento, CA: California Department of Education, Career-Vocational Division and Far West Laboratory for Educational Research and Development.

Ferrara, S., & McTighe, J. (1992). Assessment: A thoughtful process. In A. L. Costa, J. Bellanca, & R. Fogarty (Eds.), *If minds matter: A foreword to the future, Vol. II* (pp. 337-348). Palatine, IL: IRI/Skylight Publishing.

Fingered, H. (1993). *It belongs to me: A guide to portfolio assessment in adult education programs.* Durham, NC: Literacy South.

Florida Merit Achievement Program. (1998). Tallahassee: Florida Department of Education.

Fogarty, R. (1994). *The mindful school: How to teach for metacognitive reflection.* Palatine, IL: IRI/Skylight Publishing.

Fogarty, R. (1998). *Balanced assessment.* Arlington Heights, IL: Skylight Training and Publishing.

Fogarty & Bellanca. (1987). *Pattern for thinking: Patterns for transfer.* Palatine, IL: IRI/Skylight Publishing.

Fogarty, R., Perkins. D., & Barell, J. (1992). *The mindful school: How to teach for transfer.* Palatine, IL: IRI/Skylight Publishing.

Frazier, D., & Paulson, F. (1992). How portfolios motivate reluctant writers. *Educational Leadership, 49*(8), 62-65.

Gardner, H. (1993). *Frames of mind: The theory of multiple intelligences.* New York: Basic Books.

Glaser, R. (1988). Cognitive and environment perspectives on assessing achievement. In *Assessment in the service of learning: Proceedings of the 1987 ETS Invitational Conference.* Princeton, NJ: Educational Testing Service.

Goodrich, H. (1997). Understanding Rubrics. *Educational Leadership, 54*(4), 14-17.

Gronlund, N. E., & Linn, R. L. (1995). *Measurement and evaluation in teaching* (7th ed.). New York: Macmillan.

Guskey, T. R. (1994). Making the grade: What benefits students? *Educational Leadership, 52*(2), 14-20.

Guskey, T. R. (1994). What you assess may not be what you get. *Educational Leadership, 51*(6), 51-54.

Hamayan, E. V. (1995). Approaches to alternative assessment. *Annual Review of Applied Linguistics, 15*, 212-226.

Hammond, L. D., Ancess, J., & Falk, B. (1995). *Authentic assessment in action: Studies of schools and students at work.* New York: Teachers College Press.

Han, E. P. (1995). Reflection is essential in teacher education. *Childhood Education, 71*(4), 228-230.

Herman, J. L. (1998, Dec.). The state of performance assessments. *School Adminstrator.* [On-line]. Available: http://www.aasa.org/publications/sa/1998_12/herman.htm

Herman, J. L., Aschbacher, P. R., & Winters, L. (1992). *A practical guide to alternative assessment.* Alexandria, VA: Association for Supervision and Curriculum Development.

Hills, J. R. (1991). Apathy concerning grading and testing. *Phi Delta Kappan, 72*(2) 540-545.

Hoachlander, E. G. (1998). Is there a better way to test? Assessing assessment. *Techniques, 73*(3), 14-16.

Hoachlander, E. G., & Rahn, M. L. (1994). National skill standards: Everyone agrees on the destination. Getting there is another story. *Vocational Education Journal, 69*(1), 21-23, 47.

Huck, R., Meyers, R., & Wilson, J. (1989). *Adapt: A developmental activity program for teachers* (2nd ed.). Pittsburgh, PA: Allegheny Intermediate Unit.

Huerta-Macias, A. (1995). Alternative assessment: Responses to commonly asked questions. *TESOL Journal, 5,* 8-10.

Hunt, J. (1996). Grades: Helpful or harmful? *Natural Life, 51,* 13.

Hyerle, D. (1996). *Visual tools for constructing knowlwedge.* Alexandria, VA: Association for Supervision and Curriculum Development.

Jamentz, K. (1994). Making sure that assessment improves performance. *Educational Leadership, 51*(6), 55-62.

Johnson, D. W., Johnson, R. T., & Holubec, E. J. (1990). *Circles of learning.* Edina, MN: Interaction Book Company.

Jones, K., Miederboff, J. W., & Wood, J. W. (1990). Adapting the teacher made test for students mainstreamed into vocational education. In K. H. Jones (Ed.), *Career education for transition: Curriculum implementation* (pp. 67-74). Athens, GA: The University of Georgia, Department of Vocational Education.

Kilpatrick, W. H. (1918). The project method: The use of the purposeful act in the educative process. *Teachers College Record, 19*(4), 319-315.

Knowles, J. G., Cole, A. L., & Presswood, C. S. (1994). *Through preservice teachers' eyes: Exploring field experience through narrative and inquiry.* New York: Macmillan College Publishing Company.

Kohl, H. (1998). *The discipline of hope: Learning from a lifetime of teaching.* New York: The New Press.

Kohn, A. (1994). Grading: The issue is not how but why. *Educational Leadership, 52*(2), 38-41.

Lund, J. (1997). Authentic assessment: Its development and application. *Journal of Physical Education, Recreation and Dance, 68*(7), 25-28.

Mabry, L. (1999). *Portfolios plus: A critical guide to alternative assessment.* Thousand Oaks, CA: Corwin Press.

Mannie, K. (2000). Coaching feedback, Its why and where. *Coach and Athletic Director, 69*(8), 18, 20.

Maoris, P. A. (1993). *The educator's guide to the Americans with Disabilities Act.* Alexandria, VA: American Vocational Association.

Marzano, R. J. (1994). Lessons from the field about outcome-based performance assessments. *Educational Leadership, 51*(6), 44-57.

Marzano, R. J., Pickering, D., & McTighe, J. (1993). *Assessing student outcomes.* Alexandria, VA: Association for Supervision and Curriculum Development.

Meyer, C. (1992). What's the difference between authentic and performance assessment? *Educational Leadership, 49*(8), 39-42.

Mitchell, R. (1992). *Testing for learning: How new approaches to evaluation can improve American schools.* New York: The Free Press, Division of Macmillian.

Moses, M. (1991). How to create a performance assessment. *Vocational Education Journal, 66*(6), 26.

Moskal, B. (2000). Scoring rubrics: What, when and how? *Practical Research & Evaluation, 7*(3).

National Advisory Commission on Work-Based Learning (1990). *Skill standards and certification: A fact sheet for action.* Washington, DC: Author.

National Center on Education and the Economy. (1990). *America's choice: High skills or low wages.* Washington, DC: Author.

National Commission on Secondary Vocational Education. (1984). *The unfinished agenda.* Columbus, MO: National Center for Research in Vocational Education.

National Commission on Testing and Public Policy. (1990). *From gatekeeper to gateway: Transforming testing in America.* Chestnut Hill, MA: National Commission on Testing and Public Policy, Boston College.

The national education goals report: Building a nation of learners. (1993). Washington, DC: National Education Goals Panel.

National Forum on Assessment. (1995). *Principles and indicators for student assessment systems.* Cambridge, MA: Fair Test.

National Skill Standards Board. (2001). [On-line]. Available: http://www.nssb.org

Neill, D. M. (1997). Transforming student assessment. *Phi Delta Kappan, 79*(1), 34-40.

Newman, F. (1991). Linking restructuring to authentic student achievement. *Phi Delta Kappan, 73*(6), 458-463.

O'Neil, H. F., Allread, K., & Baker, E. L. (1993). *Measurement of workforce readiness competencies: Design of prototype measures.* Los Angeles, CA: National Center for Research on Evaluation, Standards, and Student Testing (CRESST).

O'Neil, J. (1994). Aiming for new outcomes: the promise and the reality. *Educational Leadership, 51*(6), 6-10.

Parnell, D. (1990). *Dateline 2000: The new higher education agenda.* Washington, DC: American Association of Community Colleges.

Paulson, F. L., Paulson, P. R., & Meyer, C. A. (1991). What makes a portfolio a portfolio? *Educational Leadership, 48*(5), 60-63.

Perkins, D., & Salomon, G. (1992). The science and art of transfer. In A. L. Costa, J. A. Bellanca, & R. Fogarty (Eds.), *If minds matter: A foreward to the future, Volume I* (pp. 201-209). Palatine, IL: IRI/Skylight Publishing.

Piper, J. W., Smith, E., & Wiblin, J. H. (1994). Impacts of industry standards. *Vocational Education Journal, 69*(3), 39.

O'Conner, K. (1999). *The mindful school: How to grade for learning.* Arlington Heights, IL: Skylight Professional Development.

Ogle. D. (1986). K-W-L group instruction strategy. In A. Palincsar, D. Ogle, B. Jones, & E. Carr (Eds.), *Teaching techniques as thinking (Teleconference resource guide).* Alexandria, VA: Association for Supervision and Curriculum Development.

Ordover. E. L., & Annexsteine, L. T. (1999). *Ensuring access, equity, and quality for students with disabilities in school-to-work systems: A guide to federal law and policies.* Washington, DC: Center for Law and Education.

Popham, W. J. (1997). What's wrong and what's right with rubrics. *Educational Leadership 55*(2), 72.

Ravitch, D. (1992). In *Workforce 2020: Action report school-to-work opportunities national voluntary skill standards.* Leesburg, VA: National Association of Trade and Industrial Education.

Reedy, R. (1995). Formative and summative assessment: A possible alternative to the grading-reporting dilemma. *NASSP Bulletin, 79*(573), 47-51.

Resnick, L. B., & Resnick, D. P. (1991). Assessing the thinking curriculum: New tools for educational reform. In B. G. Gifford & M. C. Conner (Eds.), *Changing assessments: Alternative views of aptitude, achievement, and instruction* (pp. 37-75). Boston: Kluwer Academic Publishers.

Rojewski, J. W., Pollard, R. R., & Meers, G. D. (1990). Practices and attitudes of secondary industrial education teachers toward students with special needs. *Journal of Industrial Education, 27*(3), 17-32.

Rose, M. (1999). Make room for rubrics. *Instructor, 108*(6), 30-31.

Ryan, J. M., & Miyasaka, J. R. (1995). Current practices in testing and assessment: What is driving the changes? *NASSP Bulletin 79*(573), 1-10.

Scott, J. L. (1993). Cognitive Achievement Evaluation. In L. G. Duenk (Ed.), *Improving vocational curriculum* (pp. 145-172). South Holland, IL: The Goodheart-Willcox Company.

Secretary's Commission on Achieving Necessary Skills (SCANS). (1992). *Learning a living: A blueprint for high performance.* Washington, DC: U.S. Department of Labor.

Seely, M. M. (1994). The mismatch between assessment and grading. *Educational Leadership, 52*(2), 4-6.

Shephard, L. A. (1989). Why we need better assessments. *Educational Leadership 46*(7), 4-5.

Siegel, J., & Shaughnessy, M. F. (1994). An interview with Howard Gardner: Educating for understanding. *Phi Delta Kappan, 75*(7), 563-566.

Sperling, D. H. (1994). Assessment and reporting: A natural pair. *Educational Leadership, 52*(2), 10-13.

Stecher, B. M., Rahn, M. L., Ruby, A., Alt, M. N., Robyn, A., & Ward, B. (1997). *Using alternative assessment in vocational education.* Berkeley, CA: National Center for Research in Vocational Education.

Stiggins, R. J. (1988). Revitalizing classroom assessment: The highest instructional priority. *Phi Delta Kappan, 69*(5), 363-368.

Stiggins, R. J. (1991). Assessment literacy. *Phi Delta Kappan 72*(7), 534-539.

Stiggins, R. J. (1992). in R. Mitchell, *Testing for learning: How new approaches to evaluation can improve American schools.* New York: The Free Press, Division of Macmillian.

Stiggins, R. J. (1994). *Student-centered classroom assessment.* New York: Merrill.

Stiggins, R. J. (1999). Barriers to effective student assessments. *Education Digest 64*(6), 25-29.

Szetela, W., & Nicol, C. (1992). Evaluating problem solving in math. *Educational Leadership, 49*(8), 42-48.

Terenzi, P. T. (1989). Assessment with open eyes: Pitfalls in studying student outcomes. *Journal of Higher Education, 60*, 644-664.

Todd, S. S., Fiske, K. J., & Dopico, H. A. (1994). Vocational assessment for LEP students. *Journal for Vocational Special Needs Education, 16*(1), 16-28.

Torrance, E. P. (1994). *Norms-technical manual: Torrance tests of creative thinking.* Lexington, MS: Ginn and Co.

U. S. Congress, Office of Technology Assessment. (1992, February). *Testing in American schools: Asking the right questions.* (OTA-SET-519). Washington, DC: U. S. Government Printing Office.

Vavrus, L. (1990). Put portfolios to the test. *Instructor, 100*(1), 48-52.

VICA Professional. (1994). *National project reflects U.S. need for skill standards.* Leesburg, VA: Vocational Industrial Clubs of America, 28(8), 1-2.

Vitali, G. J. (1993). *Factors influencing teacher assessment and instructional practices in an assessment-driven educational reform.* Unpublished doctoral dissertation, University of Kentucky.

Vocational Education Weekly. (1994). Electronics association unveils voluntary industry skill standards. Alexandria, VA: American Vocational Association, *VI*(4), 1-3.

Vocational Education Weekly. (1994). Goals 2000 passes congress: President signs into law. Alexandria, VA: American Vocational Association, *VII*(5), 1-2.

Vocational Education Weekly. (1994). President signs school-to-work opportunities act into law. Alexandria, VA: American Vocational Association, *VII*(7), 1-2.

Weber, E. (1999). *Student assessment that works: A practical approach.* Boston: Allyn and Bacon.

Wiggins, G. (1989). A true test: Toward more authentic and equitable assessment. *Phi Delta Kappan, 70*(9), 703-714.

Wiggins, G. (1993). *Assessing student performance.* San Francisco: Jossey-Bass Publishers.

Wiggins, G. (1994). Toward better report cards. *Educational Leadership, 52*(2), 28-37.

Wiggins, G. (1997). Work standards: Why we need standards for instructional and assessment design. *NASSP Bulletin, 8*(590), 56-64.

Wiggins, G., & McTighe, J. (1998). *Understanding by design.* Alexandria, Virginia: Association for Supervision and Curriculum Development.

Workforce Skills Program. (1994). *The certificate of initial mastery: A primer.* New York: National Center on Education and the Economy.

Workforce 2020: Action report school-to-work opportunities and national voluntary skill standards. (1994). Leesburg, VA: National Association of Trade and Industrial Education.

Wolf, D. P. (1989). Portfolio assessment: Sampling student work. *Educational Leadership, 46*(7), 35-40.

Wolf, D. P. (1992). *What works in performance assessment. Proceedings of the 1992 CRESST Conference.* Los Angeles: UCLA Graduate School of Education.

Wolf, K. (1991). The school teacher's portfolio: Issues in design, implementation and evaluation. *Phi Delta Kappan, 73*(2), 129-36.

Worthen, B. R. (1993). Critical issues that will determine the future of alternative assessment. *Phi Delta Kappan, 74*(6), 444-454.

Zappardino, P. H. (1995). Fair test: Charting a course for testing reform. *Clearing House, 68*(4), 248-252.

Career and Technical Student Organizations

INTRODUCTION

Career and technical student organizations (CTSOs), formerly called vocational student organizations (VSOs) and called vocational and technical student organizations in the Carl D. Perkins Vocational and Technical Education Act of 1998, play an essential role in career and technical education programs. These organizations provide a unique mix of instructional programs and activities that provide middle and junior high, secondary, postsecondary, adult, and collegiate learners with opportunities for leadership and career development, motivation to learn and achieve, and recognition for effort and progress. The mission of CTSOs is to provide the best learning environment and preparation possible so learners can enhance their leadership and technical skill development in their chosen occupational areas. Today, 10 national CTSOs are recognized by the U.S. Department of Education.

Career and technical student organizations have been important to career and technical education for over 66 years. Soon after the passage of the Smith-Hughes Act of 1917, which provided federal support for vocational programs, leaders recognized the need to provide organized clubs for career and technical education learners that would provide them with social and recreational activities, motivate them to take full advantage of their instructional programs, and provide them opportunities to showcase their skills. A number of local student organizations developed and as career and technical education became more widespread, each major service area of career and technical education developed a national CTSO. In recent years, some of these organizations have changed their names and all of them have changed their programs, activities, and resources to better meet the career and leadership skill needs of all learners, including those from special populations.

Learners who participate in CTSOs, and especially learners from special populations, are provided with many benefits. These benefits include opportunities to develop positive self-concepts, social skills, problem-solving skills, communication skills, leadership skills, and occupational skills, all of which are valued universally by employers. Learners also benefit from the satisfaction of belonging to a student organization, which helps satisfy the basic need of belonging to group of people.

Even though CTSO activities are considered an integral part of the regular instructional program, a number of real or perceived barriers inhibit learners from active participation. The challenge of making these activities attractive and accessible to all learners is being accepted by leaders at the national, state, and local school levels. Today, an increasing number of learners from special populations are learning and developing important occupational, social, academic, and leadership skills through participation in CTSO programs and activities.

This chapter presents information about the development and characteristics of 10 CTSOs and a National Honor Society, the benefits and advantages of active participation in CTSOs, CTSO programs and activities, and how advisors and teachers can involve all learners in CTSOs. It presents information that can be used by career and technical education teachers and support personnel to make modifications or provide necessary support services to help learners from special populations participate in meaningful ways.

OUTLINE

OBJECTIVES

After completing this chapter, the reader should be able to accomplish the following:

1. Describe how CTSOs were developed and describe their purposes and their relationships to career and technical education programs.
2. Identify some of the benefits and advantages that are provided by active CTSOs for learners, teachers, schools, and communities.
3. Describe the federal legislation that has guaranteed all learners the right to participate in CTSO activities.
4. Identify some of the real and perceived barriers that learners from special populations can experience in becoming involved in CTSOs.
5. Identify some of the CTSO activities in which learners from special populations and other learners can participate.
6. Identify instructional strategies that teachers and CTSO support team members can use to increase the participation of learners from special populations in CTSO activities.
7. Identify modifications that can be made to regular CTSO activities that can increase the participation of learners from special populations.
8. Identify and describe the 10 CTSOs that are recognized by the U.S. Department of Education.
9. Describe the National Vocational-Technical Honor Society and how it differs from CTSOs.
10. Describe the characteristics, programs, and services provided by the CTSO in a chosen occupational field.
11. Describe how to involve all learners in a CTSO.
12. Identify some of the key advisor functions involved in providing leadership to a CTSO.
13. Identify and describe the common programs and activities of CTSOs.
14. Describe business and industry partnerships for CTSOs.
15. Describe how to involve learners from special populations in CTSOs.
16. Describe some of the activities of a CTSO support team for members of special populations.
17. Describe some of the specific advisor functions involved in working with learners from special populations.

TERMS

career and technical student organization (CTSO)	integral	special education teacher
chapter	interpreter	state association
chapter advisor	modification	state director
	self-esteem	support team

DEVELOPMENT OF CAREER AND TECHNICAL STUDENT ORGANIZATIONS

Student organizations have been a part of career and technical education programs since the passage of the Smith-Hughes Act of 1917, which provided federal support for vocational education programs. These organizations were not mentioned in the Smith-Hughes Act, but funds were provided for training teachers whose duties would later include advising and supervising vocational student organizations. The George-Barden Act of 1946 was the first to mention a vocational student organization, the vocational agriculture student organization that was founded in 1928. This act stated that funds could be used for vocational agriculture teacher activities related to the vocational student organization. Four years later in 1950, another federal law, the Act to Incorporate the Future Farmers of America (commonly known as PL 740), officially chartered the Future Farmers of America (FFA). This established the integral relationship of the organization to the educational instruction program and directly involved the U.S. Office of Education in supporting vocational student organizations. This act set the precedent for all VSOs to be recognized as essential components of a quality vocational education program (Vaughn, Vaughn, & Vaughn, 1993, p. 4).

Other federal acts included references to VSOs. The Vocational Education Act of 1963 along with its amendments of 1968 and 1976 broadened vocational education by eliminating specific occupational categories and provided a specific definition of vocational instruction that included activities for VSOs. The amendments of the 1963 Act reaffirmed that these organizations were an essential part of instruction and specified which activities were to be considered integral (for which federal funds could be used) and which activities were not (Vaughn, 1999, p. 4).

The Carl D. Perkins Vocational Education Act of 1984 (PL 98-524) included vocational student organization activities in its definition of vocational education. The definition of vocational education according to the act was organized educational programs directly related to preparing learners for paid or unpaid employment in such fields as agriculture; business occupations; marketing and distributive occupations; technical and emerging occupations; modern industrial and agriculture arts; and trade and industrial occupations or for additional preparation for a career in such fields and occupations requiring other than a baccalaureate or advanced degree, with vocational student organization activities as an integral part of the program.

Vocational student organizations, as defined by the Carl D. Perkins Vocational and Applied Technology Act of 1990, were those organizations for individuals enrolled in vocational education programs that engaged in activities as an integral part of the instructional program. Such organizations may have state and national units that aggregate the work and purposes of instruction in vocational education at the local level (American Vocational Association [AVA], 1990).

Career and technical student organizations were called vocational and technical student organizations in the Carl D. Perkins Vocational and Technical Act of 1998 and were defined as the following: "organizations for individuals enrolled in a vocational and technical education program that engages in vocational and technical activities as an integral part of the instructional program." These organizations may have state and national units that aggregate the work and purposes of instruction in vocational and technical education at the local level. Section 135 of the 1998 Perkins Act includes assisting vocational student organizations in its permissible uses of local funds (AVA, 1998, p.92).

Finally, the School-to-Work Opportunities Act (STWOA) of 1994 continued the recognition of the value of VSOs by including them in the definition of local partnerships. A local partnership consists of an entity that is responsible for local school-to-work opportunities programs consisting of employers, representatives of local educational agencies, local postsecondary educational institutions (including representatives of area career and technical education schools where applicable), local educators (such as teachers, counselors, or administrators), and representatives of labor organizations or non-managerial employee representatives and learners and may include such entities as vocational student organizations. The act requires states to include in their state plans information on how they will continue to obtain the involvement of the statewide school-to-work opportunities system of employers and other interested parties, such as locally elected officials, vocational student organizations, state or regional cooperative education associations, and human service agencies.

The National Vocational Advisory Council on Vocational Education in its historic 7th Report (1972) acknowledged the work that vocational student organizations had done and made six recommendations to the U.S. Secretary of Health, Education and Welfare for the further development of these organizations. Undoubtedly influenced by the advisory committee report, the U.S. Office of Education (now the Department of Education) recognized the vital role that vocational student organizations play in vocational education and developed a policy statement that acknowledged that these organization activities were intracurricular and that federal monies could be used to support certain activities of the organization.

On February 11, 1990 The U. S. Department of Education released a policy statement describing its position on vocational student organizations as being an integral part of vocational-technical instructional programs. A new U.S. Department of Education policy statement was released in 1999 identifying the 10 nationally recognized career and technical student organizations and affirming continuing support for these organizations as an integral part of vocational and technical education instructional programs. See Figure 10-1.

In 1996 the National Association of State Directors of Vocational Technical Education Consortium issued a similar policy statement to the one issued by the U.S. Department of Education in 1990. This statement was entitled *Statement of Policy: Career and Technical Student Organizations*. This policy statement was revised in 1999 to reflect changes in the name of vocational student organizations to career and technical student organizations. The policy statement recognizes 10 career and technical student organizations that are integral to regular career and technical education programs and provide learners with employabil-

ity skills, business partners, community outreach opportunities, school-to-career solutions, and comprehensive programs in career majors (The National Coordinating Council for Career and Technical Student Organizations, 1999).

In 1998, the 105th Congress of the United States recognized the importance of the FFA as an integral part of the program of vocational agriculture and passed Public Law (PL) 105-225, which included technical amendments to

---

Policy of the United States Department of Education For Career and Technical Student Organizations

The United States Department of Education maintains a close relationship with ten career and technical student organizations and welcomes their cooperation and support in strengthening programs of vocational and technical education. Recognizing that the past performance and future potential of these ten organizations are compatible with the overall purposes and objectives of education today, the United States Department of Education strongly endorses their objectives and seeks to involve their thinking in the improvement of vocational and technical education.

In view of this, these policies represent the position of the United States Department of Education:

1. The United States Department of Education recognizes the educational programs and philosophies embraced by the following career and technical student organizations as being an integral part of vocational and technical education instructional programs:

    Business Professionals of America
    National DECA
    Future Business Leaders of America-Phi Beta Lambda
    National FFA Organization
    Family, Career and Community Leaders of America
    Health Occupations Students of America
    National Postsecondary Agricultural Student Organization
    National Young Farmer Educational Association
    Technology Student Association
    SkillsUSA-VICA

2. The United States Department of Education recognizes the concept of total student development as being necessary for all vocational and technical education students to assume successful roles in society and to enter the labor market.

3. The United Stated Department of Education will facilitate technical and supportive services to assist career and technical student organizations through State agencies in their efforts to improve the quality and relevance of instruction, develop student leadership, enhance citizenship responsibilities, overcome sex and race discrimination and stereotyping, and serve students of special populations, especially with respect to efforts to increase the participation of students who are members of special populations.

4. The United States Department of Education recognizes the responsibility for vocational and technical instructional programs and related activities, including career and technical student organizations, rests with the State and local education agencies.

5. The United States Department of Education approves of Federal and State grant funds for vocational and technical education to be used by the States to give leadership and support to these career and technical student organizations and activities directly related to established vocational and technical education instructional programs at all levels under provisions of approved State plans for vocational and technical education.

Efforts on the part of the State and local education agencies to recognize and encourage the growth and development of these career and technical student organizations are highly important and deserve the support of all leaders in American education.

Figure 10-1. The U.S. Department of Education policy statement recognizing CTSOs as an integral part of career and technical education programs.

PL 81-740 passed in 1950 that granted a federal charter to the Future Farmers of America (FFA). These new amendments spelled out in detail the purposes of the FFA as a corporation and included information on membership, governing body, national officers, powers, exclusive rights to its name, seals, emblems, badges, and other operational information. This new law reveals that Congress recognizes the value of CTSOs like the FFA in the preparation of youth for careers in the workforce.

Federal legislation has provided the foundation for career and technical education programs, and the inclusion of career and technical student organizations in legislative acts and the support of the U.S. Department of Education have made it possible for these organizations to become a vital part of local career and technical education programs. Career and technical education teachers are expected to include in their curriculum information and activities that relate directly to these CTSOs.

Over the years, each major service area of career and technical education, such as vocational agriculture and trade and industrial education, has developed a national student organization to serve learners enrolled in their programs.

The vocational agriculture educators were the first to establish a CTSO by founding the Future Farmers of America in 1928. By 1988, nine other national CTSOs had been formed (*Vocational Student Organizations: A Reference Guide*, 1990). Today, CTSOs are more than simply an organized activity to provide social and recreational opportunities for learners; they are an integral part of every career and technical education program. They have become a major instructional tool for teachers to provide the leadership, citizenship, and occupational skills and knowledge required to prepare learners for jobs and careers in our fast-changing technological society. They have become the highly visible component of career and technical education in America and therefore have provided the vehicle for business, industry, and community involvement in the educational process in our nation's secondary and postsecondary schools.

Federal Legislation and Career and Technical Student Organizations

Since the first national vocational legislation in 1917 known as the Smith-Hughes Act and continuing today under the Carl D. Perkins Vocational and Technical Education Act of 1998, the federal government, in partnership with state departments of education and local educational agencies, has provided funding for vocational and technical education programs. Today the field of vocational and technical education has evolved into career and technical education. The Perkins Act provides funding for career and technical education through the years 1999-2003 and contains mandates and options for state and local educational agencies that CTSOs can help carry out (The National Coordinating Council for Career and Technical Student Organizations, 1999).

According to this act, mandated use of funds for state leadership activities include (1) professional development, (2) support for career and technical education programs that improve academic and career and technical skills of learners, and (3) support for forging partnerships between local education agencies, higher education, adult education, employers, labor, and parents, which encourages learners to achieve state academic standards. Professional development activities at state, regional, and national conferences are provided by CTSOs. These programs and activities are an integral part of the regular instructional programs, which help learners develop both academic and technical skills. Career and technical student organizations operate by establishing partnerships with education, business, industry, labor unions, community leaders, and parents to support their programs and activities (The National Coordinating Council for Career and Technical Student Organizations, 1999).

The Perkins Act also provides states with options to use federal funds to improve career guidance, support CTSOs, and support business/education partnerships. Each CTSO has programs and activities that are integrated into the curriculum to enhance the career development of learners. States have the flexibility of using funds to support CTSO activities, such as travel for chapter advisors and learners and the purchase of instructional materials, as long as the expenditure of these funds leads to improvement of the career and technical education programs. These organizations provide opportunities for learners to become involved in school-to-work programs, which operate as partnerships between education and business and industry (The National Coordinating Council for Career and Technical Student Organizations, 1999).

Local educational agencies also have mandated the use of funds specified in the Perkins Act. These uses include strengthening the academic and career and technical skills of learners and providing learners with a variety of experiences in an industry. CTSOs are an integral part of career and technical education programs at the local school level and their integrated programs and activities provide learners with real-world learning experiences and recognition for achievement. Learners can become involved in school-to-work programs such as apprenticeship, cooperative education, or job shadowing to learn all aspects of a chosen career area while developing leadership and technical skills through integrated CTSO activities (The National Coordinating Council for Career and Technical Student Organizations, 1999).

Local education agencies can choose leadership activities listed under optional use of funds in the Perkins Act including (1) involving parents, business, and labor organizations in the design, implementation, and evaluation of career and technical education programs, (2) providing career guidance, (3) providing work-related experiences, and (4) supporting CTSOs. Organization programs and activities require the involvement of parents and business and industry leaders to make them successful, such as parents serving as chaperons for leadership conferences and business and industry leaders assuming the leadership roles in designing and conducting competitive events. All CTSOs have enhancing career guidance and career development as a goal or objective. Members and learners can develop work experience in a realistic work environment through participation in school-to-work programs like apprenticeship and cooperative education. Local education agencies, like states, can use federal funds to support certain CTSO activities provided the activities enhance the quality of career and technical education programs (The National Coordinating Council for Career and Technical Student Organizations, 1999).

Purposes of Career and Technical Student Organizations

Most CTSOs were formed to serve learners in a specific career and technical service area with the exception of Future Business Leaders of America (FBLA), which was originally open to all business education learners at the secondary level. All CTSOs carry on activities as an integral part of their respective career and technical education programs. All CTSOs have similar purposes and focus on the following areas:

- developing leadership skills
- cultivating personal growth
- exploring careers
- improving home and family
- developing citizenship and patriotism
- improving scholarship and vocational preparation
- improving school and community
- developing respect for the dignity of work
- developing high ethical and moral standards
- participating in cooperative efforts
- developing creativity
- developing social skills and worthy use of leisure time

Each CTSO has a motto and creed stating its basic beliefs and guiding its actions. Also, each CTSO has an emblem and official colors that are symbolic of its organization and serve to remind members of its purpose.

One of the basic needs of individuals is a sense of belonging, a feeling of being accepted. CTSOs provide the basic vehicle for learners to meet this need of belonging and becoming a part of an organized group. Other reasons why learners join groups or organizations are recognition, expanded opportunities, helping others, making new friends, security, being involved in a worthwhile cause, developing leadership abilities, and self expression. They provide opportunities for learners to meet friends, to work together with learners in a specific interest field, to gain individual and group recognition for achievements, to develop leadership and occupational skills required for entrance into a chosen career, and to render services to school and community by making them better places in which to learn, live, and work. Learners who belong to CTSOs are afforded an opportunity to compete in leadership and skills contests that give them a valuable learning experience in which they can demonstrate their knowledge and skills before competent technical chairpersons and judges from business and industry. These leadership and skills contests also showcase learner achievement before potential employers in a realistic work setting.

Straight talk from a learner who experienced involvement in a CTSO clarifies the value of student organizations. Katrina Miller describes her experience of attending a Technology Student Association (TSA) meeting at the invitation of a friend at the start of seventh grade. The meeting was a dialogue between learners and CTSO advisers. The TSA advisor gave her a nudge that made all the difference in her education and career outlook for the future. She was encouraged to attend the TSA Fall Leadership Conference where she listened to a presentation from a former TSA president who provided an overview of the offices she had held and her achievements in TSA competitive events. Katrina noticed how poised and passionate the former TSA learner was and she knew right then that she could do these things too. Katrina credits her career and technical courses, involvement in TSA activities, and the influence of her TSA adviser with helping her to become technologically literate, to acquire confidence in her abilities, and to move forward in pursuit of her education and career goals (Miller, 2000).

The members of SkillsUSA-VICA (the national organization for learners enrolled in trade, technical, industrial, and health occupations programs) approved a VICA Bill of Rights in 1992 that can serve as a compact for quality for all career and technical education students. This bill represents an agreement between teachers and learners as they work together in the interest of their schools and communities. SkillsUSA-VICA's 10 basic rights are as follows:

1. To be respected for our occupational choices;
2. To meet occupational standards set by employers and to be proficient in workplace basics;
3. To receive a world-class academic education;
4. To earn credentials and degrees that qualify us for further education and work;
5. To receive career guidance that fits our interests and aptitudes and allows for freedom of choice;
6. To work in the occupations for which we have trained;
7. To study in safe and stimulating schools;
8. To serve our communities;
9. To learn from competent instructors committed to the success of their learners;
10. To meet face to face with business, industry, and organized labor.

Relationship of Career and Technical Student Organizations to Career and Technical Programs

Career and technical student organizations are not "clubs" or extracurricular organizations to which only a few select individuals belong. Rather, a CTSO is a powerful instructional tool that works best when integrated into the career and technical education curriculum and classroom by a teacher who is committed to the total development of learners. Career and technical education teachers have long recognized the need to provide learners with more than technical knowledge and skills; they recognize the need to provide authentic, interesting activities for learners so the learners can develop personal, social, leadership, and employability skills (*Vocational Student Organizations: A Reference Guide*, 1990).

While a few educators may view CTSOs as extracurricular organizations (organization activities take place outside of the instructional program), most recognize CTSO activities as an integral part of career and technical education programs that contribute to the comprehensive learning experiences of learners. In actual practice, CTSO activities are scheduled along with other classroom and laboratory learning experiences. CTSO activities often complement and reinforce learning experiences for the learner, thereby adding another dimension to the instructional program.

All learners, including learners from special populations, can participate and benefit from CTSO activities. The overriding purpose of all student organizations is to provide learning experiences, opportunities, and recognition for achievement that contributes to the maximum development of individual learners. Of no less importance is the preparation of learners for active participation in our democratic and free enterprise society.

There are a number of techniques that CTSO advisors can use to integrate the CTSO into the regular career and technical education classroom. The following techniques were presented in *Vocational Student Organizations: A Reference Guide* (1990) as typical of the role that the CTSO can play in the classroom and laboratory. The advisor can do the following:

- Review professional oaths as well as the oaths of CTSOs.
- Elect chapter officers and use them to call the class to order, take roll call, maintain financial records, monitor class protocol and member behavior, prepare bulletin board and posters, and prepare articles and news releases.
- Establish committees for CTSO and classroom functions and encourage all learners to participate in them.
- Use parliamentary procedures to enable the class to arrive at decisions in an orderly manner.
- Prepare chapter newsletters so learners can practice many important communication skills.
- Emphasize professional dress and grooming as important to personal and career success.
- Sponsor field trips and involve CTSO members in planning and coordinating the trips.
- Encourage members to attend civic, professional, or trade meetings to learn the importance of contributing to the community and their profession. Have members share their experiences in class with others learners who were unable to attend.

- Assign CTSO members the task of interviewing selected business and industry leaders and have them share their findings with other learners. Learners can learn how to develop and use interview questionnaires to gather data in an organized manner.
- Assign learners the task of preparing for and delivering extemporaneous talks. The CTSO contest rating sheets for extemporaneous speaking can be used to evaluate and provide feedback to the presenter.
- Assign learners the task of preparing for and presenting a talk to community groups. Most CTSOs have a prepared speech contest rating instrument that can be used to prepare learners. Communication skills will help them accelerate their career advancement.
- Arrange for learners to participate in mock interviews to enable them to better market themselves in actual job interviews.
- Encourage members to participate in CTSO team competitions, which build enthusiasm and provide opportunities for them to learn to cooperate with other members of a group.
- Encourage members to get involved in collecting funds for worthwhile organizations (i.e., Muscular Dystrophy, March of Dimes).
- Encourage members to help prepare for implementing the Special Olympics in their community.
- Encourage members to adopt a mentally disabled or elderly person and attend to this person's needs.
- Encourage members to become involved in the many worthwhile school and community projects to provide them a variety of learning experiences. Involvement also demonstrates that CTSO members support their schools and community.

General Characteristics of Career and Technical Student Organizations

The organizational structure of CTSOs is similar to a national organization, state association, and local chapter. At the national level, they are incorporated and listed under the Internal Revenue Service code for nonprofit organizations. They are governed by a board of directors and managed by an executive director and staff who execute the policies established by the organization. DECA, a national association of marketing education learners and a learner-directed CTSO, is governed by a set of national officers who form the National Executive Council. The council receives direction from a delegate assembly that convenes annually at the national conference. Most CTSOs have a third organizational form, a foundation, which enables business, industry, organizations, and individuals to cooperate in enhancing and furthering the their programs.

State CTSOs are chartered by their national organizations and consist of a set of state officers who form the executive council under the guidance of a state director.

This is usually a member of the state Department of Education in the CTSO service area. State associations support the national organization's goals, purposes, policies, and activities and provide leadership to organizational structures below it such as districts, regions, areas, and local chapters.

Local chapters are learner-directed through a set of elected officers under the guidance of the career and technical education teacher who serves as the advisor. Local chapters also plan programs of work that list the various activities required to accomplish the purposes of the organization and the national program of work.

The activities that make up programs of work are usually selected from the following major categories: professional, leadership, personal growth, civic and community, social, service, safety, public relations, cooperation, financial, and scholastic or educational.

Membership in CTSOs is open to all learners enrolled in career and technical education programs or those who have been enrolled during the school year. Most CTSOs have several types of membership that include active member, honorary member, alumni member, associate member, professional member, and collegiate member. Active members are those learners presently enrolled in career and technical education programs and those who have been enrolled during the school year.

Members have many opportunities available to them to develop the knowledge and skills required to become leaders in their chosen career fields. Leadership, communication, and social skills can be developed through participation in meetings, conferences, special seminars, and a variety of career fields. Leadership, occupational skills, and knowledge can be further developed through participation in the individual competition, team competition, and chapter events offered by most CTSOs. Winners in these competitive events are recognized in a variety of ways. They receive trophies, plaques, medals, pins, certificates, newspaper coverage, and recognition at meetings and banquets. Members can be identified by their official dress consisting of a colored blazer, sweater, or jacket with the emblem of the organization attached to the left breast pocket, white shirts and blouses, appropriately colored tie, slacks, skirts, shoes, and socks.

The national CTSO office provides many interesting and informative materials to support local chapter activities. All CTSOs publish learner magazines such as *Teen Times*, the official magazine of the Family, Career and Community Leaders of America (FCCLA); *School Scene*, the magazine of the TSA; the *VICA Professional*, the official newsletter for secondary learners of SkillsUSA-VICA; *Tomorrow's Business Leader* of the Future Business Leaders of America (FBLA); and *New Horizons*, the magazine for FFA members. CTSOs also provide communications for advisors like *Connect*, the newsletter for advisers of SkillsUSA-VICA, and *Adviser Hotline* of FBLA.

National CTSOs have additional publications and mediated materials listed in educational materials catalogs such as newspapers, newsletters, brochures, posters, instructional aids, and a wide variety of chapter materials such as handbooks, computerized programs, videotapes, competitive events guides, and recognition certificates. All CTSOs have Internet sites that contain information about the organization, and some have their publications catalog on-line like SkillsUSA-VICA's *Educational Materials Catalog*. National CTSOs also work with suppliers, such as the SkillsUSA-VICA supply service, and the Midwest Trophy Manufacturing Company, Inc., to provide other CTSO support materials such as blazers and other clothing, pennants, awards, certificates, pins, and other memorabilia.

BENEFITS AND ADVANTAGES OF CAREER AND TECHNICAL STUDENT ORGANIZATIONS

When CTSOs are organized as an integral part of an educational program and when that organization is properly implemented, they can be very influential in the following ways:
- increasing program enrollment
- enhancing program visibility
- involving employers and community leaders
- securing commitment of important support people and groups
- motivating both career and technical education teachers and learners to higher levels of individual and group performance
- recognizing effort and achievement
- providing the means by which personal and career goals become achievable for all career and technical education learners (*Vocational Student Organizations: A Reference Guide*, 1990)

Benefits to Learners

Harris and Sweet (1981) and Vaughn (1999) identified a number of benefits provided through active participation in CTSOs. These benefits apply to all learners, including learners from special populations. These benefits are as follows:
- civic responsibility
- interest in vocational education
- leadership skills
- development of social skills through committee work and recreational activities
- respect for the dignity of work
- effective use of free time
- understanding of employer/employee relationships
- spirit of healthy competition
- vocational understanding
- recognition and prestige
- enthusiasm for learning

- firsthand knowledge of the democratic process
- home improvement skills
- employability skills
- sense of independence and accomplishment
- opportunity to plan and carry out an idea
- opportunity to see adult sponsors as role models
- self-improvement and scholarship
- occupational competence

This list of benefits includes most of the desirable behaviors needed by all learners, but several of them reflect critical needs of many learners from special populations, notably a sense of independence and accomplishment and an enthusiasm for learning.

Sarkees (1983) identified some advantages of participating in CTSO activities that are important for learners from special populations. Participation helps the learner to build self-confidence, develop interpersonal relationship skills, improve vocational-related and employability skills, increase motivation to learn, gain valuable information about citizenship and living independently in our democratic society, develop leadership skills, and participate in effective learner-teacher interaction.

Organization activities were developed so that the learner could improve self-concept, develop respect for work and pride in a chosen occupation, develop high ethical and moral values, create an understanding and appreciation of the work ethic, and develop a sense of cooperation with others in accomplishing chapter activities and school and work assignments. Active participation in CTSO activities helps learners from special populations to develop a strong identity, a feeling of belonging, a sense of independence, and a healthy relationship with fellow learners and adults (Sarkees, 1983).

The personal, social, and academic benefits of involvement in CTSOs go hand in hand. Learners from special populations get to know other learners and their teachers on a personal basis through individual activities and cooperative teamwork. At the same time they strengthen their commitment to the goals, objectives, and learning experiences of the career and technical education program and become motivated to succeed in classroom and laboratory activities (Sarkees, 1983). Learners can also expand their network of contacts by participating in CTSO meetings, conferences, and competitive events. This network may prove helpful in obtaining and holding a job.

These organizations reinforce workplace basics. *Vocational Student Organizations: A Reference Guide* (1990) provides the following information on how participation in activities helps a learner develop workplace basics:

- Knowing how to learn–CTSOs encourage learner-directed learning and experimentation, thereby requiring members to absorb, process, and apply new information quickly and effectively. Employers place great value on people who are capable of learning on their own.
- Reading, writing, and computation–CTSOs provide a variety of opportunities to apply and refine reading, writing, and computational skills by operating the learner-led

"chapter" and by participating in the professional development and national competitive events programs.
- Communicating effectively-CTSOs encourage the application and refinement of speaking, listening, and feedback skills in chapter meetings, committee work, and in preparation for competitive events.
- Creative thinking and problem solving-CTSO members are provided with opportunities to practice and refine their problem-solving skills through groups or committees conducting chapter management activities. By learning how to work cooperatively as members of a team, members will be better prepared when they become employees to discover new solutions to existing problems that might otherwise serve as barriers to improved quality of products, productivity, and competitiveness.
- Personal management-CTSOs contribute greatly to the improvement of a member's personal management skills. They encourage heightened self-esteem, goal-setting, and goal achievement and provide career direction, education, and training analysis. They also provide real situations in which more "authentic skills" for creating a productive and competitive workforce can be developed.
- Group effectiveness-CTSOs are "group-oriented" and chapter activities provide opportunities for members to develop and refine interpersonal, negotiating, and team-building skills. A major objective of these organizations is to help members develop skills and attitudes that can be successfully applied in the workplace to resolve problems and foster innovation. Members who have developed these essential teamwork skills will achieve the flexibility and adaptability that America's workforce must have to remain competitive in the global economy.
- Influencing others-Exhibiting leadership potential is the hallmark of CTSOs. A major purpose of all CTSOs is to develop the leadership abilities of its members. Leadership is a learned skill that must be practiced and refined in real situations. Active involvement in organization activities provides members with numerous opportunities to develop, practice, and refine their leadership skills. In the workplace of today, leadership skills are among the most important workplace basics.

Benefits to Teachers, Schools, and Communities

In addition to providing many benefits to career and technical education learners, CTSOs provide benefits to teachers, schools, and communities. Through a CTSO, a teacher gains a valuable teaching tool, opportunities for self-improvement, opportunities to enrich instructional experiences, a means of adding excitement to daily routines, a valuable learner recruitment tool, publicity for the career and technical education program, opportunities to expand business and industry contacts through competitive events, and opportunities to improve the total school program.

Benefits to schools include motivating learners to apply themselves more to school and learning, promoting community involvement in school activities, and bringing school and life into closer harmony. Communities also receive benefits such as better-prepared citizens, services provided to citizens in need, and a source of young people who have leadership and employment skills. Finally, the United States benefits by having a source of competent workers who can work in team environments to solve problems, introduce innovation, and produce products of high quality in the most efficient and cost-effective manner possible.

BARRIERS TO INVOLVEMENT IN CAREER AND TECHNICAL STUDENT ORGANIZATIONS

With so many benefits and opportunities provided by CTSOs, it is difficult to imagine why all career and technical education learners do not belong to student organizations in their career and technical service areas. There are many reasons for this finding: (1) some career and technical education learners are denied the opportunity to become members because local school administrators too often consider CTSO activities disruptive to more formal and fashionable education and discourage their establishment (National Advisory Council on Vocational Education, 1972) and (2) career and technical education teachers often ignore the vast potential of an active student organization as an integral part of their instructional program. Career and technical education teachers give the following reasons for not starting a CTSO in their classes:

- Dues are too high for learners to pay.
- School activity periods are not provided.
- Transportation is not available for after-school activities.
- CTSO activities take up too much after-school and weekend time.
- Learners are not interested in activities.
- Parents are not supportive.
- Learners are not likely to take career and technical education courses the entire year.
- Teachers are accountable for meeting curriculum objectives and have little time for CTSOs.
- Obtaining approval for fund-raising events is difficult.
- There is a lack of preparation to become an effective CTSO advisor.
- There is a lack of state Department of Education support for CTSOs as an integral component of a quality career and technical education program.

Another major barrier limiting learner participation in career and technical student organizations is the negative attitudes and myths that some learners, career and technical educators, and administrators have toward active participation of learners from special populations in CTSO activities. Traditionally, learners from special populations avoided pursuing membership in these organizations because they lacked the motivation and self-confidence and felt inadequate to compete with other learners in organization activities, such as in competitive events. Other perceived factors that discourage learners from special populations from becoming involved in CTSO activities were identified by Birchenall and Wanat (1981) and are as follows:

- a tendency toward selective and elitist membership
- negative attitudes of administrators and supervisors concerning the integration and preparation of learners from special populations
- emphasis on competition and winning instead of learner development
- insufficient or inappropriate activities for learners from special populations
- lack of recruitment and public relations activities to encourage learners from special populations to join
- insufficient support services to accommodate the special needs of learners with disabilities
- an attempt to create separate student organizations for learners from special populations

Of all the barriers mentioned, probably the major one is simply an unwillingness on the part of some teachers to implement a CTSO in their classrooms even though it is considered an integral part of a quality career and technical education program. Certainly there are challenges that confront teachers who are considering establishing a student organization, such as learning how to get a chapter started and reviewing all of the materials available from the national office about the organization in their career and technical area. There are challenges in learning how to become an advisor and how to truly integrate the organization activities into the career and technical education program. There are challenges of how to modify CTSO activities to allow participation of learners from special populations. But then, there are challenges associated with any endeavor that is worthwhile. One teacher addressed the problems associated with CTSOs this way: "Teachers who feel that a CTSO is a pain in the neck are shortchanging their students and denying them the opportunity to gain the qualities necessary for success that are often impossible to develop in the regular classroom alone. You ask if the benefits are worth the problems? You bet they are." (Butler, 1981, p. 49)

FEDERAL LEGISLATION FOR LEARNERS FROM SPECIAL POPULATIONS

Federal legislation enacted in the past 20 years supports the rights of disabled individuals to become regular participants in CTSOs. Section 504 of the Rehabilitation Act of 1973 (PL 93-112) mandated that no otherwise qualified handicapped individual shall be excluded from participation in programs or activities supported with federal funds. Since career and technical education programs are partially supported with federal funds and CTSOs are integrated into career and technical education programs, this legislation applies to them (Sarkees, 1983).

The Education of All Handicapped Children Act (PL 94-142) specified that states shall use the mandated set-aside funds to assist handicapped learners to participate in regular career and technical education programs. This legislation also contains the concept of least restrictive environment. Many learners with disabilities are capable of succeeding in regular career and technical education programs, given appropriate support, and are capable of participating in CTSO activities (Sarkees, 1983).

Part B of the Individuals with Disabilities Education Act of 1975 required that every disabled child between 3 and 21 be provided with a free public education. It is very prescriptive and includes integration of disabled learners and the provision of assisting devices and services to help these learners succeed in regular programs, including CTSOs (Morrissey, 1993).

The Vocational Amendments of 1976 (PL 94-482) stated that CTSOs must be listed in state annual and five-year vocational education plans and that these organizations should be an integral part of vocational education supervised by qualified personnel. The amendments state that participation in CTSOs should be available to all learners in the instructional program without regard to membership in any student organization (Leonard & Elston, 1981).

The Carl D. Perkins Vocational and Applied Technology Act of 1990 required a focus on serving the needs of special populations including disabled learners. While much of the text of the Perkins Act addresses how funds are to be spent, it requires states to provide for "full participation" by members of special populations, including disabled learners in career and technical education programs including CTSOs.

The Americans with Disabilities Act (ADA) of 1990, which took effect in 1992, is the most comprehensive enactment barring discrimination against disabled individuals. The ADA is based on five key principles that include a focus on the individual, integration, equal opportunity, physical accessibility, and the provision of reasonable accommodation and auxiliary aids and services (Morrisey, 1993).

The Individuals with Disabilities Education Act (IDEA) Amendments of 1997, PL 105-17, brought many changes to PL 94-142, which was passed in 1975. It also fine-tuned the processes already laid out for schools and parents to follow in planning for and providing special education and related services to children and youth with disabilities. This included assisting them in actively participating in CTSOs as an integral part of career and technical programs (National Information Center for Children and Youth with Disabilities, 1998).

The Carl D. Perkins Vocational and Technical Education Act of 1998 eliminated some of the specific requirements for serving special populations, relegating them to other binding legislation such as IDEA. However, the act requires that state assessment must evaluate how needs of special populations are being met and how programs are designed to enable special populations to meet state levels of performance and prepare them for further learning or high skill, high wage careers. The act also requires local educational agency plans to describe how they will review, identify, and adopt strategies to overcome barriers to access and success for members of special populations. This can be interpreted to include providing assistance to special population learners in overcoming barriers that might exist to active participation in CTSOs (AVA, 1998).

The Workforce Investment Act (WIA) of 1998 provides for youth requiring assistance to complete an educational program or to secure and retain employment. The act identifies youth activities and elements that local areas can use to assist youth in preparing for employment or postsecondary education. It may be possible for learners falling under provisions of the WIA to receive economic support to enable them to participate fully in secondary and postsecondary school CTSO activities, such as when traveling to conferences and competing in events (Kaufman & Wills, 1999).

Clearly, learners from special populations are guaranteed the right to participate in CTSO activities if CTSOs are available in their career and technical education programs in local schools.

TEN NATIONALLY RECOGNIZED CAREER AND TECHNICAL STUDENT ORGANIZATIONS AND A NATIONAL HONOR SOCIETY

The United States Department of Education recognizes 10 national CTSOs and considers them to be an integral part of career and technical education instructional programs. These CTSOs share many common goals such as developing the leadership, cooperation, and citizenship of their members. They are similarly organized with national executive directors and staff, state directors, and local CTSO chapters guided by advisors (career and technical education teachers). They are provided for career and technical learners and are governed by learners through the democratic process. All of these student organizations have unique activities and instructional materials that can enhance career and technical education instructional programs at the local level. The National Vocational-Technical Honor Society (NY-THS) has been recognizing outstanding learner achievement in vocational and technical programs since 1984 and shares many of the same goals and purposes as the CTSOs.

Ten National CTSOs

The United States Department of Education issued a policy statement on CTSOs in 1990 and a revised policy statement in 1998 in which the following 10 CTSOs were recognized as being an integral part of career and technical education instructional programs:

1. National FFA Organization (FFA) (formerly Future Farmers of America)

2. Family, Career and Community Leaders of America (FCCLA) (formerly FHA, Future Homemakers of America) and Home Economics Related Occupations (HERO)
3. Future Business Leaders of America (FBLA) and Phi Beta Lambda (PBL)
4. DECA, An Association of Marketing Students (formerly Distributive Education Clubs of America) and Delta Epsilon Chi (DEC)
5. SkillsUSA-VICA (formerly VICA, Vocational Industrial Clubs of America)
6. Technology Student Association (TSA)
7. Business Professionals of America (BPA)
8. Health Occupations Students of America (HOSA)
9. National Postsecondary Agriculture Student Organization (PAS)
10. National Young Farmer Educational Association (NYFEA) See Appendix.

FFA

The Future Farmers of America was founded in 1928 to serve high school vocational agriculture learners who were preparing for careers in agricultural production, processing, supply and service, mechanics, horticulture, forestry, and national resources. In 1988, FFA changed its name, dropping "Future Farmers of America," and now uses only the letters FFA to reflect the widening diversity in the field of agriculture. Today, more than 455,000 young people are involved in FFA and are developing their potential for leadership, experiencing personal growth, and preparing for more than 300 careers. Major agricultural career areas include genetic engineering; floriculture; agriscience and engineering; agricultural marketing; merchandising and sales; management and finance; social science professions; production agriculture; education and communications; horticulture; forestry; natural resources; agricultural mechanics; and agriculture processing. Chapters of FFA can be found in all 50 states, Puerto Rico, and the Virgin Islands, with more than 11,000 teachers delivering innovative, cutting edge, integrated curricula to learners and involving them in hands-on work experiences that allow them to apply the knowledge learned in the classroom.

The mission of FFA is to make a positive difference in the lives of young people by developing their potentials for leadership, personal growth, and career success through agricultural education. Agricultural education programs/FFA provide a well-rounded, practical approach to learning through three components (1) classroom education topics such as plant and animal science, horticulture, forestry, agrimarketing, etc.; (2) hands-on supervised agricultural experiences such as starting a business or working for an established company; and (3) FFA activities integrated into the curriculum to provide leadership opportunities and opportunities for learners to test their knowledge and skills through a number of diverse programs, including competitive events. Through participation in FFA activities, learners learn how to conduct and take part in meetings, handle financial matters, speak in public, solve their own problems, develop leadership skills, compete in contests, and assume civic responsibility.

The FFA web page lists 22 different programs in which agriculture learners who are FFA members can get involved. These programs range from Agri-Entrepreneurships to proficiency awards to the Stars Program. For example, the Proficiency Award Program contains 44 different contest areas beginning with Agricultural Communications—Entrepreneurship/Placement and ending with Wildlife Management/Placement. Another example program is the Agriscience Awards and Fair Program in which learners in grades 7–12 can participate in one of five categories: biochemistry/microbiology/food science, botany, engineering, environmental sciences, or zoology.

FFA keeps members, advisors, and industry partners informed through a number of publications that can be read on-line. The *FFA News* contains information on FFA programs, conferences, members, and special events. The publication *Making a Difference* is a monthly guide for advisors containing helpful hints and useful information on teaching, the FFA, and more. *New Horizons* is the magazine for FFA members about FFA members, events, and agriculture. *Pal-to-Pal* is the newsletter for interested partners who want to provide active learning support for the agriculture program and FFA. Finally, *UPDATE* is a monthly publication containing update information from the national FFA staff.

FFA organization is linked with a number of agriculture related organizations including the National Association of Agricultural Educators, the State Leadership Center for Agriculture Education, the National Council for Agricultural Education, the National Postsecondary Agricultural Student Organization, the National Young Farmers Educational Association, the American Association for Agricultural Education, the Association for Career and Technical Education and the National Association, Supervisors of Agricultural Education, Inc. The FFA web page provides links to these supportive organizations.

FFA was the first career and technical student organization and the only one (in 1950) to receive a federal charter from Congress. It is one of the largest CTSOs and has many programs and services available to its members, who range in ages from 12 to 21. The reader can become more informed about the FFA organization by contacting the national FFA center.

Family, Career and Community Leaders of America (FCCLA)

The Future Homemakers of America (FHA) was founded in 1945 to help learners prepare for their future multiple roles as homemakers, wage earners, and community leaders. The FHA expanded its organization in 1971 to include a division of Home Economics Related Occupations (HERO) for learners studying occupational home economics. On July 6, 1999 the members of the Future Homemakers of America from across the country voted to change the name of the 54-year old national association, dropping Future Homemakers of America (FHA) and Home Economics Related Occupations (HERO) and replacing them with the new name of Family, Career and Community Leaders of America (FCCLA) to better reflect the breadth of changes within Family and Consumer Sciences Education.

The Family, Career and Community Leaders of America (FCCLA) is the national career and technical student organization for young men and women enrolled in family and consumer sciences education in public and private school through grade 12. The mission of the organization is "to promote personal growth and leadership development through family and consumer sciences education. Focusing on the multiple roles of family member, wage earner, and community leader, members develop skills for life through (1) character development, (2) creative and critical thinking, (3) interpersonal communication, (4) practical knowledge, and (5) vocational preparation" (Family, Career and Community Leaders of America, 2000).

The FCCLA has a national membership of over 222,000 young men and women in nearly 8,000 local chapters located in 53 state associations including the District of Columbia, Puerto Rico, and the Virgin Islands. An executive director leads the organization and heads the national staff that gives direction to and carries out programs, communications, membership services, and financial management. Each state has a professional designated to provide leadership to the organization, and family and consumer sciences education teachers serve as chapter advisers to give direction and support activities of local school chapters.

The FCCLA functions as an integral part of the family and consumer sciences education curriculum and operates within the school system. It is the only student organization with the family as its central focus. The FCCLA provides opportunities for active learner participation in a number of programs, projects, and activities at local, state, and national levels. Chapter projects focus on a variety of youth concerns, including teen pregnancy, parenting, family relationships, substance abuse, peer pressure, environment, nutrition and fitness, teen violence, and career exploration. Through involvement in the FCCLA, members are provided with opportunities to expand their leadership potential and develop skills for life, including planning, goal setting, problem solving, decision making, and interpersonal communications.

The FCCLA has a number of programs under the headings of family, career and community. The Families First program, one program under the family category, enables learners to become strong family members and in the process, improve their families' ability to nurture socially, emotionally, mentally and physically strong, healthy individuals. The Career Connections program, a program under the career heading, helps young people explore the important aspects of a career and start to prepare for it through a development process that can be used for a lifetime. They learn to understand and prepare for interactions among careers, families and communities. The Community Service Day Opportunities program, a new program under the heading of community, provides learners with an opportunity to tackle a local problem and make a difference in their communities. This program is linked with local Wal-Mart™ stores in providing grants to help learner with their community service projects.

The FCCLA provides several publications to keep their members and advisors informed about news, events, and activities of the organization. *Teen Times* is the official magazine of FCCLA, which is published quarterly and distributed to affiliated members. *The Advisor* is a quarterly publication that keeps advisors informed of organization activities and events and provides information on pertinent topics, such as how to deal with block scheduling. The FCCLA Week is an electronic communication that allows members to share news releases and proclamations. The FCCLA has an on-line bookstore where members can obtain publications, logos, videos, and other items required to support local chapter activities.

The FCCLA is supported primarily by learner membership dues, with additional funds raised from individuals, corporations, and foundations. It is endorsed by the U.S. Department of Education (Office of Vocational and Adult Education) and the American Association of Family and Consumer Sciences (AAFCS). Since its inception as the FHA in 1945, the FCCLA has involved more than nine million youth in its programs and the future looks even brighter for this organization.

Future Business Leaders of America (FBLA) Phi Beta Lambda (PBL)

The Future Business Leaders of America (FBLA) concept was developed in 1937, and the National Council of Business made it a sponsored national student organization in 1940. The first high school chapter was organized in 1942 in Johnson City, Tennessee. The FBLA is the career and technical student organization for learners preparing for careers in business and business-related fields. It has four divisions, FBLA for high school learners; FBLA for junior high, middle, and intermediate school learners; Phi Beta Lambda (PBL) for postsecondary learners; and the Professional Alumni Division for business people, educators, and parents who support the goals of the organization. The first Phi Beta Lambda (PBL) chapter was chartered in Iowa in 1958. The Professional Division (originally the Alumni Division) began in 1979. The FBLA Middle Level for learners grades 5-9 began in 1994.

The FBLA is a professional organization for student leaders preparing for careers and business. It functions as an integral part of the instructional program of business education to provide learners with the opportunity to apply their classroom instruction in business practices and procedures to leadership development activities and competitive events. The goals of FBLA include (1) promoting competent, assertive business leadership; (2) understanding American business enterprise; (3) facilitating the transition from school to work; (4) establishing career goals; (5) encouraging scholarship; (6) promoting sound financial management; and (7) developing character and self-confidence.

Phi Beta Lambda shares many of the same goals as the FBLA including opportunities for learners to gain personal growth, business experience, and to participate in business and community activities. It provides opportunities for postsecondary and college learners to develop vocational competencies for business and office occupations and business teacher education. It acts as an integral part of instructional programs and helps learners develop community and personal responsibility.

The FBLA-PBL provides many programs and activities to help learners accomplish the goals of the association. These include conferences and seminars and a number of competitive events.

The FBLA-PBL National Awards Program recognizes learners and chapters in a broad range of business and career areas. Learners compete at the state level in events that test their knowledge and skills and the top winners advance to national level competition. Competitive events are divided into three categories: individual, team, and chapter. The FBLA competitive events list some 28 different individual contests ranging from Accounting I and II to Word Processing I and II. There are four team events including Desktop Publishing and Parliamentary Procedure. Seven chapter events are available to recognize achievement and performance in chapter management and growth, including the American Enterprise Project and Chapter Website.

The PBL competitive events also fall into three categories: individual, team, and chapter. There are 27 individual events beginning with Accounting Principles and ending with Word Processing. There are three team events: Desktop Publishing, Emerging Business Issues, and Parliamentary Procedure. Seven chapter events are available to help learners promote chapter management and growth including the Community Service Project and a Partnership with Business Project.

The FBLA-PBL informs its members and supporters through several publications and an on-line resources service. *Tomorrow's Business Leader* is a magazine published four times during the school year for secondary and middle school members and features interviews with successful business leaders and articles on leadership, career options, postsecondary options, and more. *PBL Business Leader* is a magazine published three times during the school year for PBL members. *The FBLA Advisers' Hotline* is published three times during the school year and provides valuable information to advisors about chapter management, how

to prepare learners for competitive events, and other information to make their tasks more effective. The *Middle Level Advisers' Hotline* is published three times during the school year and provides information to teachers about FBLA middle school programs, activities, and services. Finally, *The Professional Edge* newsletter is published three times a year to inform professional division members about local, state, and national FBLA-PBL activities and events. The organization has an on-line resources service to assist members and advisors in locating publications and web sites. The FBLA-PBL has more than 240,000 members who participate in 13,000 chapters in 50 states, the District of Columbia, Puerto Rico, the Virgin Islands, U.S Territories, Canada and Department of Defense Dependent Schools worldwide.

The FBLA-PBL is headed by a president/CEO who directs the national staff and the association programs at the National Center in Reston Virginia. The center provides chapter management and promotional and educational materials for advisors and members, coordinates national conferences and seminars, and provides leadership services to the field of business education. State level associations are usually headed by a state department of education professional who coordinates state level activities. Business teachers serve as advisors to guide local chapters. The FBLA-PBL is primarily financed through member dues, but corporate and foundation grants supplement the association. It conducts national conferences and seminars; sponsors competitive events; produces national publications; and provides scholarships, programs, and other services for its members.

DECA/Delta Epsilon Chi—An Association of Marketing Students

DECA, formerly known as the Distributive Education Clubs of America, was founded in 1947 to serve learners enrolled in secondary programs of marketing, distribution, merchandising, and management. Delta Epsilon Chi (DEC), a postsecondary division of DECA, was established in 1961 to meet the needs of learners enrolled in marketing and distributive education programs in junior colleges, community colleges, colleges and universities, technical institutes and colleges, and area vocational-technical schools. In July of 1991, the organization changed its name, dropping Distributive Education Clubs of America and using only the letters DECA with a tag line of "An Association of Marketing Students." The logo of DECA was also updated and newly designed to suggest the strength, stability, and forward-looking image of the association and its members.

DECA is the national association of marketing education learners that provides teachers and members with educational leadership and development activities through integration with the classroom instructional program. DECA is not an extracurricular club but rather an integral part of the marketing education program that serves learners preparing for marketing, entrepreneurial, or management careers. Its mission is to enhance the education of learners with interests in these areas by helping them develop the skills and competencies required for marketing careers. At the same time, DECA helps learners build self-esteem, experience leadership, and practice community service. DECA serves as a strong advocate of marketing education and the development of education and business partnerships.

The goals of DECA include helping learners develop: (1) occupational competencies needed for marketing careers, (2) leadership abilities, (3) social and business etiquette, (4) an understanding and appreciation of civic responsibility, (5) an ethical behavior in personal and business relationships, and (6) an understanding of the role of free enterprise in the global economy. To accomplish its goals, DECA provides learners with publications and educational materials, leadership conferences, opportunities for on-the-job experiences, chapter projects and a number of competitive events in marketing occupational areas.

The competitive events program contains events in more than 30 occupational areas, including individual, team, and chapter events. For example, DECA offers 11 individual series events such as the Apparel and Accessories Marketing Series event and the Retail Merchandising Series, Al event. In addition, DECA has a written event series that can be entered by one or several learners such as the Marketing Research event of Food Marketing Research or the Business Ownership and Management Event of Entrepreneurship. Five chapter team events are offered such as the Civic Consciousness Project and the Learn and Earn Project. Another team event is the DECA Quiz Bowl. Information about DECA's competitive events is available on-line through accessing the *DECA Guide*.

Members and advisors are kept informed through several publications. *DECA Dimensions* is a magazine for DECA members that contains business and association news and special features on job skills, leadership development, and civic consciousness. The *Advisor* is the DECA newsletter that informs DECA advisors of association news as well as providing information to help them become more effective advisors. The *DECA Script* is a newsletter for state officers to help them develop the knowledge and skills required for leadership of their local chapters. The *DECA Guide* is the annual publication that contains information about official DECA competitive events. DECA also publishes an annual catalog, *IMAGES*, that contains items on educational materials that are useful to local DECA chapters.

DECA has over 180,000 members and faculty advisors in over 5,000 marketing education programs in secondary and postsecondary schools in the U.S., its territories and Canada. DECA has many business partners that sponsor competitive events and provide financial awards and scholarships to national winners.

The national office of DECA provides leadership training; member recognition and awards; publications for chapter advisors, members, and officers; and serves as a strong advocate for marketing education programs across the country. National DECA is headed by a CEO and professional staff who provide leadership and services to chapter members. It is headquartered in Reston, Virginia. See Appendix.

Delta Epsilon Chi is the national career and student organization for college learners preparing for careers in marketing, management, merchandising and entrepreneurship. It is a division of National DECA and is currently active throughout the United States and Canada. Delta Epsilon Chi activities are an integral part of the college curriculum in marketing education. The mission of Delta Epsilon Chi is "to nurture competent, entrepreneurial, self-reliant, cooperative leadership in a variety of professional areas with specific emphasis in the areas of marketing, management, merchandising, and entrepreneurship; to help learners make informed career choices by providing opportunities to explore fields as diverse as advertising, wholesaling, fashion/apparel, design, food/food service, sales/sales management, retail management, human resource management, financial services, advertising/promotion, sports and entertainment, hospitality/travel/tourism, international marketing, business-to-business marketing and other management and marketing-oriented occupations; to encourage business activity that demonstrates civic, social and moral responsibility; to recognize the importance of career education and to promote a willingness to use the training facilities provided by corporations to continually improve skills and knowledge in college and throughout life; to increase understanding of and appreciation for the system of free enterprise" (Delta Epsilon Chi, 2001).

Delta Epsilon Chi provides many advantages for members including an opportunity to develop leadership skills, to participate in community service projects and to receive recognition and awards through competitive events. There are over 20 competitive events in different career areas that provide learners with opportunities to showcase their knowledge and skills, to travel to conferences, and to network with peers. Like DECA, Delta Epsilon Chi publishes an annual guide to competitive events that contains updates for the current year and guidelines for each competitive event.

The *Delta Epsilon Chi Guide* contains a listing of competitive events under the categories of Business Simulations, Case Studies, and Prepared Business Presentations, as well as special activities. Some of these events are for individuals while others are team and chapter events. These events are designed to measure a participant's knowledge, skills, and attitudes in both general marketing/management and industry-specific areas. There are eight different business simulation events beginning with Apparel and Accessories Marketing and ending with Travel and Tourism Marketing/Management. Six case study events provide participants with opportunities to analyze real-world case situations and to present solutions to competent judges. Examples of case study events include Human Resource Management Decision Making and Sport and Entertainment Marketing. Prepared Business Presentation provides participants with an opportunity to prepare a written prospectus or sales presentation and to present it to a competent judge in a specialty area. Five Prepared Business Presentations are offered covering such topics as Advertising Campaign and Sales Representative. Two special activities are available for participants: the Delta Epsilon Chi Quiz Bowl and the National Management Institute.

Delta Epsilon Chi publishes three important documents for members and advisors. *The Chi Connection* is published on-line during the school year and informs the reader about activities of the association and provides information on leadership, careers, and more. *The Delta Epsilon Chi Guide* contains official information on competitive events and special activities of the association. The *Images* catalog provides information and is the resource through which members and advisors can order apparel, sample events, educational materials, and promotional materials that can be useful for the local chapter.

Delta Epsilon Chi is a national organization with a CEO and a national staff providing leadership and services to the association. It has dedicated state advisors to provide leadership for the association at the state level. Chapter advisors motivate learners to become members, provide advice, and encourage members to become actively involved in chapter activities and to take full advantage of the many professional development opportunities available. As a division of DECA, Delta Epsilon Chi is also headquartered in Reston, Virginia.

SkillsUSA-VICA

SkillsUSA-VICA was founded in May 1965 to serve learners enrolled in trade, industrial, technical, and health occupations at the secondary level. A postsecondary division of VICA was established in 1969. On July 4, 1999, the name of the Vocational Industrial Clubs of America (VICA) was changed to SkillsUSA-VICA. SkillsUSA-VICA is dedicated to providing experiences and opportunities for the total development of the individual through development of citizen and leadership qualities as well as through the development of occupational knowledge and skills. Today, SkillsUSA-VICA is the national organization for learners enrolled in trade, technical, industrial, and health occupations programs in public high schools, trade and technical schools, and junior and community colleges. SkillsUSA-VICA works directly with business and industry to maintain American productivity, quality, and competitiveness (SkillsUSA-VICA, 1999).

SkillsUSA-VICA is a national organization serving high school and college students and teachers who are enrolled in technical, skilled, and service occupations, including health occupations. The organization has more than 245,000 members in nearly 13,000 chapters located in 54 states and territorial associations. The mission of SkillsUSA-VICA is to help its members become world-class workers and responsible citizens. The goal of the organization is to provide quality education experiences for learners in leadership, teamwork, citizenship, and character development. SkillsUSA-VICA programs and activities focus on total quality at work: high ethical standards, superior work skills, lifelong education, and pride in the dignity of work. SkillsUSA-VICA members who actively participate in association programs and activities are provided with opportunities to build and reinforce self-confidence, positive work attitudes and communication skills. They are also able to gain a better understanding of the American free enterprise system and to get involved in providing community service.

SkillsUSA-VICA involves more than 15,000 teachers and educational administrators and has more than 1,000 business, industry, and labor sponsors who actively support the organization through financial aid, in-kind contributions and involvement of their people in SkillsUSA-VICA activities, such as the competitive events known as SkillsUSA Championships.

SkillsUSA-VICA has a number of programs and services besides local chapter activities to help learners develop their potential. The four major programs are: SkillsUSA Championships, the SkillsUSA-VICA Total Quality Curriculum, the Professional Development Program, and the Career Education Programs. The SkillsUSA Championships provide learners with an opportunity to compete at the local school, region, state, and national level in more than 70 different leadership and occupational areas. The *Total Quality Curriculum* is a special curriculum based on competencies identified by the U.S. Secretary of Labor's Commission on Achieving Necessary Skills, which affords organization members an opportunity to receive special preparation for the modern workplace. The Professional Development Program guides learners through 84 employability skills lessons including some that are devoted to goal setting, career planning, and community service. The Career Education Programs provide training in employability, career, and leadership skills development to learners and teachers through educational opportunities (programs, workshops, conferences, seminars), curriculum, and partnerships with stakeholders to prepare a more competitive workforce for America.

The SkillsUSA Championships are showcases for the best career and technical learners at the local, regional, state, and national level. More than 70 leadership and occupational contests are available for individual learners, teams of learners, and chapters to demonstrate their knowledge and skills before competent judges from business, industry, and labor. These contests are listed in the publication *SkillsUSA Championships: Technical Standards* and are organized under the headings of Leadership Development Contests, Health Occupations Contests,

Occupationally Related Contests and Trade, Industrial, and Technical Contests. There are 11 leadership contests, including contests such as Job Interview and Prepared Speech. There are seven health occupations contests such as First Aid/CPR and Practical Nursing. The three occupationally related contests are Principles of Technology, Related Technical Math, and Total Quality Management. There are over 40 trade, industrial, and technical contests including contests such as Automotive Service Technology, Culinary Arts, and Technical Drafting.

SkillsUSA-VICA provides members with several publications as well as a number of promotional and educational materials to support chapter activities. *SkillsUSA Professional*, available in print and on-line, is a newsletter for high school members and advisors that provides news and information about organization activities, as well as feature articles on careers, educational programs, and much more. *SHARP* is the SkillUSA-VICA newsletter for high school learners that shares information about the accomplishments of learners and contains articles to help learners develop the personal and professional skills required for success in careers and in life. *NEXT* is a newsletter for postsecondary members that contains information about postsecondary programs and activities as well as informative articles appropriate to postsecondary learners. *CONNECT* is a newsletter for college and postsecondary advisers and teachers. The *Skills USA-VICA Educational Materials Catalog* is available in printed form and on-line. It contains a wealth of materials such as chapter tools and advisor essentials, CDs and transparencies, promotional materials, and curriculum and educational materials. Finally there is a *SkillsUSA-VICA Merchandise Catalog*, which is available in printed form and on-line and provides materials such as apparel, certificates, awards, and much more.

SkillsUSA-VICA at the national level is headed by a CEO and a national staff who provide leadership for the organization; publish materials; conduct conferences, workshops and seminars; and serve as advocates for secondary and postsecondary career and technical education programs. The secondary division and postsecondary division are headed by a single or by separate state advisors who coordinate SkillsUSA-VICA activities at the state level. Each chapter has an advisor and a number of section advisors for the various occupational programs offered in local schools. These advisors are key to the success of the programs. They are the individuals who motivate learners to become actively involved in chapter activities and to spend time integrating these activities into their instructional programs.

National SkillsUSA-VICA is a dynamic organization that provides many excellent programs, activities, and services for its members and continues to add new ones each year. For example, the *Building Skills For America* campaign broadened business, industry, and government support for public career and technical education training programs by gathering over 200,000 signatures of supporters who recognize the need for skilled workers. It has an excellent web site that provides a wealth of information for anyone interested in SkillsUSA-VICA.

Technology Student Association (TSA)

The Technology Student Association (TSA), formerly the American Industrial Arts Student Association (AIASA), was officially organized in 1965 as a sponsored program of the American Industrial Arts Association (AIAA). It was officially incorporated in 1978 as the only national student organization designed exclusively to meet the needs for industrial arts learners at the elementary, junior high and middle school, and high school levels. At the national conference in 1988, delegates voted to change the name to the Technology Student Association to reflect the commitment to the dynamic field of technology and the future.

Today, the TSA is the only student organization dedicated exclusively to the needs of technology education learners at the elementary, middle school, and high school levels. More than 100,000 elementary, middle, and high school learners in over 2,000 schools in 45 states are members of the TSA and are benefiting from the integrated activities of the TSA in the regular instructional program of technology education as well as through leadership opportunities and competitive events at the regional, state and national levels.

The mission of the TSA is "to prepare our membership for the challenge of a dynamic world by promoting literacy, leadership, and problem solving, resulting in personal growth and opportunity" (Technology Student Association, 2001).

The world is rapidly changing as a result of technological advancements, and TSA programs and activities provide learners with opportunities to demonstrate their understanding of, and technical abilities related to technology. Goals of the TSA include helping learners become critical thinkers, problem solvers, and technologically literate readers.

The TSA provides leadership conferences, curriculum and educational materials, special projects and competitive events to help learners meet the goals and objectives of the association. Leadership conferences are held at the state and national levels to help TSA learners develop their leadership skills. *The Great Technology Adventure* is TSA's curriculum package for learners in grades K–6, which offers technology educators an integrated approach to technology education for elementary school children. One example of a TSA special project is the partnership they have with the American Red Cross to provide community service. Middle school and high school TSA members are provided with opportunities to become involved in a number of competitive events at the local school, regional, state, and national levels. These competitive events are detailed in the *Curricular Resources Guide* published by the national TSA.

The TSA offers a number of individual, team, and chapter competitive events for middle school and high school learners. For example, the Communication Challenge is a middle school individual contest where the participant designs, produces, and submits two printed materials. There are over 20 middle school team events, such as the Chapter Team event in which learners demonstrate parliamentary procedure skills and the Computer Applications event in which learners demonstrate knowledge of software applications. The Construction Challenge is a middle school chapter event requiring learners to identify a community need related to construction and plan and implement a course of action that includes involvement of both learners and community members. These competitive events provide active learning situations that help middle school learners develop higher-order thinking. They also allow learners to showcase their knowledge and skills in front of competent judges and to receive recognition.

There are over 29 TSA competitive events in which high school learners can demonstrate their technological knowledge and skills. There are a number of contests available for a single participant such as the Architectural Model contest in which a set of architectural plans and reference materials are produced. There are also many contests that involve two or more participants, such as the Technology Bowl and the Radio Controlled Transportation competition in which a team of two members design, fabricate, and demonstrate a radio controlled vehicle. These competitive events provide valuable learning experiences for learners in the applications of technology and allow them to showcase their knowledge and skills in front of knowledgeable judges and receive recognition through awards and prizes.

The national TSA provides publications to keep its members and advisors informed of association news, activities, and materials. *School Scene* is the official publication for TSA members and advisors and provides news about association activities and feature articles about topics of interest to technology education learners. *The TSA View* is a monthly publication in which distinguished members share their views about what TSA has meant to them. The *Curricular Resources Guide* is a publication that contains detailed information about TSA competitive events. Other publications are available that offer guidelines and ideas for TSA advisors and members such as the *Chapter Program Kit*. TSA supplies, such as patches, apparel, and gift items are available through an on-line service with Pitsco, Inc., a primary supporter of the association.

The TSA at the national level is headed by a CEO and a professional staff who provide leadership for the association, publish materials, conduct conferences, and provide other membership services. At the state level, a state department of education official in charge of technology education usually coordinates TSA activities. Technology teachers or other designated educators serve in middle school and high school chapters. These advisors are the key to the success of the TSA chapters; they must moti-vate learners to join and actively participate in TSA programs and activities that are an integral part of quality technology education programs.

The TSA is a dynamic student organization that provides many benefits to its members and advisors through leadership conferences, curriculum and educational materials, special projects, and competitive events.

Business Professionals of America (BPA)

The Business Professionals of America (BPA), formerly the Vocational Office Education Clubs of America (OEA), was founded in 1966 to serve secondary and postsecondary learners enrolled in vocational office programs. In 1988, the OEA changed to the Business Professionals of America, with a new logo, emblem, and colors. BPA is a national student association for learners enrolled in business and/or office education. The mission of BPA is "to contribute to the preparation of a world-class workforce through the advancement of leadership, citizenship, academic, and technological skills." It is a co-curricular organization that provides programs and services to BPA members, which helps them demonstrate their business technology skills, develop their professional and leadership skills, network with each other and with professionals across the nation, and become involved in community service projects (Business Professionals of America, 2000).

The BPA provides learners with the opportunity to enhance their knowledge and skills through integrated activities that are part of regular classroom instruction as well as through programs and activities outside the school. BPA members can enhance their development by participating in the Torch Awards Program, a four-level achievement program that recognizes learners for their involvement in all aspects of the organization and for their growth and achievement in leadership, service, cooperation, knowledge, friendship, love-hope-faith, and patriotism. Conferences are provided at the state and national levels to offer leadership training. The national BPA provides a comprehensive program of regional, state, and national competitive events that provide members with learning experiences and opportunities to showcase their business and office skills, leadership abilities, and chapter team efforts.

Competitive events offered by the national BPA are listed in their annual publication *Guidelines*, which is available in printed and on-line form. There are 11 contests listed under the heading Financial Services such as Fundamental Accounting and Banking and Finance. BPA members can participate in 12 contests under the heading Administrative Support such as Keyboarding, Production, and Legal Office Procedures. Under the heading Information Services/Systems, members can participate in six contests such as Basic Programmer and Network Concepts. Finally, there are 16 different contests under the heading of Management/Marketing/Human Resources ranging from the International Business contest to the Parliamentary

Procedure contest. Many of these contests are available for both secondary and postsecondary participants.

The national office provides publications and materials to inform members of association activities and to support chapter functions. *Communique* is the official journal of the association and is published four times a year. It provides information that keeps members abreast of organization news, programs and events, trends in business, and advances in technology. The *Local Adviser's Bulletin* is a bimonthly newsletter covering association news and other information that can help advisors become more effective in managing chapter activities. In addition, the national BPA publishes *It's a New Year* (chapter handbook) and *CEG* (Competitive Events Guidelines) to help members and advisors carry on chapter programs and activities. BPA offers a Related Materials Service that provides promotional and educational materials, videotapes, award certificates, computer software and numerous other chapter aids.

The BPA is headed by a CEO and professional staff who provide leadership to the association, plan and conduct leadership conferences and competitive events, and publish materials that support chapter activities. BPA activities at the state level are usually coordinated by a state department of education official in charge of business and office programs. Business education teachers serve as chapter advisors who motivate learners to join the organization and participate in the programs, activities, and services of the association.

Health Occupations Students of America (HOSA)

The Health Occupations Students of America (HOSA) was founded in 1976 to provide a student organization that exclusively serves secondary and postsecondary learners enrolled in health occupations programs. HOSA was created to become an integral part of health occupations programs and to provide health occupations learners with learning experiences that help them to develop leadership, citizenship, and occupational knowledge and skills required to enter jobs and careers in the health occupations field. Its two-part mission is to promote career opportunities in the health care industry and to enhance the delivery of quality health care to all people. The goal of HOSA is to encourage instructors and learners in all health occupations to join and be actively involved in an integrated program of HOSA activities and the regular health occupations curriculum. HOSA provides a unique program of leadership development, motivation, and recognition exclusively for secondary, postsecondary, adult, and collegiate learners enrolled in health occupations education programs.

HOSA membership has grown steadily since its inception and now reaches over 60,000 learners through 34 affiliated state associations with involvement in four unaffiliated states and 2,200 chapters. Health occupations teachers recognize that learners need more than technical skills to become health professionals; they need leadership and follower skills that will enable them to be part of a team of health providers. The programs and activities of HOSA provide a powerful instructional tool that can aid health occupations teachers at the secondary and postsecondary levels to motivate learners and get them actively involved in developing the knowledge and skills that they will need in order for them to assume leadership roles in the health care profession.

HOSA offers a number of programs, activities, competitive events, publications, and services to help chapter advisors and members enhance the instructional program. For example, The National Recognition Program is a self-paced, individualized program in which all members can participate. Members have the opportunity to move through four levels of tasks involving demonstration of leadership development, career development, community service, and personal development. A recognition certificate is awarded upon satisfactorily completing the tasks at each level.

HOSA has a national program of competitive events that enables health occupation learners to demonstrate their knowledge and skills in leadership and occupationally specific health careers. These competitive events are organized under five categories: Category I-Health Occupations Related Events has six contests beginning with Dental Spelling and proceeding to Knowledge Tests. Category II-Health Occupation Skill Events has 14 contests beginning with Administrative Medical Assisting and ending with Veterinary Assisting. Category III-Individual Leadership Events is comprised of eight contests including Extemporaneous Health Poster and Prepared Speaking. Category IV-Team Leadership Events has seven contests that begin with Community Awareness and end with Medical Reading. Finally, Category V-Recognition is comprised of eight competitions such as Outstanding HOSA Chapter and Chapter Newsletter.

The national office provides publications and materials to help inform its members of association news, programs, activities, services, and pertinent articles in the health field. The *HOSA* magazine, the official publication, informs members and advisors about HOSA activities and accomplishments and contains feature articles about careers and new advances in the health field. The *HOSA Handbook* is a resource that is used by advisors and members to organize and manage local chapters and to guide preparation for competitive events. Chapter advisors can obtain a copy of *A Guide for Integrating HOSA into the HOE Classroom*, a valuable source for curriculum planning.

HOSA is organized at the national level with a CEO and a professional staff who provide leadership and services for the association. Usually, a state department of education professional who is in charge of health occupations provides leadership and coordinates state level HOSA activities. Health Occupations teachers serve as chapter advisors and play a key role in motivating learnerss to join HOSA and become actively involved in the programs. See Appendix.

Case Study . . . Jean

Jean is an 11th grade disadvantaged student. Her father died when she was two, and she lives in a low-income housing unit with her older sister and mother. Jean's mother works long hours at a low-paying job to provide for her family. Jean has not had the opportunities afforded others, and her home life has affected her school achievement. She is functioning two grade levels below average in reading and one grade below average in math. She earned C grades in all her subjects in the 10th grade except drafting technology in which she earned a B. Jean has expressed her intentions to quit school and find employment to help with the financial difficulties at home. Jean is a shy, modest girl of average appearance and stays much to herself. She was encouraged to join her SkillsUSA-VICA section in drafting technology last year but declined because she felt she couldn't contribute.

Jean's drafting technology instructor recently met with the IVEP planning team, which identified a need for Jean to belong to some organization or group. The drafting technology instructor and disadvantaged specialist encouraged Jean to join SkillsUSA-VICA, but she was undecided. In January, several of the member students in her class and several of the club officers asked her if she would assist them in preparing an architectural display as their entry in the State Display contest. At first she declined, but eventually she agreed to work with Marla, a drafting technology student in her class and a SkillsUSA-VICA member.

The drafting technology program instructor assigned all of his students an architectural design project and arranged to let Jean and Marla develop their assignment together on the SkillsUSA-VICA display project. Jean and Marla have spent many hours over the past two months during and after school on the project. They have become good friends, and Jean has made friends with other students who are also working on the project. Jean is developing a sense of belonging, as evidenced by her change from inactivity to participation in school activities. She is now a regular SkillsUSA-VICA member, thanks to her section's fund-raising activities, which earned money for members who could not pay dues. Jean's disadvantaged specialist has obtained SkillsUSA-VICA materials such as the Leadership Handbook and the Skills USA Championships Technical Standards and is incorporating them into Jean's reading program. Jean's reading skills are showing improvement. She now realizes the importance of reading and spends many hours reading assigned materials as well as library materials she selects for herself.

The SkillsUSA-VICA chapter met two weeks ago and designated Jean to be their representative in the State Display contest. Jean's teachers are working with her on the public-speaking and interview techniques required for the contest. Jean has taken an exceptional interest in preparing for this contest and has shown noticeable improvement in her drafting technology class. Last week Jean attended the State SkillsUSA-VICA Conference. It was the first time she ever stayed away from home in a motel and she was glad to have her friend, Marla, and two other girls as roommates. Jean and her SkillsUSA-VICA chapter came in second in the contest, but Jean took it in stride with the comment, "Wait till next year."

Jean's attitude, personality, and behavior have changed drastically. She has improved her reading, math, and other course grades. She earned an A in drafting technology, the first A she earned in high school. Jean is talking about applying for summer employment in drafting technology at a local engineering firm. Her teacher is assisting her with the contact persons and has helped set up an interview. Jean has established many friendships and now feels part of the group. Some of her teachers and friends ask her what caused her to change. She replies with a confident smile, "Joining SkillsUSA-VICA helped me to feel needed and gave purpose to school. It is the best thing that ever happened to me."

National Postsecondary Agricultural Student Organization (PAS)

The National Postsecondary Agricultural Student Organization (PAS) was founded in 1980 to provide individual growth, leadership, and career preparation for postsecondary learners enrolled agriculture, agribusiness, horticulture, and natural resources. The values of the PAS include (1) developing individual leadership abilities, (2) promoting intellectual growth, (3) developing technical competencies, (4) fostering strong personal ethics, (5) encouraging lifelong learning, (6) recognizing that synergy exists in diversity, and (7) uniting education and industry (National Coordinating Council for Career and Technical Student Organizations, 1999).

The PAS is one of 10 CTSOs approved by the U.S. Department of Education as an integral part of career and technical programs. One of its major purposes is to give learners opportunities to develop leadership through activities, course work, and employment programs. The membership of the PAS is over 1,115 members from 56 chapters located in 18 states.

The PAS provides a national conference, publications, and competitive events to help its members accomplish the goals of the organization. Each year a national conference provides learners with opportunities to develop leadership skills, receive training, and participate in a number of competitive events. Members earn the right to participate in competitive events at the national level by competing at the local and state levels. The *PAS Leadership Handbook* contains a wealth of information about the organization including details about competitive events.

The Award Program is the title for the competitive events of the PAS. Members can compete in contests under the headings of Ag Machinery, Curriculum Specialists, Employment, Individual Student Program, Leadership, and College Bowl. In addition, a new Ag Awareness Awards Program is available that is designed to promote awareness to agriculture and/or nonagriculture audiences. In the Ag Machinery contest a team of two learners troubleshoot and repair various components of agricultural machinery. In the curriculum specialists area, teams of learners can compete in one of four areas: Crops Specialists, Dairy Specialists, Livestock Specialists, and Ornamental Horticulture Specialists. A team of two participate in the Crop Specialists contest. In the employment area, learners can compete in employment interviews in 12 career areas ranging from Ag Equipment Service to Feeds and Animal Science. In the Individual Student Program area, learners can demonstrate their career planning abilities in one of 28 different areas such as crop protection or animal health/technology. In the Leadership area participants demonstrate their skills in either impromptu or prepared speaking. Finally, teams of learners compete in the College Bowl to demonstrate their knowledge gained in their instructional programs.

The PAS keeps its members and supporters informed through *PAStimes*, a newsletter published three times a year. This letter contains information about organization activities and features articles on careers and new advances in the broad field of agriculture. In addition, the PAS has a web site providing information about the organization. The *PAS Handbook* is a major publication of the organization and contains information about it and how to establish and manage an active chapter. The *PAS Handbook* also contains information about PAS programs, including the competitive events.

The PAS is affiliated with other agricultural organizations including FFA. The PAS is headed by an executive director and staff who provide leadership to the organization and provide for programs and activities of the organization at the national level. State PAS programs and activities are coordinated by a state advisor, usually a state department of education official in charge of postsecondary agricultural education. Teachers of agricultural and agricultural related programs/courses serve as chapter advisors and play a vital role in building interest in the organization and getting postsecondary learners actively involved in organization programs and activities.

National Young Farmer Educational Association (NYFEA)

The National Young Farmers Education Association (NYFEA) was founded in 1982 to enhance the development of agricultural leaders and help recruit new people into agricultural careers. It is the official student organization for adult education in agriculture as recognized by the United States Department of Education. Today, more than 3,500 members ages 18 and over are involved in the NYFEA in 22 state chapters and over 500 local chapters (National Coordinating Council for Career and Technical Student Organizations, 1999).

The mission of the organization is to promote the personal and professional growth of all people involved in agriculture. The NYFEA has a long list of goals including to (1) refine leadership skills, (2) improve business skills, (3) inform farmers, ranchers, foresters, business persons, and consumers of the diverse issues facing agriculture, (4) win positive media attention for agriculture and forestry, (5) concentrate on education and agricultural awareness, not politics, (6) provide for travel to achieve firsthand knowledge of a place, (7) define issues, recognize problems, and implement solutions, (8) support children while helping them develop an appreciation for agriculture, (9) strengthen local agricultural awareness through public service projects, (10) assist needy people in local communities through service activities, and (11) encourage new entrants into the highly competitive world of agricultural careers.

To meet its goals, the national NYFEA has developed a long range plan for the organization, "Education for American Agriculture" (EAA), that includes conferences and seminars at the state and national level to train individuals in leadership and business management; programs and activities such as competition and contests; and projects that allow individuals to apply what they have learned in community service projects.

The NYFEA provides programs for members to get involved in organization activities and to receive recognition for their efforts. For example, the EAA Degree Recognition Program is designed to provide recognition for members who have completed a designated number of educational programs, contests, and community service projects. Participants can earn a degree in the areas of leadership, management, and instructor. The NYFEA's Education for American Agriculture plan includes opportunities for members of get involved in contests and competitive events. Currently, the NYFEA has nine different contests that are available for members to compete in at the local, state, and national levels including the contest of Spokesperson for Agriculture Program and the Chapter Community Service Project of the Year.

The national organization provides several publications to keep its members informed of organization activities and the changes in the field of agriculture. *The Leader for Agriculture* is a magazine sent to each NYFEA household as well as to the corporate community and prospective young farmers or agriculture leaders. *The Young Farmer and Ag Leaders UPDATE* is a newsletter printed four times annually to provide current leadership information to members and to motivate members to participate in organizational events. *Taking Action* is a newsletter that provides an in-depth look at current leadership topics such as communication, time and stress management, economic trends, and other issues. The *NYFEA Contest Handbook* provides members with the tools they need to become leaders. Finally, The NYFEA homepage is another resource for information about the organization and it programs, publications, and services.

The national organization is led by an executive vice president who is responsible for the day-to-day operations of the organization. A president's council provides leadership and direction for the organization. State associations are organized in similar fashion under the direction of a state executive vice president. Local chapters are the workhorses of the organization and are usually headed by a professional who coordinates the programs and activities of the organization.

National Vocational-Technical Honor Society (NV-THS)

The National Vocational-Technical Honor Society (NV-THS) was founded in 1984 to recognize outstanding achievement in career and technical education. The purpose of the NV-THS is "(1) to reward excellence in workforce education, (2) to develop self-esteem, pride and encourage learners to reach for higher levels of achievement, (3) to promote business and industry's critical workplace values—honesty, responsibility, initiative, teamwork, productivity, leadership, and citizenship, (4) to help schools build and maintain effective partnerships with local business and industry, and (5) to champion a stronger, more positive image for workforce education in America." Today over 1,500 schools and colleges throughout the United States and its territories are affiliated with the NV-THS (National Vocational-Technical Honor Society, 2000).

The NV-THS is different in many respects from a career and technical student organization. It is mainly an honor society and members must meet certain qualifications established by schools and colleges. One qualification (usually) is a grade point average of at least a 3.0, or B average. Student candidates are recommended by members and are usually persons who have demonstrated scholastic achievement, skills development, leadership, honesty, responsibility, and good character. Learners benefit primarily from attending local chapter activities and from personal recommendations for employment, college admission, and scholarships provided by the NV-THS national headquarters. Schools that have local NV-THS chapters benefit from a positive school image, opportunity to build and maintain active partnerships with local business and industry, recruitment of more qualified learners for workforce education programs, involvement of parents and family in the educational process, and involvement of learners in service learning activities.

The NV-THS publishes *Artisan,* the official newsletter of the society, which is available in print form and on-line, to inform members of society activities and to share the successes of its members. An *Advisor's Handbook* is made available for chapter advisors to help them organize their chapters and manage chapter activities.

INVOLVING ALL LEARNERS IN CAREER AND TECHNICAL STUDENT ORGANIZATIONS

Learners often need to be encouraged to become involved in career and technical student organization programs and activities. Given encouragement by career and technical teachers as well as support personnel, all learners can be involved in CTSO activities that will help them to develop the knowledge, skills, attitudes, and work habits needed to compete for employment and to live independent, productive lives in their communities.

Learners should be actively recruited by CTSO members, the teacher/advisor, and support personnel. The teacher/advisor relationship and communication with learners is often the determining factor of CTSO involvement or rejection. Teachers can consult with staff or other school personnel, parents, and other advocacy groups to obtain information that might be helpful in attracting learners to a student organization. While personal invitations are probably the most effective method for getting learners to join a CTSO, an active chapter program of work that showcases many activities in which learners can become involved is also a powerful recruitment tool. Chapter advisors need to encourage learners to take full advantage of the many programs, activities, and projects that are structured for them by the national headquarters of a given CTSO, and they need to integrate them into the curriculum so all learners, not just members, can learn.

Chapter Advisor Functions

The key to an effective CTSO chapter that involves all learners is a dedicated, informed, learner-oriented career and technical education teacher acting as chapter advisor. Since student organizations are an integral part of the educational program and curriculum, teachers should obtain materials from their national CTSO headquarters to help them learn about the duties and responsibilities of chapter advisors and how to integrate CTSO materials into the instructional program.

All CTSOs have materials and publications for advisors such as the *Advisors Success Kit (ASK) 2000* CD-ROM available from SkillsUSA-VICA, the *Survival Guide for Class and Club Advisors* available from FBLA, HOSA's *Guide for Integrating HOSA into the HOE Classroom*, and the *Chapter Program Kit* available from TSA. Advisors can obtain current information about organizations activities through periodical publications produced for them such as *The Advisor* of FCCLA and *Making a Difference* of FFA. In addition to resources for advisor training, some CTSOs have curriculum materials that can be integrated into the regular instructional program such as the *Total Quality Curriculum* and *Professional Development Program* available from SkillsUSA-VICA and the Great Technology Adventure available from TSA.

In their publication *Career and Technical Student Organizations: A Reference Guide* (1999), the National Coordinating Council for Career and Technical Student Organizations (NCC-CTSO) has identified the following functions advisors should perform when working with a CTSO:
- Understand the important role the CTSO has in furthering the goals of career and technical education.
- Develop, refine, and evaluate materials, methods, and techniques used by local, state, and national organizations.

- Encourage learners to be active members of CTSOs.
- Allow the chapter to be learner-led.
- Collaborate with support groups that can facilitate CTSOs and career and technical education programs.
- Actively promote career and technical education and CTSOs in the community.
- Provide a learning environment that will complement and reinforce—rather than compete with or duplicate—career and technical education training.
- Work cooperatively with learners and teachers to develop skilled leaders.
- Encourage learners to learn from both successful and not-so-successful activities.
- Help chapter leaders carry out their responsibilities.
- Obtain current information on CTSO-related policies, documents, publications, procedures, etc.
- Assist with the fiscal management of the CTSO chapter.
- Review the career and technical education and determine how best to fully integrate CTSO activities into the classroom.
- Encourage learner members to employ group consensus-making principles in an effort to overcome difficult problems facing the chapter.
- Encourage members to elect an officer team that is able and willing to provide leadership to the chapter.
- Assist in the development of an effective officer team.
- Facilitate the development of a meaningful program of work that will guide the chapter for the membership year.
- Encourage members to take full advantage of the benefits of CTSO membership.
- Encourage members to participate in state and national competitive events.
- Facilitate participation in local, district, state, and national competitions.
- Help members plan, organize, and conduct fund-raising projects that will finance chapter activities not supported by school funds.
- Use chapter activities to develop leader and follower skills.
- Encourage parents to get involved in chapter projects and activities.
- Secure approval for activities, etc., from local, state, and national agencies when appropriate.
- Provide ongoing counsel and advice to chapter members and officers.
- Provide advice, support, and service to state and national CTSOs.

The list of advisor functions presented can be useful in helping career and technical education teachers provide leadership to CTSOs. Advisors can obtain both on-line and printed information from their CTSO headquarters such as the *Advisor's Success Kit* of SkillsUSA-VICA. In addition, advisors can obtain a copy of the *Handbook for Advisors of Vocational Student Organizations,* 4th Edition, published by AAVIM. Chapter advisors occasionally have to modify their functions and make modifications to CTSO activities to accommodate learners from special populations.

Career and Technical Student Organization Programs and Activities

Career and technical student organizations have many common programs and activities. Following are some examples:
- program of work
- chapter calendar
- chapter section meetings
- individual achievement/degree programs
- leadership development programs
- district, state, and national conferences
- competitive events
- career development
- community service
- fund-raising
- social/recreation
- communication/public speaking
- public relations

These activities and programs are interwoven into the regular educational program in such a manner as to make it difficult to tell what is career and technical program content and what is CTSO program activity. These CTSO programs and activities are supported with professionally prepared materials such as handbooks, workbooks, resource kits, secretary and treasurer's books, audio-visuals, instructional aids, and certificates. These are available through the national organization or the organization's official supplier. Information and programs and activities are available on-line on the official web sites of each CTSO.

The opportunities for all learners to become involved in CTSO activities are extensive. There are so many possible activities that it is impossible for a chapter to engage in all of them in a school year. Therefore, chapters usually use the national program of work major activities as a guide to developing their own program of work and work calendar.

When appropriate support services are available, learners with special needs can participate in most CTSO activities, and it is important that they be encouraged to do so. A balanced CTSO program of work contains the activities that learners need to participate in to further develop the knowledge and skills required to obtain satisfying employment and lead independent, productive lives.

Career and Technical Student Organization Program of Work

National CTSOs have recognized the importance of well-prepared, balanced programs of work and have developed them with major topics that are related to the goals of the organization. Examples of these major program of work topics include personal growth, leadership development, social development, competitive events, community service, fund-raising, and career development.

The chapter program of work includes all of those activities in which members want to participate. Members can identify and select activities that meet their needs and the needs of the organization, with consideration given to meeting the needs of the school and community. For example, one of the easiest topics to develop is social development. Examples of activities in this category that members can select include skating and swimming parties, dance, talent show, cookout, picnic, hayride, athletic activity, orientation of new members, school open house, and trip to an amusement park or other interesting sites.

Through active participation in the program of work planning process, learners are provided with an overview of the broad range of opportunities. They have the opportunity to select activities that are of interest to them and that meet individual needs in such areas as community service, safety, public relations, social skills, recreational skills, and competitive events. These learners are also provided with opportunities to improve their interpersonal and group participation skills and long range planning skills through active involvement in chapter meetings and committee assignments. Learners can receive special assistance in developing long-term and short-term goals related to the program of work and effective strategies to meet these goals (e.g., using time management and planning calendars).

The program of work serves as an outline of activities covering a definite time period, usually an entire school year. It should contain a listing of specific goals/activities, strategies for accomplishing them, persons responsible for each activity, and provisions for monitoring and evaluating each activity in relation to its goal.

In developing the program of work, it is good practice to prepare members for the planning meeting by providing them beforehand with copies of the last year's program and programs of work from other chapters if available. Learners can be given exercises in developing the program of work by completing program of work worksheets. See Figure 10-2. Career and technical student organization advisors can also ensure involvement of all learners by talking with those who will be presiding during the program of work planning meeting and asking them to call on as many learners as possible, especially learners with special needs.

During the planning meeting all learners are given an opportunity to brainstorm and identify possible activities under each major program of work topic. After the group makes a tentative selection of activities, a program of work committee should be appointed, and subcommittees should be formed to develop activities under each major topic area. All learners should have the opportunity to learn how committees operate and how to actively participate in them. Advisors should make sure that all learners are members of one or more committees during the school year.

The program of work committee presents the tentative program of work for review at a meeting of the entire CTSO membership. Revisions and editorial work are performed on the tentative plan, and it is sent on to the school administration for approval. Once the program receives administrative approval, the program of work is brought before the CTSO members again for formal adoption and to assign permanent committees to further plan and conduct program of work activities.

The program of work activity provides many learning experiences for special needs learners and other learners. These experiences should be identified by the CTSO advisor and support team and become short-term instructional objectives in the individualized education program (IEP) and individualized vocational education program (IVEP) for special needs learners.

EXAMPLE PROGRAM OF WORK WORKSHEET

CTSO _____   20 _____ Program of Work   Date _____

School _____   Program _____

Major Topic: Activities/Projects	Date	Strategies for Accomplishing	Members Responsible	Evaluation Procedures

Figure 10-2. A program of work worksheet for including students in the planning process.

Chapter Calendar

Career and technical student organizations carry on many activities during the year but so do other organizations in the school, as well as the school itself. It is important that a calendar of events be developed that allows adequate time for program of work activities to be planned and strategically scheduled. For example, early in the year organizational activities take precedence over other activities. Early activities include the CTSO orientation meeting, election of officers, appointment of standing committees, training CTSO officers and chairpersons, membership drive, planning the program of work, collecting dues, ordering needed supplies and materials, and sending reports and articles to the state association and national headquarters.

Planning the chapter calendar can be a valuable learning experience. Every learner needs to know how to develop a schedule of events and establish realistic time frames for the occurrence of these events. Advanced planning is often one of the most important factors in whether an activity is successful or not.

Advisors and support team members can provide instruction to learners about budgeting time and scheduling activities. Organizations have materials available to help learners and advisors plan chapter calendars, such as the planning calendar available from SkillsUSA-VICA. Examples of previous CTSO chapter calendars can be presented and reviewed by learners in preparation for a calendar of events planning meeting.

Chapter Meetings

The majority of CTSO activities that occur in chapters take place at the local level, and one of the most important activities is the chapter meeting. Members of CTSOs are given the opportunity to make decisions and to see the consequences of those decisions. Some members will be elected to the leadership team to guide their class and chapter, while others will be able to experience firsthand the challenges that face leaders and their followers. Chapter meetings involve a type of "workforce team" that must work together to plan and implement a balanced program of work.

One of the most powerful instructional tools provided by CTSOs is the chapter meeting. Many new members will have never participated in formal business meetings, and the experience is a great opportunity for learning. Our society conducts business through millions of meetings every day. It is important that every student learn how to function effectively as leaders or members of all types of groups.

Most CTSOs have excellent materials to help advisors and officers plan for and conduct effective chapter meetings, such as the *Meetings Kit* available from the national SkillsUSA-VICA and the *Chapter Program Kit* available from the national TSA. Advisors can use these materials to help members learn meeting skills, such as planning agendas, preparing for meetings, using parliamentary procedure, making introductions, participating in committees, inviting and introducing guests, speaking in front of groups, and using effective team building and group dynamic skills.

Membership Campaign

One of the first activities that occurs in the beginning of a chapter year is the membership campaign. This activity is critical, for the purpose of any CTSO is to involve all learners in leadership and career development activities through the integration of CTSO programs, events, activities, and materials into the regular career and technical education curriculum. While learners do not have to be dues-paying members to benefit from classroom CTSO activities, they cannot participate in everything that is offered unless they become members.

Obtaining new members is a high priority with all the national career and technical student organizations, and these organizations are devising new ways to reach teachers and members by providing on-line membership services and special membership campaigns. One such campaign is the National Membership Recruitment Campaign of DECA, which challenges chapters to recruit new members while providing incentives that make the recruitment effort exciting and worthwhile. FCCLA has the Member Quest 2001 program in which chapters can compete for the best recruitment program and earn financial support to send their members to the national conference. Career and technical student organization advisors and leaders have a number of on-line as well as written and media materials available from these organizations to help promote membership. Advisors and leaders have a number of written and media materials available from their respective national organizations to help promote membership. All CTSOs have magazines available that members receive upon joining. SkillsUSA-VICA has a 100% chapters program that gives national recognition to chapters that enroll every eligible learner in the instructional program, with members receiving certificates, gold membership cards, and attractive 100% chapter pins to wear on their clothing.

Organization chapters need to develop or adopt a membership campaign that includes some of the following features identified by Sarkees and Sullivan (1989):

- daily announcements through available media
- central bulletin board with membership "thermometers"
- competitive sports events, such as a volleyball tournament for chapters with 100% membership, with the winning chapter challenging the teachers
- special fund-raising activities to pay dues for those who are unable to pay them
- assembly programs for all learners, with guest speakers addressing school-to-work transition followed by an announcement of the membership campaigns for CTSOs represented in the school
- membership poster contest with a prize for the best poster

- a membership computer or videotape program contest with the winner receiving a prize
- a local school CTSO web page that describes the organization and invites learners to join

Officer Elections/Training

The elections of CTSO section and chapter officers are exciting events in which all learners can participate. It is a natural occasion to teach leadership skills. Most student organizations have materials that can be used by members and advisors to develop the leadership abilities of the members and to help conduct the election of officers. One excellent example of such materials is the Leadership Techniques booklet produced by Business Professionals of America. This source covers topics such as (1) what is a leader? (2) opportunities for developing leadership, (3) the election and installation of officers, and (4) officer responsibilities and leadership training. Chapter seven of the *Advisor's Success Kit* produced in CD-ROM form by SkillsUSA-VICA is an example of an excellent source of information for training officers. Other CTSOs have similar officer training materials. In addition to officer training materials available from the national CTSOs, chapter advisors can encourage their learners to attend state level leadership conferences, and if they have a learner who is a state CTSO officer, encourage him or her to attend national leadership conferences such as the Washington Leadership Training Institute (WLTI). The WLTI is the premier leadership training activity for learner leaders across the United States.

Budget Preparation and Fund-Raising

All CTSOs must develop a budget to plan for income and expenditures for the year and identify fund-raising activities to generate income. These two processes are important learning experiences for all learners. Preparing budgets and planning for fund-raising can reinforce math skills, personal finance concepts, and teamwork skills.

The CTSO advisor must play a key role in helping learners anticipate major expenses and identify sources of income that will support chapter activities. Typical expense categories identified by Sarkees and Sullivan (1989) include state and national dues, organization publications, conference registrations, office supplies, transportation, awards, CTSO clothing, and committee funds. Income for these expenses is usually generated through membership dues, fund-raising activities, and donations. A tentative budget is prepared by the officers with input from the advisor and presented to and adopted by the membership at a chapter meeting.

Once a budget is adopted, the process of raising funds to generate income should begin. There are usually school policies that govern fund-raising activities with some schools forbidding them entirely, while other schools allow as many as necessary to support the CTSO if the activities can be scheduled without conflict. Fund-raising activities are suggested by the chapter, but before they can be accepted they need to meet certain criteria. They need to adhere to school policy, have educational value, be profitable, involve all members, be short in duration, provide incentives and rewards for outstanding work, not be competitive with local schools and merchants, and have the potential to start a tradition.

Learners with special needs may need some assistance in understanding the procedures for preparing budgets and fund-raising. Advisors, with the assistance of special needs support personnel, need to work individually with learners with special needs to solve specific problems, such as the availability of money to pay dues or obtain CTSO clothing (e.g., blazers, sweaters, jackets). It may also be helpful for advisors to employ the "buddy" system of having other CTSO members work closely with special needs learners to help them perform their roles in the fund-raising assignment. Learners from special populations can benefit greatly from the social interaction that is the natural outcome of total CTSO member involvement when planning and preparing budgets and fund-raising activities.

Achievement/Degree Programs

Career and technical student organization activities are designed to function as an integral part of the regular instructional program. Several CTSOs have provided integration tools, such as the *Professional Development Program (PDP)* of SkillsUSA-VICA that has specific requirements in the regular career and technical program as well as requirements of chapter knowledge and leadership abilities. Learners progress through these programs on a self-paced basis and are recognized for their accomplishments during degree ceremonies. Additional examples of these achievement/degree programs include (1) the Proficiency Award Program of FFA, (2) the Star Events Program of FCCLA, and (3) the National Recognition Program of HOSA. These programs provide structured learning experiences in which individual learners compete against predetermined standards rather than against fellow classmates. Learners often participate in these achievement/degree programs in order to earn certificates and pins and stripes to wear on their CTSO jackets and blazers.

Competitive Events

One of the most visible programs offered by a career and technical student organization is its competitive events program. Every CTSO has such a program, with events in leadership and occupational areas in individual and group contests. These contests take place in the local school and at the district, state, and national levels. They are designed to provide opportunities for learners to compete with themselves and others through demonstrating the leadership abilities and occupational skills they have acquired in their career and technical education programs. These competitive events provide a powerful incentive for learners to excel in their occupational preparation programs.

Career and technical student organization competitive contests are available as individual events or as team and chapter events. For example, most organizations have an individual contest on extemporaneous speaking and an organization business procedures contest for a group of members. The variety of competitive events available in each CTSO should make it possible for every learner to become involved in these incentive programs. Every learner wants to be a winner—to receive recognition through compliments from parents and classmates, as well as through medals, ribbons, trophies, plaques, and cash awards. Every learner who participates is a winner, whether the learner receives awards or not.

An example competitive event in which learners from special populations and others have participated successfully is the SkillsUSA-VICA job skill demonstration contest. This contest involves demonstrating a skill and explaining the topic and process through the use of examples, experiments, and displays. The advantage of this contest is that it offers contestants a chance to pick the content for the contest and an opportunity to practice it many times before they are evaluated by competent judges. Another advantage of this contest is that it is only five to seven minutes in length, which requires much less physical stamina than other contests of a skills nature, some running one to four hours.

National CTSOs provide information, both on the Internet and in printed form, detailing their competitive events. For example, each student organization has a competitive events information page on its web site as well as information on competitive events either as part of its official handbook or as a separate document, such as the *DECA Guide* or the *SkillsUSA Championships: Technical Standards* of SkillsUSA-VICA.

Leadership Conferences

Career and technical student organizations provide regional, state, and national leadership conference activities that provide excellent opportunities for members to compete in leadership and occupational skill contests; participate in leadership skills and officer training workshops; serve as delegates representing their schools, districts, and states; travel to new cities and states and meet new people; share ideas and develop new attitudes toward cooperation and national pride; and receive inspiration to further achievement in their CTSO.

All learners who serve as delegates should be prepared to represent their schools or states on matters of common concern. If delegates are to introduce motions or make remarks they should be prepared to do so before arriving at the conference. Delegates and others attending leadership conferences should be reminded of expected behavior, since the way they participate in these conferences reflects on their chapters, districts, and state associations as well as their school. CTSO advisors should share the conference agenda with learners and prepare them for conference activities to ensure maximum participation.

Not every CTSO member can attend leadership conferences, so learners earn the right to represent their local chapter by actively participating in chapter activities. Some learners may lack experience in traveling to conferences and spending nights away from home in hotels or at camps. CTSO advisors should work with the learners, parents, and appropriate support personnel to prepare these learners for the trip. If these learners are to participate in the conferences as contestants or presenters, the IEP and IVEP support team should prepare them thoroughly ahead of time. The following suggestions and requirements should be given to all learners who attend leadership conferences:

- Obtain a parent's permission and provide a liability release form.
- Develop a list of clothing and other equipment and materials needed for each learner to bring to the conference.
- Go over expected conference behavior and regulations.
- Go through a dry run of registering for the conference and conference lodging.
- Upon arriving at the room, unpack clothing and organize it to avoid conflict with other learners.
- Check to see where emergency exits and fire extinguishers are located.
- Review the conference agenda and mark those events you must be at and those you wish to attend.
- Walk with friends or your advisor to the locations of meetings that you plan to attend.
- Walk with friends or your advisor to the restaurants in or near the hotel where you plan to eat.
- Be in your room when you are expected to be there.
- Be prepared to report your activity to fellow classmates when you return from the conference.
- Be sure you know what to do in the event that a roommate gets sick or another emergency occurs.

Building Business/Industry/Labor Partnerships

One of the important goals of all career and technical student organizations is gaining the support of business, industry, and labor. The national CTSOs, like SkillsUSA-VICA, have staff persons who are dedicated to promoting beneficial partnerships among business, industry, labor, and education, which enhances the quality of training for America's technical workforce. Business, industry, and labor leaders recognize the potential that CTSOs have for improving the leadership, interpersonal, and technical skills of learners; these skills can make them future business and industry leaders. Business and industry are willing to support CTSOs in a number of ways including (1) providing financial and technical assistance for competitive events, (2) providing prizes and scholarships for competitive event winners, (3) providing equipment and work gear for local programs of career and technical education, (4) serving as advocates for career and technical education programs at the local, state, and national levels, (5) participating in career fairs held in conjunction with national conferences, and (6) funding mission-related projects and programs. All national CTSOs are supported by partners from business, industry, and labor organizations. National SkillsUSA-VICA reports over 1,000 national corporations, businesses, associations, and labor unions support the organization at the national level with thousands more supporting state and local SkillsUSA-VICA activities (SkillsUSA-VICA, 2001).

Leaders of CTSOs at the national, state, and local levels are actively campaigning to promote awareness of America's need for a skilled workforce and the need for partnerships among education, business, industry, and labor to improve leadership and skills training for secondary and postsecondary learners. SkillUSA-VICA launched the Building Skills for America National Awareness Campaign in 1999-2000 to provide a way for learners to talk directly with community employers and local leaders about the shortage of skilled workers and the need to support public career and technical education as a way of providing well-trained workers who can fill entry-level positions in U.S. companies. As a part of this campaign, members collected over 220,000 endorsements and signatures from their community leaders, who in turn pledged support for training programs in the learners' high schools and postsecondary institutions. In the process of obtaining endorsements, signatures, and proclamations, SkillsUSA-VICA learners had a chance to tell community leaders how participation in career and technical education programs and the student organization have provided them with specific skills to earn a living and made a difference in their lives (SkillsUSA-VICA, 2001).

State CTSO directors and local chapter advisors recognize the importance of contributions from business, industry, and labor to the success of their programs of work. State CTSO directors and state officers actively recruit involvement from business and industry leaders to sponsor competitive events and to participate in determining contest standards, planning the contests, securing equipment, and running the events. Local chapter advisors and members follow a similar course of action to involve business and industry leaders in assisting local school competitive events and in determining who has successfully completed CTSO achievement/degree programs.

Chapter advisors can access their organization's national web site to obtain a listing of business, industry, association and labor union sponsors. They can contact the local, regional, and state representatives of these contributors to obtain support for local, district, and state CTSO activities. They can utilize members of their advisory committees to assist them in obtaining additional business and industry support for their programs of work. Career and technical student organization members can make presentations at business, industry, and community organization meeting and extend the invitation for support of career and technical education programs as well as CTSOs.

Involving Special Needs Learners in Career and Technical Student Organizations

One of the perceived barriers to involvement of learners from special populations in CTSOs is that some learners with disabilities may not be able to participate successfully in regular programs and activities. This barrier may well be more perceived than real since most career and technical teachers who have successfully involved special needs learners in CTSO activities indicate that most aspects of the organization require little or no modification. The following ideas may be useful in better meeting the unique needs of learners from special populations (Sarkees and Sullivan, 1985, 1989).

- Learners with special needs may have difficulty reading CTSO materials. These materials may be adapted for use by these learners by rewriting them in simpler language, by recording them on tape, by presenting them in larger written type, or by scanning materials into the computer and presenting them in larger type fonts. For example, materials that may be difficult to read include emblem ceremonies, officer installation programs, competitive events handbooks, and learner handbooks.
- Instructional strategies used in CTSO activities may need to be carefully selected to meet the various learning styles of learners. Learners with special needs often profit from action-oriented strategies such as role-playing, video demonstrations of events, observing others, working with another learner in the buddy system, etc.
- Disabled learners may experience physical barriers in facilities where meetings and contests are held. These facilities should be checked for barriers before they are selected for organization activities and events. Appropriate modifications may be needed to overcome a barrier in a facility should other facilities be unavailable.
- Organization leadership activities, such as serving as an officer, often require memorization and oral recitation, which may be a problem for some learners from special populations. These problems can be overcome by providing learning experiences in the trouble areas ahead of time and by working with support teachers to reinforce instruction in these areas. For example, FBLA learner officers must learn their parts to participate in the emblem ceremony. Career and technical education teachers can videotape this ceremony ahead of time and use it to help learners learn their parts. Special needs teachers can borrow the tapes and use them in their classes as a demonstration of public speaking skills. Overhead or computer slide projections of officer speeches can be displayed on a screen as well.

- Many competitive events require learners to read directions and other materials. Some learners from special populations may be able to perform the contest activity well but may not be able to read the directions. Directions may need to be printed in larger type, be converted to a prerecorded audiotape, or be given orally. Directions can also be written in simpler terms and made more readable by drawings and illustrations.

- Hearing-impaired and limited English-proficient learners can participate in CTSO activities and competitive events if the service of interpreters or signers is provided. For example, interpreters, as well as signers, have been provided at national SkillsUSA-VICA contests to enable hearing impaired learners to participate.

- Many learners who compete in CTSO activities and events experience high levels of anxiety and tension. Learners from special populations may experience even higher tension and anxiety levels because of their low self-esteem and confidence. There is no substitution for preparation for competitive activities. Career and technical education teachers and support personnel need to provide repetition and practice for all learners to promote overlearning of the knowledge and skills required for a competitive task. This usually results in lower levels of anxiety and apprehension.

- Participating as a contestant in an area, region, state, or national CTSO contest is a new and stressful experience for most learners. It is not uncommon for learners to get lost in meeting facilities and to fail to attend required briefings for competitive contests. Career and technical student organization advisors should arrive at the contest sites early and provide a dry run experience for learners so they know where to go and what to expect. Contest designers can facilitate logistical concerns by using appropriately displayed posters and signs and by color-coding contest signs, numbers, and materials.

- Some contest judges might not have experience in judging learner effort in competitive events. Contest judging can be made more objective if a contest rating briefing is conducted in which judges are informed about the nature of learner contestants, their school programs (without naming schools), their learning characteristics, and their needs.

- One of the logistical problems for all CTSO advisors is providing transportation and supervisory services for learners to meetings, conferences, and competitive events. Special consideration should be given to the unique needs of learners from special populations in these two areas. For example, the advisor may find it desirable to make room assignments so that one or more mature, responsible learners are paired with a learner with a special need. Additional adult supervision may be required when bus transportation is provided to competitive events. Funds for travel need to be raised through chapter activities so all eligible learners can participate in out-of-school activities.

- Learners from special populations often have low self-esteem and self-confidence. It is a good practice to encourage these learners to participate in committee work and group activities so they can experience success before they venture into individual activities. Another good practice is to encourage learners who want to become committee chairpersons or officers to serve as apprentices to past or present officers and chairpersons to "learn the ropes."

- Learners from special populations sometimes need more time to complete a project, activity, or contest because of disabilities. Special consideration should be given to time limits that would allow all learners to participate, tempered with realistic work expectations.

- Learners with special needs may require more sequenced, structured activities and materials than other learners. It is a good practice to review the use of meeting materials in advance by using a meeting agenda planning form, which can be completed by participating learners. Learners with special needs who are to present before a group should be provided with appropriate note cards and possibly scripts to reduce anxiety and ensure success. When planning CTSO activities, the advisor should help learners outline the steps required to complete the activities. Contracts for project completion should be carefully prepared with clearly defined goals, objectives, steps, and directions that are appropriate to the unique needs and abilities of learners from special populations.

- Learners from special populations often have trouble participating in meetings for a variety of reasons including poor self-image, lack of confidence, and lack of general meeting and leadership skills. Advisors, with assistance from special needs support personnel, should set aside time and present instruction to help learners develop these important meeting and leadership skills. Most student organizations have excellent materials, such as the SkillsUSA-VICA Meetings Kit, to support instruction in this area.

- Learners from special populations, along with other learners, can profit from individualized or self-paced instructional materials covering aspects of CTSOs. Career and technical education teachers can prepare individualized learning packages on a number of topics such as chapter meetings, opening ceremonies, parliamentary procedures, preparing and presenting speeches, etc. Most CTSOs have a variety of well-prepared materials that can be used to support individualized learning.

- Some competitive events employ written tests, which may cause problems for some learners from special populations. These written tests can be modified as needed by converting them to audiotapes, by reading the items aloud, by allowing oral responses instead of written responses, by delivering tests on the computer, and by substituting hands-on demonstrations for written tests.

- Career and technical student organization activities and competitive events are an integral part of the instructional program. All learners should be given the opportunity to compete in some portion of their instructional program as a learning experience at the local school level. The CTSO advisor and support team can plan and hold the local competition so that all learners can participate. All learners should receive recognition, not just the winners. All CTSOs have certificates and awards that can be given to learners who enter competitions and do their best.
- Learners from special populations learn a great deal from other learners. CTSOs emphasize working together to accomplish goals and projects. Advisors should promote the buddy system (pairing a learner with special needs with a capable learner) as a method of learner development. This helps build a sense of self-confidence for learners with special needs and increases their level of participation.
- Many local schools have more than one career and technical student organization. Organization advisors and support team personnel should plan and work co-operatively to conduct leadership seminars for officers and committee chairpersons on such leadership topics as conducting chapter meetings and fund-raising activities, etc.
- It is often helpful to develop or secure certificates of merit or achievement for learners who have actively participated in CTSO activities to the best of their abilities.
- In order for learners from special populations to be successfully integrated into a CTSO, the advisor may need to make appropriate modifications in some activities.

Sarkees and Sullivan (1985) present the following suggestions for advisors to consider for integrating learners with special needs into CTSOs:

- Assign learners with special needs to committees and/or activities where they will experience success in order to build their confidence and self-esteem.
- Award certificates of merit or participation to learners who are actively involved in VSO activities.
- Publicize the accomplishments (e.g., becoming officers, committee members, competitors, winners in contests, project leaders) of special needs learners in newsletters, school newspapers, and other local publications.
- Set aside time to help learners with special needs develop planning and decision-making skills.
- Be flexible and allow extended time limits for projects when necessary.
- Use advisor-learner contracts for project completion. Plan these carefully to meet the needs and ability levels of each learner. Write in clearly defined goals, directions, and criteria. Reinforce this information periodically and share it with support personnel.
- Allow learners to refer to notes or scripts when they address a group. This will help them develop confidence.

- Encourage learners to become involved in community service projects such as sponsoring families in need, writing letters to shut-ins, or visiting nursing homes.
- Work with local administrators to encourage a positive, flexible, supportive philosophy regarding the integration of learners who have special needs into CTSO activities. Close coordination may also be needed in order to provide appropriate support services for these learners.
- Reinforce the relationship between CTSO activities and career goals.
- Recommend resource materials for support personnel who can help to reinforce CTSO information.
- Invite support personnel to become actively involved in the CTSO (e.g., organization co- advisor, committee chairperson, chairperson, or judge for district or state contests).

This list of ideas to increase the involvement of learners from special populations in CTSO activities and events is not exhaustive. Career and technical education teachers, with assistance from the special needs support team members, can come up with many more ways to improve the match between the capabilities of learners with special needs and CTSO activities. One good technique for teachers in encouraging learners from special populations to join a CTSO is to find one particular talent that a learner with special needs has and encourage the learner to apply that talent to a specific activity. Participation in CTSOs should be a major component in the IEP for disabled learners and the IVEP for other learners from special populations and should be jointly planned by all parties involved.

Career and Technical Student Organization Support Team

Career and technical student organization advisors are often successful in involving learners from special populations in chapter activities, but it is helpful to build a support team as well. Collaborative efforts should be encouraged between the career and technical education teacher/advisor and support personnel. Suggested team members might include special populations (transition) coordinators, special education teachers, English teachers, remedial teachers, administrators, peers, parents, community agencies, school psychologists, counselors, interpreters, and representatives from business and industry.

Examples of approaches for CTSO collaborative teams were identified by Sarkees (1983) and Sarkees and Sullivan (1985) and include the following:

1. Conduct cross-training in-service sessions. Special education teachers can utilize vocational assessment information and share it with CTSO advisors to assist in identifying appropriate modifications for activities, projects, assignments, and contests when necessary. They can also provide information to advisors on preferred learning styles. CTSO advisors can provide support team

members with information about the role of the student organization in the instructional program, including how and when organization activities are implemented, the nature of activities and competitive events, and how team members can assist learners from special populations in selected CTSO activities. See Figure 10-3.

2. Jointly conduct leadership seminars for learners from special populations that would help them develop participation skills and attributes, such as the ability to speak in front of a group, accepting responsibility, delegating duties, accepting and giving constructive criticism, working together as a team, and executing the decision-making process through parliamentary procedure. Informal techniques such as simulation and peer tutoring can be used to deliver instruction in these seminars. For example, CTSO advisors in a school or school district and special education personnel can plan a leadership seminar to meet one evening during the week to focus on the topic of public speaking. Most CTSOs have a prepared speech and an impromptu or extemporaneous speaking contest. These contests usually feature speeches on topics related to the organization's goals and current programs and are supported with rating sheets that include specific criteria used to evaluate speeches.

   In addition, some CTSOs have materials on the topic of public speaking that can be used in a seminar. Seminar content could include an overview of the importance of public speaking skills; an example speech delivered by an experienced CTSO learner volunteer; an illustrated talk on each of the components of public speaking such as opening, voice quality, platform deployment, etc.; a preparation of scripts for learners to follow when speaking in front of groups; assigning learners with special needs to work in small groups with CTSO learner volunteers, advisors, and special education personnel to develop and present components of speeches; videotaping practice speeches given by learners with special needs and reviewing and critiquing them together; and awarding each participant a certificate of achievement for participating in the seminar.

3. Share career and technical education assessment information that may be relevant in the selection and modification of activities and competitive events for a given learner, such as manipulative skills, learning styles, perceptual impairment, and disability.

4. Incorporate CTSO participation into the IEP for disabled learners and IVEP for other learners from special populations. Input should be provided by the CTSO advisor, support personnel, parent/guardian, and learner.

5. Jointly publicize and recognize learners with special needs (without using labels) who have been successful as chapter officers, project leaders, committee chairpersons, and participants in competitive events. The CTSO advisor and support team can discuss ways to recognize the achievement of learners with special needs in activities. For example, special education personnel and career and technical education teachers can develop a CTSO learner recognition program such as the learner of the week or award and publicize this accomplishment on bulletin boards in the classroom and at other appropriate locations throughout the school.

Publishing newsworthy articles on such items as the election of officers, community and school service projects, and attendance at leadership conferences and meetings also provides an excellent opportunity to list the names of learners with special needs who are involved in these activities. First, second, and third place winners of competitive events receive recognition for their accomplishments, but additional awards can be given to others who meet high standards of performance, such as the SkillsUSA-VICA certificates of honor, merit, and accomplishments.

CTSO CROSS-TRAINING MEETING AGENDA

1. Introduce the participants (special educators/CTSO advisor)
2. Explain meeting purpose
   A. Share plans for building a CTSO support team
   B. Dicuss how special education personnel can participate on a team
   C. Discuss how CTSO advisors can give and request information
3. Present a motivational film on each CTSO in the school or district
4. Present brief overviews on each CTSO in the school or district
5. Have a CTSO advisor present a case study problem on a special needs student who has been integrated into CTSO activities
6. Have a special education instructor discuss working with a CTSO advisor regarding an individual with special needs
7. Present a summary of areas where CTSO advisors and support team participants can work together, such as tutoring, chaperoning, judging, co-advising, assisting in modifying materials, contests, and rating devices, etc.
8. Develop a plan of action to establish CTSO support teams
9. Summarize the meeting
10. Share the refreshments

Figure 10-3. Information for special education teachers to share with CTSO advisors to assist in identifying appropriate modifications for activities and programs.

Information about CTSO activities and benefits needs to be shared with parents, who should be encouraged to become actively involved when possible, even if it is only in a "cheerleading" role. Every effort should be made to creatively think of ways to publicize accomplishments of learners from special populations since such recognition helps these learners improve self-concept and build confidence in their abilities to succeed in other areas.

6. Work cooperatively to prepare learners with special needs for competitive events and to modify contest directions, contest procedures, written test items, and response modes as necessary to compensate for disabilities while still adhering to the high standards of performance expected by other learners. CTSO advisors can inform other teachers who are working with a learner with special needs about the learner's decision to enter a competitive event and provide these teachers with information and materials about the contest.

If needed, a CTSO support team meeting can be conducted to explore ways to modify contests, materials, and procedures to allow for full participation of learners with special needs. Such strategies as enlarging the print of directions and test items; providing an auditory tape of contest directions, test directions, and test items; allowing learners to respond orally to test items; and substituting hands-on demonstrations when possible for written test items can be employed to enable learners with special needs to compete in contests.

If there are learners who are hearing impaired or speak limited English, interpreters and signers can be provided to assist as needed. Practice sessions can be arranged to provide learners with opportunities to rehearse their leadership and hands-on skills in simulated environments.

7. Encourage support personnel for learners from special populations to become involved in the following capacities in chapter meetings and activities:
- co-advisor of the chapter or section
- chairperson to plan and conduct a CTSO contest
- interpreter for disabled learners in contest setting
- judge of a CTSO contest
- chairperson for field trips and overnight meetings
- speaker at CTSO chapter/organization meetings
- host or hostess at social or recreational events
- resource person to provide special services to CTSO learners such as remedial assistance in basic skills
- team advisor in civic and community service projects
- support observer for learners involved in contests
- co-teacher in the career and technical education classroom and laboratory
- CTSO support team member
- assistant in leadership seminars
- assistant in publicizing achievement of learners from special populations

8. Work cooperatively with administrators and other faculty to develop positive attitudes toward active participation of learners from special populations in CTSOs. Perhaps the greatest barrier to the involvement of these learners in student organizations is the negative or indifferent attitudes held by these learners, career and technical education teachers, academic teachers, administrators, and parents. These attitudes can only be changed by supplying information to these groups and by creating examples out of learners from special populations who have profited from involvement in CTSO activities. It is necessary to address these negative or indifferent attitudes in the IEP and IVEP planning process and identify specific strategies to make these attitudes more positive toward the involvement of learners from special populations in career and technical student organizations.

Career and Technical Student Organization Special Advisor Functions for Learners from Special Populations

In order for learners from special populations to be successfully integrated into CTSOs, the advisor may need to make appropriate modifications to regular chapter advisor functions. Sarkees and Sullivan (1989) present the following suggestions to CTSO advisors when working with learners from special populations:

- Advise and guide learners from special populations in selecting CTSO activities in which they have interest and a high probability of success in order to build self-esteem and confidence. It is important for some of these learners to engage in group activities first and advance to more demanding individual ones.
- Provide supervision of activities to help learners understand the interrelationship of career and technical education instruction and their CTSO.
- Provide necessary instruction for learners in the steps of planning, preparing for, executing, and evaluating CTSO activities and projects.
- Provide assistance to learners in developing leadership, human relationships, and communication skills in the classroom and in CTSO activities.
- Provide assistance in helping learners set realistic goals for self-improvement.
- Provide assistance to learners who are competing against standards in professional development and achievement programs and those who are preparing for competitive events.
- Provide encouragement to learners to run for CTSO officer positions and to volunteer to chair and/or serve on committees.
- Provide specialized training for learners who are serving as officers and chairpersons.
- Recommend or prepare resources and resource materials that will help learners to participate fully in CTSO activities.

- Suggest resources to finance and implement chapter and individual activities so that economically disadvantaged learners can participate fully in these activities.
- Inform the school administration, faculty, learners, parents, career and technical education advisory committee members, and the community about the involvement of learners from special populations in individual and CTSO chapter activities.
- Arrange for transportation for learners to and from CTSO meetings.
- Devote extra time to advise out-of-school CTSO activities for all learners.
- Form CTSO support teams to help learners benefit fully from CTSO activities.
- Promote the "buddy" system between learners with special needs and other learners involved in CTSO activities.
- Invite support personnel to become actively involved in the CTSO and chapter co-advisors, committee chairpersons, chairpersons, or judges for competitive events.
- Encourage all learners to become involved in community service projects such as sponsoring families in need, writing letters to shut-ins, or visiting senior citizen homes.
- Encourage learners to refer to notes if needed when they are addressing large groups.
- Develop and use advisor-learner contracts for project completion. This will engage learners in carefully determining realistic goals and developing directions, criteria, and timelines for project completion.
- Set aside time to help learners develop planning, problem-solving, and decision-making skills.
- Publicize the accomplishments of learners in newsletters, school newspapers, and local publicity (e.g., officers, committee chairpersons and members, competitive event contestants and winners, and project leaders).
- Assist all learners in learning from both successful and unsuccessful CTSO activities.
- Allow the CTSO chapter to be learner-led rather than instructor-led.
- Facilitate the development of a meaningful program of work that will guide the chapter for the membership year and involve all members in CTSO activities.

Creative Activities to Supplement Career and Technical Student Organization Activities for Learners from Special Populations

Career and technical education teachers often duplicate national CTSO activities, awards programs, and competitive events because these experiences are well established, organized, and supported with written materials. There is nothing wrong with this practice, but career and technical education teachers and CTSO support team personnel should consider other worthy activities to meet the unique needs of learners from special populations, while at the same time, providing benefits to other learners.

One activity that can be developed is the formation or sponsorship of career or job groups. This activity organizes learners into a group that investigates all the factors involved in locating, obtaining, and making progress on a career or job. Activities may include uncovering the hidden job listing through use of the telephone, direct contact with employment sources, and networking with friends, parents, and relatives. Learners can role-play how to open and close job bids, how to respond to tough questions in an interview, how to meet employer's expectations, and how to adjust to supervision styles. CTSO materials, such as job interview contest materials, can be used to support this activity. The national SkillsUSA-VICA has a job program that may be used as a source of ideas for this activity. In addition, there are many commercially available materials on the topic of finding and keeping jobs that can be obtained for this activity.

Another activity that can be developed is the creation of a futuristic community. Learners could gather information from written materials and interview community leaders to determine what the community might look like 20 years in the future. Learners then recreate the community in model form, applying new technological advances in transportation, energy, communications, housing, agriculture, business, industry, government, and health care. All learners can be actively involved in cooperating on and creating this project.

Another example is the implementation of the total quality management approach to classroom instruction and the organization and implementation of CTSOs. An excellent source of information is the *Total Quality Curriculum* available from national SkillsUSA-VICA. This resource is composed of 17 chapters that begin with a discussion, followed by activities that put quality concepts into practice. Implementing a total quality curriculum will help learners develop the skills needed for tomorrow's workers, such as creativity, problem solving, teamwork, and decision making.

A final example of creative activity is engaging the learners in the development of a chapter web page. This will give them an opportunity for creative expression. It will help them identify and organize important information, utilize marketing principles, and develop technical skills in using digital cameras and computer software programs.

These four activities are only examples of what can be developed to capture learner interest and provide opportunities for learners to gain new knowledge and skills. These activities also provide opportunities for learners to apply what they have learned in an interest area.

SUMMARY

Beginning around the time of the Smith-Hughes Act, career and technical education program leaders recognized the need for forming student organizations to provide learners with opportunities to develop leardership, social, and communication skills in a career area. The first program area to form a student organization was agriculture with the FFA. Currently, there are 10 nationally recognized CTSOs serving the major service areas for secondary and postsecondary learners. Active CTSOs provide many benefits to learners, teachers, schools, and communities. These organizations have developed many functions and activities that are interesting to learners while providing them with motivation to enhance their technical knowledge and skills, their leardership abilities, and their social and communication skills.

All career and technical education learners, including those from special populations, need to be given the opportunity to develop their potentials through active participation as members of a CSTO. Many individuals from special populations can participate in regular CTSO activities with little or no modifications, but some will need intervention services and accommodations to benefit fully from organizational activities. CTSO advisors, with the help of support team members, can make the necesssary modifications in most of these activities. There are perceived barriers that some learners from special populations have about participating in CTSO activities, but these are often more perceived than real. Career and technical education instructors can utilize many of the recommendations presented in this chapter to encourage learners from special populations to become active CTSO members and to involve them in significatnt ways in the many positions, functions, and activities of these organizations.

SELF-ASSESSMENT

1. When, why, and how did CTSOs develop?
2. What are some of the benefits and advantages CTSOs provide to learners, teachers, schools, and communities?
3. What are the missions and purposes of CTSOs?
4. How can participation in CTSOs help learners develop workplace basics?
5. Identify and briefly describe the 10 nationally recognized career and technical student organizations and the National Vocational-Technical Honor Society.
6. What are some of the major advisor functions in implementing career and technical student organizations as an integral part of the instructional program?
7. How can teachers or support people obtain information and materials to help them initiate, organize, and manage a career and technical student organizations as an integral part of a career and technical education program?
8. How can career and technical education teachers integrate career and technical student organization programs, events, and activities into the regular instructional program?
9. What are some modifications that advisors may need to make to accommodate learners with special needs in career and technical student organization activities?

ASSOCIATED ACTIVITIES

1. Select a CTSO web site that is of interest to you and become familiar with the facts about the organization, including its motto, creed, purpose and objectives, programs, services, publications, and special events.
2. Obtain CTSO materials from national headquarters on topics like leadership development, communication skills, and team-building skills and incorporate them into your instructional program.
3. Attend CTSO leadership workshops and conferences that may be offered locally, regionally, or at the state and national levels.
4. Visit a school with career and technical education programs and observe how CTSO activities are incorporated as an integral part of the curriculum.
5. Using information obtained from the web page or from the national or state office of a selected CTSO, prepare a promotional report to deliver to a chosen audience that would inform them and spark their interest in the organization.
6. Write an article supporting CTSOs for publication in a CTSO magazine or another professional journal.

REFERENCES

American Vocational Association. (1990). *The AVA guide to the Carl D. Perkins Vocational and Applied Technology Education Act of 1990.* Alexandria, VA: Author.

American Vocational Association. (1998) *The official guide to the Perkins Act of 1998.* Alexandria, VA: Author.

Birchenall, J., & Wanat, J. (1981). Serving the handicapped in vocational student organizations. *Vocational Education, 56*(3), 51-54.

Business Professionals of America. (2000). [On-line] Available: http://www.bpa.org

Butler, T. (1981). What's in it for the teacher? *Vocational Education, 56*(6), 47-49.

Delta Epsilon Chi. (2001). [On-line] Available: http://www.delta-hq.org

Family, Career and Community Leaders of America. (2000). [On-line] Available: http://www.fcclainc.org

Harris, T., & Sweet, G. (1981). Why we believe in vocational student organizations. *Vocational Education, 56*(6), 33-35.

Kaufman, B. E., & Wills, J. L. (1999). *User's guide to the Workforce Investment Act of 1998. A companion to the law and regulations* Alexandria, VA: Association for Career and Technical Education.

Leonard, L. L., & Elston, B. (1981). Second thoughts about federal support for vocational student organizations. *VocEd Journal of the American Vocational Association, 56*(6), p. 22.

Miller, K. (2000). Straight from the source. *Techniques, 75*(1), 24.

Morrissey, P. (1993). *The educator's guide to the Americans with Disabilities Act.* Alexandria, VA: American Vocational Association.

National Advisory Council on Vocational Education. (1972). *Vocational student organizations, 7th report.* Washington, DC: Author.

The National Coordinating Council for Career and Technical Student Organizations. (1999). *Career and technical student organizations: A reference guide.* Washington, DC: National Association of State Directors of Vocational and Technical Education Consortium.

National Information Center for Children and Youth with Disabilities. (1998, June). *NICHCY News Digest 26.* Washington DC: Author.

National Vocational-Technical Honor Society. (2000). [On-line] Available: http://www.nvths.org

Sarkees, M. D. (1983). Vocational student organizations: Benefits for handicapped students. *Teaching Exceptional Children, 16*(1), 60-64.

Sarkees, M. D., & Sullivan, R. L. (1985). Special needs students and vocational student organizations: A winning team. *Vocational Education, 60*(5).

Sarkees, M. D., & Sullivan, R. L. (1989). Learners with special needs in vocational student organizations. *The Journal for Vocational Special Needs Education, 12*(1), 21-26.

SkillsUSA-VICA. (1999). *SkillsUSA-VICA leadership handbook.* Leesburg, VA: Author.

SkillsUSA-VICA. (2001). [On-line] Available: http://www.skillsusa.org

Technology Student Association. (2001). [On-line] Available: http://www.tsawww.org

Vaughn, P. R. (1999). *Handbook for advisors of vocational student organizations.* Winterville, GA: The American Association for Vocational Instructional Materials.

Vaughn, P. R., Vaughn, R. C., & Vaughn, D. L. (1993). *Handbook for advisors of vocational student organizations.* Athens, GA: American Association for Vocational Instructional Materials.

Vocational student organizations —"A reference guide." (1990). National Coordinating Council for Vocational Student Organizations. (Available from National SkillsUSA-VICA, P.O. Box 3000, Leesburg, VA 20177-0300).

Coordinating Student Services

INTRODUCTION

Student services are defined as those services provided by an educational institution to facilitate learning and the successful transition of learners from school to lasting and rewarding careers and lifelong learning. A variety of services are available for learners from special populations. However, coordinating these services and deciding which institution or agency will provide them for a specific learner is not always accomplished easily. Without school-based teaming efforts and interagency collaboration, many services may be excluded or duplicated.

The goal of educators who work with learners from special populations is to organize an active, participative team that can facilitate success for all learners. Once necessary services have been identified they should be coordinated and planned through a student services plan that can be used to facilitate services necessary for a specific learner.

The collaboration of educators in school-based settings is necessary in order for a comprehensive system of student services to be organized and made available to learners from special populations who are enrolled in career and technical programs.

Over the past decade, cooperation and coordinated planning between education and agencies have been recognized as effective and efficient methods to serve individuals from special populations. Interagency networking can include collaboration between education and agencies, service organizations, business and industry, and community services. Interagency linkage helps reduce gaps in service delivery, minimizes duplication of services, and reduces unnecessary expense. In addition, interagency linkage has been identified as a crucial component in helping these learners make a successful transition from school to employment or postsecondary programs. Local linkages should investigate services needed by learners with special needs so that their career potential can be developed, determine which agency can provide which services, and determine to what extent these services can be shared in a cost-effective manner.

OUTLINE

OBJECTIVES

After completing this chapter, the reader should be able to accomplish the following:

1. Provide a rationale for coordinating student services for learners from special populations who are enrolled in career and technical education programs.
2. Discuss the importance of teambuilding in providing student services to learners from special populations who are enrolled in career and technical education programs.
3. Identify student services frequently available at secondary and postsecondary institutions for learners from special populations.
4. Identify methods of communication to facilitate school-based teaming.
5. Discuss the importance of collaborative planning with agencies and organizations to provide student services for learners from special populations.
6. Identify methods to promote interagency linkage for student services for learners from special populations.
7. Describe the importance of local interagency linkage teams in providing student services for learners from special populations.
8. Describe the importance of collaborative planning with business and industry in providing student services for learners from special populations.

TERMS

agency	networking	student services
interagency agreement	one-stop career center	student services plan
interagency cooperation	paraprofessional/paraeducator	teacher support team
interagency linkage	resource directory	team
local advisory committee	school-based student services	telementoring
mentoring	special education personnel	transition coordinator

OVERVIEW OF STUDENT SERVICES

The need to relate education and work more effectively cannot be overemphasized. All learners need much assistance to become competitive in today's and tomorrow's world market. To keep pace with rapidly changing technology and other workplace demands, educators, businesses, parents, and the community have to collaborate to provide all learners with a high-quality education and training system that includes the delivery of essential student services (Maddy-Bernstein & Cunanan, 1996).

Student services are those services provided by an educational institution to facilitate learning and the successful transition of learners from school to lasting and rewarding careers and lifelong learning. High-quality, comprehensive, and coordinated student services systems can make a difference in every learner's educational and occupational future.

Student services are crucial for at-risk learners work. Keeping learners in school is one of the challenges that educators face today. Statistics show that a huge proportion of high school students are unable to complete high school or choose to drop out. At-risk learners include those who are

- not learning to read or compute;
- learning to hate school;
- dropping out of school;
- becoming hooked on drugs;
- drifting into crime;
- becoming sexually active too soon;
- getting pregnant;
- becoming despondent and suicidal;
- failing to acquire skills needed for employment;
- failing to acquire the understanding needed for citizenship;
- failing to acquire habits of work;
- drifting into and remaining in poverty;
- becoming dependent on welfare throughout life; and
- placing their own children in future cycles of risk.

Forces that place learners as risk include those that (1) stem from society (e.g., poverty, hardships that come with minority status, weakening of home influence); (2) originate with the school and educational programs (e.g., the troubled curriculum, unsuitable standards for large numbers of learners); and (3) come from within the learner (e.g., emotional factors that lower self-esteem).

While there is no single approach that works best to provide essential student services effectively, the following are guidelines that schools can use to build a student services system:

- Use all available resources, including those in the school, the educational system, and the community. Parents, students, business and industry representatives, school administrators, faculty, counselors, and all school staff, as well as community service providers must work cooperatively and collaboratively.
- Assess the needs of every learner. Assessment is imperative in determining how to serve the learner best and avoid duplication of programs and services.
- Implement a comprehensive management system to ensure that all learners are receiving needed services.
- Use the developmental approach. Through this approach, each learner, while in the process of progressing through some common growth stages, is still recognized as unique.
- Involve administrators, parents, teachers, and other school staff members in the change process. High schools can combat potential resistance to the concept of building a comprehensive student services system by gaining the support and collaboration of those working with learners.
- Design and conduct staff development activities that will prepare the school and the community for the work ahead. Workshops or seminars can focus on the following topics: how the new system works, curriculum integration, team building, time management, and others.
- Keep the communication lines open among all key players. This will help break down the traditional barriers between levels of education and between student services personnel and other school staff.
- Resolve issues that can impede the implementation of an inclusive student services system (e.g., coordinating several services, providing time for personnel to work together, and funding).
- Conduct ongoing evaluation and follow-up for program improvement and to determine student services.
- Organize a student services team (SST). As a team, student services personnel can effectively provide the necessary student services (Maddy-Bernstein & Cunanan, 1996).

EXEMPLARY PROGRAM COMPONENTS

In 1989, The National Center for Research in Vocational Education conducted an extensive review of related literature on how exemplary vocational special needs programs were identified and designed a framework consisting of 20 components that characterize exemplary programs. A pilot test of the framework was conducted through 1994. See Appendix. These 20 components include

1. administrative leadership and support;
2. financial support;
3. professional development;
4. formative program evaluation;
5. summative program evaluation;
6. individualized curriculum modifications;
7. integration of academic and vocational curricula;
8. appropriate instructional settings;
9. cooperative learning experiences;
10. assessment of vocational interests and abilities;
11. instructional support services;
12. career guidance and counseling;
13. family/parental involvement and support;
14. notification of both students and parents regarding vocational opportunities;

15. vocational educator's involvement in individualized educational planning;
16. formalized transition planning;
17. intra- and interagency collaboration;
18. work experience opportunities;
19. job placement services; and
20. follow-up of graduates and nongraduates (Matias et al, 1995).

SECONDARY PROGRAMS

High schools today face the challenge of ensuring success for all learners. To prepare all high school students for rewarding careers, schools must offer essential student services in addition to sound curricular offerings. An efficient, coordinated, and comprehensive student services system is a key component in enhancing the chances of success for every learner (Maddy-Bernstein & Cunanan, 1996).

Maddy-Bernstein and Cunanan, (1996) identified the following three stages of attendance during which learners may need core services:

1. pre-enrollment, when the learner is preparing to enroll in a secondary school
2. enrollment, when the learner is enrolled
3. post-enrollment, when the learner has left the program, whether he or she has advanced to the next level or withdrawn

The principle driving this model is that schools must assist all learners in realizing their educational and career goals. Learners need some services during all three levels and others at different stages of enrollment. See Figure 11-1. Some of these services, such as counseling, food services, transportation services, safety and security services, and medical/nursing services, are often taken for granted by learners and parents. Other basic or fundamental services include child-care assistance, psychological services, social work/social services, and special accommodations.

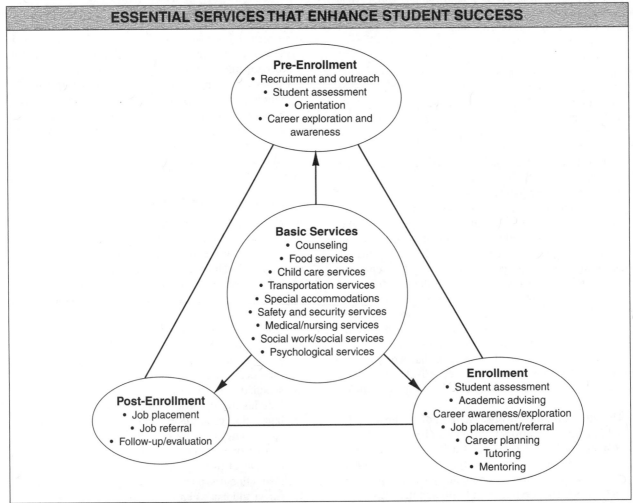

Source: Maddy-Bernstein, C., & Cunanan, E. (1996, October). *Student Services: Achieving Success for All Secondary Students.* Berkeley, CA: National Center for Research in Vocational Education.

Figure 11-1. A model of services to be delivered during different phases of a learner's school experience.

During the pre-enrollment stage, learners need certain services to facilitate their movement to the next level (e.g., middle to high school, high school to college, education to work). Activities and programs at this stage are designed to help learners be familiar with and adjust to another level of school life or, ultimately, to work. Orientation to their new school is very helpful. Appropriate assessment should take place, as well as career awareness and exploration activities. Learners will benefit from career/educational counseling prior to entering a high school program.

During enrollment, most learners will continue to need educational/career counseling, including career exploration and awareness, career/transition planning (including financial aid), and additional assessment. Some learners will need tutoring, most will benefit from a mentor, and almost all can use academic advisement. Job-referral and job-placement services help ensure a learner's smooth transition from school to gainful employment.

While graduates and those who leave school early traditionally have minor contact with the former institution, many of them would still profit from job referral, job placement, and counseling. There seems to be a growing trend for former learners in the post-enrollment stage to return frequently to their previous school to serve on advisory councils, to act as mentors to current learners, to offer jobs to learners, and to provide other assistance.

POSTSECONDARY PROGRAMS

Services provided by postsecondary schools address learner needs that range from typical, developmental needs common to many learners at a particular age—like the inability to determine a career choice—to atypical, severe problems such as clinical depression. Student services professionals in colleges and universities respond to each case by understanding the continuum of problems and correct responses through meetings with learners or through referrals from others who know the learners.

Pacifici and McKinney (1997) identified several barriers that learners from special populations may encounter in seeking and effectively utilizing student services at the postsecondary level:

- In contrast to the K-12 sector, learners in higher education must initiate a referral for themselves. In this situation, awareness of the availability of the services is critical to referral. In addition to knowing that services are available, other factors may influence a learner to seek services, such as individual motivation, perception of ability and need for services, and willingness to accept the assistance. Any one of these factors could be a substantial barrier to obtaining service.
- Often, learning disabilities are the only disability category for which colleges complete the assessment, and learners with other types of disabilities must be assessed through an outside agency such as a hospital or reha-

bilitation department, or a private consultant. Although the college will generally direct learners to these outside agencies, transportation, time, and financial constraints may make it difficult for learners to obtain the assessments on which their services depend.
- Faculty and staff perceptions and training are an important part of the provision of student services. The elimination of attitudinal barriers is critically linked to the knowledge and support of faculty and staff.
- The introduction of computer technology to many campuses may require that additional services be instituted to ensure that learners with disabilities are able to utilize them effectively. It may also increase the demand for more technologically advanced and expensive equipment such as speech synthesizers and word predictor software.

Services offered through student services at the postsecondary level may include
- registration assistance;
- academic advisement to remove academic deficiencies, help with selecting appropriate courses, major advisement, and financial aid counseling;
- monitoring grade point averages and academic progress for learners who are not accustomed to identifying what the academic needs in college will be;
- personal and academic supportive counseling for learners who have not practiced setting academic and career goals, and those experiencing adjustment problems;
- graduation and graduate/professional school advisement for learners remaining in college without definitive plans;
- instruction in study skills, time management, and negotiating the college experience for learners who have poor habits in these areas;
- developing strategies to help learners maintain acceptable grade point averages;
- career and technical or transitional guidance;
- loan of equipment;
- note taking assistance;
- sign language interpreting;
- special classroom seating arrangements;
- reading assistance/taped texts;
- referrals to community resources;
- advocacy with campus instructors and staff;
- testing accommodations;
- tutoring (face-to-face, on-line, individual, group);
- study groups;
- assistance in participating in campus organizations;
- assistance to enhance peer contact and support;
- financial aid;
- veterans affairs;
- service learning;
- international learner concerns;
- testing center;
- technology resources; and
- personal counseling and support groups.

When discussing the needs of learners with disabilities and the obligations of institutions that serve them, it is not uncommon for someone to ask, "Who's going to pay for all this?" Nowhere has this question been more hotly debated over time than between the higher education community and the vocational rehabilitation system. More specifically, the issue of responsibility for payment of sign language interpreter services and, by extension, other auxiliary aids and services, has been at the heart of an escalating debate for several years.

Colleges and universities will typically access other agencies, such as the state's division of vocational rehabilitation, in helping to mitigate the costs for services whenever possible. It is assumed that other existing agencies can be looked to as a means of holding down the cost involved in providing services to learners with disabilities in higher education. An interagency agreement may be developed between higher education and a state's division of vocational rehabilitation for individuals with disabilities.

COORDINATING SCHOOL-BASED STUDENT SERVICES

The first step in planning and facilitating student services for learners from special populations is to identify essential services that each learner will need in order to successfully participate and succeed in career and technical education programs. See Figure 11-2. Once necessary services have been identified for a specific learner, they should be coordinated and planned through a student services plan. See Figure 11-3.

When instructional assistance, student services, and other services are provided to address specific needs of learners from special populations, change occurs. Student services have proven effective in helping to build the technical skills and work behaviors necessary for career success and gainful employment. Some specific outcomes for the learner who receives these services include

- acquiring positive study habits and skills;
- improving self esteem;
- accepting responsibility;
- setting realistic goals;
- adjusting successfully to change;
- developing effective assertiveness skills;
- developing decision-making skills;
- realizing and being able to discuss one's own vocational strengths and learning styles with instructors or employers;
- improving attendance;
- building positive employable-worker traits;
- working successfully with others;
- consistently completing assignments;
- developing leadership skills;
- using time effectively;
- using effective test-taking skills;

- participating in career and technical student organization activities and meetings;
- competing in and/or winning a competition in skill contests (e.g., career and technical student organization competition);
- investigating postsecondary training programs;
- obtaining and retaining employment in a chosen occupational area;
- passing a licensing board examination;
- completing job applications; and
- experiencing successful work experience (Maryland State Department of Education, 1984).

ROLES AND RESPONSIBILITIES OF SCHOOL-BASED STUDENT SERVICES

Career and technical education personnel cannot be expected to accept the full responsibility of planning, implementing, and evaluating appropriate programming for learners with special needs. Cooperative planning is essential if necessary services are to be provided. The success of these learners in career and technical education programs depends to a large degree on the collaborative relationships established among school-based personnel. A team approach is usually the best method to ensure that these learners receive appropriate guidance and counseling services, supplemental services, instructional materials, occupational competencies, evaluation activities and job placement opportunities. See Figure 11-4. Following are suggested roles and responsibilities of select school-based team members, including academic teachers, administrators, guidance and counseling personnel, and paraprofessionals/paraeducators.

Academic Teachers

Academic teachers can play a key role in working with learners from special populations who are enrolled in career and technical education programs. Some services that can be provided by academic teachers include

- sharing ideas, insights, and expertise with the career and technical education instructors;
- helping blend academic concepts with career and technical education content in an effort to make learning experiences more realistic and meaningful for all learners in their classes; and
- reporting to the rest of the school-based team members any problems or concerns that may arise in their classroom regarding learners with special needs.

Administrators

The administrator's role in planning, implementing, and evaluating career and technical education programs to meet the needs of learners from special populations is very important in the collaborative planning process. The administrator's role in formulating cooperative agreements is very important. Policies used to determine how programs will be coordinated and monitored to include learners with special needs are usually formulated by administrators at state and local levels. With administration support in the cooperative planning process, the following services can be provided:

- appropriate service delivery options
- student services necessary to assist learners
- flexible scheduling opportunities, such as extended time in programs and open entry/open exit arrangements
- staff development/professional development activities to develop cooperative relationships among school-based personnel
- funds to purchase instructional materials
- elimination of environmental barriers, modification of machinery and equipment, and modification of classroom/laboratory facilities for accessibility.

In order for learners with special needs to achieve success, it is important that administrators

- clarify the district/campus/institution philosophy of providing career and technical education for learners from special populations;
- demonstrate belief in career and technical education for all learners and develop policies and guidelines to support this philosophy;
- become well informed about the requirements mandated by federal and state legislation concerned with career preparation of learners from special populations;
- work toward implementing these mandates, especially equal access to career and technical education programs for learners from special populations;
- annually survey the school district/campus to locate and identify individuals with special needs who are eligible for career and technical education programs and notify them of the programs and student services available within the district;
- consider necessary student services for learners from special populations as a factor in the process of educational planning for each learner;
- provide services for learners with special needs (e.g., counseling services, registration assistance, career development activities, orientation and mobility instruction, transportation assistance, interpreters, special materials and equipment, and academic remediation assistance);
- identify roles and responsibilities of personnel in the district/campus/institution in providing career and technical education for learners from special populations;
- periodically share the progress of the district/campus/institution in meeting the established goals for providing career and technical education for learners from special populations;
- provide for professional development/staff development to assist personnel in meeting the needs of learners from special populations enrolled in career and technical education programs;

- emphasize and facilitate continuous collaboration among school-based personnel, community resources, agencies, business/industry, and parents in the planning, implementation, and evaluation of individual education plans/transition plans for learners;
- share information about needs of learners from special populations as they relate to future career demands; and
- actively promote public relations activities describing the goals of the district/campus/institution in making career and technical education accessible to learners from special populations as well as the student services available to help them succeed.

Guidance and Counseling Personnel

Counseling and guidance personnel should be instrumental in providing guidance, counseling, and career development activities to learners from special populations. Some services that can be provided by counselors include

- administering or supervising vocational assessment activities;
- reviewing vocational assessment data, interpret the results, and making recommendations for services for learners from special populations;
- providing and supervising the provision of guidance counseling and career development activities designed to facilitate the transition from school to postsecondary training or to post-school employment and career opportunities;
- cooperating with student services personnel;
- coordinating career and technical education activities and services with special education, compensatory education, bilingual or ESL programs to provide services needed by learners from special populations who are enrolled in career and technical education programs;
- providing information about the local job market;
- providing assistance in helping learners make decisions about job alternatives related to their interests, values, and capabilities;
- counseling learners regarding their work adjustment development;
- developing support groups for learners;
- providing information on work-study opportunities;
- providing parental/family counseling as well as personal counseling;
- providing information about local community resources;
- creating job clubs for learners to assist them in developing job-seeking and job-retention skills;
- facilitating school-based cooperative team meetings to plan for and evaluate educational programs developed for learners; and
- conducting exit interviews with learners as they leave the educational system and refer them to agencies and services within the community that will assist them in reaching their transition goals.

STUDENT SERVICES FOR LEARNERS FROM SPECIAL POPULATIONS

In order to plan appropriate career and technical education programming for learners from special populations, essential support services must be identified for each student. Suggested support services include

- Advisement (academic, career, vocational, personal)
- Applied academics
- Bilingual career and technical instruction and/or materials
- Campus accessibility for individuals with disabilities
- Career development activities
- Changes in time allowed to complete courses or programs
- Changes in time spent in the lab/classroom for additional instruction
- Classroom accommodations
- Communication skills development
- Coordination of academic work with the curriculum in the career and technical education program
- Counseling/guidance services
- Curriculum modification activities
- Diagnostic/prescriptive services
- Equipment/facilities modifications
- Free/reduced fees or materials
- Financial assistance (e.g., tuition fees for postsecondary programs)
- Follow-up to evaluate transition plans/services
- Functional living skills
- In-school work experiences (paid or unpaid)
- Instructional material modifications
- Interpreters
- Job clubs, placement assistance, seeking and retention skills, follow-up assistance, and readiness instruction
- Medical services
- Modification of instructional strategies involving changes in
  - ~ reading requirements
  - ~ math requirement
  - ~ methods of instruction
  - ~ sequence of topics
  - ~ classroom environment
  - ~ project or report requirements
  - ~ methods of testing student competencies
- Note-taking assistance
- Occupational therapy
- Paraprofessional/teacher aide assistance
- Parent counseling and training
- Physical therapy
- Postsecondary placement follow-up assistance
- Postsecondary program orientation
- Psychological services
- Reader and interpreter assistance
- Referral assistance to agencies
- Remedial academics
- Social skills development
- Specialized instructional materials and equipment
- Study skills
- Summer work experience
- Supplementary services for limited English-proficient learners
- Testing accommodations
- Transfer assistance (e.g., middle school to high school, high school to postsecondary programs)
- Tutoring
- Work experience programs

Figure 11-2. A list of student services that may be necessary for specific learners from special populations.

STUDENT SERVICES PLAN

Student's Name _____ **Grade Level** _____ **Age** _____

Based on career interest and aptitude assessment data, this student is recommended for placement in the following program area:

_____Agricultural Science and Technology

_____Industrial Technology

_____Office Education

_____Career Investigation

_____Marketing Education

_____Consumer and Family Science Education

_____Health Science Technology

_____Trade and Industrial Education

Specific Class: _____

Characteristic of Student

Vocational assessment data show deficits in the following areas:

__ Communication skills
  __ Reading
  __ Writing
  __ Composition
__ Math skills
__ Vocational behaviors
__ Work attitudes
__ Career awareness
__ Is below grade level
__ Other (describe)
_____
_____
_____
_____

Support Services Needed

Items checked are the programs or services necessary for the student to succeed in the program:

__ Specialized career counseling
__ Extended community involvment
__ Use of teacher aides
__ Tutorial services and assistance
__ Integration of basic education and vocational subject matter
__ Team teaching in career and technical education programs
__ Curriculum modifcation (implemenation, not development)
__ Adaptations in the career/employment goals for individual students
__ Changes in the rules regarding
  __ a. time allowed to complete a course or program
  __ b. time spent in the lab or classroom
__ Changes in the course of study in an individual student's program
__ Changes in the way program accomplishments are reported
__ Programmed and individualized instruction
__ Special teachers
__ Special teachers for job readiness (prevocational) instruction
__ Arrangements for transportation
__ Specialized equipment
__ Other (describe)
_____
_____
_____
_____

Check modifications of courses necessary for student participation:

__ Changes in reading requirements
__ Changes in listening requirements
__ Changes in math requirements
__ Changes in the methods of instruction
__ Changes in the pace of instruction
__ Changes in the sequence of topics
__ Changes in tools, equipment, or machinery used in the classroom
__ Changes in the classroom environment
__ Changes in project or report requirements
__ Changes in the way tests are given

Source: Mikulin, E., & Patterson, R. (1992). *Guide for Serving Members of Special Populations in Vocational and Applied Technology Education*. Austin, TX: Texas Education Agency, Vocational and Applied Technology.

Figure 11-3. A sample of a student services plan for learners from special populations participating in career and technical education programs.

SCHOOL-BASED PERSONNEL

- administrators
- academic instructors
- bilingual personnel
- career and technical personnel
- cooperative education personnel/work study coordinators
- counselors
- curriculum coordinators
- interpreters, direct readers, note-takers
- itinerant personnel
- job coaches
- learners from special populations as self-advocates
- media specialists
- nurses/medical personnel
- occupational therapists
- paraprofessionals/paraeducators
- parents as partners in education
- physical therapists
- psychologists
- rehabilitation services personnel (coordinating the IWRP with the IEP)
- remedial academic personnel
- social workers
- special education personnel
- speech therapists/communication specialists
- transition coordinators
- vocational assessment personnel

Figure 11-4. A list of school-based personnel who can provide student services for learners from special populations.

Paraprofessionals/Paraeducators

Paraprofessionals or paraeducators are employees (1) whose positions are either instructional in nature or who deliver other direct or indirect services to learners and/or their parents and (2) who work under the supervision of teachers or other professional personnel who have the ultimate responsibility for (a) the design and implementation of education and related student services programs, and (b) the assessment of their impact on learners' progress and other education outcomes.

Paraprofessionals can play an important role in providing necessary student services to learners from special populations enrolled in career and technical education programs. Suggested responsibilities of paraprofessionals include

- providing tutorial services to learners or small groups of learners in career and technical education classrooms who have difficulty comprehending the program content or who need more attention given to assigned tasks or related materials;

- providing assistance to learners in laboratory activities and assignments;
- selecting and utilizing available instructional materials in coordination with the instructor and the transition coordinator;
- modifying instructional materials;
- giving suggestions to learners for self-improvement in a supportive way;
- assisting with record keeping and filing to keep learners' progress updated;
- documenting student competency profiles/portfolios;
- facilitating group activities;
- observing behaviors and participating in behavior management strategies;
- giving tests and quizzes;
- supervising learners in off-campus instructional programs (e.g., cooperative education settings); and
- serving as a liaison between school and community.

Ensuring that paraprofessionals' work contributes appropriately to achieving the school's mission requires the following five important factors:

1. Clear definitions of paraprofessional roles and responsibilities–Aligning diverse responsibilities, time allocations, teacher direction, and formal supervision can generate clear expectations for teaching assistants and lay the foundation for teamwork between them and their teacher colleagues. Because paraprofessionals now play many diverse educational roles, they need clearly defined responsibilities, or they risk being pulled in different directions by those who direct and supervise them. For instance, a teaching assistant whose job is to manage a computer lab may be regularly asked to patrol the halls or deliver audio/visual equipment to various teachers, leaving her/his assignment uncovered. Those who work closely with paraprofessionals suggest that role overload and role conflict are more often the rule than the exception.

2. Appropriate job qualifications–Concerns about the qualifications of teaching assistants were raised after studies commissioned by the U.S. Department of Education found that some assistants were assuming roles normally reserved for teachers. To help prevent such problems, 26 states have established specific education or experience guidelines for hiring paraprofessionals in regular education. For example, recommended standards for paraprofessional licensing include a high school diploma; district-sponsored training that includes initial pre-service and ongoing in-service education; and demonstrated competency in areas directly bearing on paraprofessionals' assignments, such as instructional methods and behavior management.

3. Ongoing professional development–Awareness of the value of professional development is growing at school and classroom levels and among policy makers at state and local levels. Developing a good training program begins by identifying which skills and

knowledge are most important for paraprofessionals to cultivate. Experts recommend that professional development programs include topics that not only provide the foundation for instructional support activities but also build a shared professional language for collaborating with teachers. These topics include learning principles and instructional strategies; classroom and behavior management strategies; school policies, legal and ethical issues, and confidentiality protection; school governance issues related to school or district practices; and maintenance of a safe and secure environment.

4. Organizational support for paraprofessionals' work–Roles designed for paraprofessionals should be performed under the supportive direction of a certified teacher. Effective programs and schools provide the conditions that enable paraprofessionals to learn the duties required of them, receive evaluation that helps them excel in their positions, and become more aware of the important role they play on the instructional team.

5. Development of effective career ladders–Career ladders, which most often support the transition from paraprofessional to teacher, are an increasingly popular strategy for recruiting qualified teachers and improving the diversity of the teacher labor force. Some programs, conducted by school or district staff, lead to salary increments and promotions within the role of teaching assistant. Others, often co-managed by districts and colleges or universities, lead to degrees and certification.

For many paraprofessionals studying to become certified teachers, their college enrollment is a first in their families' history. Participants in such programs report that they need and want family support, but their families often do not understand the nature and extent of program demands. Programs that celebrate participants' small successes through periodic informal social events for families have discovered that such gatherings nurture family support (Policy Studies Associates, 2001).

Morgan and Ashbaker (2001) suggested the following for instructors who work with paraeducators:

- Set aside a regular time to meet with your paraeducator and plan work together: Situations change, so schedules need to be adjusted to allow for meetings throughout the school year.
- Be sure that you have a clear idea of what you wish to accomplish with your students before you share your plans with your paraeducator and ask for her suggestions. Keep an open mind and be prepared to incorporate her suggestions, as she will bring a new perspective and her own rich experience to your work together for student success.
- Prepare a written job description for your paraeducator. For each role you assign her, include details of what the role includes and what it does not include so that she knows exactly what the limits of her responsibilities are.

- Check school and district policies and procedures regarding the employment and supervision of paraeducators to ensure that you are assigning responsibilities that your paraeducator should not assume.
- Clearly explain to your paraeducator what her role is in relation to parents—what information she should or should not share with them—and whether she will be invited to parent-teacher conferences. It may be useful to put this in writing so that she can refer to it during the school year.
- Ask your paraeducator to list her previous experience and what skills/assets she thinks she brings to the job. Ask her if there are additional responsibilities she believes she could take on in the light of these skills/assets.
- Check whether your paraeducator has the necessary skills before you assign her roles. This may mean that initially you assign simple tasks and then add more complex roles as you observe her work and see how well she handles each additional responsibility.
- Be aware of your paraeducator's strengths and preferences. For example, some people prefer to have things written down. They may not tell you, but you will notice that tasks do not get done if they are not written down. Other people may need to have instructions explained several times. Express your needs and preferences to your paraeducator so that you can both respect each other's strengths.
- If a task or teaching assignment is not performed the way you expected, before you challenge your paraeducator, ask yourself "Did I give clear directions?" "Did I misunderstand what she said she would do?" or "Were there other factors I was not aware of that prevented her completing the assignment?"
- Be honest with your paraeducator. If you do not agree with the way she does something in particular, then let her know. But remember to also let her know about what she does that you do like and agree with.
- Be specific in the feedback you give your paraeducator. If she has done something particularly well, tell her exactly what it is rather than expressing your approval in general terms. If you need to ask her to change what she does, be specific about what you would like her to do instead and provide a rationale for the new behavior or method.
- Ask your paraeducator to observe you as you teach so that you can model effective instructional practices for her. In order to focus her attention on one specific aspect at a time, ask her to take data on your performance so that you can discuss the data afterwards and explain why you do certain things that you would also like her to do.
- Although it may feel that you cannot do without your paraeducator, even for a day, remember that you will not be able to provide all of the training she needs. Do what is necessary to ensure that she can take advantage of training opportunities offered outside your classroom.
- Get in the habit of holding 'professional dialogue' with your paraeducator: Her relationship with the students may be different from yours, and she may see them in a

different context if they live in the same community or she supervises recess. Seek her perspective on students' strengths and abilities and on new ways of meeting their individual needs.

- Be supportive of your paraeducator, especially in front of students. As far as is possible, uphold her decisions. If you disagree or feel that you need to correct or change what she does, do it privately and in an appropriate manner.
- Get into the personal habit of monitoring your own classroom practices and setting goals for improvement. This will set an excellent example for your paraeducator of the need to constantly seek better ways to meet student needs.
- Be an advocate for your paraeducator with the school administration. Do what you can to see that she has a mailbox (or that her name is put on yours) so that any information that comes to the school relating to paraeducators can be routed to her; find out what training opportunities may be available for her; ask that she be allowed planning time or be paid to attend IEP meetings or parent-teacher conferences.
- Share items from your professional journals and publications with your paraeducator: Let her know that the school subscribes to journals, and tell her how she can access them.
- If you work with more than one paraeducator, make sure that they all understand the others' roles and responsibilities and what they can expect of each other.
- Remember that the students' best interests come first. All of the decisions you make with and in regard to your paraeducator and her work should be based on considerations of whether or not they will enhance student success. (pp. 230-231)

Tasks performed by teachers to effectively integrate paraprofessionals into the instructional team and supervise their work may include

- planning, scheduling, and assigning specific duties for paraprofessionals based on their experience, level of training, and demonstrated competency to perform a task;
- directing and monitoring the day-to-day work of the paraprofessionals;
- delegating appropriate tasks to paraprofessionals;
- using effective communication and problem-solving techniques to reduce interpersonal or other problems that may occur in the classroom;
- providing feedback about the paraprofessional's job performance; and
- planning and providing structured on-the-job coaching based on the identified training needs of the paraprofessionals.

Special Education Personnel

Special education means specially designed instruction, at no cost to the parent, to meet the unique needs of eligible learners with disabilities. Special education teachers usually do not have a background in career and technical education

programs. Their primary responsibility is to provide instruction and other related services to learners with disabilities who are involved in special education programs. See Figure 11-5. Suggested responsibilities of special education personnel include

- providing prevocational and career development experiences for learners;
- ensuring that career assessment is conducted for learners;
- ensuring that appropriate career goals and objectives are written into the individualized education plans (IEPs) for learners;
- making certain that transition statements written into the IEP are related to the career and technical education instruction the learner is receiving in the career and technical education program;
- providing learners with opportunities to learn appropriate work attitudes and behaviors;
- providing data on academic, personal, and social skills;
- suggesting modifications and adaptations in curriculum, instruction, materials, and equipment to the career and technical education instructor; and
- reinforcing math, reading, and communication skills intrinsic in the career and technical education curriculum.

Transition Coordinators

The major objective of the transition coordinator is to provide support for learners from special populations who are having difficulty participating in and succeeding in career and technical education programs. See Figure 11-6. The services for special populations provided by the transition coordinator may include, but not be limited to

- insuring that all members of special populations are provided equal access in recruitment, enrollment, and placement activities leading to enrollment in career and technical education programs available to individuals who are not members of special populations;
- planning the program placement and supplemental services for all learners who are members of special populations including linguistically appropriate vocational assessment, instruction and services for individuals of limited English proficiency, student services for individuals participating in nontraditional occupationally specific training, the implementation of the IEP for eligible learners with disabilities, reviewing learners' education programs for consistency with their IEP, providing transitional services for learners with disabilities, and reviewing the education program for consistency with the IEPs of learners in special education;
- monitoring the provision of career and technical education to ensure that learners with disabilities, educationally disadvantaged learners, learners of limited English proficiency, migrant learners, and learners participating in nontraditional occupationally specific training have access to career and technical education in the most integrated setting possible;

- assisting in the development and dissemination of the required career and technical education program information for learners who are members of special populations and their parents concerning the opportunities available in career and technical education, requirements for eligibility for enrollment in such programs, specific courses that are available, employment opportunities, and placement options;
- assisting in the preparation of applications relating to admission to career and technical education programs;
- assisting in fulfilling the transitional services requirements of the individual transition plans, including provision of career awareness, counseling and guidance, and developing a four or more year plan for enrolling in an appropriate sequence of courses leading to the development of occupational and daily living skills;
- assessing the career interests and aptitudes of learners from special populations;
- providing counseling activities based on the data obtained in the career interest and aptitude assessment;
- insuring that the required supplementary services for all members of special populations are provided including (a) curriculum modification, (b) equipment modification, (c) classroom modification, (d) supportive personnel, and (e) instructional aids and devices;
- monitoring guidance, counseling, and career development activities conducted by professionally trained counselors and teachers;
- providing counseling and instructional services designed to facilitate the transition from school to postschool employment and career opportunities; and
- coordinating the delivery of services with other service providing agencies.

Learners from Special Populations

Learners should develop self-advocacy skills and become involved in the planning and implementation of their own career goals. Responsibilities of learners include

- participating in establishing long- and short-term goals toward a transition plan, including postschool plans;
- developing effective self-advocacy skills;
- becoming actively involved in self-monitoring progress in the career and technical education program; and
- providing feedback about the student services provided by the district/campus/institution.

Support Personnel

Support personnel are a crucial part of the school-based support team for learners from special populations. Individuals included in this category include special education teachers, diagnosticians, psychologists, therapists, social workers, bilingual specialists, and others who provide services for individuals from special populations. The use of support personnel is crucial to

the success of many learners with special needs. These learners generally require the expertise of more than one professional. Support personnel can assume the following responsibilities in working with learners with special needs:

1. Assisting career and technical education teachers who have students from special populations enrolled in their programs.
2. Providing direct instruction to students.
3. Helping to determine the interests, abilities, and needs of students.
4. Evaluating and documenting student performance.
5. Counseling students in career planning and transition from school into the community.
6. Creating linkages between the school and the home.
7. Assisting in developing, implementing, and evaluating Individualized Education Plans for students.
8. Networking with community agencies that can offer appropriate services.
9. Providing remedial assistance or related academic instruction to students.
10. Participating in ongoing, professional development activities concerning effective practices in meeting the needs of students from special populations.
11. Assisting career and technical education teachers in identifying specific learning styles of students and selecting appropriate instructional strategies.
12. Consulting and working with parents.
13. Conducting career assessments.
14. Acting as liaison for students within school-based settings.
15. Facilitating collaboration with other educators regarding the development of basic academic skills, social skills, self-awareness skills, and career development skills.
16. Incorporating career development and counseling experiences in the delivery of student services to students.
17. Emphasizing the correlation between school and the world of work to students.
18. Incorporating problem-solving and decision-making skills, stress management, and interpersonal skills into their work with students. (Sarkees-Wircenski, 1991, pp. 207-208)

Career and Technical Education Instructors

Career and technical education instructors have the major responsibility of teaching their curriculum to their learners. It is often difficult for them to meet the special needs of learners from special populations while they are trying to teach the entire class. Therefore, it is essential that they learn as much as possible about curriculum modification techniques and coordinate with support personnel who can assist these learners while they are participating in career and technical education programs. See Figure 11-7.

ROLES AND RESPONSIBILITIES OF SPECIAL EDUCATION PERSONNEL								
In cooperation with...	Career and Technical Education Instructor	Transition Coordinator	School Support Personnel	Administrators	Vocational Rehabilitation	Community Agencies	Business/ Industry	Parent/ Guardian
SPECIAL EDUCATION PERSONNEL (Working with eligible learners with disabilities in special education):								
1. Provide learners with prevocational personal adjustment and career development experiences	X	X	X					X
2. Provide learners with opportunities to learn appropriate work attitudes and behaviors	X	X	X				X	
3. Promote teacher/administrator awareness of the purpose of vocational assessment and the appropriate use of the results	X	X	X	X				
4. Arrange for vocational assessment to be conducted		X	X	X				X
5. Assist in interpreting the results of vocational assessment	X	X	X					X
6. Share vocational assessment results with the learner, parent, support personnel, and career and technical education instructor	X	X	X					X
7. Promote the use of assessment results in planning for delivery of career and technical education instruction	X	X	X					
8. Provide counseling to learners and parents	X	X	X					X
9. Involve career and technical education instructor in the development of the career and technical education component of the IEP/ITP	X	X	X					X
10. Make certain that transition statements written in the IEP are related to the career and technical education instruction the learner is receiving in the program	X	X						X
11. Provide data on learner academic, personal, and social skills to the career and technical education instructor and other support personnel	X	X	X					X
12. Assist the career and technical education instructor in identifying appropriate career pathways for the learner	X	X	X					X
13. Suggest appropriate instructional materials	X	X	X					
14. Suggest appropriate methods of modifying existing instructional materials	X	X	X					
15. Assist in modifying instructional materials	X	X	X					
16. Share information about appropriate instructional strategies to meet individual learner needs	X	X	X					
17. Share information about alternative evaluation techniques (e.g., authentic assessment)	X	X	X					
18. Identify appropriate behavior management strategies when necessary	X	X	X					X
19. Monitor learner progress during participation in career and technical education program	X	X	X					X
20. Reinforce math, reading, and communication skills intrinsic in the career and technical education program	X	X	X					X
21. Reinforce career and technical education instruction with student	X	X	X					
22. Provide student with study skills and test-taking skills	X	X	X					X
23. Review/evaluate learner progress and record in student portfolio and/or IEP	X	X	X					
24. Provide in-service workshops for colleagues regarding effective strategies for working with learners with disabilities	X	X	X	X				
25. Work with employers to facilitate job engineering and job redesign		X	X				X	
26. Work with state Vocational Rehabilitation agencies to provide appropriate services		X			X			X
27. Coordinate the IEP/ITP with the IWRP	X	X			X			X
28. Coordinate services from outside agencies for transition from school to postschool activities		X			X	X		X
29. Introduce learners to postsecondary institutions in the geographic area and the appropriate admission process		X				X		

Figure 11-5. Suggested roles and responsibilities of special education personnel in collaborating with others to provide student services.

ROLES AND RESPONSIBILITIES OF TRANSITION COORDINATORS . . .

In cooperation with...	Career and Technical Education Instructor	Special Ed. Coordinator	School Support Personnel	Administrators	Vocational Rehabilitation	Community Agencies	Business/ Industry	Parent/ Guardian
TRANSITION COORDINATOR:								
1. Work with school administrators to create a positive philosophy and environment for learners from special populations				X				
2. Establish communication channels and coordinate information to all those in the school who work with learners with special needs	X	X	X	X				
3. Develop a referral procedure for learners who exhibit learning problems	X	X	X	X				X
4. Coordinate academic testing and other diagnostic testing for referred learners		X	X					
5. Assist learner and parent in making informed career decisions and developing an appropriate career pathway	X	X						X
6. Provide individualized counseling		X	X					X
7. Make certain that equity and access to career and technical education programs are provided for each learner	X	X			X			X
8. Provide each learner with equal access in recruitment, enrollment, and placement activities in career and technical education	X	X			X			X
9. Place learner in the least restrictive and most appropriate career and technical education program	X	X			X			X
10. Work closely with school guidance personnel to assure that each learner receives counseling and career development		X				X		
11. Provide career development services and activities	X	X	X				X	
12. Relate career and technical education program tasks to the interests and abilities of the learner	X	X	X					X
13. Teach and reinforce specific prevocational competencies	X	X	X					X
14. Listen to career and technical education instructors as they find necessary	X	X	X					X
15. Provide diagnostic testing services necessary for learners to participate in the program	X	X	X					X
16. Work with staff to maintain rapport and communication	X	X	X	X				X
17. Develop a comprehensive vocational assessment process to include interests, abilities, and aptitudes		X	X	X				X
18. Assist in referral of student for vocational assessment prior to placement in a career and technical education program		X	X					X
19. Participate in the vocational assessment process		X	X					
20. Maintain continuous contact with career and technical instructors	X	X	X					X
21. Develop a system for monitoring the progress of each learner	X	X	X					
22. Keep records of each learner's progress	X	X	X					
23. Provide each learner and parent/guardian with information about career and technical education program opportunities	X	X	X	X				X
24. Participate in the IEP conference for learners in special education programs	X	X	X	X				X
25. Assist the student to take an active part in planning the educational program	X	X	X					X
26. Monitor/evaluate/update learner progress according to the contents of the IEP	X	X	X					
27. Review effectiveness of curriculum modifications as noted in the IEP	X	X	X					
28. Assist the career and technical instructor in making curriculum modifications	X	X	X					
29. Assist the career and technical education instructor in selecting instructional materials	X	X	X					

...ROLES AND RESPONSIBILITIES OF TRANSITION COORDINATORS

In cooperation with...	Career and Technical Education Instructor	Special Ed. Coordinator	School Support Personnel	Administrators	Vocational Rehabilitation	Community Agencies	Business/ Industry	Parent/ Guardian
TRANSITION COORDINATOR:								
30. Assist the career and technical education instructor in modifying instructional materials	X	X	X					
31. Tape audio versions of written vocational materials	X	X	X					X
32. Help individual learners to complete program assignments	X	X	X					X
33. Read tests orally to individual learners	X	X	X					
34. Assist in making physical adaptations in the classroom and laboratory environment	X	X	X					
35. Assist in identifying each individual's learning style	X	X	X					X
36. Assist career and technical instructors in blending the learning style of the learner with appropriate teaching strategies	X	X	X					
37. Assist career and technical education instructors in utilizing behavior management strategies	X	X	X					X
38. Assist career and technical education instructors in utilizing alternative evaluation strategies	X	X	X					
39. Maintain regular contact with other support personnel	X	X	X					
40. Coordinate individualized instruction experiences	X	X	X					X
41. Provide one-on-one instruction in related career and technical education classes	X	X	X					
42. Provide one-on-one instruction in laboratory settings	X	X	X					
43. Assist learners in learning how to properly operate equipment and machinery in career and technical education laboratory settings	X	X	X					
44. Provide learners with study skills and test-taking skills	X	X	X					X
45. Assist learners in developing and using problem-solving skills	X	X	X					
46. Monitor learner progress on a continuous basis to identify potential problems	X	X	X					X
47. Coordinate additional support services for the learner to succeed in the career and technical education program	X	X	X	X	X	X		X
48. Encourage learner involved in career and technical education student organizations	X	X	X	X				X
49. Keep records of contact with learners, parents, instructors, and other school personnel	X	X	X					
50. Establish and utilize an advisory committee	X	X	X	X	X	X	X	X
51. Help organize and coordinate the activities of a transition team	X	X	X	X	X	X	X	X
52. Develop a transition agreement to assure the coordination of all services needed for each learner	X	X	X	X	X	X	X	X
53. Coordinate transitional services from school to post-school situations	X	X	X	X	X	X	X	X
54. Coordinate employment placement and follow-up services	X	X	X		X	X	X	X
55. Refer each learner to appropriate agencies for referral/services		X	X		X	X		X
56. Provide professional development sessions for colleagues	X	X	X	X		X	X	
57. Maintain contact with parents	X	X	X					X
58. Assist learners in completing applications, resumes, and other job-related forms	X	X	X				X	X
59. Assist in identifying potential employment opportunities	X	X			X	X	X	X
60. Assist in job placement	X	X			X	X	X	X
61. Provide pertinent information regarding postsecondary opportunities	X	X						X

Figure 11-6. Suggested roles and responsibilities of transition coordinators in collaborating with others to provide student services.

ROLES AND RESPONSIBILITIES OF CAREER AND TECHNICAL EDUCATION INSTRUCTORS								
In cooperation with...	Transition Coordinator	Special Ed. Personnel	School Support Personnel	Administrators	Vocational Rehabilitation	Community Agencies	Business/ Industry	Parent/ Guardian
CAREER AND TECHNICAL EDUCATION INSTRUCTOR:								
1. Refer learners who are exhibiting learning problems for assessment	X	X	X					
2. Allow learners to explore in career and technical education programs prior to actual enrollment	X	X	X					
3. Participate in developing the career and technical education component of the IEP for learners with disabilities	X	X	X					X
4. Review vocational assessment results with respect to program requirements so that support services and curriculum modification strategies can be identified for the learner	X	X	X					X
5. Identify program requirements and share them with the learner, parents, and support personnel	X	X	X	X			X	X
6. Identify competencies delivered in program curriculum and share these with the learner, parents, and support personnel	X	X	X	X			X	X
7. Identify multiple exit points for which the program can prepare individuals and share them with the learner, parents, and support personnel	X	X	X	X			X	X
8. Allow for open-entry/open-exit arrangements	X	X	X	X				
9. Assure that barrier-free facilities are provided as needed for learners with disabilities	X	X	X					
10. Adapt and modify tools, equipment, and machinery as necessary	X	X	X					
11. Assist in diagnosing the instructional levels, strengths, and limitations demonstrated by the learner	X	X	X					X
12. Identify technical terms necessary for successful participation in the program	X	X	X					
13. Identify and secure appropriate instructional materials	X	X	X					
14. Modify existing instructional materials for learner use	X	X	X					
15. Allow for extended time requirements	X	X	X	X				
16. Identify the learning style for each learner	X	X	X					X
17. Plan instructional techniques to blend with learning styles of each learner	X	X	X					
18. Utilize alternate methods of assessing learner performance	X	X	X					
19. Integrate and reinforce academic concepts throughout the curriculum	X	X	X					
20. Coordinate with support personnel to identify and provide necessary services for each learner	X	X	X	X				
21. Monitor learner progress and share results with the learner, parents, and support personnel	X	X	X					X
22. Encourage participation in career and technical student organization activities	X	X	X	X				X
23. Participate in cooperative meetings with other school-based personnel to share information and exchange ideas	X	X	X					
24. Make contact and establish linkages with business and industry	X					X	X	
25. Collect input from advisory committee members	X					X	X	
26. Provide cooperative education opportunities	X	X	X	X				X
27. Analyze the job market for placement options	X				X	X	X	X
28. Assist in job development activities	X	X			X	X	X	
29. Provide employment follow-up	X	X			X	X	X	X
30. Provide information about postsecondary programs and opportunities	X	X	X					X
31. Participate in planned staff development sessions	X	X	X	X				

Figure 11-7. Suggested roles and responsibilities of career and technical education instructors in collaborating with others to provide student services.

Major responsibilities of career and technical education instructors who work with learners from special populations include

- referring learners who are having difficulty in their classes as soon as possible so that they can be assessed and provided with assistance;
- coordinating with resource personnel to identify services that learners need and deciding how these services can be provided;
- assisting in diagnosing the instructional levels, strengths, and limitations of learners in relationship to program standards and objectives;
- coordinating with support personnel in developing individualized education program goals for learners;
- integrating and reinforcing academic concepts within the career and technical education curriculum;
- monitoring learner progress and sharing the results with other members of the school-based team; and
- participating in cooperative meetings with other school-based personnel to share information, exchange ideas, and plan for learners with special needs.

Vocational Rehabilitation Services Counselors

Although not considered to be school-based personnel, vocational rehabilitation services counselors work closely with personnel in the schools to serve eligible learners with disabilities. Eligibility for vocational rehabilitation services is generally based on the existence of a physical or mental disability, the existence of a substantial disability to employment, or a reasonable expectation that vocational rehabilitation services would lead to gainful employment. Vocational rehabilitation can offer eligible individuals the following services:

- vocational evaluation
- medical services
- referral to other agencies
- technical aids and devices/special equipment
- prosthetic devices
- placement service
- follow-up services.

An individualized written rehabilitation plan (IWRP) is written for each eligible individual with a disability who becomes a client of vocational rehabilitation. The elements of an IWRP include

- background information about the individual learner;
- type of program planned for learner (e.g., extended evaluation, occupational cluster/grouping, specific career goal);
- vocational objective;
- intermediate objectives including contributing services (e.g., funding source, type of services necessary), projected initiation and completion dates, and evaluation criteria;
- client and/or family participation and other resources (responsibilities and conditions); and
- views of the client regarding the program.

The IWRP should be coordinated with the IEP, which is developed in the school by special education personnel, especially in the statement of transition plans for learners with disabilities. These two documents are not necessarily drafted at the same time, due to planning considerations and timelines; however, the contents of the two plans should be parallel. The IWRP can become a vehicle to provide for the transfer of services for learners leaving high school so they can enroll in a postsecondary training program or make a transition to the world of work.

DELIVERING SCHOOL-BASED STUDENT SERVICES

The collaboration of educators in school-based settings is necessary in order for a comprehensive system of student services to be organized and made available to learners from special populations who are enrolled in career and technical education programs. The National Center for Research in Vocational Education (1993) identified the following benefits from this collaboration:

1. Through formal and informal training sessions, study groups and conversations about teaching, instructors and administrators get the opportunity to "get smarter together."
2. Teachers are better prepared to support one another's strengths and accommodate weaknesses. Working together, they reduce their individual planning time while greatly increasing the available pool of ideas and materials.
3. Schools become better prepared and organized to examine new ideas, methods, and materials. The faculty becomes adaptable and self-reliant.
4. Teachers are organized to ease the strain of staff turnover, both by providing systematic professional assistance to beginners and by explicitly socializing all newcomers, including veteran teachers, to staff values, traditions, and resources. (p. 1)

Student services can be divided into two categories—direct student services and indirect student services. Direct student services refers to working directly with learners in the career and technical education classroom or laboratory while providing parallel instruction based on the career and technical education curriculum; teaching concepts; redesigning handouts; outlining chapter questions; highlighting and color-coding texts; assisting with the completion of daily assignments; checking weekly assignments; motivating learners in the class; providing study sheets; reading tests to the learners; and giving further explanations or demonstrations of what has been taught.

Indirect student services extend beyond directly instructing learners. Services in this category include conducting in-service or professional development sessions to let other individuals in the school-based setting know how career and technical educators and support personnel collaborate. Another example is conducting follow-up reviews of learners during their participation in a career and technical education program as well as after they leave to monitor their progress and provide them with appropriate student services as necessary.

Support personnel can provide indirect support to career and technical education instructors by

- suggesting methods that may help to ensure success for learners using competency-based curricula, motivational techniques, adapting instructional strategies, teaching techniques and evaluation methods;
- helping plan lessons and activities;
- helping with instruction;
- developing class review sheets that reinforce the instructor's lessons;
- writing tests;
- proctoring tests;
- operating audiovisual equipment; and
- taking learners on field trips to reinforce a lesson they may have had in class (Wisconsin Department of Public Instruction, 1993a).

Ideally, student services are centrally located or found in areas with good access. To coordinate the various services, a director is needed. Commitment and collaboration from among the different student services professionals are essential to organizing and implementing a comprehensive student services system. Members of a unified team collaborate with one another to make the various components work as one. They strive toward one goal—to prepare every learner for successful careers and lifelong learning.

TEAM BUILDING PROCESS

A team is a collection of people who must rely on collaboration if each member is to experience ultimate success and goal achievement. Sarkees-Wircenski (1991) stated that as our country moves into a future that will demand so much from our youth, one of the critical issues that will have to be addressed is the organization of our educational system and the growing numbers of learners from special populations. Flexible programs will have to be developed to meet the needs of each learner. Educators must assume that every learner has the potential to succeed. Professional collegiality will be necessary to meet this challenge, including support, cooperation, and sharing. In addition, a strong coalition must be developed to support the public schools, one that joins business, labor, and civic leaders with parents, educators, and school boards. A team effort will be essential in order to accomplish this projected agenda.

Buchholz and Roth (1987) described the three essential phases of team development:

1. Collection of individuals–This phase brings together a number of individuals who ultimately will form a team. Each of these individuals brings a unique background of professional preparation, educational perspectives, and experiences. In this first phase, members tend to be more individually oriented than group oriented. Responsibility is not always shared. Many people will avoid change and dealing with conflict that may arise.

   It is important during Phase 1 that individuals start to define the purpose of the team, recognize the skills of other members, and address ways that members can work together effectively. All newly established groups start out at Phase 1. Even groups that have been together for a long time may be in the early phases of team development if group dynamics have not developed in a positive direction.

2. Groups–Individuals begin to form into a group during this phase of team development. This occurs when the members establish a group identity, formulate the purpose of the group, and develop a pattern of working together. A leader usually emerges who provides direction, assigns tasks to members, facilitates communication, and oversees group performance.

3. Team–During this phase the team becomes purpose oriented. Members understand the goal of the group and dedicate their commitment to it. Actions and decisions are based on this goal. This is the most difficult end to attain.

Collaborative teams should be aware of both variables that inhibit group cohesiveness and those that enhance team development so that members can work effectively to meet the needs of learners with special needs. Dyer (1977) identified the following problems in team building:

- Even though people are aware that a problem exists, they don't know how to address it.
- The group members do not have a common goal to which everyone is committed.
- Some people do not want things to change, while others are actively searching for new methods.
- Some people never accept their role and responsibilities in relation to the team's goals.
- Some people are intimidated by the team leader(s) and therefore pretend to know things that they should be asking questions about.
- Decisions are made by the team, but some people disagree with the decision or procrastinate about following through with the decision.
- Tension or friction among team members makes it difficult for them to work together.

The goal of educators who work with learners from special populations is to organize an active, participative team that can facilitate success for all learners. Buchholz and Roth (1987) reported that typically there are eight characteristics of a successful, high-performance team:

1. Participative leadership–Members of a team participate in planning and decision-making and openly collaborate with others.

2. Shared responsibility–The team creates an atmosphere in which all members feel a professional responsibility for the performance of the team.

3. Aligned on purpose–All members share a common purpose regarding the function that the team serves and the reason it was created.

4. High communication–The team builds a climate of trust, as well as open, honest, communication among all team members.

5. Focused on future–Team members recognize and accept change as an opportunity for growth and improvement.

6. Focused on task–Team members keep the focus during team meetings on performance toward stated goals and objectives.

7. Creative talents–Team members apply individual talents toward the common goals of the team.

8. Rapid response–Team members recognize and act on opportunities that arise that can help to move the team toward successful completion of its goals.

In order for teams to perform to the height of their collective potential each member must participate and make a contribution. A number of variables increase the participation levels of team members, such as the following:

1. There is a clear definition of the team's purposes, including what the goals are and what team members are to do.

2. There is careful control of the time commitment necessary for team members and there is enough time allowed to get the work done.

3. Team members listen to and respect the opinions of others and are sensitive to their needs.

4. There is an informal, relaxed atmosphere rather than a formal environment.

5. There is good preparation by the team leadership, so that necessary materials and resources are available.

6. Team members have an interest in and a commitment to the goals of the team.

7. Records are kept of team meetings and actions, so that decisions are not lost.

8. The team periodically stops and assesses its performance, so that changes and improvements can be made.

9. Recognition and appreciation are awarded to team members for their efforts so that they feel they are really making positive contributions.

10. The work of the team is accepted and used by the institution that brought the group together and presented it with a goal to accomplish. (Buchholz & Roth, p. 75)

The following support teams can be commissioned to assist learners from special populations:

• Collaboration team–This team consists of grade level, departmental, or school improvement members seeking to learn and implement strategies that result in effective collaborative work.

• Topical study group–This team consists of two or more educators, committed to meeting at least monthly for the purpose of collaborating to learn about and implement one or more promising educational practices.

• Instructional team–This team consists of general, career technical education, and special education teachers who teach and support learners in common. The team commits to weekly meetings and seeks assistance in collaborating to generate and implement differentiated lesson plans that actively engage all learners in both the general education and the career and technical education classes or subjects.

• Community-based career and technical education team–This team consists of at least one special education teacher and the following, as negotiated: one or more career and technical education teacher, career and technical education supervisor, special education supervisor, principal, and career and technical education school director, all of whom are committed to meeting once every two weeks. The purpose of this team is to collaborate to design and implement a system of community work sites that sample the array of career and technical education clusters available.

• Special education team–This team consists of all special education teachers and support personnel, where possible, committed to meeting at least monthly for the purpose of collaborating to use each person's expertise to problem-solve strategies for unifying special education services. This team's main focus is to develop and implement a plan to reallocate their services to yield effective and efficient educational supports for all learners within inclusive settings. This involves redesigning special education from the placement model to a service model. Special educators become grade level or subject area learning specialists for learners and provide a wide range of support needs.

• Positive behavior support team–This team consists of interested persons and major stakeholders in the life of a learner with significant behavioral and/or emotional difficulties. The team commits to weekly meetings for the purpose of collaborating to develop and implement a positive behavior support plan, within inclusive settings, for a specific learner. The team facilitates the (a) completion of a thorough functional assessment to determine the variables associated with the challenging behavior, (b) generation of hypothesis(es) concerning the functions of the challenging behavior, (c) implementation of positive behavior support strategies, and ongoing evaluation of the behavior support plan.

• Interagency transition team–This team consists of school administrators, teachers, parents, adult service representatives, employers, and others, as appropriate, meeting on a routine basis. The purpose of this team is to collaborate to develop, implement, and evaluate an action plan that coordinates a wide range of goods and services that facilitate smooth transitions for learners from school to employment including supported work, supported employment, and continuing educational options (Butterworth, 1999).

• Student services team–This team consists of professionals who specialize in providing counseling, job placement, consulting, assessment, and other related services to ensure the career, educational, social, emotional, intellectual, and healthy development of all learners. Typically, a student services team consists of the school counselor, social worker, psychologist, nurse, and other related professionals, as well as special education resource teachers, transition coordinators, assessment specialists, paraprofessionals, and rehabilitation counselors.

- Teacher support teams–This team consists of a select group of teachers at the building or campus level whose role is to provide teachers in the educational environment who work with learners from special populations with suggestions of alternative instructional strategies that would assist these learners to succeed. Members of the teacher support team should include an administrator, the instructor requesting assistance, additional classroom teachers in the building or on campus, and support personnel (e.g., counselors, transition coordinators, special education teachers, social workers, remedial staff members).

Other school services personnel who should be included on the team are transition specialists, school-to-work coordinators, multicultural services professionals, tutors, academic advisors, job coaches, and recruitment representatives. Local service providers should also be represented. Inclusion of employment, health and social services, welfare, and other community services will further strengthen the team. Representatives from food service, child care, and transportation providers could also meet periodically with the team.

Teacher Support Teams

Teacher support teams are school-based, problem-solving groups whose purpose is to provide a vehicle for discussion of issues related to the specific needs of teachers or learners and to offer consultation and follow-up assistance to the staff. The team can respond to short-term consultation, continuous support, or the securing of information, resources, or training for those who request its service. By providing problem-solving support and assistance to individuals and groups, the team can help teachers and other professionals to become more skillful, gain confidence, and feel more effective in their work with learners. This support model is built on the assumption that teachers in regular classroom settings have the ability to resolve many instructional and behavioral problems and that they deserve the cooperation and support of others within their buildings.

Harden (1989) suggested the following responsibilities of the team:

1. The team assists the requesting classroom teacher with an identification and clarification of the difficulties the student is experiencing. Examples of information that could be shared with the team are group achievement test results, samples of classroom work, results of classroom observations, and a review of interventions which have been tried.

2. Data provided by the classroom teacher, and forwarded to the team by the Team Coordinator, is carefully reviewed by the Teacher Support Team. If data are lacking, the Team Coordinator should request this information before the team studies the background information.

3. After adequate information has been collected, a plan of intervention is developed. The team assists and supports the teacher in developing a plan which might include modification of curricula or materials, changes in grouping procedures or classroom management, the use of alternative instructional strategies, development of a behavior management program, or other recommendations.

4. The classroom teacher is assisted in determining the effectiveness of the recommendations and in making modifications in the interventions as needed. The team has an obligation to continue to support the teacher as he/she implements intervention procedures. Therefore, after a trial period has been set, another meeting is held with the teacher to evaluate the student's progress and to make additional recommendations and modifications as needed. The effectiveness of the intervention program can be determined only after a reasonable amount of time in the program has elapsed.

5. The team should make any recommendations for additional services deemed desirable. After the team becomes familiar with the student's special needs, members might recommend a remedial or counseling program within the district. (pp. 20-21)

MAKING SCHOOL-BASED TEAMS WORK

The National Center for Research in Vocational Education (1993) identified six dimensions that make teacher collaboration work. These dimensions include the following:

1. Symbolic endorsements and rewards that place value on cooperative work–The schools where teachers work together best are those in which the administration and leadership conveys their faith in the power of interdisciplinary teams to make the school better for all students.

2. School-level organization of assignments and leadership–For collaborative teams to be effective, leadership must be broadly distributed among teachers and administrators. In some schools, teachers are given reduced teaching loads in exchange for being a working member of a collaborative team which has a curricular charge to make the program and school better able to meet needs of all students.

3. Latitude given to teachers for influence on crucial matters of curriculum and instruction–Teachers' investment in team planning appears to rest heavily on the latitude they have to make decisions in areas of curriculum, materials selection, student assignments, instructional grouping, and the assessment of student progress. Teaming for the sake of teaming leads to disillusionment; teaming must be about matters of compelling importance.

4. Time–Common planning periods, regularly scheduled team or subject-area meetings, and released time for collaborative work all support cooperative work among teachers. The opportunities for collaborative work are either enhanced or eroded by the master schedule.

5. Training and assistance–Since it is a radical departure from the usual, cooperative relationships place unfamiliar and pressing demands on teachers. Teacher work groups succeed in part by mastering specific skills and by developing explicit agreements to govern their work together. Task-related training and assistance bolsters confidence of teachers to work with one another outside of classrooms.

6. Material support–The quality and availability of reference texts and other materials, adequate copying facilities and equipment, consultants on selected problems, and other forms of human and material support appear to be crucial contributors to teachers' ability and willingness to work together successfully. (p. 3)

A study conducted by Greenan (1986) identified the following suggestions to facilitate effective networking so that student services can be provided to learners from special populations in career and technical education programs:

1. Conferences are a very effective networking strategy. Individuals can be provided with relevant information while at the same time share what they are doing with others.

2. University/college and other personnel responsible for preservice, in-service, and certification activities need to enhance their networking capabilities to adequately serve prospective teachers and current practicing teachers.

3. Conferences, regional resource centers, and/or instructional materials centers can be an effective networking activity for career and technical education instructors, support personnel, and other direct service/instruction providers.

4. Newsletters can be used as a resource to enhance networking with support/ancillary personnel such as psychologists, counselors, vocational assessment personnel, and parents/advocates.

5. Computer linkages can be considered as an effective and useful networking strategy/resource. State and national computer linkage systems should be expanded to include universities, local education agencies, resource centers, and others.

6. Hotlines are of particular interest to career and technical education instructors, support personnel, and state supervisors/coordinators.

7. Network planning for minority group concerns should strongly consider consortia activities. (p. 20)

Case Study . . . Ms. Foster

Ms. Aleene Foster is a consumer and family science instructor at the secondary level. She has a number of learners from special populations enrolled in her classes. Initially, Ms. Foster did not feel that she could adequately meet the needs of these learners without some assistance. Since there is a local interagency agreement in the district where Ms. Foster teaches, a number of school-based personnel and community-based agencies were identified to help her work with these learners. Ms. Foster began working with the transition coordinator, who helped coordinate the services of a psychologist, social worker, other support personnel, counselors, agency representatives from the local community, and the special education teacher.

The school-based collaborative team worked together to develop individual education plans for learners with special needs who were enrolled in Ms. Foster's program. An effective communication network was established among the team members with every member of the team aware of the career goals and special needs of each learner. Periodic team meetings were held to share information about learner progress, techniques that were used in the classroom, curriculum modification procedures that were implemented, support services that were provided, and additions and revisions that were needed in each learner's IEP.

Each team member brought a different contribution to the collaborative team process. The special education teacher conducted vocational assessment activities, assisted learners in reinforcing information taught in the home economics program, converted information to audio cassettes for several auditory learners, conducted study skills seminars for learners, and provided oral testing. The counselor developed a job club for learners, kept team members informed about resources in the local community, and worked directly with parents. Building administrators pledged their support and ordered some special materials for Ms. Foster to use with learners with special needs. In addition, a series of ongoing professional development activities was planned for the entire faculty focusing on successful strategies for working with learners from special populations.

Ms. Foster is working with her program advisory committee to secure cooperative workstations as well as available employers to develop shadowing activities. She has received several commitments from advisory committee members to hire several special needs learners who will be graduating this year. The parents of the learners from special populations have been very supportive and enthusiastic about Ms. Foster's program. They have volunteered to come to her class to tutor and spend time in the evening reinforcing material covered in class. They have even formed an informal support group to encourage each other. The cooperative planning process has been successful in meeting the needs of learners from special populations in Ms. Foster's program.

COMMUNICATING TO FACILITATE SCHOOL-BASED TEAMING

It is important that members of a school-based team communicate with one another when planning, implementing, and evaluating individualized career programming for learners from special populations. Time for communication and collaboration to share information about learners from special populations is often limited. It is imperative that a system of communication be established among the members of the school-based team. Progress reports, such as a learner progress report, can be used by the career and technical education instructor to communicate information to a transition coordinator and other support personnel about how the learner is progressing in the program. This tool can help to identify problems as they arise so that appropriate assistance can be provided immediately. See Figure 11-8. A teacher-to-teacher progress report can provide information about the progress of a group of learners to be communicated between multiple instructors. See Figure 11-9.

An individual option plan can be used by the school-based team to identify teaching options and strategies that can be used to meet the needs of a specific learner, especially if the learner is having difficulty in the career and technical education program. Areas that can be addressed in an individual option plan include classroom management, instruction, and evaluation issues. A collaborative approach to developing and facilitating this plan is usually best because it combines the expertise and ideas from a number of professionals. See Figure 11-10.

A collaborative planning sheet can be used by the school-based support team to identify deficiencies demonstrated by a specific learner with special needs who is enrolled in a career and technical education program. Once a deficiency has been identified, the support team should identify methods, activities, and resources that can be structured to remediate the deficiency. Remedial assistance from academic teachers is often helpful. See Figure 11-11.

An overview of adapted activities can be used to assist learners with special needs in a career and technical education program. The school-based support team should review the activities in relationship to learner deficiencies that have been demonstrated in the career and technical education program. The team should determine what activities would be best for the learner and decide on responsibilities that will be assumed by various team members in providing specified student services. See Figure 11-12.

LEARNER PROGRESS REPORT . . .

NAME _____ CLASS _____ DATE _____

I. ATTITUDE

A. Toward class
1. ____ Enthusiastic
2. ____ Cooperative
3. ____ Indifferent
4. ____ Not Cooperative
5. ____ Disruptive

B. Toward others
1. ____ Gets along well with others
2. ____ Quiet, rarely interacts with others
3. ____ Occasional problems with coworkers
4. ____ Argumentative

1. ____ Accepts supervision readily
2. ____ Occasional problems accepting supervision
3. ____ Hostile towards others

II. CLASS PROGRESS

A. ____ Mastering competencies   OR
1. ____ On schedule
2. ____ Ahead of schedule

B. ____ Not mastering competencies
1. ____ Poor attendance
2. ____ Lack of effort and/or interest
3. ____ Limited ability to master skills

III. WORK HABITS

A. Initiative
1. ____ Finds tasks to do when assigned work is completed
2. ____ Needs reminders to stay busy
3. ____ Wastes time when assigned task is done

B. Safety
1. ____ Always works safely
2. ____ Needs reminders to work safely
3. ____ Does not use good safety habits

...LEARNER PROGRESS REPORT

IV. PROBLEM AREAS

1.____ None
2.____ Following instructions
3.____ Speed and accuracy
4.____ Completing written work on time
5.____ Written tests

6.____ Performance tests
7.____ Daily points earned
8.____ Staying on assigned task
9.____ Grooming
10.____ Other (Please specify _____)

V. ATTENDANCE

Dates absent _____

Dates tardy _____

Second Hour
First Quarter _____
Second Quarter _____
Semester _____

VI. COMMENTS

Strengths:

_____
_____
_____

Weaknesses:

_____
_____
_____

Additional Comments:

_____
_____
_____

INSTRUCTOR'S SIGNATURE _____

STUDENT'S SIGNATURE _____

Figure 11-8. A sample learner progress report form that can be filled out by an instructor working with a learner from a special population.

TEACHER-TO-TEACHER PROGRESS REPORT

Week of _____

DIRECTIONS: Please check the appropriate spaces for the students listed below:

Name	Period	Progressing Satisfactorily	Completing Homework
1. (Jeanne)			
2. (Jill)			
3. (Renee)			
4. (Nel)			
5.			

Please check how the following students are experiencing difficulty:

Name	Period	Progressing Unsatisfactorily	Incomplete Homework	Difficulty Reading	Inadequate Preparation for Tests	Inadequate Note Taking
1. (Jeanne)						
2. (Jill)						
3. (Renee)						
4. (Nel)						
5.						

1. I am planning a test this week for my _____ class. The test will be on: _____

2. The test will cover the following text pages: _____

3. The test will be in this format: _____

4. ____ I am not planning any tests this week.

Source: Huck, R., Myers, R., & Wilson, J. (1989). *ADAPT—A Developmental Activity Program for Teachers* (2nd ed.). Pittsburgh, PA: Allegheny Intermediate Unit.

Figure 11-9. A sample progress report form that can be filled out by an instructor to inform support personnel and others of the progress made by students from special populations.

INDIVIDUAL OPTION PLAN

DATE _____

NAME _____ TEACHER _____

DISTRICT _____ SCHOOL _____

SUBJECT _____ GRADE LEVEL _____ PERIOD _____

DIRECTIONS: List problems the student has in each assessment area as indicated on the assessment summary. Then list teaching options to meet those needs.

AREAS	STUDENT PROBLEMS:	TEACHING OPTIONS:
CLASSROOM MANAGEMENT	*needs a planned system of rules* *has difficulty asking for help in class* *needs an individual reward system*	
INSTRUCTION	*has difficulty listening to lectures* *has difficulty taking notes* *needs hands-on experience*	
EVALUATION	*has difficulty with written tests* *has difficulty answering completion questions* *needs alternative grading procedures*	

Source: Huck, R., Myers, R., & Wilson, J. (1989). *ADAPT-A Developmental Activity Program for Teachers,* (2nd ed.). Pittsburgh, PA: Allegheny Intermediate Unit.

Figure 11-10. An individual option plan format that can be used to determine potential teaching options in classroom management, instruction, and evaluation for students who exhibit problems.

COLLABORATIVE PLANNING SHEET

Student Name _____ Instructor Name _____

Date	Deficiencies Identified by Career and Technical Education Instructor	Methods, Activities, Resources to be Utilized in Remediating Differences	Results	Support from Academic Remediation Team Where Applicable

Figure 11-11. A format for planning collaborative student services for learners from special populations.

ADAPTED ACTIVITIES FOR LEARNERS WITH SPECIAL NEEDS . . .

Activity	The Student has Difficulty	The Student Needs
Structured study guide–Provides structure and location clues to help learners read for understanding and information	• Listening to lectures • Taking notes • Organizing information • Participating in class discussion • Reading the text • Using complicated study guides • Completing work independently • Locating information • Recalling information	• Consistent routine • Practice and review • Structure
Information organizer–Presents information in chart, graph, or pictorial form to help learners organize information, understand relationships, categorize information, sequence events, or identify cause and effect	• Listening to lectures • Taking notes • Organizing information • Reading the text • Completing in-class assignments independently • Studying for tests independently • Locating information • Sequencing information • Making comparisons • Understanding relationships	• Visual presentation • Concrete approach • Structure
Skeletal outline–Provides a visual structure to accompany a lecture or text	• Listening to lectures • Using advance organizers • Organizing information • Reading the text • Completing written assignments • Writing legibly	• Structure • Taking notes • Practice and review
What-You-Need-to-Know chart–Provides a list of important terms and concepts contained in each chapter or unit	• Organizing information • Reading the text • Completing work independently • Defining new vocabulary • Locating information • Recalling information • Understanding relationships	• Consistent routine • Structure
Concept activity–Presents abstract concepts in a concrete manner using graphics or advance organizers	• Listening to lectures • Taking notes • Participating in class discussion • Reading silently • Studying for tests independently • Defining new vocabulary • Recalling new information • Understanding relationships • Understanding abstract concepts	• Visual presentation • Advance organizers • Concrete approach
Application activity–Encourages students to organize and apply learned information in a structured format (i.e., making a poster, conducting an interview, building a model or making a collage)	• Communicating through written expression • Applying information • Demonstrating understanding through written tests	• Structure • Hands-on activities • Concrete approach • Small group interaction • An alternative to written assignments

... ADAPTED ACTIVITIES FOR LEARNERS WITH SPECIAL NEEDS		
Activity	**The Student has Difficulty**	**The Student Needs**
Game–Encourages students to practice and review facts and concepts using board games, card games, class interaction games, and puzzles	• Organizing information • Participating in class discussion • Reading the text • Completing the homework • Completing class assignments independently • Studying for tests independently • Recalling information • Applying information	• Positive reinforcement • Small group interaction • Intermediate feedback • Hands-on activities • Additional practice and review
Manipulative–Provides a kinesthetic approach for applying, categorizing, and relating information in the form of pocket charts or study cards	• Taking notes • Organizing information • Reading the text • Completing homework • Completing in-class assignments independently • Studying for tests independently • Writing legibly • Making comparisons • Understanding relationships • Answering completion questions	• Hands-on activities • Visual reinforcement • An alternative to written tests

Source: Huck, R., Myers, R., & Wilson, J. (1989). *ADAPT-A Developmental Activity Program for Teachers* (2nd ed.). Pittsburgh, PA: Allegheny Intermediate Unit.

Figure 11-12. Suggested adapted classroom activities for learners from special populations.

WORKING WITH PARENTS

Parents and guardians are very important in the collaborative planning process. They know the learner better than any professional in the school system and are influential in the growth and development of the learner. Willis (1989) identified the following research conclusions regarding the involvement of parents in the educational planning process:

• The family provides the primary educational environment.
• Involving parents in their child's formal education improves that learner's achievement.
• Family involvement is most effective when it is comprehensive, long-lasting, and well-planned.
• Benefits are not confined to early childhood or the elementary level. Strong effects result from family involvement throughout high school.
• Involving parents in their child's education at home is not enough. To ensure that high quality schools are institutions serving the community, they must participate at all levels.
• Children from low-income and minority families have the most to gain. Any parent can help regardless of socioeconomic level, education, or background.
• The school and the home are not isolated; they interconnect with each other and with the community.

It is advantageous to involve parents in the collaborative planning process; they can lend encouragement and reinforcement at home that will help motivate the learner. They can apply behavior management techniques, assist the learner in related instruction, lead and participate in career guidance discussions, and report any problems that arise at home that may impact their participation in the career and technical education program. See Figure 11-13.

Parents often have valid questions and concerns that should be addressed when planning an instructional program for the learner, such as the following:

• Does the career and technical education program meet the needs of the learner?
• Is the career and technical education program the best placement for the learner? Have all realistic options been discussed? Has the learner been provided with appropriate career exploration activities and counseling?
• Will necessary learner services be provided to help the learner succeed in the program? Will the learner be able to keep up with others in the program? Will extended time in the program be allowed if necessary?
• Will the learner be accepted by peers in the program?
• Will the career and technical education instructor understand the needs of the learner? Will the instructor discriminate against the learner?
• Will the learner have a job once the program is completed? Will the learner have the technical skills for competitive employment?

QUESTIONS FOR PARENTS TO ASK DURING TRANSITION PLANNING

- Do I see my child as a worker?
- Do I help my child see himself/herself as a worker?
- Do I help my child to share dreams about who he/she wants to become?
- Do I serve as a role model?
- Do I know workers who can be role models for my child?
- Do I dare to allow my child greater independence?
- Do I assign work responsibilities at home and expect my child to complete tasks in a reasonable time?
- Do I encourage independence in daily living activities (i.e., transportation, managing money, socializing)?
- When my child is unable to master a complete task or skill, do I encourage mastery of whatever part he/she can do or do I complete the task for him/her?
- Can I allow my child to experience times of failure as he/she learns new skills?
- Do I encourage my child to pursue his/her own interests, not just the things I would like to see him/her do?
- Do I help my child to explore occupations (i.e., reading, visiting workers and workplaces, using job information resources)?
- Am I open-minded about what my child may be able to do for a career?
- Can I help to arrange volunteer or paid work experiences for my child?
- In what kind of job would I like to see my child working?
- Are there jobs I would not want my child to have where physical safety, emotional well-being, and personal dignity might be at a risk?
- Do I help my child recognize every person as a possible employer and every place as a possible worksite?
- What difficulties does my child have which would interfere with employment?
- Do I help my child explore community resources (i.e., libraries, stores, shopping centers, recreational facilities)?
- Am I aware of post-school agencies which may provide career services to my child after graduation?
- Is there a person who can assist me and my child in preparing for the transition from school to post-school environments?
- Do I know the legal rights of learners and workers with special needs?
- Does my child know his/her legal rights and participate in transition planning meetings whenever possible?
- After leaving the public school, what do I anticipate my child's living situation will be?
- Have I talked with other parents and case managers to learn what options are available for independent or supported living arrangements in the community?
- Have I visited available programs with my child to determine which options are most appropriate?
- If my child is considering higher education which will involve living away from home, have I contacted or visited schools to ask what types of support is available?
- What other activities (besides a career) would I like to see my child participate in after he/she leaves school?

Figure 11-13. A list of questions for parents to consider when participating in the collaborative planning process.

A progress update form can be used to communicate information to parents about how the learner with special needs is progressing in the career and technical education program. It is important that an open channel of communication be maintained between school and home. See Figure 11-14.

Sarkees (1989) stated that parent education programs are an effective way to keep parents informed about the educational program that is being implemented for their son or daughter. Suggested parent education program topics include
- stages of career development;
- components of career development programs;
- career development activities for use in the home;
- interpretation of pertinent legislative assurances;
- role of parents as a resource in the school;
- secondary and postsecondary career and technical education program opportunities available in the geographic area;
- career exploration opportunities available;
- generalizable skills needed for successful employment;
- SCANS Workplace Know-How competencies necessary for successful employment;
- employability skills for successful employment;
- vocational assessment services in the district;
- career and technical education curriculum modification strategies used in the district for students from special populations;
- student services in the district available to students from special populations;
- skills and attitudes expected by employers;
- advocacy and professional organizations available in the community;
- community agencies available;

- adult service providers available;
- vocational components of Individualized Education Plans and Individualized Transition Plans;
- community based employment settings available in the geographic area;
- potential employment opportunities;
- transition services available in the district; and
- independent living skills necessary for successful transition to the community. (p. 20)

The following strategies can lead to effective collaboration with parents:

1. Conduct meetings to increase parents' understanding of curricula and activities being offered in the school for learners from special populations (i.e., links between subject matter and careers, cooperative programs between schools and local business and industry).
2. Conduct joint meetings of parents, educators, community organization representatives, and business/industry persons to address the need for basic skills, employability skills, SCANS (Secretary's Commission for Achieving Necessary Skills) competencies, and specific job skills for learners with special needs.
3. Publish informational materials that provide parents with suggestions and activities for providing (home-based) career experiences that will parallel those offered in school.
4. Provide parents with opportunities to serve as career resource persons in their children's classrooms.
5. Provide parents with opportunities to assist school personnel in obtaining, cataloging, and updating career development resource materials.
6. Open up business and industry settings on weekends for field trips for youth with special needs and their parents who are interested in learning more about competitive employment options. (Illinois State Board of Education, p. 10)

PARENT PROGRESS UPDATE

Quarter   1   2   3   4

To the Parent/Guardian of: _____

Grade: _____   School: _____

The purpose of this communication is to inform you of your child's progress at this point in the quarter. Currently he/she is making a grade of _____ in _____. Below I have checked comments which I feel represent his/her situation at this point in time.

_____ Is doing a good job	_____ Needs to improve attendance
_____ Exhibits a positive attitude	_____ Needs to improve arriving to class on time
_____ Has shown improvement	_____ Needs to better utilize lab/class work time
_____ Needs more preparation for exams	_____ Should talk less to classmates
_____ Needs to increase class participation	_____ Should seek more teacher help
_____ Needs to increase lab participation	_____ Quality of work needs improvement
_____ Has not completed all work assignments	_____ Instructional equipment is missing

Teacher's Comments: _____
_____
_____

I would welcome the opportunity to talk with you and will be available during my conference period each day from _____ to _____. You may call _____ to arrange an appointment

Teacher's Signature: _____

Please sign and return to: _____

Parent's Signature: _____

Figure 11-14. A sample format to report learner progress to parents.

Providing parents with a transition checklist is another way of helping them become actively involved in the collaboration process. The checklist should contain a transition activities that the parents and their children should consider when preparing transition plans. The learner's skills and interests will determine what items on the checklist are relevant. The parents can use the checklist to ask themselves whether or not these transition issues should be addressed at transition meetings. The checklist can also help identify who should be part of the transition team. Responsibility for carrying out the specific transition activities should be determined at the transition meetings. See Figure 11-15.

PARENT TRANSITION CHECKLIST

FOUR TO FIVE YEARS BEFORE LEAVING THE SCHOOL DISTRICT
- Identify personal learning styles and the necessary accommodations to be a successful learner and worker
- Identify career interests and skills, complete interest and career inventories, and identify additional education or training requirements
- Explore options for postsecondary education and admission criteria
- Identify interests and options for future living arrangements, including supports
- Learn to effectively communicate interests, preferences, and needs
- Be able to explain the disability and needed accommodations
- Learn and practice informed decision-making skills
- Investigate assistive technology tools that can increase community involvement and employment opportunities
- Broaden experiences with community activities and expand friendships
- Pursue and use local transportation options outside of family
- Investigate money management and identify necessary skills
- Acquire identification card and the ability to communicate personal information
- Identify and begin learning skills necessary for independent living
- Learn and practice personal health care

TWO TO THREE YEARS BEFORE LEAVING THE SCHOOL DISTRICT
- Identify community support services and programs (vocational rehabilitation, county services, independent living centers, etc.)
- Invite adult service providers, peers, and others to the IEP transition meeting
- Match career interests and skills with career and technical education course work and community work experiences
- Gather more information on postsecondary programs and support services offered and make arrangement for accommodations to take college entrance exams
- Identify health care providers and become informed about sexuality and family planning issues
- Determine the need for financial support (supplemental security income, state financial supplemental programs, Medicare)
- Learn and practice appropriate interpersonal, communication, and social skills for different settings (employment, school recreation, with peers, etc.)
- Explore legal status with regards to decision making prior to age of majority
- Begin a resume and update it as needed
- Practice independent living skills (e.g., budgeting, shopping, cooking, housekeeping)
- Identify needed personal assistant services and, if appropriate, learn to direct and manage these services

ONE YEAR BEFORE LEAVING THE SCHOOL DISTRICT
- Apply for financial support programs (supplemental security income, independent living services, vocational rehabilitation, and personal assistant services)
- Identify postsecondary schools and arrange for accommodations
- Practice effective communication by developing interview skills, asking for help, and identifying necessary accommodations at postsecondary and work environments
- Specify desired job and obtain paid employment with supports as needed
- Take responsibility to arrive on time to work, appointments, and social activities
- Assume responsibility for health care needs, (making appointments, filling and taking prescriptions, etc.)
- Register to vote and for selective service (if male)

Source: Washington State Department of Social and Health Services. (1996). *Transition Guide for Washington.* Olympia, WA: The Office of Superintendent of Public Instruction.

Figure 11-15. A checklist of transition activities that parents and their children may wish to consider when preparing transition plans.

One way to involve parents in collaborative planning activities is to establish a parent support group. This support group is operated cooperatively by school systems and parents of learners from special populations. There are a number of characteristics that describe an effective parent support group:

- The group is a collaborative effort between parents and school-based personnel. Everyone should join together to work for an appropriate educational plan for learners from special populations.
- The primary focus of the group is for parents to provide support for one another. Parent-to-parent support may take the form of resource sharing, activity planning, or peer coaching to solve specific problems and to achieve identified goals.
- The group provides a forum for parents and school-based personnel to communicate on a regular basis and to share information and concerns. The support group is a vehicle for communication that allows all participants to remain consistently in contact with each other. Critical issues and concerns can be dealt with as soon as they arise.
- The group is a structured body. Regularly scheduled meetings are publicized to have maximum attendance. Sometimes meetings are open to everyone. At other times, special meetings can be held to train a small core group of parents who are on call to provide individual support to other parents and learners with special needs in the educational system.
- The group is a school-sponsored entity separate and distinct from other parent-teacher or community groups. Specific goals are established for the group.

Parent support groups can create a regularly scheduled opportunity for parents and school-based staff to communicate on a positive and mutually supportive basis. They allow both parents and educators to understand more clearly the difficulties that they are confronting. Parents who are members of these groups can provide the school district and agencies with a way to directly communicate with one another. There are definite indications that these groups represent a cost effective way of promoting parent/professional cooperation in school systems and agencies. District administrators involved with support groups have indicated that they can help to alleviate costly and time consuming formal conflicts between the school and the home.

Programs designed to involve families in school need to respond to today's realities. For example, the family where the father works at a job and the mother works at home is no longer common. Additional family structures include single-parent families, families of noncustodial parents, families with two wage earners, blended families (whose kids may be the father's, the mother's, or both), homeless families, families undergoing breakup (divorce primarily, but could also include the death of a parent), foster parent families, and families headed by one or two teenage parents. Culture, ethnicity, income, and class also affect family structures.

School policy seeking to involve families must reflect the time and resource constraints and the stress that many families now face. School policy that promotes family involvement should facilitate it by

- involving itself in before- and after-school day care;
- holding meetings at alternative times (e.g., evenings) and providing child care;
- allowing open enrollment so children can attend school closer to their parents' work places; and
- preventing school cancellation (or delays) at the last minute except in catastrophic emergencies, to avoid leaving working parents with no way to provide care for their children.

In addition, administrators should provide

- written policies at the district and school levels that establish the legitimacy of family involvement efforts;
- three types of support: designated funding in the main budget; materials, equipment, and meeting space; and assigned staff to carry out program efforts;
- training for school staff and parents to help them develop skills;
- joint planning, goal setting, and assessment by teachers, parents, and administrators;
- frequent communication between home and school;
- connections with other programs, information systems, and resources that serve families; and
- regular evaluations and program revisions of the family involvement programs to meet changing needs (Wisconsin Department of Public Instruction, 1993b).

MENTORING

Research indicates that retention of learners in educational programs increases when there is a linkage of learners to a significant other. This is often a crucial factor in keeping them in school. Mentoring relationships can include sharing social, personal, and academic information. Mentoring is a supportive relationship between a youth or young adult and someone senior in age and experience who offers support, guidance, and assistance as the younger partner goes through a difficult period, enters a new area of experience, takes on an important task, or corrects an earlier problem. The primary objective for mentoring is to keep learners from special populations in school. These learners often need to build self-esteem and identify realistic career and academic goals. Mentors can serve a variety of functions for learners from special populations. They can

- assist in identifying learner's interests;
- show learners that they are taken seriously by an adult;
- regularly offer reassurance;
- help learners to define who they are;
- foster possibilities for career and personnel development;
- provide guidance in solving everyday problems; and
- help learners to develop problem-solving and critical-thinking skills.

A variety of individuals can serve as mentors, including
- business and industry volunteers;
- teachers;
- college students;
- parents;
- community volunteers;
- representatives from business and industry;
- representatives from service organizations and clubs;
- Chamber of Commerce volunteers;
- postsecondary educational institution volunteers; and
- community education program volunteers.

Reilly (1992) provided guidelines for identifying potential mentors, identifying the specific roles of mentors, and providing reasons for business and industry to contribute time as mentors. In identifying potential mentors, the following questions should be addressed:
- Is the prospective mentor flexible?
- Does the potential mentor have good people skills? Is this individual people-oriented and enthusiastic?
- Is the potential mentor comfortable with teenagers and/ or young adults?
- Is the potential mentor sensitive to learners' needs and in setting expectations for them?
- Is the potential mentor willing and able to help identify potential problems and find solutions with learners?
- Can the potential mentor provide constructive evaluation and feedback to nurture learner growth?
- Does the potential mentor perceive possible benefits of the mentoring experience to the learners, business, and community?

The role of the mentor can include a variety of responsibilities. Mentors may be asked to
- shape the circumstances of the learning environment when they are with the learner;
- shape the environment, both physical and emotional, that the learner will interact with them;
- encourage dialogue and focus on appropriate details of feelings and perceptions of a situation;
- generate problems for the learner to ponder and suggest original solutions;
- provide regular feedback on all aspects of the mentor relationship (e.g., clarify the learner's questions and their responses, select the appropriate moment for feedback);
- provide role modeling (e.g., share their educational and work backgrounds, model a path for an eager learner to pursue, model personal traits such as a positive attitude and work ethic);
- establish connections between other professionals and the learners they are mentoring (e.g., introducing the learner to other staff, accompanying the learner to a professional conference, allowing the learner to sit in on a meeting, or requesting an appointment with a colleague who might further develop the learner's knowledge or an area of mutual interest); and
- advocate for the learners (e.g., give advice, guide them in their learning process).

Business and industry can provide valuable resources for the mentoring process. The following several questions need to be answered before these individuals are ready to provide commitment and time for this effort:
- Why should business be willing to be involved as a partner with education in a mentoring endeavor?
- What educational needs does the business have and what needs must be met within the community's schools? What is the company's stake in education and in the community at large?
- What is the business willing to offer in the partnership?
- Who within the business will be a direct participant? In what capacity?
- Can staff time be allocated?
- Can the business offer access to its facilities and specialized equipment?
- Is security or confidentiality an issue?
- Will the business absorb certain expenses?
- What does the business expect in return?
- How will the business know if the partnership has met their expectations?

Sometimes mentors will come into classrooms. They should work with the instructor to determine what is going to be covered and how the information will relate to the program. A worksheet may be helpful for both the instructor and the mentor in planning a classroom visit. See Figure 11-16. Feedback from mentors about the learner's performance during the mentoring experience as well as overall feelings about their role in the process can be instrumental in making changes in the mentor program. Providing the mentor with an evaluation form to use after the visit is one effective way to collect this feedback. See Figure 11-17.

The world is rapidly changing and with this change comes new dimensions in mentoring options. On-line communications via the Internet, known as *telementoring*, offer a new dimension to the mentor process that may help educators to overcome the obstacles presented by traditional mentoring programs.

Telementoring programs require several elements in order to be considered legitimate mentoring programs versus information-seeking or friendship activities. First, the relationship should have established learning objectives. The mentor should work with the learner toward a final goal. For example, a goal for a learner might be to find out about what possible occupational opportunities exist within an area in which the mentor has familiarity. Mentoring should also be more than just sharing information. The mentor should try to advise or guide the learner to help him or her make connections between their shared knowledge and applications of the knowledge to the real world. Finally, mentor relationships should be long-term partnerships that last at least a year and hopefully continue during the high school years and into the learner's post secondary activities. The mentor should not just supply some information and advise and move on. The relationship needs to be active and ongoing (Wheeldon & Lehmann, 1999). See Figure 11-18.

MENTOR WORKSHEET FOR CLASSROOM VISITS

Purpose. At the end of my talk, the students will be able to _____.

Opening. Should satisfy the four following requirements.

    1. Gets attention.

    2. Relates to topic.

    3. Helps learners think about what they already know about the topic.

    4. Summarizes major points.

    My opening: _____

_____

Information. Stick to no more than six main points.

    1. _____

    2. _____

    3. _____

    4. _____

    5. _____

    6. _____

Delivery. You should use at least two different techniques.

    _____ lecture   _____ ask the learners

    _____ handout   _____ bring things to show

    _____ write on the board   _____ use overhead transparencies

    How I will share this information: _____

_____

Activity. Be sure it suits your purpose as stated above.

    My activity. _____

_____

Supplies. Things to bring or the school will provide (e.g., chalk, overhead projector, recorder, handouts, paper, pencils, rulers, magazine cutouts, things to show).

Closure. Summarize main points.

Source: Reilly, J. (1992). *Mentorship: The Essential Guide for Schools and Business.* Dayton, OH: Ohio Psychology Press.

Figure 11-16. A sample worksheet for mentors to use when preparing for classroom visits.

MENTOR EVALUATION FORM . . .

Mentor _____   Date _____

Student _____   Instructor _____

Please comment and also circle the most accurate description.

1. Comment on the quality of student work on the project.

_____

_____

    Surpassed Expectation   Met Expectation   Not Up to Expectation

2. Comment on the work habits that the student exhibited (independence, punctuality, initiative, etc.).

_____

_____

    Surpassed Expectation   Met Expectation   Not Up to Expectation

3. Comment on the student's skill employed to communicate about the project.

_____

_____

    Surpassed Expectation   Met Expectation   Not Up to Expectation

...MENTOR EVALUATION FORM

4. Comment on the learning challenge that the project provided for the student. Did it stretch him/her beyond what he/she already knew?

_____

_____

| Surpassed Expectation | Met Expectation | Not Up to Expectation |

5. Check all the items that describe what the student learned.

_____ Technical skills   _____ Independent work skills   _____ Advanced research skills

_____ Advanced subject matter   _____ Other (specify) _____

6. On a scale of 1–10, how worthwhile was the learning experience for the student?

1	2	3	4	5	6	7	8	9	10
Useless				Worthwhile					Useful

7. Based on your comments above, what grade would you give the student for his/her overall performance at your worksite? (You may use +'s and –'s)

| **A** Excellent | **B** Good | **C** Average | **D** Below Average |

---

1. My responsibilities were described adequately.

| Strongly disagree | Disagree | Uncertain | Agree | Strongly agree |

2. The informational material was helpful.

| Strongly disagree | Disagree | Uncertain | Agree | Strongly agree |

3. The informational meeting(s) was (were) helpful.

| Strongly disagree | Disagree | Uncertain | Agree | Strongly agree |

4. The mentor/student relationship was meaningful in terms of discussions held, ideas exchanged, and experiences shared.

| Strongly disagree | Disagree | Uncertain | Agree | Strongly agree |

5. My participation did not cause significant inconvenience in the performance of my job.

| Strongly disagree | Disagree | Uncertain | Agree | Strongly agree |

6. I would consider being a mentor to a future student.

| Strongly disagree | Disagree | Uncertain | Agree | Strongly agree |

Source: Reily, J. (1992). *Mentorship: The Essential Guide for Schools and Business.* Dayton, OH: Ohio Psychology Press.

Figure 11-17. A sample evaluation form to be filled out by a mentor regarding the mentoring experience.

The following are a number of identified key points about providing telementoring experiences:

- Once the telementoring program's goals and intentions are established and a pool of mentors has been matched to learners, the relationship must be sustained through commitment by all parties—the mentor, the learner, and the instructor. Each must find time to build the relationship. Rules clarifying topics to be discussed and contact schedules provide a framework for early e-mail interactions.
- Mentors should be screened before they are paired with learners. The use of a survey that helps sort and match mentors and learners by gender and interests is important. Besides asking questions about time commitments, personal philosophies of mentoring, potential mentors are also asked what they do for fun in their spare time and to list some of the books and magazines they read. These questions pro-

vide some biographical information that can forge links between learners and mentors. Matching the learner's interests to the mentor is necessary in creating a meaningful, lasting relationship.

- Telementoring can help to dispel the stereotypes that some learners hold about adults. A learner who has had negative experiences with a parent or teacher may feel that adults cannot relate to or understand them. Because telementoring is not face-to-face and not confrontational, it may provide a safer environment from which a learner-adult relationship can be forged.
- Mentor relationship increases the mentor's own professional development. For example, mentors must question their own practices when helping others to reflect on motivations, values, and needs, thereby improving their performance and evaluation skills.

- Because it is difficult to anticipate all possible difficulties, the educators must monitor interactions. Monitoring activities includes helping mentors and learners become acquainted with one another, anticipating problems, supporting learners academically in terms of reading and writing e-mail messages, infusing new ideas when on-line interactions seem to wane, and assuring confidentiality and mutual respect between all involved parties.

- Telementoring relationships have other practical values in their ability to link rural or isolated learners to diverse ideas as well as mainstream cultural themes that may not be present in learners' hometowns. Since telementoring partnerships take place via phone connections the possibilities for distant and diverse relationships are virtually limitless. Mentors who are skilled at navigating the World Wide Web can teach their protégés through web links about subjects beyond their fields of expertise. Although the concept of telementoring is still fairly new, the rapid expansion of the Internet and computer capabilities should bring about more programs using some form of telementoring to connect learners with professionals.

- There are a number of barriers to providing learners with mentors including locating a pool of potential mentors in the community, creating time for the mentor relationship, addressing the special needs of some learners, and overcoming the geographic isolation of some schools (Wheeldon & Lehmann, 1999).

STEPS FOR ESTABLISHING A TELEMENTORING PROGRAM

PLANNING
- Articulate program purpose
- Design program format
- Define educator role
- Contact potential businesses

IMPLEMENTATION
- Identify suitable mentors
- Match mentors with learners
- Prepare learners
- Begin e-mail conversation

EVALUATION
- Measure learners' and mentors' satisfaction
- Monitor learners' attendance and grades
- Evaluate learners' occupational knowledge and computer proficiency
- Revise/refine program accordingly

Adapted from: Wheeldon, R., & Lehmann, J. (1999, Spring). Establishing a Telementoring Program That can be Used in Vocational Classes. *The Journal for Vocational Special Needs Education, 21*(3), 32-37.

Figure 11-18. A list of steps to plan, implement, and evaluate a telementoring program.

ADVISORY COMMITTEES

Local advisory committees are groups of individuals from the community that advise career and technical educators about planning, implementing, and maintaining programs. Members of career and technical education advisory committees should come from a variety of community areas. The major portion of the committee should be representatives from the business and industrial sector. Other sources include

- Chamber of Commerce representatives;
- labor department representatives;
- labor union representatives;
- state and community agency representatives;
- employers of program completers;
- prospective employers;
- local government representatives;
- clergy;
- local newspaper representatives;
- parents;
- successful graduates from special populations;
- community-based organization representatives;
- parents of current learners; and
- representatives of apprenticeship councils.

The collaboration between education and the community is best exemplified when advisory committees demonstrate certain characteristics, such as the following:

1. Membership is representative of the major groups concerned with and involved in improving education, training, and competitive employment opportunities for individuals with special needs. For instance, collaborative activities and directions should be established which will join and serve more than two sectors (e.g., special education, career and technical education, vocational rehabilitation services, business/industry). Advisory committees should treat the collaborating institutions/agencies as equal partners. Although in particular instances, the strength and interest of one or two organizations may predominate, the goal of the committee should be to meet multiple purposes rather than the interests of a few organizations.

2. Advisory committees are self-organized. The committee, once organized, should be responsible for its continuity. The agenda should not be led by any one of the committee members. Over time, responsibility for leadership of the committee should be rotated and shared appropriately.

3. Advisory committees are performance-oriented. The membership should develop their own agenda and approaches to addressing employment and education needs and concerns of individuals enrolled in career and technical education programs. Although a major role may be advisory, committees may engage in activities which include fact-finding, program development, and program evaluation.

4. Responsibility for implementing the action plans developed by the committee is shared. Because the members comprising the committee are the active leaders

in their respective organizations, the effectiveness of collaborative efforts is greatly enhanced when shared interest results in mutual action. Examples of such activities include

- conducting a needs assessment of the local community's perceptions of education and training needs of learners from special populations (research);
- developing and publishing a newsletter that highlights exemplary education and industry training programs for individuals with special needs (public awareness);
- facilitating site visits to business and industry by high school and community college students for on-site shadowing and interaction with people at work (student development);
- working with career and technical education instructors, support personnel, and counselors to modify their curriculum and instructional processes to meet the career development and skill training needs of individuals from special populations (staff development); and
- establishing school/business partnerships (e.g., equipment donation and/or sharing program) which will actively work to expand and enrich the students' career development and training experiences (administrative policy concerns). (Illinois State Board of Education, n.d., p. 8)

Cooperative planning with advisory committees can help career and technical education personnel provide appropriate opportunities for learners with special needs. Specific services that can be provided by this valuable resource include

- assistance in planning programs that would be appropriate and realistic for learners from special populations;
- advice concerning appropriate program objectives, curriculum content, and occupational competencies to be included in programs;
- identification of community resources that may help learners succeed in programs;
- assessing the educational and labor market needs of the community (possibly through a needs survey);
- identification of entry-level job proficiencies;
- establishing and promoting positive community public relationships;
- advice concerning equipment, laboratory, and facility modifications for learners with special needs;
- assistance in locating potential on-the-job training sites for learners who require further assistance during or after completion of a specific program; and
- assistance in identifying job placement situations for learners with special needs.

COLLABORATIVE PLANNING WITH AGENCIES AND ORGANIZATIONS

Services are available for learners with special needs to provide technical skills and prepare them for the transition to the working world. However, coordinating these services and deciding which institution or agency will provide specific services to an individual is not always easily accomplished.

An agency is a governmental or non-governmental body organized around the needs of a specific population or group with certain functions designed to benefit that population or group. Greenan (1980) defined interagency cooperation as coordination of the available resources of both public and private agencies whose objective is to provide career and technical education instruction and services to learners from special populations. Efficient and effective delivery of vocational assessment, career and technical education instruction, student services, and other essential related services depends upon coordination among various service providers.

Over the past decade, cooperation and coordinated planning between education and agencies has been recognized as an effective and efficient method to serve individuals from special populations. Interagency cooperation reduces gaps in service delivery, minimizes duplication of services, and reduces unnecessary expense. In addition, interagency cooperation has been identified as a crucial component in helping these learners make a successful transition from school to employment or postsecondary programs.

Educational institutions, job training programs, rehabilitative agencies, employment services, community services, and business and industrial services are often available to develop skills necessary for independence for individuals from special populations. However, the full force of the combined potential of these resources is seldom seen because they are frequently fragmented and separated. Thus, the need for interagency collaboration is crucial.

According to Ferrini et al. (1980), interagency cooperation provides a variety of benefits to each cooperating party including the following:

Education
- access to a wider range of expertise, information, and contacts when serving learners with special needs
- development of cost-efficient services
- development of a reputation for responsiveness to community needs

Government Agencies
- access to a larger and wider range of clients from special populations
- access to more job placements for learners with special needs
- greater community understanding of the mandates of specific agencies as well as the services available

Service Organizations for Individuals from Special Populations
- development of greater community visibility and impact
- establishment of greater community awareness of the needs and capacities of individuals with special needs

- opportunities to promote individualized approaches to educational services for clients; and
- ability to address the "whole life needs" of clients with special needs

Business and Industry

- opportunity to better prepare workers
- access to referrals and support systems for individuals from special populations
- vehicle with which to comply with Section 504 of the Rehabilitation Act of 1973
- opportunity to improve their community image

The following agencies are frequently involved in collaborative planning:

- Division of Vocational Rehabilitation (DVR)–Offers vocational assessment and counseling, and rehabilitation planning and services, to achieve job placement. This agency also provides an Independent Living Program (ILP) designed for people with disabilities who want to increase their independence. The ILP may assist with attendant care management, counseling and advocacy, living arrangements, skill training, and services to the participant's family.
- Division of Developmental Disabilities (DDD)–Offers a wide range of services and supports to eligible individuals. Such services include employment training and placement, assistance in accessing the community and participation in leisure activities, residential options that include minimal support to full 24-hour support for people with severe challenges to live in the community.
- Division of Mental Health–Offers diagnostic services, residential programs that provide a range of support to citizens in order to remain in their own homes and function in the community, job training and placement, individual and group therapy, support to families of citizens with mental illness, and medication management.
- Division of Alcohol and Substance Abuse (DASA)–Offers diagnostic services, residential rehabilitation programs that includes inpatient rehabilitation, placement into a community program that may include short-term residential support such as a halfway house, follow-along treatment, educational programs for schools and for the community.
- Aging and Adult Administration–Offers community residential resources focused on allowing citizens to remain in their own homes with appropriate medical and physical care. Among these, chore services is one of the most important resources funded through this agency. In addition, the agency provides adult family home placement and monitoring for citizens who cannot remain in their own homes, respite care, access to nursing home care, and adult protection.
- Department of Employment Security–Offers employment, training programs, and job placement services for people who are unemployed. Services are available to all citizens including those who have disabilities.

- Community and Technical Colleges–Offers technical, educational, and skills training for careers requiring other than a baccalaureate degree for entry into a profession and for career enhancement. Many programs include people with disabilities.
- Division of Children and Family Services–Offers protection to children who are identified as at risk, counseling for children and their families to preserve the integrity of the family unit, and foster care placement. Eligibility is based on identified need for services.
- Medical Assistance Administration–Offers Medicaid health insurance to eligible applicants.
- Community Services Division–Offers monthly grants for basic living requirements, Medicaid, food stamps, employment referral services to the Department of Employment Security, and other job training and placement resources.
- Department of Services for the Blind–A state agency that provides training and placement of visually impaired and/or blind adults. This program assists in transition of high school learners into vocational rehabilitation services of the agency: counseling, guidance, adaptive skill training, career and technical education exploration, academic and career and technical education tuition assistance, job development, and accommodations relevant to employment.
- Social Security Administration–A federal agency that offers financial assistance for people with disabilities to achieve an independent lifestyle. Eligibility depends on severity of disability. Supplemental Security Income (SSI) and Social Security Disability Insurance (SSDI) are two of the major programs. Transition students who have a disability are most likely to benefit from SSI. Each program has its own eligibility criteria.

Becoming familiar with these and other organizations in your local community that support children and adults with disabilities is essential for effective planning and coordination of services for individuals. The time to know about these resources is before they are needed to provide ongoing support for continued employment, independent living, or in-home support.

One-Stop Career Center System

Since the introduction of one-stop employment systems funded by the U.S. Department of Labor (DOL), many states have attempted to merge traditional employment and training services to provide consolidated programs, supervised by states and local communities, to enable easy customer access to services. After 1994, a number of states began creating one-stop career centers, but no federal legislative mandate existed to help implement them. The Workforce Investment Act (WIA), passed in 1998, requires the formation of locally based one-stop service delivery systems to deliver many employment and training services funded by the federal government.

What before was a voluntary movement to a more integrated employment and training system has now become a legislative mandate.

The WIA requires that one-stop centers provide core services, intensive services, and training services. Core services, expected to be made available to all who are interested, include access to career information resources such as local labor market data, Internet job listings and information about education and training providers. Intensive services are those that require some staff assistance and include counseling, case management, and short-term prevocational services. Training services are reserved only for those who are unable to benefit through core and intensive services, with priority given to public assistance recipients and low-income individuals.

The following four principles guide the development of the one-stop system:

1. Universal access–One-stop centers are to make core work force development services available to all population groups, including job seekers and employers. Eligibility for specific programs is not a criterion for receiving services.
2. Customer choice–Because customers can select services based on their needs, centers can compete for customers based on their understanding of both job seekers and employers.
3. Service integration–Work force development services provided by local, state, and federal programs will be consolidated in one-stop centers.
4. Accountability–Centers will be evaluated on the basis of measurable outcomes with future funding tied to the results of services provided to customers.

The WIA identifies specific programs and activities that must provide their services through one-stop centers. Each one-stop center integrates the services of federally funded programs targeting adults, youth, dislocated workers, job corps, Native Americans, migrant and seasonal farm workers, and veterans.

These employment and training programs have specific eligibility criteria and target certain audiences. Contact a local one-stop center to get more information on what is available locally. Available programs may include the following:

- Job service–This provides assistance for job seekers to find jobs and for employers to find qualified workers.
- Adult education and literacy–This provides assistance for adults to become literate and obtain the knowledge and skills necessary for employment and self-sufficiency.
- Vocational rehabilitation–This includes assistance for people with disabilities to prepare for, obtain, or keep meaningful employment.
- Welfare to work–This is employment-based assistance for long-term welfare recipients and those with characteristics associated with welfare dependency.
- Senior Community Service Employment Program (SCSEP)–This is a part-time program providing help

for persons aged 55 and older to find jobs, increase incomes, and learn new skills.
- Postsecondary career and technical education–This provides training for adults for high-skill, high-wage jobs in emerging occupations.
- North American Free Trade Agreement (NAFTA)/Transitional Adjustment Assistance (TAA)–This includes employment services to persons whose firms are affected by layoff or threatened layoff due to competition from foreign countries.
- Veterans' employment and training services–This offers specialized employment and training services for qualified veterans and other eligible persons.
- The Office of Community Services community services block grant–This is federal funding for nonprofit agencies for the purposes of creating and promoting job opportunities for low-income individuals.
- The Department of Housing and Urban Development (HUD) employment and training activities–Employment opportunities and necessary training and supportive service programs through several HUD-funded programs.
- Unemployment insurance–This consists of benefits paid for a duration of time to individuals who are involuntarily unemployed.
- Job clubs–These provide career counseling, job search techniques, resume writing, interviewing skills, and job search resources (e.g., job listings, career resource libraries, telephones, computers and printers, fax machines).
- Job retraining–This provides basic remedial and high-tech skills to people in the classroom or on the job. Instruction can be provided to individuals or groups in a classroom format or through self-paced computer programs. Advantages include specialized and individualized training, and customized training programs may be developed in partnership with employers.

COMMUNITY RESOURCES

Community agencies, organizations, and advocacy groups can often offer services that are not readily available in the educational system. Educators should make initial contacts with outside agencies and community services, especially when they can effectively supplement career development activities. Community resources can be divided into four categories: federal and state agencies; community agencies and organizations; citizen and special interest groups; and business, industry, and labor organizations. See Figure 11-19. Each agency, organization or group can provide specific contributions to individuals with special populations. See Figure 11-20.

Taking learners into the community and bringing community representatives into the schools can provide learners from special populations with positive learning opportunities. The relevance between school and the working world can be established or reinforced.

Sarkees-Wircenski (1991) identified the following strategies that the community can use to make a contribution to the school-based support team:

1. Local business and industry can establish partnerships with schools and work actively with educators to plan effective programs for learners with special needs. Advice can be offered about necessary employability and job-seeking skills that should be incorporated into school curricula. Equipment can be donated to schools. Adopt-A-School, Adopt-A-Program, and Adopt-A-Student arrangements can be made through which visitations to local industrial sites can be arranged, volunteers can visit students in classes to talk about the world of work, and shadowing experiences can be scheduled.
2. Community volunteers can act as mentors for students.
3. Scholarships, part-time paid employment, and other financial assistance can be provided by the community.
4. Information about valuable community resources can be shared with members of the school's support team.
5. Community representatives can serve on advisory committees for specific programs in the school system.
6. Volunteer tutorial services can be provided.
7. Information about potential job placement opportunities for students can be provided.
8. Volunteers can help with student events, vocational [career and technical] student organization activities, and other extracurricular activities and encourage students to become involved in them.
9. Members of the community can work in the classrooms as teacher volunteers. This can be an ongoing service throughout the year or can represent a one-time experience. (pp. 211-212)

COMMUNITY RESOURCES ...

FEDERAL AND STATE AGENCIES

These provide services to their local and regional offices. Such services include financial support, job training and placement programs, housing, health, youth programs, consumer information, and legal aid. Examples include the following:

- Legal services
- Armed services
- State employment services
- State agency or school for the visually impaired
- State agency or school for the hearing impaired
- State Department of Welfare
- Mental health agency
- U.S. Immigration and Naturalization Services (INS)
- Department of Veterans Affairs (VA)
- Social Security Administration (SSA)
- Job Training Partnership Act (JTPA)
- Community Action Partnership
- Legal and judicial agencies
- Public health services/programs
- U.S. Department of Health & Human Services
- State agency for economic opportunity or development
- Civil service programs
- Rehabilitation Services Administration (RSA)
- Employment services
- National Park Service
- Adult basic education programs
- Migrant programs
- Correctional facilities
- Governors'/Mayors' committees for employment of the disabled
- Law enforcement agencies
- Bureau of Indian Affairs (BIA)

COMMUNITY AGENCIES AND ORGANIZATIONS

These provide such services as youth recreation, counseling and tutoring, employment and job training, foster care placement, and leadership development. Examples include the following:

- Chamber of commerce
- YMCA/YWCA
- Drug and alcohol abuse centers
- American Red Cross
- Child abuse/women's centers
- Urban League
- Adult continuing education programs
- Student financial aid programs
- League of Women Voters
- Mental health clinics
- Probation and parole services
- Children and youth services
- Foster homes
- Halfway houses
- Community action agencies
- Migrant programs
- Bilingual programs
- Dropout prevention programs
- Parent-teacher organizations
- American Legion
- Veterans of Foreign Wars
- Salvation Army
- Jaycees
- Optimist Clubs
- Goodwill Industries

... COMMUNITY RESOURCES

CITIZEN AND SPECIAL INTEREST GROUPS

These typically offer scholarship programs, legal aid, day care, and transportation. Examples include the following:

- Lions Club
- Rotary Club
- Churches
- Women's and men's clubs in the community
- Crisis intervention centers
- Hospitals
- Girl Scouts
- Camp Fire USA
- Planned Parenthood

- Big Brothers Big Sisters
- Boy Scouts of America
- Indian Guides
- Knights of Columbus
- Sertoma Club
- Elks Lodge
- Retired citizens
- Volunteer tutor groups

BUSINESS, INDUSTRY, AND LABOR ORGANIZATIONS

These are good sources of field trips, guest speakers, job opportunities, and occupational and product information. Examples include the following:

- Trade and labor unions
- Advisory committee members
- Employers

- Personnel offices
- Industrial supervisors

Figure 11-19. A list of potential resources from federal and state agencies; community agencies and organizations; citizen and special interest groups; and business, industry and labor organizations.

INTERAGENCY LINKAGES

Interagency linkage is formal interagency cooperation that includes collaboration of public and private agencies to promote the best use of available services through interagency agreements. The services that learners from special populations may need to prepare for and use to successfully make the transition to postsecondary education, further technical training, apprenticeship training, or employment may include

- career development opportunities;
- career assessment services;
- career guidance and counseling services;
- curriculum modification;
- specific skill training;
- remedial academic assistance;
- employability skills training;
- diagnostic and related services; and
- placement and follow-up services.

Without interagency planning, many services may be excluded or duplicated. A collaborative process must be established at the state and local level. Collaborating agencies on the local level should investigate needed services, determine which agency can provide these services, and determine to what extent these services can be shared in a cost effective manner.

Getzel, Salin, and Wacker (1982) listed several factors that prompt the need for interagency linkage agreements:

- A number of different agencies may provide the same or similar services.
- Few agencies possess all the necessary resources to meet the totality of client needs.
- A scarcity of resources and funds demands the most effective use of available services.

- High quality services provided in sufficient quantity and in an orderly fashion require case management techniques.
- A well-coordinated and systematic delivery of services facilitates the identification of gaps and barriers.

McNulty and Soper (1983) identified a variety of ways that local interagency linkage can be effective:

- Communication–The ability of the participants in the cooperative endeavor to accurately and adequately share information, ideas, feelings, and values greatly influences the outcome of the cooperative effort.
- Group dynamics and group behavior–In dealing with cooperative efforts, the group becomes an entity in itself as well as a composite of the entities of the individuals within the group. Group dynamics, group behavior, and individual behavior within the group, are all crucial elements to the success of interagency cooperation.
- Conflict resolution strategies–The type of problem-solving approach or conflict resolution strategy used in decision-making is one of the most crucial elements for successful group endeavors.
- Management of transition–Interagency linkage by definition necessitates change on the part of the agencies and individuals involved. If systems and procedures do not change in the process of developing interagency coordination, the collaborative efforts serve no purpose.
- Sharing needs and common goals–There can be little incentive to initiate interagency linkage activities unless participants involved perceive that they have common problems, needs, and/or goals that can be dealt with effectively by a combining their resources and efforts.
- Definition of roles and responsibilities–As a function of developing and maintaining commitment to the process

of interagency linkage, the roles and responsibilities of each participant should be defined and acknowledged. Adequate resources should be provided to the participants to allow them to effectively meet their responsibilities.

- Leadership identification and roles–Interagency collaborative efforts cannot be successful without effective, flexible, and strategic leadership.
- Commitment of time and resources–In addition to a commitment to the concept and process of interagency linkage, the agencies involved must be willing and able to commit the time and resources required to implement cooperative endeavors.
- Knowledge of external forces and influences–The planning process and any resulting interagency linkage agreements must fit the state legislative and budgetary process.
- Identification of and focus on target population–Participants in interagency linkage activities must agree upon the population to benefit from a coordinated effort.
- Evaluation procedures–A critical aspect of interagency linkage is the need to develop a framework for analyzing the effects of the collaboration.

Probably the most critical step in working collaboratively with different people and agencies is determining who the critical groups are in the locality. A framework for identifying organizations and individuals to consider for interagency planning would be helpful in accomplishing this. See Figure 11-21.

Wehman (1996) identified the types of information that can be incorporated into an interagency agreement:
- mission statement or purpose of agreement
- number and names of agencies involved
- measurable goals to be accomplished by core team as preliminary activities to creating the agreement
- definitions of terms
- descriptions of roles and responsibilities of each agency in agreement implementation
- descriptions of eligibility determination processes for each agency
- delineation of referral procedures for each agency's services
- description of staffing allocations from each agency for transition and interagency operations
- implementation procedures
- plan for disseminations of agreement
- plan for interagency in-service
- time overlapping/service coordination
- list of service options available (direct or purchase)
- procedure for development of new services
- provisions for individual with severe disabilities
- time-limiting and ongoing service provision
- cost sharing
- data sharing (formative and evaluative)
- procedures for information release and confidentiality policy
- attendance of IEP/ITP meetings
- schedule for implementation

- schedule for renegotiation or modification of agreement terms
- policy on service delivery (e.g., duplication, repeating, initiation dates)
- identification of agency liaisons to participating agencies
- schedule of interaction between liaisons
- desired outcomes of agreement
- dissemination of services available to parents and candidates
- procedure and schedule for ongoing needs assessment

COMMUNITY RESOURCE SUPPORT

Listed below are some of the many agencies, groups, and individual contacts that can be used as resources.

DIRECT SERVICES TO LEARNERS
- Community agencies
- Parents and personal advocates
- Local education agency support/auxiliary staff
- Volunteer and service organizations
- Placement services
- Postsecondary programs and personnel
- Transitional services
- Other school-based personnel

CONSULTATIVE AND TECHNICAL ASSISTANCE
- Professional organizations
- Service organizations
- Parent organizations
- Advisory groups
- State education agency personnel
- Business/industry personnel and programs
- Other vocational support services teams
- Local colleges and universities
- Career and technical education research and development resource center(s)

INFORMATION AND REFERRAL
- Career counseling centers
- Work experience and job placement services
- School and private psychologists
- Tutors
- Recreational programs
- Employers
- Employment services
- Community agencies for counseling or health services
- New schools (transfer students)
- Division of vocational rehabilitation
- Job training partnership program

Source: Maryland State Department of Education. (1984). *Handbook for Vocational Support Service Teams in Maryland.* Annapolis, MD: Division of Vocational-Technical Education.

Figure 11-20. An example of collaborative services for individuals from special populations including direct services, technical assistance, and information and referral services.

POSSIBLE LOCAL ORGANIZATIONS AND INDIVIDUALS AVAILABLE FOR INTERAGENCY COLLABORATION

Other Local Community
Organizations

_____

_____

_____

_____

Parent, Consumer, and
Civic Organizations

_____

_____

_____

_____

Education Agencies
and Organizations

_____

_____

_____

_____

**YOUR LOCAL
COMMUNITY**

Business and Industrial
Organizations

_____

_____

_____

_____

Social Service Agencies
and Organizations

_____

_____

_____

_____

Rehabilitation Agencies
and Organizations

_____

_____

_____

_____

Figure 11-21. A framework for identifying organizations and individuals to consider for interagency planning.

The following steps can be taken to identify existing and duplicated services for individuals from special populations:

1. Sharing agency information–Before collaborative planning can take place, the members of the team must understand the role, function, and operating procedures of the other agencies involved. An agency collaboration worksheet can provide an overview of such things as goals, clients served, eligibility criteria, and services provided for each contributing agency. See Figure 11-22.
2. Identifying necessary services–The services needed for learners with special needs to participate and succeed in career and technical education programs as well as job-seeking and job-retention must be defined. A worksheet can be used in interagency planning to identify necessary student services and also to determine whether these services are unavailable or are available through one or more agencies. This list is a general list of services, and some services may not be appropriate for every local interagency collaboration plan. Any additional services should be added by the team. See Figure 11-23.
3. Identifying shared services–Once necessary services have been identified it must be determined whether or not there is a gap or duplication of services. A special delivery worksheet can be used to determine how ser-

vices will be delivered. If the service is unavailable, plans should be made for one agency to make provisions for it, or two or more agencies may share responsibility for the service. In the case of duplicated services, it should be determined which agencies will share the responsibility for making the service available and what part of the cost each shall assume. See Figure 11-24.

Ferrini, Matthews, Foster, and Workman (1980) stated that interagency linkages and agreements promote the

- sharing of organizational perspectives on clients' needs;
- sharing of information about services currently offered to clients;
- identification of the most crucial unmet needs of clients;
- identification of new programs or new linkages between existing programs that would meet these crucial client needs;
- identification and sharing of organizational resources which could be pooled to develop needed new programs;
- planning and implementation of new programs by key staff from organizations holding needed resources; and
- development of long-term collaborative relationships among these organizations to insure continued community-wide efforts to identify needs and develop programs for their common clientele. (p. 30)

AGENCY COLLABORATION INFORMATION				
Area of Concern	Career and Technical Education	Special Education	Rehabilitation Services	Other Agencies (Specify)
I. Philosophy and goals for agency				
II. Clients served (description)				
III. Age ranges for providing services				
IV. Eligibility criteria for services				
V. Services provided (see "identifying necessary services" worksheet)				
VI. Staffing patterns and ratios				
VII. Funding sources and patterns				
VIII. Source of evaluating services provided				
IX. Data collected for reports, etc.				
X. Terminology relevant to agency				

Figure 11-22. A format for collecting and synthesizing information about necessary support services provided by agencies that work with learners from special populations.

INTERAGENCY TEAMS AND AGREEMENTS

A number of barriers can complicate effective team building in the interagency collaboration process, including the following:
- The roles and responsibilities among members of a team working together may be poorly understood.
- A single individual may dominate the team operation (personality styles and group dynamics).
- Job-related stress may result from unclear goals and objectives.
- Individuals may find it difficult to link their expertise to those of the other team members.
- Trust and respect may be missing among team members.
- Administrative barriers may be present.
- Philosophical differences may often exist among agency representatives.
- A lack of commitment to identified interagency roles and responsibilities of team members may exist.
- A perception may exist on the part of one or more team members that another member is less qualified than the remainder of the group representatives.
- A diversity in the amount or level of professional training of team members may exist.
- Poor communication among individuals from different professional backgrounds may be present.
- A lack of flexibility of team members or the agencies

they represent may be present (e.g., inflexible schedules, limited planning time, lack of support from supervisors).
- An inability of team members to delegate and share responsibilities based on the various strengths of team members may be a barrier.
- Individuals on the team may lack skills in decision making, problem solving, and conflict resolution.

- There may be a lack of authority on the part of team members.
- There may be feelings of territoriality on the part of team members (e.g., rivalry, professional insecurity).
- New and different terminology used by various team members, especially from different agencies or disciplines, may present a barrier.

IDENTIFYING NECESSARY SERVICES WORKSHEET . . .

Service	Necessary or Supplemental Service	Unavailable	Availability of Service (amount, frequency, and cost)			
			Career and Technical Education	Special Education	Rehabilitation Services	Other Agencies (specify)
Personal counseling						
Family counseling						
Career counseling						
Career exploration						
Vocational assessment						
Career and technical education training						
Work adjustment program						
Work experience or co-op						
Job placement						
On-the-job training						
Faculty/staff in-service training						
Employer/employee sensitization						
Public awareness						
Employability skills						
Prevocational skills						
Independent living skills						
Transition services						
Academic remediation						
Academic diagnostic assessment						
Providing adaptive equipment/aids						
Transportation (e.g., to work site)						
Referral services						
Guidance services						
Psychological services						
Medical services						
Occupational therapy services						

Service	Necessary or Supplemental Service	Unavailable	Availability of Service (amount, frequency, and cost)			
			Career and Technical Education	Special Education	Rehabilitation Services	Other Agencies (specify)
Physical therapy services						
Remedial reading services						
Remedial math services						
Technical tutoring services						
Homebound instructional services						
Job seeking and job keeping skill development services. Job follow-up services						
Work experience and career exploration						
Curriculum modification and development services						
Equipment/facilities modification and development services						
Instructional material modification and development services						
Social and recreational experiences						

...IDENTIFYING NECESSARY SERVICES WORKSHEET

Figure 11-23. A format to identify the availability and providers of necessary support services for learners from special populations.

SERVICE DELIVERY WORKSHEET

Services Not Available from Any Agency	Duplicated Services	Services More Appropriately Provided Through Cooperative Planning		
		Service	Agency/Agencies to Provide Service	Cost to Each Agency

Figure 11-24. A format to identify duplicated and unavailable student services as well as collaborative approaches to providing services.

The North Central Regional Educational Laboratory (1996) identified the following collaboration implementation pitfalls:

- Projectitis–The rush to implement a plan or project exacerbates the tendency for collaborators to develop "projectitis." Collaborators become so absorbed in creating new projects and programs that they fail to identify and lobby for needed changes in the policies, attitudes, and staff behaviors of major community institutions. While new services are often necessary, the day-to-day, across-the-board operation of existing systems must change to support, respect, and engage learners and families more effectively. Add-on programs, even when they are highly successful, are often short-lived and have limited impact. Most rely on soft money and are limited to single sites. They are seldom replicated broadly throughout the community or incorporated as a permanent line item in institutional budgets.

- Time constraints–For most school staff, participating in collaborative activities adds to an already jammed schedule. In the beginning, doing double duty may be inevitable, but success over the long haul depends on making sure that participants are supported in their efforts. Collaborators operating at the policy level may hire staff, or partners may assign existing personnel to do collaborative work on a full- or part-time basis. At the service delivery level, substantial innovation may be necessary to ensure that teachers and other frontline staff have the time to participate. Surveys suggest that time-finding strategies in schools focus on (1) taking time that is now scheduled for other things, (2) adding additional time to the school day and/or school year, or (3) altering staff utilization patterns.

- Unequal power relations–Turf issues are inevitable among groups that come to the table with different professional orientations, organizational agendas, and resources. Having unequal power relations is a more serious matter. It stems from perceived inequalities in status among members and results in the reduced capacity of some groups to initiate and influence collaborative actions. This imbalance frequently occurs when representatives of large institutions with sizable budgets try to work together with parents or community members. When these latter groups bring essential resources—namely their ability to provide information about what is needed, what strategies are likely to be well received, and their ability to marshal community support—that are not acknowledged or valued, the legitimacy and effectiveness of the collaboration is severely undermined. Open conflict can erupt; more frequently, the participation of parents and community representatives gradually erodes as their frustration and alienation grows.

- Confidentiality–Agencies serving the same learner and/or family often must share relevant information if they are to provide services more effectively and efficiently. Administrators and frontline staff who have never worked together may be concerned about infringing on their clients' privacy rights. In addition, some partners see sharing information as an encroachment on professional privilege. Conflict can be minimized if partners (1) assume early on that strategies to protect privacy and to share essential information do exist; and (2) agree to postpone further discussion until they have designed their initiative and know what kind of information, under what circumstances, they want to share.

Interagency linkage teams that effectively work together possess many of the following characteristics:

1. Participants work together to identify problems which are common to the group. They consider the student, labor, equipment, knowledge of services to be provided, and monies available.
2. They explore all possible solutions and choose those solutions which will be most beneficial to the learner.
3. There is a constant desire to keep commitment alive and to expand the interagency linkages when and where necessary to benefit the student.
4. Ideas are shared between local and state levels.
5. Interagency team encourages and supports local level service providers and individuals from special populations.
6. A good community spirit exists toward the education and employment of individuals from special populations.
7. There is a desire to decrease the overlap in services, and the fear of losing prestige or jobs by eliminating overlapping services is not dominant.
8. The objectives of cooperating agencies are compatible and agency personnel feel cooperation will be of mutual benefit.
9. Agencies have a referral system which sends clients to the agency with the best resources to help the individual. (Greenan, 1980, p. 62)

Many factors contribute to an agency's decision to collaborate with other agencies. However, for successful planning of a cooperative program it is essential that the central goal be to help individuals from special populations achieve maximum potential. In order to achieve this goal, agencies must collaborate to improve their services. There is no single model of successful coordination between various agencies. When considering planning for different coordination practices, it is important to realize that it is impossible to completely transplant a model and expect it to work for every situation. Programs demonstrating practices in interagency coordination generally fall into three different planning categories:

- State-level cooperative agreements followed by state-wide training, local agreements, and the development of local cooperative programs
- State-initiated pilot projects leading to program expansion, local agreements, and sometimes state-level agreements
- The development of cooperative programs through local initiative See Figure 11-25.

LOCAL COOPERATIVE PLAN FOR PROVISION OF SERVICES TO LEARNERS WITH SPECIAL NEEDS ...		
Identified Need	**Necessary Services**	**Services Provider(s)**
Physical modifications–facilities, equipment, tools	1. Removing physical barriers by making entrances and facilities accessible 2. Modifying machinery (jigs, etc.) so physically handicapped students can use them 3. Providing lower level reading materials when needed 4. Providing interpreters (oral or manual) 5. Providing note takers and readers 6. Providing specialized equipment such as reading machines, tape recorders, writing aids, etc.	1. Federal, state and local agencies 2. Rehabilitative services 3. Service organizations 4. Private sector agencies 5. Engineers, technicians, and architects 6. Advocacy groups
Curriculum modification	1. Basic skills 2. Career awareness 3. Pre-vocational 4. Independent living skills 5. Identification of multiple exit points in each vocational area 6. Prepared pretests and post-tests 7. Utilization of appropriate instructional techniques (e.g., task analysis) 8. Utilization of instructional materials 9. Utilization of evaluation techniques 10. Adequate time allowed	1. Special education personnel 2. Transition coordinators 3. Career and technical education personnel 4. Administrators 5. Career and technical education evaluators 6. Career and technical education counselors 7. University personnel 8. Parents

In-service	1. Provision of in-service for all personnel, including:
	  a. Special ed. teachers
	  b. Career and technical education teachers
	  c. Related transition coordinators
	  d. Administrators
	  e. Paraprofessionals
	  f. Counselors
		1. Administrators
		2. University personnel
		3. State Department of Education
		4. Local school systems
		5. Consultants
		6. Resource people
		7. Agencies

Job placement and follow-up	1. Job placement services 2. Observation 3. Data collection 4. Job site evaluation checklist 5. Vocational adjustment counseling	1. Special education teachers 2. Transitional coordinators 3. Rehabilitation service counselors 4. Co-workers and employers 5. Other appropriate school personnel
Counseling	1. Career and technical education counseling 2. Personal counseling (individual and group therapy)	1. School counselors 2. Career and technical education counselors 3. Special education 4. Related career and technical education personnel 5. Rehabilitation counselors 6. Employers 7. Parents 8. Psychologists of appropriate services

...LOCAL COOPERATIVE PLAN FOR PROVISION OF SERVICES TO LEARNERS WITH SPECIAL NEEDS...		
Identified Need	**Necessary Services**	**Services Provider(s)**
Work experience	1. Career and technical education programs/ occupational training classes 2. Workshop settings 3. Work stations within industry 4. Rehabilitation services/facilities	1. Rehabilitation services personnel 2. Business and industry 3. Sheltered employment programs

Funding
  1. Administrative support
  2. Public and private
	1. Additional staff, equipment, materials, transportation, and modification to equipment and physical facilities	1. Federal, state, local, private agencies

Assessment
  1. Psychological
  2. Medical
    a. Vision
    b. Hearing
  3. Intellectual capacities
    a. Communication
    b. Language and speech
    c. Comprehension
  4. Interest inventories
  5. Personal and social skills
    a. Daily living skills
    b. Survival skills
    c. Employability skills
  6. Aptitude
  7. Mobility
  8. Vocational background
  9. Work sample experiences
  10. On-the-job training experiences
	1. Psychological testing
	2. Medical examinations
	3. Rehabilitation services
	4. Testing, observation
	5. Interest inventories
	6. Behavior management
	7. Counseling (personal, vocational)
		1. Psychologists/psychometrists
		2. Medical staff
		3. Rehabilitation services
		4. Special educators/appropriate school personnel
		5. Records
		6. Work activity centers
		7. Sheltered employment staff
		8. Therapists
		9. Clinicians

Parental involvement	1. Parent and staff sessions (discussion and training sessions 2. Encourage involvement in staffings and IEP updates 3. Solicitation of parent participation, such as parent advocacy and parent to parent	1. Educational and training staff 2. Consultants 3. Parents

Transportation	1. Transportation to and from:
	  a. On-the-job training sites
	  b. Competitive employment sites
	  c. Assessment sites
	  d. Medical services sites
	  e. Mobility training services sites
		1. Local education agency
		2. Local employers
		3. Parents
		4. Rehabilitation services personnel
		5. Volunteer staff
		6. Local/city/state governments
		7. Community service organizations

...LOCAL COOPERATIVE PLAN FOR PROVISION OF SERVICES TO LEARNERS WITH SPECIAL NEEDS		
Identified Need	**Necessary Services**	**Services Provider(s)**
Medical services	1. Physical exams 2. Psychological testing 3. Counseling 4. Occupational therapy 5. Physical therapy 6. Speech therapy 7. Vision/hearing testing 8. Medicaid/Medicare services	1. Nurses 2. Psychologists 3. Psychiatrists 4. Occupational therapists 5. Physical therapists 6. Speech therapists 7. Rehabilitation services 8. Doctors 9. Local health department or trained personnel within the school system 10. Social Security Administration
Public relations–community business and industrial awareness	1. In-service session for staff 2. Identification of jobs available in community 3. Canvassing of skills needed for job 4. Public service announcements on radio, TV, and newspapers 5. Addresses at business group meetings 6. Addresses at civic organization meetings 7. Radio and TV interviews 8. Job fairs	1. School staff 2. Business and industrial personnel 3. Media 4. Civic group offices and members

Adapted from: Sarkees, M., & Stephens-Fleuren, S. (Eds.). (1984). *Working with Moderately and Severely Handicapped Students in Vocational Education.* Athens, GA: University of Georgia, Division of Vocational Education.

Figure 11-25. An example of a local interagency plan for providing student services.

An interagency planning guide may be helpful in collaborating student services for learners from special populations. See Figure 11-26. A memorandum of understanding (MOU) may be necessary to facilitate collaboration between agencies.

COLLABORATIVE PLANNING WITH BUSINESS AND INDUSTRY

Collaborative ties with business and industry are crucial if learners are to be prepared for transition from school-based settings into business and industrial jobs. Educators should take every opportunity to work jointly with representatives from the business sector. Contributions that may be provided by business and industry include the following:

- Adopt-A-School–Business and industry can provide tangible goods and services to schools such as guest speakers, employee tutors, small grants, computers, and/or management-training for school administrators.
- Adopt-A-Program–Business and industry can provide specific support for an individual career and technical education program including visits to the class, arranging for industrial field trips, sharing equipment and

facilities, arranging for guest speakers for class sessions, and participating in mock job interviews for individual learners or groups.

- Adopt-A-Learner–Business and industry can provide specific support and services to an individual learner including mentoring, industry visits, shadowing opportunities, incentives to stay in school, summer employment, and periodic get-togethers.
- Recognition for instructors and/or learners–Business and industry can provide recognition to instructors who have successfully worked with learners with special needs during the year and/or the learners themselves for completing the school year.
- Grants–Business and industry can provide grants to school districts, specific programs, or instructors for use in purchasing equipment and materials or funding field trips and career and technical student organization activities.
- Mentoring–Business and industry can provide individuals who will mentor individual learners.
- Career speakers–Business and industry can provide individual representatives of various occupations, both employers and employees, to come to school and talk to small groups of learners.

- Career days–Business and industry can provide representatives from diverse occupations to come to a school-sponsored program to present information about the occupational outlook in their field and prerequisite training and qualifications.
- Site visits–Business and industry can invite groups of learners to visit a workplace for an on-site presentation of occupational information and a chance to see and interact with people at work.
- Shadowing–Business and industry can invite learners to be paired with a worker for a day or part of a day to gain firsthand experience in a particular occupation.
- Internships–Business and industry can provide situations where a learner can work without pay on certain aspects of a job at regular intervals in order to gain hands-on exploratory experience in an occupation.
- Work-study opportunities–Business and industry can provide situations where a learner is released early from school and works at a part-time, entry-level job.
- Alternative semesters–Business and industry can provide opportunities for learners to engage in a series of career-related activities instead of attending regular subject matter classes.
- Contract apprenticeships–Business and industry can provide structural learning experiences for learners, under contract with the local school or work-study linkage.
- Learner-operated businesses–Business and industry can provide leadership in assisting learners to create and operate their own business.
- Community resource banks–Business and industry can provide time to talk individually or in small groups with interested learners outside the school setting.
- Community visitation days–Business and industry can take time to visit classrooms and exchange information with teachers and administrators regarding the infusion of career-related concepts into the curriculum.
- Community forums–Business and industry can host pertinent forums where specific education-to-work issues are discussed and linkage agreements developed between education and industry.

Developing a Local Business and Industry Resource Directory

The specialized experiences and knowledge provided by community-based resources can provide enriching experiences, both school-based and on-the-job, for learners with special needs. Full use of all resources in the community provides and improves educational and training programs for these learners. In order to use these resources to the fullest capacity, they must first be identified. Available resources are often not used because of a lack of awareness of their existence. An inventory of services and resources can offer new and expanded opportunities including counseling services, employability skills training, job-seeking and retention simulation experiences, tutorial services, apprenticeship projects, and career exploration activities.

A resource directory is a tool that can assist educators in developing interagency collaboration when preparing learners for the adult roles they will assume. A resource directory will benefit educators who are involved in providing student services and developing transition plans for learners from special populations. It can also be a valuable aid to learners looking for services upon leaving the school setting. Parents can benefit from an organized listing of services because it will better inform them about services in their community and can assist them in being more effective advocates for their children. Local agencies might also be interested in helping to produce a directory and would benefit from educators, parents, and learners understanding the services that they provide.

One source of entries for the directory can be provided by advisory committee members associated with the local career and technical education program. Members of advisory committees can provide information about available community services. Another resource is a community survey conducted either by mail, in person, by phone, or through a combination of these techniques. Surveys help identify additions to the directory that can provide career development, training, job placement, or supplementary resources for special populations. Community resource directories such as those developed by social service agencies can also be useful in identifying entries for the directory. It is important that the information in these directories is validated and updated prior to entering it in a local business and industry directory.

Resources placed in a local business and industry directory can be categorized into the areas of human resources and material resources. Human resources refer to individuals willing to share their expertise and training with school-based personnel (e.g., seminars, on-site technical assistance, topical workshops) and learners with special needs (e.g., shadowing experiences, classroom lectures, industrial tours). Material resources refer to financial assistance or material contributions to be used for scholarships, field trips, project supplies, tuition, equipment, and other needs.

The format of a local business and industry directory should reflect the following information:
- name of the company/organization
- address, phone number, and fax number of the company/organization
- type(s) of available resources
- purpose(s) of available resources
- restriction(s) to availability of resources
- name of contact person
- special considerations

A form can be used for collecting, recording, and organizing information regarding community resources for use in developing a directory. See Appendix. The local business and industry directory should be updated regularly.

INTERAGENCY PLANNING GUIDE . . .			
	Component in Place	**Component Needs Modification**	**TA Required/ Requested**
Group Composition (Possible team members) — Student			
School district staff			
Advocacy groups (ARD, PAVE)			
Social clubs, churches, civic organizations			
Private employers, chamber of commerce			
Housing authority			
Peer support groups			
Parent/guardian			
Consumer representatives			
Postsecondary education representative			
State division of vocational rehabilitation			
State division of developmental disabilities			
Employment security			
Post-School Linkages (Planning for adult services linkages occurs pre-graduation) — The student is involved in adult services linkages planning			
Interagency agreements exist between group members			
Meetings occur regularly and are time specific			
Meetings have an agenda and minutes are kept			
Meetings have a facilitator or group leader			
Group has a vision statement (may include goals)			
Group has procedures to ensure all persons' comments are heard and valued (active listening is practiced)			
Group has participated in linking activities			
Group has developed a method for dealing with conflict			

... INTERAGENCY PLANNING GUIDE		Component in Place	Component Needs Modification	TA Required/ Requested
Group Activities (Causing change)	Effective exchange of agency information			
	Identify local funding sources			
	Financial issues (PASS, IRWE)			
	Futures planning, guardianships, trusts			
	Transportation issues			
	Natural supports (immediate and ongoing)			
	Volunteering (participation on boards, committees, etc.)			
	Community access (full inclusion in community activities)			
	Residential options			
	Recreational options			
	Developing postsecondary training options			
	Employment options or support needs			
Follow-Up Activities (Follow-up data is collected on learners starting six months after exiting high school)	Group has an annual review of activities			
	The annual review directs and/or modifies future activities			

Source: Washington State Department of Social and Health Services. (1996, October). *Transition Guide for Washington.* Olympia, WA: The Office of Superintendent of Public Instruction.

Figure 11-26. A guide for collaborating student services when planning a cooperative program of interagency linkages.

SUMMARY

Student services must be provided to learners from special populations to allow them to have equitable participation and successful completion in career and technical education courses in the most integrated setting possible. Student services for learners with special needs enrolled in career and technical education programs have proven effective in helping build the technical skills and work behaviors necessary for success and gainful employment.

Career and technical education personnel cannot be expected to accept the full responsibility of planning, implementing, and evaluating appropriate career and technical education programming for learners from special populations. Cooperative planning is essential if necessary services are to be provided. The success of these learners in career and technical education programs depends to a large degree on the collaborative relationships established among school-based personnel. A team approach is usually the best method to ensure that learners receive appropriate guidance and counseling services, supplemental services, appropriate instructional materials, occupational competencies, evaluation activities, and job placement opportunities.

Interagency linkage is the coordination of the available resources of both public and private agencies whose objective is to provide career and technical education instruction and services to learners from special populations. Educational institutions, job training programs, rehabilitative agencies, employment services, community services, and business and industry services can often assist learners with special needs to develop the skills necessary for success in the world of work. Often the potential for assistance from these resources is not realized due to fragmented efforts. Thus, the need for collaboration and cooperation among agencies is crucial.

SELF-ASSESSMENT

1. What is the rationale for coordinating student services for learners from special populations enrolled in career and technical education programs?
2. What is the importance of team building in providing student services for learners from special populations who are enrolled in career and technical education programs?
3. What is the role of academic teachers in school-based support team efforts?
4. What is the role of administrators in school-based support team efforts?
5. What is the role of guidance personnel in school-based support team efforts?
6. What is the role of the paraprofessional or paraeducator in school-based support team efforts?
7. What is the role of special education personnel in school-based support team efforts?
8. What is the role of the transition coordinator in school-based support team efforts?
9. What is the role of learners from special populations in school-based support team efforts?
10. What is the role of support personnel in school-based support team efforts?
11. What is the role of career and technical education instructors in school-based support team efforts?
12. What is the role of the vocational rehabilitation services counselor in school-based support team efforts?
13. How can mentoring serve as a model for providing school-based student services?
14. What are some successful methods of communication that can facilitate school-based teaming?
15. Why is it important to collaborate with agencies and organizations to provide student services for learners from special populations?
16. What are some successful methods of promoting interagency linkage so that student services can be provided for learners from special populations?
17. What is the importance of local interagency linkage teams in providing student services for learners from special populations?
18. What is the importance of collaborative planning with business and industry in providing student services for learners from special populations?
19. What is the role of career and technical program advisory committees in providing student services for learners from special populations?
20. What is the process for developing a local business and industry resource directory?
21. What are some effective strategies for working with parents as members of the collaborative team to provide student services for learners from special populations?

ASSOCIATED ACTIVITIES

1. Identify and contact appropriate personnel in the school district and/or on campus, and incorporate these individuals in the collaborative planning process for learners with special needs enrolled in your program.
2. Work with other staff members to develop a professional development workshop for other personnel in your school that is relative to working with learners with special needs. Stress what these people can do to assist learners from special populations.
3. Check to see whether your state and/or local district has developed a cooperative interagency linkage agreement. What are the responsibilities of career and technical education personnel, student services personnel, and agencies involved in the agreement?
4. Obtain a copy of your local interagency linkage agreement and familiarize yourself with the identified roles and responsibilities associated with your position in the school.
5. Identify agencies and state and local organizations that can help provide services for learners in your program.
6. Work cooperatively with the local advisory committee members in your program area to determine the services and assistance they provide for learners with special needs.
7. Contact the parents or guardians of the learners from special populations in your program and involve them in cooperative planning for these learners.

REFERENCES

Buchholz, S., & Roth, T. (1987). *Creating the high performance team.* New York: John Wiley.

Butterworth, J. (1999). *LRE for LIFE project ongoing staff development and technical assistance.* Knoxville, TN: University of Tennessee.

Dyer, W. (1977). *Team building: Issues and alternatives.* Reading, MA: Addison-Wesley.

Ferrini, P., Matthews, B., Foster, J., & Workman, J. (1980). *The interdependent community: Collaborative planning for handicapped youth.* Cambridge, MA: Technical Education Research Center.

Getzel, E., Salin, J., & Wacker, G. (1982). Developing local agreements. In Tindall et al., *Handbook on developing effective linkage strategies.* Madison, WI: Wisconsin Vocational Studies Center.

Greenan, J. (1980). *Interagency cooperation and agreements.* Champaign, IL: University of Illinois, Leadership Training Institute/Vocational and Special Education.

Greenan, J. (1986). Networking needs in vocational special education. *Journal for Vocational Special Needs Education, 8*(3), 15-20.

Harden V. (1989). *A guide to alternative intervention strategies.* Jefferson City, MO: Missouri Department of Elementary and Secondary Education.

Huck, R., Myers, R., & Wilson, J. (1989). *ADAPT—A developmental activity program for teachers* (2nd ed.). Pittsburgh, PA: Allegheny Intermediate Unit.

Illinois State Board of Education. (n.d.). *Industry-education collaboration for special needs youth and adults.* Springfield, IL: Author.

Maddy-Bernstein, C., & Cunanan, E. (1996, October). *Student services: Achieving success for all secondary students.* Berkeley, CA: National Center for Research in Vocational Education.

Maryland State Department of Education. (1984). *Handbook for vocational support service teams in Maryland.* Annapolis, MD: Division of Vocational-Technical Education.

Matias, L., Maddy-Bernstein, C., & Kantenberger, J. (1995). *Profiles and best practices: Exemplary vocational special populations programs.* Berkeley, CA: National Center for Research in Vocational Education.

McNulty, B., & Soper, E. (1983). *Perspectives on interagency collaboration.* Washington, DC: U.S. Department of Education, Special Education Programs.

Mikulin, E., & Patterson, R. (1992). *Guide for serving members of special populations in vocational and applied technology education.* Austin, TX: Texas Education Agency, Vocational and Applied Technology.

Morgan, J., & Ashbaker, B. (2001, March). Work more effectively with your paraeducators. *Intervention in School and Clinic, 36*(4) 230-231.

National Center for Research in Vocational Education. (1993). Teacher collaboration in secondary schools. *Centerfocus, 2,* 1-4.

North Central Regional Educational Laboratory. (1996). *Critical issue: Linking at-risk students and schools to integrated services.* [On-line]. Available: http://www.ncrel.org/sdrs/areas/issues/students/atrisk/at500.htm

O'Leary, E., & Paulson, J. (1991). *Developing and writing transition services within the IEP process.* Des Moines, IA: Drake University, Mountain Plains Regional Resource Center.

Pacifici, T., & McKinney, K. (1997). *Disability support services for community college students.* Los Angeles, CA: ERIC Clearinghouse for Community Colleges. ED 409972.

Policy Studies Associates. (2001). *Roles for education paraprofessionals in effective schools: 1997.* [On-line]. Available: http://www.ed.gov/pubs/Paraprofessionals/summary.html

Reilly, J. (1992). *Mentorship: The essential guide for schools and business.* Dayton, OH: Ohio Psychology Press.

Sarkees, M. (1989). Developing effective assistance programs for parents of at-risk students. *Journal for Vocational Special Needs Education, 11*(2), 17-21.

Sarkees, M., & Stephens-Fleuren, S. (Eds.). (1984). *Working with moderately and severely handicapped students in vocational education.* Athens, GA: University of Georgia, Division of Vocational Education.

Sarkees-Wircenski, M. (1991). The school at-risk team. In West, L. (Ed.). *Effective strategies for dropout prevention of at-risk youth.* Gaithersburg, MD: Aspen Publishers.

Washington State Department of Social and Health Services. (1996, October). *Transition guide for Washington.* Olympia, WA: The Office of Superintendent of Public Instruction.

Wehman, P. (1996). *Life beyond the classroom.* Baltimore, MD: Paul H. Brookes Publishing.

Wheeldon, R., & Lehmann, J. (1999, Spring). Establishing a telementoring program that can be used in vocational classes. *The Journal for Vocational Special Needs Education, 21*(3), 32-37.

Willis, M. (1989). *Mobilizing parents to better serve children at-risk*. Madison, WI: Wisconsin Department of Public Instruction.

Wisconsin Department of Public Instruction. (1993a). *Designated vocational instruction: A cooperative process for change*. Milwaukee, WI: Author.

Wisconsin Department of Public Instruction. (1993b). *Designated vocational instruction: A resource and planning guide*. Milwaukee, WI: Author.

Workforce Investment Act of 1998, Pub. L. No. 105-220, United States Statutes at Large, (112), 937. Washington, DC: U.S. Government Printing Office.

The Transition Process

INTRODUCTION

Satisfying and sustained employment is a critical aspect of adult life. The ability to obtain and hold a job indicates the capacity to participate fully in our society. To individuals from special populations, employment brings status and respect. Years of education are of little value to these individuals unless they can become productive and self-sufficient.

Transition is a term being used by individuals who are involved in the educational reform movement. It is one of the most important components of the new paradigm of providing education for our nation's youth. Transitions are an essential part of every person's life. They require modifications at various times to new roles and relationships. Transitions are necessary when an individual moves from preschool to kindergarten, from kindergarten to elementary school, from elementary school to middle school, from middle school to high school and from high school to beyond. Transition planning is designed to increase the probability of success in the next environment. Transition planning should occur at all stages of an individual's life.

The educational system plays an important role in the ongoing process of preparing individuals for a life of work and learning. The educational experience should provide a solid foundation of skills and knowledge to prepare individuals for meaningful employment and continuing education. The attention of all educators should be focused on assessing the unique needs of individual learners, establishing learning environments that support learner needs, teaching skills and knowledge that have a direct bearing on life after high school, and counseling learners for a smooth transition to jobs and higher education.

OUTLINE

THE WORKFORCE OF THE FUTURE
PREPARING TODAY'S LEARNERS FOR THE FUTURE WORKFORCE
WHAT IS TRANSITION?
TRANSITION OPTIONS
COMPONENTS OF EFFECTIVE TRANSITION SYSTEMS
DEVELOPING INDIVIDUALIZED TRANSITION PROGRAMS (ITP)
IMPROVING URBAN AND RURAL SCHOOL COMMUNITIES
PROFESSIONAL DEVELOPMENT FOR EDUCATORS
SUMMARY
SELF-ASSESSMENT
ASSOCIATED ACTIVITIES
REFERENCES

OBJECTIVES

After completing this chapter the reader should be able to accomplish the following:
1. Describe competencies that will be needed by all workers in the future in order to be prepared for the workforce.
2. Define and discuss *transition*.
3. Identify barriers to successful postschool opportunities that frequently confront learners from special populations.
4. List appropriate transition options.
5. Define an *individualized transition program* and discuss its components.
6. Identify components of effective transition systems for individuals from special populations.
7. Discuss the important issues related to serving individuals from special populations in transition systems.

TERMS

all aspects of the industry
apprenticeship
business/industry linkage
career development
community-based vocational
  instruction (CBVI)
cooperative education program
internship
Job Accommodation Network (JAN)

job coach
job redesign
job shadowing
mentoring
multiple exit points
National Skill Standards
placement profile
portfolio

school-based enterprise
service learning
supported employment
tech-prep
transition
transitional employment
work-based learning
youth apprenticeship

THE WORKFORCE OF THE FUTURE

American society is based on work. A job is the price of admission to the American way of life and a means of realizing the American Dream. The work that one does affects nearly every dimension of life: personal sense of accomplishment, type of dwelling and neighborhood in which one lives, standard of living and educational opportunities provided to one's family, one's circle of friends, the organizations in which one participates, the extent of community involvement, a sense of security both now and in the future, and a sense of belonging and importance. Those who are not able to get and keep a job eventually tend to drop out of family and community life. Even worse, those not able to function in the American economy may become involved in substance abuse, crime, and violence. For some youth, the inability to maintain satisfying employment creates alternative cultures such as gangs, cults, and other groups that threaten the mainstream of American communities (Carnevale & Porro, 1994).

Americans expect our schools to prepare learners with the knowledge and skills required to enter and succeed in the world of work and to take on the responsibility of self-sufficiency. When young people fail to enter the workforce and maintain steady employment, society concludes that schools have failed, parents have failed, or individuals have failed (West, 1988).

The American economy, the workplace, and work are in the midst of change. New ways to organize and manage the workplace and new ways to work are becoming more common. These changes represent profound challenges to how we think about work and the workplace. As work and the workplace change, public policies and employment practices must change as well. Regardless of their causes, these changes present both new challenges and new opportunities for employers, employees, and policymakers:

- Companies are getting smaller–Large companies are giving way to smaller and leaner organizations. The typical business establishment today employs about 15 persons.
- Across all industries, smaller establishments are growing faster compared to larger establishments.
- Boundaries among companies are blurring–More and more companies are involved in networks, partnerships, and alliances with other companies and sometimes even across national boundaries. The number of industrial technology alliances in the U.S. has increased rapidly.
- New patterns of work are emerging–More persons are working at home or on flexible work schedules. However, the share of the workforce in alternative or contingent employment relationships has remained stable over the last couple of years.
- Companies support employee development by investing in education and training–Investments in education and training rose by over 30% between 1990 and 1998 (National Alliance of Business, 1999).

At the same time, new forms of workplace organization and management are beginning to replace hierarchical, chain-of-command organizations. Team-based workplaces and decentralized "flatter" organizations with cross-functional groups are replacing the old, rigid, organizations. See Figure 12-1.

SHIFTS IN ORGANIZATION AND MANAGEMENT		
Element	**Old System**	**New System**
Workplace organization	Hierarchical Function/specialized Rigid	Flat Networks of multi/cross-functional teams Flexible
Job design	Narrow Do one job Repetitive/simplified/standardized	Broad Do many jobs Multiple responsibilities
Employee skills	Specialized	Multi/cross-skilled
Workforce management	Command/control systems	Self-management
Communications	Top down Need to know	Widely diffused Big picture
Decision making responsibility	Chain of command	Decentralized
Worker autonomy	Low	High
Employee knowledge of organization	Narrow	Broad

Source: U.S. Department of Commerce et al. (1999). *21st Century Skills for 21st Century Jobs*. Washington, DC: U.S. Government Printing Office.

Figure 12-1. Attributes of the old and new organizational systems of business and industry.

The United States is the only industrialized nation in the world that has no institutionalized school-to-work transition system to help its young people navigate successfully between their learning and work experiences. The lack of a comprehensive and effective school-to-work transition system has a serious impact on many learners. It also means significant costs to business and our economy as a whole. A skill-deficient workforce hampers the nation's economic growth, productivity, and ability to compete in an international economy.

Through the following points, Charner (1996) provided a rationale for developing strong transition processes in our nation's educational system:

- Rapid changes in technology and increasing international competition have led employers to seek new strategies for producing goods and providing services.

These changes require a high-performance organization where all workers have more responsibility and decision-making functions. Such organizations need employees who are well trained and possess the skills and knowledge necessary for their new functions. In addition, as learning becomes an integral part of the work itself, workers will need to be better prepared to avail themselves of training and learning opportunities in the workplace.

- One challenge faced by educators and employers is how to prepare learners for their changing roles in the workplace and how to ensure that the economy uses the full capacity and potential of our youth. At a point in our history when education beyond high school is increasingly viewed as necessary to meet the educational and skill requirements of many current and emerging careers, approximately one half of U.S. youth do not attend college and about half of those who do will not complete their studies. For many of these youth, particularly those who are members of the growing underclass, the transition between school and work has become problematic. Many graduate high school with few or no job-related skills; often their academic preparation is weak.
- Many of those who drop out before high school graduation are caught up in an inescapable world of poverty. They have limited job and career prospects. Until the age of 25, these youth are likely to move from job to job, usually in the service sector of the economy where they find jobs that are low skilled, poorly paid, and offer few opportunities for further training or advancement.
- The result for some young people is a life of poverty. For many others the prospect is employment that pays less than a living wage and offers neither self-respect nor a future.
- Related to these employment patterns are the prospects for further training and career mobility. Employers tend to invest training dollars in their best-educated employees. Only 45% of high school dropouts received training from their employers compared to 71% of high school graduates and 79% of college graduates. Also, those who are trained on one job are more likely to be trained on subsequent jobs.
- Recent attention to the "forgotten half" of learners who do not follow the traditional high school to college sequence stems from changes in the economy and the inadequate response by schools, businesses, and government. A number of factors make the transition issue critical at this time.
- The changing demographics of the U.S. population find fewer young people and a general aging trend. A set of changes in the labor market suggests a shift from manufacturing to a service economy with the resulting reduction in low-level high-pay jobs in manufacturing and growth in the low-skilled low-pay jobs in the service sector of the economy.

- An increasing number of young people are "at-risk" of not becoming productive members of society.
- As the institutions of family and community have changed dramatically, society once again has turned to the schools to carry out the transition process, an enormous role for which schools have not received the resources or the required training. Critics argue that while our education system is in need of major improvement, business has done much to contribute to the American worker's lowered competitiveness and offers little in the way of an economic agenda aimed at absorbing the highly skilled workers it is demanding from the schools.

Economic, legislative, and educational data document the national concern for the plight of a large percentage of America's youth. Many face unemployment and underemployment. Others remain dependent on society. This results in an economic drain on our country as well as a huge loss of individual potential. The ability to obtain and retain employment and advance up the career ladder throughout one's life is dependent on a combination of basic skills development, pre-employment skills, career counseling, and specific training. A combination of programs and services are needed to remediate deficiencies and achieve stable employment outcomes for individuals from special populations.

No one transition program or technique will work for all learners. Good school-to-work transition will require systemic processes. Research suggests systemic implementation of the following concepts is especially beneficial in helping learners make the transition from school to post-school opportunities:

1. Work force readiness will be enhanced if exposure to career options begins in kindergarten and continues through high school.
2. All students should be taught good reading, mathematical, writing, listening, and speaking skills. All students should be taught higher-order thinking skills and learn group problem-solving skills.
3. Students will be better prepared for life outside of school if school activities are made more relevant to the real world.
4. Young people who do not plan to attend college are in urgent need of new or enhanced programs which develop their workplace skills and prepare them for life outside of school.
5. Schools, businesses, and communities must strive to help all students meet the same high academic standards.
6. Students will gain a better grasp of what the real world expects of them if assessments emphasize performance-based practices, such as task performance and portfolio assessments, rather than multiple-choice examinations.
7. Schools, businesses, and communities must intensify efforts to recover learners who have dropped out of high school, and help them re-enroll in regular school or alternative programs.

8. Experts suggest that America should develop national performance-based assessments, all benchmarked to the same high standards, to ensure that all schools and students are striving to meet the same high goals. These assessments should lead to certificates of competency.
9. Schools, businesses, and communities should strive to help all students successfully complete high school with the skills necessary to pursue a college degree or further technical training.
10. An African proverb says, "It takes an entire village to educate a child." Parental, business and community involvement in students' education is crucial. (Texas Education Agency Clearinghouse, 1993, p. 3)

PREPARING TODAY'S LEARNERS FOR THE FUTURE WORKFORCE

Former United States Secretary of Education Richard Riley (1998) challenged educators to prepare for the future:

> Consider, in 1969 there were just four primitive web sites in the world. By 1990, there were 333,000. Today, there are almost 20 million. How many will there be in the year 2000? It's all quite extraordinary. Scientists can land the Sojourner space vehicle on Mars with pinpoint accuracy. At the same time, a cloned sheep named Dolly is chewing her cud in Scotland while world leaders ponder the implications for humankind.

> Expanding the horizons of knowledge and giving our children the power to use that knowledge wisely are at the very center of this new Education Era. We cannot sit still rooted in the chalkboard and pencil at a time when a 12-year old can literally touch his or her mouse pad and travel from web site to web site around the world.

> This is why I am so encouraged by the vibrancy and growing spirit of innovation that comes with charter schools, new technology in the classroom and the demand for high achievement. At the same time, American education has a deep responsibility to pass on to the next generation the essential elements of good citizenship and mastery of the basics as a stepping-stone to more advanced skills.

> And this I know for sure—we are in a new time with new challenges—and none is more important than this: never has this nation been confronted with the task of teaching so much to so many while reaching for new high standards. That is the state of American education and America's first challenge. (pp. 2-8)

Ferguson and Blumberg (2001) studied the following reports:

1. The National Longitudinal Transition Study, SRI International (1987, 1990)
2. The National Association of Industry-Education Cooperation (1992)
3. The National Council of Chief State School Officers (1995)
4. National Organization on Disability/Harris Survey (1998)
5. U.S. Department of Education, Office of Special Education Programs, Annual Report to Congress (1996, 1999)

They then synthesized the following information relative to transition planning for individuals with disabilities:

- More than one-third (36%) of all youth with disabilities served by public mandated special education programs drop out of high school prior to graduation. This represents a significantly higher dropout rate than the national average of 12%. A higher percentage of learners with disabilities in urban school (36.6%) drop out of high school than their peers in suburban areas (24%) and rural schools (31.4%).
- It is widely recognized that poverty may place youth at greater risk of poor school performance. A recent study indicated that 47% of youth with disabilities lived in households with an annual income of less than $12,000. Family structure and parent education levels are important predictors of learner success. Research indicates that only 10% to 25% of urban learners with disabilities live in two parent households.
- Outcome data indicate that the average time spent on urban secondary learners in regular education classrooms was 41%, compared to 56% for suburban learners, and 59% for rural learners.
- Three to five years after graduating from high school, only 37% of youth with disabilities had ever attended any kind of postsecondary school, compared with 68% of high school graduates in the general population.
- Nearly one in five youth with disabilities was not employed and not looking for work three to five years after exiting high school. A 1992 survey of 13 million working-age people in the U.S. revealed that only 34% of adults with disabilities worked full- or part-time, compared to 79% of adults without disabilities.
- The employment rates for high school graduates were nearly double that of nongraduates. Sixty-five percent of high school graduates with disabilities were employed 3 to 5 years out of high school compared to 37% of learners with disabilities who had not graduated from high school.
- Sixty-one percent of white youth with disabilities were employed 3 to 5 years after secondary school, compared with peers who were African-American (47%) and Hispanic (50%). African-American youth have made the greatest gains in employment. Previous outcome data suggest that these same youth were nearly twice as likely to be employed in 1990 as they were in 1987.

- A prominent theme of transition initiatives nationwide is the inclusion of all learners in typical educational and training programs. Outcome studies suggest that for those learners who were able to complete high school, inclusion in regular classes was related to a higher probability of competitive employment, higher earnings, and enrollment in postsecondary education and training.

- Outcome studies suggest that minority learners have made significant gains in education and employment during the past decade. However, minority learners with disabilities, particularly African-American learners, continue to lag behind white learners with disabilities on many outcome measures.

- School-based learning experiences such as career awareness, career exploration, and counseling services help learners to identify their interests, goals, and career majors. These learning experiences should be started at the earliest possible age, but no later than the seventh grade. They should include regularly scheduled evaluations for determining the needs of learners.

Wentling and Waight (2000) provided a prospective look into the impact of individuals from minority populations on the workforce of the future:

- According to the U.S. Bureau of the Census projections, during the next 10 years non-Hispanic whites will contribute to only one-quarter of the total population growth. From 2030 to 2050, the non-Hispanic white population will contribute nothing to the nation's population growth because it will be declining in size. African-Americans, Asians, and Hispanics will outnumber whites in the U.S. in the next millennium. By 2010, Hispanics are expected to supplant African-Americans as the nation's largest minority group. The rapid growth of minorities has been and will continue to be marked by an increasing diversity in terms of practices as new immigrant groups (e.g., Vietnamese, Cambodians, Dominicans, Nicaraguans) join earlier immigrants (Mexicans, Cubans, Chinese and Japanese).

- An increasing number of youth in the 16- to 24-year old age group are entering the job market. They are likely to be more ethnically diverse than workers in today's workforce. African-American and Hispanic birthrates are four and seven times respectively that of whites. The proportion of African-American youth population, ages 14 to 24, will increase from 5,859,000 in 1990 to a projected 7, 411,000 by the year 2010. Likewise, Hispanics will increase from 4,791,000 to 9,666,000. This increase in the numbers of minority youth will require business organizations to consider hiring more African-American and Hispanic employees.

- After two-and-a-half decades of local, state, and federal efforts to improve urban education for low-income and minority children, achievement in inner-city schools continues to lag behind national norms, and dropout rates in inner-city high schools, especially among African-American and Hispanic youth, remain distressingly high. At the same time, many of those who do graduate are often poorly prepared and are unable to compete successfully in the labor market. The Business-Higher Education Forum underlines the joblessness issue for African-Americans and Hispanics by saying that in any given month, Hispanic unemployment is about 50% higher than the rate of whites, and African-American unemployment is 2.5 times higher than that of Hispanics.

- Racial and linguistic biases continue to stifle employment opportunities for minority youth, including Native American or Alaskan native, Asian or Pacific Islander, African-American, Hispanic, and other racial minorities between the ages of 16 and 24. Schools have not fully developed nor have workplaces fully utilized the talents of minority youth. Minority youth have a greater probability of being poor, living in poverty, or being otherwise disadvantaged. An increasing number of young people are diverging from the white middle-class pattern. Educational institutions and workplaces must adapt to changes in the youth population. Education and workplace training that are typically effective with advantaged youth will not necessarily enable disadvantaged youth to reach their full potential.

- The unemployment struggle that minority youth face has an overpowering effect on America. Prior unemployment often leads to a high risk of unemployment later. In addition, it poses huge financial and societal challenges to the competitive advantage of America. Responding to the poor school-to-work transition of minority youth is an expensive undertaking in itself. With more than 20% of high school learners dropping out and with a dropout rate of 50% in the cities, more than one-third of America's frontline labor force is at stake.

- As we move into the next decade, it is imperative that we identify what initiatives continue to support and assist the successful transition of minority youth into the workplace. In addition, to ensure that the larger, more diverse youth of the next decade are prepared to do the work of the new decade and new century, the barriers that they encounter must be determined and addressed so that their transition into the workplace can be made more smoothly and efficiently.

- Minority youth who are in the transition from school to work face a variety of problems and barriers. Discrimination, lack of appropriate educational programs, poverty, lack of transportation, low self-efficacy, peer pressure, poor job networking, poor basic work skills, unemployment, lack of parent involvement, cultural differences, and unavailability of workplace training are some of the barriers that hinder their successful school-to-work transition.

At the start of the 21st century in America, we face a series of challenges that include (1) increasing secondary-aged learners' access to relevant and rigorous curricula and information technology while also increasing the proportion of learners who successfully complete a high school program as a result of the national investment in our pubic secondary schools; (2) expanding options for career and employment for youth and young adults who choose to work upon graduation from high school; (3) improving access to postsecondary educational experiences for learners after exiting a secondary education program; (4) ensuring a range of educational and/or employment alternatives for out-of-school youth and young adults (i.e., those who do not complete a high school program); and (5) increasing the level of accountability of government funded programs for human service outcomes such as secondary and postsecondary education, career training, and employment (National Council on Disability, 2000).

America faces an imposing but not impossible set of challenges in terms of the academic and work preparation of its youth and young adults and their entry into the world of adulthood. This is as true for those who receive special education services as it is for learners who are in general education. Public secondary schools are slowly beginning to recognize that general education must change. For example, the traditionally dominant purpose of American high schools—perform well on tests and get learners admitted to a university—serves a small fraction of learners, and many of them not very well when we consider that up to 50% of college freshmen receive remediation in the basic skills. High schools that, in the past, have been organized around isolated academic disciplines use a lecture-based format, and the formats are ineffective. We see ineffectiveness in the increasing numbers of learners who drop out of general education and those who prematurely exit special education services. For those learners who manage to graduate from high school and enter college, the little-known truth is that very few of them actually graduate. The largest majority of them enter technical training, complete a year or two of career-focused education at a community college, or go directly into the workplace or try to obtain work (National Council on Disability, 2000).

There is a pressing need to connect secondary school curricula and structure with the realities and demands of life beyond high school. If one of the primary purposes of high school—and transition planning, services, and supports—is to successfully prepare young people for the adult world, then (a) we should implement transition planning and service delivery mandates with fidelity, and (b) the high school experience should resemble the world of adulthood. The goals, accommodations, linkages, and services learners incorporate into their transition programs must be adhered to and implemented in a timely manner. What we ask learners to learn, how we ask them to learn it and how they are tested, should correspond to the ways in which they will demonstrate proficiency on the job, in lifelong education activities, in their families and in the community. High school should position every graduate

to successfully begin the next major steps in life—whether going to a university, entering a community college, or beginning a job or career. A high school education, basically, should contribute toward competence in learners' various roles as adults. In short, a learner completing 12 years or about 14,000 hours of public education culminating in a high school diploma should not face shock, frustration, and powerlessness upon entering the world that many of today's graduates and dropouts face (National Council on Disability, 2000).

WHAT IS TRANSITION?

In 1990, the Individuals with Disabilities Education Act (IDEA), PL 101-476, defined transition as

> A coordinated set of activities for a student, designed within an outcome-oriented process, which promotes movement from school to postschool activities including postsecondary education, vocational training and education, integrated employment (including supported employment), continuing and adult education, adult services, independent living, or community participation. The coordinated set of activities shall be based upon the individual student's needs taking into account the student's preferences and interests, and shall include instruction, community experiences, and development of employment and other post-school adult living objectives, and when appropriate, acquisition of daily living skills and functional vocational evaluation.

In the Individuals with Disabilities Education Act Amendments of 1997, PL 105-17, the definition for transition services remained the same as in the IDEA of 1990 (Section 602), with the exception that the coordinated set of activities could include the related services of transportation, support services such as speech and language pathology and audiology services, psychological services, physical and occupational therapy, recreation, social work services, counseling services (including rehabilitation counseling), orientation and mobility services, and medical services (for diagnostic and evaluation purposes). Providing related services may be especially significant to learners with more significant disabilities who participate in community-based transition programs from the age of 21 (or 22) (Sitlington, Clark & Kolstoe, 2000).

Transitions are an essential part of every person's life. Transition is necessary when an individual moves from preschool to kindergarten, from kindergarten to elementary school, from elementary school to middle school, from middle school to high school, and from high school to postschool activities. Transition planning is designed to increase the probability of success in the next environment and should occur at all stages of an individual's life. See Figure 12-2.

EXAMPLES OF CAREER TRANSITIONS AND THE NEED FOR EMPLOYMENT-RELATED SERVICES

Examples of Employment-Related Services	Major Career Transitions					
	Home to Work	School to Work	Work to School	Work to Work	Work to Retirement	Retirement to Work
Job search assistance	●	●		●		●
Basic education	●	●	●	●		●
Vocational training	●	●	●	●		●
Career passports	●	●	●	●		●
Internship–coop. programs	●	●		●		●
JTPA assistance	●		●	●		
Unemployment insurance			●	●		
Testing/self-assessment	●	●	●		●	●
Displaced worker assistance	●		●	●	●	
2 + 2 programs		●				
Individual education plans	●	●	●			
Resume/interview preparation	●	●	●	●		●
Cross-training				●		●
Apprenticeship programs	●	●	●	●		●
Social security benefits					●	●
Career counseling	●	●	●	●	●	●
Medicare-Medicaid					●	●
Employment assistance	●	●	●	●	●	●
Volunteer assistance	●				●	●

● = Match between a likely need and available assistance.

Source: Pratzner, F. (1994). Career Transition: Coordinated One-Stop Shopping for Employment Services. *Journal of Industrial Teacher Education, 31*(3), 5.

Figure 12-2. An overview of the employment-related services that individuals may need as they experience transitions in life.

In 1984, Madeline Will, then Assistant Secretary of the Office of Special Education and Rehabilitative Services (OSERS), recognized transition as a much-needed extension of the work-study and career education movements of the 1970s. She launched a campaign to include transition services in PL 94-142, stressing the multiple services required by youth with disabilities in school-to-work transitions and pushed for cooperation among individuals and agencies attempting to meet the needs of these youth. Will realized that school-based career education and similar services for youth with disabilities were ineffective without the connection to adult service programming. Will described transition as a bridge between secondary education and the challenges of postschool life. McCarty-Warren and Hess-Grabill (1989) used the concept of a bridge to organize components of an effective transition process for individuals from special populations. Work experience, job placement and follow-up services are an integral part of this model. See Figure 12-3.

Transition from school to employment has been made a national priority for educational reform. It is a concept that has tremendous potential for improving the vocational preparation for individuals from special populations and for assisting them in obtaining and retaining satisfying employment. See Figure 12-4.

The roles and responsibilities of all individuals involved in transition planning must be established. Working linkages will have to be developed between parents, the school, and community agencies to ensure a continuum of nonduplicated services for learners with special needs. Every effort will have to be made to identify the barriers to effective transition for each individual and to find solutions that result in reducing or eliminating these barriers.

The challenge for educators and others involved in transition planning is to build broad-based, cooperative, and multifaceted transition programs which are flexible enough to assist learners individually and collectively from high school to postsecondary education, employment, or further training opportunities. These programs should build upon earlier career development activities and experiences. In the process, they need to actively involve such individuals as students, family members, secondary and community college counselors, resource specialists, instructors, transition coordinators, agency personnel, and business and industry staff (McCarty & Hess-Grabill, 1989. p. 4).

Elliott, Schalock, and Ross (1988) identified a number of key elements that should be considered in establishing a transition process and corresponding procedures:

1. The process should be individualized, planned, and systematic, with specific outcomes in mind.
2. Locally available options for transition should be explored and utilized.
3. Personnel from the school district, multiple disciplines, and adult community service delivery systems must participate.
4. Parent participation and early involvement is essential.
5. Transition planning should begin at as early an age as possible.
6. Transition planning should focus on a planning process that includes independent living skills, social skills, employability skills, and employment skills.
7. The importance of school programs should be established as a foundation for successful transition to adult life.

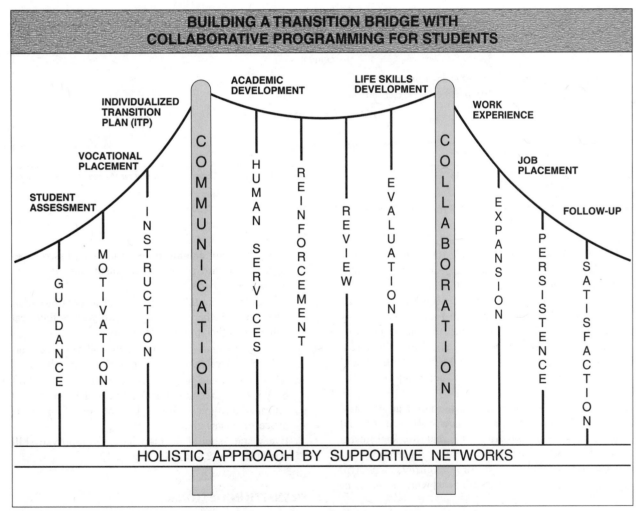

Source: McCarty-Warren, T., & Grabill-Hess, D. (1989). *Postsecondary Vocational Special Needs Coordinators Handbook*. Normal, IL: Illinois State University, Office of Specialized Vocational Research.

Figure 12-3. Components of a collaborative process for delivering transition services to learners from special populations.

COMPETITIVE EMPLOYMENT TRANSITION MODEL

Phase I: Career Planning
Personnel: Career/Technical teachers/Guidance counselors/Parents

Individual transition plan development
Individual education plan
Vocational assessment
Individual career plan development

Phase II: Career/Technical preparation
Personnel: Career/Technical teachers/Counselors/Support professionals

School-based career/technical preparation
Job shadowing/Tryouts
Supported job search
Career portfolio development
Employability training

Phase III: Initial placement/Follow-up
Personnel: Placement and follow-up specialists/Job coaches/Mentors/Job club leaders

Stabilized employment
Initial work site adjustment training
Follow-up
Placement

Phase IV: Unsupported or supported employment
Personnel: Work site mentors/Job coaches/Job club leaders

Job advancement
Job change
Job adjustment

Adapted from: Neubert, D., & Tilson, G. (1987). The Critical Stage of Transition: A Challenge and an Opportunity. *Journal for Vocational Special Needs Education, 10*(1), 3-7.

Figure 12-4. Components of a competitive employment transition model.

Dykman (1994) stated that while school-to-work plans may differ on some points, many appear to have the same framework, which contains the following formula:

1. Improved counseling should be incorporated at all levels of education, with a big focus in elementary and middle school. Guest speakers and counselors can expose elementary school students to different types of occupations. Junior high students should experience job shadowing and mentoring for a true taste of careers.

2. Applied academics should be the norm in all classrooms. Students should learn how math, science, and communication skills are used in real life. Their learning must be geared toward results. Students are assessed on how well they achieve specific requirements such as the ability to work in teams or exhibit critical thinking skills.

3. High school teachers and coordinators, especially those in vocational and applied technology [career and technical] education, will be expected to forge strong ties with employers to set up work-based experiences and with postsecondary institutions to ensure smooth transitions.

4. All students should be encouraged to continue their education; whether in a one-year, two-year, or four-year college or other training programs.

5. All state programs should have some follow-up elements to keep track of students' progress after high school.

6. All states should help to promote local partnerships by providing technical assistance and labor market information, typically through some sort of statewide office or clearinghouse.

7. Every state should develop industry approved skill standards (pp. 25-26). See Figure 12-5.

TRANSITION OPTIONS

There are a variety of options that are available to learners as they prepare to leave school and transition into postschool experiences. See Figure 12-6.

INITIATING ACTIVITIES FOR THE TRANSITION PROCESS . . .

A school-based transition coordinator is ideal for initiating and facilitating transition programming for students from special populations. When this is not possible, guidance counselors and other educators connected to program services for special needs students may be designated to coordinate transition initiatives.

The activities below are several that transition coordinators can initiate in local educational agencies (LEAs), community agencies, and with transition teams.

Students can participate in the process as indicated by the student symbol.

LEAs	COMMUNITY AGENCIES	TRANSITION TEAMS

Step 1: Survey transition activities currently in place

 Gather data for complete picture of students' needs from individual and collective assessment results, interviews, and previous records

Determine internal service, personnel, and financial resources

Survey job and career training possibilities

Gather data for complete picture of workforce needs from businesses, industries, and service organizations

Determine external service, personnel, and financial resources

Survey job and career training possibilities

Form transition team with representatives from education, families, community agencies, businesses, and industries

Collaborate to record transition program services using a matrix of transition services

Locate transition service gaps and compare them to student and workforce needs

Step 2: Evaluate existing transition activities

 Review effectiveness of communication methods between students and staff regarding transition activities and job/career opportunities

Evaluate degree of administrative support

 Review effects of collaborative activities upon students

 Review data from transition activities to determine effectiveness for students

Review methods for assessing students' progress as they proceed through transition activities

Check effectiveness of communication with community personnel

Evaluate degree of support from agencies' administration

 Evaluate benefits to community of collaborative activities to date

 Evaluate performance of students participating in transition activities to determine value of activities

Review methods for assessing students' progress as they proceed through transition activities

Evaluate effectiveness of communication among agencies, including educational institutions

Evaluate degree of power given by administration

Compare overall collaboration benefits and determine areas needing improvement

Compare student data from LEA and community agencies to decide what activities are to be replaced or strengthened

Evaluate the effectiveness of the assessment process to determine future assessment activities and policies

Step 3: Expand transition programming based upon findings from the survey and evaluatory steps

Frequently communicate information about transition activities to inform staff and students in accordance with transition team decisions

Include administrators in decision making and inform them of transition team decisions

Design cooperative LEA and agency projects, bringing new personnel into supportive roles as possible

Distribute information about available transition activities in accordance with transition team decisions

Include agency administration in planning and decision making for transition activities to aid students and community-at-large

Connect student needs with community agencies when possible

 Set transition program goals and objectives

Decide communiques needed and who needs to receive the information

Plan meetings which include and inform administration

... INITIATING ACTIVITIES FOR THE TRANSITION PROCESS		
LEAs	**COMMUNITY AGENCIES**	**TRANSITION TEAMS**
Implement plans with students, opening doors, and easing the way	Implement plans with students	Enlist new participants for the team as desirable to increase support and link community, students, and educational institution
Review progress regularly and refer students to relevant resources	Review progress regularly and refer students to relevant resources	Choose transition activity priorities
Follow through with students as further skill building activities are needed	Follow through with students as placement is accomplished	Plan transition activities and assign responsibilities
		Review progress of overall goals and objectives regularly and revise as needed
		Plan strength-building reinforcements to follow students

Adapted from: McCarty, T., & Hess-Grabill, D. (1989). *Transition for Disadvantaged Students*. Normal, IL: Illinois State University, Office of Specialized Vocational Research.

Figure 12-5. Activities for implementing transition programming for learners from special populations.

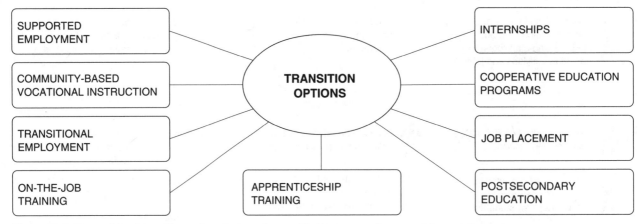

Figure 12-6. The variety of transition options that can be provided to learners from special populations.

Supported Employment

Supported employment is paid work with ongoing support for as long as necessary in settings with nondisabled peers for individuals traditionally denied access to such opportunities. In other words, individuals with disabilities decide what type of career they want with the support of their family and friends. They search for a job that matches the things they like and their skills.

Once they find the right job, they are offered ongoing support and training for as long as necessary at the job. Employment specialists and coworkers offer this support.

In most cases, the employer pays the worker with the disability and the employment specialist is paid by a provider agency. An employment specialist also may help a person using supported employment services determine job preference. Then the employment specialist may help

find that job and provide additional training at the job site until the worker is comfortable with the natural supports. Natural supports are those people or coworkers who are not paid to work with the individual.

Since the early 1970s, supported employment has evolved and expanded. Prior to its development, there was a belief that persons with disabilities needed life-long support and training to be employed. In the 1950s, vocational programs for persons with disabilities were instituted. These services consisted of training in a segregated setting, where persons with disabilities attempted to get "ready" to go to work. The system anticipated that the individual would progress from one program to the other and would someday be prepared for a job.

Vocational assessments that focused on what the person could not do rather than what the person could do were used to determine readiness. One of the major flaws with this model was that training was developed around simulated rather than actual job settings. Few people got regular jobs as a result of these programs and advocates began to search for a better way. In the early 1970s, vocational pioneers in the disabilities field began to experiment with new ideas.

Today there are a variety of work-based models for supported employment. Individuals with disabilities may work in various ways in a supported employment program:

- The individual model is one person, one paid job at a regular job site assigned to one employment specialist. The job may be full- or part-time. Regular contact occurs with coworkers and other persons who do not have disabilities or are not paid to work with the individual. Over time, the support of the employment specialist will fade to a minimum number of contacts per month.
- The job share model is a variation of the individual model with two persons in supported employment sharing one employment specialist and one job. The two persons may work at the same time, each doing part of the job duties. Another way is to share a full- or part-time job between two people needing part-time work. If fading is possible, the employment specialist will fade from the work site to a minimum number of contacts per month.
- Enclaves consist of eight or fewer supported employees closely working together at a regular job site or at the same job but in different locations. One or more employment specialists may provide ongoing support. Fewer opportunities for integration develop compared with the individual model because the group sometimes operates as a small contract unit.
- Mobile work crews are crews of up to eight persons with disabilities working in community businesses or other community settings. Each crew may be supervised by one or more employment specialists.
- The entrepreneurial model is a group approach to employment where up to eight people with disabilities work in a small business created specifically by or for the individual workers.
- Transition from school to work is a popular model of supported employment for school districts to provide a smooth transition from school to work for learners with disabilities. Learners explore various workstations in industry for a short time. Work can be full- or part-time. The school district has an agreement with the employer to provide training. Learners are rotated among different jobs to learn work skills and build a resume.

Community-Based Vocational Instruction (CBVI)

The concept of community-based instruction has now expanded to secondary programs for learners with disabilities in the form of community-based vocational instruction (CBVI). CBVI encourages learner participation in real work environments under the supervision of school personnel and employers. The implementation of CBVI has grown as an expanding body of research has demonstrated the benefit of CBVI in assisting learners with disabilities in securing competitive employment. Because of CBVI's success with learners with disabilities, it offers a strategy for consideration by decision makers planning transition programs for all learners.

CBVI relies on an integrated approach to school and community activities to prepare learners for postsecondary opportunities. Learners from the age of 14 participate in nonpaid vocational exploration, assessment, and training experiences to identify their career interests, assess their employment skills and training needs, and develop the skills and attitudes necessary for paid employment. After such instruction, learners may engage in cooperative vocational experiences for which they are paid.

The CBVI approach has four components: vocational exploration, vocational assessment, vocational training, and cooperative vocational education. Learner participation in each component is based on individual needs and circumstances. Learners may progress through the entire sequence or participate in only one or two components before moving to cooperative vocational education.

Vocational Exploration. Vocational exploration exposes learners to a variety of work settings to help them make decisions about future career directions or occupations. The exploration process involves investigating interests, values, beliefs, strengths, and weaknesses in relation to the demands and other characteristics of work environments. Through vocational exploration, learners gain information by watching work being performed, talking to employees, and performing work under direct supervision of school personnel. Exploration enables learners to make choices regarding career or occupational areas they wish to pursue. The learner, parents, exploration site employees, and school personnel use this information to develop the learner's individualized education program (IEP) and individualized transition program (ITP) for the remainder of the learner's educational experience.

Vocational Assessment. Vocational assessment helps determine individual training objectives for a learner. In this CBVI component, the learner undertakes work assignments in various business settings under the direct supervision of school personnel and employees. Assessment data regarding social skills, values and attitudes toward work, work tolerance, and workplace accommodations required for the learner are systematically collected. The learner rotates among various work settings corresponding to the learner's range of employment preferences as school personnel and assessment site employees complete situational assessments. As a result, learners select work settings in which they can best pursue career or occupational areas matching their interests and aptitudes. Future training objectives are matched with these selections. These training objectives become a part of the learner's subsequent IEPs.

In any industry there are a series of multiple exit points or job titles. See Figure 12-7. By comparing an individual's abilities, interests, and needs with the specific competencies required, placement and training plans can be developed. Multiple exit point guides (MEPGs) can also be used as portable profiles as the learner demonstrates required competencies.

MULTIPLE EXIT POINTS AND ENTRY LEVEL COMPETENCIES IN MASONRY

TASK LISTING BY DOT CODE

MASONRY

TASK NO.	TASK NAME	POSSIBLE EXIT POINTS / DOT DESCRIPTIONS: Cement Mason Helper (DOT NO. 869.687-026)	Bricklayer Helper (861.687-010)	Stone Mason Helper (869.687-026)	Cement Mason (844.364-010)	Stone Mason (861.381-038)	Bricklayer Construction (001.301-010)
01	Spreading mortar	X	X	X	X	X	X
02	Laying brick to a line		X				X
03	Building a brick corner						X
04	Cutting brick and block		X	X		X	X
05	Determining spacing for standard sized brick						X
06	Laying out courses to sill and cornice height						X
07	Interpreting and using a line modular rule		X	X		X	X
08	Dimensioning and scaling a working drawing						X
09	Identifying names and uses of lines and symbols on a working drawing						X
10	Identifying different views and their uses on a working drawing						X
11	Setting batter boards	X	X		X		X
12	Inspecting grading at building site				X	X	X
13	Finishing grading at building site	X	X	X	X	X	X

Figure 12-7. The relationship between multiple exit points and the competencies that are taught in a curriculum.

Vocational Training. The vocational training component of CBVI places the learner in various employment settings for work experiences. The learner, parents, and school personnel develop a detailed written plan that includes the competencies to be acquired, method(s) of instruction, and procedures for evaluating the training experience. Training is closely supervised by a representative of the school or a designated employee or supervisor. The purpose of this component is to enable learners to develop the competencies and behavior needed to secure paid employment. As the learner reaches the training objectives in a particular employment setting, the learner moves to other employment environments where additional related learning and reinforcement of current competencies and behavior occur.

Cooperative Education. Cooperative education (co-op) consists of an arrangement between the school and an employer in which each contributes to the learner's education and employability in designated ways. The learner is paid for work performed in the employment setting. The learner may receive payment from the employer, from the school's cooperative program, from another employment program operating in the community, or a combination of these. The learner is paid the same wages as regular employees performing the same work. Cooperative education, although designed as a learning experience for the learner as specified in the IEP, constitutes an employment relationship. As such, all requirements of learner employment must be met, including securing a work permit when required, as well as other provisions of the Fair Labor Standards Act (FLSA) applying to learners or minors.

The school and the employer reach a written agreement before the learner enters cooperative education. The agreement includes the work-based learning experiences to be obtained, support provided by the school and the employer, and the methods for measuring learner progress on the job, as well as a clear stipulation of the learner's wages and benefits. This agreement may also include follow-along services to ensure that the learner adjusts to the work assignments and improves performance and productivity over time.

There are as many versions of the cooperative education approach as there are school districts using it. These examples illustrate what school personnel working with secondary school learners with disabilities in community-based work settings have learned through the co-op approach:

- Cooperative education makes learners and their parents partners in decision making in the school-to-work transition process. It allows learners to experience a variety of career opportunities, provides information on learner strengths and interests, and carries out evaluation and training in real work situations. As a result of this level of participation, learners and parents can make informed decisions concerning postsecondary choices.
- Cooperative education is an effective and efficient means of assessing job-related performance and conducting job-specific training, including assessing social skills necessary to participate in the workforce.
- Cooperative education instruction by school personnel and job site personnel results in increased learning and retention of job-related skills and facilitates community and employer involvement in school-to-work programs.
- The components of co-op prepare learners to participate appropriately in cooperative education experiences (paid employment) and provide an appropriate match of learners to employment situations.
- The acquisition of generic vocational skills requires multiple job-site experiences that are best facilitated by co-op (Norman & Bourexis, 1995).

Transitional Employment

Transitional employment is designed for those who cannot enter into competitive work on their own, but who are able to handle an independent, full-wage job after training and support. In demonstration projects funded by the U.S. Department of Labor, transitional employment consists of three phases. In phase one, participants receive initial training and support services in a low-stress work environment. Phase two involves a period of on-the-job training in local firms that resembles the demands faced by other workers in the same types of jobs. Phase three consists of up to six months of follow-up services (National Information Center for Children and Youth with Disabilities, 1999).

On-the-Job Training

On-the-job training is short-term training that enables an individual to work on a job site while learning the job duties from a coworker or supervisor. This situation may be paid or unpaid, and can lead to the learner taking over the job as an employee once the training period has been successfully completed.

Apprenticeships

Changing demographics, changing technology, and increasing international competition have combined to make the preparation of workers for the workplace a critical issue today. One training strategy in particular is often cited as holding great promise for improving workplace preparation: apprenticeship. Apprenticeship has been very effective in preparing skilled workers in the United States and abroad. Apprenticeship is a combination of on-the-job training and related instruction in which workers learn the practical and theoretical aspects of a highly skilled occupation. Apprenticeship programs are sponsored by joint employer and labor groups, individual employers, and/or employer associations. There are two types of apprenticeships: registered apprenticeships and youth apprenticeships.

Wonacott (2000) provided the following information on apprenticeship programs:

- In the past, apprenticeship was often viewed as pedagogically questionable and biased toward employers' interests. Today, however, many consider it an ideal vehicle for the work-based learning necessary for the school-to-work transition. In particular, youth apprenticeships are seen as having potential to minimize youth floundering in the labor market, ensure educative work experiences, increase earnings and educational attainment, and make school more meaningful.
- Apprenticeship has become increasingly attractive to many as a means of preparing workers for today's high-tech, high-performance workplace with its demands for a blend of technological, information, interpersonal, and lifelong learning skills. Apprenticeship's direct ties to employment make it a natural element of the market-driven, customer-focused job training system envisioned by the Workforce Investment Act.
- Unions may perceive youth apprenticeship as a threat to their influence, or they may view it as a help in maintaining unions and wages. Employer participation in youth apprenticeships is a focus of many state efforts, but concerns about costs, lost trainer productivity, and liability often affect employer participation in youth apprenticeship. Employers also call for increased training and support for workplace mentors and trainers and improved coordination with schools.
- Race and gender are long-standing issues in both registered apprenticeship and youth apprenticeship. Women continue to be underrepresented and to enjoy less favorable earning outcomes, whereas African-Americans are often overrepresented but have less favorable completion rates and employment and earnings outcomes.
- There is concern about low learner awareness of apprenticeship as an option as well as general career and labor market awareness. In addition, participation may be limited by the perception among both learners and parents that apprenticeship is a low-prestige alternative to college or university placement.

There are eight essential components for apprenticeship experiences:

1. Apprenticeship is sponsored by employers and others who can hire and train individuals in the workplace, and it combines hands-on training on the job with related theoretical instruction.
2. Workplace and industry needs dictate key details of apprenticeship programs—training content, length of training, and actual employment settings.
3. Apprenticeship has a specific legal status and is regulated by federal and state laws and regulations.
4. Apprenticeship leads to formal official credentials—a certificate of completion and journeyperson status.
5. Apprenticeship generally requires a significant investment of time and money on the part of employers or other sponsors.
6. Apprenticeship provides wages to apprentices during training according to predefined wage scales.
7. Apprentices learn by working directly under master workers in their occupations.
8. Apprenticeship involves both written agreements and implicit expectations. Written agreements specify the roles and responsibilities of each party. Implicit expectations include the right of program sponsors to employ the apprentice, recouping their sizable investment in training, and the right of apprentices to obtain such employment.

Registered Apprenticeships. Registered apprenticeships are formal programs registered with the U.S. Department of Labor, Bureau of Apprenticeship and Training or with an approved state apprenticeship agency. These programs follow strict guidelines as to the types of training and amount of training time an apprentice receives and lead directly into occupations requiring such training for entry. Registered apprenticeships are typically paid work experiences.

Registered apprenticeship program sponsors identify the minimum qualifications to apply into their apprenticeship programs. The eligible starting age can be no less than 16 years of age; however, individuals must usually be 18 to be an apprentice in hazardous occupations. Program sponsors may also identify additional minimum qualifications and credentials necessary to apply (e.g., education, ability to physically perform the essential functions of the occupation, proof of age). All applicants are required to meet the minimum qualifications. Based on the selection method utilized by the sponsor, additional qualification standards, such as fair aptitude tests and interviews, school grades, and previous work experience may be identified.

Through the Apprentice Agreement, an apprentice, as an employee, receives supervised, structured on-the-job training combined with related technical instruction. The on-the-job training provides the diversity of training required to perform at a highly skilled level and the related instruction provides the technical knowledge required to perform at a highly skilled level. Some registered apprenticeship programs also have dual accreditation through postsecondary institutions, which apply credit for apprenticeship completion towards an associate's degree.

A progressively increasing schedule of wages is based on the journeyworker's hourly wage in the apprentice's occupation. These increases occur with satisfactory progress in both related instruction and on-the-job training until wages reach 85% to 90% of the rate paid the journeyworker.

Upon completing a three- to five-year (2,000 hours to 8,000 hours) apprenticeship, the worker receives an apprenticeship completion certificate and is recognized as a qualified journeyworker nationwide. This certificate is one of the oldest, most basic, and most highly portable industry credentials in use today. The certificate is issued by a federally approved state apprenticeship council or agency or, in those states not having such an agency, by the Bureau of Apprenticeship and Training.

Youth Apprenticeships. Youth apprenticeships are typically multiyear programs that combine school- and work-based learning in a specific occupational area or occupational cluster and are designed to lead directly into either a related postsecondary program, entry-level job, or registered apprenticeship program. They may or may not include paid work experiences.

Youth apprenticeship is a learning program for young people ages 16 and older that combines on-the-job learning with classroom instruction, bridges secondary and postsecondary schooling, and results in certification of mastery of work skills. There has been a renewed interest in school-to-apprenticeship in the past few years. Most youth apprenticeship programs

- require participants to come to school;
- give learners on-the-job training with up-to-date equipment;
- provide school credit for the on-the-job training as experimental learning;
- involve employers in the planning of programs and in the development of related instruction to meet the training needs of both employers and apprentices; and
- assist in addressing labor shortages in certain skills areas.

The process for participation in a youth apprenticeship program is as follows:

1. The apprentice enters a high school/youth apprenticeship program in junior or senior year.
2. The apprentice works on a part-time basis during the school year and full-time in the summer.
3. The apprentice's work-based learning is monitored and evaluated by the employer.
4. Related academic and technical instruction is coordinated by the school to connect work-based and school-based learning.
5. After graduating from high school, the learner moves into an adult apprenticeship program while continuing education, usually at a local technical/community college.

6. When the apprentice successfully completes the required number of hours of work-based learning and related classroom instruction, certification of occupational and academic mastery is awarded.
7. The apprentice has the option of entering the workforce and/or continuing in school.

Registered school-to-apprenticeship programs assist youth in the 11th and 12th grades who plan to enter the workforce directly after high school. The apprentice and the sponsor sign an apprenticeship agreement. The apprentice agrees to perform the work and complete the related study, and the sponsor agrees to make every effort to keep the apprentice employed and to comply with the standards established for the program. If this agreement meets all the standards of registered apprenticeship, it is then registered with the Bureau of Apprenticeship and Training or a state apprenticeship council or agency. The registered school-to-apprenticeship program is designed to provide the flexibility the high school apprentice needs to continue with the school-based related instruction component and the part-time structured on-the-job training component. After graduating from high school, the apprentice is employed full time and continues with the occupational on-the-job training and related instruction. See Figure 12-8.

Internships

Internships are situations where learners work for an employer for a specific period of time to learn about a particular industry or occupation. Learners' workplace activities may include special projects, a sample of tasks from different jobs, or tasks from a single occupation. These may or may not include financial compensation.

Whether they are provided during the summer or school year, internships provide structured work experiences for learners in career fields that are of interest to them. Although an internship is usually short-term, its duration varies and so does the complexity of knowledge and skills the learner is required to master at each placement. The learner's internship objectives are built around skill development, gaining a broader knowledge of the occupation, career awareness and development, and personal development.

YOUTH APPRENTICESHIP AGREEMENT . . .

Mutual Expectation Agreement
Cornell Youth Apprenticeship Demonstration Project

1. Parties to the Agreement

Apprentice Name _____   School _____

Apprenticeship Title _____   Employer _____

Parent/Guardian _____

2. Expectations for Apprentices
The apprentice agrees to . . .
* Complete assigned work tasks
* Abide by company policy (e.g., to notify manager if late or absent)
* Seek assistance for personal and workplace problems
* Participate in the academic components of the apprenticeship offered by the school and the workplace, including
    - Continue to pursue related academic courses
    - Participate in an advisory group
    - Complete a special project in the senior year
    - Maintain a journal
    - Maintain a training notebook
3. Expectations for School
* Offer a school-based curriculum for apprentices that enriches their learning, including
    - Academic courses related to the apprenticeship
    - Special project help
    - Regular meeting with advisory group
* Assist with course selection, time use, scheduling, and career pathway decisions
* Assign a school apprenticeship coordinator who will foster effective communication links among the school, parents, and guardians and the apprentice
* Assist in solving problems

...YOUTH APPRENTICESHIP AGREEMENT

4. Expectations for the Employer

   The employer agrees to . . .

   - Structure learning by assigning appropriate work tasks
   - Enable the apprentice to learn the occupational area described in an attached training document
   - Evaluate the apprentice's progress periodically each year, sending at least one progress report to the school and to Cornell each semester
   - Accord the apprentice equal opportunity in all phases of the apprenticeship employment and training, without discrimination because of race, color, religion, national origin, age, sex, disability, or marital status

5. Expectations for Parents and Guardians

   The parent or guardian agrees to . . .

   - Support the apprentice's effort
   - Help him or her meet the terms of the contract (e.g., attendance, attire, academic courses, and so on)

6. Termination

   - The employer may terminate an apprentice for any reason
   - An apprentice may terminate his or her employment for any reason
   - Ordinarily, termination will only occur after serious efforts by all parties to resolve difficulties

7. Special Arrangements

   The following documents are attached:

   - Apprenticeship training documents _____ yes _____ no
   - Employer policies and procedures _____ yes _____ no
   - Orientation material _____ yes _____ no

8. Hours, Duration

   Start date _____   Program length _____   Hours per week _____

   Holidays _____   School vacation _____   Summer hours _____

   - Apprentices may choose not to attend work during special exams (e.g., SAT), snow days, and so on. They should notify their employer about schedule changes in advance

9. Compensation

   - Pay and progression (pay progression is not automatic; it depends upon the apprentice's skills and increasing value to the employer)

     1st year _____   2nd year _____   3rd year _____   4th year _____

   - Other compensation (benefits, tuition assistance, and so on)

10. Signatures

_____	_____
Apprentice	School Apprentice Coordinator
_____	_____
Address	Address
_____	_____
Date	Date
_____	_____
Parent or Guardian	Firm Apprentice Coordinator
_____	_____
Address	Address
_____	_____
Date	Date

Source: Rahn et al., (1995). *Getting to Work: Module 3 – Learning Experiences.* Berkeley, CA: National Center for Research in Vocational Education.

Figure 12-8. Sample agreement for a youth apprenticeship.

Following are steps for beginning an internship program:

1. Identify and recruit employers willing to provide internship sites. Consider what employers want. Several surveys indicate that employers want roles and responsibilities to be clearly defined. For example, they want to know what the benefits are for participation and how they can serve your needs while avoiding conflicts with unions and employee groups. Employers want to discuss up front the training and liability issues associated with learners at the workplace.
2. Complete a company profile of the internship site as it is confirmed. See Figure 12-9.
3. Match learners with internship sites according to career pathway and career objectives. Identify a specific internship objective and an outline of internship experiences.
4. Develop an internship training plan in conjunction with the industry internship supervisor.
5. Prepare the industry internship supervisor with training and appropriate guidelines for supervising the intern.
6. Prepare the learner for the internship. See Figure 12-10.
7. Assign learners a weekly journal activity to record internship experiences.
8. Evaluate the internship experience. See Figure 12-11.

Cooperative Education Programs

Cooperative education (co-op) is a program that combines academic study with paid, monitored, and credit-bearing work. It was established around the turn of the century as part of a movement to create experience-based education. In fact, the first co-op program looked more like what we now would call an apprenticeship. The four-year program, which led to beginning journeyman status, began with a year in which learners studied only academic subjects; in the following three years, learners alternated weeks between shop and school.

Today, cooperative education is concentrated in the career and technical areas of marketing, trade and industry, and business. Although the programs are national, specific arrangements are worked out locally between individual employers and school staff and are subject to state laws and local customs. In contrast to German apprenticeships, to which they are often compared, high school cooperative education in this country generally only lasts a year or less (U.S. General Accounting Office, 1991). Although a few co-op programs alternate days or weeks of school with work or allow learners to work in the morning, the most common arrangement is to schedule the morning at school and the afternoon in a paid job. Co-op learners usually take traditional academic and career and technical education classes with noncooperative-education learners, although particular courses may be recommended to the learners by the school cooperative education coordinator. In addition, good co-op programs include a special related class in which learners are able to reflect on and integrate their job experiences.

COMPANY PROFILE FORM

Internship Program – Company Profile

Name of company: _____
Industry: _____ # Years in business: _____
Principal contact: _____ Title: _____
Address: _____
Phone: _____ Fax: _____
Email: _____ Business hours: _____
Locations: Local _____ Regional: _____ National: _____ Int'l: _____
Employees at location: _____ Dress code: _____
Business of company (briefly describe): _____

Typical client/customers: _____

Internship position: _____
Internship job description: _____

Intern qualities/qualifications required: _____

Intern reports to: _____ Date: _____
Profile created by: _____ Date: _____

Adapted from: Carrollton-Farmers Branch Independent School District. (n.d.). *Technology Internship Program Handbook.* Carrollton, TX: Author.

Figure 12-9. Sample company profile for an internship program.

INTERNSHIP PROGRAM RULES FOR PARTICIPANTS

Internship Attendance

- Call the business sponsor and the coordinator if unable to attend class or your internship
- Absences from your internship are consistent with school policy
- If you are aware of an absence in the future, a memo needs to be written to the business sponsor and to the coordinator as soon as possible
- Make-up work needs to be turned in a week following your absence. Check with a classmate or your teacher for make-up work assignments

Evaluations

- Business sponsors will evaluate you according to your performance. Evaluation due dates are marked on your school calendar. Instructions will be given in class as to logistics of collection and return

Intern Performance

- If there are concerns of any nature relating to class or intern assignments, you are responsible for contacting me
- Small problems tend to become BIG problems
- A large portion of your intern experience is learning how to be responsible for taking the initiative to fulfill the objectives of the program (refer to TIP brochure)
- Keep me informed on your progress

Signature_____   Date_____

Adapted from: Carrollton-Farmers Branch Independent School District. (n.d.). *Technology Internship Program Handbook.* Carrollton, TX: Author

Figure 12-10. Sample internship program rules.

Ascher (1994) made the following relevant points concerning co-op programs:

1. The recent drive to create apprenticeships and work-based education for high school learners makes it imperative that the long and largely fruitful experiences of cooperative education be taken seriously. This experience has shown that worthwhile co-op programs have not been cheap and that there must be money for promotion and recruitment as well as training of both teachers/coordinators and employers. Teachers need to know how to work with industry, and employers have to understand the benefits of hiring and working with these learners. Although strong evidence supports the benefits of school-supervised work experiences, we know little about what learning goes on in the workplace and how to maximize it. Finally, some form of certification must recognize skill attainment in co-op education or any new school-supervised work experience program for it to be part of a school-to-work transition strategy.

2. Cooperative education is not an inexpensive program. Typically, cooperative education teachers/coordinators are given only three courses, of which one is a special co-op course related to learners' work assignments. In return for three periods of released time, the teachers/coordinators are responsible for screening learners for eligibility, as well as developing employment agreements and training plans, finding jobs, and monitoring the field experience (for the 15-20 learners for whom they are ultimately responsible), through monthly or even biweekly visits. In periods of budget constraints, high schools find it difficult to absorb the costs of this released time. As a consequence, co-op programs have diminished in size and effectiveness.

3. Budget cuts have also made it more difficult for teachers/coordinators to market their co-op programs to prospective employers. Ironically, successful programs, in which learners become permanent employees after completing their co-op experience, involve the most work for coordinators, who must find new placements each year.

4. In the most effective and common high school cooperative education model, a teacher/coordinator handles all the work placements and teaches a course related to the learners' work assignments. The traditional preparation for becoming a teacher/coordinator has been through a special career and technical education course offered in teacher training institutions.

5. For co-op or any other workplace training program to succeed, it is important to have someone at the work site responsible for workplace learning. This includes mentoring and coaching to pass on the culture of the workplace, as well as transmitting real knowledge and skills.

6. If co-op only provided learners with money, it would be no better than unsupervised youth employment experiences. However, a five-year longitudinal study comparing learners in unsupervised jobs with learners enrolled

in school-supervised work programs (predominately co-op) found that learners in supervised programs had higher-quality jobs and more contact with adults. These co-op and other school-supervised work experiences provide learners more supervision on the job, more challenge, and more work that is meaningful.

7. Relative to learners in regular classrooms, learners in experimental education programs like co-op make gains on moral reasoning, self-esteem, social and personal responsibility, attitudes toward adults and other, career exploration, and empathy/complexity of thought.

Equally important, the single strongest factor explaining these changes is the weekly reflective learning session in their related class, during which learners integrate their learning on the job with classroom learning.

The way in which learners are prepared at school before they leave for work determines more than any single factor how successful their work-based learning will be. Learners need a training plan that begins at school, carries over into the workplace, and contains clear expectations of what learners, teachers, and employers are expected to do. See Figure 12-12.

INTERNSHIP PERFORMANCE EVALUATION

Intern _____   Due Date _____

Internship/Sponsor _____

Please rate your intern on the extent to which he/she has exhibited the following work habits.

	Low		Average		High
Knowledge of Work	1	2	3	4	5
Does the student strive to understand all phases of his/her work and related matters?					
Quality of Work	1	2	3	4	5
High level of work					
Dependability	1	2	3	4	5
Attendance, punctuality, accepts responsibility, works without supervision					
Attitude	1	2	3	4	5
Interest in job, eager to learn, positive feeling about internship					
Initiative	1	2	3	4	5
Ability to develop constructive ideas, works without supervision					
Thoroughness	1	2	3	4	5
Accurate, completion of work, follows directions correctly, practices safety					
Personal Appearance	1	2	3	4	5
Neat, dressed appropriately					
Manners	1	2	3	4	5
Courteous, considerate, respectful, open-minded					
Ability to Get Along with Others	1	2	3	4	5
Friendly, cooperative, ability to accept criticism					
Communication Skills	1	2	3	4	5
Ability to receive and give information					
Overall Job Performance	1	2	3	4	5

Intern's Best Qualities:

_____

_____

Areas Which Need Improvement:

_____

_____

Adapted from: Carrollton-Farmers Branch Independent School District. (n.d.). *Technology Internship Program Handbook.* Carrollton, TX: Author.

Figure 12-11. Sample performance evaluation for an internship.

DESCRIPTION OF SPECIFIC AND RELATED OCCUPATIONAL TRAINING

The specific occupation essential elements listed below are provided as a convenience to assure that the required minimum training is made available. Additional space is available to add specific individual training opportunities not identified as essential elements. *NOTE:* Occupational training objectives having no identified essential elements will require the training plans to be individually developed.

Required Essential Elements	To Be Done		Related Study Assignments
	On the Job	Related Class	
Additional Occupational Experiences	On the Job	Related Class	

Figure 12-12. Training plan for learners in a co-op program.

A training plan is necessary for each learner in order to specify roles and responsibilities of everyone concerned. The following considerations should be addressed when developing and implementing a training plan:

- A list of learner outcomes to be measured in the classroom and workplace describing what learners should be able to do and the level at which learners should be able to do it should be created.
- Work samples or some other reflection of work where the learner is involved in activity that contributes to the overall profitability and efficiency of the employer should be required.
- A skills plan that the employer can verify should be created. If both the school and employer agree upon the skills that the learner needs, the employer can check off the skills the learner develops over time. It may be a check-off sheet or a rating system with a specified level of performance.
- All aspects of the industry activities should be included. The aspects defined by legislation include planning, management, finance, technical and production skills, underlying principles of technology, labor issues, community issues, and health, safety, and environmental issues. The training plan should specify how the learner is going to receive broad understanding and experience in the industry during classroom learning, work, or both.
- Reflection time, oral and written, should be built into the work-based experience. Learners who take time at work to write about what they observe and learn can reflect on and absorb knowledge. Learners should share their reflections with workplace supervisors, teachers, and peers (Rahn et al., 1995).

From the insights of several studies, Ascher (1994) suggested a number of features of quality cooperative education programs:

- quality co-op placements in which the learner is allowed to perform work that both provides opportunities to develop new competencies and contributes to the productivity of the organization
- teachers/coordinators with appropriate occupational experience related to the industry associated with their program, as well as professional preparation for operating a school-supervised work education program
- close supervision at the work site by a training supervisor, as well as a mechanism by which the supervisor can share professional expertise with the co-op learner
- at the onset, an accurate and realistic description of the job for the learner as well as accurate expectations by the employer of the skills the learner brings to it
- strong links between job training and related instruction, which might include an individualized, written training plan that is correlated to the learners' in-school curriculum
- frequent and specific informal and formal evaluations of the learners' progress by the teacher/coordinator, with feedback and follow-up to improve performance
- involvement of parents or guardians
- placement of graduates in full-time positions, or referrals for additional instruction, and follow-up of graduates after three and five years
- strong administrative support for the program

Job Placement

Demographic changes in the workforce and federal legislative mandates have forced employers to redefine their labor pool. Increasing numbers of employers are recruiting individuals from special populations for a variety of reasons, including recognition that these individuals can become loyal, productive employees, that they are usually carefully prepared and screened before seeking employment, and that follow-up services are available to help them adjust to new jobs.

Thousands of employers are now offering support to local schools. Employers are investing in education for reasons other than philanthropy. They want a labor pool of graduates with a strong work ethic and appropriate skills, and they realize that their communities must be economically strong for companies to succeed. Employers recognize that a well-trained workforce is more productive and flexible, can solve work-related problems, assimilates new knowledge and skills, and is necessary to maintain and increase a business's performance and competitiveness. Businesses train people and provide work-based learning sites for learners at their own expense because they view training as a priority investment with high, long-term economic and social returns (*Workforce 2020*, 1994).

Employers are interested in forming partnerships with schools because they believe it is the best way to ensure a steady supply of qualified workers. According to Carnevale and Porro (1994), employers value education for four important reasons: (1) Education is the means of disseminating knowledge and skills that ultimately result in the creation of new technology, new machines, and new products, (2) increased years of education correlate positively with a stronger work ethic, (3) education is a major provider of job-related skills, with one-third of all workers who need preparation for their jobs obtaining some or all of that preparation from schools and about 13% of employed workers who need skill improvement securing those skills from educational institutions, and (4) the results of education in terms of educational attainment, work ethic, and skills provide employers with information that can assist them in choosing among job seekers.

Job placement should be viewed as a process, not an event. Job placement for learners from special populations should be viewed as a critical element of the transition process that prepares learners to find their own jobs and to maintain steady employment with appropriate support services. The goal of job placement programs should be to assist individuals to secure and make progress in meaningful work that provides adequate income, job satisfaction, opportunities for continuing education and personal growth, means of independent living, and opportunities for participation in community activities. The job placement process involves a number of components combined with an effective follow-up program that should be coordinated and delivered by trained placement team members.

One of the first steps in job placement is to assess the local employment situation and to identify jobs for which learners from special populations can be prepared and placed. This can be done by conducting a job information search through a variety of sources. The results of the job information search can be used to compile a listing of potential employers. A recommended way to organize information obtained in the job search is to place it on file cards or on computer diskettes. Such information should include the name, address, and telephone number of the employer; the person to contact; the type of job; the job performance requirements; the hiring requirements and procedures; the contract requirements (hours of work, wages paid, and referral instructions); who to see; and when to apply. See Figure 12-13. Job information cards and diskettes can be placed into a master file and used in job placement as a source for mail-outs and follow up. The master job file must be periodically reviewed and kept up to date.

Once an exhaustive job search has been completed, the next step is to conduct a selected employer survey to determine more detailed information about jobs in which learners from special populations may be placed and the willingness on the part of the employer to consider job redesign and job development. The employer survey should be designed to obtain detailed information about the type of jobs, the availability of on-the-job training, the job turnover rate, and other information needed to prepare job profiles as well as an overview of job tasks and requirements. It is usually necessary to follow up the employer survey with a prearranged visit to the company. There is no better way to facilitate job development than to meet the potential employer and to observe firsthand the actual work environment.

In preparation for visits to companies, the placement staff should learn as much as possible about the company and the products or services it provides. This can be accomplished by reviewing printed and media materials on the company such as career guidebooks, trade journals, employer directories, public relations literature, and annual reports. In addition, information about companies can be obtained through talking with current employees of the firm and with other employers who may purchase products and services from the company or provide it with products and services.

When visiting employers, job placement personnel must be well prepared, confident, assertive, and positive. They

---

TYPICAL JOB INFORMATION CARD

Side 1

Name of Company: _____

Address: _____

_____

Phone (   )   Fax (   )

Person to Contact: _____

Types of Jobs (what, where, how, why)

_____
_____
_____

Willing to Redesign Jobs (Yes _____ No _____)

- -

Side 2

Worker Performance Requirements:

_____
_____

Work Ecology (physical, social, and organizational)

_____
_____

Hiring Requirements (age, training, experience, license, screening exams, career portfolio, resume, placement file)

_____
_____

Contract Requirements (wages, work hours, full or part-time, work site)

_____
_____

Referral Instructions (whom to see, where to apply)

_____
_____

Figure 12-13. An example of a job information card for collecting pertinent information about a specific job.

must present themselves in a professional and courteous manner. Conversation should employ business terminology and focus on increasing employer awareness about the school's job placement program and the benefits of hiring persons from special populations. Positive factors should be stressed, such as convincing employers that hiring these individuals results in more benefits than costs. Placement professionals must be prepared to reason in a positive manner when confronted with cost myths such as increased accident rates, absenteeism, and lowered productivity. Placement personnel need to emphasize the preplacement training and screening that learners receive before they are referred for placement and the services that will be provided when they are employed. Employers should be informed that a major goal of the placement program is to help them find qualified job applicants to meet their needs.

How to Conduct a Job Analysis. A job analysis is a logical process to determine the job's purpose, its essential functions, its setting, and its necessary qualifications. A job analysis describes the job, not the person who fills it. The following questions can help analyze each job in an organization:

Purpose

• What are the particular contributions of the job toward the accomplishment of the overall objective of the unit or organization?

Essential Functions

• What three or four activities actually constitute the job? Is each really necessary?
• What is the relationship between each task? Is there a special sequence that the tasks must follow?
• Do the tasks necessitate sitting, standing, walking, climbing, running, kneeling, lifting, carrying, digging, writing, operating, talking, interpreting, analyzing, coordinating, etc.?
• How many other employees are available to perform the job function? Can the performance of that job function be distributed among any other employees?
• How much time is spent on the job performing each particular function? Are the tasks performed less frequently as important to success as those done more frequently?
• Would removing a function fundamentally alter the job?
• What happens if a task is not completed on time?

Job Setting

• What is the location of the job? Where are the essential functions of the job carried out?
• How is the work organized for maximum safety and efficiency? How do workers obtain necessary equipment and materials?
• What movement is required of employees to accomplish the essential functions of the job?
• What are the physical conditions of the job setting (hot, cold, damp, inside, outside, underground, wet, humid, dry, air-conditioned, dirty, greasy, noisy, etc.)? What are the social conditions of the job (work alone, work around others, work with the public, work under close supervision, work under minimal supervision, work under deadlines, etc.)?

Worker Qualifications

• What are the physical requirements (lifting, driving, cleaning, etc.)?
• What are the general skills needed for the job (ability to read, write, add, etc.)?
• What specific training is necessary? Can it be obtained on the job?
• What previous experience, if any, can replace or be substituted for the specific training requirements?

Other Ways of Locating Jobs. In addition to locating jobs through employer surveys followed by personal visits, the placement team should actively seek the services of out-of-school agencies. The local Office of Employment Services, an agency of the Department of Labor, should be contacted. This agency has given priority to the placement of persons from special populations. It can often provide job leads as well as special guidance and assistance to these individuals.

• Job banks–The job bank system in each state should be used to identify local job opportunities. This is a system for locating jobs through the use of a computerized listing of available jobs throughout the state. Individuals can scan these listings until they find a potential job for which they qualify. They can then be sent to the local Labor Department office for a referral to the job.

The central processing hub for state employment security agencies and their local offices, as well as for hundreds of colleges and libraries, is America's Job Bank. This is a computerized network accessed through the U. S. Department of Labor's nationwide employment service that provides information on work opportunities in the United States and other locations worldwide. The database is updated weekly as jobs are filled and new job listings become available. Users can select from four search modes: search by military code, search for federal job listings, search by job code, and search by occupational preference through the self-directed search mode. Information on salary, employer requirements, job duties, and job locations are available.

• Civil service agencies–Another excellent source for obtaining information about job opportunities is the civil service agencies that exist within most communities. Contact should be made with these agencies to determine current job listings as well as testing procedures to help prepare learners for the various civil service examinations.

• Job networks and networking–In order to help learners from special populations find jobs, placement team members must use their contacts in the community to obtain job leads or information about available jobs. For example, teachers should maintain close contact with the employers in their specific field to keep informed of job openings. This information should be forwarded to the placement staff for further action. Follow-up studies indicate that teachers are often directly involved in the placement of individuals with special needs.

It has been estimated that up to 75% of job openings are filled by word of mouth, networking, and direct contact (Kimeldorf & Tornow, 1984). One reason for this is that many job openings (approximately 60% to 70%) are not formally advertised or listed but are communicated through informal local notices (e.g., notices posted on the doors, windows, and bulletin boards of firms) that are highly visible to a large network of people. There are two main reasons why employers do not advertise job vacancies. First is the financial cost and time involved in formally advertising positions and screening the usual flood of applicants. Second, many employers prefer the informal network approach to filling positions because they believe this approach yields more and better qualified job seekers who tend to be more productive and stay with the firm longer. Employers are usually very interested in talking with job candidates whom others have recommended because the weight of a personal recommendation is far more significant than a reference letter in the candidate's file. They prefer to hire people who have known qualities and proven track records of satisfactory job performance.

Jobs that haven't been formally advertised are labeled "hidden jobs." It is essential for the placement team to identify job openings in the announced job market as well as to penetrate the hidden job market to enhance placement opportunities for learners from special populations. Learners and placement team members can receive valuable job leads from the informal network of parents, relatives, and friends.

In today's competitive job market, job seekers must pursue all possible sources of job information. One of the most valuable sources is the informal network composed of family, friends, and neighbors. A network is simply a list of people a job seeker knows. Networking uses and expands this list of contacts and brings a job seeker's name and qualifications to the attention of many people. A strong personal network provides information about employers and job openings even though the people in the network are not usually potential employers.

In establishing a network, job seekers need to consider all possible resources including (1) family (parents, cousins, aunts, uncles, siblings); (2) friends (neighbors and parents of classmates); (3) school (classmates, teachers, counselors, alumni, administrators, school support staff); (4) employment (employers, colleagues, customers, competitors); (5) professionals (lawyers, doctors, clergy, practicing professionals participating in a career field); and (6) community (business people, clubs, associations, chamber of commerce, religious groups, placement agencies, advocacy groups) (*Placement Manual*, 1993-94).

- Job clubs–One technique for identifying jobs in the hidden job market is through job clubs. Placement team members in a school can sponsor and form job clubs that can meet during or after school. Job club members are taught how to uncover the hidden job listings through use of the telephone, fax, Internet, direct contact with employment sources, and networking strategies. Job club participants are taught how to open and close job bids, how to respond to tough questions, how to respond appropriately to objections or reservations from interviewers, and how to meet employer expectations. Job clubs provide training sessions to assist members in developing job seeking skills within the confines of a peer support group.

- Job fairs–A final activity through which job seekers can make themselves visible to potential employers and gather information about many organizations and their career opportunities is attending job or career fairs. Secondary and postsecondary institutions and some associations sponsor job or career fairs in which employer representatives are invited to "sell" their organizations to job seekers and job seekers have an opportunity to "sell" their qualifications to potential employers. Potential employers generally meet with interested job seekers for a short period (5 to 15 minutes) and determine if they want to invite an individual for a more formal interview. Career or job fairs allow information sharing, product marketing, and opportunities for expanding the informal job network.

Preparing Placement Profiles. An important part of the placement process is the collection of descriptive and evaluative information on each learner and the organization of this information into a job placement profile. Job placement profiles showing the interests and capabilities of each learner can then be matched with the job profiles described earlier and used to make placement decisions.

There are at least two types of job placement profiles currently being used by job placement specialists. The first is a simple placement profile containing the following types of information: (a) a listing of tasks that learners have mastered, (b) a listing of demonstrated basic skills and abilities, and (c) a rating of personal-social behaviors.

Another type of placement profile is much more comprehensive. This profile consists of the following components: (a) educational/psychological information, (b) physical/medical information, (c) social/interpersonal relationship skills information, (d) prevocational/vocational/career information, and (e) employment related information.

Regardless of the type of placement option selected, the placement staff will need to collect learner background and evaluative information from career and technical education teachers, transition personnel, and other appropriate placement team members. This information should be compiled into a placement profile that presents an accurate picture of the learner's interests, abilities, and special needs.

While the primary purpose of the job placement profile is to provide a basic source of information for the placement staff to use in matching learners to jobs, it also has several other uses. It can be used to determine whether or not learners are ready for placement or if they should be given additional training in an identified area of weakness. Proponents of supported employment emphasize the need to classify individuals as either "job ready" or "not job ready" (Rogan & Hagner, 1990). Job placement profiles are useful in the follow-up program in determining areas that may cause problems as measures can then be taken to prevent these problems.

There are two major approaches that can be used for job placement of individuals from special populations. The first and most common approach is to find a job first and then select qualified candidates to apply for it. This approach emphasizes fitting individuals into existing jobs. The second approach is to find and/or develop a job suitable for a given learner. This approach is sometimes called the "person-centered approach" (Karan, 1992) or the "consumer-driven approach" (Martin & Mithaug, 1990). Both approaches make use of placement profiles/career portfolios and job profiles in the matching process, but placement procedures are different for each approach.

The second placement approach, finding a specific job or creating one (job development), may be the more effective. The approach provides the placement team with sufficient time to develop and assess the potential of learners while they are in the career and technical education program as well as time to locate appropriate jobs for them when they are ready for placement. This technique also provides time for the placement staff to identify a number of potential employers who would be willing to redesign jobs.

The job redesign technique can be used to provide jobs for learners who have difficulty obtaining jobs in their preferred occupational area. In redesigning jobs, employers must be willing to have their present job categories analyzed and reorganized to accommodate individuals from special populations. Few employers will be willing to try this venture unless they can see how job redesign will improve productivity. They must be shown how job redesign will release their more experienced and skilled workers to perform job activities that require higher skill levels, thereby increasing overall worker effectiveness.

Job Redesign and Accommodation. In assisting a willing employer with job redesign, the placement staff should analyze the employer's job structure and use the results of this analysis to zero in on a group of similar jobs that can be redesigned. Each of the jobs in this cluster must be analyzed or broken down into tasks and worker requirements and then sequenced according to ability levels. The final step is to assist the employer in making the necessary physical and managerial accommodations and in retraining the displaced workers for their new job activities.

Accommodations that may be necessary for job redesign include (a) altering existing facilities to make them accessible, (b) restructuring the job (rearranging tasks and task elements), (c) modifying work schedules (including break times), (d) reassigning existing workers to a vacant position, (e) modifying examinations, training materials, and supervision policies, (f) acquiring or modifying equipment or other devices, (g) developing job performance aids that ensure consistency of job performance to standards, (h) providing qualified readers or interpreters, (i) acquiring assistive technology devices, and (j) providing mentors or job coaches to assist individuals with special needs when necessary. Job placement personnel and employers can receive assistance in making job accommodation by contacting the Job Accommodation Network, a service of the President's Committee on Employment of People With Disabilities.

The Job Accommodation Network (JAN) is an international toll-free consulting service that provides information about job accommodations and the employability of people with functional limitations. The mission of JAN is to assist in the hiring, retraining, retention, or advancement of individuals with disabilities by providing accommodation information. Calls are answered by consultants who understand the functional limitations associated with disabilities and who have instant access to the most comprehensive and up-to-date information about accommodation methods, devices, and strategies. JAN preserves the confidentiality of communication between caller and consultant.

JAN helps employers hire, retain, and promote qualified employees with disabilities; reduce worker's compensation and other insurance costs; address issues pertaining to accessibility; and provide accommodation options and practical solutions. It helps rehabilitation professionals facilitate placement of clients through accommodation assistance; find local resources for workplace assessment; and discover resources for device fabrication and modification. It helps individuals with disabilities acquire accommodation information and discover other organizations, support groups, government agencies, and placement agencies.

Placement Team. The placement team must have an organizational structure with a number of players who work together cooperatively. Team members must be willing to move out of familiar roles, give up some control, provide resources, and devote time and energy to the placement process. There must be a game plan. For some learners from special populations, this plan is the IEP. For other learners from special populations, it is the ITP. For the team to be successful, it must have support from everybody involved.

Placement and follow-up services begin the day that learners enter a career and technical education program and conclude only after a learner is successfully employed and living independently. The placement and follow-up process must be a team effort with members selected from the entire school staff and supplemented with outside assistance from agencies and organizations.

Suggested team members and their responsibilities in the placement and follow-up process include the following:

1. Career and technical administrators–The success or failure of the placement and follow-up process depends greatly upon the efforts and cooperation of career and technical administrators. In addition to supporting the placement and follow-up process by supplying staff, supplies, and an operation budget, administrators should perform the following duties:

   - keep all teachers and school staff informed and involved concerning the purpose, goals, and activities of the program
   - assist in establishing a placement and follow-up advisory committee and insure placement is addressed by various craft or technical committees
   - provide release time for school staff who engage in placement program public relations activities and become involved in these activities when appropriate
   - initiate and maintain contact with employers who have hired learners from special populations
   - promote support for placement and follow-up program with other school administrators, community leaders, and special populations advocacy groups
   - work with state and federal agencies in administering the program
   - inform all school staff of their responsibilities and duties in the placement and follow-up process
   - utilize placement and follow-up data to make appropriate changes in the school's total program

2. Learner personnel specialists and counselors–It is essential that counselors and other learner personnel specialists work closely with placement team members in providing services for learners from special populations. Career counseling is viewed by many as the key in forging the connection between school and work. Yet, career guidance is one of the most neglected services provided today in American schools (U.S. Department of Education, 1992). Career counseling must involve the three areas of career development, personal counseling services, and assistance in placement. Counselors and school personnel specialists should perform the following duties:

   - participate in a schoolwide effort to provide learners with career development activities
   - obtain current information about the local job market and the types of jobs that career and technical education learners may enter after program completion
   - provide current, factual job placement information to career and technical education teachers, learners, and their parents so they can examine job possibilities
   - provide information to learners regarding the assistance they can receive from the school and community agencies to help them prepare for and obtain jobs

   - assist learners in making decisions about job alternatives related to their interests and capabilities
   - counsel learners regarding their work adjustment development in such areas as work attitudes, work habits, grooming and dress, and job performance
   - assist career and technical education teachers in making any modifications to their laboratory environments by serving on the assessment team
   - assist the job placement staff in preparing learner placement profiles and career portfolios
   - participate in follow-up visits to work sites where learners and former learners are employed
   - inform learners and their parents, as well as placement team members, concerning legislative mandates dealing with guidance and placement

3. Vocational assessment/evaluation personnel–Vocational assessment information is essential in order to help prospective career and technical education learners identify their areas of occupational interest and their capabilities. Vocational assessment personnel should perform the following duties as members of the placement team:

   - assist counselors and learner personnel specialists in determining the interests and capabilities of learners from special populations
   - provide the job placement staff with information about new employer contacts and leads about possible job openings
   - assist career and technical education teachers, transition personnel, and cooperative and work-based education coordinators in providing work adjustment training
   - assist career and technical education teachers in identifying work environment barriers as members of the barrier assessment team
   - assist placement team members in the identification of generalizable work skills and work skills identified as important by employers and professional and industrial organizations

4. Career and technical education instructors–Career and technical education instructors are in the placement business daily as they prepare their learners for employment. Through cooperative planning and joint effort with other placement team members, they can help learners from special populations complete their desired program and improve their chances for successful job placement. These teachers, along with transition personnel, interact daily with learners with special needs and usually know their interests, capabilities, and limitations. They maintain continuous contact with employers and are often called when job openings become available. They are familiar with job requirements in their technical area and can determine if the capabilities of learners with special needs are compatible. Career and technical education teachers should perform the following placement and follow-up duties:

- develop and maintain a good working relationship with all members of the placement and follow-up team
- assist the placement and follow-up staff in identifying potential employers
- assist the placement and follow-up specialist in analyzing identified jobs and developing job profiles
- maintain continuous contact with local employers and provide meaningful feedback to the placement team
- provide an orientation for all learners, stressing job placement as the ultimate goal of the instructional program and informing them of the placement services that are available to help them prepare for and obtain employment
- maintain an active advisory or technical committee and involve them in the placement and follow-up program
- provide basic skills and employability skills as well as technical skills in instructional programs
- maintain a laboratory environment similar to that found in industry
- encourage all learners to visit employers and observe what workers do as they perform their daily work activities
- arrange field trips to various industries and businesses to provide learners with firsthand information about jobs and job opportunities
- refer learners with special needs to other school staff for special guidance and supplementary services
- participate in career and technical and professional organizations to keep abreast of the changing nature of work in your teaching area
- refer learners to the placement and follow-up staff for part-time and full-time placement assistance
- work with special needs personnel, learners, and parents in developing the IEP/ITP for learners with disabilities and ITP for other learners from special populations
- assist learners in the development of career portfolios
- participate in follow-up visits to present and former learners who are involved in work-based training or in initial employment

5. Cooperative education/work-based and work-study coordinators–Cooperative education and work-based education coordinators can make important contributions to the job placement and follow-up program. Coordinators spend about one-half of their day working with employers and learner-employees at the place of employment. They are able to provide valuable information regarding employer contacts, job leads, and information about the nature of jobs in the community. In addition, these coordinators are experienced job placement specialists who continually try to develop jobs for their learners and match them with available jobs. Cooperative education and work-based education coordinators should perform the following duties:

- assist learners from special populations enrolled in programs in finding work-study placement
- provide information to job placement staff regarding employer contacts, job leads, and specific information about the nature of jobs in the community
- assist job placement staff in analyzing jobs and preparing job profiles
- assist job placement staff in promoting public relations for the placement program
- assist in providing training to job supervisors, job coaches, and mentors to make them more effective in working with learners with special needs

6. Transition personnel–Transition coordinators, support personnel, and specialists also play a key role in the job placement and follow-up effort of a career and technical education program. They provide instruction and support services for learners from special populations. They also work closely with career and technical education teachers to provide remedial and support instruction in a given technical area. Transition personnel should perform the following placement duties:

- work with learners with disabilities and other learners from special populations, their parents, and career and technical teachers in planning the IEP/ITP and ITP respectively
- assist career and technical education teachers and other placement team members in understanding the nature and needs of learners from special populations
- assist career and technical education teachers in providing appropriate instruction
- provide work adjustment skill training to learners
- assist career and technical education teachers in assessing classroom and laboratory environments to make suggestions for appropriate modifications for learners with disabilities
- assist career and technical education teachers in obtaining appropriate aids and devices to eliminate identified barriers
- participate in training sessions for job supervisors, job coaches, and work site mentors to make them more effective in working with individuals with special needs
- assist learners with the development of career portfolios
- participate in follow-up visits to work sites where individuals are placed

7. Job placement and follow-up staff–Placement and follow-up specialists also have specific duties to perform as placement team members, but their chief responsibility is to coordinate the entire placement and follow-up effort and to gain the assistance of all involved. These professionals "hit the streets" and talk placement wherever they go. They serve as liaisons between the school and the community and are directly involved with employers in matching the vocational competencies of learners from special populations with the personnel qualification needs of employers.

Job placement and follow-up staff may have a variety of different titles and perform a broad spectrum of duties or serve in a more narrow specialty area. For example, job development is one of the primary duties of job placement specialists but some school systems have created a job developer position in which a placement specialist reviews want-ads, calls on local businesses, attends job fairs, and informs learners of job opportunities in the area (Stern et al., 1994).

Another placement specialty area is the job coach or employment specialist. Job coaches are trained individuals employed by the school system, community agency, and sometimes by the employer to assist newly placed employees adjust to the work environment and become productive as soon as possible. Job coaches make regular on-site visits to employees, make phone calls, and use supervisor evaluation and employee progress reports to monitor work adjustment problems and provide needed services.

Test et al. (1988) noted that job coach duties fall under the two functions of job-site training and advocacy. Job-site training includes direct instruction on worker tasks along with a cadre of work adjustment skills such as interpersonal skills, social skills, and utilizing transportation systems. Advocacy involves interventions on behalf of the new employee and may include arranging transportation, counseling the employer and coworkers, assisting in altering job elements, and providing assistance in performing job tasks until they can be mastered by the individual.

Depending upon need, job coaches should be available at the work site on a daily basis until the new employee has made critical adjustments to the job and eventually fade services until they are no longer needed. If individuals are in need of supported services for an extended period of time, job coaches should work with agencies, advocacy groups, or employers to provide the ongoing assistance to help them maintain productive employment. See Figure 12-14.

A final example of a placement specialist is a paraprofessional "tracker." Trackers often (a) support career and technical education teachers on campus, (b) develop and teach some lessons, (c) evaluate learners' skills, (d) arrange field trips and job shadowing experiences, (e) contact and visit businesses to promote job development for learners with special needs, (f) arrange job interviews, (g) follow-up learners who are placed in employment, and (h) coordinate all facets of learner performance.

Job placement and follow-up staff should perform the following duties:

- develop and maintain a team-oriented job placement and follow-up program
- prepare for and conduct a continuous public relations program to promote the placement effort
- develop contacts and placement opportunities

- visit potential employers to initiate and promote learner placement
- work with employers in developing job profiles and, if possible, in redesigning jobs or developing jobs for learners with special needs
- establish and maintain a placement and follow-up advisory committee
- work with out-of-school agencies that provide special services to enhance the job placement and follow-up effort
- obtain data on learners and work with other placement team members in preparing learner job placement profiles
- provide career and technical education teachers and other placement team members with information related to the placement and follow-up of program completers
- coordinate preplacement training for those learners who have been referred
- provide placement and referral services to learners from special populations who are ready for placement
- follow up former learners from special populations who have been placed to smooth the transition between school and employment
- maintain records of all activities of the placement and follow-up program
- provide job coach and/or employment specialist services to newly employed individuals with special needs
- conduct continuous job development activities

8. Learners from special populations–Learners from special populations are at the very heart of the placement and follow-up process. Every activity that is carried on is directly or indirectly related to learner placement upon program completion. Since job placement is unique for each individual, each learner must be actively involved as a team member. Successful placement is not simply putting individuals from special populations to work, but rather it is placing learners in employment according to their capabilities and interests. Placement is successful only when individuals stay employed, not simply during the follow-up period when they are receiving time-limited supportive service. Learners from special populations can perform the following duties:

- participate in the development of the IEP/ITP
- become as informed as possible about entrance requirements and job requirements in the chosen area of interest by using printed materials and computerized occupational information systems
- visit employers and observe workers firsthand
- take advantage of all the services offered by the helping system to prepare for and enter employment
- learn self-directed job search skills
- volunteer for nonpaid work in the community to get work experience
- begin developing a career portfolio

- participate in career and technical student organization (CTSO) activities
- take advantage of opportunities to become involved in school-based enterprises, cooperative education, work-based programs, job shadowing, internships, and job tryouts
9. Advisory committees–Placement and follow-up advisory committees and career and technical advisory committees can provide services to the placement and follow-up effort. Advisory committee members should perform the following duties:
- provide information about job leads and employer contacts
- identify employers who have previously hired individuals from special populations
- promote the job placement of learners from special populations among colleagues, employers, and business associates
- assist in helping to remove attitudinal and physical barriers confronting job applicants with special needs
- become involved in the community to encourage entrepreneurship for learners with special needs
10. Agencies and special needs advocacy groups–There are a number of agencies, foundations, institutes, and special groups that can provide services for the placement effort. These agencies should be contacted to determine what services they can provide. They can often perform the following duties:
- provide suggestions for helping learners from special populations to make the transition from school-to-work
- provide job placement services when appropriate
- provide specific helping services in line with their respective programs
- assist in overcoming barriers to the employment of individuals from special populations.
- provide job leads
- assist in support services (time-limited and long-term) to employed individuals with special needs.

Follow-up Services. An important component of an effective job placement program is a timely, continuous follow-up of both the newly employed or rejected individual with special needs and the employer. Heal et al. (1988) reported that follow-up support is closely related to placement success. Initial follow-up visits help smooth the transition to regular employment for the successful placement candidate and help employers meet productivity demands. Immediate follow-up services provided to the rejected candidate can lead to the identification of problem areas and appropriate actions. Follow-up services help to assure that program completers do not disappear into the ranks of the labor market or unemployment rolls. Follow-up services to employers reassure them of the placement agency's commitment to achieving a satisfactory placement situation. Follow-up services should also assist newly employed individuals with transition to independent living and accessing community services and programs.

JOB COACHING STRATEGIES

To prepare to assist individuals from special populations at work sites, job coaches should do the following

- Visit the job site to begin a detailed analysis of the job tasks and routines (job analysis)
- Observe how current employees perform various tasks and routines
- Interview and get to know supervisors and coworkers
- Shadow workers at job site and have someone teach you routines and procedures for specific jobs
- Try out the job tasks that are not familiar so that they can be demonstrated to learners receiving coaching at the job site
- Document the amount of supervision necessary and/or available at the site for specific jobs
- Note the complexity of routines and the potential for using cues and other forms of coaching to teach and/or reinforce independent job performance
- Write detailed task analyses, job inventories, and associated instructional cues to prepare individuals with special needs for the job
- Identify appropriate job redesign methods and job modification strategies
- Identify training strategies and motivational strategies for specific individuals so that they can be utilized during coaching sessions at the work site
- Develop a training plan for the individual with special needs once an appropriate job site and job title have been identified
- Include employers, supervisors, coworkers, advocacy volunteers, and agency representatives in training sessions and long range planning as appropriate
- Make arrangements for the individual with special needs to have a comprehensive job site/job orientation. Specific information that should be provided might include company culture, dress code, jargon and technical terms, facility tour, rules and regulations of the employer, specific job procedures, and where to go for assistance
- Be available to coach and assist the individual with special needs at the job site when necessary
- Use constructive feedback during coaching sessions
- Serve as a conduit between employers, supervisors, coworkers, and the individual with special needs
- Utilize behavior modification techniques as necessary at the job site
- Document learner progress at the job using the training plan for direction
- Introduce the individual with special needs to agencies and advocacy groups in the community that can be called upon for assistance if job upgrading or retraining becomes necessary

Figure 12-14. Job coaching strategies that can assist learners from special populations who are placed at work sites.

Follow-up services must be provided simultaneously to both the newly placed individuals with special needs and to the employer. Information must be obtained from employees who have special needs to determine their adjustment to the work environment. Following are some of the questions that should be asked of these employees:

- Are you performing the work tasks at the rate and quality expected by your employer?
- Have you encountered any barriers caused by the facilities, equipment, or lack of training?
- Have you encountered any difficulties in getting along with your supervisor or fellow workers?
- What do you like best about your job?
- What do you like least about your job?
- Are you experiencing any problems in getting to work on time?
- Are you experiencing any problems in understanding your work assignments or in communicating with others?
- Are you experiencing any problems in independent living?

It is just as important to provide follow-up services to the employer as to the new employee. Employers who have hired individuals with special needs for the first time often feel uneasy in supervising them. They often have misconceptions about these individuals that sometimes influence their behavior toward them in an adverse way. An open discussion of any identified problems between employee and employer can help to keep such problems from reaching a level that could result in early termination of employment.

Follow-up specialists should obtain information from employers about the level of work performance and adjustment of new employees from special populations. In collecting information from employers, the following questions can be asked:

- Is the new employee performing job tasks at the rate and quality level that you expect of other employees?
- Is the employee punctual in getting to work and returning from breaks?
- Do you feel the employee understands the job requirements?
- Can you communicate clearly with the new employee?
- Is the employee having any trouble using the machinery or equipment or moving about in the work environment?
- Does the employee interact successfully with his direct supervisor and with fellow workers?
- Have you assigned a fellow worker to help the new employee make the transition to work?
- What do you like best about the employee?
- What do you like least about the employee?
- Have any problems surfaced that you think the placement and follow-up team can help overcome?
- Have you noticed any area(s) in which the employee seems to lack training?

Typically, follow-up services are provided at the end of the first day of employment and weekly for the first month.

After this critical period of employment, follow-up services are provided monthly for six months and annually thereafter. In the case of individuals from special populations who need continuous support services to maintain employment, school follow-up personnel (job coach or mentor) will need to assist the employer in providing the needed support services and/or assist in obtaining these services from helping agencies.

Follow-up procedures are an integral part of any placement program. The following list is an example of a procedure plan:

1. Near the end of the first day of employment, visit with the new employee and employer. Emphasize the positive achievements during the first workday but also try to identify any problem areas and take measures to resolve them.
2. At the end of the first week, and more often as needed, contact the new employee and employer by phone or personal visit to obtain responses from both parties to the questions presented earlier. Counsel the employee and employer if necessary to work out any problems that have occurred.
3. During the latter part of the second week of employment, visit the company and talk with both the new employee and employer. Observe firsthand the employee's job performance and recommend any required modifications. Obtain additional information about job satisfaction and worker adjustment from both parties.
4. At the end of the third week, repeat the procedures described in number three.
5. Visit the employer at the end of the first month of employment to assess the employee's progress on the job. Try to determine if the employer is satisfied with the employee's work performance and adjustment to work. Following the visit to the employer, meet with the employee and obtain similar information. Counsel the employee on the basis of information received from both parties.
6. At the end of the second month, visit the company again to observe job performance and to obtain information from the employee and the employer regarding job satisfaction and work adjustment.
7. At the end of the third through the ninth month of employment, make contact with the employee and employer by phone or visit the job site to monitor progress on the job and to recommend any required modifications.
8. At the end of one year and annually thereafter, make contact with the employee and employer by phone, mail-in postcard or survey form, or by personal visit to obtain summary information about the placement.

Once a follow-up plan has been developed, it is essential that this plan be discussed with both the employee and the employer. Learners from special populations need to know that follow-up services are available to help them make adjustments to the work environment. Maintaining contacts with employers assures the employers that services are available to help resolve any potential problems that may arise during the early stages of employment.

Postsecondary Education

Transition systems are designed to provide all youth with access to a broad range of opportunities after their secondary education is completed. Options can include direct entry into the workforce or enrollment in a postsecondary institution. These postsecondary institutions include career, technical, two-year colleges, and four-year colleges or universities, and all can take active roles in supporting the transitioning of learners to successful paths after high school. Postsecondary institutions offer a wealth of research and applied knowledge and a variety of other resources to transition learners and to assist high schools when designing education and career preparation systems.

Three-quarters of America's high school learners end up in the workforce without baccalaureate degrees. Many of these learners leave high school with poor academic skills, narrow or nonexistent work preparation, and little understanding of how they fit into the adult world. By contrast, in most other industrialized countries young people have clear systems that connect their schooling to a range of postsecondary work and learning options. Our lack of such a system has harmful effects for business competitiveness, school effectiveness, and learners' future options and incomes.

The U.S. Department of Education (2001) disclosed the following information about postsecondary education:

- Education is the keystone to continuing the success for both individuals and society at large. Increasingly, in the information age, postsecondary education is a necessity. Yet, the value of a postsecondary education goes beyond mere economics. As the problems and questions society faces become more complicated and complex, postsecondary education prepares citizens to be thoughtful participants in decisions and debates, passes on the best of our heritage, and helps every new American discover what it means to be a citizen in this country. It has always done this. If it is to continue to do so, it must adapt to the rapid pace of change facing all segments of society.
- America's universities, two- and four-year colleges, community colleges, technical schools, and other postsecondary institutions face numerous other challenges in adjusting to the changing environment. Increased enrollment, assessment and outcome questions, financial and access issues, technological advances, and international developments are all changing the education landscape rapidly.
- In the fall of 2000, approximately 15.1 million learners enrolled at postsecondary institutions. More than 40% of these learners are enrolled part-time, and a similar proportion is older than 24 years of age, This fall enrollment figure, which is substantially less than year-round, is projected to reach 17.5 million by 2010. Additionally, more Americans are taking adult courses and certificate programs. In 1998, 50% of adults participated in formal learning.
- Unfortunately, about one-third of learners who enter college or technical school drop out before they earn a certificate or degree. The problem is acute among minorities: 29% to 31% of African-Americans and Hispanics drop out of college in their first year compared to 18% of whites. All Americans deserve access to postsecondary education, and the message must be clear that the expectation is that everyone will finish.

The National Alliance of Business (2001) provided an overview of the diversity of postsecondary populations of the future and the necessity for changes in education:

- Today's jobs demand more education and training than in the past. Professions that once hired employees with high school diplomas now require them to possess more education. As a result, college enrollment is growing rapidly. College attendance for recent high school graduates is about 66%.
- If trends continue, up to 75% of new high school graduates in 2010 will enroll in some type of postsecondary education. These trends translate into significant challenges for the education system.
- All learners must experience a rich K–12 curriculum and must achieve high standards and meet high expectations. They must be able to demonstrate their readiness for higher education. Standards and expectations must be applied across a student body that is growing more culturally and ethnically and is socially diverse in both K–12 and higher education.
- Higher education institutions, therefore, need to help prepare diverse entrants. They must seize the opportunity, as they have before, of educating learners for a world of accelerating changes and new job realities. The importance of a solid K–12 education to ensure success in higher education has never been greater.
- The nation's population is astonishingly young and diverse. There are 73.2 million children under age 18, a statistic very evident in today's crowded K–12 schools. In 2008, the largest group of high school seniors in U.S. history will graduate. By 2015, the college-age population—made up of 18- to 24-year-olds already born by 1998—is projected to grow by 4.3 million to 31 million. Of these, 16 million are expected to enroll in postsecondary education, up from 13 million now—a 20% enrollment increase.
- The college-age population will be radically different in terms of race, ethnicity, and readiness for higher education. College-age racial and ethnic minorities will increase by 40%, to 3.5 million.
- During the next decade, colleges and universities will have to provide quality education to a larger pool of learners, many of whom are not adequately prepared

for higher education and will need stronger academic support than most colleges have given in the past.

• Reforms are needed to help learners before they even get to college. Learners who might enroll in postsecondary institutions by 2015 have not yet entered the K–12 education system. Based on promising trends in many states and local districts, it will take systemic reforms, an emphasis on quality teaching, and targeted interventions to significantly close the educational gap between minority and majority learners.

• The business community clearly has a role to play in bringing together state policymakers and higher education leaders to address the demographic and educational reform implications on postsecondary education. Specifically, business can convince states and higher education that preparing for the coming influx of college-age learners is an urgent national priority; help states and higher education institutions improve the quality of higher education using strategies such as high standards, assessments and accountability; and bring business principles and models of effectiveness and efficiency to bear on higher education.

As the nature of the nation's workforce continues to change rapidly because of technological developments, demographic shifts of the population, and increased competition in international markets, there will be a big demand to train and retrain adults for new jobs. Postsecondary institutions such as baccalaureate conferring institutions, community and junior colleges, technical schools, and postsecondary area vocational schools can prepare workers to meet the changing employment needs of our nation. It is reasonable to expect that competition for rewarding jobs will increase in the future, putting individuals from special populations at a greater disadvantage than ever before. One of the important goals of postsecondary institutions must be to provide learners from special populations with a sound educational experience, accompanied with appropriate transition services so that they can compete with others for satisfying jobs.

The National Council on Disability (2000) reported that

1. Data about participation rates among youth and young adults with disabilities in postsecondary education have been uneven. Youth and young adults with disabilities have been less likely than their peers in the general population to participate in postsecondary education. However, the percentage of all freshmen entering college who reported disabilities quadrupled between 1978 and 1991—from 2.2 % to 8.8%. The Department of Education data suggested that, among youth with disabilities, 16.5 % enrolled in academic postsecondary programs while 14.7 % enrolled in vocational postsecondary programs within 3 years after graduating from high school.

2. The National Center for Education Statistics (NCES) conducted a survey with 21,000 college learners the 1995–96 academic year. Of these, 6% reported having a disability. Among college learners with disabilities, 29% had a learning disability, 23% had an orthopedic disability, 16% had a noncorrectable vision impairment, 16% were deaf or hard-of-hearing, and 3% had a speech impairment. Learners with disabilities, when compared to nondisabled learners, were more likely to be male, older, non-Hispanic white, and to be enrolled in subbaccalaureate institutions, mostly public two-year colleges. They were less likely to have taken advanced placement courses in high school and more likely to be in remedial mathematics and English courses. In addition, as a group, they tended to have a lower high school grade point average and average SAT scores than learners without disabilities.

3. In a more recent study, the HEALTH Resource Center published its data about freshmen college learners with disabilities. One in 11 first-time, full-time freshmen entering college in 1998 reported a disability. This translates to about 9% of the total, or about 154,520 learners who reported disabilities described as hearing, speech, orthopedic, learning, health-related, partially sighted or blind, or other conditions. According to the published data, there were some major differences between learners who did and did not report disabilities. Among the findings reported in 1998 by freshmen with disabilities were that they were more likely than their peers to

• be male;

• be 20 years or older;

• come from families with slightly lower median incomes;

• have earned Cs and Ds in high school;

• have not met or exceeded the recommended years of high school study in math, foreign languages, or biological and physical sciences;

• have spent more time between high school graduation and entry to college;

• be attending two-year colleges;

• predict that they would need extra time to complete their educational goals;

• aspire toward career/technical or associate's degrees rather than bachelor' s or master's degrees; and

• rate themselves lower in measures of self-esteem, emotional health, and academic or physical ability.

The National Center for Education Statistics (1999) collected and analyzed data from two-year and four-year postsecondary education institutions regarding learners with disabilities enrolled in their programs. The results indicated that almost all (98%) of the institutions that enrolled learners with disabilities in 1996–97 or 1997–98 had provided at least one support service or accommodation to learners with disabilities. Most institutions (88%) had provided alternative exam formats or additional time, and 77% provided tutors to assist with ongoing course work. Readers, classroom note takers, or scribes were provided by 69% of the institutions, and registration assistance or priority class registration was provided by 62%. Institutions also frequently provided adaptive equipment or technology, such as assistive listening devices or talking computers (58%) and textbooks on tape (55%). Sign language interpreters/translators were provided by 45% of the institutions, and course substations or waivers by 42%. Various other support services were provided by one-third or fewer of the institutions.

The center also found that, in general, public two-year and four-year institutions were more likely than private two-year and four-year institutions to have provided a service or accommodation, and medium and large institutions were more likely than small institutions to have provided a service or accommodation. Large institutions were also more likely than medium institutions to have provided many of the services (The National Center for Education Statistics, 1999).

Day and Edwards (1996) identified several reasons for the increase in the number of learners with disabilities entering postsecondary institutions:

- The passage of Section 504 of the Rehabilitation Act of 1973 mandated accessibility to postsecondary education for learners with disabilities and required postsecondary institutions to provide "auxiliary aids to learners with disabilities."
- Legislation mandated special education programs and services for elementary and secondary learners with disabilities; as a result, more of these learners are completing high school and view attending college as the next step.
- Many learners, as a result of being placed in a least restrictive environment, have taken the prerequisite academic course work for college entrance requirements.
- Learners with disabilities have become increasingly attractive to college admission officers as a viable learner market.
- Advocacy groups and postsecondary guidebooks have made these learners aware of both their need and their rights in regard to college options.
- The increased availability of computers and other compensatory technology has resulted in greater learner independence in a college setting.

Examples of services that may be needed for individuals from special populations as they participate in postsecondary programs include the following:

Special Admission Criteria
- foreign language waiver
- interview
- class rank or transcript analysis
- placement test time extended
- determination of reasonable accommodations
- special orientation accommodations
- letter of recommendation from learning disability specialist
- admission on probation status
- performance contract

Program Modifications
- part-time schedule or modified course allowance
- longer time to complete program
- ability to repeat classes without penalty
- waiver of language requirements
- late course withdrawal without penalty
- priority registration
- additional time to complete courses
- course substitution

Instructional Accommodations
- note taking modification or note takers provided
- tape recorded lectures and books
- typing or word processing service
- test and testing accommodations
- assistive technology
- listening aids
- speech synthesis system
- speech recognition system
- proofreading service
- syllabus available before class begins
- lecture outline
- large print

Almost all (95%) of the institutions that enrolled learners with disabilities in 1996–97 or 1997–98 provided at least one kind of educational material or activity for faculty and staff designed to assist them in working with learners with disabilities. Most of these institutions (92%) provided one-on-one discussions with faculty and staff who requested information and assistance, 63% provided workshops and presentations to faculty groups, 62% had information resources available for faculty and staff use, 41% had a faculty/staff handbook, and 32% did annual mailings to faculty and staff (National Center for Educational Statistics, 1999). See Figure 12-15.

One successful model of postsecondary articulation is tech-prep programs. Tech-prep education is a four-year planned sequence of study for a technical field, beginning in the junior year of high school. The sequence extends through two years of postsecondary career and technical education or an apprenticeship program of at least two years following secondary instruction and culminates in a certificate or associate's degree. See Figure 12-16.

Tech-prep requires a formal and program-specific articulation agreement between the secondary and postsecondary institutions involved. An articulation agreement is a formal mechanism by which secondary and postsecondary institutions commit to jointly develop and implement tech-prep curricula and instruction. Tech-prep is made available to all secondary learners—those preparing for college, those who have elected career and technical training, and those in the so-called general track. Tech-prep prepares learners for direct entry into the workplace as technically skilled employees or for further education leading to baccalaureate and advanced degrees.

QUESTIONS TO ASK A POSTSECONDARY INSTITUTION – GUIDELINES FOR INDIVIDUALS WITH DISABILITIES

1. What are the college's admissions requirements?
2. Are ACT and/or SAT scores required? If so, what minimum score is required for admission?
3. What grade point average is needed?
4. What class rank is needed?
5. Are letters of recommendation required?
6. Is an entrance exam offered with testing accommodations?
7. Are there any special admissions programs such as EOP/HEOP athletics, special talents, or a program for non-high school graduates?
8. Where is the Disabled Student Services office on campus?
9. How is the office staffed? Full-time? Part-time? Are there evening hours?
10. What kind of services are available through the Disabled Student Services office?
11. How are services obtained?
12. How are faculty told about accommodations?
13. Are services limited to students with disabilities or for all students?
14. What paperwork or proof is required to prove a disability and to whom should it be given? Who has access to this paperwork?
15. Is there help available for choosing courses and making schedules?
16. Who does academic advisement?
17. Is there an orientation for new students?
18. Is there an orientation for new students with disabilities?
19. Who supervises accommodated tests? Student Disability Services office? Faculty member? Testing center?
20. Is there a summer preparation program? When is it?
21. Is there a disabled student group on campus? How do I get in touch with it?
22. Who is the college's 504 coordinator? What is the grievance process?
23. Is tutoring available? Who tutors? Professionals? Peer tutors? Is tutoring available in small groups? Specific subjects? General study skills for all students? Specifically for students with disabilities? Is there a charge for tutoring?
24. How are note takers and readers made available, selected, or arranged?
25. Are sign language interpreters available? How are they arranged?
26. Is there a TDD (telephone device for the deaf) on campus? What is the number? Where is it located?
27. Who arranges for taping of books or ordering of recorded books?
28. Who arranges for tape recording of classes?
29. What are the alternative testing arrangements?
30. How accessible are the classrooms, labs, buildings, etc?
31. What is the college policy for waiving graduation requirements or arranging substitute courses?
32. What adaptive equipment is available for student use?
33. What is the extent of use of computers and where are they?
34. Are there any special adaptive features on the computers?
35. What word processing programs are available?
36. How does one make special room arrangements for resident students?
37. Are personal attendants available on campus? If yes, how are they contacted?
38. What are the rules about equipment and electrical use?
39. Are there physically accessible residence halls including toilet and bathing facilities?
40. Are buildings equipped with auditory fire alarms?
41. Where is the parking for those with disability permits?
42. Are there signs showing the accessible entrances to buildings and elevators? Is there a snow removal policy as it relates to mobility routes?
43. Is there personal counseling available?
44. Is there a written policy regarding disability services?

Adapted from: Burgstahler, S. (1994). *Effective College Planning – Transition.* Seattle, WA: University of Washington.

Figure 12-15. Relevant questions relating to learners with disabilities who are entering postsecondary institutions.

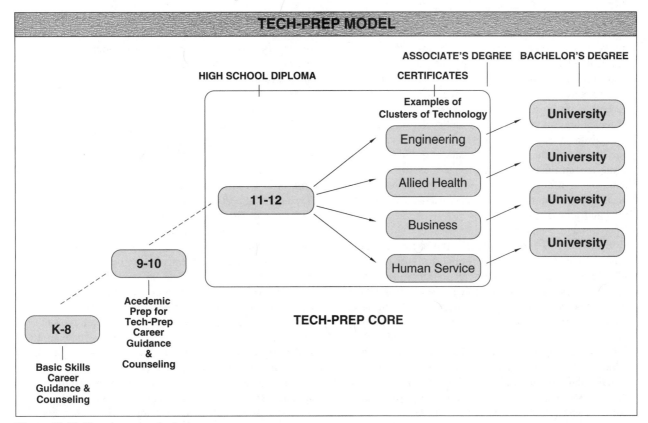

Figure 12-16. The elements of a tech-prep program.

COMPONENTS OF EFFECTIVE TRANSITION SYSTEMS

There are a variety of components of effective transition systems to help learners through the transition process. See Figure 12-17.

Career Development

Learners, parents, government, and the business community have been telling schools for a long time that they are dissatisfied that learners are inadequately trained for the high-tech jobs of today and tomorrow, or for the reality of repeated career change. There is also strong social pressure for greater equity in career opportunity. More females, visible minorities, children of economically disadvantaged parents, and physically challenged learners are expected to be able to acquire occupations that are associated with higher earning power, more security and prestige, and higher job satisfaction.

Historically, the place of career education in the educational agenda has not been clear. No shared belief exists as to how schools ought to prepare learners for adult life. The patchwork of programs such as transition-to-work, technological education, employability skills, and cooperative education are important, but they do not adequately address the career development needs of learners.

The new vision is that schools will make a significant contribution towards seeing that the future labor force is well prepared for adult and working life, is able to make informed career decisions, is capable of managing successful career transitions, and is committed to lifelong personal development, education, and training. This means that schools must act deliberately to ensure that all learners have access to current and accurate information about careers. Teachers must also understand the importance of providing learners with learning experiences outside of the school walls and must understand that teaching learners decision-making strategies is crucial to helping them make successful transitions to work, further education, and training.

The following should be the outcomes of the career development process:

• Self-awareness–Learners will be able to analyze changing personal attitudes, values, and abilities and explain how they relate to a range of choices; describe a personal accomplishment and specify the skills that were used in this achievement; recognize and develop ways of dealing with stereotyping, discrimination, and racism; develop and apply skills for studying, organizing, managing time, planning, researching, accessing school and community resources, and goal setting; and explain the interrelationship of personal responsibility, good work habits, and career opportunities.

• Opportunity awareness–Learners will be able to explain basic concepts about the economy and work, such as market forces, entrepreneurship, responsibilities, commitments of employers and employees, and the role of trade unions; identify types and levels of work performed across a broad range of occupations and in a variety of settings; describe the present and future role of technology in the workplace and society as a whole; analyze the value of learning as a result of visits to a variety of community settings and work sites; demonstrate the attitudes necessary for success in work and learning; and describe how gender role stereotyping, bias, and discrimination limit career choices, opportunity and achievement.

• Decision and transition learning–Learners will also be able to identify the knowledge and skills taught in school subjects that are transferable to work, community, family, and leisure activities; describe a range of opportunities for secondary and postsecondary education and training in both the immediate and long term, (and also learn how to gain access to these opportunities and where they may lead); identify ways of making decisions and apply the knowledge to specific life situations; develop an action plan to accomplish occupational, educational, leisure, and/or family goals; and develop skills for making transitions and for dealing with unexpected situations (Burke, 1993).

Career awareness activities can begin as early as kindergarten and continue through elementary school and can involve guest classroom lectures of field trips to work sites to expose young people to a variety of career and occupational options. In upper elementary and junior high school, career development programs can turn more toward career exploration activities in which learners examine specific careers more closely. In this stage, learners can participate in job shadowing or mentoring experiences with workers or work on classroom projects that apply academic concepts to the careers they are examining. In high school, learners can participate in activities that expose them to careers, including work-based learning experiences that focus on a specific job or occupation. Through these experiences, young people not only learn about a variety of careers and occupations, but they can also begin to identify what skills are required to succeed in these areas and can start making informed career decisions.

Career development programs can be successful only if up-to-date career and occupational labor market information is provided regularly. Labor market information includes information on the jobs and occupations available both within and outside of a learner's community, advantages and disadvantages of specific jobs and careers, and the growth potential of specific occupations. It is in this area that the participation of businesses, organized labor, and community organizations is especially important as they are the partners who are best equipped to provide accurate and up-to-date labor information.

Employers and representatives from organized labor can work directly with administrators and classroom teachers to ensure that academic course work and curricula are providing young people with the information required to make informed career decisions and can assist counselors in building career development programs within a school-to-work system. Comprehensive labor market information should also cover a wide range of occupational areas in the local, state and national labor market. This can help young people recognize that there are many jobs and career opportunities for them outside of their local economy and can provide learners a chance to explore this wider range of options.

Career development programs should also work to help young people develop individualized education programs and career plans. These plans can serve as the centerpiece of a career development program by setting educational and career goals for youth and outlining the academic and occupational experiences required to meet these goals. In addition, these plans are most effective when they address both the strengths and weaknesses of youth and when they

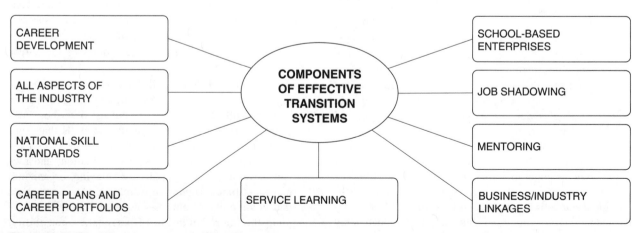

Figure 12-17. The different components of transition systems.

are evaluated and updated on a regular basis. This allows young people to develop strategies to overcome the obstacles they face in school and the workplace as well as build on their existing strengths, goals, classes, work experiences, extracurricular activities, significant accomplishments, etc. These programs and plans are important organizational tools that can be used as a "road map" to document the young person's career development.

Career development programs can greatly benefit from a centralized career center and the use of career software and technology. Career centers emphasize the importance of career development and allow career and guidance counselors to better coordinate counseling and training programs and services. For example, career centers can be used to perform career and skill assessments, operate in-service training activities, conduct career counseling and planning sessions, house labor market and postsecondary education information, and host job and career fairs.

Computerized career information systems help individuals explore career options and opportunities and relate personal characteristics (such as interests, aptitudes, and goals) to job and career possibilities. These systems contain a wealth of information on occupations and related education and training programs such as employment outlook, earning levels, working conditions, educational requirements, admissions policies, financial aid, etc. These systems are widely used at public schools, job service offices, military bases, libraries, colleges, state employment agencies, and many other sites. Access to computerized information systems provides learners with a comprehensive yet simplified method of obtaining information about any and all careers that are appropriate to their personal goals.

Effective career development programs work best when they follow a sequence of coordinated and comprehensive activities beginning in the early grades. This type of programming allows for young people to obtain continuous exposure to career options, understand the skill levels and education required for these occupations, and determine their prospects in a variety of career paths. Starting early allows for a developmental approach to career development, so career awareness, career exploration, and career planning and decision making can occur during the progression from elementary school through postsecondary education. Most career development processes are delivered in phases. See Figure 12-18.

One-stop career centers and transition programs have spurred demand for career development facilitators (CDFs). Working under the supervision of a qualified career counselor, a CDF may serve as a career group facilitator, job search trainer, career resource center coordinator, career coach, career development case manager, intake interviewer, occupational and labor market information resource person, human resource career development coordinator, employment/placement specialist, or workforce development staff person. Career development facilitators undergo training in the following competencies: helping skills, training clients and peers, program management/implementation, promotion and public relations, technology, and supervision.

The career coach, another growing specialty, assists clients in identifying core values, sense of purpose, and vision and in turning vision into a plan for life/career action. Many business professional are being "telecoached"—getting career assistance from virtual coaches through e-mail and telephone. The International Coaching Federation has established a voluntary credentialing program for coaches that offers an International Job and Career Transition Coach Certification program (Kerka, 2001).

The Partnership for Academic and Career Education (1993) provided 50 ways to increase learners' understanding of careers:

1. Establish an information resource center as part of the guidance office, with videos, brochures, and career software programs.
2. Sponsor a Career Day; invite area business people to bring handouts, do demonstrations, or show sample materials that people use in various jobs at their companies.
3. Sponsor field trips or site visits to an area business, industry, health care facility, or social service agency. (If possible, try to include small businesses as well.)
4. Assign class projects where learners "shadow" a businessperson employed in an area of interest.
5. Sponsor a "Parent Workday" where learners go to work with one of their parents; follow up with a class assignment or discussion on the kinds of jobs held by the parents.
6. Have speakers from the school's business partner or other area companies address classes, clubs, or other learner groups.
7. Design career games, puzzles, or other career-related activities (or use commercially-prepared games in classroom assignments).
8. Establish a mentoring program with an area business partner and have each learner complete a semester or yearlong project related to the career areas of the mentors.
9. Have learners research local careers by examining the classified section of the newspaper and conduct a class exercise using information gathered from different job ads. For example, have learners write four job descriptions and do reports on what is involved in the jobs, or, have learners rewrite the job descriptions to make them clearer after doing research on the careers.
10. Have learners write for free career brochures available from professional associations, such as the Tooling & Machining Association, and compile the results for a classroom or guidance office resource. Directories of professional associations are available from most public libraries and technical college libraries.

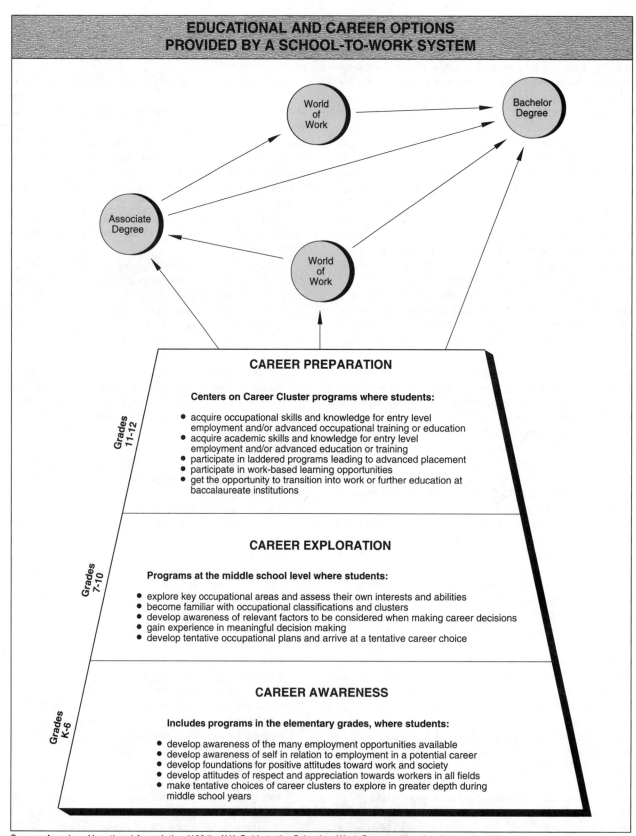

**EDUCATIONAL AND CAREER OPTIONS
PROVIDED BY A SCHOOL-TO-WORK SYSTEM**

World of Work

Bachelor Degree

Associate Degree

World of Work

CAREER PREPARATION

Grades 11-12

Centers on Career Cluster programs where students:

- acquire occupational skills and knowledge for entry level employment and/or advanced occupational training or education
- acquire academic skills and knowledge for entry level employment and/or advanced education or training
- participate in laddered programs leading to advanced placement
- participate in work-based learning opportunities
- get the opportunity to transition into work or further education at baccalaureate institutions

CAREER EXPLORATION

Grades 7-10

Programs at the middle school level where students:

- explore key occupational areas and assess their own interests and abilities
- become familiar with occupational classifications and clusters
- develop awareness of relevant factors to be considered when making career decisions
- gain experience in meaningful decision making
- develop tentative occupational plans and arrive at a tentative career choice

CAREER AWARENESS

Grades K-6

Includes programs in the elementary grades, where students:

- develop awareness of the many employment opportunities available
- develop awareness of self in relation to employment in a potential career
- develop foundations for positive attitudes toward work and society
- develop attitudes of respect and appreciation towards workers in all fields
- make tentative choices of career clusters to explore in greater depth during middle school years

Source: American Vocational Association (1994). *AVA Guide to the School-to-Work Opportunities Act.* Alexandria, VA.

Figure 12-18. An overview of a career development process delivered through three phases.

11. Arrange tours of area career centers, two-year colleges, and/or four-year colleges. Have learners ask specific questions about the career fields related to the specific departments that they visit.

12. Conduct role-playing simulations in which learners act out the role of career advisors to their peers.

13. Conduct interactive career exploration activities with a panel of businesspersons.

14. Encourage learners to take occupational courses at the high schools or career centers.

15. Ask school alumni to make presentations to classes or learner groups.

16. Design a bulletin board featuring one or more careers or assign teams of learners to design a new career bulletin board every month.

17. Have learners write to different companies in their area and request career brochures to be kept in a binder as a classroom resource.

18. Obtain copies of professional or technical journals. Have learners read selected articles and report on career-related aspects of their assigned articles.

19. In collaboration with a businessperson, develop applications for various academic concepts using career-related examples from the company.

20. Develop a career newsletter or include a section on careers in an existing high school newsletter or publication.

21. Using a career software program, develop a career data bank folder to be maintained by learners.

22. Conduct a "problem bucket" exercise in which learners anonymously contribute concerns or fears about choosing a career, entering a career in a specific field such as electronics, or continuing their education after high school. Conduct a class discussion to address common fears and concerns.

23. Develop a "tips sheet" to help learners consider career interests when choosing part-time employment In addition, delineate how they could expand their career awareness through their current part-time employment.

24. Sponsor a learner summer internship program with area businesses.

25. Encourage learners to volunteer with hospitals or social/community agencies in order to explore career fields in the health and human services area.

26. Have career materials available in the library, or feature new materials in the library for a specified period of time before they are transferred to the guidance office.

27. Load career exploration software on PCs in computer classroom or in open computer labs.

28. Have the guidance office or library subscribe to career magazines such as *Career Opportunities News.*

29. In high school academics or occupational classes, have learners conduct research on careers of interest and then have them design information sheets or brochures for middle school learners.

30. Have learners interview someone from the school's business partner about the position the person holds and how it relates to the product or service offered by the company. Then, have the learner write an article for a class or school publication (or have the learner submit the article to the company newsletter as a feature on one of their employees).

31. Have teams of learners develop "career spots" with one learner interviewing someone in a career field of interest while another learner videotapes the interview. Career spots could be broadcast during Career Awareness Week.

32. As a class activity, have learners list careers not typically held by males and careers not typically held by females. Have them identify persons not traditionally employed in these fields and invite them to speak to the class.

33. Have learners identify unusual career fields and ask them to guess what the salary and educational requirements might be for these areas. Then, have learners conduct research and compare what they learned to what they originally had thought about these careers.

34. Ask each learner to write down two careers of interest. Identify the top two or three choices. As a class project, have learners research these careers, identifying five positive and five negative aspects of each career.

35. Assign learners into groups of two and have one play the role of peer career counselor for the other. After the learners identify and discuss current career plans, interests, and goals, reverse the roles. Let the class discuss the results.

36. Have learners identify a product made in their geographic area. Have them identify all the jobs involved in converting this product from raw materials into a finished good.

37. Have learners read a series of futuristic articles and ask them to project the types of careers required to support the changes predicted in the articles. For example, how would a cashless society, in which people used only credit cards, affect careers in the banking industry?

38. Have learners identify a product developed 100 years ago and still used today. Then, have them trace this product's growth and development in terms of careers and technology.

39. Conduct a "career charades" game for elementary or middle school learners. Have high school learners use costumes or props to reflect a career area. Be sure to select careers that are not immediately obvious (e.g., police officer) or that are not too obscure for young children (e.g., surface process mount technician). Have younger learners ask questions to try and identify each career area.

40. Have learners choose a prime time drama or situation comedy to watch. Ask learners to identify the professions of the four main characters. Discuss these careers and possible stereotypes and have them compare television to reality.

41. Have learners interview a businessperson who works in a totally different career field from the one in which that person started. Ask learners to determine why the person changed fields and what, if anything, the person would do differently in hindsight. Assign written or oral reports based on the interview project.

42. Assign learners to identify career areas in which they are interested and to design and use persuasive advertising materials in order to convince others of the value of a particular career.

43. Divide learners into groups. Assign each group a "glamour career" to research (e.g., football player, actor, lawyer, or model). Since each team will already know the positive side of their assigned career, ask them to identify the negative aspects of the career. Compare results from each group and lead a classroom discussion about their results. Help learners realize that it's important to understand both positive and negative aspects of potential careers.

44. Divide learners into groups and ask them to identify everything that they would hate in a job. Ask teams to identify realistic ways of avoiding the things they would not like in a job or career field.

45. Have learners develop a mock company that would produce a specific product. Ask them to identify and research all the jobs required to produce that product, obtaining information from a local company that produces a similar product.

46. Ask learners to watch a movie video of their choice and identify five movie-related jobs by watching the credits at the end of the movie. Have learners do research on these careers for a written or oral project.

47. Ask learners to watch one of the local news shows and identify one or two career fields (other than reporter) associated with producing the news show. Have learners do research on those careers, or conduct a site visit to the television studio so that learners can learn more about these fields.

48. For a class or club project, let two-person teams of learners identify and interview a businessperson employed in a position or career field that the learners find interesting. Have each team trace all the jobs that the person has held, leading up to the individual's current position. Let the group of learners discuss their findings and conclusions.

49. Have teams of learners identify all the jobs or career fields associated with operating the school, the district, or other agencies that work closely with the school system. Let the class discuss the findings of each team.

50. Ask learners to list two career fields that they are considering. Then ask learners to list two hobbies or outside activities that they enjoy. Assign learners to groups for information sharing. Ask them to examine whether or not a relationship exists between their career interests and their outside interests. Have each group discuss whether there should be a relationship between the two or how a vocation and an avocation can be combined.

All Aspects of the Industry

The major changes in the American workplace environment have profound implications for education systems. Transition systems emphasize the importance of an all aspects of the industry (AAI) approach to learning. This approach integrates career and technical and academic education for the purpose of producing well-rounded individuals prepared to continue learning in either postsecondary institutions or the workplace. All career-related opportunities should provide for exploration of and experiences in all aspects of the industry or industry sector a learner is preparing to enter, including planning, management, finances, technical and production skills, underlying principles of technology, labor and community issues, health and safety issues, and environmental issues. This helps learners gain a better understanding of an industry as a whole and the many roles they can play in it (National School-to-Work Office, September 1997). See Figure 12-19.

The AAI approach improves learners' chances for success in the workplace. As employees, learners trained to perform a variety of functions across an industry can adapt when advances in technology make job-specific skills obsolete. Because they have learned how to learn, these individuals are more open to the idea of continual development throughout their working lives. Armed with a variety of skills and an understanding of how these skills can be applied throughout an industry or transferred to other industries, youth with basic experiences in all aspects of an industry are better informed to make initial career choices and may have more options throughout their careers.

The nine aspects of an industry are identified below with suggested competencies for learners:

Planning
- Describe why industries respond to customer wants and expectations.
- List differences in how companies deliver products versus services.
- Describe ways a worker can influence company decision making.
- Identify benefits in anticipating technology and market trend changes.
- Identify an example of how regulatory laws can impact how a business operates.
- Identify an example of how a political organization can impact how a company operates.

Management
- Identify key components of a company's mission statement.

- Identify how a corporate chain of command works.
- Describe the significance of a company's corporate culture.
- Describe how a company organizes its departments.
- List typical ways company departments communicate.
- Cite examples of why a worker should adjust to different management styles.
- Cite an example of how companies are dependent upon the national economy.
- Cite an example of how a company is dependent upon the local economy.
- Describe the importance of achieving internal and external customer satisfaction.
- Identify examples of how cultural diversity can affect an industry.
- Identify key differences in how private companies and government agencies operate.
- List reasons why written policies are used in industry.
- Identify resources available from professional organizations.
- Identify how roles and responsibilities in a family business are different than in larger companies.
- List the benefits of worker participation in meetings.
- Describe how a company's marketing affects all its employees.

Finance

- List typical ways a business obtains capital.
- Describe the importance of accounting in a business.
- Describe key implications for a company that grants credit.
- Describe how a company estimates and bids for a contract.
- Describe how paycheck deductions affect a worker.
- Describe the importance of cost containment in a company.

Technical and Production Skills

- Demonstrate basic math ability.
- Demonstrate the ability to measure quickly and accurately.
- Demonstrate the ability to speak and write the English language effectively.
- Demonstrate the ability to listen effectively.
- Demonstrate the ability to use effective negotiation skills.
- Demonstrate the ability to manage time effectively.
- Demonstrate the ability to read blueprints and/or drawings.
- Demonstrate the ability to perform basic computer operations.
- Demonstrate the importance of deadlines and schedules.
- Demonstrate the ability to use team player skills.
- Demonstrate the ability to use supervisory and delegation skills.
- Demonstrate the ability to utilize good public speaking skills.

- Describe the importance of using troubleshooting techniques.
- Cite one example of a job that is interrelated with another job.
- Demonstrate the ability to obtain technical information.
- Identify certification requirements of a specific job.

Principles of Technology

- Describe the key characteristics of the technology used in an industry.
- Describe the importance of analyzing new equipment for possible use.
- Describe the importance of continuously upgrading one's job skills.
- Describe the importance of adaptability and learning from experience.
- Describe the importance of acquiring and analyzing information effectively and making sound decisions.
- Describe the importance of cross-training.

Labor

- Describe the importance of a written job description.
- Describe the importance of knowing your rights as a worker.
- Describe the role labor organizations play in an industry.
- List advantages/disadvantages of hourly and salaried pay.
- List differences between being a self-employed worker and a worker employed by a company.
- Describe the importance of participating in quality improvement programs.
- Describe the importance of understanding why a worker is asked to occasionally work longer hours.
- Describe the importance of cultural sensitivity.

Community

- Describe the importance of recognizing that a worker may contribute special skills through volunteer work.
- Identify key ways a company helps its community.
- Identify key ways a community helps a company.
- Identify an impact of buying outside the community.
- Describe how a company's public perception is important.
- Describe the importance of providing for the access needs of the physically challenged.

Health, Safety, and Environment

- Describe the importance of complying with state and federal agency regulations.
- Describe why it is important to avoid job-specific health threats.
- Read and comprehend major components of a material safety data sheet (a listing of components and relative hazards of common chemicals).
- Identify basic safety training techniques.
- Describe the importance of participating in preventive medicine programs.
- Describe the importance of handling stress effectively.
- Describe the importance of good workplace ergonomics.

- Identify any effects weather could have on an industry.
- Describe the importance of management's responsibility for a safe workplace.

Personal Conduct

- Describe the importance of recognizing the dignity of all workers.
- Describe the importance of producing quality work.

- Describe the importance of being fit for duty (no drugs, no alcohol).
- Describe the importance of exhibiting good attitude, enthusiasm, and integrity.
- Describe the importance of exhibiting good grooming and appearance.
- Describe the importance of good personal financing.

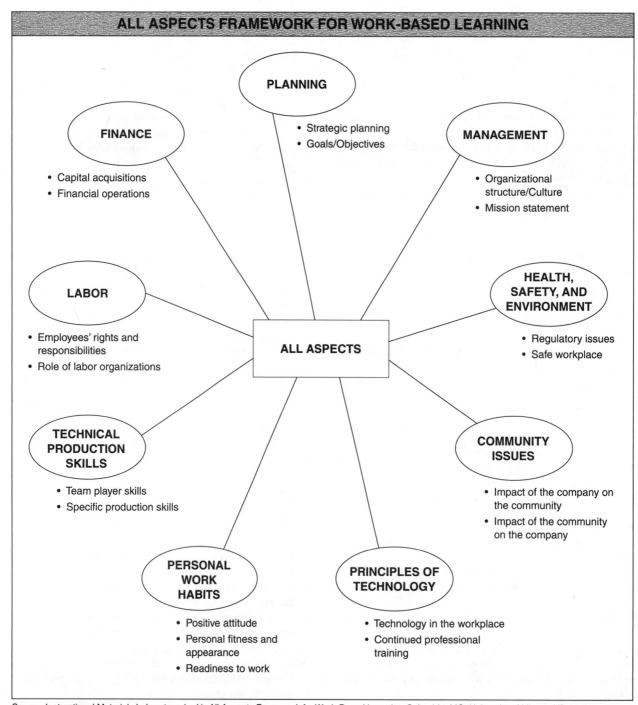

Source: Instructional Materials Laboratory. (n.d.). *All Aspects Framework for Work-Based Learning.* Columbia, MO: University of Missouri-Columbia.

Figure 12-19. Aspects of an industry and their components.

Examples of the use of AAI include the following:

- Tenth grade learners hold a car wash every year to raise money for a class trip. Teachers could incorporate AAI into this activity by involving learners heavily in planning, management, marketing, finance, labor relations, and environmental safety. Learners might be asked to break the overall process into tasks and schedule shifts and assignments. They could help choose a location for their venture and negotiate with the owners. They could identify production needs (hoses, buckets, soap, wash mitts, towels), research the costs of different products available in the market and make recommendations while being cognizant of environmental and worker safety impacts. Learners might estimate a price for their services, based on a reasonable projection of business levels, costs of production, and a comparison of prices in the market. Learners might create a marketing campaign advertising the car wash. Lessons in social studies, science, English, and math could be linked to provide learners with the knowledge and abilities to make decisions about the car wash.

- A learner interested in art might decide to intern at a museum, intending to gain experience in art restoration or as a curator. A creative employer, by systematically rotating the learner through different departments upon skill mastery in each, presents the learner with many more options. The learner could gain experiences as a tour guide, an exhibit or graphic designer, an administrator, or maybe a teacher if the museum offers classes. The learner could experience aspects of marketing, sales, and finance unique to the art industry. The learner might take an interest in working with potential donors on developing the collection.

- Many learners work after school and on weekends for experience or money, independent of school-arranged opportunities and placements. In some cases, AAI can make these extracurricular activities more meaningful. Teachers might ask a learner to explore an interest in terms of the particular industry in which the learner works. For example, a learner interested in law, working for a lawn service, could examine worker safety or environmental laws and talk with people at the lawn service to determine how they remain in compliance.

- Work-based learning may be more easily integrated with various academic disciplines when defined in relation to AAI. For example, if English teachers find it difficult to provide a context for instruction to learners studying auto mechanics, they might relate reading and writing exercises to activities focused on broader, but associated, themes, such as transportation or entrepreneurship. Learners could be tasked with writing advertisements or training manuals linking an applied exercise in an English course to other aspects of the industry.

- School-based enterprises, actual businesses run by learners, can illustrate the connections among different aspects of an industry. When learners are involved in all aspects of a school-based enterprise, they often have an opportunity to take on a variety of workplace responsibilities, giving immediate relevance to classroom lessons. For example, learners can assess the effects of marketing on their own business and witness firsthand the impacts of laws, technology, and labor issues on the balance sheet. In addition, learning how to establish and run a business may foster a sense of entrepreneurship in some learners, opening the door to new career options, including possibilities for self-employment.

- Learners can create portfolio work samples that demonstrate their knowledge, understanding, and application of the different aspects of industry and how they relate to a particular industry. Teachers can incorporate AAI into guidelines for portfolios to help learners reflect on the different activities they have undertaken.

- Teachers do not need to be experts on all aspects of an industry, but they may find it easier to connect classroom concepts to workplace applications if they can relate them back to their own practical experiences. Teachers may also find it easier to communicate with employers, other educators, and learners if everyone shares a degree of common knowledge. Some teachers may be better able to support their learners involved in all aspects of an industry if they are able to speak about their own accomplishments and frustrations in the workplace.

- Cooperation with area businesses and a local community college offers K–12 teachers an opportunity to participate in a business/industry fellowship program. Through this type of program, teachers are placed in local businesses for six weeks of the summer, learning about the workplace and gaining exposure to all aspects of the industry. Teachers are awarded two graduate credits upon completion of the program.

- Job rotations, one technique for expanding work-based learning opportunities, provide learners with introductory training in a range of occupations and departments, broadening their knowledge of the industry. Job rotations work best if activities are coordinated within and across departments. In some cases, each department defines the skills the learner will be exposed to in the course of the stay in the department and then becomes responsible for providing the learner with certain preestablished experiences to ensure broad coverage overall (National School-to-Work Office, 1997).

National Skill Standards

There is clearly widespread need for a skilled workforce. Workplaces change constantly. Jobs that used to be relatively simple now require high performance work processes and enhanced skills in order to compete globally. Because skill standards reflect these changing realities, standards are essential in helping applicants and employees enjoy greater career opportunities and economic security. Also, with the shelf life of skills shrinking, up-to-date standards provide benchmarks that help educators and corporate trainers decide what skills are necessary, allowing them to make better education and training investments for their workers.

Created by Congress through the National Skill Standards Act of 1994, the National Skill Standards Board (NSSB) is a national organization, comprised of a host of interest groups, that wants to encourage the creation and adoption of a national system of skill standards to enhance the ability of the U.S. workforce to compete effectively in the rapidly changing global economy. This is the first time that business, labor, educators, civil rights, and community-based organizations have come together in this setting to develop a national skill standards system.

A skill standard is a description of the work to be performed, how well the work must be performed, and the level of knowledge and skill required to perform that work. The skill standards are developed by industry, which includes business, labor unions, and employee and employer organizations, in cooperation with educators and public interest groups.

The standards will be flexible, portable, and continuously updated and improved. In today's environment, change is the only constant. New technologies are creating new jobs, new industries, and new ways of working. If skill standards are to effectively articulate these changing workplace realities and help workers anticipate change, the standards themselves must be continuously updated and improved.

The NSSB has categorized the workforce into 15 industry sectors that are assembling skill standards, assessment, and certification for their respective industries:

- Agriculture, Forestry and Fishing
- Business and Administration Services
- Construction
- Education and Training
- Finance and Insurance
- Health and Human Services
- Manufacturing, Installation and Repair
- Mining
- Public Administration, Legal and Protective Services
- Restaurants, Lodging, Hospitality and Tourism, and Amusement and Recreation
- Retail Trade, Wholesale Trade, Real Estate and Personal Services
- Scientific and Technical Services
- Telecommunications, Computers, Arts and Entertainment, and Information
- Transportation
- Utilities and Environment and Waste Management.

As a stand-alone tool, the standards allow employers and unions to do a better job of communicating skill needs to workers, educators, and trainers. Employees can better communicate their skills and knowledge to employers, and can seek out training for career advancement. Educators can start to plan curricula and communicate to learners the skills expected by employers. See Figure 12-20.

Skill standards do not tell teachers how to teach. They are used by schools as a framework to design curricula that integrate academic and career and technical learning in occupational contexts and to provide benchmarks for learner achievement. Teachers and schools have the flexibility to create materials and use teaching methodologies that draw upon their strengths and best suit their needs.

Assessment based on occupationally relevant standards can result in more equitable and efficient judgments about learner performance. Standards allow for the measurement of performance in relation to established criteria rather than in comparison to other learners. With the aid of standards, assessments can measure much more than course completion—they can measure learners' ability to actually perform functions they will be expected to perform in the working world. Learners are able to create a record of achievement and receive a credential that employers will recognize and value.

The NSSB cannot ensure access to good jobs, but it intends to improve access to these jobs for all Americans by making sure that the skills needed to get these jobs are clearly spelled out to learners, new entrants to the job market, current workers, laid-off workers, and people trying to re-enter the work force. By clearly and simply spelling out the skill needs of employers, both horizontal and vertical career movement will result. This will make it easier for workers to see how their skills can be transferred laterally from one industry or job area to another, as well as ease the transition from novice to expert worker.

Career Plans and Career Portfolios

An individualized career plan (ICP) is a formalized written plan that fits the learner's unique, specific needs. It relates learning experiences to career goals. The plan is designed to facilitate the transition of the learner from high school to future learning or employment. It should be a comprehensive document based on both formal and informal assessment of the individual. The ICP should also include the areas in which the learner most needs to increase knowledge and skills in order to reach the identified goal. See Figure 12-21.

Cunanan and Maddy-Bernstein (1995) suggested the following components for inclusion in a learner's individualized career plan:

1. Personal data–Learner's name, birth date, address, social security number or learner identification number, middle grade or high school level, and telephone number are essential information.
2. Career and educational goals–This section contains a statement of the tentative career and educational goals of the learner. Results from aptitude, career interests, and other relevant assessment instruments as well as the learner's extracurricular activities can guide the setting of goals. Career goals must be outcome-oriented and flexible based on changing learner preferences.

3. Assessment information–Data about the learner's career interests, educational and vocational aptitudes, achievements, and special needs are reported in this section to provide counselors, transition specialists, and career and technical educators baseline information. Assessment information is key in matching careers with the learner's abilities, interests, and preferences.

4. High school course plan–Courses required for graduation as well as those that will lead to the achievement of the learner's post–high school career and educational goals must be determined. Establish a clear understanding of academic areas where the learner is progressing and any areas where the learner is not making adequate progress.

HOW TO USE SKILL STANDARDS

If you are a(n):	Value of Stand-alone Skill Standards	Value of Skill Assessments and Certifications
Employer	Help establish high-skilled jobs Establish career paths Benchmark manufacturing processes to best practices Plan organizational redesign Develop job descriptions Work with line managers, unions, and employees to conduct training needs analyses Develop and/or improve training programs Work with local schools to develop curriculum and programs to prepare students for good manufacturing jobs	Recruit or hire staff Help your employees assess their skills and develop an individual training plan Compare job profiles and interviewees
Student or employee	Plan your career path Upgrade your existing skills Learn high-performance skills Learn about the skills employers need Describe your skills to an employer Support and promote best practices in your workplace	Assess your skills against the skill standards Obtain portable credentials for existing skills Obtain portable credentials for advancement
Educator/Trainer	Work with local manufacturers and unions to develop curriculum that meets skill needs Identify teacher/trainer qualifications Identify space and equipment needs Advise students on high-skilled career opportunities in manufacturing	Assess proficiency Recommend certification
Union representative	Encourage employers to develop or improve training programs Bargain training dollars and programs for your members Develop or improve union training programs for members and other workers Negotiate new career paths for members Help leverage public training dollars for training in manufacturing skills	Get members recognition for existing knowledge and skills Assess members skills and provide assistance in education/career planning Credential members and workers in skill standards Work with employers and public agencies to place union credentialed workers in good manufacturing jobs
Workforce development professional	Work with employers and unions to incorporate standards into local labor market information and economic development systems Build capacity of training providers to help workers attain standards Build the use of standards into criteria for funding public job training programs	Assess and credential participants in skill standards Use credentials in job placement

Adapted from: National Skills Standards Board. (2001). *How to Use the MSSC Skill Standards.* Washington, DC: Author.

Figure 12-20. An example of the value of using skill standards.

INDIVIDUALIZED CAREER PLAN . . .

Personal Data

Last Name _____   First Name _____   M.I. ____   Date of Birth _____

Address _____   Student ID Number _____

City _____   State _____   Zip Code _____   Social Security Number _____

Projected Graduation Date _____

Home Phone Number _____

Career/Educational Goal(s)

9th Grade	**10th Grade**	**11th Grade**	**12th Grade**
Career Goal(s)	*Career Goal(s)*	*Career Goal(s)*	*Career Goal(s)*
_____	_____	_____	_____
_____	_____	_____	_____
Educational Goal(s)	*Educational Goal(s)*	*Educational Goal(s)*	*Educational Goal(s)*
_____	_____	_____	_____
_____	_____	_____	_____

Assessment Data

	Name of Test/Inventory	**Date Administered**	**Results**
ACHIEVEMENT	_____	_____	_____
APTITUDES	_____	_____	_____
VOCATIONAL ASSESSMENT	_____	_____	_____
LEARNING STYLES	_____	_____	_____
CAREER INTERESTS	_____	_____	_____
OTHER TESTS	_____	_____	_____

PSAT: V _____   M _____   ACT Composite Score: _____   Date Taken: _____

Tentative High School Course Plan

9th Grade		**10th Grade**		**11th Grade**		**12th Grade**	
Courses	Credit	Courses	Credit	Courses	Credit	Courses	Credit
_____	___	_____	___	_____	___	_____	___
_____	___	_____	___	_____	___	_____	___
_____	___	_____	___	_____	___	_____	___
_____	___	_____	___	_____	___	_____	___
_____	___	_____	___	_____	___	_____	___
Total Credits ___		Total Credits ___		Total Credits ___		Total Credits ___	

Student's Signature Date   Student's Signature Date   Student's Signature Date   Student's Signature Date
Comments: _____   Comments: _____   Comments: _____   Comments: _____

Interests

Grade	School Activities (clubs, organizations, sports, committees)	Community Activities (clubs, committees, organizations)	Interests/Hobbies
9th	_____	_____	_____
10th	_____	_____	_____
11th	_____	_____	_____
12th	_____	_____	_____

... INDIVIDUALIZED CAREER PLAN

Employment History

Employer & Address	Dates Employed	Type of Work & Responsibilities	Comments
_____	_____	_____	_____
_____	_____	_____	_____
_____	_____	_____	_____

Career Preparation Activities
TO PREPARE FOR MY CAREER, I NEED TO

☐ Enroll in a magnet program or Career Center.
Area of interest: _____

☐ Learn how to market my experiences and abilities. (Resume writing, letter of application writing, thank you letter writing, interview)

☐ Pursue an on-the-job training program. (Bureau of Apprenticeship, job fair, job placement counselor)
Training desired: _____

☐ Enlist in the military service. (ASVAB, ROTC, recruiter visit)
Area of interest: _____

☐ Attend a trade, technical, or vocational school. (Career college fair, school visits, financial aid)
Area of study: _____
School(s) considered: _____

☐ Go to work full-time. (Job fair, shadowing, job placement counselor)
Type of work: _____

☐ Attend a two-year college to prepare for work. (Articulation agreement(s), career college fair, school visits)
Area of study: _____
School(s) considered: _____

☐ Attend a two-year college and transfer to a four-year college. (Career college fair, school visits, college workshops)
Area of study: _____
School(s) considered: _____

☐ Enroll in a four-year college. (PSAT, ACT, SAT, achievement tests, financial aid application, college fairs)
Area of study: _____
School(s) considered: _____

Career and Technical Training
Name of Courses/Program

Business Education/Marketing _____
Health Science Technology _____
Family and Consumer Science _____
Trade & Industrial Occupations _____
Agriculture and Natural Resources _____

Future Plans (After High School)

Employment
☐ Full-time job
☐ Part-time job
☐ Military

Education
☐ Career and technical training
☐ Apprenticeship
☐ On-the-job training
☐ Community college – 2 year
☐ University – 4 year

References

Name	Address	Phone
_____	_____	_____
_____	_____	_____
_____	_____	_____

Adapted from: Cunanan, E., & Maddy-Bernstein, C. (May, 1995). Individualized Career Plans: Opening Doors for All. *Office of Student Services Brief, 7*(1). Berkeley, CA: National Center for Research in Vocational Education.

Figure 12-21. A sample individualized career plan.

5. Employment history–This part reflects the learner's work experience. This can include employment (paid and unpaid) gained through internships, apprenticeships, or part-time work. List employer's name and address, type of work, and dates of employment.

6. Career development activities–Examples of career-related activities that can help the learner develop an unbiased perspective and self-confidence include exploring occupational and educational options, investigating job requirements, writing resumes and letters of application, filling out application forms, participating in mock interviews, completing assignments in an accurate and timely manner, and communicating effectively with others.

A career portfolio contains detailed documentation of the learner's progress and should include work samples, certificates of completion including competencies mastered, and other indicators of actual work. Career portfolios are important for the following reasons:

- Educational systems are charged with preparing learners for productive employment in a global economy and success in life.
- Career development is an ongoing process, not a singular event. Schools need to systematically help learners with career decisions by facilitating the process and modeling appropriate ways to make sound decisions.
- The personalized portfolio helps learners take responsibility for and have ownership of their career decisions.
- Many large companies are now requesting transcripts and portfolios for documentation of work-based learning skills when hiring employees.
- The portfolio model is now being used in many schools as a viable alternative to objective and standardized testing to assess learner progress.
- The portfolio serves to educate learners about the many facets of career decision making, while serving as a repository for their work.
- The comprehensiveness of the portfolio requires that learners use higher-level analysis, synthesis, and evaluation skills.
- Learners often need a tangible means of seeing their progress and direction.
- The purpose of the portfolio's sequential planning activities is for better linkage of education to future career plans.
- The portfolio allows for a variety of activities, procedures, products, and opportunities, which contribute to a better understanding of the overall picture.
- All learners deserve the opportunity to develop individualized career plans (Ettinger, 1995).

Portfolios are both a process and a product. The career portfolio product is basically a manila folder or an accordion folder that expands as work is added to it, a file kept on microcomputer disks, or any other type of holder for information. The contents of a career portfolio are dependent upon the functions it is to serve and are limited only by the theme and the developer's imagination and creativity. Most portfolios contain materials arranged under major headings such as resumes, grade transcripts, career interests, and certificates and awards received.

The range of work that goes into portfolios is deliberately diverse due to individual learner differences and school/program/course requirements. Some of the common items that appear in portfolios include the following:

- learner narratives about how they developed the portfolio contents and about what they have learned
- classroom and laboratory assignments
- works learners develop to show their interests and abilities
- reflections about themselves
- observations and comments from teachers, parents, and significant others
- rough drafts and finished papers and reports
- best and worst tests
- records of books or magazine articles read
- samples of homework completed
- physical accomplishments
- artistic achievements
- career development plan including resumes, completed application forms, letters of recommendation, cover letters for applicants, letters from past and present employers, and future-oriented career plans
- documentation of employability skills
- recognition awards and honors
- performance appraisals from teachers
- transcripts with class descriptions and grades for related classes
- photographs or videotapes of completed projects and other events
- learner-published materials
- project reports
- selected daily work
- copies of important documents such as driver's licenses, first aid training cards, and insurance cards
- daily schedule of classes
- selected excerpts from personal diaries
- record of participation in learner and community organizations
- cooperative education training programs and agreements

Ettinger (1995) identified the following benefits of using the career planning process and career portfolios:

Benefits for Learners

- provides learners with written documentation of their career development to take with them when they graduate
- personalizes the planning process
- provides a vehicle (or process) for integrating various aspects of their career development
- helps learners relate their educational experiences, including the activities of a comprehensive school counseling program, to future work competencies
- gives learners a sense of accomplishment
- promotes personal accountability

Benefits for the School

- provides a process of accountability and documentation
- aligns the school with national models of excellence
- offers a vehicle for articulation among school levels
- provides validation of the school's efforts to address learners' affective, educational, and career planning needs
- offers an excellent opportunity for the school to integrate its curriculum
- provides a basis for teacher/advisor and student advocacy programs
- establishes a consistent approach for all learners

Benefits for the Community

- helps prepare learners for the workforce
- addresses the need for more positive work attitudes
- involves the parents and the community in the implementation process
- helps learners develop responsibility for their career success
- identifies parents and community members as key players in the career planning process
- provides the opportunity for learners to bring tangible evidence of their skills accomplishments, and perspectives to the job search

Service Learning

Service learning and transition efforts are both designed to connect learners to their communities—service learning through community service and transition through workforce participation. Both promote an approach through which learners apply academic and career skills to real-life work situations while developing the attitudes, values, and behaviors that will lead them to become informed citizens and productive workers. See Figure 12-22.

Service learning is a strategy in which learners grow and develop through active participation in thoughtfully organized service experiences that

- are conducted in and meet the needs of a community;
- are coordinated between the school and the community;
- are integrated into and enhance the learners' curriculum;
- provide structured time for learners to reflect on the service experience;
- provide learners with opportunities to use newly acquired skills and knowledge in real-life situations in their own communities; and
- enhance what is taught in schools by extending learning into the community, thereby fostering the development of a sense of caring for others.

SELECTED BEST PRACTICES FOR SUSTAINING SERVICE LEARNING PROGRAMS

Students	Faculty	Institution	Community
Start small	Start small	Start small	Start small
Hold an orientation	Hold an orientation	Create advisory boards	Hold an orientation
Involve students in process	Use service learning as a teaching strategy	Connect to existing initiatives	Develop resource handbooks
Use a team approach	Focus on academic rigor	Write service learning into course competencies	Develop public relations
Empower students to do projects alone	Offer mini-grants	Combine student services with academic affairs	Celebrate local culture
Organize student learning communities	Organize faculty learning circles	Use a team approach	Make government/ corporate connections
Hold group reflection sessions	Develop resource handbooks	Combine structure and flexibility	Fund service scholarships
Note service learning on transcripts, in catalogs	Develop contracts	Co-locate with volunteer center	Create spin-off partnerships
Identify student ambassadors	Suggest faculty perform service as part of orientation	Develop public relations	Connect with Learn and Serve K-12 programs
Let students be advocates	Appoint a faculty coordinator	Hire student assistants	Connect with tech-prep
Conduct pre/post surveys	Use a team approach	Apply student fees to support program	Identify student ambassadors
	Obtain faculty senate support	Consider service learning as accreditation criteria	
	Conduct pre/post surveys	Make presentations to board of trustees	
		Network with other colleges	

Adapted from: Robinson, G., & Barnett, L. (1998). Best Practices in Service Learning: Building a National Community College Network 1994-1997. *American Association of Community Colleges Project Brief, (3),* 3.

Figure 12-22. Suggestions for different entities involved in service learning programs.

Self-confidence, competence, and empathy for others are some of the personal benefits learners realize through service learning. Additionally, by engaging in problem solving and by working cooperatively and collaboratively with others, learners are able to build skills needed for employment in today's workplace.

The National School-to-Work Office (May 1996) identified four key elements central to service learning programs:

1. Integrated curriculum–Integrating the service being performed and classroom learning is a natural extension of the interdisciplinary nature of community service and operates under the same premise as other work-based components. For example, if learners are working to remove graffiti, environmental classes could focus on the damage that graffiti causes, science classes could discuss various methods for removing graffiti, and civics courses could address the issues of citizenship and personal responsibility. Other course work could focus on setting up teams to clean the graffiti, gathering data to determine which area of the city to clean, and coordinating with local officials to start the project This cross-curricular approach not only links classroom learning to the real world, but also exposes youth to a variety of career paths and options.

2. Time for reflection–Any service learning experience is enhanced when reflected upon, both during the experience and afterwards. In service learning, reflection is an essential component that affords young people the opportunity to think, write, and talk about their service and how it relates to the classroom, how it benefits them personally, and how it benefits others. Receiving feedback from supervisors, those served, and peers provide youth with the opportunity to share their thoughts with others while considering different perspectives on service. This further promotes the learning aspect of service learning by helping young people analyze the broad array of skills and knowledge they have gained from their experience.

3. Building community partnerships–Service learning involves schools, learners, community-based organizations, local government officials, and the public in program development and promotes cooperation and collaboration among these institutions. The active involvement of each sector also helps ensure that program services are meeting individual and community needs. Through this strategy, service learning can expand the scope of transition to provide an opportunity for young people to address the needs of their community and incorporate a unique youth perspective into the development of local community services.

4. Diverse activities–Through its base in community service, service learning expands the opportunities and learning experiences available to young people beyond the constraints of work-based learning. As a result, young people benefit from exposure to a wide variety of experiences from which they may take different but equally important lessons. For example, working with the elderly can teach young people about intergenerational issues such as aging and changes in society, while mentoring preschool or elementary school learners can develop communication skills. Other service, such as work in a neighborhood soup kitchen, can provide lessons about hunger and homelessness. This type of diversity develops a broader range of interpersonal skills while offering youth the opportunity to learn about experiences different from their own.

Service learning projects can meet diverse learner, school, and community needs in social services, the environment, education, and safety. Examples include

- community gardens with learners and community partners to meet nutritional needs;
- intergenerational programs with an integrated reading and writing component to develop learner literacy;
- community history projects where learners utilize primary sources to establish and maintain historical exhibits;
- watershed reclamation projects with learners and community members working together to restore habitat and maintain water quality;
- health and human services projects where high school health learners enrich their academics by volunteering in a local hospital; and
- civic studies projects that allow high school government learners to learn firsthand about citizenship, democracy, and leadership.

In the past, teachers did not ask their learners to make any connection between their volunteer service experiences and their academic course work. This meant that volunteer administrators did not have to concern themselves with linking service activities to academic pursuits. Generally they were asked only to comment on the quality of a learner's service and on whether each learner had fulfilled the time requirement.

Teachers who never thought that volunteer service time was anything but "learning-to-serve" time are recognizing that they have missed some golden opportunities to help the types of learners who thrive when what they do correlates with what they study. These teachers can be tremendous assets. Following are a few examples:

- Typing teacher in a business skills class–These learners need to learn how to create mailing labels. Almost every nonprofit agency needs up-to-date mailing lists and must generate new mailing labels. The learners also need letter-perfect practice writing text material. All nonprofit agencies need letters processed and directed to multiple audiences.
- English composition teacher–These learners need practice summarizing material in news form. Almost every nonprofit agency needs shortened, summarized articles for newsletters. The learners must learn how to take

oral data and transfer this information to the written essay form. Almost every nonprofit agency preserves historical data for its clients.

- Chemistry teacher–These learners need to learn the difference between the physical characteristics of potable and nonpotable water. Every residential facility needs to have its water supply checked for potability.
- Math teacher–These learners need to know how to synthesize relationships in understandable charts and graphs. Every nonprofit organization's annual report needs explanatory charts and graphs.

School-Based Enterprises

Growing interest in transition and new models of youth apprenticeship have drawn attention to the existence of school-based enterprises (SBEs), which engage learners in school-based activities that produce goods or services

for sale or use to people other than the learners involved. In high schools and two-year colleges, these activities range from Junior Achievement mini-enterprises to learners building houses, running restaurants, managing retail stores, repairing and selling cars, raising crops and livestock, staffing child care centers, publishing books and periodicals, conducting studies of environmental quality or energy conservation, reconstructing local historical landmarks, and engaging in small-scale manufacturing. These activities have most often been associated with career and technical education, giving learners an opportunity to apply knowledge and skills taught in classes. School-based enterprises in high schools or two-year colleges are analogous to practices at the postgraduate level where law learners produce law review journals or doctoral learners help run research studies. Teaching hospitals associated with medical schools are school-based enterprises at an advanced level. See Figure 12-23.

SCHOOL-BASED ENTERPRISES					
Name of Business	Product/ Service	Student Responsibilities	Start-up Costs/ Materials Needed	Student Scheduling	Monitoring and Evaluation
Apple Cart Espresso Bar	Coffee drinks Baked goods	Preparing specialty drinks Maintaining product inventory Selling products to customers	$5,000 for purchasing espresso cart, cups, coffee, flavored syrups, paper products, and other food supplies	2-hour blocks 5 days per week	Students complete 6 to 10 week training program and meet competencies in • money handling • communication • customer service
Comets Classic Carry-out	Take-out needs	Planning menus Shopping for groceries Preparing and packaging meals	$300 for kitchen equipment and food supplies	1 class period per day	Students receive individual and group instruction in • accounting • comparison shopping • nutrition/meal planning • safety/hygiene
WildBunch Seed Company	Wholesale and mail order seed packets	Collecting and identifying wildflower seeds Packaging seeds Developing catalogs and marketing materials	$150 for seeds and envelopes	90-minute block 2 or 3 days per week	Students receive career education and work experience credit for completing specific assignments in • horticulture • consumer math • business accounting
Winter Garden	Organic produce	Planning garden layout and preparing soil	$850 for seeds, garden tools, and materials for greenhouse	Twice a week after school	Students complete curriculum addressing • organic gardening • business/marketing

Adapted from: Lindstrom, L., Benz, M., & Johnson, M. (March-April, 1997). An Introduction to School-Based Enterprises. *Teaching Exceptional Children,* 21-24.

Figure 12-23. Sample school-based enterprises and their requirements.

School-based enterprises provide learners with invaluable experience for the workplace through the following:
- brainstorming
- ordering necessary materials
- designing and creating the product
- developing an advertising plan
- selling the product
- placing and setting up a delivery date
- delivering the product to the customer
- problem solving
- keeping accurate records of cost and profit.

Turning a good idea into reality takes a lot of planning and hard work. This is an ideal opportunity to involve learners and other interested staff in thinking through all of the details involved in developing, operating, and maintaining a real business on the school grounds. During this planning stage, the following questions should be addressed:
- What product or service will you offer?
- Whom does your market survey suggest are your potential customers?
- What kind of advertising strategies will you need?
- How will you staff and run the business?
- What are the initial and ongoing costs of operating the business?

Before moving ahead with starting the enterprise, it is essential to have administrative support within the school. Set up a meeting with school administrators to obtain their support for the business plan. At the meeting, describe the product to be sold, the learners and staff who will be involved in operating the business, any research that has been done on licensing and liability issues, and the unique benefits of operating a school-based enterprise.

The following are guidelines for developing SBEs:
- Select learners to participate–You may decide to have all of the learners enrolled in a particular class or program participate in the business or only those learners who have an interest in learning the career skills associated with the business. Learner participation will also be influenced by existing class and work schedules. As much as possible, provide opportunities for learners to be involved in management decisions so that they can experience the entire process of developing and operating a business. Also, consider involving other career and technical education learners in your venture. These learners may be interested in helping you with the day-to-day tasks of operating the business, or they may want to be involved only in certain special projects such as developing a marketing strategy.
- Develop the materials needed to run a successful small business–Most small businesses require a certain amount of paperwork to ensure that the business runs smoothly. In addition, because you are developing a school-to-work training program, you will need to develop materials that will structure and support these additional training activities. Materials may include

(a) training materials, (b) advertising or marketing information, and (c) accounting and inventory materials.
- Advertise your product–You must get the word out about your product, even if your business is school-based and geared toward learner customers. Use the flyers or catalogs you have developed to provide information to your potential customers. You may want to develop some special promotional materials to prepare customers for the grand opening of your new business.
- Providing training to learners as needed–Before you actually serve your first customer, you will need to provide some hands-on training to learners to teach them specific tasks involved in operating the business such as making change, packaging materials, or taking orders. Some school districts have worked with local employers to develop curriculum packages geared to the demands of a specific industry. The type and amount of training you provide will depend on the skill level of your learners and the needs of your business. Once the training is complete, develop a daily schedule for learners and staff who will be operating the business.
- Staff and run the business–When you have finished purchasing all your supplies, preparing all of your paperwork, and providing training to your learners, you can finally get down to opening your business. This is the time when all your preparation finally pays off and you can begin to sell your product or service to real customers. Remember that although one of your goals is certainly to make a profit, you are really in business to help your learners learn valuable skills. Be flexible enough to allow your learners to make important business decisions and experience the impact of these decisions. These "real-world" experiences will help to prepare them for the transition into community employment.
- Evaluate the success of the business–The final step in developing any new program is to evaluate its impact. Creating a school-based enterprise from scratch is not easy, so give yourself some time before you evaluate your program too harshly. When you are ready, program staff can collect information from customers and learners to help determine the success of the venture. You will certainly want to consider the profits made as one marker of success, but also remember the intangible benefits that learners receive from participating in the development and operation of a brand-new business. Staff and learners should discuss the need to modify operating procedures and ultimately decide if it is feasible (and profitable) to continue to operate the business.

Job Shadowing

When it comes to their career plans, some learners' minds are made up while other learners are undecided. The challenge is to find ways to help learners learn about occupations so they can make their own decisions about the future. One device is job shadowing, an increasingly popular mode of experiential learning for learners exploring careers. Job shadowing at the secondary school level differs from job shadowing at the college level, but the fundamentals remain the same. Learners observe workers performing the normal duties of their occupations in a particular setting. The learners see for themselves what a job is like and probe for more information by asking questions.

Job shadowing is one of the most popular work-based learning activities because it provides learners with opportunities to gather information on a wide variety of career possibilities before deciding where they want to focus their attention. Classroom exercises conducted prior to and following the job shadow help learners connect their experience to their course work, career pathways, related skills requirements, and future educational options.

Once the career investigation is complete, then a learner chooses a more personally tailored career path. Modern day job shadowing allows future workers to better their chances of finding and maintaining employment, lowers their chances of dropping out, and primes them for the transition from a school environment to a competitive, fast-moving workforce that will continue to be ever changing.

Characteristics of job shadowing include

- arranging time commitments for shadowing experiences;
- providing learners with realistic views of a specific jobs;
- allowing learners to observe employees on the job;
- allowing learners time to ask questions; and
- requiring learners to complete related class assignments (journal, focused questions, etc.).

Following are examples of the kinds of assignments learners may be asked to complete as a result of their job shadow:

- written report on a specific career
- information about the job shadowing site such as emergency procedures, site fire plan, diagram of the facility, site personnel names and titles within department/floor
- supervisor interview
- journal entry describing the site, the people, the work, and the environment or classroom
- oral presentation on careers represented at the job-shadowing site

Implementing a job shadowing program requires time and commitment. The following steps should be employed:

1. Establish goal(s) for the program.
2. Develop the structure for the job shadowing experience.
3. Recruit employers.
4. Develop learner outcomes.
5. Create forms and procedures for the program (including parental consent forms, accident procedures, supervisory evaluation forms, and timesheets).
6. Develop an orientation for learners and supervisors.
7. Develop activities for learners.
8. Develop guides for both learners and employers.

Formal job shadowing programs often include the following components:

1. Interest survey–Learners fill out a survey to identify their career interests and the kind of job shadow they might want to do. Sometimes this step includes extensive career explorations.
2. Matching process–A coordinator matches each learner with a volunteer who has agreed to serve as a job shadow host. Local organizations, such as chambers of commerce or rotary clubs, help identify volunteer hosts in a variety of occupations. Coordinators try to match learners with hosts working in certain careers, according to learner interests.
3. Orientation activities–Learners prepare questions for their host and learn how to conduct themselves properly in the workplace. Learners are coached on details like using telephone manners, making eye contact, giving a proper handshake, and knowing when to ask questions. Some job shadowing experiences call for extra preparation.
4. Learner confirmation–After a coordinator schedules the job shadows, learners call their host to introduce themselves and confirm the schedule. It's important to make a good first impression and to be interested in the host's work. Learners must also obtain permission from their parents/guardian to take part in a job shadow.
5. The shadow–Learners spend a specified amount of time on the job with a host worker in a certain occupation. The learners observe closely and ask questions. They inquire about training, the role of technology, and necessary math and communication skills.
6. Follow-up–Learners write a letter thanking the host and think about what they have learned. A job shadow host may prove helpful as a contact in the future, and a thank-you letter strengthens the relationship. Learners may also have to fill out evaluations, write brief reports, or make oral presentations to underscore what they have learned. They may discuss their experience with a coordinator or counselor as well.

Specific roles and responsibilities should be determined for all participants involved in job shadowing:

1. Teacher responsibilities–The teacher will be responsible for seeing that all learners participating in the job shadowing experience have met all of the criteria required prior to the placement of learners on job shadowing sites. They will

- ensure that job shadowing paperwork is completed, including insurance documentation by the school district prior to any learner assignment;
- schedule learners and keep records of the learner names, dates of shadowing, sites, and supervisors;
- follow up with work sites for feedback on the job shadow;
- monitor completion of learner assignments; and
- be available in emergency situations.

2. Learner responsibilities–As part of the job shadowing experience, learners will
   - dress according to the standards of the particular site;
   - arrive at the site at the agreed upon time;
   - call the site before the scheduled time if unable to attend on the appointed day;
   - follow all guidelines and policies of the site;
   - complete any school assignments related to the job shadowing experience; and
   - complete all required paperwork (permission, medical authorizations, etc.).

3. Host responsibilities–It is important for the supervisor to understand learners are not present to work. They are there to observe and ask questions. Upon agreeing to take a job shadowing learner, the supervisor will
   - inform the learner of any relevant policies or regulations at the work site;
   - answer any relevant questions about the profession or facility;
   - direct learners to the areas of their career interest;
   - arrange for the actual job shadowing experience(s); and
   - monitor the learner and contact the teacher should there be any problems.

The following activities should be conducted prior to the job shadowing experience:

- Learners should have been exposed to certain information and skills prior to the job shadowing experience.
- An orientation session is essential to the success of the program. It is important that all participants understand their roles and expected outcomes of the activity. See Figure 12-24.
- Administrators, teachers, parents and school coordinators involved must have a good understanding of the entire job shadowing process. The work in school before the site visit and post-visit activities are as important as the job shadowing itself.
- Learners must complete and return a preliminary survey before the job shadowing day. This allows learners to be placed according to their interests, and the information is very useful to the workplace mentor and the school coordinators when planning the day. See Figure 12-25.
- The school must plan to transport the participating learners to each site.

The following activities should be conducted during the job shadowing experience:

- The job-shadowing day should begin with a welcome session, including a brief overview of the company, safety rules, introduction of personnel, and information about the schedule for the day. See Figure 12-26.
- The job shadowing experience should allow learners to explore the world of work—it should not overwhelm learners with too many details of the job they are shadowing. A list of guided questions should be made available. See Figure 12-27.

- Learners learn by doing. Make sure that they are engaged in the experience.
- If the shadowing occurs during lunch, arrangements need to be made to provide a facility for eating at the site.
- The experience is most meaningful to learners when they engage in reflection activities both on-site and back at school. Reflection activities should be fun for the learners—not intimidating.

LEARNER ORGANIZATION AGENDA

   I. Introduction: What is job shadowing?

  II. Goals and purpose of job shadowing

      A. You will observe what really happens in the world of work.

      B. You will see how what you learn in school is used on the job.

      C. You will learn what skills are needed for a job.

      D. You will meet interesting people in our community.

 III. Guided tour of the program

      A. Before your visit to the site

         1. Game plan and timeline

         2. Roles and responsibilities

         3. Program orientation

         4. Student survey

         5. Consent form

         6. Tips for succeeding in the workplace

      B. During the job shadowing day

         1. Game plan and timeline

         2. Roles and responsibilities

         3. Student questionnaire

         4. Reflection activities

         5. Program evaluations

      C. After returning from the site

         1. Student reflection form

         2. Thank-you letters

 IV. Things to remember while you're at the site

      A. The importance of professional behavior

         1. How to dress

         2. Expectations while at workplace

         3. Workplace policies and procedures

      B. How to learn the most you can

         1. Make careful observations

         2. Listen

         3. Ask questions

      C. Courtesy to others

  V. Wrap-up: Question and answer period

Figure 12-24. Sample agenda for a job shadowing orientation session.

- Observe safety procedures. Make sure that learners are not exposed to prohibited occupational areas. See child labor laws.
- Provide an opportunity for learners to reassemble at the end of the day to provide immediate feedback. This is helpful in the event any concerns arose during the job shadowing experience.

The following activities should be conducted after the job shadowing experience:

- Learners should complete a job shadowing experience report and share results with other learners, transition coordinators, counselors and parents.
- Feedback should be collected from the workplace supervisor relative to the shadowing experience.

- After the job-shadowing day, the school should keep the employer updated on reflection activities done at school and the impact of the job shadowing experience. Employers are often interested in hearing directly from the learners about what they learned. Thank you notes are a key to building a strong relationship between the school and business site.
- The work-based mentors and any other individuals who participated on behalf of the employer should also receive thank you notes from the learners.
- Publicity media should be utilized to publicize employers' participation in the job shadowing experience. This will help encourage employers' future participation.

LEARNER PRELIMINARY SURVEY

This is a student survey designed to give your workplace mentor — your guide throughout your visit at the workplace — some introductory information about you and your interests.

Your name: _____

School: _____

Grade: _____

1. What are you favorite subjects at school?

_____

_____

2. What are your favorite hobbies, sports or activities?

_____

_____

_____

3. What careers interest you?

_____

_____

4. Have you had any previous job shadowing experiences? If so, where?

_____

_____

_____

5. Do you have any work experience? What jobs have you had? Do you currently have a job?

_____

_____

_____

6. At what type of business would you like to shadow and why?

_____

_____

_____

7. What are your goals for your job shadowing experience?

_____

_____

_____

Figure 12-25. Sample preliminary job shadowing survey.

SUGGESTED SHADOWING ACTIVITIES FOR THE EMPLOYER

Name: _____   Home Phone: _____

School: _____   School Phone: _____

Coordinator: _____

Shadowing Agency: _____

Shadowing Supervisor: _____

Shadowing Occupation: _____

SUGGESTED ACTIVITIES:

1. Introduce the learner to the staff.
2. Explain the occupation being observed.
3. Tour the facility (if possible/practical).
4. Create a small activity for the learner to perform that is related to the career. This activity can be planned in advance of the learner's arrival.
5. Expose the learner to the same routine a new employee would experience.
6. Answer questions that the learner has regarding the job.

OFFER ANSWERS TO THE FOLLOWING QUESTIONS:

1. What is your occupation (what are your duties)?
2. What are the working conditions associated with your position (physical working conditions, amount of overtime required, stress level, amount of responsibility, amount of travel required, etc.)?
3. What is your educational background? What school subjects do you feel would be most helpful to prepare for this position?
4. What do you enjoy most about this position?
5. What do you find most difficult or stressful about this position?
6. What recommendations would you offer to someone who is interested in entering a similar position?
7. In your opinion, what type of attitude, personality traits, or personal characteristics are important in order to be successful in this career field?
8. What opportunities are there for advancement in this career field?
9. What is your role in supervision?
10. What are the starting salaries and education requirements at the company for persons who hold positions similar to the one that the learner is observing today?
11. What does this company do to encourage it employees to continue their education?
12. What are some good ways for the learner to find out about this career?

Figure 12-26. Sample activities and questions to help the employer during a job shadow.

Mentoring

Mentoring is generally defined as a relationship in which adults offer support and encouragement to a younger person. In recent years, mentoring initiatives have emerged in workplaces across the country. A workplace mentor is an employee who helps a learner acquire the skills, knowledge, and work habits that lead to a successful career. The mentor instructs the learner, critiques the learner's work, and challenges the learner to perform well.

Mentoring has been defined, most generally, as a relationship between a young person and an adult in which the adult offers support and guidance as the youth goes through a difficult period, enters a new area of experience, takes on important tasks, or attempts to correct an earlier problem. Mentoring is thought to be useful in particular for providing positive adult contacts for youth who are isolated from adults in their schools, homes, communities, and workplaces (Stern et al., 1994).

The new importance of mentoring in youth programs is partly a function of the conditions in which young people increasingly live in America—in urban America in particular. Widespread family breakdown, erosion of neighborhood ties, and time demands of parents' work have created a situation in which few young people have even one significant close relationship with a nonparental adult before actually reaching adulthood. For inner-city youth, the problem of not having positive adult role models is compounded by the relatively higher rates of single-parent homes, the strength of youth gangs, and more prevalent substance abuse. Mentorship programs for youth have been designed to help fill this need for positive adult role models, support, and guidance (Stern et al., 1994).

JOB SHADOWING GUIDE: EXAMPLES OF QUESTIONS TO ASK DURING A JOB SHADOW

INTRODUCTION

- What is your occupation and job title?
- How did you become interested in this type of work?
- Why did you choose this career?
- How did you get your job with this company?

QUALIFICATIONS

- What types of education and/or training were required for this job?
- What classes did you take in high school that prepared you for your job?
- Did you have to interview, take any tests, or complete an internship or apprenticeship for this position?
- What kind of experience was required for this job?
- What personality traits are important for this job?
- What kind of technical knowledge is required for this job?
- How are technology demands increasing or changing for this job?

DUTIES

- How many hours do you work in a typical week?
- Are certain times of the month or year busier than other times?
- What kinds of things are you required to do?
- Are you required to supervise other employees as part of your job?
- Do you have to depend on others in order to perform your job?
- Do you take work home?
- Do you work a shift? What choices do you have in making your work schedule?

SALARY AND BENEFITS

- What are the salary ranges for different levels in this field?
- What types of fringe benefits are offered to you for this job?
- How are raises earned?
- What is the opportunity for advancement in this area?

PERSONAL SATISFACTION

- What do you like best about your job?
- What don't you like about your job?
- How has your company kept up with technology and progressive business management techniques?
- How does your job affect your time away from work?
- What are the job opportunities for this area of work?
- What kind of personal satisfaction do you get from your job?

MISCELLANEOUS

- What advice would you give a learner interested in this career?
- What changes do you see in this area within the next 5 to 10 years?

Figure 12-27. Sample questions to ask during a job shadow.

Mentors can play an important role in helping young people reach their full potential. Over the past several years, a number of studies have shown that mentoring relationships are linked to improved grades, lower dropout rates, and higher enrollment in college. Mentoring initiatives have also been shown to address wider social concerns, including a greater regard for people of other races and socioeconomic backgrounds and a reduction in drug use.

Employer participation in mentoring initiatives often stems from concern for young people, but mentoring also provides benefits to employers. Mentoring fosters an atmosphere of learning, teamwork, and flexibility in the workplace and can reduce the costs of recruiting, screening, selecting, and training new workers. Employers can obtain firsthand information on the skills, abilities, and work habits of learners in mentoring programs and often hire learners based on this information.

Workplace mentoring also provides a number of benefits to individual mentors. Employees who serve as mentors can develop supervisory skills and learn to work with young people. In the process of determining key workplace learning elements and job-specific skills they want to convey, mentors may find ways to improve their own performance. In addition, the satisfaction mentors feel when working with young people often translates into improved work habits and productivity. But perhaps the most important benefit to a mentor is the recognition that they can make a difference in the lives of young people.

The National School-to-Work Office (September 1996c) identified successful practices of mentoring experiences:

1. A recruitment plan for mentors–Developing mentoring initiatives requires a sustained effort to recruit employers and mentors. Employer recruitment plans often identify CEOs or high-level executives in organizations who are most likely to participate in mentor programs. These individuals, with the assistance of transition coordinators, teachers, and parents, can then help build participation throughout the community. Successful recruitment plans also devise methods to recruit mentors within an organization once an employer has committed to participation.

2. Eligibility screening for mentors and learners–Practitioners stress the importance of a well-defined application and screening process to determine the suitability of an individual for a mentoring initiative. Unsuccessful mentor relationships can result from a variety of causes, such as lack of time, commitment, and communication. These problems can disillusion mentors and participants and reduce their chances of subsequent participation. An effective screening mechanism can significantly reduce the probability of problems caused by individuals who cannot fulfill the responsibilities of a mentoring program.

Staff members should select eligibility criteria to keep these occurrences at a minimum. For mentors, criteria such as commitment, time, knowledge of job-specific and general workplace skills, and the absence of a criminal history are often used in the screening process. Learners' grades, attendance, behavior, and motivation or willingness to participate are the primary determinants of their eligibility. See Figure 12-28.

3. Mentor training–Many training sessions focus on the balance of challenge and support that mentors must provide in an active, work-based learning experience. Training should help mentors set challenging yet realistic goals, plan projects to meet these goals, select appropriate instruction techniques, and assess learner progress. Mentors should also be trained to support learners. Supportive mentors understand the different stages of adolescent development, recognize learning preferences, encourage communication, and provide feedback. Training should also help mentors avoid potential problems or learn to work through the problems that may develop in a mentoring relationship. See Figure 12-29.

Training should help mentors become familiar with program expectations, school district policies, work schedules, review processes, support services, and the roles they will be expected to fulfill. Mentors will become role models, nurturing the learners and helping them adapt to the culture of the workplace. A mentor may also be called upon to assume the role of coach, instructing a learner in specific occupational skills and evaluating their performance. In some mentoring initiatives, one person is expected to fulfill both of these roles. Other organizations use several different coaches as a learner rotates through different jobs while maintaining one mentor. They provide training for all of these individuals.

The design of a mentoring program must contain guidelines for prospective mentors. An effective mentor

- understands time commitments;
- provides a support structure;
- respects young people;
- understands the challenges that face today's youth, both in and out of school (e.g., peer pressure, cultural differences);
- demonstrates a willingness to be as nonjudgmental as possible;
- assists learners in developing goals;
- is a good listener;
- is consistent; and
- communicates at the learners' level.

Training sessions can help learners define their objectives and roles in mentoring initiatives and prepare them for entry into the workplace. Learners should understand what will be expected of them in the workplace and should be reminded that their appearance, attitude, and behavior will influence the nature of their mentor relationship and their success in the workplace. Training should also clarify what to reasonably expect from their mentors and what not to expect. See Figure 12-30.

4. A monitoring process and ongoing support and training–Monitoring should consist of regular meetings that include school-to-work staff, mentors, participants, and, whenever possible, parents. These meetings should monitor learner progress in school and the workplace and address the learner's social development. A formal, written record of these meetings can provide information to improve the individual relationship and the mentoring initiative as a whole.

Ongoing support, including recognition of achievements and peer support groups for both mentors and learners, is essential to maintaining long-term mentoring relationships. In addition, school-to-work staff can provide support assistance and training that should continue for the duration of the relationship. Ongoing training can help mentors and learners work through problems and provide new activities or approaches to learning as relationships mature and learners develop new areas of interest.

5. Closure steps–All mentoring relationships should include a private and confidential formal meeting between learners, mentors, staff, and parents. These exit interviews should include evaluations of both the program and the mentoring relationship based on the individual and program goals. They should also help learners plan for the fixture and include a clearly stated policy for further contact between mentor and learner.

Business/Industry Linkages

The National Alliance of Business (1999), in affiliation with the National Association of Manufacturers, U.S. Chamber of Commerce, and Committee for Economic Development and the American Business Conference, filed a joint statement on transition initiatives:

We strongly support school-to-career initiatives as a way of motivating individuals to reach higher levels of academic excellence and equip themselves to succeed in the future. Transition initiatives combine demanding core academic curriculum with practical work-based application. Research tells us that all students learn more when given the opportunity to apply knowledge and skills to "real world" challenges. The transition preparation process, linked to high academic standards, can provide better education, workforce preparation, and the ability to learn throughout a lifetime.

APPLICATION FOR MENTOR PROGRAM—LEARNER FORM

Name: _____   Date: _____

Address: _____   Phone: _____

School: _____   Best time to contact: _____

If employed, where? _____   Supervisor: _____

Interests and Hobbies (Circle all that apply)

Art	Camping	Dancing	Games	Martial Arts
Baseball	Cars	Fashion	Golf	Music
Basketball	Cooking	Football	Hiking	Shopping

Other: _____

Current GPA: _____   Anticipated date of graduation: _____

Career pathway/occupational interests: _____

Why would you like to have a mentor? _____

_____

Please list two people who have known you at least two years. By supplying this information you are granting permission for us to contact the individuals below.

Name _____   Job employer _____

Home address _____

Home phone _____   Business phone _____

Name _____   Job employer _____

Home address _____

Home phone _____   Business phone _____

What characteristics would you want your mentor to have? (For example: patience, knowledge of many different jobs, etc.)

_____

_____

Terms of the mentor program:

1. Spend at least _____ hour(s) a week with your mentor for _____ (length of time).
2. Attend an orientation session that will prepare you to work with a mentor and set goals for what you want to accomplish.
3. Follow through with activities agreed upon with your mentor.
4. Complete a brief evaluation at the end of the mentor program period.

I agree to all the conditions stated above and confirm that I am not presently engaged in any criminal activities. I also agree that the mentor can contact my parent(s)/guardian(s) and my school if a concern arises during the mentoring period.

_____   _____

Signature   Date

Please return this form to: Mentor Program Coordinator

Name: _____

Address _____

Adapted from: Boyer-Stephens, A. (n.d.). *Employer as Mentor.* Columbia, MO: University of Missouri-Columbia, Institute for Workforce Education.

Figure 12-28. Sample application for learners for the mentor program.

APPLICATION FOR MENTOR PROGRAM — MENTOR FORM

Name: _____   Date: _____

Department: _____   Phone: _____

Job Title: _____   Best time to contact: _____

Home Address: _____   Supervisor: _____

Interests and Hobbies (Circle all that apply)

Art	Camping	Dancing	Games	Martial Arts
Baseball	Cars	Fashion	Golf	Music
Basketball	Cooking	Football	Hiking	Shopping

Other: _____

Educational background: _____
_____

List previous work and/or experiences with young people. _____
_____

Please list two people who have known you at least two years. By supplying this information you are granting permission for us to contact the individuals below.

Name _____   Job employer _____

Home address _____

Home phone _____   Business phone _____

Name _____   Job employer _____

Home address _____

Home phone _____   Business phone _____

What special characteristics do you feel you have to offer a young person to help in his/her personal and career development? _____
_____

How did you hear about the mentoring program? _____

Terms of the mentor program:

1. Spend at least _____ hour(s) a week with the learner for _____ (length of time).
2. Attend an orientation session that will prepare you to work with the learner and set goals for what you want to accomplish.
3. Follow through with activities agreed upon with the learner.
4. Complete a brief evaluation at the end of the mentor program period.

I agree to all the conditions stated above and confirm that I am not presently engaged in any criminal activities. I also grant permission to the Mentor Program Coordinator to check with appropriate authorities (courts, youth agencies, police, and motor vehicle), if necessary, upon matters of record regarding my background.

_____   _____
Signature   Date

Please return this form to: Mentor Program Coordinator

Name: _____

Address: _____

Adapted from: Boyer-Stephens, A. (n.d.). *Employer as Mentor.* Columbia, MO: University of Missouri-Columbia, Institute for Workforce Education.

Figure 12-29. Sample application for mentors for the mentors program.

```
╔══════════════════════════════════════════╗
║          TRAINING TOPICS FOR MENTORS       ║
╠══════════════════════════════════════════╣
```

1. Definition: What is Mentoring?
   - Description
   - Research finding – what works?
2. Issues for Mentors
   - Roles and responsibilities, expectations
   - Potential benefits
   - Attitudes toward youth (myths, realities, prejudices, values, fears, concerns)
   - The cycle of the relationship
3. Understanding Youth
   - Adolescent development (psychosocial and cognitive)
   - Youth culture (typical behaviors, pressures, and so on)
   - Profile for youth (increased self-esteem, goal setting, decision making and assertiveness skills, completion of high school, future planning)
4. Mentor/Protégé Relationships
   - Developing rapport
   - Building trust
   - Communicating effectively (listening, supporting, advising, problem solving)
   - Overcoming differences (race, culture, age, socioeconomic background, values)
   - Letting go
5. Program Issues
   - Policies and guidelines (confidentiality, accountability, agency expectations)
   - Program development/activities
   - Parent involvement (creating and supporting it)
   - Community resources (finding and using them)
   - Measuring success
6. Issues Affecting Youth
   - Self-esteem
   - Sexuality (feelings, facts, decisions)
   - Teenage pregnancy and parenthood
   - Substance abuse
   - Violence
   - Special needs of groups
   - Emotional problems
   - Family stress
   - Life planning and career education
7. Training for Specific Program Models

Source: Wilson, J., & Wilson, P. (1990). *Mentoring Manual: A Guide to Program Development and Implementation.* Baltimore, MD: Abell Foundation.

Figure 12-30. A sample list of mentoring topics to help mentors understand roles and issues.

Successful transition initiatives are part of the main, academically rigorous path of education for all learners. They expose learners to career options they might not know about otherwise, give participants skills that can be applied and adapted to any career of their choice, and prepare learners to choose any course of endeavor, including further education. Transition initiatives are not plans to divert learners away from school and into the workplace. They are not separate paths designed for "slow learners" nor tracking systems that force learners into certain jobs. They are not dependent on federal funding or programmatic direction.

An effective transition initiative emphasizes the following:

- A primary goal is higher academic achievement–Transition programs are intended to ensure that all learners, college and noncollege bound, meet challenging academic standards. Learners should be prepared to succeed in an associate or baccalaureate degree program. In the best of these programs, learners can only participate in the work experience component if they stay in school, take a core curriculum, maintain satisfactory grades, and make reasonable progress toward completing a degree.

- Local communities design the programs–A transition initiative can succeed only if based on voluntary, local decisions resulting in partnerships between educators, employers, local officials, and, ultimately parents and learners.

- School-based and work-based learning are coordinated–Academic curriculum and workplace experiences reinforce each other to enhance overall educational achievement. Work site learning involves practical demands for mathematics, science, reading, writing, social studies, and computer skills. Work site learning also develops skills that traditional classroom learning does not develop as well, such as problem-solving skills, management of time and resources, responsibility, initiative, and communication skills. Learners participating in effective transition programs tend to take more courses in advanced math and science, increase their grades, graduate at higher rates, go on to postsecondary education at higher rates, and are better prepared to succeed in jobs. In addition, youth who might otherwise drop out of school are more likely to stay in school and complete their education.

- Employer participation adds relevance–Employers should inform schools of the knowledge and skills demanded by the economy of the future and provide the necessary learning experiences.

The appeal of working with youth and participating in the community drives many businesses to provide learners with work-based learning experiences or become involved in transition in other ways. In a recent survey of employer participation in school-to-work, the Institute for Educational Leadership found that over 75% of employers, particularly those from large establishments, agreed that they were motivated by an interest in performing a community service (National School-to-Work Office, September 1996a).

But an appeal solely to an employer's sense of civic duty will not, on its own, produce a nationwide school-to-work system that provides work-based learning opportunities for all learners. A critical supplement to engagement efforts focusing on an employer's sense of civic duty lies in demonstrating the economic and financial benefits of participation in transition efforts to employers. The American economy is changing in response to heightened international competition and the development of new technologies. Increasingly, the success of a company depends on the knowledge, skills, and abilities of its workers, necessitating a better link between education and work.

The National School-to-Work Office (September 1996a) provided a variety of strategies to recruit employers for school-to-work/transition initiatives:

1. Articulate the benefits of school-to-work to employers–School-to-work initiatives can offer many benefits to employers, including the following:

- School-to-work initiatives can reduce the costs of recruiting, screening, selecting, and training new workers. Schools are the principal supplier of employees for many businesses. When employers work collaboratively with schools, they can reduce their costs. School-to-work systems help employers avoid having to rely on uncertain information and costly methods of recruitment and selection. Employers can obtain evidence of a potential employee's skills and abilities through work-based learning programs, skill certificates, or portfolios of learner work. In addition, if employers in school-to-work systems hire learners from their own structured work-based learning initiatives, they reduce training costs. There is also evidence that school-to-work can reduce turnover costs for employers.

- School-to-work initiatives can improve the performance of existing employees, particularly work site supervisors and mentors. The process of developing work-based learning experiences for learners can lead work site supervisors to examine their own activities in the workplace. In the process of determining key workplace learning elements and processes for learners, employees may find ways to improve their own performance. Individuals in the workplace who work with learners also have an opportunity to develop managerial and supervisory skills.

- School-to-work initiatives help meet the demand for new skills required by rapid technological change. Many learners currently in high school have considerable computer and technology skills because they have grown up working with computers and high-tech electronics. In many instances, they can share this knowledge and experience with current workers.

- School-to-work initiatives improve community relations. Community involvement is good business practice. Not only do employers receive the satisfaction of interacting with young people and contributing to their educational development, but they also benefit from an improved local education system and a positive image projected throughout the community.

2. Provide a range of opportunities for involvement–Employers consistently report that a wide range of well-defined roles and responsibilities encourages participation. Successful school-to-work systems do not attempt to channel employers into prescribed activities. Instead, they offer employers a continuum of choices, ranging from career awareness, career exploration, and job shadowing, to more intensive activities such as mentoring, apprenticeships, and other structured work-based learning opportunities. Employers can also provide input in the development of integrated curriculum, develop and recognize skill standards, serve on planning and governance bodies, and recruit other employers. The intensity and nature of employer involvement in these activities depend upon the specific resources available in local labor markets and the goals of both the employer and the school-to-work system.

3. Target key employers and industries–Local school-to-work partnerships can begin to build employer involvement by targeting businesses and industries in high growth areas and those that have prior involvement in business and education partnerships or other community-based activities. Other factors that may help in targeting employer recruitment efforts include the extent to which the employers have a record of hiring young people, skill shortages among entry-level workers, cooperative labor-management relations, or a commitment to employee training and diversity. While all area employers should be addressed in a recruitment effort, targeting the industry sectors and types of firms most likely to participate is an effective way to initiate a recruitment strategy. The visible engagement of these employers can serve as a springboard for expanding school-to-work among other employers.

4. Foster employer ownership–Employer participation on advisory boards and in developing skill standards, curriculum, and assessment tools provides businesses with a sense of "ownership" of a school-to-work system. The National Alliance of Business explains that school-to-work initiatives provide employers an opportunity to help shape education systems and the preparation of young people for productive futures. Through school-to-work systems, employers can help to identify growth industries and the skills required to fill jobs in them, articulate an education reform agenda that reflects current and future workforce needs, and advocate policies that ensure global competitiveness. Business involvement in school-to-work ensures that programs are responsive to industry needs, that skill

standards are current with high performance workplaces and technology, and that learners are able to find jobs in their chosen fields.

5. Address employers' concerns about liability issues–A number of business partners have raised questions regarding child labor laws and the Fair Labor Standards Act. Many local school-to-work initiatives use intermediary organizations as the "employers of record" for learners, absorbing liability and administrative costs associated with work-based learning experiences.

6. Build local networks of employers–Developing networks among schools, community organizations, labor, and employers is critical to the success of school-to-work systems. Employers emphasize that they respond more readily to other employers than they do to government officials or educators. Encouraging CEOs or high-level managers to champion school-to-work, both within their own company and with other employers in the community, is a key element of strategies to build employer involvement. Practitioners can promote employer networking by encouraging participation on advisory boards, arranging presentations, and providing employers with school-to-work materials for distribution.

Activities that business and industry can become involved in include

• providing learners with work-based knowledge and skills;
• providing tours of the facilities;
• hosting open houses;
• making classroom presentations;
• providing work experience opportunities for instructors and counselors;
• providing work-based learning experiences and internships for learners;
• participating as team teachers;
• teaching classes in their settings;
• providing or loaning equipment;
• speaking at career days or other special events;
• assisting in determining performance standards (curriculum validation);
• agreeing to priority hiring for graduates;
• sponsoring scholarships for learners;
• guaranteeing placement of qualified graduates;
• providing industry training for instructors and counselors;
• participating in Adopt-a-School activities;
• participating in Adopt-a-Program activities;
• participating in Adopt-a-Teacher activities;
• participating in Adopt-a-Learner activities;
• participating in youth apprenticeship programs;
• providing grants and materials to programs/classes;
• participating in school-run enterprises;
• mentoring;
• providing for job shadowing; and
• providing cooperative education sites.

Before connecting learners with employers, there are several steps that will make the school and work partnership more comfortable and beneficial to all parties. Churchill, Morales and O'Flanagan (1994) suggested the following:

• Encourage employers to visit and participate in school activities. This will help employers understand the school culture in which teachers and learners interact every day.

• Encourage teachers to participate in internships or job shadowing experiences in industry to begin to understand the skills and knowledge requirements. Some community college courses are another effective way to gain industry knowledge.

• Form a committee with employers and teachers to prepare written materials that provide directions to learners' supervisors. If possible, field test the materials with a small group.

• Appoint a coordinator or industry liaison to arrange, schedule, and oversee learner work placements. This provides one contact for work site supervisors if they have questions or problems.

• Appoint a work site coordinator for each firm involving groups of learners and a supervisor for each learner.

• Use advisory boards to design curriculum and training plans, as well as orienting new employers to the program.

• Conduct formal orientation sessions for employers who will be working directly with learners. Often supervisors will need tips on how to work, teach, and possibly supervise adolescents. Provide clear expectations and possibly role-playing exercises.

• Conduct formal orientations for teachers who will be supervising or visiting their learners regularly at the work site.

• Involve employers in classroom activities. Prepare newsletters or other forms of communication to keep participants up to date on events.

• Ask business and industry volunteers to serve as guest speakers. In order to prepare them for this activity, a guide of relevant information should be provided for them. See Figure 12-31.

DEVELOPING INDIVIDUALIZED TRANSITION PROGRAMS (ITP)

The ITP is a written document that describes the long-range career and occupational goals of individuals with special needs and the skills and services they will need to secure and maintain satisfying employment leading to independent living and personal growth. The ITP may be separate from other individualized plans, such as individual career plans (ICPs), or it may be developed as a component of the IEP.

The Individuals with Disabilities Education Act (IDEA) requires that a statement of needed transition services be included as a component of the IEP for learners with disabilities, beginning at age 16 and each year thereafter, and to the extent appropriate, in the IEPs of learners with disabilities who are 14 years of age or younger.

GUIDE FOR GUEST SPEAKER

This guide is provided to assist you in planning and preparing your presentation to our class. This is an example of the type of information that the students will be interested in obtaining.

1. Why did you decide on your career?
2. Where did you learn about your career?
3. How long have you worked at your job?
4. What things did you learn in school that helped you in this career?
5. Is there a subject area you wish you had studied more about in school?
6. What type of special training, if any, do you need for your career?
7. What special equipment or tools, if any, do you use?
8. How many hours do you work each day?
9. Are you required to work more hours if needed?
10. Is your job ever dangerous?
11. Do you have a boss?
12. What skills do you feel are most important in getting along with others?
13. Does your career relate to your hobbies?
14. With what type of people do you work daily?
15. Are you required to move often? If so, what problems does it create?
16. What does the future look like for your career?
17. Is there an opportunity for advancement in your career?
18. Does your employer provide fringe benefits? If so, what?
19. What personal qualities are needed to be successful in your career?
20. If someone wanted to pursue a career similar to yours, what advice would you give that person?

Figure 12-31. Sample questions for a guest speaker to use as criteria for a presentation.

Whether transition planning begins for a learner at age 14 or 16 or later, the IEP must include a coordinated set of activities for each of the following areas:

- Instruction–This is typically provided in schools (e.g., general education classes, academic instruction, tutoring arrangements). There may be other ways to deliver skill development utilizing other agencies, adult education, and postsecondary schools.
- Community experiences–This is provided outside the school building in community settings, or perhaps by schools or other agencies and includes community-based work experiences, job site training programs, banking, shopping, transportation, community counseling, recreational services, independent living, etc.
- Development of employment and other postsecondary adult living objectives–These are services that lead to a

job or career, such as work experience or job site training, and important adult activities that are done occasionally, such as registering to vote, filing taxes, accessing medical services, etc. This type of training may be provided by schools or other agencies.

When appropriate the ITP may include the following:

- Daily living skills–This is training in tasks or activities adults do every day, such as preparing meals, paying bills, etc. This training may be provided by schools or other agencies.
- A functional vocational evaluation–This provides information about job or career interests and aptitudes and skills. Information may be gathered through observation or formal measures. It should be practical. The evaluation may be conducted by the school or other agencies.

Planning transition services cannot be done is isolation but must reach beyond the school boundaries into the community. Planning must also reach beyond a learner's limitations to explore the learner's strengths, interests, hopes and dreams. Transition planning is, first, to help learners and families think about the life of the learner after high school and identify long-range goals, and second, to design the high school experience to ensure that learners gain the skills and connections they need to achieve those goals.

IEP/Transition Planning Team

A learner's IEP/transition planning team should be put together by the IEP manager in consultation with the learner and family. The learner and parent(s) may identify key individuals that are already involved in their lives, such as a relative, county case manager, mental health counselor, or parole officer. Learners and their parents should be given information about available postschool services and community resources so that they can make decisions about the individuals they want on the team. See Figure 12-32.

In order to ensure compliance with the IDEA, certain members must be present at the IEP/transition planning meeting. In addition, certain individuals must be invited to attend; others may be included as appropriate. The following team members must be present:

- An administrator or designee–The administrator may be the school principal or director of special education; an administrative designee may be a special educator authorized by the principal to commit district resources. When a learner's parents reside in a district other than the providing district, an administrator or designee from the resident district must be invited to the meeting. The resident district may appoint a member of the providing district as its administrative designee.
- The learner's regular education teacher–An appropriate representative may be the school principal or

director of special education; an administrative designee may be a special educator authorized by the principal to commit district resources. The resident district may appoint a member of the providing district as its administrative designee.

- A special education teacher–This is the teacher holding the license of the learner's primary disability.

The following individuals must be invited:

- The learner must be invited to the planning meeting. Learners should always be involved in their transition planning and encouraged to attend all the meetings.
- One or both parents must also be invited to any meeting where transition services will be discussed, and they must be informed that the purpose of the meeting is to discuss transition planning.
- A member of the assessment team must be invited. This may be the learner's teacher, a representative of the district, or some other person who is knowledgeable about the assessment procedures used with the learner.

The following individuals may be invited to attend, as appropriate:

- Related service providers such as an occupational therapist, physical therapist, audiologist, psychologist, adaptive physical education instructor, doctor or nurse, rehabilitation counselor, or social worker.
- Representatives of nonschool agencies such as a division of rehabilitation services counselor, county case manager, health care provider, residential service provider, supported employment service provider, community leisure service provider, or postsecondary education support service facilitator.
- Other individuals at the discretion of the parent(s) and learner. Parents and learners need to be informed of their right to bring anyone of their own choosing to the meeting.
- Representatives from an outside district, agency, or school when the assessment team summary report recommends placement options outside the resident district.

Case Study . . . Juan

Juan is an academically and economically disadvantaged learner enrolled in a masonry program. He is a bilingual student whose family came from Puerto Rico seven years ago. There are ten people in the family. Juan's father sometimes finds employment doing odd jobs. Most of the time, however, he is unemployed. The family is on public assistance. Spanish is spoken in the home.

When Juan first entered public schools in this country, he was given a psychological test. His difficulty in understanding English resulted in a low score, which automatically placed him in a special education class for the mentally retarded. When it came time for his periodic reevaluation, he had developed a sufficient proficiency in English to test out of the special education class. The psychologist was also bilingual and was able to administer the test questions in Spanish and English.

Currently Juan is registered in regular classes at school. He works with a bilingual teacher several times a week and attends a class in a resource room each day for assistance in remedial academics. His reading and math levels are three levels below his peers. The district social worker also has Juan on her caseload and visits the home periodically in order to keep an open channel of communication between the school and the family. She is also looking into the possibility of enrolling Juan in a summer youth employment program run by a local JPTA sponsored agency.

An ITP has been developed specifying the activities required to help Juan succeed in a masonry program and to obtain employment in the construction occupation. Particular attention has been devoted to transition enhancing activities in the ITP that will assist Juan in finding employment so he can help to support his family. Juan is succeeding in the skills development phase of the masonry program. He has demonstrated proficiency in laying brick, making bonds and ties, building footings and arches, and working with a variety of materials such as glass, brick, cement blocks, and artificial stone.

The guidance counselor and the masonry instructor are assisting Juan with the development of a career portfolio that will enable him to realize the progress he is making in school and give him the opportunity to document his strengths and recognize areas requiring more work. Juan has really taken an interest in his career portfolio and is involving his parents, classmates, and friends in its development. He is developing the important skill of self-reflection, as evidenced by his evaluation of experiences in his portfolio.

Juan has been having difficulties in keeping up with the classroom lectures and reading assignments in the areas of construction theory and printreading. The resource room teacher and the bilingual teacher are both working cooperatively with the program instructor to help him in these areas.

Juan's career and technical education teacher has taken him along on several visits to job sites where masonry workers are employed. One of these workers took an interest in him after overhearing the masonry instructor talking with the supervisor about Juan's capabilities. This worker agreed to let Juan help him in the evenings after school on part-time jobs to help him further develop his masonry skills and to experience work in an authentic environment. The guidance counselor and career and technical education teacher are working on establishing a job shadowing experience for Juan with a local masonry contractor.

The guidance counselor has assisted Juan in using the school's computerized career information system to find additional information about the construction trades and particularly the masonry trade. Arrangements are being made to help Juan find summer employment with a masonry contractor and to establish a work site that can be developed into a work-based learning site for him when school begins in the fall.

POTENTIAL PARTICIPANTS IN TRANSITION PLANNING	
Potential Consultant	**Relationship to Transition Services**
Adult education rep	Provides information about lifelong education options
Advocacy organization(s) rep	May offer self-advocacy training or support groups for young adults
Assistive technology rep	Provides expertise on devices that can open doors to opportunities
At-risk/Prevention specialist	Offers counseling and support on teen pregnancy, alcohol, and drugs
Business-education partnership rep	Provides links between schools and local businesses and industry
Community action agency rep	May link team to resources for traditionally underrepresented groups
Correctional education staff	Provides incarcerated youth with continued learning opportunities
Employer	Offers insight into expectations; promotes hiring of people with disabilities
Employment specialist	Provides job development, placement, coaching
Extension service agent	Offers programs in parenting, homemaking, independent living
Health department	Provides guidance on community health services and health care advice
Higher education rep	Provides information on postsecondary services to learners with disabilities
Housing agency rep	Assists in developing housing options
Leisure program rep	Knows available program options within the community
Literacy council rep	Coordinates volunteers to teach basic reading and writing skills
Local government rep	Funds many local services; can provide information on local services
Local disability rep	Provides information and training (often serves all disabilities, not just one)
Parent training information center rep	Provides training on transition planning and advocacy services to families
Religious community member	Can provide social support to young adults and their families
Residential service provider	Can help access specialized housing
Social worker	Provides guidance and arranges for case management, support, respite care
Special Olympics rep	Provides sports training, competition, and recreational opportunities for youth
Therapists	Provides behavioral, physical, occupational, and speech services in the community
Transportation rep	Offers expertise about transportation options and training
United Way rep	Funds many community programs that may offer options for young adults
YMCA/YWCA	Offers recreations and leisure programs

Figure 12-32. A listing for learners, parents, and other interested parties of potential participants on an IEP/transition planning team.

Roles of IEP/Transition Planning Team Members

Team members all have specific roles to play in developing the IEP and its transition plan.

Learner. Involving learners in making decisions about their own lives is extremely important. It is not enough for a learner simply to attend the meeting. Individuals who are active participants in the planning of their futures are more likely to be committed to reaching their goals. All learners, regardless of their disabilities, should be encouraged to advocate for themselves. Some learners have had limited experience in expressing personal preferences. Teachers and parents can help prepare learners to participate in the meeting by talking about the meeting's purpose, describing what goes on and who typically attends, and discussing transition issues before and after the meeting occurs.

Some learners may benefit from rehearsing certain parts of the meeting, such as how to greet team members or the way to express preferences or suggest alternatives. The ultimate goal is for learners to assume control, with appropriate levels of support, over their education and transition and identify and manage its various components. The role of learners in developing their IEP/transition plan includes

- providing information about their future adult goals to the team;
- determining their strengths and challenges and communicating them to the team;
- expressing a desire for certain program components;

- contributing information about their preferences; and
- collaborating in the decision-making process.

Family Members. One of the most important responsibilities of parents is to prepare their children to be independent and successful adults regardless of the child's disability. Because learners with disabilities are likely to encounter a variety of obstacles, transition to life as an adult may have to be more carefully planned. Families bring a wealth of information about the child that is critical to effective transition planning. Family members can assist in the development of transition plans by

- sharing information about "what has worked," family strengths and resources, incentives that school cannot offer, and most important, their dream of the future of their child;
- becoming informed about quality transition planning and services in the community that can assist and support their child in achieving success as an adult;
- assisting in the implementation of identified transition activities;
- assigning specific duties to the child around the home; emphasizing good grooming, physical fitness, and social and communication skills;
- making sure that the intentions of agreements and collaborative efforts between various agencies are fully met;
- providing an assessment of their child's skills outside of the school environment;
- actively supporting efforts to provide training in a variety of community settings and sharing contacts to assist in securing training sites; and
- providing a variety of community experiences for their child.

Parents as Partners. As the first teachers of their children, parents have a unique opportunity to provide early career exploration and the basic skills necessary to succeed in school and the workplace. As children progress through school, parents can help them learn in the home, monitor school assignments, and encourage career-related activities after school, on weekends, and in the summer. Programs have been developed to help parents understand the dynamics of child and adolescent development and teach the attitudes and skills their children will need to lead a successful life.

As children grow older, the role of parent becomes a balancing act between providing support and encouraging independence. Learners gradually assume more responsibility and greater control over their lives as they progress through school towards work. In order to assume adult responsibilities, children need and deserve the opportunities provided by transition systems to interact with and earn the respect of adults. Parents play a key role in this process by providing support and working with counselors, teachers, and employers to develop career opportunities for youth. Parents and guardians who become engaged in transition systems not only improve the future prospects of their children but also contribute valuable insight to transition partnerships and can serve as community advocates for a transition system.

An involved parent is a teacher's ally, coordinating learning in the home with schoolwork, helping the child stay on track in school, and cooperating with teachers to resolve problems encountered along the way. In many high schools, infrequent communication between parent and teacher means that a learner is doing acceptable work, because under current policies, high school contacts families mainly to discuss serious academic or behavioral problems.

A strong relationship between parent and career counselor can help learners select, develop, and follow through on their educational and career goals. Counselors who give parents access to career information and involve them in individual planning sessions for their children have experienced great success in fostering such relationships. Because career counselors are often overwhelmed by sheer numbers of learners, many administrators have made the commitment to support counselors by offering staff development and by establishing lower learner-career ratios, flexible scheduling, and easier access to career and labor market information.

Many school-to-work systems require that parents co-sign training agreements, a step that initiates communication between parents and employers. Some parents take the next step, actually visiting work sites and conferring with employers and supervisors to gain firsthand information with which to encourage and support their children. Many employers say they would welcome such contact from parents but are often unsure how to proceed. Some need encouragement from school personnel or parents; others need specific advice and training in how to structure contact with parents.

Partnerships between parents and employers can benefit both parties, particularly where an agreement is worked out with school personnel that provides some structure or procedures. These relationships work both ways: Parents call or visit the work site to learn about progress and problems, and work sites contact parents, either directly or through the school, to share information or request help.

Similar to IEPs developed for learners with disabilities, individualized education and career plans have been utilized in school-to-work systems. Many learners and parents do not understand the requirements for learner educational and career goals. The development of learner plans provides structured time for parents to discuss education and career options with learners, counselors, and teachers. The typical plan includes periodic meetings to discuss plans, career exploration, testing, and establishment of a course of study to meet career goals.

Transition practitioners can encourage employers to support their employees who are parents. Flexible work scheduling arrangements, such as part-time work, flexible time, job-sharing, and telecommuting, also encourage parent involvement in school-to-work. Developers of school-to-work systems can ask businesses to support practices that provide opportunities for parents to play an active part in their children's future.

School-to-work should operate as a community-wide effort, recognizing that parents bring invaluable perspectives to the partnerships that guide local systems. Parents who serve on governing bodies can speak with informed voices regarding the experiences of their children in school-to-work. They are in a position to advocate and work for better information, services, and other resources for their children, and to become leaders and catalysts for other parents. (National School-to-Work Office, September 1996b).

Parents should also

- help their child identify skills and further education necessary to enter potential career fields;
- help their child make appropriate decisions, matching interests, skills, and expectations with program offerings;
- consider the possibility of learner placement in their place of work;
- work with teachers and program staff to offer feedback about their child's experience in transition planning;
- help other parents understand the value of the program for their children;
- offer to assist with fund-raising activities, mailings, and recruitment of employers; and
- after graduation from the program, remind their child to complete and return postgraduation evaluation surveys and questionnaires so the program can continue to improve.

Educators and Other School Personnel. Educators prepare learners for adult life. The role of educators and related service personnel includes

- informing learners and family members about transition planning;
- preparing learners by teaching skills that can be used in work, living, and leisure activities outside of school;
- assisting learners in the selection of accommodation and assistive technology that may increase independence or participation in activities;
- coordinating IEP/transition planning and assessment, as well as the delivery of both direct and indirect services as designed by the team;
- educating families about support alternatives available in the community;
- involving learner and family members in the design and implementation of a written, formal transition plan;
- incorporating modifications used in the classroom into the transition planning process (e.g., testing considerations, physical accommodations, or taped texts); and
- encouraging family members to allow learners to practice making choices and to follow through on decisions.

Community Service Providers. Community service providers are an important link to community resources and can assist in accessing services. They are responsible for working with the learners and parents to achieve work, residential, social, and leisure goals both before and after graduation.

Team members do not necessarily have to come from social service agencies. Learners and their families may also invite a relative, friend, or advocate who can provide emotional support, access to their personal networks, or other unique expertise. If possible, it is also helpful to have team members from similar language and cultural backgrounds as the learner. These members can help the team understand how cultural or language issues impact the transition process. Some typical transition outcomes, such as going away to college, getting a paying job, moving out of the family home, and making decisions independently of the family, are valued differently in different cultures. Transition planning is a long-range process. It is often helpful to establish a transition planning timeline. See Figure 12-33.

IMPROVING URBAN AND RURAL SCHOOLS AND COMMUNITIES

Although rural and urban areas also differ in factors such as population density and the presence or absence of natural-resource-based industries, they are fundamentally connected by the economic system, labor markets, population migration, legal and political systems, and broad cultural values. Both urban and rural communities and their schools have been caught up in several trends that have opened the way for education reform, including:

- Community and neighborhood decay following national and global economic restructuring that caused job and population declines and increased poverty.
- Changes in federal policy that increased pressure on states and local communities to deal with their own problems, raising questions about equity and local social capacity to deal with vital issues such as education, welfare reform, and workforce investment.
- State-level systemic education reform largely based on higher standards, stricter accountability, and school-based governance. These efforts put many schools at the brink of a historic moment that continues to demand that local communities change the way children are educated. In many cases, these reforms came about as a result of state-level lawsuits brought by poor urban and rural school districts.
- The realization that having relatively large numbers of poorly educated adults damages the economy, puts a heavy burden on state and federal budgets, and saps communities of their civic and economic vitality.
- A growing yearning for a sense of community coupled with efforts to bolster citizen participation in civic life and manifested by movements to have more public input into public schools. (Collins & Flaxman, 2001, p.2)

TRANSITION PLANNING TIMELINE — SUGGESTED ACTIVITIES

GRADE 8

- Teach and reinforce strategies to improve study habits, time management, and general organization skills.
- Prepare students for active involvement in their IEP meetings and begin to explore future goals in all transition areas. Teach students to be self-advocates.
- Assist students in selecting courses that will allow them to explore career interests and skills through school-to-work activities.
- Teach and reinforce learning strategies in academic areas.
- Prepare students to take basic graduation standards tests.
- Explore the use of a variety of school, home, and community accommodations with students.
- Offer opportunities for students to learn about high school courses, activities, and services.
- Encourage involvement in community organizations, extracurricular activities, and school-to-work organizations.
- Encourage students to select general education courses that offer service learning opportunities.
- Assist students in developing a personal transition file in which to collect important information such as school and medical records, IEPs samples of academic work, evaluation information, transcripts and test scores, records of school-based, work-based, and service learning school-to-work activities.

GRADES 9 AND 10

- Assist students in clarifying the exact nature of their disabilities. This could be done by sharing with students their assessment results (interpret as needed so students understand).
- Assist students in developing a profile of their own unique strengths and limitations.
- Assist students in understanding how their disabilities affect their lives.
- Help students understand their legal rights under the Americans with Disabilities Act and Section 504 of the Rehabilitation Act, especially as related to their legal right to accommodations.
- Assist students in selecting and using learning strategies and accommodations that are most effective for them.
- Teach students to request appropriate accommodations in school, home, work, and community environments.
- Assist students in pinpointing specific academic needs and developing goals to address them.
- Assist students in refining their future goals in all transition areas and selecting performance measures within graduation standards that will help them successfully meet their goals.
- Assist general educators in adapting and modifying graduation standards performance measures to meet unique student goals and needs.
- Continue to encourage involvement in community organizations, extracurricular activities, and school-to-work activities.
- Assist students in developing and following through with solutions to academic and social difficulties.
- Continue to assist student in collecting resources and organizing and using their personal transition files.

GRADES 11 AND 12

- Assist students in collecting information about institutions of higher education if postsecondary education is one of their future goals.
- Encourage students to contact postsecondary institutions of interest to find out about services offered for students with disabilities.
- Continue to develop and refine future adult goals in all transition areas.
- Assist students in taking charge of their own transition-focused IEP meetings.
- Assist students and families in applying for postschool support services (rehabilitation services, social services, health services, social security, etc.).
- Support students in continuing to use and improve skills and learning strategies developed in previous years, such as determining and following through with solutions to academic and social difficulties they encounter in the general education settings.
- Continue to assist students in selecting performance measures within graduation standards that will help them successfully meet their transition goals. Assist general educators in adapting and modifying performance measures to meet unique student goals and needs.
- Continue to encourage involvement in community organizations, extracurricular activities, and school-to-work student organizations.
- Continue to assist students in selecting courses that will allow them to refine career interests and skills through school-to-work activities.

Adapted from: Area Special Education Cooperative. (2001). *Interagency and Community Relations*. East Grand Forks, MN: Author.

Figure 12-33. Sample of transition planning activities at each grade level.

Full Service Schools

Dryfoos (1994) described a full service school as a school committed to serving the needs of the community; specifically, it improves the welfare of children and youth by coordinating the fragmented services necessary for the development and the educational, social, and economic success of both youth and their families. Such an engagement in the life of the community is a tradition in urban American schooling; historically, the school has been the agent of civic and moral education, the Americanization of immigrants, the preparation of youth for work and adult education, and the provider of social and health services to children and families in need. But now the urban school is assuming a different role by becoming a partner with other community members—agencies, organizations, and families—in a complex arrangement, jointly and collaboratively formed to improve the welfare of children and families and to build the capacity of the urban community to serve its own ends. The venue for this collaboration is the community school.

> Full service schools vary in comprehensiveness and depth. Some schools have only one component, provide only one service, or engage in only one collaboration or partnership; others are more complex, provide more services, and involve more parts of the community. Full service is defined by the particular school or community itself. Fortunately, almost all schools can plan and participate in the governance of coordinated services, especially when the services are based in the school building itself. Services are typically provided outside of the school, but ideally close by. Such schools provide various health services—including mental health, social, and family and student education support services—through a number of venues, groups, programs, and partnerships. (Flaxman, 2001, p.7)

One of the strongest direct links between the school and the community is made by parents or other responsible family members and schools collaborating to improve the academic outcomes and social development of the children and youth for whom they are commonly responsible. Today, purposeful efforts to involve parents and families in the education of their children are becoming as much a part of schooling as curriculum and teaching, school management, learner assessment, or student services. Increasingly, educators are becoming convinced of the value of involving parents in the formal education of their children (Flaxman, 2001).

Strategies that are successful in facilitating practical family involvement in reform-based educational programs include

- overcoming time and resources constraints (for example, through home-school liaisons and the use of parent co-ordinators and volunteers to handle time-consuming, routine tasks; released time and extra compensation for teachers; holding parent conferences near the home rather than just at school; and providing transportation and child care services so that parents can attend evening and weekend parent workshops and other school-related events);
- providing parents and school staff involved in collaborative efforts with the information and training that historically they both have lacked, which can help them overcome their misconceptions of each other's attitudes and motives;
- offering parents various workshops, classes, and other opportunities, often through family resource centers, to further develop their parenting skills (especially for supporting learning at home) and other skills (for example, literacy, including computer literacy) and to prepare them to take a role in school decision making;
- devising mechanisms for keeping parents regularly informed about school affairs;
- developing and maintaining professional development activities in schools to train staff in the practice of parent involvement and to remove any misperceptions and stereotypes they may have about parents and families that could interfere with forging effective partnerships;
- restructuring schools to support parent involvement by making them less hierarchical and bureaucratic and more responsive to family needs and creating new organizational structures that make parents full partners in school decision making;
- bridging family-school differences resulting from language and cultural differences or the misperception that parents with little formal education cannot be full partners in their children's education (for example, by including organized efforts to promote cultural understanding);
- drawing on external agencies such as local businesses, social and health agencies, and colleges and universities to support the partnerships; and
- seeking district and state assistance in the form of policies and funding to support training and services that can contribute to effective family-school partnerships (Funkhouser, Gonzales & Moles, 1997).

Decker and Decker (2000) argued that both administrators and teachers who are actively part of the school side of the collaboration need highly developed listening and communication skills; must respect diversity, build consensus, and motivate others; must be able to take risks and manage conflict; and must be decisive, reflective, empowering, and flexible. In addition, the relationship between families and the school has to be credible and characterized by shared concerns; arrive at a consensus of goals and activities; and build trust and share decisions among all members in the collaboration, especially about outcomes that can be achieved and evaluated early.

Rural Program Issues

Rural communities and schools occupy an important position in the effort to link school and work and expand economic opportunities for all learners. Rural populations are found in every state throughout the country, and make up over 40% of our nation's workforce. School-to-work systems can help to ensure the vital contribution of these communities and their schools to the nation's economy.

Current momentum in improving relationships between rural schools and their communities may continue for some time to come. However, if experts are correct about the breadth and depth of changes under way in rural areas, rural citizens today face challenges much different from those in the past. Deteriorating conditions and the erosion of communities in some rural areas has led to the emergence of the "rural ghetto." Other communities are experiencing an influx of immigrants, which has challenged schools to serve learners with cultures and needs that are different from those they were accustomed to seeing. Meanwhile, rural schools face costly demands for accountability and higher standards with few additional resources (Davidson, 1996).

Jolly and Deloney (1996) offered suggestions to help school officials begin a school-community engagement process:

- Staff at rural schools who may be relatively isolated need firsthand opportunities to see working models of school-community partnerships so they can see how to adapt the models to their own circumstances.
- There must be staff support. Staff needs to be interested in participating in the collaboration and convinced that it is relevant and compatible with the school's operations and that it has been field tested in similar areas.
- Information documenting the effectiveness of school-community partnerships must be widely disseminated.
- School officials like to hear success stories from other officials who have implemented school-community partnerships.
- A support network is needed when new programs are being adopted.
- Staff development opportunities must exist.
- Schools need constant technical assistance to help build a culture of continuous learning and improvement.

A review of the rural education literature suggests at least four trends:

- A healthy relationship between rural communities and their schools is crucial to school effectiveness and the communities' quality of life.
- Although it is impossible for rural communities to alter global changes that put them at risk, they can have broad-based local discussions; develop agreed-upon policies; and pursue educational, civic, and economic activities that enhance their sustainability and growth.
- Rural students must be prepared to work, learn, and live well, not only as participants in the global economy but also as citizens in their own communities.

- Rural schools, as central institutions in rural life, must assume a role in community economic development. (Collins, 2001, p. 15-16)

Rural communities face significant economic and demographic challenges. Shifting employment patterns in the global economy have caused a significant level of poverty in rural areas, and many rural schools have a limited capacity to adapt to the changing economy. The economics of rural communities are often focused on one industry, such as manufacturing or farming, and individuals not interested in those careers may have limited career paths and opportunities for work-based learning experiences. As a result, many learners leave their communities upon completing high school or college to move to communities with more job opportunities. In addition to the economic challenges facing rural communities, geographic isolation and limited educational resources pose a problem in building transition systems. Learners may have a difficult time researching or obtaining information for class or career development activities due to limited library resources.

Veir (1990) illustrated the growing problem, which is mounting in American rural public education:

- Approximately 10 million learners are enrolled in rural schools, comprising 12,000 of the 15,000 schools in the country. The poverty rates of rural areas exceed those of urban sectors.
- Approximately 15 million individuals with disabilities, many of school age, reside in rural areas and would benefit from career and technical education programming that could assist them in developing salable skills for competitive employment.
- Low educational attainment, high rates of functional illiteracy, and increasing dropout statistics place many learners in rural areas at risk of not becoming contributing members of society.
- A growing number of language minority and multicultural learners are isolated in rural communities and quite often left without the resources needed to ensure success in school or employment.
- Each year, it is estimated that 500,000 people leave rural areas to seek employment and new hope in urban areas.

The National School-to-Work Office (December 1996) identified the following strategies for rural programs:

- Start early–In many rural communities, learners often think their only pathway to success is to leave their community upon completing their education. Rural transition partnerships can work to show learners and their families that there are ample opportunities for success in their own communities, and that transition systems can help develop these opportunities. In addition, incorporating transition principles as early as kindergarten and elementary school helps learners begin to develop responsibility, confidence, and teamwork skills and promotes awareness of a broad range of careers.

- Identify educational and economic opportunities in the community–If learners are trained and prepared for occupations that exist or can be improved upon in their communities, they will be more likely to remain instead of leaving for jobs elsewhere. Transition systems can help learners and community leaders identify the existing and potential opportunities for economic growth and work-based learning experiences by undertaking an analysis of community strengths and needs. Learners and community leaders can identify opportunities for improving existing businesses; potential opportunities for entrepreneurship and small business development; and public sector jobs and community service initiatives that can provide a variety of work-based learning experiences. In this process, learners learn how to make practical use of data collection and analysis while building knowledge of the community. Transition systems can then help prepare learners to take advantage of these opportunities, fulfilling their educational needs and helping build community economic development.

- Provide entrepreneurial experiences–Many rural transition initiatives emphasize the effectiveness of entrepreneurial activities in rural areas. The community analysis described earlier can help learners identify and establish businesses that actually create jobs and meet community needs. Learning how to establish and run a business provides immediate relevance to learners' school experience, can create additional economic activity in a community, and is a lifelong skill that continues to pay benefits. But these school-based entrepreneurial activities must supplement, rather than threaten, established local businesses. Competition between area businesses and student-run businesses that are often subsidized can create animosity and damage school-community relations.

- Take advantage of community service learning–Rural transition partnerships can also utilize community service learning experiences in the work-based learning component of the transition process. Service learning projects help meet community needs and provide learners with hands-on learning experiences that allow them to use the academic skills being developed in the classroom. For example, environmental projects provide learners an opportunity to develop and apply their knowledge of math, science, environmental studies, and civics, while promoting a sense of responsibility for the environment and return to the community.

- Utilize computer/technology skills–Many rural transition initiatives emphasize the critical role of technology in assisting rural partnerships to prepare learners for lifelong learning and success. Technology helps rural communities overcome their geographic isolation by providing them with access to information from all over the world. As a result, the effective use of technology

"evens the playing field" between rural and urban or suburban communities by ensuring that learners in rural areas have equal access to a wealth of information and opportunities. Through the Internet, learners have been able to obtain not only research but also assistance from educators and professionals throughout the world. Many schools have helped learners design and develop their own home pages, or the school home page, providing an opportunity for learners to learn a marketable skill while in school. Other technologies available for rural schools include distance learning, telecommunication technologies, e-mail, interactive television, and electronic bulletin boards.

- Build networks among rural schools–Networks among rural schools can help synthesize and disseminate information and methods of building transition partnerships in rural areas. Newsletters, conference calls, and electronic bulletin boards can all facilitate the formation of networks among rural schools. Organizations such as the National Rural and Small Schools Network and the National Rural Education Association provide educators, administrators, and staff an opportunity to exchange information with other small and rural schools.

Urban Program Issues

Individuals who reside in urban areas face many challenges. The National Center for Education Statistics reported that learners who live in urban areas are more likely to drop out than learners from nonurban areas (Kaufman & Frase, 1990).

West and Penkowsky (1994) cited a number of issues in urban environments that impact on serving learners in educational institutions:
- poverty
- dislocated families
- high rate of teen pregnancies
- poor job prospects
- physical state of school buildings
- overcrowded classrooms
- neighborhoods with crime, drugs, and parent absenteeism

> In almost every urban area across the country, evidence of school reform can be found. Urban schools need to coordinate or broker the myriad of services necessary to assist students in their increasingly complex environment. Cooperative efforts with outside agencies enable the educational system to meet the changing needs of the community through a wider range of services. In response to the need for collaborative school reform, outside agencies and public schools have increasingly entered into formal and informal partnerships. (Repetto, 1990, p. 2)

Neubert (1990) identified a number of strategies to ensure that urban learners from special populations have equal access to and successful participation in career and technical education programs, including

- collaborative and flexible approaches to scheduling;
- class release time for teachers to develop community-based experiences;
- stimulating prevocational programs that prepare learners for a range of vocational opportunities;
- exploratory programs for students to observe vocational and applied technology [career and technical] education programs in secondary and postsecondary settings;
- outreach and recruitment efforts in alternative settings (e.g., church and community centers);
- vocational assessment experiences beginning at the middle school level;
- periodic assessments of vocational and applied technology [career and technical] education programs to assess enrollment patterns and relevance for learners from special populations;
- flexible instructional programming;
- pilot programs and alternative programs which allow students to earn credit in academic areas while placed in community-based work sites;
- flexible support services to ensure successful completion of vocational and applied technology [career and technical] education programs;
- case management framework for providing services to learners as they exit vocational and applied technology [career and technical] education programs; and
- implementation of "multiple added-chance opportunities" or "second-chance opportunities" for education, training, and employment. (pp. 2-3)

PROFESSIONAL DEVELOPMENT FOR EDUCATORS

Professional development is a broad, inclusive term referring to the full range of activities that help educators learn, improve their ability to teach, and interact with other partners in a transition system. As these systems evolve across the nation, educators will assume a variety of new roles and responsibilities. The collaborative nature of transition requires greater interaction between educators and other partners in schools and the community. Educators are often asked to assume a greater role in system governance and work with employers and other educators to develop integrated curricula. Innovative approaches to work-based, applied systems are significant departures from traditional teaching practices. An effective professional development system must be in place in order for teachers to embrace these changes. Professional development activities must provide educators with what they need to know and be able to do to make a transition system work.

Teacher shortages, new technologies, and transition certification demands are directing attention to the need for the professional development of career and technical education teachers. Brown (2000) made the following observations about professional development for educators:

- Changes in the workplace require continual professional development as a means of skill upgrading, even for teachers with degrees in education. New ways of teaching and learning are requiring teachers to assume the roles of coach and facilitator and to situate learning in real-world contexts. New transition programs are requiring teachers to collaborate with business representatives in the community and partner with employers and with other educators to develop integrated curricula. Teachers must be able to use new technologies, which are continually changing the ways that people live, work, and learn. To respond to these changing roles and responsibilities, teachers need an effective professional development plan that can help them keep current and embrace new ways to improve their practice.
- Work site experiences afford opportunities for teachers to gain firsthand knowledge of what is happening in the workplace and observe ways that workers are integrating knowledge, concepts, and skills from a variety of disciplines to solve complex problems of their industry. Through these contextual learning experiences (experiences that situate learning in the context of its use), teachers can observe how skills become multidimensional when used to solve problems in the workplace. Such real-world experiences provide a basis from which teachers can begin to create learning experiences that are authentic and engage learners in the use of complex reasoning skills, work-related attitudes, cooperative skills, job-specific knowledge, and academic knowledge required in the workplace. Three professional development activities that teachers can use to connect to the workplace are internships, tours, and externships.
- Linking with colleagues to discuss the trials and challenges of teaching and share instructional strategies can result in "nuggets of wisdom" that teachers can immediately apply in the classroom. Teacher networks, teacher unions, and professional organizations offer opportunities for teachers to leave the isolation of their classrooms to meet with colleagues to learn what is happening in the field (e.g., current standards affecting the industry, the direction of the market, and economic and employment trends).

Professional development activities are most effective if they incorporate the key elements of the continuous improvement process—planning, implementation, and evaluation. Professional development planning should be a collaborative process that takes into account the timing, scope, and impact of a variety of different activities. Conducting a needs assessment that identifies gaps in abilities or knowledge can improve professional development planning. Teachers, in collaboration with other partners in the transition system, can then choose specific professional development activities to help them achieve individual and system goals. To complete the continuous improvement cycle, both process and impact evaluations can help teachers incorporate lessons from their experiences into subsequent professional development activities.

Teachers are critical to the success of transition systems. From integrating academic and work-based curricula to building collaborative relationships with employers and other partners, teachers play a key role in the effort to prepare learners for further education and work. Teacher internships are an innovative professional development strategy that can help educators fulfill these new and often unfamiliar roles.

Educator Internships

While many professional development opportunities for teachers involve interaction and learning within the academic community, the work-based nature of transition systems necessitates a greater emphasis on learning activities that occur in the workplace. Teacher internships place educators in the workplace so that they can experience, firsthand, the skills, abilities, and knowledge that their learners will need at work. In these temporary work placements, teachers gain a greater understanding of the practical applications of classroom concepts and an appreciation of the learning potential of work-based activities for learners. Taken back to the school, these experiences encourage teachers to enhance instructional strategies and incorporate applied academics into a work-based curriculum.

Teachers benefit from an increased knowledge of both occupation-specific and general workplace requirements. Through internships, teachers can deepen their subject area knowledge through experience-based learning and develop applications for use in the classroom. Working directly with employers can help educators observe and develop workplace readiness skills, such as working in teams, which they can then incorporate into their curriculum. In addition to industry or career related knowledge, teachers are able to observe general workplace competencies, such as the SCANS skills, and incorporate them into classroom instruction. Finally, in many teacher internships, teachers can gain graduate credit for their workplace experiences.

Employers also benefit from teacher internships. Teachers bring a variety of skills to the workplace that can boost productivity. Their external opinion can bring an unbiased viewpoint to planning, implementation, and evaluation of workplace practices, and encourage "out-of-the-box" thinking.

Teacher internships are not simply isolated components of a transition initiative. Working directly with employers can give educators insight into the business viewpoint. Conversely, employers can become more connected with education. By physically frequenting a workplace, teachers and employers build a relationship and forge channels of communication. The most obvious follow-up after completing an internship is to incorporate newly learned material into the learners' curriculum. Another option resulting from strengthened channels of communication is the possibility of engaging the employer in classroom activities. Employers may begin to host learners from the class as interns while the teacher prepares a complementary curriculum. This foundation of communication between the teacher and employer may result in the employer's, as well as the teacher's, expanded involvement in the governance of system-wide transition activities. Likewise, hosting teachers as interns may help employers to see the relevance of becoming more involved in the development of school curriculum, in addition to having already developed a personal contact to facilitate this process (National School-to-Work Office, January 1997).

There are many ways in which teachers involved in industry internships may benefit at both a personal and professional level. Some of them include

- a broadening of their knowledge of the world of work;
- an opportunity to design and deliver curriculum that incorporates contemporary work practices and directions;
- a greater confidence in advising learners about careers and general work-related issues; and
- the opportunity to contribute to the professional development of their teaching colleagues by sharing their work site experiences.

Workshops and Conferences

Workshops and conferences can be an effective way to disseminate information to a large number of teachers. Many effective workshops and conferences use a "train-the-trainer" approach in which teachers develop training skills and share information from these activities with fellow teachers and other partners working to develop transition systems. The most effective sessions make use of the interactive, applied, and integrated approaches that teachers will be expected to use with their learners. Rather than traditional one-way lectures, these professional development activities include ample opportunities for participants to experiment with new concepts and techniques.

Another way to maximize the benefit of workshops and conferences begins with a solicitation of proposals for attendance from teachers. Through a competitive process, one of the teachers is selected to attend the workshop or conference. Other teachers can then pose specific questions that the attending teacher can ask the presenters or bring up in discussions. Returning to the school, the attending teacher can not only provide a summary of the key issues but can also address the specific questions of other teachers, sharing the benefits of attendance.

SUMMARY

Satisfying and sustained employment is a critical aspect of adult life. The ability to obtain and hold a job indicates the capacity to participate fully in our society. To individuals from special populations, employment brings status and respect. Years of education are of little value to these individuals unless they can become productive and self-sufficient.

Transition is a term frequently being used by individuals who are involved in the educational reform movement. It is one of the most important components of providing education for our nation's youth. Transitions are an essential part of every person's life. Transitions are necessary when an individual moves from preschool to kindergarten, from kindergarten to elementary school, from elementary school to middle school, from middle school to high school, and from high school to beyond. Transition planning is designed to increase the probability of success in the next environment. Transition planning should occur at all stages of an individual's life.

The educational system plays an important role in an ongoing process of preparing individuals for a life of work and learning. The educational experience should provide a solid foundation of skills and knowledge to prepare individuals for meaningful employment and continuing education. The attention of all educators should be focused on assessing the unique needs of individual learners, establishing learning environments that support learner needs, teaching skills and knowledge that have a direct bearing on life after high school, and counseling learners for a smooth transition to jobs and higher education.

A growing number of follow-up studies consistently show that individuals from special populations can work successfully and contribute to the American economy if they are provided with quality secondary and postsecondary career and technical training, followed with career guidance, job placement, and follow-along and follow-up services. Job placement personnel need to do more than simply choose capable learners for existing jobs. They need to work with employers in analyzing existing jobs to determine training requirements, to assist employers in job redesign, and to work with other school personnel in implementing programs to help learners from special populations make the transition from school-to-work. They need to work with community agencies to provide the follow-up services that will help these individuals stay employed, live independently, and participate in continuing education and community activities.

SELF-ASSESSMENT

1. Describe the competencies that will be needed by all workers in the future in order to be prepared for the workforce.
2. Define and discuss transition.
3. Identify barriers to successful postschool opportunities that often confront individuals from special populations.
4. List appropriate transition options.
5. Define an individualized transition program and discuss the components.
6. Discuss the important issues relative to serving individuals from special populations in transition systems.

ASSOCIATED ACTIVITIES

1. Conduct a literature search for current articles in journals and books that contain practical information on transition planning for individuals from special populations.
2. Attend workshops, seminars, and professional development activities offered locally, regionally, statewide, or nationally that focus on transition-related topics.
3. Identify the transition options that are available in your geographic area for individuals from special populations. Provide a vehicle at the local level for making this information available to learners and parents.
4. Visit the local employment office and obtain information about services that can be provided for individuals from special populations to assist in job seeking and/or retention.
5. Contact state organizations that collect employment data for specific information about current and projected job openings.
6. Identify employers who have hired individuals with special needs and contact them to act as speakers, mentors, and role models for the community.
7. If a placement team approach is not being used at your school, meet with administrators and discuss the possibility of establishing this system.
8. Explore postsecondary programs available in your geographic area. Create linkages with admissions and learner services personnel. Make arrangements for learners to visit these institutions/programs. Share this information with parents.
9. Explore possible business/industry linkages in your geographic area. Talk to representatives to see how partnering activities can be established or strengthened.
10. Identify schools/institutions that have established transition and school-to-work systems. Visit these schools/institutions to observe components and operational procedures. Share this information with learners, parents, colleagues, administrators, and others in the community.

REFERENCES

American Vocational Association. (1994). *AVA guide to the School-to-Work-Opportunities Act.* Alexandria, VA: Author.

Area Special Education Cooperative. (2001). *Interagency and community relations.* East Grand Forks, MN: Author.

Ascher, C. (1994, January). Cooperative education as a strategy for school-to-work transition. *Center Focus 3,* 1-7. Berkeley, CA: National Center for Research in Vocational Education.

Blumberg, R., & Ferguson, P. (2001). *On transition services for youth with disabilities.* National Transition Alliance for Youth with Disabilities. [On-line]. Available: http://www.edc.org/urban/op_Tra.htm

Boyer-Stephens, A. (n.d.). *Employer as mentor.* Columbia, MO: University of Missouri-Columbia, Institute for Workforce Education.

Brown, B. (2000). Vocational teacher professional development. *Practice Application Brief No. 11.* [On-line]. Available: http://www.ericacve.org/textonly/pubs.asp ED 442994.

Burgstahler, S. (1994). *Effective college planning—transition.* Seattle, WA: University of Washington.

Burke, M. (1993). *Career education: It's for life.* North York, ON: North York Board of Education.

Carnevale, A., & Porro, J. (1994). *Quality education: School reform for the new American economy–Executive summary.* Washington, DC: U.S. Department of Education, Office of Educational Research and Improvement.

Carrollton-Farmers Branch Independent School District. (n.d.). *Technology internship program handbook.* Carrollton, TX: Author.

Charner, I. (1996, October). *Study of school-to-work initiative.* Washington, DC: U.S. Department of Education, Office of Educational Research and Improvement.

Churchill, A., Morales, D., & O'Flanagan, M. (1994, March). *School-to-work toolkit.* Cambridge, MA: Jobs for the Future.

Collins, T. (2001, Winter). Rural school and communities: Perspectives on interdependence. *The ERIC Review, 8*(2), 15-18.

Collins, T., & Flaxman, E. (2001, Winter). Improving urban and rural schools and their communities. *The ERIC Review, 8*(2), 2-4.

Cunanan, E., & Maddy-Bernstein, C. (1995, May). Individualized career plans: Opening doors for all. *Office of Student Services Brief, 7*(1). Berkeley, CA: National Center for Research in Vocational Education.

Davidson, O. (1996). *Broken heartland: The rise of America's rural ghetto.* Iowa City, IA: University of Iowa Press.

Day, S., & Edwards, B. (1996, September). Assistive technology for postsecondary students with learning disabilities. *Journal of Learning Disabilities, 29*(5), 486-492.

Decker, L., & Decker, V. (2000). *Engaging families and communities: Pathways to educational success.* Fairfax, VA: Decker and Associates.

Dryfoos, J. (1994). *Full service schools: A revolution in health and social services for children, youth and families.* San Francisco, CA: Jossey-Bass.

Dykman, A. (1994). Let the reforms begin. *Vocational Education Journal, 69*(7), 24-26, 66.

Elliott, B., Schalock, R., & Ross, I. (1988) *Handbook for transition planning and implementation.* Hastings, NE: Educational Service Unit #9.

Ettinger, J. (1995). *Improving career counseling service.* Madison, WI: University of Wisconsin at Madison, Center on Education and Work.

Flaxman, E. (2001, Winter). The promise of urban community schooling. *The ERIC Review, 8*(2), 5-14.

Funkhouser, J., Gonzales, M., & Moles, O. (1997). *Family involvement in children's education: Successful local approaches—An idea book.* Washington, DC: Office of Educational Research and Improvement, U.S. Department of Education.

Heal, L., Haney, J., DeStefano, L., & Rusch, F. (1988). *A comparison of successful and unsuccessful placements of secondary students with mental handicaps into comprehensive employment.* Champaign, IL: University of Illinois, Transition Institute at Illinois.

Individuals with Disabilities Education Act of 1990, Pub. L. No. 101-476, United States Statutes at Large, (104), 1103. Washington, DC: U.S. Government Printing Office.

Individuals with Disabilities Education Act Amendments of 1997, Pub. L. No. 105-17, United States Statutes at Large, (111), 37. Washington, DC: U.S. Government Printing Office.

Instructional Materials Laboratory. (n.d.). *All aspects framework for work-based learning.* Columbia, MO: University of Missouri-Columbia.

Jolly, D., & Deloney, P. (1996). *Integrating rural school and community development: An initial examination.* Austin, TX: Southwest Educational Development Laboratory.

Karan, O. (1992). The need for ethical guidelines, *The P.C. Brief, 4,* 2.

Kaufman, P., & Frase, M. (1990). *Dropout rates in the United States: 1989.* Washington, DC: Office of Educational Research and Improvement.

Kerka, S. (2001). Capstone experiences in career and technical education. *Practice Application Brief No.6.* [On-line]. Available: http://www.ericacve.org/textonly/pubs.asp ED 456333.

Kimeldorf, M, & Tornow, J. (1984). Meeting the challenge of unemployment. *Journal of Vocational Special Needs Education.*

Lindstrom, L., Benz, M., & Johnson, M. (1997, March/April). An introduction to school-based enterprises. *Teaching Exceptional Children,* 21-24.

Martin, J.E., & Mithaug, D.E. (1990). Consumer directed placement. In F. Rusch (Ed.), *Supported employment: Models, methods, and issues.* Sycamore, IL: Sycamore Publishing.

McCarty-Warren, T., & Hess-Grabill, D. (1989). *Postsecondary vocational special needs coordinators handbook.* Normal, IL: Illinois State University, Office of Specialized Vocational Research.

McCarty-Warren, T., & Hess-Grabill, D. (1989). *Transition for disadvantaged students.* Normal, IL: Illinois State University, Office of Specialized Vocational Research.

National Alliance of Business. (1999, Spring). *New work: The revolution in today's workplace.* Washington, DC: Author.

National Alliance of Business. (2001, June). *Work America.* Washington, DC: Author.

National Center for Education Statistics. (1999, August). *An institutional perspective on students with disabilities in postsecondary education.* Washington, DC: U.S. Department of Education.

National Center for Education Statistics. (2000). *NCES Fast Facts.* [On-line]. Available: http://nces.ed.gov

National Council on Disability. (2000, November). *Transition and post-school outcomes for youth with disabilities: Closing the gaps to post-secondary education and employment.* Washington, DC: Social Security Administration.

National Information Center for Children and Youth with Disabilities. (1999). *Transition planning: A team effort.* Washington, DC: Author.

National School-to-Work Office. (1996, May). *School-to-work and service learning.* Washington, DC: U.S. Department of Education.

National School-to-Work Office. (1996a, September). *Engaging employers in school-to-work systems.* Washington, DC: U.S. Department of Education.

National School-to-Work Office. (1996b, September). *The role of postsecondary institutions in school-to-work.* Washington, DC: U.S. Department of Education.

National School-to-Work Office. (1996c, September). *Workplace mentors in school-to-work systems.* Washington, DC: U.S. Department of Education.

National School-to-Work Office. (1996, December). *Building school-to-work systems in rural areas.* Washington, DC: U.S. Department of Education.

National School-to-Work Office. (1997, January). *School-to-work and professional development for teachers.* Washington, DC: U.S. Department of Education.

National School-to-Work Office. (1997, September). *All aspects of an industry.* Washington, DC: U.S. Department of Education.

National Skill Standards Board. (2001). *How to use the MSSC skill standards.* Washington DC: Author.

Neubert, D. (1990, December). Serving urban youth with special needs in vocational education: Issues and strategies for change. *Technical Assistance for Special Populations Program (TASPP) Bulletin.* Berkeley, CA: National Center for Research in Vocational Education.

Neubert, D., & Tilson, G. (1987). The critical stage of transition: A challenge and an opportunity. *Journal for Vocational Special Needs Education, 10*(1), 3-7.

Norman, M., & Bourexis, P. (1995). *Including students with disabilities in school-to-work systems.* Washington, DC: Council of Chief State School Officers.

Partnership for Academic and Career Education. (1993). *Summer institute '93 resource handbook for teachers and counselors.* Pendleton, SC: Author.

Placement manual. (1993-1994). Athens, GA: The University of Georgia, Career Planning and Placement Center.

Pratzner, F. (1994). Career transition: Coordinated one-stop shopping for employment services. *Journal of Industrial Teacher Education, 31*(3), 5.

Rahn, M., lt, M., Emanuel, D., Ramer, C., Hoachlander, G., Holmes, P., Jackson, M., Klein, S., & Rossi, K. (1995, December). *Getting to work: Module 3—learning experiences.* Berkeley, CA: National Center for Research in Vocational Education.

Repetto, J. (1990, December). Issues in urban vocational education for special populations. *Technical Assistance for Special Populations Program Brief.* Berkeley, CA: University of California, National Center for Research in Vocational Education.

Riley, R. (1998, February 17). *Education first: Building America's future.* The Fifth Annual State of American Education Speech. Seattle, WA. [On-line]. Available: http://www.ed.gov/Speeches/98a.html

Robinson, G., & Barnett, L. (1998). Best practices in service learning: Building a national community college network 1994-1997. *American Association of Community Colleges Project Brief,* (3), 3.

Rogan, P., & Hagner, R. (1990). Vocational evaluation in supported employment. *Journal of Rehabilitation, 56,* 45-51.

Sitlington, P., Clark, G., & Kolstoe, O. (2000). *Transition education & services for adolescents with disabilities* (3rd ed.). Boston, MA: Allyn and Bacon.

Stern, D., Finkelstein, N., Stone, J., Latting, J., & Dornsife, C. (1994). *Research on school-to-work transition programs in the United States.* Berkeley, CA: National Center for Research in Vocational Education.

Test, D., Keul, P., & Grossi, T. (1988). Transitional services for mildly handicapped youth. *Journal for Vocational Special Needs Education, 10*(2), 7-10.

Texas Education Agency Clearinghouse. (1993). *School-to-work transition: A Texas perspective.* Austin, TX: Texas Education Agency, Office of Education of Special Populations and Adults.

U.S. Department of Commerce, U.S. Department of Education, U.S. Department of Labor, National Institute of Literacy, & Small Business Administration. (January, 1999). *21st century skills for the 21st century jobs.* Washington, DC: U.S. Government Printing Office.

U.S. Department of Education. (1992). *Here is what we must do to get our students ready for work: Blueprint for a school-to-work system.* Washington, DC: U.S. Department of Education, Office of Vocational and Adult Education.

U.S. Department of Education. (2001). *A turning point for postsecondary education.* Washington, DC: Author.

U.S. General Accounting Office. (1991). *Transition from school-to-work: Linking education and worksite training.* Washington, DC: U.S. Government Printing Office.

Veir, C. (1990). Serving special populations in rural America. *The Journal for Vocational Special Needs Education, 12*(2), 3-4.

Wentling, R., & Waight, C. (January, 2000). *Initiatives that assist and barriers that hinder the successful transition of minority youth into the workplace.* Berkeley, CA: National Center for Research in Vocational Education.

West, L. (1988). Designing, implementing, and evaluating transition programs. *Journal for Special Needs Education, 11*(1), 3.

West, L., & Penkowsky, L. (1994). Special problems for rural youth in transition. In A. Pautler Jr. (Ed.), *High school to employment transition: Contemporary issues* (pp.167-168). Ann Arbor, MI: Prakken Publications.

Will, M. (1984). *Supported employment services. An OSERS position paper.* Washington, DC: Department of Education.

Wilson, J., & Wilson, P. (1990). *Mentoring manual: A guide to program development and implementation.* Baltimore, MD: Abell Foundation.

Wonacott, M. (2000). Apprenticeship. *Trends and Issues Alert No. 19.* [On-line]. Available: http://www.ericacve.org/textonly/pubs.asp ED 448288.

Workforce 2020: Action report, school-to-work opportunities national voluntary skill standards. (1994). Leesburg, VA: National Association of Trade and Industrial Education (NATIE), p.7.

Appendix

CHRONOLOGICAL CHART ...	
2½ Million B.C.	In the Paleolithic Period, people learned to develop and use stone tools, learned to use fire, made weapons (bow and arrow, spears), developed bone needles, and invented the body parts system of measurement. Work education was provided through the father-son, mother-daughter, trial-and-error system of learning.
9000 B.C.	People learned to improve stone and wood tools, domesticate animals, and plant and harvest grains. Crafts such as pottery making, spinning and weaving, basket making, brick making, boat-building, house building, and farming were practiced.
6000 B.C.	The great river civilizations developed along the Nile, Tigris, and Euphrates Rivers. Animals were domesticated for work and food. The ox-drawn wooden plow was invented, ushering in agricultural civilization. People learned to irrigate fields and to grow grains like barley, wheat, and flax. A system of telling time was developed and by 4200 B.C. the Egyptians had developed a calendar and a form of picture writing from which an alphabet later emerged.
4200 B.C.	This period is known as the Bronze Age or Age of Metals, when bronze drills and the bow-drilling technique were invented, and bronze axes, knives, files, scraping tools, adzes, and saws were developed. People learned to build large structures of stone, and molded kiln-dried bricks. New trades were developed including carpentry, masonry, brick making, pattern making, and boat-building. Trades were learned through the trial-and-error method of passing along knowledge and skills from parents to children.
2000 B.C.	Egyptians developed an alphabet and recorded business transactions on clay tablets. Later a system of writing using a pen, writing fluid, and papyrus (an early form of paper) was developed which led to the establishment of the first organized schools for scribes who recorded literature or served as clerks to record business transactions. Crafts became organized and a system of legalized apprenticeship came into being during the Babylonian Age.
1200 B.C.	The Hebrew people settled in Palestine and adapted themselves to new types of work in businesses and the trades. They held manual labor in high regard and established religious doctrine which required children to attend religious school and learn a trade, thus establishing the earliest form of compulsory education.
1000 B.C.	The discovery of iron making in Greece led to improved tools and weapons of war including drills, gouges, broadaxes, knives, skews, files, scrapers, shaper-planes, metal-cutting saws, and calipers and dividers. The Greek civilization perpetuated a caste system with second-class citizens and slaves performing the work and first-class citizens holding and managing the wealth of the country. Greek schools were established in Sparta and Athens for children of first-class citizens, and a university system was established to prepare engineers and professionals. The dual system of education was born, one type of education for culture and another type of education for workers.
1000-200 B.C.	The Roman civilization included the development of banks, currency, and shares in commercial enterprises. Roads, aqueducts, drainage systems, and massive structures were constructed using ideas borrowed from the Greek civilization, but with new twists of the Romans'. A system of public law and education was developed for Roman citizens and their children. The educational system consisted of the three levels of elementary, secondary, and higher education.
A.D. 300-1300	The Middle Ages constituted a period of nearly 1000 years when little progress was made to advance civilization, and the Christian monasteries carried the banner of education for culture and work. Manual labor was held in high regard and monks were expected to work at a trade for seven hours each day.
1000-1100	Merchant and craft guilds were formed to regulate the buying and selling of goods and to regulate the quality and quantity of goods produced. The guilds established the practice of indentured apprenticeship, which was both a way of life for a young person and a means of general education and preparation for skilled work. The indentured apprenticeship is considered the earliest form of vocational education. Although it probably had antecedents that were successively refined during the Egyptian, Babylonian, Greek, and Roman civilizations, it was re-emphasized as an honorable form of education by the craft guilds.
1300-1550	The Renaissance and Reformation periods of history featured the rediscovery of great literature and the formation of a new spirit of human dignity which led to geographical and scientific discovery. Firearms and cannons were invented, and great ships were built both for commerce and for war through naval

. . . CHRONOLOGICAL CHART . . .

	power. Most notably, this period produced great works of sculpture and art and the printing of books, written first in Latin and later in the vernacular, through the invention of the printing press. During this period, towns increased in size into small cities and the merchants' and crafts' guilds flourished. The Reformation brought on religious revolt leading to the establishment of Protestant churches led by Martin Luther in Germany and a number of other religious leaders in other countries. The religious revolt included challenges to the type of education offered in church schools.
1483-1546	Martin Luther advocated that education should be the responsibility of the state and even recommended compulsory education for part of the day for both boys and girls, with the balance of the day devoted to learning a trade or occupation.
1483-1553	Rabelais advocated educational reform in the churches of France, which involved redirecting education away from a heavy concentration on the abstract to teaching subjects through natural events and situations of life. His ideas would be expanded by many other educational reformers centuries later.
1562	The Statute of Artificers was passed in England, taking the power to regulate apprenticeship away from guilds and placing the guilds under government control, thus establishing a national apprenticeship system. This same type of action would occur in France years later.
1531-1611	Richard Mulcaster maintained that the hand and eye are the greatest instruments to receive learning. He is credited as being the first educator to make drawing one of the fundamental subjects of his Merchant Taylor's School in England.
1561-1626	Francis Bacon was the first educator to use the term "manual arts" in his theory of realism in which he advocated improving learning through the study of nature and involvement in experiments with common objects and real-world experiences.
1592-1670	John Amos Comenius introduced a practical method of education and founded the sense-realism movement which emphasized that learning should be accomplished through experiences and investigation of objects according to the course of nature. He advocated formal schooling for both boys and girls in the form of infant schools in every home, a public elementary school, a gymnasium or secondary school, and a university. He is known as the "father of modern pedagogy" because of his work in school structure and teaching methodology.
1600-1670	Samuel Hartlib conceived the idea of agricultural colleges in England and the "office of address," which was an agency to help people find employment, an idea that has evolved into our labor departments and local employment service offices.
1601-1642	English Poor Laws were enacted to place pauper children into apprenticeships, which gave apprenticeship a bad name. The Comprehensive Apprenticeship Law was passed in Massachusetts.
1642-1727	John Locke, a member of the Royal Society, presented his views on a new form of education that would fit youngsters for practical life. He advocated a dual system of practical training, with poor children to receive occupational preparation and wealthy children to study the classics and engage in practical arts education in the mechanical trades as a form of physical activity and recreation. He strongly favored a type of education that emphasized the development of thinking skills and discovery through the scientific method. Locke's *Essays on Human Understanding* is regarded as the cornerstone of modern empirical psychology.
1647	Sir William Petty advocated the establishment of literary workhouses for children and guilds for tradesworkers in England. He recommended industrial education be made an integral part of school.
1647	Massachusetts passed a law requiring every town of 50 households to hire a schoolmaster to teach reading and writing. A town of 100 households was required to establish a Latin grammar school to prepare selected youngsters for college.
1648	The Royal Society of London, a group of famous scholars of the day, expanded the philosophy of realism proposed earlier by Francis Bacon, which emphasized discovery of knowledge through methods of research such as observation, comparison, and experiment. This society included the study of manual arts in their writings. The creative works of these scholars were instrumental in opening a new age of scientific discovery.

... CHRONOLOGICAL CHART ...

1648	The French Academy of Painting and Sculpture was founded.
1663-1727	August Hermann Francke founded a school for poor children, a Latin school for the wealthy, a seminary for training teachers, and a publishing house to print copies of the Bible. He included instruction in several of the manual arts in his schools as a means of individual development and as a means of keeping students occupied in worthwhile pursuits.
1685	Thomas Budd proposed a plan of setting aside land to support public education in Pennsylvania and New Jersey.
1699	The Royal College of Art was established in Berlin.
1707-1768	Johann Hecker founded a new type of secondary school, the "realschule," in which he expanded Francke's school curriculum and methods of instruction to emphasize instruction in science, art, and the trades and industries. His school, and its practical curriculum, was the prototype for the non-classical secondary school curriculum in Germany.
1712-1778	Jean-Jacques Rousseau rebelled against the classical curriculum and methods of education of his day and recommended that much of education should be taught through nature study and the manual arts. He advocated manual arts instruction as a means of mental training, which was in direct line with the tenets of faculty psychology of his day. He is known as the "father of Industrial Arts."
1738-1779	A number of inventions came into use such as James Watt's steam engine, which altered textile work forever and paved the way for the Industrial Revolution. With new steam-powered machinery, factory towns sprang up and the need for skilled workers emerged.
1746-1827	Johann Heinrich Pestalozzi, the "father of instructional analysis and manual labor schools," introduced a number of educational principles and methods which have common acceptance today. He is believed to have been the first to apply psychology to the learning process in his recognition of the stages of development of the individual. He used the technique of analysis to order learning tasks derived from the study of objects from the natural and humanmade environment. His principle of instruction was key to the establishment of manual training in Europe and eventually in America. His children learned by engaging in real-life activities around them, and the results of their learning could produce articles that could be sold to provide economic support for the children's own schools, which introduced the concept of manual labor schools.
1747	Moravians established a public school for children up to age 12 and a type of separate industrial school for boys and girls age 12 and over where common trades were taught.
1751	The Franklin Academy of Philadelphia was established to teach academic subjects as well as subjects of a practical nature, which served as a prototype for other academies. Soon afterwards, academies were established in other parts of the country.
1776-1841	Johann Herbart advocated the inclusion of workshops in elementary schools so that every youngster would learn to use their hands. He advocated manual training as a means of teaching other, more abstract subjects.
1783-1852	Fredrich Froebel placed unity and interconnection at the center of his educational philosophy and maintained that the three elements of reception, reflection, and student response in the form of some creative production were critical of the learning process. His educational methods, which involved the selection and construction of objects in a wide variety of mediums and according to the ability and interest level of the youngster, earned him the title "the father of the kindergarten."
1787	Cokesbury College in Maryland was one of the first manual labor schools in America to teach gardening and carpentry, which served as a prototype for other manual labor schools that emerged 40 years later.
1787	The Northwest Ordinance authorized land grants for the establishment of educational institutions.
1789	The Massachusetts Education Act of 1789 led to the development of the first urban school system that did not prohibit African-American children from attending.

...CHRONOLOGICAL CHART...	
1790s	The first urban system of education in America was established in Boston.
1790s	Since there were no compulsory school laws, church schools, private schools, charity schools, and reform schools served students whose parents wanted them to get an education or students who needed a moral education to escape poverty.
1791	The Constituent Assembly abolished the guilds in France and placed apprenticeship under government control.
1791	The Sunday School Movement, an idea borrowed from England, was introduced in Philadelphia. It brought together children from all classes, thus establishing the secular Sunday school which spread through the country.
1796	Thomas Jefferson's bill for establishment of universal education at public expense was passed.
1799	The National School of Arts and Trades was established in France to train superior skilled workers and supervisors for manufacturing industries. This school was recognized by Napoleon Bonaparte, who championed other such schools in France.
1800s	The power age of machine tools began with the invention of the lathe (1800), planer (1817), milling machine (1818), drill press (1840), band saw (1853), grinder (1880), and the first micrometer and master gauge blocks (1877).
1800s	The National Grange was formed to lobby for the interests of farmers at the state and national levels.
1800s	In the early 1800s, powerful leaders like Benjamin Rush and Horace Mann, in keeping with their belief in faculty psychology, advocated creation of a system of common schooling that would help children with moral development and the development of faculties of the mind.
1800s	Numerous charity and reform schools were established in large urban areas to help reduce crime and poverty among children whose parents worked long hours in factories and failed to provide an adequate nurturing environment for the family.
1800	Dr. George Birkbeck began his lectures in Glasgow, Scotland, to adult mechanics. This evolved into the mechanics' institute movement, which made rapid progress in Britain and America during the next 30 years.
1805	The New York Free School Society was founded by DeWitt Clinton to provide education for poor children, calling attention to the need for free public education.
1806	Lancastrian schools were established in New York City.
1807	Philip Emanuel von Fellenberg established his farm and trade school in Switzerland which utilized Pestalozzian ideas of manual labor. His school was instrumental in the establishment of three other types of schools, agricultural, industrial reform, and the manual labor school.
1812	New York state created the first position of state school superintendent.
1810	The first American periodical, the *Agricultural Museum,* was published to enhance the field of agriculture.
1816	The Infant School, an idea of Robert Owen of Scotland, was established in Boston to prepare children for grammar schools.
1818	Boston established a system of public primary schools.
1820s -1830s	Some states appointed a chief school officer to monitor education in the state, and soon thereafter a State Board of Education was formed to develop school policy for the state.
1820	The first mechanics institute in America, the General Society of Mechanics and Tradesmen of the City of New York, was established. This school marked the beginning of the mechanics institute movement in America.

	...CHRONOLOGICAL CHART...
1820	Girls were taught sewing in the primary grades of Boston schools.
1821	Boston established its first public high school.
1821	Emma Willard's Troy Female Seminary was established in Troy, New York, to teach domestic or household duties along with academic subjects to female students.
1821	The state of Ohio passed a law allowing for taxation of property in a district for the support of schools.
1823	The Gardiner Lyceum, a type of manual labor school and full-time scientific and technical school, was established in Gardiner, Maine. This was one of the earliest American schools of applied science and engineering.
1823	Bookkeeping was included in the curriculum of the English high school of Boston.
1824	Rensselaer School was established at Troy, New York, which was the second and perhaps most important of the applied science and engineering schools.
1824	The Franklin Institute of Philadelphia, the second mechanics' institute in America, was established.
1824	First girls' high school was opened in Worcester, Massachusetts.
1825	A mechanics' institute was established in Baltimore, Maryland.
1825	Robert Owen and William McClure established a new experimental school in New Harmony, Indiana, which consisted of an infant school, an elementary school, and a secondary school for youngsters over age 12. This school employed a number of Pestalozzian ideas including the concept of a manual labor school.
1826	Josiah Holbrook published a comprehensive plan for popularizing education to which he gave the title "American Lyceum of Science and Arts." He began to deliver a series of lectures on natural sciences in Worcester County, Massachusetts. This marked the beginning of the American Lyceum movement.
1827	A mechanics' institute was opened in Boston.
1827	Massachusetts law required that bookkeeping be taught in selected high schools of the state.
1827	The Oneida Institute of Science and Industry, a Presbyterian manual labor school, was established at Whitesboro, New York. This was one of the most famous academies because of its manual labor system.
1827	Massachusetts passed a law requiring the establishment of high schools in cities, towns, and districts of 500 families or more.
1827	The Lyceum movement began in America.
1831	The Society for Promoting Manual Labor in Literary Institutions was formed to advocate support for manual labor projects as part of schoolwork. This society heightened the concern for agricultural, business, industrial, and women's education.
1833	Oberlin College was founded as one of the earliest coeducational institutions of higher learning.
1835	Girls were taught sewing in the grammar schools of Boston.
1836	Drawing was established as a required subject in the high schools of Boston. Lowell Institute was established in Boston.
1837	Horace Mann became Secretary of the Massachusetts Board of Education and emerged as a tireless leader in improving the condition of education and schools in his state. He served as editor of the *Common School Journal* which presented educational ideas, described educational practices, and introduced innovation and improvements. He became a major leader in the development of free, public, universal education for all American youngsters.

	... CHRONOLOGICAL CHART ...
1839	The first normal school for the training of teachers was established in Lexington, Massachusetts.
1839	The Philadelphia Institute for Colored Youth—a manual training school— was established by the Richard Humphrey estate to offer training in the various branches of the mechanic arts and agriculture.
1841	Catherine Beecher published her *Treatise on Domestic Economy for the Use of Young Ladies*, which covered nearly every phase of homemaking and paved the way for the development of homemaking education. Augustus Wattles established manual labor schools for African-Americans with headquarters in Mercer, Ohio.
1842	The New England Female Medical College was founded.
1847	The Sheffield Scientific School was established at Yale.
1849	Avery College was established in Allegheny City, Pennsylvania, to offer academic subjects and one occupational subject for African-Americans.
1850s	The mechanical, biological, and chemical evolution of agriculture began, which was to change the American farm forever.
1851	Massachusetts passed laws making school attendance compulsory through the eighth grade.
1855	Elmira College in New York was founded and became the first women's college to require young women to take domestic science and general household affairs courses. This was the first women's college to grant degrees.
1856	Wilberforce University of Wilberforce, Ohio, was established to offer African-American students training in academic subjects, occupational subjects, and teacher preparation.
1857	The National Education Association (NEA) was organized.
1860	The first kindergarten in America was established in 1860, based on the kindergartens established in Europe by Froebel. The kindergarten was a school that stressed individual child development, motor activity as the primary teaching method, and social cooperation as its environment. Kindergartens were slow to evolve in America until after the Civil War, but by 1900 some 4,500 of them had been established in the United States.
1861	Oswego State Normal School was established to train teachers using teaching methods developed years earlier by Pestalozzi and other European educators. The Oswego movement that followed brought much-needed reform to the educational methods used in that time.
1862	The first Morrill Act was passed. This authorized public land grants to states for the establishment and maintenance of agricultural and mechanical colleges.
1865	The Freedmen's Bureau was created by Congress as the Bureau of Refugees, Freedmen, and Abandoned Lands, which set about assisting the founding and operation of a number of schools for African-Americans which included some form of industrial education.
1866	The Penn Normal and Industrial School was established on St. Helen Island, South Carolina, by Miss Laura Towne. The school was one of the earliest manual labor schools in the South, and served as a model for many others which followed.
1867	Howard Theological Seminary was founded in 1867 in Washington, DC. One year later, in 1868, its name was changed to Howard University. Howard University is believed to be the first truly African-American university. Although it was never designated as an industrial training school, it did offer industrial education courses until they were replaced by an engineering program. Howard University began as a private institution but was heavily subsidized by the federal government in 1879, a practice which continues today.
1867	The U.S. Department of Education was created, which later became known as the Office of Education. Over 100 years later, in 1980, the U.S. Department of Education became a cabinet-level entity.

... CHRONOLOGICAL CHART ...	
1868-1906	Trade schools arose in France, England, Germany, and America.
1868	Victor Della Vos established a new type of instructional program to teach the mechanical arts at the Imperial Technical School of Moscow in 1868. He developed eight principles, known as the "Russian system" of manual training, that incorporated job analysis for content identification, separate instructional shops, group instruction, and graded exercises to build skill competency. His system of instruction became the answer to instructional methodology for manual training in the United States and other countries.
1868	The Worcester County Free Institute, a manual labor school, was established in Massachusetts to provide practical training and application of scientific principles in the mechanical arts. A number of these applied science and industry institutions became engineering colleges.
1868	The Hampton Institute, one of the first manual labor trade schools in America designed to provide specific trade training supplemented with directly related academic subjects, was established in Hampton, Virginia. This institution marked the beginning of the establishment of many private trade schools.
1868	A complete graded system of drawing was instituted in Boston schools. Drawing was a required subject in all grades of Cincinnati schools.
1870	The Virginia Legislature chartered Hampton Institute as the Land-Grant College for African-Americans, which paved the way for the institution to receive federal funds from the Land-Grant Act of 1862. It received the first federal funds in 1872.
1872	The Kalamazoo Case established the right of states to collect taxes to support public education.
1872	Massachusetts authorized schools to offer courses in sewing and other industrial education subjects.
1872	R. Hoe and Company, a manufacturer of printing presses, established one of the first corporate schools to train high-quality employees for their firm.
1873	The first public school kindergarten in the U.S. was established in St. Louis, Missouri, for the purpose of dealing with urban poverty.
1874	The Kalamazoo decision of the Michigan Supreme Court clarified the legal basis for imposing taxes on the public for the support of high schools, which later led to high school vocational education programs.
1874-1907	Otto A. Salomon established a system of woodworking called sloyd in the elementary schools of Sweden to help children develop their mental and physical powers and to teach dexterity of hand and instill a general love of work. He is considered the father of the sloyd system of education, which influenced manual training and industrial arts in America.
1875	The Quincy Plan, developed by Francis Parker in Quincy, Massachusetts, reoriented the school system to an activity-centered curriculum based on the needs and interests of youngsters. This plan, based on the child-centered ideas of Pestalozzi, changed the teaching methods of elementary education in America forever.
1876	Manual arts and arts and crafts were introduced into America from England and France. The name of manual training has changed many times from manual training to manual arts, industrial arts, and now technology education.
1876	Professor John Runkle, of the Massachusetts Institute of Technology, visited the Philadelphia centennial exhibition where he saw the Russian system of manual training. Professor Runkle established the School of Mechanic Arts as part of the Massachusetts Institute of Technology in Boston using some of the Russian system of manual training to educate and train qualified grammar-school students.
1879	The Huntington Industrial Works was established at Hampton Institute to provide employment opportunities for students. This may have been one of the very first formal school-based enterprises.
1880	The first manual training high school was established in St. Louis, Missouri, by Professor Calvin Woodward. This school borrowed some of the ideas of the Russian system, using the laboratory method of instruction and graded lessons in the use of common tools of the mechanical arts.

	...CHRONOLOGICAL CHART...
1880	Charles Leland introduced arts and crafts instruction, which originated in England and France, into the schools of Philadelphia. The arts and crafts movement which followed led some manual training teachers to emphasize a wider variety of mediums for instruction and directed attention to artistic design.
1880	The Philadelphia High School for Girls offered courses in sewing, and many other manual training schools included courses in domestic science in their curriculums.
1880	Booker T. Washington founded Tuskegee Institute in Tuskegee, Alabama, which became one of the premier private colleges for African-American students, offering academic and occupational instruction as well as teacher preparation.
1880-1900	Many liberal arts colleges and universities established industrial education departments to take advantage of the Slater Fund for this type of education. Beginning in 1910 and continuing through 1920, with the withdrawal of Slater funds and for other reasons, many of these schools began to phase out industrial education.
1881	The New York Trade School was one of the first institutions established to offer specific trade training and supplemental studies for those preparing to enter employment as well as for those already employed. This was one of the first schools to utilize advisory committees.
1881	The Federation of Organized Trades & Labor Unions was formed and became the American Federation of Labor in 1886, consisting of 25 different unions and over 300,000 members.
1883	The Hebrew Technical Institute, a type of trade school, was established in New York City to provide general subjects and instruction in the mechanical trades for Jewish youngsters.
1884	The first publicly supported high school for manual training was established in Baltimore, Maryland.
1884	The Kitchen Garden Association was founded to deal with the problems of slum conditions in inner cities through education for household management.
1886	The American Federation of Labor was founded in Columbus, Ohio.
1884	New York College for the Training of Teachers was established which later became Teachers College of Columbia University. Teachers College provided important leadership to the field of industrial arts. It was the first institution to offer professional coursework in the field; it was the first institution to confine its offerings in industrial education exclusively to the graduate level; it graduated the first doctorate in industrial education; and it was the site of several important curriculum projects.
1887	The Hatch Act provided federal funds to establish and support agricultural experiment stations.
1888	Gustaf Larson established a system of sloyd instruction in Boston. Sloyd instruction emphasized developing the capacities of the child and the making of useful objects that were of interest to students. Sloyd also used only trained teachers rather than trained craftworkers. This experiment led the way to the establishment of "American sloyd" instruction in other schools of the country.
1888	St. Paul School was established in Lawrenceville, Virginia, by Reverend James Russell, an Episcopal minister and graduate of Hampton Institute. This was one of the first manual labor trade schools to offer academic subjects only at night. This school became a Virginia high school in 1923 and a normal school in 1926. In 1946 its name was changed to St. Paul's Polytechnic Institute. This school, along with Hampton and Tuskegee institutes, were the three longest-lasting industrial schools for African-Americans.
1890	The Country Life Movement began. This stimulated the development of general agriculture courses in elementary schools.
1890	The Morrill Act of 1890, also known as the Maintenance Act, extended funding for the original Morrill Act and included a provision for funding at least one Land Grant college or university for African-Americans to receive education and training in agriculture and the mechanical arts.
1891	The Williamson Free School of Mechanical Trades, a trade school that was entirely free to those who could qualify, was established in Philadelphia to offer trade training that could match the best apprenticeship programs.

... CHRONOLOGICAL CHART ...	
1892	The National Education Association Committee of Ten ruled against a two-track system of education for the college bound and the non-college bound and endorsed four different courses of study, all of which would meet college admissions requirements.
1893	Boston established its first publicly supported manual training high school.
1893	Tuskegee Institute was incorporated in the state of Alabama as the Tuskegee Normal and Industrial Institute.
1893	Professional courses for teachers of manual training were offered at Teachers College, New York.
1895	The National Association of Manufacturers was formed in 1895 and began to explore how public schools could help American manufacturers obtain a supply of manpower that could make them more competitive in a growing international market.
1895	The American Correspondence School was established in Boston, Massachusetts, by R. T. Miller, Jr. It moved to Chicago after the turn of the century.
1898	The American Technical Society was founded in 1898 to publish books for use in courses offered by American Correspondence School.
1898	One of the first technical high schools was established in Springfield, Massachusetts.
1899	Ten annual conferences for home economics were conducted at Lake Placid and Chautauqua in New York under the leadership of Ellen Richards. These conferences provided the organizational framework for programs of home economics education in schools of the late nineteenth and early twentieth century.
1900	Most states passed compulsory school laws and provided the final incentive to publicly supported high schools throughout the nation.
1900	Beginning of the vocational education movement. Also, the beginning of the comprehensive high school that combined academic and manual training in one school facility.
1900s	The social efficiency movement in education began resulting in the vocational guidance movement and debate over the type of curriculum needed in American high schools.
1901	The Baldwin Locomotive Works of Philadelphia established a corporate school serving three levels of workers.
1902	General Electric Company established a corporate school for their employees which used an apprentice-ship system that combined activities at the work site with classroom instruction.
1902	The first junior college in the United States was established in Joliet, Illinois.
1903	James Haney, director of manual training of the New York City public schools, introduced the term "manual arts" at the NEA convention.
1905	Governor Douglas appointed a Commission on Industrial and Technical Education, known as the Douglas Commission, that studied the need for some form of industrial education in Massachusetts and in 1906 reported a number of findings that sparked increased interest in establishing industrial education in schools to prepare individuals for vocations. The Douglas Commission Report attracted much attention to the need for publicly supported programs of vocational education.
1905	New York established its first seventh and eighth grade in intermediate or junior high schools and began adding the ninth grade by 1915.
1905-1906	The first cooperative education program for engineers was established by Dr. Herman Schneider at the University of Cincinnati.
1906	The National Society for the Promotion of Industrial Education was formed to promote the cause of industrial education nationwide and to assist in preparing draft legislation to be acted on by Congress.

	. . . CHRONOLOGICAL CHART . . .
1906	The Adams Act increased federal funds to states for operation of experimental stations established by the Hatch Act of 1887.
1907	Wisconsin adopted vocational education as part of its high school program.
1906	The Nelson Amendments to the Morrill Act of 1907 (PL 59-242) authorized more money for land-grant colleges and designated a portion of the funds to be used to prepare instructors for teaching agriculture and the mechanic arts.
1908	New York adopted vocational education as part of its high school curriculum.
1908	The cooperative part-time plan of trade training was initiated by Professor Herman Schneider at Cincinnati, Ohio, in connection with college engineering courses.
1908	Frank Parsons led the way for the establishment of the Vocational Bureau of Boston to deal with the problems of both youth and adults in finding suitable employment. He developed the concepts of vocational guidance and introduced the trait and factor theory of vocational guidance.
1909	The American Home Economics Association was founded.
1909	Charles Bennett, "father of manual arts" in America, outlined a classification system for elementary school manual arts to include the five areas of graphic arts, mechanic arts, plastic arts, textile arts, and book-making arts.
1909	Dean James Russell expanded the term "industrial arts" and recommended that industrial arts replace manual training in the elementary schools of the nation. Industrial arts was to be a study of the industrial processes by which raw materials are transformed into things of greater value to meet human needs and wants.
1909	The first junior high school was established in Berkley, California.
1910	The National Association for the Advancement of Colored people (NAACP) was founded in 1909 under the leadership of W. E. B. DuBois.
1909	The Manual Arts Conference of the Miscopy Valley was founded in 1909 to serve the needs of teacher educators, state department of education leaders, and leaders from big city school systems in the central states.
1911	Part-time cooperative courses were introduced into the high school of York, Pennsylvania.
1912	Charles Prosser became the Executive Secretary of the National Society for the Promotion of Industrial Education and was appointed to the Commission of National Aid to Vocation Education in 1914. In his leadership roles, Prosser was a strong advocate for publicly supported vocational education that would prepare people to better serve the society. His ideas about vocational education were incorporated into the Smith-Hughes Act of 1917 and were dominant in vocational education for over 40 years.
1913	The National Education Association Commission on the Reorganization of Secondary Education released its report of the Cardinal Principles of Secondary Education that provided the framework for the organization of the comprehensive high school.
1914	The Commission on National Aid to Vocational Education was appointed by President Wilson to study the issue of federal aid to vocational education and to assist in drafting a bill to present to Congress. This commission was instrumental in developing the language of the Smith-Hughes Act which was passed three years later in 1917.
1914	The Smith-Lever Act established cooperative extension programs in agriculture and home economics and initiated the concept of federal-state matching of funds.
1916	John Dewey published his book *Democracy and Education* in which he developed his ideas of progressive education. He was a strong advocate for vocational education of a broad nature that would help individuals understand the industrial nature of society and the nature of work as basic to social understanding. He was a strong proponent for an activity-centered program that featured problem-solving and doing activities.

	...CHRONOLOGICAL CHART...
1917	The Smith-Hughes Act was passed, authorizing federal funds for the establishment and support of secondary and postsecondary vocational training in the occupational areas of agriculture, home economics, and trades and industry. Federal funds could also be used to provide vocational teacher training.
1917	Charles R. Allen became supervisor of training for the Newport News, Virginia, shipyards and brought his idea of training workers to teach other workers, which enhanced the production of ships for the war effort. After the war, Allen worked for the Federal Board for Vocational Education as an agent and as a consultant. Charles Allen has been called the father of vocational education in America.
1918	The Smith-Sears Act provided federal funds for establishing retraining programs for World War I veterans.
1918	The Commission on Reorganization of Secondary Education issued its famous "seven cardinal principles of education," with one of the principles being development of a vocation.
1920s	The 1920s was a period for expansion of high school vocational education programs established through Smith-Hughes funds; for the establishment of vocational rehabilitation programs for war veterans and other disabled individuals; and for the expansion of research in agricultural experiment stations and service through agricultural extension programs.
1920	The Smith-Bankhead Act provided for the establishment of rehabilitation programs for non-military disabled persons in civil employment.
1920	The Smith-Fess Act established rehabilitation programs for industrially disabled persons.
1923	Gordon Bonser advocated the inclusion of industrial arts into the elementary school with a study of manufacturing industries as the curriculum base with the goal being to develop an understanding of the functioning of our industrial society. Industrial arts were to be a general education subject desirable for all to take.
1924	An Act to Extend Vocational Education to Hawaii (PL 68-35) was enacted into law on March 10, 1924.
1925	The American Association for Adult Education was organized.
1925	The Purnell Act of 1925 (PL 68-458) authorized more money for agricultural experiment stations.
1926	The American Vocational Association was formed out of the merger of the National Society for Vocational Education (formerly NSPIE) and the Vocational Association of the Middle West.
1928	The Capper-Ketcham Act of 1928 (PL 70-475) authorized additional money for the further development of agricultural extension work in Land-Grant colleges and universities.
1929	The George-Reed Act authorized additional funds for agriculture and home economics vocational programs funded by the Smith-Hughes Act of 1917, but no additional funds for trade and industrial education programs.
1930s	The 1930s was a period of increased funding and the broadening of vocational education to include marketing education as well as establishment of federal programs to reduce unemployment resulting from the Great Depression. Numerous diversified cooperative occupational programs were established under the leadership of C. E. Rakestraw, a U.S. Office of Education regional agent.
1931	The Territory of Puerto Rico Agricultural Experiment Station Act of 1931 (PL 71-856) extended vocational education to the territory and coordinated the agricultural experiment station on the island.
1932	The Civilian Conservation Corp (CCC) was established to provide work-study and vocational education to unemployed youth to counteract the Great Depression.
1932	A division of Industrial Arts was established in the American Vocational Association in 1932 with Robert W. Selvidge from the University of Missouri as its head.
1933	The administrative power of the Federal Board of Vocational Education (FBVE) was transferred to the U.S. Office of Education by executive order of President Franklin D. Roosevelt. The FBVE was abolished completely in 1946.

	...CHRONOLOGICAL CHART...
1934	The George-Ellzey Act increased supplemental funding for agriculture, home economics, and trade and industrial education programs authorized by the Smith-Hughes Act of 1917.
1935	The Social Security Act provided for vocational training of the handicapped.
1935	The National Youth Administration was established to provide vocational training and employment for unemployed youth.
1935	The Works Project Administration and Public Works Administration were established to provide vocational training, employment, and work relief.
1935	The Committee for Industrial Organization was founded in 1935 under the leadership of John L. Lewis.
1936	The Fitzgerald Act was passed by Congress to promote apprenticeship-related instruction by national agreement.
1936	The George-Deen Act increased federal support for vocational programs identified in the Smith-Hughes Act of 1917, and added the vocational areas of distributive occupations and teacher education to receive federal funds.
1937	The National Association of Industrial Teacher Trainers (NAITT) was founded in 1937. NAITT was the forerunner of The National Association of Industrial and Technical Teacher Educators.
1938	The Congress of Industrial Organizations (CIO), another large labor organization, was founded.
1939	The American Industrial Arts Association was founded in1939 as an affiliate of the National Education Association (NEA).
1940	The 1940s was a period of training people to support the war effort and helping veterans readjust to civilian life. Vocational education programs received additional funding, and state and local education agencies were given more discretion as to how federal funds could be used.
1940	The Future Business Leaders of America was made a national student organization for business education students in 1940.
1940-1946	A series of ten Vocational Education for National Defense acts were passed as war emergency measures to provide money for vocational education programs to prepare war industry workers.
1944	The Servicemen's Readjustment Act, commonly known as the GI Bill, authorized money to help World War 11 veterans make the adjustment to civilian life, and subsequent legislation allowed veterans of the Korean and Vietnam wars to receive benefits.
1945	The Future Homemakers of America (FHA) (now called Family, Career and Community Leaders of America or FCCLA) was founded prepare students for multiple roles as homemakers, wage earners, and community leaders.
1945	The U.S. joined UNESCO and participated in organization activities to provide vocational training to underdeveloped countries.
1946	The National School Lunch Act of 1946 (PL 79-396) was enacted to assist states in the expansion and operation of nonprofit school lunch programs for needy children.
1946	The George-Barden Act increased federal support for the vocational programs of agriculture, home economics, trade and industrial, and distributive education. It also added authorization for the Office of Vocational Education in Washington and vocational education for the fishery trades to receive federal funds.
1947	The Distributive Education Clubs of America (DECA) was founded.
1949	The Federal Property and Administrative Services Act of 1949 (PL 81-152) made it possible for schools with vocational programs to access government surplus equipment and supplies.

... CHRONOLOGICAL CHART ...	
1949	An Act to Incorporate the Future Farmers of America of 1950 (PL 80-740) chartered the vocational student organization and spelled out in detail the purposes, objectives, and organizational structure of the organization.
1950s	The 1950s was a period of continued expansion of vocational education programs to include those in fishery and health occupations. The most notable event was passage of the National Defense Education Act that refocused attention on the importance of educating individuals in technical and scientific areas for the defense of the country. The focus of this legislation was on postsecondary training and the preparation of workers for occupations that require higher levels of applied academics and technical skills.
1950	Federal vocational education programs were extended to the Virgin Islands by public law (PL 81-462).
1955	The American Federation of Labor (AFL) and the Committee for Industrial Organization (CIO) united to form the AFL-CIO in 1955 at a convention in New York.
1956	The Health Amendments of the George-Barden Act added practical nursing and health occupations programs to the list of vocational programs eligible to receive federal funds.
1956	The Fishery Amendments of the George-Barden Act further promoted vocational programs for the fishery industry.
1958	The National Defense Education Act provided federal support to state and local school systems for strengthening instruction in science, mathematics, foreign languages, and other critical subjects. In addition, it provided funds to support technical programs, vocational guidance and testing programs, training institutes, higher education student loans and fellowships, and statistical services.
1958	The Education of Mentally Retarded Children Act authorized federal assistance for training teachers of the handicapped.
1958	The Captioned Films for the Deaf Act authorized a loan service of captioned films for the deaf.
1958	The first chartered Phi Beta Lambda chapter was chartered in Iowa.
1960s	This decade marked the beginning of manpower legislation and employment and training programs under the direction of the U.S. Department of Labor. The vocational education act of 1963 and its amendments in 1968 changed the focus of federal vocational education from specific occupational programs to programs to meet the needs of different categories of people.
1961	The Area Redevelopment Act provided funds for retraining persons in defined redevelopment areas of the country that were severely economically depressed.
1962	The Panel of Consultants on Vocational Education, appointed by President John F. Kennedy and chaired by Benjamin C. Willis, released its report entitled *Education for a Changing World of Work* that described needed changes in federal legislation for vocational education and contained a number of recommendations that were later included in the Vocational Education Act of 1963.
1962	The Manpower Development and Training Act provided funds for training in new and improved skills for the unemployed and underemployed.
1963	The Health Professions Educational Assistance Act provided federal funds to expand teaching facilities for health programs and for loans to students preparing for the health professions.
1963	The Vocational Education Act increased federal support for vocational education, but changed the way money was allocated toward serving people rather than occupational programs. This act authorized federal funds to support residential vocational schools, vocational work-study programs, and research, training, and demonstrations in vocational education. It also included business education as a program eligible for federal funds.
1963	The Higher Education Facilities Act authorized a five-year program of federal grants and loans to colleges and universities for the expansion and development of physical facilities.

...CHRONOLOGICAL CHART...	
1964	The Civil Rights Act established basic human rights and responsibilities in the workplace and prohibited discrimination on the basis of race, gender, national origin, or handicap. Other issues addressed equal employment opportunities, voting rights, equal education, fair housing, and public accommodations.
1964	The Economic Opportunity Act of 1964 authorized federal funds to support college work-study programs for students from low-income families, education and vocational training for unemployed youth, training and work experience opportunities in welfare programs, Job Corps programs, and support for community action programs such as Head Start, Follow Through, Upward Bound, and Volunteers in Service to America (VISTA).
1965	The Elementary and Secondary Education Act (ESEA) authorized expenditure of federal funds for elementary and secondary school programs serving children of low-income families; for school library resources, textbooks, and other instructional materials; for supplementary educational centers and services; and educational research and development training.
1965	The Higher Education Act addressed some of the same issues that ESEA dealt with, only at the higher education level. Federal funds were made available to assist states and local school systems to solve educational problems through such programs as continuing education, student loans, and the establishment of the National Teacher Corps.
1965	The National Institute for the Deaf Act provided for the establishment and operation of residential schools for postsecondary education and training for the deaf.
1965	The Vocational Industrial Clubs of America (VICA) was founded in 1965.
1965	The American Industrial Arts Student Association (AIASA) was organized in 1965 and was officially recognized as the only national student organization serving industrial arts students in 1978. This organization became the Technology Student Organization in 1998.
1966	The Adult Education Act authorized grants to states to encourage expansion of educational programs for adults.
1966	The ESEA Amendments modified existing elementary and secondary programs and provided for state grants to initiate, expand, and improve programs and projects for handicapped children and youth.
1966	The Vocational Office Education Clubs of America (OEA) was founded in 1966. This organization was the forerunner of the Business Professionals of America.
1967	The Education Professions Development Act (EPA) provided federal funds to address the training of teachers in critical shortage areas, and provided fellowships for teachers and other educational professionals. This act was instrumental in providing a vital source of college and university vocational teacher educators.
1967	The ESEA Amendments authorized federal support of regional centers for education of handicapped children, model centers and services for deaf-blind children, assistance in recruitment of personnel, and dissemination of information on the education of the handicapped; technical assistance for rural education programs; and support for dropout prevention programs and for bilingual education programs.
1967	The National Association of Industrial Teacher Trainers (NAITT) changed its name to the National Association of Industrial and Technical Teacher Educators.
1967	General Report of the Advisory Council on Vocational Education released its report *The Bridge Between Man and His Work* that presented information on the status of vocational education under the provisions of the Vocational Education Act of 1963 and recommended a course of action for amending the Act that eventually was included in the Vocational Education Amendments of 1968 and subsequent amendments to the Vocational Education Act of 1963.
1968	The Vocational Amendments broadened the definition of vocational education to bring it closer to general education and provided vast sums of money to address the nation's social and economic problems. The act established a National Advisory Committee, expanded vocational education services to meet the needs of disadvantaged students, and established methods of collecting and disseminating information about vocational education. This act placed more emphasis on vocational programs at the postsecondary level. It also added cooperative education as one of the vocational education programs eligible to receive federal funds.

... CHRONOLOGICAL CHART ...	
1969	A postsecondary division of VICA was established in 1969.
1970s	The 1970s was a period of consolidation of earlier manpower legislation and the attempt to bring about change in both academic and vocational education through the career education movement. It was also a period in which both general and vocational education were to provide education and training for disabled individuals.
1971	The Comprehensive Health Manpower Training Act of 1971 (PL 92-257) increased and expanded provisions for health manpower training and facilities.
1971	The Future Homemakers of America (FHA) added a division of Home Economics Related Occupations (HERO) to its organization.
1971	Sidney Marland, U.S. Commissioner of Education, made Career Education his highest priority.
1972	The Education Amendments continued support for many of the programs established in the Vocational Act of 1963 and 1968 Amendments and introduced some new provisions important to vocational education such as special programs for the disadvantaged, and a broadened definition of vocational education to allow federal funds to be spent to support industrial arts programs and the training of volunteer firefighters. Postsecondary occupational education received more support in this act.
1973	The Rehabilitation Act reaffirmed the rights of handicapped persons in the workplace. Section 503 established affirmative action programs to hire handicapped individuals and required employers to make reasonable accommodations, while Section 504 prohibited discrimination on the basis of handicap in any private or public program or activity receiving federal funds. This act was designed to allow handicapped individuals to enter the mainstream of American life.
1973	The Comprehensive Employment and Training Act (CETA) of 1973 (93-203) consolidated earlier manpower legislation and began the federal government's drive to establish training programs for the unemployed and underemployed.
1974	The Educational Amendments encouraged the development of individualized education plans (IEPs) for children with special needs participating in Title I of the 1965 ESEA Act. These amendments also included the Women's Educational Equality Act of 1974, which was designed to assist states in bringing about educational equity for women. Other important provisions of these amendments included support for career education, establishment of the National Center for Educational Statistics, and research into the problems of providing bilingual education.
1974	The Emergency Jobs and Employment Assistance Act of 1974 (94-405) was enacted to maximize efforts to produce jobs and job training for individuals who served in the armed services and to inform all veterans about employment and education and training opportunities available to them.
1975	The Education of All Handicapped Children Act of 1975 launched an organized effort to provide a free and appropriate education for all handicapped children ages 3-21. This act spelled out the assurances for handicapped youngsters including due process, written individualized education plans, bias-free testing and assessment, and measures to protect the confidentiality of records. In addition, a number of terms related to handicapped individuals were clearly defined. This act provided a number of grants to states and local school systems to improve vocational education and related services for handicapped individuals.
1975	The Indian Self-Determination and Education Assistance Act (PL 93-638) provided for increased participation of Indians in the establishment and conduct of their own education.
1976	The Education Amendments continued the trend of omnibus legislation to extend and revise previous legislation and to redirect American education in an attempt to correct some of the nation's problems including changing the public's attitude toward the roles of men and women in society. This act required the development of programs to eliminate sex discrimination and sex stereotyping. It also required the development of a national vocational education data reporting and accounting system and required states to develop an evaluation system. It established the NOICC and SOICC Occupational Information Coordinating Committees.
1976	The Health Occupations Students of America (HOSA) was founded.

...CHRONOLOGICAL CHART...	
1977	The Youth Employment and Demonstration Projects Act established youth employment training programs promoting the education-to-work transition.
1978	The Career Education Incentive Act authorized the establishment of career education programs for elementary and secondary schools.
1978	The Education Amendments established the community schools concept to use existing educational facilities for instruction of adults and established a comprehensive basic skills program aimed at improving student achievement in reading, mathematics, and written and oral communication.
1978	The Comprehensive Employment and Training Act (CETA) Amendments revised existing manpower legislation to connect it with other related programs involved in preparing people for work, including vocational education. Prime sponsors were required to identify the services to be provided to handicapped individuals in their five-year and annual training plans.
1978	The Tribally Controlled Community College Assistance Act of 1978 (PL 95-471) provided federal funds for the operation and improvement of tribally controlled community colleges for Indian students.
1978	Kenneth Hoyt was named Director of the Office of Career Education in the U.S. Office of Education. Hoyt was one of the premier leaders of the career education movement.
1979	The Department of Education Organization Act established the U. S. Department of Education.
1980s	The 1980s marked the beginning of the school reform movement. The Carl D. Perkins Vocational and Applied Technology Education Act of 1984 was enacted to reform vocational education, to improve vocational programs, and to improve services for students with special needs. It also was a time for reform and consolidation of manpower programs of the 1970s into a new job training partnership program to provide education and training to disadvantaged youth and unemployed individuals. A new focus of federal legislation appeared in the form of programs and services to address problems of youth making the transition from school to work or continuing education. The decade of the 1980s also saw the industrial arts program evolve into technology education.
1980	The National Postsecondary Agricultural Student Organization (PAS) was founded in 1980.
1982	The Job Training Partnership Act (JTPA) significantly revised other manpower legislation to introduce a new era of collaboration between vocational education and the private sector to provide job training and related services to participants. This act provided funds to regional service delivery areas (SDAs) that used private industry councils (PICs) to determine what training programs were needed and how these programs were to be implemented. JTPA funds were not to be used for employment subsistence as was the case in previous manpower legislation, and 70% of funds were to be spent directly for training. Special summer youth employment programs were established and the successful Job Corps program was continued.
1982	The National Young Farmers Education Association was founded in 1982.
1983	The Education Handicapped Act Amendments included a number of special provisions to support and coordinate education and service programs to assist handicapped youth in the transition from secondary to postsecondary education, employment, or adult services. The act also included support for expanding preschool special education programs and early intervention programs.
1983	The *Nation at Risk: Imperative for Educational Reform* report of the National Commission on Excellence in Education focused attention on the ineffectiveness of public education and called for reform through a number of recommendations. This report made the need for educational reform a public priority.
1983	*The Unfinished Agenda: The Role of Vocational Education in the High School* report of the National Commission of Secondary Education was released in response to the *Nation at Risk: Imperative for Educational Reform* report that did not specifically address the role of vocational education in America education.
1984	The Rehabilitation Act Amendments of 1984 (PL 98-221) authorized demonstration projects to address the problems encountered by youth with disabilities in transitioning to work.

	... CHRONOLOGICAL CHART ...
1984	The Human Services Reauthorization Act of 1964 (PL 98-558) reauthorized the Head Start and Follow Through programs, and created a Carl D. Perkins Scholarship program, a National Talented Teachers Fellowship program, a Federal Merit Scholarships program, and a Leadership in Educational Administration program.
1984	The National Vocational-Technical Honor Society (NV-THS) was founded.
1984	The Carl D. Perkins Vocational Education Act continued the long-standing tradition of federal support for vocational education with two major goals in mind, one economic and one social. The economic goal was to improve the skills of the labor force and prepare adults for job opportunities. The social goal was to provide equal opportunities for adults in vocational education. This act had nine stated purposes including to expand, improve, modernize, and develop quality vocational education programs in order to meet the needs of the nation's existing and future workforce for marketable skills, and to improve productivity and promote economic growth. Educational services were to be provided to meet the needs of specific populations, including handicapped and disadvantaged individuals. The act spelled out the assurances that were to be provided to handicapped and disadvantaged individuals. This act was one of the most comprehensive in attempting to meet the vocational education needs of special populations.
1985	The Montgomery GI Bill Active Duty Act of 1985 (PL 98-525) brought about a new GI Bill for individuals who initially entered active military duty on or before July 1, 1985.
1985	The Montgomery GI Bill Selected Reserve Act of 1985 (PL 98-525) created an education program for members of the Selected Reserve (which includes the National Guard) who enlist, reenlist, or extend an enlistment after June 30, 1985, for a six-year period.
1986	The Education Handicapped Act Amendments continued and expanded discretionary programs and transition programs. It established the handicapped infant and toddler programs, and changed the age of eligibility for special education services to age three.
1986	The Handicapped Children's Protection Act provided monetary support for parents and guardian who found themselves in litigation over the rights of their children to receive a free, appropriate education.
1986	The Rehabilitation Act Amendments authorized funding for programs in supported employment services for individuals with disabilities.
1986	The *Workforce 2000: Work and Workers for the 21st Century* (Johnson and Packer, 1987) report commissioned by the U.S. Department of Labor described a shift in the economy and the need to produce more semi-skilled, skilled, and professional workers. This was one of the first of a series of U. S. Department of Labor reports to address the need for change in the way the nation trains its workers.
1987	The Southern Regional Education Board (SREB) established the "High Schools That Work" (HSTW) initiative.
1988	The Technology-Related Assistance for Individuals with Disabilities Act provided assistance to states in developing programs of technology-related assistance to individuals with disabilities and their families.
1988	The Augustus F. Hawkins–Robert T. Stafford Elementary and Secondary School Improvement Amendments of 1988 (PL 100-297) reauthorized through 1993 major elementary and secondary education programs including Chapter 1, Chapter 2, Bilingual Education, Math-Science Education, Magnet Schools, Impact Aid, Indian Education, Adult Education, and other smaller education programs.
1988	The Commission on Work, Family and Citizenship, also known as the Commission on Youth and America's Future, released two landmark reports, *The Forgotten Half: Non-College Youth in America* and *The Forgotten Half: Pathways to Success for America's Youth and Families.*
1988	The American Society for Training and Development report *Workplace Basics: The Skills Employers Want* was released, identifying seven basic foundational skills needed for learning the specific skills required for the high-performance workplace.
1988	The Vocational Office Education Clubs of America (OEA) changed its name to Business Professionals of America (BPA) in 1988.

...CHRONOLOGICAL CHART...

1989	The Children with Disabilities Temporary Care Reauthorization Act authorized funds to provide temporary care for children with a disability or chronic illness and provided crisis nurseries for children at risk of abuse and neglect.
1989	President George Bush and the nation's governors convened at the Educational Summit in Charlottesville, Virginia, and established six National Goals to guide the American educational system.
1990s	The 1990s was a period of continued reform for academic and vocational education as well as manpower training. The earlier concern of the federal government on improving the transition of youth from school to work led to the passage of the School-to-Work Opportunities Act of 1964. A new Carl D. Perkins Vocational and Technical Education Act was enacted in 1998 to bring about needed change in career and technical education. The Workforce Investment Act of 1998 along with other manpower enactments promised to reform the nation's welfare program to move large numbers of individuals and families from dependency to productive work. A number of commission reports revealed the need for focusing education on providing individuals with the essential skills needed for the 21st century.
1990	The Education of the Handicapped Amendments, more popularly known as the Individuals with Disabilities Education Act (IDEA), combined many of the programs of previous legislation for individuals with special needs. It is the most important piece of legislation ever passed by Congress for educating disabled children and youth. IDEA includes many provisions such as requiring schools to provide assistive devices to increase or maintain the functional capability of individuals with disabilities and establishing special programs on transition. The list of persons who are eligible for special education and related services was expanded from nine to eleven categories. A new structure was provided for developing IEPs and ITPs.
1990	The Americans with Disabilities Act furthered the provisions begun in the Rehabilitation Act of 1973 banning discrimination based on disability, and guaranteed equal opportunities for individuals with disabilities regardless of whether or not federal funds are involved in employment, public accommodation, transportation, state and local government services, and telecommunications. This act is the most comprehensive law ever written which identifies and protects the civil rights of Americans with disabilities.
1990	The Developmental Disabilities Assistance and Bill of Rights Act authorized grants to support the planning, coordination, and delivery of specialized services to persons with developmental disabilities.
1990	The Carl D. Perkins Vocational and Applied Technology Education Act amended and extended the previous 1984 Perkins Act authorizing the largest amount of federal funds ever for vocational education. The intent of this act was to assist states and local school systems in teaching the skills and competencies necessary to work in a technologically advanced society to all students. A major goal of this legislation was to provide greater vocational opportunities to disadvantaged individuals. The act provided funds for the integration of academic and vocational education and for Tech Prep programs, an articulated program between high schools and postsecondary institutions. The act eliminated set-asides for support services for special populations, giving states and local agencies greater flexibility in how funds are best used to serve special populations.
1990	The School Dropout Prevention and Basic Skills Improvement Act of 1990 (PL 101-600) improved secondary school programs for basic skills improvements and dropout reduction.
1990	The landmark report *America's Choice: High Skills or Low Wages* called for a single comprehensive system for general, professional, and technical education that meets the needs of everyone from high school students to dislocated workers, from the chronic unemployed to working adults who want to improve their skills.
1990	The Secretary's Commission on Achieving Necessary Skills (SCANS), in its landmark report *Learning a Living: A Blueprint for High Performance,* identified a three-part foundation of skills and five competencies believed to be essential to successful job performance and necessary preparation for all students.
1990	Tech Prep programs began to be established as a part of the Carl D. Perkins Vocational and Applied Technology Act of 1990 and continue to be among the major forms of secondary career and technical education today.
1991	The Civil Rights Act of 1991 (PL 102-66) amended the Civil Rights Act of 1964, the Age Discrimination in Employment Act of 1967, and the Americans with Disabilities Act of 1990 with regard to employment discrimination. It also established the Technical Assistance Training Institute.

...CHRONOLOGICAL CHART...	
1991	The Distributive Education Clubs of America (DECA) changed its name, dropping the Distributive Education Clubs of America and keeping the letters DECA with a tag line of "An Association of Marketing Students."
1992	The Job Training Reform Amendments revised the JTPA of 1982 to change the focus of manpower programs toward improving services to those facing serious barriers to employment, enhancing the quality of services provided, improving accountability of funds and the programs they serve, linking services provided to real labor market needs, and facilitating the development of a comprehensive and coherent system of human resources services. One of the new provisions of special interest to vocational educators was the requirement for on-the-job training contracts and the development of individual service strategies (ISSs), which are individualized employability development plans for each JTPA participant. This act is devoted to serving special populations who face the greatest employment barriers.
1993	Family and Consumer Sciences Education became the new name for Home Economics Education.
1993	The General Accounting Office (GAO) released its report *Vocational Education: Status in School Year 1990-1991 and Early Signs of Change at the Secondary Level,* which culminated a four-year study to determine how the mandates and provisions of the Carl D. Perkins Vocational and Applied Technology Education Act of 1990 were being carried out.
1994	The Technology-Related Assistance for Individuals with Disabilities Act Amendments expanded the efforts to assist states in developing and implementing a comprehensive, consumer-responsive, statewide program of technology-related assistance for individuals with disabilities of all ages.
1994	The Goals 2000: Educate America Act was a blueprint for improving America's schools through the establishment of eight national goals and the development of voluntary academic and skill standards to assist state and local agencies in helping every child learn what they need to learn in order to function as a family member, involved community member, and competent worker. The act identified ten elements which constitute a suggested framework for developing a local Goals 2000 Plan.
1994	The Improving America's Schools Act was a reauthorization of the ESEA of 1965 which placed primary emphasis on serving disadvantaged students. The major goal of Title I has been revised to improve the teaching and learning of children in high-poverty schools to enable them to meet the challenging academic and performance standards being established by the Goals 2000 Act. This act increased opportunities for vocational and applied technology education to provide input into state and local educational plans and strengthened vocational and applied technology education in 14 different areas.
1994	The School-to-Work Opportunities Act (STWOA) provided a framework to build a high-quality skilled workforce for our nation's economy through partnerships between educators and employers. This act emphasized preparing students with the knowledge, skills, abilities, and information about occupations and the labor market that facilitate the transition from school to continuing education and work. Key elements of this act included collaborative partnerships, integrated curricula, technological advances, adaptable workers, comprehensive career guidance, work-based learning, and a step-by-step approach.
1994	The Educational Research, Development, Dissemination, and Improvement Act of 1994 (PL 103-227) authorized the educational research and dissemination activities of the Office of Educational Research and Improvement. It also authorized the regional education laboratories and university-based research and development centers.
1994	The National Assessment of Vocational Education report to Congress was released, containing a wealth of information about the status of vocational education in American public high schools and postsecondary institutions.
1994	Youth apprenticeship programs were established in a number of states as part of the School-to-Work Opportunities Act of 1994.
1994	The Educate America Act of 1994 established the National Skill Standards Board.
1996	The Personal Responsibility and Work Opportunity Reconciliation Act of 1996 (PL 104-93) dramatically changed the nation's welfare system into one that requires work in exchange for time-limited assistance. This Act contains a strong work requirement combined with support for families moving from welfare to work. The Department of Health and Human Services is the federal agency that oversees this welfare-to-work program.

...CHRONOLOGICAL CHART...	
1996	Developmental Disabilities Assistance and Bill of Rights Act Amendments of 1996 (PL 104-1834) amended the Developmental Disabilities Assistance and Bill of Rights Act to extend the act, and for other purposes.
1997	The Balanced Budget Act of 1997 (PL 105-33) contained the most significant changes to the Medicare and Medicaid programs since their inception over 30 years ago. It also included provisions to supplement the welfare-to-work program begun one year earlier. Specific changes to the original welfare act include the establishment of Welfare-to-Work Challenge Fund to help states and local communities move long-term welfare recipients into long-lasting unsubsidized employment. This act was amended in 1998 with the Noncitizen Technical Amendments that restored disability and health benefits to 380,000 legal immigrants who were in this country prior to passage of welfare reform legislation. The act was amended again in 1999 to change the definition of eligible non-custodial parents to include those who were unemployed or underemployed and could not meet child support obligations or had children receiving or eligible to receive food stamps, supplemental security income, and Medicaid.
1997	The Taxpayer Relief Act of 1997 (PL 105-34) enacted the Hope Scholarship and Lifelong Learning Tax provisions into law.
1997	The Individuals with Disabilities Education Act of 1997 (PL 105-17) was the most important piece of legislation passed by Congress for educating children and youth with disabilities. It was written to ensure that special education and related services are provided to eligible individuals under the age of 22 in addition to the general curriculum and not separate from it. It identifies 13 types of disabilities that persons must have that need special education. It contains many changes to earlier legislation designed to help children and youth with disabilities so that they can receive a free and appropriate education.
1998	The Carl D. Perkins Vocational and Technical Education Act of 1998 (PL 105-332) replaced the 1990 Perkins Act and gave states and local school agencies greater flexibility to develop career and technical education programs while making them more accountable for student performance. Congress requires states and local school districts to provide information on student achievement, program completion, placement in postsecondary education and the workforce, and improved gender equity in program offerings. Congress wanted this act to further develop the academic, vocational, and technical skills of vocational and technical education students through achieving high standards; linking secondary and postsecondary programs; increasing flexibility in the administration and use of funds provided under the act; disseminating national research about vocational education; and providing professional development and technical assistance to vocational and technical educators. Distinguishing features of the new act include a focus on accountability, funding formulas, Tech Prep, school-to-work, gender equity, and students with disabilities.
1998	The Workforce Investment Act of 1998 (PL 105-220) repealed the Job Partnership and Training Act as of July 1, 2000. The act was designed to establish a framework for a unique national workforce preparation and employment system that will better meet the needs of the nation's businesses and the needs of job seekers and those who want to further their careers. Specifically, the goals of the act are to increase the employment, retention, and earnings of participants; increase occupational skill attainment by participants; improve the quality of the workforce; reduce welfare dependency; and enhance the productivity and competitiveness of our nation. Special features of this legislation include delivering services through one-stop career centers, consolidation of workforce development activities, realignment of existing programs, emphasis on youth programs, emphasis on customer information and choice, new focus on program accountability, recognizing differences in individual outcomes and the role of employers, and allowing longer periods of time for planning and service.
1998	The American Youth Policy Forum released its report *The Forgotten Half Revisited: American Youth and Young Families 1988-2008* in 1998. This report revealed what out nation had accomplished for late adolescents and young families since the Forgotten Half reports a decade ago.
1999	Amendments to the Higher Education Act of 1965 (PL 105-244) extended authorization of the Higher Education Act of 1965 and included a number of new provisions that are intended to strengthen higher education, including lowering student loan interest rates, recruiting and training qualified teachers, and promoting high quality distance learning opportunities for students.
1999	The Ticket to Work and Work Incentives Act of 1999 (PL 106-170) was intended to increase the employment opportunities of people with disabilities. It increases beneficiary choice in obtaining rehabilitation and vocational services, removes barriers that require people with disabilities to choose between health care coverage and work, and assures that more Americans with disabilities have the opportunity to participate in the workforce and lessen their dependency on public benefits. This act is administered by the Social Security Administration and promises to modernize employment-related services for individuals with disabilities.

...CHRONOLOGICAL CHART	
1999	The name of the Future Homemakers of America (FHA) was changed to the Family, Career and Community Leaders of America (FCCLA).
1999	The name of the Vocational Industrial Clubs of America (VICA) was changed to SkillsUSA-VICA, substituting merely an acronym for the Vocational Industrial Clubs of America name.
1999	The American Vocational Education Association (AVA) changed its name to the Association for Career and Technical Education (ACTE) in December of 1999.
2000s	The first decade of the 21st century can be characterized as one of unprecedented change in education, the workplace, and in society and the world. Technology continues to change every aspect of civilization. The educational system is being called on to provide individuals with high skills and the ability to actively participate in life-long learning. Business and industry are becoming more involved in the American education system to bring about change in the preparation of individuals for an increasingly complex workplace.
2000	The report of the National Center for Educational Statistics, *Vocational in the United States: Toward the Year 2000,* describes the status of career and technical education at the secondary and postsecondary levels.
2000	The *New Directions for High School Career and Technical Education in the 21st Century* Information Series No. 384, authored by Richard Lynch and published by the ERIC Clearinghouse on Adult, Career and Technical Education, Center on Education and Training for Work, describes new direction for secondary vocational education programs.
2001	The No Child Left Behind (NCLB) Act of 2001 was signed into law by President Bush. It contains the most far reaching revisions yet to the Elementary and Secondary Education Act since its passage in 1965. The act introduces major reform in the areas of accountability and testing, flexibility and local control, funding for what works, and expanded parental options.

LEGISLATIVE REFERENCE INFORMATION . . .					
Act	**Date**	**Public Law**	**Chapter**	**Statute**	
				Volume	**Page**
Morrill Act of 1862	July 2, 1862		130	12	503
Department of Education Act of 1867			158	14	434
Hatch Act of 1887	March 2, 1887		314	24	440
Morrill Act of 1890	August 30, 1890		841	26	417
Adams Act of 1906	March 16, 1906	58-74	951	34	63
Nelson Amendments to Morrill Act of 1907	March 4, 1907	59-242	34		1281
Smith-Lever Act of 1914	May 8, 1914	63-95	79	38	372
Smith-Hughes Act of 1917	February 23, 1917	64-347	114	39	929
Smith-Sears Act of 1918	June 27, 1918	65-178	107	40	617
Smith-Bankhead Act of 1920	June 2, 1920	66-236	219	41	735
Smith-Fess Act of 1920	June 2, 1920	66-236	219	41	735
An Act to Extend Vocational Education to Hawaii	1924	68-35	468	43	1202
Purnell Act of 1925	1925	68-458	308	43	970
Capper-Ketcham Act of 1928	1928	70-475	580	45	578
George Reed Act of 1929	February 5, 1929	70-702	153	45	1151
Territory of Puerto Rico Agricultural Experiment Station Act of 1931	1931	71-846	314	47	412
George-Ellzey Act of 1934	May 22, 1934	73-245	324	48	792
George-Deen Act of 1936	June 8, 1936	74-673	541	49	1488
Vocational Education for National Defense Acts (a series of ten acts)	1940-1946	76-812; 77-647; 77-843; 77-726; 78-74; 78-113; 78-156; 78-248; 78-338; 79-76	253	57	569
Servicemen's Readjustment Act of 1944	June 22, 1944	78-346*	268	58	284
George-Barden Act of 1946	August 1, 1946	79-586	725	60	775

				Statute	
Act	**Date**	**Public Law**	**Chapter**	**Volume**	**Page**
The National School Lunch Act of 1946	1945	79-396	281	60	230
Federal Property and Administrative Act of 1949	1949	81-152	288	63	377
An Act to Incorporate the Future Farmers of America of 1950	1950	81-740	823	64	563
Health Amendments Act of 1956	August 7, 1956	84-911	871	70	923
Fishery Amendment, George-Barden Act of 1956	August 8, 1956	84-911	1039	70	1126
National Defense Education Act of 1958	September 2, 1958	85-864	t	72	1580
Captioned Film for the Deaf Act	September 2, 1958	85-905	t	72	1742
Education of Mentally Retarded Children Act of 1958	September 6, 1958	85-926	t	72	1777
Area Redevlopment Act of 1961	May 1, 1961	87-27	t	75	47
Manpower Development and Traning Act of 1962	March 15, 1962	87-415	t	76	23
Health Professions Eduational Assistance Act of 1963	September 24,1963	88-129	t	77	164
Higher Education Facilities Act of 1963	December 16,1963	88-204	t	77	363
Vocational Education Act of 1963	December 18,1963	88-210	t	77	403, 1-16
Civil Rights Act of 1964	July 2, 1964	88-352	t	78	241
Economic Opportunity Act of 1964	August 20, 1964	88-452	t	78	508
Nurse Training Act of 1964	1964	88-581	t	78	908
Elementary and Secondary Education Act of 1965	April 11, 1965	89-10	t	79	27
National Technical Institute for the Deaf Act of 1965	June 8, 1965	89-36	t	79	125

... LEGISLATIVE REFERENCE INFORMATION ...

Act	Date	Public Law	Chapter	Statute	
				Volume	Page
Higher Education Act of 1965	November 8, 1965	89-329	t	79	1219
Adult Education Act of 1966	November 3, 1966	89-750	t	80	1191
Elementary and Secondary Education Amendments of 1966	November 3, 1966	89-750	t	80	1191
Education Professions Development Act of 1967	June 29, 1967	90-35	t	81	81
Elementary and Secondary Education Amendments of 1967	January 2, 1968	90-247	t	81	783
Vocational Education Amendments of 1968	October 16, 1968	90-576	t	82	1064
Nurse Training Act of 1971	November 18, 1971	92-158	t	85	465
Education Amendments of 1972	June 23, 1972	92-318	t	86	
Rehabilitation Act of 1973	September 26, 1973	93-112	t	87	355
Comprehensive Employment and Training Act of 1973	December 28, 1973	93-203	t	87	839
Education Amendments of 1974	August 21, 1974	93-380	t	88	484
Emergency Jobs and Employment Assistance Act of 1974	1974	94-505	t	90	2429
Women's Educational Equality Act of 1974	August 21, 1974	93-380	t	88	484
Education for all Handicapped Children Act of 1975	November 29, 1975	94-142	t	89	773
Education Amendments of 1976	October 12, 1976	94-482	t	90	2081
Youth Employment and Demonstration Project Act of 1977	August 5, 1977	95-93	t	91	627
Career Education Incentive Act of 1978	December 13,1977	95-207	t	91	1464

... LEGISLATIVE REFERENCE INFORMATION					
Act	Date	Public Law	Chapter	Statute	
				Volume	Page
Comprehensive Employment and Training Act Amendments of 1978	October 27, 1978	95-124	t	92	1904
Educational Ammendments of 1978	November 1, 1978	95-561	t	92	2143
Department of Education Organization Act of 1979	October 17, 1979	96-88	t	93	668
Job Training Partnership Act of 1982	October 13, 1982	97-300	t	96	1322
Education Handicapped Act Amendments of 1983	Deceber 2, 1983	98-199	t	97	1357
Rehabilitation Act Amendments of 1984	February 22, 1984	98-221	t	98	17
Carl D. Perkins Vocational Education Act of 1984	October 19, 1984	98-524	t	98	2435
Education Handicapped Act Amendments of 1986	October 6, 1986	99-457	t	100	1145
Rehabilitation Act Amendments of 1986	October 21, 1986	99-506	t	100	1807
Technology-Related Assistance for Individuals with Disabilities Act of 1988	August 19, 1988	100-407	t	102	1044
Children with Disabilities Temporary Care Reauthorization Act of 1989	October 25, 1991	101-127	t	103	770
Americans with Disabilities Act of 1990	July 26, 1990	101-336	t	104	327
Carl D. Perkins Vocational and Applied Technology Act of 1990	September 25, 1990	101-392	t	104	753
Education of the Handicapped Act Amendments of 1990	October 30, 1990	101-476	t	104	1103
Developmental Disabilities Assistance and Bill of Rights Act of 1990	October 31, 1990	101-496	t	104	1191
Job Training Reform Amendments of 1992	September 7, 1992	102-367	t	106	1021
Technology-Related Assistance for Individuals with Disabilities Act Amendments of 1994	March 9, 1994	103-218	t	108	50

LEGISLATIVE REFERENCE INFORMATION					
Act	**Date**	**Public Law**	**Chapter**	**Statute**	
				Volume	**Page**
Goals 2000: Educate America Act of 1994	March 31, 1994	103-227	t	108	125
School-to-Work Opportunities Act of 1994	May 4, 1994	103-239	t	108	568
Improving America's Schools Act of 1994	October 20, 1994	103-382	t	108	3518
Personal Responsibility and Work Opportunity Reconciliation Act of 1996	1996	104-193	t	110	2105
The Balanced Budget Act of 1997	1997	105-33	t	111	251
The Individuals with Disabilities Education Act Amendments of 1997	1997	105-17	t	111	37
The Carl D. Perkins Vocational and Technical Education Act of 1998	October 31,1998	105-332	t	112	3077
The Workforce Investment Act of 1998	July 1, 1998	105-220	t	112	937
Amendments to the Higher Education Act of 1965	1999	105-244	t	112	1581
The Ticket to Work and Work Incentive Act of 1999	1999	106-70	t	113	1031
The No Child Left Behind (NCLB) Act of 2001	2001	107-110	t	†	†

The first reference to a public law number and usage occurs on page 237, of the United States Code, 1988 Edition, Vol. 20, Statutes at Large (1789-1978), starting with the 57th Congress, January, 1902. Prior to this date, only statute and chapter locations were cited.

t Chapter designations were removed from reference citations after 1957.

* Between the 57th Congress and the 85th Congress, public laws were referenced only by the public law number (i.e. PL 347). If a congressional session carried over into another year, the public law numbers were reset to 1. For example, if a particular session of the 57th Congress carried over from 1902 to 1903, on January 1, 1903, public law numbers would be reset to 1 for a new year. Because of this practice, several public laws in the same session of Congress could have identical numbers. Starting with the 85th Congressional session, one set of public law numbers were assigned per session regardless of the length. Citations and references to the laws were designated as PL 85-864, or 85th Congressional session, public law number 864. The first reference to this practice can be found on page 651, Vol. 20, of the 1988 United States Code, 85th Congress, 1957.

~ Several citations listed may contain the same reference location in the United States Statutes. This is because a specific piece of legislation may contain amendments, enactments, or references to a number of bills and laws. The citation references the beginning of the legislation. As some statutes contain over 200 pages, some scanning of the sections of the legislation may be required.

† No publishing information is available at this time.

ACCOMMODATIONS FOR DEALING WITH SPECIFIC BEHAVIORS OF STUDENTS WITH ATTENTION DEFICIT/HYPERACTIVITY DISORDER . . .

The accommodations listed below are intended to be examples for schools to use in developing a plan to address a student's needs.

When You See This Behavior	Try This Accommodation
1. Difficulty following a plan (has high aspirations, but lacks follow through); sets out to get straight A's, but ends up with F's (sets unrealistic goals)	Assist student in setting long-range goals; break the goal into realistic parts. Use a questioning strategy with the student: Ask, "What do you need to be able to do this?" Keep asking that question until the student has reached an obtainable goal. Have student set clear time lines, and establish how much time he or she needs to accomplish each step. (Monitor student's progress frequently.)
2. Difficulty sequencing and completing steps to accomplish specific tasks (e.g., writing a book report or term paper, organizing paragraphs, solving division problems)	Break up task into workable and manageable steps. Provide examples and specific steps to accomplish task.
3. Shifting from one uncompleted activity to another without closure	Define the requirements of a completed activity (e.g., your math is finished when all six problems are completed and corrected; do not begin the next task until the previous task is finished).
4. Difficulty following through on instructions from others	Gain student's attention before giving directions. Use alerting cues. Accompany oral directions with written directions. Give one direction at a time. Quietly repeat directions to the student after they have been given to the rest of the class. Check for understanding by having the student repeat the directions. Make sure you mean it. Do not present the command as a question or favor. Place general methods of operation and expectations on charts displayed around the room and/or on sheets to be included in student's notebook. Make up job or work cards.
5. Difficulty prioritizing from most to least important	Prioritize assignments and activities. Provide a model to help students. Post the model and refer to it often.
6. Difficulty sustaining effort and accuracy over time	Reduce assignment length and strive for quality (rather than quantity). Increase the frequency of positive reinforcements. (Catch the student doing right and let him know.)
7. Difficulty completing assignments	List and/or post (and say) all steps necessary to complete each assignment. Reduce the assignment into manageable sections with specific due dates. Make frequent checks for work/assignment completion. Arrange for the student to have the phone number of a "study buddy" in each subject area.

...ACCOMMODATIONS FOR DEALING WITH SPECIFIC BEHAVIORS OF STUDENTS WITH ATTENTION DEFICIT/HYPERACTIVITY DISORDER ...

When You See This Behavior	Try This Accommodation
8. Difficulty with any task the requires memory	Combine seeing, saying, writing, and doing; student may need to sub-vocalize to remember. Teach memory techniques as a study strategy (e.g., mnemonics, visualization, oral rehearsal, numerous repetitions).
9. Difficulty with test taking	Allow extra time for testing; teach test-taking skills and strategies; and allow students to be tested orally. Use clear, readable, and uncluttered test forms. Use test format that student is most comfortable with. Allow ample space for student response. Consider having lined answer spaces for essay or short answer tests.
10. Confusion from nonverbal cues (misreads body language, etc.)	Directly teach (tell the student) what nonverbal cues mean. Model and have student practice reading cues in a safe setting.
11. Confusion with written material (difficulty finding main idea from a paragraph, attributes great importance to minor details)	Provide student with copy of reading material with main ideas underlined or highlighted. Provide an outline of important points from reading material. Teach outlining, main idea/details concepts. Provide tape of text/chapter.
12. Confusion from spoken material lecture, and audiovisual material (difficulty finding main idea from presentation, attributes too much importance to minor details)	Provide student with a copy of presentation notes. Allow peers to share carbon copy notes from presentation. (Have student compare own notes with copy of peer's notes.) Provide framed outlines of presentations (introducing visual and auditory cues to important information). Encourage use of tape recorder. Teach and emphasize key words (the following, the most important point, etc.).
13. Difficulty sustaining attention to tasks or other activities (easily distracted by extraneous stimuli)	Reward attention. Break up activities into small units. reward for timely accomplishments. Use physical proximity and touch. Use earphones and/or student carrels, quiet place, preferential seating.
14. Frequent messiness or sloppiness	Teach organizational skills. Be sure student has daily, weekly, and/or monthly assignment sheets and daily list of materials needed. Be sure student has a consistent format for papers. Have a consistent way for students to turn in and receive back papers. Reduce distractions. Give reward points for notebook checks and proper paper format. Provide clear copies of worksheets and handouts and have a consistent format for worksheets. Establish daily routine; provide models for what you want your students to do. Arrange for a peer who will help him/her with organization. Assist student to keep materials in a specific place (e.g., pencils and pens in pouch). Be willing to repeat instructions.

... ACCOMMODATIONS FOR DEALING WITH SPECIFIC BEHAVIORS OF STUDENTS WITH ATTENTION DEFICIT/HYPERACTIVITY DISORDER ...	
When You See This Behavior	**Try This Accommodation**
15. Poor handwriting (often mixing cursive with manuscript and capitals with lowercase letters)	Allow for a scribe, and grade on content, not on handwriting. Allow for use of a computer or typewriter. Consider alternative methods for mixing cursive and manuscript (accept any method of production). Don't penalize student for mixing cursive and manuscript (accept any method of production).
16. Difficulty with fluency in handwriting (e.g., good letter/word production but very slow and laborious)	Allow for shorter assignments. (Emphasize quality over quantity.) Allow for alternate method of production (computer, scribe, oral presentation, etc.).
17. Inappropriate responses in class often blurted out; answers given to the questions before they have been completed	Seat student in close proximity to teachers so that visual and physical monitoring of student's behavior can be done by the teacher. State behavior that you do want (tell the student how you expect him/her to behave).
18. Agitation under pressure and competition (athletic or academic)	Stress effort and enjoyment for self, rather than competition with others. Minimize time activities; structure class for team effort and cooperation.
19. Inappropriate behaviors in a team or large group sport or athletic activity (difficulty waiting turn in games or group situations)	Give the student a responsible job (e.g., team captain, care and distribution of the balls, score keeping); consider leadership role. Have student in close proximity to teacher.
20. Frequent involvement in physically dangerous activities without considering possible consequences	Anticipate dangerous situations and plan for them in advance. Stress Stop-Look-Listen. Pair student with a responsible peer. (Rotate responsible students so that they don't wear out!)
21. Poor adult interactions; defies authority; manipulates (passive); hangs on	Provide positive attention. Talk with student individually about the inappropriate behavior (*What you are doing is . . . A better way of getting what you want or need is . . .*).
22. Frequent self put-downs, poor personal care and posture, negative comments about self and others, low self-esteem	Structure for success. Train student for self-monitoring; reinforce improvements; teach self-questioning strategies. (What am I doing? How is that going to affect others?) Allow opportunities for the student to show his/her strengths. Give positive recognition. Remain calm, state infraction of rule, and don't debate or argue with student. Have a pre-established consequence for misbehavior. Administer consequences immediately and monitor proper behavior frequently. Enforce rules of the classroom consistently.

... ACCOMMODATIONS FOR DEALING WITH SPECIFIC BEHAVIORS OF STUDENTS WITH ATTENTION DEFICIT/HYPERACTIVITY DISORDER ...	
When You See This Behavior	**Try This Accommodation**
	Design discipline to "fit the crime" without harshness.
	Avoid ridicule and criticism. Remember, AD/HD children have difficulty staying in control.
	Avoid **publicly** reminding students on medication to "take their medicine."
	Reward more than you punish in order to build self-esteem.
	Praise immediately any and all good behavior and performance.
	Change rewards if not effective in motivating behavioral change.
	Teach the child to reward himself/herself. Encourage positive self-talk (e.g., "You did very well remaining in your seat today. How do you feel about that?"). This encourages the child to think positively about himself or herself.
23. Difficulty using unstructured time, recess, hallway, lunchroom, locker room, library, assembly	Provide student with a definite purpose during unstructured activities (e.g., *The purpose of going to the library is to check out . . . The purpose of . . . is . . .*). Encourage group games and participation (organized school clubs and activities).
24. Losing things necessary for task or activities at school or at home (e.g., pencils, books, assignments); losing things before, during and after completion of a given task.	Help students organize. Frequently monitor notebook and dividers, pencil pouch, locker, book bag, desk. (Emphasize a place for everything and everything in its place.) Provide positive reinforcement for good organization. Provide student with a list of needed materials and their locations.
25. Poor use of time (sitting, staring off into space, doodling, not working on task at hand)	Teach reminder cues (a gentle touch on the shoulder, hand signals, etc.). Tell the student your expectations of what paying attention looks like (e.g., You look like you are paying attention when . . .). Give the student a time limit for a small unit of work with positive reinforcement for accurate completion. Use a contract, timer, etc. for self-monitoring.
26. Fails to complete homework assignments and bring them back to school	Assign a peer to help the student with homework. Allow the student additional time to turn in homework assignments. Send homework assignments and materials home with someone other than the student (e.g., brother or sister, neighbor, etc.). Assign small amounts of homework initially, gradually increasing the amount over time. Set up a homework assignment notebook and have the teacher check and sign it daily. Work a few problems with the student on the given homework assignment(s) in order to serve as a model. Allow the student to keep an extra set of books at home.

...ACCOMMODATIONS FOR DEALING WITH SPECIFIC BEHAVIORS OF STUDENTS WITH ATTENTION DEFICIT/HYPERACTIVITY DISORDER	
When You See This Behavior	**Try This Accommodation**
27. Difficulty with cafeteria rules, regulations, and eating habits	Have the student/parent prepare for lunches at the beginning of the week. Set student in close proximity to an authority figure (e.g., lunchroom aide, teacher). Assign the student a special responsibility after he/she finishes lunch (e.g., assist the P.E. coach, assist in the main office, etc.). Provide positive attention. Have the school nurse discuss proper nutrition habits with the student. Encourage the student to eat lunch. Allow the student to play a quiet game at the lunch table. Seat the student next to a positive role model.
28. Difficulty on the school bus (tips for the bus driver)	Seat the student in close proximity to the bus driver. Avoid a direct confrontation with the student in front of his/her classmates. Ignore minor infractions. Use a calm but firm tone of voice when reprimanding the student. Discuss the problem privately with the student. Seat the student next to a positive role model. Provide positive attention. Alert an administrator and have them deal with the problem immediately. Develop a school/home reward system. (An administrator or guidance counselor can assist you in developing this plan.)
29. Difficulty with medication compliance and other related issues	Assign a staff member (e.g., secretary, aide) to remind the student to take medication. Provide the teacher with the child's medication schedule. Provide positive verbal praise. Have school nurse educate the student on the benefits of taking a particular medication. Have adult/peer escort the student to the office for medication. Utilize a school/home reward system for complying with medication schedule.

Adapted from: Utah State Office of Education. *Section 504/ADA Guidelines for Education.* Salt Lake City, UT: Author.

GREENAN'S GENERALIZABLE SKILLS CURRICULUM . . .

Mathematics Skills

WHOLE NUMBERS
- Read, write, and count single and multiple digit whole numbers
- Add and subtract single and multiple digit whole numbers
- Multiply and divide single and multiple digit whole numbers
- Use addition, subtraction, multiplication, and division to solve word problems with single and multiple digit whole numbers
- Round off single and multiple digit whole numbers

FRACTIONS
- Read and write common fractions
- Add and subtract common fractions
- Multiply and divide common fractions
- Solve word problems with common fractions

DECIMALS
- Carry out arithmetic computations involving dollars and cents
- Read and write decimals in one or more places
- Round off decimals to one or more places
- Multiply and divide decimals in one or more places
- Add and subtract decimals in one or more places
- Solve word problems with decimals in one or more places

PERCENT
- Read and write percents
- Compute percents

MIXED OPERATIONS
- Convert fractions to decimals, percents to fractions, fractions to percents, percents to decimals, decimals to percents, common fractions or mixed numbers to decimal fractions, and decimal fractions to common fractions or mixed numbers
- Solve word problems by selecting and using correct order of operations
- Perform written calculations quickly
- Compute averages

MEASUREMENT AND CALCULATION
- Read numbers of symbols from time, weight, distance, and volume measuring scales
- Use a measuring device to determine an object's weight, distance, or volume in standard (English) units
- Use a measuring device to determine an object's weight, distance, or volume in metric units
- Perform basic metric conversions involving weight, distance, and volume
- Solve problems involving time, weight, distance, and volume
- Use a calculator to perform basic arithmetic operations to solve problems

ESTIMATION
- Determine if a solution to a mathematical problem is reasonable

Communications Skills

WORDS AND MEANINGS
- Use plural words appropriately in writing and speaking
- Use appropriate shortened forms of words by using an apostrophe when writing and contractions when speaking
- Use appropriate abbreviations of words in writing
- Use words correctly that sound the same as other words but have different meanings and spellings
- Use words appropriately that are opposite of one another
- Use appropriate word choices in writing and speaking
- Add appropriate beginnings and endings to words to change their meaning
- Punctuate one's own correspondence, directives, or reports

... GREENAN'S GENERALIZABLE SKILLS CURRICULUM ...

READING
- Read, understand, and find information or gather data from books, manuals, directions, or other documents
- Restate or paraphrase a reading passage to confirm one's own understanding of what was read
- Read and understand forms
- Read and understand short notes, memos, and letters
- Read and understand graphs, charts, and tables to obtain factual information
- Understand the meanings of words in sentences
- Use a standard dictionary to obtain the meaning, pronunciation, and spelling of words
- Use the telephone and look up names, telephone numbers, and other information in a telephone directory to make local and long distance calls

WRITING
- Review and edit another's correspondence, directives, or reports
- Compose logical and understandable statements, phrases, or sentences to fill out forms accurately

SPEAKING
- Speak fluently with individuals or groups
- Pronounce words correctly
- Speak effectively using appropriate behaviors such as eye contact, posture, and gestures

LISTENING
- Restate or paraphrase a conversation to confirm one's own understanding of what was said
- Ask appropriate questions to clarify another's written or oral communications
- Attend to nonverbal cues such as eye contact, posture, and gestures for meanings in others' conversations
- Take accurate notes that summarize the material presented from spoken conversations

Interpersonal Relations Skills

WORK BEHAVIORS
- Work effectively under different kinds of supervision
- Work without the need for close supervision
- Work cooperatively as a member of a team
- Get along and work effectively with people of different perspectives
- Show up regularly on time for activities and appointments
- Work effectively when time tension or pressure are critical factors for successful performance
- See things from another's point of view
- Engage appropriately in social interaction and situations
- Take responsibility and be accountable for the effects of one's own judgments, decisions, and actions
- Plan, carry out, and complete activities at one's own initiation

INSTRUCTIONAL AND SUPERVISORY CONVERSATIONS
- Instruct or direct someone in the performance of a specific task
- Follow instructions or directions in the performance of a specific task
- Demonstrate to someone how to perform a specific task
- Assign others to carry out specific tasks
- Speak with others in a relaxed and self-confident manner
- Compliment and provide constructive feedback to others at appropriate times

CONVERSATIONS
- Be able to handle criticism, disagreement, or disappointment during a conversation
- Initiate and maintain task-focused or friendly conversations with another individual
- Initiate, maintain, and draw others into task-focused or friendly group conversations
- Join in task-focused or friendly group conversations

... GREENAN'S GENERALIZABLE SKILLS CURRICULUM

Reasoning Skills

VERBAL REASONING

- Generate or conceive of new or innovative ideas
- Try out or consciously attempt to use previously learned knowledge and skills in a new situation
- Understand and explain the main ideas in another's written or oral communication
- Recall ideas, facts, theories, principles and other information accurately from memory
- Organize ideas and put them into words rapidly in oral and written conversations
- Interpret feelings, ideas, or facts in terms of one's own personal viewpoint or values
- State one's point of view, opinion, or position in written or oral communication
- Define one's point of view, opinion, or position in written or oral communication
- Distinguish between fact and opinion in one's own and in others' written and oral communication
- Identify the conclusions in others' written or oral communication
- Identify the reasons offered by another and evaluate their relevance and strength of support for a conclusion
- Compile one's own notes taken on several written sources into a single report
- Compile ideas, notes, and materials supplied by others into a single report
- Carry out correctly written or oral instructions given by another
- Observe another's performance of a task to identify whether the performance is satisfactory or needs to be improved
- Ask questions about another's performance of a task to identify whether the performance is satisfactory or needs to be improved

PROBLEM SOLVING

- Recognize or identify the existence of a problem given a specific set of facts
- Ask appropriate questions to identify or verify the existence of a problem
- Enumerate the possible causes of a problem
- Use efficient methods for eliminating the causes of a problem
- Judge the credibility of a source of informaton
- Identify important information needed to solve a problem
- Identify others' and one's own assumptions relating to a problem
- Describe the application and likely consequences of alternative problem solutions and select a solution that represents the best course of action to pursue

PLANNING

- Sort objects according to similar physical characteristics including shape, color, and size
- Estimate weight of various objects of different shapes, sizes, and makeup
- Estimate length, width, height, and distance between objects
- Use the sense of touch, sight, smell, taste, and hearing
- Set priorities or the order in which several tasks will be accomplished
- Set the goals or standards for accomplishing a specific task
- Determine how specific activities will assist in accomplishing a task
- Select activities to accomplish a specific task
- Determine the order of the activities or step-by-step process by which a specific task can be accomplished
- Estimate the time required to perform activities needed to accomplish a specific task
- Locate information about duties, methods, and procedures to perform the activities needed to accomplish a specific task
- Locate information and select the materials, tools, equipment, or locate resources to perform the activities needed to accomplish a specified task
- Periodically revise or update plans and activities for accomplishing a specific task

Adapted from: Greenan, J. (1986). Curriculum and Assessment in Generalizable Skills Instruction. *The Journal for Vocational Special Needs Education, 9*(1).

TRANSITION PLANNING INTERVIEW . . .

Name _____ Date _____ D.O.B. _____ Graduation Date _____

Please check each box Yes, No, ? if uncertain, or NA if an item does not apply.

A. Employment Career Awareness and Vocational Training

Yes	No	?	NA
☐	☐	☐	☐	1. Name the top 3 careers you want 1) _____ 2) _____ 3) _____
☐	☐	☐	☐	2. Do you understand employment options: (full time, part time, etc.)
☐	☐	☐	☐	3. Do you want to be employed?
☐	☐	☐	☐	4. Do you need support to remain employed?
☐	☐	☐	☐	a. Can the support be arranged with the employer or employees?
☐	☐	☐	☐	b. Does the support require an outside agency?
☐	☐	☐	☐	5. Do you need sheltered industry? (Goodwill Center)
☐	☐	☐	☐	6. Do you want to be self-employed? If yes, doing what? _____
☐	☐	☐	☐	7. Would you like career exploration help to expand your career options?
☐	☐	☐	☐	a. Do you want or need help to obtain a career?
☐	☐	☐	☐	b. Do you want or need help to maintain a career?
☐	☐	☐	☐	8. Do you have previous work experience?

If yes, list your last two jobs _____

9. What is your social security number? _____ - _____ - _____

B. Independent Living

Yes	No	?	NA
☐	☐	☐	☐	10. Do you plan to live on your own? If yes, when? _____
☐	☐	☐	☐	11. Would you like independent living skills training?
				12. What living setting do you plan to have in the future? (Check all that apply)

☐ own home   ☐ house with friends   ☐ own apartment   ☐ apartment with friends
☐ mobile home   ☐ other (please describe) _____

Yes	No	?	NA
☐	☐	☐	☐	13. Will you need assisted living such as a group home?
☐	☐	☐	☐	14. Will you remain at home with immediate family, for a while or longer?
☐	☐	☐	☐	15. Will other family members continue care for you later on in life?

16. List any medications you take _____

C. Postsecondary Options and Training After High School

Yes	No	?	NA
☐	☐	☐	☐	17. Do you want or need postsecondary education or training?
				18. What type? (Check all the student is willing to do)

☐ 4 year college   ☐ community college   ☐ vocational/technical school
☐ Apprentice   ☐ military

Yes	No	?	NA
☐	☐	☐	☐	a. Do you need help selecting sites for the above?
☐	☐	☐	☐	b. Do you know and can you meet deadlines to enter your choice(s) above?
☐	☐	☐	☐	c. Do you meet the criteria for admission?
☐	☐	☐	☐	d. Can you contact the support services at the sites selected?
☐	☐	☐	☐	e. Can you visit sites related to your selection above on your own?
☐	☐	☐	☐	f. Can you secure financial assistance on your own?

   g. If not, who do you think could assist? _____

19. What support service for instruction do you receive now? (Circle all that are used)

Classroom resource teacher, resource, self-contained, none. Other _____

☐ | ☐ | ☐ | ☐ | 20. Can you effectively express your limits and needs related to your disability?

. . . TRANSITION PLANNING INTERVIEW . . .

D. Adult services

Yes	No	?	NA	
☐	☐	☐	☐	21. Do you need services from Developmental Disabilities?
☐	☐	☐	☐	22. Do you need services from Vocational Rehabilitation?
☐	☐	☐	☐	23. Do you need supports from the Social Security Administration?
☐	☐	☐	☐	24. Do you need assistance from Behavioral Health Services?
☐	☐	☐	☐	25. Do you need assistance from the Workforce Investment Act?
☐	☐	☐	☐	26. Do you, the student, parent, or teacher, need information about these services?
				If yes, contact the Transition Office at (623) 487-5192.
☐	☐	☐	☐	27. Do you have a casemanager assigned to you now?
				If yes, Name _____ Phone # _____

E. Functional Evaluations

Yes	No	?	NA	
☐	☐	☐	☐	28. Have you completed a SAGE evaluation?
☐	☐	☐	☐	29. Have you taken the ASVAB?
☐	☐	☐	☐	30. Have you taken the ASSET for community college placement information?
☐	☐	☐	☐	31. Have you completed the PSAT for college preparation?
☐	☐	☐	☐	32. Have you taken the SAT or ACT college entrance exam?
☐	☐	☐	☐	33. Have you completed a vocational evaluation from RSA for eligibility?

F. Community Participation

Yes	No	?	NA	
☐	☐	☐	☐	34. Do you recreate appropriately with peers?
				If not, why not? _____
☐	☐	☐	☐	35. Do you use shopping malls, theaters, post offices, libraries, etc.?
☐	☐	☐	☐	36. Do you know how to register to vote?
☐	☐	☐	☐	37. Do you know when and how to register for selective service? (males)
☐	☐	☐	☐	38. Do you participate in community activities and events appropriately?
☐	☐	☐	☐	39. Do you participate in both group and individual recreation activities?
				If not, why not? _____
☐	☐	☐	☐	40. Do you have any hobbies?
				If so, list a few _____

G. Transportation

Yes	No	?	NA	
☐	☐	☐	☐	41. Do you plan to drive (If no, check what alternate transportation you will use)
				☐ bus ☐ taxi ☐ Dial-a-Ride ☐ other _____
☐	☐	☐	☐	42. Do you have a license?
				If no, when do you plan to get a license? _____ If yes, when obtained? _____

H. Related Services

Yes	No	?	NA	
☐	☐	☐	☐	43. Do you need speech services?
☐	☐	☐	☐	44. Do you need occupational therapy services?
☐	☐	☐	☐	45. Do you need physical therapy services?
☐	☐	☐	☐	46. Do you take medications?
☐	☐	☐	☐	47. Does a doctor or casemanager monitor them?
☐	☐	☐	☐	48. Are there other medical conditions that impact your education or employment?
				List them: (e.g., asthma, allergies, epilepsy, heart problems, etc.) _____
☐	☐	☐	☐	49. Do you require specialized transportation?

... TRANSITION PLANNING INTERVIEW

I. Additional Transition Issues (Please read and identify you interest areas.)

Yes   No   ?   NA

☐ ☐ ☐ ☐   50. Do you have personal management/self help/self care issues?

If yes, list or describe _____

☐ ☐ ☐ ☐   51. Do you need social skill development?

If yes, describe _____

☐ ☐ ☐ ☐   52. Do you have difficulty with authority?

If yes, describe _____

☐ ☐ ☐ ☐   53. Do you resolve conflicts appropriately?

If not, why not? _____

☐ ☐ ☐ ☐   54. Do you demonstrate self-advocacy skills?

☐ ☐ ☐ ☐   55. Would you like to run your own IEP meeting after training?

☐ ☐ ☐ ☐   56. Do you have any questions about the move from school to adult life?

If yes, briefly describe _____

57. List any specific sites for training after high school you would like to investigate (college, voc/trade, branch of the military, etc.) _____

J. Career Planning

Yes   No   ?   NA

☐ ☐ ☐ ☐   58. Have you completed an interest inventory?

☐ ☐ ☐ ☐   59. Have you completed a vocational assessment?

☐ ☐ ☐ ☐   60. Have you completed a personality assessment?

☐ ☐ ☐ ☐   61. Do you have a plan that will result in the career of choice?

☐ ☐ ☐ ☐   62. Do you have your parent's support?

— — — — — — — — — Optional — — — — — — — — — — —

K. Advocacy & Legal Services, Independent Living, Community Participation

Yes   No   ?   NA

☐ ☐ ☐ ☐   63. Do you know your rights as a person when you become 18 years old?

☐ ☐ ☐ ☐   64. Do you need to have a legal guardian?

☐ ☐ ☐ ☐   65. Do you need to seek a conservatorship?

☐ ☐ ☐ ☐   66. Do you see a need for a power of attorney to be set up?

☐ ☐ ☐ ☐   67. Do you have any other legal or advocacy concerns?

Describe briefly _____

Date reviewed is to reflect at least annual updating

Review date _____ by _____

Review date _____ by _____

Review date _____ by _____

Review date _____ by _____

Source: Peoria Unified School District #11. (n.d.). *Transition Services.* Peoria, AZ: Special Education Department.

INDIVIDUALIZED EDUCATION PROGRAM CHECKLIST . . .

Referral and Compilation of Information for Staffing

____ Have you obtained copies of the IEP referral forms and procedures?

____ Have you attended informational meetings to become familiar with your district's referral procedures and special education resources?

____ Have you attended inservice training sessions on procedures and techniques for identifying special needs learners?

____ Are you familiar with the individual(s) in your district responsible for collecting informal data on learners from special populations? What types of information or data can you compile on the learner?

____ Standardized test scores (achievement and aptitude)	____ Results from diagnostic testing done on learners
____ Work evaluation results	____ Behavioral observation data
____ Attendance record	____ Interest inventory result
____ Progress evaluation reports	

____ Have all pertinent data on the learner been collected and forwarded to the person responsible?

____ If additional information about career and technical education programs/classes is desired, can you make available any or all of the following?

____ Exit level skills	____ Admission requirements
____ Course description	____ Desirable vocational aptitudes and interests
____ Course outline	____ Instructional materials used by learners
____ Instructional goals and objectives	____ Information regarding opportunities for job placement

____ Have you reviewed the learner's cumulative folders for the following types of information?

____ Reading and math achievement scores

____ Previous career and technical education or prevocational classes taken

____ Work or vocational evaluation results

____ Vocational interest inventory results

____ Information regarding special needs of the learner

____ Other pertinent information _____

____ Have you met with the learner's teachers (present or former) to discuss his/her progress?

____ Have you met with other resource personnel who can provide additional vocational information about the learner?

____ Parent(s) or guardian(s)	____ Principals
____ Guidance counselors	____ Referring teachers
____ School psychologist	____ School social workers
____ School nurse	____ Other specialists _____

____ Have you identified organization or agencies in the community (e.g., sheltered workshops, community colleges) where vocational testing and evaluations could be conducted?

____ Have you identified organizations and agencies necessary for transitional needs?

____ Do you have sufficient learning style information on the learner?

IEP Staffing

____ Have you considered and discussed the appropriateness of the specific career and technical education program for this learner?

____ To what extent have all career and technical education and training alternatives been examined by the team?

____ If the learner is to be placed in a regular career and technical education class, what curriculum modifications may be needed (special learning needs)?

____ To what extent may class size, equipment availability, and other factors limit the amount of individualized attention this learner receives?

____ Are the parents supportive of the proposed career and technical education class?

____ If a learner has already been placed in a regular career and technical education class, have you examined existing assessment data on the learner to determine present levels of functioning?

____ For a previously identified special needs learner, have you reviewed his/her IEP and discussed his/her progress with the special education staff and parent(s)?

. . . INDIVIDUALIZED EDUCATION PROGRAM CHECKLIST . . .

_____ Are the goals and performance objectives for the regular career and technical education program available for review by the parent(s), special education staff, and others?

_____ Have program goals and objectives been reviewed by the parent(s), special education personnel, and other support staff?

_____ To what extent have special educators and the parent(s) been involved in selecting or identifying appropriate career and technical education goals and objectives for the learner?

_____ Do the selected goals and objectives match the learner's interests, capabilities, and special needs?

_____ Are the goals and objectives written in measurable terminology with clearly stated criteria for successful performance?

_____ Have special education and other resource teachers and consultants been involved in outlining the instructional plans and learning experiences for the learners?

_____ Are the necessary support services available to ensure that this learner will receive maximum benefit from the career and technical education program? Some of the following services may be appropriate:

    _____ Special or vocational counseling

    _____ Readers/interpreters

    _____ Basic skills instruction

    _____ Instructional aids/tutors/supplemental teachers

    _____ Educational testing and diagnosis

    _____ Special transportation

    _____ Special equipment

    _____ Modification of equipment

    _____ Social work and family counseling

    _____ Curriculum adaptation

IEP Implementation

_____ To what extent are all members of the instructional team aware of the IEP plans for each class in which the learner is enrolled?

_____ Is there a systematic plan to coordinate and integrate various instructional activities (e.g., team teaching math and measurement skills as needed in the career and technical education class)?

_____ Have all needed modification (e.g., lab equipment, instructional materials, facilities) been completed for this learner?

_____ Do you have a directory of resource people to contact for specialized assistance in working with special needs learners? Such a directory might list:

    _____ Vocational rehabilitation specialists/counselors

    _____ Special education consultants (e.g., speech therapists, resource room teachers, mobility consultants)

    _____ Work adjustment coordinators

    _____ Work-study or co-op coordinators

    _____ Mental health agency

    _____ State agencies for the blind and deaf

    _____ U.S. Employment Service

    _____ Community agencies (e.g., Opportunities Industrialization Centers, Goodwill Industries)

    _____ Business, industry, and labor groups

    _____ Civic and special interest organizations (e.g., service clubs)

    _____ Parents organizations (e.g., local chapters of National Association of Retarded Citizens, Association for Children with Learning Disabilities)

_____ Do you fully understand the role that the career and technical education program plays in this learner's IEP?

_____ Is there additional information you need to gather about the learner during the early phases of implementing the IEP?

_____ Have you established dates of a schedule for meeting with other teachers involved in IEP to review learner's progress?

_____ Have you discussed with the special education staff the specific types of evaluation data you should be collecting on this learner (e.g., behavioral information, attendance, attitude development, classroom achievement)?

... INDIVIDUALIZED EDUCATION PROGRAM CHECKLIST

_____ Are there standard forms used to compile this or other evaluative information?

_____ What resources are available to assist in testing the handicapped learner (e.g., resource consultants that can read or tape record written material for the learner)?

IEP Evaluation

_____ To what extent has this learner attained the objectives and goals stated in the career and technical education section of his/her IEP?

_____ Have precautions been taken to insure the learner was appropriately tested (e.g., reading level of tests were at or below his/her reading level)?

_____ Overall, what is the learner's level of employability?

_____ Has a profile been prepared illustrating the learner's strengths and weaknesses in various areas? Areas included in the profile might encompass:

     _____ Mastery of competencies

     _____ Job readiness

     _____ Work habits

     _____ Social skills

     _____ Dexterity and strength

     _____ Communication (reading, writing, speaking)

     _____ Quantitative and math skills

     _____ Occupational interests

_____ Have meetings been held or planned for the IEP team to compile evaluative information into a composite report?

_____ To what extent were the support services the learner received adequate and effective?

_____ What changes need to be made in the learner's IEP (objectives, support services, placement)?

_____ What plan(s) have been developed to follow up special needs learners leaving the career and technical education program to learn more about their transition from school to work?

Adapted from: Center for Innovations in Special Education (formerly Missouri LINC). (n.d.). [Workshop handout]. Columbia, MO: University of Missouri, Department of Special Education and Department of Vocational Technical Education

SAMPLE COURSE SYLLABUS . . .

DEPARTMENT: CAREER AND TECHNICAL EDUCATION
COURSE TITLE: BUILDING TRADES I
COURSE NUMBER: 12879
COURSE DESCRIPTION: This course will teach the basics of carpentry, from foundations through roof framing. Other topics include masonry, tools and equipment; plumbing instruction in systems, materials, and tools and methods of installation; house wiring instruction in electrical terms, symbols, tool and steps of installation.

I. GENERAL COMPETENCIES - The learner will be able to
  A. Comprehend information received and apply information in a variety of everyday situations.
  B. Use a variety of information resources to obtain assistance and information.
  C. Know appropriate emergency responses to accidents and demonstrate preventive actions for health/safety hazards.
  D. Demonstrate skills necessary to obtain employment.
II. PERFORMANCE OBJECTIVES:
Items listed below include the objectives and their indicators for this course:
  A. Carpentry
    1. The learner will safely utilize and operate all tools and equipment.
      (a) List safety rules for each machine.
      (b) Demonstrate safety of machines and tools.
    2. The student will perform tasks using knowledge of blueprint reading, foundations, and basic framing procedures of a residential building.
      (a) Utilize knowledge of signs and symbols.
      (b) Prepare batter boards.
      (c) Identify parts of floor system.
      (d) Identify parts of wall and ceiling systems.
      (e) Identify parts of a roof system.
  B. Plumbing
    1. The learner will safely perform the installation of the sewer and supply system of a residential home.
      (a) List safety rules.
      (b) Identify parts of sewer system.
      (c) Identify parts of supply system.
  C. Masonry
    1. The learner will safely perform the operation of tools and equipment used in the basic skills of masonry.
      (a) List safety rules.
      (b) Demonstrate skills of handling trowel.
      (c) Demonstrate ability to lay brick to the line.
  D. House Wiring
    1. The student will safely utilize and operate all tools and equipment according to the proper electrical code.
      (a) List safety rules.
      (b) Demonstrate safe wiring practices.
COURSE OUTLINE
I. Carpentry
  A. Safety and Orientation
  B. Framing
  C. Blueprints
  D. Foundations
  E. Framing
  F. Interior and Exterior
  G. Cabinetmaking and Furniture
II. Plumbing
  A. Safety and Orientation
  B. Plumbing Material Identification
  C. Basic Plumbing Techniques
  D. Blueprints
  E. Sewer System
  F. Supply System
  G. Fixtures
  H. Plumbing Maintenance

...SAMPLE COURSE SYLLABUS

III. Masonry
  A. Safety and Orientation
  B. Basic Projects with Tools
  C. Foundations
  D. Layout Procedures
  E. Brick Project and Practices
  F. Block Project and Practices
IV. House Wiring
  A. Safety and Orientation
  B. Basic Writing Procedures
  C. Diagrams
  D. Service Entrance
  E. General Purpose
  F. Individual Circuit

APPLICATION TASKS

 I. Plumbing
  A. The learner will complete the tasks of installing the sewer and the supply systems of residential construction.
     1. Devise a sewer system.
     2. Devise a supply system.
     3. Install bathroom fixtures.
     4. Test systems for leaks.
 II. Masonry
  A. The learner will perform activities in laying bricks and blocks in residential masonry.
     1. Construct a 4 brick wall.
     2. Construct a corner lead.
     3. Construct a block wall.
     4. Construct a block corner.
 III. House Wiring
  A. The learner will demonstrate residential wiring practices.
     1. Prepare wiring diagram.
     2. Construct service entrance.
     3. Construct general purpose circuits.
     4. Construct individual circuits.
     5. Test electrical systems.

SUGGESTED ACTIVITIES, MATERIALS, AND EVALUATIONS

Suggested Activities
1. Teacher Demonstration
2. Teacher Lecture
3. Student Group Work
4. Live Work
5. Live Work Simulation
6. Individual Instructional Units

Materials
1. Resource Books
2. Lumber
3. Pipe
4. Wire
5. Brick
6. Blocks
7. Slides and Filmstrips
8. Teacher Handouts and Overlays
9. Adopted Text

Evaluation
1. Time and Participation
2. Accuracy
3. Tests
4. Attitude

C.I.T.E. LEARNING STYLES INSTRUMENT . . .

	Most like me			Least like me
1. When I make things for my studies, I remember what I have learned better.	1	2	3	4
2. Written assignments are easy for me to do.	1	2	3	4
3. I learn better if someone reads a book to me than if I read silently to myself.	1	2	3	4
4. I learn best when I study alone.	1	2	3	4
5. Having assignment directions written on the board makes them easier to understand.	1	2	3	4
6. It's harder for me to do a written assignment than an oral one.	1	2	3	4
7. When I do math problems in my head, I say the numbers to myself.	1	2	3	4
8. If I need help in the subject, I will ask a classmate for help.	1	2	3	4
9. I understand a math problem that is written down better than one I hear.	1	2	3	4
10. I don't mind doing written assignments.	1	2	3	4
11. I remember things I hear better than when I read.	1	2	3	4
12. I remember more of what I learn if I learn it when I am alone.	1	2	3	4
13. I would rather read a story than listen to it read.	1	2	3	4
14. I feel like I talk smarter than I write.	1	2	3	4
15. If someone tells me three numbers to add I can usually get the right answer without writing them down.	1	2	3	4
16. I like to work in a group because I learn from the others in my group.	1	2	3	4
17. Written math problems are easier for me to do than oral ones.	1	2	3	4
18. Writing a word several times helps me remember it better.	1	2	3	4
19. I find it easier to remember what I have heard than what I have read.	1	2	3	4
20. It is more fun to learn with classmates at first, but it is hard to study with them.	1	2	3	4
21. I like written directions better than spoken ones.	1	2	3	4
22. If homework were oral, I would do it all.	1	2	3	4
23. When I hear a phone number, I can remember it without writing it down.	1	2	3	4
24. I get more work done when I work with someone.	1	2	3	4
25. Seeing a number makes more sense to me than hearing a number.	1	2	3	4
26. I like to do things with my hands like simple repairs or crafts.	1	2	3	4
27. The things I write on paper sound better than when I say them.	1	2	3	4
28. I study best when no one is around to talk or listen to.	1	2	3	4
29. I would rather read things in a book than have the teacher tell me about them.	1	2	3	4
30. Speaking is a better way than writing if you want someone to understand what you really mean.	1	2	3	4
31. When I have a written math problem to do, I say it to myself to understand it better.	1	2	3	4
32. I can learn more about a subject if I am with a small group of students.	1	2	3	4
33. Seeing the price of something written down is easier for me to understand than having someone tell me the price.	1	2	3	4
34. I like to make things with my hands.	1	2	3	4
35. I like tests that call for sentence completion or written answers.	1	2	3	4
36. I understand more from a class discussion than from reading about a subject.	1	2	3	4
37. I remember the spelling of a word better if I see it written down than if someone spells it out loud.	1	2	3	4
38. Spelling and grammar rules make it hard for me to say what I want to in writing.	1	2	3	4
39. It makes it easier when I say the numbers of a problem to myself as I work it out.	1	2	3	4
40. I like to study with other people.	1	2	3	4
41. When the teachers say a number, I really don't understand it until I see it written down.	1	2	3	4
42. I understand what I have learned better when I am involved in making something for the subject.	1	2	3	4
43. Sometimes I say dumb things, but writing gives me time to correct myself.	1	2	3	4
44. I do well on tests if they are about things I hear in class.	1	2	3	4
45. I can't think as well when I work with someone else as when I work alone.	1	2	3	4

. . . C.I.T.E. LEARNING STYLES INSTRUMENT . . .

Sample Score Sheet

VISUAL LANGUAGE	AUDITORY NUMERICAL	SOCIAL-GROUP
5 _3_	7 _2_	8 _3_
13 _4_	15 _3_	16 _1_
21 _4_	23 _2_	24 _2_
29 _3_	31 _2_	32 _2_
37 _4_	39 _1_	40 _3_
Total _18_ × 2 = _36_ (Score)	Total _10_ × 2 = _20_ (Score)	Total _11_ × 2 = _22_ (Score)

VISUAL NUMERICAL	AUDITORY-VISUAL-KINESTHETIC (Combination)	EXPRESSIVENESS-ORAL
9 _4_	1 _4_	6 _3_
17 _2_	18 _3_	14 _3_
25 _4_	26 _3_	22 _3_
33 _4_	34 _3_	30 _3_
41 _3_	42 _4_	38 _3_
Total _17_ × 2 = _34_ (Score)	Total _17_ × 2 = _34_ (Score)	Total _15_ × 2 = _30_ (Score)

AUDITORY LANGUAGE	SOCIAL-INDIVIDUAL	EXPRESSIVENESS-WRITTEN
3 _2_	4 _4_	2 _4_
11 _3_	12 _2_	10 _3_
19 _3_	20 _2_	27 _2_
36 _2_	28 _4_	35 _4_
44 _3_	45 _4_	43 _4_
Total _13_ × 2 = _26_ (Score)	Total _16_ × 2 = _32_ (Score)	Total _17_ × 2 = _34_ (Score)

Score: 33 - 40 = Major Learning Style   20 - 32 = Minor Learning Style   5 - 20 = Neglibible Use

Score Sheet

VISUAL LANGUAGE	AUDITORY NUMERICAL	SOCIAL-GROUP
5 _____	7 _____	8 _____
13 _____	15 _____	16 _____
21 _____	23 _____	24 _____
29 _____	31 _____	32 _____
37 _____	39 _____	40 _____
Total ____ × 2 = ____ (Score)	Total ____ × 2 = ____ (Score)	Total ____ × 2 = ____ (Score)

VISUAL NUMERICAL	AUDITORY-VISUAL-KINESTHETIC (Combination)	EXPRESSIVENESS-ORAL
9 _____	1 _____	6 _____
17 _____	18 _____	14 _____
25 _____	26 _____	22 _____
33 _____	34 _____	30 _____
41 _____	42 _____	38 _____
Total ____ × 2 = ____ (Score)	Total ____ × 2 = ____ (Score)	Total ____ × 2 = ____ (Score)

AUDITORY LANGUAGE	SOCIAL-INDIVIDUAL	EXPRESSIVENESS-WRITTEN
3 _____	4 _____	2 _____
11 _____	12 _____	10 _____
19 _____	20 _____	27 _____
36 _____	28 _____	35 _____
44 _____	45 _____	43 _____
Total ____ × 2 = ____ (Score)	Total ____ × 2 = ____ (Score)	Total ____ × 2 = ____ (Score)

Score: 33 - 40 = Major Learning Style   20 - 32 = Minor Learning Style   5 - 20 = Neglibible Use

. . . C.I.T.E. LEARNING STYLES INSTRUMENT . . .

Profile

NAME _____

DATE _____

						MINOR						MAJOR			
	10	12	14	16	18	20	22	24	26	28	30	32	34	36	38	40

Visual Language

Visual Numerical

Auditory Language

Auditory Numerical

Auditory-Visual-Kinesthetic (Combination)

Social-Individual

Social-Group

Expressiveness-Oral

Expressiveness-Written

Analysis

The styles below are described as if the learner is a major in the particular style.

TEACHING STYLE

1. VISUAL LANGUAGE

These are students who learn well from seeing words in books, on the chalkboard, charts, or workbooks. They may even write words down that are given to them orally in order to learn by seeing them on paper. They remember and use information better if they have read it.

2. VISUAL NUMERICAL

These students have to see numbers on the board, in a book, or on paper in order to work with them. They are more likely to remember and understand math facts if they have seen them. They don't seem to need as much oral explanation.

TEACHING TECHNIQUE

These students will benefit from a variety of books, pamphlets, and written materials on several levels of difficulty. Given some time alone with a book, they may learn more than in class. Make sure important information has been given to them on paper, or that they take notes if you want them to remember specific information.

These students will benefit from worksheets, workbooks, and texts. Give them a variety of written materials and allow them time to study them. In playing games and being involved in activities with number and number problems, make sure they are visible printed numbers, not oral games and activities. Important information should be given on paper.

. . . C.I.T.E. LEARNING STYLES INSTRUMENT

TEACHING STYLE	TEACHING TECHNIQUE
3. AUDITORY LANGUAGE These are students who learn from *hearing words* spoken. You may hear them vocalizing or see their lips or throat moving as they read, particularly when they are striving to understand new materials. They will be more capable of understanding and remembering words or facts that they could only have learned by hearing.	These students will benefit from hearing audiotapes, rote oral practice, lecture, or a class discussion. They may benefit from using a tape recorder to make tapes to listen to, by teaching another student, or by conversing with the teacher. Groups of two or more, games, or interaction activities provide the sound of words being spoken that is so important to students of this learning style.
4. AUDITORY NUMERICAL These students learn from hearing numbers and oral explanations. They may remember phone and locker numbers with ease, and be successful with oral numbers, games, and puzzles. They may do just about as well without their math book, for written materials are not as important. They can probably work problems in their head. You may hear them saying numbers to themselves, or see their lips moving as they read a problem.	These students will benefit from math sound tapes or working with another person, talking about a problem. Even reading written explanations aloud will help. Games or activities in which the number problems are spoken will help. These students will benefit from tutoring another or delivering an explanation to their study group or to the teacher. Make sure important facts are spoken.
5. AUDITORY-VISUAL-KINESTHETIC (Combination) A/V/K students learn best by experience – doing, self involvement. They definitely need a combination of stimuli. The manipulation of materials along with accompanying sight and sounds (words and numbers seen and spoken) will make a big difference to them. They may not seem to be able to understand or be able to keep their mind on work unless they are totally involved. They seem to hand, touch, and work with what they are learning. Sometimes just writing or symbolic wiggling of the fingers is a symptom of the A/V/K learner.	These students must be given more than just a reading or math assignment. Involve them with at least one other student and given them an activity to relate to the assignment. Or accompany an audiotape with pictures, objects, and an activity such as drawing, writing, or following directions with physical involvement.
6. SOCIAL-INDIVIDUAL These students get more out of working alone. They think best and remember more when they have learned by themselves. They care more for their own opinions than for the ideas of others. You will not have much trouble keeping these students from over-socializing during class.	These students need to be allowed to do important learning alone. If you feel they need socializing, save it for a nonlearning situation. Let them go to the library or back in the corner of the room to be alone. Don't force group work on them when it will make them irritable to be held back or distracted by others. Some great thinkers have been loners.
7. SOCIAL-GROUP These students strive to study with at least one other student and will not get as much done alone. They value others' opinions and preferences. Group interaction increases their learning and later recognition of facts. Classroom observation will quickly reveal how important socializing is to them.	These students need to do important learning with someone else. The stimulation of the group may be more important at certain times in the learning process than at others, and you may be able to facilitate the timing for them.
8. EXPRESSIVENESS-ORAL These students can easily tell you what they know. They talk fluently, comfortably, and seem to be able to say what they mean. You may find after talking to them about their work they know more than their tests show. They are probably not shy about giving reports or talking to the teacher or classmates. The muscular coordination involved in writing may be difficult for them. Organizing and putting thoughts on paper may be too slow and tedious for these students.	Allow these students to make oral reports instead of written ones. Whether in conference, small group or large, evaluate them more by what they say than on what they write. Reports can be on tape, to save class time. Demand a minimum of written work but of good quality, and you won't be ignoring the basics of composition and legibility. Grammar can be corrected orally but is best done at another time.
9. EXPRESSIVENESS-WRITTEN These students can write fluent essays and good answers on tests to show what they know. They feel less comfortable when they have to give oral answers. Their thoughts are better organized when they are written.	These students need to be allowed to write reports, keep notebooks and journals for credit, and take written tests for evaluation. Oral transactions should be under nonpressured conditions, perhaps mainly in a one-to-one conference.

Adapted from: Babich, A., Burdine, P., Albright, L., & Randol, R. (n.d.). *C.I.T.E. Learning Styles Instrument.* Wichita, KS: Wichita Public Schools, Murdock Teachers Center.

TEACHER'S CHECKLIST OF TEXT SELECTION CRITERIA . . .

Student/Course _____   Grade(s): _____

Title: _____   Copyright: _____

Author(s): _____   Publisher: _____

Reading level: _____   Number of pages: _____   Price: $ _____

	Excellent	Above Average	Average	Below Average	Unsatisfactory	Not Applicable

I. Content

A. Expertise of author(s).
B. Relevance to curriculum.
C. Depth of coverage.
D. Range of topics.
E. Student interest level.
F. Objectivity.
G. Realism.
H. Currentness
I. Accuracy
J. Clarity of organization of text material
K. Clarity of explanations and examples.
L. Emphasis on safety.
M. Appropriateness of reading level.
N. Measurability of chapter objectives.
O. Suitability of listed vocabulary terms.
P. Meaningfulness of chapter review questions
Q. Variety of suggested learning activities.
R. Adaptability to varying ability levels.

II. Illustrations

A. Visual appeal and timelessness of cover illustration.
B. Relevance of cover illustration to content of the text.
C. Meaningfulness (adds to students' understanding of concepts).
D. Colorfulness/attractiveness.
E. Current yet classic appearance.
F. Frequency of distribution.
G. Variety (includes line drawings, diagrams, etc., in addition to photos).
H. Corresponds with copy in terms of content and placement.
I. Appropriateness of captions and callouts.
J. Relevance to students' lives (realistic, age-appropriate).
K. Emphasis on safety.
L. Representation of various races.
M. Representation of nontraditional as well as traditional sex roles.
N. Representation of handicapped individuals.
O. Clarity of charted material.

III. Reference Aids

A. Informativeness of introductory statements.
B. Descriptiveness of table of contents.
C. Clarity of glossary definitions.
D. Completeness of index.
E. Value of appendix(es).

...TEACHER'S CHECKLIST OF TEXT SELECTION CRITERIA

	Excellent	Above Average	Average	Below Average	Unsatisfactory	Not Applicable

IV. Format

A. Readability of type.

B. Prominence of vocabulary terms.

C. Attractiveness and clarity of layout.

D. Convenience of text size.

E. Quality of paper.

F. Durability of binding.

G. Value related to cost.

V. Supplemental Products

A. Correlation between teacher's materials and textbook.

B. Clarity of student objectives listed in teacher's materials.

C. Variety of suggested learning experiences teachers can provide for students.

D. Ability of teacher's materials to be used with students of varying abilities.

E. Validity of test questions provided in teacher's materials.

F. Completeness of answer key provided in teacher's materials

G. Correlation between student workbook activities and textbook materials.

H. Clarity of instructions for workbook activities.

I. Variety of activities provided in student workbook.

J. Ability of workbook to be used by students of different ability levels.

K. Convenience of size and format.

L. Other supplemental products:

_____

_____

VI. Comments

_____

_____

_____

_____

Source: Goodheart-Willcox Publishers. (1990). *A Guide to Selecting and Using Textbooks.* South Holland, IL: Author.

CLOZE PROCEDURE FOR READING COMPREHENSION

CONSTRUCTION

1. Select a representative passage from your class text of approximately 520 words. The passage should *not* have been previously read by the students. Include only the main body of the material (no captions, heading, etc.).
2. Type the entire first sentence as it is in the text.
3. Beginning with the second sentence, delete every *tenth* word. Use a fifteen space line in place of the deleted word. Number each deletion in the center of the fifteen space line.
4. Make *50* deletions.
5. Leave the last sentence exactly as it is in the text.

ADMINISTRATION

1. Prior to giving the test, demonstrate to students how to take the test. Make the following remarks (or paraphrase):

    On the next page is a sample of a new kind of test. Each of these tests is made by copying a few paragraphs from a book. Every tenth word was left out of the paragraphs, and blank spaces were put where the words were taken out. Your job will be to guess what word was left out of each space and to write that word in that space.

    It will help you in taking the test if you remember these things:

    1. Write only one word in each blank.
    2. Try to fill every blank. Don't be afraid to guess.
    3. You may skip hard blanks and come back to them when you have finished.
    4. Wrong spelling will not count against you if we can tell what word you meant.
    5. Most of the blanks can be answered with ordinary words but a few will be

        numbers like . . . . 3,427 or $12 or 1954

        contractions like . . . . can't or won't

        abbreviations like . . . . Mrs. U.S.A.

        part of hyphenated words like . . . . self- in the word self-made

2. Using an overhead projector or the chalkboard, present a short passage of three or four sentences with every tenth word deleted as an example of the activity.
3. Have the class fill in the deletions orally. Explain that while more than one word could be used, only the exact replacements will be accepted on this test.
4. Hand out the sheet to the class.
5. Answer any questions.

    Although there is no time limit, students will usually complete the test in 50 minutes.

SCORING THE TEST

A student's responses are scored correct only when they exactly match the words deleted. Minor spelling errors are scored correct as long as the response is otherwise correct. However, omission of plural or tense endings is scored incorrect as in "table" for tables or "work" for worked. Convert raw score to percentage scores by multiplying the number correct by two, when a 50-item test is used. To save time, use a window key with holes cut in a sheet of paper so that everything but the responses is masked when the sheet is placed over the test. Write the correct response beside each window.

_____ Raw Score × 2 = _____%

58% and higher - Independent level

44% to 58%   - Instructional level

below 44%   - Frustrational level

OVERVIEW OF SELECTED COOPERATIVE LEARNING APPROACHES . . .		
Approach/Method	**Brief Description**	**Functions–Academic and Social**
Round robin	In each group, each student in turn shares something with teammates.	Expressing ideas and opinions
Corners	1. Teacher determines alternatives. 2. Each student from the group moves to a different corner of the room representing a teacher determined alternative. 3. Students discuss within corners, then listen to and paraphrase ideas from other corners.	Seeing alternative hypotheses, values, problem-solving approaches
Approaches for Mastery Numbered heads together	1. The teacher has the students number off within groups, so that each student has a number: 1, 2, 3, or 4. 2. Teacher asks a question. 3. The teacher tells the students to "put their heads together" to make sure that everyone on the team knows the answer. 4. The teacher calls a number (1, 2, 3, or 4) and students with that number can raise their hands to respond.	Reviewing, checking for knowledge, comprehension
Pairs check	1. Students work in pairs within groups of four. 2. Within pairs students alternate–one solves a problem/ question while the other coaches. 3. After every two problems/questions, the pair checks to see if they have the same answer as the other pair.	Practicing skills
Approaches for Concept Development Three-step interview	1. Students form two pairs within their teams of four and conduct a one-way interview in pairs. 2. Students reverse roles; interviewers become the interviewees. 3. Students round robin; each student takes a turn sharing information learned in the interview.	Evaluation, analysis, synthesis, application, listening (anticipatory set, closure)
Think-pair-share	1. Teacher provides topic. 2. Students think to themselves on the topic. 3. Students pair up with other students to discuss it. 4. They then share their thoughts with the class.	Generating and revising hypotheses, inductive reasoning, deductive reasoning, application
Team word-webbing	1. In a team, students write simultaneously on a piece of paper. 2. On paper they draw main concepts, supporting elements, and bridges representing the relation of ideas in a concept.	Analysis of concepts into components, understanding multiple relations among ideas, differentiating concepts
Multifunctional Approaches Roundtable	1. Each student writes one answer as a paper/pen are passed around the group. With simultaneous roundtable, more than one paper/pen are used.	Assessing prior knowledge, practicing, skills, recalling, cooperatively creating

...OVERVIEW OF SELECTED COOPERATIVE LEARNING APPROACHES

Approach/Method	Brief Description	Functions–Academic and Social
Partners	1. Students work in pairs to create or master content. 2. They consult with partners from other teams. 3. They then share their products or understanding with the other partner pair in their team.	Mastery and presentation of new material, concept development
Jigsaw	1. Teacher prepares expert sheet and quiz for unit of study. 2. Each student on the learning team is a member of an "expert" group on a topic. 3. Each student works with "expert" members from other learning teams studying the same topic. 4. "Experts" return to their group to teach their learning team. 5. Students are assessed on aspects of the topic.	Acquisition and presentation of new material, review informed debate
STAD (Student Teams Achievement Division)	1. Teacher presents materials students are to learn. 2. Each team of students works together to answer the questions. 3. Team makes sure each member can answer each question correctly. 4. After work is done, administer a quiz to each individual team member to measure knowledge students have gained.	Acquisition and presentation of new materials, skills, processes, review
Coop	1. Teacher introduces unit or topic. 2. Students select teams based on interest. 3. Teams select a topic from the list generated during class discussion or brainstorming. Each team should select a topic. 4. Student analyze topic they have chosen and break it into mini-topics. 5. Each team member is responsible for gathering information on the mini-topic and sharing it. 6. Each team makes a presentation on complete topic to class. Presentation could be demonstrations, debate, hands-on activities, plays, etc.	Learning and sharing complex material, often with multiple sources; evaluation; application, analysis; synthesis
Group investigation	1. Students organize into teams of five or fewer. 2. Each team plans its own topic and strategy for studying the topic. 3. Individuals or pairs within the team select subtopics and decide how to pursue them. 4. Teacher and team plan specific learning procedures, tasks, and goals consistent with the subtopics of the problem selected. 5. Students carry out steps formulated. 6. Students analyze and evaluate the information gathered and plan how to summarize it in an interesting manner for a class presentation.	Learning and sharing complex material from multiple sources; evaluation; application; analysis, synthesis

Source: Kagan, S. (1989). *Cooperative Learning Resources for Teachers*. San Juan Capistrano, CA: Resources for Teachers.

WRITING MODIFIED TEST ITEMS . . .

TRUE-FALSE

- Use simple straightforward statements with as few words as possible
- Avoid negative or comparative words
- Underline the key words that make statements true or false
- Avoid trivial statements, ones that do not assess important knowledge
- Allow students to circle correct answers and provide an example item in the directions
- Avoid clues such as *NEVER, NOT, USUALLY,* and *ALWAYS* in statements, and if they must be used, underline and capitalize them
- Keep the number of true-false items in short sections with no more than ten

Example

Directions: Each of the statements below are about administering first aid. Circle T for true statments and F for false statements. Each item is worth (1) point.

1. T / F   The *emergency* phone number is 911.

COMPLETION

- Provide a word bank for possible answers
- Provide configuration clues for missing words
- Provide partial letter clues for missing words
- Avoid points off for spelling errors but circle errors
- Administer a separate spelling test
- Allow students to use a spelling list as a word bank
- Allow the use of books and notes
- Avoid taking statements directly out of mateirals
- Place possible answers directly under blanks to facilitate recall and allow students to circle the answer rather than writing it in the blank
- Provide large blanks for students with physical disabilities
- Write incomplete statements with one blank and avoid blanks at the beginning of statements

Examples

Directions: The statements below about administering first aid have a word or words missing. Fill in the balnk information needed to complete the sentence. Each item is worth (1) point.

The emergency action principle of checking for the person's ABC's stands for checking for a(n) _____, breathing, and circulation.

Directions: The statements below about administering first aid have a word or words missing. Circle the word that completes the statement correctly. Each item is worth (1) point.

The emergency action principle of checking for the person's ABC's stands for checking for a(n) _____, breathing, and circulation.
activity aroma airway

MULTIPLE CHOICE

- List choices in vertical columns
- Eliminate combination choices such as "all of the above," "none of the above," and "A and B"
- Reduce the number of choices from the usual five to three or less
- State the stem and choices as simply as possible
- Avoid using words unnecessary to answer the item
- Make stems and all choices grammatically consistent
- Include only one correct, or clearly the best, response
- Allow students to circle the correct response to avoid transfer problems to blank spaces or to machine scored answer sheets
- Underline the key word(s) or phrase(s) in the stem to provide clues

...WRITING MODIFIED TEST ITEMS...

Example

Directions: Each of the statements or questions below about administering first aid are followed by three possible responses that can correctly complete the statement or answer the question. Circle the letter of the correct response. Each item is worth (1) point.

What does administering CPR do?

A. Aids a choking victim to clear the throat

B. Restarts the heart of a heart attack victim

C. Supplies oxygen to the body's cells when the heart has stopped

MATCHING

- Present sets of items and answer in small groups (5-8 sets)
- Give the same number of items and answers
- Underline the key word(s) or phrase(s)
- Place sets of matching items on the same page
- Avoid having students draw lines from items to responses
- Use homogeneous materials for matching items
- Leave extra space between items in columns to be matched
- Place stems in the left column and choices in the right
- Keep matching stems and choices as brief as possible
- Keep items in logical order (alphabetical or numerical)
- Underline the key words that describe what is to be matched in directions

Example

Directions: Match the definitions of terms used in CPR in column I with the lettered terms in column II by placing the letter in the space beside each number. Each correctly matched definition is worth (1) point.

DEFINITIONS	TERMS
___ 1. Abbreviation for cardiopulmonary resuscitation	A. Artificial respiration
___ 2. Abbreviation for emergency medical services	B. Cardiac arrest
___ 3. Technique to clear airway of a conscious person	C. Chest compression
___ 4. Procedure for manually circulating blood in a person whose heart has stopped	D. CPR
___ 5. Process of breathing air into the lungs of a person who has stopped breathing	E. EMS
___ 6. Condition in which the heart stops beating	F. Heimlich maneuver

ESSAY

- Define any unclear terms
- Select item verbs that are on the domain level of students (define = knowledge, predict = application)
- Word items clearly so students know exactly what to do
- Construct item with words that are on the student's reading level
- Use restricted response (only a few responses required) items
- Check that students know the meaning of item action words such as discuss, define, describe, list, etc.
- Provide an answer sheet that lists expected components of the response

. . . WRITING MODIFIED TEST ITEMS

- Allow students to outline answers or provide an outline for them
- Use a limited number of essay items on each test
- Allow extra time for students to write responses
- Allow students to list or record the answers rather than write them
- Include the specific number of answers when asking to list information
- Give students options of answering two out of three essay items
- Review the actual essay items several days ahead of test administration and allow students to prepare an outline that they can write from
- Allow students to use books and notes to locate information
- Allow students to orally tape answers
- Provide an idea bank or list of topics to include in responses

Example

Directions: You are given an accident scenario and asked to do a primary survey to check the ABC's by filling in the blanks for each step (using clues provided below the item). This item is worth (10) points.

Scene: You have just entered the neighbor's pool upon hearing screams and find your friend bending over her brother stretched out on the pool deck. She says that she had just pulled him from the water where he was floating face down. What would you do next?

Clue: Do a primary survey to check the ABC's

1. Check for _____ (see clue below)
2. Shout for _____
3. Open the _____
4. Look, listen, and feel for _____ (see clue below)
5. Give 2 full _____
6. Check for a _____ at the side of the _____ (see clue below)
7. Have someone phone the _____ for help
8. Begin _____
9. Give 1 breath every _____ seconds (see clue below)
10. Keep the victim from moving until _____ personnel arrive and keep checking the victim's _____ and _____.

Clues:

- At Step 1, the victim is unconscious
- At Step 4, the victim is not breathing
- At Step 6, the victim has a pulse
- At Step 9, after you have given rescue breaths for 2 minutes, the victim begins to breathe on his own.

Adapted from: Huck et al. (1989). *ADAPT: A Developmental Activity Program for Teachers* (2nd ed.). Pittsburgh, PA: Allegheny Intermediate Unit., and Jones et al. (1990). *Adapting the Teacher Made Test for Students Mainstreamed into Vocational Education.* In K. H. Jones (Ed.), *Career Education for Transition: Curriculum Implementation* (pp. 67-74). Athens, GA: The University of Georgia, Department of Vocational Education.

CAREER AND TECHNICAL STUDENT ORGANIZATIONS

National FFA Center 6060 FFA Drive P.O. Box 68960 Indianapolis, IN 46268 Phone: 317-802-6050 www.ffa.org	**Business Professionals of America** 5454 Cleveland Avenue Columbus, OH 43231-4021 Phone: 614-895-7277 or 800-334-2007 www.bpa.org
Family, Career and Community Leaders of America 1910 Association Drive Reston, VA 20191-1584 Phone: 703-476-4900 www.fcclainc.org	**National HOSA** 6021 Morriss Road, Suite 111 Flower Mound, TX 75028 Phone: 800-321-HOSA www.hosa.org
Future Business Leaders of America – Phi Beta Lambda 1912 Association Drive Reston, VA 20191-1591 Phone: 800-FBLA-WIN www.fbla-pbl.org	**National PAS Organization** P.O. Box 221897 Sacramento, CA 95822 Phone: 916-395-5967 www.ffa.org/aero/pas/pas.html
National DECA 1908 Association Drive Reston, VA 20191 Phone: 703-860-5000 www.deca.org	**National Young Farmer Educational Association** P.O. Box 20326 Montgomery, AL 36120 Phone: 334-288-0097 www.nyfea.org
Delta Epsilon Chi: Where Success Begins 1908 Association Drive Reston, VA 20191 Phone: 703-860-5000 www.delta-hq.org	**National Vocational-Technical Honor Society** P.O. Box 1336 Flat Rock, NC 28731 www.ntvhs.org
SkillsUSA-VICA P.O. Box 3000 Leesburg, VA 20177-0300 Phone: 703-777-8810 www.skillsusa.org	**Technology Student Association** 1914 Association Drive Reston, VA 20191-1540 Phone: 703-860-9000 www.tsawww.org

LOCAL BUSINESS AND INDUSTRY RESOURCE DIRECTORY-SAMPLE FORMAT

Agency, Organization, or Institution Name: __Progress Industries__

Address: __1017 East Seventh Street N., P.O. Box 366, Newton, IA 50208__

Telephone: __515-555-6119__ Fax: _____

Administrator: __William Powell, President__ Phone: __515-555-6119__

Goal or Mission Statement: __To bring dignity, productivity, and independence to persons with special needs.__

Population Served:

Age
__X__ Youth (14-21)
__X__ Adult (21-over)

Sex
__X__ Male
__X__ Female

Target Clients (check all that apply):

__X__ In-School Youth
_____ Criminal offenders

_____ Dropouts
__X__ Adults/retraining

Disabilities
__X__ Mental
__X__ Physical
_____ Other

Disadvantaged
__X__ Socially
__X__ Economically
_____ Educationally
_____ Other

Other Eligibility Requirements: __Most clients need to be referred to Progress Industries by the Human Services or Vocational__ Rehabilitation office nearest them. They usually pay the fees involved. Persons can contact P.I. directly for basic intake information or other information. Contact Pat Glassford, Intake Coordinator.

Enrollment Dates:

_____ Fall _____ Winter _____ Spring _____ Summer __X__ Open entry

Types of Services and/or Support:

__X__ Career development
_____ Leisure/recreation
_____ Socialization
__X__ Residential
__X__ Continuing education/academic

_____ Financial assistance/income support
_____ Medical
__X__ Career placement
__X__ Transportation
_____ Advocate/guardian

__X__ Other (please describe)
Paid work in workshop and community, life coping skills instruction, vocational assessment/evaluation and counseling.

Adapted from: O'Leary, E., & Paulson, J. (1991). *Developing and Writing Transition Services Within the IEP Process.* Des Moines, IA: Drake University, Mountain Plains Regional Resource Center.

EXEMPLARY PROGRAM COMPONENTS...

A. Program Administration

1. Administration Leadership and Support

    In programs with strong administrative support, staff and students know who to approach to communicate ideas, problems, and other matters. A decision-making structure exists and the staff and other personnel understand this structure. There is a mutual understanding and appreciation between the administrators and staff. Many good programs use site-based management principles.

    Best Practices:

    - An organizational chart identifying operational elements and administrative personnel in charge is available.
    - Administrative support is provided in such areas as funding, advocacy, and marketing.

2. Financial Support

    Program personnel are active and creative in identifying and soliciting additional funding for the program. Coordinators are usually knowledgeable about the recurring and nonrecurring costs associated with the program, including personnel salaries, staff training, equipment and materials, and other special costs required to successfully implement and maintain the program. Most good programs have a budget with strong local/institutional support.

3. Professional Development

    Professional development activities include any preservice, inservice, and/or continuing education obtained by program staff, as well as training conducted by staff for others such as supplemental teachers, other programs or educational agencies. Staff are encouraged to participate in appropriate staff development activities.

    Best Practices:

    - Inservice or continuing education is provided for all program staff.
    - A committee of staff members oversees the planning and conducting of inservice professional development activities. The committee also controls the professional development budget.
    - Support/incentives are available for staff to attend inservice activities.

4. Formative Program Evaluation

    Formative or ongoing evaluations should be collected routinely. Staff appreciate the need for an evaluation and use the data to improve programs.

    Best Practices:

    - Data on program effectiveness is collected through surveys and other assessment methods.
    - Program evaluation reports are prepared and available at regular intervals during the year (e.g., monthly or quarterly reports).
    - Feedback on program effectiveness is obtained from teachers and other staff members, students, parents, business/community representatives, and other individuals or groups.

5. Summative Program Evaluation

    Summative evaluation should be gathered annually or biannually. It should include information about the program purpose and goals, have a design suited to the goals, and use appropriate instruments and procedures. In good programs, staff understand the need for an evaluation and appreciate the value of the data collected.

    Best Practices:

    - The evaluation is conducted by either an internal or an external evaluator.
    - Sufficient information is collected to provide evidence of effectiveness (e.g., completion rate, retention rate, number receiving services).
    - The evaluation data is used for program improvement.

B. Curriculum and Instruction

1. Individualized Curriculum Modifications

    Good programs individualize all aspects of the curriculum to fit the needs of the students. Programs which serve students with disabilities have comprehensive individualized education plans (IEPs). Programs serving other groups also have transition or career plans for students.

    Best Practices

    - The curriculum is modified through any of the following means: use of computers, writing or adapting separate lesson plans, use of other media to deliver instruction, use of teacher aides, use of tutors, and use of mentors.
    - The individualized educational planning process involves teachers, students, counselors, parents, transition specialists, and vocational educators.

2. Integration of Academic and Vocational Curricula

Integrating academic and vocational education has proven to be an extremely effective way of educating students, especially those who are at risk of failing in the traditional classroom. Programs that have an integrated curriculum require students to complete a sequence of courses and to master identified competencies or skills to complete the program. Such programs allow students with special learning needs to complete their work on an individualized time plan.

Best practices:

• Integration of academic and vocational curricula occurs through use of applied academic learning materials, integrated courses, team teaching between academic and vocational teacher, involvement in Tech Prep initiatives, and participation in career academies.

3. Appropriate Instructional Settings

Educational programs should reflect the diversity of the school's student population. The program meets the needs, backgrounds, abilities, and interests of program participants. While the number and classification of participants who are from special populations are available, other students are unaware of any special classification of their classmates.

Best Practices:

• Students who are members of special populations are fully included in regular education classes or included to the greatest extent possible.

4. Cooperative Learning Experiences

Cooperative learning experiences (i.e., students learning from other students) have proved to be an excellent way for students from special populations to learn. Good programs offer a variety of cooperative learning experiences to participants. These experiences relate to the purposes and goals of the program.

Best Practices:

• There are opportunities for, and students avail themselves of, the following cooperative learning experiences: group projects, in or out of the classroom; peer tutoring; and participation in student organizations.

C. Comprehensive Support Services

1. Assessment of Vocational Interests and Abilities

Programs that are exemplary have established a comprehensive program to assess students. They have paid close attention to the process, resources, and materials used to assess the vocational interests, aptitudes, and abilities of program participants. They also individualize the assessment process so that each student has only those assessments needed.

Best Practices:

• Each student's individual interests and abilities are assessed using a combination of instruments and techniques as needed.

• Assessment begins during 8th grade or lower.

2. Instructional Support Services

Instructional support services are vital to meeting the purposes and goals of the program. They include good resources, special materials, and/or additional personnel (e.g., teacher aides) who uniquely assist in achieving the stated goals of the program. Good programs continually seek better services to increase the chance for student success.

Best Practices

• The following services are available: tutors; mentors; rehabilitation counselors; psychologists; job coaches; adaptive devices; financial support for books, tools, and so on; and child care.

3. Career Guidance and Counseling

Career guidance and counseling services are crucial to the success of program participants. Good career guidance programs are integrated into other programs in the institution with leadership provided by qualified counselors. Each student has an individual education plan, transition plan, or individual career plan that serves as a road map to the future. Credentialed counselors should assist all students in the school/institution.

Best Practices:

• Career guidance and counseling programs are led by certified guidance counselors and integrated into the school's/institution's other programs.

• The following guidance and counseling activities are conducted: individual and group counseling, assessment of

... EXEMPLARY PROGRAM COMPONENTS ...

interests and abilities, career planning, consulting with teachers and parents, group counseling, job shadowing, field trips to various businesses, referrals, and follow-up evaluations.

- There is a realistic guidance couselor-to-student ratio.

D. Formalized Articulation and Communication

1. Family/Parental Involvement and Support

Active participation of parents in program activities has been shown to enhance student and program success. Parents are involved in general program planning and development as well as in planning for their children. Parents feel welcome and are involved in all decision-making aspects of the program.

Best Practices:

- Specific areas where parents and family members are involved include school management, new program planning, evaluation, and their children's programs.

2. Notification of Both Students and Parents Regarding Vocational Opportunities

Secondary program staff should inform potential students who are members of special populations and their parents of vocational education options available through the program. Good programs provide thorough information and have clearly defined methods, procedures, and resources to accomplish this mandate. Notification often includes information about vocational education program options, as well as available support services.

Best Practices:

- Information about vocational opportunities is available before or during the 9th grade.
- Brochures, newsletters, and other forms of information dissemination are used (e.g., radio, newspapers, presentations in community) in a format that both students and parents will understand.
- Information about the following is disseminated: available programs and specific courses, eligibility for enrollment, available special services, employment opportunities, placement, and financial assistance.

3. Vocational Educators' Involvement in Individualized Educational Planning

Vocational educators should be involved in the individual instruction planning process used by the program.

Best Practices:

- Vocational teachers of classes that students have expressed an interest in taking are informed participants in individualized educational planning meetings.
- The role of vocational teachers and others involved are clearly stated.

4. Formalized Transition Planning

An effective program should provide individual program participants with formalized transition planning. Transition is the movement of a completing student from one level or program to the next appropriate level or program (e.g., from a secondary school setting to a postsecondary vocational education program, a community-based rehabilitation program, and/or work). A comprehensive transition planning service should include the program staff involved in the transition process, outside agencies involved in the transition process, and the transitional options that generally exist for participants who are members of special populations as they exit the program. A program's involvement in Tech Prep initiatives is an important transition activity.

Best Practices:

- An individualized transition plan exists for each student preferably starting in 9th grade but no later than the 11th grade.
- The plan explains who are involved in the process and their roles, as well as the services needed to progress.
- Parents and students are actively involved in the planning process.

5. Intra- and Interagency Collaboration

Intra- and interagency collaboration serve as important avenues for funding, recruiting volunteers, and referrals. Departments and programs within the educational institution collaborate to provide support services, resources, and general assistance to the staff. Interagency cooperation is essential. All possible community resources are incorporated into the school or institution.

Best Practices:

- The employment services, rehabilitation services, health departments, agencies that operate Job Training and Partnership Act programs, and other community agencies cooperate regularly with the school/institution.
- The roles that different school departments play in the program are clearly stated.
- Involvement of the community and businesses may include the following: serving as tutors and mentors, donating cash or equipment and supplies, volunteering for various school/classroom activities, participating in advisory committees, and providing work experience and job training.

...EXEMPLARY PROGRAM COMPONENTS...

E. Occupational Experience Opportunities, Placement, and Follow-Up

1. Work Experience Opportunities

    In order to successfully transition from school to work, students must avail themselves of work experience opportunities during their enrollment within the program. School services related to work experience should include information about the type and nature of work experiences that are available to program participants, how these experiences relate to the instructional objectives of the program, and the extent to which the experiences are specific to the vocational education and training received by the students.

    Best Practices:

    - The program provides formal work experience to students.
    - Involvement in work experience is based on assessment of interests and abilities conducted by guidance counselors.
    - Work experience occurs both in and out of school and is both paid and unpaid.

2. Job Placement Services

    Job placement services help program participants make the transition into the workplace. Successful programs assist students, especially those who are members of special populations, in identifying available jobs (including full-time, part-time, and summer jobs). In addition, good programs assist students in securing employment following program completion.

    Best Practices:

    - The program is committed to a proactive search for businesses that may provide job placement to students in the program (e.g., there is a designated person with this major responsibility).
    - Training or assistance in developing resumes and job interview skill is provided.
    - A networking system exists which the school can draw upon for job placement.

3. Follow-Up of Graduates and Nongraduates

    To accurately assess a program's outcomes, data and information should be collected by program staff from graduates and from noncompleters. Information should be analyzed, reported, and used to improve the program and services.

    Best Practices:

    - Programs with good follow-up data on participants collected them during these desired intervals: upon graduation, three months after graduation, or six months to a year after graduation.
    - Reports summarizing the follow-up information are prepared and shared with the staff and other appropriate individuals.
    - Program coordinators and staff, as well as school administrators, use this information for program planning and improvement.

F. Other Characteristics

1. Belief in Students' Abilities

    Foremost, personnel involved in excellent programs are caring people who advocate for students and believe in their innate abilities. Teachers, staff, administrators, and employers all assume students are capable and take pride in their abilities, strengths, and successes. They never or rarely discuss their students' limitations or failure with us. Rather, they talk about their students' successes and how they have overcome their problems.

    Teachers involved with the program sometimes admit that they have been convinced of the program's merits. These teachers are the ones who encourage reluctant colleagues to accept students with special needs in their classrooms.

2. High Staff Morale

    Teachers, staff, and administrators have easy, comfortable relations with each other, others within the school system or college, local employers, community groups, and parents. As a result, staff and student morale are high.

3. One or a Core of People Leading the Program

    There is usually one person (or a small core of people) who is the heart of the program. This person may be an administrator, a teacher, or other staff personnel. All too often when the person leaves, the program becomes less effective. There are two lessons to be learned from this indicator:

    a. Steps should be taken to institutionalize the program so that when the person(s) leaves, it remains intact and strong.

    b. One person can and frequently does make a difference.

4. Creative Problem Solving

    People who work in outstanding programs find ways around barriers.

    "We used to have that problem until we talked our principal into . . . "

... EXEMPLARY PROGRAM COMPONENTS

"We learned to get around the 'nay sayers' by . . . "

"When we had no funding, we . . . [decided to write a grant; asked businesses for help; got the principal to free up money she was keeping for . . .]"

"We convinced the college president that the program was vital by . . . "

"In order to convince the union that we weren't weakening the contract, we . . . "

5. Use Site-Based Management Principles

   Outstanding programs usually adhere to site-based management principles although many do not know the term.

6. Professional Development Is a Priority

   Professional development activities are vital and welcomed by personnel. The program personnel seem to always seek a "better way" and never assume they have reached perfection.

7. Extensive Interactions with Business and Community

   There are many positive interactions between the school and the community/business/industry. Education activities are viewed as a shared responsibility.

Adapted from: Matias et al. (1995). *Profiles and Best Practices: Exemplary Vocational Special Populations Programs* (pp. 5-17). Berkeley, CA: National Center for Research in Vocational Education.

REFERENCES

Babich, A., Burdine, P., Albright, L., & Randol, R. (n.d.). *C.I.T.E. learning styles instrument.* Wichita, KS: Wichita Public Schools, Murdock Teachers Center.

Center for Innovations in Special Education (formerly Missouri LINC). (n.d.). [Workshop handout]. Columbia, MO: University of Missouri, Department of Special Education and Department of Vocational Technical Education.

Greenan, J. (1986). Curriculum and assessment in generalizable skills instruction. *The Journal for Vocational Special Needs Education, 9*(1).

Goodheart-Willcox Publishers (1990). *A guide to selecting and using textbooks.* South Holland, IL: Author

Huck, R., Meyers, R., & Wilson, J. (1989). *ADAPT: A developmental activity program for teachers* (2nd ed.). Pittsburgh, PA: Allegheny Intermediate Unit.

Jones, K., Miederboff, J. W., & Wood, J. W. (1990). Adapting the teacher made test for students mainstreamed into vocational education. In K. H. Jones, (Ed.). *Career education for transition: Curriculum implementation* (pp. 67-74). Athens, GA: The University of Georgia, Department of Vocational Education.

Kagan, S. (1989). *Cooperative learning resources for teachers.* San Juan Capistrano, CA: Resources for Teachers.

Matias, L., Maddy-Bernstein, C., & Kantenberger, J. (1995). *Profiles and best practices: Exemplary vocational special populations programs* (pp. 5-17). Berkeley, CA: National Center for Research in Vocational Education.

O'Leary, E., & Paulson, J. (1991). *Developing and writing transition services within the IEP process.* Des Moines, IA: Drake University, Mountain Plains Regional Resource Center.

Peoria Unified School District #11. (n.d.). *Transition services.* Peoria, AZ: Special Education Department.

Utah State Department of Education. *Section 504/ADA guidelines for education.* Salt Lake City, UT: Author.

Glossary

A

accessibility: The ability to enter a facility or building to move about freely and the ability to participate and function effectively in the work environment.

accommodation: A modification or adjustment made by classroom teachers or other school staff designed to provide free appropriate public education to a learner with special needs.

adaptive behavior: Defined by the American Association on Mental Retardation, adaptive behavior represents significant limitations in a person's ability to meet standards of maturation, learning, personal, independence, and social responsibility that would be expected of another individual of comparable age level and cultural group (Grossman, 1983).

agency: A governmental or non-governmental body organized around the needs of a specific population or group, with certain functions designed to benefit that population or group.

all aspects of the industry: The aspects of industry defined by legislation include planning, management, finance, technical and production skills, underlying principles of technology, labor issues, community issues, and health, safety, and environmental issues.

alternative assessments: Varied forms of academic assessments that supplement or replace conventional assessment formats such as tests and essays. Often these assessments require learners to construct their own responses or produce things. Advocates of alternative assessment favor a model where assessment activities are varied and many.

American Lyceum: The American Lyceum, created to serve towns in the country, was the counterpart of the mechanics institutes, which served cities and large towns. It was based on the concept that "men may improve themselves through sharing their knowledge and expertise." The lyceum was an organization in the towns of America where speeches were given to increase the knowledge of the common person. The lyceum movement, like the mechanics institute movement, was short-lived, but it served to popularize education for all and placed an emphasis on acquiring useful information. It perpetuated the idea that education was a community affair and responsibility, an idea that was critical to establishing publicly supported elementary and secondary schools (Martin, 1981).

analytic learner: A learner who reasons by analysis, logic, and deduction and excels in naming and categorizing things, symbolic abstraction, speech, reading, writing, and arithmetic (functions generally associated with the left brain). The left brain is mainly used to process languages and numbers and to deduce logic, which is very much emphasized for academic learning capabilities.

annual goal: A goal that describes what a learner with special needs can reasonably be expected to accomplish within one year. Annual goals should relate to the limitations identified from the learner's present level of educational performance.

apprenticeship: Program based on an employer-school partnership that integrates academic instruction, structured career and technical education training, and paid workplace experience. The expected program outcome is that youth apprentices will continue their career and technical preparation in a postsecondary institution or that the apprenticeship will lead to journeyperson status and permanent employment. Apprenticeship programs are sponsored by joint employer and labor groups, individual employers, and/or employer associations. There are two types of apprenticeships: registered apprenticeships and youth apprenticeships.

aptitude: The capacity and capability to acquire competencies with a given amount of formal or informal training. Aptitudes are distinguished from achievement in that aptitudes represent potential or abilities while achievement represents accomplishments.

aptitude test: A test that provides information about the level of difficulty an individual may have in performing certain tasks and learning accompanying procedures.

arts and crafts movement: An aesthetic movement that originated in England and came to the United States during the late nineteenth century. The movement emphasized artistic design, practical skill development for career and technical as well as for future work applications, the revival of artistic pursuits all but eliminated by industrial machinery, and the teaching of decorative arts to the abilities and interest of youngsters. Subjects in the arts and crafts include drawing, wood carving, clay modeling, mosaic work, leather carving, metal embossing, embroidery, carpentry, wood turning, wood inlaying, and ornamental wood sawing.

assessment: Involves using information obtained through measurement to evaluate or form judgments about a learner's performance on some realistic work task. It can be used as a verb describing a process or as a noun referring to a product (score on a test).

assistive technology (AT): Any item, piece of equipment, or product system (whether acquired off the shelf, modified, or customized) that is used to increase, maintain, or improve functional capabilities of individuals with disabilities. These devices are commonly referred to as assistive technology (AT) devices.

assistive technology (AT) device: As defined by the IDEA, any item, piece of equipment, or product system, whether acquired commercially off the shelf, modified, or customized, that is used to increase, maintain, or improve the functional capabilities of a learner with a disability.

assistive technology (AT) service: As defined by the IDEA, any service that directly assists a learner with a disability in the selection, acquisition, or use of an assistive technology device.

at-risk: At-risk describes learners associated with an increased probability of school failure and dropping out.

attention deficit/hyperactivity disorder: A disorder in which individuals have difficulty maintaining an attention span because of their limited ability to concentrate and exhibit impulsive actions (Lahey et al., 1987).

authentic assessments: Forms of educational assessment that involve the performance of tasks directly related to real-life problems. Portfolios, written scenarios, performance events, projects, interpretive events, demonstrations, computer simulations, and graphic organizers provide a means for making assessment an integral part of instruction that guides the learning process for all learners.

autism: A developmental disability significantly affecting verbal and nonverbal communication and social interaction, usually evident before age three, that adversely affects a child's educational performance. Other characteristics often associated with autism are engagement in repetitive activities and stereotyped movements, resistance to environmental change or change in daily routines, and unusual responses to sensory experiences (Individuals with Disabilities Education Act of 1990).

B

basic reading skills: The ability to read words as well as comprehend their meaning.

basic skills information: What a learner does and does not know. This is determined through basic skill inventories that measure achievement levels and competencies in the areas of reading, spelling, writing, math, and language development.

behavior management: A method of learning/teaching behavior through positive reinforcement. Its basic premise is that the acquisition of a particular behavior is contingent upon learning that its performance will be rewarded. The behavior strengthened by reinforcement may be either appropriate or inappropriate; however, if either type of behavior is rewarded, it is likely to continue.

benchmark: A model of exceptional performance that will enable both the instructor and the learners to compare and score learner performance.

blindness: Visual acuity of 20/200 or worse in the best eye with best correction, as measured on the Snellen test, or a visual field of 20% of less. Blindness can also be characterized as an educational disability. Educational definitions of blindness focus primarily on an individual's ability to use vision as an avenue for learning.

brain-based learning: A concept that seeks to classify learning methods from the perspective of where and how certain types of information are processed. It suggests there are two major types of learners–those in whom the right brain is dominant, and those with a dominant left brain.

business/industry linkage: A network among schools, community organizations, labor, and employers that is critical to the success of school-to-work systems. Linkages offer employers a continuum of choices, ranging from career awareness, career exploration, and job shadowing, to more intensive activities such as mentoring, apprenticeships, and other structured work-based learning opportunities. Employers can also provide input in the development of integrated curriculum, develop and recognize skill standards, serve on planning and governance bodies, and recruit other employers.

C

career academy: A program designed to integrate academic and career and technical education curricula organized around a theme (occupation areas such as health, aerospace, etc.) and taught as a "school-within-a-school" where learners take a sequence of courses together.

career development: Involves providing learners with learning experiences outside of the school walls and teaching learners decision-making strategies crucial to making successful transitions to work, further education, and training. Career development should promote self-awareness, opportunity awareness, and decision and transition learning.

career and technical education: The primary system through which youth and adults are prepared to enter competitive employment through programs of general labor market preparation such as technology (formerly industrial arts), family and consumer sciences, general work experience, computers, and others. Career and technical education programs are offered in many different forms at the secondary and postsecondary levels with some pre-career and technical programs provided in some school systems at the middle/junior high school level. Program curricula include materials that focus on the development of foundational skills, such as basic skills, thinking skills, and personal qualities, as well as a common core of workplace competencies and the specific skill competencies required for each occupational area. These programs make use of real-life situations in classrooms and laboratories as well as supervised work experiences in internships, practicums, cooperative education, and apprenticeships.

career and technical education component of the IEP: A component of the IEP that provides a process for educational personnel and community agencies to successfully plan for individual career and technical education training as part of the learner's overall transitional services planned for a learner with special needs.

career and technical education curriculum: Organized program content structured as a series of intended outcomes or competencies that a learner must master to attain an occupational goal. It involves the sum total of all experiences and learning activities encountered in the classroom and laboratory and encompasses what is to be taught and what is to be learned.

career and technical program exploration tryout: An exploratory experience that provides career and technical education personnel with important assessment information through observing a learner's performance on tasks associated with exit points from the specific program.

career and technical student organization (CTSO): One of the ten U.S. Department of Education recognized student organizations that serve learners enrolled in career and technical programs through activities that are an integral part of the regular instructional program.

career development: Assessment and implementation of appropriate program placement, planning procedures, activities, internships, job shadowing experiences, and support services for a learner to be successful in a chosen career according to established abilities, interests, and needs.

career pathway: A coherent course of study that prepares an individual with the academic and career specific skills needed for entry into a broad cluster of related occupations and/or admission into postsecondary education.

chapter: A generic term used to designate a local institution's career and technical student organization structure.

chapter advisor: Usually, a career and technical education teacher who assists in advising and helping organize and run a career and technical student organization in local career and technical education programs and institutions.

child abuse: Any recent act or failure to act on the part of a parent or caretaker that results in death, serious physical or emotional harm, sexual abuse or exploitation of a child, or an act or failure to act that presents an imminent risk of serious harm to a child.

common school: A school responsible for educating all children regardless of social or economic status. In the 1930s and 1940s, a movement began to promote the idea of education through common schools. The notion of developing moral character as well as intelligence through common schooling was supported by proponents of faculty psychology at that time.

community-based vocational assessment: A job analysis of the specific career goal or training site identified for a learner.

community-based vocational instruction (CBVI): Instruction that relies on an integrated approach to school and community activities to prepare learners for postsecondary opportunities. The CBVI approach has four components: vocational exploration, vocational assessment, vocational training, and cooperative vocational education.

community workforce survey: A method of collecting job analysis information by surveying local industries to determine the types and numbers of available jobs, specific skills required for each job, and working conditions.

competency-based curriculum: A curriculum approach that has two basic philosophies. The first philosophy is the notion that "human competence" is the ability to actually perform. Knowledge, attitudes, and effort are of little value without results. The second philosophy holds that almost anyone can learn almost anything if given quality instruction and sufficient time. This philosophy has also been called mastery learning, performance-based instruction, and criterion-referenced instruction.

cooperative education program: A school-based program where primary instruction takes place in the classroom and is supplemented with work site experience.

cooperative learning: A term applied to any type of instructional strategy in which learners work in teams to accomplish instructional objectives while maintaining individual accountability and group responsibility.

cooperative planning: Educational planning that involves career and technical education instructors and support personnel and allows the career and technical education instructor to work directly with the learner.

cooperative teaching: Co-teaching by two or more teachers in order to meet the special needs of a single learner or small group of learners in the classroom.

correctional facility: A place of continuous confinement for those held in lawful custody, such as a jail, prison, or juvenile detention center.

criminal offender: An individual who is charged with, or convicted of, any criminal offense, including a youth offender or a juvenile offender (The Carl D. Perkins Vocational and Applied Technology Education Act of 1990, PL 101-392).

critical thinking: Using mental processes, strategies, and representations to solve problems, make decisions, and learn new concepts.

curriculum-based assessment: The practice of obtaining direct and frequent measures of a learner's performance on a series of sequentially arranged objectives derived from the curriculum used in the classroom.

curriculum-based vocational assessment: A rating procedure designed to determine the interests, aptitudes, instructional needs, and skill development of learners based upon their ongoing performance within a career and technical education curriculum sequence.

curriculum modification: The tailoring of all experiences and activities encountered in pursuit of career and technical education preparation to meet the unique needs of the individual learner.

curriculum softening: The tendency among educators to provide access for learners by reducing requirements in career and technical education programs.

D

deafness: A hearing impairment so severe that the affected individual is impaired in processing linguistic information through hearing, with or without amplification, which adversely affects educational performance.

demonstration: An activity in which the instructor or another person uses examples, experiments, and/or other actual performances to illustrate a principle or show others how to do something.

Dictionary of Occupational Titles (DOT): An inventory of occupations within the economy prepared by the United States Department of Labor. This resource provides information about the physical demands, working conditions, and aptitudes for a specific job. It also identifies the relationships to people, data, and things. The information is collected through observation of workers and job sites by occupational analysis.

differentiated classroom: A classroom that offers a variety of learning options designed to tap into different readiness levels, interests, and learning profiles. In a differentiated class, the teacher uses (1) a variety of ways for learners to explore curriculum content, (2) a variety of sense-making activities or processes through which learners can come to understand and master information and ideas, and (3) a variety of options through which learners can demonstrate or exhibit what they have learned.

direct instruction: A complex systematic approach to instruction that can have a considerable impact on curriculum content and on instruction. Direct instruction involves clearly communicating goals for learning, structuring academic tasks for learners, demonstrating the steps necessary to accomplish a particular academic task, monitoring learner progress, providing learner practice and teacher feedback to ensure success, over-learning of skills, and holding learners accountable for their work through frequent teacher review.

disability: A physical or mental impairment that substantially limits one or more of an individual's "major life activities" (The Americans with Disabilities Act, PL 101-336).

disabled: Individuals who are identified as disabled under the Americans with Disabilities Act (ADA) (PL 101-336), which includes any individual who has a physical or mental impairment that substantially limits one or more of the major life activities, has a record of impairment or is regarded as having such an impairment; are evaluated under the Individuals with Disabilities Education Act (IDEA) (PL 101-476) and deemed in need of special education and related services; and any individual considered disabled under the Rehabilitation Act of 1973 (The Carl Perkins Vocational and Applied Technology Education Act, PL 101-392).

disadvantaged: Individuals (other than those with disabilities) who have economic or academic disadvantages and who require special services and assistance in order to succeed in career and technical education programs. The term includes members of economically disadvantaged families, migrants, individuals of limited English proficiency, and dropouts (or those identified as potential dropouts) from secondary school (The Carl D. Perkins Vocational and Applied Technology Education Act, PL 101-392).

discussion: An activity in which learners, under teacher and/or peer direction, exchange points of view concerning a topic, question, or problem in order to arrive at a decision or conclusion.

disorder: A general malfunction of mental, physical, or psychological processes defined as a disturbance in normal function.

displaced homemaker: Any person who has spent a number of years as an unsalaried homemaker and by circumstance must find gainful employment.

diversity: The quality of being composed of many different types or parts.

E

economically disadvantaged: An individual who receives, or is a member of a family which receives, cash welfare payments under a federal, state, or local welfare program; has, or is a member of a family which has, received a total family income for the six-month period prior to application for the program involved (exclusive of unemployment compensation, child support payments, and welfare payments) which, in relation to family size, was not in excess of the higher of the poverty level determined in accordance with criteria established by the Director of the Office of Management and Budget, or 70 % of the lower living standard income level; is receiving food stamps pursuant to the Food Stamp Act of 1977; qualifies as a homeless individual under section 103 of the Steward B. McKinney Homeless Assistance Act; is a foster child on behalf of whom State or local government payments are made; or in cases permitted by regulations of the Secretary, is an adult handicapped individual whose own income meets the stated requirements, but who is a member of a family whose income does not meet such requirements (The Job Training Partnership Act, PL 97-300).

The Carl D. Perkins Vocational and Applied Technology Act defined economically disadvantaged individuals as those who are determined to be low income according to the latest available data by the United States Department of Commerce or Department of Health and Human Service's Poverty Guidelines including individuals eligible for benefits under the Food Stamp Act; the program for Aid to Families with Dependent Children; Section 1005 of Title I of the Elementary and Secondary Education Act; free or reduced price meals programs; or participation in Title II of the Job Training Partnership Act. At the postsecondary level, Pell grant recipients are included.

educational achievement: The quality and quantity of an individual's learning and retention.

educationally disadvantaged: Individuals who have problems in general academic achievement. Individuals who are educationally disadvantaged often have a poor foundation in the basic academic skills, a lack of vocabulary development, difficulty putting thoughts into writing, difficulty following written directions, poor speech patterns, trouble comprehending vocabulary and technical terms, difficulty in pronouncing words, problems constructing a proper sentence, poor spelling, and difficulty in carrying on a conversation with others. Additionally, they may have difficulty applying basic mathematical concepts to problem-solving situations or task-related activities in career and technical education programs.

educational reform: A concept for restructured schools based upon the assumption that the world of the future will be governed by information, not manufacturing technologies. The model presupposes that meaningful learning is a personal experience involving self, readiness, understanding, and inquiry. A graduate of the restructured American school is a continuous learner, a flexible, caring person who is competent, can solve problems, take responsibility, process information, and make decisions.

employability skill: A skill necessary to seek and keep a job.

entry-level skill: A competency necessary to participate in a specific program.

environmental modification: A modification that needs to be made to physical facilities, equipment, and work stations in order to provide barrier-free access to all learners, particularly those with disabilities.

equal access: Making career and technical education programs accessible to all persons, including handicapped and disadvantaged persons, single parents and homemakers, adults in need of retraining and training, persons participating in programs designed to eliminate gender bias and stereotyping, and incarcerated persons.

Federal law requires handicapped and disadvantaged individuals participating in career and technical education programs be provided with equal access in recruitment, enrollment, and placement activities; equal access to the full range of career and technical education programs available to individuals without handicapping conditions or disadvantages; assessment of individual interests, abilities, and special needs with respect to successful completion of the career and technical education program; special services, including adaptation of curriculum, instruction, equipment, and facilities designed to meet the special needs of these individuals; guidance, counseling, and career development activities conducted by professionally trained counselors; and counseling services designed to facilitate transition from school to employment or career opportunities. (The Carl D. Perkins Vocational Education Act of 1984, PL 98-524, Section 204)

essential functions: Fundamental job duties that are very specialized, take a significant amount of time, may be important enough to be written into a collective bargaining contract, or produce important, negative consequences if not carried out (The Americans with Disabilities Act, PL 101-336).

evaluation: The process of determining the worth, value or quality of something. Evaluation is being practiced when information obtained through measurement is analyzed to determine how well a learner performed on a cognitive achievement test. When a career and technical education teacher compares learner performance on a written scenario against a model scenario or a scoring rubric, evaluation is being practiced.

exit skill: A competency taught through a career and technical education program that employers would expect learners to have when they apply for a job.

F

field trip: An educational trip to a place where learners can study the content of instruction directly in its functional setting.

flexible grouping: A process in which members of the class work cooperatively, rather than individually, toward common objectives under the guidance of one or more leaders.

formal assessment: Testing with instruments that have been norm-referenced and are available with detailed administrative and scoring information, including achievement tests, aptitude tests, personality tests, interest inventories, intelligence tests, dexterity tests, formal work samples, and work evaluation systems.

foster children: Children who receive, share, or are afforded parental care and nurturing from an adult who is not a legal or blood relative (The Carl D. Perkins Vocational and Applied Technology Education Act of 1990, PL 101-392).

frustration reading level: The level at which an individual cannot read or comprehend material, even with assistance.

full participation: The provision of supplementary and other services required by the Carl Perkins Act necessary for special populations to enter and succeed in career and technical education (The Carl D. Perkins Vocational and Applied Technology Education Act of 1990, PL 101-392).

functional living skill: A basic survival competency necessary to function effectively in an independent living or community work setting.

G

gang involvement: Association with or participation in a gang, which is usually comprised of a group of teens or young adults involved in hostile or unlawful activities.

gender bias: Having preconceived thoughts and opinions, either positive or negative, towards a person or group of people based on gender. Gender bias is often based on stereotypes.

gender equity: Equal and just treatment of all individuals regardless of gender.

generalizable skills: Cognitive, affective, or psychomotor traits (skill or skill area) that are basic to, necessary for success in, and transferable within and among career and technical programs and occupations. A generalizable skill represents a basic competency that is commonly believed to be necessary for success in career and technical programs and employment.

gifted and talented individual: A gifted and talented individual gives evidence of high performance capability in areas such as intellectual creative, artistic or leadership capacity, or in specific academic fields, and who requires services or activities not ordinarily provided by the school in order to fully develop such capabilities (The Jacob K. Javits Gifted and Talented Students Education Act of 1988, Elementary and Secondary Education Act, Title IV).

global learner: A learner who reasons in a nonverbal manner and excels in processing visual, spatial, perceptual, and intuitive information (functions generally associated with the right brain). For the right brain, processing happens very quickly and the style of processing is nonlinear and nonsequential. The right brain looks at the whole picture and quickly seeks to determine the spatial relationships of all the parts as they relate to the whole. This component of the brain is not concerned with things falling into patterns because of prescribed rules. On the contrary, the right brain seems to flourish dealing with complexity, ambiguity, and paradox. At times, right-brain thinking is difficult to put into words because of its complexity, its ability to process information quickly, and its nonverbal nature. The right brain has been associated with the realm of creativity.

grading: The process of assigning a number or symbol to the results of some activity or product such as a learner's performance on a test. It is the process of labeling the degree of performance in order to communicate quality, value, rank, intensity, etc. The term grading is frequently used interchangeably with the terms "marking" and "scoring." Career and technical education instructors are practicing the process of grading, marking, or scoring when they count the number of errors made on a test and assign a percentage score (and possibly a letter grade) so learners will know how they did on a test.

graphic organizer: A diagram or map that shows the relationship among concepts.

Guide for Occupational Exploration (GOE): A document used to identify groups of occupations a learner may be interested in or curious about.

H

hard-of-hearing: An individual who has a hearing impairment, whether permanent or fluctuating, that adversely affects that individual's educational performance.

health impairment: A health impairment causes individuals to have limited strength, vitality, or alertness due to chronic or acute health problems such as heart condition, tuberculosis, rheumatic fever, nephritis, asthma, sickle cell anemia, hemophilia, epilepsy, lead poisoning, leukemia, diabetes, cystic fibrosis, or AIDS which adversely affects educational performance.

hearing impairment: The entire range of hearing loss, from mild through profound conditions. The educational achievement of learners with hearing impairments may be delayed in comparison to the achievement of their hearing peers. Learners with hearing impairments have great difficulty succeeding in a system that depends primarily on the spoken word and written language to transmit knowledge (Greenberg & Kusche, 1989).

homeless individual: An individual who lacks a fixed, regular, and adequate nighttime residence or has a primary nighttime residence that is either a supervised, publicly or privately operated shelter designed to provide temporary living accommodations (including welfare hotels, congregate shelters, and transitional housing for the mentally ill); an institution that provides a temporary residence for individuals intended to be institutionalized; or a public or private place not designed for, or ordinarily used as, a regular sleeping accommodation for human beings.

I

inclusion: Educating learners with severe disabilities in the neighborhood school within the regular classroom, making sure that appropriate support services and curriculum modifications are available. The benefits to inclusion are being seen to benefit not only those with disabilities but also their nondisabled peers and the professionals who work with them.

independent reading level: The level at which an individual can read and comprehend information without assistance.

individualized education program (IEP): A written statement drawn up by the teacher, parent, and a school representative that must include: the learner's present educational level; annual goals, including short-term instructional objectives; the specific educational services to be provided and the extent to which the learner will participate in regular education programs; initiation date and length of services; evaluation procedures; and a transition services statement for learners by the age 16, or younger when appropriate. The IEP team must reconvene when any agency fails to provide transitional services (The Individuals with Disabilities Education Act of 1990, PL 101-476).

individualized instruction: Instruction tailored to meet the particular needs of each learner and allow the career and technical education instructor a variety of alternatives in delivering program instruction.

individualized transition program (ITP): A two- to four-year written plan identifying the progressive steps a learner will take to meet postgraduation goals, including the goals and benchmarks needed to achieve identified outcomes. The ITP may include related instruction in life and employability skills designed to maintain actual employment. Evaluations and assessments may be identified to assist the learner in achieving stated outcomes. The objective of an ITP is to provide all essential resources, supports and experiences needed for adult daily living and for full community participation.

individualized written rehabilitation plan (IWRP): A written plan developed for a learner with special needs who is eligible for services from vocational rehabilitation services. The IWRP states vocational rehabilitation goals, identifies objectives and services, and specifies timelines for providing services.

individual option plan (IOP): Identifies learner problems (classroom management, instruction, evaluation) and suggests teaching options for the instructor.

industrial arts: The career and technical education program that focuses on the study of technology. It is now referred to as technology education.

informal assessment: Information and data used for assessment that have not been developed on a norm-referenced, standardized basis. It is information that can be obtained from school records already on file, observation, interviews, and discussions with learners, parents, and teachers.

instructional reading level: The level at which an individual requires some assistance in identifying new words and/or in comprehending new content.

integral: The state of being an important internal part of instructional programs of career and technical education.

interagency agreement: A written agreement between agencies, both public and private, that details collaboration of the agencies in order to promote the best use of available services and resources.

interagency cooperation: Coordination of available resources of both public and private agencies whose objective is to provide career and technical education instruction and services to learners from special populations.

interagency linkage: A formal type of interagency cooperation, which includes collaboration of public and private agencies to promote the best use of available services through interagency agreements.

interest inventory: A personal survey designed to ask individuals to rank different types of activities based on their personal interests. There are no right or wrong answers. Individuals are usually asked to register their preferences on a scale ranging from most liked to least liked.

internship: A planned instructional experience designed to provide a learner with additional technical competencies at a work site.

interpreter: A support person, usually for the deaf, who uses finger-spelling and/or sign language to translate what is being said for the impaired individual.

interview: A meeting with the learner to collect important information about interests, abilities, goals, and history. Interviews can help to establish rapport between the learners and the educators who will be working with them.

J

Job Accommodation Network (JAN): An international toll-free consulting service that provides information about job accommodations and the employability of people with functional limitations. The mission of JAN is to assist in the hiring, retraining, retention, or advancement of individuals with disabilities by providing accommodation information.

job analysis: A procedure providing information on what a worker does, how the job is done, and why it is necessary.

job coach: A trained individual employed by the school system, community agency, and sometimes by the employer to assist newly placed employees adjust to the work environment and become productive as soon as possible.

job redesign: A technique that can be used to provide jobs for learners who have difficulty obtaining jobs in their preferred occupational area. In redesigning jobs, employers must be willing to have their present job categories analyzed and reorganized to accommodate individuals from special populations.

job shadowing: An activity that makes it possible for a learner (usually in middle or high school) to go to a work site and observe or shadow an employee for one or more days to learn about a job of interest to the learner. Job shadowing is a capstone type of experience that follows career awareness or career exploration instruction.

L

learner profile: Information gathered to provide relevant background information pertaining to a learner. The profile should be used for career counseling, placement decisions, career and technical education program planning, and identification of necessary resources and support services.

learning disability: A disorder in one or more of the basic psychological processes involved in understanding or using spoken or written language, which may manifest itself in an imperfect ability to listen, think, speak, read, write, spell, or to do mathematical calculations. Learning disabilities include such conditions as perceptual disabilities, brain injury, minimal brain dysfunction, dyslexia, and developmental aphasia. Learning disabilities do not include learning problems that are primarily the result of visual, hearing, or motor disabilities; mental retardation; or environmental, cultural, or economic disadvantage (Individuals with Disabilities Education Act, PL 101-476).

learning logs and journals: Learning logs usually consist of short, objective entries under specific headings such as problem solving, observations, questions about content, lists of outside readings, homework assignments, or anything than lends itself to record keeping. Journals, in contrast to logs, which are usually brief, factual, and impersonal, tend to include information written in narrative form, are more subjective, and deal more with feelings, reflections, opinions, and personal experiences.

learning style inventory: A formal tool used to ask learners how they feel they learn best.

learning style modalities: Modalities that describe how learners learn through the senses of sight, sound, and touch. Different learning style modalities include visual learners, auditory learners, and tactile/kinesthetic learners.

levels of vocational assessment (I, II, III): Level I vocational assessment activities include reviewing and compiling all previously existing information related to a learner's abilities, level of functioning, and other pertinent facts into a format that can be utilized for preparing a vocational plan for a specific learner. Level II vocational assessment activities are used to obtain more information about a learner who has difficulty identifying interests in a specific career and technical education program or demonstrating strengths on the paper-pencil inventories that indicate general interests and abilities. Level III vocational assessment is necessary when school personnel cannot identify long-range goals or place a learner in a specific career and technical education program based on the information gathered from Levels I and II.

limited English-proficient learner: An individual who: was not born in the United States or whose native language is a language other than English; comes from an environment where a language other than English is dominant; or is American Indian or Alaskan Native and who comes from an environment where a language other than English has had a significant impact on the level of English language proficiency; and by reason thereof, has sufficient difficulty speaking, reading, writing, or understanding the English language as to deny such individual the opportunity to learn successfully in classrooms where the language of instruction is English or to participate fully in our society (The Carl D. Perkins Vocational and Applied Technology Education Act of 1990, PL 101-392).

local advisory committee: A group of individuals from the community that advises career and technical education instructors about planning, implementing, and maintaining programs.

M

major life activity: An activity such as caring for oneself, performing manual tasks, walking, seeing, hearing, speaking, breathing, learning, working, and participating in community activities.

manual arts: An educational subject area encompassing underlying principles and practices of industrial occupations, which later came to be known as industrial arts.

manual labor: A movement first introduced in order to integrate regular school subjects with agriculture training. Later, manual labor was used as a means of providing physical activity, reducing the cost of education by selling student labor or the products of that labor, promoting a respect for all kinds of honest work, building individual character, promoting originality, stimulating intellectual development, and increasing the wealth of the country.

manual training: A program of shopwork for engineering students began in 1898 so they could become more versed in the application of engineering principles through the use of tools and machines, based on the theory that learners should have access to shop courses and that a combination of academics and shopwork would increase learner interest in school and provide a means of supplementing the mostly liberal education of the day. Manual training provided instruction in mathematics, science, drawing, language, and literature, as well as practice in the use of tools.

mastery learning: Learning that involves identification of segments of learning and mastery of those segments by individual learners. It is based on the philosophy that all learners can learn, but it will take some longer than others. The expectation is that learners will all succeed.

measurement: The process of collecting and ordering information. It involves assigning numbers or symbols to objects or activities according to written rules. Anything that exists in some quantity can be measured through a variety of measurement methods. Measurement refers to quantity and addresses the question, "How much?" A measurement example is a performance test score that provides information that can be evaluated to determine how well a learner with special needs performed on a work task.

mechanics institute: An institute designed to provide adult workers with an education that encompassed technical and industrial instruction. The mechanics institutes were short-lived, with a few of them developing into technical or trade schools and the vast majority of them dying as a result of ineffective teaching and the formation of the land-grant colleges, American high schools, and private trade schools. These institutes conducted classes in the evenings for workers and played a significant role in the establishment of evening programs for adults in community colleges and the technical schools of today.

mental retardation: Significantly subaverage intellectual functioning, existing concurrently with related limitations in two or more of the following applicable adaptive skill areas: communication, self-care, home living, social skills community use, self-direction, health and safety, functional academics, leisure, and work. Mental retardation manifests before age 18 (American Association on Mental Retardation, 1992).

mentoring: A supportive relationship between a youth or young adult and someone more senior in age and experience, who offers support, guidance, and concrete assistance as the younger partner goes through a difficult period, enters a new area of experience, takes on an important task, or corrects an earlier problem. In general during mentoring, learners identify with, or form a strong interpersonal attachment to, their mentors.

metacognition: The ability of an individual to regulate cognitive behavior.

metacognitive assessment: The process of assessing what one knows, how it is known, and why it is known. This may include feelings, attitudes, and dispositions because thinking involves not only cognitive operations but also the dispositions to engage in them when and where appropriate.

migrant: An individual, or the child of such an individual, who has moved within the past 12 months (or has had a pattern of moving within the past five years) for the purpose of obtaining temporary or seasonal employment in an agricultural or fishing activity (The Carl D. Perkins Vocational and Applied Technology Education Act, PL 101-392).

mobility: An individual's ability to move in an environment.

modification: The act of altering or changing some process or object to make it more functional. Modification also refers to a change in a part of a career and technical education facility or some type of equipment, furniture, tool, or instructional strategy in an instructional program in order to minimize or eliminate a barrier for a learner with special needs.

motivation: The needs and desires that move an individual to do something that will satisfy those needs and desires.

multiple exit points: Specific required competencies for a particular job. Multiple exit point guides (MEPGs) can be used as portable profiles as the learner demonstrates required competencies.

multiple intelligences: A psychological theory that all human beings have multiple forms of intelligence. These multiple intelligences can be nurtured and strengthened, or ignored and weakened, and they each respond to different types of stimuli. The theory was advanced by psychologist Howard Gardner of Harvard in the mid 1980s, who identified eight specific intelligences: visual/spatial, logical/mathematical, verbal/linguistic, musical/rhythmic, bodily/kinesthetic, interpersonal/social, intrapersonal/introspective, and naturalist.

N

national skill standards: A voluntary national system of skill standards, assessment, and certification systems to enhance the ability of the United States workforce to compete effectively in a global economy.

networking: The process of gathering and sharing employment information among individuals in the school and community.

nontraditional training and employment: The study of or employment in an occupation or field of work for which individuals from one gender comprise less than 25% of the individuals employed in that particular occupation or field of work. (The Workforce Investment Act of 1988, PL 105-220).

O

Occupational Outlook Handbook (OOH): A nationally recognized source of career information designed to provide valuable assistance to individuals making decisions about their future work.

one-stop career center: A facility or agency that merges traditional employment and training services to provide consolidated programs, supervised by states and local communities, which enable easy customer access to services. One-stop centers should provide core services, intensive services, and training services.

O*NET: A unique, powerful source of continually updated occupational information and labor market research. The O*NET database includes information on skills, abilities, knowledge, work activities, and interests along with occupations. This information can be used to facilitate career exploration, career and technical education counseling, and a variety of human resources functions, such as developing job orders and position descriptions and aligning training with current workplace needs.

orthopedically impaired: Individuals having a physical disorder that may interfere with an individual's mobility and coordination. The disorder may also affect the capacity to communicate, learn, and adjust. These disorders or physical impairments are usually diagnosed early in the individual's life and as he or she grows older, the treatment program may involve professionals from many different disciplines including medicine, psychology, education, and vocational rehabilitation.

P

paraprofessional/paraeducator: An employee (a) whose position is either instructional in nature or who delivers other direct and indirect services to learners and/or their parents, and (b) who works under the supervision of a teacher of another professional staff member responsible for the overall conduct of the class, the design and implementation of individualized education programs, and the assessment of the effect of the program on learner progress.

partially sighted: Individuals who have a visual acuity greater than 20/200 but not greater than 20/70 in the best eye after correction. The field of education also distinguishes between blind and partially sighted in order to determine the level and extent of additional support services required by a learner. Partially sighted individuals are able to use their vision as a primary source of learning.

peer and cross-age tutoring: A system of instruction in which one learner helps another to learn the curriculum for a specific course.

peer assessment: A form of educational assessment whereby learners are evaluated by their peers and receive feedback.

performance assessment: A form of educational assessment that focuses on a learner's ability to apply skills and knowledge to real-world problems. Learners are provided with clear guidelines about teacher expectations, effective use is made of teacher judgment, the assessment reflects real-life challenges, and assessment allows for differences in learning style and interests. Performance assessments range from performance events such as projects or written scenarios to a collection of a learner's work over time, such as in portfolio assessments.

performance event: A project or written scenario that allows learners with special needs to work over a longer time period than most other curricular activities and provides learners with an opportunity to emphasize their strengths.

performance project: A form of alternative educational assessment involving the execution and completion of an assigned project.

performance standards: Specific guidelines as to how well learners must perform their work.

personality assessment: An assessment that attempts to measure a whole host of personality factors that may affect an individual's behavior at work, attitude toward work, ability to operate effectively in particular environments, attitudes toward colleagues, capacity to cope with stress, etc.

physical or mental impairment: Any physiological disorder or condition, cosmetic disfigurement, or anatomical loss affecting one or more of the following body systems: neurological, musculoskeletal, special sense organs, respiratory (including speech organs), cardiovascular, reproductive, digestive, genito-urinary, hemic and lymphatic, skin, and endocrine; or any mental or psychological disorder, such as mental retardation, organic brain syndrome, emotional or mental illness, and specific learning disabilities; and also included are the following: orthopedic, visual, speech and hearing impairments, cerebral palsy, epilepsy, muscular dystrophy, multiple sclerosis, infection with the Human Immunodeficiency Virus, cancer, heart disease, diabetes, drug addiction, and alcoholism (The Americans with Disabilities Act, PL 101-336).

placement profile: A collection of descriptive and evaluative information on each learner. Job placement profiles showing the interests and capabilities of each learner can be matched with job profiles and used to make placement decisions.

portfolio: A collections of a learner's work over time. A portfolio often documents a learner's best work and may include other types of process information, such as drafts of the learner's work, the learner's self-assessment of the work, and the parents' assessment. Portfolios may be used for evaluation of a learner's abilities and improvements.

poverty: The classification of those who lack money or material possessions to an extent that places them economically beneath the accepted minimum standard of living. Conditions of poverty can range from desire for material comfort to an extreme need for basic necessities.

practicum: The placement of a learner in a work setting where the learner can observe workers in various roles and actually participate in daily work routines for a specified period of time.

present level of performance: Information from formal and informal assessment processes that summarizes both the strengths and limitations of the learner.

problem solving: A thought process structured by an instructor and employed by learners for clearly defining a problem, forming hypothetical solutions, and possibly testing the hypothesis.

project: A significant, practical unit of activity having educational value aimed at one or more definite goals of understanding and involving the investigation and solution of problems.

project-based learning (PBL): A model for classroom activity that shifts away from the classroom practices of short, isolated instructor-centered lessons and instead emphasizes learning activities that are long-term, interdisciplinary, learner-centered, and integrated with real-world issues and practices.

proximity control: Strategic positioning of the instructor in the classroom while inappropriate behavior is being displayed by learners.

Q

qualified individual with a disability: Someone who, with or without reasonable accommodation, can perform the essential functions of his or her job. A qualified person must satisfy basic job requirements (e.g., education, training, job experience, licensure or certification) required of all employees in similar jobs (The Americans with Disabilities Act, PL 101-336).

R

readability formula: A procedure used to determine the reading level of an instructional material.

reasonable accommodation: Any change or adjustment that permits a qualified individual with special needs to carry out the essential functions of a job (e.g., making existing facilities readily accessible to individuals with disabilities, job restructuring, part-time or modified work schedules, reassignment to a vacant position, acquisition or modification of equipment or devices, appropriate adjustments, and modifications of exams, training materials, or policies) (The Americans with Disabilities Act, PL 101-336).

reflection: A natural process that facilitates the development of future action from the contemplation of past and/or current events.

related services: Services to be provided for learners with special needs, including transportation and other support services, speech pathology, psychological services, physical and occupational therapy, recreation, rehabilitation counseling, social work services, and medical services needed for the individual to benefit from special education (The Individuals With Disabilities Education Act, PL 101-476).

resource directory: A tool that can assist educators in developing interagency linkages when preparing learners for the adult roles they will assume.

***Revised Handbook for Analyzing Jobs*:** A handbook filled with over 300 pages of career information beginning with an in-depth description of job analysis and its uses and principles. It also includes information on worker function, work fields, aptitudes, temperaments, the *GOE*, physical demands and environmental conditions, and writing job summaries, task descriptions, and job analysis reports.

role-playing: An activity in which learners and/or instructors take on the behavior of a hypothetical or real personality in order to solve a problem or gain insight into a situation.

rubrics: (1) Well-articulated performance standards. (2) Scoring devices (or tools) that are designed to assist in the process of clarifying, communicating, and assessing expected performance.

S

SCANS: The Secretary's Commission on Achieving Necessary Skills (SCANS) was appointed by the Secretary of Labor to determine the skills that young people need to succeed in the world of work. The commission's fundamental purpose is to encourage a high-performance economy characterized by high-skills and high-wage employment. The primary objective is to help instructors understand how curriculum and instruction must change to enable learners to develop those high-performance skills needed to succeed in the high-performance workplace.

school-based enterprise: An enterprise that provides learners with an opportunity to produce goods and services as part of their program of study and helps to develop knowledge and skills in all aspects of an industry. The primary purpose of a school-based enterprise is to help learners learn all that is involved in establishing and operating a successful business in a career focus area.

school-based student services: Services provided by an educational institution to facilitate learning and the successful transition of learners from school to lasting and rewarding careers and lifelong learning.

Section 504 accommodation plan: A plan that pertains to public institutions that receive federal funding, such as public school systems. This plan provides a summary of accommodations that a learner needs in order to have equal access to the learning process or to other programs, activities, and services.

self-assessment: The process of reflecting on one's own progress and discovering what steps can be taken to improve performance.

self-esteem: All of the feelings an individual has concerning oneself. Having high self-esteem is picturing oneself as being a good individual.

seriously emotionally disturbed: An individual exhibiting one or more of the following characteristics over a long period of time and to a marked degree that adversely affects educational performance: an inability to learn that cannot be explained by intellectual, sensory, or health factors; an inability to build or maintain satisfactory interpersonal relationships with peers and teachers; inappropriate types of behavior or feelings under normal circumstances; a general pervasive mood of unhappiness or depression; or a tendency to develop physical symptoms or fears associated with personal or school problems (The Individuals with Disabilities Education Act, PL 101-476).

service learning: A strategy in which learners grow and develop through active participation in thoughtfully organized service experiences, which are conducted in and meet the needs of a community, are coordinated between the school and the community, are integrated into and enhance the learners' academic curriculum, provide structured time for learners to reflect on the service experience, provide learners with opportunities to use newly acquired skills and knowledge in real-life situations in their own communities, and enhance what is taught in schools by extending learning beyond the classroom and into the community, thereby fostering the development of a sense of caring for others. Service learning is designed to connect learners to their communities through community service. It promotes a learning approach through which learners apply academic and career skills and knowledge to address real-life work situations while developing the attitudes, values, and behaviors that will lead them to become informed citizens and productive workers.

short-term objective: A measurable statement which provides intermediate steps between a learner's present level of performance and established annual goal(s).

simulation: A type of learning process which involves learners as participants in role-playing presentations and/or games simulating real-life situations or environments.

single parent: A mother or father of a child who is responsible for the upbringing of that child without the support and assistance of the other parent. The Perkins Act of 1998 specifically identifies single pregnant women when dealing with the special population of single parents.

situational assessment: A technique that uses observation skills to record the career and technical behaviors and work habits that learners exhibit while performing specific work tasks in a simulated or actual job situation. Learners are observed and evaluated while working in a group rather than on an individual basis.

skeletal outline: An organizational tool that helps to organize information from a lecture or discussion into a partial outline to be completed by the learner.

special education: Specially designed instruction for learners with special needs in all settings, including the workplace and training centers, provided at no cost to the parent.

special education personnel: Instructors and support staff who are charged with instructing and assisting learners with special needs.

special education teacher: An instructor employed by a school system to provide instruction and support services for learners with special needs enrolled in special education programs.

specific feedback: Information provided to learners with direct, usable insights into current performance in relation to desired performance. It also avoids feedback that may be considered general or vague.

speech and language impairment: Setbacks or disadvantages caused by abnormal speech or vocabulary-related issues. Speech is abnormal when it deviates so far from the speech of other people that it calls attention to itself, interferes with communication, or causes the speaker or the listeners to be distressed. Speech impairments may include a communication disorder such as stuttering, impaired articulation, a language impairment, or a voice impairment, all of which adversely affect an individual's educational performance.

Standard Occupational Classification Manual: A universal occupational classification system, which allows government agencies and private industry to produce comparable data. It is designed to cover all occupations in which work is performed for pay or profit, reflecting the current occupational structure in the United States. Users of occupational data include government program managers, industrial and labor relations practitioners, learners considering career training, job seekers, career and technical education training schools, and employers wishing to set salary scales or locate new plants.

state association: A state-level organization for each CTSO that is administered by the agency the state has authorized to be responsible for career and technical education–usually the State Department of Education, Division of Career and Technical Education.

state director: An individual appointed by the state agency to provide leadership for the state association of the CTSO.

student services: Services provided by an educational institution to facilitate learning and the successful transition of learners from school to lasting and rewarding careers and lifelong learning.

student services plan: A form for coordinating and planning student services used to facilitate services necessary for a specific learner.

student-teacher contract: An effective method in assisting learners from special populations to succeed in meeting program requirements, which is developed between the learners and career and technical education instructors

study skill: A skill that is used to promote learning the content of any course of study.

substance abuse: The taking into the body of any chemical substance, such as tobacco, alcohol, or other drugs, that causes physical, mental, emotional, or social harm to an individual.

supported employment: Competitive work in integrated settings for individuals who are unable to meet the demands of competitive employment.

support team: Career and technical education teachers, special education teachers, and other educational institution support personnel who work together to encourage and enhance the participation of learners from special populations in CTSOs.

T

task analysis: A technique that involves analyzing a job and the tasks required to successfully complete the job. The task should have a major goal or objective associated with it, which should be clearly described at the beginning of the task analysis.

teacher support team: A group composed of a select group of instructors at the building/campus level whose role is to provide instructors in the educational environment who work with learners from special populations with suggestions of alternative instructional strategies that would assist these learners to succeed.

team: A collection of people who must rely on collaboration if each member is to experience ultimate success and goal achievement.

technology education: Formerly known as industrial arts, technology education is sometimes viewed to be a service area of career and technical education, but it is more appropriately viewed as a vital part of general and academic education.

tech-prep: A major educational reform movement aimed at providing continuity of learning and quality educational opportunities for all learners.

teen father: A teenage male who becomes a father, often resulting in negative educational, financial, social, health, and other developmental consequences.

teen pregnancy: Teen pregnancy occurs when teenage girls bear children, and may have a negative effect on both quality of the teen mother's education and the chance that the teen mother will complete her secondary education.

teen suicide: Teen suicide is when a teenager takes his or her own life, and is the second leading cause of death among teenagers.

telementoring: A form of on-line mentoring via the Internet, where mentor and learner correspond via e-mail and chat sessions.

test: An instrument developed by the instructor, or commercially, to obtain measurements of what learners know and can do.

testing: The process of administering a test or instrument to obtain measurements of learned knowledge or skills. The most common forms of testing are (a) paper-pencil testing, used to measure knowledge, and (b) performance testing, used to measure skills.

trade school: A movement that emerged in the United States following the Civil War to provide a workable system of industrial education for all Americans. The trade school was designed to provide specific trade training supplemented with directly related academic subjects.

transition: A process involving a broad array of individuals resulting in a partnership of learners, parents, educators, community agencies and educational systems. The process builds upon a variety of personal experiences, interests, and goals (McCarty & Hess-Grabill, 1990).

A coordinated set of activities for a learner designed within an outcome-oriented process, which promotes movement from school to post-school activities including postsecondary education, career and technical training and education, integrated employment (including supported employment), continuing and adult education, adult services, independent living, or community participation. The coordinated set of activities shall be based upon the individual learner's needs, taking into account the learner's preferences and interests, and shall include instruction, community experiences, and development of employment and other post-school adult living objectives, and when appropriate, acquisition of daily living skills and functional career and technical education evaluation (The Individuals With Disabilities Education Act, PL 101-476).

A carefully planned process, which may be initiated either by school personnel or adult service providers, to establish and implement a plan for either employment or additional career and technical training of a learner with special needs who will graduate or leave school in three to five years; such a process must involve special educators, career and technical education instructors, parents and/or the learner, adult service systems representatives, and possibly an employer (Wehman, 1984).

A period which includes high school, the point of graduation, additional postsecondary education or adult services, and the initial years in employment (Will, 1984).

transitional employment: Employment designed for those who cannot enter on their own into competitive work, but who are able to handle an independent, full-wage job after training and support.

transition assessment: The ongoing process of collecting data on the individual's strengths, needs, preferences and interests as they relate to the demands of current and future working, educational, living, and personal and social environments. Assessment data serve as the common thread in the transition process and form the basis for defining goals and services to be included in the Individualized Education Program (IEP) (Sitlington, Neubert, & Leconte, 1997, p. 71).

transition coordinator: A qualified counselor or teacher who must ensure that learners from special populations are receiving adequate services and job skill training.

transition services: A coordinated set of activities for a learner, designed within an outcome-oriented process, which promotes movement from school to post-school activities including postsecondary education, career and technical training and education, integrated employment (including supported employment), continuing and adult education, adult services, independent living, or community participation. The coordinated set of activities shall be based upon the individual learner's needs, taking into account the learner's preferences and interests, and shall include instruction, community experiences, the development of employment and other post-school adult living objectives, and when appropriate, acquisition of daily living skills and functional vocational evaluation (The Individuals With Disabilities Education Act, PL 101-476).

traumatic brain injury: Rapid acceleration and deceleration of the brain, including shearing (tearing) of the nerve fibers, contusion (bruising) of the brain tissue against the skull, brain stem injuries, and edema (swelling). Injuries that do not involve penetration of the skull are referred to as closed-head or generalized head injuries.

U

undue hardship: An action requiring significant difficulty or expense (The Americans with Disabilities Act, PL 101-336).

universal design for learning: A method for learning that consists of instructional materials and activities that allow the learning goals to be achievable by learners with wide differences in their abilities to see, hear, speak, move, read, write, understand English, attend, organize, engage, and remember. Universal design for learning is achieved by means of flexible curricular materials and activities that provide alternatives for learners with disparities in abilities and backgrounds. These alternatives should be built into the instructional design and operating systems of educational materials—they should not have to be added after the fact.

universal education: The philosophy that all children should be educated in a common school system, and that education should be provided to all.

V

visual impairment: Even with correction, a vision impairment adversely affects an individual's educational performance. The term includes both individuals with partial vision and individuals who are blind.

vocational assessment: A comprehensive process conducted over a period of time, involving a multi-disciplinary team with the purpose of identifying individual characteristics, education, training, and placement needs, which provides educators with the basis for planning an individual's program.

vocational interest: An occupational interest expressed by an individual through interviews, exploratory activities or interest inventories.

W

work-based learning: A component of the School-to-Work Opportunities Act that includes such experiences as job shadowing, school-sponsored enterprises, and on-the-job training for academic credit.

work habits: The attitudinal, problem-solving, and interpersonal behaviors that are thought to be critical for learner success both in classroom settings and in employment situations. They represent behaviors which will contribute to eventual success in the world of work.

workplace inclusion: Workplace inclusion involves gaining a competitive advantage through workplace environments that accept, accommodate, and appreciate the talents of all employees and customers regardless of disability.

work-related social skill: An interpersonal skill important to a person's employability, productivity, and career success. Employers typically value verbal communications, responsibility, initiative, and interpersonal and decision-making skills.

work sample: An activity that simulates real work tasks and is closely associated with actual jobs in the labor market. It emphasizes performance skills rather than verbal or written skills, and incorporates the tools and standards associated with the actual job.

Y

youth apprenticeship: A learning program for young people, age 16 and older, that combines on-the-job learning with classroom instruction, that bridges secondary and postsecondary schooling, and that results in certification of mastery of work skills (Jobs for the Future).

Index

A

acceleration strategies, 474

accessibility, 150–151, 387

accommodation, 119, 717

acts (government). *See* legislation

adaptive behavior, 126

advisory committees, 669–670

agricultural education, 91–*93*

all aspects of the industry (AAI), 712, 732–735, *734*

alternative assessment, 519–532

  claims and shortcomings, 524–525

  connecting, 525–526, *526*

  definition, 522

  feedback, 525–526, 530–531

  reflection, 525–526, 526–*527*

  rubrics, 527–528, 528–530

  self-assessment, 526–527, 527–528

  strategies, 531–532, *533*

American Lyceum, 66

Americans with Disabilities Act of 1990, 46–48, *47*

analytic (left-brain) learners, 410–412, *411*

annual goals, 338–341, *340, 341*

  role of career and technical education personnel, 341

apprenticeship, 63, 705–707, *707–708*

  registered, 206

  youth, 706–707, *707–708*

apprenticeship programs, 84–85

aptitude, 255–257

aptitude test, 258

arts and crafts movement, 69

assessment, 513–542

  alternative, 519–532

    claims and shortcomings, 524–525

    connecting, 525–526, *526*

    definition, 522

    feedback, 525–526, 530–531

    reflection, 525–526, 526–*527*

    rubrics, 527–528, 528–530

    self-assessment, 526–527, 527–528

    strategies, 531–532, *533*

  authentic, 522–523

  confidentiality, 540–541

  considerations, 536

  definition, 521–522

  of educational progress, *195*

  IEP and ITP as guides for, 542

  language difficulty, *206*

national skill standards, 515–519

  benefits of, 518

  challenges of, 518–519

  national education goals, *516*

new strategies, 521

performance, 523–524

prospective on, 541–542

traditional, 532–536

assignments, 426, *427*

assistive technology, 272, 435–437

assistive technology device, 334–335

assistive technology service, 334–335

at-risk learners, characteristics, *184*

attention deficit/hyperactivity disorder (AD/HD), *121, 163–165*

auditory learners, *407,* 408

authentic assessment, 522–523

autism, *121,* 124–126, *125*

averaging system, 590, *591*

B

basic reading skills, 430

basic skills information, 253–255, *254, 255*

behavior management, 400–402

blindness, *121*

Bloom, Benjamin

  Bloom's taxonomy, *500*

  mastery learning, 463–465

bodily/kinesthetic intelligence, *449*

brain-based learning, 408, *410*–412

  left-brain/analytic learners, 410–412, *411*

  right-brain/global learners, 410–412, *411*

business education, 93–95, *96*

business/industry linkage, 750, 753–755, *756*

Business Professionals of America (BPA), 616–617

C

career academy, 63

career and technical education, 88–113

  agricultural education, 91–*93*

  business education, 93–95, *96*

  curriculum component in dropout prevention, 25

  definition, 80–81

  and dropout prevention, 24–25

  educational support system in dropout prevention, 25

  exemplary components, 26–28

M

Using the *Special Populations in Career and Technical Education* CD-ROM

Before removing the CD-ROM, please note that the book cannot be returned if the CD-ROM sleeve seal is broken.

System Requirements

The *Special Populations in Career and Technical Education* CD-ROM is designed to work best on a computer with a processor speed of 200 MHz or faster, running Microsoft® Windows® 95, 98, 2000, Me, NT®, or XP™. Adobe® Acrobat® Reader™ software is required for opening many resources provided on this CD-ROM. If necessary, Adobe® Acrobat® Reader™ can be installed from the CD-ROM. Microsoft® Windows® 2000, NT™, or XP™ users that are connected to a server-based network may be required to log on with administrative rights to allow installation of the application. See your Information Systems group for further information. Additional information is available from the Adobe® web site at www.adobe.com. Adobe® Acrobat® Reader™ provides the user with the ability to enlarge images for greater clarity as well as provides other navigational functions. The Internet links require Microsoft® Internet Explorer™ 3.0 or Netscape® 3.0 or later browser software and an Internet connection.

Opening Files

Insert the CD-ROM into the computer CD-ROM drive. Within a few seconds, the start screen will be displayed. Click on START to open the home screen. Information about the usage of the CD-ROM can be accessed by clicking USING THE CD-ROM. The Quick Quizzes, Interactive Glossary, Forms, and Reference Material can be accessed by clicking on the appropriate button located on the home screen. Clicking on the American Tech logo accesses the American Tech web site (www.go2atp.com) for information on related educational products. Unauthorized reproduction of the material on the CD-ROM is strictly prohibited.